The Cambridge Handbook of Psychology and Economic Behaviour

There has recently been an escalated interest in the interface between psychology and economics. *The Cambridge Handbook of Psychology and Economic Behaviour* is a valuable reference dedicated to improving our understanding of the economic mind and economic behaviour. Employing empirical methods – including laboratory and field experiments, observations, questionnaires and interviews – the *Handbook* provides comprehensive coverage of theory and method, financial and consumer behaviour, the environment and biological perspectives. This second edition also includes new chapters on topics such as neuroeconomics; unemployment; debt; behavioural public finance; and cutting-edge work on fuzzy trace theory and robots, cyborgs and consumption. With distinguished contributors from a variety of countries and theoretical backgrounds, the *Handbook* is an important step forwards in the improvement of communications between the disciplines of psychology and economics that will appeal to academic researchers and graduates in economic psychology and behavioural economics.

ALAN LEWIS is Professor of Economic Psychology at the University of Bath. He has been publishing in the area of psychology and economics for nearly forty years, and his journal articles and books have covered such topics as socially responsible investing; ethics, altruism and economic affairs; tax evasion and fiscal preferences; environmental attitudes and behaviour; economic socialisation; and credit and debt. His books include *Morals, Markets and Money* (2002) and, with Paul Webley and Adrian Furnham, *The New Economic Mind: The Social Psychology of Economic Behaviour* (1995). Alan Lewis was also Editor of the *Journal of Economic Psychology* from 1996 to 2000. He has presented papers at international conferences and seminars in many countries, including the United States, the United Kingdom, Canada, France, Italy, Spain, Sweden, Norway, Austria, the Czech Republic, Denmark and Belgium.

The Cambridge Handbook of Psychology and Economic Behaviour

Second Edition

Edited by

Alan Lewis
University of Bath

CAMBRIDGE
UNIVERSITY PRESS

CAMBRIDGE
UNIVERSITY PRESS

University Printing House, Cambridge CB2 8BS, United Kingdom

One Liberty Plaza, 20th Floor, New York, NY 10006, USA

477 Williamstown Road, Port Melbourne, VIC 3207, Australia

314–321, 3rd Floor, Plot 3, Splendor Forum, Jasola District Centre, New Delhi – 110025, India

79 Anson Road, #06-04/06, Singapore 079906

Cambridge University Press is part of the University of Cambridge.

It furthers the University's mission by disseminating knowledge in the pursuit of education, learning and research at the highest international levels of excellence.

www.cambridge.org
Information on this title: www.cambridge.org/9781316613900
DOI: 10.1017/9781316676349

© Cambridge University Press 2008, 2018

First edition published 2008

Second edition 2018

Printed in the United Kingdom by TJ International Ltd. Padstow Cornwall

A catalogue record for this publication is available from the British Library.

Library of Congress Cataloging-in-Publication Data
Names: Lewis, Alan, 1952– author.
Title: The Cambridge handbook of psychology and economic behaviour / edited by Alan Lewis, University of Bath.
Description: Second edition. | Cambridge, United Kingdom; New York, NY: Cambridge University Press, 2018. | Includes bibliographical references and index.
Identifiers: LCCN 2017040154 | ISBN 9781107161399 (hardback) | ISBN 9781316613900 (paperback)
Subjects: LCSH: Economics–Psychological aspects. | Consumer behavior.
Classification: LCC HB74.P8. C36 2018 | DDC 330.01/9–dc23
LC record available at https://lccn.loc.gov/2017040154

ISBN 978-1-107-16139-9 Hardback
ISBN 978-1-316-61390-0 Paperback

*This is dedicated to Paul Webley (1953–2016), a good friend
of economic psychology and a good friend of ours.*

Contents

Plates

The colour plate section appears between pages 648 and 649

Figures

Tables

Notes on Contributors

AARON AHUVIA is Professor of Marketing at the University of Michigan–Dearborn College of Business. His research looks at (a) consumers' love of products, activities and brands; and (b) how people can build happy lives within contemporary consumer culture. An independent analysis of research impact (Elbeck and Vander Schee, 2013) ranked him twenty-second in the world (nineteenth in the United States) for research influence in consumer behaviour.

GERRIT ANTONIDES is Professor Emeritus of Economics of Consumers and Households, Wageningen University, the Netherlands. He was Editor-in-Chief of the *Journal of Economic Psychology* from 2005 to 2010 and President of the Society for the Advancement of Behavioural Economics (SABE) from 2014 to 2016. His research focusses on consumer financial behaviour, consumer food behaviour and mental accounting.

NICHOLAS BARDSLEY is Associate Professor of Behavioural and Ecological Economics in the School of Agriculture, Policy and Development, University of Reading, United Kingdom. His recent research investigates household energy use, food norms in schools and social aspects of decision making.

LORY BARILE is Lecturer in Economics at the University of Coventry, United Kingdom. She completed her doctoral research in economics at the University of Bath, United Kingdom (2014). Prior to this, she received a PhD degree in economics from the University of Genoa, Italy (2009), an MSc degree in economics from the University of Bath, United Kingdom (2008) and a BSc degree in political sciences and economics from the University of Florence, Italy (2004). Her research interests are in the fields of behavioural and experimental economics, public sector economics, environmental economics and applied microeconomics.

RUSSELL BELK is York University Distinguished Research Professor and Kraft Foods Canada Chair in Marketing, Schulich School of Business, York University, Canada. He has over six hundred publications, and his research tends to be qualitative, visual, and cultural. It involves the extended self, meanings of possessions, collecting, gift giving, sharing, digital consumption and materialism.

BRENDAN BURCHELL is a Reader in the Social Sciences in the Department of Sociology at the University of Cambridge, United Kingdom. He is also a Fellow of Magdalene College, Cambridge. His main research interests centre on the effects of labour market conditions on well-being. Recent publications have focussed on job insecurity, work intensity, part-time work, zero-hours contracts, debt, occupational gender segregation and self-employment.

J. MICHAEL COLLINS is an Associate Professor at the University of Wisconsin–Madison, United States, with faculty positions at the School of Human Ecology and the La Follette School of Public Affairs. He also serves as a specialist for University of Wisconsin–Extension and directs the Center for Financial Security. He studies consumer decision making in the financial marketplace, including the role of public policy in influencing credit, savings and investment choices, with a focus on financial capability among economically vulnerable households and youth.

CHRISTOPHER J. COWTON is Professor of Financial Ethics at the University of Huddersfield Business School, United Kigdom,where he was Professor of Accounting from 1996 to 2016 and served as Dean from 2008 to 2016. He was Editor of *Business Ethics: A European Review* from 2004 to 2013 and has been a member of the Ethics Standards Committee of the Institute of Chartered Accountants in England and Wales since 2009.

JOHN CULLIS is Professor of Economics at the University of Bath, United Kingdom. He has published extensively on public sector issues in leading economics journals, such as *American Economic Review, Economic Journal, Journal of Health Economics, Journal of Public Economics*, and *Kyklos*. He is coauthor (with Philip Jones) of *Public Finance and Public Choice* (3rd edn, 2009).

WERNER DE BONDT is Professor of Finance and Founding Director of the Richard H. Driehaus Center for Behavioral Finance at DePaul University in Chicago. Between 1992 and 2003, he was the Frank Graner Professor of Investment Management at the University of Wisconsin–Madison. His recent work examines the value of professional financial advice, how celebrity investors influence market sentiment and volatility and the pricing of rare high-impact events.

DANIEL EHRLICH is a doctoral student in the Interdepartmental Neuroscience Program at Yale University, New Haven, Connecticut, United States. His research utilises recurrent neural network models to investigate the cortical circuitry underlying human and animal behaviour.

DETLEF FETCHENHAUER is Professor of Economic and Social Psychology, University of Cologne, Germany. He is doing research on the social psychology of trust, lay-economics and more generally on the interplay between our evolutionary past and human functioning in our current and complex environments.

GORDON R. FOXALL is Distinguished Research Professor at Cardiff Business School, Cardiff University, and a Visiting Professor in Economic Psychology at the University of Durham, United Kingdom. He has held visiting appointments at the universities of Michigan and Oxford, and is a Fellow of the Academy of Social Sciences (FAcSS); a Fellow of the British Psychological Society (FBPsS); and a Fellow of the British Academy of Management (FBAM). His principal research interests include consumer behaviour analysis (a field which his work inaugurated), the philosophical implications of the neurophilosophy of consumer choice and the theory of the marketing firm.

BRUNO S. FREY is Permanent Visiting Professor at the University of Basel and Research Director at the Center for Research in Economics, Management and the Arts (CREMA), Zurich. He has held chairs at the universities of Constance, Zurich, Chicago, Warwick and Friedrichshafen and has been awarded five honorary doctorates in five countries as well as publishing twenty-one books and more than six hundred articles in scholarly journals.

MARGARETA FRIMAN is Professor of Psychology and Director of the Service and Market Oriented Transport Research Group (SAMOT) at Karlstad University (Sweden). She is Associate Editor of the *Frontiers in Psychology: Environmental Psychology* (2016–present). In 2014, she received the Håkan Frisinger Foundation for Transportation Research Award as a prominent researcher. She is currently working on underlying psychological processes for motivating voluntary travel behaviour change.

JANA GALLUS is Assistant Professor of Strategy and Behavioral Decision Making at UCLA's Anderson School of Management. Her research interests lie in behavioural economics and strategy, with a focus on nonfinancial incentives and their effects on human decision making. She investigates how incentive schemes can be designed to enhance employee motivation and organisational performance in the private and nonprofit sectors.

DAVID GARAVITO is a JD/PhD candidate at Cornell University in Ithaca, New York, United States. He is currently working in Dr. Valerie Reyna's Laboratory for Rational Decision Making to study judgement, memory and risky decision making in adolescent and adult populations. His specific work focusses on the cognitive effects of mild traumatic brain injuries and predicting future neurodegenerative disease in at-risk populations.

TOMMY GÄRLING is Emeritus Professor of Psychology currently affiliated with the Centre for Finance and Department of Economics, School of Business, Economics, and Law, University of Gothenburg (Göteborg), Sweden. He is a Fellow of the International Association of Applied Psychology, and a former President of its Environmental Psychology Division. He has been an Associate

Editor of *Journal of Economic Psychology*. Current research in collaboration with economists includes effects on asset markets of tournament incentives to fund managers and influences of a scarcity mindset on young adults' borrowing to purchase consumer products.

JULIA GUMY is a Lecturer in Policy Studies with quantitative research methods in the Department of Social Policy at the University of Bristol. She is also a member of the Centre for the Study of Poverty and Social Justice and the QStep Centre at the University of Bristol. Her research interests lie in the study of the life course, subjective and economic well-being, gender, comparative welfare policies and the use of quantitative research methods. Her most recent work examines the impact of economic inequality on the accumulation of debt in Western Europe.

MICHAEL HALLSWORTH is a Director at the Behavioural Insights Team, a social purpose company that was formerly part of the U.K. government (sometimes known as the "Nudge Unit"). While at Her Majesty's Revenue and Customs, he was responsible for running large-scale randomised controlled trials that applied behavioural economics to increase tax compliance. He has undergraduate and postgraduate degrees from Cambridge University and a PhD from Imperial College London.

LISHENG HE is a PhD student in Behavioural Science at Warwick Business School, University of Warwick, United Kingdom. He is interested in learning, judgement and decision making.

DENIS HILTON is Professor of Social Psychology at the University of Toulouse, France. His principal interests are in social cognition, reasoning and judgement and decision making. He has collaborated extensively with economists on behavioural aspects of finance, insurance and sustainable consumption. He is currently an Associate Editor of the *European Journal of Social Psychology*.

TIM JACKSON is Professor of Sustainable Development at the University of Surrey, United Kingdom, and Director of the Economic and Social Research Council (ESRC) Research Centre for the Understanding of Sustainable Prosperity (CUSP). From 2004 to 2011, he was Economics Commissioner on the U.K. Sustainable Development Commission, where his work on the psychology of consumer behaviour was influential in framing the 'Changing Behaviours' chapter in the 2005 U.K. Sustainable Development Strategy. He is the author of Prosperity Without Growth (2009/2017), a landmark in the sustainability debate.

PHILIP JONES is Professor of Economics at the University of Bath, United Kingdom. He has published extensively on public finance and public choice in leading economics and political science journals, such as *American Economic Review, Economic Journal, Journal of Public Economics, Oxford Economic*

Papers and the *British Journal of Political Science*. He is coauthor (with John Cullis) of *Public Finance and Public Choice* (3rd edn, 2009).

BERNADETTE KAMLEITNER is Professor of Marketing, with a special focus on consumer behaviour, in the Department of Marketing, WU Vienna University of Economics and Business, Austria. She is President of the Austrian WWG Forum marketing and head of the Institute for Marketing and Consumer Research. Her most recent work examines antecedents and consequences of experiences of ownership and consumer perceptions and handling of personal data.

MINJO KANG is a PhD candidate in the School of Business, Yonsei University, Republic of Korea. As a Certified Public Accountant, he has worked at PWC and KPMG in Korea from 2006 to 2009. With the financial support of Mr. Dong-wook Shin, he participated in the handbook project on tax psychology as a visiting PhD student at the University of Vienna. His research interest lies in the application of psychology to the context of tax and accounting. His most recent work analyses the concept of tax avoidance from a psychological perspective.

INGO KASTNER works as a Senior Researcher in the Environmental Psychology Division at the Otto-von-Guericke University in Magdeburg, Germany. The main focus of his research is concerned with environmentally relevant investment decisions in households and organisations.

ERICH KIRCHLER is Professor of Economic Psychology, Faculty of Psychology, University of Vienna, Austria. He was Editor-in-Chief of the *Journal of Economic Psychology* (with Erik Hoelzl) and President of the International Association of Researchers in Economic Psychology (IAREP) of the International Association of Adminstration Professionals (IAAP) – Division 9 (Economic Psychology) and of the Austrian Psychological Association. His most recent work examines tax behaviour and financial decisions.

ANNE-SOPHIE LANG is a predoctoral Fellow at the Institute of Sociology and Social Psychology, University of Cologne, Germany. She has studied economics, political science and economic and social psychology. She is currently conducting research on the social psychology of trust.

IFAT LEVY is Associate Professor of Comparative Medicine and Neuroscience at Yale School of Medicine, New Haven, Connecticut. Her research combines neuroimaging and behavioural techniques to investigate the neural basis of decision making and valuation under uncertainty in healthy individuals and in psychopathology.

ALAN LEWIS is Professor of Economic Psychology in the Department of Psychology, University of Bath, United Kingdom. He was Editor-in-Chief of the *Journal of Economic Psychology* from 1996 to 2000 and President of the International Association of Researchers in Economic Psychology (IAREP) from 2009 to 2011. His most recent work examines cultural differences in perceptions of tax evasion, benefit fraud and discounting rates.

REBECCA MCDONALD is a postdoctoral Research Fellow in Behavioural Science at the University of Warwick, United Kingdom. She holds a PhD in economics from Newcastle University, United Kingdom. Her research involves using experiments to understand how individuals value nonmarket outcomes such as safety and health, particularly when the outcomes are risky or delayed.

EVA MARCKHGOTT is Teaching and Research Associate at the Institute for Marketing and Consumer Research, WU Vienna University of Economics and Business, Austria. She holds a master's degree in marketing and is currently pursuing her PhD in the field of consumer behaviour. Her research interests include external cues influencing consumer decision making.

JEROME OLSEN is a Research Associate at the Faculty of Psychology, University of Vienna, Austria. His PhD project focusses on value-added tax (VAT) compliance. Specifically, he investigates how VAT is socially represented by different actors in the field as well as factors influencing collaborative tax evasion of income tax and VAT by suppliers and consumers.

GODA PERLAVICIUTE is Assistant Professor in Environmental Psychology at the University of Groningen, the Netherlands. Her research focusses on public acceptability of energy sources, systems and policies. She is particularly interested in the role of people's values in their acceptability judgements.

DANIEL READ is Professor of Behavioural Science at Warwick Business School. He received his PhD from University of Toronto and has held posts in (amongst other places) the London School of Economics, Leeds University Business School and Durham University Business School and has been a visiting scholar at INSEAD and the Yale School of Management. His research includes experimental and theoretical work in intertemporal and risky choice and in research methods.

VALERIE REYNA is the Lois and Melvin Tukman Professor and Director of the Human Neuroscience Institute at Cornell University, United States. She has been elected to the National Academy of Medicine and Society of Experimental Psychologists, and is President of the Society for Judgment and Decision Making. Her research integrates brain and behavioural approaches to understand and improve judgement, decision making and memory across the lifespan. Her recent work has focussed on the neuroscience of risky decision making and its implications for health and well-being, especially in adolescents; applications of artificial intelligence to understanding cancer genetics;

and medical and legal decision making (e.g., jury awards, medication decisions and adolescent crime).

CARMEN SMITH is Centre Coordinator at the ESRC Research Centre for the Understanding of Sustainable Prosperity (CUSP) at the University of Surrey, United Kingdom. She holds a doctorate in environmental sustainability from the University of Bath. Her research focusses on the psychology of participation within ecovillages and community currency initiatives. Carmen has also contributed to the Sustainable Development Program at the United Nations Research Institute for Social Development with a paper on the social and solidarity economy.

MATTHEW SPARKES is a Teaching Associate in Sociology and Quantitative Methods, in the Department of Sociology at the University of Cambridge. He is also an Associate Fellow of the Higher Education Academy. His main research interests lie in the study of financialisation, political economy, economic inequality and social class. His most recent work examines Britain's transition to a financialised economy, and the impact of credit use and problem debt on personal identity.

CLIVE L. SPASH is Professor of Public Policy & Governance in the Department of Socio-Economics, Vienna University of Economics and Business, Austria. He is Editor-in-Chief of the *Journal Environmental Values*. From 1996 to 2006, he was first Vice-President and then President of the European Society for Ecological Economics. He has published over one hundred academic journal articles and book chapters and most recently the fifty-chapter edited volume *Routledge Handbook of Ecological Economics*. For further information. visit www.clivespash.org.

LINDA STEG is Professor of Environmental Psychology at the University of Groningen, the Netherlands. Her research focusses on factors influencing environmental behaviour and the effects and acceptability of environmental policies. She is a former President of the Environmental Division of the International Association of Applied Psychology, member of the Advisory Group on Energy for Horizon 2020 and Coordinator of the European PERSON platform (www.person.eu), which aims to integrate and strengthen socioeconomic research on the human dimensions of a sustainable energy transition.

PAUL C. STERN is a senior scholar at the U.S. National Academy of Sciences, Engineering, and Medicine and Professor II at the Norwegian University of Science and Technology. His areas of research interest include environmentally significant behaviour and governance of common-pool resources. He is a Fellow of the American Association for the Advancement of Science and the American Psychological Association.

HENDRIK THEINE is a PhD student and Project Assistant at the Institute for Institutional and Heterodox Economics, Vienna University of Economics and Business. His research and study interests are situated at the crossroads of ecological economics and political economy. He works on economic inequality in the media, distributional issues of CO_2 emissions and discursive practices in economics.

ELLEN VAN DER WERFF is Assistant Professor in Environmental Psychology at the University of Groningen, the Netherlands. Her research focusses on understanding environmental behaviour and developing effective and acceptable interventions to promote sustainable behaviour.

CHRIS VAN KLAVEREN is Associate Professor of Educational Sciences and Economics of Education, in the Department of Behavioural and Movement Sciences, VU University Amsterdam. He is also Director of the Amsterdam Center of Learning Analytics (www.acla.amsterdam). His most recent work combines insights from behavioural science, learning analytics and program evaluation methods to redesign and individualise education and influence student choice behaviour.

KARL-ERIK WÄRNERYD is Professor Emeritus of Economic Psychology at the Stockholm School of Economics. His most recent publications have been in the area of the psychology of consumer finances. He published *Stock-Market Psychology: How People Value and Trade Stocks* in 2001.

REBECCA WELDON is an Assistant Professor of Psychology at Juniata College in Huntingdon, Pennsylvania, United States. She recently completed a postdoctoral Fellowship with Dr. Valerie Reyna at Cornell University, in which her work involved using fMRI and behavioural techniques to examine risky decision making in adolescents. Her most recent work focusses on cognitive control, delay discounting and risky-choice framing.

ULRICH WITT is Director Emeritus of the Evolutionary Economics Research Group at the Max Planck Institute of Economics, Germany, and Adjunct Professor of Economics in the Griffith Business School at Griffith University, Australia. He has served as Editor-in-Chief of the *Journal of Bioeconomics* since 2012. In his research, he pursues an evolutionary approach to economics focussing, *inter alia*, on innate and learned constituents of human behaviour, especially consumer behaviour, and its influence on individual welfare and environmental problems.

INGA WITTENBERG works as a Senior Researcher in the Environmental Psychology Division at the Otto-von-Guericke University in Magdeburg, Germany. Her research interests include determinants of proenvironmental behaviour as well as energy consumption and related technologies.

KIMBERLY S. WOLSKE is a Research Associate (Assistant Professor) in the Harris School of Public Policy, University of Chicago, United States, and an affiliated researcher with the Energy Policy Institute at the University of Chicago (EPIC). Her research examines the motivations and barriers to low-carbon lifestyle choices as well as public perceptions of climate change solutions and energy-related technologies.

ALEX J. WOOD is a Researcher of work, employment and labour markets at the Oxford Internet Institute, University of Oxford, United Kingdom. His research focusses on labour market transformation, new forms of work, organisation and collective action. He is currently researching the online gig economy. He has previously published in *Human Relations* and *Industrial Relations Journal*.

Introduction

Alan Lewis

Welcome to the second edition of the *Cambridge Handbook of Psychology and Economic Behaviour*. Like the first, it is an inclusive selection of chapters written by experts in the field who variously refer to themselves as psychologists, economic psychologists, environmental psychologists, behavioural and experimental psychologists, evolutionary economists and psychologists and simply, behavioural scientists. What they all have in common is a belief that the study of economic behaviour should be an empirical one, stressing in particular the synthetic side rather that the analytic aspects of the discipline. However, the contributors are not restricted to one method alone, for example the insistence in some areas of experimental economics that participants in experiments should receive real financial incentives (Kagel and Roth, 2015), and the keenness in behavioural economics for the investigation of decision-making based on hypothetical stimulus conditions (including vignettes) in the tradition of cognitive psychology (Dhami, 2016).[1]

Instead, while experimental studies are often included there is also evidence presented from social surveys and questionnaire studies, interviews, neurological investigators and even qualitative and cultural analyses. Theoretical issues are also covered especially whether *homo economicus* could be more usefully replaced, or at least augmented by an appreciation of *homo realitus*.

The collection comprises 27 chapters most of which are entirely new and all contain updated material. Contributors come from the USA, UK, France, Austria, The Netherlands, Sweden, Germany, Switzerland and Canada.

The first part of the handbook is titled 'Introduction, theory and method' and comprises the current introduction, a piece by Denis Hilton on 'Theory and method in economics and psychology' and a contribution by Nick Bardsley 'What lessons does the 'replication crisis' in psychology hold for experimental economics'?

In his chapter, Hilton attempts to reduce the puzzlement among economists and psychologists about each sides theory and methodology. It is argued that much of economics has elements in common with the behaviourist movement in psychology which attempts to link stimulus and response without recourse to the 'black box' (variously referred to as the 'organism' or in our case *homo economicus* or *homo realitus*) where S is mysteriously converted to R. Hilton calls for more realism and scientific rigour in economics which draws on material from social and cognitive psychology, as well as, rather guardedly, neuroscience.

Nick Bardsley, in his contribution, picks up on issues of prediction and replication mentioned by Hilton. Replication studies are essential if genuine scientific progress is to be made but problems abound including missing (often procedural) details in original studies and a general editorial unwillingness to publish replication studies. Replication studies have only recently begun to appear in psychology and are still very rare in economics.

The second part of the handbook has seven chapters related to finance. The first, by J. Michael Collins, Werner De Bondt and Karl Erik Wärneryd is a review of the literature identifying how investors forecast the stock market. The authors show that 'subjective expectations' rather than 'rational expectations' with insights from cognitive psychologists and heuristics in decision making, should be taken seriously as it seems that both professionals and amateur investors make systematic and consistent errors which can have profound market consequences. This chapter is followed by a comprehensive and detailed appraisal of related research on speculative bubbles by Werner De Bondt, where it is shown how investor psychology influences the dynamics and structure of world equity markets. Even tweeting and the spiking of 'tweeter mood' can have a significant, if short-lived influence on stock returns. The next chapter by Daniel Read, Rebecca McDonald and Lisheng He is also about the future in the study of inter-temporal choice. The research convincingly shows that discounting rates are not constant and are subject to, for instance, sign, magnitude, delay and sub-additive effects where the discount rate is lower for delayed losses than gains; discount rates are higher for small options than large ones; and where people are more impatient for outcomes divided into sub-intervals. The authors conclude that while there is now a considerable literature in this area, charting discount rates is complicated as they are dependent on, among other things, a complex interaction between the person making the decision, the framing of outcomes and the situation in which the choice is made.

The two chapters that follow, on debt (Sparkes, Gumy & Burchell) and unemployment (Wood & Burchell), are more clearly psychological in nature as they have plenty to say about the psychological costs of debt and unemployment. It is clear that some people are poor money managers and may be 'financially phobic' ignoring bills even when they mount up. An attempt is made in the debt chapter to increase the realism and applicability of relevant economic models. The unemployment chapter begins with the now well-established finding that being unemployed diminishes psychological well-being. Starting from an historical perspective the authors link the literature to more contemporary work practices.

The eigth chapter by Kamleitner, Marckhgott and Kirchler explores money management in households. Becker's model of the household based on economies of scale and specialised human capital, is unpacked to reveal a wide range of different contemporary household arrangements where the 'traditional' set up is no longer broadly applicable. In the final chapter in this section, Christopher Cowton examines the economic psychology of socially responsible investing. An increasing number of people want to know how their money is invested beyond mere risk and return. While a good deal of overlap between economics and psychology draws on cognitive psychology, some aspects of social psychology are in evidence here. How might our attitudes, values and morals influence our economic decisions?

There are three chapters in Part III covering private sector consumer behaviour and the firm. The first by Aaron Ahuvia is a comprehensive review of the ever-growing literature on consumption, income and happiness. Contrary to popular notions the relationships are far from straightforward and materialists, in particular, are often far from happy. Similar themes are picked up by Gerrit Antonides and Chris van Klaveren in the piece that follows, pinpointing the importance of non-materialistic factors and postmodernism.

The final chapter in this section is rather different (Gordon Foxall) providing a thorough reframing of the theory of the marketing firm drawing on insights from behaviourist psychology.

There are three chapters in Part IV on consumer behaviour in the public sector, Olsen, Kang and Kirchler's contribution reviews the now extensive literature on tax psychology, addressing not only the psychology of the individual taxpayer but a broader perspective, illuminating the relationship between deterrent policies and trust in government agencies.

Next Michael Hallsworth assesses the effectiveness of 'Nudge' techniques (made famous by Thaler and Sunstein, 2008) and field experiments encouraging timely tax compliance. In chapter fifteen, Barile, Cullis and Jones speculate how adoption of *homo* and *femina realitus* would alter the traditional approach to public sector economics.

Part V deals with environmental issues in five chapters. Jackson and Smith kick off with a careful appraisal of the need for lifestyle change in order to address environmental problems, given such changes may be seen as a threat to individual freedom of choice. Bringing environmental questions 'home' is the subject of the contribution from Perlaviciute, Steg and van der Werff. How, for example, do you encourage householders to reduce their household energy consumption? It is not solely a question of improved technology. The authors argue that contextual structures need to be in place alongside trust and belief in pertinent government policies in order to develop an effective environmental self-identity.

The chapter by Stern, Wittenberg, Wolske and Kastner takes a different tack, as instead of seeing households as consumers of energy, it anticipates the role of households as producers of energy. The authors suggest ways in which households would be prepared to make the appropriate investments harnessing sunlight (photovoltaic energy). Returning to the more familiar theme of curbing unwelcome consumption, Gärling and Friman examine the problems associated with the motor car. A number of policy initiatives are evaluated after considering psychological and economic aspects of private car use. The final chapter in Part V, by Clive Spash and Hendrik Theine, questions the effectiveness of various voluntary carbon trading schemes in controlling greenhouse gas emissions. The authors do not shy away from taking a point of view, and argue that such markets are unlikely to have much impact in resolving environmental problems.

Part VI comprises three chapters from a biological perspective. The first by Levy and Ehrlich reviews important research on neuroeconomics. Advances in technology, e.g., positon emission tomography (PET) and functional magnetic resonance imaging (fMRI) have provided opportunities for psychologists and economists to work together investigating the neural correlates of decision making mechanisms. A clear, straightforward (and uncritical) contribution follows by Fechtenhauer and Lang, arguing that economic behaviour can be traced to our animal history. In a closely argued final piece on evolutionary economics, Ulrich Witt traces how competitive transformations can themselves be interpreted as part of an evolutionary process, e.g., changes in economic growth, the international division of labour and welfare.

One last section, Part VII, is an opportunity for authors to make the case for novel fields of enquiry. Frey and Gallus consider how awards (often not financial awards) motivate behaviour in the context of crowding-out and crowding-in effects on intrinsic motivation. Fuzzy-trace theory (FTT), as put forward by Garavito, Weldon and Reyna in the chapter that follows is a partial return to the theme of neuroeconomics; FTT is a theory of judgement, decision making across the lifespan. In an entertaining and provocative Chapter 26, Russell Belk invites us to look to the future where the distinction between robots and humans will be blurred, which has implications for consumer self-definition; raising behavioural, moral and legal questions.

The end-piece picks up on a theme covered throughout the handbook: Behaviour change. This short contribution encourages readers to consider the 'pros' and 'cons' of contemporary international 'Nudge' initiatives.

I commend this new edition to you and the efforts all the contributors have made in improving communications between the two disciplines of psychology and economics.

Note

1 The literature is now huge, and the Dhami volume, which incorporates the findings from the behavioural economics research into economic theory, runs to over 1,700 pages.

References

Thaler, R., & Sunstein, C. (2008). *Nudge: Improving Decisions about Health, Wealth and Happiness.* London: Yale University Press.

Kagel, J., & Roth, A. (Eds.). (2015). *The Handbook of Experimental Economics*, Vol. 2. Princeton, New Jersey: Princeton University Press.

Dhami, S. (2016). *The Foundations of Behavioural Economic Analyses.* Oxford: Oxford University Press.

PART I

Theory & Method

1 Theory and Method in Economics and Psychology

Levels and Depth of Explanation

Denis Hilton

1.1 Introduction

Entering the twenty-first century, economics increasingly looked to psychology and neuroscience in order to revise its assumptions about how people process information and make choices. New subdisciplines of economics sprang up such as behavioural economics, psychological economics, cognitive economics, and neuroeconomics which drew extensively on findings in psychology and neuroscience. In addition, the new field of experimental economics enabled economists to test theories about human choice behaviour directly in controlled conditions. Economists increasingly abandoned the assumption that people are fully rational in their choices, and became increasingly interested in constructing and testing models which incorporate realistic assumptions about human thought and behaviour.

This chapter will take a psychologist's point of view on these developments. Despite the fact that economists and psychologists are often addressing the same fundamental question – why humans make the choices they do – there is often puzzlement about the other side's theory and methodology. These kinds of misunderstanding may not only reflect lack of knowledge of the background and aims of the other's discipline, but also of the historical context of the social sciences.

I will try to explain the aims and methods of economics in a way that will make their theoretical orientations seem more understandable to psychologists. I will first try to chart the various ways that economists are seeking to use psychology in their work. I will then suggest that economics – even of the new psychological kind – is still strongly rooted in a metatheoretical perspective that many psychologists would recognize as behaviourist. I will accordingly address two major questions about theoretical frameworks and scientific explanation. The first is to do with the issue of levels of explanation, and whether and how psychological level explanations can inform economic questions, and in turn whether and how neuroscience can inform economics. The second has to with depth of explanation, which contrasts psychology's more realist approach to constructing and testing sociocognitive processes in scientific explanations of behaviour to the more instrumental perspective of economics. I argue that this realist approach not only can lead to improved explanation of the facts, but to greater opportunities for modification of economic behaviour at both the individual and societal level.

This chapter therefore pays attention to differences in how theories are constructed and evaluated in the two disciplines. In my view, this perspective can shed light on the recent debate about methods in economics and psychology, which has focused on experimentation (e.g., Croson, 2005; Hertwig and Ortmann, 2001; 2003; Sugden, 2005b). I will suggest, for example, that much of the heat in this debate has been generated by differences in theoretical orientations (cognitivist and realist in the case of psychology, behaviourist and instrumentalist in the case of economics). While written from a psychologist's point of view, this chapter may still be useful to economists. Through throwing a different light on their assumptions and practices, it may help economists to reflect on their own professional identity and epistemological approach, in much the same way that spending a period abroad teaches us about our own national identities, through observing what raises foreigners' eyebrows.

1.2 Rational Behaviourism in Economics

At the beginning of the twentieth century, economics and psychology (like philosophy and linguistics) were confronted with the success of the natural sciences. Both attempted to adopt the methods of the natural sciences through taking behaviourist approaches (measuring observables, such as behaviours rather than thoughts and feelings in psychology, prices and market share rather than experienced value, etc., in economics). While psychology primarily adopted the experimental methods of the natural sciences, economists retained the eighteenth-century model of *homo economicus* as motivated by rational self-interest, but adopted mathematical formalisms to render their theories more precise and 'scientific'. In addition, they adopted the revealed preference axiom which assumes that preferences will be revealed in objectively measurable phenomena such as prices and market share (Lewin, 1996).

In this section, I identify some behaviourist characteristics of economics. This can be done by measuring economics up against Lyons' (1977) checklist for identifying behaviourist theories, namely, a rejection of internal states of the organism as scientific explanations of behaviour; a tendency to see no essential difference between the behaviour of humans and other animals; an emphasis on the importance of learning and reinforcement (positive and negative) in explaining behaviour; and a penchant for instrumentalist (i.e., predictive) rather than realist (i.e., explanatory) theories of behaviour.

1.2.2 Rational Behaviourism

The 'revealed preference' assumption embodies what might be called a 'rational behaviourist' approach, as it combines the rational self-interest model of choice with a behaviourist approach to measurement. To know an agent's preferences, one does not have to ask her; one simply observes what choices she makes. In addition, there are some important symmetries between economists' models of the rational calculation of self-interest and psychologists' models of how S-R associations are formed: both assume that with experience, the organism (or agent) will learn the costs and benefits associated with actions that it (she) takes. Both approaches emphasise the importance of learning and incentives for understanding behaviour.

The rational self-interest model effectively makes the same predictions as Thorndike's (1911) Law of Effect that links reward to response – any response that leads to a reward is likely to be repeated. In the language of 'rational behaviourism', this can be expressed as the price effect in economics – an activity can be encouraged by raising the price paid for its performance. Neoclassical economics – like behaviourist psychology – assumes that human behaviour will be explained by situational costs and benefits (gain-loss matrices, reward-punishment schedules). Economics assumed that no curiosity need be expressed about the intervening cognitive processes that led from stimulus to response (it was assumed that gain-loss matrices would be calculated correctly by rational choice processes), while radical behaviourism in psychology argued that no attention should be paid to intervening cognitive processes, as they were unobservable.

Although it may seem paradoxical that economists' model of *homo economicus* drawn from the eighteenth-century Enlightenment should yield essentially the same method of analysing behaviour as early-twentieth-century psychologists' model of *Rattus Norvegicus*, that is indeed what happened. Whereas nineteenth-century economists were interested in psychology and used it to explain economic phenomena (Bruni and Sugden, 2007), from the early-twentieth century onwards the revealed preference approach held that values and preferences of decision makers are to be inferred from observing them make choices under varying conditions. Economists, like behaviourist psychologists, abhorred finding out people's values and preferences just by asking them disinterested questions. Indeed, a striking illustration of the convergence of economics and behaviourism comes from the use of revealed preference theory to infer demand curves for animal preferences (Kagel et al., 1981).

1.2.2 Experimental Procedures in Economics and Psychology: The Debate over Learning and Incentives

Tellingly, the first line of defence that economists put up against the implications of psychologists' experimental findings on bias and error (e.g., Kahneman and Tversky, 1979) was that they were based on questionnaire research with no payoffs for correct responses. Experimental economists were sceptical about whether these findings would be reproduced with experienced, financially motivated participants who fully understood their task and who had opportunities to learn. This position is a variant of the *tabula rasa* theory that underpins behaviourism, in assuming that cognitive biases are 'malleable' rather than being inherently structured, and thus can be eliminated by appropriate market conditions. And indeed markets sometimes do eliminate biases: for example, List (2004) found that the procedure devised by Kahneman et al. (1986) to demonstrate the endowment effect (involving exchanging mugs for chocolate bars) works with normal consumers but not with expert dealers in picture cards of sports stars whose behaviour approximates to that predicted by the standard neoclassical model.

Nevertheless, the major result of economists' research on human bias and error has been to demonstrate how often biases in judgment and choice observed in experimental settings generalise to both real-world economic settings (Camerer, 2000; Hilton, 2001) and to experimental settings with financial incentives (Camerer and Hogarth, 1999; Hertwig and Ortmann, 2001). These reviews show that while incentives reduce (but do not eliminate) bias and error in approximately 55 per cent of cases, they have no effect in approximately 30 per cent of cases, and have paradoxical effects (i.e., actually *increase* bias and error) in approximately 15 per cent of cases. On the whole, then, these results vindicate the cognitive programme of research of psychology, since they show that the way cognitive processes frame how people perceive reality will indeed affect their behaviour independently of learning and incentives.

1.2.3 The Costs and Benefits of the Behaviourist Stance: Instrumentalism Versus Realism in Explanation

A common puzzle for psychologists is to understand how economists can hold on to the rational self-interest model of human choice and behaviour. After all, it has been so clearly discredited by innumerable experimental studies. The clue to this puzzle may be that psychologists' aims in developing models of choice are different from those of economists. Whereas psychologists aim to develop *realist* models of cognitive processes that are accurate and testable descriptions of how the human mind works, economists' aims in building models are often much more pragmatic. In particular, economists seek models of choice that will be useful in helping them understand and explain economic questions at the collective level, concerning market behaviour, prices, laws, institutions and so on. So if many economists hold on to the rational choice model despite its evident falsity as an exact descriptive model of individual human choice, they may adhere to it for other reasons, such as its simplicity and elegance in generating more-or-less correct implications for understanding these higher-level economic questions. This *instrumentalist* position means that these economists are likely to give up the standard expected utility (SEU) model of choice only if a more psychologically plausible model enables them to make significantly better predictions about economic questions such as market share and prices, or help them write more effective contracts and legislation (cf. Sugden, 2005b).

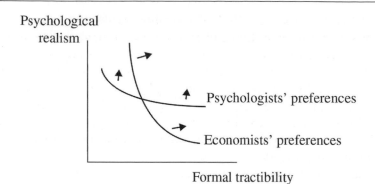

Figure 1.1. *Indifference curves for theory preferences among economists and psychologists (from Rabin, 2002).*

Rabin (2002) cleverly models these different orientations of economists and psychologists with indifference curves (see Figure 1.1). Economists' preference for models is strongly influenced by their formal properties (elegance, tractability), and less so by their realism and descriptive accuracy. For psychologists, the inverse is true.

1.3 Levels and Kinds of Explanation

We have seen that despite the diversity of ways (behavioural, psychological, cognitive, neuro- and experimental) in which economists have integrated psychological insights into economic theorising, each of these subdisciplines possesses significant assumptions that differentiate them from experimental psychology. However, I will argue that economists' use of psychology and neuroscience is likely to profit from careful attention to two questions.

The first, which I term the 'levels of explanation' question, concerns distinguishing between economic (social), psychological and neuroscientific levels of explanation, and the ways in which these levels of explanation interrelate. I will argue for a hierarchical model of scientific questions and explanation, where explanations are constrained but not determined by explanations at a lower level. I first illustrate this generative model of explanation by showing how properties of collectives (e.g., markets) may emerge from (and be explained by) lower-level properties of their components (agents). In turn, I consider how properties of agents may emerge from (and be explained by) properties of their brains. However, I conclude that economics cannot be reduced directly to neuroscience: an intermediate level of psychological explanation is necessary.

Having established the need for an autonomous psychological level of explanation, I then turn to the second 'depth of explanation' question. Here I address the need at the cognitive (psychological) level of explanation to develop theories that are explanatory in nature, and which thus offer greater power for prediction and control than 'shallow' behaviourist style explanation, which I will show to still be often favoured in psychologically inspired economics.

1.3.1 Levels of Scientific Question: Economics, Psychology and Neuroscience

Economics, psychology and neuroscience have different objects of study and pose their scientific questions at different levels. Economics typically studies the behaviour of collective phenomena such as firms, markets and prices, and asks questions like: how can markets achieve efficient allocation of goods? What causes markets to fail? Psychology typically studies the individual; individuals' personalities; the way they perceive, remember and make judgments and choices; and asks questions like: what causes depression in an individual? Why do people make irrational choices? Neuroscience typically studies brains, mapping brain anatomy and circuits, and relating this to functional processes such as vision, hearing and decision-making. So far, neuroscience seems to focus more on mapping what parts of the brain or brain circuits are associated with different psychological functions (e.g., short- vs. long-term memory; emotional vs. 'rational' decision-making) than in answering theoretically driven questions (see Table 1.1).

Of course, the picture given in Table 1.1 is something of an oversimplification, as it is easy to see points of overlap. For example, while economists following in the tradition of Hayek see economies as 'brains' that transmit information (cf. Forsyth et al., 1992), and the social psychology of group processes examines how information flows around groups in a way that is close in spirit to this kind of economic analysis (e.g., Latané and Nowak, 1991). But the important point is to see that different levels of scientific question exist, and to understand how questions at one level can be answered by facts, assumptions or hypotheses that draw on another level.

1.3.2 Generative Explanation: How Economic Phenomena Can Emerge from Psychological Characteristics

A cornerstone of classical economics has been to explain a seemingly paradoxical result: how socially desirable equilibrium states can emerge from a society of uniquely self-interested actors (Smith, 1776; Turgot, 1761). This can be explained in the following way. If there is a lack of grain at Toulouse due to crop failure but a surplus at Limoges where the harvest was good, prices will rise in Toulouse and drop in Limoges. This will have two advantages. First, the high prices in Toulouse will discourage people there from hoarding grain because it will be too expensive, thus encouraging grain to be distributed to more people. And second, the higher prices in Toulouse will attract grain from Limoges through encouraging an entrepreneur to buy low in Limoges, and

Table 1.1 *Three levels of scientific question and associated scientific disciplines*

Domains of study (level of question)	Level of explanation	Kinds of science
Market behaviour *Small group decision-making*	Human collectives	Economics Social psychology of groups
Cognitive processes in judgment and decision-making *Individual values and preferences*	Human individuals	Cognitive psychology Social cognition Artificial intelligence
Brain and body function	Brain, body parts, systems	Neuroscience

accept the cost (and risk) of shipping grain to Toulouse in order to sell high there. These classic market mechanisms make some hypotheses about human nature: namely, that some people are smart enough to spot opportunities, and greedy enough to take the risks necessary to exploit them.

In science as in common sense, questions typically arise when we need to know how something surprising or undesirable has come about (Weiner, 1985). We can see that Smith's famous example of the "hidden hand" that redistributes goods to where they are needed is so powerful because it shows how surprising properties (e.g., a socially desirable distribution mechanism) can emerge from a self-organizing system based on actors whose sole motive is rational self-interest. The point of the example is that market success occurs *because* (not *in spite*) of a psychological property of its agents – their self-interest. Smith's equilibrium model is a paradigm case of generative explanation (Harré, 1988) which shows how an effect (social welfare in the distribution of goods) can be produced by a mechanism (prices) built of components that possess specified (but unexplained) causal powers (selfish agents). The kind of explanation involved here thus seems to consist in building a model which *can* generate the effects of interest (cf. Sugden, 2000).

1.3.3 Questions about Deviations: The Logic of Contrastive Explanation

Following Smith, neoclassical economics established efficient market theory as an ideal mechanism for the distribution of goods. Subsequent theories in economics have taken *homo economicus* and efficient market theory as a foil, and have sought to explain deviations from this 'norm' (e.g., Sugden, 2005b). Such 'contrastive explanation' (Hesslow, 1983; 1988; Lipton, 1991) may seek to identify as a cause the property in the deviation model is different to standard SEU theory that 'makes the difference' between the effect observed (a market anomaly) and what should be expected according to efficient market theory. The kind of explanation involved here seems to involve counterfactual reasoning about what will happen if we *modify* a certain characteristic of the SEU/ efficient market model. Deviation models can focus either on market failures or on psychological 'irrationality' for explanations of market anomalies.

1.3.3.1 *Within-Level Explanation: Explaining Market Anomalies through Market Failure*

In a classical form of explanation in economics, questions will be resolved by explanations which stay at the same level of analysis. For example, a market anomaly will be explained by a market failure (e.g., failure of buyers and sellers to have access to the same information about the quality of the product). For example, Akerlof's (1970) analysis of 'lemons' shows that in markets of rational actors where there is asymmetric information (e.g., sellers of used cars know more about the quality of the car than potential buyers), the price of used cars will drop dramatically as buyers assume that sellers will only offer low-quality cars (lemons) leading rational buyers to refuse to pay high prices. So sellers will in turn not be motivated to sell high-quality cars, and only low-quality cars will be offered for sale. This leads to 'adverse selection' in the market, as bad products drive out good products, leading the example to be presented as showing how 'asymmetric information can result in market failure' (Pindyck and Rubinfield, 1998, p 620; see also Sugden, 2000, for a more detailed exposition of Akerlof's argument). Here the explanation for market failure is found in terms of market characteristics (distribution of information in the market), rather than in terms of the irrationalities of individuals.

Similarly, typical explanations in psychology stay 'in-house' at the same level. For example, decisions to choose a certain diet can be predicted by a weighted combination of our beliefs that the diet will work, the desirability of being thinner for us, the desirability of being thinner for important others, and our desire to please those others (Ajzen and Fishbein, 1980). However, with the advent of neurosciences, much thought has gone into how psychological-level explanations (in terms of beliefs, desires, rules of inference, etc.) can be constrained by what is known about the components of the system (serial or parallel computer, brain) on which these algorithms run (Marr, 1982). Consequently, interesting properties at one level of explanation can emerge from the properties of the components at a lower level.

1.3.3.2 *Cross-Level Explanation: Explaining Market Failure through Psychological Characteristics*

In cross-level explanation, the underlying psychological properties of market agents can also be used to explain market failure. Efficient market theory assumes that under the right market conditions (e.g., informational symmetry between buyers and sellers), markets composed of fully rational agents will allow goods to be exchanged to the benefit of both parties. However, change the nature of the component parts of the system and new properties will emerge in the system itself. For example, if we assume – following Kahneman and Tversky's (1979) prospect theory – that losses loom larger than gains in the minds of market agents – then markets can lose liquidity because of the 'disposition effect' (Shefrin and Statman, 1985), as agents refuse to trade goods of equivalent value because the experienced loss has higher disutility than the experienced gain has utility for them.

This 'disposition effect' could explain anomalies such as that observed in the British housing market in the early 1990s when a dramatic fall in house prices meant that many owners would have to sell houses at a loss compared to what they had paid before the market collapsed. Of course, because of the market collapse, they could also buy other houses cheaper. But loss aversion would explain why many would continue to live for months and even years in a house in one city (say Manchester) while commuting four hours to another (such as Edinburgh) where they had taken a job, with all the attendant commuting costs and dislocation of personal and family life. The psychological hurt that would be caused by selling a house at a loss would outweigh the gain incurred by buying one in their new place of work.

1.4 Explanation across Two Levels: Is Neuroeconomics Possible?

A question that merits consideration is whether intelligible explanations can be achieved by going down *two* levels (e.g., from economics through psychology to neuroscience). Scientific explanation often proceeds by attributing a phenomenon to some disposition of another entity, which serves as the end-point in an explanatory chain. In turn, the explanation can be expanded by attributing this disposition to the disposition of another entity at a lower level, which is attributed with a unexplained 'causal power' to produce the effects it does. As Harré (1988 p 142 writes):

> the chemical behaviour of liquids, solids and gases is explained by the behaviour of unobservables, molecules and chemical atoms … But one might well ask for an explanation of the behaviour of chemical atoms, for example why do they chum up in the proportions they do? The next level of explanation simply repeats the pattern of the level above. Drawing on the behaviour of positively and negatively electrically charged bodies as a source-model, a further step is taken, in which electrically charged electrons and protons are invoked, the story being filled out with neutral neutrons. The electrical properties of these structures explain the differences in behaviour of chemical atoms.

As we shall see in this section, this kind of reductionism across levels of explanations seems to be a pattern of explanation envisaged in what has come to be called 'neuroeconomics'.

Economists have seemed to be in two minds (brains?) about how neuro-science will inform economics: as Camerer, Loewenstein and Prelec (2005, p. 9) write:

> Some important insights will surely come from neuroscience, either directly or because neuroscience will reshape what is believed about psychology which in turn informs economics.

Other economists clearly write as if they favour the direct route. For example, Fehr et al. (2005) assert that neuroeconomic studies 'enable us to go beyond the prevailing "as if" approach in economics by uncovering the neural mechanisms behind individual decisions'. The psychological level of explanation appeared to be overlooked in this merger (cf. Rusticini, 2005). This was all the more surprising as the seminal 'neuroeconomic' studies that Fehr et al. cite (Breiter et al., 2001; Rilling et al., 2003; Sanfey et al., 2003) are in fact due to collaborations between psychologists, ethologists and neuroscientists.

Nevertheless, it is easy to see that Fehr et al.'s theoretical argumentation requires a psychological level of description (tastes, preferences), and is supported by psychological observations (questionnaire and behavioural evidence). They begin by reviewing experimental evidence that shows that people possess 'other-dependent preferences' that are inconsistent with the rational self-interest model. For example, they establish the accuracy of this psychological level description of human nature through reviewing relevant experimental evidence which persistently shows that people have 'a taste for revenge', that is, they will forgo personal rewards in order to punish people who transgress social norms in experimental games. They then ask the question:

> Why do we observe these strong deviations from the predictions of the standard model? What are the driving decisions behind the decision to trust, to reciprocate trust, and to punish non-reciprocation?

They then describe a study by De Quervain et al. (2004) in which one participant (player A) was given the opportunity to punish a partner (player B) who had abused her in a previous round of a sequential social dilemma game, even though this would incur financial cost. Noting that 'questionnaire and behavioural evidence indicates that player A indeed had a strong desire to punish the defector', they argue that punishment of the defector has intrinsic utility for her because it is associated with activation in the dorsal striatum, a zone associated with pleasure and reward in the primate brain. Neuroscience evidence is thus used to support the psychological level assertion that people have a taste for revenge on those who have wronged them.

1.4.1 The Autonomy of Levels of Explanation

The Dequervain et al. study is informative about the origin of a psychological taste for revenge. It does not support the idea, for example, that people learn to take revenge for reputational reasons, and may therefore be relevant to economic theories about how people come to acquire this taste (see Fehr and Schmidt, 2006, for a review). But it does not obviate the necessity of a psychological level explanation, as I show in this section.

To answer this question, the appropriate test requires counterfactual reasoning. If experiments on social control had turned out differently (say people were not prepared to pay to punish transgressions of social norms), we could not conclude that people had a taste for revenge, and we would not be able to use this concept to explain economic phenomena. However, if Dequervain et al.'s (2004) results had turned out differently (no difference was found in brain functioning in the dorsal striatum as a function of opportunities to take revenge), this result would of course necessitate a new theory of how taste for revenge comes to be a human characteristic. However, it would have no implication for the first link in the chain of explanation: economic anomalies could still be explained by a psychological taste for revenge. This example shows that the psychological level of explanation is autonomous, and cannot be reduced to (i.e., substituted by) a neuroscientific one.

It is easy to see that a similar intransitivity of causation will arise in other examples. For example, we have seen in the preceding how asymmetric reaction to gains and losses modelled by prospect theory can explain the disposition effect, thus illustrating how economic phenomena at the market level can be explained through reference to the psychological properties of the agents in that market. In turn, we might seek to explain this asymmetry in valuing gains and losses in terms of the differential reaction of the fronto-median area of the cortex, which shows twice as much brain activity in reaction to losses as compared to gains (Gehring and Willoughby, 2002). One may speculate that if fronto-median activity vehicles experienced utility, then this may explain why losses loom larger than gains. But once again, even if Gehring and Willoughby's results had turned out differently, this would not invalidate prospect theory, which could still explain the disposition effect in market behaviour. It would not matter at all to prospect theory's relevance to explaining economic behaviour if its value function were found to be calculated in the left knee rather than the right knee. Indeed, the fact that prospect theory has been developed in psychology and applied to economics before the relevant neuroscience theories have been performed serves to illustrate the limitations of neuroscientific level theories for economic theories per se.

1.4.2 Neuroeconomics as Social Cognitive Neuroscience

While neuroeconomics offers the promise of many important insights, its import for economics will not bypass the need for a psychological level of explanation. Its importance for economists will be to buttress explanations of economic behaviour motivated by psychological assumptions, and in this chapter we will review recent work by economists in this vein. The recent revival of interest in explaining economic behaviour through reference to underlying psychological processes is not new in economics. As Bruni and Sugden (2007) show, nineteenth-century economists hypothesised that psychological phenomena could explain economic behaviour. For example, the law of diminishing marginal utility, which states that as consumption of any commodity increases, the increment of pleasure produced by a given increment of its consumption falls, was seen as a special case of the Weber–Fechner law of psychophysics. Bruni and Sugden suggest that economics' attempt to dispense with underlying psychological levels of explanation for economic phenomena came in with Wilfred Pareto in the 1930s and 1940s and has now run its course.

For psychologists, neuroeconomics might best be thought of as a subbranch of social cognitive neuroscience, with a particular interest in economic questions and use of experimental economic techniques (such as experimental games) to induce emotional states such as envy, guilt and desire for revenge. In contrast, social psychologists have studied emotions such as shame, regret and guilt through asking participants to imagine such scenarios (e.g., Smith et al., 2002), and neuroscience studies have used similar scenario techniques (Berthoz et al., 2002). However, *experimental* games of the kind devised by economists allow researchers to generate real emotional states in controlled conditions. In this sense, the more behavioural orientation of economists has opened up an exciting line of inquiry for psychologists interested in the study of emotion (e.g., de Hooge, Zeelenberg, and Breugelmans, 2007; Mazar and Zhong, 2010).

1.5 Depth of Explanation: On Creating and Testing Cognitive Theories in Economics

Having proposed a hierarchical structure that may help understand the scope of economic, psychological and neuroscientific levels of explanation, and how they may fruitfully be demarcated from and interact with each other, I will now concentrate on the cognitive level of explanation. I will first attempt to explain why economists and psychologists formulate and test cognitive theories in systematically different ways. I begin by setting the present dialogue between economists and psychologists in a historical context, notably the rise of behaviourism in the twentieth century, which I will argue is still more influential in contemporary economics than in psychology. I then attempt to clarify what are each discipline's fundamental 'paradigms' (in a Kuhnian sense, i.e., preferred research questions, frameworks and techniques).

Economics has been essentially a deductive science (if that is possible), which works from axioms to deduce 'results' (e.g., about what a market equilibrium price should be, etc.). For economists, a 'result' is very often a theoretical prediction about what behaviour should be expected given a set of assumptions, and which is mathematically derived from a set of axioms. For example, Biais and Pouget (1999) prove that in the trading game devised by Plott and Sunder (1988) there should be no trading at all if all actors in the game are fully rational (Bayesian), as all rational actors will recognise that in these markets with asymmetric information, only offers that lose the agent money will be accepted by a rational counterparty. For Biais and Pouget (1999), this constitutes a 'result', even though they knew full well that it was quite wrong as a descriptive model of how humans behave (there is in fact considerable trading in these markets). The mathematical formalisation characteristic of economic theories helps spell out how the prediction must follow from the theory's presuppositions.

On the other hand, psychology (like physics, chemistry, biology etc.) is essentially inductive in nature, using experimental results to validate theories. For psychologists, a 'result' is obtained when the predictions of a theory have withstood experimental test better than the predictions of other rival theories. Although psychological theories are rarely expressed in mathematical form, psychologists generally follow the procedure of 'strong inference' in which successive explanations are generated and eliminated by a programme of experimental research.[1]

It is only recently that economics has come to adopt the method of strong inference that is characteristic of mature experimental sciences (Platt, 1964). To gauge this, it suffices to read the way Fehr and Schmidt (2006) introduce their experimental research programme on other-dependent preferences. Having described the existence of various alternatives to choice models that depend purely on rational self-interest, they write:

> One of the exciting aspects of this development is that the newly developed theories of other-regarding preferences were tested in a new wave of experiments, sometimes before they were published ... These experiments ... show that it is possible to discriminate between different motivational assumptions.

No contemporary psychologist would have felt it necessary to write such a passage for his peers. Indeed, many psychologists would find it hard to believe that theories could be published in respectable scientific journals without accompanying experimental tests. In fairness to economics, it should be noted that deriving predictions about market behaviour from assumptions about the characteristics of agents is often not a trivial affair, and often a significant scientific contribution in its own right. Indeed, the programme of research described by Fehr and Schmidt (2006) combines the best of both worlds: mathematical rigour in deriving nontrivial predictions from theories, and experimental rigour in seeking the observations that will discriminate between those theories.

1.6 Depth of Explanation: The Cognitive Revolution in Psychology

While economics still adopted a behaviourist position, psychology increasingly drew on analogies with computer science that demonstrated the reality of cognitive processes, and inspired by Broadbent, Bruner, Chomsky, Piaget, Simon and others, the discipline underwent a cognitive revolution. Psychology at this point sought inspiration from artificial intelligence and formal linguistics to create cognitive theories with a strong structuralist flavour that typically distinguish information-processing systems (automatic vs. controlled; short vs. long-term memory systems; visual vs. auditory vs. articulatory short-term memory stores; 'modules' for language, social cognition etc.). This was accompanied by a distinctive kind of theory building and testing, which aims at 'deep' explanations, which posit unobservable entities which *generate* the observed phenomena in question. I attempt to describe how such deep explanation using hypothesised causal models that generate behaviour differs from 'shallow' behaviourist explanation below.

The story I am about to tell is apocryphal, and may or may not be true. No matter, as it will still serve to illustrate why psychologists abandoned behaviourist theories for the kind of cognitive theories that enable explanatory models of the kind they build and test today. According to the story, psychologists discovered that Welsh-speaking children were poorer at mental arithmetic than English-speaking children. A behaviourist should be satisfied with this discovery, for he could specify a set of externally observable stimulus conditions (S, speaking Welsh vs. speaking English) which would predict how well a child would respond (R) on an externally observable task (problems requiring mental arithmetic). The explanation would satisfy the classic schema of behaviourism:

$$S \rightarrow R$$

There were, however, some problems with this explanation. Although predictive, it lacks explanatory power: we still don't know *why* Welsh children are worse at mental arithmetic than English children. Another is one of coherence: since mental arithmetic is taken as a sign of mental ability, difference in performance would seem to imply that Welsh children have less ability than English ones, which seems implausible (even though I am English).

The puzzle can however be easily resolved by a cognitive theory in terms of limited working memory capacity. The Welsh words for numbers are longer than the English ones (which are generally monosyllabic), and therefore take up more space in verbal working memory, causing less items of information to be rehearsed, thus leading to less effective performance on the mental arithmetic tasks. The explanation now includes an O term that represents mental operations that intervene between stimulus and response and takes the form:

S->O->R

The explanation is more satisfying: it explains why performance is different in Welsh and English children in positing a *mechanism* that shows *how* the difference can be produced. It also resolves the question of coherence: the worse performance of the Welsh-speaking children is attributed to their language, not to their intelligence. The cognitive explanation is in the sense 'deeper' as it *explains how* the phenomenon comes about. The behaviourist explanation is 'shallow', since it only *predicts* when the phenomenon should be observed.

In addition, the hypothesised mechanism suggests some simple experiments to test the theory: find a group of bilingual children and, using a counterbalanced experimental design, ask them to solve matched sets of problems in Welsh and English. Here, according to the theory, differences in performance should be expected in the same children. Another experiment would be to suppress verbal rehearsal in both Welsh- and English-speaking children, for example by asking them to perform a concurrent verbal task while doing the arithmetic. Here, according to the theory, differences in performance should be eliminated.

This is how psychologists typically use strong inference to test a theory. They use the theory to generate hypotheses that are tested through controlled experimentation, allowing causal induction through application of Mill's (1872/1973) method of difference, the fundamental canon of scientific induction. They therefore vary the presence and absence of the putative cause (speaking Welsh vs. speaking English while doing mental arithmetic) to see if it has the expected effects on the effect of interest (performance on the mental arithmetic task). They also use techniques to interfere with the operation of the cause when present (e.g., distraction to block mental rehearsal). This is because they believe short-term memory buffers to be *real* entities, which can be knocked out by appropriate procedures. In this, they seem no different to physicists who believe in the reality of atoms, nuclei and electrons, but who infer their existence through theory-laden experimental observation techniques because they cannot observe them directly (Hacking, 1983).

This has led psychology to a blend of cognitive theorising and experimental validation which favours "mini-models" which can explain a set of experimentally controlled observations. Models are tested by manipulating the presence and absence of hypothesised causal factors (and disablers) that the theory predicts should have an effect. In this way, psychologists seek to demonstrate their understanding of a phenomenon by constructing experiments in which they can make a phenomenon appear and disappear as the result of appropriate manipulations predicted by the theory being tested. As an example of this 'now you see, now you don't' approach to explaining a phenomenon, framing effects support prospect theory because presenting a gamble in terms of gains induces risk aversion, whereas framing it in terms of losses produces risk seeking. For psychologists, it is usually far more important to publish 'experimental results' that are predicted by a theory than to show how predictions can be deduced from that theory. Mathematics rarely comes into play, being usually considered an inessential distraction.

1.7 The Need for Cognitive Explanation: Incentives, Overconfidence and Statistical Methodology

In this section, I review two cases in detail where I argue that psychologically inspired economics could benefit from 'deeper' cognitive theories in two domains that have attracted substantial attention from psychologically inspired economists: incentives and overconfidence. Finally, I discuss how the disciplines appear to favour statistical tests that favour their metatheoretical orientations.

1.7.1 The Behaviourist Economics of Incentives: Rediscovering the Need for Cognitive Theories

Psychology cast off the mantle of behaviourism in the 1950s, in part due to demonstrations that Thorndike's Law of Effect cannot explain significant parts of human behaviour. A notable example is Festinger and Carlsmith's (1959) work on the paradoxical effects of reward, which showed that increasing payment for a boring task could actually lead to *less* motivation to perform it, which they interpreted in terms of reduction of cognitive dissonance. Later research in psychology has pointed to the importance of 'intrinsic motivation' in performing many tasks, and the fact that external incentives can undermine this intrinsic motivation (a phenomenon called 'crowding out' by economists).

An economist who has done much to call the attention of his colleagues to the implications of relevant work in psychology on the 'crowding out' of motivation is Frey (1997). But even here – in an economist who is both very knowledgeable about and sympathetic to psychology – the theoretical statements have a distinctly behaviourist feel in the way they detail a set of conditions in which crowding out should and should not occur. Following his review of the literature, Frey suggests that incentives "crowd out" intrinsic motivation when there is:

- Intrinsic interest of the task
- Personal relationship of principal and agent
- Participation of agent in principal's decisions
- And when employees
  - are only rewarded for doing the work specified (no promotions, honours, prizes etc.)
  - Perceive rewards as 'controlling' rather than 'supportive'

Although this is a very useful summary of when intrinsic motivation is crowded out, it gives little in the way of specifying psychological mechanisms that bind these conditions into a single, coherent explanation that explains *how* and *why* crowding out occurs. Four of the five conditions given specify situational characteristics, and only one refers to cognition (perception of the intention behind the reward).

An experimental field study on incentives gives an even clearer example of how a behaviourist orientation still appears to guide psychologically inspired economic theorising and research. Gneezy and Rusticini (2000) have shown that fining parents for coming late to collect their kids from school actually causes them to come late even more often than a control group that was not fined. This is a classic demonstration of a paradoxical effect of a (dis)incentive, of the kind identified by Festinger and Carlsmith (1959). But while Festinger and Carlsmith used their data to sound the death knell of behaviourism in psychology, arguing that cognitive processes (e.g., dissonance reduction) have to be invoked, Gneezy and Rusticini do not go beyond their demonstration to develop and test rival cognitive theories that explain *why* they get their effect.[2]

Gneezy and Rusticini are quite aware of the kinds of cognitive theories that could explain the paradoxical effects of incentives in their study. One hypothesis that they evoke (but do not test) is that offering money changes the participants' perception of the exchange relationship. For example, one can predict, following the Durkheimian analysis proposed by Tetlock et al. (2000), that in *sacred* domains (e.g., giving blood, giving time to help immigrant children), offering money for a greater engagement would be perceived as insulting, as it would call into question the actor's generosity. However, in *profane* domains (e.g., working overtime for an accountancy firm, taking on more responsibilities in an office), offering an incentive for more work would be perceived as a compliment by the employee because it confirms the perceived competence of the worker. These hypotheses were confirmed in a questionnaire study using hypothetical scenarios (Buscato et al., 2004). The fact that offering money can be perceived negatively by the intended recipient has been documented by Burgoyne and Routh (1991), in their study of the unacceptability of money as a gift, for example, at Christmas. Insights such as these have led some economists to develop cognitive models that allow predictions to be made about when crowding out effects are likely to occur (see section 1.8.1).

1.7.1.1 *Explanation, Prediction and Control*

Based on economic research on incentives, we would have some predictive statements we can make. Based on a simple induction from empirical studies (Camerer and Hogarth, 1999; Hertwig and Ortmann, 2001), we could predict (say) that incentives work 55 per cent of the time, have no effect 30 per cent of the time and have paradoxical effects 15 per cent of the time. We could be still more specific and note that paradoxical effects are obtained only in tasks using judgments and decisions, and never in games and markets (cf. Hertwig and Ortmann, 2003). Or we could use Frey's (1997) typology to specify when we would expect incentives to work, and when we should get paradoxical effects. But we would be still lacking a theory about an underlying mechanism that explains why we should get normal incentive effects in some cases, and paradoxical effects in others. For example, Bénabou and Tirole (2003) suggested that parents' decisions about when to propose incentives to their children will be based on experience about when they work. But this 'explanation' still seems to fall short for a cognitive theorist – it is a bit like explaining language learning through 'experience' – but what exactly would this tell us about the grammatical rules that are being learned here?

In more recent work, Bénabou and Tirole (2006) have proposed more detailed models which draw heavily on psychological research and attempt to model the implicit trade-off between motivation and accuracy in belief formation among economic agents. While drawing on similar roots (e.g., cognitive dissonance theory) and taking an essentially similar position to psychological models of self-enhancement and self-protection (e.g., Alicke and Sedikides, 2009), there has recently been a substantial effort to use this perspective to test predictions about economic behaviour (Bénabou and Tirole, 2016). As in recent social psychological theorising about the self, this approach assumes that people want to see themselves (and to be seen by others) as attractive, competent and good. Importantly, new predictions have been made through drawing on distinctively economic analyses, such as contract theory, which enables the prediction that if an employer proposes a high wage for performing a task, then an employee can infer that the task is difficult or unpleasant. Significantly, this inference is only justified if the employee believes that the employer has information about the difficulty of the task – and when told that the employer has no such information, the effect is eliminated (Bremzen et al., 2015). Other work suggests that offering extrinsic financial incentives for a prosocial task (earning money for a socially approved charity) will lead an agent to work less hard for that charity when it is disclosed to others than when it is not (Ariely et al., 2009). This is because when the agent's financial interest in performing a prosocial behaviour is made public, the agent may have an incentive to appear altruistic to observers by not working too hard.

To a social psychologist, the preceding kind of phenomena studied – whereby inferences are made about the motives of the employer (or principal) and the employee (or agent) – are of course very reminiscent of the preoccupations of attribution theory. In this regard, it is no accident that a major impulse to attribution theory was given by the challenge of understanding how experimental participants would react to incentives in cognitive dissonance experiments (Hilton, 2012). It may be that attribution theory may have a role to play in offering a theoretical clarification of how incentives and disincentives are *perceived* and *interpreted*, thus placing researchers in a better position to predict their effects and to propose ways of framing them such that they will be perceived in a way that will make them work. A similar situation exists in research on whether an initial (im)moral action should lead an actor to engage in more of the same (consistency effects such as the foot-in-the-door effect; Freedman and Fraser, 1966) or to less of the same (inconsistency or 'compensation' effects such as moral licensing; Mazar and Zhong, 2010; see also Joosten et al., 2014). Knowing when an initial act will lead to more subsequent moral (e.g., proenvironmental) behaviour and when it will lead to less should be useful information to managers and policy makers, but addressing this question needs psychological theories which explain when and why one of these effects should occur.

In conclusion, we have seen that there has been a movement in the last twenty years from documenting the existence of 'paradoxical' economic behaviour (notably the crowding-out phenomenon whereby adding a financial incentive actually decreases the propensity to perform that behaviour) to proposing cognitive models that explain *why* these effects occur and make testable predictions about *when* they occur. The usefulness of this cognitive level of analysis no doubt helps explain why textbooks on organisational behaviour abound with policy recommendations based on psychological research, just as consumer behaviour textbooks make extensive use of cognitive models of persuasion to make recommendations about how to design messages.

1.7.2 From Overconfidence to Kinds of Overconfidence

A cognitive hypothesis that received much attention from behavioural economists is that overconfidence leads investors to lose money on financial markets. Using theoretical arguments, Odean (1998; see also Benos 1998; Daniel, Hirshleifer and Subrahmanyam,1998) showed that overconfidence (in two distinct senses: [a] considering oneself to have better information than other market players; and [b] overestimating the precision of one's information) should lead to poor performance in financial markets. In addition, Barber and Odean (2001) produced a behavioural 'demonstration' of overconfidence using a database on private investors obtained from a large bank, and found that men tend to trade more than women and incurred greater losses due to failure to make profits that offset transaction costs. Using gender as a proxy for overconfidence, they argued that this result demonstrates that men are more overconfident than women, and that this overconfidence leads to lower trading profits.

Let us consider the logic of these demonstrations. First, while the theoretical demonstrations that the two kinds of overconfidence (in oneself compared to others, or in the precision of one's information) will lead to suboptimal performance provides two sufficient causes for the losses observed by Barber and Odean (2001), there is no independent evidence that they were indeed the effective causes. Second, Barber and Odean obtained no direct measure of overconfidence (in either sense) in their market participants, but used gender as a proxy for overconfidence. As research has persistently failed to find gender differences in miscalibration (Gigerenzer, Hoffrage and Kleinbolting, 1991), miscalibration (overestimating the precision of one's information) cannot explain the difference in male and female trading behaviour. Either it is overconfidence in the second sense (in oneself compared to others) that explains this effect, or something else yet again. The theoretical demonstrations that suboptimal performance should result from overconfidence in either sense are only demonstrations that these *can* be causes of a particular effect; they are not demonstrations that these processes *are* the *actual* causes in a particular observed case.

To obtain evidence that these processes actually are causes of the effect in question, we need to use experimental methods combined with scientific realism to verify the presence of the hypothesised underlying processes. Using an experimental financial market with asymmetric information, Biais et al. (2005) replicated Barber and Odean's finding that men trade more than women. However, Biais et al. (2005) found no correlation between gender and overconfidence in judgment. Biais et al. (2005) used a quasi-experimental method to study the effect of overconfidence, which they operationalised using a questionnaire test of miscalibration, where participants were required to answer general knowledge questions through setting 90 per cent confidence intervals on their responses (Alpert and Raiffa, 1982). This gave them an independent means to classify participants as high or low in miscalibration (i.e., the tendency to overestimate the precision of one's judgments), and thus allowed them to show that miscalibration did not explain overall differences in male and female earnings. Finally, Biais et al. (2005) sought to pass the 'Now you see it, now you don't' test by showing that miscalibration (as predicted) hurt traders in 'winner's curse traps' (situations where the stated price was a poor indicator of real asset value) but not when prices were good signals of real asset value.

To summarise: while gender affects trading behaviour, and overconfidence in judgment leads to lower profits in an experimental financial market, there is no evidence (*pace* Barber and Odean) that gender produces lower profits in men due to their greater miscalibration of judgment. It is of course possible that gender causes lower profits in men through another *kind* of overconfidence than miscalibration in judgment. In fact, Odean's (1998) theoretical model contains two parameters for overconfidence: one representing overconfidence in the precision of one's knowledge (i.e., underestimating conditional uncertainty); and another representing a belief that one has better information than other agents. Miscalibration of judgment appears to correspond to the first kind of overconfidence, whereas 'positive illusions' (Taylor and Brown, 1988) that the self is superior to others, has high control over outcomes and such, appear to correspond to the second kind of overconfidence. In fact, psychologists have since shown that the tendency to make miscalibrated judgments is not correlated with the tendency to entertain positive illusions such as the better-than-average effect, unrealistic optimism and high perceptions of personal control (Hilton et al., 2011; see also Moore and Healy, 2008).

Distinguishing kinds of overconfidence and careful operationalisation of these constructs allows more fine-grained predictions to be made (as predicted in the first edition of this chapter). For example, the distinction between positive illusions and judgmental overconfidence is consistent with Glaser and Weber's (2007) finding that traders who believe that they are better than others will trade more while there is no corresponding tendency for traders who are highly miscalibrated to trade more (see Hilton, 2006, for further discussion of the potential implications of this distinction).

1.7.3 Statistical Methods for Testing Causal Models: Interacting and Mediating Variables

Finally, economists and psychologists' different theoretical orientations seem to show up in the preferences for statistical tests shown by editors in the respective fields, which Croson (2005) calls 'surprisingly parochial'. She notes that economists prefer regression analyses whereas psychologists prefer analysis of variance (ANOVA) despite the close formal similarity of these techniques. Psychologists probably favour ANOVA because, for example, the different levels of a variable can reflect the levels of experimental manipulations. In addition, ANOVA automatically calculates interaction terms which reveal the 'now you see it, now you don't' nature of causal production/prevention of an effect (e.g., risk aversion vs. risk seeking) depending on facilitating/blocking conditions (e.g., gain vs. loss framing).

On the other hand, experimental economists prefer regressions, probably because this is the preferred method for expressing predictions in the field. Croson (2005) notes correctly that they steer away from interaction terms – an observation confirmed by our own experience. In Biais et al. (2005), we originally used an interaction term in our regression analysis to show that miscalibration hurt traders' earnings in winner's curse traps but not in other market situations. However, the editor supported a reviewer who requested that we calculate two separate regressions for winner's curse traps and other market situations.

Finally, a statistical method that has spread like wildfire in social psychology and organizational behaviour in the last thirty years is causal path analysis (Baron and Kenny, 1986; Preacher and Hayes, 2008). Psychologists have adopted path analysis in droves because it allows them to make strong tests of S-> O -> R causal chains. Specifically, it allows them to test whether the hypothesised intervening variables (Os) may mediate the effect of independent variables (Ss) on dependent variables (Rs). For example, Valenzuela, Srivastava and Lee (2005) show that the kind of (personality vs. situational constraint) attributions made for an opponent's behaviour seems to mediate the effects of different cultural orientation (United States vs. Korea) in accepting hypothetical offers in an ultimatum bargaining game. Despite its widespread use in psychology (as evidenced by the citation patterns of the Baron and Kenny and

Preacher and Hayes papers), these mediation analyses are hardly ever used by economists (for a rare example, see Panzone et al., 2016). No doubt this will come, as economists build, operationalise and test theories about the intervening effect of cognitive variables (such as attributions, perceptions of fairness etc.) on economic behaviour.

1.8 Conclusions

I have a confession to make. I started professional life as an attribution theorist in social psychology, and indeed, old habits die hard, as I have written other handbook chapters on this very topic (Hilton, 2006; 2017). Attribution theory describes the way we explain others' behaviour, and shows that we typically search for explanations when we are surprised by others' behaviour. In addition, these explanations tend to be *contrastive* in nature: They often focus on *abnormal conditions* – causal factors that differentiate the target case being explained from the normal case of our experience. So while an important part of science in both disciplines is mastering the key literature, going to conferences and asking questions about human choice processes, these cannot explain the difference between the disciplines as both do it. Contrastive explanations are achieved by focussing on what is different between the two.

So it is that I have spent much of my time in recent years asking the ethnocentric but (for me) natural question: *Why can't an economist be more like a psychologist?* The chapter you have read gives my current answer. In part, the differences are due to situational constraints, namely the different kinds and levels of questions that economists and psychologists address. But I cannot escape the feeling that there are deeply ingrained subcultural traditions about what constitutes 'good work' in the fields, and that economists will continue to take an instrumentalist tack when modelling choice processes, whereas psychologists will take a realist one. This will not change overnight, although the experimental approach is making progress in economics. Interesting work will continue to have occasional difficulties in crossing disciplinary barriers. Editors with behaviourist orientations in economics may continue to reject psychological work that does not incentivise subjects. Conversely, it is easy to imagine that editors with cognitive orientations in psychology would reject much experimental economics as being 'mere' demonstrations that lack strong inference tests of rival models of underlying cognitive processes.

1.8.1 *Homo Economicus*: Now You See Him – Now You Don't

The other feature of economics that differentiates it from psychology has been the dominance of a single theoretical model – *homo economicus*. This has made economics essentially deductive in nature, as the principal theoretical challenge has been either (a) to make interesting new deductions from this rational model (e.g., about what should follow from it in certain specified market conditions); or (b) show how minor changes in assumptions will lead to different deductive consequences. Economists will find these 'deviation' models (Sugden, 2005b) attractive if they are able to use simple assumptions to offer a wide range of new predictions in domains that interest them. A paradigm case of explanatory power combined with theoretical parsimony is prospect theory (Kahneman and Tversky, 1979), and this no doubt helps explain its success in economics. Part of the reason for the success of prospect theory in economics is that it makes simple additional assumptions (e.g., it is changes of state that matter, not final wealth), which explains a widespread phenomenon – the differences in reactions to gains and losses.

The continuing erosion of the dominance of *homo economicus* has prompted a change of tack by some economists, who no longer consider it possible to adhere to the grand project of applying a single kind of economic analysis based on *homo economicus* to all domains of life (cf. Becker, 1993). This audacious project seems to have gone as far as it can (and further), and may have to beat a well-organised retreat. For example, if economists accept that people are *sometimes* self-interested, and *sometimes* sensitive to others' welfare (cf. Fehr and Schmidt, 2006), then they may begin to build causal models that tell us *when* and *why* we expect them to be one or the other. Similarly, we will need causal models to tell us when and why incentives work or backfire, when optimism is likely to be productive rather than counterproductive and so on.

As we have seen in the preceding, some economics work is now moving to the 'now you see it, now you don't' approach by proposing theories that specify how situational characteristics (e.g., the employer's knowledge about a task, the private or public nature of a financial incentive) interact with cognitive mechanisms to produce (or prevent) the effects in question (e.g., informational effects of incentives, crowding out of intrinsic motivation). As we have seen, these theories lead quite naturally to experimental tests that allow the relevant factors to be manipulated to see whether the effects in question occur or not. They thus resemble models and tests in social and cognitive psychology. As microeconomic and psychological models of choice seem to be converging, there may also be interesting opportunities for cross-fertilization. For example, psychologists may ask whether the paradoxical effect of offering high wages for experimental participation in classic cognitive dissonance studies (e.g., Festinger and Carlsmith, 1959) only occurs if participants assume that their employer knows that the task proposed is difficult. And economists may find attribution theory helpful in predicting how incentives are perceived. More generally, the related trend in psychology to contingent models of decision-making is worth noting, where task characteristics and informational environments 'select' optimal strategies (Gigerenzer et al. 1991; Payne, Bettman and Johnson, 1993). These approaches help specify the conditions under which people are fully Bayesian or utility maximisers (as presupposed by the classical economic approach), or use more heuristic approaches to evaluating options.

1.8.2 The Prediction Crisis in Economics

The 2008 economic crash has led to some self-questioning in economics as well as criticism from outside the discipline, as very few economists foresaw the crash, or could propose corrective measures once it came. Indeed, the Queen of England's question, *Why didn't anyone see it coming?* posed when opening an expensive new building for the London School of Economics in 2008 could be interpreted as a challenge to academic economics to earn its keep, as so few economists had predicted the meltdown. The prediction crisis is perhaps not new, as London dustmen performed as well as finance ministers and bankers in *The Economist's* financial prediction task back in 1994 (Hilton, 2001). Moreover, once the crisis had hit, economics did not seem to have a consensual approach to resolving the problems – opinions seem to be divided between noninterventionist approaches (let the banks fail) and interventionist ones (requiring the state to guarantee failing banks) with no clear guidance which approach to apply in which circumstances (Lewis, 2010). So we may fruitfully ask whether the comparison of economic theory and method with that of psychology (or biology) can afford useful insights for economists seeking to reengineer their discipline. In the following, I discuss how the analysis given in the preceding may illuminate the challenges contemporary economics faces in order to become a more empirically based scientific discipline.

A first challenge is that empirical research shows that economic actors are often less rational than classical theory supposes, even when those actors are highly rewarded 'experts' (Hilton, 2001). For example, Attia and Hilton (2013) show that both the failure of Long Term Capital Management (LTCM) in 1999 (despite being supervised by Nobel Prize–winning economists) and the subprime crisis of 2007 can be attributed to building mathematical models that are based on insufficient data. In the case of LTCM, its models predicted that the maximum it could lose in a single day was $35 million, yet on two occasions in 1998 LTCM lost over half a billion dollars. Both the LTCM experts and the property market analysts committed the error of insufficient sampling – well known to psychologists – which leads to underestimation of variability in market conditions and hence overconfidence in the capacity of economic models to work in all conditions, thus leading to an underestimation of the probability of extreme 'black swan' events. For example, in the 2007–2008 subprime crisis, analysts had based their predictions on the Housing Price Appreciation (HPA) index, whose data on house prices only went back to 1998 (thus incorporating only five years' worth of data), and failed to exploit data bases that went back to the beginning of the 1990s. Had they done so, they would have been less prone to assume that house prices would continue rising, an essential component of their business model. To add insult to injury, subprime mortgages exploited a known irrationality in consumers' financial decision-making. This is because banks were offering extremely low interest rates for the first two years of their mortgage, before locking them into much higher interest rates.

Given the human propensity to focus too much on short-term advantages over long-term costs due to insufficient temporal discounting, these 'teasers' succeeded in tempting low-income clients into taking out mortgages which they would later not be able to pay, unless they remortgaged their home (which the analysts using the HPA index assumed would have gone up in value in the meantime).[3] Here the challenge for economists is to develop more realistic models of individual and group choice which can in turn guide policy recommendations (for a start on this project, see Bénabou and Tirole, 2016).

A second challenge is that academic economists themselves seem sometimes to be overconfident about their own models, with a corresponding lack of attention to facts that might contradict them. This can manifest itself in various forms. First, economists may propose models without supporting data for them as long as the phenomena to be explained seem intuitively plausible (at least to the authors, and to journal editors and reviewers). Related to this, models are sometimes proposed to account for 'stylized facts', which are generalizations of the kind 'more years of education leads to higher salary', which gloss over (potentially informative) exceptions. Third, when empirical evidence exists, it may be overinterpreted. Examples include our previous discussion of research on overconfidence, but similar criticisms have been made of economists' use of other psychological theories (cf. a critique by McKenzie, 1997) of the weak level of evidence provided by Thaler to support his claim that endowment effects explain market anomalies). Fourth, even when data are provided in support of an argument, not enough attention may be paid to the rigours of empirical analysis. A prominent case in point comes in Reinhart and Rogoff's (2010) paper, which argues that it is best for states not to borrow more than 90 per cent of their GDP because it would inhibit growth. This conclusion is based on a pattern obtained from their data analysis, which appeared to show a neat inverse linear relation between level of public debt in advanced countries and growth. Their analysis was used to support austerity measures in various European countries after the 2008 crisis with – some would say – disastrous consequences in countries such as Greece which cut their debt but whose economies still continued to contract. In fact, a reanalysis showed that there are numerous problems with the data analysis in this paper (Herndon et al., 2013). First, data were excluded from countries whose behaviour did not fit the claimed pattern (e.g., postwar Australia, Canada and New Zealand) without explanation, whereas data from other countries from the same period that fit the authors' claim were included (United States). Second, some other countries (Austria, Belgium and Denmark) were omitted due to an alphabetical coding error. Third, weights were used such that one year of data from New Zealand (1951) that fit their claims (–7.6 per cent negative growth) was weighted equally to the United Kingdom, which was also in the highest debt category but averaged 2.4 per cent growth over nineteen years. When these errors were eliminated or controlled for, the sample showed that countries with over 90 per cent debt averaged 2.2 per cent growth, not the –0.1 per cent growth claimed by Reinhart and Rogoff (2010). In fact, the data set has very different implications for austerity policies to that claimed by Reinhart and Rogoff. While Reinhart and Rogoff are to be commended for sharing their data with others, an outsider may still wonder how it is possible that such an accumulation of elementary errors in the analysis of publicly available data could have passed muster and be published in the premier journal in academic economics.[4]

A third challenge is that economic models may need to incorporate the causal structure and empirical sophistication that enable life sciences to make useful predictions (see Chen and Pearl, 2013, for related arguments). While progress in this direction is being made in the construction and testing of models of individual and group choice that incorporate plausible assumptions about human psychology (cf. supra), considerable challenges also exist for the modelling of macroeconomic behaviour (e.g., patterns of growth, inflation, and unemployment). An instructive contrast is the way that epidemiologists in 2008 were able to predict the contagion path that a Mexican swine flu outbreak in humans In Mexico would take. They correctly predicted that the next outbreaks would be in New York and Madrid, and then London. This was because epidemiologists had a model of microbes and vectors of contagion. Thus New York and Madrid are the most popular airline destinations from Mexico, and London the joint most popular destination from Mexico, New York and Madrid. In contrast, even when the Florida subprime crisis has been detected in 2007, there were no equivalent predictions made about which banks or banking sectors would be affected due to the 'opacity' of the derivative financial products that were the vehicle of this crisis. But it behoves us to reflect on the nature of 'opacity'. Before the work of Lister and Pasteur, microbes were not just opaque, they were (and still are) invisible to the naked eye. However, what has rendered their behaviour and spread intelligible and predictable is the combination of theory and instrumentation, combined with assiduous field work. The development of a similar realist attitude (Hacking, 1983) should help modern economics develop comparable models and instruments for predicting and measuring the behaviour of real-life economic systems.

In sum, the analysis given in this chapter suggests that to surmount the prediction problem, economics will need to develop greater scientific realism and empirical rigour. Theories of economic choice will not only have to incorporate psychological concepts that describe how decisions are made, but show how these can be operationalised and empirically tested. Theories about macroeconomics should build richer causal models of how particular markets *actually* work, in much the same way that biologists may model particular ecosystems, and seek out the data that enable them to evaluate the accuracy of their models. Whereas social psychology, echoing Bruner and Tagiuri (1954), can be criticized for 'excess of empirical enthusiasm and a deficit of theoretical surmise', economics seems to have suffered from the reverse problem, an excess of theoretical surmise and a deficit of empirical enthusiasm.

Since the first edition of this handbook, there have been some encouraging signs of progress in the development of experimental economics to test theories about individual and small group choice. This development has contributed to the recognition that classic economic incentives are not the be-all and end-all for motivating economic behaviour, which in turn has led to the growing popularity of 'nudges' with policy makers. Although introduced into the public policy area by an economist and a lawyer (Thaler and Sunstein, 2008), this approach clearly has its roots in the theories, findings and methods of experimental psychology. There are also signs of a more empirical approach in macroeconomic research through careful use of historical archives to support macroeconomic theses, such as those concerning the transmission of inequality in wealth across generations (Piketty and Saez, 2014). While their analysis of the causes of inequality has attracted considerable controversy, alternative hypotheses are now healthily constrained by these data. Finally, the Institute for New Economic Thinking (in part funded by billionaire finance guru George Soros, himself a staunch Popperian) supports research that questions some of the basic assumptions in economic theory in a way compatible with the analysis given in this chapter.

It may be that a more scientific approach to economics will evolve not only through adopting psychologically plausible theories of judgment and choice, but also by adopting a more thoroughgoing empirical approach which combines observational rigour, strong inference, an experimental approach and the capacity to model the behaviour of complex systems in the manner of successful scientific disciplines such as biology. Time will tell.

1.9 Acknowledgements

I would like to acknowledge the unstinting hospitality of the Economics Department at the University of Toulouse, which has given me remarkable opportunities to talk with economists and to listen to them discussing their work among themselves. This was greatly facilitated by a research fellowship from the French CNRS between 2001 and 2003. In particular, I would like to thank Laure Cabantous, Bruno Frey, Rom Harré, Robin Hogarth, John McClure, Steven Sloman and Bernard Walliser for helpful comments on previous drafts, and Bruno Biais, Guido Friebel, Philip Hemmings, Bruno Jullien, Luca Panzone, Sébastien Pouget, Paul Seabright, Marcela Tarazona, Jean Tirole, Nicolas Treich and Alistair Ulph for many instructive discussions concerning economics and psychology. Special thanks to Roland Bénabou for his comments on the revision of this chapter.

Notes

1 The sense of induction that I use here is essentially the hypothetico-deductive method as described by Mill (1872/1973). Mill regarded induction as a 'method of proof' of theories that had already been generated, and provided canons for the elimination of hypotheses, principally based on the methods of agreement and difference that are still used in strong inference to this day.

2 Indeed, Gneezy cheerfully sees this as a job for psychologists (Gneezy, personal communication)!

3 Evidence that securities analysts in the property sector themselves fell prey to their biased judgment can be adduced from the fact that they continued to buy homes for themselves right up to the crash. Indeed, their house purchases performed *worse* over this period than lawyers or securities analysts in other domains with a comparable income level, indicating that their financial education and access to inside information was no protection against poor judgment (Cheng et al., 2014).

4 Social psychology of course has its own methodological crisis in the form of repeated data frauds (Stroebe, Postmes and Spears, 2012) and a worryingly low replication rate for published experiments(Open Science Collaboration, 2015). That these problems concern the real value of published experimental evidence is nevertheless testament to the strong empiricist slant in the field. See Bardsley (this volume) on this controversy, and its implications for experimental economics.

1.10 References

Ajzen, I., & Fishbein, M. (1980). *Understanding Attitudes and Predicting Social Behaviour*. Englewood Cliffs, NJ: Prentice Hall.

Akerlof, G. A. (1970). The Market for "Lemons": Quality Uncertainty and the Market Mechanism. *Quarterly Journal of Economics*, 84, 488–500.

Alicke, M. and Sedikides, C. (2009). Self-enhancement and Self-protection: What They Are and What They Do. *European Review of Social Psychology*, 20(1), 1–48.

Alpert, M. and Raiffa, H. (1982). A Progress Report on the Training of Probability Assessors, in D. Kahneman, P. Slovic and A. Tversky (eds.), *Judgement under Uncertainty: Heuristics and Biases*. Cambridge: Cambridge University Press, pp. 294–305.

Ariely, D., Bracha, A. and Meier, S. (2009). Doing Good or Doing Well? Image Motivation and Monetary Incentives in Behaving Prosocially. *American Economic Review*, 99, 544–555.

Attia, C. Hilton, D. (2013). *Finance sur le divan*. Paris: Optrakan Editions.

Barber, B. M. and Odean, T. (2001). Boys Will Be Boys: Gender, Overconfidence, and Common Stock Investment. *Quarterly Journal of Economics*, 116, 261–292.

Baron, R. M. and Kenny, D. A. (1986). The Moderator–Mediator Variable Distinction in Social Psychological Research: Conceptual, Strategic, and Statistical Considerations. *Journal of Personality and Social Psychology*, 51, 1173–1182.

Becker, G. (1993). Nobel Lecture: The Economic Way of Looking at Behavior. *Journal of Political Economy*, 101, 385–409.

Bénabou, R. and Tirole, J. (2003). Self-Knowledge and Self-Regulation: An Economic Approach, in I. Brocas and J. D. Carrillo (eds.), *The Psychology of Economic Decisions: Volume 1: Rationality and Well-being*. Oxford: Oxford University Press, pp. 137–168.

Bénabou, R. and Tirole, J. (2006). Incentives and Prosocial Behavior. *American Economic Review*, 96, 1652–1678.

Bénabou, R. and Tirole, J. (2011). Identity, Morals and Taboos: Beliefs as Assets. *Quarterly Journal of Economics*, 126(2), 805–855.

Bénabou, R. and Tirole, J. (2016). Mindful Economics: The Production, Consumption, and Value of Beliefs. *Journal of Economic Perspectives*, 30, 141–164.

Benos, A. V. (1998). Aggressiveness and Survival of Overconfident Traders. *Journal of Financial Markets*, 1(3), 353–383.

Berthoz, S., Armony, J. L., Blair, R. J. and Dolan, R. J. (2002). An fMRI Study of Intentional and Unintentional (Embarrassing) Violations of Social Norms. *Brain*, 125, 1696–1708.

Biais, B. and S. Pouget (1999). Microstructure, Incentives and Convergence to Equilibrium in Experimental Financial Markets. Working paper, Toulouse University.

Biais, B, Hilton, D., Pouget, S. and Mazurier, K. (2005). Judgmental Overconfidence, Self-Monitoring and Trading Performance in an Experimental Financial Market. *Review of Economic Studies*, 72, 297–312.

Breiter, H. C., Aharon, I., Kahneman, D., Dale, A. and Shizgal, P. (2001). Functional Imaging of Neural Responses to Expectancy and Experience of Monetary Gains and Losses. *Neuron*, 30(2), 619–639.

Bremzen, A., Khokhlova, E., Suvorov, A. and Van de Ven, J. (2015). Bad News: An Experimental Study on the Informational Effects of Rewards. *Review of Economics and Statistics*, 97(1), 55–70.

Bruni, L. and Sugden, R. (2007). The Road Not Taken: How Psychology Was Removed from Economics, and How It Might Be Brought Back. *Economic Journal*, 117(516), 146–173.

Bruner, J. S., and Tagiuri, R. (1954). The Perception of People. In G. Lindzey (ed.), *Handbook of Social Psychology*, Vol. 2. Cambridge, MA: Addison-Wesley, pp. 634–654.

Burgoyne, C. B. and Routh, D. A. (1991). Constraints on the Use of Money as a Gift at Christmas: The Role of Status and Intimacy. *Journal of Economic Psychology*, 12, 47–69.

Buscato, T., Noury, F., Raynaud, M. and Rocher, A. (2004). Effets des incitations financières sur la motivation dans les domaines sacrés et profanes. *Mémoire de recherche*, University of Toulouse-II.

Camerer, C. (2000). Prospect Theory in the Wild: Evidence from the Field, in D. Kahneman and A. Tversky (eds.), *Choices, Values and Frames*. Cambridge: Cambridge University Press, pp. 288–300.

Camerer, C. and Hogarth, R. M. (1999). The Effects of Financial Incentives in Experiments: A Review and Capital–Labor–Production Framework. *Journal of Risk and Uncertainty*, 19, 7–42.

Camerer, C., Loewenstein, G. and Prelec, D. (2005). Neuroeconomics: How Neuroscience Can Inform Economics. *Journal of Economic Literature*, 43, 9–64.

Chen, B. and Pearl, J. (2013). Regression and Causation: A Critical Examination of Six Econometrics Textbooks. *Real-World Economics Review*, (65), 2–20.

Cheng, I-H., Raina, S. and Xiong, W. (2014). Wall Street and the Housing Bubble. *American Economic Review*, 104(9), 2797–2829.

Croson, R. (2005). The Method of Experimental Economics, in P. Carnevale and C. W. de Dreu (eds.), *International Negotiations: Research Methods in Negotiation and Social Conflict*, 10, 131–148.

Daniel, K., Hirshleifer, D. and Subrahmanyam, A. (1998). Investor Psychology and Security Market Under- and Overreactions. *Journal of Finance*, 53, 1839–1885.

De Bondt, W. and Thaler, R. (1985). Does the Stock Market Overreact? *Journal of Finance*, 40(3), 793–808.

De Hooge, I. E., Zeelenberg, M. and Breugelmans, S. M. (2007). Moral Sentiments and Cooperation: Differential Influences of Shame and Guilt. *Cognition and Emotion*, 21(5), 1025–1042.

De Quervain, D., Fischbacher, U., Treyer, etc. (2004). The Neural Basis of Altruistic Punishment. *Science*, 305, 1254–1258.

Fehr, E., Fischbacher, U., & Kosfeld, M. (2005). Neuroeconomic Foundations of Trust and Social Preferences, IZA Discussion Papers, No. 1641.

Fehr, E. and Schmidt, K. M. (2006). The Economics of Fairness, Reciprocity and Altruism – Experimental Evidence and New Theories. *Handbook of the Economics of Giving, Altruism and Reciprocity*, 1 615–691.

Festinger, L. and Carlsmith, J. M. (1959). Cognitive Consequences of Forced Compliance. *Journal of Abnormal and Social Psychology*, 58, 203–210.

Forsyth, R., Nelson, F., Neumann, G. R. and Wright, J. (1992). Anatomy of an Experimental Stock Market. *American Economic Review*, 82, 1142–1161.

Freedman, J. L. and Fraser, S. C. (1966). Compliance without Pressure: The Foot-in-the-Door Technique. *Journal of Personality and Social Psychology*, 4(2), 195–202.

Frey, B. S. (1997). *Not Just for the Money: An Economic Theory of Personal Motivation*. Cheltenham: Edward Elgar.

Frey, B. S. and Stutzer, A. (2002). *Happiness and Economics: How the Economy and Institutions Affect Human Well-being*. Princeton: Princeton University Press.

Gehring, W. J. and Willoughby, A. R. (2002). The Medial Frontal Cortex and the Rapid Processing of Monetary Gains and Losses. *Science*, 295, 2279–2282.

Gigerenzer, G., Hoffrage, U. and Kleinbölting, H. (1991). Probabilistic Mental Models: A Brunswikian Theory of Confidence. *Psychological Review*, 98, 506–528.

Glaser, M. and Weber, M. (2007). Overconfidence and Trading Volume. *Geneva Risk and Insurance Review*, 32(1), 1–36.

Gneezy, U. and Rusticini, A. (2000). Pay Enough or Don't Pay At All. *Quarterly Journal of Economics*, 115(3), 797–810.

Hacking, I. (1983). *Representing and Intervening: Introductory Topics in the Philosophy of Natural Science*. Cambridge: Cambridge University Press.

Harré, R. (1988). Modes of Explanation, in D. J. Hilton (ed.), *Contemporary Science and Natural Explanation: Commonsense Conceptions of Causality.* Brighton: Harvester Press and New York: New York University Press, pp. 129–144.

Herndon, T., Ash, M. and Pollin R. (2013). Does High Public Debt Consistently Stifle Economic Growth? A Critique of Reinhart and Rogoff. *Cambridge Journal of Economics,* 1 of 23 doi:10.1093/cje/bet075

Hertwig, R. and Ortmann, A. (2001). Experimental Practices in Economics: A Methodological Challenge for Psychologists. *Behavioral and Brain Sciences,* 24, 383–451.

Hertwig, R. and Ortmann, A. (2003). Economists' and Psychologists' Experimental Practices: How They Differ, Why They Differ, and How They Could Converge, in I. Brocas and J. D. Carrillo (eds.), *The Psychology of Economic Decisions: Volume 1: Rationality and Well-being.* Oxford: Oxford University Press, pp. 253–272.

Hesslow, G. (1983). Explaining Differences and Weighting Causes. *Theoria,* 49 (2), 87–111.

Hesslow, G. (1988). The Problem of Causal Selection, in D. J. Hilton (ed.), *Contemporary Science and Natural Explanation: Commonsense Conceptions of Causality.* Brighton: Harvester Press, pp. 11–32.

Hilton, D. J. (2001). Psychology and the Financial Markets: Applications to Trading, Dealing and Investment Analysis. *Journal of Psychology and Financial Markets,* 2, 37–53.

Hilton, D. J. (2006). Overconfidence, Trading and Entrepreneurship: Cognitive and Cultural Processes in Risk-Taking, in R. Topol and B. Walliser (eds.), *Cognitive Economics: New Trends Contributions to Economic Analysis,* Volume 280, pp. 225–235.

Hilton, D. J. (2007). Causal Explanation: From Social Perception to Knowledge-Based Attribution, in A. Kruglanski and E. T. Higgins (eds.), *Social Psychology: Handbook of Basic Principles* (2nd edition). New York: Guilford Press, pp. 232–253.

Hilton, D. J. (2012). The Emergence of Cognitive Social Psychology: A Historical Analysis. In W. Stroebe and A. Kruglanski (eds.), *Handbook of the History of Social Psychology.* Philadelphia: Psychology Press, pp. 45–80.

Hilton, D. J. (2017). Social Attribution and Explanation, in M. Waldmann (ed.), *The Oxford Handbook of Causal Reasoning.* Oxford: Oxford University Press, pp. 645–674.

Hilton, D. J., Regner, I., Cabantous, L., Charalambides, L. and Vautier, S. (2011). Do Positive Illusions Predict Overconfidence in Judgment? A Test Using Interval Production and Probability Evaluation Measures of Miscalibration. *Journal of Behavioral Decision Making,* 24, 117–139.

Joosten, A., van Dijke, M., Van Hiel, A. and De Cremer, D. (2014). Feel Good, Do-Good!? On Consistency and Compensation in Moral Self-Regulation. *Journal of Business Ethics,* 123 (1), 71–84.

Kagel, J. H., Battalio, R. C., Rachlin, H. and Green, L. (1981). Demand Curves for Animal Consumers. *Quarterly Journal of Economics,* 96, 1–13.

Kahneman, D. E., Knetsch, J. L. and Thaler, R. E. (1986). Experimental Tests of the Endowment Effect and the Coase Theorem. *Journal of Political Economy*, 98, 25–48.

Kahneman, D. E. and Tversky, A. (1979). Prospect Theory: An Analysis of Decision under Risk. *Econometrica*, 47, 263–291.

Lewin, S. B. (1996). Economics and Psychology: Lessons for Our Own Day from the Early Twentieth Century. *Journal of Economic Literature*, 34, 1293–1323.

Lewis, A. (2010). The Credit Crunch: Ideological, Psychological and Epistemological Perspectives. *Journal of Socio-Economics*, 39, 127–131.

Lipton, P. (1991). Contrastive Explanation and Causal Triangulation. *Philosophy of Science*, 58(4), 687–697.

Lyons, J. (1977). *Semantics*, Vol. 1. Cambridge: Cambridge University Press.

List, J. A. (2004). Neoclassical Theory vs. Prospect Theory: Evidence from the Marketplace. *Econometrica*, 72, 615–625.

Marr, D. (1982). *Vision: A Computational Investigation into the Human Representation and Processing of Visual Information*. San Francisco, CA: W. H. Freeman.

Mazar, N. and Zhong, C.-B (2010). Do Green Products Make Us Better People? *Psychological Science*, 21 (4), 494–498.

McKenzie, C. (1997). What Are the Motives? A Problem with Evidence in the Work of Richard Thaler. *Journal of Economic Psychology*, 18, 123–135.

Mill, J. S. (1872/1973). System of Logic, in J. M. Robson (ed.), *Collected Works of John Stuart Mill* (8th ed., Vols. 7 and 8). Toronto: University of Toronto Press. (Original edition published 1872).

Moore, D. A. and Healy, P. J. (2008). The Trouble with Overconfidence. *Psychological Review*, 115, 502–517.

Nowak, A., Szamrej, J., and Latané, B. (1990). From Private Attitude to Public Opinion: A Dynamic Theory of Social Impact. *Psychological Review*, 97(3), 362.

Odean, T. (1998). Volume, Volatility, Price and Profit: When All Traders Are Above Average. *Journal of Finance*, 53, 1887–1934.

Open Science Collaboration. (2015). Estimating the Reproducibility of Psychological Science. *Science*, 349(6251), aac4716.

Panzone, L., Hilton, D., Sale, L. and Cohen, D. (2016). Socio-demographics, Implicit Attitudes, Explicit Attitudes, and Sustainable Consumption in Supermarket Shopping. *Journal of Economic Psychology*, 55, 77–95.

Payne, J., Bettman, J. W. and Johnson, E. J. (1993). *The Adaptive Decision Maker*. Cambridge: Cambridge University Press.

Piketty, T. and Saez, E. (2014). Inequality in the Long Run. *Science*, 344(6186), 838–843.

Pindyck, R. S. and Rubinfield, D. L. (1998). *Microeconomics*, 4th edition. Upper Saddle River, NJ: Prentice Hall.

Platt, J. R. (1964). Strong Inference. *Science*, 146, 347–353.

Plott, C., and S. Sunder, 1988. Rational Expectations and the Aggregation of Diverse Information in Laboratory Security Markets. *Econometrica*, 56(5), 1085–1118.

Popper, K. R. (1971). *Objective Knowledge*. Oxford: Oxford University Press.

Preacher, K. J. and Hayes, A. F. (2008). Asymptotic and Resampling Strategies for Assessing and Comparing Indirect Effects in Multiple Mediator Models. *Behavior Research Methods*, 40(3), 879–891.

Rabin, M. (2002). A Perspective on Psychology and Economics. *European Economic Review*, 46: 657–685.

Reinhart, C. M. and Rogoff, K. S. (2010). Growth in a Time of Debt. *American Economic Review*, 100(2), 573–578.

Rilling, J. K. Sanfey, A. G., Aronson, J. A., Nystrom, L. E. and Cohen, J. D. 2003. Opposing Bold Responses to Reciprocated and Unreciprocated Altruism in Putative Reward Pathways. *Neuroreport* 15(16), 239–243.

Rusticini, A. (2005). Introduction. Neuroeconomics: Present and Future. *Games and Economic Behavior*, 52, 201–212.

Sanfey, A. G., Rilling, J. K., Aronson, J. A., Nystrom, L. E. and Cohen, J. D. (2003). The Neural Basis of Economic Decision-Making in the Ultimatum Game. *Science*, 300, 1755–1758.

Shefrin, H. and Statman, M. (1985). The Disposition to Sell Winners Too Early and Ride Losers Too Long: Theory and Evidence. *Journal of Finance*, 40, 777–790.

Smith, A. (1759/2002). *The Theory of Moral Sentiments*, 6th edition (ed. K. Haakonssen). Cambridge: Cambridge University Press.

Smith, A. (1776/1993). *An Inquiry into the Nature and Causes of the Wealth of Nations* (ed. K. Sutherland). Oxford: Oxford University Press.

Smith, R. H., Webster, J. M., Parrott, W. G. and Eyre, H. L. (2002). The Role of Public Exposure in Moral and Nonmoral Shame and Guilt. *Journal of Personality and Social Psychology*, 83 (1), 138–159.

Stroebe, W., Postmes, T. and Spears, R. (2012). Scientific Misconduct and the Myth of Self-Correction in Science. *Perspectives on Psychological Science*, 7(6), 670–688.

Sugden, R. (2000). Credible Worlds: The Status of Theoretical Models in Economics. *Journal of Economic Methodology*, 7, 1–31.

Sugden, R. (2005a). Experiments as Exhibits and Experiments as Tests. *Journal of Economic Methodology*, 12(2), 291–312.

Sugden, R. (2005b). Experiment, Theory World: A Symposium on the Role of Experiments in Economics. *Journal of Economic Methodology*, 12(2), 177–184.

Taylor, S. and Brown, J. (1988). Illusion and Well Being: A Social Psychological Perspective on Mental Health. *Psychological Bulletin*, 103, 193–210.

Tetlock, P. E., Kristel, O. V., Elson, S. B., Green, M. C. and Lerner, J. S. (2000). The Psychology of the Unthinkable: Taboo Trade-offs, Forbidden Base-Rates, and Heretical Counterfactuals. *Journal of Personality and Social Psychology*, 78, 853–870.

Thaler, R. and Sunstein, C. R. (2008). *Nudge: Improving Decisions about Health, Wealth, and Happiness*. New Haven, CT: Yale University Press.

Thorndike, E. L. (1911). *Animal Intelligence*. New York: Macmillan.

Turgot, A. R. J. (1761). Le commerce des grains. Reprinted in P. Vigreux (ed., 1947), *Turgot: Textes choisis*. Paris: Dalloz.

Valenzuela, A., Srivastava, J. and Lee, S. (2005). The Role of Cultural Orientation in Bargaining under Incomplete Information: Differences in Causal Attributions. *Organizational Behavior and Human Decision Processes*, 96, 72–88.

Weiner, B. (1985). "Spontaneous" Causal Thinking. *Psychological Bulletin*, 109, 74–84.

2 What Lessons Does the 'Replication Crisis' in Psychology Hold for Experimental Economics?

Nicholas Bardsley

2.1 Introduction

In recent years, psychology has come under considerable critical scrutiny concerning the soundness of its experimental results. There has been concern over outright academic fraud, following Diederik Stapel's public exposure in 2011. Stapel was a leading social psychologist who had worked at the universities of Amsterdam, Groningen and Tilburg, with a prolific research and publication record. He was found to have fabricated data, and a scandal ensued receiving significant national and international media attention. Consequently, he lost his post and became an academic and social outcast (Bhattacharjee, 2013). An investigating commission set up by three Dutch universities found that fifty-five papers should be retracted and evidence indicating fraud in ten further articles, from the corpus of 137 Stapel publications (Levelt et al., 2012). At the time of writing (November 2016), 58 of his publications are documented as retracted by the website Retraction Watch.

In many cases of academic fraud, retracted papers continue to be cited many years after their retraction (Borneman-Cimenti et al., 2016), exacerbating the pollution of a field. Of perhaps much greater import than spectacular but rare cases such as Stapel's, however, is the likelihood that careers built upon fraud are indicative of wider failures of a discipline to enforce appropriate critical and academic standards (Levelt et al., 2012). Relatedly, there has also been concern over more subtle but plausibly more pervasive problems of selection bias, publication bias, selective presentation of data, overreliance on small samples, data mining and so on. The problems are a combination of 'questionable research practices' by researchers and 'questionable publication practices' by journal editors and reviewers. Attempts to replicate results plausibly provide one indicator of the health of an experimental discipline, facilitating detection of spurious findings regardless of their origin. Though problems in academic processes extend to a variety of fields, including for example medical studies (Ioannidis, 2005), psychology has been subject to particular scrutiny, with several recent systematic replication efforts. The results are generally seen as problematic, with low rates of replication and effect sizes that fall far short of those of the original studies. This chapter provides an overview of these replication initiatives and considers in comparison the situation obtaining in experimental economics.[1]

Replication efforts themselves have sometimes proved controversial, given alleged publication incentives to disconfirm the original results, and the high stakes involved given that authors' professional reputations may be tied to the outcomes. Two positions are analysed that have featured significantly in discussion. The first states that authors ought to be extensively consulted during the design phase of a replication study in order that there is sufficient similarity between procedures (hereafter the 'authorial inclusion issue'). It is argued that the methods sections of experimental reports are typically too lacking in detail to enable adequate similarity to be achieved. The second holds that 'Critiquing [a replication study] After the Results are Known' has diminished force (hereafter the 'CARKing issue'). This might be taken to imply that peer review of replication studies should only take place *ex-ante*.

Finally, consideration is given to the links between economics experiments and theory, which may mark a key difference concerning the situation in the two fields. The issue is approached from the perspective described in Bardsley et al. (2010), where a critique was developed of model-implementing experiments. It is proposed that the kinds of theory-proximity prevalent in experimental economics may favour replications with limited confirmatory power.

The following section deals with some preliminaries, including concepts of replication and the role of repeatability in accounts of science. Section 2.3 gives an overview of replication efforts in the two fields. Sections 2.4 and 2.5 consider the authorial inclusion and CARKing issues respectively. Section 2.6 then considers a difference between the generality of experimental economics and psychology designs, namely the theory-centric character of the former, and its bearing on replication. Section 2.7 concludes.

2.2 Preliminary Considerations

2.2.1 Direct and Conceptual Replication

An important distinction has been drawn between two types of replication: direct and conceptual. Other schema have been proposed, but the remaining distinctions seem less fundamental. Schmidt (2009) provides a useful discussion, and his definitions are followed here. A direct replication can be defined as 'repetition of an experimental procedure'. A conceptual replication consists of 'repetition of a test of a hypothesis or result of earlier research work with different methods' (Schmidt, 2009 p. 91). Schmidt goes on to note that the desirable characteristics of a replication depend on which goal is being pursued, and that there is a variety of possible goals. These include checking that some result obtains; checking its robustness; checking for its boundary conditions or generality; and seeing whether it, or its theoretical interpretation, can be confirmed using different procedures entirely.

For direct replication, the general aim is often to check that a certain result in fact obtains and is not the result of a failure of experimental validity. On some views, for example Brandt et al. (2014), a direct replication should seek to mimic the original as closely as possible concerning every detail of the original setting. At the ideal limit, only the sample drawn and academic personnel involved would vary, along with some difference in timing. A failure to replicate will presumably either signify Type 1 error, academic malpractice or perhaps rapid social change.

In practice, working understandings of direct replication seem far looser than this, and it is perhaps unclear why one would wish to check only for this very narrow set of problems. It seems perhaps impossible to repeat exactly all bar three aspects of a behavioural or cognitive experiment, and this is generally seen as no bad thing since it allows for the robustness of results to be explored. However, the more aspects are varied, the more this opens the door to a predictable reaction to a failed replication attempt, that it introduced problematic deviations from the original design, which explains the absence of the original findings. We consider such objections further in section 2.4, where we consider which kinds of deviation from the original design are sensible in direct replication. For Schmidt, checking for generalisability by running a design on another category of participant, or another sample of stimuli, is also a case of direct replication.

In contrast, conceptual replication seeks to confirm a particular hypothesis by implementing different procedures and conditions. The aim is to reproduce the same phenomena abstracted from their original setting. This requires a different experimental procedure. Schmidt (2009) gives the example of Rosenthal and Fode's (1963) study of experimenter effects, in which students were given different information about the abilities of rats they were given to train in maze tasks. In reality, the information was randomly allocated, but those rats labelled as higher ability completed the mazes faster than those labelled as lower ability. The phenomenon of an experimenter effect was reproduced using teachers and school pupils, for example, in Rosenthal and Jacobson (1963), a completely different experimental setting, but with a similar manipulation of expectations about the trainee's capacities. Here teachers were given false information about scores on an IQ test, with the false information being randomly allocated. Subsequent use of the same IQ test demonstrated larger gains for the pupils who had been arbitrarily deemed more successful in the initial test. The very different setting and sample confirms the underlying hypothesis that an experimenter's expectancy can influence the behaviour of experimental subjects.

A basic example of conceptual replication in experimental economics is, arguably, Battalio et al.'s (1985) demonstration of risk aversion in rats, which necessarily uses a completely different experimental setup to the corresponding (monetary gamble-based) tasks which demonstrate this for people. The authors set up prospects for the rats using two levers, which released food in a probabilistic manner. Lever pairs were implemented offering either a high chance of a smaller quantity of food or a smaller chance of a larger amount of food, with the same expected (mean) quantity. The rats generally preferred the former. In this way, the authors were also able to test for, and find, the common ratio effect in rats. That is, preferences switch from a safer to a riskier gamble when the probability components of each are scaled down by a common factor.

Recent replication initiatives both in psychology and experimental economics have concentrated on direct replication, whereas previous replication activity in social sciences has arguably tended towards conceptual replication. The confirmatory power of conceptual replication is high, but comes at a price. For if a conceptual replication fails, it may be relatively unclear what we learn from this failure. Conversely, if a direct replication succeeds, it has limited confirmatory power, the more limited the closer the design is to the original. But failures of direct replication are correspondingly informative.

2.2.2 The Role of Repetition in Science: Essential in Theory but Not in Practice?

Arguably, the replication crisis sits uneasily with classical accounts of scientific activity offered in the history and philosophy of science. On empiricist views, following for example Hume (1739–40), science is a process of collating repeated observations and distilling from these invariant regularities, or laws, where 'constant conjunctions' of events are evident. On such views, there is nothing particularly special about a replication study; it merely adds to the stock of available observations. However, the emphasis here on repetition seems to imply that there should be many instances of corroborating observation before something can be accepted as a scientific finding.

In contrast, realists (for example, Bhaskar, 1978) see experimentation as revealing causal powers or tendencies, which can be manifested by just a single act of experimental closure. From this point of view, the role of repetition is to confirm a previous finding in a controlled setting, that is, providing confirmation that the setting was adequately isolated and controlled (Greenwood, 1982, pp. 227–31). Causal powers or tendencies are normally hidden from observation because so much is going on simultaneously in any naturally occurring setting. On this view, the observations that constitute scientific results are necessarily outcomes of rather unusual situations. Very few confirming instances may be required for a finding to count as a result, but they are still required. Consequently, initial replications or failures to replicate may be highly significant, but additional direct replications have little scientific value once a result has been established.

The empiricist account seems difficult to reconcile descriptively with the situation obtaining in scientific publishing in many fields. The situation seems rather to be that many findings are accepted as results, with relatively few, or even no, direct replications. Indeed, the 'news value' of disappointing replication studies results has stemmed from the fact that a body of findings with nonprovisional status in the relevant field has low reproducibility the first time direct replications are tried. This nonprovisional status of scarcely-replicated results does not seem to be confined to psychology. In the *Handbook of Experimental Economics Results*, for example, explicit inclusion criteria were that the authors found the results in question important, not that they had been repeatedly observed (Plott and Smith, 2008, preface). The extent of corroboration is frequently addressed in the volume nonetheless. On the other hand, even if the realist account holds, any nonreplicated finding ought to count within a given field as a provisional, not bona fide, result.

Both camps, arguably, tend to offer an idealised view of science, abstracting from human and institutional failings. Such defects are factors which the replication movement must in contrast consider as central. For if the correct explanation of low replicability is shortcomings in research and publication practices, the same flawed processes would normally govern replication attempts. And secondly, the broader aim is not only to measure replicability but to improve it. As will be outlined, replication initiatives have also sought to innovate to improve the integrity of the review and publication process. We note, however, that further controversy, beyond the scope of this chapter, has centred on whether critique based on unsuccessful replication should be conducted outside of peer review processes, via social media or blogs. See, for example, Fiske (2016) and, ironically, the online commentary to the digital edition of that article. The issue hangs partly on the extent and speed with which practices can be improved. On the one hand, there is no quality control over potential insinuations or allegations of malpractice, which can cause unjustified reputational damage, in self-published media. On the other hand, if journal publication processes lack sufficient integrity, it seems unlikely that sufficient critique will take place in peer-reviewed formats alone (Coyne, 2016).

2.3 Overview of Recent Replication Studies

Key attributes of recent substantial replication efforts are shown in Table 2.1. Works are included which bring together many attempts at direct replication of a range of results, in one outlet, following a common approach and sampling regime. Stand-alone studies and attempts to replicate a single

Table 2.1 *Recent initiatives on direct replication in psychology and experimental economics*

Study	Field	Replication rate	Effect size quotient	N (samples)	Preregistered	Target selection
Open Science Collaboration (OSC), 2015	Psychology	36%	0.49	100	No	Quasirandom
Klein, Ratliff and Vianello, 2014	Psychology	77%	1.26	36	Yes	Nonrandom
Special Issue contributions to *Social Psychology* vol. 45(3), 2014	Psychology	8%	–	13	Yes	Nonrandom
Camerer et al., 2016	Economics	61%	0.66	18	No	Nonrandom

Note: The replication rate for *Social Psychology* 45(3) is based on the author's collation of the results reported in each study. One study is excluded from this count because of equivocal results.

finding or a single author's work are excluded. For psychology, the studies comprise a journal special issue with preregistered designs, a panel data study deploying numerous labs to study thirteen effects across each of thirty-six samples, and an attempt to replicate one hundred findings across independent samples.

The 'replication rate' is the reported proportion of effects that replicated with a significant effect in the same direction, at the 5 per cent level, as the original. Whilst this is not the only or necessarily best indicator of replicability, it is perhaps the main 'headline' figure. Klein et al. (2014) is published in *Social Psychology* 45(3) but merits inclusion in its own right because it seeks to replicate a set of findings repeatedly using numerous samples, a 'many labs' approach. The 'effect size quotient' is the mean effect size of the replication studies divided by the mean effect size of the original studies, and is another widely cited indicator of replicability. A replication protocol counts here as preregistered if prospective replication attempts were subject to peer review and an editorial decision taken either by journal editors or project organisers before data were collected.

A notable feature of these studies is the wide variation in the replication rate, which ranges from one in thirteen to ten in thirteen successes. This is a huge range which seemingly gives the lie to the simple 'headline' view that psychology experiments are unlikely to replicate. However, we should also ask what the replication rate *ought* to be in the absence of questionable research practices. For there will inevitably be false positives in any corpus of experimental studies, arising from sampling variation alone. It can be shown that the probability of a replicated rejection of a null hypothesis equals

$$\frac{\alpha^2 p + \beta^2 (1-p)}{\alpha p + \beta (1-p)}$$

where β is the power of a trial, α is the threshold significance level applied and p is the probability that any given null hypothesis selected for investigation is true (Appendix).[2] Thus, if $\alpha = 0.05$, $p = 0.5$ (an uninformative prior) and all trials had 90 per cent power, a commonly used benchmark for experimental quality, one would expect a replication rate of approximately 86 per cent. So estimated replication rates in Table 2.1 are uniformly lower than they seemingly ought to be, but variable. It is worth noting that this is sensitive to the value of p, however. For expected replication of significant results to be less than 80 per cent requires p > 0.7, a field in which researchers study unlikely effects.

Large variation is also apparent for effect sizes. OSC (2015) reports lower effect sizes in the replication studies, whereas Klein et al. (2014)'s figures imply that on average (mean) they are larger, albeit using a different measure of effect size. For this study, effect sizes are reported in Cohen's d units, whilst the other studies report Pearson's r. Also, the mean effect size is influenced by extreme values; the corresponding ratio of median effect sizes is ~1 (Klein et al. 2014, Table 2.1, cols. 1 and 4). For the other papers in *Social Psychology* vol. 45(3), calculation of an overall effect size quotient would require work with the data from each paper. Ironically, though perhaps inevitably, these large replication efforts used quite different procedures, which may help explain the variation.

None of the studies in Table 2.1 used a pure random sampling method. In OSC (2015), in which the effect selection protocol is described as 'quasirandom' sampling, authors could choose which of an available set of studies to propose to replicate. The available studies initially consisted of the first twenty articles in three leading psychology journals for 2008. The last reported finding in each study was the target to be replicated. In this manner, the set of studies available at any particular time was restricted to reduce selection bias. As the set depleted, the project team helped allocate remaining studies to replicators. But it remains the case that initially authors could choose which study to attempt to replicate. Assuming there is greater news value in producing an unsuccessful replication, this could result in a lower replication rate than would occur under random sampling and assignment. In that case, one might choose a study which one expects not to replicate, and these expectations might, even subliminally, influence the conduct of the research. Teams might also apply motivated by scepticism of a particular study, or even, conceivably, personal and professional grudges, selection effects which would again tend to lower the replication rate.

The problem just outlined seems exacerbated in the case of *Social Psychology* issue 45(3). Here, authors self-proposed a study to replicate, and then submitted a research design for peer review. If the research design was deemed of high enough quality, the replication attempt proceeded. There is more scope for selection effects to operate than in OSC (2015) because the set of targets for replication was also determined by prospective replicators.

In Klein et al.'s (2014) 'many labs' study, in contrast, with the much higher replication rate, the sampling procedure to select target effects is not fully documented. But four selection criteria are specified: suitability for online presentation, length of a trial, simplicity of design and diversity of effects (ibid., p. 143). A priori, it seems reasonable to expect short and simple trials to replicate better than long, complicated ones, if only for the mundane reason that there are fewer details that have to be correctly implemented.

The first lesson to draw for experimental economics seems to be that it is not entirely clear from the preceding whether the 61 per cent replication rate of Camerer et al. (2016) suggests a better or worse situation than that obtaining in psychology. This is somewhat uncertain, even if we restrict attention to the target of comparison, OSC (2015). If we ignored the nonrandom selection of studies, conventional 95 per cent confidence intervals for the two studies would range from 39 per cent to 84 per cent, and from 27 per cent to 48 per cent, overlapping. For OSC (2015), if we restrict attention to the replications which had sample sizes sufficient for at least 90 per cent power, we obtain an improved 46 per cent replication rate, and if we further restrict to the top journal it increases to 52 per cent (author's calculations, using the publicly available dataset). In Camerer et al. (2016), the findings to be replicated were again not randomly selected and assigned. Only between-subject designs were used, and the finding that the author declared most important was selected. The allocation of target findings to teams is not reported. Thus, whilst this study is a landmark contribution to the field, systematic replication efforts in experimental economics are still at a very initial stage. It seems desirable for a random selection and assignment protocol to be used, which would give a better idea of the general direct replicability of results. However, as Gilbert et al. (2016) point out, in commentary on OSC (2015), this would presuppose a defensible definition of the population of studies from which to draw samples.

Regarding stand-alone direct replication studies, few of these seem to have been conducted in experimental economics. A past editor of the journal *Experimental Economics* has informed the author that during his tenure, not a single direct replication article had been submitted, despite it being the policy of the journal to welcome such submissions.[3] The *Journal of the Economic Science Association* has also solicited replications but with disappointing response. This does not imply that the field is bereft of replication, since it is relatively common for researchers to include a baseline treatment which directly replicates a progenitor study. Such studies are often described as 'follow-up' studies.

However, it is possible that in these cases the inclusion of the baseline replication may also be with the motivation to provide credibility for the subsequent, original, manipulation. In that case, the assumption seems to be that the original findings *ought* to be reproduced, which is not the case in a pure replication study.[4] In this mode of operation, a field may conceivably be prone to 'bad equilibria', in which an effect that is not actually robust may acquire the status of an expected outcome.

A second lesson for the field, then, is that more is required than journal policy statements to elicit replication attempts from authors. Preregistered designs, in which peer review and a provisional publication decision take place before a design is implemented, may increase authors' confidence of being able to publish replications of findings which have standing in the field. The fears which are countered are rejection because of lack of originality in case of a positive result, and because of perceived reputational damage to other researchers, in the case of a null or negative result. The other researchers in question may also be reviewers or associates of reviewers, a prospect potential replicators will doubtless be wary of. Combining a special journal issue with preregistered designs as with *Social Psychology* 45(3) seems a good strategy, and if it could be combined with randomised effect selection and assignment, would be considerably strengthened with regard to obtaining a general picture of how likely results are to hold.

2.4 Which Factors Can Be Varied in Direct Replication?

2.4.1 The Authorial Inclusion Issue

In response to the enfolding controversy, Nobel laureate Daniel Kahneman issued a call for a 'new etiquette' for replication studies:

> Authors should be guaranteed a significant role in replications of their work … In the myth of perfect science, the method section of a research report always includes enough detail to permit a direct replication. Unfortunately this seemingly reasonable demand is rarely satisfied in psychology, because behaviour is easily affected by seemingly irrelevant factors. For example, experimental instructions are commonly paraphrased in the methods section, although their wording and even the font in which they are printed are known to be significant.
> … the original author should have detailed advanced knowledge of what the replicator plans to do. [Since] authors will generally be more sensitive than replicators to the possible effects of small discrepancies of procedure (Kahneman, 2014).

Kahneman goes on to argue that the burden of justification should lie on replicators in the event that they deviate from any experimental detail advocated by the originator in pretrial correspondence.

This intervention seems to have been especially contentious. Perhaps one reason for this is because it puts power squarely back in the hands of original authors, since it increases the burden of planning and preparation for would-be replicators and increases the scope for adversarial confrontation, between researchers with probably unequal status, prior to a replication attempt. Since that objection concerns power relations, it is not epistemic, however. That is, it does not follow from this consideration that authorial involvement is not necessary or best scientifically for replication studies. Since the power relations aspect is plausibly negative, a factor which is likely to suppress valid critique, we need to consider whether there is a credible epistemic counterpoint.

Kahneman's plea actually echoes an earlier argument by Schmidt (2009). Schmidt gives an example from the natural sciences of a paper on laser construction. Apparently, several authors attempted to reproduce the laser in question following the methods and procedures set out in the paper, but were unable to do so without help from the original author. Schmidt concludes that there is often a substantial element of tacit knowledge involved in producing a result, which it is not possible to set out completely in a scientific paper, and that it is reasonable to conclude that the same is likely in the social sciences. On this basis, he advocates authorial involvement by the original author in a direct replication study, but specifically for cases where the setup is complex.

Both authors argue from a premise that methods sections of journal articles lack sufficient information to conduct direct replications and conclude that *ex-ante* authorial involvement is necessary (at least in some cases) to supply the missing information. However, Schmidt goes on to point out a consequent danger that experimental artefacts in the original study (other than Type 1 errors) will be reproduced in the replications.

That danger seems to this author especially likely given the kinds of thing that Kahneman actually mentions as missing. It seems there are epistemic asymmetries between the laser case and social science experiments which lie behind Schmidt's concern, that require analysis. Firstly, in the former case, the result is not necessarily in doubt, since once a laser has been produced it can be independently inspected and tested. In the latter case, in contrast, all we have is a reported finding. Secondly, in the case of the laser, one can well imagine that there are details with a physical basis that have to be right, even if these are not yet fully understood by the inventor. For example, a laser inventor might conceivably recommend a particular type of glass, even if they did not understand fully why this seemed superior. It would seem to be a different matter if the original author were to communicate that, for example, the laser should only be constructed on a Tuesday evening, after everyone involved has danced the Tango. If *that* were the missing information, perhaps one could reasonably conclude that the originator has happened on the result by chance, and does not really understand what is going on in the supposedly controlled setting.

A strong authorial inclusion norm therefore seems potentially counterproductive from the point of view of perpetuating possible experimental artefacts. There may be some special cases that are analogous to Schmidt's laser example where complex technical details have not been described in sufficient detail to enable replication, where authorial consultation is needed. In general, however, as commentators have argued, if methods and procedures sections are typically inadequate, a logical response is for authors to write them better, and for editors to enforce this, on pain of a replicator being unable to reproduce the results.[5] This means that all relevant details should be included if one wishes others to be able to corroborate the result. The mere mention by an author of a particular experimental detail does not make it relevant. What then does count as relevant?

2.4.2 Relevant and Irrelevant Details

The notion that there are seemingly irrelevant details that have to be right to reproduce certain psychology results is iterated in Stapel's (2014) confessional autobiography. Stapel writes, of an earlier and supposedly innocent period in which he had been reproducing other authors' results,

> My colleagues from around the world sent me piles of instructions, questionnaires, papers, and software.
>
> Now I saw what was going on. In most of the packages there was a letter, or sometimes a yellow Post-It note stuck to the bundle of documents, with extra instructions:
>
> 'Don't do this test on a computer. We tried that and it doesn't work. It only works if you use pencil-and-paper forms.'
>
> 'This experiment only works if you use "friendly" or "nice". It doesn't work with "cool" or "pleasant" or "fine". I don't know why.'
>
> 'After they've read the newspaper article, give the participants something else to do for three minutes. No more, no less. Three minutes, otherwise it doesn't work.'
>
> 'This questionnaire only works if you administer it to groups of three to five people.
>
> No more than that.'
>
> Stapel (2014, p. 69)[6]

I am inclined to think that something sets apart these kinds of detail from *bona fide* missing technical details and puts them instead on a par with the Tuesday Tango. A potential candidate for a demarcation criterion here is that the suspect requirements are irrelevant given the state of knowledge. Both Tuesdays and the Tango are social constructions with no basis in physics, and so are strictly theoretically irrelevant to producing a physical effect or working apparatus. Font choice, whilst it may have certain psychological effects, seems similarly orthogonal to (for example) the availability heuristic, cognitive dissonance, or a hypothesised relationship between moral judgements and cleanliness. Also, any explanation of how font selection might mediate a purported treatment effect would have to deal with the fact that the font selected for the experimental instructions will be the same in each experimental treatment.

For these reasons, it seems almost certain that if any of the effects just mentioned required use of a certain font for written instructions, publication of this fact would appear to undermine the result as originally described. For it would appear to be impossible to explain the influence of font in a manner that preserves unaltered either generality for the purported result, or any theoretical explanations of it considered in the relevant papers. Historians of science have argued that experimental results are unlikely to achieve significant status within a field without a theory which explains how the results came about. In the absence of this, they are likely to remain just numbers. According to realists, the theory in successful cases sets out a generating mechanism (Pawson and Tilley, 1997). Mystery factors like the Tuesday Tango could play no useful role in such a theory, serving instead as a 'ghost in the machine'.

This demarcation criterion, which we may term epistemic considerations, also seems relevant to deciding which of the *specified* details of a design are essential to repeat in order to effect a direct replication. It is uncontroversial that repetition of all details except the sample drawn is practically impossible. This seems impossible even with extensive authorial involvement, since without a photographic memory the original author will not remember such details as the exact colour of the carpet in a laboratory, the course of the weather through each experimental session or how many times the experimenter and his assistants happened to blink. Nonetheless. it presumably makes sense to speak of conducting 'the same' experiment, as this and cognate expressions are used routinely in replication literature. This paradox, that the same experiment is implemented with many details changed, seems to be an instance of the old philosophical puzzle of Theseus's ship. The ship in question remains the same vessel despite each of its timbers being replaced over time. How is this possible?

An influential answer to this question comes from philosopher Robert Nozick, in his *Philosophical Explanations* (Nozick, 1981). Nozick explains that if someone regards Theseus's ship as unchanged, we are weighting factors highly other than its material substance in our conception of its identity. Such factors might include who owns it and its general physical form, for example. The identity of something is thus akin to a weighted sum of distance scores over several types of characteristic.[7] Which weights apply may be different in different circumstances. To an archaeologist interested in dating the construction of the ship, the fact that all the timbers have changed is crucially important. To the Athenians who allegedly maintained the ship in a seaworthy condition for centuries as an act of thanks to the Gods, this factor was assigned far less weight than its physical continuity and form.

In the context of direct replication, it seems that criteria of identity for an experiment derive in part from theoretical considerations. Thus, for example, if a particular explanation is proposed for an experimental result, the procedural details employed in the original study should be consistent with this. A replication study should give equal chance for the explanations proposed to operate as did the original. This may also enable some 'gap filling' to take place in relation to missing procedural details. To take an economic example, if a purported explanation for a finding comes from the theory of finitely repeated games, one may infer that subjects were informed about the existence and timing of a final round. If this matter is not explicitly clarified in procedures, as it ought ideally to be, and full (verbal plus written) instructions are not available, this is a reasonable inference.[8] But it will not be of interest which font was used in the instructions unless, as seems improbable, font is implicated in a theory explaining the finding, and it will not be a serious objection that a different font was used.

Under theoretical considerations, far more can be included than the specific social science theories referred to as being tested or providing explanations of results, however. There is also the general theory of experimentation and experimental traditions informed by a theoretical background in particular social sciences. A more general 'theory' of experimentation includes such aspects as which factor(s) were changed between treatments, which factors operative in a naturally occurring setting were excluded from the experimental setting, the content of information, graphical or display factors, sampling procedure and subject pool, allocation to treatment, time and place of experiment, communication protocol, anonymity protocol and 'blinding' procedures. In economics experiments, considerations which would normally be relevant also include the nature and level of incentives, one shot or repeated setting and so on.

If we vary factors that are theoretically *ir*relevant and obtain the same results, this form of replication has greater confirmatory power than an exact replication would. In common parlance amongst behavioural economists, we see that the finding is more 'robust'. The pronouncement by Nosek and Lakens (2014, p7) seem apposite here:

> A direct replication is the attempt to duplicate the conditions and procedure that existing theory and evidence anticipate as necessary for obtaining the effect ... Successful replication bolsters evidence that all of the sample, setting, and procedural differences presumed to be irrelevant are, in fact, irrelevant.

This coincides with the demarcation criterion of epistemic considerations, with the proviso that the factors mentioned as evidenced are not ones that are ruled out in (well-established) theory. Another anecdote from Stapel (2014) may be illuminating here. Stapel claims inside knowledge that a particular, prized, effect in social psychology does not replicate under the conditions as described by researchers in their reports. Terror Management Theory (TMT) posits that individuals normally go about in a state of suppression of knowledge of their own death (Solomon et al., 1991). Consequently, effects are observable when experimental subjects are asked to reflect on their own death, in particular, bold, assertive statements are likely which serve to restore the participant's sense of well-being and security. Stapel claims that an unnamed research team tried repeatedly and unsuccessfully to replicate key findings in this literature, and that the difference between themselves and a laboratory which did produce the phenomena lay in the experimenters' 'alternative' subculture orientation, in particular their clothing. Specifically, in the latter laboratory, the experimenters tended to wear black clothes, heavy metal t-shirts and so on, rather than well-ironed shirts, ties, suits and so on.

The story stretches credulity, particularly because the evidence for TMT derives from a large set of research teams, not one laboratory (Burke et al., 2010). But supposing that it were true, for the sake of argument, this detail would not count as epistemically irrelevant, because it suggests a closely related priming effect. Interacting with the nihilistically dressed researchers and assistants, that is, may provide subtle cues of mortality which enable the experimental manipulation to be more effective. However, at the current state of knowledge, no such priming effect has been posited in TMT studies, so authors would be fully justified in not implementing this detail in a replication attempt. They would also be justified, it seems, in reporting a failure to replicate even if they knew about the nihilistic clothing anecdote, and even if they had strong private grounds for believing it to be true, on the preceding discussion. Thus, prior to anything being published on it, the clothing detail would not count amongst the conditions that the existing evidence identifies as necessary. On the other hand, continuing to produce the result with the aid of nihilistic clothing without reporting the matter would be detrimental to the field, because this omission would make the effect seem more robust than it really is. In psychologists' parlance, we would be suppressing knowledge of the boundary conditions for the finding in question.

Depending on our goals, however, and following Schmidt (2009), what counts as an irrelevant factor may change. Nosek and Lakens's aforementioned formulation of what can be changed leaves on the face of it considerable latitude for factors which might or might not be varied in a direct replication. The original instructions will include many factors ('Good morning. Welcome to the experiment ...') that existing theory and evidence suggest can be changed. It is normal practice in direct replication, notwithstanding this, including for the studies in Table 2.1, to use the original instructions and materials if these are available. This has the virtue of minimising omission of anything that is possibly epistemically relevant. It probably also reflects a relatively narrow goal, however, to confirm that something is there worthy of the attention of the research community, with relatively less emphasis on robustness checking.

A different goal obtains if we wish to see whether a result generalises beyond its initial context, and this may mean different criteria of identity for 'the same' experiment. It may well be defensible to argue that existing theory and evidence point to a particular context as being necessary to produce a result, but we wish to go beyond this by applying the same procedure elsewhere or differently. In doing so, however, it seems we are not necessarily in the realm of conceptual replication, where the more variation is applied to test the same hypothesis or reproduce the same phenomenon the better, and we will still be essentially repeating a procedure in a new setting. To take an economic example, we might ask whether the result of the dictator game is robust. To have a variety of designs all of which found positive transfers in the dictator game, all of which used different instructions, gives us greater confidence in this result than if everyone had used the same instructions verbatim. Or one might have found that, for example, members of a particular religious group give more than subjects in general in the dictator game. Existing evidence might, at that point, be taken to suggest that use of this particular group was necessary to produce the effect, but one would still be amply justified in using a different religious denomination to see if the result generalised, and in reporting this as 'the same' experiment for this purpose.

2.5 HARKing and CARKing

'HARKing' stands for 'hypothesising after the results are known' and is a conventionally (albeit not universally) regarded as poor academic practice. The arguments for and against HARKing are thoughtfully discussed by Kerr (1998), who argues that the costs of HARKing clearly outweigh the benefits. 'CARKing, critiquing after the results are known, seems' to have been coined by Nosek and Lakens (2014). By analogy, it means presenting a criticism of a design as one that you would have made in advance of the results being known, which is in fact a criticism made in reaction to unwelcome results. A CARKing criticism therefore seems to be one that the reviewer would not have made had the results been favourable, whether the critic is conscious of this fact or not.

It is usually seen as making a crucial difference to the validity of statistical testing whether the hypothesis is advanced prior to the knowledge of the data or not. Kerr (1998) considers objections to HARKing from both classical and Bayesian statistics viewpoints. Many of the objections from a classical perspective amount to the charge that it increases the likelihood of Type 1 error beyond the specified p-value of a reported test statistic. To put this more strongly, virtually any real dataset will contain some pattern that is 'significant' according to some statistical test if one collects enough covariate and outcome data, and so can be misrepresented after the fact as testing and confirming a hypothesis posited *ex-ante*. Under HARK-ing, then, one is almost guaranteed a high enough test statistic even if there are no genuine effects behind the data. This makes a nonsense of hypothesis testing since the real p-value should in that case, by definition, be close to 1.[9]

From a Bayesian statistics perspective, the objection Kerr (1998) relates is not temporal but substantive. That is, HARKing gives rise to *ad hoc* theorising in the sense that nothing but the data to hand are likely to support the hypothesis. In that case, by definition, it has a very low prior probability. By disguising the *post hoc* nature of a hypothesis, authors conceal the likelihood that it is *ad hoc* from the reader and so exaggerate its plausibility.

No general parallel argument to the classical objection applies, it seems, in the case of CARKing, however, since it is not an exercise in pattern finding or rationalisation, but in criticism of a piece of research. Let us suppose for clarity that the reviewer is not testing a further hypothesis, which would amount to HARKing. *When* a criticism is advanced is not strictly relevant, in itself, to the soundness of a criticism. Implicit in the concern over CARKing, therefore, seems to be the view that criticisms prompted by 'motivated reasoning' are particularly likely to be spurious. Since all acts of reasoning are, arguably, motivated, what this refers to is reasoning motivated other than by a desire to further the scholarly objectives of the research field, such as the quest for knowledge. Most obviously, the original author or their associates, followers or admirers may want to protect a result to limit reputational damage, or perhaps to protect ongoing and future research projects, if a finding has not been reproduced. Since it is not possible to exactly replicate a study, imperfectly motivated reviewers will predictably insist that some detail ought to have been implemented, and will have a menu of options to choose from.

This concern seems to mirror the Bayesian objection to HARKing. It is not the timing of the criticism per se that is worrying but the likelihood that, if an objection is made that would not have been made prior to the results being known, it is likely to be an objection with little to recommend it. In short, CARKing is probably carping. In an ideal scenario where editors have time to dispassionately evaluate reviewers' criticisms of a study, this might be of little consequence, since reasons motivated or not can still be independently evaluated in terms of evidential support and logic. But in the messy, real world where busy editors lack sufficient time for this, they are likely to take reviewers' advice to a significant extent on trust. Perhaps most academics sense this who have bothered to argue with an editor. Thus, concern about CARKing seems pragmatically reasonable.

For an earnest reviewer to guard against CARKing ('Would I have made that criticism if I had not seen the results?') seems to imply an overly exacting standard of self-knowledge. Preregistering designs (in general) must help with both CARKing and HARKing. In particular, it is simply not possible to CARK as a reviewer if one does not get to see the results, and so attention is more likely focussed on the epistemically important details of the design. The same menu of differences between the original and replication is available for the reviewer as material for objections, but as Nosek and Lakens argue (2014, p138), insistence on minor details risks trivialising a result. *Ex-ante*, that is, even an imperfectly motivated reviewer faces a trade-off between protecting a cherished result and allowing the study to find that seemingly unimportant details do not matter.

Under preregistration, a provisional decision is made on publication prior to data collection, and normally the only subsequent check is that the data were collected as planned, for example with sufficient sample size to achieve the prespecified statistical power.

However, does it follow from the motivated reasoning concern, and the availability of preregistration as a reviewing protocol, that criticism of a replication study made after the fact should never preclude publication? I think it does not. An example, which was the subject of heated controversy, may help to clarify the matter. The example is not introduced with a view to taking sides on the dispute over the particular study but to illustrate the existence of kinds of concern which are legitimate and can only arise after the data are known.

One of the findings targeted for replication in *Social Psychology* 45(3) was that judgements of an ethical nature tend to be less extreme if the person making them is clean, as reported in Schnall et al. (2008). In the original study, conducted in the United Kingdom and published in *Science*, participants either washed their hands (treatment) or did not (control) after experiencing disgust (implemented by a video screening) and before being asked to make moral judgements using a rating scale. A priming manipulation also found the same effect: when primed with the concept of physical cleanliness, subjects made more lenient judgements. The replication attempt (Johnson et al., 2014) used the same materials as the original study, and sample sizes far larger, but failed to reproduce either effect at a statistically significant level. The effect size (Cohen's d) estimated in each case is almost zero, but as seems the norm in replication studies, the authors conclude only that the true effect sizes 'are substantially smaller than the estimates generated from the original … studies' (Johnson, Cheung and Donellan, 2014), and that researchers in the field should therefore use very large samples. This might be read as a joke, since the sample sizes for an effect size close to zero would be truly enormous to achieve a design with adequate power.[10] With the reported $d = 0.01$, for example, a two-tailed, two-sample t-test would require more than 400,000 subjects in total to achieve power of 90 per cent. Good luck with obtaining funding for that!

On the face of it, this seems a very informative replication failure. Since the authors used the original materials, all of the epistemically relevant factors would appear to be held constant, including any flaws in the original design, alongside many irrelevant factors. In the authors' response to this replication (Schnall, 2014), however, it is pointed out that there were many more responses in the replication study close to the ceiling of the rating scale than obtained in the original study. Schnall argues that respondents in the United States may exercise more severe moral judgements than their UK counterparts on the scale used, for the particular stimuli deployed. The subsequent debate focussed on whether or not this made observing the purported effect too unlikely, whether observations near the ceiling can be dropped without too much detriment to the analysis and so on. But the replicators also invoked the dangers of CARKing as a response to Schnall's observation.

Whether or not the replicators are right in this specific case that the statistical analysis still goes through in the absence of the observations close to ceiling, it is generally the case that having too many observations at the ceiling of a scale could preclude any effect being observed. At the limit, with 100 per cent of observations in the treatment group at the ceiling, one could only observe an effect in one direction or a null result. There is also no reason a priori to expect moral judgements to be equally severe across different populations. So this kind of objection must be valid in principle. Further, it is inappropriate to invoke a prohibition on CARKing here since this kind of flaw cannot possibly be identified prior to the data being collected. The flaws in question, as a general class, are features of the data that either render it implausible or that undermine the proposed analysis. Consider another, hypothetical, example. A replication study that collected income data from participants, and then reported that they were all billionaires, has implausible data, is not a credible piece of research and ought not to be published to the extent that it relies on unbiased measurement of income. A strict adherence to a CARKing prohibition, and quality control only prior to data collection, will allow any such cases to go through, and might even contribute to poor-quality data collection.

Since editors do often exercise an element of quality control even with pre-registered designs after the data have been collected, it seems arbitrary to this author to rule out checks on data quality. As a formal extra step in a replication protocol, this would increase time and effort necessary to complete the publication process, however. Assuming this could be done, additional measures to guard against the reintroduction of problematically motivated reasoning might be necessary. For example, reviewers might be instructed not to comment on design features in an ex-post review, except in so far as they explain a data quality problem.

2.6 Closeness to Theory in Experimental Economics – a Double-Edged Sword?

We should perhaps be less surprised if findings turn out not to be repeatable, the less plausible or well specified is the theory set out whereby conditions A should produce effect or phenomenon B. In some of the replication failures from psychology, the theory supporting the core hypothesis seems underdeveloped. For example, consider the purported result that sensations of physical warmth affect people's tendency to exhibit selfishness as opposed to altruism. This finding was reported experimentally by Williams and Bargh (2008), and a replication attempt was conducted by Lynott et al. (2014), which failed to reproduce the effect. There is a theory section in the original study developed to motivate the research, glossed by the replicators as follows: 'The basic idea is that physical feelings of warmth translate to greater interpersonal warmth.'

As a theory, this seems to involve a pun on 'warmth', since in the latter expression warmth is a linguistic metaphor for either an emotional state or a personality disposition. If there is a general body of knowledge implying specific causal connections between the two, it should be invoked. Although motivating literature is presented in the original article, it takes a more impressionistic form than this. Evidence is cited that physical warmth is important in infant contact with early carers and subsequent healthy development; it is asserted that because of such contact that physical warmth and psychological warmth should be associated mentally, and finally that the insula is involved in processing sensations of both interpersonal and physical warmth (Williams and Bargh, 2008 p606).[11] Thus, arguably, the theory reads more as a chronology of factors that led to the formulation of a hypothesis rather than as a purported mechanism which would demonstrably produce the hypothesised effect, as realists would have it,[12] or even as a set of premises that logically imply the hypothesis.

Similar comments apply for the hypothesis linking moral judgements and cleanliness. At a risk of painting too clear and simple a picture, in economics, in contrast, theory development carries much prestige, and experimental work usually has very close ties to theory. It would be tempting to assume, then, that economics is in a better position in this respect, and that therefore a better replication record can be expected to follow.

In one respect, this seems unexceptional. There is an emphasis on deductive derivation of hypotheses from theories in modern economics which, plausibly, serves to discipline researchers against loose theorising. In other respects, however, it is debatable whether certain common kinds of tie between theory and experiment are necessarily healthy or good news for replication.

To see this, consider that most designs implement a setting that resembles in some way the ontology of economic theory. For example, rational choice theory is populated by independent decision makers, whose choice problems are represented as mathematical structures, such as well-defined probability and utility/value components. In the laboratory, independent decision-making is implemented by having subjects sit and make decisions at workstations, blind to what others are doing. (There are also good statistical reasons for doing this.) And they typically choose (in parametric choice experiments) between lotteries with monetary payoffs and specific known probabilities. In terms developed by Cubitt (2005), whilst a theory may have an *intended* domain which is very broad and inclusive of settings where ambiguity or radical uncertainty reign and communication is free, its legitimate *testing* domain may still include highly stylised settings. What matters for testing is whether the theory makes predictions for that setting, and this is a matter of what can be deduced from the theory. Using choice problems which resemble the relevant theories' representations helps, it seems, to make sharp predictions. If the theory fails in that setting, arguably, this is a particularly bad failure, since it should be more likely to work in a setting that resembles the theory. The downside to this is that if the theory performs well in such a setting, we still lack evidence for how well it performs in its intended domain (Schram, 2005).

Given a preference for working in such stylised environments, it is likely that the kinds of replication that take place in follow-up studies tend towards direct replication. Grether and Plott's (1979) famous study of the robustness of preference reversals, for example, consisted of repeating the P versus $ bet choice and valuation tasks, characterised by monetary prizes and well-defined probabilities, in a variety of modified settings. However, this is a choice, and it is also possible to run economics experiments closer to the intended domain. Ball, Bardsely and Ormerod (2012) for example, study (and find) classic preference reversals in tasks which have neither known probabilities nor known consequences. Arguably this sits closer to the conceptual replication end of the spectrum, despite the fact that choice and valuation task procedures are repeated.

However, a second common way in which experimental economists stick to theory is by 'implementing' an economic model as closely as possible, in order to test the theory associated with the model. Bardsley et al. (2010) argue that this approach commits the 'fallacy of misplaced concreteness', originally posited by A. N. Whitehead (1925). This fallacy occurs when an abstraction is mistaken for the concrete thing that it is ostensibly derived from or represents. For an economic model is essentially a mathematical structure that is used in the course of theorising *about something else*. The theory is not *about* the model.

If so, attention should be paid to implementing the something else, that which that the theory is about, rather than the model. Only in this way will the theory make predictions about the experimental environment, and therefore only in this way can the theory be tested or usefully developed by experiment. A classroom experiment which maximally implements the assumptions of, for example, Cournot duopoly theory is one in which there is no firm in the natural language sense of the word. For this natural language is not part of the formal model, despite the fact that the theory forms part of 'theory of the firm' or 'industrial organisation'. There are limits to implementation, however, if subjects really are to choose how to behave. What is really being studied in such cases, according to Bardsley et al.'s (2010) critique, is that which is not implemented, namely assumptions about motivation and interaction. By maximally implementing the Cournot model, therefore, what one actually studies is a behavioural game, and what one actually tests is a joint hypothesis comprising a game-theoretic solution concept and motivational assumptions.

A model-implementing experiment can clearly be subject to direct replication, since any procedure can be repeated, with irrelevant details such as the instruction fonts, wall colours and so on changed, and can also be found to be robust (or not) to levels of incentives, variations in samples, degree of repetition and so on. But it seems that it is difficult to specify what would constitute a conceptual replication. To stick with the same example, if we aim to reproduce a result about Cournot duopoly in a radically different setting, by implementing the same model, it is not clear what can constitute the different setting.

For if the model has to be implemented, this determines the setting, and the same model then implies essentially the same setting, and there seems to be no real room for manoeuvre. If we introduced potential for subjects to compete on quality and/or price, for example, this contradicts the Cournot model. To implement a different model would supposedly test a different theory.

Alternatively, under the interpretation of these experiments as actually constituting decision- and game-theoretic experiments, it is relatively straightforward to specify what would count as a conceptual replication. A test of Nash equilibrium can be carried out in a huge range of strategic situations. To take one finding, there is evidence of convergence to Nash equilibrium in several settings involving repetition and random rematching. One might try to reproduce this convergence using animals and children, using nonmonetary rewards, for example. And indeed this has been attempted with some success (inter alia Lee et al., 2004; Sanabria and Thraikill, 2009; Sher et al., 2014). Arguably, it does not make sense for a finding only to admit of direct replication attempts.

The theory-centric character of many economics experiments therefore seems to be double-edged. On the one hand, it is plausible to expect a greater degree of direct replicability in experimental economics than perhaps obtains in psychology (on average), given the consequent uniformity of experimental designs and the logically tight derivation of hypotheses from formally specified theories. On the other hand, the more stylised and less rich are the experimental designs, the less we are likely to learn about how the results generalise to settings that the theories are intended to apply to. The more extreme version of closeness to theory, implementing theoretical models in the laboratory, seems to preclude the possibility of conceptual replication. This may be an indicator of a conceptual mistake underlying this approach, but the problem disappears if we reinterpret the designs as research exercises in the behavioural, as opposed to applied economics, domain.

2.7 Conclusions

Systematic replication efforts have only recently been conducted in psychology and are still more recent and nascent in experimental economics. Although the indications are that the replicability in either field is less than what would obtain under ideal conditions of scholarship, research and publishing, the extent of this problem is actually currently unclear in either field. There is wide variation in replication rates in the recent literature. No general case was found for authorial involvement in direct replication efforts, though it may be necessary in some cases if potentially relevant information has been omitted. There are legitimate concerns over CARKing, in that it may consist in motivated reasoning which journal editors as a practical matter may not be in a good position to guard against. On the other hand, a complete prohibition on data-based criticism seems unjustified. There appears to be a perceived lack of incentives to conduct direct replications, which may stem partly from motivated reasoning issues on the part of reviewers. Preregistered designs and journal special issues help with the incentives to replicate problems. But there would appear to be enhanced value in randomising both selection of findings to replicate and the assignment of each target finding to a replication team, to give a clearer idea of the general extent of replicability in a field. Concerning which details should be replicated, this chapter argues that what counts are the goals of the replication and epistemic features of the original designs, relative to which some details will be irrelevant.

A key characteristic of experimental economics that may to some extent distinguish it from experimental psychology is the tight relationship most designs have to theory. It seems that experimental economics may in one sense be well served by such proximity, in terms of the avoidance of underdeveloped theorising supporting a hypothesis. But sticking closely to environments which are isomorphic to economic theory arguably comes at a cost in terms of the informativeness of designs about a theory's intended domain, which can be seen as a potential deficit in conceptual replication. When this closeness to theory consists of implementing an economic model, it seems that conceptual replication is precluded. This seems likely to be an indicator that the approach involves conceptual error.

Notes

1 It is not the author's intention to draw a sharp distinction between 'behavioural' and 'experimental' economics, but to the extent there is a set of research and publication practices distinct from those in experimental psychology, centred around incentivised experiments and a close relationship between laboratory and theory, the latter term seems more applicable.

2 I owe this point and the derivation in the Appendix to Kelvin Balcombe (personal communication). The calculation assumes that power is equal in original and replication designs. Rates of replicated rejection of null hypotheses should be higher if original designs are of lower power.

3 Personal communication with Professor Tim Cason.

4 According to Collins (1991), replication disputes are always concerned to establish what the results of an experiment *ought* to be. This seems consistent with the correct factual outcome being a logically prior matter for resolution, however, which Collins seems at pains to deny.

5 See, for example, Wilson (2014) and the ensuing online exchange.

6 It is possible that Stapel exaggerates the role of such mystery factors in order to make his fraudulent activity seem less extreme. Stapel also asks what the alleged sensitivity to mystery factors implies about the scientific value of the purported results, but does not provide an answer (Stapel, 2014, p. 72).

7 See Glass (2000), who discusses the identity issue and Nozik's solution in the context of meta-analysis.
8 It is not an infallible inference, since ideas from the theory of finitely repeated games may have traction in settings which do not perfectly instantiate the way such games are modelled.
9 By analogy. every time one strikes a match, the pattern of flame produced is unique in the history of the universe. The *ex-ante* probability of that particular pattern is vanishingly small, but one is guaranteed to produce some pattern that has negligible likelihood.
10 Other seemingly modest pronouncements in this genre include the statement that the conditions necessary to produce the effect in question are 'not yet fully understood'.
11 The weakness of the neurological component of this sequence lies in the fact that specific parts of the brain, including the insula, are typically implicated in a wide range of cognitive and affective processes. See Poldrack (2006) for critical discussion.
12 Realists would presumably not endorse the 'as-if' interpretation of economic theories, nor the conscious production of theories which only sustain an 'as if' reading, however.

Appendix

Definitions

p the probability that a null hypothesis selected for investigation is true
T the event that the null hypothesis is true
$\sim$ Not
r the event that an original trial rejected H_0
R the event that H_0 is rejected in a new trial
α significance threshold
β power of replication design

By definition, $P(T) = p$, and by assumption the original and new trials are independent.

Under precise replication of the experiment

$$P(r|T) = P(R|T) = \alpha$$

$$P(r|\sim T) = P(R|\sim T) = \beta$$

$$P(R) = P(R, T) + P(R, \sim T) = P(R|T)P(T)$$

$$+P(R|\sim T)P(\sim T) = \alpha p + \beta(1-p)$$

With no biases in reporting,

$$P(R) = \alpha p + \beta(1-p) = P(r)$$

$$P(T|r) = \frac{\alpha p}{\alpha p + \beta(1-p)} = P(T|R)$$

$$P(\sim T|r) = \frac{\beta(1-p)}{\alpha p + \beta(1-p)} = P(\sim T|R)$$

Rates of replicated rejection of H_0 are therefore given by

$$
\begin{aligned}
P(R|r) &= P(R, T|r) + P(R, \sim T|r) \\
&= P(R| T, r)P(T|r) + P(R|\sim T,r)P(\sim T|r) \\
&= P(R|T)P(T|r) + P(R|\sim T)P(\sim T|r) \\
&= \frac{\alpha^2 p + \beta^2 (1-p)}{\alpha p + \beta(1-p)}
\end{aligned}
$$

2.8 References

Ball, L., Bardsley, N. and Ormerod, T. (2012). Do Preference Reversals Generalise? Results on Ambiguity and Loss Aversion. *Journal of Economic Psychology*, 33, 48–57.

Bardsley, N., Cubitt, R., Loomes, G., Moffatt, P., Starmer, C. and Sugden, R. (2010). *Experimental Economics: Rethinking the Rules*. New Jersey: Princeton University Press.

Battalio, R. C., Kagel, J. H. and MacDonald, D. N. (1985). Animals' Choices over Uncertain Outcomes: Some Initial Experimental Results. *American Economic Review*, 75, 597–613.

Bhaskar, R. (1978). *A Realist Theory of Science*. Hassocks: Harvester Press.

Bhattacharjee, Y. (2013). The Mind of a Con Man. *New York Times*, 26 April.

Bornemann-Cimenti, H., Szilagyi, I. S. and Sandner-Kiesling, A. (2016). Perpetuation of Retracted Publications Using the Example of the Scott S. Reuben Case: Incidences, Reasons and Possible Improvements. *Science and Engineering Ethics*, 22, 1063–1072.

Brandt, M. J., Ijzerman, H., Dijksterhuis, A., Farach, F., Geller, J., Giner-Sorolla, R., …, and van't Veer, A. (2014). The Replication Recipe: What Makes for a Convincing Replication? *Journal of Experimental Social Psychology*, 50, 217–224.

Burke, B. L., Martens, A., and Faucher, E. H. (2010). Two Decades of Terror Management Theory: A Meta-analysis of Mortality Salience Research. *Personality and Social Psychology Review*, 14, 155–195.

Camerer, C. F., Dreber, A., Forsell, E., Ho, T. H., Huber, J., Johannesson, M., …, and Wu, H. (2016). Evaluating Replicability of Laboratory Experiments in Economics. *Science*. DOI: 10.1126/science.aaf0918

Collins, H. (1991). The Meaning of Replication and the Science of Economics. *History of Political Economy*, 23, 123–142.

Coyne, J. (2016). Replication Initiatives Will Not Salvage the Trustworthiness of Psychology. *BioMed Central Psychology*, 4, 28.

Cubitt, R. P. (2005). Experiments and the Domain of Economic Theory. *Journal of Economic Methodology*, 12, 197–210.

Fiske, S. T. (2016). A Call to Change Science's Culture of Shaming. *Association for Psychological Science Observer*, 29(9), 5–6.

Gilbert, D. T., King, G., Pettigrew, S. and Wilson, T. D. (2016). Comment on 'Estimating the Reproducibility of Psychological Science'. *Science*, 351, 1037.

Glass, G. V. (2000). Meta-Analysis at 25. Retrieved 15 August 2016 from www.gvglass .info/papers/meta25.html

Greenwood, J. D. (1982). On the Relation Between Laboratory Experiments and Social Behaviour: Causal Explanation and Generalisation. *Journal of the Theory of Social Behaviour*, 12, 225–249.

Grether, D. and Plott, C. (1979). Economic Theory of Choice and the Preference Reversal Phenomenon. *American Economic Review*, 69, 623–638.

Hume, D. (1739–40 [2007]) *A Treatise of Human Nature*, ed. D. F. Norton and M. J. Norton. Oxford: Clarendon Press.

Ioannidis, J. P. A. (2005). Why Most Published Research Findings Are False. *Public Library of Science – Medicine*, 2, e124.

Johnson, D. J., Cheung, F. and Donellan, M. B. (2014). Does Cleanliness Influence Moral Judgements? A direct Replication of Schnall, Benton and Harvey (2008). *Social Psychology*, 45, 209–215.

Kahneman, D. (2014). A New Etiquette for Replication. *Social Psychology*, 45, 310–311.

Kerr, N. L. (1998). HARKing: Hypothesizing After the Results Are Known. *Personality and Social Psychology Review*, 2, 196–217.

Klein, R. A., Ratliff, K., Vianello. M. et al. (2014). Investigating Variation in Replicability: A 'Many Labs' Replication Project. *Social Psychology*, 45, 142–152.

Lee, D., Conroy, M. L., McGreevy, B. P. and Barraclough, D. J. (2004). Reinforcement Learning and Decision Making in Monkeys a Competitive Game. *Cognitive Brain Research*, 22, 45–58.

Levelt, W. J. M., Drenth, P., and Noort, E. (Eds.). (2012). *Flawed Science: The Fraudulent Research Practices of Social Psychologist Diederik Stapel*. Tilburg: Commissioned by Tilburg University, the University of Amsterdam and the University of Groningen.

Lynott, D., Corker, K. S., Wortman, J., Connell, L., Donnellan, M. B., Lucas, R. E., and O'Brien, K. (2014). Replication of 'Experiencing Physical Warmth Promotes Interpersonal Warmth' by Williams and Bargh (2008). *Social Psychology*, 45, 216–223.

Nosek, B. A. and Lakens, D. (2014). Registered Reports: A Method to Increase the Credibility of Published Results. *Social Psychology*, 45, 137–141.

Nozick, R. (1981). *Philosophical Explanations*. Cambridge, MA: Harvard University Press.

Open Science Collaboration (2015). Estimating the Reproducibility of Psychological Science. *Science*, 349, aac4716. doi: 10.1126/science.aac4716

Pawson, R. and Tilley, N. (1997). *Realistic Evaluation*. London: Sage.

Plott, C. R. and Smith, V. L. (2008). *Handbook of Experimental Economics Results. Volume 1.* Amsterdam: North Holland Press.

Poldrack, R. A. (2006). Can Cognitive Processes Be Inferred from Neuroimaging Data? *Trends in Cognitive Sciences*, 10, 59–63.

Rosenthal, R. and Fode, K. L. (1963). The Effect Experimenter Bias on the Performance of the Albino Rat. *Behavioral Science*, 8, 183–189.

Rosenthal, R. and Jacobson, L. (1963). Teachers' Expectancies: Determinants of Pupils' IQ Gains. *Psychological Reports*, 19, 115–118.

Sanabria, F. and Thraikill, E. (2009). Pigeons (*Columba livia*) Approach Nash Equilibrium in Experimental Matching Pennies Competitions. *Journal of the Experimental Analysis of Behavior*, 91, 169–183.

Schmidt, S. (2009). Shall We Really Do It Again? The Powerful Concept of Replication Is Neglected in the Social Sciences. *Review of General Psychology*, 13, 90–100.

Schnall, S. (2014). Commentary and Rejoinder on Johnson, Cheung and Donnellan (2014a). Clean Data: Statistical Artefacts Wash Out Replication Efforts. *Social Psychology*. Online article; doi: 10.1027/1864–9335/a000204

Schnall, S., Benton, J. and Harvey, S. (2008). With a Clean Conscience: Cleanliness Reduces the Severity of Moral Judgements. *Psychological Science*, 19, 1219–1222.

Sher, I., Koenig, M. and Rustichini, A. (2014). Children's Strategic Theory of Mind. *Proceedings of the National Academy of Sciences*, 111, 13307–13312.

Schram, A. (2005). Artificiality: The Tension between Internal and External Validity in Economic Experiments. *Journal of Economic Methodology*, 12, 225–237.

Solomon, S., Greenberg, J. and Pyszczynski, T. (1991). A Terror Management Theory of Social Behavior: The Psychological Functions of Self-Esteem and Cultural Worldviews. *Advances in Experimental Social Psychology*, 24, 93–159.

Stapel, D. (2014). Faking Science: A True Story of Academic Fraud. Translated by N. J. L. Brown. Available at errorstatistics.files.wordpress.com/2014/12/fakingscience-20141214.pdf

Whitehead, A. N. (1925). *Science and the Modern World.* Cambridge: Cambridge University Press.

Williams, L. E. and Bargh, J. A. (2008). Experiencing Physical Warmth Promotes Interpersonal Warmth. *Science*, 322, 606–607.

Wilson, A. (2014). Psychology's Real Replication Problem: Our Methods Sections. Online article at psychsciencenotes.blogspot.co.uk/2014/05/psychologys-real-replication-problem.html accessed 01.08.2016

PART II

Finance

3 Looking into the Future

How Investors Forecast the Stock Market

J. Michael Collins, Werner De Bondt
and Karl-Erik Wärneryd

> Human nature has no role to play in how subatomic particles interact with
> one another. Our propensities related to fear, euphoria, herding, and cul-
> ture, however, virtually define finance.
>
> Alan Greenspan
> *The Map and the Territory: Risk, Human*
> *Nature, and the Future of Forecasting* 2013b, p. 6.

The 2007–2008 financial crisis and its aftermath signified "an existential crisis" for economic forecasting. This is the judgment of Alan Greenspan, the
former chief of the U.S. Federal Reserve system, in his book *The Map and the
Territory* (2013b). Before the crisis, Greenspan (2007) viewed animal spirits
as "random irrationalities" not readily integrated into economic models. In
contrast, a key theme of his latest work is *predictable error* and behavioral
economics grounded in psychology. About the integration of irrationality into
economic theory, Greenspan does not worry too much. "From the perspective
of a forecaster, the issue is … not whether behavior is rational but whether it
is sufficiently repetitive and systematic to be numerically measured and predicted" (Greenspan, 2013a, p. 14).

Even so, much of modern financial economics continues to be based on the
concept of *rational expectations*. The term stands for mathematical expectation
and is devoid of any connection to psychology. A great deal of modern-day
research in psychology, however, originates in thinking that first arose in Gestalt
psychology, an approach in which the concept of *subjective expectation* is key.

Prognostications of business and market developments, and the risks and
returns associated with particular assets and asset classes, are formed on the
basis of public and private data gathered from personal experience, newspapers, social networks, and so on. Individuals respond to information in distinctive, often systematic, ways. For some, their forecasts amount to firm
convictions and strong hopes or fears. For others, expectations are mere conjectures, colored by mood and made with little confidence.

In this chapter, we discuss how individual investors, as well as experts, use
expectations. We propose a simple model of expectation formation; and we
highlight other factors that influence financial decision-making processes and
outcomes. Many of the studies that we review focus specifically on stock market forecasts, often for U.S. markets. The research fits into a broader program

that explores how human psychology drives the economy (Selten, 1998; Akerlof and Shiller, 2009).

3.1 The Investor and the Market

What forces shape investor forecasts? Professional investors usually examine aggregate and cross-sectional data that reveal what has recently happened. One purpose is to develop explanations at the level of the market, industries, and individual firms. The state of the market, that is, the behavior of other investors, also matters but it is more often than not of secondary interest, as it only introduces noise to standard models.

The concept of expectation as discussed in this chapter is based on a *psychological* model. Mainstream economic theory allows for individual differences in decision-making under risk and uncertainty, such as diverse levels of risk tolerance, but economic theory generally does not address differences in how future expectations are formed across individuals. All investors are assumed to have *rational* expectations, with some error spread around the mean. In reality, different segments of investors may well use thoroughly dissimilar mechanisms to formulate guesses about the future. These behaviors are predictable and systematic. Understanding psychological concepts can offer insights into how investors form and act upon influences that are not readily explained by the rational expectations model.

3.2 The Use of Psychology in the Study of Finance

Since individual investors exhibit varying psychological characteristics that are linked to their particular prognoses and behavior, any attempt to understand the differences between investors is worthwhile. Hypotheses and findings from modern psychology are useful in this task.

John Stuart Mill (1843, p. 7) saw the aim of science as explanation with as few laws as possible ("to diminish as much as possible the catalogue of ultimate truths"). In an ideal world, every phenomenon could be seen as an individual case of a general law subsuming all others. This thinking prompted the notion of *homo economicus* – rational economic man equipped with the single motive of maximizing economic utility. In contrast, the field of psychology looks more like a dining hall offering many entrees; with regard to forecasting, there is a choice among multiple behavioral laws, each subject to contingencies: "It all depends." In fact, the rich assortment of laws on hand may lead researchers to underrate the contingent conditions.

Besides the notion of heuristics (Shefrin, 2000; Ariely, 2008; Kahneman, 2011), probably the most popular loan from psychology to economics is prospect theory. This alternative to expected utility theory is beautifully simple and comprehensive (Kahneman and Tversky, 1979). Theories in *behavioral economics and finance* may be characterized as explanations of behavior that in some way, perhaps only marginally, deviate from the classical rational actor model. For example, some behavioral models of expectations and markets (e.g., Shleifer, 2000) recognize two categories of investors – well-informed, rational investors ("professional traders") and poorly informed noise traders ("laymen" or "amateurs") – but pay almost no attention to the psychological processes that cause and sustain the disparity in performance.

In general, psychological explanations are either cognitive (see, e.g., Neisser, 1976), affective (Zajonc, 1980; Loewenstein et al., 2001; Loewenstein and Lerner, 2003; Slovic et al., 2004), motivational (Maslow, 1954; McClelland, 1961; Baumeister and Tierney, 2011), or sociopsychological (Ross and Nisbett, 1991; Epley, 2014).

3.3 Psychological Expectations: A Simple Model

To a cognitive psychologist, expectations are subjective, belong to people, and can be investigated as characteristics of people. During the nineteenth century, many economists, psychologists, and other commentators asked about the nature and wisdom of expectations. Later, in the twentieth century, this type of study was rejected, but in recent years it has bounced back (see, e.g., Tetlock, 2005; Tetlock and Gardner, 2015).

A notable exception to the twentieth-century neglect was Gestalt psychology. Researchers in this sphere observed perceptual phenomena and formulated laws of perceptual organization. Essentially, the laws concerned how humans form predictions through completing trends and tendencies. Basing themselves on earlier experience, people are disposed to fill in gaps in incomplete perceptions. Gestalt psychology emphasizes wholes rather than parts, in stark contrast with behaviorist psychology.

People fill in gaps because they expect closure, either because things are tangibly close together, because they are similar, or because they are perceived as belonging together. Likewise, people often neglect abrupt changes in trends. Katona (1975) offers three specific insights from this area of psychology:

1. Past experience tends to dominate our expectations and results in routine behavior;
2. New information, if strong enough, may overcome these tendencies;
3. Habitual behavior may be upgraded through insight, problem-solving, and learning.

Katona's insights constitute a model of how people form expectations (Warneryd, 1997):

$$EXP_{t+1} = w_1 B_{Pt} + w_2 B_{At} + w_3 B_{It}$$

where EXP_{t+1} = expectation about period $t + 1$ stated at time t_0, B_{Pt} = beliefs based on extrapolation of past experience, B_{At} = beliefs due to discrepancies between expectations and outcomes, B_{It} = beliefs based on new information, and w_P, w_A, w_I are weights that vary between 0 to 1.

The idea is that forecasts are formed and revised on the basis of (1) *past experience* with a phenomenon (or similar phenomena, involving generalization); (2) *learning* from prior forecast errors; and (3) *new information* in the individual's immediate or more distant environment.

Most expectations are founded on past experience. (In terms of the preceding Warneryd model, this means that the other two sets of beliefs have weights that are close to or equal to zero.) For example, momentum strategies that are built on the continuation of trends dominate the thought processes of many investors. When people expect "more of the same," economists talk about extrapolative expectations. Keynes (1936, p 24) stressed the significance of earlier experience:

> [A] large part of the circumstances usually continues substantially unchanged from one day to the next. Accordingly, it is sensible for producers to base their expectations on the assumption that the most recently realized results will continue except in so far as there are definite reasons for expecting a change.

B_A represents "error-learning." This set of beliefs operates primarily when the expectation is similar to a goal or plan. In other words, it is an intentional expectation. Expectations are contingent when the outcome cannot be affected by anything the holder of the expectation does. This distinction is already noted by James Mill (1829, p. 256):

> In contemplating pains and pleasures as future; in other words, anticipating them, or believing in their future existence; we observe, that, in certain cases, they are independent of our actions; in other cases, that they are consequent upon something which may be done, or left undone by us.

Mill also notes the difference between assessments of the past and expectations of the future. Expectations are not singly based on past experience. The model encompasses the fact that an investor may learn from earlier mistakes in expectation formation and may try to adjust what direct extrapolation suggests. In turbulent times, underestimates resulting from interpolations of earlier experience are often corrected. Forecasts become adaptive but may remain underestimates, for instance, because people often misjudge exponential growth (Stango and Zinman, 2009). The learning component reinforces and hastens the development of revised expectations. What happens when expectations are confronted with outcomes is no doubt of great interest, and some of it has been studied under the label of surprise (Teigen and Keren, 2003).

B_I represents beliefs based on new information. In most cases, new information, perhaps pertaining to the economy as a whole or to fluctuations in marketwide sentiment (as in Baker and Wurgler 2007), has to be quite spectacular to overrule earlier experience – so that other sets of beliefs get zero weight. Euphoric or, at the other extreme, panic reactions are examples of such situations. They are typically associated with very large trading volumes, and become somewhat more probable after a protracted period of nerve-wracking uncertainty. In this context, a vital question for investors is when a bear market will turn into a bull market and vice versa.[1]

3.4 Heuristics and Biases

Various cognitive and motivational mechanisms, streamlining information processing, are also related to the three components of the Warneryd expectation model.

The term *heuristic* refers to a simple intuitive strategy, deliberate or not, that produces immediate assessments and forecasts. One symptom of this type of mental operation is the relative neglect of many plausible considerations in favor of others that are easily accessible (Tversky and Kahneman, 1983a). A heuristic is effectively a shortcut, that is, a frugal but fragile problem-solving procedure that reduces the number of possible solutions in a systematic, predictable way. Many financial economists link the utilization of heuristics with regimented deviations from rationality, that is, predictable cognitive errors that produce systematic bias (Shefrin, 2000; Ariely, 2008).

At this juncture, our focus is on how most people form forward expectations about a firm's cash flows, such as revenues, costs, and profits. Of necessity, the starting point is each individual's past subjective experience. Information processing starts with selective attention to whatever is happening in the world and includes many ways for storing and retrieving data that diverge from what is "objectively true."[2] Looking back at previous stock prices or company earnings, a person may well recall something that is pretty close to what actually transpired, but the reality may also have been quite different, especially as we move further back into the past. This is why extrapolative models of investors' hopes put extra weight on recent developments.

Three psychological heuristics have important consequences for retrieving data from memory: availability, representativeness, and conservatism.[3]

3.4.1 Availability

The availability heuristic explains a large number of everyday experiences. It is employed whenever a person estimates probability or frequency by the ease with which instances or associations can be brought to mind. More recent events are easy to recall; instances of large classes are recalled better and faster than instances of less frequent classes; likely occurrences are easier to imagine than unlikely ones; and associative connections are strengthened when two events frequently occur together (Tversky and Kahneman, 1982b; Rothman and Hardin, 1997).

Stephan (1999) distinguishes between (1) experience-based, (2) memory-based, and (3) imagination-based availability. *Experience-based* availability means that people rely on what they have seen or heard. They neglect the fact that their samples probably have been small and biased. If unemployed workers answer a question about how many workers are unemployed, or social workers about how many families need social relief, they tend to overestimate the numbers. They derive their estimates from their own experience, which involves frequent contacts with the relevant groups, and they are likely to exaggerate the actual number. Ask a stock owner how many households own stocks, and you can expect that the answer will be an overstatement or at least be higher than what a nonowner of stocks would estimate.

Memory-based availability depends on the ease with which memories can be brought to mind. It is related to factors such as (a) how intense initial attention was, (b) the salience of the impression, (c) its vivacity, (d) its familiarity to the subject, and (e) spatial and temporal propinquity. For example, Frieder and Subrahmanyam (2005) conclude that the demand for well-known brand-name companies is stronger for individual investors than for institutional investors. Furthermore, Seasholes and Zhu (2010) show that individual investors tend to favor locally based firms.

Imagination-based availability arises as a consequence of how easy it is to imagine something. For example, the stock price of a company seems more apt to go up when the firm announces a new sales contract, even though the value of the contract may be insignificant in relation to total sales volume. Also, investors may not evaluate the risk of different investments based solely on the historical standard deviation of returns. They may impute extra "risk" to foreign investments because they know less about foreign markets, institutions, and firms (French and Poterba, 1991).

A person may see the addition of something familiar to an uncertain event as raising the probability of that event when that additional information actually decreases it. Experiments show that a scenario that includes a possible cause and an outcome could appear more probable than the outcome on its own (Tversky and Kahneman, 1983b). For example, publicity about an event that is favorable to a company may result in overly positive forecasts, even when objective information is easy to obtain and apply to forecasts.

A related phenomenon is herding, where investors appear to follow popular investment choices even if the fundamental, objective information is not supportive of demand. Nofsinger and Sias (1999) show that even institutional investors engage in this pattern. Ivković and colleagues (2007) show this among individual investors. The authors find investors have an increased likelihood of buying a stock if their neighbor owns that stock, especially in more socially connected communities. They conclude word-of-mouth communication drives a substantial portion of stock purchases. Of course, information from neighbors is still new information, but this likely mainly represents a focus of attention rather than fundamental facts that drive expectations. Individual investors also show patterns of being contrarians, at least in the short run (Kaniel, Saar, and Titman, 2008). Individual investors are more likely to buy stocks following declines and sell after price increases, for example, again forming expectations based on heuristics. Individual investors also show patterns of investing in, and bidding up prices for, stocks that have a high rate of Internet searches, especially among small firms with high rates of individual investors. This initial price increase rapidly declines, however, as more fundamental information is incorporated into market expectations (Da, Engelberg and Gao, 2011).

3.4.2 Representativeness

Kahneman and Tversky (1973) demonstrate that people have a tendency to neglect base rate or statistical information in favor of similarity judgments. In a typical study, subjects are asked to predict the field of study of a graduate student or the profession of someone on the basis of a brief sketch that highlights personality traits characteristic of a stereotype, say, lawyers or engineers. As it happens, the subjects' judgments are greatly influenced by the degree of similarity between the description and the stereotype. This is the case even when the participants are made familiar with the base rates, that is, the frequencies of law and engineering students and professionals in the population. This is the so-called base-rate fallacy.[4]

This heuristic is often equated with the heuristic of representativeness: an event is judged probable to the extent that it represents the essential features of its parent population or of its generating process. It means, among other things, that people in situations of uncertainty tend to look for familiar patterns and are apt to believe that the pattern will repeat itself. The neglect of base rates is more general than representativeness and cannot always be explained by this heuristic.

Gigerenzer and Hoffrage (1995) suggest some reasons why base rates are neglected and intimate that in many inference problems base rates are uninteresting. It is not always erroneous to neglect base rates. Interestingly, people tend to find it more natural to handle frequencies than probabilities. Gigerenzer and Hoffrage ask subjects to guess the probability that a woman with a positive mammogram actually had breast cancer. The respondents perform better with data presented as frequencies. However, less than half of the subjects use algorithms classified as Bayesian reasoning.

Fiedler et al. (2000) finds that frequencies were better handled in some situations. They explain the problem in terms of the "sampling hypothesis." When making a judgment, people sample information from memory and from the environment and then make inferences on the basis of sample information. The requested probability is referred to as the "criterion" and the conditional as the "predictor." According to the results, a sample that is focused on the criterion leads to more neglect of base rates than a sample focused on the predictor. The authors stress that the neglect of base rates is primarily associated with low base-rate probabilities. They also find that in addition to focusing on criterion or predictor, the size of the cognitive sample is important.

In Shefrin and Statman's (1994) behavioral capital asset pricing model (CAPM) noise traders are assumed to underweight base-rate information. They make forecasts by overweighting recent events and by underweighting more distant events that form the base rate. Noise traders look at the most recent patterns and believe that those will be repeated in the future.

The base-rate fallacy no doubt occurs, but may be less common than has been assumed in behavioral finance. Some findings may have suffered from methodological lack of clarity (see Fiedler, 2000; Fiedler et al., 2000). Gigerenzer and Hoffrage (1995) as well as Fiedler et al. (2000) talk of natural rather than probabilistic situations and assert that people are not inclined toward logical inference and deductive reasoning. Investors, like most other people, may not construe situations in the way the experimental designs presume.

While the neglected use of base-rate data has been amply studied and discussed, less attention has been bestowed on the likely case that, when the base-rate probability is high, there could be a tendency to overlook the specific symptoms. Judging from newspaper stories, a patient with indistinct symptoms of pneumonia may sometimes be misclassified as having the flu at times when almost everyone else seems to be affected by it. In finance, undue attention to the base rate may occur when the majority of stocks go up. Details about a specific firm are neglected and investors may believe in its stock without grounds. When, say, tech stocks fall, other stocks, including those for which there is good news, tend to join. When the majority of stocks go up, a positive effect spreads to stocks that may not deserve it because of bad news. The sudden cascades of information that some economists have propounded may be cases of undue attention given to base rates: investors at first do not heed the information from their own experience and immediate environment, but concentrate on earlier developments, that is, on the base rates of stock prices. This may be seen as the reverse of the base-rate fallacy. The base rate dominates the specifics.

The phenomenon, well known in the psychology of learning, is called "generalization" (or, in experimental psychology, "stimulus generalization"). Generalization is a kind of inference about the unknown. What is known to be true about the known members of a class of objects is assumed to be true of all members including those not yet observed. The converse is "discrimination." In this case, differences, especially minor ones, are attended to. An interesting finding is that when people are anxious, they tend to generalize more, that is, to include more stimuli and too discriminate less. Exuberance may have similar effects. Irrational exuberance may thus be explained as being caused by failures to discriminate due to strong positive or negative emotions (Shiller, 2000b).

Johnson and Tellis (2005) show that expectation heuristics interact depending on the time frame (see also Sonsino and Regev, 2013). Individuals behave as if they believe in the "hot hand" fallacy in the short run. Thus, expectations become more positive based on recent success. In the long run, however, individuals succumb to the gambler's fallacy of reversion to the mean. This behavior is consistent with short-run pricing momentum and long-run price reversals. History shows that, by and large, when past price patterns are a cause for optimism (as measured by surveys of amateur investors), the U.S. stock market tends to disappoint (Greenwood and Shleifer, 2014).[5]

Barber and Odean (2000, 2001) also find that individual investors tend to be overly confident in their expectations and use of information. Overconfidence leads them to trade at higher than optimal trading levels and to accumulate costs that cut into investment performance.[6] The authors refute other explanations of high trading volumes, such as liquidity requirements. Investors trade speculatively due to a combination of boldness and any entertainment value they receive from the activity of investment and investment monitoring (Peng and Xiong, 2006).

In general, people tend to overrate their accomplishments, and poor performers appear to suffer a double curse in the sense that their self-evaluations are only a tad less positive than those of top performers. This is the so-called Dunning–Kruger effect. It has been demonstrated in many contexts, such as automobile drivers who self-assess their competence (Dunning, Heath, and Suls, 2004).

Low performers may overrate themselves because they are not cognizant of all the factors that matter. How unaware the unskilled truly are continues to be debated; see, for example, Schlösser et al. (2013). Several researchers (e.g., Hayward, Shepherd, and Griffin, 2006) refer to hubris as a key factor in explaining the formation of new business ventures and the high failure rate of existing ones. Without doubt, confidence and wishful thinking have benefits as well as drawbacks. For instance, an optimistic outlook on life enables entrepreneurs to downplay uncertainty. But delusions of success also do damage, for example each time overconfidence excuses the escalation of commitment to a losing course of action. What is crucial, submits Trevelyan (2008), is that people are able to attune their confidence levels and to be self-critical.[7]

3.4.3 Conservatism

Delays in reactions to information have been attributed to various factors; in behavioral finance, for example, such delays are ascribed to *conservatism*. The concept was suggested by the psychologist Ward Edwards (1982) and involves slow updating of models in the face of new evidence. People's behavior is not Bayesian, but may get closer to it by successive attempts. Edwards points to "human misaggregation of data" as the major cause of conservatism.

The use of the concept in finance was rejected by, among others, Fama (1998), who is critical of its use (and the use of other psychological concepts in finance). Many authors appeal to conservatism to explain stock market underreaction to economic (earnings) news. Financial analysts too are inclined to make only partial adjustments at first, and they are slow to arrive at the actual numbers ultimately reported. Barberis, Shleifer, and Vishny (1998) and Shleifer (2000) suggest that the presence of under- and overreactions of stock prices can be explained by conservatism and representativeness.

The representativeness heuristic has been held to be inconsistent with conservatism. Conservatism (which is sometimes labeled under confidence) and overconfidence are not compatible in the sense that they cannot occur at the same time for one individual. The question then arises under what circumstances overconfidence occurs and under what circumstances conservatism prevails. Griffin and Tversky (1992) tried to reconcile overconfidence, which is close to representativeness, and underconfidence, which is similar to conservatism. The hypothesis they tested was that people focus on the strength or extremeness of the available evidence with insufficient regard for its weight or credence. This mode of judgment yields overconfidence when strength is high and weight is low, and underconfidence when strength is low and weight is high. The assumption is that people update their beliefs depending on the strength and weight of new evidence. The strength of the evidence is inferred from aspects such as salience and extremity, whereas weight has to do with such factors as sample size.

3.5 Learning from Experience

Expectations of outcomes may differ more or less from what actually happens, and people are surprised, negatively or positively as the case may be. Since expectations seem mostly based on past experience, such surprise may lead to adaptations of future expectations of the same kind as the learning factor in the model. Surprises are usually classified as emotions and are not always evaluated in a purely rational way. It is thus possible that a smaller gain is a more pleasant surprise than a larger gain if the former derives from an unexpectedly high rise in price and the latter arose from a smaller gain than expected. Similarly, a loss can involve a pleasant surprise if the loss is lower than expected.

In cognitive psychology, expectations have often been quantified in probabilities. According to this interpretation, unexpected events can simply be described as low-probability outcomes, and the surprise follows when they occur (Teigen and Keren, 2003). In financial economics, surprise is used to describe unexpected turns in firm earnings, and it is often explained as a result of shock. Business firms are more or less forced to state their expectations of future earnings in their quarterly and annual statements. Studies indicate that U.S. firms are carefully trying to avoid giving rise to negative surprises. They show a tendency to understate their expected earnings and get the advantage of a positive surprise (Brown and Higgins, 2005; Burgstahler and Eames, 2006).

3.5.1 Hindsight bias

It is not always easy to learn from experience. Hindsight bias is a threat to real insight. Fischhoff and MacGregor (1982, p 168) describes the bias as follows:

> In hindsight, people consistently exaggerate what could have been anticipated in foresight. They not only tend to view what has happened as having been inevitable, but also to view it as having appeared "relatively inevitable" before it happened. People believe that others should have been able to anticipate events much better than was actually the case. They even misremember their own predictions so as to exaggerate in hindsight what they knew in foresight.

Hindsight depends on memory, and memory is fallible. Retrieving memories is a constructive process. Memory traces are deficient because of errors in impressions, limitations in storage capacity, and interference in recall processes. While this does not mean that memories are always incorrect, it points to the need for caution. Looking back, one tends to find patterns in random events and seemingly useful explanations. One aspect of the relationship between confidence and hindsight is the "knew-it-all-along effect."

> [E]vents that the best-informed experts did not anticipate often appear almost inevitable after they occur. Financial punditry provides an unending source of examples. Within an hour of the market closing every day, experts can be heard on the radio explaining with high confidence why the market acted as it did. A listener could well draw the incorrect inference that the behavior of the market is so reasonable that it could have been predicted earlier in the day (Kahneman and Riepe, 1998, p. 54).

Hoffrage and Hertwig (1999, p. 194) argue that hindsight should not be seen as an error in information processing. It is "a by-product of two generally adaptive processes: first, updating knowledge after receiving new information; and second, drawing fast and frugal inferences from this updated knowledge." Three views of hindsight bias are reviewed. The first, in the literature the most common view focuses on the potential harmful effects. A second view stresses the adaptive aspects, since hindsight bias may contribute to the esteem we enjoy from others and from ourselves. The third view, which is the main point, maintains that memory must be selective and that recall when memory has sorted out certain traces is a constructive, adaptive process. The process is the updating of information, which as a by-product may have hindsight bias.

Forming memories of earlier decision situations may involve leaving out trivial details and pulling out the essential factors in the situation, which can then be used for future decision-making. Like any other type of learning, hindsight can lead to better preparation for the future (Fischhoff 1982). In this view, despite the fact that unsatisfactory outcomes may occur, the hindsight bias, like other heuristics, implies adaptive behavior that should not be classified as flaws or errors. Hindsight may be useful to the individual or it may be harmful, depending upon the circumstances.

Hindsight usually outperforms foresight, since events tend to become clear, and causal structures appear disentangled when one is looking back. Part of the superiority may be specious due to hindsight bias. Ostensibly successful decisions in the past may lead an investor to believe in her or his own ability and serve as a guide for future decisions. It should not surprise anyone that stories about how successes were achieved or failures avoided in the stock market may be far from objective accounts, even with no intention to lie on the part of the storyteller. For example, Biais and Weber (2009) show that hindsight bias negatively impacts investment choices, both in experiments and in real-world investment decisions.

Hindsight bias is rarely fully conscious. Hindsight, with or without bias, may give rise to strong feelings such as pride or regret. Such emotional hindsight, though often biased, may influence the disposition to act in future situations and, if inducing pride, perhaps lead to buying or, if producing regret, to selling at the wrong moment (Watts, 2011).

3.6 How People Handle New Information

New information, if attended to at all, is interpreted and treated using simplifying heuristics. Many types of heuristics are applicable to information processing, but two are worthy of attention related to investor decisions: *anchoring and adjustment* and *illusion of control.*

3.6.1 Anchoring and Adjustment

Anchoring bias means that people make estimates by starting from an initial value that is subjected to *adjustment* before the final answer is arrived at. The initial value may be given by the formulation of the problem or partial calculation.[8] Due to the anchoring in the first place, the later adjustments are usually insufficient. Consequently, different starting points yield different estimates that are biased toward the initial values (Tversky and Kahneman, 1982a). The first figure apparently serves as an anchor, and later adjustments are insufficient, more so when the anchor is low. When investors make forecasts of future stock values, their forecasts may be affected by the value that they use as a starting point even if they do not believe in it and make adjustments. Studies show that when investors are asked to give confidence intervals for probability estimates, the intervals are often too narrow, which is ascribed to the effect of anchoring (Stephan and Kiell, 2000).

If there are anchoring effects, financial analysts could be expected to be slow upgrading their evaluations when there are sudden increases in earnings. George and Hwang (2004) believe that many investors use the 52-week high of a stock price as an anchor and consider changes relative to that high price. Investors may also be slow to update their reference point used as an anchor (Baucells, Weber, and Welfens, 2011).

Stephan (1999) also found that there were anchoring effects from tasks that were unrelated to the crucial forecasts. People who had worked on discriminating a certain number in a series of numbers flashed on a screen showed anchoring effects when they, with a different experimenter and in a different setting, were asked to forecast a future stock exchange value. Stephan warns that overestimation of the probability of favorable environmental conditions may lie behind many individual failures in financial markets. The anchors have in such cases been too high, especially for young investors who grew up in a predominantly bull market.

Knowledge about anchoring effects may protect an investor from too easily accepting an offer to buy stocks. It happens that a less serious broker offers a client stocks that the broker knows are above the financial capacity of the client. When the client says "no," an offer of a more reasonably priced bundle of stocks is made. In relation to the anchor that the first offer established, the second offer will appear favorable. There will also, according to Cialdini (1988), be strong pressure on the client to accept the new offer because of the demands of reciprocity. The broker has made a concession when dropping the first offer in favor of the second, lower-price offer, and this calls for an appropriate concession on the part of the client, who is more likely to buy than if there had been no high-price offer.

3.6.2 Illusion of Control

Perceived control is a key factor in the theory of planned behavior formulated by Ajzen (1991). If a person perceives that there is no control of means to achieve a desired purpose, a positive attitude toward the act does not produce the commensurate behavior. Perceived control can produce self-confidence, although it may be an illusion. Langer (1982) theorizes that perceived skill in chance situations causes people to feel improperly confident. Illusion of control refers to higher estimated probabilities than the objective probability would warrant. People behave as though chance events are subject to control. The illusion may have some basis in fact, but generally the label is used when there are indications of superstition.[9]

Langer notes that many dice players behave as if they are controlling the outcome of the toss. They throw the dice softly if they want low numbers and to throw hard for high numbers. They also believe that effort and concentration pay off. Langer's studies show that people do not properly distinguish chance- from skill-determined events even if they are aware of chance factors.[10]

Why is it that people who are ordinarily sensible hesitate to make bets after a die has been thrown, but not yet read, while they are willing to place bets before the die is thrown? It cannot be just overconfidence in one's own ability. Tversky and Heath (1991) let participants choose between two alternatives:

(1) A stock is selected at random from the *Wall Street Journal*. The participant must guess whether it will go up or down tomorrow, winning $5 if they are correct. (2) A stock is selected at random from the *Wall Street Journal*. The participant mist guess whether it went up or down yesterday, without checking. Again, winning $5 if they are correct. Two-thirds of the subjects select the first alternative. The illusion of control makes people believe that they can influence future events even if they have no such power and have to rely on the magic of good or bad luck. The illusion of control and overconfidence in ability coincide to some extent, but not completely. A simulation study of stock traders found that there was illusion of control in varying degree among traders and that it was maladaptive in this context (Fenton-O'Creevy et al., 2003). *Illusion of prediction* and *illusion of knowledge* are other phenomena of overconfidence. In fact, people's perception of their ability to predict outcomes may surpass their perceived ability to control outcomes.

3.7 Affective Influences

On April 13, 2000, the Nasdaq index dropped 9.7 percent and the Dow Jones almost 6 percent. Commentators on TV, in several countries, used almost the same expression: "Now it is all psychology." What did they mean? Do stock markets then have feelings? While stock markets do not have feelings or moods, investors do. The use of metaphors for the feeling of the market is an aggregation of behaviors into familiar categories or labels. But, even when most stock prices plummet and the market is said to be pessimistic, there are buyers and sellers, each with differing expectations, completing transactions. Investors have more feelings than they think. This also holds for professional investors and nonexpert casual investors.

Developments at the stock exchange are often described in terms that are taken from everyday psychology. Investors have feelings and moods, and this influences individual and aggregate decisions (Hirshleifer and Shumway, 2003; Nofsinger, 2005; Statman, Fisher, and Anginer, 2008). While cognitive psychology has informed behavioral finance, the psychology of emotions and motivation has received much less attention in finance until recently.

Feelings and motivation include emotions, affects, and moods. Mood is often referred to in reviews of financial markets. Psychological studies of an individual's mood help us understand how emotions influence investors. Gasper (2004) investigates how mood influenced information processing. She deals with three problems: (1) the speed of the processing, (2) the role of stimuli or the circumstances (ambiguous vs. unambiguous), and (3) individuals' ability to decrease mood effects. The results indicated that judgments of unambiguous situations were less influenced by mood differences. Information with some ambiguity may lead to differing outcomes depending on which moods prevail.

Both positive and negative effects of emotions or moods can influence behavior (see, e.g., McGraw, Mellers, and Ritov, 2004). Loewenstein and Lerner (2003) distinguish between moods that are immediate or anticipatory, especially related to intertemporal choices involving risk or uncertainty. This is a different mechanism than immediate moods, which might be quite mild, but still influence choices at the time of the decision. The *affect heuristic* is an example of the latter, and *affective forecasting* is an example of the former; both are ways that moods may impact investor decisions.

3.7.1 The Affect Heuristic

The *affect heuristic* concept emanates from an ongoing debate as to what extent there can be an affective reaction that consistently precedes cognitive evaluation of a (strong) stimulus. The question is whether an affective reaction can precede and rule out cognitive evaluation altogether or delay it. If there is a primary affective reaction, people may be more ruled by emotions than is generally assumed in rationality discussions.

Zajonc (1980) maintains that there is a primary affective reaction that evaluates the stimulus as good or bad before the stimulus is cognitively checked. He rejects the idea of most contemporary theories that affect is postcognitive, that is, that it occurs only after considerable cognitive operations are accomplished. Zajonc pointed out differences between judgments based on affect and those based on perceptual and cognitive processes. A strongly threatening stimulus leads to attempts to distance oneself as quickly as possible without really thinking until it is too late. Certainly, many discussions of herd behavior hint at primary affective reactions without conscious evaluation (Nofsinger and Sias, 1999).

The ideas about a primary affective reaction, explored by Slovic et al. (2004), have met with opposition. These authors suggest that affect may serve as a cue for many important judgments related to risk and uncertainty, as well as attention to information. An overall, readily available affective impression is an easy escape from weighing the pros and cons or retrieving from memory any relevant examples. This holds especially when the required judgment or decision is complex or the recourse to mental resources is limited. The affect heuristic is a mental shortcut similar to availability and representativeness.

There is accordingly a human tendency for primary affective reactions and subsequent cognitive handling of the stimulus information. The affect heuristic may warn the investor to be overly cautious when analyzing information about stocks and stock events or lead to overexuberance. Emotions color the initial and ongoing continued information processing. If the reaction is extremely strong and there is no cognitive elaboration, panic or exuberance can drive choices.

3.7.2 Affective Forecasting

"Foreseeing the future is one of the most appealing of all psychic powers" (Wilson and Gilbert, 2003, p. 345). Like other choices, selecting stocks involves forecasts. It is generally assumed that the forecasts have to do with utility in terms of economic value. It is well known and accepted, although little considered, that emotions, including mood at the time of the decision, affect the estimates of value. It is less recognized that prediction of the feelings that will follow after a certain outcome may affect the decision:

> Anyone who has ever made an important decision knows that emotions play a role. Not only do immediate emotions, or those experienced while making a choice, shape decisions but also anticipated emotions about future consequences. Anticipated feelings of guilt, dread, and excitement allow people to simulate what life would be like if they made one choice or another (Mellers, 2000, p. 910).

People apparently base many decisions on affective forecasts: predictions about their emotional reactions to future events influence their choices, including regrets for being "wrong." Affective forecasts often display an *impact bias*, meaning that people overestimate the intensity and duration of their emotional reactions to future events. One cause of the impact bias is *focalism*, the tendency to underestimate the extent to which other events will influence one's thoughts and feelings. The pleasure paradox (Wilson et al., 2005) is that people make sense of their worlds in a way that speeds recovery from emotional events and that this sense-making process is largely automatic and nonconscious. These processes are described by the acronym AREA: attend, react, explain, adapt. People attend or orient to novel, relevant events; they react emotionally to the events; they explain or make sense of the events; and as a result they adapt to them, in that they think about them less and have a less intense emotional reaction when they do.

People fail to anticipate how quickly they will make sense of things that happen to them in a way that speeds emotional recovery. This is especially true when predicting reactions to negative events. This research brings up two things for investor consideration in connection with stock market transactions: (1) imagining the feelings that would accompany a great gain will probably lead to overestimation of the degree of happiness, and (2) loss aversion embodies an overestimation of the negative effects of a loss. In both cases, people tend later to make sense of what happened, a process that is governed by other events. This sense-making process is highly similar to hindsight biases (Wilson et al., 2005).

A related issue influencing individual investors behavior and the formation of expectations is myopia. Benartzi and Thaler (1999) describe the problems of "myopic loss aversion," where long-term investors tend have a greater sensitivity to losses than to gains and a tendency to evaluate investment outcomes too frequently. Despite long-term goals, investors frequently check prices, and take actions that are focused on short-run, not long-run, goals. Individuals overreact to short-term movements in prices, and that may drive selling in a panic rather than as part of a careful plan.

3.8 Forecasting the Stock Market

Vissing-Jorgensen (2004) argues that subjective financial expectations affect individual stockholdings, especially those who are not wealthy, and that subjective forecasts are useful for understanding stock prices. But the measurement of expectations is challenging. In principle, it is possible to assess values of the three components in the expectation formation model through interview surveys. The University of Michigan Index of Consumer Sentiment, launched by George Katona in 1952, is now broadly accepted and has good standing as a predictor of consumer purchases in the short run. Perhaps the longest series of data on *investor expectations* are provided by the Yale School of Management Stock Market Confidence Indexes™. Professor Robert Shiller has been collecting data on expectations since 1984, using questionnaires that cover a number of aspects: (a) the one-year Confidence Index (the percent of the population expecting an increase in the Dow in the coming year), (b) the Buy-On-Dips Confidence Index (the expectation that the stock exchange index will go up the next day after a fall of more than 3 percent one day), (c) the Crash Confidence Index (the percent of the population who attach little probability to a stock market crash in the next six months), and (d) the Valuation Confidence Index (the percent of the population who think that the market is not too high). Similar measures include the University of Michigan Investor Survey, and the De Nederlandsche Bank (DNB) survey by CentER at Tilburg University.

The explanatory value of these indexes seems good, but the predictive capacity is open to some doubts. Shiller (2000a), who analyzed stock market bubbles, concluded that there was evidence that while bubbles and investor confidence among institutional investors varied over time, the variations were often significant though not enormous. Dominitz and Manski (2007) analyzed investor expectations for the covariation between the indexes and actual stock-price development. They conclude large-scale population surveys are too limited and that only lengthy interviews can adequately measure investor expectations.

A special difficulty with forecasts of stock market developments should be noted: if the forecasts are believed, they can be suspected of being self-fulfilling. If the forecast predicts that prices will rise, investors will have fewer doubts, sell less, and buy more, thereby implementing the prediction. If falling prices are predicted, there will be more sellers and more hesitant buyers and prices will fall, all on the proviso that investors believe in the forecast results. For good reasons, regular forecasts of stock markets as a whole are rare, whereas forecasts for individual firms are common.

In sum, there is now evidence that some measures of reported expectations can help explain what happens to stock market returns. There remains significant uncertainty about the possibilities of using the data for predicting turning points in total financial markets, however. The use of these or other population-based measures may as yet only be supplementary to other techniques.[11]

3.9 Individual Differences

A fundamental tenet of economic psychology is that there may be critical differences among consumers.[12] By and large, financial economists recognize two categories of investors: those who are informed and rational, and the others, often called noise traders, who disturb the predictive value of efficient market theory. Individual levels of financial knowledge, skills, and capability are one factor that influences how well investors can plan, form expectations, and then recognize and confront common psychological biases (FINRA, 2016).

Measurements of economic and financial literacy are a relatively recent phenomenon, starting with prominent work by Lusardi and Mitchell as summarized in their review (2014). Researchers have used Lusardi and Mitchell's five standardized financial knowledge questions (compound interest, inflation, risk and diversification, bond prices and interest rates, and loan terms and payment amounts) in a variety of survey populations and countries, consistently finding that lower levels of measured financial literacy are correlated with lower levels of wealth, less diversification, and other investment behaviors. More but different evidence of poor U.S. economic and financial literacy is found in Blinder and Krueger (2004) and Vissing-Jorgensen (2004). Van Rooij, Lusardi, and Alessie (2011) show that weaker financial literacy is associated with lower levels of overall stock market participation in the Netherlands. Similar patterns have been shown in still other countries and contexts, again controlling for wealth, income, education level, age, and so on (Lusardi and Mitchell, 2011).[13]

The ability of people to learn about finance and then shift behaviors is less well established. In one review, Fernandes and colleagues (2014) conclude that financial literacy interventions have very small effects on learning or behavior. However, studies of financial literacy are highly heterogeneous, ranging from brief courses to intensive courses on topics ranging from basic banking to investments and retirement planning. Studies of well-designed and targeted programs find more positive effects on investment behavior (Collins and Urban, 2016). More recent work suggests people's measured, objective financial literacy is related to people's subjective sense of their own financial knowledge, but subjective literacy levels are actually more predictive of financial behaviors in some contexts (Hadar et al., 2013).

One way investors with low financial literacy might be able to overcome psychological biases is through the use of a professional advisor (Collins, 2012).

Financial planners and counselors could learn in the course with working with multiple clients and then redirect investors to make better decisions. However, surveys show that the use of advisors increases as people have higher levels of financial knowledge, even controlling for wealth, income, and education levels (Calcagno et al., 2015). Investors effectively select to pay advisors to take on cognitive tasks they could otherwise complete, but prefer to transfer to a professional (Hackethal, Haliassos, and Jappelli, 2012).

People with lower financial literacy levels present the potential for manipulation and exploitation (Akerlof and Shiller, 2015). One critique of public policies promoting investor financial education is that the policies are often ineffective and that they undermine the requirement for strong market regulation (Willis, 2009). Heterogeneous levels of financial literacy create a situation where relatively knowledgeable actors can use information asymmetries to mislead less informed investors. Sunstein (2016) argues that this is a pervasive condition in financial and other markets; Posner (2015) counters that the government restricts manipulation in order to maintain efficient markets, including remedies for fraud.

Age is another factor that can influence the formation of expectations. Older investors have more experience, and can better use, or counteract various heuristics and biases (Christelis, Jappelli, and Padula, 2010). While older investors are more likely to invest, the quality of investment decision-making as people age declines (Korniotis and Kumar, 2011). This decline appears worse among lower education levels and minority racial groups. With time, the positive attributes of experience deteriorate as cognitive ability declines.

Wärneryd (2001) proposes four types of investors: (1) *well-to-do investors*, who invest part but not all of their wealth in risky securities and tend to buy and hold stocks; (2) *really wealthy investors*, who systematically trade in securities and have both short- and long-term goals and more volatile expectations; (3) *speculating investors*, who make frequent transactions in the stock market and have very short-term goals and expectations combining information, intuition, and feelings; and (4) *naive investors*, who are enticed by the marketing of financial services firms for potential profits in the stock market, and their expectations are based on their hopes and feelings rather than information. The size and distribution is important when analyzing stock market reactions and developments. A preponderance of longer-term investors adds to stability and predictability. As the proportion of shorter-term investors prevails, expectations can become more unpredictable using observable information.

Wärneryd (2001) also argues that professional investors use similar heuristics and yield to the same type of social factors as ordinary investors. Given that humans are far from perfect information processors, as psychological theory suggests, the question arises: are there people who consistently do better than others and, if so, under what circumstances? Research has shown that experts may not do too well on a task although they are seen as experts and believe in themselves as experts on the basis of their knowledge and experience (Ericsson and Lehmann, 1996). Many studies indicate that financial experts have difficulties outperforming private investors in the stock market (Wärneryd, 2001). At any rate, they do not consistently make better predictions or outperform ordinary investors, but some experts may do it sometimes (Porter, 2004; Stotz and von Nitsch, 2005).

3.10 Concluding Remarks

We end this chapter with a final thought about Alan Greenspan and his remarkable change of heart, now giving important weight to psychology in forecasting and economic analysis. In his legendary 1996 speech, Greenspan asked, "How do we know when irrational exuberance has unduly escalated asset values, which then become subject to unexpected and prolonged contractions?" At the time, this sentence reflected the Fed chair's concern about the potential of an Internet stock bubble. That bubble burst five years later, even though his comment did briefly arrest the growth of the bubble. In *The Age of Turbulence*, published in 2007, Greenspan reflected upon these events and observed that "sudden eruptions of fear or euphoria are phenomena that nobody anticipates" but that financial markets, as well as the economy, are "more stable and forecastable over the long run." Thus, in 2007 he still rather confidently argued that "we can" anticipate what lies ahead. Our judgments are "not always right, but they have manifestly been good enough" (Greenspan, 2007, pp. 466–467).

Plainly, since September 2008, not only Greenspan's views (2013b) but general opinion about the relevance of psychology for financial forecasting and for finance theory and practice have evolved a great deal. "The times they are a-changin'" (in the words of Bob Dylan, 1964). Academic research is contributing to this development. As our survey shows, the economic psychology of investors, amateurs as well as experts, encompasses many studies that are of profound interest to observers and financial professionals who want to understand what lies behind the shifts in markets. Research in this area is still growing but shows strong promise in theory and applications.

Notes

1 Studies of the influence of experience on expectation formation and risky choice include Hertwig et al. (2004); Malmendier and Nagel (2011); Hertwig (2012); and Lejarraga et al. (2016). Taleb (2007); Taleb, Goldstein, and Spitznagel (2009) and Barberis (2013) look specifically at the psychology of rare, high-impact events.

2 See, e.g., Schneider and Shiffrin (1977) and Loibi and Hira (2009). Of necessity, attention is zero-sum: if people pay more attention to one subject, they must

pay less attention elsewhere. Compared to professionals, individual investors have access to fewer resources and are prone to indulge in attention-driven asset purchases (Barber and Odean, 2008). Limited attention has important implications for financial reporting and how asset prices react to accounting information (Hirshleifer, Lim, and Teoh, 2011; Hirshleifer et al., 2003).

3 Heath and Heath (2007) discuss the principles of memorability (or what these authors label "stickiness") in the specific context of business communication and marketing. Sticky messages draw their power from qualities such as concreteness or surprise. In related work, Berger (2013) examines the traits of ideas that become contagious. For example, simple narratives that trigger emotion are easily remembered, and people often want to share such stories with others. Memory itself may be thought about as a catalogue of stories.

4 Yet, people do not always neglect base rates as, e.g., when they are waiting for the bus (Teigen and Keren, 2007).

5 However, based on U.S. survey and market return data going back to the early 1950s, DeBondt (1991) finds that this result may not hold true for top-ranked economic experts.

6 Overconfident investors often tilt their stock portfolios toward high-beta, small, value stocks, and they pay a large price for aggressive trading. More active traders underachieve than those who trade less. The predicament afflicts men more than women. In the United States, trading losses and costs may amount to as much as 2 percent a year. Using a complete trading history of all equity market investors in Taiwan between January 1995 and December 1999, Barber et al. (2009) find that the aggregate portfolio of individuals suffers an annual penalty of 3.8 percent, equivalent to 2.8 percent of total personal income. (In contrast, Taiwan institutions enjoy an annual performance boost of 1.5 percent.) In most cases, investment performance is made even worse by the fact that people like to sell past winner stocks but are reluctant to realize losses (Odean, 1998).

7 People often try to dodge responsibility for bad choices and foolish beliefs by justifying them (Tavris and Aronson, 2007). They do not own up. Hypocrisy and self-deception are more easily recognized in others than in oneself. Among the engines of self-justification is willful blindness, partly explained by cognitive dissonance and/or conflicts of interest. We literally do not see what we do not want to see (Heffernan, 2011). In addition, when people seek new information, they are often prejudiced in favor of self-serving data that sustain previously held beliefs or desired conclusions (Ditto and Lopez, 1992; Jonas et al., 2001).

8 Epley and Gilovich (2006) propose a specific cause for the insufficient adjustment. They suggest that people stop adjusting once their adjusted estimate falls within a range of plausible values. Therefore, the estimate lies near the anchor side of the range, but the true value often lies closer to the middle of the range.

9 In related work, Langer questions more broadly whether people continually exercise conscious, intentional control as they engage in a particular course of action. Bargh and Chartrand (1999, p. 462) review different forms of automatic self-regulation and conclude that nonconscious mental systems

"perform the lion's share of the self-regulatory burden, beneficently keeping the individual grounded in his or her current environment." In this context, see also Chartrand and Bargh (1999) on the chameleon effect: "Monkey see, monkey do." Perhaps the polar opposite of automatic self-regulation is the view, formulated by economists such as Brunnermeier and Parker (2005) and Benabou and Tirole (2016), is that forward-looking agents *knowingly* choose beliefs so as to optimally balance the utility benefits of optimism (i.e., overestimating the chances of success) against its costs. In this literature on motivated reasoning, people attach value to false beliefs that fulfill certain psychological needs.

10   Bovi (2009) studies the dynamics of forecast errors in consumer confidence surveys for ten European countries. Deaves, Luders, and Schroder (2010) examine the dynamics of overconfidence for stock market forecasters.

11   Since the 1990s, there is also a promising new literature on probabilistic survey expectations of significant personal events, e.g., the likelihood of suffering unemployment. See Manski (2004) for more discussion.

12   For example, Dominitz and Manski (2007) and Hurd, van Rooij, and Winter (2011) find substantial heterogeneity in asset return expectations of, respectively, U.S. and Dutch households, and Hadar et al. (2013) report ample heterogeneity for various consumer financial decisions. Brown and Taylor (2014) link differences in economic psychology to personality traits.

13   Evidently, besides literacy, financial product complexity greatly affects the quality of decisions. Bernard (2016) offers an interesting case study entitled "Even Math Teachers Are at a Loss Understanding Annuities." As a rule, all businesses, not only in finance, have an incentive to screen for behavioral biases and to shroud some aspects of the products that they offer (Gabaix and Laibson, 2006). Ru and Schoar (2016) suggest that U.S. credit card companies exploit the time inconsistency of their customers by offering low introductory annual percentage rates (APRs) but high late fees, penalty interest rates, and over-limit fees. Lastly, besides literacy (perhaps enhanced by advice) and product complexity, institutional factors play a key role. Regulators can modify the way in which people solve problems and "nudge" decision outcomes in a specific direction. For example, in Los Angeles, prominently displayed hygiene grade cards, providing information to consumers, have led restaurants to upgrade hygiene and improve public health (Zhe and Leslie, 2005). For more discussion of behavioral interventions and paternalism, see Camerer et al. (2003), Engel and Weber (2007), and Sunstein (2014).

3.11 References

Ajzen, I. 1991. "The Theory of Planned Behavior." *Organizational Behavior and Human Decision Processes*, 50, 179–211.

Akerlof, G. A. and R. J. Shiller. 2009. *Animal Spirits: How Human Psychology Drives the Economy, and Why It Matters for Global Capitalism*. Princeton: Princeton University Press.

Akerlof, G. A. and R. J. Shiller. 2015. *Phishing for Phools: The Economics of Manipulation and Deception*. Princeton: Princeton University Press.

Ariely, D. 2008. *Predictably Irrational. The Hidden Forces That Shape Our Decisions.* New York: HarperCollins.

Baker, M. and J. Wurgler. 2007. Investor Sentiment in the Stock Market. *Journal of Economic Perspectives*, 21(2), 129–151.

Barber, B. M. and T. Odean. 2000. "Trading Is Hazardous to Your Wealth: The Common Stock Investment Performance of Individual Investors." *Journal of Finance*, 55(2), 773–806.

Barber, B. M. and T. Odean. 2001. "Boys Will Be Boys: Gender, Overconfidence, and Common Stock Investment." *Quarterly Journal of Economics*, 116(1), 261–292.

Barber, B. M. and T. Odean. 2008. "All That Glitters: The Effect of Attention and News on the Buying Behavior of Individual and Institutional Investors." *Review of Financial Studies*, 21(2), 785–818.

Barber, B. M., Y.-T. Lee, Y.-J. Liu, and T. Odean. 2009. "Just How Much Do Individual Investors Lose by Trading?" *Review of Financial Studies*, 22(2), 609–632.

Barberis, N. 2013. "The Psychology of Tail Events: Progress and Challenges." *American Economic Review*, 103(3), 611–616.

Barberis, N., A. Shleifer, and R. Vishny. 1998. "A Model of Investor Sentiment." *Journal of Financial Economics*, 49, 307–343.

Bargh, J. A. and T. L. Chartrand. 1999. "The Unbearable Automaticity of Being." *American Psychologist*, 54(7), 462–479.

Baucells, M., M. Weber, and F. Welfens. 2011. "Reference-Point Formation and Updating." *Management Science*, 57(3), 506–519.

Baumeister, R. F. and J. Tierney. 2011. *Willpower: Rediscovering the Greatest Human Strength.* New York: Penguin Press.

Benabou, R. and J. Tirole. 2016. "Mindful Economics: The Production, Consumption, and Value of Beliefs." *Journal of Economic Perspectives*, 30(3), 141–164.

Benartzi, S. and R.H. Thaler, 1999. "Risk Aversion or Myopia? Choices in Repeated Gambles and Retirement Investments." *Management Science*, 45(3), 364–381.

Berger, J. 2013. *Contagious: Why Things Catch On.* New York: Simon & Schuster.

Bernard, T. S. 2016. "Even Math Teachers Are at a Loss to Understand Annuities." *New York Times*, October 28.

Biais, B. and M. Weber. 2009. "Hindsight Bias, Risk Perception, and Investment Performance." *Management Science*, 55(6), 1018–1029.

Blinder, A. S. and A. B. Krueger. 2004. "What Does the Public Know About Economic Policy and How Does It Know It?" *Brookings Papers on Economic Activity*, 1, 327–397.

Bovi, M. 2009. "Economic Versus Psychological Forecasting: Evidence from Consumer Confidence Surveys." *Journal of Economic Psychology*, 30, 563–574.

Brown, L. D. and H. N. Higgins. 2005. "Managers' Forecast Guidance of Analysts: International Evidence." *Journal of Accounting and Public Policy*, 24(4), 280–299.

Brown, S. and K. Taylor. 2014. "Household Finances and the Big Five Personality Traits." *Journal of Economic Psychology*, 45, 197–212.

Brunnermeier, M. and J. Parker. 2005. "Optimal Expectations." *American Economic Review*, 95(4), 1092–1118.

Burgstahler, D. and M. Eames. 2006. "Management of Earnings and Analysts' Forecasts to Achieve Zero and Small Positive Earnings Surprises." *Journal of Business Finance & Accounting*, 33(5–6), 633–652.

Calcagno, R. and C. Monticone. 2015. "Financial Literacy and the Demand for Financial Advice." *Journal of Banking & Finance*, 50, 363–380.

Camerer, C. F., S. Issacharoff, G. Loewenstein, T. O'Donoghue and M. Rabin. 2003. "Regulation for Conservatives: Behavioral Economics and the Case for 'Asymmetric Paternalism'." *University of Pennsylvania Law Review*, 151, 1211–1254.

Chartrand, T. L. and J. A. Bargh. 1999. "The Chameleon Effect: The Perception-Behavioral Link and Social Interaction." *Journal of Personality and Social Psychology*, 76(6), 893–910.

Christelis, D., T. Jappelli, and M. Padula. 2010. "Cognitive Abilities and Portfolio Choice." *European Economic Review*, 54(1), 18–38.

Cialdini, R. B. 1988. *Influence: Science and Practice.* 2nd edition. Glenview, IL: Scott Foresman.

Collins, J. M. 2012. "Financial Advice: A Substitute for Financial Literacy?" *Financial Services Review*, 21(4), 307.

Collins, J. M. and C. Urban. 2016. "The Role of Information on Retirement Planning: Evidence from a Field Study." *Economic Inquiry*, 54(4), 1860–1872.

Da, Z., J. Engelberg and P. Gao. 2011. "In Search of Attention." *The Journal of Finance*, 66(5), 1461–1499.

De Bondt, W. F. M. 1991. "What Do Economists Know About the Stock Market?" *Journal of Portfolio Management*, Winter, 84–91.

De Bondt, W. F. M. 1998. "A Portrait of the Individual Investor." *European Economic Review*, 42(3), 831–844.

De Bondt, W. F. M. 2005. "The Values and Beliefs of European Investors." In K. Knorr Cetina and A. Preda (eds.). *The Sociology of Financial Markets.* New York: Oxford University Press, pp. 163–186.

Deaves, R., E. Luders, and M. Schroder. 2010. "The Dynamics of Overconfidence: Evidence from Stock Market Forecasters." *Journal of Economic Behavior & Organization*, 75, 402–412.

Ditto, P. H. and D. F. Lopez. 1992. "Motivated Skepticism: Use of Differential Decision Criteria for Preferred and Nonpreferred Conclusions." *Journal of Personality and Social Psychology*, 63(4), 568–584.

Dominitz, J. and C. F. Manski. 2007. "Expected Equity Returns and Portfolio Choice: Evidence from the Health and Retirement Study." *Journal of the European Economic Association*, 5(2–3), 369–379.

Dunning, D., C. Heath, and J. M. Suls. 2004. "Flawed Self-Assessment. Implications for Health, Education and the Workplace." *Psychological Science in the Public Interest*, 5(3), 69–106.

Edwards, W. 1982. "Conservatism in Human Information Processing." In D. Kahneman, P. Slovic, and A. Tversky (eds.), *Judgment under Uncertainty: Heuristics and Biases*, Cambridge: Cambridge University Press, pp. 359–369.

Engel, C. and E. U. Weber. 2007. "The Impact of Institutions on the Decision How to Decide." *Journal of Institutional Economics*, 3(3), 323–349.

Epley, N. 2014. *Mindwise: How We Understand What Others Think, Believe, Feel, and Want.* New York: Alfred A. Knopf.

Epley, N. and T. Gilovich. 2006. "The Anchoring-and-Adjustment Heuristic: Why the Adjustments Are Insufficient." *Psychological Science*, 17(4), 311–318.

Ericsson, K. A. and A. C. Lehmann. 1996. "Expert and Exceptional Performance: Evidence of Maximal Adaptation to Task Constraints." *Annual Review of Psychology*, 47, 273–305.

Fama, E. F. 1998. "Market Efficiency, Long-Term Returns, and Behavioral Finance." *Journal of Financial Economics*, 49(3), 283–306.

Fenton-O'Creevy, M., N. Nicholson, E. Soane, and P. Willman. 2003. "Trading on Illusions: Unrealistic Perceptions of Control and Trading Performance." *Journal of Occupational and Organizational Psychology*, 76, 53–68.

Fernandes, D., J. G. Lynch Jr, and R. G. Netemeyer. 2014. "Financial Literacy, Financial Education, and Downstream Financial Behaviors." *Management Science*, 60(8), 1861–1883.

Fiedler, K. 2000. "Beware of Samples! Cognitive-Ecological Sampling Approach to Judgment Biases." *Psychological Review*, 107(4), 659–676.

Fiedler, K., B. Brinkmann, T. Betsch, and B. Wild. 2000. "A Sampling Approach to Biases in Conditional Probability Judgments: Beyond Base Rate Neglect and Statistical Format." *Journal of Experimental Psychology: General,* 129(3), 399–418.

FINRA (Financial Investor Regulatory Authority) Investor Education Foundation. 2016. *Financial Capability in the United States 2016*.

Fischhoff, B. 1982. "Debiasing." In D. Kahneman, P. Slovic, and A. Tversky (eds.), *Judgment Under Uncertainty: Heuristics and Biases*. Cambridge: Cambridge University Press.

Fischhoff, B. and D. MacGregor. 1982. "Subjective Confidence in Forecasts." *Journal of Forecasting*, 1(2), 155–172.

French, K. R. and J. M. Poterba. 1991. "Investor Diversification and International Equity Markets." *American Economic Review*, 81(2), 222–226.

Frieder, L. and A. Subrahmanyam. 2005. "Brand Perceptions and the Market for Common Stock." *Journal of Financial and Quantitative Analysis* 40(1), 57–85.

Gabaix, X. and D. Laibson. 2006. "Shrouded Attributes, Consumer Myopia, and Information Suppression in Competitive Markets." *Quarterly Journal of Economics*, 121, 505–540.

Gasper, K. 2004. "Do You See What I See? Affect and Visual Information Processing." *Cognition and Emotion*, 18(3), 405–421.

George, T. and C. Hwang. 2004. "The 52-Week High and Momentum Investing." *Journal of Finance*, 59, 2145–2176.

Gigerenzer, G. and U. Hoffrage. 1995. "How to Improve Bayesian Reasoning Without Instruction: Frequency Formats." *Psychological Review*, 102, 684–704.

Greenspan, A. 2007. *The Age of Turbulence: Adventures in a New World*. New York: Penguin Press.

Greenspan, A. 2013a. *The Map and the Territory. Risk, Human Nature, and the Future of Forecasting*. New York: Penguin Press.

Greenspan, A. 2013b. "Never Saw It Coming. Why the Financial Crisis Took Economists by Surprise." *Foreign Affairs*, November/December, 88–96.

Greenwood, R. and A. Shleifer. 2014. "Expectations of Returns and Expected Returns." *Review of Financial Studies*, 27(3), 714–746.

Griffin, D. and A. Tversky. 1992. "The Weighing of Evidence and the Determinants of Confidence." *Cognitive Psychology*, 24(3), 411–435.

Hackethal, A., M. Haliassos, and T. Jappelli. 2012. "Financial Advisors: A Case of Babysitters?" *Journal of Banking & Finance*, 36(2), 509–524.

Hadar, L., S. Sood, and C. R. Fox. 2013. "Subjective Knowledge in Consumer Financial Decisions." *Journal of Marketing Research*, 50(3), 303–316.

Hayward, M. L. A., D. A. Shepherd, and D. Griffin. 2006. "A Hubris Theory of Entrepreneurship." *Management Science*, 52(2), 160–172.

Heath, C. and D. Heath. 2007. *Made to Stick: Why Some Ideas Survive and Others Die.* New York: Random House.

Heffernan, M. 2011. *Willful Blindness: Why We Ignore the Obvious at Our Peril.* New York: Walker.

Hertwig, R. 2012. "The Experience and Rationality of Decisions from Experience." *Synthese*, 187, 269–292.

Hertwig, R., G. Baron, E. U. Weber and I. Erev. 2004. "Decisions from Experience and the Effect of Rare Events in Risky Choice." *Psychological Science*, 15(8), 534–539.

Hirshleifer, D., and T. Shumway. 2003. "Good Day Sunshine: Stock Returns and the Weather." *Journal of Finance*, 58(3), 1009–1032.

Hirshleifer, D. and S. H. Teoh. 2003. "Limited Attention, Information Disclosure, and Financial Reporting." *Journal of Accounting and Economics*, 36(1), 337–386.

Hirshleifer, D., S. Lim, and S. H. Teoh. 2011. "Limited Investor Attention and Stock Market Misreactions to Accounting Information." *Review of Asset Pricing Studies*, 1(1), 35–73.

Hoffrage, U. and R. Hertwig. 1999. "Hindsight Bias: A Price Worth Paying for Fast and Frugal Memory." In G. Gigerenzer, P.M. Todd, and the ABC Research Group (eds.), *Simple Heuristics That Make Us Smart*, Oxford: Oxford University Press, pp. 191–208.

Hurd, M., M. van Rooij, and J. Winter. 2011. "Stock Market Expectations of Dutch Households." *Journal of Applied Economics*, 26(3), 416–436.

Ivković, Z. and S. Weisbenner. 2007. "Information Diffusion Effects in Individual Investors' Common Stock Purchases: Covet Thy Neighbors' Investment Choices." *Review of Financial Studies*, 20(4), 1327–1357.

Johnson, J. and G. J. Tellis. 2005. "Blowing Bubbles: Heuristics and Biases in the Run-up of Stock Prices." *Journal of the Academy of Marketing Science* 33(4), 486–503.

Jonas, E., S. Schulz-Hardt, D. Frey, and N. Thelen. 2001. "Confirmation Bias in Sequential Information Search After Preliminary Decisions: An Expansion of Dissonance Theoretical Research on Selective Exposure to Information." *Journal of Personality and Social Psychology*, 80(4), 557–571.

Kahneman, D. 2011. *Thinking, Fast and Slow.* New York: Farrar, Straus and Giroux.

Kahneman, D. and M. W. Riepe. 1998. "Aspects of Investor Psychology." *Journal of Portfolio Management*, 24(4), 52–65.

Kahneman, D. and A. Tversky. 1973. "On the Psychology of Prediction." *Psychological Review*, 80, 237–251.

Kahneman, D. and A. Tversky. 1979. "Prospect Theory: An Analysis of Decision Under Risk." *Econometrica*, 47, 263–291.

Kaniel, R., G. Saar, and S. Titman. 2008. "Individual Investor Trading and Stock Returns." *Journal of Finance*, 63, 273–310.

Katona, G. 1975. *Psychological Economics.* New York: Elsevier.

Keynes, J. M. 1936. *The General Theory of Employment, Interest and Money.* New York: Harcourt, Brace & World, Inc.

Korniotis, G. M. and A. Kumar. 2011. "Do Older Investors Make Better Investment Decisions?" *Review of Economics and Statistics*, 93(1), 244–265.

Langer, E. J. 1982. "The Illusion of Control." In D. Kahneman, P. Slovic, and A. Tversky (eds.), *Judgment Under Uncertainty: Heuristics and Biases.* Cambridge: Cambridge University Press, pp. 231–238.

Lejarraga, T., T. Pachur, R. Frey, and R. Hertwig. 2016. "Decisions from Experience: From Monetary to Medical Gambles." *Journal of Behavioral Decision Making*, 29, 67–77.

Loewenstein, G. F., C. K. Hsee, E. U. Weber, and N. Welch. 2001. "Risk as Feelings." *Psychological Bulletin*, 127(2), 267–286.

Loewenstein, G. F. and J. S. Lerner. 2003. "The Role of Affect in Decision Making." *Handbook of Affective Science* 619, 642, 3.

Loibi, C. and T. K. Hira. 2009. "Investor Information Search." *Journal of Economic Psychology*, 30, 24–41.

Lusardi, A. and O. S. Mitchell. 2011. "Financial Literacy Around the World: An Overview." *Journal of Pension Economics and Finance*, 10(4), 497–508.

Lusardi, A. and O. S. Mitchell. 2014. "The Economic Importance of Financial Literacy: Theory and Evidence." *Journal of Economic Literature*, 52(1), 5–44.

Malmendier, U. and S. Nagel. 2011. "Depression Babies: Do Macroeconomic Experiences Affect Risk Taking?" *Quarterly Journal of Economics*, 126(1), 373–416.

Manski, C. F. 2004. "Measuring Expectations." *Econometrica*, 72(5), 1329–1376.

Maslow, A. 1954. *Motivation and Personality*. New York: Harper & Row.

McClelland, D. 1961. *The Achieving Society*. New York: D. Van Nostrand.

McGraw, A. P., B. A. Mellers, and I. Ritov. 2004. "The Affective Costs of Overconfidence." *Journal of Behavioral Decision Making*, 17(4), 281–295.

Mellers, B. A. 2000. "Choice and the Relative Pleasure of Consequences." *Psychological Bulletin*, 126(6), 910–924.

Mill, J. [1829] 1869. *Analysis of the Phenomena of the Human Mind.* 2nd edition. London: Longmans, Green.

Mill, J. S. 1843. 'The Logic of the Moral Sciences." In *A System of Logic, Ratiocinative and Inductive.* London: Longman, Green.

Neisser, U. 1976. *Cognition and Reality. Principles and Implications of Cognitive Psychology.* San Francisco: W. H. Freeman.

Nofsinger, J. R. 2005. "Social Mood and Financial Economics." *Journal of Behavioral Finance*, 6(3), 144–160.

Nofsinger, J. R., and R. W. Sias. 1999. "Herding and Feedback Trading by Institutional and Individual Investors." *Journal of Finance*, 54(6), 2263–2295.

Odean, T. 1998. "Are Investors Reluctant to Realize Their Losses?" *Journal of Finance*, 53(5), 1775–1798.

Peng, L. and W. Xiong. 2006. "Investor Attention, Overconfidence and Category Learning." *Journal of Financial Economics*, 80(3), 563–602.

Porter, G. E. 2004. "The Long-Term Value of Analysts' Advice in the Wall Street Journal's Investment Dartboard Contest." *Journal of Applied Finance*, 14(2), 52–65.

Posner, E. A. 2015. "The Law, Economics, and Psychology of Manipulation." University of Chicago, Coase-Sandor Institute for Law & Economics Research Paper #726.

Ross, L. and R. E. Nisbett. 1991. *The Person and the Situation: Perspectives on Social Psychology.* New York: McGraw-Hill.

Rothman, A. J. and C. D. Hardin. 1997. "Differential Use of the Availability Heuristic in Social Judgment." *Personality and Social Psychology Bulletin*, 23(2), 123–138.

Ru, H. and A. Schoar. 2016. "Do Credit Card Companies Screen for Behavioral Biases?" National Bureau of Economic Research Working Paper #22360.

Schlösser, T., D. Dunning, K. L. Johnson, and J. Kruger. 2013. "How Unaware Are the Unskilled? Empirical Tests of the 'Signal Extraction' Counterexplanation for the Dunning–Kruger Effect in Self-Evaluation of Performance." *Journal of Economic Psychology*, 39, 85–100.

Schneider, W. and R. M. Shiffrin. 1977. "Controlled and Automatic Human Information Processing: I. Detection, Search, and Attention." *Psychological Review*, 84(1), 1.

Seasholes, M. S. and N. Zhu. 2010. "Individual Investors and Local Bias." *The Journal of Finance*, 65(5), 1987–2010.

Selten, R. 1998. "Features of Experimentally Observed Bounded Rationality." *European Economic Review*, 42, 413–436.

Shefrin, H. 2000. *Beyond Greed and Fear: Understanding Behavioral Finance and the Psychology of Investing.* Boston, MA: Harvard Business School Press.

Shefrin, H. and M. Statman. 1994. "Behavioral Capital Asset Pricing Theory." *Journal of Financial and Quantitative Analysis*, 29(3), 323–349.

Shiller, R. J. 2000a. "Measuring Bubble Expectations and Investor Confidence." *Journal of Psychology and Financial Markets*, 1(1), 49–60.

Shiller, R. J. 2000b. *Irrational Exuberance.* Princeton, NJ: Princeton University Press.

Shleifer, A. 2000. *Inefficient Markets.* Oxford: Oxford University Press.

Slovic, P., M. L. Finucane, E. Peters, and D. G. MacGregor. 2004. "Risk as Analysis and Risk as Feelings: Some Thoughts About Affect, Reason, Risk, and Rationality." *Risk Analysis*, 24(2), 311–322.

Sonsino, D. and E. Regev. 2013. "Informational Overconfidence in Return Prediction. More properties." *Journal of Economic Psychology*, 39, 72–84.

Stango, V. and J. Zinman. 2009. "Exponential Growth Bias and Household Finance." *Journal of Finance*, 64(6), 2807–2849.

Statman, M., K. L. Fisher, and D. Aiginer. 2008. "Affect in a Behavioral Asset-Pricing Model." *Financial Analysts Journal*, 64(2), 20–29.

Stephan, E. 1999. "Die Rolle von Urteilsheuristiken bei Finanzentscheidungen: Ankereffekte und kognitive Verftigbarkeit." In L. Fischer, T. Kutsch, and E. Stephan (eds.), *Finanzpsychologie.* Muenchen und Wien: R. Oldenbourg Verlag, pp. 101–137.

Stephan, E. and G. Kiell. 2000. "Decision Processes in Professional Investors: Does Expertise Moderate Judgmental Biases?" In E. Holz (ed.), *IAREP-ISABE*

Conference Proceedings: Fairness and Competition. Vienna: Universitatsverlag, 41, 6–20.

Stotz, O. and R. von Nitzsch. 2005. 'The Perception of Control and the Level of Overconfidence: Evidence from Analyst Earnings Estimates and Price Targets." *Journal of Behavioral Finance*, 6(3), 121–128.

Sunstein, C. R. 2014. "Nudges vs. Shoves." *Harvard Law Review Forum*, 127(April), 210–217.

Sunstein, C. R. 2016. "Fifty Shades of Manipulation." *Journal of Marketing Behavior*, 1(3–4), 213–244.

Taleb, N. N. 2007. *The Black Swan: The Impact of the Highly Improbable.* New York: Random House.

Taleb, N. N., D. G., Goldstein, and M. W. Spitznagel. 2009. "The Six Mistakes Executives Make in Risk Management." *Harvard Business Review*, 39–41.

Tavris, C. and E. Aronson. 2007. *Mistakes Were Made but Not By Me: Why We Justify Foolish Beliefs, Bad Decisions, and Hurtful Acts.* New York: Harcourt.

Teigen, K. H. and G. Keren. 2003. "Surprises: Low Probabilities or High Contrasts?" *Cognition*, 87, 55–71.

Teigen, K. H. and G. Keren. 2007. "Waiting for the Bus: When Base-Rates Refuse to Be Neglected." *Cognition*, 101, 337–357.

Tetlock, P. E. 2005. *Expert Political Judgment. How Good Is It? How Can We Know?* Princeton: Princeton University Press.

Tetlock, P. E. and D. Gardner. 2015. *Superforecasting: The Art and Science of Prediction.* New York: Crown Publishing Group.

Trevelyan, R. 2008. "Optimism, Overconfidence and Entrepreneurial Activity." *Managerial Decision*, 46(7), 986–1001.

Tversky, A. and C. Heath. 1991. "Preferences and Beliefs: Ambiguity and Competence in Choice Under Uncertainty." *Journal of Risk and Uncertainty*, 4, 5–28.

Tversky, A. and D. Kahneman. 1982a. "Judgment Under Uncertainty: Heuristics and Biases." In D. Kahneman, P. Slovic, and A. Tversky (eds.), *Judgment Under Uncertainty: Heuristics and Biases.* Cambridge: Cambridge University Press, pp. 3–22.

Tversky, A. and D. Kahneman. 1982b. "Evidential Impact of Base Rates." In D. Kahneman, P. Slovic, and A. Tversky (eds.). *Judgment Under Uncertainty: Heuristics and Biases.* Cambridge: Cambridge University Press, pp. 153–162.

Tversky, A. and D. Kahneman. 1982c. "Availability: A Heuristic for Judging Frequency and Probability." In D. Kahneman, P. Slovic, and A. Tversky (eds.). *Judgment Under Uncertainty: Heuristics and Biases.* Cambridge: Cambridge University Press, pp. 163–178.

Van Rooij, M., A. Lusardi, and R. Alessie. 2011. "Financial Literacy and Stock Market Participation." *Journal of Financial Economics*, 101(2), 449–472.

Vissing-Jorgensen, A. 2004. "Perspectives on Behavioral Finance: Does 'Irrationality' Disappear with Wealth? Evidence from Expectations and Actions." *NBER Macro Annual 2003.* Cambridge, MA: MIT Press.

Wärneryd, K.-.E. 2001. *Stock-Market Psychology. How People Value and Trade Stocks.* Cheltenham, UK and Northampton, MA: Elgar.

Wärneryd, K.-E. 1997. "Demystifying Rational Expectations Theory Through an Economic-Psychological Model." In G. Antonides, W.F. van Raaij, and S. Maital (eds.), *Advances in Economic Psychology*. Chichester: Wiley & Sons, pp. 211–236.

Watts, D. J. 2011. *Everything Is Obvious: Once You Know the Answer*. London: Atlantic.

Willis, L. E. 2009. "Evidence and Ideology in Assessing the Effectiveness of Financial Literacy Education." *San Diego Law Review*, 46, 415.

Wilson, T. D. and D. T. Gilbert. 2003. "Affective Forecasting." In M. P. Zanna (ed.), *Advances in Experimental Social Psychology*, 35, 346–411. New York: Academic Press.

Wilson, T. D., D. B. Centerbar, D. A. Kermer, and D. T. Gilbert. 2005. "The Pleasures of Uncertainty: Prolonging Positive Moods in Ways People Do Not Anticipate." *Journal of Personality and Social Psychology*, 88(1), 5–21.

Zajonc, R. B. 1980. "Feeling and Thinking: Preferences Need No Inferences." *American Psychologist*, 35(2), 151–175.

Zhe, G. and P. Leslie. 2005. "The Case in Support of Restaurant Hygiene Grade Cards." *Choices*, 20(2), 97–102.

4 Speculative Bubbles

Insights from Behavioral Finance

Werner De Bondt

Hardly any topic in economics has received as much detailed scientific investigation as the behavior of asset prices, that is, the prices of stocks, bonds, and real estate. Economists are interested because of the role of security prices in guiding resource allocation. "Perfection" is a competitive capital market in which rational prices instantaneously and accurately reflect all available information and sustain economic efficiency (Hayek, 1945; Grossman, 1989; Turner, 2016).

In contrast, the attention of amateur and expert investors is more practical. They seek early access to news, develop trading rules, or carry out fundamental analysis in hopes of attaining superior investment performance. Their aim is to construct a portfolio of assets that earns a higher return than a portfolio of arbitrarily selected securities with comparable risk, liquidity, tax burden, et cetera. Empirical research in modern finance – exemplified by the seminal contributions of Fama (1965a, 1965b, 1970, 1976) – focused on the futility of these efforts, especially if search and trading costs are taken into account. For example, stock prices were shown to be responsive to news and to approximately follow a random walk.[1]

Beginning in the mid-1960s, modern finance theory became exceptionally influential. For four decades, it shaped the thinking of millions of investors, bankers, business executives, policy makers, academics, and university students (Fama, 2013). The paradigm earned several Nobel Prizes, first with Harry Markowitz, Merton Miller, William Sharpe, Robert Merton, and Myron Scholes, and later with Lars Peter Hansen and Eugene Fama. The continuing world crisis that began in the United States and the United Kingdom changed everything, however.

4.1 After the Crisis

We are now coming near to the tenth anniversary of the September 2007 bank run on Northern Rock, a U.K. bank, oddly at the very moment that the Bank of England was hosting a gleeful conference on "the great moderation," an idiom describing the economic success of the 1980s and 1990s, allegedly produced by improved monetary, financial, and macroeconomic policies that were rules-based. The term was much loved by former Federal Reserve Chair Ben Bernanke.[2] But aggregate demand and investment depend to a degree on views of the future that can change radically and abruptly (Keynes, 1936). Time and again, after years of good economic times, agents begin to believe that such conditions will last and for this reason take ever larger risks in order to capture ever larger returns (Minsky, 1986). This type of optimistic overconfidence (or "disaster myopia") commonly leads to financial disorder (Guttentag and Herring, 1984). So, in 2007 and 2008, the great moderation all of a sudden turned into "the great recession."[3] This is a softer phrase than "the great depression" of the 1930s, but, in retrospect, it is an historical episode with strikingly similar social and political costs.[4]

Today, after the early panic, the liquidity squeeze, the bailouts, and the credit crunch, and after years of weak growth, a poor labor market, near-zero interest rates, and escalating income inequality, economic thought as well as refined public opinion is shifting.[5] The shift is gradual but firm. It impinges on every fragment of the so-called Washington consensus, which for many years favored globalization, privatization, and deregulation. The debate about whether free, unfettered markets are efficient, self-correcting, stable, and fair has been reopened. In finance theory, important new questions to be answered have to do with the size, profitability, and welfare contribution of the financial service sector (asking, for instance, whether under any circumstances financial innovation and increased market liquidity are beneficial); with the origins and effects of speculative asset bubbles; and with the issue of how to cope with bubbles and their aftermath, from a modeling as well as a policy perspective. There is broad agreement that finance needs to be integrated into macroeconomics since neither field of study can be fully appreciated without considering the other (see, e.g., Borio and Drehmann, 2009, and Taylor, 2014).

A rethink is never easy. Neoclassical economists highlight that pure logic, in various ways, can reconcile asset bubbles with rational economic man. But many others believe that the exercise lacks surface plausibility. Even as the institutional context carries great weight (e.g., financial innovation stimulated by globalization, the liberalization of capital flows, and deregulation), asset bubbles are in essence a manifestation of "animal spirits." In other words, bubbles are generated by saving and investment decisions that often reflect pervasive self-reinforcing misconceptions. Therefore, asset risks and returns are distorted and so is the macroeconomy (Keynes, 1936, 1937; Kindleberger, 1978; Minsky, 1977, 1986; Akerlof, 2002; Akerlof and Shiller, 2009).

Before 2008, the psychology of finance did not appear on macroeconomists' radar screen. Indeed, finance itself was often viewed as a factor that may be safely ignored in business cycle studies. Standard models had "real business cycle" foundations and, as needed, were augmented with nominal rigidities and other frictions. The cycle was thought to be caused by random exogenous shocks, possibly spread, magnified, and made persistent by finance but not caused by it (see, e.g., King and Plosser, 1984; Bernanke, Gertler, and Gilchrist, 1999).

In contrast, Borio (2014a) and others list some key findings with respect to the interaction between finance and the business cycle that recently have been discovered or revived. The chief new "fact" is the existence of an irregular financial cycle with a life of its own, that is, one unconnected to the shorter business cycle. The financial cycle is linked to changing perceptions of value and risk and gives rise to booms that predictably go bust. A parsimonious portrayal, Borio suggests, is in terms of property prices and credit that is vital in funding construction activity and land purchases. The peaks of financial cycles overlap with financial crises. Cycle contractions characteristically take longer than recessions. During the boom, easy credit distorts resource allocation and enables a buildup of financial imbalances. In due course, too much debt, the legacy of the preceding boom, forces agents to cut expenses (Reinhart and Rogoff, 2009).[6]

Two elements mark the new approach. First is the presence of quasirational beliefs and disagreement among agents. People's simple models are frequently mistaken, a Keynesian notion in line with behavioral theories of asset pricing elaborated since the 1980s (Akerlof, 2002; Akerlof and Shiller, 2009). The root cause is fundamental uncertainty: we can only speculate about what lies ahead for us. Much of it is utterly unanticipated. Disparate beliefs about likely future scenarios allow for booms and busts that may be made more powerful by time-varying risk attitudes and investor herding.[7] Second is the fragility and instability of an "excessively elastic" monetary economy where saving and financing do not coincide and where loans can create additional nominal purchasing power for some agents without reducing it for others. This means that the financial system does not always put the brakes on booms that may turn out to be unsustainable. Debt expansion is a threat to economic stability (Mises, 1912; Fisher, 1933; Minsky, 1977; Kaufman, 1986; Davis, 1995).[8]

This raises the problem of the so-called financialization of capitalism, that is, the extent to which over the last thirty years the global economy has become dependent on overgrown financial activities (Konczal and Abernathy, 2015). Nowadays, the financial sector in the advanced economies is larger than ever. Among others, Krippner (2011), Stockman (2011, 2013), Kay (2015), Admati (2016), Foroohar (2016), and Turner (2016) describe the historical and political origins of the rise of finance –also depicted by Greenspan (2005, 2007) but from a much more favorable point of view.[9] As a general rule, the proponents of financialization assert that "Wall Street" has prospered at the expense of "Main Street," with dreadful results for the financial system itself, corporate governance and innovation, and long-term economic health (i.e., growth, stability, and justice).[10]

Haldane (2009), Philippon (2015), and others argue that, while the financial services industry is very profitable, it does not serve society well. "Finance has grown fat," and is becoming technologically "obsolete," according to Smith

(2016). The literature on financialization also challenges the beliefs of central bankers that we need credit growth to fuel economic growth, and that rising debt is acceptable as long as consumer price inflation remains low. Instead, it says that banking, left to itself, will inevitably create credit "in excessive and unstable amounts" (Turner, 2016, p. 174). Too much credit slows economic growth (Cournède and Denk, 2015). Interestingly, credit aggregates help to predict the chances of future financial crises.[11]

Of course, there is a limit to how much borrowing, relative to income, economic agents such as households can service, such as to avoid delinquency and foreclosure. Eventually, excess debt must lead to deleveraging and a slowdown in spending. In that sense, crises are credit booms gone wrong (Schularick and Taylor, 2012). Commenting on the credit expansion between 1920 and 1929, Persons (1930) wrote that "a considerable volume of sales recently made were based on credit ratings only justifiable on the theory that flush times were to continue indefinitely ... When the process of expanding credit ceases ... there must ensue a painful period of readjustment" (1930, pp. 188–189). Likewise responding to contemporary events, Fisher (1933) advanced a debt-deflation theory of "Booms and Depressions" (also the title of his 1932 book on the subject). He said that "over-investment and over-speculation are often important; but they would have far less serious results were they not conducted with borrowed money ... The same is true as to over-confidence" (1933, p. 341).[12] Fisher painted the chronology of depressions in ten steps (including plummeting asset and commodity prices, rising pessimism, distress sales, bank runs and failures, hoarding, and reductions in output), and he called attention to a vicious circle: "[W]hen over-indebtedness is so great as to depress prices faster than liquidation, the mass effort to get out of debt sinks us more deeply into debt" (p. 350).[13]

To sum up, overheating in credit markets reflects ebbs and flows in the preferences and beliefs of borrowers and lenders, perhaps propelled by actual past changes in wealth and their extrapolation into the future. But a second key aspect is "easy money" and the reality that many decisions are made by delegated agents inside financial firms who face distinct compensation and governance structures, accounting standards, and regulations (Stein, 2013).[14] In a highly competitive environment, well-defined but rigid rules may well encourage agents to take on unsafe risks (e.g., longer durations) and to embrace financial "innovation" that boosts short-range returns in ways that elude easy measurement, such as the sale of insurance against tail events (Rajan, 2005).[15] Evidently, if many bad loans are financed by short-term claims that investors may abruptly pull back, the credit boom becomes even more of a financial stability concern (Kay, 2015).

4.2 Excess Volatility and Predictability

Even before the financial crisis, our understanding of asset pricing was incomplete and unsatisfactory. Since the late 1970s, financial economists have compiled many empirical anomalies that baffle the mind. For example, Ball and Brown (1968), Latane and Jones (1977), and Watts (1978) were among the first scholars to document a systematic drift in returns after earnings announcements. Around the same time, Charest (1978) noticed how it can take months before the full impact of changes in dividends is impounded in prices. (See also Michaely et al., 1995.) Analogous observations were made by Givoly and Lakonishok (1979, 1980) with respect to analyst forecast revisions of earnings per share.[16] Over the years, the list of abnormalities has expanded greatly. Some patterns in security prices are related to the calendar, such as the month (Rozeff and Kinney, 1976), the turn of the year (Givoly and Ovadia, 1983; Roll, 1983), and the day of the week (Gibbons and Hess, 1981; French, 1983). Other anomalies come into view in the cross-section of companies. Small firms earn unusually large returns (Banz, 1981; Reinganum, 1981), as do firms with low price-earnings (PE) ratios (Basu, 1977), firms that are neglected by investors (Arbel and Strebel, 1983).[17]

Modern finance responds to the challenge of return predictability in different ways. For instance, it questions the pervasiveness and robustness of the new facts (Fama, 1998) or it reinterprets them as nonanomalous (e.g., Timmerman, 1993; Brav and Heaton, 2002). One way to play down the significance of the findings is to cast doubt on the valuation models that must unavoidably be part of every test of the efficient markets hypothesis. This is the position taken by, for example, Jensen (1978) and Ball (1978). The Sharpe–Lintner capital asset pricing model (CAPM) states that the expected return for any stock (in excess of the risk-free rate) equals beta times the expected market risk premium. Skepticism about this model runs deep.[18] It stems from unfavorable empirical tests as well as from hesitation about the model's testability (Roll, 1977). The theoretical studies of Merton (1973) and Ross (1976) laid the groundwork for multifactor models. These authors propose that the compensation for bearing risk is comprised of several risk premiums rather than one. However, the consumption-CAPM (Breeden, 1979) and the arbitrage pricing theory do not *a priori* specify the relevant state variables.[19] Based on U.S. data, Fama and French (1992, 1996) first added two factors (size and value) to the market risk premium. Later, they put in a momentum factor. Their most recent work includes two more factors capturing profitability and investment (Fama and French, 2015, 2016).[20] Whether multifactor models greatly enhance our practical understanding of the determination of stock prices is a matter of debate. However, once the five Fama–French factors are taken into account, some stock price anomalies lose strength, and the "excess" returns that are earned may be thought about as fair payment for time-varying risk (Fama, 2013; Fama and French, 2016).

Some researchers have taken a different approach and have asked whether price levels, rather than rates of return, can be reconciled with valuation models built on the joint assumptions of rational utility-maximizing agents and frictionless markets. Prominent among the expectations models of asset prices is the Miller-Modigliani (1961) view of stock prices as the appropriately dis-counted present values of expected future cash flows (LeRoy, 1982). Shiller (1981, 1989, 2000, 2013) finds that stock price fluctuations cannot be solely attributed to movements in dividends around the historical trend. Over the last century, he says, dividends simply did not vary enough to rationally justify the price movements (see also LeRoy and Porter, 1981). There is excess vola-tility or, as former Federal Reserve chair Alan Greenspan put it, "irrational exuberance."

Yet, the extraordinary variability of stock prices may also reflect changes in the rates of return that investors require. The consumption variability associ-ated with expected fluctuations in economic activity induces stock price var-iability, the magnitude of which depends on the level of risk aversion of the representative investor. Grossman and Shiller (1981) estimate the degree of risk aversion that would validate the observed stock price volatility. The postwar data imply implausibly high estimates. Also, the historical price movements in bonds, land, or housing do not match those of stocks (Shiller, 1989). Still, that is what should happen if asset price fluctuations chiefly reflect changes in discount rates.

Shiller's findings of excess stock price volatility disagree with the assump-tion of rational expectations.[21] Changes in stock prices are strongly correlated with changes in corporate earnings that follow about one or two years later. Maybe investors perceive short-term developments to be of great consequence for the long-term outlook of the economy? The trouble is that the argument is in conflict with the trendiness of dividends for over a century. So, it implies that investors grossly overreact to new information or, alternatively, that they are myopic.[22]

The hypothesis of stock market overreaction is not a radical departure from past belief. In *The General Theory*, Keynes argued that "day-to-day fluctua-tions in the profits of existing investments, which are obviously of an ephemeral and non-significant character, tend to have an altogether excessive, and even an absurd, influence on the market" (Keynes, 1936, pp. 153–154). In various forms, the theory is also found in Taussig (1921), Macauley (1938), Williams (1938), and Working (1949, 1958). With the prosperity of the 1920s, the crash and the depression in mind, Williams (1938) notes that security prices "have been based too much on current earning power, too little on long-run dividend paying power" (p. 19).[23]

Over its history, economics has produced many scholars – ranging from Thorstein Veblen, Vilfredo Pareto, Wesley Mitchell, or George Katona to Herbert Simon, George Akerlof, and Daniel Kahneman – who sought to introduce behavioral assumptions. Still, a good number of economists keep their distance. For instance, the search for rational microfoundations of mac-roeconomics that originated in the 1970s was a shift that is 180 degrees in the opposite direction. In 1976, Barro and Fisher stated that "… the rational expectations assumption may be excessively strong … but it is more persuasive

... than the alternative of using a rule of thumb for expectations formation that is independent of the stochastic properties of the time path of the variable about which expectations are formed. A fundamental difficulty with theories of expectations that are not based on the predictions of the relevant economic model ... is that they require a theory of systematic mistakes" (Barro and Fisher, 1976, p. 163).

In the remainder of this chapter, I first appraise the theory of rational and efficient markets, and I support tests of efficiency that compare stock prices with "intrinsic values" of companies as in Graham and Dodd (1934). Against Barro and Fisher, I contend that at this moment in time the groundwork for a theory of systematic bias exists. The failure of rationality as a descriptive model matches the findings of behavioral science. Much of this breakdown may be understood in terms of a limited number of psychological mechanisms, such as mental frames and heuristics, that shape human cognition, emotion, and social interaction. Thus, behavioral finance gives positive content to such concepts as investor sentiment, crowd opinion, or animal spirits that, by themselves, look inoperative and hollow. The rise of behavioral finance does not mean, however, that we must abandon economic man *in toto*. Since the behavioral model is one of bias, the rational approach retains some of its normative allure.[24] Economic agents are seen as boundedly rational, that is, they are thought to act sensibly within the decision-making context and within the limits of their cognitive and emotional abilities.

Next, I turn to the empirical evidence. I discuss how investor psychology influences the structure and dynamics of world equity markets. In particular, Iemphasize investor over- and underreaction, and the remarkable performance of value stocks compared to glamour stocks. The overreaction effect was discovered in the context of the study of the price-earnings ratio anomaly. In the cross-section of securities, stocks with low PE ratios earn significantly higher risk-adjusted returns than high PE stocks.[25] The overreaction hypothesis says that this happens because, relative to their intrinsic value, many high PE stocks are temporarily overpriced. Investors, the contention is, get inappropriately optimistic about the business prospects of these firms. Similarly, low PE stocks are underpriced because the market is in appropriately pessimistic. Once false beliefs take hold, however, only a great deal of opposing news (e.g., a series of negative earnings surprises) succeeds in turning prices around, and this behavior generates drifts in stock prices. (Investors do not easily change attitude. They tend to discount any news report that opposes "what they know to be true," and they give extra weight to confirming information.) Thus, trends and reversals in share price are dissimilar but connected aspects of the same phenomenon. Both the initial overreaction and the later underreaction differ from the reaction that Bayes' theorem defines as best. What is decisive is that deviations from optimality can be detected and predicted by statistics (such as past return performance) that are correlated with investor sentiment. In this chapter, I develop the overreaction hypothesis in more detail, and I review many empirical studies. A large majority of them use data for the United States and other G-7 countries. On balance, the evidence indicates that investor psychology is a significant determinant of security prices. In sum, I conclude that the stock markets of the world's leading industrialized nations are not rational and efficient, that is, there are systematic and measurable disparities between the stock prices and fundamental values of large publicly traded corporations.[26] The concept of overreaction may well embody a pervasive trait of human conduct that applies under general, identifiable circumstances – in market as well as nonmarket contexts.[27]

4.3 Rational and Efficient Markets

While the notion of rational and efficient capital markets is a cornerstone of modern finance, significant ambiguities are associated with its meaning. The concept may be analyzed from the perspective of economic outcomes, investor beliefs, or equilibrium prices free from arbitrage opportunities. That many individual investors act in ways that are less than fully rational does not create controversy. Some researchers closely associated with the rational expectations (RE) approach, such as Muth (1961) or Mishkin (1981), plainly state that RE is not a descriptive assumption.[28] In spite of this, they stress that as long as arbitrageurs eliminate profit opportunities, market behavior corresponds to the concept of economic man. So, it is not investor folly per se that drives the conclusion that actual market prices often differ from rational prices.[29] We need to argue additionally that in the price formation process there are significant institutional and economic limits on the degree to which experts can offset the actions taken by less sophisticated investors. A well-known paradox of full informational efficiency is that it destroys any incentive to spend resources on costly information (Grossman and Stiglitz, 1980).[30]

If the market is inefficient, false security prices impinge on traders' wealth positions, and episodes of mispricing have systemic welfare implications that extend far beyond the boundaries of any specific market.[31] From this angle, the standard definitions put forward by Fama (1970) – which distinguish between weak, semistrong, and strong form market efficiency and which encourage the study of price movements in reaction to historical, publicly and privately available information – are problematic. Fama's taxonomy hints that more information is better than less, but this is contradicted by welfare economics.[32]

The Miller–Modigliani (1961) characterization of market efficiency, which defines rational stock prices as the sums of the discounted values of subsequent cash flows (and which is the starting point for Shiller's volatility tests), can be defended in a variety of ways. One justification weighs the true value received *ex post* by long-term buy-and-hold investors who collect dividends against the prices paid and received *ex ante* by short-term speculators. History teaches us that there have been times when the market index put a price of $2 on $1 of true value, and that there have been times when the price was only 50 cents. If there is a persistent pattern in the deviations from value (e.g., excess price volatility) that cannot be traced to evolving risk attitudes or Bayesian learning, a blend of investor foolishness and market frictions may be the cause. A second rationalization for the model refers to Tobin's q. Corporate investment is powerfully influenced by the ratio of the market value of the capital stock to its replacement cost.

The Miller–Modigliani model has been criticized, however, for its restrictive emphasis on business fundamentals, such as its disregard of the "greater fool theory." Some authors hold as rational any investor beliefs that if generally acted upon are self-confirming (Azariadis, 1981; Froot and Obstfeld, 1991). In their view, the market may rationally launch itself onto an arbitrary self-fulfilling price bubble. Nonuniqueness is a general feature of dynamic models involving expectations (McCallum, 1983). While there is no choice-theoretic rationale for singling out solutions that do not suffer from extrinsic uncertainty ("sunspots"), these are the only Pareto-optimal allocations (Cass and Shell, 1983).

Another critique of the Miller–Modigliani view of stock prices says that the question of market efficiency cannot be solved by reference to the price and cash flows of individual assets but only by examining whether there are identifiable arbitrage opportunities – that is, violations of the law of one price – between securities (Long, 1981; Lamont and Thaler, 2003). However, in a stock market bubble, many assets may be overpriced all at once. Therefore, the absence of arbitrage opportunities does not imply efficiency in the Miller–Modigliani sense. Also, the definition of a pure arbitrage opportunity has nothing to do with the particular content of the information reflected in prices. Therefore, the successful or unsuccessful search for such opportunities is not a test of the efficiency of market prices with respect to diverse sets of data.

In sum, Miller–Modigliani market efficiency is not implied by a lack of arbitrage opportunities. Neither does it follow from the assumptions of rational behavior and rational expectations. The wealth allocations to which rational prices lead are no more and no less desirable than most other allocations. Still, the Miller–Modigliani view of market efficiency corresponds to an intuitive notion shared by investment professionals around the world, namely, that asset prices should reflect intrinsic values.

4.4 How Is Rationality in Markets Achieved?

A key question in finance is how rational and efficient markets can possibly come about. What are the dynamics of the price formation process? I now want to briefly examine the microfoundations of RE models from a theoretical perspective.[33] Blume, Bray, and Easley (1982) provide a useful overview of some relevant literature. Equilibrium is the starting point. From there, the models work backward to the restrictions that the existence, uniqueness, and stability of equilibrium put on the behavior of individual economic agents. Nearly every analysis investigates the internal consistency of the rational expectations hypothesis with other informational assumptions. Typically, the authors search for forecast rules that lead to convergence to a self-fulfilling equilibrium. For example, Cyert and DeGroot (1974) show how a Bayesian learning process can generate rational expectations. (Other models include Grossman, 1989; Townsend, 1978; DeCanio, 1979; Friedman, 1979; Bray, 1982; Frydman, 1982). In general, the search is disappointing. Not only are the models extremely demanding in terms of the information processing capacity of agents, there is no guarantee that, even if traders revise their expectations in an appropriate way, prices rapidly, if at all, converge to a revealing rational expectations equilibrium.

A weaker characterization of market efficiency (that guides us to a partial answer in response to the key question) is the notion of consensus beliefs (CB) (Rubinstein, 1975; Beaver, 1981). A market is efficient with respect to an information set A if the prices it generates are identical to the prices of an otherwise identical economy in which A describes the information available to every investor. The consensus belief is the homogeneous belief induced by knowledge of A. Provided that A is the union of all private information sets and that traders have CB, the market reaches full information efficiency even if traders do not condition their actual beliefs on equilibrium prices.[34]

The concept of consensus beliefs resembles the theory of market efficiency in Verrecchia (1979). This paper offers sufficient conditions so that prices achieve full informational efficiency and vary as if all investors knew the objective return distributions. The analysis neither requires revealing rational expectations nor costless information. Verrecchia's main theorem states that the dispersion of prices converges to the true underlying dispersion function as the number of market participants rises.[35] The theorem stirs interest in part because, in the author's words, it is based upon "a relatively weak set of assumptions" (p. 79). The set is weak since no economic or institutional constraints on market participation will produce prices that are biased. Apart from technicalities, there are five assumptions: (1) all traders are expected-utility (EU) maximizers; (2) they are risk-averse; (3) they are Bayesian decision makers; (4) their assessments of uncertain future prospects are unbiased; and (5) their assessments are pairwise independent. As a group, the first four of Verrecchia's assumptions add up to a convenient definition of rational economic man. Suppose we concede to Verrecchia that his short list of assumptions suffices to justify a theory of efficient markets: are they plausible descriptions of individual behavior?

4.5 "Rational Economic Man" Reexamined

Many economists will be inclined to answer in the affirmative. However, behavioral science advises otherwise.[36] Nisbett and Ross (1980), Kahneman et al. (1982), Tverky and Kahneman (1986), Baron (1988), Gilovich (1991),

Plous (1993), Conlisk (1996), Schwartz (1998), Rabin (1998), Hastie and Dawes (2001), Gilovich et al. (2002), Tetlock and Mellers (2002), and Baddeley (2010) offer surveys of a vast literature.

Numerous studies question the descriptive validity of the EU axioms. For instance, Kahneman and Tversky's (1979) prospect theory includes a certainty effect: people overweigh outcomes that are certain relative to outcomes that are merely probable. This effect helps to explain the Allais paradox. As a second example, Tversky (1969) documents systematic violations of transitivity. According to Schoemaker (1982), the failure of the EU model stems from "an inadequate recognition of various psychological principles of judgment and choice" (p. 548).[37]

In general, behavioral theories stress the limits of people's computational abilities and knowledge. Man seeks cognitive simplification. A central insight is that the nature of a decision task is a prime determinant of behavior. Problem solving is not easily understood by studying final choices without consideration of the decision process (Payne, 1976). It is often modeled as a selective search based on rules-of-thumb and a variety of cognitive schemata ("mental frames").[38] Three widely known rules-of-thumb are the availability, representativeness, and anchoring-and-adjustment heuristics (Tversky and Kahneman, 1974). On the whole, heuristics and knowledge structures are very useful; mental life could scarcely be managed without them. Sometimes, however, they produce misunderstanding and illogical behaviour; for example, alternative frames of what is objectively one and the same problem can produce reversals in preference (Grether and Plott, 1979). Hogarth (1980) lists thirty-seven sources of bias. Nisbett and Ross (1980) mention even more. The biases touch both experts and nonexperts. They have some bearing on every stage of the decision process – be it attention, perception, memory, analysis, simulation, output, or feedback.

Framing effects highlight the pivotal role of reference points and aspiration levels in evaluating outcomes and risk taking (Kahneman and Tversky, 1984). Targets are related to the notions of satisficing (Simon, 1945, 1957), disappointment, and regret (Loomes and Sugden, 1982). Whereas in EU theory, various actions are assessed in terms of their impact on final wealth, prospect theory defines the value function over gains and losses relative to a reference point that depends on the structure of the task. The value function is concave for gains and convex for losses, implying risk-seeking preferences for below-target outcomes.

The empirical evidence on risk attitudes of financial professionals and executives (Libby and Fishburn, 1977; Laughhunn et al., 1980; MacCrimmon and Wehrung, 1986; March and Shapira, 1987) confirms that they are related to the failure to obtain a target return. Note that in EU-theory, risk preference is viewed as a personality characteristic. However, the data suggest that risk taking is partly situationally determined (Vlek and Stallen, 1980). A dozen studies listed by Slovic (1972a) indicate little correlation, from one setting to another, in a person's preferred level of risk taking. Schoemaker (1993) and Weber and Milliman (1997) review alternative conceptualizations of decision-making under risk.

It may be thought that in view of the fallibility of judgment, people often lack decision confidence. Yet, many studies show the opposite (Einhorn and Hogarth, 1978; Langer, 1975). This contradiction focuses our attention on the link between learning and experience and on the descriptive validity of Bayes' theorem. Why do mistakes persist in the face of contrary experience? In some circumstances, new information has too little influence on opinions already formed ("conservatism"). In other circumstances – where the representativeness heuristic is at work – individuals nearly ignore base-rate knowledge (Tversky and Kahneman, 1974; Grether, 1980). Other factors restrict our ability to learn. Because of hindsight bias, outcomes often fail to surprise people as much as they should (Fischhoff, 1975). People also tend to attribute success to skill and failure to chance. Finally, in some decision situations, poor heuristic decision rules are reinforced with positive outcome feedback (Einhorn, 1980).

The biases relating to forecasting and subjective probability assessment are of special interest since they bear on the issue of the rationality of expectations. To repeat, experimental studies leave little doubt that man is mediocre as an intuitive statistician.[39] Hence, the actual forecasting performance of economic agents merits examination. Hogarth and Makridakis (1981) provide a wide-ranging survey that draws on more than forty studies. There is ample evidence of habitual miscalculation. Over a wide range of problems, mechanistic time series models are more accurate than intuitive procedures. Some studies examine predictions made by economic and financial experts (e.g., Friedman, 1980; Lakonishok, 1980; Brown and Maital, 1980; Ahlers and Lakonishok, 1982; De Bondt and Thaler, 1990; De Bondt, 1991). The data typically show large and systematic forecast errors. Once again, many individual forecasts do not improve upon the predictions of naïve models.

Group mean (consensus) forecasts are on average more exact than individual predictions – through the cancellation of errors of opposite sign, it would seem (Hogarth, 1975; Zarnowitz, 1984). This result matters because it is easy to think of the market price as a weighted average of traders' expectations. However, much inaccuracy remains after aggregation. The likely explanation is that, contrary to Verrecchia's assumption number 5, people's predictions are highly correlated. Forecasters often base their opinions on shared information. In addition, many fall victim to the same decision errors. Finally, if people worry how they come across to others, there is pressure toward conformism (Asch, 1955; Janis, 1972). Social pressures may force people to conform to popular thinking even when they privately disagree. The more problematical the decision to be made (e.g., when there are few objective guidelines, and/or the potential losses are large), the more perilous bad results can be for reputation.[40] Classic works in sociology that explore these phenomena include LeBon (1895/1977), Canetti (1962) and Smelser (1963).[41]

With few exceptions, economists and psychologists alike have looked upon risky decision-making as a cognitive activity. The survey papers of Loewenstein et al. (2001), Slovic (2002), and Loewenstein and O'Donoghue (2005) suggest that the emotional reactions to risk often conflict with their cognitive assessments. Consider, for example, fear of flying. Sometimes, people "are of two minds." Emotions distort cognitive appraisals, and appraisals give rise to emotion. The risk-as-feelings hypothesis emphasizes "gut feelings," that is, what is felt at the moment of decision.[42] The findings tie in with the work of brain scientists such as Damasio (1994) or LeDoux (1996). Loewenstein et al. (2001) list many phenomena that resist easy explanation in cognitive-consequentialist terms. (For example, sudden loud noise can cause fear well before we uncover the source of the noise.) Notably, a series of studies suggest that differences in emotional responsiveness, associated with age and gender, are linked to differences in the willingness to take risks.

So far, I have evaluated the premises underlying various models of market efficiency based on experiments. However, in addition, numerous archival and field studies (based on interviews and trading records) reveal that people's shortcomings in judgment and choice matter for the real-world financial behavior of households and institutions.[43] For instance, investors often ignore basic principles when they build investment portfolios. In her study of asset allocation, Bange (2000) finds that many people buy and sell stocks as if they extrapolate recent market movements into the future. (They are so-called positive feedback traders.) Huberman (2001) shows that people overinvest in what is familiar to them and do not diversify as much as they should. The familiarity bias reflects in part the imagined exploitation of informational advantage. It implies comfort with what is well known and discomfort with what is foreign. Lastly, De Bondt (2005c) illustrates how, among European investors, differences in cultural values and beliefs help to explain differences in asset allocation. Evidently, self-interest is modeled after the conduct of reference groups.[44]

Warneryd's (2001) survey details many nonlogical practices and idiosyncrasies in real-world investment behavior. Kahneman and Riepe (1998) and De Bondt (1998) offer checklists of classic illusions and errors "that every investor and financial advisor should know about." For now, I conclude that models of stock prices have to acknowledge (1) the likely impact of nonrational traders on prices, and (2) the essential role and the limits of arbitrage activity.[45]

4.6 Sentiment and Arbitrage

The heart of any behavioral theory of asset pricing is the idea that nonfundamental movements in prices are not primarily caused by exogenous shocks but are endogenous to financial markets and a reflection of investor sentiment, that is, widespread self-reinforcing misconceptions of value (see, e.g., Baker and Wurgler, 2005, and Prechter, 2016).[46] An important question is how to measure sentiment. Sentiment can be pertinent at the level of the economy as a whole (e.g., consumer, business, and voter sentiment), of markets (e.g., stock market sentiment), of industries, and of individual firms. It may be different for amateur and expert investors, such as the writers of investment newsletters. Sentiment is frequently measured with surveys. Baker and Wurgler (2005, 2007) build a composite index that uses inputs from as many as twelve different factors, including mutual fund flows, closed-end fund discounts, the volume and first-day returns of initial public offerings, and so on. Next, Baker and Wurgler estimate "sentiment betas" for individual stocks, measured relative the composite market sentiment index.[47]

Clarke and Statman (1998) employ the fraction of newsletter writers who are bullish on stocks as a sentiment index. The index is positively correlated with short-term contemporaneous changes in prices. It has little forecast power for S&P-500 index returns, however. Fisher and Statman (2000) compare the forecast power of sentiment indexes for individual investors, newsletter writers, and Wall Street strategists. Once again, in each case, the correlation with concurrent changes in stock prices is high and forecast power is low. The strategists' stock predictions are quite different from those of the other two groups. The most interesting result is that all three indexes are contrarian indicators. This agrees with the hypothesis that crowd sentiment is excessively volatile or, in other words, that the crowd "overreacts." Brown and Cliff (2004, 2005) and Lemmon and Portniaguina (2006) examine different sentiment indexes and time periods with more refined econometric methods. In the end, they reach the same conclusion as the two Statman studies, that is, they find an inverse relationship between investor/consumer confidence and returns, either for the market or selected portfolios.

Bollen et al. (Bollen, Mao, and Zheng, 2010; Bollen, Mao, and Pepe, 2011) analyze the sentiment of about 10 million tweets distributed on Twitter during the second half of 2008, a tumultuous period for large banks. They use a psychometric instrument that extracts tension, depression, anger, vigor, fatigue, and confusion. It appears that major economic, social, political, and cultural events create short-lived but dramatic mood spikes. Twitter mood is a significant predictor of stock returns.

At the present time, sentiment tracking is becoming widespread. It often relies on specific combinations mood indicators and data sets (e.g., Twitter feeds, Google search engine queries, or daily surveys). This makes it difficult to tell measurement effects apart from core psychological factors that may influence markets (see, e.g., Mao et al., 2011 and 2015 for more discussion). One technique is textual analysis. It is based on word categories and word counts and it examines the tone of corporate reports, press releases, message boards, as well as old-fashioned newspaper articles. Examples in academic research include Tetlock (2007), Tetlock et al. (2008), and Garcia (2013). Garcia finds that the fraction of positive and negative words in *New York*

Times financial columns (1905–2005) helps to predict stock returns at the daily frequency but that the forecast power of sentiment is concentrated in recessions. It is important to recognize that there are many hazards in parsing text, such as imprecision and misclassification. Loughran and McDonald (2011 and 2016) discuss these methodological issues at length and illustrate them with vivid examples.

What are the limits to arbitrage? In the following paragraphs, I list several reasons why the trading behavior of professional arbitrageurs does not nullify the price impact of unsophisticated traders. First, as investors with superior forecasting ability or inside information purchase (or sell) undervalued (overvalued) stock, they assume increasing amounts of diversifiable business risk (Levy, 1978). In addition, arbitrageurs with short investment horizons must worry about the unpredictability of "noise trader" sentiment and of future resale prices (Shleifer and Summers, 1990; Shleifer and Vishny, 1997; Shleifer, 2000). Abreu and Brunnermeier (2002, 2003) discuss a related problem: synchronization risk. Since any rational trader cannot remedy mispricing alone, he has to guess when a critical proportion of his peers will attempt to exploit an arbitrage opportunity and cause a price correction. Competition pushes the arbitrageur not to wait too long to act, but holding costs stop him from acting too early. This leads to delayed arbitrage.

Secondly, institutional factors also impede full price adjustment. For example, the sale of stock can force a trader to incur capital gains taxes, and restrictions on short sales have an asymmetric impact on investors with favorable and unfavorable information. As stated by Miller (1977), the net result is that, among individual traders, the optimists sway a company's stock price more than the pessimists. Specifically, strong heterogeneity of investor beliefs is associated with high prices and low expected returns in the cross-section of firms. (Jarrow, 1980) dissects Miller's arguments.) The empirical work of Figlewski (1981); Diether, Malloy, and Scherbina (2002); Chen, Hong, and Stein (2002); Ofek and Richardson (2003); and others is consistent with Miller's position.[48] The prices of stocks for which there is more negative information – measured by short interest – tend to be too high. Note that, in theory, a full price correction not only fails to happen, it is unachievable. Arbitrageurs cannot take into account what is known by those who do not trade. The heart of the matter is that, in a world with nontrivial trading costs and disagreement, every individual not only chooses the size of his holdings in each asset, but also in which assets to invest (Mayshar, 1983). As a general rule, prices depend in a complex manner on the structure of transaction costs and beliefs across investors. Sometimes, it happens that only information held by marginal investors matters. Full information efficient prices, however, ought to be independent of the distribution of private information among investors.

The previous line of reasoning presupposes that arbitrageurs take an investment stance opposite to the position taken by less skilled traders. However, it may be sensible for investors with superior talent to ride the trend rather than to go against it (Keynes, 1936). Harrison and Kreps (1978) show that, with short-sales restrictions, some investors may logically bid up the price of a stock in anticipation of selling it as at higher price than they themselves think it is worth. Surprisingly, it follows that, if an equilibrium price is to be found, it must exceed what any investor is willing to pay for the asset if obliged to hold it forever. In sum, arbitrage does not prevent rational speculative bubbles (see also Tirole, 1982).

Lastly, we may hope that noise traders will somehow learn over time and stop stumbling.[49] This is a psychological argument, not an economic one. As we have seen, the evidence for it is weak. Its weight is further diminished by the fact that, in markets (as in the rest of life), there is a continual inflow of youngsters and and outflow of older – presumably, wiser – folks. A related justification for efficient markets is a Darwinian natural selection process by which, over time, wealth is gradually redistributed from investors with poor forecasting ability to those with superior information or competence: "Only the fit survive." Among others, Figlewski (1978, 1982) and Blume and Easley (1992) show that such weeding out does not lead to full information efficiency, in the short or in the long run. Blume and Easley show that fit investment rules need not be rational, and that rational investment rules need not be fit.

4.7 The Price-Earnings Ratio Anomaly

As long as security analysis has been a profession, that is, since the days of Graham and Dodd (1934), many investment advisors have counseled their clients to invest in low PE (value) stocks and to avoid high PE (glamour) stocks.[50] Evidently, this approach embodies nonconformist, contrarian thinking that runs against mass sentiment.[51] Oppenheimer and Schlarbaum (1981) report the returns earned by a so-called defensive investor who follows the specific rules recommended by Benjamin Graham in his book *The Intelligent Investor* (Graham, 1949). Corrected for trading costs, the strategy earns an average risk-adjusted rate of return that is 2 to 2½ percent per annum higher than the market return. Basu (1977) examines the PE strategy for about 1,400 firms listed on the NYSE between 1956 and 1971, and obtains similar results. Reinganum (1981) forms high and low PE portfolios with identical CAPM-beta risk. The portfolios are updated both annually and quarterly. Using quarterly PE ratios for NYSE and AMEX stocks between the 1955 and 1977, he finds a mean difference in annualized returns in the order of 30 percent. With annual PEs for the period 1962–1975, the discrepancy is roughly 7 percent. Other studies include McWilliams (1966), Nicholson (1968), Peavy and Goodman (1983), Basu (1983), Dreman (1977, 1982), Jaffe et al. (1989), Fuller et al. (1993), Lakonishok et al. (1994), and Dreman and Berry (1995).[52]

Why does the PE strategy work? There are at least two explanations. They are not mutually exclusive. One explanation is that the excess returns and the risk of the strategy are measured wrongly because of misspecification of the capital asset pricing model. Ball (1978) points to the effect of omitted risk factors. PE ratios may proxy for such variables and seemingly explain differences in securities' rates of return.[53] The trouble with Ball's argument is that it is untestable as long as one does not spell out which variables are omitted.

The next explanation is behavioral. It is due to, among others, Graham (1949) and Dreman (1977, 1982). The explanation has three parts. First, it is assumed that waves of investor optimism and pessimism have an effect on the stock market as well as the price movements of individual stocks. The profitability of the contrarian strategy is believed to be attributable to transitory blips in (relative) PE ratios. Many naïve investors systematically over- or underestimate the growth prospects of individual firms – either because they extrapolate current earnings trends, or because they extend the latest price trends, or for other reasons. For instance, over a short period of time, masses of investors may fall in love with an investment theme that promises immense future profits even though there is no demonstrated past record of sales and earnings growth.[54] Barth, Elliot, and Finn (1999) show that firms with patterns of increasing (or nondecreasing) earnings, lasting five years or longer, have higher PEs than other firms, and that the PEs fall significantly when the pattern is broken. In sum, to the extent that the motives to trade are security-specific, investor overreaction can raise or lower the price and the PE ratio of one stock relative to other stocks.

Second, sophisticated traders who grasp what is going on either are not powerful enough to drastically change the price (say, because of short-sales constraints or other institutional frictions) or they prefer to bet on the continuation rather than on the reversal of past trends. For instance, in an historical study of the South Sea Bubble and the trading records of Hoare's Bank in London, Temin and Voth (2004) show that the bank greatly benefited from riding the bubble. Likewise, Brunnermeier and Nagel (2003) report that the exposure of hedge funds to technology stocks peaked in September 1999, approximately six months before the peak of the Internet bubble.[55] Further, sophisticated agents may also stoke the fire (or keep quiet) because bullish (or bearish) market sentiment affects their personal interests indirectly, say, as brokers, analysts, corporate insiders, venture capitalists, auditors, and so on.[56]

The third and final part of the hypothesis is that, sooner or later, competitive market forces take over. Success invites rivalry in the product markets. Failure causes internal pressure to hire new management and to restructure the business. It also induces mergers and acquisitions. As a result, the realized growth in corporate earnings-per-share (EPS) diverges from the false beliefs impounded in security prices. Changes in EPS larger or smaller than the median change, history shows, do not persist over time beyond what is predicted by chance (Chan, Karceski, and Lakonishok, 2003). Therefore there is no valid pretext for movements in PEs that assume many years of extraordinarily large or small earnings growth. Investments in high PE stocks are disappointing because actual earnings trail projected earnings. The reverse is true for low PE stocks. A large segment of the investing public is surprised – it did not anticipate the competitive push toward average returns – and various price corrections ensue. Depending on the scale of the initial euphoria or hysteria and other factors, the price correction process may take just months or several years.[57]

4.8 Price and Value on Wall Street

The evidence that relative stock returns can be forecasted by factors that seem incompatible with rational asset pricing theory has been mounting for years. The PE, book-to-market, and size factors discussed before are simply among the statistical factors that are best known. Haugen and Baker (1996) fit a model to the returns of the firms in the Russell 3000 stock index (1979–1993) that uses twelve key factors.[58] Equity returns are surprisingly predictable over short horizons. Similar results apply to the United Kingdom, Japan, Germany, and France. There is a startling commonality in the key factors worldwide. On the other hand, there is no sign that the differences in realized returns are risk-related. Haugen and Baker believe that the return differentials come as a surprise to investors and that they are evidence of systematic mispricing.

In contrast to Haugen and Baker's statistical approach, De Bondt and Thaler (1985) motivate their tests for mispricing with the representativeness heuristic of Tversky and Kahneman (1974). De Bondt and Thaler assume that many investors, in violation of Bayes' rule, overreact to news and that as a result the stock market also overreacts. They look for predictable price reversals over two- to five-year horizons. For instance, in a typical analysis, they rank the returns of extreme past winner and loser stocks listed on the New York Stock Exchange at the end of 1930 and every year thereafter. Next, they use a five-year test period to compare the performance of the fifty NYSE stocks that did the worst during the previous five years (the rank period) and the fifty stocks that did the best. When risk is controlled for, the difference in test period return is on average about 8 percent a year.[59] Much of the price correction happens in the first three years after portfolio formation, but the drift in prices continues for as long as five years.[60]

What is noteworthy about De Bondt and Thaler's 1985 paper is that it was the first rejection of the efficient markets hypothesis predicted by a behavioral theory. The empirical methods (i.e., comparing the returns, and other variables of interest, of winner and loser stocks for several years before and after portfolio formation) have become standard in asset pricing research. Interestingly, the 1985 paper not only documents price reversals but also finds price momentum (in table I) and momentum followed by predictable reversals (in table I and figure II) – facts that Thaler and I did not emphasize and that were rediscovered afterward by Jegadeesh and Titman (1993, 2002) and others.

Jegadeesh and Titman (1993) find price momentum, that is, over three- to twelve-month horizons, firms with high past returns (winners) continue to outperform firms with low past returns (losers).[61] A significant part of the puzzle is the further evidence that supports underreaction to earnings news. If companies are ranked on the basis of earnings surprises (surrounding the day of their earnings announcements), companies with positive earnings news are much better subsequent investments than are companies that report bad news. The effect lasts for several months, possibly as long as a year. Part of the explanation is that both analyst earnings forecasts and stock prices are "functionally fixated," that is, they fail to reflect the implications of current earnings news for future earnings (Abarbanell and Bernard, 1992; Bernard and Thomas, 1990).[62] Surprisingly, the strategy has reliably paid off for many years (Latane and Jones, 1977; Rendleman et al., 1982; Bernard, 1993). Chordia and Shivakumar (2006) propose that earnings momentum subsumes price momentum.

How do we reconcile overreaction with underreaction, and price reversals with earnings and price momentum? Perhaps many people initially share a cognitive frame that is wrong. Between 1998 and 2002, for example, the prices of Amazon, Yahoo, and eBay were highly correlated because traders classified all three firms as Internet firms even though they had very different business models (Cornell, 2004). Investors and their advisors freely talk about "growth firms" and "declining industries" even though statistical analysis provides little evidence of reliable time-series patterns in annual earnings changes (except in the tails of the distribution). In other words, all too often, labels and categories that are wrong "stick," that is, they persuade. No wonder, then, that when an earnings surprise hits, many investors refuse to believe it. Mental frames take time to adjust, and this slow correction process is reflected in prices.[63] Consistent with this analysis of the data, long-term past stock market losers are found to experience an unusually large number of positive earnings surprises. Past market winners go through an unusually large number of negative surprises (Chopra, Lakonishok, and Ritter, 1992). Also, compared to growth stocks, value stocks experience more good earnings news (LaPorta et al., 1997).

How do security prices respond to news? The answer depends in part on how investors' simple psychological models are influenced by new information. There are two effects. The first has to do with the short-term impact of the news – say, an earnings surprise – in light of the consensus forecast of the future that is already built into prices. The second effect depends on how the news changes the perceived odds that one future scenario rather than another will come true. At times, minor pieces of news trigger a change in consensus opinion and lead to a big price reaction. In agreement with this point of view, Dreman and Berry (1995) find that positive and negative earnings surprises affect high PE and low PE stocks in an asymmetric manner. Good news for low PE stocks and bad news for high PE stocks (so-called event triggers) generate much bigger (absolute) price reactions than good news for high PE stocks and bad news for low PE stocks. Substantially similar findings but for a larger sample of U.S. firms appear in Skinner and Sloan (2002).

What causes the winner/loser price reversals? A likely explanation is that many traders naïvely extrapolate past earnings trends.[64] Overreaction to earnings is a broad concept that appears in a variety of studies and that has been tested in different ways. De Bondt and Thaler (1987) find that past three- to five-year price movements predict reversals in earnings growth. In other words, past loser firms see their profits grow much faster than past winners. This finding strongly argues that many investors fail to recognize mean reversion in earnings. Lakonishok et al. (1994) use past sales growth (separately or combined with the book-to-market ratio, the earnings yield, and the cash flow-to-price ratio) to rank stock into portfolios. The fact that this strategy has some success (i.e., low-growth stocks beat high-growth stocks) again supports extrapolation bias.[65]

Still one more test of the extrapolation theory is to bet against security analysts' forecasts of earnings growth. This would be lucrative if analyst earnings forecasts are too extreme, and if their forecasts capture market sentiment.[66] Apparently, an arbitrage strategy that buys the 20 percent of firms for which security analysts' predictions of earnings growth are most pessimistic, and that finances the purchases by selling short the 20 percent of firms for which analysts' forecasts are most optimistic, earns consistent profits. The abnormal returns grow with the length of the forecast period; for example, they are much greater for five-year forecasts than for one-year forecasts (De Bondt, 1992). Comparable results appear in Bauman and Dowen (1988), LaPorta (1996), Dechow and Sloan (1997), and Ciccone (2003). Based on U.S. data, Dechow and Sloan cannot substantiate the view that the forecasts embedded in share prices are consistent with the simple extrapolation of past earnings and revenue growth (as suggested by Lakonishok et al., 1994). On the other hand, they do find that share prices give too much weight to exceedingly optimistic analyst forecasts of long-term earnings growth.

Is the evidence for price reversals and momentum robust? De Bondt (2000) offers a survey with tests for fourteen countries. Among many other studies (including Fama and French, 1998), Schiereck et al. (1999) and Rouwenhorst (1998) examine whether the results for the United States may be due to chance (or, what is the same, collective data snooping). Schiereck et al. document the profitability of contrarian and momentum strategies in Germany between 1961 and 1991. Rouwenhorst documents price momentum in each of twelve European countries during the period 1980–1995. Six-month past winners outperform past losers by approximately 1 percent per month. The evidence is stronger for small firms. Jegadeesh and Titman (2002) confirm the robustness of their earlier findings in a separate way. They extend the sample period for the United States by eight years (1990–1998). In addition, they show that the performance of the strategy is negative between month thirteen and month sixty after the time of portfolio formation. This effect ties in with the point of view that share prices are influenced by delayed overreactions to news that are eventually reversed.

Some researchers have begun to develop theoretical models that aim to explain price momentum and price reversals within the same analytical framework. One perspective, already discussed, is that the speculative dynamics of stock prices are driven by false expectations of future profitability, that is, overreaction followed by underreaction (De Bondt and Thaler, 1985, 1987; Barberis, Shleifer, and Vishny, 1998). A different view, emphasized by Hong and Stein (1999), is that firm-specific information diffuses little by little among investors, and that traders cannot easily extract information from prices. Hong et al. (2000) offer evidence that supports the theory. Price momentum strategies appear to be most rewarding for stocks with low market capitalization and low analyst coverage. The effect of low coverage is especially significant for firms that are in financial distress. (With low coverage, it is easier for management to hide what happened.) Thus, "bad news travels slowly."[67]

Finally, other researchers have produced interesting new and related facts. First, Lee and Swaminathan (2000) believe that past trading volume provides a link between momentum and reversal strategies. For instance, firms with high past turnover exhibit glamour characteristics, that is, they undergo negative earnings surprises and perform poorly. Teh and De Bondt (1997) and Scott et al. (2003) report parallel findings but offer different interpretations. Also, past trading volume predicts the magnitude and the persistence of price trends; for example, high volume winners experience faster momentum reversals. The market, it seems, is surprised by the disappointing earnings of high-volume firms. Lee and Swaminathan link their conclusions – described as the "momentum life cycle hypothesis" – to the work of Bernstein (1993). It may be that stocks move through periods of glamour and neglect, and that trading volume helps to identify where a stock is in the cycle. Share prices initially underreact but ultimately overreact to news.

Second, Asness (1997) and Piotroski (2000) present refinements of the winner-loser contrarian strategy. Asness' empirical analysis shows that, if the past is any indicator, it would be best for speculators to go long in cheap stocks that have started to turn upward and to go short in expensive stocks that have suffered a setback. This approach combines the insights of the contrarian and momentum strategies. Piotroski tries to improve the contrarian strategy by eliminating stocks from the portfolio that are likely to suffer financial distress. The Fama–French interpretation of value investing suggests that this may be costly, since the most risky firms should earn the highest returns. In fact, the opposite is true.

4.9 Actual and Predicted Earnings per Share

I now discuss some additional evidence related to the hypothesis of investor overreaction that is based on investigations of actual and predicted earnings per share. One way to evaluate the theory is to compare the stochastic process of annual earnings with the market expectation of that process implicit in stock prices. Many studies fail to reject the view that annual accounting earnings of U.S. companies follow a random walk with drift (e.g., Ball and Watts, 1972; Watts and Leftwich, 1977). Two other well-known studies, both analyzing U.K, data, are Little (1962) and Whittington (1971). However, the analysis of Brooks and Buckmaster (1976) indicates that in some cases the random walk hypothesis must be amended. They study all U.S. firms on Compustat with annual earnings data for nine or more years between 1954 and 1973. When the sample is stratified according to distance of a given observation from normal income, the earnings series in the outer strata revert to the preceding income levels. Fama and French (2000) reach similar conclusions.[68]

That the forecasts of earnings embedded in security prices are too extreme is indicated by the wide cross-sectional dispersion of PE multiples. This wide range appears illogical. It is difficult to reconcile with rational expectations and the Gordon growth model. Suppose that investors have no information other than the historical time series of earnings and that, for any individual firm, the discount rate can be expected to remain constant over time. Assume further that earnings growth rates do not deviate much between firms in the long run (say, over ten years) even if they vary significantly in the short run. In this case, unanticipated movements in earnings should leave PE ratios largely unchanged. The cross-sectional range in PE ratios should also be relatively steady. In addition, the range should be narrow since, by and large, it reflects the distribution of investor required rates of return.

Of course, all these conjectures are false if PE multiples predict corporate earnings with more precision than is possible on the basis of past income data alone. However, PE ratios are weak indicators of earnings growth. Beaver, Lambert, and Morse (1980) construct a PE-based forecast model. When the model's accuracy is compared with that of a naïve random walk with drift, the PE model is marginally superior. Security prices behave "as if earnings are perceived to be dramatically different from a simple random walk process" (1980, p. 3). Cragg and Malkiel (1968, 1982) show that PEs and financial analyst forecasts usually move together but that neither variable is strongly correlated with realized earnings growth. Analogous results appear in Murphy and Stevenson (1967), who decide that "if the market judges future growth through the PE-ratio, it is not a good judge" (p. 114).[69]

In many instances, the market forecast of earnings overreacts because it is a simple extrapolation of current trends – in the same way that security analyst and management forecasts are extensions of current trends (McEnally, 1971; Cragg and Malkiel, 1968; Fried and Givoly, 1982).[70] The research on the relative precision of analyst, management, and time-series forecasts has generated much conflicting evidence. The safest conclusion is that they are about equally accurate and that disparities, if they exist, do not endure.[71] What looks certain is that analyst forecast errors are large (Dreman and Berry, 1994). The forecasts suffer from persistent optimism and overreaction bias, that is, actual changes in EPS, up or down, are less than predicted changes (see, e.g., McDonald, 1973; Crichfield, Dyckman, and Lakonishok, 1978; Malkiel and Cragg, 1970; Fried and Givoly, 1982; Elton et al., 1984; De Bondt and Thaler, 1990; Easterwood and Nutt, 1999). Finally, a series of studies find serial dependence in consecutive analyst forecast errors and forecast revisions (Givoly and Lakonishok, 1979; Amir and Ganzach, 1998; Nutt et al., 1999). The work of Bernard and Thomas (1990) and Abarbanell and Bernard (1992) particularly influential in this regard.

When forecasting future EPS, analysts have a tendency to underestimate the permanence of past earnings shocks. This error is seen as an underreaction.[72] Easterwood and Nutt (1999) also conclude that analysts are too optimistic. Analysts overreact to positive earnings news but underreact to negative news. Givoly and Lakonishok (1984) and Brown (1996; 1997) offer useful surveys of what has become a vast literature.

Analyst and management forecasts are significant to research in behavioral finance because they are produced by experts who have professional experience, time, resources, and incentives to be more accurate than other market participants.[73] Also, their individual projections are sold, directly or indirectly, to unsophisticated investors. Therefore, the mean of the estimates, that is, the consensus forecast, seems bound to influence market prices. It is our closest proxy for the unobservable market expectation. Consonant with this conjecture, earnings surprises (Niederhofer and Regan, 1972; Fried and Givoly, 1982; Rendleman et al., 1982) and changes in consensus forecasts (Peterson and Peterson, 1982) are key determinants of stock price movements. Zacks (1979) and Elton et al. (1981) show that the payoff from being able to assess the errors and revisions in the consensus estimate of EPS is larger than the payoff from a precise forecast of EPS itself.

Analysts are usually thought of as "smart money." The efficient markets hypothesis becomes less plausible, however, if experts too are subject to bias. Based on U.K. data, De Bondt and Forbes (1999) suggest that security analysts herd in the sense that there is too little disagreement between them.[74] Nonetheless, analysts' earnings forecasts are persistently very wide off the mark. Yet, analysts keep offering extreme predictions. At once, the data show excessive optimism, an unwillingness to deviate from the consensus, and a reluctance to accept news that runs against current beliefs. If this behavior also characterizes many investors – and, ultimately, the market – we should not be surprised that stocks are systematically mispriced.

4.10 Conclusion

This chapter goes over some key elements of the psychology of asset prices, with special emphasis on the quality of judgment and choice.

Experimental, empirical, and theoretical research in behavioral science sheds light on many aspects of what happens in world financial markets. The short-comings of human intuition play a decisive role in speculative asset bubbles. For instance, naïve beliefs about corporate earnings growth appear to be related to predictable momentum and reversals in equity markets. Asset bubbles, especially housing bubbles, become more dangerous for the macroeconomy if they are fueled by easy money and painless access to debt financing.

That investor preferences, beliefs, and actions are not easily reconciled with rationality is deeply problematic for mainstream economic theory (Arrow, 1982). But shifting fashions, especially if they are illusions, matter a great deal for investment performance. In many ways, crowd sentiment is the lifeblood of financial markets. Examples of investors becoming obsessed with a specific asset class, industry, or firm abound. Many people fall into the trap of buying at market highpoints and selling at low points. Akerlof (2002), Akerlof and Shiller (2009), and Shiller (1990, 2000, 2013) emphasize trading motivated by "confidence" produced by popular models, that is, simple narratives that often mislead.

Behavioral finance is a valuable framework for research in asset pricing. It continues to produce many new ideas and facts. With its emphasis on the realism of modeling assumptions, such as the replication of laboratory find-ings, it introduces discipline. With its guidelines for wise decision-making, it is pragmatic. Lastly, behavioral research has meaningful policy implications. For instance, it warns experts, including top bankers and central bankers, against hubris (Ho, 2009; Greenspan, 2013; Haldane, 2014). Also, many "good peo-ple" get hurt in bubble episodes. The financial services industry and govern-ment may be able to limit future harm with improved business models (e.g., more bank equity capital) and better monetary, financial, and macropruden-tial policies. Investors can benefit from education, counseling, strict product standards, supervision of sales incentives, mandatory disclosure, paternalism (e.g., a social security system that guarantees retirement income), and so on.[75] As Levitt (1998) and Stout (2002) explain, such policies strengthen financial markets, which only exist and thrive "through the grace of investors."

Acknowledgments

This manuscript extends, updates, and revises "Stock Prices: Insights from Behavioral Finance," published in 2008. Much of the new material was first examined and debated in "The Psychology of Financial Markets," a graduate course that I teach regularly at DePaul University. I thank multiple cohorts of students as well as the participants of the investment symposia held in Chicago (April 2015); Gent, Belgium (June 2016); Madison (May 2015); and San Francisco (April 2015). Lastly, I am grateful to Richard and Inese Driehaus for financial support.

Notes

1 The random walk is approximate since expected price changes are nonzero if there is an equilibrium positive trade-off between risk and return. Since genuine news is unpredictable, the random walk evidence is often presented in support of the hypothesis of rational markets. However, as Shiller (1984) emphasizes, it also agrees with inefficient markets. Lorie and Hamilton (1973) and Fama (2013) narrate the history of modern finance. Mandelbrot and Hudson (2004) assess the random walk evidence.

2 See Bernanke (2004) and, in particular, his discussion of output and inflation volatility and the Taylor principle. The expression first appeared in Stock and Watson (2002). Taylor (2011, 2012) offers a "rules vs. discretion" interpretation of past U.S. economic performance. The Federal Reserve's recent departure from a rules-based monetary policy has fueled economic instability, Taylor maintains.

3 The financial crisis was largely unanticipated with the exception of Case and Shiller (2003), who worried about a housing bubble, and a few others such as Bogle (2005, 2008), who became progressively more nervous about the upsurge in short-term speculation with derivatives, a.k.a. "financial weapons of mass destruction," in Warren Buffett's terminology. In general, the thinking of economists who did foresee instability put emphasis on non-optimizing behavior, excessive debt, and wealth creation through soaring asset prices (Bezemer, 2011). In contrast, at the 2006 Annual Meeting of the American Economic Association, Calomiris (2006) paid tribute to Federal Reserve Chair Alan Greenspan as as "very constructive regulator" and "institutional innovator." And, in a speech for the Deutsche Bundesbank, Mishkin (2007) concluded that advances in "the science of monetary policy [were] an important reason for the policy successes that so many countries have been experiencing in recent years." As late as May 17, 2007, Bernanke predicted that "the effect of the troubles in the subprime [mortgage] sector on the broader housing market will likely be limited, and we do not expect significant spillovers from the subprime market to the rest of the economy or to the financial system." In his 2008 testimony to the U.S. Congress and in various publications (2013, 2014), Greenspan later confessed his misjudgments, saying that he himself "especially" had been "in a state of shocked disbelief."

4 Barr et al. (2012), Case and Deaton (2015), Chetty et al. (2016), and De Bondt (2016) evaluate the costs of the great recession. Brunnermeier (2001), O'Hara (2008), Brunnermeier and Oehmke (2012), and Claessens and Kose (2013) review the literature on different types of bubbles and financial crises.

5 Lowenstein (2008), Brunnermeier (2009), Haldane (2009), Wray (2009), Lewis (2010), Sinn (2010), Greenspan (2010, 2013), Keoun and Kuntz (2011), and Wolf (2014) portray the immediate causes and chief effects of the 2007–2008 crisis. They also try to distill its essential lessons. Bernanke (2012) separates the structural *vulnerabilities* of the U.S. financial system, e.g., shortcomings of regulation, from the *triggers* of the crisis in U.S. housing and mortgage markets. Earlier, Bernanke et al. (2011) drew attention to the "global savings glut" hypothesis and strong international capital flows into the United States

as its financial institutions turned risky mortgage loans "into apparently safe, AAA-rated securities" (p. 16). Krueger (2012), Wolff (2014), Piketty (2014), and Piketty et al. (2016) examine trends in income and wealth inequality. Sinn (2010) and Turner (2014a) believe that people living beyond their means and rising inequality have been major drivers of credit growth since the 1980s.

6   More prominent research like this includes, for the United States, Mian and Sufi (2010, 2014) and, based on international data for advanced countries, Jorda et al. (2013, 2014, 2015, 2016), Schularick and Taylor (2012), and Taylor (2014). With respect to emerging market economies, Lamfalussy (2000) is noteworthy. He analyzes the crises in Latin America (1982–1983), Mexico (1994–1995), East Asia (1997–1998), and Russia (1998). A buildup of short-term debt was at the heart of each bubble, with the exuberance of lenders and investors from the developed world playing a major role. Other studies of financial crises in emerging economies include Kahler (1998), Pettis (2001), Mendoza and Terrones (2008), Caballero (2012), and Gourinchas and Obstfeld (2012). Moskow (2000) formulates policy principles for governments of emerging economies hit by banking crises that go hand in hand with currency crises. Kaminsky et al. (2003) study the factors that lead to financial contagion across borders. Contagion is often linked to substantial capital inflows that end in a sudden stop and surprise crisis (see also Kynge and Wheatley, 2015). Sinn (2016) states that the introduction of the Euro and later policies of the European Central Bank (ECB) provoked a credit bubble in Mediterranean Europe. The current asset purchases of the ECB ("quantitative easing") are now causing a property boom in Austria, Germany, and Luxembourg, Sinn maintains.

7   Pech and Milan (2009) appraise the psychological insights of Keynes in the light of later behavioral research. Akerlof (2002, p. 428) refers to John Maynard Keynes' General Theory as "the greatest contribution to behavioral economics before the present era."

8   Consider, for instance, today's soaring real estate market in China (Barboza, 2015) or the new U.S. market for subprime car loans (Corkery and Silver-Greenberg, 2015). Two further comments are in order. First, in the canonical model of the "real" economy, exchange take place as in a barter economy. Money is redundant, and the sum of desired consumption and investment exhaust total output. However, this is not true in a today's credit economy, a problem already looked at by Wicksell (1898). Borio and Disyatat (2011) give a full explanation. Second, central banking policy truly aims for both monetary (price) and financial stability. For example, before 1914, monetary policy under the classic gold standard was mostly passive but stable. Yet, outsized financial cycles were common at that time. After the 1970s, price stability has been regained in most industrialized countries but financial stability has diminished. In a seminal paper, Bernanke and Gertler (1999) argue that price and financial stability are mutually consistent policy objectives to be pursued in a regime of flexible inflation targeting. See Borio (2014b) for more discussion.

9   Ho's (2009) ethnographic study explores the everyday experiences and opinions of Wall Street professionals during the 1990s and 2000s. Maurer (2006)

and Graeber (2011) offer an anthropological perspective on the evolution of money and credit systems in history.

10 A range of commentators nowadays find fault with different segments of the financial system. For example: (1) Lewis (2014) says that the U.S. stock market is today a multivenue trading system, rigged in favor of high-speed electronic trading firms, injuring many traders. (Fox et al., 2015, criticize Lewis but advance desirable reforms.) (2) Omarova (2013) examines how large U.S. banks (Morgan Stanley, Goldman Sachs, and JP Morgan Chase) have become global merchants, physically storing oil and other commodities and manipulating their prices. (3) Ayres and Curtis (2015) show that pension plans establish investment menus that lead current or future retirees to hold high-fee portfolios. (4) Mukunda (2014) and Galston and Kamarck (2015) warn against corporate short-termism and the proliferation of share repurchases, made worse by activist investors, executive pay in the form of stock awards, and fixation on quarterly earnings.

11 To repeat, this agrees with Kindleberger (1978) and Minsky (1977, 1986). But, before the Second World War, bank liabilities were mostly monetary and showed a stable relationship to total credit. Thus, central bankers could influence lending by steering money. Starting in the 1970s, deregulation and financial innovation broke the link, and debt (e.g., bank loans) exploded relative to gross domestic product (GDP). As Schularick and Taylor (2012) express it, the age of money became the age of credit.

12 Jorda et al. (2015) study equity market and housing bubbles in seventeen countries over the past 140 years. In agreement with Fisher, they find that "what makes some bubbles more dangerous than others is credit" (p. S1). In related work (Jorda et al. 2013), they show that credit-intensive business cycle expansions pave the way for deeper recessions and slower recoveries. Importantly, growth in mortgage lending, in response to "loose monetary conditions," is the driving force behind bubbles (Jorda et al., 2014). This type of lending also appears to have instigated the increase in the size of the financial sector ("financialization") since, relative to GDP, nonmortgage lending to businesses and households has remained fairly stable (Jorda et al., 2016).

13 Even so, Andrew Mellon, Herbert Hoover's treasury secretary, is mostly remembered for his liquidationist doctrine: "Liquidate labor, liquidate stocks, liquidate the farmers, liquidate real estate. It will purge the rottenness out of the system. High costs of living and high living will come down. People will work harder, live a more moral life. Values will be adjusted, and enterprising people will pick up the wrecks from less competent people." (Krugman, 2011)

14 Similarly, Bernanke's (1983) analysis of the length and depth of the great depression lays emphasis on the malfunctioning of financial institutions and the effects of a credit squeeze on aggregate demand. Bernanke (2007) reviews subsequent research on the credit channel and the financial accelerator.

15 Whether the chances of a tail event are over- or underestimated appears to depend on how easy it is for people to recall instances of past similar events (Taleb, 2007; Barberis, 2013). Gennaioli et al. (2012) make the case that "neglected" risks inspire much financial innovation that produces fragility.

16 Likewise, there was a return drift after analyst revisions of stock recommendations. But, since the start of high-frequency algorithmic trading, this drift is no longer significant (Altinkiliç, Hansen, and Ye, 2016).

17 Other perplexing findings initially recorded in the 1970s and 1980s include (1) investment advice offered by *Value Line* may be the basis for exceptional returns (Copeland and Mayers, 1982); (2) the secondary dissemination of analyst recommendations in the *Wall Street Journal* affects stock prices (Lloyd-Davies and Canes, 1978); (3) changes in the *National Bureau of Economic Research (NBER) Index of Leading Indicators* predict changes in stock prices, and assets appear to be overvalued during economic expansions and undervalued during contractions (Umstead, 1977); and (4) long-term nonlinear dependence in stock returns (Greene and Fielitz, 1977). Keim and Ziemba (2000) offer a broad survey of anomalies in worldwide equity markets.

18 It is emblematic of our lack of understanding that Fama and French (2004), too, are skeptics.

19 For this reason, arbitrage pricing may be no more testable than the CAPM (Shanken, 1982).

20 Jagannathan et al. (2010) and Nagel (2013) offer up-to-date surveys of asset pricing research. See also Cochrane (2000) for an notable summary of past work.

21 Friedman (1980) and Lovell (1986) also assess rational expectations critically.

22 Other hypotheses are that the historical standard deviation of dividends (around the trend) is a poor measure of the subjective uncertainty about dividends or that the market is rightfully concerned with a low-probability, high-loss event, e.g., war or nationalization. Both of these arguments inherently depend on unobservables. The "rare disaster" literature goes back to Rietz (1988) who offers it as a rational solution to the equity premium puzzle of Mehra and Prescott (1985). That puzzle leads Siegel (2014), Shen (2003, 2005), and others to recommend stocks as an ideal investment for the long run. (See, however, Benartzi and Thaler, 1995, and Siegel and Thaler, 1997, for alternative behavioral explanations of the high returns earned by stocks.) Rare disasters and their impacts have been studied by Barro (2009), Barro and Jin (2016), and Gabaix (2012). One apparent difficulty with the Rietz–Barro–Gabaix theory is that the base rate for a severe, single-day stock market crash is much lower than surveys of subjective beliefs of individual and institutional investors indicate. Goetzmann et al. (2016) argue that the media increase the salience of adverse events. In a related study, Bracha and Weber (2012) offer an account of financial panic in the tradition of dual process theory (Kahneman, 2011). Barberis (2013) reviews the psychology of tail events, positive as well as negative. If the return distribution of an asset is positively skewed, investors may be willing to overpay for the outside, small chance of becoming rich. This behavior implies a lower average return (Barberis and Huang, 2008).

23 Allen (1931) gives a detailed account of the great bull market of the 1920s and its aftermath. Klein (2001) critically reviews most major studies of the 1929 crash. Persons (1930) depicts the interrelated 1920s credit boom. Kindleberger

(1978) develops a general model of financial crises and confronts it with history. Reinhart and Rogoff (2009) go over eight centuries of financial folly.

24 However, how much of its normative status the rational model can retain is a matter of debate in decision theory and philosophy. See, e.g., Elster (1979), Nozick (1993), Simon (1983), Searle (2001), and Smith (2008).

25 Likewise, firms with low market value–to-book value (MB) ratios beat stocks with high MB ratios, and firms that greatly underperformed the market index over the previous three to five years, i.e., past losers, beat past winners. Other commonly used sorting variables that appear to capture the same effect include the price-to-sales ratio, the cash flow yield, and dividend yield.

26 The survey of Daniel, Hirshleifer, and Teoh (2002) also finds that there is "fairly definitive proof" (p. 141) that equity markets are subject to mispricing, and Shleifer (2000) chooses "inefficient markets" as the title of his book on the subject. Other surveys of behavioral finance and various aspects of investor psychology include De Bondt (1989, 2000, 2002, 2005b), De Bondt and Thaler (1995), Shefrin (1999, 2001, 2005), Hirschleifer (2001), and Baker and Nofsinger (2010). Fama (1998) and Rubinstein (2001) criticize behavioral finance. They also offer an orthodox analysis of the empirical evidence in favor of stock market rationality. According to Rubinstein (2001, p. 18), "the belief in rational markets stems from a long cultural and scientific heritage probably dating back to the Greeks, who elevated 'reason' as the guide to life." In sharp contrast, Turner (2010) says that many financial professionals accept market efficiency as a guiding philosophy because it unconsciously reassures them "that they must in some subtle way be doing God's work" rather than serving private interests.

27 For example, overreaction agrees with (1) findings in the market for government bonds: when long-term interest rates are high relative to short rates, they move down in the next period (Shiller, 1979); (2) findings in the market for corporate bonds: low-grade (high-yield) (junk) bonds outperform high-grade bonds (Hickman, 1958); (3) the rewards of investing in distressed or bankrupt companies with illiquid debt (Rosenberg, 1992; Gilson, 1995); (4) the steep fall and later steep recovery of the prices of low-mileage used cars during the 1973–1974 energy crisis (Daly and Mayor, 1983); and (5) journalists' observations on the fickleness of public opinion and political reporting: "British political reporters can be as mercurial as American ones. After a by-election in a South London district, the press here began to write off Labour and prophesy the disappearance of its leader, Michael Foot. Then a few weeks later Labour retained its seat in another by-election. The political writers thereupon resurrected both the party and Mr. Foot. This inconstancy in reading tea-leaves illustrates a constant tendency in human nature from which journalists, British or American, don't escape. That's a tendency to overvalue the latest in a series of events, particularly if it is unexpected or dramatic" (Royster, 1983).

28 Nonetheless, RE is often interpreted as a behavioral assumption. For example, Lucas assumes in his 1975 model of the business cycle that individual agents form their forecasts by minimizing the expectation of the forecast error (based on the equilibrium probability distribution), conditional on the

information available to them. See also the discussion in Lovell (1986) and Conlisk (1996).

29 Hayek (1948) also takes "the antirationalistic approach which regards man not as a highly rational and intelligent but as a very irrational and fallible being" (p. 8). He says that "human Reason, with a capital R, does not exist in the singular, as given or available to any particular person, ... but must be conceived as an interpersonal process in which anyone's contribution is tested and corrected by others" (p. 15). Thus, the market process transcends the bounded rationality of individual agents.

30 Verrecchia (1982) presents a model in which optimal information acquisition and equilibrium prices are determined simultaneously. Traders' conjectures about how much information prices reveal are fulfilled by their own acquisition activities. Hellwig (1982) shows that the Grossman–Stiglitz paradox can be overcome if investors only learn only from prices at which transactions have actually been completed. In this case, the return to being informed is nonzero.

31 How does a boundedly rational resource allocation compare to an allocation that obtains if all agents are fully informed and fully rational? It is unclear. Both equilibria may be subjectively Pareto-optimal. However, Pareto-optima for different configurations of information and decision expertise cannot be ordered in a simple way (Easley and Jarrow, 1982). Presumably, amateur investors are better off if they make portfolio choices free from cognitive error; fully rational agents are worse off, however, since they can no longer gain wealth at the expense of amateurs. In a fascinating paper, De Franco, Lu, and Vasvar (2007) present dollar estimates of the wealth transfers during the Internet stock bubble caused by deceptive analyst reports.

32 The analysis in Grossman (1989) is similar to Fama. Within the context of a revealing rational expectations equilibrium, traders condition their beliefs on prices and thereby infer the information available to other traders. Hellwig (1980) stresses that rational agents will neglect their own private information and look at price only. In equilibrium, investors' beliefs are homogeneous and they represent the best possible assessment of an asset's worth.

33 An alternative approach is to set up experimental laboratory markets, as pioneered by Vernon Smith. For instance, Smith et al. (1988) study bubbles, crashes, and the evolution of subjects' price expectations. Their aim is to characterize the price process and its convergence to fundamental value. Smith et al. find expectations to be adaptive, but prices do converge toward levels consistent with rational expectations, mainly when all traders are experienced. The most common outcome is a market characterized by a price bubble.

34 Verrecchia (1980) studies the exact conditions under which (i) each investor acquires what he perceives to be an optimal amount of information and (ii) the degree of precision implicit in CB is no less than the precision in any individual assessment, i.e., no informed investor can earn excess returns. Easley and Jarrow (1983) argue that an efficient CB equilibrium generically fails to exist.

35 Figlewski (1982) derives a similar "law of large numbers" result in a more restrictive setting.

36 Hereafter, I acknowledge but I do not return to the argument that Verrecchia's assumptions are only meant to be "as if" representations of individual behavior, i.e., rationality is truly an equilibrium concept. Neither do I discuss the normative status of the assumptions of rationality; their practical utility in building simple models that may be predictive; or the tautological claim that, if it is modeled appropriately, all behavior is rational (Becker, 1976).

37 The failure of the EU-model is also easily seen outside the laboratory. Consider, e.g., the extraordinary business success of the gaming industry in the United States (state lotteries, sports betting, etc.). Field studies produce more puzzling evidence. For example, in an investigation of flood and earthquake insurance, Kunreuther et al. (1978) find that almost half of the respondents (who are well informed about the availability of government-subsidized insurance) act contrary to subjective expected utility maximization. Eisner and Strotz (1961) discuss perplexing facts relating to flight insurance.

38 Cohen and Lou (2012) find more stock return predictability for complicated firms that are more difficult to value. Complexity is a friction that impedes information processing, the authors conclude.

39 Well-documented judgment biases include insensitivity of probability estimation to sample size; the belief that small samples are highly representative of the population from which they are drawn; the overestimation of small probabilities and underestimation of large probabilities; poor calibration; unrealistic optimism; wishful thinking; and various misconceptions related to random sequences and regression toward the mean.

40 Money managers never stop worrying about their image. Consider for instance the two quotes from the *Wall Street Journal* that follow. The first (November 30, 1982) illustrates compliance in a bull market: "When the market surged in August, (money) managers feared being left behind. 'Whether you were bullish or bearish, you couldn't stay out', Mr. Ehrlich says." (Ehrlich was the chair of Bernstein–Macauley, a money management firm.) The second quote (March 26, 1982) shows the same in a bear market: "Once a stock starts to collapse, it collapses completely, because no institutional manager can afford to show it in his portfolio at the end of the quarter. As long as the stock isn't there on April 1, you don't know whether he sold it January 2 or March 30. At some point in the slide, the managers sell the stock because they know the other managers are selling the stock because nobody wants to show it in the portfolio at the end of the quarter. Now, you may say this isn't rational, but the quarterly report is the time horizon we have to work with."

41 There is a great deal of related research in political science and economics. For example, Devenow and Welch (1996) survey rational herding models in financial economics. Mutz (1998) studies how perceptions of mass opinion affect individual political judgment, e.g., when a candidate for U.S. president gains momentum in the primaries because of favorable preelection polls.

42 Slovic (2002) gives many examples from business, e.g., how firms market consumer products by attaching emotional tags such as "new," "improved," "100% natural," and so on. Perhaps the same mechanism was at work

during the Internet bubble when many U.S. firms changed their name to a "dotcom" name. Cooper, Dimitrov, and Rau (2001) find that investors earned as much as 53 percent in abnormal stock returns for the five days around the announcement date. The value increase was not transitory and its magnitude was unrelated to the fraction of the firms' business derived from the Internet.

43 Well-designed experiments have the advantage that they allow us to analyze people's motives as well as their decisions. The danger is that experiments may lack external validity and/or that they induce demand effects, i.e., subjects try to please the experimenter. DellaVigna (2009) offers a broad survey of field studies of psychology and economics.

44 Zingales (2015, p. 1) agrees that *homo economicus* is "embedded in a cultural context." But, a cultural perspective "should not be taken as rejection of the fundamental assumptions of economics," he says.

45 Hayek (1948) agrees: "The statement that, if people knew everything, they are in equilibrium is true simply because that is how we define equilibrium. The assumption of a perfect market in this sense ... does not get us any nearer an explanation of when and how (an equilibrium) will come about ... we must explain by what process (people) will acquire the necessary knowledge ... We have to deal here with assumptions about causation, so that what we assume must not only be regarded as possible (which is certainly not the case if we just regard people as omniscient) but must also be regarded as likely to be true ... these apparently subsidiary hypotheses ... that people do learn from experience, and about how they acquire knowledge, ... constitute the empirical content of our propositions ... (T)he nature of these hypotheses is ... rather different from the more general assumptions from which the Pure Logic of Choice starts ..." (p. 46).

46 Besides, asset price movements also amplify and propagate shocks.

47 Of course, it is more convincing to investigate the effects on asset returns of purely exogenous mood changes. This is why Edmans et al. (2007) study stock market reactions to losses by national soccer, rugby, cricket, and basketball teams for a large group of countries. Losses lead to significant price declines, especially for stocks of small firms. There is no evidence, however, of a corresponding reaction to wins.

48 For instance, in their analysis of the Internet bubble, Ofek and Richardson (2002, 2003) document both (i) diversity of opinion between institutional and retail investors and (ii) significant market frictions. The authors link the bursting of the bubble to an unparalleled level of insider selling and lockup expirations (which correspond to the loosening of short sales constraints). For more anomalous evidence and a general discussion of the factors that prevent arbitrageurs from enforcing the law of one price, see Lamont and Thaler (2003).

49 Timmerman (1993), Lewellen and Shanken (2002), Markov and Tamayo (2006), and Brav and Heaton (2002) are examples of this type of argument. Brav and Heaton rationalize trends and reversals in stock prices. They assume that the representative investor is a rational Bayesian information processor, but that he does not have full knowledge of the fundamental structure of the

economy. In my comments on Brav and Heaton (De Bondt, 2002b), I explain in detail why the rational learning approach is inadequate.

50 PE multiples continue to be used extensively by financial practitioners to value companies, and explain stock prices remarkably well. See, e.g., Liu et al. (2002) and Anderson (2012). The PE multiple is the ratio of the price paid per share of stock (P) to the EPS over a fiscal year or quarter. EPS are measured in various ways. Some studies use proxies for "normalized" earnings that would obtain "if the company were experiencing normal operations" (Malkiel and Cragg, 1970, p. 605). Other studies look into the determinants of PE ratios (e.g., Molodovsky, 1953; Benishay, 1961; Bell, 1974; Beaver and Morse, 1978). Usually, they start from the Gordon growth model. This model is similar but not identical to the Miller–Modigliani model (Gordon, 1994). In its simplest form, the model asserts that – in a world of certainty and perfect markets – the price of a security is the sum of the present values of a dividend stream that grows at a constant rate g over an infinite horizon, $P/E = D/(r-g)$, where D symbolizes a constant dividend payout rate, and r is the risk-free discount rate. The Gordon model is not easily extended to uncertainty. Only under restrictive assumptions may one replace D, r, and g by their respective mathematical expectations (LeRoy, 1982).

51 Humphrey Neill (1954), a business journalist of the 1930s and 1940s sometimes referred to as "America's No. 1 Contrarian," justifies contrarian investing with references to the writings of William Stanley Jevons, Gustave LeBon, Gabriel Tarde, and Jean-Jacques Rousseau, among others.

52 Fuller et al. (1993) and Dreman (1998) divide the sample universe of stocks into industries. Within each industry, they judge the later returns of high PE stocks agains the returns of low PE stocks. In most cases, low PE stocks do better – regardless of industry and market performance.

53 For instance, Reinganum (1981) makes the case that the size effect discovered by Banz (1981) subsumes the PE effect and that both are related to the same missing factor. This requires further study since the cross-sectional rank of the PE ratio of a typical firm varies a great deal over time whereas the rank of its market value does not. Basu (1983) disputes Reinganum's findings. Cook and Rozeff (1984) and Jaffe et al. (1989) reexamine the problem but do not reach definitive conclusions.

54 A notable example is the story of ENMD (Huberman and Regev, 2001). Andreassen (1987) examines the key role played by "story telling" in the stock market. Causal attributions first made by journalists lead many investors to detect trends in earnings or prices that they would not see otherwise. Stock market rumors have a similar sense-making function (Rose, 1951). Related experimental research appears in Schmalensee (1976), Eggleton (1976, 1982), De Bondt (1993), and Maines and Hand (1996). Bloomfield and Hales (2002) present subjects with time series graphs for company earnings. The subjects behave as if the earnings process shifts between a mean-reverting and a trending regime. They underreact to changes that are preceded by a lot of reversals, and they overreact to changes preceded by few reversals.

55 To repeat, such destabilizing speculative behavior may be quite rational, e.g., because of synchronization risk. Another argument often encountered in the

business press refers to financial incentives in delegated portfolio management. It says that many money managers feel pressured by clients to generate fast gains. With quarterly performance reviews, there is a constant threat of dismissal (or removal of a portion of the money under management). On the other hand, the operation of investment management firms involves high fixed and low variable costs. Once the break-even point is reached, new business improves profitability rapidly. All these factors shorten the manager's time frame. Independent thinking is discouraged. Also, by law and business custom, certain standards of prudent behavior are to be maintained. Portfolio managers buy recent winners because they are "fearful of looking silly if they missed a big bull market" (*Wall Street Journal*, October 7, 1982). Similarly, in a bear market, the pressure is intense to sell recent losers.

56 Perkins and Perkins (1999) take a compelling, behind-the-scenes look at the investment bankers that created the IPO mania of the late 1990s. The book offers extensive bubble value calculations for 133 Internet companies. The authors advised the shareholders of these 133 companies "to get out now" (p. 231). They predicted accurately that a "shakeout" of the Internet stock market was "imminent" (p. 9).

57 Also in agreement with the behavioral view, PE ratios change how earnings surprises influence share prices (Basu, 1978). Over the twelve months that lead up to the date of the annual earnings announcement, positive earnings surprises boost the prices of stocks with low PEs more than the prices of stocks with high PEs. In the same way, negative surprises depress the prices of high PE stocks more than the prices of low PE stocks. Subsequent to earnings announcements (either of positive or negative sign), low PE stocks once again beat high PE stocks (Basu, 1975).

58 Haugen and Baker start their analysis with nearly fifty factors, but they continue with the most important ones. Evidently, the various statistical factors are correlated. There is no reason to think that each factor represents a different economic determinant of stock returns.

59 Numerous articles have discussed the methods to measure the risk of winners and loser stocks. Some of this literature is reviewed in De Bondt and Thaler (1987, 1989) and in Lakonishok et al. (1994). Much of the evidence suggests that the risk of long-term losers is less than the risk of long-term winners, and that the contrarian strategy is profitable in bear as well as in bull markets. A reason for the book-to-market premium suggested by Fama and French (1992) is that high book-to-market (BM) firms have a greater chance of financial distress. Griffin and Lemmon (2002) find, however, that among firms with high distress risk the difference in returns between high and low BM firms is too large to be explained by the Fama–French model. Firms with high distress risk also experience large price reversals around earnings announcements.

60 In an early study with U.K. data (1967–1972), Jones et al. (1976) assess a model based on two stylized facts established by Little (1962) and Whittington (1971): the profitability of individual firms tends to revert toward industry-wide means, and PE ratios do not reliably predict earnings growth. Jones et al. suggest a strategy of selling companies with a history of above-average

profitability and high PE ratios and using the proceeds to shares in corporations with a history of below average profitability and low PE ratios. While the strategy is profitable, "there was no fortune to be made" (p. 89).

61   The debate about price momentum (or "relative strength") goes back to Levy (1967) and Jensen and Benington (1970). Moskowitz and Grinblatt (1999) find industry momentum, i.e., industries that performed well over the recent past (three to twelve months) continue to beat industries that performed poorly. In addition, Chen and De Bondt (2004) report style momentum for stocks that are part of the S&P-500 index, e.g., small-cap value stocks may go on to outperform large-cap growth stocks over three- to twelve-month horizons if they did so in the past.

62   Sloan (1996) looks at a different type of earnings fixation. Based on U.S. data for 1962–1991, he finds that stock prices behave as if investors do not differentiate between the cash and accrual components of current earnings. The accrual component of earnings exhibits lower persistence over time, however. Hence, stock prices overreact. Companies with high (low) levels of accruals experience negative (positive) abnormal stock returns around subsequent earnings announcements. Important later work on earnings quality, cash, and accruals includes Richardson et al. (2005), Chan et al. (2006), and Ball et al. (2016).

63   Security analysts' earnings forecasts, discussed later in this chapter, are a good example.

64   Thus, stock market overreaction is thought to be linked to foreseeable errors in investor and market forecasts of future cash flows that are corrected afterward. (A broader version of the same hypothesis says that the market is sometimes too optimistic and sometimes too pessimistic, but that the extreme beliefs are not linked to cash flows in the recent past or in the near future.) There are, however, two other behavioral interpretations of the overreaction evidence. The first theory stresses irrational risk perceptions. Many stocks with low PEs certainly look riskier than high PE-stocks. The second theory puts the accent on herding behavior. At times, the market takes on a life of its own, when many traders jump on or off the bandwagon in reaction to what they believe other traders are doing. Prices aggregate information. If news disseminates slowly, it may be beneficial to look for patterns in prices (Hirshleifer et al., 1994). All three behavioral theories may be true to some degree: the theories are not mutually exclusive. Finally, it may be that there is also some variation over time in risk premia that is rationally justified.

65   The evidence is supportive but relatively weak. See Dechow and Sloan (1997) and Zarowin (1989).

66   Both assumptions are correct. However, it is not the case that analyst earnings forecasts extrapolate past trends in stock prices or in the book-to-market ratio. See Klein (1990) and Doukas, Kim, and Pantzalis (2002).

67   A third behavioral theory is the overconfidence model formulated by Daniel et al. (1998). A fourth model is Barberis and Huang (2001). These authors' model the equilibrium behavior of firm-level stock returns (1) when the representative investor is loss averse over the price fluctuations of individual stocks, or (2) when he or she is loss averse over the value of his equity portfolio. (The

extent of narrow framing is a matter of mental accounting.) With individual stock accounting, the discount rate can change as a function of its past return performance. A stock that performed well will be seen by investors as less risky; a stock that performed poorly, more risky. The model accounts for a wide range of empirical facts. For instance, firm-level returns are excessively volatile and are predictable from lagged variables. Individual stock accounting also reproduces a value premium in the cross-section of firms.

68 Clearly, the fact that many time-series studies fail to reject the random walk hypothesis does not imply that changes in EPS cannot be predicted. It only means that such movements cannot be forecasted on the basis of current and past EPS data. Among others, Chant (1980) and Freeman et al. (1982) present models that improve upon time-series forecasts by including variables such as industry stock price indexes, the money supply, and the book rate-of-return.

69 Likewise, Malkiel and Cragg (1970) conclude "that if one wants to explain (stock) returns over a one-year horizon it is far more important to know what the market will think the growth rate of earnings will be next year rather than to know the realized long-term growth rate" (p. 616).

70 For that reason, some studies (e.g., Ball and Brown, 1968; Watts, 1978) let a naïve time-series model proxy for the market expectation of earnings.

71 See, e.g., Cragg and Malkiel (1968); Elton and Gruber (1972); Basi, Carey, and Twark (1976); and Imhoff and Pare (1982). Only Brown and Rozeff (1978) find that analyst forecasts are superior. But Mikhail et al. (1997) suggest that analysts produce better forecasts, and better stock recommendations, as they gain firm-specific experience, and that market prices reward competence. Loh and Mian (2006) also find that the quality of earnings forecasts and stock recommendations move together and that accuracy has positive investment value for investors.

72 Elgers and Lo (1994) find that prior stock returns and earnings changes can be used to modify analyst predictions in a way that meaningfully improves their precision. For instance, for firms with poor earnings performance, analysts forecast greater reversals than are demonstrated by actual earnings. Markov and Tamayo (2006) offer a rational explanation for the predictability in analysts' forecast errors. Serial correlation in analysts' quarterly earnings forecast errors agrees, they say, with an environment in which analysts face parameter uncertainty but learn rationally over time.

73 As the various financial scandals of the last decade demonstrate (Partnoy, 2003; Berenson, 2004; Bogle, 2005), conflicts of interest permeate Wall Street, and experts may have powerful incentives to mislead. For instance, analysts, investment bankers, journalists, and others may be keen to maintain good relations with corporate management. If they issue negative reports, they lose business. For telling anecdotes in this regard, see Gallant (1990) and Browning (1995). Hong and Kubik (2003) find a empirical link between analyst optimism and career success. A long-standing Wall Street adage says that "you start as an analyst, but you end as an ambassador."

74 Cornell (2001) discusses the case of Intel. In the summer of 2000, nearly all analysts were very enthusiastic about Intel. In September 2000, however, Ashok Kumar, a superstar analyst, stated his belief that the demand for

personal computers would grow at about 6 percent (rather than the 12 percent that was forecast). Also, on September 21, Intel management issued a press release warning that revenue growth for the third quarter would be positive but less than forecasted. In response, the stock price dropped 30 percent and $120 billion of shareholder value was lost – a number so large that no reasonable discounted cash flow analysis can justify it. Yet, fewer analysts recommended Intel after the price drop than before.

75 In addition, behavioral and network research appears to support a regulatory response to systemic risk grounded in market fragmentation, a lesser amount of homogeneity across agents, modularity, and simplicity (Turner, 2014b; Haldane and May, 2011). Homogeneity, e.g., many banks using the same value-at-risk models, breeds fragility. Complexity increases the cost of cognition, and hence generates uncertainty. It may be better to restrict a certain type of risk taking than to try to price it properly (Haldane, 2012). For more discussion of risk management, see Power (2007).

4.11 References

Abarbanell, J. and V. L. Bernard, "Tests of Analysts' Overreaction/Underreaction to Earnings Information as an Explanation for Anomalous Stock Price Behavior," *Journal of Finance*, 47, 3, 1181–1207, July 1992.

Abdel-khalik, A. R. and B. B. Ajinkya, "Returns to Informational Advantages: The Case of Analysts' Forecasts Revisions," *Accounting Review*, 57, 4, 661–680, October 1982.

Abreu, D. and M. K. Brunnermeier, "Synchonization Risk and Delayed Arbitrage," *Journal of Financial Economics*, 64, 341–360, 2002.

Abreu, D. and M. K. Brunnermeier, "Bubbles and Crashes," *Econometrica*, 71, 173–204, 2003.

Admati, A. R., "It Takes a Village to Maintain a Dangerous Financial System," Working Paper, Graduate School of Business, Stanford University, May 2016.

Agarwal, S., I. Ben-David and V. Yao, "Systematic Mistakes in the Mortgage Market and Lack of Financial Sophistication," *Journal of Financial Economics*, 123, 42–58, 2017.

Ahlers, D. and J. Lakonishok, "A Study of Economists' Consensus Forecasts," *Management Science*, 29, 10, 1113–1125, 1982.

Akbas, F., W. J. Armstrong, S. Sorescu, and A. Subrahmanyam, "Smart Money, Dumb Money, and Capital Market Anomalies," *Journal of Financial Economics*, 118, 355–382, 2015.

Akerlof, G. A., "Behavioral Macroeconomics and Macroeconomic Behavior," *American Economic Review*, 92, 3, 411–433, June 2002.

Akerlof, G. A. and R. J. Shiller, *Animal Spirits: How Human Psychology Drives the Economy, and Why It Matters for Global Capitalism*, Princeton: Princeton University Press, 2009.

Albuquerque, R., M. Eichenbaum, D. Papanikolaou, and S. Rebelo, "Long-Run Bulls and Bears," *Journal of Monetary Economics*, 76, S21–S28, 2015.

Ali, A., A. Klein, and J., "Analysts' Use of Information About Permanent and Transitory Earnings Components in Forecasting Annual EPS," *Accounting Review*, 67, 1, 183–198, 1992.

Allen, F. L., *Only Yesterday: An Informal History of the 1920s*, New York: Perennial Library, 1931.

Altinkiliç, O., R. S. Hansen, and L. Ye, "Can Analysts Pick Stocks for the Long Run?" *Journal of Financial Economics*, 119, 371–398, 2016.

Amir, E. and Y. Ganzach, "Overreaction and Underreaction in Analysts' Forecasts," *Journal of Economic Behavior and Organization*, 37, 3, 333–347, November 1998.

Anderson, K., *The Essential P/E: Understanding the Stock Market through the Price-Earnings Ratio*, Harriman, 2012.

Andreassen, P. B., "On the Social Psychology of the Stock Market: Aggregate Attributional Effects and the Regressiveness of Prediction," *Journal of Personality and Social Psychology*, 53, 3, 490–496, 1987.

Arbel, A. and P. Strebel, "Pay Attention to Neglected Firms! Even When They're Large," *Journal of Portfolio Management*, 9, 2, 37–42, Winter 1983.

Arce, O. and D. Lopez-Salido, "Housing Bubbles," *American Economic Journal: Macroeconomics*, 3, 212–241, January 2011.

Arrow, K. J., "Risk Perception in Psychology and Economics," *Economic Inquiry*, 20, 1–9, January 1982.

Asch, S., "Opinions and Social Pressure," *Scientific American*, 193, 5, 31–35, 1955.

Asness, C., "The Interaction of Value and Momentum Strategies," *Financial Analysts Journal*, 53, 2, 29–36, March–April 1997.

Avramov, D., T. Chordia, G. Jostova, A. Philipov, et al., "Dispersion in Analysts' Earnings Forecasts and Credit Rating," *Journal of Financial Economics*, 91, 83–101, 2009.

Ayres, I. and Q. Curtis, "Beyond Diversification: The Pervasive Problem of Excessive Fees and 'Dominated Funds' in 401(k) Plans," *Yale Law Journal*, 124, 1476–1552, 2015.

Azariadis, C., "Self-Fulfilling Prophecies," *Journal of Economic Theory*, 25, 380–396, 1981.

Baddeley, M., "Herding, Social Influence and Economic Decision-Making: Socio-psychological and Neuroscientific Analyses," *Philosophical Transactions of the Royal Society B*, 365, 281–290, 2010.

Baik, B. and G. Jiang, "The Use of Management Forecasts to Dampen Analysts' Expectations," *Journal of Accounting and Public Policy*, 25, 531–553, 2006.

Baker, H. K. and J. R. Nofsinger, *Behavioral Finance. Investors, Corporations and Markets*. Wiley, 2010.

Baker, M. and J. Wurgler, "Investor Sentiment and the Cross-section of Stock Returns," *Journal of Finance*, 61, 4, 1645–1680, 2006.

Baker, M. and J. Wurgler, "Investor Sentiment in the Stock Market," *Journal of Economic Perspectives*, 21, 2, 129–151, Spring 2007.

Ball, R., "Anomalies in Relationships Between Securities' Yields and Yield-Surrogates," *Journal of Financial Economics*, 6, 23, 103–126, June-September 1978.

Ball, R. and P. Brown, "An Empirical Evaluation of Accounting Income Numbers," *Journal of Accounting Research*, 6, 2, 159–178, Autumn 1968.

Ball, R., J. Gerakos, J. Linnainmaa and V. Nikolaev, "Deflating Profitability," *Journal of Financial Economics*, 117, 225–248, 2015.

Ball, R., J. Gerakos, J. Linnainmaa and V. Nikolaev, "Accruals, Cash Flows, and Operating Profitability in the Cross Section of Stock Returns," *Journal of Financial Economics*, 121, 28–45, 2016.

Ball, R. and R. Watts, "Some Time Series Properties of Accounting Income," *Journal of Finance*, 27, 3, 663–681, June 1972.

Bange, M. M., "Do the Portfolios of Small Investors Reflect Positive Feedback Trading?" *Journal of Financial and Quantitative Analysis*, 35, 2, 239–255, June 2000.

Bange, M. M. and W. F. M. De Bondt, "R&D Budgets and Corporate Earnings Targets," *Journal of Corporate Finance*, 4, 153–184, 1998.

Banko, J. C., C. M. Conover, and G. R. Jensen, "The Relationship Between the Value Effect and Industry Affiliation," *Journal of Business*, 79, 5, 2595–2616, 2006.

Banz, R., "The Relationship Between Return and Market Value of Common Stocks," *Journal of Financial Economics*, 9, 3–18, 1981.

Barberis, N., "The Psychology of Tail Events: Progress and Challenges," *American Economic Review*, 103, 3, 611–616, 2013.

Barberis, N., A. Shleifer, and R. Vishny, "A Model of Investor Sentiment," *Journal of Financial Economics*, 49, 307–343, 1998.

Barberis, N., A. Shleifer, and J. Wurgler, "Comovement," *Journal of Financial Economics*, 75, 283–317, 2005.

Barberis, N. and M. Huang, "Mental Accounting, Loss Aversion, and Individual Stock Returns," *Journal of Finance*, 56, 4, 1247–1292, August 2001.

Barberis, N. and M. Huang, "Stocks as Lotteries: The Implications of Probability Weighting for Security Prices," *American Economic Review*, 98, 5, 2066–2100, 2008.

Barboza, D., "In China, a Building Frenzy's Fault Lines," *New York Times*, March 13, 2015.

Baron, J., *Thinking and Deciding*, Cambridge: Cambridge University Press, 1988.

Baron, M. and W. Xiong, "Credit Expansion and Neglected Crash Risk," Working Paper, Princeton University, October 2014.

Barr, B., D. Taylor-Robinson, A. Scott-Samuel, M. McKee and D. Stuckler, "Suicides Associated with the 2008–2010 Economic Recession in England: Time Trend Analysis," *BMJ,* 345, e5142, August 14, 2012.

Barro, R.J., "Rare Disasters, Asset Prices, and Welfare Costs," *American Economic Review*, 99, 1, 243–264, March 2009.

Barro, R. J. and S. Fisher, "Recent Developments in Monetary Theory," *Journal of Monetary Economics*, 2, 2, 133–167, April 1976.

Barro, R. J. and T. Jin, "Rare Events and Long-Run Risks," National Bureau of Economic Research (NBER) Working Paper #21871, January 2016.

Barth, M. E., J. A. Elliot, and M. W. Finn, "Market Rewards Associated with Patterns of Increasing Earnings," *Journal of Accounting Research*, 37, 387–413, 1999.

Bartov, E., D. Givoly, and C. Hayn, "The Rewards to Meeting or Beating Earnings Expectations," *Journal of Accounting and Economics*, 33, 173–204, 2002.

Bartov, E., S. Radhakrishnan, and I. Krinsky, "Investor Sophistication and Patterns in Stock Returns After Earnings Announcements," *Accounting Review*, 75, 1, 43–63, January 2000.

Basi, B., K. Carey and R. Twark, "A Comparison of the Accuracy of Corporate and Security Analysts' Forecasts of Earnings," *Accounting Review*, 51, 2, 244–254, April 1976.

Basu, S., "The Information Content of Price-Earnings Ratios," *Financial Management*, 53–64, 4, 2, Summer 1975.

Basu, S., "Investment Performance of Common Stocks in Relation to Their Price-Earnings Ratios: A Test of the Efficient Market Hypothesis," *Journal of Finance*, 33, 3, 663–682, June 1977.

Basu, S., "The Effect of Earnings' Yield on Assessments of the Association Between Annual Accounting Income Numbers and Security Prices," *Accounting Review*, 53, 3, 599–625, July 1978.

Basu, S., "The Relationship Between Earnings' Yield, Market Value and Return for NYSE Common Stocks: Further Evidence," *Journal of Financial Economics*, 12, 1, 129–156, June 1983.

Bauman, W. S., C. M. Conover, and R. E. Miller, "Growth Versus Value and Large-Cap Versus Small-Cap Stocks in International Markets," *Financial Analysts Journal*, 54, 2, 75–89, March–April 1998.

Bauman, W. S. and R. Dowen, "Growth Projections and Common Stock Returns," *Financial Analysts Journal*, 44, 4, 79–80, July–August 1988.

Bayer, P., K. Mangum, and J. W. Roberts, "Speculative Fever: Investor Contagion in the Housing Bubble," NBER Working Paper #22065, March 2016.

Beaver, W., "Market Efficiency," *Accounting Review*, 56, 1, 23–37, January 1981.

Beaver, W., R. Lambert, and D. Morse, "The Information Content of Security Prices," *Journal of Accounting and Economics*, 2, 3–28, 1980.

Beaver, W. and D. Morse, "What Determines Price–Earnings Ratios?" *Financial Analysts Journal*, 34, 4, 65–76, July–August 1978.

Becker, G., *The Economic Approach to Human Behavior*, Chicago: University of Chicago Press, 1976.

Bell, F. W., "The Relation of the Structure of Common Stock Prices to Historical, Expectational and Industrial Variables," *Journal of Finance*, 29, 1, 187–197, March 1974.

Benartzi, S. and R. H. Thaler, "Myopic Loss Aversion and the Equity Premium Puzzle," *Quarterly Journal of Economics*, 110, 73–92, 1995.

Benishay, H., "Variability in Earnings Price Ratios of Corporate Equities," *American Economic Review*, 51, 1, 81–94, March 1961.

Berenson, A., *The Number: How the Drive for Quarterly Earnings Corrupted Wall Street and Corporate America*, New York: Random House, 2004.

Berkman, H., V. Dimitrov, P. C. Jain, P. D. Koch, and S. Tice, "Sell on the News: Differences of Opinion, Short-Sales Constraints, and returns Around Earnings Announcements," *Journal of Financial Economics*, 92, 376–399, 2009.

Bernanke, B. S., "Nonmonetary Effects of the Financial Crisis in the Propagation of the Great Depression," *American Economic Review*, 73, 3, 257–276, June 1983.

Bernanke, B. S., "The Great Moderation," Speech, Annual Meeting of the Eastern Economic Association, Washington, D.C., February 20, 2004.

Bernanke, B. S., "The Subprime Mortgage Market," Speech, 43rd Annual Conference on Bank Structure and Competition, Chicago, Illinois, May 17, 2007.

Bernanke, B. S., "The Financial Accelerator and the Credit Channel," Speech, Conference on "The Credit Channel of Monetary Policy in the Twenty-First Century", Federal Reserve Bank of Atlanta, Atlanta, Georgia, June 15, 2007.

Bernanke, B. S., "Some Reflections on the Crisis and the Policy Response," Speech, Conference on "Rethinking Finance: Perspectives on the Crisis," Russell Sage Foundation and the Centure Foundation, New York, April 13, 2012.

Bernanke, B. S., C. Bertaut, L. Pounder DeMarco, and S. Kamin, "International Capital Flows and the Returns to Safe Assets in the United States, 2003–2007," Board of Governors of the Federal Reserve System, International Finance Discussion Papers #1014, February 2011.

Bernanke, B. S. and M. Gertler, "Monetary Policy and Asset Price Volatility," *Federal Reserve Bank of Kansas City Economic Review*, 17–51, 4th quarter, 1999.

Bernanke, B. S., M. Gertler, and S. Gilchrist, "The Financial Accelerator in a Quantitative Business Cycle Framework," in J. Taylor and M. Woodford (eds.), *Handbook of Macroeconomics*, 1, part C, 1341–1393, Amsterdam: Elsevier–North Holland, 1999.

Bernard, V. L., "Stock Price Reactions to Earnings Announcements: A Summary of Recent Anomalous Evidence and Possible Explanations, in R. Thaler (ed.), *Advances in Behavioral Finance*, New York: Russell Sage Foundation, 1993.

Bernard, V. L. and J. K. Thomas, "Evidence that Stock Prices Do Not Fully Reflect the Implications of Current Earnings for Future Earnings," *Journal of Accounting and Economics*, 13, 305–340, 1990.

Bernstein, R., "The Earnings Expectations Life Cycle," *Financial Analysts Journal*, 49, 2, 90–93, March–April 1993.

Bezemer, D. J., "The Credit Crisis and Recession as a Paradigm Test," *Journal of Economic Issues*, 45, 1, 1–18, March 2011.

Bidder, R. M. and M. E. Smith, "Robust Animal Spirits," *Journal of Monetary Economics*, 59, 8, 738–750, 2012.

Billings, B. K. and R. M. Morton, "Book-to-Market Components, Future Security Returns, and Errors in Expected Future Earnings," *Journal of Accounting Research*, 39, 2, 197–219, September 2001.

Bloom, N., "The Impact of Uncertainty Shocks," *Econometrica*, 77, 3, 623–685, May 2009.

Bloom, N., "Fluctuations in Uncertainty," *Journal of Economic Perspectives*, 28, 2, 153–176, Spring 2014.

Bloomfield, R. and J. Hales, "Predicting the Next Step of a Random Walk: Experimental Evidence of Regime-Shifting Beliefs," *Journal of Financial Economics*, 65, 397–414, 2002.

Blume, L. E., M. M. Bray, and D. Easley, "Introduction to the Stability of Rational Expectations Equilibrium," *Journal of Economic Theory*, 26, 313–317, 1982.

Blume, L. E. and D. Easley, "Evolution and Market Behavior," *Journal of Economic Theory*, 58, 9–40, 1992.

Bogle, J. C., *The Battle for the Soul of Capitalism*, New Haven: Yale University Press, 2005.

Bogle, J. C., "The New Global Economy," Speech, Combined Columbia University/MIT Association, April 10, 2008.

Bollen, J., H. Mao, and A. Pepe, "Modeling Public Mood and Emotion: Twitter Sentiment and Socio-economic Phenomena," *Proceedings of the Fifth International AAAI Conference on Weblogs and Social Media*, 450–453, 2011.

Bollen, J., H. Mao, and X.-J. Zeng, "Twitter Mood Predicts the Stock Market," *Journal of Computational Science*, 2, 1, 1–8, 2010.

Borio, C., "The Financial Cycle and Macroeconomics: What Have We Learnt?" *Journal of Banking and Finance*, 45, 182–198, 2014a.

Borio, C., "Monetary Policy and Financial Stability: What Role in Prevention and Recovery?" *Capitalism and Society*, 9, 2, 1, 2014b.

Borio, C. and P. Disyatat, "Global Imbalances and the Financial Crisis: Link or No Link?" Bank for International Settlements Working Paper #346, May 2011.

Borio, C. and M. Drehmann, "Financial Instability and Macroeconomics: Bridging the Gulf," Paper presented at the 12th Annual International Banking Conference cosponsored by the Federal Reserve Bank of Chicago and the World Bank, September 24–25, 2009.

Bracha, A. and E. U. Weber, "A Psychological Perspective of Financial Panic," Working Paper, Federal Reserve Bank of Boston, September 2012.

Branch, W. A. and G. W. Evans, "Learning About Risk and Return: A Simple Model of Bubbles and Crashes," *American Economic Journal: Macroeconomics*, 3, 159–191, July 2011.

Brav, A. and J. B. Heaton, "Competing Theories of Financial Anomalies," *Review of Financial Studies*, 15, 2, 575–606, 2002.

Bray, M. M., "Learning, Estimation and the Stability of Rational Expectations," *Journal of Economic Theory*, 26, 318–339, 1982.

Breeden, D., "An Intertemporal Asset Pricing Model with Stochastic Consumption and Investment Opportunities," *Journal of Financial Economics*, 7, 265–296, 1979.

Brooks, L. D. and D. A. Buckmaster, "Further Evidence on the Time Series Properties of Accounting Income," *Journal of Finance*, 31, 5, 1359–1373, December 1976.

Brown, B. W. and S. Maital, "What Do Economists Know? An Empirical Study of Experts' Expectations," *Econometrica*, 49, 2, 491–504, 1980.

Brown, G. W. and M. T. Cliff, "Investor Sentiment and the Near-Term Stock Market," *Journal of Empirical Finance*, 11, 1–27, 2004.

Brown, G. W. and M. T. Cliff, "Investor Sentiment and Asset Valuation," *Journal of Business*, 78, 2, 405–440, 2005.

Brown, L. D., "Analyst Forecasting Errors and Their Implications for Security Analysis: An Alternative Perspective," *Financial Analysts Journal*, 52, 1, 40–47, January–February 1996.

Brown, L. D., "Earnings Surprise Research: Synthesis and Perspectives," *Financial Analysts Journal*, 53, 2, 13–19, March–April 1997.

Brown, L. D., "Analyst Forecasting Errors: Additional Evidence," *Financial Analysts Journal*, 53, 6, 81–88, November–December 1997.

Brown, L. D. and M. L. Caylor, "A Temporal Analysis of Quarterly Earnings Thresholds: Propensities and Valuation Consequences," *Accounting Review*, 80, 2, 423–440, 2005.

Brown, L. D. and H. N. Higgins, "Managing Earnings Surprises in the U.S. Versus 12 Other Countries," *Journal of Accounting and Public Policy*, 20, 373–398, 2001.

Brown, L. D. and M. S. Rozeff, "The Superiority of Analysts Forecasts as Measures of Expectations: Evidence from Earnings," *Journal of Finance*, 33, 1, 1–16, March 1978.

Brown, L. D. and M. S. Rozeff, "Univariate Time-Series Models of Quarterly Accounting Earnings: A Proposed Model," *Journal of Accounting Research*, 17, 1, 179–189, 1979.

Brown, P. and R. Ball, "Some Preliminary Findings on the Association Between the Earnings of a Firm, Its Industry and the Economy," *Empirical Research in Accounting: Selected Studies*, 1967. Supplement to *Journal of Accounting Research*, 5, 1–14, 1967.

Browning, E. S., "Please Don't Talk to the Bearish Analyst," *Wall Street Journal*, May 2, 1995.

Brunnermeier, M. K., *Asset Pricing Under Asymmetric Information: Bubbles, Crashes, Technical Analysis, and Herding*, Oxford: Oxford University Press, 2001.

Brunnermeier, M. K., "Deciphering the Liquidity and Credit Crunch 2007–2008," *Journal of Economic Perspectives*, 23, 1, 77–100, Winter 2009.

Brunnermeier, M. K. and C. Julliard, "Money Illusion and Housing Frenzies," *Review of Financial Studies*, 21, 1, 135–180, January 2008.

Brunnermeier, M. K. and S. Nagel, "Hedge Funds and the Technology Bubble," *Journal of Finance*, 59, 2013–2040, 2003.

Brunnermeier, M. K. and M. Oehmke, "Bubbles, Financial Crises, and Systemic Risk," NBER Working Paper #18398, September 2012.

Caballero, J., "Do Surges in International Capital Inflows Influence the Likelihood of Banking Crises?" Working Paper #305, Inter-American Development Bank, May 2012.

Calomiris, C. W., "The Regulatory Record of the Greenspan Fed," *American Economic Review*, 96, 2, 170–173, May 2006.

Canetti, E., *Crowds and Power*, New York: Viking Press, 1962.

Capstaff, J., K. Paudyal, and W. Rees, "A Comparative Analysis of Earnings Forecasts in Europe," *Journal of Business Finance and Accounting* 28, 531–562, 2001.

Case, A. and A. Deaton, "Rising Morbidity and Mortality in Midlife Among White Non-Hispanic Americans in the 21st Century," www.pnas.org/cgi/doi/10.1073/pnas.1518393112, September 17, 2015.

Case, K. E. and R. J. Shiller, "Is There a bubble in the Housing Market?" *Brookings Papers on Economic Activity*, 2, 299–362, 2003.

Cass, D. and K. Shell, "Do Sunspots Matter?" *Journal of Political Economy*, 91, 2, 193-227, April 1983.

Cerra, V. and S. C. Saxena, "Growth Dynamics: The Myth of Economic Recovery," *American Economic Review*, 98, 1, 439–457, 2008.

Chan, K., L. Chan, N. Jegadeesh, and J. Lakonishok, "Earnings Quality and Stock Returns," *Journal of Business*, 79, 3, 1041–1082, 2006.

Chan, L., J. Karceski, and J. Lakonishok, "The Level and Persistence of Growth Rates," *Journal of Finance*, 58, 2, 643–684, April 2003.

Chan, W., "Stock Price Reaction to News and No-News: Drift and Reversal After Headlines," *Journal of Financial Economics*, 70, 223–260, 2003.

Chant, P. D., "On the Predictability of Corporate Earnings per Share Behavior," *Journal of Finance*, 35, 1, 13–21, March 1980.

Charest, G., "Dividend Information, Stock Returns and Market Efficiency," *Journal of Financial Economics*, 6, 297–330, 1978.

Chen, H.-L. and W. F. M. De Bondt, "Style Momentum Within the S&P-500 Index," *Journal of Empirical Finance*, 11, 483–507, 2004.

Chen, J., H. Hong, and J. C. Stein, "Breadth of Ownership and Stock Returns," *Journal of Financial Economics*, 66, 171–205, 2002.

Chernenko, S., S. G. Hanson, and A. Sunderam, "Who Neglects Risk? Investor Experience and the Credit Boom," *Journal of Financial Economics*, 122, 248–269, 2016.

Chetty, R., D. Grusky, M. Hell, N. Hendren, R. Manduco, and J. Narang, "The Fading American Dream: Trends in Absolute Income Mobility Since 1940," NBER Working Paper #22910, December 2016.

Chopra, N., J. Lakonishok, and J. R. Ritter, "Measuring Abnormal Performance: Do Stocks Overreact?" *Journal of Financial Economics*, 31, 235–268, 1992.

Chopra, V. K., "Why So Much Error in Analysts' Earnings Forecasts?" *Financial Analysts Journal*, 54, 6, 35–42, November–December 1998.

Chordia, T. and L. Shivakumar, "Earnings and Price Momentum," *Journal of Financial Economics*, 80, 627–656, 2006.

Ciccone, S., "Does Analyst Optimism About Future Earnings Distort Stock Prices?" *Journal of Behavioral Finance*, 4, 2, 59–64, 2003.

Claessens, S. and M. A. Kose, "Financial Crises: Explanations, Types and Implications," International Monetary Fund Working Paper 13/28, January 2013.

Clarke, R. G. and M. Statman, "Bullish or Bearish?," *Financial Analysts Journal*, 63–72, May–June 1998.

Cochrane, J. H., *Asset Pricing*, Princeton: Princeton University Press, 2000.

Cohen, L. and D. Lou, "Complicated Firms," *Journal of Financial Economics*, 104, 383–400, 2012.

Coller, M., and T. L. Yohn, "Management Forecasts: What Do We Know?" *Financial Analysts Journal*, 54, 1, 58–62, January–February 1998.

Conlisk, J., "Why Bounded Rationality?" *Journal of Economic Literature*, 34, 669–700, 1996.

Cook, T. J. and Rozeff, M. S., "Size and Price-Earnings Anomalies: One Effect or Two?" *Journal of Financial and Quantitative Analysis*, 19, 4, 449–466, December 1984.

Cooper, M., "Filter Rules Based on Price and Volume in Individual Security Overreaction," *Review of Financial Studies*, 12, 4, 901–935, 1999.

Cooper, M., O. Dimitrov, and P. R. Rau, "A rose.com by Any Other Name," *Journal of Finance*, 56, 6, 2371–88, December 2001.

Copeland, T. E. and D. Mayers, "The Value-Line Enigma (1965–1978): A Case Study of Performance Evaluation Issues," *Journal of Financial Economics*, 10, 289–321, 1982.

Corkery, M. and J. Silver-Greenberg, "Investment Riches Built on Subprime Auto Loans to Poor," *New York Times*, January 26, 2015.

Cornell, B., "Is the Response of Analysts to Information Consistent with Fundamental Valuation? The Case of Intel," *Financial Management*, 30, 1, 113–136, Spring 2001.

Cornell, B., "Comovement as an Investment Tool," *Journal of Portfolio Management*, 30, 3, 106–111, Spring 2004.

Cournède, B. and O. Denk, "Finance and Economic Growth in OECD and G20 Countries," OECD Economics Department Working Paper #1223, 2015.

Cragg, J. G. and B. G. Malkiel, "The Consensus and Accuracy of Some Predictions of the Growth of Corporate Earnings," *Journal of Finance*, 23, 1, 67–84, March 1968.

Cragg, J. G. and B. G. Malkiel, *Expectations and the Structure of Share Prices*, Chicago: University of Chicago Press, 1982.

Crichfield, T., T. Dyckman, and J. Lakonishok, "An Evaluation of Security Analysts' Forecasts," *Accounting Review*, 53, 3, 651–668, July 1978.

Cronqvist, H., S. Siegel, and F. Yu, "Value Versus Growth Investing: Why Do Different Investors Have Different Styles?" *Journal of Financial Economics*, 117, 333–349, 2015.

Cyert, R. M. and M. H. DeGroot, "Rational Expectations and Bayesian Analysis," *Journal of Political Economy*, 82, 521–536, 1974.

Da, Z., J. Engelberg, and P. Gao, "The Sum of All FEARS Investor Sentiment and Asset Prices," *Review of Financial Studies*, 28, 1, 1–32, 2015.

Daly, G. G. and T. H. Mayor, "Reason and Rationality During Energy Crises," *Journal of Political Economy*, 91, 168–181, 1983.

Damasio, A., *Descartes' Error: Emotion, Reason, and the Human Brain*, New York: G. P. Putnam's Sons, 1994.

Daniel, K., D. Hirshleifer, and A. Subrahmanyam, "Investor Psychology and Security Market Under- and Overreactions," *Journal of Finance*, 53, 1839–1885, December 1998.

Daniel, K., D. Hirshleifer, and S. H. Teoh, "Investor Psychology in Capital Markets: Evidence and Policy Implications," *Journal of Monetary Economics*, 49, 139–209, 2002.

Daniel, K. and T. J. Moskowitz, "Momentum Crashes," *Journal of Financial Economics*, 122, 221–247, 2016.

Das, S., C. B. Levine, and K. Sivaramakrishnan, "Earnings Predictability and Bias in Analysts' Earnings Forecasts," *Accounting Review*, 73, 2, 277–294, April 1998.

Davis, E. P., *Debt, Financial Fragility and Systemic Risk*, Oxford: Clarendon Press, 1995.

Davis, M. A. and M. G. Palumbo, "The Price of Residential Land in Large US Cities," *Journal of Urban Economics*, 63, 352–384, 2008.

De Bondt, W. F. M., "A Behavioral Theory of the Price/Earnings Ratio Anomaly," Working Paper, Cornell University, March 1983.

De Bondt, W. F. M., "Stock Price Reversals and Overreaction to News Events: A Survey of Theory and Evidence," in R. M. C. Guimaraes, B. G. Kingsman, and S. J. Taylor, *A Reappraisal of the Efficiency of Financial Markets*, New York: Springer, 1989.

De Bondt, W. F. M., "What Do Economists Know About the Stock Market?" *Journal of Portfolio Management*, 18, 84–91, Winter 1991.

De Bondt, W. F. M., *Earnings Forecasts and Share Price Reversals*, monograph, Charlottesville, VA: AIMR, 1992.

De Bondt, W. F. M., "Betting on Trends: Intuitive Forecasts of Financial Risk and Return," *International Journal of Forecasting*, 9, 3, 355–371, 1993.

De Bondt, W. F. M. "A Portrait of the Individual Investor," *European Economic Review*, 42, 831–844, 1998.

De Bondt, W. F. M., "The Psychology of Underreaction and Overreaction in World Equity Markets," in D. B. Keim and W. Ziemba (eds.), *Security Market Imperfections in Worldwide Equity Markets*, 65–89, Cambridge: Cambridge University Press, 2000.

De Bondt, W. F. M. "Bubble Psychology", in W. Hunter and G. Kaufman (eds.), *Asset Price Bubbles: Implications for Monetary, Regulatory, and International Policies*, Chapter 13, 205–216, Cambridge, MA: MIT Press, 2002a.

De Bondt, W. F. M., "Discussion of 'Competing Theories of Financial Anomalies'," *Review of Financial Studies*, 15, 607–613, 2002b.

De Bondt, W. F. M., "Global Macro-economic Arbitrage: The Investment Value of High-Precision Forecasts," *Revue bancaire et financière*, 423–429, 2005a.

De Bondt, W. F. M. (ed.), *The Psychology of World Equity Markets*, Camberly, UK: Edward Elgar, 2005b.

De Bondt, W. F. M., "The Values and Beliefs of European Investors," in K. Knorr Cetina and A. Preda (eds.), *The Sociology of Financial Markets*, 163–186, Oxford and New York: Oxford University Press, 2005c.

De Bondt, W. F. M. (ed.), *Financial Accounting and Investment Management*, Cheltenham, UK: Edward Elgar, 2009.

De Bondt, W. F. M., "Asset Bubbles: Insights from Behavioral Finance," in D. D. Evanoff, G. Kaufman, and A. G. Malliaris (eds.), *New Perspectives on Asset Price Bubbles*, 318–321, New York: Oxford University Press, 2012.

De Bondt, W. F. M., "Crisis of Authority," in A. G. Malliaris, L. Shaw, and H. Shefrin (eds.), *The Global Financial Crisis and Its Aftermath. Hidden Factors in the Meltdown*, 302–339, Oxford: Oxford University Press, 2016.

De Bondt, W. F. M. and M. M. Bange, "Inflation Forecast Errors and Time Variation in Term Premia," *Journal of Financial and Quantitative Analysis*, 27, 4, 479–496, December 1992.

De Bondt, W. F. M. and W. Forbes, "Herding in Analyst Earnings Forecasts: Evidence from the United Kingdom," *European Financial Management*, 5, 143–163, 1999.

De Bondt, W. F. M. and R. H. Thaler, "Does the Stock Market Overreact?" *Journal of Finance*, 40, 3, 793–805, July 1985.

De Bondt, W. F. M. and R. H. Thaler, "Further Evidence on Investor Overreaction and Stock Market Seasonality," *Journal of Finance*, 42, 557–581, July 1987.

De Bondt, W. F. M. and R. H. Thaler, "A Mean-Reverting Walk Down Wall Street," *Journal of Economic Perspectives*, 3, 1, 189–202, Winter 1989.

De Bondt, W. F. M. and R. H. Thaler, "Do Security Analysts Overreact?" *American Economic Review*, 80, 2, 52–57, May 1990.

De Bondt, W. F. M. and R. H. Thaler, "Financial Decision Making in Markets and Firms: A Behavioral Perspective," in R. A. Jarrow et al. (eds.), *Handbook of Finance*, 385–410, Amsterdam: Elsevier–North Holland, 1995.

DeCanio, S. J., "Rational Expectation and Learning from Experience," *Quarterly Journal of Economics*, 92, 47–57, 1979.

Dechow, P. M. and D. J. Skinner, "Earnings Management: Reconciling the Views of Accounting Academics, Practitioners, and Regulators," *Accounting Horizons*, 14, 2, 235–250, 2000.

Dechow, P. M. and R. G. Sloan, "Return to Contrarian Investment Strategies: Tests of Naïve Expectations Hypotheses," *Journal of Financial Economics*, 43, 3–27, 1997.

De Franco, G., H. Lu, and F. P. Vasvar, "Wealth Transfer Effects of Analysts' Misleading Behavior," *Journal of Accounting Research*, 45, 1, 71–110, March 2007.

Degeorge, F., J. Patel, and R. Zeckhauser, "Earnings Management to Exceed Thresholds," *Journal of Business*, 72, 1, 1–33, January 1999.

DellaVigna, S., "Psychology and Economics: Evidence from the Field," *Journal of Economic Literature*, 47, 22, 315–372, 2009.

Desai, H. and P. Jain, "An Analysis of the Recommendations of the Superstar Money Managers at Barron's Annual Roundtable," *Journal of Finance*, 50, 4, 1257–1273, September 1995.

Desai, M. A., "The Degradation of Reported Corporate Profits," *Journal of Economic Perspectives*, 19, 4, 171–192, Fall 2005.

Devenow, A. and I. Welch, "Rational Herding in Financial Economics," *European Economic Review*, 40, 603–615, 1996.

Dichev, I., "Is the Risk of Bankruptcy a Systematic Risk?" *Journal of Finance*, 53, 3, 1131–1147, June 1998.

Diether, K., C. J. Malloy, and A. Scherbina, "Differences of Opinion and the Cross-section of Stock Returns," *Journal of Finance*, 57, 5, 2113–2141, October 2002.

Doukas, J. A., C. Kim, and C. Pantzalis, "A Test of the Errors-in-Expectations Explanation of the Value/Glamour Stock Returns Performance: Evidence from Analysts' Forecasts," *Journal of Finance*, 57, 5, 2143–2165, October 2002.

Doukas, J. A., C. Kim, and C. Pantzalis, "Divergence of Opinion and Equity Returns," *Journal of Financial and Quantitative Analysis*, 41, 3, 573–606, 2006.

Dowen, R. J., "Analyst Reaction to Negative Earnings for Large Well-Known Firms," *Journal of Portfolio Management*, 23, 1, 49–55, Fall 1996.

Dreman, D. N., *Psychology and the Stock Market*, New York: Amacom, 1977.

Dreman, D. N., *The New Contrarian Investment Strategy*, New York: Random House, 1982.

Dreman, D. N., *Contrarian Investment Strategies: The Next Generation*, New York: Simon & Schuster, 1998.

Dreman D. N. and M. A. Berry, "Analyst Forecast Errors and Their Implications for Security Analysis," *Financial Analysts Journal*, 51, 3, 30–41, May–June 1994.

Dreman, D. N. and M. A. Berry, "Overreaction, Underreaction, and the Low-P/E Effect," *Financial Analysts Journal*, 51, 4, 21–30, July–August 1995.

Easley, D. and R. Jarrow, "The Meaning and Testing of Market Efficiency: A Synthesis," Working Paper, Cornell University, October 1982.

Easley, D. and R. Jarrow, "Consensus Beliefs Equilibrium and Market Efficiency," *Journal of Finance*, 38, 3, 903–911, June 1983.

Easterwood, J. C. and S. R. Nutt, "Inefficiency in Analysts' Earnings Forecasts: Systematic Misreaction or Systematic Optimism?" *Journal of Finance*, 54, 5, 1777–1797, October 1999.

Edelen, R. M., O. S. Ince, and G. B. Kadlec, "Institutional Investors and Stock Return Anomalies," *Journal of Financial Economics*, 119, 472–488, 2016.

Edmans, A., D. Garcia, and O. Norli, "Sports Sentiment and Stock Returns," *Journal of Finance*, 62, 4, 1967–1998, August 2007.

Eggleton, I., "Patterns, Prototypes, and Predictions: An Exploratory Study," *Studies on Information Processing in Accounting*, Supplement to *Journal of Accounting Research*, 14, 68–131, 1976.

Eggleton, I., "Intuitive Time-Series Extrapolation," *Journal of Accounting Research*, 20, 1, 68–102, Spring 1982.

Einhorn, H., "Learning from Experience and Suboptimal Rules in Decision Making," in T. Wallsten (ed.), *Cognitive Processes in Choice and Decision Behavior*, Hillsdale, NJ: Lawrence Erlbaum, 1980.

Einhorn, H. and R. Hogarth, "Confidence in Judgment: Persistence of the Illusion of Validity," *Psychological Review*, 85, 395–476, 1978.

Eisner, R. and R. H. Strotz, "Flight Insurance and the Theory of Choice," *Journal of Political Economy*, 69, 4, 355–368, August 1961.

Elgers, P. T. and M. H. Lo, "Reductions in Analysts' Annual Earnings Forecast Errors Using Information in Prior Earnings and Security Returns," *Journal of Accounting Research*, 32, 2, 290–303, Autumn 1994.

Elgers, P. T., M. H. Lo, and R. J. Pfleifer, "Delayed Security Price Adjustments to Financial Analysts' Forecasts of Annual Earnings," *Accounting Review*, 76, 4, 613–632, 2001.

Elliott, J. A. and J. D. Hanna, "Repeated Accounting Write-offs and the Information Content of Earnings," *Journal of Accounting Research*, 34, 135–155, Supplement 1996.

Elliott, J. A., D. R. Philbrick, and C. I. Wiedman, "Evidence from Archival Data on the Relation Between Security Analysts' Forecast Errors and Prior Forecast Revisions," *Contemporary Accounting Research*, 11, 2, 919–938, Spring 1995.

Elster, J., *Ulysses and the Sirens: Studies in Rationality and Irrationality*, Cambridge and New York: Cambridge University Press, 1979.

Elton, E. J. and M. J. Gruber, "Earnings Estimates and the Accuracy of Expectations Data," *Management Science*, 18, 409–424, 1972.

Elton, E. J., M. J.,Gruber, and M. N. Gultekin, "Expectations and Share Prices," *Management Science*, 27, 975–987, 1981.

Elton, E. J., M. J. Gruber, and M. N. Gultekin, "Professional Expectations: Accuracy and Diagnosis of Errors," *Journal of Financial & Quantitative Analysis*, 19, 4, 351–363, December 1984.

Esponda, I., "Behavioral Equilibrium in Economies with Adverse Selection," *American Economic Review*, 98, 4, 1269–1291, September 2008.

Fama, E. F., "The Behavior of Stock Market Prices," *Journal of Business*, 38, 1, 34–105, January 1965a.

Fama, E. F., "Random Walks in Stock Market Prices," *Financial Analysts Journal*, 21, 5, 55–59, September–October 1965b.

Fama, E. F., "Efficient Capital Markets: A Review of Theory and Empirical Work," *Journal of Finance*, 25, 2, 383–417, May 1970.

Fama, E. F., *Foundations of Finance*, New York: Basic Books, 1976.

Fama, E. F., "Market Efficiency, Long-Term Returns, and Behavioral Finance," *Journal of Financial Economics*, 49, 283–306, 1998.

Fama, E. F., "Two Pillars of Asset Pricing," Lecture, Sveriges Riksbank Prize in Economic Sciences in Memory of Alfred Nobel, December 8, 2013.

Fama, E. F. and K. R. French, "The Cross-section of Expected Stock Returns," *Journal of Finance*, 47, 2, 427–465, June 1992.

Fama, E. F. and K. R. French, "Size and Book-to-Market Factors in Earnings and Returns," *Journal of Finance*, 50, 1, 131–155, March 1995.

Fama, E. F. and K. R. French, "Multifactor Explanations of Asset Pricing Anomalies," *Journal of Finance*, 51, 1, 55–84, March 1996.

Fama, E. F. and K. R. French, "Value Versus Growth: The International Evidence," *Journal of Finance*, 53, 6, 1975–1999, December 1998.

Fama, E. F. and K. R. French, "Forecasting Profitability and Earnings," *Journal of Business*, 73, 161–175, 2000.

Fama, E. F. and K. R. French, "The Capital Asset Pricing Model: Theory and Evidence," 18, 3, 25–46, *Journal of Economic Perspectives*, 2004.

Fama, E. F. and K. R. French, "A Five-Factor Asset Pricing Model," *Journal of Financial Economics*, 116, 1–22, 2015.

Fama, E. F. and K. R. French, "Dissecting Anomalies with a Five-Factor Model," *Review of Financial Studies*, 29, 1, 69–103, 2016.

Fielding, D. and J. Rewilak, "Credit Booms, Financial Fragility and Banking Crises," *Economics Letters*, 136, 233–236, 2015.

Figlewski, S., "Market Efficiency in a Market with Heterogeneous Information," *Journal of Political Economy*, 86, 4, 581–597, August 1978.

Figlewski, S., "The Informational Effects of Restrictions on Short Sales: Some Empirical Evidence," *Journal of Financial and Quantitative Analysis*, 16, 4, 463–476, November 1981.

Figlewski, S., "Information Diversity and Market Behavior," *Journal of Finance*, 37, 1, 87–102, March 1982.

Fischhoff, B., "Hindsight Does Not Equal Foresight: The Effect of Outcome Knowledge on Judgment Under Uncertainty," *Journal of Experimental Psychology, Human Perception and Performance*, 1, 288–299, 1975.

Fisher, I., "The Debt-Deflation Theory of Great Depressions," *Econometrica*, 1, 4, 337–357, October 1933.

Fisher, K. L. and M. Statman, "Investor Sentiment and Stock Returns," *Financial Analysts Journal*, 56, 2, 16–23, March–April 2000.

Foroohar, R., *Makers and Takers. The Rise of Finance and the Fall of American Business*, New York: Crown Business, 2016.

Fostel, A. and J. Geanakoplos, "Leverage Cycles and the Anxious Economy," *American Economic Review*, 98, 4, 1211–1244, September 2008.

Fox, M. B., L. R. Glosten, and G. V. Rauterberg, "The New Stock Market: Sense and Nonsense," *Duke Law Journal*, 65, 2, 191–277, November 2015.

Frankel, R. and C. M. C. Lee, "Accounting Valuation, Market Expectation, and Cross-sectional Stock Returns," *Journal of Accounting and Economics*, 25, 283–319, 1998.

Freeman, R. N., J. A. Ohlson, and S. H. Penman, "Book Rate-of-Return and Prediction of Earnings Changes: An Empirical Investigation," *Journal of Accounting Research*, 20, 2, 639–653, Autumn 1982.

French, K. R., "Stock Returns and the Weekend Effect," *Journal of Financial Economics*, 8, 1, 55–69, March 1983.

Fried, D. and D. Givoly, "Financial Analysts' Forecasts of Earnings," *Journal of Accounting and Economics*, 4, 85–107, 1982.

Friedman, B., "Optimal Expectation and the Extreme Informational Assumptions of Rational Expectations Macromodels," *Journal of Monetary Economics*, 5, 24–41, 1979.

Friedman, B., "Survey Evidence on the 'Rationality' of Interest Rate Expectations," *Journal of Monetary Economics*, 6, 453–465, 1980.

Froot, K. and M. Obstfeld, "Intrinsic Bubbles: The Case of Stock Prices," *American Economic Review*, 81, 1189–1217, 1991.

Frydman, R., "Towards an Understanding of Market Processes: Individual Expectations, Learning, and Convergence to Rational Expectations Equilibrium," *American Economic Review*, 72, 4, 652–668, September 1982.

Fuller, R. J., L. C. Huberts, and M. J. Levinson, "Returns to E/P Strategies, Higgledy-Piggledy Growth, Analysts' Forecast Errors, and Omitted Risk Factors," *Journal of Portfolio Management*, 20, 13–24, Winter 1993.

Gabaix, X., "The Granular Origins of Aggregate Fluctuations," *Econometrica*, 79, 3, 733–772, May 2011.

Gabaix, X., "Variable Rare Disasters: An Exactly Solved Framework for Ten Puzzles in Macro-finance," *Quarterly Journal of Economics*, 127, 2, 645–700, 2012.

Gallant, D., "The Hazards of Negative Research Reports," *Institutional Investor*, 73–80, July 1990.

Galston, W. A. and E. C. Kamarck, "Against Short-Termism," *Democracy Journal*, 38, 10–24, Fall 2015.

Garcia, D., "Sentiment During Recessions," *Journal of Finance*, 58, 3, 1267–1300, June 2013.

Gennaioli, N., Y. Ma, and A. Shleifer, "Expectations and Investment," BIS Working Papers #562, May 2016.

Gennaioli, N., A. Shleifer, and R. Vishny, "Neglected Risks, Financial Innovation, and Financial Fragility," *Journal of Financial Economics*, 104, 452–468, 2012.

George, T. J. and C.-Y. Hwang, "The 52-Week High and Momentum Investing," *Journal of Finance*, 54, 5, 2145–2176, October 2004.

Gibbons, M. R. and P. Hess, "Day of the Week Effects and Asset Returns," *Journal of Business*, 54, 4, 579–596, October 1981.

Gilovich, T., *How We Know What Isn't So: The Fallibility of Human Reason in Everyday Life*, New York: Free Press, 1991.

Gilovich, T., D. Griffin, and D. Kahneman, *Heuristics and Biases: The Psychology of Intuitive Judgment*, New York: Cambridge University Press, 2002.

Gilson, S. C., "Investing in Distressed Situations: A Market Survey," *Financial Analysts Journal*, 51, 6, 8–27, November–December 1995.

Givoly, D. and C. Hayn, "Rising Conservatism: Implications for Financial Analysis," *Financial Analysts Journal*, 58, 1, 56–74, January–February 2002.

Givoly, D. and J. Lakonishok, "The Information Content of Financial Analysts' Forecasts of Earnings," *Journal of Accounting and Economics*, 1, 165–185, 1979.

Givoly, D. and J. Lakonishok, "Financial Analysts' Forecasts of Earnings," *Journal of Banking and Finance*, 4, 221–233, 1980.

Givoly, D. and J. Lakonishok, "The Quality of Analysts' Forecasts of Earnings," *Financial Analysts Journal*, 40, 5, 42–47, September–October 1984.

Givoly, D. and A. Ovadia, "Year-End Tax-Induced Sales and Stock Market Seasonality," *Journal of Finance*, 38, 1, 171–185, March 1983.

Goetzmann, W. N., D. Kim, and R. J. Shiller, "Crash Beliefs from Investor Surveys," NBER Working Paper #22143, April 2016.

Gordon, M., *Finance, Investment and Macroeconomics*, Hants, UK: Edward Elgar, 1994.

Gourinchas, P.-O. and M. Obstfeld, "Stories of the Twentieth Century for the Twenty-First," *American Economic Journal: Macroeconomics*, 4, 1, 226–265, 2012.

Graeber, D., *Debt: The First 5,000 Years*, Brooklyn: Melville House, 2011.

Graham, B., *The Intelligent Investor: A Book of Practical Counsel*, New York: Harper, 1949.

Graham, B. and D. L. Dodd, *Security Analysis*, 1st ed., New York: McGraw-Hill, 1934.

Graham, J. R., C. R. Harvey, and S. Rajgopal, "The Economic Implications of Corporate Financial Reporting," *Journal of Accounting and Economics*, 40, 3–73, 2005.

Greene, M. T. and B. D. Fielitz, "Long-Term Dependence in Common Stock Returns," *Journal of Financial Economics*, 4, 339–349, 1977.

Greenspan, A., "Risk Transfer and Financial Stability," Speech, Federal Reserve Bank of Chicago, 41st Annual Conference on Bank Structure, May 5, 2005.

Greenspan, A., *The Age of Turbulence: Adventures in a New World*, New York: Penguin Press, 2007.

Greenspan, A., "The Crisis," *Brookings Papers on Economic Activity*, 201–261, Spring 2010.

Greenspan, A., *The Map and the Territory. Risk, Human Nature, and the Future of Forecasting*, New York: Penguin Press, 2013.

Greenspan, A., "How to Avoid Another Global Financial Crisis," *The American*, March 6, 2014.

Greenwood, R. and A. Shleifer, "Expectations of Returns and Expected Returns," *Review of Financial Studies*, 27, 3, 714–746, 2014.

Grether, D. M., "Bayes Rule as a Descriptive Model: The Representativeness Heuristic," *Quarterly Journal of Economics*, 95, 3, 537–557, November 1980.

Grether, D. M. and C. Plott, "Economic Theory of Choice and the Preference Reversal Phenomenon," *American Economic Review*, 69, 4, 623–638, September 1979.

Griffin, J. M. and M. L. Lemmon, "Book-to-Market Equity, Distress Risk, and Stock Returns," *Journal of Finance*, 57, 5, 2317–2336, October 2002.

Griffin, J. M., X. Ji, and J. S. Martin, "Momentum Investing and Business Cycle Risk: Evidence from Pole to Pole," *Journal of Finance*, 58, 6, 2515–2547, December 2003.

Griffin, J. M., J. H. Harris, T. Shu, and S. Topaloglu, "Who Drove and Burst the Tech Bubble?" *Journal of Finance*, 64, 4, 1251–1290, August 2011.

Grossman, S. J., *The Informational Role of Prices*, Cambridge, MA: MIT Press, 1989.

Grossman, S. J. and R. J. Shiller, "The Determinants of the Variability of Stock Market Prices," *American Economic Review*, 71, 2, 222–227, May 1981.

Grossman, S. J. and J. Stiglitz, "On the Impossibility of Informationally Efficient Markets," *American Economic Review*, 70, 3, 393–408, June 1980.

Guttentag, J. M. and R. J. Herring, "Credit Rationing and Financial Disorder," *Journal of Finance*, 39, 1359–1382, 1984.

Hague, W., "Central Bankers Have Collectively Lost the Plot: They Must Raise Interest Rates or Face Their Doom," *Daily Telegraph*, October 18, 2016.

Haldane, A. G., "Small Lessons from a Big Crisis," Speech, Federal Reserve Bank of Chicago Conference on "Reforming Financial Regulation," May 8, 2009.

Haldane, A. G., "The Dog and the Frisbee," Speech, Federal Reserve Bank of Kansas City Policy Symposium, Jackson Hole, Wyoming, August 31, 2012.

Haldane, A. G., "Central Bank Psychology," Speech, Royal Society of Medicine Conference on "Leadership: Stress and Hubris," London, November 17, 2014.

Haldane, A. G. and R. M. May, "Systemic Risk in Banking Ecosystems," *Nature*, 469, 351–355, January 20, 2011.

Harrison, J. M. and D. M. Kreps, "Speculative Investor Behavior in a Stock Market with Heterogeneous Expectations," *Quarterly Journal of Economics*, 92, 2, 323–336, May 1978.

Hastie, R. and R. Dawes, *Rational Choice in an Uncertain World: The Psychology of Judgment and Decision-Making*, Thousand Oaks, CA: Sage, 2001.

Haugen, R. and N. Baker, "Commonality in the Determinants of Expected Stock Returns," *Journal of Financial Economics*, 41, 401–39, 1996.

Hayek, F. A. von, "The Use of Knowledge in Society," *American Economic Review*, 35, 4, 519–530, September 1945.

Hayek, F. A. von, *Individualism and Economic Order*, Chicago: University of Chicago Press, Chicago, 1948.

Hellwig, M. F., "On the Aggregation of Information in Competitive Markets," *Journal of Economic Theory*, 22, 477–498, 1980.

Hellwig, M. F., "Rational Expectations Equilibrium with Conditioning on Past Prices: A Mean-Variance Example," *Journal of Economic Theory*, 26, 279–312, 1982.

Hickman, W. B., *Corporate Bond Quality and Investor Experience*, Princeton: Princeton University Press, 1958.

Hirshleifer, D., A. Subrahmanyam and S. Titman, "Security Analysis and Trading Patterns When Some Investors Receive Information Before Others," *Journal of Finance*, 49, 5, 1665–1698, December 1994.

Hirshleifer, D., "Investor Psychology and Asset Pricing," *Journal of Finance*, 56, 1533–1597, August 2001.

Ho, K., *Liquidated. An Ethnography of Wall Street*, Durham: Duke University Press, 2009.

Hogarth, R. M., "Cognitive Processes and the Assessment of Subjective Probability Distributions," *Journal of the American Statistical Association*, 70, 350, 271–289, June 1975.

Hogarth, R. M., *Judgment and Choice, The Psychology of Decision*, New York: Wiley, 1980.

Hogarth, R. M. and S. Makridakis, "Forecasting and Planning: An Evaluation," *Management Science*, 27, 2, 115–138, February 1981.

Hong, H. and J. D. Kubik, "Analyzing the Analysts: Career Concerns and Biased Earnings Forecasts," *Journal of Finance*, 58, 1, 313–351, February 2003.

Hong, H., T. Lim, and J. C. Stein, "Bad News Travels Slowly: Size, Analyst Coverage, and the Profitability of Momentum Strategies," *Journal of Finance*, 55, 1, 265–295, February 2000.

Hong, H. and J. C. Stein, "A Unified Theory of Underreaction, Momentum Trading, and Overreaction in Asset Markets," *Journal of Finance*, 54, 2143–2184, 1999.

Huang, A., "The Cross-section of Cash Flow Volatility and Expected Stock Returns," *Journal of Empirical Finance*, 16, 409–429, 2009.

Huberman, G., "Familiarity Breeds Investment," *Review of Financial Studies*, 14, 3, 659–680, Fall 2001.

Huberman, G. and T. Regev, "Contagious Speculation and a Cure for Cancer: A Non-event that Made Stock Prices Soar," *Journal of Finance*, 56, 1, 387–396, February 2001.

Huberts, L. C., and R. J. Fuller, "Predictability Bias in the U.S. Equity Market," *Financial Analysts Journal*, 51, 2, 12–28, March–April 1995.

Imhoff, E. A. and P. V. Pare, "Analysis and Comparison of Earnings Forecast Agents," *Journal of Accounting Research*, 20, 2, part 1, 429–439, Autumn 1982.

Jaffe, J., D. B. Keim, and R. Westerfield, "Earnings Yields, Market Values, and Stock Returns," *Journal of Finance* 44, 1, 135–148, 1989.

Jagannathan, R., E. Schaumburg, and G. Zhou, "Cross-sectional Asset Pricing Tests," *Annual Review of Financial Economics*, 2, 49–74, December 2010.

Janis, I. L., *Victims of Groupthink*, Boston: Houghton Mifflin, 1972.

Jarrow, R., "Heterogeneous Expectations, Restrictions on Short Sales, and Equilibrium Asset Prices," *Journal of Finance*, 35, 5, 1105–1113, December 1980.

Jegadeesh, N. and S. Titman, "Returns to Buying Winners and Selling Losers: Implications for Stock Market Efficiency," *Journal of Finance* 48, 65–91, 1993.

Jegadeesh, N. and S. Titman, "Profitability of Momentum Strategies: An Evaluation of Alternative Explanations," *Journal of Finance*, 56, 2, 699–720, April 2001.

Jensen, M. C. and G. A. Benington, "Random Walks and Technical Theories: Some Additional Evidence," *Journal of Finance*, 25, 2, 461–482, May 1970.

Jensen, M. C., "Some Anomalous Evidence Regarding Market Efficiency," *Journal of Financial Economics*, 6, 95–101, 1978.

Jensen, M. C., "The Agency Costs of Overvalued Equity and the Current State of Corporate Finance," *European Financial Management*, 10, 4, 549–565, 2004.

Jones, C. J., D. Tweedie, and G. Whittington, "The Regression Portfolio: A Statistical Investigation of a Relative Decline Model," *Journal of Business Finance & Accounting*, 3, 71–92, 1976.

Jones, C. P. and R. H. Litzenberger, "Quarterly Earnings Reports and Intermediate Stock Price Trends," *Journal of Finance*, 25, 1, 143–148, March 1970.

Jorda, O., M. Schularick, and A. M. Taylor, "When Credit Bites Back," *Journal of Money, Credit and Banking*, 45, 2, 3–28, December 2013.

Jorda, O., M. Schularick, and A. M. Taylor, "Betting the House," Working Paper, Federal Reserve Bank of San Francisco, June 2014.

Jorda, O., M. Schularick, and A. M. Taylor, "Leveraged Bubbles," *Journal of Monetary Economics*, 76, 1–20, 2015.

Jorda, O., M. Schularick, and A. M. Taylor, "The Great Mortgaging: Housing Finance, Crises, and Business Cycles," *Economic Policy*, 31, 85, 107–152, 2016.

Kahler, M. (ed.), *Capital Flows and Financial Crises*, Manchester: Manchester University Press, 1998.

Kahneman, D., *Thinking, Fast and Slow*, New York: Farrar, Straus and Giroux, 2011.

Kahneman, D. and M. Riepe, "Aspects of Investor Psychology," *Journal of Portfolio Management*, 24, 4, 52–65, Summer 1998.

Kahneman, D., P. Slovic, and A. Tversky, *Judgment Under Uncertainty: Heuristics and Biases*, New York: Cambridge University Press, 1982.

Kahneman, D. and A. Tversky, "Prospect Theory: An Analysis of Decision Under Risk," *Econometrica*, 47, 263–291, March 1979.

Kahneman, D. and A. Tversky. "The Psychology of Preferences," *Scientific American*, 246, 1, 160–173, January 1982.

Kahneman, D. and A. Tversky, "Choices, Values, and Frames," *American Psychologist*, 39, 4, 341–350, 1984.

Kaminsky, G.L., C.M. Reinhart and C.A. Vegh, "The unholy trinity of financial contagion," *Journal of Economic Perspectives*, 17, 4, 51–74, Fall 2003.

Kasznik, R. and M.F. McNichols, "Does Meeting Earnings Expectations Matter? Evidence from Analyst Forecast Revisions and Share Prices," *Journal of Accounting Research*, 40, 3, 727–759, June 2002.

Kaufman, H., "Debt: The Threat to Economic and Financial Stability," *Federal Reserve Bank of Kansas City Economic Review*, 3–11, December 1986.

Kay, J., *Other People's Money. Masters of the Universe or Servants of the People?*, Profile Books, 2015.

Ke, B., S. Huddart and K. Petroni, "What Insiders Know about Future Earnings and How They Use It: Evidence from Insider Trades," *Journal of Accounting and Economics*, 35, 315–346, 2003.

Keane, M. P., and D. E. Runkle, "Are Financial Analysts' Forecasts of Corporate Profits Rational?" *Journal of Political Economy*, 106, 4, 768–805, August 1998.

Keim, D. B and W. Ziemba (eds.), *Security Market Imperfections in Worldwide Equity Markets*, Cambridge: Cambridge University Press, 2000.

Keoun, B. and P. Kuntz, "Wall Street Aristocracy got $1.2 trillion in Secret Loans," *Bloomberg News*, August 22, 2011.

Keynes, J. M., *The General Theory of Employment, Interest and Money*, New York: Harcourt Brace Jovanovich, 1936.

Keynes, J. M., "The General Theory of Employment," *Quarterly Journal of Economics*, 51, 209–223, 1937.

Kindleberger, C., *Manias, Panics, and Crashes: A History of Financial Crisis*, New York: Basic Books, 1978.

Kindleberger, C., "Manias and How to Prevent Them," *Challenge*, 40, 6, 21–31, November–December 1997.

King, R. and C. Plosser, "Money, Credit and Prices in a Real Business Cycle," *American Economic Review*, 74, 363–380, June 1984.

Kinney, W., D. Burgstahler, and R. Martin, "Earnings Surprise Materiality as Measured by Stock Returns," *Journal of Accounting Research*, 40, 5, 1297–1329, December 2002.

Kiyotaki, N., "Credit and Business Cycles," *Japanese Economic Review*, 49, 1, 18–35, March 1998.

Kiyotaki, N. and J. Moore, "Credit Cycles," *Journal of Political Economy*, 105, 2, 211–248, 1997.

Klein, A., "A Direct Test of the Cognitive Bias Theory of Share Price Reversals," *Journal of Accounting and Economics*, 13, 2, 155–166, 1990.

Klein, M., "The Stock Market Crash of 1929: A Review Article," *Business History Review*, 75, 2, 325–351, Summer 2001.

Konczal, M. and N. Abernathy, *Defining Financialization*, New York: Roosevelt Institute, July 27, 2015.

Kothari, S. P. and J. Shanken, "Book-to-Market, Dividend Yield, and Expected Market Returns: A Time-Series Analysis," *Journal of Financial Economics*, 44, 169–203, 1997.

Krippner, G. R., *Capitalizing on Crisis. The Political Origins of the Rise of Finance*, Cambridge, MA: Harvard University Press, 2011.

Krueger, A. B., "The Rise and Consequence of Inequality in the United States," Speech, Center for American Progress, January 112, 2012.

Krugman, P., "The Mellon Doctrine," *New York Times*, March 31, 2011.

Kunreuther, H., R. Ginsberg, L. Miller et al., *Disaster Insurance Protection: Public Policy Lessons*, New York: Wiley, 1978.

Kynge, J. and J. Wheatley, "Emerging Markets: The Great Unravelling," *Financial Times*, April 1, 2015.

Lakonishok, J., "Stock Market Return Expectations: Some General Properties," *Journal of Finance*, 35, 4, 921–931, September 1980.

Lakonishok, J., A. Shleifer and R. W. Vishny, "Contrarian Investment, Extrapolation, and Risk," *Journal of Finance*, 49, 1541–1578, December 1994.

Lamfalussy, A., *Financial Crises in Emerging Markets. An Essay on Financial Globalisation and Fragility*, New Haven: Yale University Press, 2000.

Lamont, O.A. and R.H. Thaler, "The Law of One Price," *Journal of Economic Perspectives*, 17, 4, 191–202, Autumn 2003.

Langer, E., "The Illusion of Control," *Journal of Personality and Social Psychology*, 32, 311–328, 1975.

Lansing, K. J., "Lock-in of Extrapolative Expectations in an Asset Pricing Model," Federal Reserve Bank of San Francisco Working Paper, October 2005.

LaPorta, R., "Expectations and the Cross-section of Stock Returns," *Journal of Finance*, 51, 5, 1715–1742, December 1996.

LaPorta, R., J. Lakonishok, A. Shleifer, and R. Vishny, "Good News for Value Stocks: Further Evidence on Market Efficiency," *Journal of Finance*, 52, 2, 859–874, June 1997.

Latane, H. A. and C. P. Jones, "Standardized Unexpected Earnings – a Progress Report," *Journal of Finance*, 32, 5, 1457–1465, December 1977.

Laughhunn, D. J., J. W. Payne, and R. Crum, "Managerial Risk Preferences for Below-Target Returns," *Management Science*, 26, 12, 1231–1249, December 1980.

LeBon, G., *The Crowd. A Study of the Popular Mind*, New York: Penguin, 1977 (originally published in 1895).

LeDoux, J., *The Emotional Brain*, New York: Simon & Schuster, 1996.

Lee, C. M. C., J. Myers, and B. Swaminathan, "What Is the Intrinsic Value of the Dow?" *Journal of Finance*, 54, 5, 1693–1741, October 1999.

Lee, C. M. C. and B. Swaminathan, "Price Momentum and Trading Volume," *Journal of Finance*, 55, 5, 2017–69, October 2000.

Lemmon, M. and E. Portniaguina, "Consumer Sentiment and Stock Prices," *Review of Financial Studies*, 19, 4, 1499–1529, 2006.

LeRoy, S. F., "Expectations Models of Asset Prices: A Survey of Theory," *Journal of Finance*, 37, 1, 185–217, March 1982.

LeRoy, S. F. and R. Porter, "The Present Value Relation: Tests Based on Implied Variance Bounds," *Econometrica*, 49, 3, 555–574, May 1981.

Levis, M. and M. Liodakis, "Contrarian Strategies and Investor Expectations: The U.K. Evidence," *Financial Analysts Journal*, 57, 5, 43–56, September–October 2001.

Levitt, A., "The Numbers Game," Remarks by the Chair of the Securities and Exchange Commission, New York University Center for Law and Business, September 28, 1998.

Levy, H., "Equilibrium in an Imperfect Market: A Constraint on the Number of Securities in the Portfolio," *American Economic Review*, 68, 4, 643–658, September 1978.

Levy, R., "Random Walks: Reality or Myth," *Financial Analysts Journal*, 23, 6, 69–77, November–December 1967.

Levy, R. and S. Kripotos, "Earnings Growth, P/E's and Relative Price Strength," *Financial Analysts Journal*, 25, 6, 60–67, November–December 1969.

Lewellen J. and J. Shanken, "Learning, Asset Pricing Tests, and Market Efficiency," *Journal of Finance*, 57, 3, 1113–1145, 2002.

Lewis, M., *The Big Short: Inside the Doomsday Machine*, New York: W. W. Norton, 2010.

Lewis, M., *Flash Boys: A Wall Street Revolt*, New York: W. W. Norton, 2014.

Li, J. and J. Yu, "Investor Attention, Psychological Anchors, and Stock Return Predictability," *Journal of Financial Economics*, 104, 401–419, 2012.

Libby, R. and P. C. Fishburn, "Behavioral Models of Risk Taking in Business Decisions: A Survey and Evaluation," *Journal of Accounting Research*, 15, 2, 272–292, Autumn 1977.

Little, I. M. D., "Higgledy Piggledy Growth," *Bulletin of the Oxford University Institute of Economics and Statistics*, 24, 4, 387–412, November 1962.

Liu, J., D. Nissim, and J. Thomas, "Equity Valuation Using Multiples," *Journal of Accounting Research*, 40, 1, 135–172, March 2002.

Lloyd-Davies, P. and M. Canes, "Stock Prices and the Publication of Second-Hand Information," *Journal of Business*, 51, 1, 43–56, 1978.

Loewenstein, G. F., E. U. Weber, C. K. Hsee, and N. Welch, ' "Risk as Feelings," *Psychological Bulletin*, 127, 2, 267–86, 2001.

Loewenstein, G. and T. O'Donoghue, "Animal Spirits: Affective and Deliberative Processes in Economic Behavior," Working Paper, Department of Social and Decision Sciences, Carnegie-Mellon University, May 2005.

Loh, R. K. and G. M. Mian,"Do Accurate Earnings Forecasts Facilitate Superior Investment Recommendations?" *Journal of Financial Economics*, 80, 455–483, 2006.

Long, J. B., Jr., "Discussion," *Journal of Finance*, 36, 2, 304–307, May 1981.

Loomes, G. and R. Sugden, "Regret Theory: An Alternative Theory of Rational Choice Under Uncertainty," *Economic Journal*, 92, 368, 805–824, December 1982.

Lorie, J. and M. Hamilton. *The Stock Market: Theories and Evidence*, Homewood, IL: Irwin, 1973.

Loughran, T. and B. McDonald, "When Is a Liability Not a Liability? Textual Analysis, Dictionaries, and 10-Ks," *Journal of Finance*, 66, 1, 35–64, February 2011.

Loughran, T. and B. McDonald, "Textual Analysis in Accounting and Finance: A Survey," *Journal of Accounting Research*, 54, 4, 1187–1230, September 2016.

Lovell, M. C., "Tests of the Rational Expectations Hypothesis," *American Economic Review*, 76, 110–124, 1986.

Lowenstein, R., "Triple-A Failure," *New York Times*, April 27, 2008.

Lowry, M., "Why Does IPO Volume Fluctuate So Much?" *Journal of Financial Economics*, 67, 3–40, 2003.

Lucas, R. E., "An Equilibrium Model of the Business Cycle," *Journal of Political Economy*, 83, 6, 1113–1144, December 1975.

Macauley, F. R., *Some Theoretical Problems Suggested By The Movement of Interest Rates, Bond Yields and Stock Prices In The United States Since 1856*, Cambridge, MA: NBER, 1938.

MacCrimmon, K. R. and D. A. Wehrung, *Taking Risks: The Management of Uncertainty*, New York: Free Press, 1986.

Maines, L. A. and J. R. M. Hand, "Individuals' Perceptions and Misperceptions of Time Series Properties of Quarterly Earnings," *Accounting Review*, 71, 3, 317–336, July 1996.

Malevergne, Y., P. Santa-Clara, and D. Sornette, "Professor Zipf Goes to Wall Street," NBER Working Paper #15295, August 2009.

Malkiel, B. G. and J. G. Cragg, "Expectations and the Structure of Share Prices," *American Economic Review*, 60, 4, 601–617, September 1970.

Mandelbrot, B. and R. L. Hudson, *The (Mis)behavior of Markets*, New York: Basic Books, 2004.

Mao, H. S. Counts, and J. Bollen, "Predicting Financial Markets: Comparing Survey, News, Twitter and Search Engine Data," arxiv.org/abs/1112.1051, December 2011.

Mao, H., S. Counts, and J. Bollen, "Quantifying the Effects of Online Bullishness on International Financial Markets," Working Paper, European Central Bank, July 2015.

March, J. G. and Z. Shapira, "Managerial Perspectives on Risk and Risk Taking," *Management Science*, 33, 11, 1404–1418, November 1987.

Markov, S. and A. Tamayo, "Predictability in Financial Analyst Forecast Errors: Learning or Irrationality," *Journal of Accounting Research*, 44, 4, 725–761, September 2006.

Matsumoto, D. A., "Management's Incentives to Avoid Negative Earnings Surprises," *Accounting Review*, 77, 3, 483–514, July 2002.

Maurer, B., "The Anthropology of Money," *Annual Review of Anthropology*, 35, 15–36, 2006.

Mayshar, J., "On Divergence of Opinion and Imperfections in Capital Markets," *American Economic Review*, 73, 1, 114–128, March 1983.

McCallum, B. T., "On Non-uniqueness in Rational Expectations Models," *Journal of Monetary Economics*, 11, 139–168, 1983.

McDonald, C., "An Empirical Evaluation of the Reliability of Published Predictions of Future Earnings," *Accounting Review*, 48, 3, 502–510, July 1973.

McEnally, R. W., "An Investigation of the Extrapolative Determinants of Short-Run Earnings Expectations," *Journal of Financial and Quantitative Analysis*, 6, 2, 687–706, March 1971.

McWilliams, J.D., "Prices, Earnings, and PE Ratios," *Financial Analysts Journal*, 22, 3, 137–142, May–June 1966.

Mehra, R. and E. Prescott, "The Equity Premium: A Puzzle," *Journal of Monetary Economics*, 15, 145–161, 1985.

Mendoza, E. and M. Terrones, "An Anatomy of Credit Booms: Evidence from Macro Aggregates and Micro Data," NBER Working Paper #14049, May 2008.

Merton, R. C., "An Intertemporal Capital Asset Pricing Model," *Econometrica*, 41, 5, 867–887, September 1973.

Mian, A. and A. Sufi, "The Great Recession: Lessons from Microeconomic Data," *American Economic Review*, 100, 2, 1–10, 2010.

Mian, A. and A. Sufi, *House of Debt*, Chicago: University of Chicago Press, 2014.

Miao, J., P. Wang, and J. Zhou, "Asset Bubbles, Collateral, and Policy Analysis," *Journal of Monetary Economics*, 76, S57–S70, 2015.

Michaely, R., R. H. Thaler, and K. L. Womack, "Price Reactions to Dividend Initiations and Omissions: Overreaction or Drift?" *Journal of Finance*, 50, 2, 573–608, June 1995.

Miller, E., "Risk, Uncertainty and Divergence of Opinion," *Journal of Finance*, 32, 4, 1151–1168, September 1977.

Miller, M. H. and F. Modigliani, "Dividend Policy, Growth and the Valuation of Shares," *Journal of Business*, 34, 411–433, October 1961.

Minsky, H. P., "The Financial Instability Hypothesis: An Interpretation of Keynes and an Alternative to 'Standard' Theory," *Nebraska Journal of Economics and Business*, 16, 1, 5–16, Winter 1977.

Minsky, H. P., "Can 'It' Happen Again? A Reprise," *Challenge*, 25, 3, 5–13, July–August 1982.

Minsky, H. P., *Stabilizing an Unstable Economy*, New Haven: Yale University Press, 1986.

Mikhail, M. B., B. R. Walther, and R. H. Willis, "Do Security Analysts Improve Their Performance with Experience?," *Journal of Accounting Research*, 35, 131–157, 1997.

Mises, L. von, *Theorie des Geldes und der Umlaufsmittel*, 1912 (*The Theory of Money and Credit*, New Haven: Yale University Press, 1953).

Mishkin, F. S., "Are Market Forecasts Rational?" *American Economic Review*, 71, 3, 295–306, June 1981.

Mishkin, F. S., "Will Monetary Policy Become More of a Science?" Deutsche Bundebank Conference "Monetary Policy over Fifty Years," Frankfurt am Main, Germany, September 21, 2007.

Molodovsky, N., "A Theory of Price-Earnings Ratios," *Analysts Journal*, 9, 5, 65–80, November 1953.

Moskow, M. H., "Disruptions in Global Financial Markets: The Role of Public Policy," Speech, Global Finance Conference, DePaul University, Chicago, April 21, 2000.

Moskowitz, T. J. and M. Grinblatt, "Do Industries Explain Momentum?" *Journal of Finance*, 54, 4, 11249–1290, August 1999.

Mukunda, G., "The Price of Wall Street's Power," *Harvard Business Review*, 70–78, June 2014.

Murphy, J. E., Jr., and H. W. Stevenson, "Price/Earnings Ratios and Future Growth of Earnings and Dividends," *Financial Analysts Journal*, 23, 6, 111–114, November–December 1967.

Muth, J. F., "Rational Expectations and the Theory of Price Movements," *Econometrica*, 29, 3, 315–335, July 1961.

Mutz, D. C., *Impersonal Influence: How Perceptions of Mass Collectives Affect Political Attitudes*, Cambridge: Cambridge University Press, 1998.

Myers, J. N., L. A. Myers, and D. J. Skinner, "Earnings Momentum and Earnings Management," *Journal of Accounting, Auditing and Finance*, 22, 1, 249–284, 2007.

Nagel, S., "Empirical Cross-sectional Asset Pricing," *Annual Review of Financial Economics*, 5, 167–199, November 2013.

Neal, R. and S. M. Wheatley, "Do Measures of Investor Sentiment Predict Returns?" *Journal of Financial and Quantitative Analysis*, 33, 4, 523–547, December 1998.

Neill, H. B., *The Art of Contrary Thinking*, Caldwell, ID: Caxton Printers, 1954.

Nicholson, F., "Price Ratios in Relation to Investment Results," *Financial Analysts Journal*, 24, 1, 105–109, January–February 1968.

Niederhoffer, V. and P. Regan, "Earnings Changes, Analysts' Forecasts, and Stock Prices," *Financial Analysts Journal*, 28, 3, 65–71, May–June 1972.

Nisbett, R. and L. Ross, *Human Inference: Strategies and Shortcomings of Social Judgment*, Englewood Cliffs, NJ: Prentice Hall, 1980.

Nofsinger, J. R. and R. W. Sias, "Herding and Feedback Trading by Institutional and Individual Investors," *Journal of Finance*, 54, 6, 2263–2295, December 1999.

Novy-Marx, R., "The Other Side of Value: The Gross Profitability Premium," *Journal of Financial Economics*, 108, 1–23, 2013.

Nozick, R., *The Nature of Rationality*, Princeton: Princeton University Press, 1993.

Nutt, S. R., J. C. Easterwood, and C. M. Easterwood, "New Evidence on Serial Correlation in Analyst Forecast Errors," *Financial Management*, 28, 4, 106–117, Winter 1999.

Ofek, E. and M. Richardson, "The Valuation and Market Rationality of Internet Stock Prices," *Oxford Review of Economic Policy*, 18, 3, 265–287, Autumn 2002.

Ofek, E. and M. Richardson, "DotCom Mania: The Rise and Fall of Internet Stock Prices," *Journal of Finance*, 58, 3, 1113–11137, June 2003.

O'Hara, M., "Bubbles: Some Perspectives (and Loose Talk) from History," *Review of Financial Studies*, 21, 1, 11–17, January 2008.

Omarova, S. T., "The Merchants of Wall Street: Banking, Commerce, and Commodities," *Minnesota Law Review*, 98, 265–355, 2013.

Oppenheimer, H. R. and G. G. Schlarbaum, "Investing with Ben Graham: An Ex Ante Test of the Efficient Markets Hypothesis," *Journal of Financial and Quantitative Analysis*, 16, 3, 341–360, September 1981.

Partnoy, F., *Infectious Greed: How Deceit and Risk Corrupted the Financial Markets*, New York: Henry Holt, 2003.

Payne, J. W., "Task Complexity and Contingent Processing in Decision Making: An Information Search and Protocol Analysis," *Organizational Behavior and Human Performance*, 16, 366–387, 1976.

Peavy, J. W. and D. A. Goodman, "The Significance of P/Es for Portfolio Return," *Journal of Portfolio Management*, 9, 43–47, Winter 1983.

Pech, W. and M. Milan, "Behavioral Economics and the Economics of Keynes," *Journal of Socio-Economics*, 38, 891–902, 2009.

Penman, S. H., "The Quality of Financial Statements: Perspectives from the Recent Stock Market Bubble," *Accounting Horizons*, 17, Supplement, 77–96, 2003.

Penman, S. H., S. A. Richardson, and I. Tuna, "The Book-to-Price Effect in Stock Returns: Accounting for Leverage," *Journal of Accounting Research*, 45, 2, 427–467, May 2007.

Peng, L. and W. Xiong, "Investor Attention, Overconfidence and Category Learning," *Journal of Financial Economics*, 80, 563–602, 2006.

Perkins, A. B. and M. C. Perkins, *The Internet Bubble*, New York: HarperBusiness, 1999.

Persons, C. E., "Credit Expansion, 1920 to 1929, and Its Lessons," *Quarterly Journal of Economics*, 45, 1, 94–130, November 1930.

Peterson, D. and P. Peterson, "The Effect of Changing Expectations upon Stock Returns," *Journal of Financial and Quantitative Analysis*, 17, 5, 799–813, December 1982.

Pettis, M., *The Volatility Machine. Emerging Economies and the Threat of Financial Collapse*, Oxford and New York: Oxford University Press, 2001.

Philippon, T., "Has the US Finance Industry Become Less Efficient? On the Theory and Measurement of Financial Intermediation," *American Economic Review*, 105, 4, 1408–1438, 2015.

Piketty, T., *Capital in the Twenty-First Century*, Cambridge, MA: Belknap Press, 2014.

Piketty, T., E. Saez, and G. Zucman, "Distributional National Accounts: Methods and Estimates for the United States," NBER Working Paper #22945, December 2016.

Piotroski, J. D., "Value Investing: The Use of Historical Financial Statement Information to Separate Winners from Losers," *Journal of Accounting Research*, 38, 1–41, 2000.

Piotroski, J. D. and E. C. So, "Identifying Expectation Errors in Value/Glamour Strategies: A Fundamental Analysis Approach," *Review of Financial Studies*, 25, 9, 2841–2875, September 2012.

Plous, S., *The Psychology of Judgment and Decision-Making*, New York: McGraw-Hill, 1993.

Power, M., *Organized Uncertainty. Designing a World of Risk Management*, Oxford and New York: Oxford University Press, 2007.

Prechter, R. R., *The Socionomic Theory of Finance*, Gainesville, GA: Socionomics Institute Press, 2016.

Rabin, M., "Psychology and Economics," *Journal of Economic Literature*, 36, 11–46, 1998.

Rajan, R. G., "Has Financial Development Made the World Riskier?" NBER Working Paper #11728, November 2005.

Reinganum, M. R., "Misspecification of Capital Asset Pricing: Empirical Anomalies Based on Earnings' Yields and Market Values," *Journal of Financial Economics*, 9, 19–46, 1981.

Reinganum, M. R., "The Significance of Market Capitalization in Portfolio Management over Time," *Journal of Portfolio Management*, 26, 39–50, Summer 1999.

Reinhart, C. M. and K. S. Rogoff, *This Time Is Different: Eight Centuries of Financial Folly*, Princeton: Princeton University Press, 2009.

Rendleman, R. J., C. P. Jones, and H. A. Latane, "Empirical Anomalies Based on Unexpected Earnings and the Importance of Risk Adjustments," *Journal of Financial Economics*, 10, 269–287, 1982.

Richards, A. J., "Winner-Loser Reversals in National Stock Market Indices: Can They Be Explained?" *Journal of Finance*, 52, 5, 2129–2144, December 1997.

Richardson, S. A., R. G. Sloan, M. T. Soliman, and I. Tuna, "Accrual Reliability, Earnings Persistence, and Stock Prices," *Journal of Accounting and Economics*, 39, 437–485, 2005.

Rietz, T. A., "The Equity Premium Puzzle: A Solution," *Journal of Monetary Economics*, 22, 117–131, 1988.

Roll, R., "A Critique of the Asset Pricing Theory's Tests," *Journal of Financial Economics*, 4, 129–176, 1977.

Roll, R., "Vas ist das? The Turn-of-the-Year Effect and the Return Premia of Small Firms," *Journal of Portfolio Management*, 9, 18–28, Winter 1983.

Rose, A. M., "Rumor in the Stock Market," *Public Opinion Quarterly*, 15, 3, 461–486, Autumn 1951.

Rosenberg, B., K. Reid, and R. Lanstein, "Persuasive Evidence of Market Inefficiency," *Journal of Portfolio Management*, 11, 9–17, 1985.

Rosenberg, H., *The Vulture Investors*, New York: HarperBusiness, 1992.

Ross, S. A., "The Arbitrage Theory of Capital Asset Pricing," *Journal of Economic Theory*, 13, 341–360, 1976.

Rouwenhorst, K. G., "International Momentum Strategies," *Journal of Finance*, 53, 1, 267–84, February 1998.

Roychowdhury, S., "Earnings Management Through Real Activities Manipulation," *Journal of Accounting and Economics*, 42, 335–370, 2006.

Royster, V. "An Innocent Abroad," *Wall Street Journal*, April 20, 1983.

Rozeff, M. S. and W. R. Kinney, "Capital Market Seasonality: The Case of Stock Returns," *Journal of Financial Economics*, 3, 379–402, October 1976.

Rozeff, M. S. and M. A. Zaman, "Overreaction and Insider Trading: Evidence from Growth and Value Portfolios," *Journal of Finance*, 53, 2, 701–716, April 1998.

Rubinstein, M., "Securities Market Efficiency in an Arrow-Debreu Economy," *American Economic Review*, 65, 812–824, 1975.

Rubinstein, M., "Rational Markets: Yes or No? The Affirmative Case," *Financial Analysts Journal*, 57, 3, 15–29, 2001.

Schiereck, D., W. De Bondt, and M. Weber, "Contrarian and Momentum Strategies in Germany," *Financial Analysts Journal*, 55, 6, 104–116, November–December 1999.

Schmalensee, R., "An Experimental Study of Expectation Formation," *Econometrica*, 44, 1, 17–41, January 1976.

Schmeling, M., "Institutional and Individual Sentiment: Smart Money and Noise Trader Risk," *International Journal of Forecasting*, 23, 127–145, 2007.

Schmeling, M., "Investor Sentiment and Stock Returns: Some International Evidence," *Journal of Empirical Finance*, 16, 394–408, 2009.

Schoemaker, P. J. H., "The Expected Utility Model: Its Variants, Purposes, Evidence and Limitations," *Journal of Economic Literature*, 20, 2, 529–563, June 1982.

Schoemaker, P. J. H., "Determinants of Risk-Taking: Behavioral and Economic Views," *Journal of Risk and Uncertainty*, 6, 49–73, 1993.

Schularick, M. and A. M. Taylor, "Credit Booms Gone Bust: Monetary Policy, Leverage Cycles, and Financial Crises, 1870–2008," *American Economic Review*, 102, 2, 1029–1061, 2012.

Schultz, P. and M. Zaman, "Do the Individuals Closest to Internet Firms Believe That They Are Overvalued?" *Journal of Financial Economics*, 59, 3, 347–381, March 2001.

Schwartz, H., *Rationality Gone Awry? Decision-Making Inconsistent with Economic and Financial Theory*, Westport, CT: Praeger, 1998.

Scott, J., M. Stumpp, and P. Xu, "News, Not Trading Volume, Build Momentum," *Financial Analysts Journal*, 59, 2, 45–54, March–April 2003.

Searle, J. R., *Rationality in Action*, Cambridge, MA: MIT Press, 2001.

Shanken, J., "The Arbitrage Pricing Theory: Is It Testable?" *Journal of Finance*, 37, 5, 1129–1140, December 1982.

Shefrin, H., *Beyond Greed and Fear: Understanding Behavioral Finance and the Psychology of Investing*, New York: Oxford University Press, 1999.

Shefrin, H. (ed.), *Behavioral Finance*, London: Edward Elgar, 2001 (in 3 volumes).

Shefrin, H., *A Behavioral Approach to Asset Pricing*, Amsterdam: Elsevier Academic Press, 2005.

Shen, P., "The P/E Ratio and Stock Market Performance," *Federal Reserve Bank of Kansas City Economic Review*, 85, 4, 23–36, 2000.

Shen, P., "Market Timing Strategies That Worked," *Journal of Portfolio Management*, 29, 2, 57–68, Winter 2003.

Shen, P., "How Long Is a Long-Term Investment?" *Federal Reserve Bank of Kansas City Economic Review*, 5–32, 1st quarter 2005.

Shiller, R. J., "The Volatility of Long-Term Interest Rates and Expectation Models of the Term Structure," *Journal of Political Economy*, 87, 6, 1190–1219, December 1979.

Shiller, R. J., "Do Stock Prices Move Too Much to Be Justified by Subsequent Changes in Dividends?" *American Economic Review*, 71, 3, 421–436, June 1981.

Shiller, R. J., "Stock Prices and Social Dynamics," *Brookings Papers on Economic Activity*, 2, 457–510, 1984.

Shiller, R. J., "Theories of Aggregate Stock Price Movements," *Journal of Portfolio Management*, 10, 2, 28–37, Winter 1984.

Shiller, R. J., *Market Volatility*, Cambridge, MA: MIT Press, 1989.

Shiller, R. J., "Speculative Prices and Popular Models," *Journal of Economic Perspectives*, 4, 2, 55–85, Spring 1990.

Shiller, R. J., *Irrational Exuberance*, Princeton: Princeton University Press, 2000.

Shiller, R. J., "Bubbles, Human Judgment, and Expert Opinion," *Financial Analysts Journal*, 58, 3, 18–26, May–June 2002.

Shiller, R. J., "Speculative Asset Prices," Lecture, Sveriges Riksbank Prize in Economic Sciences in Memory of Alfred Nobel, December 8, 2013.

Shleifer, A., *Inefficient Markets*, New York: Oxford University Press, 2000.

Shleifer A., and L. H. Summers, "The Noise Trader Approach to Finance," *Journal of Economic Perspectives*, 4, 2, 19–33, Spring 1990.

Shleifer, A. and R. W. Vishny, "The Limits of Arbitrage," *Journal of Finance*, 52, 35–55, March 1997.

Siegel, J. J., *Stocks for the Long Run*, New York: McGraw-Hill, 2014 (5th edition).

Siegel, J. J. and R. H. Thaler, "Anomalies: The Equity Premium Puzzle," *Journal of Economic Perspectives*, 11, 1, 191–200, Winter 1997.

Simon, H. A., *Administrative Behavior: A Study of Decision-Making Processes in Administrative Organization*. New York: Free Press, 1945.

Simon, H. A., *Models of Man: Social and Rational*, New York: Wiley, 1957.

Simon, H. A., *Reason in Human Affairs*, Stanford: Stanford University Press, 1983.

Sinn, H.-W., *Casino Capitalism*. Oxford: Oxford University Press, 2010.

Sinn, H.-W., "Europe's Emerging Bubbles," *Project Syndicate*, March 28, 2016.

Skinner, D. J. and R. G. Sloan, "Earnings Surprises, Growth Expectations, and Stock Returns, or Don't Let an Earnings Torpedo Sink Your Portfolio," *Review of Accounting Studies*, 7, 289–312, 2002.

Sloan, R. G, "Do Stock Prices Fully Reflect Information in Accruals and Cash Flows About Future Earnings?" *Accounting Review*, 71, 3, 289–315, July 1996.

Slovic, P., "Information Processing, Situation Specificity, and the Generality of Risk-Taking Behavior," *Journal of Personality and Social Psychology*, 22, 128–134, 1972a.

Slovic, P., "Psychological Study of Human Judgment: Implications for Investment Decision-Making," *Journal of Finance*, 27, 4, 779–799, September 1972b.

Slovic, P., "The Affect Heuristic," in T. Gilovich, D. Griffin and D. Kahneman (eds.), *Heuristics and Biases: The Psychology of Intuitive Judgment*, 397–420, Cambridge: Cambridge University Press, 2002.

Smelser, N. J., *Theory of Collective Behavior*, New York: Free Press of Glencoe, 1963.

Smith, N., "Peak Finance Looks Like It's Over," *Bloomberg View*, September 27, 2016.

Smith, V. L., G. Suchanek, and A. Williams, "Bubbles, Crashes, and Endogenous Expectations in Experimental Spot Asset Markets," *Econometrica*, 56, 5, 1119–1151, September 1988.

Smith, V. L., *Rationality in Economics: Constructivist and Ecological Forms*, New York: Cambridge University Press, 2008.

Stambaugh, R., J. Yu, and Y. Yuan, "The Short of It: Investor Sentiment and Anomalies," *Journal of Financial Economics*, 104, 288–302, 2012.

Statman, M., K. Fisher, and D. Alginer,"Affect in a Behavioral Asset-Pricing Model," *Financial Analysts Journal*, 64, 2, 20–29, March–April 2008.

Stein, J. C., "Overheating in Credit Markets: Origins, Measurement, and Policy Responses," Speech, Federal Reserve Bank of St. Louis Research Symposium on "Restoring Household Financial Stability After the Great Recession," February 7, 2013.

Stickel, S. E., "Common Stock Returns Surrounding Earnings Forecast Revisions: More Puzzling Evidence," *Accounting Review*, 66, 2, 402–416, April 1991.

Stickel, S. E., "Reputation and Performance Among Security Analysts," *Journal of Finance*, 47, 5, 1811–1836, December 1992.

Stock, J. and M. Watson, "Has the Business Cycle Changed and Why?" *NBER Macroeconomics Annual*, 17, 159–224. Cambridge, MA: MIT Press, April 2002.

Stockman, D. A., "The End of Sound Money and the Triumph of Crony Capitalism," Henry Hazlitt Memorial Lecture, Mises Institute, March 12, 2011.

Stockman, D. A., *The Great Deformation. The Corruption of Capitalism in America*, New York: PublicAffairs, 2013.

Stout, L. A., "The Investor Confidence Game," 9th Annual Abraham L. Pomerantz Lecture, Brooklyn Law School, 2002.

Szyszka, A., *Behavioral Finance and Capital Markets: How Psychology Influences Investors and Corporations*, New York: Palgrave Macmillan, 2013.

Taleb, N. N., *The Black Swan: The Impact of the Highly Improbable*, New York: Random House, 2007.

Taussig, F. W., "Is Market Price Determinate?" *Quarterly Journal of Economics*, 35, 3, 394–411, May 1921.

Taylor, A. M., "The Great Leveraging," in V. V. Acharya et al. (eds.), *The Social Value of the Financial Sector: Too Big to Fail or Just Too Big?* Singapore: World Scientific Studies in International Economics, 29, 33–36, 2014.

Taylor, J. B., "The Cycle of Rules and Discretion in Economic Policy," Speech, Joint Luncheon of the American Economic Association and the American Finance Association (January 7, 2011), *National Affairs*, 7, 55–65, Spring 2011.

Taylor, J. B., *First Principles. Five Keys to Restoring America's Prosperity*. New York: W. W. Norton, 2012.

Teh, L. and W. F. M. De Bondt, "Herding Behavior and Stock Returns: An Exploratory Investigation," *Swiss Journal of Economics and Statistics*, 133, 293–324, 1997.

Temin, P. and H.-J. Voth, "Riding the South Sea Bubble," *American Economic Review*, 94, 5, 1654–1668, December 2004.

Tetlock, P. C., "Giving Content to Investor Sentiment: The Role of Media in the Stock Market," *Journal of Finance*, 63, 3, 1139–1168, June 2007.

Tetlock, P. C., "All the News That's Fit to Reprint: Do Investors React to Stale Information?" *Review of Financial Studies*, 24, 1481–1512, 2011.

Tetlock, P. C., M. Saar-Tsechansky, and S. Macskassy, "More Than Words: Quantifying Language to Measure Firms' Fundamentals," *Journal of Finance*, 63, 3, 1437–1467, June 2008.

Tetlock, P. E. and B. A. Mellers, "The Great Rationality Debate," *Psychological Science*, 13, 1, 94–99, January 2002.

Timmerman, A., "How Learning in Financial Markets Generates Excess Volatility and Predictability in Stock Prices," *Quarterly Journal of Economics*, 108, 1135–1145, 1993.

Tirole, J., "On the Possibility of Speculation Under Rational Expectations," *Econometrica*, 50, 5, 1163–1181, September 1982.

Townsend, R.M., "Market Anticipations, Rational Expectations, and Bayesian Analysis," *International Economic Review*, 19, 2, 481–494, June 1978.

Turner, A., "The Uses and Abuses of Economic Ideology," *Project Syndicate*, July 15, 2010.

Turner, A., "Debt and Demand," *Project Syndicate*, January 10, 2014a.

Turner, A., "In Praise of Fragmentation," *Project Syndicate*, February 18, 2014b.

Turner, A., *Between Debt and the Devil. Money, Credit, and Fixing Global Finance*, Princeton: Princeton University Press, 2016.

Tversky, A., "Intransitivity of Preferences," *Psychological Review*, 76, 31–48, 1969.

Tversky, A. and D. Kahneman, "Judgment Under Uncertainty: Heuristics and Biases," *Science*, 185, 1124–1131, 1974.

Tversky, A. and D. Kahneman, "Rational Choice and the Framing of Decisions," *Journal of Business*, 59, 67–94, October 1986.

Umstead, D. A., "Forecasting Stock Market Prices," *Journal of Finance*, 32, 2, 427–441, May 1977.

U.S. House of Representatives, "The Financial Crisis and the Role of Federal Regulators," Hearing before the Committee on Oversight and Government Reform, 110th Congress, Second session, October 23, 2008.

Verrecchia, R. E., "On the Theory of Market Efficiency," *Journal of Accounting and Economics*, 1, 77–90, 1979.

Verrecchia, R. E., "Consensus Beliefs, Information Acquisition, and Market Information Efficiency," *American Economic Review*, 70, 5, 874–884, December 1980.

Verrecchia, R. E, "Information Acquisition in a Noisy Rational Expectations Economy," *Econometrica*, 50, 6, 1415–1430, November 1982.

Vlek, C. and P. J. Stallen, "Rational and Personal Aspects of Risk," *Acta Psychologica*, 45, 273–300, 1980.

Walther, B. R., "Investor Sophistication and Market Earnings Expectations," *Journal of Accounting Research*, 35, 157–192, Autumn 1997.

Wang, P. and Y. Wen, "Speculative Bubbles and Financial Crises," *American Economic Journal: Macroeconomics*, 4, 3, 184–221, 2012.

Wang, Y.-H., A. Keswani, and S. J. Taylor, "The Relationships Between Sentiment, Returns and Volatility," *International Journal of Forecasting*, 22, 109–123, 2006.

Warneryd, K.-E., *Stock-Market Psychology: How People Value and Trade Stocks*, Cheltenham, UK: Edward Elgar, 2001.

Watts, R., "Systematic Abnormal Returns After Quarterly Earnings Announcements," *Journal of Financial Economics*, 6, 127–150, 1978.

Watts, R. and R. Leftwich, "The Time Series of Annual Accounting Earnings," *Journal of Accounting Research*, 15, 2, 253–271, Autumn 1977.

Weber, E. U. and R. A. Milliman, "Perceived Risk Attitudes: Relating Risk Perception to Risky Choice," *Management Science*, 43, 2, 123–144, February 1997.

Wermers, R., "Mutual Fund Herding and the Impact on Stock Prices," *Journal of Finance*, 54, 581–622, 1999.

Whittington, G., *The Prediction of Profitability and Other Studies of Company Behaviour*, Cambridge: Cambridge University Press,1971.

Wicksell, K., *Geldzins und Güterpreise*, Jena: Gustav Fischer, 1898.

Williams, J. B., *The Theory of Investment Value*, Amsterdam: North-Holland, 1956 (reprint of the 1938 edition).

Wolf, M., *The Shifts and the Shocks: What We've Learned and Have Still to Learn from the Financial Crisis*, New York: Penguin Press, 2014.

Wolff, E., "Household Wealth Trends in the United States, 1962–2013: What Happened over the Great Recession?" NBER Working Paper #20733, December 2014.

Working, H., "The Investigation of Economic Expectations,"*American Economic Review*, 39, 3, 150–166, May 1949.

Working, H., "A Theory of Anticipatory Prices," *American Economic Review*, 49, 2, 188–199, May 1958.

Wouters, T., *Style Investing: Behavioral Explanations of Stock Market Anomalies, Rijksuniversiteit Groningen*, Ridderkerk, Netherlands: Ridderprint, 2006.

Wray, L. R., "The Rise and Fall of Money Manager Capitalism: A Minskian Approach," *Cambridge Journal of Economics*, 33, 807–828, 2009.

Wright, B., "In the Topsy-Turvy World of Negative Interest Rates Even Gold Investment Start to Make Sense," *Daily Telegraph*, February 4, 2015.

Yu, J., "Disagreement and Return Predictability of Stock Portfolios," *Journal of Financial Economics*, 99, 162–183, 2011.

Yuan, Y., "Market-wide Attention, Trading, and Stock Returns," *Journal of Financial Economics*, 116, 548–564, 2015.

Zacks, L., "EPS Forecasts – Accuracy Is Not Enough," *Financial Analysts Journal*, 35, 2, 53–55, March–April 1979.

Zarowin, P., "Does the Stock Market Overreact to Corporate Earnings Information?" *Journal of Finance*, 44, 5, 1385–1399, December 1989.

Zarnowitz, V., "The Accuracy of Individual and Group Forecasts from Business Outlook Surveys," *Journal of Forecasting*, 3, 11–26, 1984.

Zingales, L., "The Cultural Revolution in Finance," *Journal of Financial Economics*, 117, 1–5, 2015.

Zuckerman, E. W., "The Categorical Imperative: Securities Analysts and the Illegitimacy Discount," *American Journal of Sociology*, 104, 5, 1398–1438, March 1999.

Zuckerman, E. W., "Structural Incoherence and Stock Market Activity," *American Sociological Review*, 69, 3, 405–432, June 2004.

5 Intertemporal Choice

Choosing for the Future

Daniel Read, Rebecca McDonald and Lisheng He

5.1 Introduction

Perhaps the majority of our choices are *intertemporal* ones, in which the options under consideration differ in their timing as well as (perhaps) a host of other things. Often these demand we choose between 'smaller sooner' (SS) and 'larger later' (LL) options, in which receiving more or better outcomes comes at a cost in timing. We make such a choice when deciding between immediately going on a short trip or saving our holiday allowance towards a longer but later getaway; or when choosing between getting the current version of a smartphone today or the next version once it is released. More broadly, you might choose to spend your money on consumption today, or invest the money to let yourself consume more later (since your investment will earn you interest). Choices might not even be between similar things: you might deliberate between buying a new TV now or saving towards a new car in a few months' time or having a more comfortable retirement. This choice is still intertemporal, though the options differ in many ways apart from their timing and magnitude.[1]

Discussion of intertemporal choice has a long history. In around 450 BC, Plato provided a surprisingly modern account in his dialogue *Protagoras*. He suggested (through his spokesperson Socrates) that outcomes further away in time are diminished in perception just as are objects farther away in *space*. Plato considered this a bias, asserting that the correct way to choose between was to ignore outcome delay and focus on outcome size, just as we should ignore distance when estimating the heights of distant objects:

> 'Do not objects of the same size appear larger to your sight when near, and smaller when at a distance? … And the same holds of thickness and number; also sounds, which are in themselves equal, are greater when near, and lesser when at a distance … Now suppose doing well to consist in doing or choosing the greater, and in not doing or avoiding the less, what would be the saving principal of human life? Would it be the art of measuring or the power of appearance?' (Plato, translated 1956, Section 356d).

Plato's *normative* account is based on the view that it is rational to take the larger of two outcomes, regardless of when they occur.

> 'If anyone says … the pleasure of the moment differs widely from future pleasure and pain, to that I should reply: And do they differ in anything but

in pleasure and pain? There is nothing else ... If you weigh pleasures against pleasures, you of course should take the more and greater; or if you weigh pains against pains, you should take the fewer and the less; or if pleasures against pains, then that course of action should be taken in which the painful is exceeded by the pleasant, whether the distant by the near or the near by the distant; and you should avoid that course of action in which the pleasant is exceeded by the painful' (Plato, translated 1956, Section 357b).

However, Plato's *psychological* account is one in which people, if insufficiently trained, are governed by their current time perspective and prefer sooner things ('seeing' them as if they were closer) rather than later. The issues Plato identified, involving the conflict between normative and descriptive accounts of decision-making, remain a central part of current discussions of intertemporal choice.

Many terms have been used for the driving force behind intertemporal choice, including delay of gratification, delay discounting, time discounting, impatience and time preference. All these terms capture, in a general sense, the rate at which people are willing to exchange earlier for later consumption. In economics, this is called the marginal rate of intertemporal substitution. The core concept is that outcomes are intrinsically less important to us the later they occur.

Before continuing, try making an intertemporal choice of your own. Imagine you are offered a choice between $100 today, or $120 in one year. You can be sure because of the integrity of those making the offer (i.e., the authors of this chapter) that you will receive the chosen sum at the chosen time. Would you take *SS* ($100 today) or *LL* ($120 in one year)? Exactly how much would the later amount have to be for you to be just willing to wait? Put your answer in the blank:

I would be indifferent between $100 today and $_____ in one year.

We will refer to the number you gave as X. By telling us X, it should be as though you were telling us, 'For any amount less than $X, I would choose *SS* over *LL*, but for any amount more than $X, I would choose *LL* over *SS*.'

Using X, you can now work out your personal discount rate for money.[2] Set up a fraction with X as the numerator and the earlier amount of $100 as the denominator, and subtract one from that fraction. For example, if you demanded $110 a year, then your discount rate would be 10 per cent, or 110/100 – 1 (in percentage terms). Our guess is that many readers will have wanted even more than the $120, implying a discount rate of at least 20 per cent.

5.2 The Normative Model

Let us analyse the choice between $100 now and $120 in one year. According to conventional economic analysis, there are three influences on whether you would take the $120. These are (1) the amount of interest the $100 today could have earned during the year; (2) the amount of interest it would cost you to borrow $100 and pay it back in one year; and (3) *the experimental interest rate*, which is given by $(X/100)-1$, in this case, 20 per cent.[3] To see why these are the only things that matter, imagine your bank offers a 5 per cent rate of return on savings, and charges a 25 per cent rate of interest on borrowing. (The savings rate of 5 per cent is a bit high by current standards, but the 25 per cent is about what it costs to borrow using a credit card.) If you take the $100 now, you can save it and then have $105 to spend in one year's time. So you should not specify X less than $105. In general, you should never take LL over SS if by doing so you would earn less than your best alternative (in this case, taking $100 and saving it in the bank).

What if the experimental interest rate was higher than your borrowing rate in the market? Then you should always choose LL. You should reject our $100 today, borrow $100 from the bank to spend instead and then in one year pay back the bank loan (plus the 25 per cent interest) with X, making a profit from the difference between X and the amount you owe the bank. If the experimental interest rate is less than 5 per cent or more than 25 per cent, the decision is easy. When you specified X, you *should not* have given a value less than the amount you would earn by investing the money, or greater than the amount it would cost you to borrow the money, regardless of how patient or impatient you are about consumption now and later.

What if the experimental interest rate is in between 5 per cent and 25 per cent, as it is when X is $120? Then what you should choose depends. Mostly it depends on your personal financial circumstances. If you are currently saving money at 5 per cent, and you can get a return of 20 per cent on some money, you should take LL. The reason is that even if you want to spend the money right now, you would be better off withdrawing $100 from your savings at the bank and spending that, and then depositing the $120 in the bank in one year. You will then be $15 better off, having spent $100 now, than if you had taken SS from the experimenter. If, on the other hand, you are currently in debt and paying 25 per cent interest, then you should take the $100 now and reduce your debt by that amount. That way you will pay $5 less in interest over the coming year.

But suppose you have no savings and no debt? This situation is a bit more complicated, because it depends on your consumption preferences. The basic intuition is clear. Roughly, if you would prefer to consume $100 now over $120 in one year, you should take SS; otherwise, you should take LL. More precisely, what you should choose depends on which option brings you to the highest indifference curve (discussed next). Since the person with no savings and debt can achieve different distributions of consumption by taking SS or LL, it is possible for either option to lead to the better distribution for them. A thorough discussion of these issues can be found in Cubitt and Read (2007). It should be emphasised, however, that this intermediate case will only apply to those people who are not currently saving or holding debt, and who are offered a choice implying an interest rate between their best saving and borrowing opportunity.

In reality, people do not have perfect access to saving and borrowing opportunities, so the choice of X might violate the economic predictions to some degree. To illustrate, if you are offered $100 in cash now as opposed to a direct deposit of $120 in one year, and you want to spend the $100, and would have to walk to an ATM to withdraw that amount, you might be willing to forego some future money to save yourself the walk. Or if you had to fill out a form and wait to borrow $100, you might forego some interest to not have to fill out the form. But these violations are likely to be quite minor, so the scale of violations typically observed in experiments and surveys (and, perhaps, in your own introspection when you previously specified X) is difficult to reconcile with the economic model. This is particularly true since the overwhelming majority of these violations imply discount rates that are *too high* (see Frederick, Loewenstein and O'Donoghue, 2002). Explaining this observation is one of the key objectives of behavioural economics. For instance, many people will prefer SS even when the experimental interest rate is greater than the rate of interest on their credit cards.

Let us take a step up in generality and consider a framework first formalised by Irving Fisher (1930) in the *Theory of Interest*. Imagine a person with a stock of resources. If they used up all their resources today, they would enjoy consumption at an amount C_1. Alternatively, those resources could all be saved up for tomorrow. Assume a *single* external rate for saving and borrowing, r, and that there are no additional costs to saving and borrowing. So if all of the resources were saved up, consumption next period could be $C_2 = C_1(1 + r)$. Alternatively, consumption can be spread out between the two periods. This gives an *intertemporal budget constraint* that describes all possible ways to distribute consumption over the two periods, given that any consumption not taken in Period 1 grows at interest rate r until it is consumed in Period 2.

The optimal point on the intertemporal budget constraint depends on the person's indifference curves for consumption across the two periods. The indifference curve plots all equally desirable combinations of C_1 and C_2, so the slope of the curve reflects their marginal rate of substitution (i.e., the rate they are willing to trade off) between consumption at times 1 and 2. For simplicity, let us first suppose a decision maker has a stable discount rate r^*, regardless of the allocation to each period. If her personal discount rate is equal to the external discount rate (i.e., $r^* = r$), her indifference curves are straight and parallel with the budget constraint line. Thus they are equally happy at any point along the budget constraint. If $r^* > r$, she will allocate all to C_1, and if $r^* < r$, she will allocate all to C_2. However, people usually prefer to smooth their consumption, and thus their indifference curve will be convex to the origin (i.e., $C_1 = C_2 = 0$), because when their consumption is concentrated in one period, they will forego quite a lot of it in that period for a small increase in consumption in the other period. As usual for optimisation problems, the highest attainable indifference curve is the one that is at a tangent to the budget constraint.

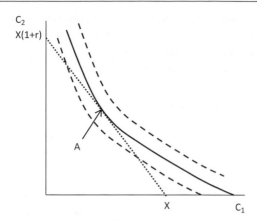

Figure 5.1. *How consumption is allocated across two time periods.*

Figure 5.1 illustrates such a case. This person will choose to allocate his or her consumption at point A.

Fisher (1930) assumed each person's time preference is determined by personal characteristics.[4] He also assumed that actual behaviour (intertemporal choices) would be influenced by each individual's current consumption circumstances and the individual's expectation of future consumption circumstances (since this would influence that person's perceived endowment of consumption in later periods, and hence his or her budget constraint). For example, a university student with a low current income might expect to earn more after graduation. She may therefore 'borrow' from her future self to smooth her consumption over time. Her choices might appear to give more weight to present than future consumption and be interpreted as showing a high level of impatience. Later, the same person might enjoy a good salary, but expect to retire in the next few years, when her income would be much lower. She may then reduce her consumption in the present and reallocate it to her future, retired self. This behaviour looks patient, as though she gives future consumption more weight in her decisions than present consumption. But conceivably, her private discount rate over this lifetime might be unchanged (she may be as impatient for dessert at age fifty as she was at age twenty). This demonstrates a nuance of intertemporal choice that is often overlooked in simple models of time preference: even if a person has positive, stable underlying time preferences, she may act in ways that appear (to a naïve observer) to be inconsistent so as to smooth her lifetime consumption.[5]

5.3 The Core Findings in Intertemporal Choice Research

The rational theory of intertemporal choice just laid out has important implications. One is that an individual's personal degree of impatience will not influence the intertemporal decisions he or she makes for money, at least not for relatively small amounts. We cannot describe this implication more concisely than Richard Thaler (1981):

> In the case of perfect capital markets, everyone behaves the same way *at the margin* since firms and individuals borrow or lend until their marginal rate of substitution between consumption today and consumption tomorrow is equal to the interest rate (p. 201, italics added).

As a corollary to this, each person's discount rate will be approximately the same in all settings involving monetary choice. The best known findings in intertemporal choice are called 'anomalies' because they are inconsistent with this economic model, or close relatives of that model similarly designed to reflect economic rationality (see Thaler, 1981; Loewenstein and Thaler, 1989; Roelofsma, 1996).

Most anomalies concern how differences in options influence preferences in ways that generate deviations from the predictions of a model based on a constant discount rate. There are two classes of anomalies: in the first class, differences in the objective properties of options influence preferences over those options; in the second class, economically irrelevant variations in choice circumstances or option description produce variations in preference. Here we give a brief tour of both classes of anomaly. In all cases, we will be discussing the *discount rate*, defined as the experimental interest rate which would render the decision-maker indifferent between an option now and an option later. For example, as discussed previously, someone indifferent between $100 now and $120 in one year will be said to display a 20 per cent discount rate for that decision.

5.3.1 The Sign Effect

The *sign effect* is that the discount rate is lower when choosing among delayed losses than delayed gains (Thaler, 1981). For instance, if we compare two choices, between *receiving* $100 today or $120 in one year, and between *paying* $100 today or $120 in one year, we would find a much higher proportion would pay today than would receive in one year. This contradicts the view that a single rate governs all decisions since anyone with a discount rate of less than 20 per cent would take the later money in the first choice and pay today in the second, while anyone with a rate greater than 20 per cent would show the reverse preference. The sign effect is even more extreme than this, since many people will prefer to pay now rather than to pay later, even if there is no financial advantage in waiting and indeed even if the amount to be paid is *greater* now than later (e.g., Hardisty, Appelt and Weber, 2013; Yates and Watts, 1975). Hardisty and Weber (2009) found that some domain differences in intertemporal choice (e.g., quantities of health are discounted at a different rate than quantities of money) are partly attributable to the differences in outcome signs, with health changes typically described as losses, and monetary changes described as gains.

5.3.2 The Magnitude Effect

The *magnitude effect* is that the discount rate is higher when choosing among small options than larger ones (Thaler, 1981). For instance, if we compare choices between receiving $100 today or $120 in one year, or receiving $1,000 today or $1,200 in one year, we would find a much higher proportion would choose to receive the larger delayed outcome than the smaller one. Again, this contradicts the idea of a single rate that governs all intertemporal decisions.

5.3.3 The Delay Effect

The *delay effect* is that people require lower rates of interest for long delays than for short ones (Thaler, 1981). For example, someone indifferent between $1,000 today and $1,200 in one year (implying a required interest rate of 20 per cent per annum) will prefer $1,440 in two years to $1,000 today (implying a required interest rate lower than 20 per cent per annum). Although the delay effect is often interpreted as evidence for hyperbolic discounting, it confounds hyperbolic discounting with subadditive discounting (Read, 2001), which is illustrated in the following section.

5.3.4 Subadditive Discounting

Subadditive discounting occurs when people are more impatient when the delay to an outcome is divided into subintervals than when it is undivided (e.g., Kinari, Ohtake and Tsutsui, 2009; McAlvanah, 2010; Read, 2001; Read and Roelofsma, 2003; Scholten and Read, 2006; 2010). Reconsider the example for the delay effect discussed in the preceding section. The preference for $1,440 in two years over $1,000 today could be due to a lower required interest rate for the interval between one year later and two years later (i.e., hyperbolic discounting) or a lower required interest rate for the two-year delay when it is undivided, relative to when it is divided into two one-year intervals (i.e., subadditive discounting).

5.3.5 The Common Difference Effect (and Its Reversal)

The *common difference effect* is that discounting over an interval changes as a function of the onset of the interval (Loewenstein and Prelec, 1992), with less discounting the later the interval begins. Tests of the common difference effect serve as evidence for hyperbolic discounting, free from the confusion of subadditive discounting. However, existing evidence has shown a mixture of constant impatience (e.g., Halevy, 2015; Read, 2001), decreasing impatience or hyperbolic discounting (e.g., Bleichrodt, Gao and Rohde, 2016; Green, Myerson and Macaux, 2005; Kinari et al., 2009; Read and Read, 2004; Read and Roelofsma, 2003; Scholten and Read, 2006; Sopher and Sheth, 2006) and increasing impatience or antihyperbolic discounting (e.g., Attema et al., 2010, 2016; Holcomb and Nelson, 1992; Read, Olivola and Hardisty, in press; Sayman and Öncüler, 2009).

5.3.6 Sequence Effects

Intertemporal choices between sequences of positive outcomes have been shown to be different from those between single-dated outcomes. Most compellingly, *negative time preference*, which means a preference for a positive outcome to take place later rather than earlier, has been frequently observed when subjects choose between intertemporal sequences (Loewenstein and Prelec, 1993; Loewenstein and Sicherman, 1991; Read and Powell, 2002; Rubinstein, 2003), but is rarely observed when they are asked to choose between two single-dated outcomes. However, this preference for increasing sequences is not at all a universal phenomenon (Gigliotti and Sopher, 1997; Manzini, Mariotti and Mittone, 2010; Scholten, Read and Sanborn, 2016). More research is needed to determine when people prefer increasing sequences, and when they prefer to take rewards early.

5.3.7 Framing Effects Versus Procedural Invariance

Normatively equivalent elicitation methods should elicit the same preferences for the same choice options (Tversky, Sattath and Slovic, 1988). However, diverse framing effects found in intertemporal choice have demonstrated violations of this principle of *procedural invariance*. The *delay/speed-up asymmetry* is that people tend to be more impatient when an intertemporal choice is described as SS being delayed to LL than when it is described as LL being expedited to SS (Loewenstein, 1988; Scholten and Read, 2013; Weber et al., 2007). The *date/delay effect* is that people tend to be less impatient when time is described with calendar dates than with the length of delays (LeBoeuf, 2006; Read et al., 2005). *Outcome framing effects* are that people exhibit different degrees of impatience when the outcomes are framed in different terms, such as an interest rate, the gross interest earned or the total amount earned (Read et al., 2005; Read, Frederick and Scholten, 2013). The *(asymmetric) hidden-zero effect* is that the explicit display of getting nothing at a later time in the SS option reduces impatience (e.g., Magen, Dweck and Gross, 2008; Read et al., in press; Wu and He, 2012). This research is in line with an argument put forward by Ebert and Prelec (2007) that the impact of time is uniquely 'fragile', meaning that small manipulations can markedly increase the impact of time on choice, or reduce that impact almost to nothing.

5.3.8 A Brief Note on Neuroeconomics

The wide range of anomalies just described illustrates just how much even monetary discounting (which theoretically should be constant for all outcomes and roughly constant across people) is highly malleable, and contingent on a wide range of cognitive and affective processes (see Lempert and Phelps, 2016, for a further review). An important approach to understanding intertemporal choice is through the relatively new field of neuroeconomics (Loewenstein, Rick and Cohen, 2008). This approach attempts to look directly at processes occurring in the brain to pinpoint physiological drivers of intertemporal choice. Much neuroeconomics has focussed on whether intertemporal choice is governed by dual systems (Faralla et al., 2015; McClure et al., 2004, 2007;) or a unitary system (Kable and Glimcher, 2007, 2010). A second line of studies tries to reveal the neural underpinnings that determine individual differences in impatience by comparing brain-lesion patients with healthy people (Manuck et al., 2003; Sellitto, Ciaramelli and di Pellegrino, 2010), associating activation in certain brain regions with impatience measures from intertemporal choice (Hariri et al., 2006; Kayser et al., 2012; Smith et al., 2016) or external control of certain brain regions (Figner et al., 2010; Kayser et al., 2012). The neural evidence is growing rapidly but yet remains inconclusive (see Kable, 2013, for a review). It is likely, however, that in future versions of this chapter the classic anomalies in intertemporal choice will be further clarified by greater understanding of the physiological processes that lead to choice in intertemporal settings.

5.4 Functional Forms and Inconsistency

In the previous section, we discussed empirical anomalies to the Fisher model. Here we return to the idealised economic models and go more deeply into the problem of dynamic inconsistency. The original, convenient and elegant model of time preference is exponential, formalised by Paul Samuelson in 1937. This model assumes that time preference can be captured by a single parameter, the discount rate. This is applied through an exponential function, so consumption worth X after a delay of t years is worth $\dfrac{X}{(1+r)^t}$ today with an annual discount rate of r. This model is analytically tractable and also provides a normative framework, since it will lead to consistency over time in decision-making ('dynamic consistency'). To illustrate dynamic consistency, imagine a person today who has a 10 per cent discount rate, applied exponentially. She will be indifferent between receiving consumption worth 110 utils[6] in one year or 121 utils in two years, since her present value of both 110 utils in one year and 121 utils in two years is precisely the same at 100 utils. Now imagine that one year passes. Will she still be indifferent between the options she had considered the previous year? The 110 utils are now available. The 121 are now due in one year, and given exponential discounting also have a present value of 110 utils. So her relative present value of the two outcomes is unchanged by the passage of time, and her choices will be dynamically consistent.

We discussed preferences over utils here, rather than over amounts of money, but experiments often involve people choosing between money. To interpret discount rates elicited from money amounts as revealing and underlying discount rate over consumption (or even utils), these studies make two assumptions. The first is that there is a direct link between monetary experimental receipts and consumption (or utils), so that £1 today gives £1 of consumption (or its equivalent utils) today, while £100 in one year gives £100 of consumption (or its equivalent utils) in one year, or at least it gives anticipated or perceived consumption of those utils at those times. Second, they assume 'narrow bracketing' in which respondents think about the choices in isolation, ignoring the opportunity costs of their decisions as determined by financial markets, as discussed in the earlier section.

The exponential discounting model and the dynamic consistency it implies is not, and indeed was never expected to be, descriptively accurate. To see how, let us return to *Protagoras*. In it, Plato describes a person who follows 'the power of appearance' rather than 'the art of measuring'. Plato is not optimistic about how this will turn out. Speaking of the power of appearance, he asks:

> Is it not that deceiving art which makes us wander up and down and take at one time the things of which we repent at another, both in our actions and in our choice of things great and small? But the art of measurement would invalidate the power of appearance and, showing the truth, would fain teach the soul at last to find lasting rest in the truth, and would thus save our life (Plato, translated 1956, Section 356d).

We can illustrate with an example of comparing the heights of two skyscrapers, where the taller is slightly farther. When both are distant, the taller correctly appears to be taller. However, if you walk towards the skyscrapers, eventually the relative heights of the skyscrapers will reverse in your perception, so the closer but shorter one will appear to be largest, until the farther but taller one disappears. This is a powerful metaphor for time inconsistency and impatience.

While we are in conversation with the ancients, consider Odysseus and the sirens. Odysseus longs to hear the sirens, but their song is deadly as it lures sailors to crash their ships onto the rocks of their island. It is in Odysseus's long-run interests to hear the song of the sirens without crashing, and we can think of 'hear the song, don't crash the ship', as his original plan.[7] However, Odysseus knows that in the heat of the moment, he would not be able to resist the temptation to run his ship onto the rocks. That is, he cannot trust his short-run self to carry out the original plan. This is the classic failure of dynamic consistency.

This passage from the Odyssey motivates Robert Strotz's (1955) classic paper 'Myopia and Dynamic Inconsistency in Dynamic Utility Maximization'. He

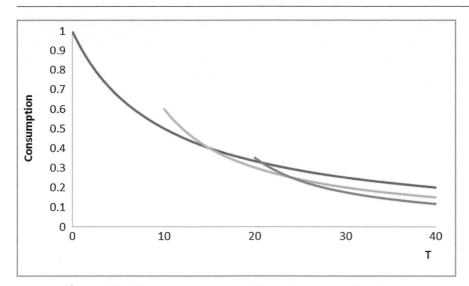

Figure 5.2. *How consumption is reallocated over time (based on Strotz, 1955).*

describes the behaviour he would expect of an agent, like Odysseus, with dynamically inconsistent preferences. He proposes this agent starts life with a stock of resources which must last his entire life. He makes a consumption plan for those resources. The plan involves relatively even spreading, with some privilege given to earlier consumption, so that the consumption plan declines over time. This is the initial plan, which is depicted as the darkest line in Figure 5.2. Strotz suggests that when this agent has the opportunity to reevaluate his plan, he will reallocate his consumption, favouring his (then) current interests over those of his future selves. This allows a little less consumption for later. Subsequent reevaluations will repeat this, with the agent drawing more and more consumption from his future selves into the present.

Strotz proposes that someone who does not recognise this tendency in himself will behave as a 'spendthrift' or else as a 'miser', 'his behaviour being inconsistent with his plans' (Strotz, 1955, p. 165). O'Donoghue and Rabin (1999) refer to these unaware actors as *naïfs*, contrasted with *sophisticates* who anticipate their potential inconsistency. Sophisticates can adopt one of two broad classes of strategy to alleviate or forestall their inconsistency. The first is the use of consistent planning in which knowledge about future behaviour is taken into account at the time of the initial plan. That is, the initial plan is made such that even the impatient future self will leave the plan unchanged. The second strategy is precommitment. For example, the agent could lock her resources into a pension plan that can only be released at a much later time, so the greedy early selves cannot pilfer it. This second type of strategy is the one chosen by Odysseus, who had his sailors plug their ears with wax so they were not tempted by the Sirens' song. Then he had them bind him to the mast of his ship, ears unplugged, so he could hear the song without being able to default on the original plan (i.e., 'don't crash the ship'). Odysseus, indeed, found a way to cheat the system by having his cake and eating it too, by hearing the Sirens without crashing the ship. Here is a passage from the translation by Lawrence of Arabia (T. E. Lawrence) himself:

> Only myself may listen [to the sirens], after you have so fastened me with tight-drawn cords that I stand immovably secured against the tabernacle of the mast ... and if I beg or bid you to let me loose, then must you redoubly firm me into place with yet more bonds (Homer, translated 1932, p. 217).

A little introspection will provide plenty of examples where we might behave like Strotz's agent, or like Odysseus would have if not fastened to the mast. Consider any time you have decided to eat healthily, then given in to a slice of cake, or planned to save carbon by taking the bus, but succumbed to the temptation to drive instead. There are also occasions where we employ a strategy of consistent planning: we might stuff ourselves with healthy snacks so we do not want any cake, or plan our travels for times when the roads will be so busy we will not want to drive. We might instead precommit, by giving the cake away to our colleagues, or buy a week's bus pass in advance and hand our car keys over to a friend.

Given the power of the metaphor and the abundance of real-life examples, it is not surprising that situations where we might expect violations of the predictions of the exponential model have been extensively studied. As mentioned earlier, this has often been done using SS-LL monetary amounts, although these studies have not been so conclusive. In nonmonetary domains, however, evidence for Odysseus-like violations are widespread as in the earlier-mentioned papers by Shapiro (2005) and Read and Van Leeuwen (1998).

Here we briefly outline some models of intertemporal choice that attempt to account for this type of behaviour. Hyperbolic discounting models, first named by Chung and Herrnstein (1961) and strongly advocated by Ainslie (1975, 2001), are the best established class of models to account for Strotz-like preference reversals (for a review, see Andersen et al., 2014). In these models, the discount rate declines with the time horizon between now and the event, approaching zero as that horizon becomes very remote. The most familiar variant of hyperbolic discounting is the one proposed by Mazur (1987), where

consumption worth X today is worth $\dfrac{X}{1+kt}$ after a delay of time t. This has

two major consequences. First, when we look into the future and compare two distant outcomes with one more delayed to the other, these outcomes are discounted to a very similar extent, and so we may choose the larger later outcome. However, the same difference separating outcomes close to us in time generates a much bigger difference between the present values, so we might wish to choose the smaller sooner outcome.

An alternative form, which has become extremely influential in economics, is quasi-hyperbolic (or, 'β-δ') discounting (O'Donoghue and Rabin, 2000; Phelps and Pollak, 1968; Elster, 1979; Laibson, 1997). Additional weight is placed on the current period, but the rest of the time horizon is characterised by exponential discounting. This allows preference reversals as proposed by Strotz, but is mathematically convenient. The format for this model is exponential discounting, but with an additional weight $\beta < 1$ that applies to every period after the current one, giving a 'present bias'. Formally:

$$\frac{X}{(1+r)^t} = X \qquad \text{if} \quad \text{t=0}$$

$$\frac{\beta X}{(1+r)^t} \qquad \text{if} \quad \text{t>0}$$

Quasi-hyperbolic discounting differs from 'true' hyperbolic discounting in that it does not lead people to discount far-future outcomes at a very low marginal rate. To illustrate, imagine someone evaluating two future outcomes – the loss of 1,000 lives in 20 years, or the loss of 1,000 lives in 40 years. For a quasi-hyperbolic discounter, the proportional reduction in value for each additional year would be the same regardless of when that year occurs (as long as it was not the first, which would be discounted more). For a true hyperbolic discounter, however, the proportional reduction in value is less for each year of additional delay. True hyperbolic discounting entails that people will care more than they 'should' about outcomes delayed for a very long time, as well as less than they 'should' about outcomes delayed for a very short time.

It is often claimed that the delay until an outcome drives a decline in the discount rate, which motivates the hyperbolic models we discussed. However, there is an alternative interpretation. Declining discount rates are observed in SS-LL studies where SS is now and LL is increasingly later. But this design confounds the delay from now until LL with the interval between S and L. What if the interval was driving the declining rates, and not the delay? This proposition motivated the development of subadditive discounting models (e.g., Read, 2001).

Subadditive models assume that the per-period discount rate elicited from SS-LL choices when a long interval separates them is lower than the per-period discount rate elicited from the same interval when it is subdivided. The discounting function is then given by $\dfrac{X}{(1+r)^{(t_L - t_S)^{\psi}}}$, where ψ captures the non-linear perception of time (individuals perceive short intervals as longer than they are, and long ones as shorter than they are, as explained in Read, 2001). The difference $t_L - t_S$ captures the delay until the later and earlier outcome (and hence the interval between them) and r is, as usual, the discount rate.

The subadditive model is consistent with a wide range of empirical results (Glimcher, Kable and Louie, 2007; Kable and Glimcher, 2010; McAlvanah, 2010; Read, 2001; Read and Roelofsma, 2003), although it may be that both subadditive and hyperbolic discounting work together (see Scholten and Read, 2006). The idea that distortions in time perception drive intertemporal choice (at least in part) is now well established (Takahashi, 2005; Zauberman et al., 2009).

These are by no means the only models proposed to explain behaviour that cannot be captured in an exponential discounting framework (see the review in Doyle, 2013). Here, we have highlighted the role for nonexponential models of discounting that may apply across domains and in many real-world applications. However, the majority of existing nonexponential models are designed to accommodate relatively few effects and mostly focus on explaining the purported tendency to prefer SS in choices between now and later, but LL when the choices are between later and even later (i.e., the common difference effect). These models frequently ignore the abundance of evidence for other violations of the normative model.

So far, we have considered discounting for money, consumption or utility. Under standard economic theory, if commodities, experiences and outcomes can be translated into one another (i.e., if they are fully fungible), then there is no need to look any further than discounting for utility, since agents will distribute their resources into a consumption stream that maximises discounted utility. However, it is an open empirical question whether a single-time preference rate for each person is sufficient to explain behaviour across all contexts, or whether discounting could be domain-specific. We take up this question next.

5.5 Commodity Specific Discounting

To think about discounting for different commodities (e.g., candy and money), we need information about how someone would be willing to trade across commodities and across time. We first need to distinguish between the own-rate and money-rate of discount. The own-rate is the discount rate of a good measured in terms of itself. For instance, if Heather thinks six candies one year from now are as good as three now, her candy-rate of interest is 100 per cent. The money rate of discount depends on what Heather is willing to pay for candies. Suppose she is indifferent between $1.00 worth (to her) of candies today and $1.50 worth of candies in one year. Her money rate of discounting for candies is 50 per cent. For this analysis, we do not mind how many candies this equates to. However, to see whether her money rate and her own-rate of discounting are consistent, we need to add this information.

Suppose Heather is willing to pay $1.00 for three candies today. If she is consistent and rational (in economic terms), we can make four inferences. First, since she is indifferent between three candies today and six the next year, and indifferent between three candies today and $1 today, she will also be indifferent between $1.50 next year and six candies next year. She will be willing to pay $1 today for six candies next year and will be willing to pay $1.50 in one year to get three candies *today*. Finally, she will treat paying $1 today as equivalent to paying $1.50 in one year, so her discount rate for money is the same as her money discount rate for candies. For Heather, all four outcomes are exactly as good as one another.

A similar analysis can be carried out when there is market for a good. We can analyse that market to determine what the commodity's own-rate and its money-rate should be. You can think of this as a scaled-up version of Heather's preferences, with the difference that these are now market prices as opposed to her private willingness to pay – the equivalences are between market prices and quantities of a commodity. If the market perfectly clears, it will imply consistency between the outcomes over time. Like for Heather, in the market, the four outcomes are precisely equivalent in their value. Figure 5.3 shows forward interest rates (the price to transform outcomes at one time to outcomes at a different time) and spot rates (the price to transform outcomes of one kind into outcomes of another kind).

Why do the own-rates of interest differ from commodity to commodity? Keynes (1936) described three determinants of discount rates: The *yield*, the *carrying cost* and the *liquidity premium*. The yield is the benefit from using a good. For some goods, earlier receipt is better because you can start using them right away and get more total use out of them. This can apply to durables such as houses, land and radios, but usually not to consumables such as candies that are likely to be consumed at the same rate regardless of when they are received and will then be largely forgotten. *Carrying cost* refers to the costs of having to hold on to something for a period of time, and includes things such as storage, obsolescence, spoilage and wastage. An increased carrying cost will decrease the discount rate because if you want to consume something in the future, you prefer not to have it until then – it is better not to receive tomorrow's dinner today. The third determinant is the *liquidity premium*. This refers to how easily something can be converted into something else. Cash money is the most liquid, since it can be easily converted into other types of consumption. But if that money is invested in a pension, it cannot easily be converted into other consumption (at least, not until you retire). Keeping money liquid, therefore, is worth something.

A separate issue, which might make a larger amount proportionally less attractive than a smaller, is *satiation*.[8] For example, imagine a choice between two donuts today and four in one year. Suppose you take the two donuts today. This does not mean you discount the pleasure-from-donuts at a rate of 100 per cent or more (as one might naïvely assume from your choice of SS). Instead, the later donuts are less valuable because of your *diminishing marginal utility for donuts* as well as your *donut discount rate*. These two reasons can be tricky to disentangle empirically, although recent studies have tried to address this by

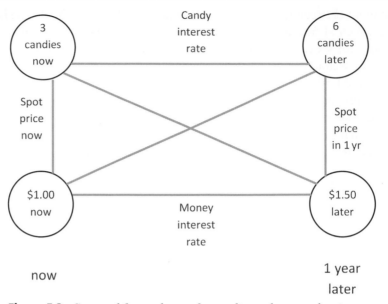

Figure 5.3. *Spot and forward rates for candies and money showing equivalence between outcomes.*

either double elicitation of both utility curvature and the discounting function (Andersen et al., 2008) or avoiding utility curvature through their experimental design (Attema et al., 2010; Laury, McInnes and Swarthout, 2012).

5.6 Approaches to Measuring Commodity-Specific Discounting

We have discussed various reasons, compatible with rational decision-making, that could generate different strengths of preference for sooner and later receipt across different goods even if the underlying discount rates are identical. This line of reasoning is often not pursued by researchers investigating the discounting of different goods, and yet these issues pervade all types of intertemporal choices. Indeed, a large number of results show domain-specific discounting can be easily accounted for by Keynesian factors and satiation. Further, after taking account of diminishing marginal utility, liquidity, carrying costs and yields, the normative models have at their heart the assumption that there is one 'true' underlying discount rate. This can be thought of as the discount rate for utility over time. (We are using 'utility' in the sense of a measure or index of good that can be added up, as in Edgeworth (1879), though we recognise there are many different interpretations of the concept).[9] However, many scholars take the view there are intrinsic differences between the discount rate for different commodities. For example, Berns, Laibson and Loewenstein (2007) suggest a key role for the determinants of intertemporal choice that are unrelated to discounting per se. They focus on anticipation, self-control and representation and argue for a unifying theory of intertemporal choice that accounts for these effects. But to explore these issues and develop such a theory, we need a way to compare discount rates across different commodities. We can conceive of four possibilities.

The first possibility is to examine the amount of a good that, if received today, is equivalent to receiving some other amount at a later date (Option 1). This is the essence of the SS-LL experimental paradigm, but is vulnerable to all the practical constraints we have discussed so far: it requires a proportional relationship between quantities of the good and their value and perfect divisibility of goods. This often renders the approach unsuitable. For example, remember Heather, who is indifferent between three candies today or six candies in one year. Imagine she is also indifferent between two pens today or three pens in one year. If we can say for sure that six candies are valued twice as highly as three candies, or that three pens are 1.5 times as good as two pens, then we can infer that her discount rate for candies is 100 per cent while that for pens is 50 per cent. But we cannot be sure about this relationship. A more fundamental question is whether there is any meaningful comparison between the 100 per cent for pens and the fifty for candies. If these numbers represent the proportional loss of 'utility' that arises from a one-year delay to each of them, they would be comparable, and this is the approach often taken in the literature (e.g., Chapman, 1996, elicits proportional loss for health and for money and directly compares these). But it is an open question whether these numbers can really be compared directly. Another serious problem with this approach is that it restricts us to looking at divisible goods, and ones for which we can assume constant marginal utility (or else correct for nonlinearity).

Since the first possibility – eliciting own-rate discounting – seems problematic, we next consider approaches that share the same foundation: making use of some common currency or 'numeraire' to allow comparison of discounting across commodities.

The first of these is to find the 'numeraire equivalent' value of an outcome occurring today (Option 2). We can then ask, if I delay the outcome by t days, what is the 'numeraire equivalent' of this delayed outcome? That is, how much of the numeraire today would be equivalent to receiving the good after the delay? By taking the proportion of the numeraire that is lost when delaying different commodities, we have elicited the *numeraire-rate* of discounting for each of them. These discount rates are directly comparable to one another, although the rate of discount for different numeraires will not necessarily be the same.[10] Crucially, however, the ordering of the magnitude of discount rates should be the same regardless of the numeraire. The alternative numeraire approach is to elicit a value (in terms of the numeraire) of different levels of the commodity. We can ask what amount of the commodity now is equally preferred to a fixed quantity of that commodity after a specified delay, translate these commodity amounts into the numeraire and calculate the implied rate of discount. Doing this for a range of commodities permits us to *compare* them in terms of the amount to which they are discounted.

A variant on the numeraire approaches is the Delayed Compensation Method (DCM) introduced in Cubitt, McDonald and Read (in press) (Option 3). This method asks what amount of money, received after a delay, would be enough to make a person indifferent between their most preferred out of two options and their least preferred plus the money amount. The benefit of the DCM is that the options can be any goods available at any dates. The DCM approach does not require the outcomes to be divisible, nor do they have to satisfy nonsatiation. We can, for instance, ask how much money you would require to delay the receipt of a Ferrari by one year. So this approach opens up the possibility for a wide range of research questions in intertemporal choice that have previously been closed. However, the method does not directly give an estimate of the discount rate, instead giving comparative information about how heavily things are discounted.

A final option is to avoid the elicitation of discount rates altogether, but instead to see how the relative preference for two options changes over time (Option 4). Take two goods that are equally preferred. To make it concrete, imagine someone is indifferent between two pens and three candies, if they could have them right now. If candies and pens are discounted at the same rate, then delaying the receipt of *both* the candies and the pen by one year will not change the relative preference between them: the person will still be indifferent. Now suppose pens are actually discounted by more than candies. In that case, if both the pens and the candies are delayed by one year, then the person will now prefer the candies (from the perspective of the present).

5.7 Prior Research into Commodity-Specific Discounting

We have just explained several potential pitfalls to avoid when investigating intertemporal choices for non-monetary goods. We have made clear our reservations about Option 1, which was to find out what proportion of its value something loses as a function of delay by matching quantities of an outcome over time. Nonetheless, the majority of existing studies have drawn on versions of Option 1. We will outline some of the major contributions to the literature and discuss whether they can be interpreted as revealing respondents' underlying discount rates.

Ubfal (2016) used Option 1 to elicit the discount rate for different goods, including money. The goods were chosen to be divisible in some way, such as meat, sugar and bottles of perfume, or else were described in monetary terms such as vouchers for school supplies and phone airtime. In other conditions, the goods were described in '$-worth' terms, as in '$1 worth of meat'. Ubfal found rates ranging from 66 per cent to 110 per cent per month, with discounting for money on the higher end of that range (90 per cent per month). The use of $-worth values aims to avoid problems with unobservable value functions, but does not fully accomplish this because the relevant money amount is actually the individual's willingness to pay for options, rather than the market price of those options.[11] For instance, if a person is given a choice between a Bic pen now (costing $1) and a Mont Blanc pen in one year (costing $500) and they take the Bic pen, this does not mean that they have a discount rate of 50,000 per cent for pens. More likely, they do not perceive the fancy pen to be 500 times as valuable to them as the Bic. Ubfal (2016) did attempt to control for this by eliciting a utility curvature estimate for money and then applying this across all goods, but of course the problem is not the utility function for money, but for the goods being discounted. Ubfal suggested an interesting next step would be to do this on a good-specific basis.

Weatherly and Ferraro (2011) also used Option 1 to elicit and compare discount rates for different commodities. They explored outcomes such as debts owed and money won, federal legislation on education, having your ideal body and even finding the love of your life. They used the Area Under the Curve (AUC) method (see Myerson, Green and Warusawitharana, 2001), finding differences in discount rates across commodities. They made no concession for how much the outcomes are liked in the first place. However, their results indicate different domains of outcomes, where discounting is related within the domain but not between domains. This idea fits well with the suggestion that discounting will depend on a range of factors, such as visceral influences, satiation and so on, which might be expected to apply similarly within outcome domains.

Knapman and Tronde (2011) investigated closely related, yet not identical rewards. They found that different rewards from hypothetical airline schemes are discounted differently. However, their study demonstrates the difficulty in finding convincing divisibility in nonmonetary rewards, since in their quest to find divisible outcomes they have to assume constant marginal utility of the distance of a reward flight. For example, they calculate discounting on the basis of choices such as 'I would accept a free flight of __ km in 1 month in lieu of a free flight of 17000 kilometres in two months'. It is likely, for instance, that a free flight to the middle of the Pacific Ocean is worth less than half that to an airport even closer, and someone whose relatives live 500 kilometres away might not want a 2,000 kilometre flight.

Other scholars have taken an approach much more aligned with our Option 4 and investigated time preferences without eliciting a discount rate per se. Some examples include Read, Loewenstein and Kalyanaraman (1999), who examined preference reversals for high- and low-brow movie rentals and lotteries, and Read and van Leeuwen (1998), who investigated preference reversals for snack foods under hot and cold states. Another is Kirby and Herrnstein (1995), who used consumer goods and titrated the delay until preferences were reversed, providing evidence that different consumer goods have different discount rates – in Kirby and Herrnstein's case, either because the goods were differentially delayed in time, or because they were different goods. In none of these studies were the authors able to directly measure the discount rates for goods, since there was no common currency with which to do so. From their results, however, we can conclude that (for instance) junk food snacks have higher discount rates than healthy snacks (Read and Van Leeuwen, 1998), that low-brow movies have higher discount rates than high-brow ones (Read et al., 1999), and that immediate average-quality goods have lower discount rates than delayed higher-quality goods (Kirby and Herrnstein, 1995).

To get around the problems of yield and carrying costs, some innovative researchers have considered 'directly consumable rewards'. In the early work in this area, subjects were usually drug addicts and rewards were hypothetical. Bickel and Marsch (2001) reviewed the literature, and found that in most cases drug abusers discount the drug they abuse more than they discount money.[12] More recently, research has tended to focus on food choices with real incentives (i.e., the food or drink is consumed in the experiment). For example, Estle and colleagues (2007) compared the discounting of candy and drinks (i.e., soda and beer) and concluded that people discount the consumption of candy and drinks far more steeply than money. Reuben, Sapienza and Zingales (2010) compared the discounting of money and chocolate. To avoid satiation, they picked small, fancy chocolates that were not easily available on the market. They found the discount rates for money and chocolates are moderately correlated, but could not compare those rates directly. Tsukayama and Duckworth (2010) elicited discount rates for chips, candy, beer and money and measured impatience with Area Under the Curve. Although they argued that directly consumable goods (i.e., chips, candy and beer) are discounted more steeply than money, they did not match utility across goods, so it is hard to know if the discount rates are truly comparable. However, Tsukayama and Duckworth (2010) drew a second line between directly consumable goods and money by showing that the correlation between discount rates of money and that of consumable goods are lower than the correlation of discount rates among different directly consumable goods. Food is a useful vehicle for studying intertemporal choice because the associated utility gain is received as soon as the food is consumed (and in the laboratory this can be tightly controlled). There are no concerns about storage or yield. There is another category of outcomes that fill this brief as well. These are *experienced* outcomes.

George Loewenstein has been highly innovative in this area, and has shown how apparently divergent discount rates for different goods can be consistent with the same underlying discount rate for utility. He has proposed the consumption of nonmonetary goods is associated with violations of additive separability, the assumption that the receipt of an outcome has no impact on the value placed on a future outcome. Loewenstein and Prelec (1993) proposed that people like their experiences to improve rather than to get worse over time, even if individually the experiences are the same. Later work (e.g., Frederick and Loewenstein, 2008) showed that a preference for improvement is not universal, and identified a wide range of motives for sequence preferences: (1) anticipation and dread, (2) contrast effects, (3) extrapolation, (4) uncertainty, (5) opportunity cost, (6) pure time preference, (7) diminishing marginal utility, (8) equity among selves and (9) the divide equally heuristic. Among them, 1 through 3 are factors favouring improving sequences, 4 through 6 are factors favouring deteriorating sequences and 7 through 9 are factors favouring flat sequences. Read and Powell (2002) similarly proposed (and demonstrated the existence of) a wide range of motives for sequence preferences, which also implied that a wide range of patterns could be observed.

Loewenstein (1987) and Rick and Loewenstein (2008) also proposed that future good and bad experiences could be augmented by anticipation. Knowing that you are going to have a positive experience in the future produces savouring, which may make you prefer to delay the experience rather than take it right away; and knowing you will have a negative experience can make you so anxious that you want to get it over with. Many researchers have since shown that dread, in particular, is a powerful motivator. People often want to get unpleasant experiences out of the way, and will even take a worse bad experience now in exchange for a better bad experience later (as predicted by Loewenstein, 1987). This produces high rates of apparent 'negative discounting' (Casari and Dragone, 2011; Harris, 2012; Story et al., 2013). Loewenstein (1987) suggested these effects are a legitimate part of a behaviourally accurate discounting model.

> Since DU [discounted utility] does not ordinarily incorporate savouring or dread, and since both of these factors attenuate devaluation, conventional estimates of discount rates should be biased downward, especially in situations where savouring or dread significantly affect devaluation ... The bias in estimation of discount rates will be especially serious if savouring and dread are different for different categories of consumption. If this were the case, then the general assumption that 'the discount rate is independent of the category of consumption goods for which it is calculated' (Landsberger, 1971, p. 1351) would be invalid.

Clearly, scholars of intertemporal choice for consumer goods have struggled with the restrictions of divisibility and satiation. They have also been restricted by the fact that the consumer goods have market prices, and participants might have some ability to 'game' the choices in their experiments to take advantage of buying and selling opportunities in the market (much like we discussed early on with regard to the choice of SS and LL money amounts in the presence of a banking sector). One way to sidestep this latter concern is to use hypothetical outcomes, as in Loewenstein's (1987) paper, where he offered hypothetical kisses from one's favourite movie star. In fact, there are many domains where there exists no market for the outcomes, so that arbitrage is not possible. A good example is the domain of health.

In some respects, health outcomes are the best conceivable vehicle for finding the 'true' discount rate, if such a thing exists. They are directly experienced
and cannot be bought or sold. Arguably, there is unlikely to be satiation in
health. This is not to say that there is constant marginal utility from improvements to health: for example, improving the quality of life from a health state
close to death may be much more valuable than improving an already good
health state by the same amount. But it might be legitimate to assume linearity
in the *duration* of a health state (holding its severity constant). For instance,
imagine comparing a moderate headache lasting ten hours that starts now, and
a moderate headache lasting twelve hours that starts in one week, where the
intensity of the headache is identical. We might assume *temporal additivity*,
which is that each hour of headache is just as bad as the other, and so we can
obtain the total (dis)utility of the headache by multiplying its 'badness' by its
duration. There are obviously limits to temporal additivity for health states,[13]
but they are arguably less than those limits for any other domain.

Under this assumption, many researchers conduct matching studies that
are, essentially, variants of Option 1, in which the duration of a health state
is traded off against the delay until it would be experienced (Chapman and
Elstein, 1995; Chapman, 1996; Van der Pol and Cairns, 2001). Unusually,
Bleichrodt and Johanneson (2001) control for the nonlinearity of the duration of health states, to obtain discount rates that are not confounded by
these nonlinearities. Overall, these papers show that many of the phenomena reported in intertemporal choices for money also are found for health
states, including decreasing discounting with delay (cf. Bleichrodt et al.,
2016, though McDonald et al., 2017, found that the declining discount rates
observed in their data were better explained by subadditive than by hyperbolic discounting).

The theoretical benefits of health as an outcome in the elicitation of intertemporal choice, in combination with its successful implementation in the
studies we mentioned, make it an attractive option for the investigation of
intertemporal choice. Health may allow us to learn about an individual's 'true'
discount rate. However, this depends on whether there exists a 'true' discount
rate to be measured. Evidence is mixed regarding the domain-generality of discount rates for health and for other outcomes. Evidence in favour was found by
some (Moore and Viscusi, 1990; Cropper, Aydede and Portney, 1994) but not
by others. Evidence that money is more discounted than health was reported
by Cairns (1992), while a gain/loss effect was found by Cairns (1994) and by
Hardisty and Weber (2009), with health gains discounted more than health
losses. Papers directly estimating the correlation between health and money
discounting typically find low but positive correlation (Chapman and Elstein,
1995; Chapman, 1996). However, for the reasons discussed earlier, since
the health and financial discounting measures do not use the same numeraire, we cannot conclude absolutely that health and money are discounted at
different rates.

There are also reasons to think that health behaviour does depend on a general discounting trait: Many studies show a correlation between time preference measured using money, and real-world health-related outcomes such as obesity, smoking and drug addiction (e.g., Chabris et al., 2008; Estle et al., 2007; Kirby, Petry and Bickel, 1999; Robles, 2010; Smith, Bogin and Bishai, 2005). The low correlations between health and monetary choices, however, underline a major issue in intertemporal choice research: these choices depend on a wide range of factors that researchers have only begun to investigate.

5.8 Conclusion

Researchers often assume the standard smaller sooner (SS) versus larger later (LL) paradigm – usually involving monetary amounts – provides a direct window on an underlying intertemporal discount rate for all goods, as if this is a 'trait' associated with the person, and not a rich interaction between the outcomes being evaluated, the way those outcomes (and delays separating outcomes) are represented, the situation in which the choice is made, as well as the person making the evaluation. We argued that a single experimental paradigm, or even a narrow class of such paradigms, may be insufficient to capture this richness, and researchers will need to find different ways to address both theoretical and empirical questions.

We focussed on the problem of how to measure time preference in a broader range of settings. Because the notion of time preference concerns utility from consumption, rather than the ratio between receipts, the standard methods do not help us very much. Even if we find, for instance, that someone is indifferent between ten bananas now and fifteen bananas in one month, we cannot say anything about their discount rate until we know how much consumption utility they will get from ten and fifteen bananas and how that utility will be distributed over time. We spent much of this chapter explaining the challenges involved in making the link between raw receipts and consumption, as well as the problems in comparing rates of discounting elicited for different goods and in different contexts. We suggested different approaches that researchers can take to alleviate these problems. As is clear from our examples, these methods need not be technically complex, but do require us to think of the measurement problem as being about something other than eliciting points of indifference between SS and LL. Indeed, as we discussed, relative discount rates can be assessed when two options are available at the same time, if we observe preferences between the options at different future points (and if preferences between them reverse). We also described a general method, the delayed compensation method (Cubitt et al., in press), for eliciting comparative rates of discounting. Other new methods include that of Attema et al. (2010, 2016), which enables discount rates to be measured directly without knowledge of the utility function.

While intertemporal choice has already received much attention, there is yet a great deal to be done. There is clearly a rich unexplored terrain for research in this area, and with clear reference to the normative theories, and insights from psychology and behavioural science, we will be able to exploit them and better understand a wide array of human decision-making.

Notes

1 Strictly speaking, intertemporal choice is not always between SS and LL. For example, people might choose between having a child now (putting their careers on hold) and waiting to have a child later (prioritising their careers in the meantime). This is more likely to be viewed as a struggle about when is the best time to schedule a good thing. Later we will take a broader view of intertemporal choice.

2 Strictly speaking, this is a personal interest rate r, or the rate at which money must grow to make you indifferent between now and later. The term *discount rate* is sometimes reserved for a simple transformation of this interest rate, $r/(1+r)$, but in this chapter (following convention), we will use *discount rate* to refer to both the personal interest rate and the personal discount rate.

3 The general formula for this rate is given by $\left(\dfrac{L}{S}\right)^{1/t} - 1$ where L and S are, respectively, the larger and smaller amount, and t is the interval separating them. In our example, $1/t = 1$, so it drops out.

4 Fisher identified these as foresight, self-control, habit, life expectancy, concern for the lives of others and fashion. This list covers many of the most prominent elements of behavioural economic models of intertemporal choice.

5 According to Fisher (1930), pure time preference is the rate of substitution when the allocations to the two periods are equal (i.e., the slope of the indifference curve on points $C_1 = C_2$ in Figure 5.1). Pure time preference defined in this way is often not observable and is different from measured time preference elicited in experiments. Thus, if not specially stated, time preference (or discount rate) in this chapter refers to the measured rate of time preference (or discount rate).

6 A *util* is a measure of the benefit or utility from consumption. A related term in the literature is 'instantaneous' utility, referring to the utility experienced at a given moment, which could be expressed in utils.

7 Note that it might not have been in his interest to not hear the song and not crash – it is not clear he did his sailors a favour by denying them the opportunity to hear the Sirens even at the cost of their lives.

8 Keynes was concerned with aggregate demand, not individual preferences. In the aggregate, satiation is a less important issue since it takes a lot of a commodity to satiate everybody.

9 See Kahneman, Wakker and Sarin (1997) and Read (2007) for reviews of the concept of utility in the context of modern behavioural economics.

10 Chapter 17 of Keynes (1936) discusses the issues here in the context of a whole economy and the determinant of interest rates. So important is this chapter that we were tempted to quote it in its entirety.

11 Though the market price will provide an indication of the population's willingness to pay, it cannot be assumed to accurately capture the individual willingness to pay for all respondents.

12 This occurs when the street value of the drug is matched to the money value – a reasonable decision if the addicts will certainly use *at least that much* of the drug. Many studies involve addicts in treatment programs, who may actively wish not to use drugs in the future and so sharply devalue future drugs.

13 For instance, each day of a lengthy illness, even if not associated with worsening symptoms, can nonetheless be worse than the day before.

5.9 References

Ainslie, G. (1975). Specious Reward: A Behavioral Theory of Impulsiveness and Impulse Control. *Psychological Bulletin*, 82(4), 463–496.

Ainslie, G. (2001). *Breakdown of Will*. Cambridge: Cambridge University Press.

Andersen, S., Harrison, G. W., Lau, M. I. and Rutström, E. E. (2008). Eliciting Risk and Time Preferences. *Econometrica*, 76(3), 583–618.

Andersen, S., Harrison, G. W., Lau, M. I. and Rutström, E. E. (2014). Discounting Behavior: A Reconsideration. *European Economic Review*, 71, 15–33.

Attema, A. E., Bleichrodt, H., Rohde, K. I. and Wakker, P. P. (2010). Time-Tradeoff Sequences for Analyzing Discounting and Time Inconsistency. *Management Science*, 56(11), 2015–2030.

Attema, A. E., Bleichrodt, H., Gao, Y., Huang, Z, and Wakker, P. P. (2016). Measuring Discounting Without Measuring Utility. *American Economic Review*, 106(6), 1476–1494.

Berns, G. S., Laibson, D. and Loewenstein, G. (2007). Intertemporal Choice: Toward an Integrative Framework. *Trends in Cognitive Sciences*, 11(11), 482–488.

Bickel, W. K. and Marsch, L. A. (2001). Toward a Behavioral Economic Understanding of Drug Dependence: Delay Discounting Processes. *Addiction*, 96(1), 73–86.

Bleichrodt, H., Gao Y. and Rohde, K. I. (2016). A Measurement of Decreasing Impatience for Health and Money. *Journal of Risk and Uncertainty*, 52(3), 213–231.

Bleichrodt, H. and Johannesson, M. (2001). Time Preference for Health: A Test of Stationarity Versus Decreasing Timing Aversion. *Journal of Mathematical Psychology*, 45(2), 265–282.

Casari, M. and Dragone, D. (2011). On Negative Time Preferences. *Economics Letters*, 111(1), 37–39.

Cairns, J. (1992). Discounting and Health Benefits: Another Perspective. *Health Economics*, 1(1), 76–79.

Cairns, J. A. (1994). Valuing Future Benefits. *Health Economics*, 3(4), 221–229.

Chabris, C. F., Laibson, D., Morris, C. L., Schuldt, J. P. and Taubinsky, D. (2008). Individual Laboratory-Measured Discount Rates Predict Field Behavior. *Journal of Risk and Uncertainty*, 37(2–3), 237–269.

Chapman, G. B. (1996). Temporal Discounting and Utility for Health and Money. *Journal of Experimental Psychology: Learning, Memory, and Cognition*, 22(3), 771–791.

Chapman, G. B. and Elstein, A. S. (1995). Valuing the Future Temporal Discounting of Health and Money. *Medical Decision Making*, 15(4), 373–386.

Chung, S. and Herrnstein, R. J. (1961). Relative and Absolute Strengths of Response as a Function of Frequency of Reinforcement. *Journal of the Experimental Analysis of Animal Behavior*, 4(3), 267–272.

Cropper, M. L., Aydede, S. K. and Portney, P. R. (1994). Preferences for Life Saving Programs: How the Public Discounts Time and Age. *Journal of Risk and Uncertainty*, 8(3), 243–265.

Cubitt, R. P., McDonald, R. and Read, D. (in press). Time Matters Less When Outcomes Differ: Uni-modal Versus Cross-modal Comparisons in Intertemporal Choice. *Management Science*.

Cubitt, R. P. and Read, D. (2007). Can Intertemporal Choice Experiments Elicit Time Preferences for Consumption? *Experimental Economics*, 10(4), 369–389.

Doyle, J. R. (2013). Survey of Time Preference, Delay Discounting Models. *Judgment and Decision Making*, 8(2), 116–135.

Ebert, J. E. and Prelec, D. (2007). The Fragility of Time: Time-Insensitivity and Valuation of the Near and Far Future. *Management Science*, 53(9), 1423–1438.

Edgeworth, F. Y. (1879). The Hedonical Calculus. *Mind*, 4, 394–408.

Elster, J. (1979). *Ulysses and the Sirens: Studies in Rationaltiy and Irrationality.* Cambridge: Cambridge University Press.

Estle, S. J., Green, L., Myerson, J. and Holt, D. D. (2007). Discounting of Monetary and Directly Consumable Rewards. *Psychological Science*, 18(1), 58–63.

Faralla, V., Benuzzi, F., Lui, F., Baraldi, P., Dimitri, N. and Nichelli, P. (2015). Neural Correlates in Intertemporal Choice of Gains and Losses. *Journal of Neuroscience, Psychology, and Economics*, 8(1), 27–47

Figner, B., Knoch, D., Johnson, E. J., Krosch, A. R., Lisanby, S. H., Fehr, E. and Weber, E. U. (2010). Lateral Prefrontal Cortex and Self-control in Intertemporal Choice. *Nature Neuroscience*, 13(5), 538–539.

Fisher, I. (1930). *The Theory of Interest*. New York: Macmillan.

Frederick, S. and Loewenstein, G. (2008). Conflicting Motives in Evaluations of Sequences. *Journal of Risk and Uncertainty*, 37(2–3), 221–235.

Frederick, S., Loewenstein, G. and O'Donoghue, T. (2002). Time Discounting and Time Preference: A Critical Review. *Journal of Economic Literature*, 40(2), 351–401.

Gigliotti, G. and Sopher, B. (1997). Violations of Present-Value Maximization in Income Choice. *Theory and Decision*, 43, 45–69.

Glimcher, P. W., Kable, J. and Louie, K. (2007). Neuroeconomic Studies of Impulsivity: Now or Just as Soon as Possible? *American Economic Review*, 97(2), 142–147.

Green, L., Myerson, J. and Macaux, E. W. (2005). Temporal Discounting When the Choice Is Between Two Delayed Rewards. *Journal of Experimental Psychology: Learning, Memory, and Cognition*, 31(5), 1121–1133.

Halevy, Y. (2015). Time Consistency: Stationarity and Time Invariance. *Econometrica*, 83(1), 335–352.

Hardisty, D. J., Appelt, K. C. andWeber, E. U. (2013). Good or Bad, We Want It Now: Fixed-Cost Present Bias for Gains and Losses Explains Magnitude Asymmetries in Intertemporal Choice. *Journal of Behavioral Decision Making*, 26(4), 348–361.

Hardisty, D. J. and Weber, E. U. (2009). Discounting Future Green: Money Versus the Environment. *Journal of Experimental Psychology: General*, 138(3), 329–340.

Hariri, A. R., Brown, S. M., Williamson, D. E., Flory, J. D., de Wit, H. and Manuck, S. B. (2006). Preference for Immediate over Delayed Rewards Is Associated with Magnitude of Ventral Striatal Activity. *Journal of Neuroscience*, 26(51), 13213–13217.

Harris, C. R. (2012). Feelings of Dread and Intertemporal Choice. *Journal of Behavioral Decision Making*, 25(1), 13–28.

Holcomb, J. H. and Nelson, P. S. (1992). Another Experimental Look at Individual Time Preference. *Rationality and Society*, 4(2), 199–220.

Homer (Translated 1932). *The Odyssey*, T. E. Lawrence (translator). London: Macmillan Collectors Library (this edition published 2004).

Kable, J. W. (2013). Valuation, Intertemporal Choice, and Self-Control. In P. W. Glimcher and F. Ernst (Eds.), *Neuroeconomics: Decision Making and the Brain* (pp. 173–192): London: Academic Press.

Kable, J. W. and Glimcher, P. W. (2007). The Neural Correlates of Subjective Value During Intertemporal Choice. *Nature Neuroscience*, 10(12), 1625–1633.

Kable, J. W. and Glimcher, P. W. (2010). An 'as Soon as Possible' Effect in Human Intertemporal Decision Making: Behavioral Evidence and Neural Mechanisms. *Journal of Neurophysiology*, 103(5), 2513–2531.

Kahneman, D., Wakker, P. P. and Sarin, R. (1997). Back to Bentham? Explorations of Experienced Utility. *Quarterly Journal of Economics*, 112(2), 375–405.

Kayser, A. S., Allen, D. C., Navarro-Cebrian, A., Mitchell, J. M. and Fields, H. L. (2012). Dopamine, Corticostriatal Connectivity, and Intertemporal Choice. *Journal of Neuroscience*, 32(27), 9402–9409.

Keynes, J. M (1936). *The General Theory of Employment, Interest and Money*. London: Macmillan (reprinted 2007).

Kinari, Y., Ohtake, F. and Tsutsui, Y. (2009). Time Discounting: Declining Impatience and Interval Effect. *Journal of Risk and Uncertainty*, 39(1), 87–112.

Kirby, K. N. and Herrnstein, R. J. (1995). Preference Reversals Due to Myopic Discounting of Delayed Reward. *Psychological Science*, 6(2), 83–89.

Kirby, K. N., Petry, N. M. and Bickel, W. K. (1999). Heroin Addicts Have Higher Discount Rates for Delayed Rewards Than Non-Drug-Using Controls. *Journal of Experimental Psychology: General*, 128(1), 78–87.

Knapman, A. and Tronde, J. (2011). *Temporal Discounting of Different Commodities in Airline Customer Reward Programs*. (MBA), Blekinge Institute of Technology. Retrieved from www.diva-portal.org/smash/get/diva2:829832/FULLTEXT01.pdf

Laibson, D. (1997). Golden Eggs and Hyperbolic Discounting. *Quarterly Journal of Economics*, 112(2), 443–477.

Landsberger, M. (1971). Consumer Discount Rate and the Horizon: New Evidence. *Journal of Political Economy*, 79(6), 1346–1359.

Laury, S. K., McInnes, M. M. and Swarthout, J. T. (2012). Avoiding the Curves: Direct Elicitation of Time Preferences. *Journal of Risk and Uncertainty*, 44(3), 181–217.

LeBoeuf, R. A. (2006). Discount Rates for Time Versus Dates: The Sensitivity of Discounting to Time-Interval Description. *Journal of Marketing Research*, 43(1), 59–72.

Lempert, K. M. and Phelps, E. A. (2016). The Malleability of Intertemporal Choice. *Trends in Cognitive Sciences*, 20(1), 64–74.

Loewenstein, G. (1987). Anticipation and the Valuation of Delayed Consumption. *Economic Journal*, 97(387), 666–684.

Loewenstein, G. (1988). Frames of Mind in Intertemporal Choice. *Management Science*, 34(2), 200–214.

Loewenstein, G. and Prelec, D. (1992). Anomalies in Intertemporal Choice: Evidence and an Interpretation. *Quarterly Journal of Economics*, 107(2), 573–597.

Loewenstein, G. and Prelec, D. (1993). Preferences for Sequences of Outcomes. *Psychological Review*, 100(1), 91–108.

Loewenstein, G., Rick, S. and Cohen, J. D. (2008). Neuroeconomics. *Annual Review of Psychology*, 59, 647–672.

Loewenstein, G. and Sicherman, N. (1991). Do Workers Prefer Increasing Wage Profiles? *Journal of Labor Economics*, 9(1) 67–84.

Loewenstein, G. and Thaler, R. H. (1989). Anomalies: Intertemporal Choice. *Journal of Economic Perspectives*, 3(4), 181–193.

Magen, E., Dweck, C. S. and Gross, J. J. (2008). The Hidden-Zero Effect Representing a Single Choice as an Extended Sequence Reduces Impulsive Choice. *Psychological Science*, 19(7), 648–649.

Manuck, S. B., Flory, J. D., Muldoon, M. F. and Ferrell, R. E. (2003). A Neurobiology of Intertemporal Choice. In G. Loewenstein, D., Read and R. Baumeister (Eds.), *Time and Decision: Economic and Psychological Perspectives on Intertemporal Choice* (pp. 139–172). New York: Russell Sage.

Manzini, P., Mariotti, M. and Mittone, L. (2010). Choosing Monetary Sequences: Theory and Experimental Evidence. *Theory and Decision*, 69(3), 327–354.

Mazur, J. E. (1987). An Adjusting Procedure for Studying Delayed Reinforcement. In M. L. Commons, J. E. Mazur, J. A. Nevin and H. Rachlin (Eds.), *The Effect of Delay and of Intervening Events on Reinforcement Value: Quantitative Analyses of Behavior* (pp. 55–73). Hillsdale, NJ: Lawrence Erlbaum.

McClure, S. M., Ericson, K. M., Laibson, D. I., Loewenstein, G. and Cohen, J. D. (2007). Time Discounting for Primary Rewards. *Journal of Neuroscience*, 27(21), 5796–5804.

McClure, S. M., Laibson, D. I., Loewenstein, G. and Cohen, J. D. (2004). Separate Neural Systems Value Immediate and Delayed Monetary Rewards. *Science*, 306(5695), 503–507.

McAlvanah, P. (2010). Subadditivity, Patience, and Utility: The Effects of Dividing Time Intervals. *Journal of Economic Behavior & Organization*, 76(2), 325–337.

McDonald, R., Chilton, S., Jones-Lee, M. W. and Metcalf, H. (2017). Evidence of Variable Discount Rates and Non-standard Discounting in Mortality Risk Valuation. *Journal of Environmental Economics and Management*

Moore, M. J. and Viscusi, W. K. (1990). Models for Estimating Discount Rates for Long-Term Health Risks Using Labor Market Data. *Journal of Risk and Uncertainty*, 3(4), 381–401.

Myerson, J., Green, L. and Warusawitharana, M. (2001). Area Under the Curve as a Measure of Discounting. *Journal of the Experimental Analysis of Behavior*, 76(2), 235–243.

O'Donoghue, T. and Rabin, M. (1999). Doing It Now or Later. *American Economic Review*, 89(1), 103–124.

O'Donoghue, T. and Rabin, M. (2000). The Economics of Immediate Gratification. *Journal of Behavioral Decision Making*, 13(2): 233–250

Phelps, E. S. and Pollak, R. A. (1968). On Second-Best National Saving and Game-Equilibrium Growth. *Review of Economic Studies*, 35(2), 185–199.

Plato. (trans. 1956). *Protagoras*. in B. Jowett and M. Ostwald (Trans.), G. Vlastos, (Ed.). Indianapolis: Bobbs-Merrill.

Read, D. (2001). Is Time-Discounting Hyperbolic or Subadditive? *Journal of Risk and Uncertainty*, 23(1), 5–32.

Read, D. (2004). Intertemporal Choice. In D. J. Koehler and N. Harvey (Eds.), *Blackwell Handbook of Judgment and Decision Making* (pp. 424–443). New Jersey: Blackwell.

Read, D. (2007). Experienced Utility: Utility Theory from Jeremy Bentham to Daniel Kahneman. *Thinking & Reasoning*, 13(1), 45–61.

Read, D., Frederick, S., Orsel, B. and Rahman, J. (2005). Four Score and Seven Years from Now: The Date/Delay Effect in Temporal Discounting. *Management Science*, 51(9), 1326–1335.

Read, D., Frederick, S. and Scholten, M. (2013). DRIFT: An Analysis of Outcome Framing in Intertemporal Choice. *Journal of Experimental Psychology: Learning, Memory, and Cognition*, 39(2), 573–588.

Read, D., Loewenstein, G. and Kalyanaraman, S. (1999). Mixing Virtue and Vice: Combining the Immediacy Effect and the Diversification Heuristic. *Journal of Behavioral Decision Making*, 12(4), 257–273.

Read, D., Olivola, C. Y. and Hardisty, D. (in press). The Value of Nothing: Asymmetric Attention to Opportunity Costs Drives Intertemporal Decision Making, *Management Science*, dx.doi.org/10.1287/mnsc.2016.2547

Read, D. and Powell, M. (2002). Reasons for Sequence Preferences. *Journal of Behavioral Decision Making*, 15(5), 433–460.

Read, D. and Read, N. L. (2004). Time Discounting over the Lifespan. *Organizational Behavior and Human Decision Processes*, 94(1), 22–32.

Read, D. and Roelofsma, P. H. (2003). Subadditive Versus Hyperbolic Discounting: A Comparison of Choice and Matching. *Organizational Behavior and Human Decision Processes*, 91(2), 140–153.

Read, D. and Van Leeuwen, B. (1998). Predicting Hunger: The Effects of Appetite and Delay on Choice. *Organizational Behavior and Human Decision Processes*, 76(2), 189–205.

Reuben, E., Sapienza, P. and Zingales, L. (2010). Time Discounting for Primary and Monetary Rewards. *Economics Letters*, 106(2), 125–127.

Rick, S. and Loewenstein, G. (2008). The Role of Emotion in Economic Behavior. In M. Lewis, J. M. Haviland-Jones and L. F. Barrett (Eds.), *Handbook of Emotions* (pp. 138–156). New York: Guilford Press.

Robles, E. (2010). Delay and Loss of Subjective Value. *Journal of Behavior, Health & Social Issues*, 2(1), 105–118.

Roelofsma, P. H. (1996). Modelling Intertemporal Choices: An Anomaly Approach. *Acta Psychologica*, 93(1), 5–22.

Rubinstein, A. (2003). 'Economics and Psychology'? The Case of Hyperbolic Discounting. *International Economic Review*, 44(4), 1207–1216.

Samuelson, P. A. (1937). A Note on Measurement of Utility. *Review of Economic Studies*, 4(2), 155–161.

Sayman, S. and Öncüler, A. (2009). An Investigation of Time Inconsistency. *Management Science*, 55(3), 470–482.

Scholten, M. and Read, D. (2006). Discounting by Intervals: A Generalized Model of Intertemporal Choice. *Management Science*, 52(9), 1424–1436.

Scholten, M. and Read, D. (2010). The Psychology of Intertemporal Tradeoffs. *Psychological Review*, 117(3), 925–944.

Scholten, M. and Read, D. (2013). Time and Outcome Framing in Intertemporal Tradeoffs. *Journal of Experimental Psychology: Learning, Memory, and Cognition*, 39(4), 1192–1212.

Scholten, M., Read, D. and Sanborn, A. (2016). Cumulative Weighing of Time in Intertemporal Tradeoffs. *Journal of Experimental Psychology: General*, 145(9), 1177–1205.

Sellitto, M., Ciaramelli, E. and di Pellegrino, G. (2010). Myopic Discounting of Future Rewards After Medial Orbitofrontal Damage in Humans. *Journal of Neuroscience*, 30(49), 16429–16436.

Shapiro, J. M. (2005). Is There a Daily Discount Rate? Evidence from the Food Stamp Nutrition Cycle. *Journal of Public Economics*, 89(2), 303–325.

Smith, C. T., Wallace, D. L., Dang, L. C., Aarts, E., Jagust, W. J., D'Esposito, M. and Boettiger, C. A. (2016). Modulation of Impulsivity and Reward Sensitivity in Intertemporal Choice by Striatal and Midbrain Dopamine Synthesis in Healthy Adults. *Journal of Neurophysiology*, 115(3), 1146–1156.

Smith, P. K., Bogin, B. and Bishai, D. (2005). Are Time Preference and Body Mass Index Associated? Evidence from the National Longitudinal Survey of Youth. *Economics & Human Biology*, 3(2), 259–270.

Sopher, B. and Sheth, A. (2006). A Deeper Look at Hyperbolic Discounting. *Theory and Decision*, 60(2–3), 219–255.

Story, G. W., Vlaev, I., Seymour, B., Winston, J. S., Darzi, A. and Dolan, R. J. (2013). Dread and the Disvalue of Future Pain. *PLoS Computational Biology*, 9(11), e1003335.

Strotz, R. H. (1955). Myopia and Inconsistency in Dynamic Utility Maximization. *Review of Economic Studies*, 23(3), 165–180.

Takahashi, T. (2005). Loss of Self-Control in Intertemporal Choice May Be Attributable to Logarithmic Time-Perception. *Medical Hypotheses*, 65(4), 691–693.

Thaler, R. (1981). Some Empirical Evidence on Dynamic Inconsistency. *Economics Letters*, 8(3), 201–207

Tsukayama, E. and Duckworth, A. L. (2010). Domain-Specific Temporal Discounting and Temptation. *Judgment and Decision Making*, 5(2), 72–82.

Tversky, A., Sattath, S. and Slovic, P. (1988). Contingent Weighting in Judgment and Choice. *Psychological Review*, 95(3), 371–384.

Ubfal, D. (2016). How General Are Time Preferences? Eliciting Good-Specific Discount Rates. *Journal of Development Economics*, 118, 150–170.

Urminsky, O. and Zauberman, G. (2015). The Psychology of Intertemporal Preferences. In G. Wu and G. Keren (Eds.), *The Wiley Blackwell Handbook of Judgment and Decision Making* (pp. 141–181). Malden, MA: Wiley-Blackwell

Van der Pol, M. and Cairns, J. (2001). Estimating Time Preferences for Health Using Discrete Choice Experiments. *Social Science & Medicine*, 52(9), 1459–1470.

Weatherly, J. N. and Ferraro, F. R. (2011). Executive Functioning and Delay Discounting of Four Different Outcomes in University Students. *Personality and Individual Differences*, 51(2), 183–187.

Weber, E. U., Johnson, E. J., Milch, K. F., Chang, H., Brodscholl, J. C. and Goldstein, D. G. (2007). Asymmetric Discounting in Intertemporal Choice a Query-Theory Account. *Psychological Science*, 18(6), 516–523.

Wu, C. Y. and He, G.-B. (2012). The Effects of Time Perspective and Salience of Possible Monetary Losses on Intertemporal Choice. *Social Behavior and Personality*, 40, 1645–1653.

Yates, J. F. and Watts, R. A. (1975). Preferences for Deferred Losses. *Organizational Behavior and Human Performance*, 13(2), 294–306.

Zauberman, G., Kim, B. K., Malkoc, S. A. and Bettman, J. R. (2009). Discounting Time and Time Discounting: Subjective Time Perception and Intertemporal Preferences. *Journal of Marketing Research*, 46(4), 543–556.

6 Debt

Beyond *Homo Economicus*

Matthew Sparkes, Julia Gumy and Brendan Burchell

'Neither a borrower nor a lender be.'

6.1 Introduction

Debt is difficult to understand. There are many ways to think about debt, and what seems like common sense from one perspective looks inaccurate or incomprehensible from another point of view. Psychologists, economists, sociologists, political scientists, historians, bankers, theologians and moral philosophers have all addressed the puzzles and paradoxes of debt in a myriad of ways.[1] In the public imagination, debt has negative connotations, because it is deemed to reflect some form of financial problem. However, in his book *Debt: The First 5,000 Years*, Graeber (2011) argues rather convincingly that civilisation would not have been possible without debt, which has existed for far longer than money.

From an economic viewpoint, 'credit' and 'debt' are often taken to be the same thing. They refer to an agreement between a lender and a borrower in which money has been loaned and is repaid on the agreed date. The agreement can be *secured* against property – such as a house purchase mortgage, car loan or equity release loan – or *unsecured* – such as a credit card, bank loan, overdraft, store card, hire purchase loan or payday loan.[2] In this chapter, we will stay with the economic convention by using the term 'credit-debt' to refer to any *formal* agreement in which money has been borrowed and payments are being made by the consumer when they are due. We will refer to a situation in which due payments have not been made as 'problem debt'; in other words, problem debt equals default or arrears (Ford, 1991). This distinction is helpful because it implies credit-debt is regarded as unproblematic, even as something positive, whereas problem debt is deemed to indicate a negative occurrence in the individual's financial situation.

Unfortunately, though, the terms are used differently in different literatures, and to further complicate matters, the terms 'debt', 'problem debt', 'heavy debt burden', 'unmanageable debt' and 'overindebted' are used to mean similar things in different contexts. The blurred conceptual boundaries do point to distinctions both nationally and internationally in how debt is perceived by different stakeholders, which we will explore in this chapter. We have outlined the distinction between credit-debt and problem debt in order to make sense of all of the different ways of looking at debt. However, despite national discrepancies in how debt is perceived, at the heart of contemporary economics is a theoretical model that homogenises explanations for why credit-debt is used by individuals and for what ends.

This chapter, like others in this handbook, embraces a number of different aspects of the overlap between psychology and economics. The first is an attempt to make economic models (in this case, concerning debt) more realistic (replacing *homo economicus* with *homo realitus*) by adding components of psychology to existing economic models. This is exemplified by the Behavioral Life Cycle Hypothesis (BLCH) (Shefrin and Thaler, 1988), which adds findings from cognitive psychology to the existing Life Cycle Model (LCM). The second component comprises 'softer' elements, such as individual differences (whether people are financially 'phobic' or not) as well as aspects from social psychology, including social norms, attitudes and values, and the wider economic and sociocultural context. The third aspect is more purely psychological in the sense that it examines the psychological consequences of debt in terms of subjective well-being and mental health. Finally, the fourth aspect addresses debt collection practices and policy questions drawing, to some extent, on both disciplines.

6.2 Theories on Debt Accumulation

6.2.1 The Life Cycle Model

Since the Global Financial Crisis of 2008, there has been a proliferation of studies attempting to understand why individuals accumulate debt. Yet, within economic theory a consensus has persisted for the last five decades that the take up and accumulation of debt can be explained by the LCM, first proposed by Ando and Modigliani in 1963. In Ando and Modigliani's (1963) model, individuals 'dissave' or borrow to smooth consumption patterns based on flows of income during their life, particularly when current income is insufficient to meet their consumption needs. Without considering model imperfections, the theory states that individuals should be able to juggle their finances in an optimal way so that by the end of their lives positive fluctuations of income compensate for the negative ones, producing a zero-sum game. In this model, age is taken as a baseline to demonstrate how borrowing patterns are influenced by age-specific characteristics of individuals. In line with the theory, some research has shown that young and old individuals are more likely to borrow than middle-aged individuals, as their income levels are more likely to fall below their level of needs (Webley and Nyhus, 2001). Contrarily, middle-aged individuals are more likely to be reaching their labour market maturity and therefore display larger incomes and accumulated assets, making borrowing less likely. The saving and consumption life cycle is conceived as a process of generation, maturation and death, almost resembling a biological process (Harris, 1987; O'Rand and Krecker, 1990). Credit-debt thus arises in situations in which current monetary resources do not match monetary outgoings. Debt problems arise when individuals are not able to service their debt due to lack of economic resources or financial illiquidity, which is often the result of sudden income drops, or because of an excessive accumulation of debt. If the inability to repay is persistent over time, individuals' living standards could deteriorate rapidly, thus putting families at economic risk. This is, in turn, linked to poor psychological well-being (as we will discuss in Section 6.3).

The LCM is not only a dominant economic theory, but has also been at the heart of financial and monetary policy in many countries over the last four decades. In the United Kingdom, for example, its emergence as conventional thinking is signified in a speech given by the then-governor of the Bank of England, Leigh-Pemburton, when he discussed how credit could underpin the British economy:

> As a nation, our attitude to credit is typically ambivalent. There is a tendency to think of credit as something intrinsically reprehensible ... But at the same time it is very hard to envisage the effective functioning of the economy without credit to oil the wheels. Its role is to allow flexibility in the timing of expenditures, enabling them to be separated in time from the receipt of income ... credit performs [a] function for consumers, enabling them to make large purchases or investments at a convenient or opportune time, and to pay for them in accordance with their expected pattern of income. I find nothing reprehensible about that – indeed rather the reverse ... It must be an advantage for the individual to have more choice between different types of borrowing facility, and greater flexibility over the timing of his expenditure and in the arrangement of his portfolio of assets and liabilities (Leigh-Pemburton, 1988, p. 48).

As the statement by Leigh-Pemburton mplies, credit is assumed to provide 'flexibility in the timing of expenditures', it allows 'consumers' to make larger 'purchases or investments' than their income at that moment would permit, thus enabling 'more choice' in the arrangement of 'consumers' portfolio of assets and liabilities'. As the semantics expose, this view is one of a 'rational' and 'knowing' economic agent making strategic, sensible and logical decisions in their financial management, and credit provides an additional tool in the performance of this role. The LCM is thus built on the traditional rational actor model of behaviour that postulates individuals are 'highly rational, hold coherent, well-informed, and justified beliefs, and pursue their goals effectively, with little systematic error and no need for help' (Mullainathan and Shafir, 2009, p. 121). Through the rational actor model and LCM, economists have dominated both the study of individual financial decision-making and the study of credit-debt.

6.2.2 The Behavioural Life Cycle Hypothesis (BLCH)

The literature in economics on debt-related decisions has been heavily influenced by Paul Samuelson's (1937) classic paper on the 'Discounted Utility Model', which spawned many theoretical and empirical contributions to try and understand the rationale for the decisions individuals make to prefer a given sum of, say, $100 now to a larger sum, say $150, in twenty-four months' time. Despite the fact that different experiments yielded very different discounting rates and hyperbolic curves, and these curves were different for different people and different goods (for instance, cash or a meal in an expensive restaurant), economists seem to have been fascinated by the fact that intertemporal choices could be predicted by a precise model. Such a model was assumed to have important implications for a wide variety of phenomena, such as the greater accumulated wealth of some nations over others or the huge variability in risks that people are prepared to endure for instant rewards. This literature is reviewed critically by Frederick, Loewenstein and O'Donoghue (2002), who conclude by stating:

> [W]e believe that economists' understanding of intertemporal choices will progress most rapidly by continuing to import insights from psychology, by relinquishing the assumption that the key to understanding intertemporal choices is finding the right discount rate (or even the right discount function), and by readopting the view that intertemporal choices reflect many distinct considerations and often involve the interplay of several competing motives (p. 394).

Like the LCM, the BLCH recognises that there is a rational 'planner' in all of us, yet there is also a rather shortsighted (myopic) 'doer' who wants to live now and pay later. A large body of research in behavioural economics has convincingly shown that discount rates are not constant over time but instead decline over time (Frederick et al., 2002; see also Read, McDonald and He in the current volume). This shortsighted weakness is somehow known by the 'planner' through some mysterious metacognitive process, and just as Ulysses had himself tied to the mast as he knew he could not otherwise resist the allure of the sirens, the 'planner' has ways of keeping the 'doer' in check. The main way this is achieved is by the employment of 'mental accounts'. Whilst from the point of view of economic theory the form that money takes should not influence how it is treated (i.e., that it is 'fungible'), persuasive empirical work has however revealed that money is saved or spent quite differently depending on how it is 'framed' (i.e., it is 'nonfungible') (Thaler, 1990). For instance, windfall gains more readily encourage spending compared to regular income, whilst pension funds are more likely to be saved (Shefrin and Thaler, 1988;

Thaler, 1990). Thus, excessive spending (and presumably debt accumulation) can be avoided by placing funds in compartments where the 'marginal propensity to consume' is reduced.

However, Shefrin and Thaler (1988) recognise that criticising LCM and other similar models on the grounds that they are unrealistic is not sufficient in itself; as has been pointed out, models have some predictive merit based on their aggregate 'as if' assumptions. Shefrin and Thaler (1988) nonetheless claim that their model provides better predictions by adding a little psychology, yet it remains a conundrum just how the 'planner' can overcome the myopic 'doer' to such an extent that saving and spending can be streamed over a lifetime.

6.2.3 Life Course, Gender, Socialisation and Personality

In contrast to life *cycle* theories, where the main emphasis of study is on individuals' life stages and related outcomes at each stage, life *course* theories may be a better way to approach the question of debt. Life course theories focus on the timing and sequencing of stages and the social meaning of individuals' changes over their life course (O'Rand and Krecker, 1990). Research has shown that – although common – not all households pool their income (Browning et al., 1994; Lancaster and Ray, 2002; Manser and Brown, 1980), and that family financial arrangements are diverse and vary between men and women and between household types, often being a reflection of labour market circumstances (Pahl, 1989, 1995; Vogler and Pahl, 1993; Vogler, Brockmann and Wiggins, 2006). These studies challenge the traditional concept of the household economy and highlight the need to focus on the individual to examine intrahousehold financial inequalities. Individuals' characteristics do matter in determining levels of debt. For instance, Kan and Laurie (2010) and Westaway and Mckay (2007) find that women in the United Kingdom have lower levels of debt than men. Some studies (Grable, 2000; Jianakoplos and Bernasek, 1998; Powell and Ansic, 1997) link the accumulation of debt to the concept of risk. For instance, women have been found to be more risk averse than men, thus leading them to undertake greater financial planning and limit investments, which may lead to lower accumulation of debt. These levels do however depend on traditional economic roles that men and women adopt in the private sphere, which are often a reflection of inequalities both in the labour market and in the household. Furthermore, despite reporting lower levels of debt than men, women are actually found to be more at risk of experiencing debt problems, due to lower earning potential and restricted labour market opportunities (Scott and Dex, 2009), particularly after critical life events, such as divorce (Jarvis and Jenkins, 1999). Moreover, childbirth and unemployment affect debt burdens in a different manner; thus, expected events do not have the same effects as unexpected events. It is this evidence that moves us on to considering whether life course theories may be better at capturing debt use than the LCM. Life course theories are useful insofar as they represent an integrated framework of analysis that allows the interplay between individuals' life course changes and the structural context (e.g., country) to be observed. The theories emphasise the importance of life trajectories and sequences of events and changes of state (Elder, 1985) and are therefore useful to theoretically frame and empirically test how different events impact on individuals' debts.

Just as the financial decisions faced by men and women are different, so are those facing individuals with varying personalities. One study, using surveys, semistructured interviews and focus groups identified a psychological syndrome that consisted of avoiding information about personal finance (Burchell, 2004), sometimes called 'financial phobia' in the popular media. A mild tendency to avoid financial information is very common, but in more extreme cases individuals had piles or boxes of unopened bank and credit card statements. Such individuals were not necessarily in debt, but were usually managing their money poorly; for instance, in some cases they had large amounts of money in current accounts that were not receiving any interest. This syndrome did not seem particularly related to an inability to understand finance; in some cases, individuals managed large budgets very carefully in their working lives, but could not do the same for their own personal money. In-depth interviews suggested that there might be several reasons that individuals develop high levels of financial aversion. In some cases, it seemed to be related to a more general level of procrastination. Fortunately, psychological research has increased understanding of procrastination and its treatment. (See, for instance, Wohl, Pychyl and Bennett, 2010.) Some other cases seemed to be linked to difficulty or unease in understanding financial information; 'small print' is particularly mentioned as a block to getting to grips with finance. But the most common cause for this puzzling syndrome seemed to be 'frustrated prudence'.

A common theme in much research on economic socialisation is that socioeconomic values, such as each individual's preferred level of financial caution, are learned in childhood and become emotionally laden (Inglehart, 1977, 2008). A number of individuals with the highest scores on the financial aversion scale recounted major life events where they acted in a way that they thought was careful, but their plans were thwarted. In some cases, this was because a financial product previously considered safe failed (such as an endowment mortgage), sometimes it was linked to crashes in the housing market leading to negative equity and in other cases to spendthrift relatives who needed financial rescuing. In occasional cases, this mismatch was reversed, for instance when a windfall rescued someone from poverty. The mismatch between deeply held socioeconomic values and experiences caused a dissonance that was managed by avoidance of personal finance.

The nature of this phenomenon became clearer when it was subject to laboratory investigation. Shapiro and Burchell (2012) found that a modified Emotional Stroop Test (EST) and Dot-Probe Paradigm (DPP) were both found to correlate with scores on the self-reported financial avoidance questionnaire.[3] It seemed that, even before they were consciously processed, those words with a financial resonance were avoided by participants with high levels of financial avoidance. Furthermore, financial anxiety was shown to be a separate construct from depression or general anxiety. These findings suggest that the term 'financial phobia' may be quite appropriate, as financial anxiety is behaving in a similar manner to phobias in these tests. This gives a good indication of how financial anxiety could be treated. Other phobias (such as social phobia) tend not to self-extinguish, nor do they respond well to therapies based on empathy, but they can be treated effectively and enduringly by cognitive behavioural therapy (CBT) (Carlbring, Nordgren, Furmark, and Andersson, 2009).

Another, complementary approach to understanding how individuals make decisions about loaning money from banks and other financial institutions is to carefully study the way in which individuals make decisions, both by experimental manipulations of the information available to them and also by tracking the process they go through as they arrive at a judgement (see Schulte-Mecklenbeck, Kühberger, and Ranyard, 2011). This can be done by a number of different high-tech and low-tech methods, such as tracking the movements of their computer mouse, search behaviour or their eye movements, or getting them to talk out loud as they make decisions. An excellent example of this is the research of Ranyard and colleagues, who sought to understand the role of individual financial decision-making in the mis-selling of payment protection insurance (PPI), which was a hugely profitable financial product that created billions of pounds for financial institutions in the United Kingdom at the expense of consumers, who were misled about the disproportionately high costs of such products. Their detailed accounts of consumer understanding of the costs and benefits of PPI (Ranyard and McHugh, 2012) were an important contribution to the governmental enquiry that led to banks having to repay their vast profits from PPI mis-sales (see Ranyard, 2014). Later in this chapter, we further explore the practices of financial institutions in the processes of debt accumulation (see Section 6.2.7) and its repayment (see Section 6.3.3). But before we can explore the interplay between individual and structural factors in a more systematic way, it is important to first set the context by detailing the different ways debt is measured.

6.2.4 Objective Versus Subjective Measures

How debt is measured affects our understanding of this phenomenon, and studies rely on either *objective* or *subjective* measurements. An assessment of households' level of debt as compared to their income is used to provide an objective way of quantifying debt levels. Debt-to-income (DTI) ratios are commonly used to assess households' credit worthiness, excessive burden of debt and vulnerability to problem debt in the event of an income or expenditure shock. They measure the proportion of monthly or annual debt with regards to monthly or annual income. For instance, in the United Kingdom, households with a DTI ratio of 60 per cent or more to their annual income are classified as 'highly vulnerable' (TUC, 2016, p. 27). Debt servicing cost to income ratio (DSR) is a second, and more current, measure of overindebtedness that focusses on the repayment to gross income ratio. Households with a DSR of 25 per cent are commonly identified as overindebted, although a recent Trade Union Congress (TUC) report used a ratio of 40 per cent as a measure of 'extreme over-indebtedness' (TUC, 2016, p. 27). Studies also rely on indicators that measure whether households are falling behind their scheduled payments (e.g., utility bills, rent, mortgage payments, etc.) as they can indicate households' lack of economic resources (Betti et al., 2001).

Objective debt provides an indication of individuals' or a household's levels of economic well-being, but subjective perceptions of debt (i.e., their perception of their own financial situation) may have a bigger impact on individuals' subjective well-being and also provide a window into national variations and contexts. In many ways, individuals' perceptions about their finances are the main mediating factor between individuals' objective economic situation and their well-being (Sinclair et al., 2010), although other threats to well-being, such as the behaviour of debt collectors, will be linked more closely to objective finances in Section 6.3.

Surveys often measure subjective debt burden by asking individuals whether their – secured or unsecured – debts are a burden. Response categories are typically 'not a problem', 'somewhat of a burden' and 'a heavy burden'. Individuals' perceptions about debt, or in other words their subjective debt burden, can capture individuals' ability to cope with their financial situation, and such perceptions are therefore suggested to measure individuals' experience of debt more accurately than objective forms of debt.[4] Intriguingly, when observing individuals' levels of debt and their subjective debt burden, a few studies (del Río and Young, 2005; Georgarakos, Lojschova and Ward-Wamedinger, 2010; Keese, 2012) have shown that individuals' understanding of their finances is only weakly correlated to their objective financial information. That is, individuals' *objective* debt burden often does not coincide with individuals' *subjective* or perceived debt burden. For instance, del Río and Young (2005) found that although levels of unsecured debt increased between 1995 and 2000 in the United Kingdom, individuals' perceptions about debt did not worsen. In other words, individuals did not perceive themselves financially worse off despite higher objective levels of debt. In a further study conducted in the United Kingdom, Kempson and Atkinson (2006) found that many individuals who seemed to the researchers to be struggling with their finances reported living well within their means. These were typically young individuals with high levels of debt, low savings and a tendency for compulsive consumption. This mismatch gives us a clue as to how individuals' subjective over- or underestimation of their *real* financial situation might lead to money mismanagement and further accumulation of debt. The discrepancy between objective and subjective measures may also give us some indication of the psychological and sociocultural factors influencing debt perceptions. As we will show in this chapter, individuals' attitudes towards debt, culture, personality traits or lifestyle expectations, amongst others, are factors that influence how individuals perceive and experience their debt. To begin to frame this argument, we will now explore factors influencing subjective debt burden.

Perceptions are a representation of how individuals understand the surrounding environment, and they are shaped through life by various socioeconomic and psychological factors (Veenhoven, 2007). As noted previously, individuals are said to be subjectively debt burdened if they perceive their debt, either secured or unsecured, to be a burden or a heavy burden. Part of their assessment will include information on their 'real' financial situation. The remaining part is affected by factors that are unrelated to their finances (Keese, 2012). When asked about their financial situation, individuals will attempt to recall their level of debt and compare that figure to what they consider is an acceptable level of debt. The comparison process will determine whether their debt is perceived to be a burden or not (Kamleitner and Kirchler, 2007). The recall process requires the individual to be knowledgeable about his or her finances to accurately estimate the amount of debt owed. The increase in confidence derived from an increased level of financial literacy does affect individuals' attitudes and behaviour. Lusardi and Tufano (2009), for instance, find that individuals with low financial literacy are less able to judge their debt position. The financial transactions of these individuals are also more costly as they tend to use products with higher interest rates. Different credit products may also yield different estimations of debt. Several studies have pointed out how the use of nontangible money products, such as credit cards, affect mental accounting. Studies have shown how the use of credit cards reduces individuals' ability to keep track of their finances whilst tangible forms of money (i.e., notes, coins) help individuals keep better track of their spending patterns (Chatterjee and Rose, 2012; Hirschman, 1979). Kamleitner and Kirchler (2007) also find that the burden of debt may be perceived differently depending on the source of debt considered, credit card debt being the most satisfying to pay off. In addition to accurately estimating the level of debt, the process of evaluating one's debt will also depend on individuals' attitudes towards debt, either of acceptance or rejection, as well as how individuals perceive their finances in the context of what is socially acceptable. Figure 6.1 shows the percentage of individuals living in households with critically high and medium levels of debt in the twenty-seven countries of the European Union (EU-27) in 2008.[5] These data are extracted from the European Union Statistics on Income and Living Conditions (EU-SILC) Overindebtedness module (2008), which aimed to provide detailed information on households experiencing problem debt. According to these data, a household is critically in debt if the household's debt is above 66 per cent of the monthly household disposable income. Although both debt and income are self-reported measures in the survey, this indicator could be understood as an objective measure of problem debt. The data show that the United Kingdom, Germany and Cyprus had the

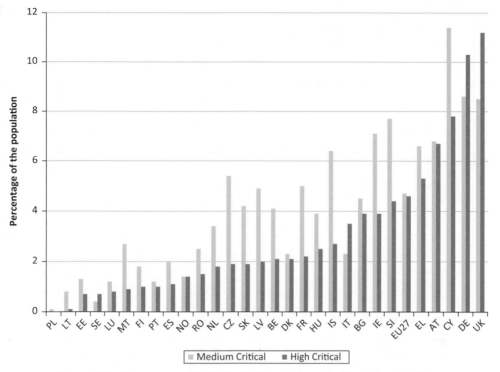

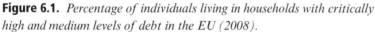

Figure 6.1. *Percentage of individuals living in households with critically high and medium levels of debt in the EU (2008).*

Key: EU27 – European Union (twenty-seven countries); BE – Belgium; BG – Bulgaria; CZ – Czech Republic; DK – Denmark, DE – Germany; EE – Estonia; IE – Ireland; EL – Greece; ES – Spain; FR – France; IT – Italy; CY – Cyprus; LV – Latvia; LT – Lithuania; LU – Luxembourg; HU – Hungary; MT – Malta; NL- Netherlands; AT – Austria; PL – Poland; PT – Portugal; RO – Romania; SI – Slovenia; SK – Slovakia; FI – Finland; SE – Sweden; UK – United Kingdom; IS – Iceland; NO – Norway. Note: The measure is based on an index of financial difficulties, created by Eurostat, which consists of the amount of money owed in arrears (housing bills/repayment, consumption loan/credit repayment and other nonhousing bills). It also includes outstanding amounts from bank overdrafts and credit and/or store card(s). A household is in a medium critical debt situation if the total debt is at least higher than 66 per cent of the monthly household disposable income. A household is in a high critical debt situation if the total debt is higher than 100 per cent of the monthly household disposable income. Source: Eurostat-SILC (2015); data extracted from the EU-SILC overindebtedness module for 2008.

highest percentage of individuals living in households with medium and high critical debt. Some Eastern European countries, such as Poland, Lithuania and Estonia, had the lowest percentage.

Figure 6.2 shows the percentage of households that report the repayment of unsecured debt a financial burden in the EU-27 in 2008.[6] It is, hence, a

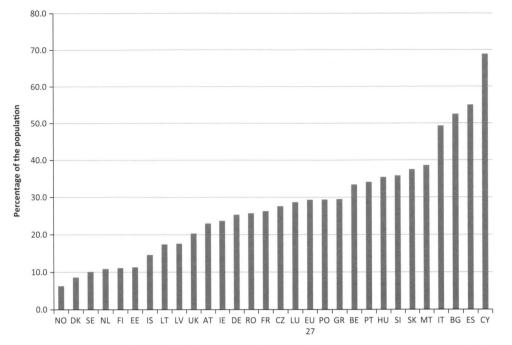

Figure 6.2. *Percentage of households that report the repayment of debt from hire purchases or loans a financial burden in the EU-27 (2008). Key: EU27 – European Union (twenty-seven countries); BE – Belgium; BG – Bulgaria; CZ – Czech Republic; DK – Denmark, DE – Germany; EE – Estonia; IE – Ireland; EL – Greece; ES – Spain; FR – France; IT – Italy; CY – Cyprus; LV – Latvia; LT – Lithuania; LU – Luxembourg; HU – Hungary; MT – Malta; NL- Netherlands; AT – Austria; PL – Poland; PT – Portugal; RO – Romania; SI – Slovenia; SK – Slovakia; FI – Finland; SE – Sweden; UK – United Kingdom; IS – Iceland; NO – Norway. Source: Eurostat SILC (2015); data extracted from the EU-SILC overindebtedness module for 2008.*

subjective measure of problem debt. Some of the Mediterranean (e.g., Cyprus, Spain, Italy) and some Eastern European countries (e.g., Bulgaria, Slovakia) had the highest percentage of households reporting their debts to be a burden. Norway and Denmark had the lowest percentage. The comparison of both graphs reveals that although there appears to be some correlation between the objective and the subjective indicator, the two indicators are clearly not interchangeable. The United Kingdom is the clearest example where, despite having a high percentage of individuals living in households with problem debt, it does not rank amongst the highest for subjective debt. In a further study, Gumy (2013) compared objective and subjective debt indicators for Germany and the United Kingdom and found that similar debt-to-income ratios yielded different subjective debt burdens, with German individuals perceiving their debts to be a burden at lower debt-to-income ratios than the United Kingdom.

This evidence raises some important questions: Why does this discrepancy between subjective debt and objective debt occur? What explains differing levels of debt accumulation and the subjective responses to that behaviour? In order to make sense of these anomalies, we can seek answers by focussing on the effects of (amplifying) inequality in societies, (shifting) attitudes towards credit-debt and the cultural context that shapes narratives around credit-debt, and finally macrostructural processes that influence the availability of credit-debt. We will deal with each in turn.

6.2.5 Social Comparison and Norms

In the preceding sections, we outlined the discrepancy between objective debt levels and subjective perceptions. Ultimately, this discrepancy places a spot-light on the LCM and its homogenising notion that rationality is driving the use of credit-debt. To make a start on exploring this discrepancy, in this section we wish to touch upon some factors that are influencing why individuals seek credit-debt in the first place. There is recognition that a small proportion of individuals show a compulsive urge to buy (D'Astous, 1990; Faber, 1988) and, hence, to accumulate debt no matter how societies are structured. Tokunaga (1993) found that the psychological characteristics underlying this compulsive behaviour were similar to those found in drug abuse. Nonetheless, in the social sciences, many arguments relate to individuals' need to meet their material necessities. Berthoud and Kempson (1992) and Ford (1988) suggest that hardship and consumerism are the two paths into debt. Low levels of income produce hardship, and this can lead to accumulation of debt. High levels of income promote consumerism, and that in turn can lead to accumulation of debt. The use of debt for the achievement of desired living standards denotes a relative component to the accumulation of debt. In other words, individuals' living standards are determined in the society in which they live and interact and, hence, individuals will accumulate debt to achieve those living standards.

The 'relative standards model', first developed by Campbell, Converse and Rogers (1976), could be applied to better understand these processes. In this theory, individuals' satisfaction is determined by comparison of their standing to relevant standards. Upwards comparisons would yield low satisfaction, whilst downwards comparison would yield high satisfaction. It is argued that individuals' financial satisfaction is low when the person's aspired and actual financial situation do not match. In this context, Lown and Ju (1992) and Plagnol (2011) argue that debt can be seen as a mechanism to increase material well-being when financial satisfaction is low. Thus, financially satisfied individuals may be less likely to report high subjective debt burdens, even though their level of debt may be high. Keese (2012) argues that young people are more likely to report lower subjective debt burdens, as it is more natural for them to be indebted due to higher material needs. How individuals perceive their debts at different ages or life stages may reflect the expenses that each age group is confronted with at different points in time but also their level of tolerance towards debt.

In a similar fashion, Festinger's (1954) 'social comparison theory' provides further insights into how individuals might perceive their financial and material situation, and how credit-debt can emerge as a reflexive response. The comparison with other members in society induces individuals to evaluate their position by comparing themselves to a reference group (e.g., their peers). Downwards comparisons are considered self-enhancing, as individuals compare themselves to others in a lower status position, whilst upwards comparisons are most detrimental to their well-being. Hence, upwards comparisons would not only yield lower well-being but may induce individuals to behave differently and accumulate more debt. In this context, individuals are more likely to accept behaviours if they are shared with people in the reference group. Various empirical studies support the view that inequality induces increased consumption to maintain social position (Heffetz, 2011; Krueger and Perri, 2002; Morgan and Christen, 2003; Wilkinson and Pickett, 2009). Substantiating this point, Frank, Levine, and Dijk (2010) argue:

> [P]eople do not exist in a social vacuum … The rich have been spending more … their spending shifts the frame of reference that shapes the demands of those just below them, who travel in overlapping social circles. So this second group, too, spends more, which shifts the frame of reference for the group just below (p. 4).

In other words, an individual's consumption habits affect other individuals as they draw information about the subject's social position through those practices. This, in turn, influences their own consumption choices as they seek to maintain standards relative to others. Furthermore, this process intensifies when inequalities amplify (Sparkes, 2015).

As a result of the Global Financial Crisis, a spate of studies by economists investigated the associations between amplifying inequality, macroeconomics, the increasing importance of the financial sector and its role in the financial crisis, and the overwhelming finding to emerge is that growing income inequality has been a driver behind the rise in unsustainable debt (see, for example, Frank et al., 2010; Kumhof, Rancière and Winant, 2015; Milanovic, 2009; Rajan, 2010; Skott, 2013; Stiglitz, 2013; Van Treeck, 2014). This research highlights that in countries with high levels of income inequality individuals are more likely to pursue cultural and lifestyle practices with credit-debt to advance social positions relative to others.. Conversely, 'countries with more equal income distributions tend to have significantly longer growth spells' than countries with more unequal income distributions (Berg and Ostray, 2011), not to mention higher levels of trust and well-being amongst adults and children, and lower levels of mental health, drug addiction, obesity and, more importantly, debt (Wilkinson and Pickett, 2009). Thus, cultural and social-structural factors do play a major part in the use and accumulation of debt, as we will illuminate in more detail in this chapter.

6.2.6 The Role of Attitudes and the Sociocultural Context

Attitudes towards debt are considered to be an important underlying factor affecting individuals' perceptions. Attitudes describe individuals' tendency to observe social phenomena and to behave in a certain way based on individuals' own experiences (Allport, 1935). Attitudes towards debt are typically manifested through individuals' approval or disapproval of debt. In a study conducted in the United Kingdom, Livingstone and Lunt (1992) measured attitudes by asking survey respondents whether they were pro- or anti-credit. Procredit individuals would see debt as useful, convenient and part of modern life and a way to satisfy their needs and wants. Anticredit individuals would find debt as shameful and a source of problems, so they would rather save money to satisfy their lifestyle needs than run up debts. In this regard, attitudes towards debt may be a factor affecting individuals' behaviour by denoting a certain willingness or propensity to borrow (Godwin, 1997). Rammstedt (2009) argues that perceptions are not considered to vary substantially except when serious life events, such as unemployment, occur. Gumy (2013) investigated whether subjective debt burden worsened after three life course events, namely unemployment, childbirth and partnership dissolution in three countries: the United Kingdom, Germany and Luxembourg. The results show that subjective debt burden increased after these events, yet differently between men and women, suggesting that there are gender-specific effects. Importantly, the study showed that the same events that alter objective levels of debt also affect subjective levels of debt. This highlights again the need to consider the question of debt dynamically by using a life course theoretical framework that can allow a more comprehensive interpretation of individuals' objective and subjective debt outcomes. It also reiterates the need to observe this phenomenon from an individual point of view to assess intrahousehold inequalities and changes over individuals' lives.

As noted earlier, a life course approach is useful insofar as it represents an integrated framework of analysis which allows the interplay between individuals' life course changes and the structural context (e.g., country) to be observed. Following this approach, we propose that attitudes towards debt may change over time, influenced by the changing socioeconomic context surrounding credit-debt within different nations. In this regard, taking the United Kingdom and the United States as case studies may explain why we see such a large disconnect between the high percentage of individuals living with problem debt and the low percentage of those who regard it as a burden.

Free-market economists in the United Kingdom have long fervently expressed the benefits that credit can bring to the economy. In 1959, a document entitled *Hire Purchase in a Free Society* was published by the free-market think tank the Institute of Economic Affairs (IEA).[7] At the time of the document's publication, the state controlled hire purchase financing in order to maintain a steady money supply and guard against inflationary pressures. The document's authors, Harris, Seldon and Naylor, were scathing towards this position:

> One day ... the notion that hire purchase restrictions could be even a partial substitute for control over the money supply ... will be recognised as the short-sighted delusion it always was ... There is enormous scope for extending the

use of instalment credit for all kinds of goods and services ... Popular prosperity ... increases demand for credit facilities by awakening the individual's ambition and ability to extend his possessions (Harris, Seldon and Naylor, 1959, p. 146)

The importance they place on credit is due mainly to its central role as a medium to enable the widespread pursuit and acquisition of private property. Throughout the 1980s, Margaret Thatcher and the Conservatives proselytised the benefits of homeownership: 'Wherever we can we shall extend the opportunity for personal ownership and the self-respect that goes with it' (Thatcher, 1982). The proliferation of credit was instrumental to meeting this objective. This period signifies a key shift in the way credit was viewed in the United Kingdom amongst those charged with managing the monetary systems. Rather than it being perceived negatively as the 'frittering away of money' that is 'reprehensible' (Leigh-Pemburton, 1988, p. 48), as it once was before under Keynesian demand management, it became infused with many positive features. As a result, since the 1980s the United Kingdom has observed continuously expanding levels of credit lending for both secured and unsecured agreements. Figure 6.3 details the percentage growth in total debt outstanding in the United Kingdom and the United States up to April 2016, with 1987 levels representing the base figure for both countries in order to standardise trends across time.

In 1987, the total levels of debt outstanding equalled £177.4 billion in the United Kingdom. By 2008, the year the financial crisis started, it had reached £1,394.3 billion, representing a 786 per cent increase on 1987 levels. This expansion meant there was an increase in homeowners as a proportion of housing tenures from 55.4 per cent in 1980 to 69.6 per cent in 2002 (Office for National Statistics, 2015). Although the levels of debt outstanding have levelled in recent years, expanding by only a further 98 per cent on 1987 figures since 2008, to £1,568.8 billion in 2016, credit-debt still forms a major part of how British economic and social life functions. Given this situation, perhaps it is unsurprising that within hours of the British EU referendum result, the governor of the Bank of England, Mark Carney, was beamed across television screens reassuring 'markets' there is 'substantial capital and huge liquidity' in reserve that will give 'banks the flexibility they need to continue to lend to UK businesses and households' (Carney, 2016).

In the United States, we observe a process that shares many parallels with the United Kingdom. Total levels outstanding in 1987 stood at $2,426.9 billion, rising 589 per cent to $13,978.8 billion by 2008. Although much larger in real terms – the US figure was fourteen times larger than the UK figure in 1987 – Figure 6.3 shows that the US total debt grew at a smaller rate than experienced in the United Kingdom. Nonetheless, as was the case in the United Kingdom, this growth was driven by a political and economic imperative to increase the number of homeowners. In a speech given in 2002, President George Bush captures this imperative:

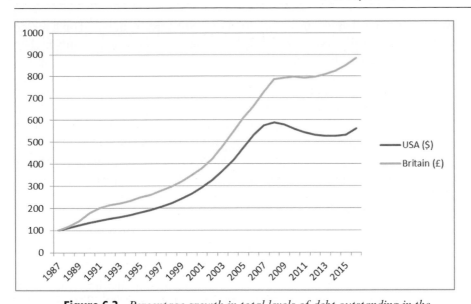

Figure 6.3. *Percentage growth in total levels of debt outstanding in the United Kingdom and the United States, with 1987 figures as the base. Note: Outstanding debt levels represent the combined growth in levels of unsecured and secured forms of debt. The Bank of England first started publishing statistics on credit lending and total debt levels in 1987, which is why this date is used as the base for comparison purposes. Source: UK growth is calculated from data on levels of secured debt, unsecured credit and student loans outstanding published by the Bank of England (2016). US growth is calculated from data on levels of secured debt, unsecured credit and student loans outstanding, published by the US Federal Reserve (2016a, 2016b).*

> We can put light where there's darkness, and hope where there's despondency in this country. And part of it is working together as a nation to encourage folks to own their own home ... Part of economic security is owning your own home (cited in Becker, Stolberg and Labaton, 2008).

The semantics used by George Bush mirrors the language adopted by Margaret Thatcher in the United Kingdom twenty years earlier, mainly because it was driven by the same economic and political rationality.[8] Bush's politicisation of homeownership transformed into an economic plan that aimed to increase the number of minority and low-income homeowners by 5.5 million (Becker et al., 2008), and together this strategy resulted in homeownership levels as a proportion of housing tenures reaching 69.2 per cent in 2005, the highest figure ever recorded in the United States (US Census Bureau, 2017, p. 6).

However, from the early 2000s an increasing proportion of house purchase loans in the United States were of a subprime quality. Subprime lending is the tailoring of financial and credit products to individuals with low incomes. In practice, subprime lending involves a loan or credit agreement based on a teaser rate of interest for the first period of the agreement, before a significantly higher interest rate and monthly repayment is triggered for the remainder of the agreement. This policy creates the potential for a payment shock to the borrower and in consequence a significantly enhanced risk of default (Montgomerie, 2010). The move towards subprime lending was fuelled by a combination of advances in technological capabilities for granting credit, the excess production of credit through securitisation[9] and lender demands for higher rates of interest on loans, and, hence, higher profit margins. Indeed, the root of the Global Financial Crisis emerged in the US subprime housing market, as individuals began defaulting when the teaser rate ended and repayments could not be made. The number of foreclosures in 2005 stood at 530,000, but at their peak in 2011 they had increased to 3.6 million (Statistic Brain, 2016). In a study on the foreclosure crisis, Ross and Squires (2011, p. 140) concluded that many of these subprime mortgage loans were of a 'deceptive or predatory nature'.

However, it would be mistaken to assume that it was just mortgage debt that proliferated in the United States. Draut and Silva (2003) note that the per cent of low-income families with credit cards doubled between 1983 and 2001 from 20 per cent to 40 per cent, and this coincided with an increase in the proportion of low-income families with credit card balances more than twice their monthly incomes from one in thirty to one in eight (cited in Tach and Sternberg-Greene, 2014, p. 2). In 2007, unsecured credit had reached 30 per cent of disposable income in the United States, and by 2008, 61 per cent of adults had outstanding consumer debt (Trumbull, 2014, p. 2, 4). To put this into perspective, at its peak in 2005 unsecured credit as a proportion of income reached just 11 per cent in France (Trumbull, 2014, p. 2).[10]

Taking a wider perspective, no government in the United Kingdom or the United States since the 1980s has acted to slow down the accumulation of debt by individuals who are borrowing to buy houses and other goods and services (Payne, 2013). The dissemination of credit-debt is thus a major part of how these economies are governed, and it is no coincidence that the forced reduction in growth of debt since 2008 in both countries also corresponds with declining living standards, the reduction in the number of homeowners as a proportion of housing tenures, significant political and social changes and increases in labour market insecurity. The term 'credit crunch' that came to signify this reduction captures a crucial economic reality in which the once unhindered growth in credit-debt reached a crux moment, which has subsequently brought with it sharp economic, social, cultural and political changes and consequences.

In essence, what we are saying is that the proliferation of credit-debt in both the United Kingdom and the United States was not unintentional but followed a careful economic rationality with specific political objectives. When economic and political thinking views widespread access to credit as a beneficial platform for society, it provides a case for understanding why a larger proportion of individuals in the United Kingdom and the United States drew upon credit to build their lives and did not regard it as a subjective burden when doing so. There is further empirical evidence to support this position. Previously, we noted how Gumy (2013) had found that German individuals perceive their debt to be a burden at lower debt-to-income ratios than individuals in the United Kingdom. This was indeed attributed to cultural differences in saving patterns. Consistent with this analysis, in a study of fifteen European countries, Georgarakos et al. (2010) found that subjective debt burdens are lower in countries where the percentage of mortgage holders is high. Widespread access to credit, as it has been the case of the United Kingdom and the United States since the 1980s, portrays debt as a more acceptable financial tool, hence affecting how individuals perceive their finances. This stresses the importance of taking cultural aspects into account when evaluating individuals' subjective accounts of finances. Attitudes predispose individuals to certain debt behaviours, whilst the context in which individuals interact shapes how they perceive themselves and their financial status in society. The higher use of credit in the United Kingdom and the United States – amongst other countries – in recent years highlights how an expanding consumer society and use of credit has stimulated individuals to become more tolerant towards debt accumulation, consolidating what some authors have called a 'debt culture' or 'indebted society' (Brown and Taylor, 2008; Draut and Silva, 2007; Ford, 1988). In societies or social groups where credit is widely accessible and where most of the population live in debt, individuals are not reporting their debts to be a 'heavy burden' in the same proportions as those in countries that have greater restrictions on access to credit.

6.2.7 Macro-Level Factors

We have discussed the case studies of the United Kingdom and the United States, in which changing economic perceptions of the benefits of credit-debt became integrated into monetary governance from the 1980s. In referring back to the Life Cycle Model, we must therefore question the validity of an argument that proposes individuals 'rationally' turn to the financial markets to smooth over income and expenditure flows, when, at the same time, a growing number of households accumulate credit beyond the point that is deemed prudent. Indeed, the links between macroeconomic policies and *problem* debt have been established by a number of researchers. For instance, drawing on various data from debt charities and the UK government, Gathergood (2011, p. 2) found that a 1 per cent increase in the unemployment rate is associated with an additional 60,000 debt advice enquires per quarter, and a 1 per cent increase in the average interest rate on a £10,000 loan is associated with an additional 40,000 debt advice queries per quarter.

The build-up of debt can cultivate over a long period of time, and therefore the movement between a manageable and unmanageable financial situation can also take many years to develop (see Marron, 2007; O'Loughlin and Szmigin, 2006). This process is influenced by the way creditors sometimes deal with individuals who are reaching their credit limits. To elaborate, an individual may start with a credit card; they may then obtain a second one to pay off the first; maybe another to pay off the second; then perhaps a personal loan to pay off all three; and finally a consolidation loan to pay off the credit cards, overdrafts and loans that have accumulated. If an individual owns a property, the option is present for the mortgage loan to be remortgaged in order to release equity and clear the unsecured credit that has accumulated. This was indeed a common theme prior to the financial crisis. In May 2007, 34 per cent of mortgages taken out in the United Kingdom were 'interest-only' compared to just 12 per cent in June 2003; of these interest-only mortgages, 27 per cent did not have a specified repayment plan in place (The Money Charity, 2007, p. 5). Bernthal, Crockett and Rose (2005, p. 139) refer to this as 'shuffling practices', whereby individuals request 'additional credit ... once their credit limit has been reached rather than having to face being "maxed out" on their credit agreements and risk the possibility of having to scale back their consumption'. The consolidation of credit agreement(s) can act as a 'clean slate' and can lead to the same credit-induced habits and routines continuing despite an accumulating credit-debt balance. Rarely do banks interject by informing their customers of potential 'stress signals' in their financial accounts, and instead promote 'revolving credit' (Griffiths, 2008, p. 187) as a solution to accumulating credit. Moreover, creditors sometimes increase credit limits without any solicitation by their clients. According to Walker et al. (2014, p. 10), these practices are implicated in the attempt to create 'specific types of economic subjects', a group referred to as 'responsibilised revolving debtors', who rely on a continuous supply of credit and, by implication, provide a continuous stream of profit to credit lenders because they do not pay off their credit balances. The spend, consolidate, spend, consolidate cycle is the materialisation of these systemic processes, which in turn are encouraged through a 'form of economic management' that sustains individuals 'as revolving debtors' (Walker et al., 2014, p. 5).

The problem of consumer credit-debt has increased in many countries as the providers of debts have developed new 'products' to tempt individuals into situations which quickly become unmanageable (Packman, 2014). Over recent years, there has been a rapid increase in payday or online credit companies, termed 'legal loan sharks' by those who have been calling for greater control of these markets. Indeed, in 1992 there were three hundred payday loan companies in the United States; by 2000, there were ten thousand (Manning, 2000, cited in Burton, 2008, p. 17). Some of these companies have high street premises, some operate only through the Internet. Some offer loans to employees on the basis that they will be repaid at the end of the month when the borrower is paid by his or her employer. Others will consider any short-term loan, even for quite small amounts, for example as little as £50 for a few days. Such loans are easy to procure via the Internet, and the cost of just a few pounds for a short-term loan seems very reasonable in some ways, but typically equates to annualised percentage rates (APRs) of well over 1,000 per cent (much higher than the APRs offered by bank loans or credit cards). This signifies a move within credit markets to high-frequency lending in which individuals are not only able to apply for credit online at greater speeds, but the nature of the credit agreement instils a form of borrowing that is short term and frequent.

These companies justify their business by pointing out that people often need loans for short periods – for instance, to purchase a new tyre for a car following a puncture, where the car is essential to travel to work each day. But, in practice, research has shown that these companies deliberately target vulnerable customers who repeatedly take out high-interest loans, and often take out one short-term loan to pay off another short-term loan from another provider (Ali, McRae and Ramsay, 2015). This typically leads to a cycle of debt that can have major psychological implications (described in Section 6.3.2) and in extreme cases to house or car repossession. One might question why otherwise 'rational' people would get involved with such obviously inferior products. There are a number of ways of answering this question. For some people with poor credit ratings (because they have defaulted on previous debts, or because they are migrants who have just arrived in a country), other financial products are not available to them, and they do not have friends or family who are able or willing to loan them money. They may also have different decision-making styles, relying more on affective than factual information. Lamming's (2011) analysis of Internet forums where individuals post recommendations for Internet loans shows that the discussions were rarely about interest rates but were often about nonquantifiable aspects of the transaction such as the friendly greeting from the sales representatives of these short-term loan companies, who seemed to be very sympathetic of their situations – a welcome change from the stigma or belittling they had experienced from financial institutions in the past. These payday and short-term loan companies have developed this friendly and welcoming persona through advertising and even (controversially) sponsoring UK sports teams, such as Wonga.com's sponsorship of Newcastle United Football Club (Cooper Wognsen, 2013). In the United States, companies such as the Dollar Loan Center[11] have been more restrained in their advertising. However, in the United Kingdom, the combination of less regulated online gambling, Internet loans and sports sponsorship seems like a particularly toxic mix.

Fortunately, the situation in the United Kingdom has improved considerably due to the tighter regulation of such companies (see West, 2016). This has involved capping the interest rates they can charge at 0.8 per cent per day; restricting the amount that loans can be increased after default to no more than twice the amount borrowed; and making it more difficult for loans to be continually 'rolled over' (West, 2016).[12] The politician who drove this legislation through the UK parliament, Stella Creasy (MP), drew upon the research on debt by economic psychologists in her contributions to the Consumer Rights Bill (2014).[13] These changes have not been without criticism: Rowlingson, Appleyard and Gardner (2016) argue that the increased activity by payday lenders has been driven not only by financialisation but also by increased demand for loans brought about by labour market flexibility (such as zero-hours contracts – see Wood and Burchell in the current volume), a wider gap between the rich and the poor and reductions in welfare spending. This is further acerbated by the Coalition Government's decision in 2013 to end the Social Fund Loan system, the only mechanism that permitted vulnerable individuals to borrow from the state in times of need. Without realistic alternatives, Rowlingson et al. (2016) argue that people will be forced to borrow from other less regulated services such as doorstep lenders.

Credit unions seem a better alternative to payday lenders. Credit unions are mutual, not-for-profit organisations that encourage members to save money and then have access to loans. They also see their role as providers of education in financial literacy and in urging individuals to develop good long-term goals for their finances. Although, in the narrow sense, credit unions do not provide high rates of interest to savers, the 'social return on investment' in credit unions is high in ameliorating the hidden costs of debts to individuals and to society (McKillop and Wilson, 2015).

6.3 Problem Debt and Its Psychological Effects

6.3.1 Debt Morality

Despite a range of factors influencing the take-up and accumulation of debt, and also the discrepancy between objective and subjective debt, there are dominant discourses that circulate across national contexts when debt problems arise (in other words, the point at which an individual defaults on their agreement(s)). Here we move on to the question of perceived morality. Morality significantly influences how individuals shape their understanding of debt and consequently their behaviour. Historical evidence suggests that the concept of debt has often carried a negative connotation and that the lack of repayment of debt could be understood as an individual's life failure, lack of responsibility, dishonesty and personal fault (Ford, 1988; Sullivan, Warren and Westbrook, 1999). The legal and social norms that regulate debt situations play a major role in shaping individuals' attitudes towards debt. Individuals are legally (and morally) obliged to repay their debts. Failure to do so may be interpreted as dishonesty on the part of the borrowers, which makes them responsible for their acts (Huls, 1993). The phrase at the top of this chapter, 'Neither a borrower nor a lender be', is often assumed to originate from the Bible or to have a religious genesis. In fact, the Bible, particularly the New Testament, has very little to say about debt. The only time Jesus is reported as using violence was to eject the money lenders (not borrowers!) from the temple, but this was because he thought the temple was an inappropriate setting for commerce of any sort. This phrase is actually spoken by Polonius in Shakespeare's *Hamlet*; Polonius is usually seen as a rather comical windbag who thinks himself rather cleverer than his words or actions indicate, suggesting that Shakespeare thought it to be nonsensical. Yet, the widely held belief that 'bad debtors' are deserving of our distain and shaming is deeply rooted in some societies. Furthermore, the penalties associated with the lack of repayment, which in the past also included imprisonment, contributed over time to the stigmatisation of debt, so that debt could be a factor producing embarrassment and shame for the individual, thus strengthening sentiments of rejection, aversion and anxiety (Drentea, 2000). The stigma attached to debt is most salient when trying to study debtors. Numerous surveys collecting information on individuals' finances are indicative of individuals' unwillingness to share their financial information, resulting in low response rates or in the underreporting of information. Ford (1988) suggests that in societies where debt problems are seen as an individual failure, respondents may feel stigmatised and would not want to disclose their debts.

Although problem debt and the demand for debt advice are found to be significantly correlated with developments in the macroeconomy, there are still a number of economists in the United Kingdom and the United States who consider problem debt to be caused by the moral failure of people, particularly those who they believe knowingly take out loans and mortgages they cannot afford (e.g., Booth, 2009; Gregg, 2009). Put simply, this line of reasoning argues that problem debt and the social issues it creates are predominantly the consequences of the choices individuals have made (Orton, 2009). Therefore, in this line of reasoning, problem debt is viewed as the failings of irresponsible, undisciplined and immoral debtors who have abused the opportunities afforded to them through greater access to credit. These types of explanations behind the causes of problem debt were advanced in a more aggressive way after the 2008 Global Financial Crisis by free-market economists in both the United Kingdom and the United States. Booth, the editorial and programme director for the IEA, set the tone of this narrative:

> If we do not look for the underlying, as opposed to the popularly assumed, causes of the financial crash ... it is quite possible to so seriously misdiagnose the causes ... that diametrically wrong conclusions are reached as to the appropriate policy action (Booth, 2009, p. 35).

In considering the 'causes' of the financial crisis, Booth (2008) bluntly states, 'we should not forget the consumer', before going on to argue, 'when it comes down to it, individuals need to take responsibility, whatever the pressure from salesmen or their peers'. Gregg, director of research at the Acton Institute, a Michigan-based think tank that integrates Christian principles with free-market economics, adds to this denunciation by suggesting there have been few 'moral critiques' of individuals who 'lied … about their assets, income and liabilities in order to obtain loans and mortgages' (Gregg, 2009, p. 149). In light of this, Gregg (2009) suggests we need to recognise the economic significance of particular moral habits, such as the 'virtue of prudence', as an 'adequate control mechanism for keeping personal borrowing under control' (p. 150). When issues of morality are promoted as the underlying causes of problem debt, it is unsurprising that individuals internalise this line of reasoning and perceive their own predicament within the frame of language to which they are subjected. Edwards (2003, p. 48), for instance, illustrates that 'many people with debt problems think that when they seek advice they will be judged', and that 'they often feel it is their fault for not being able to manage their money effectively'. Additionally, Ross and Squires (2011) found those at risk of losing their home internalise the situation as a personal failure. It is interesting to ask why moral failure is one of the most publicly visible ways in which problem debt is perceived. We will explore this facet after we detail the individual consequences of this discourse.

6.3.2 The Psychological Effects of Debt

Up to this point, we have explored the psychology of debt, and for that we have discussed issues concerning theories, measures, perceptions, attitudes and macro-level factors. However, so far little attention has been given to the psychological *effects* of having problem debt. Several studies have in fact found a strong association between self-reported measures of financial difficulties and *psychological depression* (Bridges and Disney, 2010; Brown, Taylor and Wheatley Price, 2005; Drentea and Reynolds, 2012; Fitch et al., 2011; Jenkins et al., 2008; Reading and Reynolds, 2001), *suicidal ideation and behaviour* (Hintikka et al., 1998; Meltzer et al., 2011; Yip et al., 2007) and *physical impairment and mental health* (Balmer et al., 2005; Dossey, 2007; Drentea and Lavrakas, 2000; Matthews and Gallo, 2011; Sweet et al., 2013). These associations have been confirmed by Richardson, Elliott and Roberts' (2013) meta-analysis of more than sixty studies, although due to a lack of longitudinal studies the researchers conclude it is difficult to demonstrate causality. Nonetheless, an increase in the percentage of individuals reporting financial stress (i.e., worry about finances) has prompted studies to focus on the factors influencing this rise. For example, Dunn and Mirzaie (2016) used a psychological measure of stress tied to the individual's debt (e.g., worry over debt) to examine whether debt stress increased during the Great Recession in the United States. They find that unsecured debt (i.e., nonmortgage debt) created the most stress, and this has increased during the recession mostly due to an upwards shift in the percentage of consumers taking unsecured debt, as opposed to secured debt.

The other aspect of this relationship missing from the economic and psychological accounts is an awareness of the social mechanisms that facilitate these health 'effects', particularly, as discussed previously, the role of stigma that is concomitant with problem debt. In the final section of this chapter, we wish to draw attention to the process through which debt morality is mobilised to create shame and fear amongst problem debtors in order to change economic behaviour. We will do this by probing the practices of debt collectors to show how debt morality is used to shape debtors' self-perceptions and also their strategies to deal with their debt. Subsequently, we shed light on some major factors underpinning the psychological and physiological effects of problem debt that are omitted from contemporary research in economic psychology.

6.3.3 Debt Collection Practices

As noted earlier, default on household utility bills or credit agreement(s) is the trigger that moves an individual from an *unproblematic* credit user to a *problematic* debtor. At the point default occurs, creditors become inimical towards their clients; they send letters eliciting the full balance of the debt, and these letters signify 'danger'. The language used and the implicit threats made create uncertainty, mainly because there is generally a lack of lay knowledge regarding the powers creditors possess to reclaim the debt along with a lack of awareness of the consequences of nonpayment. Although repossession of a home and/or other possessions is a real possibility when default occurs, it is generally a last resort for creditors.[14] Instead, Edwards (2003, p. 32) found that creditors take the view 'that "informal" pressure on individuals' to make a payment 'is more effective than court action'. For instance, when collecting unsecured debts, creditors often place on their correspondence that a 'representative' or 'debt collector' will be sent to the property, and although they have no legal powers to take goods or payments, creditors are aware their clients often take them to be bailiffs, and thus they become imbued with powers they do not possess. Creditors use this misclassification to construe specific possibilities in the minds of those with problem debt. They want the threat of losing one's home, possessions and/or assets to create anxiety and uncertainty. As a result, Poster (2013, p. 225) suggests individuals 'are victims of many kinds of deception' by credit providers, as their 'workers "trick" them with their words, or omit crucial information' about their practices and wider legal issues.

This illuminates a key question: what behavioural affects are these practices intended to procure? Poster (2013, p. 216) reveals that debt collectors, or 'emotional hitmen', as she refers to them, draw on a preexisting set of social norms regarding immoralities to affect the individual, one of which is the attempt to humiliate their client for falling into debt in order to generate shame and fear for transgressing a dominant notion of responsibility: repaying debt. Returning to the arguments put forward by Gregg will substantiate this point. Gregg (2009, p. 150) explored the etymology of the word 'credit' and traces it back to the Latin word *credere*, meaning 'to believe' and 'to trust'. Gregg (2009,

p. 151) subsequently uses this context to argue that 'providing people with credit means that you trust and believe' in such borrowers to keep their 'promise' and pay the money back (Gregg, 2009, p. 151). We see an attempt here to produce a specific 'morality' surrounding debt, a 'morality of the *promise* to honor one's debt' (Lazzarato, 2011, p. 30). Booth supports this position: 'The important thing is that those who make the decisions bear the cost when things go wrong: there should be no bail-out of borrowers [and] there should be no bail out of shareholders' (Booth, 2007). In this context, there is an attempt to train 'the governed to "promise" to honor their debt' (Lazzarato, 2011, p. 46). Walker et al. (2014, p. 58) refer to the tactics adopted by debt collectors as a kind of 'mental warfare' that is used to maintain credit 'organisations' competitiveness in the marketplace'. There is empirical evidence to support this position. After rising bankruptcy and foreclosure rates in the United States, creditors inferred these figures suggest individuals are more willing to pursue insolvency because of a diminution of social stigma (see Cohen-Cole and Duygan-Bump, 2008). For instance, Visa USA specified in testimony at a congressional hearing on bankruptcy law, that 'surely one reason [for increases in bankruptcy] is that bankruptcy no longer appears to carry the social stigma it once did', which means an increasing number of people 'choose bankruptcy as the "solution" to their financial difficulties rather than as a "last resort"' (Consumer Debt Hearing, supra note 77, at 428–429, cited in Efrat, 2006, p. 384). As we saw previously, the rise in bankruptcy and foreclosure rates in the United States was mainly triggered by 'deceptive and predatory' lending, but this example reveals how stigma is also seen as a vital tool in the creditors' arsenal.

At the macro level, debt and the possibility of nonpayment threatens the functionality of markets, consumption and, more importantly, profitability. In a move conceptualised by Walker (2012) as the 'discourse of individual financial responsibility', it is clear how those with problem debt are 'publicly constituted and acted upon'. The 'discourse' is utilised in an attempt to produce a normative social influence regarding problem debt. Stigma is often mobilised against those who default on their agreements in an attempt to intensify the psychological effects of debt so, firstly, the individual knows and feels they have failed; and, secondly, to make sure that the only 'rational' option is to repay the money that is owed, even in cases when insolvency is a better financial option (Sparkes, 2015). Against this backdrop, Edwards (2003) found many individuals contacting the Citizens Advice Bureau (CAB) for debt advice could not cope with their finances and were feeling in crisis. The consequences of the stigma surrounding problem debt for psychological health can be devastating. For instance, Meltzer and colleagues (2011, p. 771) found that after controlling for sociodemographic and lifestyle factors, those with problem debt were twice as likely to think about suicide.

One thing that is missing from economic and psychological accounts is how insecurity is mobilised as a debt collection tactic. Although debtors are free to make their own choices, the discourse that debt problems are the result of immoral behaviour stigmatises those with problem debt, creating shame and humiliation, which 'pushes' debtors to act in such a way to make sure they honour their debts (Lazzarato, 2011, p. 31). The psychological and economic accounts of debt and their effect for psychological and/or physiological health would do well to pay head to the social mechanism of stigma and morality as an 'affective' strategy and tactic that is intended to induce individuals into a certain engagement with their problem debt.

Ultimately, the discourse that prevails at explaining personal indebtedness is crucially important. As Booth indicates, the prevailing discourse dictates the types of governmental, charitable and private sector policies that are imagined to deal with individuals with problem debt, but also it heavily influences how those individuals understand themselves and the steps they take to get themselves out of problem debt. The discourse of debt and immorality is all too easily ignored by financial institutions when encouraging individuals to take out loans, but then is used as a weapon when enforcing repayment. Hamilton (1980, p. 767) argued that, rather than considering individuals as intuitive psychologists, scientists or statisticians, our thought processes are more akin to those of an 'intuitive lawyer', apportioning blame rather than apportioning cause. Psychologists and economists might do well to think about debt as being a study of lay understandings of virtue and blame.

6.4 Conclusion

Given the strong links between debt and financial and psychological well-being, the study of debt needs to be a core topic for economic psychology. It is an excellent example of a topic where laboratory and field research combined with analysis of large datasets complements the insights of practitioners dealing with people and households with financial difficulties. Yet the study of debt cannot be complete if it is based on a narrow perspective: psychology, sociology and economics are important, but so are history and ethics to understand the cultural baggage that comes with the study of debt. We need to understand how households use debt to cope with the life course, and how financial institutions make money as providers of credit-debt that can lead to problem debt. The gulf between debtors' actual, objective debts and their perceptions of those debts is essential to understand the effects of debts on individuals' well-being and behaviour. Values, attitudes, personality and cultural influences give insights into that gap. We need to understand the rationality of debt, and simultaneously why individuals and families do not behave in accordance with 'rational' expectations. This chapter has, hopefully, made some advances in pulling these strands together.

Notes

1 Note that this chapter is only interested in 'personal debt' held by individuals and households. The debts held by countries, 'national debts', are a completely different phenomenon.

2 Debt can also be taken up informally, by borrowing from family or friends, and does not always require an agreed date for repayment, although there is an expectation of repayment; however, this type of debt is not the focus of this chapter.

3 The EST and DPP are both methods used to detect the avoidance of some words, typically presented as part of a reaction-time task on a computer screen. In the EST, words are presented in different font colours; the time taken to report the colour is longer for words associated with negative emotions for that participant. The DPP measures selective attention to words flashed onto a screen. After the two words disappear, a dot appears on the screen. Participants are instructed to press a button as soon as they see the dot. The reaction time will be slower if the dot appears in the same location as a word that they subconsciously avoided looking at. Both tasks showed that participants with high levels of financial aversion took longer to process or avoided words such as 'debt' or 'bank'.

4 Finding objective questions that individuals will answer to give an indication of their actual debts is more challenging, particularly for individuals with 'financial phobia' who actively avoid information on their own finances.

5 More up-to-date data are not available.

6 More up-to-date data are available but the 2008 data was used for comparability with Figure 1.

7 The IEA was established in 1955, and its mission statement is 'to improve understanding of the fundamental institutions of a free society by analysing and expounding the role of markets in solving economic and social problems' (Institute of Economic Affairs, 2016).

8 The politicisation of homeownership and the various policies that have supported it – Right-to-Buy and Help-to-Buy in the United Kingdom and the Community Reinvestment Act (CRA) and the Federal Housing Administration's homeownership subsidies in the United States – are built from free-market economic theory and represent its materialisation as a form of governmentality.

9 In 1986, a phenomenon referred to as the financial 'Big Bang' took place, and it involved fundamental transformations in the markets for securitised debt. Securitised debt, or asset-backed bonds, is the bundling together by credit providers of existing credit instruments into larger tradeable assets in which investors can buy shares and receive interest payments (Bank of England, 1991; Marron, 2007, 2014). With securitisation, any credit agreement made can be resold (Hyman, 2012), and thus securitisation represents a key structural development in the capacity of financial institutions production of credit-debt.

10 The exponential increase in both unsecured and secured lending observed in the United States between 1987 and 2008 did not continue after the Global

Financial Crisis. Total levels outstanding actually decreased by 63 per cent of the levels touched in 2008, reaching $12,898.5 billion in 2013, but have since rebounded somewhat, reaching $13,600.8 billion in 2016 (a figure representing a 560 per cent increase on 1987 figures, and an amount ten times larger than in the United Kingdom).

11 See www.dontbebroke.com.

12 Regulation of payday or 'subprime' loans has also been tightened in the United States and Canada.

13 www.publications.parliament.uk/pa/cm201314/cmpublic/consumer/140306/pm/140306s01.htm.

14 In 2013, there were 667,168 County Court Judgements, 47,769 Charging Orders, and just 222 Order of Sales issued in UK county courts (StepChange Debt Charity, 2015). Although an Order of Sale is very rare (in 2013, just 0.47 per cent of Charging Orders got to this stage), the fact that this prospect even exists can cause anxiety amongst homeowners with problem debt.

6.5 References

Ali, P., McRae, C., and Ramsay, I. (2015). Payday Lending Regulation and Borrower Vulnerability in the United Kingdom and Australia. *Journal of Business Law*, (3), 223–255.

Allport, G. W. (1935). Attitudes. In E. Murchison (Ed.), *Handbook of Social Psychology* (pp. 798–844). Worcester, MA: Clark University Press.

Ando, A., and Modigliani, F. (1963). The 'Life Cycle' Hypothesis of Saving: Aggregate Implications and Tests. *American Economic Review*, 53(1), 55–84.

Balmer, N., Pleasence, P., Buck, A., and Walker, H. C. (2005). Worried Sick: The Experience of Debt Problems and Their Relationship with Health, Illness and Disability. *Social Policy and Society*, 5(1), 39–51.

Bank of England. (1991). Developments in International Banking and Capital Markets in 1990: Asset-backed Bonds. *Bank of England Quarterly Bulletin*, Q2, 234–245. Retrieved 11 September 2013, from www.bankofengland.co.uk/archive/Documents/ historicpubs/qb/1992/qb92q2190198.pdf

Bank of England. (2016). Quarterly Total Lending to Individuals (Including Student Loans). Retrieved 14 November 2016, from www.bankofengland.co.uk/boeapps/iadb/index.asp?first=yes&SectionRequired=A&HideNums=-1&ExtraInfo=false&Travel=NIxSTx

Becker, J., Stolberg, S. G., and Labaton, S. (2008). White House Philosophy Stoked Mortgage Bonfire. Retrieved 15 January 2016, from www.nytimes.com/2008/12/21/business/worldbusiness/21iht-21admin.18841556.html

Berg, A., and Ostry, J. (2011). Inequality and Unsustainable Growth: Two Sides of the Same Coin? *International Monetary Fund Staff Discussion Note*, 1–21.

Bernthal, M. J., Crockett, D., and Rose, R. L. (2005). Credit Cards as Lifestyle Facilitators. *Journal of Consumer Research*, 32(1), 130–145.

Berthoud, R., and Kempson, E. (1992). *Credit and Debt. The PSI Report*. United Kingdom: PSI.

Betti, G., Dourmashkin, N., Rossi, M. C., Verma, V., and Yin, Y. (2001). *Study of the Problem of Consumer Indebtedness: Statistical Aspects*. Commision of European Union No. B5-1000/00/000197. Retrieved 4 August 2017, from www.iaclaw.org/Research_papers/iff_OverindebtednessandConsumerLaw .pdf

Booth, P. (2007). Rocky Road Ahead. *Media Post*. Institute of Economic Affairs. Retrieved 10 March 2015, from https://iea.org.uk/in-the-media/media-coverage/rocky-road-ahead

Booth, P. (2008). Bishops Should Tread Carefully in Their Response to the Financial Crash. *Media Post*. Institute of Economic Affairs. Retrieved 30 March 2015, from www.iea.org.uk/in-the-media/media-coverage/bishops-should-tread-carefully-in-their-response-to-the-financial-crash

Booth, P. (2009). The Causes of the Crash. In P. Booth (Ed.), *Verdict on the Crash: Causes and Policy Implications.* (pp. 25–36). London: Institute of Economic Affairs.

Bridges, S., and Disney, R. (2010). Debt and Depression. *Journal of Health Economics*, 29(3), 388–403.

Brown, S., and Taylor, K. (2008). Household Debt and Financial Assets: Evidence from Germany, Great Britain and the USA. *Journal of the Royal Statistical Society. Series A: Statistics in Society*, 171(3), 615–643. doi.org/10.1111/ j.1467-985X.2007.00531.x

Brown, S., Taylor, K., and Wheatley Price, S. (2005). Debt and Distress: Evaluating the Psychological Cost of Credit. *Journal of Economic Psychology*, 26(5), 642–663.

Browning, M., Bourguignon, F., Chiappori, P. A., and Lechene, V. (1994). Income and Outcomes: A Structural Model of Intrahousehold Allocation. *Journal of Political Economy*, 102(6), 1067–1096.

Burchell, B. J. (2004). Identifying, Describing and Understanding Financial Aversion: Financial Phobes. *Argent: Journal of the Financial Services Forum*, 2(3), 22–26.

Burton, D. (2008). *Credit and Consumer Society*. London: Routledge.

Campbell, A., Converse, P. E., and Rogers, W. L. (1976). *The Quality of American Life: Perceptions, Evaluations, and Satisfactions*. New York: Russell Sage.

Carlbring, P., Nordgren, L. B., Furmark, T., and Andersson, G. (2009). Long-term Outcome of Internet-Delivered Cognitive-Behavioural Therapy for Social Phobia: A 30-Month Follow-up. *Behaviour Research and Therapy*, 47(10), 848–850. doi.org/10.1016/j.brat.2009.06.012

Carney, M. (2016). EU Referendum: Statement from Bank of England Governor Mark Carney. Retrieved 24 June 2016, from www.bbc.co.uk/news/business-36618560

Chatterjee, P., and Rose, R. L. (2012). Do Payment Mechanisms Change the Way Consumers Perceive Products? *Journal of Consumer Research*, 38(6), 1129–1139.

Cohen-Cole, E., and Duygan-Bump, B. (2008). Household Bankruptcy Decision: The Role of Social Stigma vs. Information Sharing. Federal Reserve Bank Boston, Quantitative Analysis Unit Series Paper No. QAU08-6. Retrieved 13 March 2015, from faculty.washington.edu/jhcook/seminar/cohen-cole stigma and information in bankruptcy_10sept.pdf

Cooper Wognsen, T. P. (2013). *It'd Be Weird Without McDonald's*. Aalborg Universitet.

D'Astous, A. (1990). An Inquiry into the Compulsive Side of 'Normal' Consumers. *Journal of Consumer Policy*, 13, 15–31.

del Río, A., and Young, G. (2005). The Impact of Unsecured Debt on Financial Distress Among British Households. Bank of England, Working Paper No. 262. Retrieved 4 August 2017, from www.bankofengland.co.uk/archive/Documents/historicpubs/workingpapers/2005/wp262.pdf

Dossey, L. (2007). Debt and Health. *Explore: The Journal of Science and Healing*, 3(2), 83–90. doi.org/10.1016/j.explore.2006.12.004

Draut, T., and Silva, J. (2003). *Borrowing to Make Ends Meet: The Growth of Credit Card Debt in the '90s*. New York: Demos.

Draut, T., and Silva, J. (2007). *Borrowing to Make Ends Meet: The Growth of Credit Card Debt in the '90s*. New York: Demos.

Drentea, P. (2000). Age, Debt and Anxiety. *Journal of Health and Social Behavior*, 41(4), 437–450. doi.org/10.2307/2676296

Drentea, P., and Lavrakas, P. J. (2000). Over the Limit: The Association Among Health, Race and Debt. *Social Science and Medicine*, 50(4), 517–529.

Drentea, P., and Reynolds, J. R. (2012). Neither a Borrower nor a Lender Be: The Relative Importance of Debt and SES for Mental Health Among Older Adults. *Journal of Aging and Health*, 24, 673–695.

Dunn, L. F., and Mirzaie, I. (2016). Consumer Debt Stress, Changes in Household Debt, and the Great Recession. *Economic Inquiry*, 54(1), 201–214.

Edwards, S. (2003). *In Too Deep: CAB Clients' Experience of Debt*. London: Citizens Advice.

Efrat, R. (2006). The Evolution of Bankruptcy Stigma. *Theoretical Inquiries in Law*, 7(2), 365–393.

Elder, G. H. (1985). *Life Course Dynamics. Trajectories and Transitions, 1968–1980*. Ithaca, NY: Cornell University Press.

Eurostat – SILC. (2008). 2008 Module: Over-indebtedness and Financial Exclusion. Retrieved 22 November 2016 from ec.europa.eu/eurostat/web/income-and-living-conditions/data/ad-hoc-modules

Faber, R. (1988). Compulsive Consumption and Credit Abuse. *Journal of Consumer Policy*, 11, 97–109.

Festinger, L. (1954). A Theory of Social Comparison Processes. *Human Relations*, 7(2), 117–140.

Fitch, C., Hamilton, S., Bassett, P., and Davey, R. (2011). The Relationship Between Personal Debt and Mental Health: A Systematic Review. *Mental Health Review Journal*, 16(4), 153–166.

Ford, J. (1988). *The Indebted Society: Credit and Default in the 1980s*. New York: Routledge.

Ford, J. (1991). *Consuming Credit: Debt and Poverty in the UK*. London: Child Poverty Action Group (CPAG).

Frank, R. H., Levine, A. S., and Dijk, O. (2010). Expenditure Cascades. *SSRN Electronic Journal*, 1–30. doi.org/10.2139/ssrn.1690612

Frederick, S., Loewenstein, G., and O'Donoghue, T. (2002). Time Discounting and Time Preference: A Critical Review. *Journal of Economic Literature*, 40, 351–401.

Gathergood, J. (2011). Demand, Capacity and Need for Debt Advice in the United Kingdom. *Money Advice Trust*. Retrieved 4 August 2017, from, http://www .moneyadvicetrust.org/SiteCollectionDocuments/Research%20and%20 reports/demand_and_capacity.pdf

Georgarakos, D., Lojschova, A., and Ward-Wamedinger, M. (2010). Mortgage Indebtedness and Household Financial Distress. European Central Bank, Working Paper No. 1156.

Godwin, D. H. (1997). Dynamics of Households' Income Debt and Attitudes Toward Credit, 1983–1989. *Journal of Consumer Affairs*, 31(2), 303–325.

Grable, J. E. (2000). Financial Risk Tolerance and Additional Factors That Affect Risk Taking in Every Day Money Matters. *Journal of Business and Pyschology*, 14(4), 625–630.

Graeber, D. (2011). *Debt. The First 5,000 Years*. Brooklyn: Melville House.

Gregg, S. (2009). Moral Failure: Borrowing, Lending and the Financial Crisis. In P. Booth (Ed.), *Verdict on the Crash: Causes and Policy Implications* (pp. 145–56). London: Institute of Economic Affairs.

Griffiths, M. (2008). Guest Editorial: Themed Issue: Consumer Issues in Credit and Debt. *International Journal of Consumer Studies*, 32(3), 187.

Gumy, J. M. (2013). The Impact of Unemployment, Childbirth and Partnership Dissolution on Perceived Problematic Debt in the UK, Germany and Luxembourg. Thesis, University of Cambridge.

Hamilton, V. L. (1980). Intuitive Psychologist or Intuitive Lawyer? Alternative Models of the Attribution Process. *Journal of Personality and Social Psychology*, 39(5), 767–772.

Harris, C. (1987). The Individual and Society: A Processual Approach. In A. Bryman, B. Bytheway, P. Allatt, and T. Keil (Eds.), *Rethinking the Life Cycle*. London: Macmillan Press.

Harris, R., Seldon, A., and Naylor, M. (1959). *Hire Purchase in a Free Society*. London: Institute of Economic Affairs.

Heffetz, O. (2011). A Test of Conspicuous Consumption: Visibility and Income Elasticities. *Review of Economics and Statistics*, XCIII(4), 1101–1118.

Hintikka, J., Kontula, O., Saarinen, P., Tanskanen, A., Koskela, K., and Viinamäki, H. (1998). Debt and Suicidal Behaviour in the Finnish General Population. *Acta Psychiatrica Scandinavica*, 98(6), 493–496. doi.org/10.1111/j.1600-0447.1998. tb10125.x

Hirschman, E. C. (1979). Differences in Consumer Purchase Behavior by Credit Card Payment System. *Journal of Consumer Research*, 6(1), 58–66.

Huls, N. (1993). Towards a European Approach to Overindebtedness of Consumers. *Journal of Consumer Policy*, 16(2), 215–234. doi.org/10.1007/BF01418377

Hyman, L. (2012). The Politics of Consumer Debt: U.S. State Policy and the Rise of Investment in Consumer Credit, 1920–2008. *Annals of the American Academy of Political and Social Science*, 644, 40–49.

Inglehart, R. (1977). *The Silent Revolution: Changing Values and Political Styles Among Western Publics*. Princeton: Princeton University Press.

Inglehart, R. (2008). Changing Values Among Western Publics from 1970 to 2006. *West European Politics*, 31(1–2), 130–146. doi.org/10.1080/0140238070 1834747

Institute of Economic Affairs. (2016). Mission Statement. Retrieved 22 November 2016, from iea.org.uk/about-us

Jarvis, S., and Jenkins, S. P. (1999). Marital Splits and Income Changes: Evidence from the British Household Panel Survey. *Population Studies*, 53(2), 237–254.

Jenkins, R., Bhugra, D., Bebbington, P., Brugha, T., Farrell, M., Coid, J., et al. (2008). Debt, Income and Mental Disorder in the General Population. *Psychological Medicine*, 38(10), 1485–1493. doi.org/10.1017/S0033291707002516

Jianakoplos, N. A., and Bernasek, A. (1998). Are Women More Risk Averse? *Economic Inquiry*, 36(4), 629–630.

Kamleitner, B., and Kirchler, E. (2007). Consumer Credit Use: A Process Model and Literature Review. *Revue européenne de psychologie appliquée/European Review of Applied Psychology*, 57(4), 267–283. doi.org/doi: DOI: 10.1016/j.erap.2006.09.003

Kan, M.-Y., and Laurie, H. (2010). Savings, Investments, Debts and Psychological Well-being in Married and Cohabiting Couples. ISER Working Paper Series. Essex.

Keese, M. (2012). Who Feels Constrained by High Debt Burdens? Subjective vs Objective Measures of Household Debt. *Journal of Economic Psychology*, 33(2), 125–141.

Kempson, E., and Atkinson, A. (2006). *Overstretched: People at Risk of Financial Difficulties*. Bristol: Genworth Financial.

Krueger, D., and Perri, F. (2002). Does Income Inequality Lead to Consumption Inequality? Evidence and Theory. NBER Working Paper 9202. Retrieved 15 April 2015, from www.nber.org/papers/w9202.pdf

Kumhof, M., Rancière, R., and Winant, P. (2015). Inequality, Leverage, and Crises. *American Economic Review*, 105(3), 1217–1245. doi.org/10.1257/aer.20110683

Lamming, A. (2011). 'My Old Friend Wonga': Experiences of Using Payday Loans as Revealed in Online Forums. Thesis. University of Cambridge.

Lancaster, G., and Ray, R. (2002). Tests of Income Pooling on Household Budget Data: The Australian Evidence. *Australian Economic Papers*, 41(1), 99–114.

Lazzarato, M. (2011). *The Making of the Indebted Man: An Essay on the Neoliberal Condition*. Los Angeles: Semiotext.

Leigh-Pemburton, R. (1988). Personal Credit in Perspective. Governor's Speech at the Annual Luncheon of the Newspaper Conference. *Bank of England Quarterly Bulletin*, Q1, 48–50. Retrieved 24 August 2013, from www.bankofengland.co.uk/archive/Documents /historicpubs/qb/1988/qb88q14850.pdf

Livingstone, S. M., and Lunt, P. K. (1992). Predicting personal debt and debt repayment: psychological, social and economic determinants. *Journal of Economic Psychology*, 13(1), 111–134. doi.org/10.1016/0167-4870(92)90055-c

Lown, J. M., and Ju, I. (1992). A Model of Credit Use and Financial Satisfaction. *Financial Counseling and Planning*, 3, 105–125.

Lusardi, A., and Tufano, P. (2009). Debt Literacy, Financial Experiences and Overindebtedness. NBER Working Paper No. 14808.

Manning, R. (2000). *Credit Card Nation: The Consequences of America's Addiction to Credit*. New York: Basic Books.

Manser, M., and Brown, M. (1980). Marriage and Household Decision-Making: A Bargaining Analysis. *International Economic Review*, 21(1), 31–44.

Marron, D. (2007). 'Lending by Numbers': Credit Scoring and the Constitution of Risk Within American consumer Credit. *Economy and Society*, 36(1), 103–133.

Matthews, K. A., and Gallo, L. C. (2011). Psychological Perspectives on Pathways Linking Socioeconomic Status and Physical Health. *Annual Review of Psychology*, 62, 501–530.

McKillop, D., and Wilson, J. (2015). Credit Unions as Cooperative Institutions: Distinctiveness, Performance and Prospects. *Social and Environmental Accounting Journal*, 35(2), 96–112.

Meltzer, H., Bebbington, P., Brugha, T., Jenkins, R., McManus, S., and Dennis, M. S. (2011). Personal Debt and Suicidal Ideation. *Psychological Medicine*, 41(4), 771–778.

Milanovic, B. (2009). Two Views on the Cause of the Global Crisis. *YaleGlobal Online*, 11–13. Retrived 13 April 2015, from at: http://yaleglobal.yale.edu/content/two-views-global-crisis

Montgomerie, J. (2010). Neoliberalism and the Making of Subprime Borrowers. In M. Konings (Ed.), *The Great Credit Crash* (pp. 103–118). London: Verso.

Morgan, R., and Christen, M. (2003). Keeping Up with the Joneses: The Effect of Income Inequality on Demand for Consumer Credit. Insead. Retrieved 23 July 2014, from flora.insead.edu/fichiersti_wp/inseadwp2003/2003–67.pdf

Mullainathan, S., and Shafir, E. (2009). Saving Policy and Decision-Making in Low-Income Households. In R. Blanc and M. Barr (Eds.), *Insufficient Funds: Saving, Assets, Credit, and Banking Among Low-Income Households* (pp. 121–146). New York: The Russell Sage Foundation.

Office for National Statistics. (2015). Housing and Home Ownership in the UK. Retrieved 14 November 2016, from visual.ons.gov.uk/uk-perspectives-housing-and-home-ownership-in-the-uk/

O'Loughlin, D., and Szmigin, I. (2006). 'I'll Always Be in Debt': Irish and UK Student Behaviour in a Credit Led Environment. *Journal of Consumer Marketing*, 23(6), 335–343. doi.org/10.1108/07363760610701878

O'Rand, A. M., and Krecker, M. L. (1990). Concepts of the Life Cycle: Their History, Meanings, and Uses in the Social Sciences. *Annual Review of Sociology*, 16(1), 241–262.

Orton, M. (2009). Understanding the Exercise of Agency Within Structural Inequality: The Case of Personal Debt. *Social Policy and Society*, 8(4), 487–498.

Packman, C. (2014). *Payday Lending: Global Growth of the High-Cost Credit Market*. London: Palgrave Macmillan.

Pahl, J. (1989). *Money and Marriage*. London: Palgrave Macmillan.

Pahl, J. (1995). His Money, Her Money: Recent Research on Financial Organisation in Marriage. *Journal of Economic Psychology*, 16, 361–376.

Payne, C. (2013). *The Consumer, Credit and Neoliberalism*. London: Routledge.

Plagnol, A. (2011). Financial Satisfaction over the Life Course: The Influence of Assets and Liabilities. *Journal of Economic Psychology*, 32(1), 45–64. doi.org/10.1016/j.joep.2010.10.006

Poster, W. R. (2013). Hidden Sides of the Credit Economy: Emotions, Outsourcing, and Indian Call Centres. *International Journal of Comparative Sociology*, 54(3), 205–227.

Powell, M., and Ansic, D. (1997). Gender Differences in Risk Behaviour in Financial Decision-Making: An Experimental Analysis. *Journal of Economic Psychology*, 18(6), 605–628.

Rajan, R. (2010). *Fault Lines: How Hidden Fractures Still Threaten the World Economy*. Princeton: Princeton University Press.

Rammstedt, B. (2009). Subjective Indicators. RatSWD Working Paper Series No. 119. Berlin. Retrieved 4 August 2017, from www.ratswd.de/download/RatSWD_WP_2009/RatSWD_WP_119.pdf

Ranyard, R. (2014). The Psychology of Consumer Credit Risk Management: Impact on the UK Payment Protection Insurance (PPI) Market. Impact Case Study. University of Bolton. Retrieved 4 August 2017, from impact.ref.ac.uk/casestudies2/refservice.svc/GetCaseStudyPDF/27159

Ranyard, R., and McHugh, S. (2012). Bounded Rationality in Credit Consumers' Payment Protection Insurance Decisions: The Effect of Relative Cost and Level of Cover. *Journal of Risk Research*, 15(8), 937–950. doi.org/10.1080/13669877.2012.686050

Reading, R., and Reynolds, S. (2001). Debt, Social Disadvantage and Maternal Depression. *Social Science and Medicine*, 53(4), 441–453.

Richardson, T., Elliott, P., and Roberts, R. (2013). The Relationship Between Personal Unsecured Debt and Mental and Physical Health: A Systematic Review and Meta-analysis. *Clinical Psychology Review.* doi.org/10.1016/j.cpr.2013.08.009

Rosenbleeth, R. (2008). A Credit-Crunch Reader: Free-Market Blog and Think-Tank Responses to the Crash of 2008. IEA Current Controversies Paper No. 29. London. Retrieved 10 March 2015, from www.iea.org.uk/publications/research/a-credit-crunch-reader-web-publication

Ross, L., and Squires, G. (2011). The Personal Costs of Subprime Lending and the Foreclosure Crisis: A Matter of Trust, Insecurity, and Institutional Deception. *Social Science Quarterly*, 92(1), 140–163.

Rowlingson, K., Appleyard, L., and Gardner, J. (2016). Payday Lending in the UK: The Regul(aris)ation of a Necessary Evil? *Journal of Social Policy*, 1–17. doi.org/10.1017/S0047279416000015

Samuelson, P. (1937). A Note on the Measurement of Utility. *Review of Economic Studies*, 4(2), 155–161.

Schulte-Mecklenbeck, M., Kühberger, A., and Ranyard, R. (2011). The Role of Process Data in the Development and Testing of Process Models of Judgment and Decision Making. *Judgment and Decision Making*, 6(8), 733–739.

Scott, J., and Dex, S. (2009). Paid and Unpaid Work. In J. Miles and R. Probert (Eds.), *Sharing Lives, Dividing Assets: An Interdisciplinary Study* (pp. 41–59). Oxford: Hart.

Shapiro, G. K., and Burchell, B. J. (2012). Measuring Financial Anxiety. *Journal of Neuroscience, Psychology, and Economics*, 5(2), 92–103. doi.org/10.1037/a0027647

Shefrin, H. M., and Thaler, R. H. (1988). The Behavioral Life Cycle Hypothesis. *Economic Inquiry*, 26(4), 609–643. doi.org/10.1111/j.1465–7295.1988.tb01520.x

Sinclair, R. R., Sears, L. F., Probst, T., and Zajack, M. (2010). A Multilevel Model of Economic Stress and Employee Well-being. In J. Houdmont and S. Leka

(Eds.), *Contemporary Occupational Health Psychology: Global Perspectives on Research and Practice* (pp. 1–20). West Sussex: Wiley-Blackwell.

Skott, P. (2013). Increasing Inequality and Financial Instability. *Review of Radical Political Economics*, 45, 478–488.

Sparkes, M. (2015). *Borrowed Identities: Credit, Debt and Classificatory Struggles in Neoliberal Britain*. Thesis, University of York. Retrieved 29 March 2016, from etheses.whiterose.ac.uk/11360/

Statistic Brain. (2016). Home Foreclosure Statistics. Retrieved 21 October 2016, from www.statisticbrain.com/home-foreclosure-statistics/

StepChange Debt Charity. (2015). England and Wales Court Action. Retrieved 14 July 2015, from www.stepchange.org/Debtinformationandadvice/Whatyour creditorscando/Courtaction/EnglandWalescourtaction/Chargingorder.aspx

Stiglitz, J. (2013). *The Price of Inequality*. London: W. W. Norton.

Sullivan, T. A., Warren, E., and Westbrook, J. L. (1999). *As We Forgive Our Debtors*. New York: Beard.

Sweet, E., Nandi, A., Adam, E., and McDade, T. (2013). The High Price of Debt: Household Financial Debt and Its Impact on Mental and Physical Health. *Social Science and Medicine*, 91, 94–100.

Tach, L., and Sternberg-Greene, S. (2014). 'Robbing Peter to Pay Paul': Economic and Cultural Explanations for How Lower-Income Families Manage Debt. *Social Problems*, 61(1), 1–21.

Thaler, R. H. (1990). Anomalies: Saving, Fungibility, and Mental Accounts. *Journal of Economic Perspectives*, 4(1), 193–205. doi.org/10.1257/jep.4.1.193

Thatcher, M. (1982). Leaders Speech: Conservative Party Conference. Retrieved 28 August 2013, from www.britishpoliticalspeech.org/speech-archive .htm?speech=128

The Money Charity. (2007). Debt Facts and Figures. Retrieved 20 August 2015, from themoneycharity.org.uk/media/august-2007.pdf

Tokunaga, H. (1993). The Use and Abuse of Consumer Credit: Application of Psychological Theory and Research. *Journal of Economic Psychology*, 14(2), 285–316.

Trade Union Congress. (2016). Britain in the Red: Why We Need Action to Help Over-indebted Households. London. Retrieved 15 November 2016, from www.tuc .org.uk/sites/default/files/Britain-In-The-Red-2016.pdf

Trumbull, G. (2014). *Consumer Lending in France and America: Credit and Welfare*. Cambridge: Cambridge University Press.

US Census Bureau. (2017). Quarterly Residential Vacancies and Homeownership. Retrieved 4 August 2017, from www.census.gov/housing/hvs/files/currenthvs press.pdf

US Federal Reserve. (2016a). Consumer Credit Outstanding (Levels), Historical Data. Retrieved 14 November 2016, from www.federalreserve.gov/releases/G19/ HIST/cc_hist_sa_levels.html

US Federal Reserve. (2016b). Mortgage Debt Outstanding. Retrieved 4 August 2017, from www.federalreserve.gov/econresdata/releases/mortoutstand/mortout stand2016.htm

Van Treeck, T. (2014). Did Inequality Cause the U.S. Financial Crisis? *Journal of Economic Surveys*, 28(3), 421–448. doi.org/10.1111/joes.12028

Veenhoven, R. (2007). Subjective Measures of Well-Being. In M. McGillivray (Ed.), *Human Well-Being, Concept and Measurement* (pp. 214–239). Houndsmills: Palgrave Macmillan.

Vogler, C., Brockmann, M., and Wiggins, R. D. (2006). Intimate Relationships and Changing Patterns of Money Management at the Beginning of the Twenty-First Century. *British Journal of Sociology*, 57(3), 455–482.

Vogler, C., and Pahl, J. (1993). Social and Economic Change and the Organisation of Money Within Marriage. *Work, Employment and Society*, 7(1), 71–95.

Walker, C. (2012). Neoliberal Ideology and Personal Debt in the United Kingdom. In C. Walker, K. Johnson, and L. Cunningham (Eds.), *Community Psychology and the Socio-economics of Mental Distress: International Perspectives* (pp. 49–61). London: Palgrave Macmillan.

Walker, C., Hanna, P., Cunningham, L., and Ambrose, P. (2014). 'A Kind of Mental Warfare': An Economy of Affect in the UK Debt Collection Industry. *Australian Community Psychologist*, 26(2), 54–67.

Webley, P., and Nyhus, E. K. (2001). Life-cycle and Dispositional Routes into Problem Debt. *British Journal of Psychology*, 92(3), 423–446.

West, M. (2016). City Watchdog Takes Over Control of Credit Industry. Retrieved 18 November 2016, from www.thisismoney.co.uk/money/bills/article-2578978/Payday-lenders-face-cap-charges-year-City-Watchdog-takes-control-consumer-credit

Westaway, J., and Mckay, S. (2007). *Women's Financial Assets and Debts*. London. Retrieved 4 August 2017, from www.friendsprovidentfoundation.org/wp-content/uploads/2014/07/Womens-Financial-Assets-and-Debts.pdf

Wilkinson, R., and Pickett, K. (2009). *The Spirit Level: Why More Equal Societies Almost Always Do Better*. London: Penguin.

Wohl, M. J. A., Pychyl, T. A., and Bennett, S. H. (2010). I Forgive Myself, Now I Can Study: How Self-Forgiveness for Procrastinating Can Reduce Future Procrastination. *Personality and Individual Differences*, 48(7), 803–808.

Yip, P. S. F., Yang, K. C. T., Ip, B. Y. T., Law, Y. W., and Watson, R. (2007). Financial Debt and Suicide in Hong Kong SAR. *Journal of Applied Social Psychology*, 37(12), 2788–2799.

7 Unemployment and Well-Being

Alex J. Wood and Brendan Burchell

7.1 Introduction

Research by psychologists and others has consistently found that employees experience better psychological well-being than those who are unemployed. This finding has proven remarkably robust across time and across countries, and seems to affect all groups regardless of their age, gender or social class. Finding a theoretical framework to understand the negative psychological consequences has, on the other hand, generated a lot of controversy despite many decades of serious research on the subject. There is consensus that unemployment cannot be understood in simply economic terms, but requires psychological insight. Some theorists have focussed on the good things about being in paid work, others on the distinctly negative things about unemployment. This chapter will describe some of the most influential theories, and how well they are supported by empirical evidence, before considering their applicability in a wider variety of settings. The theories were generated in a time when employment in industrialised countries was more homogeneous; people went to the factory or office, worked and then went home. Now many employees' lives have moved beyond this. The shift away from manufacturing to service industries combined with the Internet and mobile technologies such as laptops and phones has softened the boundaries around workplaces so that employees can increasingly work from anywhere. And the rise of zero-hour contracts and other flexible forms of work scheduling have detracted from the security and predictability of paid work that is central to many psychological theories of well-being. A growing awareness of the very different labour markets that exist in developing countries, where the boundaries between employment, self-employment and work within the family have also challenged the applicability of our understanding of employment and unemployment. This chapter will provide a solid coverage of the conventional material in this area as well as a critical analysis of its global applicability in the twenty-first century.

7.2 Unemployment and Mental Health

Some people enjoy being unemployed. It can provide them with more leisure time than they had been used to as an employee or a student, and it can be a welcome relief from an unpleasant job. Some people use a spell of unemployment as an opportunity to achieve a goal that they previously did not have time to do such as voluntary work, political activism or a sporting achievement, or to spend more time caring for young or elderly relatives.

Unfortunately, such people are rare. Having large numbers of willing and able workers idle is an illogical or absurd situation from many perspectives. Economically, it is a wasted resource; idle workers do not contribute to the output of the nation, do not pay taxes and consume welfare benefits. The results of a large body of research extending over many decades leaves us in no doubt that the more typical reaction to unemployment is not only economic hardship but also a challenge to individuals' well-being in the form of symptoms of anxiety and depression, low self-esteem and an inability to enjoy life or to 'flourish'. At any one point in time over the past forty years, unemployment is being experienced by tens of millions of people in Europe alone. It is a source of such misery on such an enormous scale that it deserves to be taken very seriously by psychologists, economists and policy makers.

The literature linking unemployment to poor mental health has been systematically reviewed on a number of occasions. Paul and Moser's (2009) international review concluded that there was very strong evidence not only that unemployment was correlated with poor psychological health but also that the unemployment caused the poor psychological health. This effect seemed to hold across a wide variety of different types of person and situations, but the effects were always negative. Men, particularly blue-collar men, fared worse than women.

Another international meta-analysis published by McKee-Ryan et al., (2005) came to similarly unequivocal conclusions, although they tended to emphasise the psychological attributes that could moderate the effects of unemployment; individuals who held work to be less central to their lives and individuals with better coping strategies seemed to be somewhat protected from the negative effects.

Socially, unemployment is seen as unjust and exacerbates a variety of social problems, including inequality, crime (Hagan, 1994), homelessness and divorce (Lampard, 1994), to name but a few. Additionally, many of the individuals who experience unemployment themselves suffer problems of poverty as well as poor physical and psychological health. It is psychological health which is mainly considered here, although it will be argued that one cannot fully understand the psychological effects of unemployment without also understanding the social and economic correlates of employment and unemployment. We should also be aware that there is good evidence that the individual deprived of paid work is not the only person to suffer negative consequences; there is also strong evidence that the psychological health of the spouse or partner can suffer, as can the psychological and educational development of children in the household (Fagin and Little, 1984).

In fact, there cannot be many other areas of psychology where there is so much consensus as the effect of unemployment on well-being. But if we are going to be able to intervene to offset the worst effects of unemployment, we need to be able to understand *why* unemployment has such negative effects. This has proven to be a far harder task and has generated many different theories and much argument.

Before we move on to examining those theories that attempt to explain this link between unemployment and mental health, we will take a few words to define employment and unemployment.

7.3 Definitions

Employment should be fairly easy to define as a relationship between two individuals, an employee who sells his or her labour in exchange for a wage and an employer. It is assumed that this is an enduring state, unlike paying a self-employed person for job that only lasts for a few hours or days, but there are large grey areas here, for instance people on zero-hours contracts or franchisees and in the growing digital platform mediated 'gig economy'.

People who are not employed or self-employed can be in a whole variety of other economic statuses, such as being retired, a full-time student, stay-at-home dad, housewife, playboy or unemployed. Unemployment can be differentiated from these other statuses by the fact of wanting and looking for paid work. Again, there are grey areas; some disaffected unemployed people realise that they stand no chance of finding employment, so stop looking for work. Others may only be half-heartedly looking for paid work because they, for whatever reason, prefer not to be employed. But perhaps the most misused word is 'work', particularly when it is used to mean 'employment'. Much work is unpaid, particularly work inside the household to cook, clean and care for others, and even today the majority of that work is done by women (Smith et al., 2013). And 'work' is a very difficult thing to define. Sometimes it is unpleasant (what economists call a 'disutility'), but actually most people report liking their jobs. Sometimes it is paid, but not always. The best definitions usually suggest that the difference between work and other activities is that we do not just do work for intrinsic pleasure, but to achieve something else, such as a wage, or to care for friends and relations, or to bring about some other desired outcome such as work for a charity. Some think of work as a morally virtuous activity (as in the 'Protestant work ethic'), but we should perhaps remind ourselves that, by most definitions, conmen and thieves are both performing work!

7.4 The Social-Environmental Model of Employment

The most influential approach for understanding the ways in which paid work benefits psychological health is Marie Jahoda's social-environmental

Table 7.1 *Jahoda's (1982) categories of experience provided by employment*

	Function
Manifest	Income
Latent	Time structure
	Enforced activity
	Social contact
	Collective purpose
	Status and identity

model of employment (also known as her 'latent consequences', 'deprivation' or 'functionalist' theory). This theory has roots in Jahoda's studies of unemployment in Austria in the 1920s, and has been refined and debated by Jahoda right up until her death in 2001 – a remarkable career as a social psychologist spanning seven decades. The central tenet of this approach is the view that employment is a dominant social institution in modern societies (Jahoda, 1992). This social institution provides an important role in contemporary market societies, not only fulfilling our material needs by providing a wage but also furnishing our psychological needs. Those who are excluded from this institution thus tend to suffer severe psychological deprivation. Jahoda argues that while gaining an income is the manifest function of employment, employment also provides five latent functions, or, more precisely, five categories of experience which fulfil psychological needs (see Table 7.1). These five latent (or 'incidental') functions are: time structure; enforced activity; social contact outside of the family; collective purpose; and status/identity (Jahoda, 1982).

Jahoda used detailed ethnographic research to illustrate how employment fulfils and reinforces a need for habitual time structures. Jahoda argued that time structures take a rigid form in contemporary societies, and are shaped and impressed upon individuals from a young age by public institutions such as school and the family. Jahoda goes on to argue that public institutions not only create the need for rigid time structures, they also inscribe the need for individuals to fill their days with planned activities. Without the enforced activities provided by employment, people risk boredom and idleness. In fact, as Jahoda stated, employment provides a collective purpose that transcends our individual purposes. Jahoda (1987) details how the major collective purpose instilled in individuals in a capitalist society is that of earning a cash income, so much so, that nonpaid work cannot adequately provide status and identity or inclusion within the collective purposes of the larger society in the absence of employment (Jahoda, 1982: 32).

Despite the importance of individualism in contemporary society, people's 'individualism needs to be embedded in a social context ... [and that] outside of the nuclear family, it is employment that provides for most people this social context' (Jahoda, 1982: 24). Without social contact, people are left socially isolated, as employment forces everyone to observe habits, opinions and life experiences different from their own. Jahoda (1982) supports this with the evidence that women who give up employment to look after children often speak of the deprivation of losing social contact outside the family. The final category of status and identity is, in fact, the combination of two categories of experience. For Jahoda (1982), status and identity are conceptually distinct. An individual's identity is a personal notion of an image of themselves, and status is anchored in the value system of society. But they are, Jahoda argues, nonetheless closely intertwined because people tend to adopt the status ascribed to a position by society as an element of their identity. In contemporary society, status is largely defined by the job you have. This socially ascribed status then forms one clear way that individuals define themselves and support their self-identity.

In spite of its influence, the social-environmental model of employment has not been without criticism (Cole, 2007; 2008; Ezzy 1993; Fryer, 1986; 2013; Nordenmark and Strandh, 1999; Strandh, 2000). We will therefore assess the strengths and weaknesses of the model through elucidating the functions which employment is held to provide while considering each major criticism in turn.

At the most basic level, it has frequently been asserted that Jahoda's framework marginalises the importance of income (Cole, 2007; 2008; Fryer, 1986; Fryer, 2013). However, this line of criticism is somewhat peculiar, as Jahoda (1982) identifies income as the first of employment's six functions. Moreover, income is the only function of employment which is manifest, that is, recognised by the population at large. The importance of income can be seen in the fact that Jahoda (1987) focusses upon it to explain why the unemployed she studied during 1937–1938 in Monmouthshire, Wales, suffered significantly less psychological distress than the unemployed she studied six years previously in Marienthal, Austria. According to Jahoda (1982; 1987), the size and permanence of unemployment benefits constitute the principal explanation. The widely held criticism that Jahoda's framework ignores income, and thus poverty, is perhaps a misreading; her work is most illuminating when discussing the other 'latent' functions which employment provides, and thus it is these sections which draw the reader's attention.

Beyond the lack of attention to income, the social-environmental model has been criticised on other theoretical grounds (empirical support is discussed later in this chapter). One important criticism which led Jahoda to clarify her approach was the absence of the psychological need to exercise agency (Fryer, 1986). Indeed, Jahoda (1982: 23) argues that most people are unable to:

> single-handedly overthrow the compelling social norms under which we all live and which provide a supportive frame within which individuals shape their individual lives. There are at all times only a few who can manage without it.

However, Jahoda (1986: 28) would later recognise the 'specification of "agency" as an attribute of being human ... but the tendency to shape one's life from inside-out operates within possibilities, and constraints of social arrangements ... in this sense we are both active and passive.' The idea that we are both active and passive hints towards a notion of duality of structure, which lies at the heart of the structuration (Giddens, 1976; 1979). Furthermore, Jahoda (1986: 110) points out that implicit in the five latent functions is a sixth: personal control – a concept clearly linked to agency and its suppression.

A further criticism is Jahoda's uncritical acceptance of the benefits of employment, seeing all employment as equally fulfilling necessary psychological needs but paying little attention to the quality of jobs (Fryer, 1986). Cole (2007, 2008) argues that Jahoda sees employment as a telos, an end in itself, due to a hidden normative commitment to the assumed 'supra-economic' benefits. This simplicity in the theory may have been politically expedient in arguing that mass unemployment was unequivocally a cause of mass human misery, and that providing employment (any employment) was a principal duty of any good government. Yet this minimalism may have had unintended consequences, as that sort of argument was used to deregulate labour markets (for instance, by removing health and safety legislation, or weakening safeguards against long work hours) under the guise of creating more jobs.

This portrayal is not entirely accurate, for Jahoda (1981) does state on at least one occasion in her extensive writings that, while most employment provides these positive functions, in some cases it may not provide them to a satisfactory degree. For example, the time structure could be too rigid, the purpose unclear or unacceptable, the status too low or the activity either boring or too exhausting. Jahoda may well have been implicitly referencing a more uniform type of factory or office work which was ubiquitous in most of the twentieth century but is now less pervasive.

Building upon Jahoda's reflections on both the variability in latent functions and upon control and agency, Warr (1987) developed a more refined social-environmental model termed the 'vitamin model' which elaborated on Jahoda's theory in a number of ways.

7.5 Warr's Vitamin Model

Peter Warr's (1987) vitamin model represents an extension on the core of Jahoda's social-environmental model and overcomes many of the problems identified. Following an extensive review of relevant research, Warr (1987, 1999) proposes nine different sets of determinants of whether both employment and unemployment lead to better or worse mental health: opportunity for control; skill use; interpersonal contact; external goal and task demands; variety; environmental clarity; availability of money; physical security; and valued social position. Finally (in his later writings), he added other 'vitamins', such as supportive supervision (Warr, 1999). As can be seen, many of Warr's determinants are remarkably similar to Jahoda's categories of

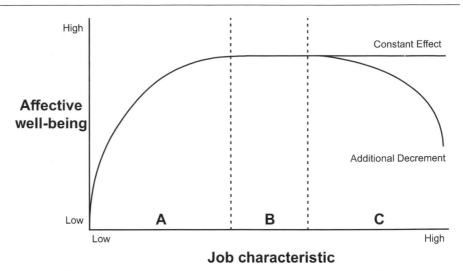

Figure 7.1. *Relations between level of intake and level of well-being in Warr's model.*
Source: Reproduced from Warr (1987: 234).

experiences. However, of particular importance with regards to the criticisms of Jahoda's theory is the inclusion of opportunity for control and environmental clarity, as both assume the physiological need for agency. The analogy to vitamins in Warr's model is particularly ingenious. Warr proposes that the determinants which he identifies act in a manner similar to the ways in which two different sets of vitamins affect our physical health. With all vitamins, too little is harmful, so if we have been deprived of vitamins it is beneficial to increase our intake of any and all of them. An optimal state will be reached, other things being equal, well before high consumption is reached. Once the optimum plateau has been reached, further increases in vitamin intake will neither improve nor damage our health at least for some time. For some vitamins (e.g., vitamins C and E), this continues to be the case no matter how high the intake, that is, they continue to have Constant Effects. But with other vitamins (e.g., A and D), too high an intake becomes poisonous, that is, they result in harmful Additional Decrements. Warr claims that the three vitamins relating to money, physical security and valued social position have constant effects and the other vitamins have additional decrements. The hypothesised differences in the relations between level of intake and level of well-being is depicted in Figure 7.1. Warr also suggested that each individual differed in their own need for each of these vitamins; for instance, introverts would have less need for social contact compared to extroverts.

7.6 Essentialism, Functionalism and Social Construction

Warr's vitamin model represents an important refinement of Jahoda's model, yet it does not overcome all criticism of the social-environmental approach. A more fundamental critique has been levelled at the social-environmental model, highlighting its essentialist character. Jahoda (1982: 59) cites the anthropological work of Sahlins (1974) to argue that the psychological functions that she identified are not time-bound or culture-bound but are enduring needs of human beings. She claims that these needs have been met in societies without employment (such as preindustrial societies) by 'rituals, religious and community practices' (Jahoda, 1982: 59). However, as Cole (2007: 1143) points out, the functions are 'contingent social constructs cut through with gendered and class-based assumptions', and, therefore, Nordenmark and Strandh (1999: 2–3) are insightful in the general thrust of their comment that:

> the possibility that people have different psychological needs, or that needs can change for individuals and for humans in general, is not something which is easily introduced into the perspective. From a sociological viewpoint, we must be able to incorporate the notion of a changing society and a changing individual.

Warr is likewise criticised by the social anthropologist Ezzy (1993) for focussing on objective environmental contexts while ignoring how these influence subjective understandings (the importance of which can be seen later in this chapter with regards to job insecurity research). Nordenmark and Strandh (1999) are correct to argue that psychological needs must be considered as social constructs rather than essential human needs. In fact, Jahoda (1982, 1987) herself paradoxically provides an alternative account in which psychological needs are not essential but rather the specific result of conditioning social institutions: school, the family, market exchange and employment itself. Jahoda (1987) documents how unemployed Welsh miners' lived experience of a collective purpose, status and identity were shaped by the imperative of a market society for people to measure themselves against others according to level of income. As highlighted previously, it is also argued that the school and the family 'impress on the young the value of punctuality and the need to fill the day with planned activities' (Jahoda, 1982: 22). That institutions in capitalist society generate a psychological need for experiences which can best be fulfilled through employment follows logically from Jahoda's argument that employment is a dominant institution in contemporary society. If employment were unsupported and not intermeshed with other institutions, it would be unlikely to have persisted for the last four hundred years. Jahoda would not claim that employment in its modern form was created deliberately as a psychologically beneficial environment as a philanthropic act by factory owners in the early industrial revolution, but rather she claims that its survival over the centuries is testament to its compatibility with human needs. As Wright (2010: 193) argues, 'social structures and institutions … require vigorous mechanisms of active social reproduction in order to be sustained over time.'

Elaborating the social-environmental model in this way opens it up to another criticism, that of being a functionalist explanation. In fact, Nordenmark and Strandh (1999) and Strandh (2000) confusingly suggest that Jahoda's framework is 'functionalistic'. Cohen (2002) points out that the terms 'functionalism', 'functional explanation' and 'function' are the source of serious confusion amongst social scientists. Functionalism is a theoretical conception of society within which all the elements reinforce one another. This is quite different from both 'functional explanations' and 'explanations of functions'. However, functionalist explanations are usually criticised due to this confusion. Unlike functionalism, there is no reason for functional explanations of social reproduction to be automatic, and they can equally be the result of unintentional and dynamic societal conflicts. As Wright (2010: 276) puts it, 'if there are strong tendencies for particular institutions to contribute functionally to social reproduction, this is the result of the history of struggles over social reproduction and the resulting process of institution building, not some automatic, functional logic of the system.' Cohen (2002: 282) demonstrates this point with the example of religion. Imagine that ten societies required a religion, and each was visited by a prophet, but of the ten only one accepted the prophet's teaching. However, they accepted him not because they needed him but rather because they liked his looks; the other nine societies would then perish, leaving only the society with a religion. This shows that in this example that while 'there is a religion, and it is needed, it does not show that there is a religion because it is needed' (Cohen, 2002: 282). Likewise, in showing that there is employment and *that it is needed* to fulfil psychological functions, Jahoda does not necessarily show that there is employment *because it is needed* to fulfil psychological functions.

Another important difference between the approaches of Warr and Jahoda is in the scope of their intended applicability. Jahoda was narrowly focussed on accounting for the difference between employment and unemployment. Warr had greater aspirations, to be able to account for not only the psychological effects of employment and unemployment, but also to be able to understand the positive and negative effects of other environments, such as being a student, a stay-at-home parent or retired. He was also optimistic that a knowledge of the effects of different economic environments on well-being could lead to our ability to improve those environments, not only to improve the quality of jobs, but also to think what 'good unemployment' might look like.

We have argued that the criticisms of the social-environmental model can be overcome. Doing so requires that it be elaborated in line with Warr's (1987; 1999) vitamin model while stressing the socially constructed, contingent and subjective nature of the psychological needs which employment fulfils. We now consider some of the empirical support for Warr's vitamins model.

In the next section of this chapter, the various sources of evidence concerning the psychological health of individuals in the workforce are discussed. The reasons why individuals seem to depend on employment to maintain their psychological well-being will then be considered.

7.7 Researching Environmental Functions and 'Vitamins'

As outlined, the social-environmental model of employment postulates that paid work provides a healthier environment for the individual. It also suggests that the unemployed person, without the benefits which commonly accrue from such an environment, will suffer psychological ill-health. Warr's vitamin model (1987) and Jahoda's 'latent functions' or 'deprivation' framework (1982), both described earlier in this chapter, both attribute the poor psychological health found amongst the unemployed to their lack of access to the good things about employment. Although Warr's model was largely derived from his own systematic review of many hundreds of empirical reports on employment and well-being, it is difficult to definitively demonstrate the causal link between functions/vitamins and unemployment.

One methodological challenge facing the researcher is to separate the direct causes of unemployment from an alternative account known as the 'selection hypothesis', whereby the association between poor well-being and unemployment is due to people with poor health being more likely to lose their job or remain unemployed for longer (Buffel, Missinne and Bracke, 2016). For this reason, the best empirical evidence for the effects of unemployment cannot rely on simple cross-sectional studies but typically compares the same individuals when they are employed and unemployed, or tracks changes in public health at an aggregate level and correlates that with rates of employment and unemployment.

The methodological problems of testing theories as to *why* unemployment affects well-being can be more difficult to overcome. Here the causal ordering is even more difficult to detect. For instance, a correlation between a lack of social contact or enforced activity might well cause depression, as Jahoda would predict. Alternatively, withdrawing from activities and social contact are known to be symptoms of depression, so that could also account for a correlation between depressive symptoms and unemployment. There are, however, a number of empirical studies which are highly suggestive that the causal link between unemployment and lower psychological health is mediated by the restricted access to Jahoda's functions and Warr's vitamins.

Waters and Moore (2002), using a sample of 201 unemployed and 128 employed participants, find that the unemployed reported higher perceived latent deprivation, higher depressive affect and lower self-esteem. Creed et al. (2001) also find significant associations amongst their sample of 248 unemployed people between both the latent benefits (time structure, activity, status, collective purpose and social contact) and well-being, and between the manifest benefits (financial strain) and well-being. Financial strain was the largest contributor to well-being, followed by status, time structure and collective purpose. Using a representative survey of the German population, Paul and Batinic (2009) also find (N = 998) that employed people reported higher levels of time structure, social contact, collective purpose and activity than the unemployed, and that reduced latent functions correlated with psychological distress.

Buffel et al. (2016) show that amongst their sample of fifty- to sixty-five-year-old European men (N = 11,789) and women (N = 15,118), unemployment is associated with depression. However, this effect is lessened for men when they are a displaced worker, that is, someone who has lost their job due to business closure. It is argued that this can be explained with reference to what they term 'employment based social norms' – norms which are shared by other people and partly sustained by their approval and disapproval. Therefore, the lower levels of depression amongst displaced workers are seen as a consequence of the fact that they will have lost their job together with a group of colleagues while the cause of their unemployment will appear as obviously structural rather than their own fault. Thus, Buffel et al. (2016: 16) argue that their study 'confirms that as the financial situation of respondents has been taken into account, unemployment captures not only the loss of income, but also several socio-psychological factors, such as a loss of status and self-esteem, social isolation and the lack of time structure ... These lead to a deterioration of mental health.'

Qualitative studies that are rich in detail also provide support for the importance of employment to identity. For example, Kirk and Wall's (2010) qualitative studies of teachers and bank employees illustrate how employment leads to self-affirmation of identity. Teachers affirm their identity through the creation of a 'teacherly-self', while bank call centre workers use the nonmanual nature of their employment to affirm their identity as moving away from the manual working class. Kirk and Wall argue that, through employment, self-affirmation of identity takes place as a result of people's capacity to perform labour, their desire for recognition and as an act of commitment to others. They identify the intersection of four overlapping influences that give rise to employment identity: cultural representations; employment social relations; social location (family, generation and class); and civil engagement.

Researchers have also empirically investigated Warr's (1987) overall vitamin model, albeit to a lesser extent than Jahoda's framework. This is perhaps to be expected, as Warr's model was based much more directly on a large number of empirical studies, whereas Jahoda's theory emerged more organically from her research and personal experiences. De Jonge and Schaufeli's (1998) study is the most explicit test of Warr's model; 1,437 Dutch nurses and nurse's assistants found that job demands were associated with job-related depression (occupational burnout and emotional exhaustion). While this relationship was linear rather than being the expected curvilinear relationship, job autonomy and workplace social support did exhibit the expected curvilinear relationship.

A standardised scale has been developed by Muller et al. (2005) to aid the systematic investigation of Jahoda's theory. Known as the Latent and Manifest Benefits (LAMB) scale, it enables researchers to use standardised measures for all six of Jahoda's (1982) original latent and manifest functions of employment. Muller and Waters (2012) report that the LAMB scale has been administered to 5,692 participants across thirteen studies. All of Jahoda's functions have been found to relate to well-being in at least two or more of these LAMB studies, with financial strain, social contact/support and time structure being the most frequently related to well-being. Muller and Waters (2012: 35) summarise these studies as having:

> consistently predicted that lack of access to the latent and manifest benefits of employment is associated with decreased psychological well-being. This pattern has held across various samples, such as in low-wage earners, people with spiritual beliefs, people who are unemployed or out of the labour force, and people with negative and positive future perspective.

These cross-sectional studies are supported by longitudinal ones, such as Wanberg, Griffiths and Gavin (1997) and Selenko, Batnic and Paul (2011). Wanberg et al. (1997) investigate the relationship amongst time structure, (un)employment and mental health. They find that perceived time structure increases as individuals move from unemployment into employment. For those who remain unemployed, reduced time structure two months after job loss leads to lower mental health three months later. Selenko et al. (2011) used a sample of 1,026 German respondents (which reduced to 285 by T4) and measured their employment status, psychological health and access to manifest and latent functions according to the LAMB scale at four time periods each separated by six months. Across the four waves of their study, they found that someone who reports a decrease in latent benefits at one time point will probably report a decrease in psychological health six months later. After twelve or eighteen months, the effect of latent benefits was no longer detectable. However, their cross-sectional results only find that financial benefits, social contact and time structure affected psychological health. The lack of effect for collective purpose, enforced activity and status may in part be explained by issues in translating these more abstract functions from the English LAMB scale into German.

In summary, there is ample empirical support for Jahoda's (1982) assertion that employment fulfils manifest and latent functions, and their restriction is associated with psychological well-being. Moreover, there is some evidence to suggest that the relationship between the functions and mental health is curvilinear, as suggested by Warr's (1987) vitamin model. The more difficult task is establishing causality, given the potential for people with poor health being more likely to lose their job or remain unemployed for longer. However, there are some longitudinal studies which indicate that those moving from unemployment into employment report higher perceived levels of at least some manifest and latent functions (financial benefits, social contact and time structure), and that the unemployed who report lower levels of these functions at one point in time will also report lower levels of psychological well-being in the future. That causal evidence only exists for some of the latent functions lowering psychological health probably reflects the abstract nature of collective purpose, enforced activity and status and identity, this in turn make them hard to capture in survey items.

7.8 Environmental Clarity and the Rise of Job Insecurity

Warr's 'Environmental Clarity' vitamin relates to job security, or more generally to the predictability of the future of one's job. Burchell (2002) demonstrates how, in the United Kingdom, job insecurity increased substantially between 1970 and 1980, after which it remained fairly constant in the 1990s and up until 2007. Since 2007, a series of severe economic crises (the credit crunch, the Euro crisis and austerity) have affected many parts of our planet, leading many more employees to feel unsure of what the future holds for their jobs. For example in 2012, 25 per cent of the UK workforce reported that they felt at some risk of job loss (Gallie et al., 2016). Warr (1987: 149) argues that:

> Predictability is valued because anticipation of the nature and timing of potentially aversive events permits possible coping responses … Uncertainty about whether or not undesirable events are likely to occur inhibits these preparatory responses, and has been widely shown in the laboratory and field investigations to give rise to anxiety and other forms of low affective well-being.

This uncertainty has become known as job insecurity. De Witte's (2005: 1) review of the psychological literature on job insecurity determines that:

> What typifies this subjective conceptualisation of job insecurity is that it concerns insecurity about the future: Insecure employees are uncertain about whether they will retain or lose their current job. They are 'groping in the dark' as far as their future within the organisation or company is concerned.

As suggested by the preceding quote, research into job insecurity often focusses upon potential loss of employment. However, job insecurity does not only involve fear and worry pertaining to potential job loss. In fact, threat to valued job features was also central to Greenhalgh and Rosenblatt's (1984: 441) now classic conceptualisation of 'job insecurity', in which they state 'loss of valued job features is an important but often overlooked aspect of job insecurity.' Greenhalgh and Rosenblatt (1984: 441–442) suggest that 'the job features principally associated with job insecurity' are career progress, income stream, status/self-esteem, autonomy, resources and work community. Subsequent research has tended to overlook the perceived threat to valued job features, perhaps due to Greenhalgh and Rosenblatt (1984: 442) arguing that the threat to job features 'is less severe because organisational membership and all that such membership means to the individual is not lost'. Thus Gallie et al. (2016) refer to the insecurity relating to job features as the 'hidden face of job insecurity'. With threat to job features ignored, Burchell (2002) argues that job insecurity has conventionally been conceptualised only in terms of continued

Table 7.2 *Standing's (1999) eight-point typology of economic insecurity*

- **Employment insecurity** – when the employer can dismiss or lay off workers, or put them on short time without difficulty or costs.

- **Job insecurity** – when the employer can shift workers from one job to another at will or where the content of the job can be altered or reduced.

- **Work insecurity** – where the working environment is unregulated, polluted or dangerous in some way, so that the ability to continue to work is at risk.

- **Income insecurity** – when earnings are unstable, or when transfer payments are contingency-based, not guaranteed.

- **Working-time insecurity** – when the employer can impose fragmented, shortened or irregular hours without difficulty or costs.

- **Representation insecurity** – when the employer can impose change in the labour process and refuse to negotiate with effective trade unions and other institutions protecting workers' collective interests.

- **Skill reproduction insecurity** – when opportunities to gain and retain skills through access to education and training is impeded.

- **Labour market insecurity** – represented by labour surplus conditions, so that the probability of securing employment is low, with workers readily available wherever jobs arise.

(Adapted from Burchell, 2002: 63)

existence of employment. Thus, it has been conceptualised as *employment insecurity* – the threat to continued employment and the connected threat of becoming unemployed – rather than as *job insecurity* – the threat to a specific job role, its content and its characteristics. Employment insecurity has thus been operationalised through survey items such as 'In the next twelve months, how likely is it that you will lose your job?'

Burchell (2002) suggests that as the loss or erosion of job features can also trigger feelings of job insecurity, 'in today's labour market, many employees are worried not only because they might lose their jobs *per se* but because they are threatened with the loss of valued job features' (Burchell, 2002: 70). In support of this theory, Burchell (2002: 70–71) highlights that analysis of the 1997 British Skills Survey of 2,500 employed and self-employed respondents finds that 40 per cent of workers who experienced secure employment (they felt it was unlikely they would lose their job in the next twelve months) and 11 per cent of workers who experienced *very* secure employment (they felt it was very unlikely that they would lose their job in the next twelve months) still did not describe their *job* as being secure. Therefore, Burchell (2002) states that 'this clearly demonstrates that non-specific feelings of insecurity are more pervasive than feelings of impending job loss, and probably include several other aspects of job insecurity'. Researchers often refer to Standing's eight-point classification of economic insecurity (1999; see Table 7.2) to clarify the diverse ways in which individuals can experience insecurity; worrying about total job loss is only one of the ways insecurity is a potential threat to well-being. This will become more apparent later in this chapter's discussion of zero-hours contracts.

De Witte et al. (2010) also demonstrate that this traditional focus upon employment insecurity alone is problematic. It is only recently that research has taken the insecurity related to valued job features seriously. De Witte et al. (2010) term this perceived threat to valued job features as 'qualitative job insecurity'. Their study of 7,146 Belgian employees in the banking sector finds threats to job features to be just as harmful to well-being as threats to continued employment. Additionally, Gallie et al. (2016) highlight the prevalence of what they term 'job status insecurity'. Job status insecurity is, they contend, comprised of anxieties surrounding unfair treatment at work or having less say, less opportunities to utilise skill, less pay or less interesting work. Gallie et al. find that 23 per cent of the UK workforce in 2012 were *very* anxious about at least one of these items.

7.9 Employment Insecurity: Evidence for the Harm to Well-being

The quantitative conceptualisation of job insecurity (threats to continued employment) has consistently been shown to be highly detrimental to individual mental and physical health. For example, a meta-analysis by Cheng and Chan (2008) of 172 independent samples amounting to 132,927 employees demonstrated that job insecurity is negatively correlated to psychological health ($r = -0.28$) and physical health ($r = -0.23$). The strength of this effect varies between studies. In some extreme cases, the stress of job insecurity might have had an even more negative effect on well-being than unemployment, but the meta-analysis tends to show that insecure jobs are better for psychological well-being than unemployment, but not as protective as secure jobs. The negative effects of job insecurity also seem to affect most demographic groups equally, regardless of gender, income or social class. Some studies report a nonlinear age effect, such that those at the very start and end of their employment careers are less affected by job insecurity than those in midcareer.

7.10 Schedule Insecurity and Zero Hours Contracts

The discussion so far is based on a literature that developed when the assumption was that most jobs were fairly standardised with regard to type of contract and hours of work, with occasional 'atypical' exceptions. Many researchers claim that the labour market has changed through the repeated recessions that have hit most developed countries since the end of a 'golden era' of capitalism that lasted from the late 1940s until the early 1970s. Theorists such as Standing (2014) and Beck (2000) have argued that contemporary labour markets are characterised by precarious jobs, where, arguably, the literature based on the works of Jahoda and Warr are less applicable.

A recent notable labour market trend has been the growth of temporal flexibility in the workplace. For many, working time is now seemingly unstable and irregular. The perceived growth of temporal flexibility has been a source of considerable public comment and, in some cases, concern. A case in point is that of the increasing numbers of people in the United Kingdom reporting that they are employed on zero hours contracts. Zero hours contracts refer to an employment situation which does not guarantee employees any hours of work. This leaves workers with little choice but to accept whatever hours they are given, even when hours are offered to them at extremely short notice. Although difficult to measure, reliable figures suggest that around 801,000 (ONS, 2016) to 1.3 million (Watt, 2014) people are employed in the United Kingdom on zero hours contracts. The perceived increase in the number of people working in this way has become a major political issue in the UK, with a leader of the opposition Labour Party declaring the country to be 'Zero-Zero Britain – a country of zero hours contracts for the poor and zero tax for the rich' (Watt, 2014). In response to the public concern regarding zero hours contracts, the UK government held a public consultation on the issue in 2014. However, the growth of temporal flexibility is not limited to nonstandard employment such as zero hours contracts; standard permanent, and even full-time, workers also experience flexible working time (Wood, 2016). Nor is the pervasiveness of temporal flexibility limited to the United Kingdom. In the United States, Golden (2005) found that 28 per cent of workers report having schedules with variable start and end times. In Canada, one-third of part-time workers learned of their work schedule with one week or less notice (McCrate, Lambert and Henly, 2012). A similar situation exists across Europe, where around 35 per cent of workers report facing changes in their work schedule (Parent-Thirion et al., 2012). Rubery et al. (2005) suggest that temporal flexibility may represent a new regulation of working time which has spread far beyond contingent work. In fact, Wood (2016) posits that, while in the past the 'flexible firm' was based upon the numerical flexibility of contingent workers, today's firm flexibility may be based upon a generalised temporal flexibility.

So, how does increasing temporal flexibility relate to job insecurity? Burchell's (2002: 63) highlighting of Standing's (1999) typology is important, as it includes 'working time insecurity – when the employer can impose fragmented, shortened or irregular hours without difficulty or costs.' Moreover, De Witte et al. (2010) include 'worry that hours of work will get worse' as one of their ten features of 'qualitative job insecurity'. Additionally, in the case of hourly paid workers, temporal flexibility can be related to job insecurity and thus environmental clarity in a second manner. Greenhalgh and Rosenblatt (1984) argue that income stream is one of the job features principally associated with job insecurity. The income stream of hourly paid workers is linked directly to scheduling, as their pay is determined by the quantity of hours they work. Accordingly, temporally flexible jobs may be associated with two forms of job insecurity identified in the extant literature: working-time insecurity and income insecurity. The term *schedule insecurity* is used to denote the confluence of these two forms of insecurity.

Temporal flexibility itself can take two forms: manager-controlled and worker-controlled. Worker-controlled flexible scheduling tends to be introduced to benefit employees by improving their work-life balance. The same is not true for manager-controlled flexible scheduling, which tends to be introduced to contain costs by tightly matching labour supply to demand (Wood, 2016). Lambert (2008) argues that employers are increasingly unwilling to pay for labour which exceeds demand on an hourly or daily basis. In these circumstances, staffing outlay budgets are tightly linked to customer demand, with frontline managers expected to closely enforce staffing budget. Research suggests that, despite government and employer claims to the contrary, flexible scheduling cannot be both manager-controlled and worker-controlled (Wood, 2016). For example, Hyman, Scholarios and Baldry (2005: 719–720) find that ' "flexible" working time patterns were only flexible for the employers and actually undermined workers' own coping arrangements.' Lambert, Haley-Lock and Henly (2012: 304) state that 'the zero-sum game created among workers when employers apply strict limits to total labour hours means that control granted to one employee tends to lessen control enjoyed by co-workers.'

As insecurity is related to uncertainty, it is manager-controlled flexible scheduling which is likely to act as a source of schedule insecurity. This proposition is supported by the findings of Wood and Burchell (2014) whose qualitative research into the experiences of temporal flexibility amongst retail workers supports a causal link between frequent unpredictable changes to workers' schedules and job insecurity. Workers were found to experience both working-time and income insecurity as a consequence of frequent irregular and unpredictable alterations to their schedules. A clear theme of the interviews which Wood and Burchell (2014) draw upon is the importance of environmental clarity for mental health, with the lack of environmental clarity afforded by manager-controlled flexible scheduling causing stress, anxiety and depressed well-being. Some informants also suggested that these psychological effects could manifest into psychosomatic complaints. Henly and Lambert (2014) provide quantitative support for the proposition that schedule insecurity damages mental health. Using a sample of 256 retail workers, they find unpredictable scheduling, particularly last-minute changes to schedules, was associated with lower psychological well-being.

There is currently no national-level data on schedule insecurity within the European Union. However, Wood and Burchell's (2015) analysis of the 2005 and 2010 waves of the European Working Conditions Survey (EWCS) provides a unique time series on the number of workers who have their schedules altered regularly by their employer. Analysis of these data finds that manager-controlled flexible scheduling increased significantly – more than 2 percentage points – in eleven out of the fifteen Western European countries. The biggest increase was in the United Kingdom, where the number of workers experiencing this practice increased by more than 5 percentage points to close to 20 per cent of the workforce. These findings suggest that schedule insecurity might be increasingly widespread across many Western European countries. Furthermore, analysis of the data for tens of thousands of employees surveyed in the 2010 EWCS shows that there is a direct linear relationship between the imposition of unsocial (e.g., evenings, nights and weekends), variable or unpredictable working hours and the low well-being of employees.

7.11 Active Labour Market Policies

Research on and theorising about unemployment is rarely done as a purely academic exercise. One hopes that it gives us some evidence as to what can be done to reduce the effects of unemployment. Economists have, at various times over the past seventy years, claimed to have ways of controlling the economy such that mass unemployment is eliminated from boom-and-bust business cycles; unfortunately, such optimism has proven unfounded. So, if we have to live with unemployment, what can be done to make it less destructive to human well-being?

Jahoda was one of the first psychologists to attempt to research alternative ways of living for otherwise unemployed individuals that would ameliorate the negative effects of unemployment. Having read her research, a group of wealthy benefactors sought to recreate the positive features of work through other cooperative community activities for unemployed coal miners in Britain in the 1930s. Despite these schemes being well funded, they (by her own admission) failed. Warr was also optimistic that, with his understanding of the important psychological 'vitamins' for a good life, it should be possible to engineer environments that are jobless but healthy. But, not for the lack of trying, nothing has been found that is as effective in curing the effects of unemployment as a good job (Coutts, Stuckler and Cann, 2014).

Perhaps the best evidence we have of a policy that is effective against unemployment is a type of intervention called Active Labour Market Policies (ALMPs). Rather than just passively giving out benefits to unemployed individuals to cover the basic cost of living, ALMPs try to intervene in a way to deal with the problem, for instance by teaching individuals skills for more effective job search, providing training to increase their employability and giving them coping strategies to deal with the setbacks and challenges of unemployment. There is now a growing body of evidence that many of these schemes not only help unemployed people to get back into employment, but also that these schemes themselves improve the psychological health of the participants even if they don't lead to employment. Coutts et al. (2014) argue that some of these

ALMPs seem to be effective because they recreate some of Warr's 'vitamins' or Jahoda's 'categories of experience'; some make individuals more resilient to negative life events, and others may be effective because they provide more optimism for the future.

7.12 A Global Perspective

Psychologists have often been accused of doing research in a few locations, all in developed Western countries, and much of it in the United States of America, and then disseminating research findings as if they applied to humans everywhere. Research on unemployment is vulnerable to this criticism. There have been relatively few studies of the experience of unemployment in less developed countries – for instance Gonzo and Plattner's (2003) study of street unemployment in Namibia. Gonzo and Plattner try to use the same theoretical perspectives (such as Jahoda's model of latent functions) to understand unemployment in Namibia, where the lack of any recognisable welfare system forces jobless people onto streets in search for casual employment. This creates a completely different everyday environment to the social isolation experienced by many people in richer countries.

Unemployment presupposes that individuals are given some payments (usually from the state or possibly from their family) to search for employment but otherwise to be idle. In many parts of the world, such as most of sub-Saharan Africa, this is far from the norm (Burchell et al., 2016). Analysis of the economic status and work histories of people up to the age of thirty showed that some of the more highly educated individuals do have more Western-style careers of employment, sometimes punctuated by spells of unemployment. But for many sections of society in developing countries, their trajectories do not include spells identifiable as unemployment. Rather, they alternate between periods of self-employment (often linked to a family business); informal employment; and periods where they are 'family workers', helping with domestic, agricultural or some other family business and being provided with meals and accommodation by the family.

This suggests that we actually know little about unemployment as it is experienced in developing countries. Its nearest equivalent, family work, could be very different in its psychological consequences of Western-style unemployment; time structure and enforced activity might be better, but the economic dependence and lack of control could be far worse.

Other indications about the relative demerits of unemployment in richer and poorer countries are mixed. Paul and Moser's (2009) meta-analysis of the psychological effects of unemployment suggested that the wider economic climate can be an important moderating variable; less developed countries, countries that have more unequal income distributions and countries that spend less on benefits could make the experience of unemployment harsher. Patel and

Kleinman (2003) argue that the link between poverty and mental disorders in developing countries is actually caused more by the low levels of education rather than income levels per se. On the other hand, Powdthavee (2007) compared the experience of unemployment in different parts of South Africa and found that where the rate of unemployment was higher, the individual impact was slightly less than in situations where unemployment was relatively rare. Unfortunately, there is a stark contrast between the plethora of evidence on the relationship between economic status and psychological well-being in rich countries and paucity of research in the rest of the world.

7.13 Unemployment, Job Insecurity, Political Attitudes and Islamic Radicalisation

Whilst the main thrust of this chapter has been on the individual misery that can be caused by unemployment and job insecurity, it is by no means the only way that individuals and societies can be threatened by economic insecurity. In the United Kingdom in the 1980s, when unemployment peaked at close to 4 million (its highest level since before the Second World War), there was much political concern that this extremely high level of unemployment would make the country ungovernable and lead to a left-wing revolution. This did not happen – in fact, it was a period of electoral success for a right-wing conservative party. So, perhaps the opposite is true: unemployment and job insecurity are more likely to favour extreme right-wing parties, as argued by Flecker (2016). As Flecker points out, the mass unemployment in Germany in the 1930s was seen as a major factor leading to the election and then political domination of Hitler.

More careful empirical tests of this hypothesis find little support for a direct link between unemployment or job insecurity and popular support for extreme right-wing parties. There do seem to be a few extreme political parties that have gained some popular support by blaming immigrants for 'stealing jobs', leading to unemployment, but this only seems to happen sporadically (Oesch, 2008). In fact, careful empirical analysis of aggregate levels of unemployment, job insecurity and elections suggests that there is more support for the opposite effect. Arzheimer and Carter (2006) analysed actual elections that took place between 1984 and 2001 in the European countries with more established extreme right parties. Somewhat surprisingly, they found that support for extreme right-wing parties was negatively correlated with levels of unemployment in Europe. This finding has been replicated by other authors; it seems that voting for extremist parties is more strongly linked to threatened cultural identities than individuals' economic or employment status.

More recently, research on the political implications of unemployment has shifted to another perceived threat – radicalisation and acts of political violence or 'terrorism' connected to Islamic fundamentalist groups. Although the number of sympathisers of political violence for Islamic causes in Western countries is very small even amongst Islamic ethnic groups (and the number of fatalities is also relatively small compared to the public health impact of economic crises), the political impact of fundamentalist Islamic terrorism has been significant. A number of studies have looked at the radicalisation process (see, for instance, Githens-Mazer's 2008 study of North Africans living in the United Kingdom), and they tend to conclude that political mobilisation through historic accounts of injustice are more important than poverty and economic deprivation. This has been supported by a large survey of young people of Muslim heritage living in London and Bradford; Bhui, Warfa and Jones (2014) found that being young, healthy and being in education rather than employment were three predictors of sympathising with Islamic political violence. Of those in employment, those with the highest incomes (over £75,000 per year) were more likely to be sympathisers of violent protest and terrorism. Beyond this, neither unemployment, nor the psychological outcomes of unemployment such as isolation or symptoms of depression and anxiety disorders, predisposed individuals towards Islamic extremism. Nevertheless, one of the defining characteristics of modern democratic states is that employment is the normal and stabilising link between individuals and the capitalist system, so without mass employment, civilisation as we know it would change fundamentally.

7.14 The End of Work?

Just as the employment relationship between an employer and an employee is a relative novelty in the context of human existence, there is increasing concern that we will see its demise in the next few decades.

There have been a large number of predictions that this system should already have collapsed, but these predictions have, so far, proven to be premature. Some of these predictions are based on what are claimed to be fundamental flaws or contradictions in the socioeconomic systems based on capitalism. Although capitalism has experienced a number of crises, it has also shown itself, up until now, to be resilient and able to recover from crises.

The other claims for the 'end of work' are based on advances in the technologies that can substitute for humans, thus reducing the need for people to be employed in a whole range of agricultural, extraction, manufacturing and service industries. Indeed, this 'end of work' argument has been made repeatedly with the introduction of new spinning and weaving machines, tractors on farms, computers to replace clerks and so on. To give one example, the number of farmers and farm labourers accounted for 33 per cent of all employment in the United States in 1910, but by the year 2000 it had declined to only 1.2 per cent (Wyatt and Hecker, 2006). Far from leading to mass unemployment, the proportion of adult populations in employment in Western countries has actually increased in most countries (albeit they are working shorter hours than a century ago); at the same time as some occupations such as farm labouring were in decline, other occupations have been expanding just as rapidly. For instance, the highly skilled occupations, such as 'Professional, Technical and Kindred' occupations, have increased from about 5 per cent of employees in 1910 to about 24 per cent of the US workforce by the end of the twentieth century.

One might draw the conclusion from this that all such 'end of work' predictions will be proven wrong, because as we do away with some jobs, we create other jobs, often to supply luxury goods to ever-wider sections of society. However, in the past year, a number of authorities in the field of technology and employment have become increasingly concerned that this 'doomsday scenario' whereby jobs disappear at an alarming rate, rendering even the majority of the working-age population unemployed, might be about to happen. The reason for this concern is that many experts are confidently predicting that we are on the edge of a revolution in machine learning and big data. Over the next ten or twenty years, many cognitive skills that had been considered as only doable by humans, such as driving, teaching, accounting and so on, will now be performed more economically and to a higher standard by intelligent machines. It is predicted that, when we hit the point of exponential increases in machine intelligence, and those machines are developing their own intelligence, the speed of change will be far more dramatic than anything we have seen before, and the effects on employment could be catastrophic. The latest controversial predictions by Frey and Osborne (2016) are that 57 per cent of jobs in the richest countries (the Organisation of Economic Cooperation and Development [OECD]) will be taken over by artificial intelligence. If we can no longer provide employment to sustain the well-being of the population, societies will need to find an alternative type of economic system if we are to avoid calamitous levels of individual misery and political instability.

7.15 Conclusions

Unemployment, as experienced in Western societies, is a colossal source of misery. We now have a large body of evidence that helps us to understand what it is about employment that protects individuals' well-being. Where there is the political will to help rather than to blame the jobless, we can use this knowledge to ameliorate the suffering associated with unemployment. We should be mindful that not all jobs are good jobs: for instance, insecure and zero-hour contracts do not provide as many of the benefits as better quality jobs.

In richer industrialised and postindustrial countries, we have become used to societies where full-time employment is the normal activity for adults between leaving education and retiring. There is now good reason to worry that this era might be coming to an end, and we will need to find some alternative socioeconomic systems for a future where the amount of paid work halves. Maintaining stability and well-being in such a scenario will provide the biggest challenge yet for economic psychologists.

7.16 References

Arzheimer, K. and Carter, E. (2006) Political Opportunity Structures and Right-Wing Extremist Party Success. *European Journal of Political Research* 45(3): 419–443.

Beck, U. (2000) *The Brave New World of Work*. Cambridge: Polity.

Bhui, K., Warfa, N. and Jones, E. (2014) Is Violent Radicalisation Associated with Poverty, Migration, Poor Self-Reported Health and Common Mental Disorders? *PLoS ONE*. 9(3): e90718.

Buffel, V., Missinne, S. and Bracke, P. (2016) The Social Norm of Unemployment in Relation to Mental Health and Medical Care Use: The Role of Regional Unemployment Levels and of Displaced Workers. *Work, Employment and Society*. 31(3): 501–521.

Burchell, B. J. (2002) The Prevalence and Redistribution of Job Security and Work Intensification. In (Eds) Burchell B. J., Ladipo, D. and Wilkinson, F., *Job Insecurity and Work Intensification*. London: Routledge, 61–76.

Burchell, B. J., Coutts, A., Hall, E. and Pye, N. (2016) Self-Employment Programmes for Young People: A Review of the Context, Policies and Evidence. Employment Working Paper No. 198. Geneva: International Labour Organisation.

Cheng, G. and Chan, D. (2008). Who Suffers More from Job Insecurity? A Meta-analytic Review. *Applied Psychology* 57(2):72–303.

CIPD (Charted Institute for Personnel Development) (2015) *Zero Hours and Short Hours Contracts in the UK: Employer and Employee Perspectives*. Policy Report. CIPD: London.

Cohen, G. A. (2002) *Karl Marx's Theory of History: a Defence*, 2nd Edition. Princeton, NJ: Princeton University Press.

Cole, M. (2007) Re-thinking Unemployment: A Challenge to the Legacy of Jahoda et al. *Sociology* 41(6): 1133–1149.

Cole, M. (2008) Sociology Contra Government? The Contest for the Meaning of Unemployment in UK Policy Debates. *Work, Employment and Society* 22(1): 27–43.

Coutts A. P., Stuckler D. and Cann D. J. (2014) The Health and Wellbeing Effects of Active Labor Market Programs. *Wellbeing* 6:2(13):1–18.

Creed, P. A. and Macintyre, S. R. (2001) The Relative Effects of Deprivation of the Latent and Manifest Benefits of Employment on the Well-being of Unemployed People. *Journal of Occupational Health Psychology* 6:(4): 324–331.

De Jonge, J. and Schaufeli, W. (1998). Job Characteristics and Employee Well-Being: A Test of Warr's Vitamin Model in Health Care Workers Using Structural Equation Modelling. *Journal of Organizational Behavior* 19(4): 387–407.

De Witte, H. (2005) Job Insecurity: Review of the International Literature on Definitions, Prevalence, Antecedents and Consequences. *Journal of Industrial Psychology* 4: 1–6

De Witte, H., De Cuyper, N., Handaja, Y., Sverke, M., Näswall, K. and Hellgren, J. (2010) Associations Between Quantitative and Qualitative Job Insecurity and Well-being. *International Studies in Management Organisations* 40(1): 40–56.

Ezzy, D. (1993) Unemployment and Mental Health: A Critical Review. *Social Science and Medicine* 37(1): 41–52.

Fagin, L. and Little, M. (1984) *The Forsaken Families*. Harmondsworth: Penguin.

Flecker, J. (2016) (Ed) *Changing Working Life and the Appeal of the Extreme Right*. Abingdon: Routledge.

Frey, C. B. and Osborne M. (2016) *Technology at Work v2.0: The Future Is Not What It Used to Be*. Citi GPS: Global Perspectives and Solutions.

Fryer, D. (1986) Employment Deprivation and Personal Agency During Unemployment: A Critical Discussion of Jahoda's Explanation of the Psychological Effects of Unemployment. *Social Behaviour* 1: 3–24.

Fryer, D. (2013) Labour Market Disadvantage, Deprivation and Mental Health. In (Eds) Wolff, C., Drenth, P. J. D and Henk, T. *Handbook of Work and Organizational Psychology, Vol 2*. Hove: Pychology Press Ltd.

Gallie, D., Felstead, A., Green, F. and Inanc, H. (2016) The Hidden Face of Job Insecurity. *Work, Employment and Society*. 26(5): 806–821.

Giddens, A. (1976) *New Rules of Sociological Method: A Positive Critique of Interpretative Sociologies*. London: Hutchinson

Giddens, A. (1979). *Central Problems in Social Theory: Action, Structure, and Contradiction in Social Analysis*. Los Angeles, CA: University of California Press.

Githens-Mazer, J. (2008) Islamic Radicalisation Among North Africans in Britain. *British Journal of Politics and International Relations* 10(4): 550–570.

Golden, L. (2005) The Flexibility Gap: Employee Access to Flexibility in Work Schedules. In (Ed) Zeytinoglu, I. U. *Flexibility in Workplaces: Effects on Workers, Work Environment and the Unions*. Geneva: International Industrial Relations Association and International Labour Organisation, 38–56.

Gonzo, W. and Plattner, I. E. (2003). *Unemployment in an African Country: A Psychological Perspective*. Windhoek, Namibia: University of Namibia Press.

Greenhalgh, L. and Rosenblatt, Z. (1984) Job Insecurity: Toward Conceptual Clarity. *Academy of Management Review* 9(3): 438–448.

Hagan, J. (1994) *Crime and Disrepute*. Thousand Oaks, CA: Pine Forge Press.

Henly, J. R. and Lambert, S. J. (2014) Unpredictable Work Timing in Retail Jobs Implications for Employee Work–Life Conflict. *ILR Review* 67(3): 986–1016.

Hyman, J., Scholarios, D. and Baldry, C. (2005) Getting On or Getting By? Employee Flexibility and Coping Strategies for Home and Work. *Work, Employment and Society* 19(4): 705–725.

Jahoda, M. (1981) Work, Employment, and Unemployment: Values, Theories, and Approaches in Social Research. *American Psychologist* 36(2): 184–191.

Jahoda, M. (1982) *Employment and Unemployment: A Social-Psychological Analysis*. Cambridge: Cambridge University Press.

Jahoda, M. (1986) In Defence of a Non-reductionist Social Psychology. *Social Behaviour* 1: 25–29.

Jahoda, M. (1987) Unemployed Men at Work. In Fryer, D. and Ullah, P. (Eds) *Unemployed People: Social and Psychological Perspectives*. Milton Keynes: Open University Press.

Jahoda, M. (1992) Reflections on Marienthal and After. *Journal of Occupational and Organizational Psychology* 65(4): 355–358.

Kirk, J. and Wall, C. (2010) *Work and Identity: Historical and Cultural Contexts.* Basingstoke: Palgrave Macmillan.

Lambert, S. J. (2008) Passing the Buck: Labor Flexibility Practices That Transfer Risk onto Hourly Workers. *Human Relations* 61(9): 1203–1227.

Lambert, S. J, Haley-Lock, A. and Henly J. R. (2012) Schedule Flexibility in Hourly Jobs: Unanticipated Consequences and Promising Directions. *Community, Work and Family* 15(3): 293–315.

Lampard, R. (1994) An Examination of the Relationship Between Martial Dissolution and Unemployment. In (Eds) Gallie, D., Marsh, C. and Volger, C. *Social Change and the Experience of Unemployment.* Oxford: Oxford University Press.

McCrate, E., Lambert S. and Henly, J. R. (2012) Schedule Instability and Unpredictability as Sources of Underemployment Among Hourly Workers in Canada. Paper presented at the Work and Family Researchers Network Conference, New York.

McKee-Ryan, F. L., Song, Z., Wanberg, C. R. and Kinicki A. J. Psychological and Physical Well-being During Unemployment: A Meta-analytic Study. *Journal of Applied Psychology* 90(1): 53–76.

Muller, J. J., Creed, P. A., Waters, L. E. and Machin M. A (2005) The Development and Preliminary Testing of a Scale to Measure the Latent and Manifest Benefits of Employment. *European Journal of Psychological Assessment* 21(3): 191–198.

Muller, J. J. and Waters L. E. (2012) A Review of the Latent and Manifest Benefits (LAMB) Scale. *Australian Journal of Career Development* 21(1): 31–37.

Nordenmark, M. and Strandh, M. (1999) Towards a Sociological Understanding of Mental Well-Being Among the Unemployed: The Role of Economic and Psychosocial Factors. *Sociology* 33(3): 577–597

Oesch, D. (2008) Explaining Workers' Support for Right-Wing Populist Parties in Western Europe: Evidence from Austria, Belgium, France, Norway, and Switzerland. *International Political Science Review* 29(3): 349–373.

ONS (Office for National Statistics) (2016) *Contracts That Do Not Guarantee a Minimum Number of Hours: March 2016.* London: Office for National Statistics.

Parent-Thirion, A., Vermeylen, G., van Houten, G., Lyly-Yrjänäinen, M., Biletta, I. and Cabrita, J. (2012) *Fifth European Working Conditions Survey – Overview Report.* Brussels: Eurofound.

Patel, V. and Kleinman, A. (2003) Poverty and Common Mental Disorders in Developing Countries. *Bulletin of the World Health Organization* 81(8): 609–615.

Paul, K. I. and Batinic, B. (2009) The Need for Work: Jahoda's Latent Functions of Employment in a Representative Sample of the German Population. *Journal of Organizational Behavior* 31(1): 45–64.

Paul, K. I. and Moser, K. (2009) Unemployment Impairs Mental Health: Meta-analyses. *Journal of Vocational Behavior* 74(3): 264–282.

Powdthavee, N. (2007) Are There Geographical Variations in the Psychological Cost of Unemployment in South Africa? *Social Indicators Research* 80(3): 629–652.

Rubery, J., Ward, K., Grimshaw, D. and Beynon, H. (2005) Working Time, Industrial Relations and the Employment Relationship. *Time and Society* 14(1): 89–110.

Sahlins, M. (1974) *Stone Age Economics.* Hawthorne, NY: Walter de Gruyter.

Selenko, E., Batnic, B. and Paul, K. (2011) Does Latent Deprivation Lead to Psychological Distress? Investigating Jahoda's Model in a Four-Wave Study. *Journal of Occupational and Organizational Psychology* 84(4): 723–740.

Smith, M., Piasna, A., Burchell, B., et al. (2013) *Women, Men and Working Conditions in Europe*. Luxembourg: Publications Office of the European Union.

Standing, G. (1999) *Global Labour Flexibility: Seeking Distributive Justice*. Basingstoke: Palgrave Macmillan

Standing, G. (2014) *The Precariat: The New Dangerous Class*. London: Bloomsbury.

Strandh, M. (2000) Different Exit Routes from Unemployment and Their Impact on Mental Well-being: The Role of the Economic Situation and the Predictability of the Life Course. *Work, Employment and Society* 14(3): 459–479.

Wanberg, C., Griffiths, R. and Gavin, M. (1997) Time Structure and Unemployment: A Longitudinal Investigation. *Journal of Occupational and Organisational Psychology* 70(1): 75–95.

Warr, P. (1987) *Work Unemployment and Mental Health*. Oxford: Oxford University Press.

Warr, P. (1999) Well-being and the Workplace. In (Eds) Kahneman, D., Diener, E. and Schwarz, N. *Well-being: The Foundations of Hedonic Psychology*. New York: Russell Sage Foundation.

Waters, L. and Moore, K. (2002). Reducing Latent Deprivation During Unemployment: The Role of Meaningful Leisure Activity. *Journal of Occupational and Organizational Psychology* 75(1): 15–32.

Watt, N. (2014) Embattled Miliband Vows to Challenge Britain's 'Zero-Zero' Economy. *The Guardian* 12 November 2014. www.theguardian.com/politics/2014/nov/12/miliband-fightback-labour-victims-zero-zero-britain.

Wood, A. J. (2016) Flexible Scheduling: Degradation of Job Quality and Barriers to Collective Voice. *Human Relations* 69(10): 1989–2010.

Wood, A. J. and Burchell, B. J. (2014) *Zero Hour Contracts as a Source of Job Insecurity. Report Submitted to the UK Government Department of Business Innovation and Skills Consultation on Zero Hour Contracts*. Cambridge: University of Cambridge Individual in the Labour Market Research Group Reports.

Wood, A. J. and Burchell, B. J. (2015) Zero Hours Employment: A New Temporality of Capitalism? *Reviews and Critical Commentary (CritCom)*, September. http://councilforeuropeanstudies.org/critcom/zero-hours-employment-a-new-temporality-of-capitalism/

Wright, E. O. (2010) *Envisioning Real Utopias*. London: Verso.

Wyatt, I. D. and Hecker, D. E. (2006) Occupational Changes During the 20th Century. *Monthly Labor Review*. March: 35–57.

8 Money Management in Households

Bernadette Kamleitner, Eva Marckhgott
and Erich Kirchler

8.1 Introduction

Private households dispose of a major part of a nation's financial resources. Consequently, financial decisions taken by households affect a nation's overall welfare. Regulators, marketers, consumer protectionists, businesses and economists are in need of knowledge about how households operate if they are to understand and shape household decisions. Economic models that fail to take account of systematic variations in household financial practices will inevitably be less accurate in predicting the impact of policies aimed (for example) at enhancing the well-being of children, encouraging debt avoidance or combatting poverty.

The standard economic concept of a household has perhaps been best described by Becker (1973). He applied the notion of maximisation of (human) capital to the household level and described the stereotypical roles of male breadwinner and female carer as a rational use of human capital. His thesis was that households as exemplified by marriage offer gains in trade and economies of scale by means of specialised human capital. Since women have a 'comparative advantage' in bearing and caring for children, they should invest primarily in domestic capital. To date, it makes economic sense for couples to adhere to this pattern when male earnings are (typically) higher than women's and the latter bear the children (Burgoyne et al., 2007). This normative economic ideal contrasts with the reality of households which are driven by multiple factors beyond the maximisation of economic benefits through role specialisation. Psychologists, in particular, have been concerned with describing financial household dynamics as a multidetermined set of socially negotiated practices.

But what is a household? The concept is widely used as the main unit of analysis by researchers and policy makers, yet few present a clear definition. Given that most people share a household, we are interested in households composed of more than one member. Such multiperson households have either been broadly defined as 'a group of people who share resources, activities and expenditures' (Casimir and Tobi, 2011, p. 503) or, more pragmatically, as all persons living together in a housing unit (United Nations, 2016).

Regardless of which definition is being used, various compositions of households exist. Households come in a variety of sizes and may consist of romantically or economically attached, legally bound, related or unrelated members of both sexes at various ages. Due to societal and economic developments, the potpourri of household compositions is ever changing, and they affect the financial decisions households make. Beyond being influenced by the relationships household members have with each other (Kirchler et al., 2001), households are influenced by a multifacetted interplay of their context (e.g., culture, economic situation) and the individual characteristics (e.g., Donnelly, Iyer and Howell, 2012) household members bring into the situation (Kamleitner, Mengay and Kirchler, 2017). Together, these factors determine a household's resources and who in the household disposes of these resources, that is, they determine a household's money management (van Raaij, 2016).

In this chapter, we review and discuss how households manage money. We start our review by providing evidence on the multifacetted reality of household compositions. Before that background, we proceed to address the question of how households manage the money available to them and whether the assumption of the household as a unit is at all warranted. After unveiling essential dynamics shaping money management, we briefly address how the financial practices of a household may in turn influence its members and their interplay. We end the chapter with a juxtaposition of various insights across different household compositions and a systematic identification of what appear to be the most significant themes, implications, gaps and research directions in the study of household money management.

8.2 Composition of Households

The boundaries of households are fuzzy and they may shift over time (Kirchler et al., 2001). For example, the arrival and departure of children or movements in and out of the labour market affect a household's composition and activities. The household is thus a dynamic concept that comes in many guises.

In many Western societies, the average household size has been declining. The reasons are manifold and include decreasing fertility rates, high divorce rates and a trend towards living alone (Eurostat, 2015). To name an example, in the European Union (EU) the average household comprises 2.4 persons, but single-person households account for almost one-third (32 per cent) of households. Another third (32 per cent) of households comprises two persons, and it is only roughly a third of households (36 per cent) that comprises at least three persons. It is only among this last segment that the proverbial family comprising a breadwinning husband, a wife and one or more children can be found. This 'traditional' household format has been steadily declining (Antonides and van Raaij, 1998), as in 2008 only 21 per cent of households in the EU consisted of a couple with children (Iacovou and Skew, 2011).

Another change to households that affects money management and that we know little about to date (for initial insights, see Burgoyne et al., 2006, 2007) is a decline in the formal bond of marriage. In most Western societies, marriage used to be a 'societal prerequisite'. Now it is often just an option (Sweeney, 2010). In the EU, the marriage rate has nearly halved between 1964 and 2011 and the age at which people get married has increased (Eurostat, 2015). Many women now spend time developing a career before considering marriage and giving birth to children (Mills et al., 2011). Moreover, a substantial number of women continue in paid employment thereafter, which entails an increase in multiple-income households. For example, in both the United Kingdom (UK) and the United States (US), working wives contribute an average of close to 40 per cent of the family's income (Bureau of Labor Statistics, 2015; Cory and Stirling, 2015).

Marriage also used to be an enduring civil state. It no longer is. Following the liberalisation of divorce laws, divorce and remarriage have become more common. In the EU, today almost 50 per cent of marriages end in a divorce; that is twice as many as in the 1970s (Eurostat, 2015). In the United States, where remarriage is fairly widespread, three-quarters of divorced persons go on to remarry, and 65 per cent of these remarriages include children from one or more previous marriages (Bramlett and Mosher, 2001; van Eeden-Moorefield et al., 2007). Beyond the immediate implications to the prior household, as we shall see, such disruptions influence how individuals behave in a new household (van Eeden-Moorefield et al., 2007).

Alternatives to marriage have also become more acceptable and widespread (Barlow et al., 2008). Cohabitation is no longer a simple prelude to marriage. It has become a legitimate alternative and 'a normal context in which to bear and parent children' (Kennedy and Bumpass, 2008, p. 1686). For example, in the United Kingdom 14 per cent of dependent children were living with unmarried, cohabiting parents in 2015, and more than a third of the population had been in a cohabiting relationship at some point (Office for National Statistics, 2015).

A further household composition pattern results from the increasing acceptability of same-sex unions. Some countries have adopted laws which offer marriage for same-sex couples in a similar way to heterosexual couples. At the time of writing, same-sex marriage is possible in Argentina, Belgium, Brazil, Canada, Colombia, Denmark, England/Wales, Finland, France, Greenland, Iceland, Ireland, Luxembourg, Mexico, Netherlands, New Zealand, Norway, Portugal, Scotland, South Africa, Spain, Sweden, the United States and Uruguay (Pew Research Center, 2015).

Though the decrease in fertility rates tends to decrease average household size, there is another trend opposing this effect: a trend back towards extended-family households with at least two adult generations. In 2008, 16 per cent of the total US population lived in such extended-family households, that is, one-third more than in 1980 (Pew Research Center, 2010; Taylor et al., 2010).

In Europe, extended households are also increasing, though their prevalence sees strong variations, ranging from 7 per cent in northern Europe to up to 40 per cent in some eastern European countries such as Bulgaria (Iacovou and Skew, 2011).[1] In many Western societies, the average age at which young adults leave their parents' house has also increased (Kins et al., 2009). Both the rising number of extended-family households and the trend of young adults living with their parents are at least in part a response to the economic situation. Economic crises, which have not equally hit all parts of Europe, often lead to an increase in housing costs, and hit the younger generation harder than their parents' generation (e.g., Manacorda and Moretti, 2006), forcing them to stay home. How the increasing reality of multiple generations in a household affects households' money management is an interesting but largely open question.

Some countries also experience an increase in households consisting of non-related adults who are neither married nor cohabiting partners. In the United States, for example, such shared households were reported to account for 19 per cent of all households, and the trend is rising (Mykyta and Macartney, 2012). Once again, challenging economic circumstances and the subsequent urge to reduce the costs of living have been suggested to underlie such developments (Steinführer and Haase, 2009). What such household compositions imply for the way money is managed across the different household members has yet to be established.

All in all, we see an increase in the flexibility and the variety of household composition. Marriage has almost become a lifestyle choice. Its nature, meaning and practice have been shifting in parallel with other social and economic changes, all of which are likely to affect the dynamics at play when making decisions within and as a household. In the upcoming sections, we use this initial backdrop to review what economic psychology currently knows about money management within households.

8.3 Who Owns and Handles a Household's Resources?

The resources owned by a household consist of members' wealth and infrastructure (e.g., house, furniture) as well as their recurring income. In order to understand how money is managed in the household, we have to understand which resources are owned and handled by which household member. Overall, we know quite well how households deal with recurring income. In comparison to the literature on the management of recurring income, literature on the ways in which households perceive and handle wealth and infrastructure is limited. We first discuss the knowledge we hold on how households handle more permanent assets such as wealth and infrastructure. We then review and discuss the considerably broader base of knowledge on how different households handle recurring income.

8.3.1 Holding Possessions – Wealth and Infrastructure

From a legal viewpoint, possessions of a household are either individually or jointly owned, rented, leased or borrowed[2] by one or several members of the household. In case of joint entitlements, household members share ownership rights and obligations regarding the target object.

The way household members actually behave towards resources is, however, also a matter of the extent to which they experience 'psychological ownership', that is, the feeling that something is 'mine' (Pierce, Kostova and Dirks, 2003) or 'ours' (Kamleitner and Rabinovich, 2010; Pierce and Jussila, 2010), over the respective resource. The psychological experience of ownership affects how objects are being handled and decided on (Brasel and Gips, 2014; Brough and Isaac, 2012).

Owning things jointly rather than individually likely affects the extent to which a person feels psychological ownership for an object. On the one hand, joint ownership entails having less control over the object (e.g., in case of a jointly owned car the freedom to use the car at any time). This leads to a decrease in *individual* psychological ownership ('my-ness') and reduced object care. On the other hand, joint ownership can lead to *collective* psychological ownership ('our-ness'). This could cause a more careful handling of the target object. In case of a poor co-owner relationship, it can happen that neither collective nor individual psychological ownership are strongly experienced. Such situations result in low levels of object care (Kamleitner and Rabinovich, 2009).

Situations of low psychological ownership for a household's assets are especially likely for households comprising of cohabiting nonrelated persons. Within these households, jointly owned objects might easily become a source of conflicts both during the cohabitation as well as at the dissolution of the household. More generally, blurred or entangled ownership relations might complicate the division of household items when one or more household members leave the household. Despite an increasing prevalence of the real-world phenomenon, we know little about how different household compositions handle such situations. Rather than looking at the resources that are already at a household's disposition, most scientific attention has been devoted to the recurring resource of household income.

8.3.2 Handling Recurring Income – Money Management

A household may obtain recurring income through any of its members. In essence, most recurring income enters a household through the labour of an individual household member. A question that has received considerable interest in the psychological research community is how and whether it is then turned into a resource for the entire household, that is, who is in charge of and manages the recurring income? Notably, deciding on a certain money management system also affects psychological ownership. Households that pool all their resources are more likely to be explicit about treating all resources collectively, and to say that all of the money is 'ours' (Ashby and Burgoyne, 2009).

Jan Pahl (1989) identifies the following money management systems:

a. *The female whole wage system*: where the wife manages all household money apart from the husband's personal spending money; this system tends to be practiced by less affluent households (Pahl, 1995).
b. *The male whole wage system*: in which the husband manages all finances; this can leave a stay-at-home wife with no access to any money and tends to be practiced by higher-income households (Pahl, 1995).
c. *The housekeeping allowance system:* where the main earner gives his or her partner a sum to cover household expenses and retains control of the rest.
d. *The joint or total pooling system:* where all the household income is combined, often in a joint account; some transfer small amounts purely for personal spending money into separate personal accounts (Burgoyne et al., 2006; Burgoyne et al., 2007).
e. *The partial pooling system:* where some of the household income is combined to cover collective expenses, while the rest is kept separate. An essential difference between joint and partial pooling is that in partial pooling partners usually have their earnings paid directly into their individual accounts, and then transfer an agreed sum (or proportion) into a joint account for shared expenses. Many keep considerable sums of money and other assets separately. Partial pooling is motivated mainly by a desire to achieve independence, autonomy and some financial privacy as well as a sense of financial 'identity' (Burgoyne et al., 2006, 2007).
f. *The independent management system:* where each partner keeps his or her income in a separate account. This system is more typical for dual-earner couples. In independent management, the boundaries between 'mine', 'yours' and 'ours' are blurry. Couples using independent management are 'less individualistic and private than the label ... suggests' (Evertsson and Nyman, 2014, p. 65). They do not necessarily spend their own money without considering the couple's and the partner's financial situation. Often partners only feel free to spend their money as they wish after joint expenses have been paid. Couples might have to negotiate how much money each partner contributes (and from which account), what is defined as a joint expense and who ensures that bills are paid. This can be even more tricky when there is a large disparity in earnings (Ashby and Burgoyne, 2005; Elizabeth, 2001). Though perceived as fair, independent management does not provide much protection to the economically weaker partner (Elizabeth, 2001).

An astonishing finding across the body of research building on this typology has been that all money management systems have the potential to replicate financial inequalities at the household level. One reason lies in an important distinction inherent to Pahl's typology: that between overall control of money (or strategic power) and management (or executive power). Making a significant financial contribution is visible and it is accorded privilege (such as greater access to money for personal use and more 'say' in decision-making) than other types of input such as housework or childcare, thus yielding strategic power. In turn, access to money is not the same as the right to allocate money for different purposes. Thus, the female whole wage system may leave overall control in the hands of a male breadwinner who can set priorities for the use of the money that his wife manages on a day-to-day basis. Pooling likewise is often more apparent than real, with the potential for one partner to have more say on how the money is to be used (Vogler, Lyonette and Wiggins, 2008b). Money is not only an economic medium of exchange, but has an ideological and social value (Pahl, 1989). Even if partners have a joint account, and try to treat money as a collective resource, it might still be 'laden with meaning' (Nyman, Reinikainen and Stocks, 2013, p. 647), and the source of that income – that is, who has earned or contributed it – is difficult to ignore (Burgoyne et al., 2006, 2007).

Although Pahl's typology covers most ways in which money may be managed within a household, the use of the terms 'wife' and 'husband' already suggests that this work was done at a time with less heterogeneity in household compositions. It was guided by money management in traditional heterosexual marriage with the husband being the main breadwinner. Given the aforementioned diversification of households and the shift towards less traditional gender roles within heterosexual relationships (Lindsey, 2015), several scholars have since been reinvestigating actual practices (e.g., Ashby and Burgoyne, 2008; Vogler, Brockmann and Wiggins, 2006). To highlight how differences in household compositions may affect money management practices, we will start by summarising what is known about the money management practiced by heterosexual married couples and go on to juxtapose it with insights on money management practiced in other household compositions.

8.3.2.1 *Money Management in Households Bound by 'Traditional' Heterosexual Marriage*

Heterosexual marriage used to be the traditional unit of analysis and hence received the highest amount of scientific attention (Bennett, 2013). It dominated the reality of households in the past century (Cunningham, 2008), and though it is declining this organisational unit is still widespread. In particular, it remains a stereotype and benchmark for how households are supposed to function.

The classical economic stereotype is that of role specialisation including a male breadwinner and a female carer (Becker, 1973). While this stereotypical practice makes economic sense if the unit of analysis is the household (Burgoyne et al., 2007), the entailed division of labour exposes women to economic risk (e.g., Burgoyne, 2004; Vogler et al., 2006). Despite a public rhetoric depicting

(Western) marriage as a partnership of equals (Reibstein and Richards, 1993), few seem to achieve this ideal in practice (Burgoyne, 2004; Webley et al., 2001). To date, men are more likely to start off with higher earnings (e.g., Maume and Ruppanner, 2015) than their wives and are more likely to become the principal breadwinners when a couple has children (Berghammer, 2014). The resulting disparity between male and female incomes can result in a lower standard of living for wives than husbands within the same household, and less say in decision-making. In societies with a high divorce rate, it can make women even more financially vulnerable. In particular, the situation for mothers who reduce their earning power tends to deteriorate over time as their labour market human capital diminishes (James, 1996; Webley et al., 2001).

This vulnerability could potentially be offset by the way that a couple chooses to manage income and other financial assets. Surveys in the United Kingdom during the 1990s (e.g., Laurie and Rose, 1994) show that around half of all couples were pooling their money, typically in a joint account, about 36 per cent used a whole wage system, 11 per cent used a housekeeping allowance system and around 2 per cent practiced independent management. More recent studies (e.g., Pahl, 2008; Vogler, Brockmann and Wiggins, 2008a) show a clear shift towards individualisation of money management. The number of couples using independent management and partial pooling has been rising, while the number of couples opting for joint pooling has remained comparably stable. Whole wage systems, which once were the second most used money management system, are now only used by a small fraction of couples, and housekeeping allowances are no longer popular either. While older couples are more likely to use a male-dominated money management system (Bisdee, Daly and Price, 2013), younger and more affluent couples are increasingly keeping all or parts of their income separate (Pahl, 2005). Longitudinal studies with newly-weds (Burgoyne et al., 2006, 2007) show, however, that marriage still can act as a prelude to pooling income. One year after marriage, the number of couples using total pooling had tripled. Merging finances is, however, often prompted by economic factors, such as taking on a mortgage or starting a family. Mostly couples are likely to go only as far as partial pooling unless there is also a commitment to shared ownership of household resources, that is, a high sense of collective psychological ownership. To some extent, the trend towards individualisation may also reflect the reality of increasing divorce rates. Doubts about a relationship and its stability make couples less likely to see money as collectively owned (whatever system they use) (Vogler et al., 2006), thus strengthening existing inequalities in earning potentials. Finally, market forces, too, are pushing for individualised practices with payment methods such as individualised credit cards being on the rise (Pahl, 2008).

The extent to which couples may subscribe to a traditional view of marriage and of marital roles may also foster financial inequalities within households (Burgoyne, 1990). Gender sets the parameters for several behaviours in households dominated by heterosexual couples. Married couples still practice stereotypical purchasing patterns. Much like in the 1970s (Davis and Rigaux, 1974), the wife of the twenty-first century still tends to be in charge of buying cleaning products, while the man has more say in the purchase of a car (Belch and Willis, 2002; Kamleitner et al., 2017; Lakshmi and Murugan, 2008; Meier, Kirchler and Hubert, 1999; Xia et al., 2006). The more households subscribe to traditional roles as opposed to egalitarianism, the less they decide jointly and the more influence the man has (Ford, LaTour and Henthorne, 1995; Ganesh, 1997; Norvilitis et al., 2006). Stereotypes also appear able to describe some of the forces at play when it comes to allocating resources. Men are more likely to allocate benefits on the basis of equity, whereas women are more likely to opt for equality (Burgoyne and Lewis, 1994). Even in a country such as Sweden, which is renowned for its attention to equality, Nyman (1999) argues that 'real' equality will remain just an ideal when men are still able to set the overall agenda for money management and women (are expected to) put the interests of the family before their own. In Nyman's study, the couples had arranged to cover all household expenses jointly, leaving each partner with an equal amount of money for personal use. However, as the wives had day-to-day responsibility for meals and childcare, they tended to use their own personal spending money as a buffer to even out household expenses, and this was not accounted for. The men seemed able to ignore their wives' pleas to change the way that these expenses were managed, and the women seemed reluctant to press the issue if it might lead to conflict. Thus, systems of management that should leave these dual-income partners with equal access to personal spending money paradoxically led to the familiar inequalities associated with gender.

We have discussed a number of possible explanations for inequalities in marriage. But do people really think that household money should be shared equally, even when partners are contributing different amounts? This issue was investigated in two studies by Burgoyne and Routh (2001) and Sonnenberg, Burgoyne and Routh (2011). They used a series of vignettes describing (a) a couple who are getting married, and (b) a couple about to have their first baby. In both types of vignette, the relative incomes of the partners were varied so that sometimes they earned equally and sometimes one partner earned more than his or her partner. Participants in Burgoyne and Routh's (2001) study were asked to choose the 'best' and 'fairest' of a list of possible systems of money management (based upon Pahl's typology). Overall, regardless of relative income, the most frequently chosen 'best' option was pooling all money and making joint decisions about it. Respondents also tended to identify their choice as the 'fairest'. However, for a significant minority, the partner earning relatively more money was deemed to be entitled to more personal spending money. A similar pattern of results was obtained by Sonnenberg et al. (2011). One noteworthy new finding was that when the woman was depicted in the role of mother, her income was seen as being by default for the family, with less individual freedom to own and control it. In contrast, the man in the role of father seemed to be accorded a higher degree of financial autonomy. This echoes earlier findings that women typically contribute a larger proportion of their income to the family (Nyman, 1999; Pahl, 1995). Some work on bargaining experiments also supports gender differences: both sexes expect women to be more generous in their allocations and to be content with receiving less (Solnick, 2001).

Thus far, we have seen that equality in marriage is not always achieved, though people generally endorse it and – in principle – would opt for a system of money management that gives both partners a relatively equal say in how the household income is used. Given these insights from a traditional context, a question begs asking: Do other household compositions manage money differently?

8.3.2.2 *Money Management in 'Nontraditional' Households*
A household composition that is similar to that of traditional marriage is the fast-growing population of cohabiting couples. The challenge in studying this population is its heterogeneity. Some couples regard cohabitation as a valid alternative to marriage and feel that they are as good as married already, others see it as a less binding form of relationship and these perceptions may vary over time (Ashby and Burgoyne, 2005; Barlow et al., 2001). To some extent, this is reflected in the broader circumstances the cohabitants face. Kiernan and Estaugh (1993) distinguish between never-married childless cohabitants, never-married cohabiting parents and postmarital cohabitants. In particular, never-married cohabiting parents behave in a similar manner to married respondents, with more than 50 per cent of cohabiting parents using pooling (Vogler et al., 2008a). In contrast, both cohabiting parents without children and postmarital cohabitants are more likely to keep money partly or completely separate. They primarily opt for partial pooling or independent management (Vogler et al., 2008a). On balance, however, gender inequalities in access to finances are reported to be just as likely in cohabiting unions as in marriage (Avellar and Smock, 2005).

One essential difference between cohabitation and marriage is the lack of legal rights and explicit responsibilities of cohabiting partners (Barlow, 2008). Again, this comes primarily to the detriment of the financially worse off partner, usually the woman. Cohabiting women's concerns about their financial future are reported to be deeper and more salient than those of married women. They are also more likely to express fears about becoming a burden for their partner (Malone et al., 2010). Women's fears appear warranted. After dissolution of the partnership, women's income is likely to drop by 33 per cent (compared to 10 per cent for men). Although this drop is somewhat less than for women getting divorced, who interestingly have fewer fears initially, the differences are relatively small when the women have custody of children (Avellar and Smock, 2005).

Taken together, insights on cohabitation paint a picture similar to that of marriage with a tendency for more independence. The main point these insights highlight is that households need to be regarded in their entirety. Just looking at the union of the primary couple is insufficient to explain the financial dynamics within a household. The moment children arrive, households founded by a romantically attached couple appear to behave similarly regardless of whether they are married or not. Likewise, the propensity for women to be worse off within a household remains untouched by whether the partners are legally bound to each other or not.

Given the importance of earning money, that is, strategic power within a household, it is interesting to ask what happens if, in contrast to the model of the male breadwinner, the *female partner is the main breadwinner.* This is the case for more than a third of working wives in the United States (Bureau of Labor Statistics, 2015). The insights available suggest that gender opposes strategic power. A husband's financial satisfaction declines as his wife's income rises (Bonke, 2008). Women who earn more than their husbands have accordingly been observed to downplay their role as the main breadwinner. To achieve this, both husband and wife extend their notion of providing for the family to other tasks that are not related to breadwinning (e.g., meeting emotional and physical needs of family members) (Tichenor, 2005). To bolster the male identity of provider, they also tend to avoid total pooling systems in which the husband's share would show up as minor. Rather, they tend to adopt partial pooling, which enables the husband to incur expenditures with symbolic meaning (e.g., mortgage payments) out of his own account, thus resembling his traditional role as the breadwinner (Commuri and Gentry, 2005). Even in cases of disagreement, women tend to refrain from exercising the power their financial position would afford them. Couples with female main breadwinners tend to disrupt the link between money and power for the female partner, but maintain the possibility of such a link for the male partner (Tichenor, 2005). In a nutshell, this composition is a showcase for the pervasive role of gender stereotypes.

A household composition which teaches something about the role of experience and enhanced relationship complexities is that of *remarriage.* Despite the high rate of remarriage, research on economic behaviour in such couples is somewhat scanty (Allen et al., 2001). In sum, it appears that experience is able to trump gender stereotypes to some extent, although remarriage is unlikely to help combat the effects of income inequalities. Generally, money management in remarriage tends to be more separate than in first marriage (Burgoyne and Morison, 1997; Raijas, 2011; Singh and Morley, 2011). Remarried couples are most likely to use a kind of partial pooling system with some accounts kept separate and others comingled (van Eeden-Moorefield et al., 2007). There appear to be several reasons for this. For one, divorce always entails the question of who is entitled to what, plus it makes the threat of future separation more salient. This appears to sometimes shift the perceptions of psychological ownership of money. Some of the men feel that they have been 'ripped off' in divorce settlements with former wives and want to keep control of both recurring income and assets they bring into the second marriage. For the women's part, although generally less wealthy than their new partners, many have learned to cherish more independent access to resources than in their first marriages. As a consequence, women are also more involved in money management in a remarriage compared to a first marriage (Burgoyne and Morison, 1997). Another relevant factor is of a more financial nature. Remarried couples may have to deal with maintenance payments or debts to or because of former spouses (Malone et al., 2010). Some couples avoid merging money because they want to keep their current partner out of assessments for maintenance payments (Burgoyne and Morison, 1997). Finally, in particular when children are involved the ensuing range of potential step-relationships can result in complex intrahouseholds relationships and money flows (Singh and Bhandari, 2012). Separation of accounts in remarriage is also observed to occur with children in mind; those with children from previous relationships feel that they are holding resources 'in trust' for their own children (Burgoyne and Morison, 1997). Moreover, remarried partners tend to feel that they are financially responsible for the expenditures of their own biological children (Raijas, 2011; Singh and Morley, 2011).

In sum, insights on remarriage suggest that experience is able to break stereotypes. The ideal of the male breadwinner seems to become somewhat trumped by the experienced need for financial autonomy, and once again the presence of children seems to make a difference. On the whole, however, remarriage is not well suited to remedying intrahousehold income inequalities.

The potential for an interesting point of contrast with regard to inequalities and stereotypes lies in households composed of *same-sex couples*. Similar to heterosexual cohabitation, there is a variety of ways in which same-sex couples live together, ranging from short-term cohabitation to marriagelike relationships. In general, same-sex partners tend to be particularly sensitive to power imbalances (Weeks, Heaphy and Donovan, 2001), and thus more egalitarian in their decision-making (Reiss and Webster, 1997; Solomon, Rothblum and Balsam, 2005). Joint decisions are seen as both a necessity to fulfil the desire for equality and a pleasurable aspect of the relationship (for lesbian couples, see Wilkes and Laverie, 2007). Since it is important that each partner can actively contribute to joint decisions as an egalitarian partner, it is necessary that each partner remains in charge of his or her own financial stake. Similar to heterosexual cohabiting couples without children (Burgoyne, Clarke and Burns, 2011; Vogler et al., 2008a), few lesbian and gay couples pool all their income, though a majority pool some money to cover joint expenses (Burgoyne et al., 2011; Burns, Burgoyne and Clarke, 2008). Income disparities between most partners necessitate the adoption of a system of proportional contributions to joint expenses, and to joint expenses only (Burns et al., 2008).

A frequent theme in same-sex couples is the avoidance of financial dependence on one's partner. This does, however, not equate to unwillingness to support each other. Most members of same-sex households state that they are prepared to support each other financially if necessary. Still, such support seems in many cases to be time-limited, and many seemed to endorse an ethic of co-independence rather than mutual dependence (Burns et al., 2008). Eventually, the money management practiced by same-sex couples tends to reproduce financial inequalities between the partners. Although couples attempt to equalise outcomes, an underlying norm of equality (characterised by equal contributions where feasible) paradoxically (re)produces the status and control of the higher earner in most cases.

8.3.3 Themes Guiding Money Management

The juxtaposition of existing insights on different household compositions suggests that – even in romantic relationships – money management is more than a reflection of the relationship quality of the household members. It follows the rules governing economic exchange as much as those of social exchange (Curtis, 1986; Webley et al., 2001). In particular, three themes emerged: 'power through resources', 'psychological entitlement through relationship' and 'stereotypes versus values'. We discuss them in turn.

8.3.3.1 *Power Through Resources*

The perhaps most dominating theme identified is that of a link between power and resources (e.g., Vogler et al., 2008b). Whoever brings in more resources, in particular monetary resources, also tends to end up with more resources and more say about how the households' resources are to be used. This even holds for children (Flurry, 2007). The influence of monetary contributions is pervasive. Household members earning higher wages are even deemed entitled to more leisure time (Browning and Gørtz, 2012). Moreover, couples who face more inequality in terms of income or education tend to have a more clear-cut division of decision-making, ending in fewer joint decisions (Schneebaum and Mader, 2013). Given that it is still mostly the women who earn less, more income and other resources tend to beget men having more say (Antman, 2014; Carlsson et al., 2013; Lakshmi and Murugan, 2008; Sultana, 2011).

The link between financial contributions to and power within a household appears to be intuitively understood. Its effect on bigger societal phenomena is potentially profound. For example, it may affect how households decide to contribute to the labour market (Knowles, 2013). Given the narrowing of the gender-wage gap, Knowles wondered why it can be that the increase in female wages did not lead to a corresponding reduction in male labour supply. Drawing on longitudinal time-use surveys, he suggests that the answer lies in the bargaining power that income affords men within the household.

8.3.3.2 *Psychological Entitlement Through Relationship*

Although household members appear to be generally aware of who brings what into the household, they differ in terms of whose money they feel this is. Pooling of money – along with high intimacy and quality of the members' relationship – often results in the experience of collective psychological owner-ship of household resources (Ashby and Burgoyne, 2009), which in turn might counteract intrahousehold inequalities. It is this mechanism that distinguishes the money management practiced by many households from that of purely economic units. An intimate relationship alone does, however, not always appear to suffice to make things 'ours'. Significant joint decisions and acquisi-tions (e.g., buying a house) may be a necessary catalyst.

One such catalyst is the arrival of children. Though their presence disrupts the woman's earning potential, it facilitates or even necessitates pooling of resources (Vogler et al., 2008a), in particular when children are younger.

One might assume that there is an increase in collective psychological own-ership – after all, we live in an age in which the term 'sharing' has become a buzzword (Belk, 2014). In fact, there are no signs that intrahousehold sharing, collective psychological ownership of resources and factual pooling are on the rise. On the contrary, several authors have observed a shift to individual finan-cial independence. Household members appear to become less rather than more likely to pool their resources (e.g. Pahl, 2008; Vogler et al., 2008a).

8.3.3.3 *Stereotypes Versus Values*

One explanation for the trend towards autonomy is an increase in the endorsement of egalitarian values (Reiss and Webster, 1997; Solomon et al., 2005). In particular, in households that are not subject to traditional role stereotypes, values of egalitarianism appear to play an important role. They are also more strongly endorsed in households that are particularly well endowed; there they tend to extend to all household members, includ-ing children (Flurry, 2007). At the surface level, this has had positive con-sequences. For example, with an increase in egalitarian values in a society, women have started to receive somewhat more say in financial decisions, such as the purchase of a car (Belch amd Willis, 2002). But where there is light, there is shadow. The drawback of egalitarian values is that they also tend to involve equal financial obligations. Not all household members are equally well suited to shoulder these.

Stereotypes are a powerful force counteracting egalitarian values. As much as people strive to deny them, stereotypes remain a sculptor of actual behav-iours. In particular, gender roles permeate money management and household decision-making in a way that benefits the male provider. Given that stereo-types reflect cultural meanings, cultural notions such as the worth and role of women, children and the elderly are likely to shape what parts they take in household decisions. Values and stereotypes are likely the main factors explaining cultural differences in money management (cf., Xia et al., 2006).

8.4 How Does Money Management Affect the Household?

The quality of the relationship between household members affects how households decide to deal with money (Kirchler et al., 2001).The reverse holds also true. The way households manage money and make financial decisions affects the relationship between household members and their well-being.

The potential for negative consequences of money management is evident. The household is a prime site for cooperation but also for the negotiation of conflicts of interest and settlement of disagreements. Many issues concern money (Kirchler et al., 2001; McGonagle, Kessler and Schilling, 1992), making money management a potential factor in bringing about separation and divorce (Gottman, 2014) and, therefore, the dissolution of the household.

The way households manage money can, however, also bring about positive consequences for its members and society at large. In particular, the process of making joint decisions has been reported to have a positive effect on relationships (Vogler et al., 2008b). Couples who make financial decisions jointly are more satisfied with their relationship compared to couples where either partner controls spending autonomously. This matters because the more satisfied people are with their relationship, the happier they are with life in general. Combined with Kirchler et al.'s (2001) insight that satisfaction with the relationship is directly connected to the tactics used to persuade one's partner, we see a virtuous or vicious circle. Partners who are satisfied with the overall quality of their relationship are more likely to use cooperative tactics, which in turn increases satisfaction with the relationship. On the other hand, dissatisfied couples might opt for less cooperative tactics, which result in a decrease in satisfaction.

Living in the same household implies getting to know each other well. One could assume that people who have decided to spend (a part of) their lives together are able to take each other's preferences into account; over time, this should reduce the need to decide jointly in order to remain happily together. Some evidence suggests that this assumption is not warranted. Couples are surprisingly bad at predicting each other's preferences to begin with and get no better at doing so with relationship duration (Scheibehenne, Todd and Mata, 2011). Even long-term couples can, thus, only ensure that both partners' interests are accounted for if they actively partake in joint decisions.

Apart from happiness and satisfaction, the way households manage money can affect the health of household members. At least in developing countries, the inclusion of women in money management and decision-making has been shown to positively affect their body mass index and chronic energy deficiency (Hindin, 2000). While there is likely a direct effect of financial empowerment, there are also hints at indirect effects. A recent study in Kenya reveals a positive effect of women's decision-making power in the household on household sanitation (Hirai, Graham and Sandberg, 2016), which in turn affects the health of household members. Similarly, research in China shows that an increase in women's income results in more bargaining power in the relationship, which in turn has a positive impact on the survival rate of daughters and educational attainment of both daughters and sons (Qian, 2008).

8.5 Discussion

Money management in the household determines who has access to and control over monetary resources. Consequently, it permeates other financial decisions made by a household's members. A frequent assumption by policy makers and researchers has been that households are an income-pooling entity with a common standard of living. This review has shown that such an assumption is misguided (cf. Lise and Seitz, 2011). Across various household compositions, different dynamics are at play. In particular, three themes have been identified:

a. The higher the resource inequalities between household members to begin with, the more likely it becomes that those members that bring in most resources also control most of the household's monetary resources.
b. The more household members engage in joint endeavours with significant financial implications (e.g., buying a house, getting children), the more likely they are to pool the household's income.
c. The more the household members subscribe to egalitarianism and the more independent they are from role stereotypes, the more likely they will manage their income independently.

Jointly, these themes feed into multiple nuanced practices through which, at the end of the day, intrahousehold inequalities frequently prevail. Often this comes to the detriment of the woman who more or less willingly partakes, for example, by helping to keep stereotypes of the male provider alive. Experience from prior household membership (in particular, in remarried relationships) but also trends towards egalitarian understandings of relationships seem to lead to more (perceived and desired) financial autonomy but to no fewer financial inequalities. Intrahousehold inequalities could only be remedied by total factual and mental pooling of the household's resources, a practice that has seen a decrease rather than an increase in popularity.

The main implication resulting from these insights is that public policy has to aim at the individual as well as the household if it is to affect financial decisions within households. Individual's actual or threatened poverty, in particular, is likely to often go unnoticed if a household's total income is used as a benchmark (Webley et al., 2001).

The insights garnered also enable us to derive informed guesses as to what happens in those household compositions that have still escaped scientific scrutiny. One such composition is that of extended, multiple-generation households. A primary question in these households is whether they perceive themselves and act as one big household or rather as two (or more) largely independent subhouseholds. All themes identified are likely to play a role. They entail such questions as the following: Who is bringing what into the household? Specifically, how does one account for the natural head start of the parent generation? Who feels psychologically entitled to resources? Specifically, do children feel automatically entitled to resources brought in by their parent generation? Who takes on which roles? Specifically, do stereotypes of the giving parent, the innovative younger generation or the wise elder prevail in who has a say? In short, money management in extended-family households is a largely open field that is potentially ripe with new insights.

One such potentially more generic insight relates to how households deal with an increase in income-generating members. It often happens, and it does so through multiple routes. For example, the woman may start to work after a child break, a child may turn into a money-earning adult or a new related or unrelated member may be accepted into the household for economic or social reasons. Given that resources amount to power within households, it is likely that the addition of a new member also affects the money management system in place. Based on what is known, it may often lead to even more independent money management practices.

An interesting subquestion is how the mere anticipation of an increase in financially contributing household members (e.g., children taking over the family home) influences the way a household manages its resources. Existing investigations are very much focussed on current household composition. How they behave may be as much driven by who is expected to be there in the future.

Another potential research avenue for which extended-family households are fertile ground is the question of what resources lead to power. Does it always have to be money? The likely answer is that money is the dominating factor. For example, recent insights from Africa suggest that retired women have more influence if they receive higher pensions (Ambler, 2016). It would be interesting to find out to which extend other 'resources' such as health or experience may yield power in different types of households.

There are also multiple research avenues that households composed of unrelated and romantically unattached members may open up. The last avenue we address here is one of 'shared space'. There is an increase in the phenomenon of 'living apart – together', where partners do not share space on an everyday basis. Almost a quarter of British adults who are not married and do not cohabit opt for a 'living apart – together' relationship (Duncan, 2015). At the same time, communication and interaction are increasingly becoming independent of space. In state-of-the art 'smart homes' (Harper, 2006), it is even possible to be in another continent and still switch on or off the lights or determine what is available in the fridge. Relationships may increasingly play out across multiple sites and homes that are only partly physically shared. To date, we know next to nothing about how such 'virtual' households manage their money and household practices. It is, however, likely that they will do so even more independently. The reality of living apart and of technologies facilitating this opens up the question as to how much one space actually needs to be physically shared to still be considered a household by policy makers. To date, homes housing virtual households may be considered as smaller than they are, determined only by those members living there permanently.

8.6 Concluding Remarks

To conclude, we know that a combination of recent trends fosters the desire for individual financial autonomy. It also fosters the appearance of household compositions that are founded on other than romantic motives. Yet, it is romantically attached households that we know most about. Through these households, we know that there are multiple, partly counteracting mechanisms at play (resources as power; relationship strength; and collective ownership, stereotypes and values). These mechanisms play out through different money management systems (from independent to total pooling) which are put in place through nuanced practices. It is these practices that ensure that households replicate and sometimes even foster intrahousehold inequalities across money management systems. In particular, the link between power and money and pervasive role stereotypes are able to turn the desire for more egalitarianism into a reality of inequality. Still, we also know that it is beneficial for households to try and overcome trends for separation. Most evidence suggests that joint decisions and the active inclusion of multiple household members benefit the well-being of the entire household and society at large.

Notes

1 Note that the statistical basis for determining the prevalence of extended households differs between the United States and Europe. The definition used in Europe does not include households with adult children. The figures stated here result from merging all categories considered extended family in the United states. Furthermore, note that the baseline used for the United States is the entire population while for Europe it is households. The figures may thus be similarly high.
2 For the sake of simplicity, we will refer to all of these types of (temporary) ownership as 'owning'.

8.7 References

Allen, E. S., Baucom, D. H., Burnett, C. K., Epstein, N., and Rankin-Esquer, L. A. (2001). Decision-Making Power, Autonomy, and Communication in Remarried Spouses Compared with First-Married Spouses. *Family Relations*, 50(4), 326–334. doi:10.1111/j.1741-3729.2001.00326.x

Ambler, K. (2016). Bargaining with Grandma: The Impact of the South African Pension on Household Decision Making. *Journal of Human Resources,* 51(4), 900–932. doi: 10.3368/jhr.51.4.0314-6265R1

Antman, F. M. (2014). Spousal Employment and Intra-household Bargaining Power. *Applied Economics Letters,* 21(8), 560–563. doi:10.1080/13504851.2013.875101

Antonides, G., and van Raaij, F. (1998). *Consumer Behaviour: A European Perspective.* Chichester: Wiley.

Ashby, K., and Burgoyne, C. (2005). Independently Together: An Exploratory Study of Money Management in Cohabiting Couples. Paper presented at the 30th Annual Congress: International Association for Research in Economic Psychology: Absurdity in the Economy, Prague, Czech Republic.

Ashby, K., and Burgoyne, C. (2008). Separate Financial Entities? Beyond Categories of Money Management. *Journal of Socio-Economics,* 37(2), 458–480. doi:http://dx.doi.org/10.1016/j.socec.2006.12.035

Ashby, K., and Burgoyne, C. (2009). The Financial Practices and Perceptions Behind Separate Systems of Household Financial Management. *Journal of Socio-Economics,* 38(3), 519–529.

Avellar, S., and Smock, P. J. (2005). The Economic Consequences of the Dissolution of Cohabiting Unions. *Journal of Marriage and Family,* 67(2), 315–327.

Barlow, A. (2008). Cohabiting Relationships, Money and Property: The Legal Backdrop. *Journal of Socio-Economics,* 37(2), 502–518.

Barlow, A., Burgoyne, C., Clery, E., and Smithson, J. (2008). Cohabitation and the Law: Myths, Money and the Media. *British Social Attitudes,* 24, 29.

Barlow, A., Duncan, S., James, G., and Park, A. (2001). Just a Piece of Paper? Marriage and Cohabitation. *British Social Attitudes,* 29–58.

Becker, G. S. (1973). A Theory of Marriage: Part I. *Journal of Political Economy,* 813–846.

Belch, M. A., and Willis, L. A. (2002). Family Decision at the Turn of the Century: Has the Changing Structure of Households Impacted the Family Decision-Making Process? *Journal of Consumer Behaviour,* 2(2), 111–124. doi:10.1002/cb.94

Belk, R. W. (2014). You Are What You Can Access: Sharing and Collaborative Consumption Online. *Journal of Business Research,* 67(8), 1595–1600. doi: dx.doi.org/10.1016/j.jbusres.2013.10.001

Bennett, F. (2013). Researching Within-Household Distribution: Overview, Developments, Debates, and Methodological Challenges. *Journal of Marriage and Family,* 75(3), 582–597.

Berghammer, C. (2014). The Return of the Male Breadwinner Model? Educational Effects on Parents' Work Arrangements in Austria, 1980–2009. *Work, Employment and Society,* 28(4), 611–632.

Bisdee, D., Daly, T., and Price, D. (2013). Behind Closed Doors: Older Couples and the Gendered Management of Household Money. *Social Policy and Society,* 12(1), 163.

Bonke, J. (2008). Income Distribution and Financial Satisfaction Between Spouses in Europe. *Journal of Socio-Economics,* 37(6), 2291–2303.

Bramlett, M. D., and Mosher, W. D. (2001). First Marriage Dissolution, Divorce, and Remarriage. Retrieved from www.cdc.gov/nchs/data/ad/ad323.pdf

Brasel, S. A., and Gips, J. (2014). Tablets, Touchscreens, and Touchpads: How Varying Touch Interfaces Trigger Psychological Ownership and Endowment. *Journal of Consumer Psychology*, 24(2), 226–233. doi:10.1016/j.jcps.2013.10.003

Brough, A. R., and Isaac, M. S. (2012). Finding a Home for Products We Love: How Buyer Usage Intent Affects the Pricing of Used Goods. *Journal of Marketing*, 76(4), 78–91. doi:10.1509/jm.11.0181

Browning, M., and Gørtz, M. (2012). Spending Time and Money Within the Household. *Scandinavian Journal of Economics*, 114(3), 681–704. doi:10.1111/j.1467-9442.2012.01711.x

Bureau of Labor Statistics. (2015). Women in the Labor Force: A Databook. Retrieved from www.bls.gov/opub/reports/womens-databook/archive/women-in-the-labor-force-a-databook-2015.pdf

Burgoyne, C. (1990). Money in Marriage: How Patterns of Allocation Both Reflect and Conceal Power. *Sociological Review*, 38(4), 634–665.

Burgoyne, C. (2004). Heart-Strings and Purse-Strings: Money in Heterosexual Marriage. *Feminism and Psychology*, 14(1), 165–172.

Burgoyne, C., Clarke, V., and Burns, M. (2011). Money Management and Views of Civil Partnership in Same-Sex Couples: Results from a UK Survey of Non-Heterosexuals. *Sociological Review*, 59(4), 685–706.

Burgoyne, C., Clarke, V., Reibstein, J., and Edmunds, A. (2006). 'All My Worldly Goods I Share with You?' Managing Money at the Transition to Heterosexual Marriage. *Sociological Review*, 54(4), 619–637.

Burgoyne, C., and Lewis, A. (1994). Distributive Justice in Marriage: Equality or Equity? *Journal of Community and Applied Social Psychology*, 4, 101–114.

Burgoyne, C., and Morison, V. (1997). Money in Remarriage: Keeping Things Simple – and Separate. *Sociological Review*, 45, 363–395.

Burgoyne, C., Reibstein, J., Edmunds, A., and Dolman, V. (2007). Money Management Systems in Early Marriage: Factors Influencing Change and Stability. *Journal of Economic Psychology*, 28(2), 214–228.

Burgoyne, C., and Routh, D. (2001). Beliefs About Financial Organization in Marriage: The 'Equality Rules OK' Norm? *Zeitschrift für Sozialpsychologie*, 32(3), 162–170.

Burns, M., Burgoyne, C., and Clarke, V. (2008). Financial Affairs? Money Management in Same-Sex Relationships. *Journal of Socio-Economics*, 37(2), 481–501.

Carlsson, F., Martinsson, P., Qin, P., and Sutter, M. (2013). The Influence of Spouses on Household Decision Making Under Risk: An Experiment in Rural China. *Experimental Economics*, 16(3), 383–401. doi:10.1007/s10683-012-9343-7

Casimir, G. J., and Tobi, H. (2011). Defining and Using the Concept of Household: A Systematic Review. *International Journal of Consumer Studies*, 35(5), 498–506.

Commuri, S., and Gentry, J. W. (2005). Resource Allocation in Households with Women as Chief Wage Earners. *Journal of Consumer Research*, 32(2), 185–195.

Cory, G., and Stirling, A. (2015). *Who's Breadwinning in Europe?: A Comparative Analysis of Maternal Breadwinning in Great Britain and Germany*: London: Institute for Public Policy Research.

Cunningham, M. (2008). Changing Attitudes Toward the Male Breadwinner, Female Homemaker Family Model: Influences of Women's Employment and Education over the Lifecourse. *Social Forces*, 87(1), 299–323.

Curtis, R. F. (1986). Household and Family in Theory on Inequality. *American Sociological Review*, 168–183.

Davis, H. L., and Rigaux, B. (1974). Perception of Marital Roles in Decision Processes. *Journal of Consumer Research*, 1(1), 51–62. doi:10.2307/2488954

Donnelly, G., Iyer, R., and Howell, R. T. (2012). The Big Five Personality Traits, Material Values, and Financial Well-being of Self-Described Money Managers. *Journal of Economic Psychology*, 33(6), 1129–1142. doi:10.1016/j.joep.2012.08.001

Duncan, S. (2015). Women's Agency in Living Apart Together: Constraint, Strategy and Vulnerability. *The Sociological Review*, 63(3), 589–607.

Elizabeth, V. (2001). Managing Money, Managing Coupledom: A Critical Examination of Cohabitants' Money Management Practices. *Sociological Review*, 49(3), 389–411.

Eurostat. (2015). People in the EU – Statistics on Household and Family Structures. Retrieved from ec.europa.eu/eurostat/statistics-explained/index.php/People_in_the_EU_%E2%80%93_who_are_we_and_how_do_we_live%3F

Evertsson, L., and Nyman, C. (2014). Perceptions and Practices in Independent Management: Blurring the Boundaries Between 'Mine', 'Yours' and 'Ours'. *Journal of Family and Economic Issues*, 35(1), 65–80.

Flurry, L. A. (2007). Children's Influence in Family Decision-Making: Examining the Impact of the Changing American Family. *Journal of Business Research*, 60(4), 322–330.

Ford, J. B., LaTour, M. S., and Henthorne, T. L. (1995). Perception of Marital Roles in Purchase Decision Processes: A Cross-cultural Study. *Journal of the Academy of Marketing Science*, 23(2), 120–131. doi:10.1177/0092070395232004

Ganesh, G. (1997). Spousal Influence in Consumer Decisions: A Study of Cultural Assimilation. *Journal of Consumer Marketing*, 14(2), 132–155. doi:doi:10.1108/07363769710166765

Gottman, J. M. (2014). *What Predicts Divorce? The Relationship Between Marital Processes and Marital Outcomes*: Hove, East Sussex: Psychology Press.

Harper, R. (2006). *Inside the Smart Home*: Springer Science and Business Media.

Hindin, M. J. (2000). Women's Poer and Anthropometric Status in Zimbabwe. *Social Science and Medicine*, 51(10), 1517–1528. doi:http://dx.doi.org/10.1016/S0277-9536(00)00051-4

Hirai, M., Graham, J. P., and Sandberg, J. (2016). Understanding Women's Decision Making Power and Its Link to Improved Household Sanitation: The Case of Kenya. *Journal of Water Sanitation and Hygiene for Development*, 6(1), 151–160.

Iacovou, M., and Skew, A. J. (2011). Household Composition Across the New Europe: Where Do the New Member States Fit In? *Demographic Research*, 25, 465–490.

James, S. (1996). Female Household Investment Strategy in Human and Non-Human Capital with the Risk of Divorce. *Journal of Divorce & Remarriage*, 25(1/2), 151–167.

Kamleitner, B., Mengay, T., and Kirchler, E. (2017). Financial Decisions in the Household. In M. Altman (Ed.), *Handbook of Behavioral Economics and*

Smart Decision-Making: Rational Decision-Making Within the Bounds of Reason (pp. 349–365). Northhampton: Edward Elgar.

Kamleitner, B., and Rabinovich, A. (2009, October 22–25). Mine Versus Ours: Does It Matter? Paper presented at the Association for Consumer Research (ACR), Pittsburgh, PA.

Kamleitner, B., and Rabinovich, A. (2010). Mine Versus Ours: Does It Matter? In M. C. Campbell, J. Inman, and R. Pieters (Eds.), *Advances in Consumer Research* (37, pp. 87–88). Duluth MN: Association for Consumer Research.

Kennedy, S., and Bumpass, L. (2008). Cohabitation and Children's Living Arrangements: New Estimates from the United States. *Demographic Research*, 19, 1663.

Kiernan, K., and Estaugh, E. (1993). *Cohabitation, Extra-marital Child-bearing and Social Policy*. London: Joseph Rowntree Foundation/Family Policy Studies Centre.

Kins, E., Beyers, W., Soenens, B., and Vansteenkiste, M. (2009). Patterns of Home Leaving and Subjective Well-being in Emerging Adulthood: The Role of Motivational Processes and Parental Autonomy Support. *Developmental Psychology*, 45(5), 1416.

Kirchler, E., Rodler, C., Hölzl, E., and Meier, K. (2001). *Conflict and Decision-Making in Close Relationships: Love, Money and daily routines*. Hove, East Sussex: Psychology Press.

Knowles, J. A. (2013). Why Are Married Men Working So Much? An Aggregate Analysis of Intra-household Bargaining and Labour Supply. *Review of Economic Studies*, 80(3), 1055–1085. doi:10.1093/restud/rds043

Lakshmi, P. V., and Murugan, M. S. (2008). The Influence of Marital Roles on Product Purchase Decision Making. *ICFAI Journal of Consumer Behavior*, 3(1), 66–77. Retrieved from search.ebscohost.com/login.aspx?direct=true&db=buh&AN=31197961&site=ehost-live

Laurie, H., and Rose, D. (1994). Divisions and Allocations Within Households. *Changing Households: The British Household Panel Survey*. Colchester: University of Essex.

Lindsey, L. L. (2015). *Gender Roles: A Sociological Perspective*. Abingdon, Oxon: Routledge.

Lise, J., and Seitz, S. (2011). Consumption Inequality and Intra-household Allocations. *Review of Economic Studies*, 78(1), 328–355.

Malone, K., Stewart, S. D., Wilson, J., and Korsching, P. F. (2010). Perceptions of Financial Well-being Among American Women in Diverse Families. *Journal of Family and Economic Issues*, 31(1), 63–81.

Manacorda, M., and Moretti, E. (2006). Why Do Most Italian Youths Live with Their Parents? Intergenerational Transfers and Household Structure. *Journal of the European Economic Association*, 4(4), 800–829.

Maume, D. J., and Ruppanner, L. (2015). State Liberalism, Female Supervisors, and the Gender Wage Gap. *Social Science Research*, 50, 126–138.

McGonagle, K. A., Kessler, R. C., and Schilling, E. A. (1992). The Frequency and Determinants of Marital Disagreements in a Community Sample. *Journal of Social and Personal Relationships*, 9(4), 507–524.

Meier, K., Kirchler, E., and Hubert, A.-C. (1999). Savings and Investment Decisions Within Private Households: Spouses' Dominance in Decisions on Various Forms of Investment. *Journal of Economic Psychology*, 20(5), 499–519. Retrieved from www.sciencedirect.com/science/article/B6V8H-3XK6XF6-1/2/100fd47a6996739ef01560a17ccef2bc

Mills, M., Rindfuss, R. R., McDonald, P., and Te Velde, E. (2011). Why Do People Postpone Parenthood? Reasons and Social Policy Incentives. *Human Reproduction Update*, 17(6), 848–860.

Mykyta, L., and Macartney, S. (2012). Sharing a Household: Household Composition and Economic Well-being: 2007–2010. *Current Population Report, US Census Bureau*. June.

Norvilitis, J. M., Merwin, M. M., Osberg, T. M., Roehling, P. V., Young, P., and Kamas, M. M. (2006). Personality Factors, Money Attitudes, Financial Knowledge, and Credit-Card Debt in College Students. *Journal of Applied Social Psychology*, 36(6), 1395–1413. doi:10.1111/j.0021-9029.2006.00065.x

Nyman, C. (1999). Gender Equality in 'the Most Equal Country in the World'? Money and Marriage in Sweden. *Sociological Review*, 47(4), 766–793.

Nyman, C., Reinikainen, L., and Stocks, J. (2013). Reflections on a Cross-National Qualitative Study of Within-Household Finances. *Journal of Marriage and Family*, 75(3), 640–650.

Office for National Statistics. (2015). Families and Households: 2014. Retrieved from www.ons.gov.uk/peoplepopulationandcommunity/birthsdeathsand marriages/families/bulletins/familiesandhouseholds/2015-01-28/pdf

Pahl, J. (1989). *Money and Marriage*. London: Macmillan.

Pahl, J. (1995). His Money, Her Money: Recent Research on Financial Organisation in Marriage. *Journal of Economic Psychology*, 16(3), 361–376. Retrieved from www.sciencedirect.com/science/article/B6V8H-3Y5FPV4-B/2/60ef7d5e9db47263735edeb696355f0e

Pahl, J. (2005). Individualisation in Couple Finances: Who Pays for the Children? *Social Policy and Society*, 4(04), 381–391.

Pahl, J. (2008). Family Finances, Individualisation, Spending Patterns and Access to Credit. *Journal of Socio-Economics*, 37(2), 577–591. Retrieved from www.sciencedirect.com/science/article/B6W5H-4N3GNWS-1/2/97234dcf7440af3761b7e955e06deb82

Pew Research Center. (2010). The Return of the Multi-Generational Family Household. Retrieved from www.pewsocialtrends.org/files/2010/10/752-multi-generational-families.pdf

Pew Research Center. (2015). Gay Marriage Around the World. Retrieved from www.pewforum.org/2015/06/26/gay-marriage-around-the-world-2013/

Pierce, J. L., and Jussila, I. (2010). Collective Psychological Ownership Within the Work and Organizational Context: Construct Introduction and Elaboration. *Journal of Organizational Behavior*, 31(6), 810–834. doi:Doi 10.1002/Job.628

Pierce, J. L., Kostova, T., and Dirks, K. T. (2003). The State of Psychological Ownership: Integrating and Extending a Century of Research. *Review of general Psychology*, 7(1), 84–107. Retrieved from <Go to ISI>://000181503400005

Qian, N. (2008). Missing Women and the Price of Tea in China: The Effect of Sex-Specific Earnings on Sex Imbalance. *Quarterly Journal of Economics*, 123(3), 1251–1285.

Raijas, A. (2011). Money Management in Blended and Nuclear Families. *Journal of Economic Psychology*, 32(4), 556–563. doi:dx.doi.org/10.1016/j.joep.2011.02.006

Reibstein, J., and Richards, M. P. M. (1993). *Sexual Arrangements: Marriage and the Temptation of Infidelity*. New York, NY: Scribners.

Reiss, M. C., and Webster, C. (1997). Relative Influence In Purchase Decision Making: Married, Cohabitating, and Homosexual Couples. *Advances in Consumer Research*, 24(1), 42–47.

Scheibehenne, B., Todd, P. M., and Mata, J. (2011). Older but Not Wiser – Predicting a Partner's Preferences Gets Worse with Age. *Journal of Consumer Psychology*, 21(2), 184–191.

Schneebaum, A., and Mader, K. (2013). The Gendered Nature of Intra-household Decision Making in and Across Europe. Department of Economics Working Paper Series. Vienna: WU Vienna University of Economics and Business.

Singh, S., and Bhandari, M. (2012). Money Management and Control in the Indian Joint Family Across Generations. *Sociological Review*, 60(1), 46–67.

Singh, S., and Morley, C. (2011). Gender and Financial Accounts in Marriage. *Journal of Sociology*, 47(1), 3–16.

Solnick, S. J. (2001). Gender Differences in the Ultimatum Game. *Economic Inquiry*, 39(2), 189.

Solomon, S. E., Rothblum, E. D., and Balsam, K. F. (2005). Money, Housework, Sex, and Conflict: Same-Sex Couples in Civil Unions, Those not in Civil Unions, and Heterosexual Married Siblings. *Sex Roles*, 52(9–10), 561–575.

Sonnenberg, S. J., Burgoyne, C. B., and Routh, D. A. (2011). Income Disparity and Norms Relating to Intra-household Financial Organisation in the UK: A Dimensional Analysis. *Journal of Socio-Economics*, 40(5), 573–582.

Steinführer, A., and Haase, A. (2009). Flexible-inflexible: Socio-demographic, Spatial and Temporal Dimensions of Flat Sharing in Leipzig (Germany). *GeoJournal*, 74(6), 567–587. doi:10.1007/s10708-008-9248-3

Sultana, A. (2011). Factors Effect on Women Autonomy and Decision-Making Power Within the Household in Rural Communities. *Journal of Applied Sciences Research*, 7(1), 18–22.

Sweeney, M. M. (2010). Remarriage and Stepfamilies: Strategic Sites for Family Scholarship in the 21st Century. *Journal of Marriage and Family*, 72(3), 667–684.

Taylor, P., Passel, J., Fry, R., et al. (2010). *The Return of the Multi-Generational Family Household*. Washington, DC: Pew Research Center.

Tichenor, V. (2005). Maintaining Men's Dominance: Negotiating Identity and Power When She Earns More. *Sex Roles*, 53(3–4), 191–205.

United Nations. (2016). Households and Families. Retrieved from unstats.un.org/unsd/demographic/sconcerns/fam/fammethods.htm van Eeden-Moorefield, B., Pasley, K., Dolan, E. M., and Engel, M. (2007). From Divorce to Remarriage: Financial Management and Security Among Remarried Women. *Journal of Divorce & Remarriage*, 47(3–4), 21–42.

van Raaij, W. F. (2016). *Money Management Understanding Consumer Financial Behavior: Money Management in an Age of Financial Illiteracy*. New York: Palgrave Macmillan US.

Vogler, C., Brockmann, M., and Wiggins, R. D. (2006). Intimate Relationships and Changing Patterns of Money Management at the Beginning of the Twenty-First Century. *British Journal of Sociology*, 57(3), 455–482.

Vogler, C., Brockmann, M., and Wiggins, R. D. (2008a). Managing Money in New Heterosexual Forms of Intimate Relationships. *Journal of Socio-Economics*, 37(2), 552–576. doi: dx.doi.org/10.1016/j.socec.2006.12.039

Vogler, C., Lyonette, C., and Wiggins, R. D. (2008b). Money, Power and Spending Decisions in Intimate Relationships. *Sociological Review*, 56(1), 117–143.

Webley, P., Burgoyne, C., Lea, S. E. G., and Young, B. M. (2001). *The Economic Psychology of Everyday Life*. Hove, East Sussex: Psychology Press.

Weeks, J., Heaphy, B., and Donovan, C. (2001). *Same Sex Intimacies: Families of Choice and Other Life Experiments*. Hove, East Sussex: Psychology Press.

Wilkes, R. E., and Laverie, D. A. (2007). Purchasing Decisions in Non-Traditional Households: The Case of Lesbian Couples. *Journal of Consumer Behaviour*, 6(1), 60–73.

Xia, Y., Ahmed, Z. U., Ghingold, M., Hwa, N. K., Li, T. W., and Ying, W. T. C. (2006). Spousal Influence in Singaporean Family Purchase Decision-Making Process: A Cross-cultural Comparison. *Asia Pacific Journal of Marketing and Logistics*, 18(3), 201–222. doi:10.1108/13555850610675661

9 Socially Responsible Investing

Christopher J. Cowton

9.1 Introduction

Socially responsible investment or investing (SRI) is the practice of integrating social, environmental and ethical (SEE) considerations into investment decisions. In particular, SRI refers to the addition of SEE criteria to conventional financial criteria in the selection and management of portfolios of shares (stocks) of companies listed on stock markets. Socially responsible (SR) investors care not only about the size of their prospective financial return and the risk attached to it, but also about its source – the nature of the company's products and services or how it does business. '[I]t matters where the money comes from' (Lewis, 2002: p. 4).

The addition of nonfinancial considerations stands in stark contrast to conventional approaches to investment. Building on the insights of Markowitz (1952), modern portfolio theory (MPT) provides an elegant, parsimonious treatment of investment decision-making in terms of expected returns (in the form of dividends or capital gains) and risk (based on covariance of returns). Similarly, popular depictions of investment activity are focussed upon the amount of money made, while recognising that past performance is not a guide to future returns and the value of investments may go down as well as up. The conventional or 'mainstream' investor would appear to be a case of *homo economicus par excellence*; morality, and other preferences in general, are not part of the picture.

Not least because of the way in which it stands in contrast to mainstream investing, SRI is a phenomenon worth understanding. Moreover, supported by institutional developments, it is clear that SRI – in different countries, at different times and with different emphases – has over the past three or four decades become an established feature of most developed stock markets. Estimates of the total funds involved vary, depending to some extent on the definition employed, but SRI has undoubtedly become significant. For example, the US SIF Foundation estimates that at the end of 2015 more than 20 per cent of sums under professional management in the United States – or nearly $9 trillion – was invested according to SRI strategies; Hendry (2013) notes claims that 'responsible investment', which might be argued to be associated with SRI, now accounts for about 20 per cent of stock market investment in

Europe; and, focussing more specifically on investment products, in October 2015, the Ethical Investment Research and Information Service (EIRIS) estimated that the amount invested in the UK's green and ethical retail funds had reached £15 billion, up from approximately £6 billion a decade earlier. SRI is no longer a quirky activity practised by a few cranks.

Since we are more interested in the attitudes and behaviours that lie behind the portfolios examined by finance researchers, the title of this chapter refers to socially responsible invest*ing*, rather than the more usual invest*ment*. The remainder of the chapter is structured as follows. First, some basic terminology and concepts are introduced and various possible approaches to incorporating SEE considerations into investment decisions are outlined. Second, the routes by which an individual investor can come to hold an SRI stake are explained. Third, the possibility that SRI entails a financial sacrifice is discussed. Fourth, the question of whether SRI makes a difference to the morality of markets is explored. Finally, the conclusion summarises the key points of the chapter.

9.2 Coming to Terms with SRI

Berry and Junkus (2013) find it 'surprising' that there is not a clear consensus on what the term 'SRI' means. However, vagueness is not unusual in human affairs, and SRI can take a number of different forms, leading to some variety in definitions (Cooper and Schlegelmilch, 1993; Frankel, 1984) and terminology too. Popular for many years, and still current in some circles, is the term 'ethical investment', which may be taken to be broadly synonymous with SRI – though there are some possible grounds for usefully distinguishing between the two terms on occasion (Sparkes and Cowton, 2004). Sometimes indicating particular strands within SRI, other terms have also been used over the years, including 'social' (Bruyn, 1987; McGill, 1984), 'divergent' (Schotland, 1980), 'creative' (Powers, 1971) and 'green' (Simpson, 1991). Indeed, the abbreviation 'SRI' is sometimes taken to refer to 'sustainable and responsible investment'.

While terminological variety can lead to some confusion, the essential feature of the investment practices being considered in this chapter is, as the introductory definition indicated, the bringing together of both moral values and conventional financial criteria in decisions over whether to purchase, hold or sell a share as part of an investment portfolio. The remainder of this section and the next section will outline the principal ways in which these two elements may be combined in investment decisions.

At the heart of much SRI, at least traditionally, is the avoidance of certain types of companies because of the nature of their products or services. Sometimes referred to as 'sin stocks' (Miller, 1991), the shares in companies involved in some or all of alcohol, gambling, tobacco and pornography are commonly absent from SRI investment portfolios. Such exclusions reflect the importance of church bodies in the antecedents and development of SRI (see Sparkes, 2002: chapter 3; Kreander, McPhail and Molyneaux, 2004), to which might now be added investors who wish to invest according to Islamic law, or Shariah (Ghoul and Karam, 2007). Military contractors might also be excluded (Cowton, 1993), and during the Apartheid regime the avoidance of companies with interests in South Africa united many SR investors in both the United States (Schueth, 2003) and the United Kingdom (Cowton, 1999a). Such exclusion is, in effect, a kind of boycott behaviour, although the precise definition of avoidance is open to some interpretation and practical challenges. Taking alcohol as an example, a brewing company would obviously be avoided, but what about a family restaurant chain or a supermarket that sells alcohol? What about a company that supplies raw materials or even information technology (IT) to a brewing company?[1] In practice, implicitly or explicitly, certain judgment calls have to be made; while not arbitrary, they do reflect acceptance that 'purity' is not possible, other than through not investing at all or severely downplaying risk criteria as a consequence of having a very constrained set of options. Thus, in practice, thresholds of acceptability (perhaps 5 per cent of turnover) rather than 'strictly binary propositions' (Rockness and Williams, 1988: p. 406) tend to be seen.

Things can become even more complex, when it comes to judging companies, if an avoidance approach involves *how* a company behaves rather than *what* it does. One way of framing this is by means of the stakeholder groups affected. For example, an SR investor might wish to avoid investing in a company that treats its staff badly (employees), is a significant polluter (environment, local community) or engages in problematic advertising practices (customers; see Cowton, 1992).

With a pure avoidance approach, an investor can build an investment portfolio using conventional financial criteria and techniques, albeit with a smaller investment universe of companies from which to choose. In other words, having ruled out some companies, an attempt can be made to construct as balanced a portfolio as possible to reflect the risk and return preferences of the investor.

'Any individual or group which truly cares about ethical, moral, religious or political principles should in theory at least want to invest their money in accordance with their principles' (Miller, 1992: p. 248). This is the *prima facie* case for SRI or ethical investment (Cowton and Sandberg, 2012). Avoidance represents a key strand in this, but it has been argued that it is, at the very least, an insufficient response to perceived problems with companies. Many commentators have suggested that there is an argument for positively selecting and hence 'encouraging' or expressing support for 'good' companies, rather than just avoiding 'bad' ones. Like an avoidance approach, such a 'supportive' approach (Cowton, 1994) can be related to what a company does or how it does it. For example, an investor might be keen to hold a stake in a renewable energy company or one that has exemplary employment practices, perhaps in relation to women or minorities.

It is common to find positive criteria, where they are employed, alongside negative criteria. There are various ways in which they can be combined. One simple method is to use the negative criteria to define the investment universe and then use some sort of scoring system to select companies, taking into account their financial characteristics too. The subsequent apparent ignoring of negative SR criteria in the detail of the investment decision might appear to treat them as relatively unimportant but, like any constraint, they can be viewed as degenerate objectives (Tocher, 1970) or expressions of overriding goals (Eilon, 1971) – that is, whatever else, *this* will not be invested in. Another way of combining the positive and the negative is to give companies negative marks rather than excluding them altogether, with sufficiently strong positive marks giving them a chance of being included in the portfolio – again while factoring in financial characteristics. Alternatively, 'really bad' companies might still be excluded, with the remainder receiving both negative and positive marks to yield an overall rating for them. Thus there are several ways in which investors can factor their ethical attitudes into SRI decisions.

Holding shares in companies which are, on the whole, good or acceptable but nevertheless possess some negative features also provides SR investors the opportunity – and some would say a duty – to use their rights as shareholders to seek to improve things. Shareholder activism (Sullivan and Mackenzie, 2006) has a long history but, with the growth in SRI, has probably become more widespread and nuanced in recent years. Much attention is focussed on high-profile issues such as apartheid (in the past), mining operations in the developing world and executive pay, where public means such as shareholder resolutions (perhaps put forward by members of a campaigning group who hold shares only for the purpose of bringing about change) and shareholder voting via proxy statements at the annual general meeting are employed. However, more private behind-the-scenes dialogue also takes place between prominent shareholders and management (Logsdon and Van Buren, 2009). Such interaction enables issues to be raised with management without the need for a public response or defence, arguably making for more constructive and productive conversations. Thus, for example, an SR investor might question the case for a proposed acquisition if the new business would alter the profile of the company in a direction deemed undesirable (Cowton, 2004).

The way in which financial criteria are combined with other considerations depends not only on the approach being taken to SEE issues, as indicated in the preceding, but also on the sophistication of the investor; not all will be able to engage in 'active risk minimisation' or 'best in class' investing, for example (see Sparkes and Cowton, 2004). Indeed, often reflecting their degree of investment sophistication, there are various possible routes by which the ordinary investor can put the general approaches previously described into practice. Those routes are discussed in the next section.

9.3 Putting SRI into Practice

Given the focus of this handbook, it is appropriate to begin with individual investors rather than, say, institutional investors or charities that hold investments. Figure 9.1 maps out the principal routes by which an SR investor can come to have stakes in companies in a manner that is intended to reflect his or her values.

The diagram makes a distinction between direct investment, whereby investors own the shares, and indirect investment, whereby they have a stake in something else (such as a pension fund) which itself owns the shares.

9.3.1 Direct Investment

The most obvious way for socially responsible investing to take place is for individuals simply to purchase shares using their savings; this is represented by the left-hand arrow (route 1) in Figure 9.1. They might undertake this activity with the help of professional advisors, just as a conventional investor might. They might engage someone, such as their stockbroker, to act on their behalf; but they still own the shares, or have the direct benefit of the shares.

One of the arguments against the feasibility of SRI many years ago, before it became more commonplace, was that it was impracticable to gather the relevant information to implement a reasonably extensive policy that was not simply focussed on a single SEE issue. As the discussion of approaches in the previous section implied, assessing and monitoring the status of a large number of complex companies against a significant set of criteria require a great deal of information, some of which will not be available in corporate annual reports – and even when it is, it might be difficult to find and interpret. Powers commented many years ago, 'There is simply a crying need for information *and* for organisations to research and compile such information (Powers, 1971: p. 170, emphasis in original). That need has been met by information intermediaries (Moizer and Arnold, 1984), such as KLD Research & Analytics in the United States and London-based EIRIS (now Vigeo EIRIS). Use of such services while investing directly in companies is indicated by route 2 in Figure 9.1.

Direct investment activity takes place in private, and so it is difficult not only to estimate how large are the funds involved but also to know what SEE considerations are taken into account and how they are factored into investment decisions. However, some studies provide useful insights. For example, in a focus group study, Lewis (2001) noted that SR investors primarily mentioned avoiding companies that manufacture munitions, are exploitative or pollute. Other studies have used questionnaires to elicit opinions on negative and positive screening, but it is not always clear which responses come from individuals who are actually engaging in SRI (e.g., Czerwonka, 2014). Berry and Junkus (2013) surveyed the 85,000 members of the American Association of

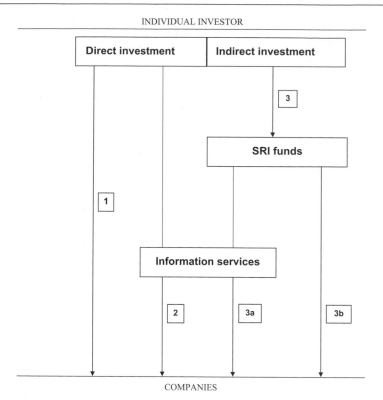

Figure 9.1. *Routes for socially responsible investing.*

Individual Investors (AAII), from which they obtained a 6 per cent response rate. Environmental issues were found to dominate, for both SR and non-SR investors. Many of the exclusion categories were consistent with other studies, but with pornography ranked first. Berry and Junkus noted that their respondents were interested in a corporation's overall behaviour in the marketplace, taking a more holistic approach than implied by the negative screening approach prevalent in SRI funds. However, their analysis, while useful, did not involve any sophisticated statistical analysis that might have yielded deeper insights from their data.

An earlier study focussed on 125 UK SRI 'pioneers', the first to use EIRIS in the mid-1980s, provided more depth of analysis (Cowton, 1999a; Anand and Cowton, 1993). Their investment activity could not be directly observed, but the advantage in terms of honest revelation of preferences was that the clients were paying a fee to obtain a list of 'acceptable' companies that would not contravene the exclusion criteria (usually more than one option for each topic area) that they selected in a questionnaire that reflected information contained in EIRIS's database. Out of the 125 clients, 120 wanted to avoid investing in companies involved in South Africa, using at least one of the criteria available. (Not surprisingly, the dominance of South Africa disappeared once the apartheid regime fell; it does not appear as a concern in Lewis, 2001, for example.) The next most objected to were military contractors (111), tobacco (87) and nuclear power (82).

Of course, the analysis was limited to the list of topics that the EIRIS database covered at that time, which was not only less extensive than it is today but also restricted to negative issues. Nevertheless, the issues covered are still familiar from SRI practice. Moreover, two further pieces of statistical analysis of the data provide deeper insights which are likely to have greater longevity. First, initial cluster analysis revealed partition into two groups (see Cowton, 1999a), the first of which (with sixty members) was more sensitive or stringent than the other; a larger proportion of the group excluded in relation to each topic. There were several topics that featured quite strongly with the sensitive group but much less so with the moderate group; advertising, animals, gambling and political donations registered with less than 40 per cent of the moderate group but more than 60 per cent of the sensitive group. Sometimes the differences were large. Further cluster analysis provided a particularly interesting split of the moderate group into two subgroups. As expected, given the overall findings, both groups had a high proportion who wanted to avoid South African involvement and military contractors. However, other than that, there were clear differences. A majority of members of one group (with thirty-two members) wished also to avoid tobacco (94 per cent), alcohol (63 per cent) and gambling (56 per cent). The only additional issue that registered with the second group, on the other hand, was nuclear power (58 per cent), with tobacco, alcohol and gambling accounting for just 9 per cent, 3 per cent and 12 per cent respectively. Although the terms are not mutually exclusive, the first group with its focus on 'sin stocks' was viewed as 'religious', whereas the second group could be seen as 'political'. They had some points of convergence but also some very clear differences (see Cowton, 1999a).

The second piece of statistical analysis sought to discern the attitudes that might underlie the choices of the 125 EIRIS clients (Anand and Cowton, 1993). Using principal component analysis, five components were found to explain more than 60 per cent of the variation in the data, with the first component accounting for almost a quarter of it (23 per cent). That first component comprised a rather large grouping of items; nuclear power, animals, military contractors, political contributions and financial institutions. A plausible interpretation is that this is a broadly left-of-centre, 'postindustrial' orientation, perhaps providing a tentative, affirmative answer to the question posed by Lewis and Cullis (1990: p. 403): 'Have the greens come of age?' The other four identified components were as follows:

- Alcohol, gambling and tobacco – a more straightforward grouping and a further sign of the 'sin' concern uniting certain characteristics
- Overseas interests and advertising – given how the underlying criteria were defined, a grouping focussed on companies' economic power, a 'mistrust' factor

- Company size and newspaper or television production – again, a grouping pointing towards power, perhaps in the form of 'undue influence'
- Military contractors and South Africa, which perhaps hint at a human rights or pacifist dimension

Although the research cited in the preceding is dated, the groups discovered through cluster analysis and the underlying structure inferred from the principal component analysis are likely to point to more enduring features, as well as providing guidance for more up-to-date analysis, if data of sufficient quality can be obtained.

However, research into SR investing has a further possible data source. While individual SR investors can make direct investments in company shares, it is also open to them to invest indirectly. The creation of this option (route 3 in Figure 9.1) has been responsible for significant growth in both the extent and visibility of SRI.

9.3.2 Indirect Investment: Using an SRI Fund

Many individual investors who are interested solely in financial considerations do not manage their own investment portfolio, even with professional advice and support, but instead invest indirectly in the stock market via collective investment vehicles such as pension funds and mutual funds (US) or open-ended investment companies (UK, formerly 'unit trusts'). Such funds levy charges, but many individual investors still choose to use them because they offer superior fund management expertise and access to information, efficient diversification and, in some cases, relatively high liquidity when compared with a conventionally owned portfolio (Draper, 1990).

As explained earlier, the informational challenges of a reasonably diverse SRI policy are likely to be considerable, thus increasing the incentives for an investor to use a fund which effectively has the information 'built in', from the individual investor's point of view, in the sense that the investment can be taken to possess characteristics in line with the stated investment policy and SR criteria. Funds can, and do, carry out their own research, but – just as they may do in relation to financial aspects – they may also make use of a specialist information service; hence the two legs of the right-hand arrow (route 3) in Figure 9.1.

SRI funds have been a feature of many economies in recent decades. The Pax World Fund was established in the United States in 1970, followed by the Dreyfus Third Century Fund in 1972. In the case of the United Kingdom, the first was Friends Provident Stewardship Trust, launched in 1984 and closely linked to the establishment of EIRIS in 1983 with backing from various religious organisations and religiously inspired charities (Cullis, Lewis and Winnett, 1992). It is sufficient that a commercial company identifies a potentially profitable market niche and seeks to match product characteristics to

SR investor preferences, perhaps taking 'innovative chances' in an attempt to distinguish its products (Lewis and Cullis, 1990, p. 401). Mackenzie (1998) refers to such funds as 'market led', though he notes that some funds are more 'deliberative', undertaking some ethical reflection and reasoning on corporate activity themselves. SRI funds can also, like any collective investment vehicle, pursue different investment policies, for example, oriented towards income (via dividends) or growth (via capital gains). However, of greater relevance to this chapter, they also differ in the SR polices that they offer. Because of their visibility as marketed and regulated products, more is known publicly about the SRI funds than about the individuals who invest in them. Many early funds in the United Kingdom, for example, focussed on exclusion, with apartheid in South Africa a prominent unifying issue. As concern about the environment grew significantly from about 1990 onwards, various other criteria came into play, including positive ones, especially around the environment (Cullis et al., 1992). 'Green' issues were particularly important for prompting the growth of SRI in much of Western Europe outside the United Kingdom.

Given the efforts that companies take in designing their investment products, it might be thought that the preferences of private investors could simply be 'read off' from the published SEE criteria. This is true up to a point, assuming that firms have judged investor concerns correctly, but there are two linked problems. First, as noted earlier, there are various ways to combine avoidance with more positive criteria, but there is relatively little agreement on what such positive issues should be and the positive criteria are often surprisingly vague; it is hard to avoid the conclusion that negative criteria tend to dominate (Schepers and Sethi, 2003). Second, although funds are usually clearer about what they avoid, even here there is a problem in inferring what actually concerns investors. This 'structural' issue stems from an underappreciated difference between positive and negative criteria in the context of collective investment.

Suppose two investors are thinking of clubbing together to form an investment portfolio. Further suppose that Investor 1 wishes to avoid companies with characteristics Xa and Xb, while Investor 2 wishes to avoid companies with characteristics Xb and Xc. Then a portfolio that does not contain Xa, Xb or Xc will satisfy their joint preferences; it is sufficient for both of them while not strictly necessary for either of them. This probably accounts for the phenomenon, observed by Lewis and Mackenzie (2000b), that funds originally launched as environmental or 'green' funds added ethical criteria in relation to arms, tobacco and gambling. Sometimes their published reasoning for doing so seemed a little contrived in trying to link to environmental issues.

Now contrast this with a situation where two investors wish to engage in positive screening (with or without complementary negative screening). Suppose Investor 3 wishes to invest in companies that display characteristics Ya and Yb, whereas Investor 4 values characteristics Yb and Yc. Then unless a portfolio can be constructed of companies that each possess all three characteristics, the satisfaction of the preferences of one investor is likely to lead to a dilution of the other investor's preferences in a joint portfolio. Perhaps this is one reason why, whatever their claims, SRI funds tend to appear more convincing on negative screening than on positive criteria. Furthermore, the greater the range of criteria, the more significant is the issue just identified.

Therefore, for many of the investors in an SRI fund, some of the negative criteria will likely be redundant. Thus, for example, Lewis (2001) found investors who cited certain concerns when the funds they were invested in almost certainly used significant other, likely redundant, negative criteria that were not mentioned by the investors. In principle, the 125 EIRIS clients analysed earlier could have had a single, restricted fund designed to meet all their SEE concerns. Thus, from the view of the firm designing the fund, there is an incentive to add negative criteria so as not to 'put off' individual investors who have certain values-based sensitivities – subject to extra informational demands and a more constrained investment universe from which to choose when delivering financial characteristics. There is also a mimetic competitive pressure in operation, since it makes sense to copy the negative criteria, or at least match the avoidance issues, of competitor firms so as not to rule out a subsection of SR investors. Perhaps this accounts for Berry and Junkus's (2013) observation that negative screening is far more prevalent amongst SRI funds than might be justified, on the face of it, from the attitudes of their survey respondents.

So far, it has been assumed not only that firms offering SRI funds are trying to match fund characteristics to investor preferences, but also that those investors are making a measured assessment of which fund to invest in based on their own particular values. However, there is evidence to suggest that individual SR investors might not approach SRI with a great deal of sophistication or attention to detail. Mackenzie and Lewis (1999) characterised the process as the expression of 'anxieties' about various issues and 'feelings' that companies engaged in these activities were behaving unethically. So it seems likely that some investors are not as clear as they might be about their moral attitudes or, at least, how they might or should attach these to the particularities of investment decisions; they are probably just content to be invested in a fund that is described as 'ethical' or 'socially responsible' and mentions some of the issues that concern them. This is a further reason (in addition to the bundling of negative criteria) for the policies of SRI funds being but a weak guide to the SEE attitudes of investors. Nevertheless, such investors in SRI funds are, in some sense, connecting their moral values to investment and therefore going beyond the parsimonious depiction of investors in theory and conventional wisdom.

Of course, most investors probably invest solely with financial goals in mind. This is not to imply that their behaviour is 'greedy' or 'selfish' and undertaken totally without consideration of others, though; Lewis (2001), for example, found that many people, SR investors and otherwise, were keen not to be a burden to others when they grew older, or they wished to leave a legacy to their loved ones. Nevertheless, it is possible that some non-SRI investors feel 'faintly embarrassed' by the notion that they are invested primarily for their own income and capital growth. Moreover, there are probably many mainstream investors who do not intentionally fail to make a connection between their ethical commitments and their investment behaviour. There might be various reasons for this attitude–behaviour gap.

One reason might be that, ignorant of the option of SRI and cognisant of the typical depictions of investment activity and goals, they are unaware of the putative connection – though the longer that SRI funds are established and the greater the profile they have, the more this explanation is likely to diminish. Nevertheless, perhaps reflecting its more recent development in Poland than some other countries, more than 40 per cent of Czerwonka's (2014) respondents stated that they had not heard of SRI. Lack of awareness, though, can take another form. Many individuals probably do not realise that they are indirectly invested, perhaps through a conventional pension fund, in companies of which they would disapprove if they were aware of it. Inertia might be another explanation, even when aware. Lewis (2001) found that even some of the SR investors had 'mixed' investments, with the non-SRI components often explained as historical accidents, such as inheritances that they had 'yet to disinfect'.

On the other hand, some individuals might be reluctant to invest in an SRI fund because they are unconvinced by their ethical status (Lewis, 2001; see Anderson, 1996) or do not trust the (profit-seeking) company to invest according to the published SR policies – though some sort of committee of reference to provide expert oversight is common (Cowton, 1999b; Cowton, 2004), especially in the case of 'deliberative' funds (Mackenzie, 1998). Alternatively, an investor might judge the criteria an insufficient match to their own preferences – though, as noted earlier, if their focus is exclusively or principally upon avoidance or if their preferences are rather vague, there should be a suitable SRI fund available. However, in such circumstances an SRI fund will almost certainly be a better match than a mainstream fund; and a particularly scrupulous or unusual investor might also consider investing directly, of course.

There might thus be several different reasons for individuals not engaging in SRI. Nevertheless, SRI has now become an established part of most, if not all, developed stock markets. However, interesting though the phenomenon might be, an obvious question that arises is: does it make a difference? Various parties might be affected, including the SR investors themselves, the wider stock market and the companies in which they invest. The next two sections consider some possibilities.

9.4 A Question of Sacrifice

As explained earlier, SRI appears, on the face of it, significantly different from conventional investing, which is depicted parsimoniously purely in terms of financial return and risk. The previous sections have shown *how* it is different as it brings into play moral (SEE) considerations. However, it is still principally a form of *investment*, so it is natural to question the possible impact that the presence of additional considerations has upon financial performance. Is a financial sacrifice involved when investors engage in SRI, and how do they view such a prospect?

In addition to the informational challenge mentioned in the previous section, it used to be asserted that SRI would entail too much financial sacrifice to be practicable. Of course, such a sacrifice would not actually prevent SRI being implemented, but the greater the sacrifice involved, the less would be its attractiveness. How much would SR investors be prepared to sacrifice profit for principle? What would be the nature and extent of the trade-offs that people would accept – their moral elasticity, so to speak? Thus SRI raises highly pertinent issues for economic psychology: are people willing to incur an opportunity loss on their investments for reasons of conscience (Lewis, 2002)?

It is investors' perception of performance, rather than the financial performance itself, that influences behaviour. In a study of two leading UK SRI funds, Lewis and Mackenzie (2000a) found that, while some perceived no difference, more than 40 per cent believed that their investments gave a lower rate of return and nearly 20 per cent considered them riskier. It is common to hold nonethical investments too, for fear of having all the eggs in one basket (Lewis, 2001); inertia, mentioned earlier, might not be the only reason for 'mixed' investments.

There is some evidence to suggest that the underlying investors in SRI retail funds are willing to accept lower financial returns as a price worth paying in order to invest in line with their conscience (see Lewis and Mackenzie, 2000a, 2000b). This 'price inelasticity' for losses has also been demonstrated in a simulated investment experiment with a 'virtual' independent financial advisor (Webley, Lewis and Mackenzie, 2001). While there is a certain pragmatism in holding a morally mixed portfolio in the first place (and investors with 100 per cent of their investments in SRI are rare), investors are loyal to the SRIs they have. It is also the case that SR investors appear to be less sensitive to past negative returns, particularly if they invest in SRI funds with negative screens, than are investors in conventional funds (Renneboog, Ter Horst and Zhang, 2011).

This begs the question of whether SRI actually does involve financial sacrifice. Proponents of SRI, sometimes in popular media, have been keen to highlight examples where investing using SEE criteria appears to lead to superior financial return – perhaps on occasions where the wider consuming public and stock market have subsequently come into line with the 'pioneering' attitudes of SR investors. Likewise, opponents have cited examples where SRI apparently leads to inferior returns or they have enthusiastically noted where investing in a portfolio focussed on one or more SEE avoidance criteria (e.g., tobacco) would have made an unusually good return over a particular time frame. The nature of the stock market means that both are possible. However, such evidence is basically anecdotal; a more systematic approach is needed.

Certainly it would be expected in theory – modern portfolio theory (MPT), that is – that the adoption of SRI criteria which restrict the investment universe would lead to lower risk-adjusted financial returns (Westerfield, 1984), to which might be added the additional cost of screening (Boatright, 1999). More generally, the addition of any objectives or constraints is bound to lead to the dilution of financial goals. Put another way, anything an SR investor can do, a financially focussed conventional investor can do too; but there are some things the SR investor is constrained or diverted from doing in the pursuit of financial goals. However, without making certain assumptions about investor SEE preferences and the associated investment criteria, it is not possible to determine empirically how large any expected sacrifice might be.

A great deal of empirical research has been conducted on financial performance, either simulating SRI portfolios or studying actual SRI funds. It has even been argued that there has been too much research of this sort (Capelle-Blancard and Monjon, 2012), while other issues in SRI have been relatively neglected – which perhaps reflects data availability and the methodological preferences of researchers. Nevertheless, carrying out the empirical research is not a methodologically straightforward matter; there are many variables and necessary assumptions when conducting such studies. However, having found in their holdings-based study of US data that SRI funds generate similar returns to conventional funds, Humphrey, Warren and Boon (2016) concluded that this was in line with previous returns-based studies. Similarly, consideration of the evidence led Louche and Lydenberg (2010: p. 399) to conclude that 'in general, social and environmental screening as recently practiced does not hurt a fund's financial performance'. Even if there is, at least sometimes, an impact on performance, it tends to be much less than was apparently supposed by early SRI sceptics.

Of course, any performance effect will tend to depend on how extensive and stringent the SEE criteria are, as discussed earlier. However, in practice – at least in large stock markets – fund managers are able construct SRI portfolios with the desired investment style attributes (Humphrey et al., 2016), particularly if they use sophisticated active risk-minimisation techniques (see Sparkes and Cowton, 2004). After all, SRI fund managers are still acutely aware of the need to 'perform' financially. SR investors are interested in both SEE considerations *and* financial features when they are investing in listed shares or share-based financial products – as opposed to 'alternative' investments, such as a social enterprise, where more philanthropic motives might have a more prominent role to play. Some may be more willing than others to sacrifice financial return, but other things being equal, all will want to make a good return; and SRI fund managers know that they are competing with other SRI funds not only on the basis of SEE characteristics but also in terms of financial performance (see Cowton, 2004).

In conclusion, while SR investors might be prepared to accept a financial sacrifice for reasons of conscience, the research tends to suggest that the loss of return or increase in risk are comparatively small, if present at all, thus opening SRI up to a much larger clientele.

9.5 Making a Difference?

The ability to construct portfolios that are perceived to have acceptable financial characteristics and to address SEE concerns adequately means that SRI has now become firmly established. Direct investment by individuals and bodies such as charities, together with indirect investment via SRI funds, might seem to offer the potential to make financial markets and even business itself 'more moral'. If so, this would enhance the ethical status of SRI, since one critique is that simply salving one's conscience (Mackenzie and Lewis, 1999) is insufficient (see Cowton and Sandberg (2012) for a review of the key arguments); making a difference, or the consequences of action, matter. While some SR investors might be seeking simply to avoid investing in companies engaged in activities that contradict their own moral values (e.g., gambling), they might also be more generally motivated to avoid other companies that they consider to do significant harm, for example in the form of environmental pollution or climate change. Moreover, some SR investors hope that the funds in which they invest actively lobby companies to improve behaviour.

However, Rivoli (2003) notes that the perfect market assumptions that underlie most finance theory would imply that SRI will not affect social outcomes. Basically, other money flows will replace any investment diverted for noneconomic reasons. Nevertheless, she notes that there is evidence of imperfections in equity markets, which means that the claim that SRI 'makes a difference' is potentially a reasonable one. However, Boatright (1999), citing the efficient markets hypothesis, argues that, even if the stock market is not perfectly efficient, share prices will tend to reflect future business profitability alone – including any gains from acting responsibly (the so-called business case), as some companies set out to do. Given that normal SRI funds and similar private investment are still probably of 'minor economic importance' (Sparkes and Cowton, 2004, p. 45), it is hard to imagine the share prices of large corporations being affected in such a way as to provide a signal that they should change their behaviour – unless that message is reinforced by, for example, a consumer boycott, as in the case of apartheid. Shareholder action (rather than avoidance of the company) might have some influence, but it is unlikely that SRI, on its own, is a significant influence on large companies.

Perhaps more significant is the indirect influence that SRI is claimed to be having. Its movement from margin to mainstream as it has, to some extent, been incorporated into conventional investment practice might be seen as its 'maturing' (Sparkes and Cowton, 2004). McCann, Solomon and Solomon (2003: p. 19) claim SRI in its current form involves a mainstream investment strategy that is being adopted increasingly by the majority of pension funds and large institutional investors. Through initiatives such as the Principles for Responsible Investment and the Stewardship Code, such investors have been encouraged to take a longer-term view, seeking long-term value by taking into account environmental, social and governance (ESG) factors and engaging more actively with companies. Advocates hope that this will not only reduce the pressure on company management to seek short-term profitability (e.g., quarterly earnings) at the expense of longer-term success, which benefits the wider economy, but also influence them to address CSR issues (Sparkes and Cowton, 2004).

While a focus on 'long-term value creation' (Louche and Lydenberg, 2010, p. 393) and some of the practices that are coming to the fore are consistent with SRI, this trend can also be seen as part of an evolution in corporate governance since the publication of the Cadbury Report in 1992 – not least if fund managers focus on the governance component of ESG. After all, good governance might be considered as important as good management. This is one reason why Hendry (2013, pp. 229, 231) is probably correct to caution against drawing too strong a conclusion regarding the mainstream advance and hence influence of SRI:

> Responsible investment now accounts for about 10 percent of funds invested in the USA and 20 percent in Europe, but the more mainstream it has become, the more the ethical and financial elements have been conflated. Terms like 'responsible investing' and 'sustainable investing' are increasingly used to describe financial strategies that are responsible and sustainable in the sense that they are relatively long term, but with no necessary connection to social responsibility or environmental sustainability.

Some of the percentages claimed for 'responsible investment' can be even higher, but Hendry's assessment is perhaps not surprising. As mentioned at the beginning of this chapter, the traditional view of investing is that it is financially oriented. A relatively early study of US pension fund and (conventional) mutual fund managers found that, while individual feelings may be very strong towards environmental control and corporate social responsibility (CSR), the fiduciary relationship and profit motives outweighed these concerns (Baker et al., 1974). Economic rhetoric, as much as evidence, has a large role to play in investment culture (O'Barr and Conley, 1992).

Further work has highlighted the barriers that might prevent fund managers from engaging in practices that are in line with niche SRI. Juravle and Lewis (2008, 2009) suggest that obstacles to the broadening of investment criteria fall into three categories: individual cognitive biases and belief systems; organisational structures, processes and cultures (including incentives based on short-term performance); and institutional impediments related to, inter alia, the structure of the investment value chain, regulatory and mimetic pressures on trustees and fund managers (including perceptions of 'fiduciary duties') and free-riding. Conventions are particularly powerful, not least because they are rarely, if at all, subject to conscious appraisal. Behaviour that threatens to contravene them requires special justification. In the case of SRI, this would tend to be in the form of a 'business case' that resonates with the dominant economic discourse.

This does not mean that there has been no 'progress'. Lewis and Juravle's (2010) interviews suggested that 'Champions in the City [of London]' have been a driving force behind what they term 'sustainable investment'. Human agency thus has a role to play. Driven by a range of religious and political beliefs and values to work against the conservatism of senior players within existing organisational constraints, the champions had helped launch new funds, influenced the investment process or changed organisational structures (including recruiting specialists) with the help of sympathetic financial insiders. The 'softening' of widespread cynical attitudes, aided by an improved ability to put forward a 'business case' in the light of evidence on financial performance and changes in the environment (e.g., the Principles for Responsible Investment and the Stewardship Code), no doubt helps. However, given that moral reasons do not have leverage, SRI-like responsible or sustainable investment still tends to be a 'side show to the main event' (Lewis and Juravle, 2010: p. 492). There are still significant risks for an individual fund manager or some other professional in the investment supply chain to support SRI without a specific mandate to do so. Even a small performance penalty matters to a fund manager.

Nevertheless, to the extent that novel or unconventional practices – which may in turn influence quoted companies – have taken root amongst institutional investors, perhaps because they are thought to be associated with longer-term financial performance, it seems reasonable to suggest that niche SRI has had a role to play. It has allowed the financial performance question to be addressed, showing what is possible, and permitted the development of infrastructure and expertise. For example, Juravle and Lewis (2009) quote an interviewee who noted that EIRIS already provided a 'fairly low-cost service', meaning that it was unnecessary to buy a team or hire a specialist when making certain alterations to mainstream investment practice. How much progress will continue to be made by niche SRI and, in the mainstream, by practices associated with SRI remains to be seen. However, the active engagement of large institutional investors on at least some of the issues considered important by SRI investors both represents a shift in mainstream investing and offers the possibility of influence on quoted companies to pay greater attention to CSR issues, principally over how they do business rather than what they do.

9.6 Conclusion

Socially responsible investment (SRI) has emerged over the past three decades or so to become a viable and visible element of investment practice. In this development, not only private investors but also specialist information providers, marketers and fund managers have had a part to play. SRI demonstrates that some investors, at least, are putting their money where their morals are (Lewis, 2002). The combination of social, environmental and ethical (SEE) considerations with conventional financial factors in investment decisions, which are more typically depicted in stark economic terms, makes it an interesting phenomenon.

A wide range of different positive and negative SEE considerations can be brought to bear on the investment decision in various ways, leading to varying degrees of possible tension with financial performance – which some investors will be more willing to countenance sacrificing than will others. Given some early commentators' scepticism regarding both the provision of relevant information and the impact on financial performance, it is something of an achievement that innovations have been sufficiently successful for SRI to become established as a significant set of niche investment practices that depart from the 'rational economic' norm.

Whether SRI thinking and practice are having a wider impact beyond the niche satisfaction of the preferences of a segment of investors, perhaps making markets more generally 'moral' in some sense, depends on the degree to which they penetrate mainstream investment practice. Although there are significant barriers in terms of conventions and perceptions, particularly regarding financial performance, amongst the fund management community and other parts of the investment chain, there are signs of possible influence, particularly where aligned with other attempts to reform institutional investment practice. At the very least, the establishment of SRI means that its tools and techniques are available to be drawn upon when considered appropriate by 'mainstream' investment practitioners.

Note

1   For discussion of a further example, military contracting, see Cowton (1993, 1999a).

9.7 References

Anand, P. and Cowton, C. J. (1993). The Ethical Investor: Exploring Dimensions of Investment Behaviour. *Journal of Economic Psychology*, 14, 377–385.

Anderson, D. (1996). *What Has 'Ethical Investment' to Do with Ethics?* London: Social Affairs Unit.

Baker, J. C., Domm, D. R., Roth, H. J. and Ryans, J. K., Jr. (1974). Institutional Investor Attitudes Toward Corporate Social Responsibility. *Arkansas Business and Economic Review*, 7, 14–20.

Berry, T. C. and Junkus, J. C. (2013). Socially Responsible Investing: An Investor Perspective. *Journal of Business Ethics*, 112, 707–720.

Boatright, J. (1999). *Ethics in Finance*. Malden, MA: Blackwell.

Bruyn, S. T. (1987). *The Field of Social Investment*. Cambridge: Cambridge University Press.

Capelle-Blancard, G. and Monjon, S. (2012). Trends in the Literature on Socially Responsible Investment: Looking for the Keys Under the Lamppost. *Business Ethics: A European Review*, 21, 239–250.

Cooper, M. and Schlegelmilch, B. B. (1993). Key Issues in Ethical Investment. *Business Ethics: A European Review*, 2, 213–227.

Cowton, C. J. (1992). The Ethics of Advertising: Do Investors Care? *International Journal of Advertising*, 11, 157–164.

Cowton, C. J. (1993). Peace Dividends: The Exclusion of Military Contractors from Investment Portfolios. *Journal of Peace Research*, 30, 21–28.

Cowton, C. J. (1994). The Development of Ethical Investment Products. In Prindl, A. R. and Prodhan, B. (Eds.), *Ethical Conflicts in Finance*: 213–232. Oxford: Blackwell.

Cowton, C. J. (1999a). Accounting and Financial Ethics: From Margin to Mainstream? *Business Ethics: A European Review*, 8, 99–107.

Cowton, C. J. (1999b). Playing by the Rules: Ethical Criteria at an Ethical Investment Fund. *Business Ethics: A European Review*, 8, 60–69.

Cowton, C. J. (2004). Managing Financial Performance at an Ethical Investment Fund. *Accounting, Auditing and Accountability Journal*, 17, 249–275.

Cowton, C. J. and Sandberg, J. (2012). Socially Responsible Investment. In Chadwick, R. (Ed.), *Encyclopedia of Applied Ethics*, 2nd Edition: 142–151. San Diego, CA: Academic Press.

Cullis, J. G., Lewis, A. and Winnett, A. (1992). Paying to Be Good? U.K. Ethical Investments. *Kyklos*, 45, 3–24.

Czerwonka, M. (2014). The Influence of Religion on Socially Responsible Investing. *Journal of Religion and Business Ethics*, 3, Article 21.

Draper, P. (1990). The Marketing of Unit and Investment Trust. In Ennew, C., Watkins, T. and Wright, M. (Eds.), *Marketing Financial Services*: 217–235. London: Heinemann.

Eilon, S. (1971). Goals and Constraints. *Journal of Management Studies*, 8, 292–303.

Frankel, T. (1984). Decision Making for Social Investing. In McGill, D. M. (Ed.), *Social Investing*: 131–162. Homewood, IL: Richard D. Irwin.

Ghoul, W. and Karam, P. (2007). MRI and SRI Mutual Funds: A Comparison of Christian, Islamic (Morally Responsible Investing), and Socially Responsible Investing (SRI) Mutual Funds. *Journal of Investing*, 16, 96–102.

Hendry, J. (2013). *Ethics and Finance: An Introduction*. Cambridge: Cambridge University Press.

Humphrey, J. E., Warren, G. J. and Boon, J. (2016). What Is Different About Socially Responsible Funds? A Holdings-Based Analysis. *Journal of Business Ethics*, 138, 263–277.

Juravle, C. and Lewis, A. (2008). Identifying Impediments to SRI in Europe: A Review of the Practitioner and Academic Literature. *Business Ethics: A European Review*, 17, 285–310.

Juravle, C. and Lewis, A. (2009). The Role of Championship in the Mainstreaming of Sustainable Investment (SI): What Can We Learn from SI Pioneers in the United Kingdom? *Organization & Environment*, 22, 75–98.

Kreander, N., McPhail, K. and Molyneaux, D. (2004). God's Fund Managers: A Critical Study of Stock Market Investment Practices of the Church of England and UK Methodists. *Accounting, Auditing & Accountability Journal*, 17, 408–441.

Lewis, A. (2001). A Focus Group Study of the Motivation to Invest: 'Ethical/Green' and 'Ordinary' Investors Compared. *Journal of Socio-Economics*, 30, 331–341.

Lewis, A. (2002). *Morals, Markets and Money: Ethical, Green and Socially Responsible Investing*. London: Pearson.

Lewis, A. and Cullis, J. (1990). Ethical Investments: Preferences and Morality. *Journal of Behavioral Economics*, 19, 395–411.

Lewis, A. and Juravle, C. (2010). Morals, Markets and Sustainable Investments: A Qualitative Study of 'Champions'. *Journal of Business Ethics*, 93, 483–494.

Lewis, A. and Mackenzie, C. (2000a). Morals, Money, Ethical Investing and Economic Psychology. *Human Relations*, 53, 179–191.

Lewis, A. and Mackenzie, C. (2000b). Green and Ethical Investment: Can It Make a Difference? In Warhurst, A. (Ed.), *Towards a Collaborative Environment Research Agenda*: 75–88. New York, NY: Macmillan.

Logsdon, J. M. and Van Buren, H.J. (2009). Beyond the Proxy Vote: Dialogues Between Shareholder Activists and Corporations. *Journal of Business Ethics*, 87, 353–365.

Louche, C. and Lydenberg, S. (2010). Responsible Investing. In Boatright, J. (Ed.), *Finance Ethics: Critical Issues in Theory and Practice*: 393–417. Hoboken, NJ: Blackwell.

Louche, C. and Lydenberg, S. (2011). *Dilemmas in Responsible Investment*. Sheffield: Greenleaf.

Mackenzie, C. (1998). The Choice of Ethical Criteria in Ethical Investment. *Business Ethics: A European Review*, 7, 81–86.

Mackenzie, C. and Lewis, A. (1999). Morals and Markets: The Case of Ethical Investing. *Business Ethics Quarterly*, 9, 439–452.

McCann, L., Solomon, A. and Solomon, J. (2003). Explaining the Recent Growth in UK Socially Responsible Investment. *Journal of General Management*, 28, 32–53.

McGill, D. M. (1984). Preface. In McGill, D. M. (Ed.), *Social Investing*: ix–xiii. Homewood, IL: Richard D. Irwin.

Markowitz, H. (1952). Portfolio Selection. *Journal of Finance*, 7, 77–91.

Miller, A. (1991). *Socially Responsible Investment: The Financial Impact of Screen Investment in the 1990s*. London: Financial Times Business Information.

Miller, A. (1992). Green Investment. In Owen, D. (Ed.), *Green Reporting: Accountancy and the Challenge of the Nineties*: 242–255. London: Chapman & Hall.

Moizer, P. and Arnold, J. (1984). Share Appraisal by Financial Analysts: Portfolio vs. Non-Portfolio Managers. *Accounting and Business Research*, 56, 341–348.

O'Barr, W. M. and Conley, J. M. (1992). Managing Relationships: The Culture of Institutional Investing. *Financial Analysts Journal*, September–October, 21–27.

Powers, C. W. (1971). *Social Responsibility and Investments*. Nashville, TN: Abingdon.

Renneboog, L., Ter Horst, J. and Zhang, C. (2011). Is Ethical Money Financially Smart? Nonfinancial Attributes and Money Flows of Socially Responsible Investment Funds. *Journal of Financial Intermediation*, 20, 562–588.

Rivoli, P. (2003). Making a Difference or Making a Statement? Finance Research and Socially Responsible Investment. *Business Ethics Quarterly*, 13, 271–287.

Rockness, J. and Williams, P. F. (1988). A Descriptive Study of Social Responsibility Mutual Funds. *Accounting, Organizations and Society*, 13, 397–411.

Schepers, D. H. and Sethi, S. P. (2003). Do Socially Responsible Funds Actually Deliver What They Promise? *Business and Society Review*, 108, 11–32.

Schotland, R. A. (1980). Divergent Investing for Pension Funds. *Financial Analysts Journal*, September–October, 29–39.

Schueth, S. (2003). Socially Responsible Investing in the United States. *Journal of Business Ethics*, 43, 189–194.

Simpson, A. (1991). *The Greening of Global Investment: How the Environment, Ethics and Politics Are Reshaping Strategies*. London: Economist Publications.

Sparkes, R. (2002). *Socially Responsible Investment: A Global Revolution*. Chichester: Wiley.

Sparkes, R. and Cowton, C. J. (2004). The Maturing of Socially Responsible Investment: A Review of the Developing Link with Corporate Social Responsibility. *Journal of Business Ethics*, 52, 45–57.

Sullivan, R. and Mackenzie, C. (2006). Shareholder Activism on Social, Ethical and Environmental Issues: An Introduction. In Sullivan, R. and Mackenzie, C. (Eds.), *Responsible Investment*: 150–157. Sheffield: Greenleaf.

Tocher, K. D. (1970). Control. *Operational Research Quarterly*, 21, 159–180.

US SIF (2016). *2016 Report on US Sustainable, Responsible and Impact Investing Trends*, 11th Edition. Washington, DC: US SIF Foundation.

Webley, P., Lewis, A. and Mackenzie, C. (2001). Commitment Among Ethical Investors: An Experimental Approach. *Journal of Economic Psychology*, 22, 27–42.

Westerfield, R. (1984). Capital Market Theory Perspectives. In McGill, D. M. (Ed.), *Social Investing*: 107–129. Homewood, IL: Richard D. Irwin.

PART III

Private Sector Consumer Behaviour and the Firm

10 Consumption, Income, and Happiness

Aaron Ahuvia

10.1 Introduction: What Is Happiness?

The relationship among wealth, consumption, and happiness is an ancient question, addressed in the early writings of major religions and philosophers. Many religious and philosophical thinkers have argued that money and the things it can buy do not generate happiness, whereas general public has seen things quite differently. Recent empirical work has allowed us to bring data to bear on this question, with fascinating results.

Most of this research on happiness (i.e., subjective well-being) is based on surveys that ask people about how "happy" they are as well as of things such as their income, what they buy, and what their most important life goals are. The term "happiness" is very broad, and in these studies can refer to several different things: life satisfaction, emotions, mental health/development, and life meaning.

- Many surveys assess a person's overall *life satisfaction* (Diener, Inglehart, and Tay, 2012) by asking questions such as "looking at your life as a whole these days, how satisfied with your life would you say you are?" Studies also sometimes assess satisfaction with various domains of life, such as people's satisfaction with their finances, health, and family life. Life satisfaction is cognitive, that is to say it is a judgment, a conscious *thought*, about how well one is doing.
- Other measures focus on emotions, that is, how people feel, rather than what they think about their lives. In one common measure, the Gallup World Poll asks people about whether they had various positive feelings (e.g., enjoyment and smiling or laughing) and negative feelings (e.g., worry, sadness, depression, and anger) the day before (Kahneman and Deaton, 2010).
- Some studies ask about *mental health* and/or *psychological development*. These studies may ask people about the level of stress they feel or they may look for symptoms of neurosis. These studies sometimes assess people's "self-actualization" on the premise that persons are mentally healthier and more mature the closer they are to being self-actualized. Although most of these measures are survey questions, researchers sometimes also use physiological measures such as testing for stress hormones in the blood (Ryff, 1989).

- Finally, some studies ask about *meaning in life* (Ryff and Keyes, 1995), asking people about the extent to which they feel their life has meaning and purpose.

The distinction between these types of measures turns out to be important. Not surprisingly, all of these things are positively correlated with each other; for example, people who report frequently feeling sad also tend to have low levels of life satisfaction, have high levels of stress, and see their lives as lacking meaning. But these measures are not always synchronized, so, for example, it is possible for a person to experience a lot of sadness and despite this still report a high level of life satisfaction, or vice versa. This is important because, as we shall see, some of the things that cause people to have high levels of life satisfaction are quite different from the things that lead them to experience positive emotions. So the question of "what makes people happy" may have a somewhat different answer depending on which of these four aspects of happiness one is talking about.

Of these four types of questions, the first two – measures of life satisfaction and feeling positive and/or negative emotions – are by far the most common. For brevity, when I use the terms "happiness" or "subjective well-being" (SWB) without further qualifications, I am referring to these common measures of life satisfaction and affect. When I am referring to mental health or life meaning measures, I will say so explicitly.

This research assumes that people can assess their own happiness with reasonable accuracy, and there is a great deal of evidence to show that this is a reasonable assumption, especially when the researcher is averaging together the answers from a large sample (Diener et al., 2012; Helliwell, Layard, and Sachs, 2012; Van Praag and Ferrer-i-Carbonell, 2010; Watson, Clark, and Tellegen, 1988). In this sense, it is no different from the overwhelming majority of psychological research, which relies on self-report measures, as well as research in economics that looks at things such as consumer sentiment or customer satisfaction. Moreover, research from neuroscience offers support for the claim that these self-reported measures of happiness are associated with the activation of reward centers in the brain (Sutton and Davidson, 1997).

While people are pretty accurate at telling whether they feel happy right now, I will discuss several examples in this chapter where people are pretty lousy at predicting which options will make them happiest in the future, or explaining why they feel the way they do. This research is particularly useful when it can answer these questions where our intuitions often lead us astray.

10.2 Time: Future => Present => Past

In this section, I review how the ways we think about our choices as consumers relate to our happiness. (For other similar reviews, see Dunn, Gilbert, and Wilson, 2011; Tatzel, 2014a, 2014b.)

It is common to hear the phrase "past, present, and future." But with regard to the consumption cycle, it works the other way around: first we anticipate a *future* purchase, then we use the product in the *present*, and then we look back on our *past* experience with the product (Koehler and Harvey, 2014; Quoidbach, Mikolajczak, and Gross, 2015b; Zauberman, Ratner, and Kim, 2009). Dunn and Weidman (2015) call these three stages *anticipatory value* (of future product use), *momentary value* (while consuming the product), and *afterglow value* (from memories of past experiences). This framework highlights the fact that it is not just the actual use of products (i.e., momentary value) that matters for happiness. As Quoidbach et al. (2015b, p. 5) point out, people "play the lottery just because buying a ticket allows them to dream about what they would do … (and people) buy souvenir pictures to help them remember how fun a roller-coaster ride was."

When a topic relates primarily (although not necessarily exclusively) to one of these stages, I have organized it by stage, as discussed in the following subsections.

10.2.1 Anticipation of Future Product Use

From a sociological perspective, Campbell (1987) wrote about the way modern consumer culture was built on and is driven by the pleasure people get from fantasizing about how great it will be when they finally buy this or that, rather than simply the utility they will get from actually using the product. Later research has shown that, indeed, the pleasure people get from anticipating future purchases can be a major source of enjoyment that people get from the marketplace (Dunn and Norton, 2013; Richins, 2013). For example, a study of people going on vacation found that their anticipated enjoyment of the vacation and their recalled enjoyment after the vacation were both higher than their actual enjoyment on the vacation (Mitchell et al., 1997). In a related study, Nawijn et al. (2010) found that this pretrip anticipation boosted the overall happiness of people about to go on a vacation. But the happiness of the vacation did not carry over into people's lives immediately after their return (with the exception of people who had an extremely relaxing vacation).

Why was there more of an emotional impact to thinking about the vacation one is about to take than there is to thinking about the vacation one just took? Caruso, Gilbert, and Wilson (2008) found that, in general, *people respond with greater emotional intensity to future events than to past events*. In a series of studies, Caruso et al. (2008) showed that mock jurors awarded less money to an accident victim who had already suffered for a year than they did to an accident victim who was going to suffer for the next year, and people also bought a less expensive "thank you" gift for someone who had already done them a favor than they did for someone who was about to do them a favor.

The pleasure of positive anticipation is powerful – powerful enough in fact that people who make a point of practicing positive anticipation tend to be happier than those who do not (Bryant, 2003). And in some cases, people do seem to know that anticipation is a good thing and act accordingly. For example, in one study students where asked how much they would be willing to pay for a kiss from the movie star of their choice, and the students indicated they would pay more for a kiss three days later than for a kiss three hours later (Loewenstein, 1987). Yet more often, people succumb to the call of present gratification and do not take full advantage of the possibilities that anticipation provides. This is because, "while the future may be more emotionally compelling than the past, nothing is as powerful as the present" (Dunn et al., 2011, p. 120). Often, people fall prey to what is called future anhedonia: "the belief that hedonic states will be less intense in the future than in the present" (Kassam et al., 2008, p. 1533). For example, when people estimate how much they will enjoy getting a gift on the day they receive it, they expect more pleasure if that day is today than if it is three months in the future.

The most straightforward way to boost anticipatory pleasure is to delay purchase, but it is not the only way to achieve that. Delaying purchase allows you to anticipate the pleasure over a longer period of time, but uncertainty (not to be confused with anxiety) leads you to have more frequent positive thoughts about the future happy event, and thus increases its impact on your mood. For example, Kurtz, Wilson, and Gilbert (2007) told some research participants that they had won one prize (certain condition); told other participants that they had won two prizes (two-gift condition); and told a third group that they had won one of two prizes, but not which of the two prizes it was (uncertain condition). Not only did people in the uncertain condition spend more time in a positive mood than did people in the certain condition, the people in the uncertain condition were even happier than people in the two-gift condition who were getting both of the possible gifts.

10.2.1.1 *Impulse Buying*

Impulse buying is the enemy of savoring the anticipation of future purchases. And it is quite widespread, as Nicholls and Li (2001) found that nearly half of all shoppers in a US mall made at least one impulse purchase while there. And Kacen and Lee (2002) report that worldwide, increasing numbers of people identify as impulse buyers. Studies have also found impulse buying to be somewhat more common in women than in men, and that like many other impulsive behaviors, it tends to decrease with age (Silvera, Lavack, and Kropp, 2008).

Impulse purchasing is not inherently bad; in some cases, it might simply reflect a shopper's healthy spontaneity and flexibility. But a chronic tendency for impulse buying is associated with numerous problems. For example, feelings of regret are so central to the impulse buying experience that they became part of the most widely used impulse buying measure (Verplanken and Herabadi, 2001). Trocchia and Janda (2002) also found buying impulsively predicted later unmet expectations and social embarrassment when using the product.

Some outcomes of impulse buying are specific to the cognitive or affective aspects of this phenomenon. The cognitive aspects of impulse buying include a lack of planning and deliberation before purchase, whereas the affective aspects include feeling excited, compelled to buy, and even out of control regarding impulse purchases (Verplanken and Herabadi, 2001). The cognitive aspects of impulse buying are associated with lower levels of life satisfaction, whereas the affective elements are positively related to negative affect and negatively related to self-esteem (Silvera et al., 2008).

10.2.2 Momentary Value from Current Product Use

One might think that the benefits we get from products while we are actually using them (as opposed to anticipating our future use or remembering our past use) would be the most widely studied aspect of the relationship between happiness and consumer behavior ... but you would be wrong. The reason momentary value is rarely directly studied is that doing so is difficult. Either you create a situation in which study participants will be using a product, such as a taste test, or you use experience sampling. In experience sampling, participants are contacted at random times during the day and asked what they are doing, how they are feeling. Experience sampling has the advantage of getting data from people using products as they normally would. But experience-sampling studies are very difficult and expensive to run.

Rather than asking people about their product experience while they are using it, it is so much more feasible to simply ask participants to remember a time they used a product, for example, "Think back to the last time you drove your car; how much fun was it?" This type of research is quite common. Unfortunately, we know that people's memories for this type of information are inaccurate (Csikszentmihalyi and Hunter, 2003; Dunn and Weidman, 2015; Mitchell et al., 1997; Weidman and Dunn, 2015). That's not to say that this type of data is useless. It does help us understand afterglow value, the good or bad feelings people have *now* because of the (correct or incorrect) ways they remember past product experiences. But it isn't an accurate measure of the feelings people were having in the past when they were actually using the product.

Despite the practical difficulties involved, there have been some studies with accurate "online" measures of consumer experience while using products (e.g., Csikszentmihalyi and Hunter, 2003; Weidman and Dunn, 2015), as well as other related studies reviewed by Zuzanek and Zuzanek (2014). In terms of overall time use, some of the least enjoyable activities are those associated with the traditional homemaker role: cleaning, cooking, and childcare. Childcare is an interesting example of something that when people are asked about their past experiences they remember as a fairly enjoyable activity, but when they are actually providing childcare and are asked how they are feeling at that moment, they report low levels of enjoyment (Zuzanek and Zuzanek, 2014).

Paid work out of the home tends to be more enjoyable than household chores, but commuting to that work tends to be a very unpleasant experience (Gallup, n.d.; Stutzer and Frey, 2008; Zuzanek and Zuzanek, 2014).

Shopping is an activity of special relevance to any discussion of consumption and happiness. Compared to other daily activities, shopping is in the middle of the pack in terms of being an enjoyable experience, with grocery shopping being slightly less enjoyable than other types of shopping (Zuzanek and Zuzanek, 2014).

The most enjoyable activities are active sports, socializing, and sex (Csikszentmihalyi and Hunter, 2003; Zuzanek and Zuzanek, 2014), so products that enable those activities can produce significant happiness. Further supporting the centrality of interpersonal relationships to consumption (Ahuvia, 2015), an activity done alone produces significantly less happiness than that same activity done with friends (Csikszentmihalyi and Hunter, 2003).

One crucially important finding is that, contrary to what one might expect, spending more time in enjoyable entertainment activities does not necessarily make a person happier overall (Zuzanek and Zuzanek, 2014). Rather, as Aristotle taught, happiness lies in a balanced life with neither too little, nor too much, time spent simply on recreation (Aristotle, 1999). Watching TV provides a good example. Watching TV is enjoyable, often more so than people like to admit. TV is the opposite of childcare in this regard; that is, when one compares (a) how much people say they are enjoying themselves at that moment while they are watching TV to (b) how much people say they enjoy watching TV in general, their actual enjoyment (a) is significantly higher than their remembered enjoyment (b). Yet people who spend a lot of time watching TV tend to be less happy than people who spend only a moderate amount of time watching TV. It is very possible to get too much of a good thing.

10.2.3 Afterglow Value from Experiences Versus Objects

A significant and rapidly growing body of research shows that, in general, people derive more happiness from purchasing experiences such as entertainment, travel, and education than from purchasing similarly priced physical goods (Carter and Gilovich, 2013; Gilovich, Kumar, and Jampol, 2015; Van Boven and Gilovich, 2003). For example, Van Boven and Gilovich (2003) asked people to recall one experiential purchase and one material purchase that they had made with "the aim of increasing your happiness." When asked which purchase made them happier, people chose the experiential purchase by an almost two to one margin (57 per cent: 34 per cent).

I am addressing this topic under the heading of afterglow value, because the overwhelming majority of this research has looked at how consumers remember past purchases (Dunn and Weidman, 2015). That said, Kumar, Killingsworth, and Gilovich (2014) found that purchasing experiences produced more anticipatory pleasure than did purchasing objects. Looking at momentary value received while using the product, some studies find that experiential purchases have the advantage here as well (Carter and Gilovich, 2010; Nicolao, Irwin, and Goodman, 2009), but Weidman and Dunn (2015) tell a slightly more complex story in which purchasing experiences produce the most intense happiness during use but purchase of objects provides more frequent momentary happiness over time.

Common sense, and the findings from Weidman and Dunn (2015), might reasonably (yet incorrectly) lead one to think that spending money on an experience, such as going to a concert, would provide only short-term happiness, whereas putting that money toward an object, such as a sophisticated audio system, would provide more afterglow happiness, since the object would still be around to provide recent positive experiences and to remind you of all the pleasant experience it has provided over time. Yet the data show just the reverse. In one study, people were asked to remember significant past purchases of either objects or experiences, and rate how much enjoyment they received both just after purchase and how much enjoyment the purchase still brings them today. "There was no difference in participants' ratings of their initial enjoyment, but participants indicated that they got much more current enjoyment from their experiences" (Carter and Gilovich, 2013, p. 52).

Beyond the staying power in memory of experiential purchases, Carter and Gilovich (Carter and Gilovich, 2013; Gilovich et al., 2015) argue that there are three main reasons why experiential purchases tend to bring more happiness than do purchases of objects. First, making competitive comparisons between ourselves and other people usually leads to unhappiness. Material purchases lend themselves to these types of comparisons much more easily than do experiential purchases (Carter and Gilovich, 2010).

Second, people also use the things they buy to help define their identity (Ahuvia, 2013), and for most people, experiential purchases tend to do this more effectively than do purchases of objects (Carter and Gilovich, 2012). However, in a paper entitled *Damned If They Do, Damned If They Do Not*, Zhang et al. (2014) found that people who have a strong tendency to purchase goods over experiences do so, in part, because they do not find the purchase of experiences to be particularly self-expressive. These people still receive relatively little happiness for the purchase of objects, but this research concludes that their happiness would not increase if they switched to purchasing experiences, because they would not receive one of the major benefits (i.e., self-expression) that other people enjoy from experiential purchases.

And third, one of the core functions of consumption is creating, strengthening, and helping manage our social relationships (Ahuvia, 2015). Experiential purchases also have the edge over objects in this regard, as experiential purchases are better at bringing people together and creating a shared sense of group identity (Carter and Gilovich, 2013; Gilovich et al., 2015; Kumar and Gilovich, 2015). This is partly because, as Caprariello and Reis (2013) found, experiential purchases are often consumed with other people whereas purchased objects are often used solo. The positive effect of consuming products in a social setting had such a powerful effect on happiness that when the effects of social versus solitary consumption were controlled for, experiences no longer showed a happiness advantage over objects.

In addition to these three explanations, I would add that *a purchase really only brings happiness to the extent that it creates an experience*. If you buy a pair of skis but never use them, all they will bring you is regret. However, Guevarra and Howell (2015) found that when the purchase of an object facilitates a meaningful experience (i.e., you actually use the skis), these objects produce similar levels of happiness to the direct purchase of an experience. Unfortunately, we often we do not make as good use of the objects we buy as we had envisioned we would. When we buy experiences, in contrast, we almost always follow through. It is easy to buy skis and never get around to learning how to use them, but if you actually buy a ski vacation, it would take an extraordinary circumstance for you not to go.

10.2.4 Time-Inconsistent Preferences

In addition to the three types of value (anticipation value, momentary value, and afterglow value) discussed in the preceding, time is also important for the relationship between consumption and happiness because of what in the academic literature are often called "time-inconsistent preferences" or "hyperbolic discounting" and in the common English are simply called temptations. "When people select goods for immediate consumption, they are tempted by 'vices,' such as fattening food and lowbrow entertainment, which produce pleasure right away but lack long-term benefits – or even carry long-term costs – for well-being" (Dunn et al., 2011, p. 120).

This is a major problem with regard to savings and debt. In terms of happiness, one of the best things you can do with your money is save it. Having savings or other investment assets has "been found to be stronger predictors of life satisfaction than income alone" (Ruberton, Gladstone, and Lyubomirsky, 2016, p. 1). And this is not limited to large stock portfolios; simply having a little readily accessible cash on hand "is of unique importance to life satisfaction, above and beyond raw earnings, investments, or indebtedness" (Ruberton et al., 2016, p. 1). In contrast, being in debt (excepting mortgages) is psychologically very harmful, and each dollar of debt is more psychologically painful than a dollar of savings is psychologically beneficial (Brown, Taylor, and Wheatley Price, 2005). People with high levels of consumer debt live in what Bernthal, Crockett, and Rose (2005, p. 137) call a psychological "debtor's prison" of guilt, rationalization, and low self-esteem (Tatzel, 2014b). And this is an all too common experience, with almost half (48 percent) of US residents telling pollsters that they are worried about their debts (Chancellor and Lyubomirsky, 2013). Yet even though many people recognize that they ought to save more, they have a hard time resisting present temptations.

Research on willpower and temptation has provided useful insights on this phenomenon. For example, Shiv and Fedorikhin (1999) assigned half the participants in their study to remember a seven-digit number and the other half to remember a two-digit number. Subsequently, the participants were offered a choice between chocolate cake and fruit salad. Participants remembering a seven-digit number were much more likely to choose the chocolate cake. Why? Resisting the temptation of the cake required mental resources, and these resources had been previously depleted by their heavier cognitive load of remembering the seven-digit number. The choice of cake or fruit, then, is partly a function of what individuals think will be best for them in the long run, and partly a function of whether they have the mental strength to resist the short-term temptations.

Research has also suggested ways for helping people limit the negative effects of temptation. First, whether employees choose to set aside part of their paychecks for retirement savings, for example, is strongly influenced by the default options on their paperwork: if "save" is the default, people are much more likely to save than if the default is "do not save," even if all they need to do is check a box on their paperwork. A simple yet powerful nudge in this case is to set the default option to "save," and in fact this measure has proven highly effective in increasing retirement savings (Thaler and Sunstein, 2008).

Second, in many ways the brain's ability to exert willpower is similar to a muscle's ability to exert physical power (Muraven and Baumeister, 2000). They both can be strengthened by exercise. Specifically, regular small exertions of willpower will strengthen your ability to resist temptation (Baumeister, Vohs, and Tice, 2007).

Third, cultivating good habits is a classic virtue that has regained public attention of late (Duhigg, 2012). In this approach to the problems of temptation, rather than resisting temptation with willpower, the individual avoids the experience of temptation by cultivating good habits and preventing the creation of bad habits (Neal, Wood, and Drolet, 2013). In this way, habits allow people to sidestep the use of willpower because their decisions have been "premade" by the habit.

Finally, it is also possible to limit the problems of temptation by more literal forms of "premaking" a decision. "Delayed consumption is more likely to promote the selection of 'virtues,' which produce more lasting (if less immediate) well-being" (Dunn et al., 2011, p. 120). This can be seen when people choose what foods to eat. When people choose between fruit and candy for a food to eat immediately, they overwhelmingly choose the candy. But when given the same choice but told they will eat the food a week later, they usually choose the fruit (Read and van Leeuwen, 1998). This also applies in the case of savings. For example, employees may not agree to have a high percentage of their current wages put into savings, but are much more likely to agree to have a high percentage of all future wage increases automatically diverted into long-term savings (Thaler and Sunstein, 2008).

10.3 Happiness: The Me and the We

10.3.1 Giving

In a now classic experiment, Dunn, Aknin, and Norton (2008) had people imagine hypothetical scenarios in which they were given either $5 or $20 and asked to spend the money either on themselves or on someone else. The researchers then asked the study participants to predict in which scenarios the recipient of the money would be happiest. Perhaps not surprisingly, most people guessed that people receiving $20 would be happier than people who received only $5, and that the people who spent the money on themselves would be happier than people who gave it away. The researchers then actually did what they had described, giving away either $5 or $20 to random people, asking half of them to spend it on themselves and the other half to give it away, and then contacting those people later that day to ask them about their mood. It turns out that commonsense predictions of what would happen got it all wrong. People who received $20 were not happier than people who received $5 (both groups were equally happy), and the people who gave the money away were actually in a *happier* mood than the people who spent the money on themselves. Thus began a long series of studies showing that, in terms of happiness, one of the best things you can do with money is give it away (Aknin et al., 2013; Dunn, Aknin, and Norton, 2014; Ricard, 2015).

Dunn et al., (2014) argue that giving creates happiness because it helps people meet what self-determination theory considers to be their basic psychological needs. Self-determination theory (Grouzet et al., 2005; Kasser, 2002a; Niemiec, Ryan, and Deci, 2009; Ryan and Deci, 2000) holds that people have basic needs for *relatedness* (i.e., close social relationships), *competence* (i.e., feeling that you are good at what you do and can make a difference in the world), and *autonomy* (i.e., being able to freely make choices about your own life). Giving enhances relatedness in many ways such as giving a gift to someone you know (Ahuvia, 2015; Belk and Coon, 1993; Giesler, 2006) or when two people become closer by working side by side on a prosocial task. Giving helps meet the giver's need to feel competent and effective when the giver can see or imagine that the gift is making a difference in someone else's life. Lastly, giving helps meet the givers' need for autonomy when they feel the gift was freely given.

Research on self-determination theory holds that people will be happier, mentally healthier, and even physically healthier (e.g., lower stress levels) when they strive to meet these needs and find some success in doing so (Dittmar et al., 2014; Niemiec et al., 2009; Sheldon and Kasser, 1998). Self-determination theory calls motivations and goals associated with meeting these needs *intrinsic motivations*. In contrast, *extrinsic motivations* are goals such as getting rich and famous that distract from, or even work against, meeting one's intrinsic needs.

As I suggested in Ahuvia (2011), self-determination theory may be most easily understood through an analogy to "psychological nutrition." In this view, lasting happiness is not the result of any particular pleasant experience but rather an outcome of psychological health. The mind has certain "psychological nutrition" needs, and intrinsic goals are those goals that, when met, fulfill these psychological nutrition requirements and thus lead to psychological health. Extrinsic goals such as gaining social prestige through conspicuous consumption are the equivalent of mental desserts – attractive and momentarily pleasing, but lacking in psychological nutrition. Obtaining these mental desserts does not promote psychological health and hence does not create long-term happiness. In fairness to desserts, whether chocolate or metaphoric in nature, they can be fun and are dependably pleasurable. Desserts are not inherently bad, but if they play too large a role in one's life, that can cause real problems. In the case of meeting one's psychological needs, an excessive emphasis on extrinsic goals (psychological desserts) has been empirically associated with a host of maladies, including anxiety, depression, neurotic physical symptoms, unpleasant emotions, drug abuse, alcohol abuse, behavioral disorders, lower levels of self-actualization, less vitality, less life satisfaction, and fewer pleasant emotions (Ahuvia and Izberk-Bilgin, 2012).

10.3.2 Materialism

Materialism is not good for happiness. The two most widely used measures of materialism come from Richins (2004), who conceptualizes materialism as (a) placing possessions and money at the center of one's life, (b) believing that money brings happiness, and (c) judging one's own and others' success based on income and possessions; and from Kasser (2002b), who defines materialism as a tendency to prioritize extrinsic goals (e.g., money, fame, and physical attractiveness) rather than intrinsic goals (e.g., building strong positive social relationships, growing as a person, and contributing to one's community). In a meta-analysis of studies on materialism, Dittmar et al. (2014) found very consistent results in which higher levels of materialism (for those two measures and others) were associated with lower levels of well-being. The meta-analyses went beyond looking at happiness per se, and found that the relationship between materialism and negative outcomes was actually stronger for risky health behaviors (e.g., drugs), problematic consumer behaviors (e.g., excessive debt), and negative self-image than it was for unhappiness (i.e., low life satisfaction and negative affect). Looking at various measures of materialism, the measures that only looked at how much a person desires money had the weakest associations with negative outcomes, whereas the measures that saw materialism as including a focus on image and social status had the strongest association with negative outcomes. Nonetheless, even studies just looking at financial aspirations can produce strong results, as in the following example:

> An important study covers a group of students who were freshmen in 1976. Soon after entering college they were asked "the importance to you personally of being well off financially." Nineteen years later they reported their income

and their overall satisfaction with life, as well as with family life, friendships, and work. At a given level of income, people who cared more about their income were less happy with life overall, with their family life, with their friendships and with their job. Of course people who care more about money also tend to earn more, and this helps to offset the negative effect of materialism. But in this study a person considering high income essential would need twice as much income to be as happy as someone considering high income unimportant (Helliwell et al., 2012, p. 73).

Does the fact that materialism is associated with unhappiness mean that materialism causes unhappiness? Pieters (2013) looked specifically at the association between materialism and loneliness and found that it was a bidirectional cycle, where materialism led to loneliness, and loneliness also led to materialism. It is likely that a similar bidirectional cycle exists between materialism and unhappiness in general.

Why is materialism associated with unhappiness? If you consider the attitudes and behaviors that have been shown so far to lead to happiness, materialists tend to strike out. Saving money for the future is associated with happiness. Yet Watson (2003) found that the higher people were in materialism, the less likely they were to save, and the more likely they were to spend money and to express positive attitudes about borrowing money for luxury goods. Giving to others has also been shown to lead to happiness (Ricard, 2015), yet materialists also tend not to be generous (Belk, 1985; Kasser, 2002b; Richins and Dawson, 1992). Much of the pleasure in consumption comes from the pleasant anticipation of a purchase, and this tends to be particularly true of materialists in that their enjoyment of a product tends to go *down* once they actually purchase it (Richins, 2013). So a wise materialist would try to extend this prepurchase period, but materialists tend to do just the opposite and are particularly prone toward impulse purchasing (Podoshen and Andrzejewski, 2012).

While those reasons are important, "perhaps the blackest mark against materialism" (Tatzel, 2014b, p. 182) is the negative effect materialism can have on one's social relationships (Ahuvia, 2015). One of the strongest findings from happiness research is the indispensable role that strong positive social relationships play in creating a happy life (Demir, 2009; Lewis et al., 2015; Myers, 1999). Materialists often neglect their close social relationships (Pieters, 2013; Wallendorf and Arnould, 1988). Materialists generally do not share well (Belk, 1985; Richins and Dawson, 1992), and Kasser (2008, p. 2) notes that "materialistic values tend to oppose values such as being "helpful" and "loyal," obtaining "true friendship" and "mature love," and having "close, committed relationships." Materialists tend to bring a competitive status orientation to their social relationships (Ahuvia, 2015). Even materialists' marital relationships tend to be "cool" rather than "warm" (Claxton, Murray, and Swinder, 1995). And to add insult to injury, materialistic people are even seen as boring to talk to, at least about materialistic topics (Van Boven, Campbell, and Gilovich, 2010). It should not be surprising, then, that materialists are relatively less satisfied with their close personal relationships (Nickerson et al., 2003).

Although purchases of experiences tend to directly produce more happiness than do purchases of objects, materialists tend to purchase objects rather than experiences. This is probably because materialists like to buy status symbols (Ahuvia, 2015; Hudders and Pandelaere, 2011; Hunt, Kernan, and Mitchell, 1996; Richins, 1994; Wang and Wallendorf, 2006), and publicly visible physical objects are usually better than experiences at conveying high social status to others (Carter and Gilovich, 2010, 2012).

The finding that materialistic people tend to purchase physical objects rather than experiences raises an important issue about the nature of materialism. Some people understand the word "materialism" as referring to people who care a lot about material (i.e., physical) objects, in which case it would be true by definition that materialists care more about objects than experiences. Elsewhere (Ahuvia, 2015) I have argued that this is a misunderstanding of the term "materialism." The root word *mater* in "materialism" originally referred to *worldly* rather than *spiritual* concerns. By this earlier religiously grounded definition, many purchased experiences (e.g., a massage) would be considered highly worldly/materialistic, whereas the purchase of some physical objects (e.g., a bible) would not be materialistic. As our culture has become more secular, this understanding that spiritual concerns are not materialistic (even if they involve physical objects) has broadened to include what our culture considers to be "higher," more "elevated" concerns, such as the arts. So, "starving artists" are widely seen as among the least materialistic members of society, even if they dedicate their lives to producing material objects. Therefore, it is incorrect to assume that *by definition* materialists are inclined to purchase material objects (Zhang et al., 2014). And this makes the finding that materialists do in fact tend toward purchases of objects all the more interesting.

Along with the preceding discussion of materialism, the topic of materialism emerges again in the following as I discuss the relationship between income and happiness.

10.3.3 Noninterpersonal Love

Brand love is not psychologically identical to interpersonal love (Batra, Ahuvia, and Bagozzi, 2012; Langner, Schmidt, and Fischer, 2015), yet it is still a deep love relationship that is far more complex than simply being a high level of liking (Ahuvia, 2005; Ahuvia, Bagozzi, and Batra, 2014; Ahuvia, Batra, and Bagozzi, 2009; Albert and Merunka, 2013; Albert, Merunka, and Valette-Florence, 2008; Bagozzi, Batra, and Ahuvia, 2016; Batra et al., 2012; Lastovicka and Sirianni, 2011). The relationship between brand love and happiness is intriguing because, on the one hand, love has a strong positive relationship to happiness (Helliwell et al., 2012), yet brand love also looks a lot like materialism, which we have just seen has a negative relationship to happiness.

Research to date on this question has been limited (Ahuvia and Rauschnabel, 2015), but the findings are interesting because they present a bit of a puzzle. This research is based on a representative sample of Facebook users in Germany and the United States collected by the market research firm GfK, as well as numerous student samples. All data are consistent with past findings that materialism is negatively related to happiness, and also show that materialism is positively related to brand love. Yet, data also consistently show that brand love is *positively* related to happiness. Why we dependably see this pattern of results is still unknown, but Ahuvia and Rauschnabel (2015) suggest what they call the "sunshine people" explanation, that is, that some consumers may have a generally positive and cheery disposition that leads them to evaluate things in a positive way. This cheery disposition would lead them to evaluate their own lives positively, leading to high scores on happiness measures, and it would lead them to evaluate brands positively, leading to high scores on brand love.

Whereas "brand love" refers specifically to loved brands, products, and services, "noninterpersonal love" refers more broadly to love of anything other than a person, such as loved places and activities. A significant body of research by Vallerand and colleagues (for review, see Vallerand, 2012) explores the relationship between passionate activities and happiness. While this literature uses the word "passion," the actual construct definitions are completely compatible with theories of noninterpersonal love (Ahuvia et al., 2009). This research shows that, in general, being involved with activities one loves is positively associated with psychological well-being. But in some cases, a loved activity can become an "obsessive passion" (Vallerand et al., 2003, p. 756), where the person feels out of control and emotionally dependent on the activity. These obsessive passions are associated with lower levels of happiness and overall psychological well-being.

10.4 Income and Happiness

Many readers look to the research on income and happiness with a question in mind: is striving for a higher income a good strategy for becoming happier? The short answer is, *if you are genuinely poor* and getting out of poverty is a realistic option, then yes, getting out of poverty is an excellent idea. But for the rest of us, treating a higher income as an important life priority is probably not an efficient strategy for becoming happier. Why? Ahuvia et al. (2015) distinguish between three types strategies for becoming happier: (1) *externalist strategies,* such as increasing one's income in order to try to change one's circumstances; (2) *internalist strategies,* such as therapy or meditation, in order to try to change one's thinking; and (3) *interactionist strategies* (the advocated approach) looking for synergistic ways of combining internal and external changes. Many people have a habit of looking immediately to externalist strategies, such as increasing one's income, without giving enough consideration to internalist approaches, or better still, considering how internalist and externalist strategies can interact with each other in a synergistic way to boost one's happiness. Furthermore, even looking within the various external-ist strategies, for most people who are not poor, externalist approaches such as improving one's social relationships are going to have a higher happiness payoff than increasing one's income (for more applied advice, see Ahuvia et al., 2013).

That said, the relationship between income and happiness is one of the most widely researched topics in positive psychology, and studies almost invariably find a small, but statistically significant, positive relationship between income and happiness. For this correlation, how small is small? In the previous work (Ahuvia, 2012; Ahuvia and Friedman, 1998), I reported that typical studies in developed economies indicate that income explains only about 3 percent of the difference in happiness between individuals, give or take a point or two. This remains true, but more recent work has revealed a much more detailed and interesting picture of the relationship between money and happiness – so much so that if all you remember is the 3 percent figure you really will not have a very useful picture of the relationships between money and happiness. Therefore, we now turn to some of the more important factors.

10.4.1 Income and One's Standard of Living

Research on the relationship between income and happiness is mostly done through finding correlations in survey data. When positive correlations are found between income and happiness (and they almost always are weak, but present), it is tempting to interpret these as revealing the impact of a higher standard of living on happiness. But there are several very plausible rival explanations for these correlations.

High-paying jobs also tend to have other rewards such as autonomy and relatively interesting work, which are associated with SWB (Argyle, 1996). Unemployment is another likely cause of spurious correlations, since unem-ployment brings both a loss in income and strong negative effects on happiness over and above the associated loss of wages (Clark, 2006). Like unemploy-ment, heavy consumer debt significantly reduces happiness regardless of income level (Ahuvia and Friedman, 1998), putting people in "a psychological 'debtor's prison' of constraint, guilt, and low self-esteem" (Tatzel, 2014, p. 177; citing Bernthal et al., 2005). And like unemployment, consumer debt is possi-ble at all income levels but is more common among those with lower incomes (Lea, Webley, and Walker, 1995).

The case of consumer debt is particularly interesting because of what it implies about consumption and happiness. Imagine three people who have the same income and all start the month with no debt and no savings. However, by the end of the month person 1 is $1,000 in debt, person 2 has broken even, and person 3 has put $1,000 away as savings. It follows that person 1 has enjoyed $1,000 more consumption than person 2 and $2,000 more consumption than person 3. If consumption leads to happiness, we would expect person 1 to be the happiest and person 3 to be the least happy. But in fact just the opposite is true; at any given income level, debt is associated with less happiness and savings (i.e., reduced consumption) is associated with greater happiness (Ahuvia and Friedman, 1998; Douthitt, 1992).

Finally, rather than wealth causing happiness, the causation could go in the other direction, as happiness "seems to foster success in the workplace" (Diener, 2012, p. 593). It seems intuitive to many people that of course success leads to happiness more so than happiness leading to success. But evidence continues to mount that a significant portion of the observed correlations between income and happiness may be due to the fact that happy people end up having higher incomes. In a direct test of this idea, researchers found that college students who rated themselves as being cheerful upon entering college ended up having higher incomes nineteen years later (Diener et al., 2002). Aspects of a happy personality, such as optimism, have been shown to lead to higher incomes (Argyle, 1996; Lucas and Diener, 2009; Myers and Diener, 1995). Other studies have found that "happy" workers are more productive (Oishi, 2012). The influence of these personality variables can be so powerful, as noted in Cummins (2000) review study, that when income is included in models, along with psychological variables such as optimism, control, and self-esteem, income does not show unique significance. However, a longitudinal study by Diener et al. (2013) found a cycle of causation in which both increased income led to happiness and increased happiness led to income.

One of the best ways to separate out the effects of income on happiness from many of these other confounding variables is to track individuals over time and see how changes in their income related to changes in their level of happiness. One such study used longitudinal West German data that tracked the income and life satisfaction of specific individuals every year since 1984 (Helliwell et al., 2012). Remarkably, this study found that "ceteris paribus, differences in income explain about 1 percent of the variance of life-satisfaction in the population" (p. 61). It should be noted, though, that West Germany is a wealthy country with a strong social safety net, so poverty of the type found in the developing world was not within the domain of the study.

10.4.2 Emotions Versus Life Satisfaction

Income has a different relationship to one's emotional experience than it does to one's life satisfaction. To understand why, suppose we took some typical happiness questions and changed them to focus on driving your car. Emotional questions would become something like, "Last time you drove your car, to what extent did you feel each of these emotions (frustration, joy, sadness, worry, excitement, happiness)?" It is likely that the things that had the biggest impact on your emotional experience while driving included whether you were in a hurry, what the traffic was like, the behavior of other drivers, or how long the drive was. Having more money would allow you to buy a better car that would probably also influence your emotional experience while driving, but not nearly as much as whether a driver suffering from road rage honked and yelled at you. This holds true when we ask not just about your emotions while driving, but about the emotions you experienced in all of your activities the day before. Having more money lets you buy nicer things, but this has only a very small relationship with the positive or negative emotions you feel throughout your day (Kahneman and Deaton, 2010).

Some recent research allows us to understand this relationship between our income and our daily emotional experience in a little more detail. True, a higher income allows one access to the finer things in life. But a higher income also has a downside in that it reduces one's ability to savor life's everyday small pleasures (Quoidbach et al., 2015a).

To the extent that having a higher income does improve one's day-to-day emotional experience, evidence suggests that it does so by reducing the severity of negative experiences rather than improving positive experiences (Kushlev, Dunn, and Lucas, 2015; cf. Diener et al., 2010). The "pain of some of life's misfortunes, including asthma, divorce, and being alone, is significantly exacerbated by poverty; even the benefits of the weekend are less for the poor. Similar results apply to stress and positive affect" (Kahneman and Deaton, 2010, p. 16491). This is also consistent with findings that even controlling for income and investments, having enough cash on hand to buffer life's unexpected problems is significantly related to happiness (Ruberton et al., 2016). (This finding finally allowed me to understand what I had previously thought was an absurd aphorism from my grandmother: "rich or poor, it is good to have money.")

Now consider a "car satisfaction" question that asked you to evaluate your car on a scale that ranged from zero (worst possible car) to ten (best possible car). How much your car cost is probably quite relevant to your answer on this question. The same occurs when respondents state where their current life would fall on a scale that ranged from zero (worst possible life) to ten (best possible life), as respondents do in the most popular life satisfaction measure, called Cantril's ladder (Cantril, 1966). In responding to this type of measure, people step back from their day-to-day experience and reflect on how their life compares to some standard they have for what constitutes a good life. Since most people see having an affluent lifestyle to be part of a good life, income has a much stronger relationship to life satisfaction than it does to one's daily experience of life as you live it (Diener et al., 2010; Kahneman and Deaton, 2010; Ng and Diener, 2014). For example, Diener et al. (2010, p. 57) found that the relationship between income and life satisfaction was over six times as strong as the relationship between income and positive or negative emotions. And even these relatively strong correlations between life satisfaction and income are, in absolute terms, weaker than many people might expect. For example, the Diener et al. (2010) study found that 80 percent of the difference in life satisfaction between people was attributable to factors other than income.

Finally, it may be helpful to note that asking people "on a scale of 1–10, how good is your life?" is similar to asking them how "successful" they are. Thus we can summarize the finding here by noting that income above a moderate level has no further impact on how happy a person feels. But higher and higher incomes continue to increase people's view of themselves as being successful.

10.4.3 The Less Income You Have, the More It Matters

The strength or the relationship between income and life satisfaction is curvilinear, where the richer one is, the less impact additional income will have on one's happiness. This curvilinear relationship holds for both affect and life satisfaction, although as stated previously, the relationship is much stronger for income and life satisfaction than it is for income and affect. We are now able to specify that the shape of the curve is roughly logarithmic, so that an extra dollar in the hands of a person earning $5,000 per year produces ten times as much happiness as a dollar in the hands of someone earning $50,000, which in turn produces ten times as much happiness as a dollar in the hands of someone earning $500,000 per year (Helliwell et al., 2012). This curvilinear relationship is consistent with the finding that people in extreme poverty report dramatically lower levels of life satisfaction than do the nonpoor (Biswas-Diener and Diener, 2001; Diener, 2012; Diener and Biswas-Diener, 2002; Galinha, Garcia-Martín, and Gomes, 2016; Thin et al., 2013). In the United States, increased income stops producing any significant improvement in the emotional experience of living one's life at about $75,000 per year, although improvements in life satisfaction are still measurable beyond this point (Kahneman and Deaton, 2010).

It was once believed that the negative effects of poverty on life satisfaction would be ameliorated somewhat by the tendency of people to compare themselves to their neighbors. So, poor people living in a poor neighborhood would mostly compare themselves to their also poor neighbors. And certainly, poor people living in poor countries would compare themselves to other typical people in their country. This may have been true in the past, but it is not true now. In today's global economy, consumers judge their lifestyle against a "world standard package of goods" (Ger and Belk, 1996), that is, their idea of what people in first world economies have. In a major study, Diener, Tay, and Oishi, (2013, p. 267) concluded that "income standards are now largely global, with little effect of national social comparison." Similarly, Becchetti et al. (2013) found that Europeans compared themselves to people in other wealthier countries, generating negative feelings that were detectable in thirty years of Eurobarometer surveys. This international standard for what a person should have is influenced by international media and advertising (Diener, 2012; O'Guinn and Shrum, 1997). It is worth noting that Ger and Belk (1996) found that people in poorer countries tended to have the *highest* expectations for what goods they saw as necessities. This suggests that rather than comparing themselves to their immediate neighbors, people in lesser-developed countries may be comparing themselves to the lifestyles they see on American television, as if reality was already bad enough.

10.4.4 Does Money Matter More Than We Formerly Thought? A Cautionary Note

Looking at the scientific literature on income and happiness over the past fifteen years, it would be easy to reach the oversimplified conclusion that we used to think that income had little impact on happiness, but now we know it has a fairly strong impact. Fortunately, the points made in the preceding allow us to see more clearly what is actually going on.

First, we have seen that income has a much greater impact on life satisfaction measures than it does on one's emotional experience of life. Some of what looks like a difference between older and newer studies is really a difference between studies looking at emotions and studies looking at life satisfaction.

Second, we know that income matters a lot more to the poor. Newer studies have done a much better job than previous work at getting representative global samples that include poorer countries and poorer people within each country. Adding poor people to the sample increases the overall relationship between income and happiness, but it does not change the fact that for the nonpoor, increased income has a weak relationship to increased happiness.

Third, older studies looked at the linear correlation between income and happiness, whereas newer studies tend to look at the relationship between log income and happiness. Because the underlying relationship is curvilinear, using log income is a more accurate way of modeling this relationship. But most readers are not accustomed to thinking in terms of logarithms and may not understand that even if we say there is a fairly strong relationship between log income and life satisfaction, if we translate this to the real world for someone earning, say, $80,000 per year, even getting a big raise to $110,000 per year would probably not be a large enough increase to make a noticeable difference in that person's life satisfaction.

10.4.5 If Money Does Not Buy Happiness, Why Do We Act Like It Does?

I began this section by noting that as a practical matter, if you are not poor, trying to become happier by increasing your income is probably not the most efficient happiness strategy. But knowing this often has little impact on people's behavior, as we frequently remain quite motivated to increase our incomes. Economists have long assumed that situations where people behave in ways that run counter to their own happiness are rare exceptions, not deserving of serious consideration. We are seeing here, though, that people make choices that do not maximize their happiness with great regularity and consequence. There are two main reasons why people might behave in ways at odds with their own happiness: biased processing and multiple goals. The biased processing approach maintains that consumers are trying to maximize happiness, but are bad at it due to various biases and heuristics (Layard, 2005). And indeed, people seem to be astonishingly bad at predicting how happy some turn of events will make them, and also seem unable to learn from their mistakes. For example, Van Praag and Frijters (1999) and Easterlin (2001) argue along the same lines in explaining why people think more money will make them happy, when in fact it does not. Essentially, people have a psychological bias that prevents them anticipating the way their aspirations will adjust to their improved circumstances. So, when they contemplate getting a raise in pay, they imagine how happy they would be with that income, if their material norm remained unchanged. Yet, time and time again, their material norm does change after receiving a raise, and we seem to have great difficulty in taking this into account when making decisions.

Frey and Stutzer (2014) further refine this view. They argue that several biases combine to cause people to overvalue extrinsic benefits (e.g., wealth and prestige) and undervalue intrinsic benefits (e.g., family time) when making decisions. (For a fuller discussion of the extrinsic/intrinsic dichotomy, see Kasser, 2002b). To illustrate this point, they use the example of making a choice to take a job that offers a higher salary, but requires a longer commute. The commute cuts into time needed to pursue intrinsically rewarding activities such as building social relationships, but provides income that can easily be translated into extrinsic rewards such as status. They suggest that decision-making biases cause people to overvalue the income and undervalue the costs of the commute, thus leading them to accept the job when they should not. As empirical support for this hypothesis, they find that after controlling for a host of demographic variables, longer commute times are closely associated with lower life satisfaction among respondents to the German Socio-Economic Panel Study (GSEPS). This runs counter to rational decision-making models, which suggest that commute times and life satisfaction should be uncorrelated, since people would only choose to take a job with a long commute if it offered other advantages that compensated for this lost time. As further evidence for the psychological mechanism that they propose to explain this phenomenon, Frey and Stutzer hypothesize that people with a more extrinsic values orientation are particularly prone to make the mistake of overvaluing income relative to the loss of free time. To demonstrate this, they divide GSEPS respondents into those who primarily value intrinsic rewards (family, friends, faith, and religion) versus those who primarily value extrinsic rewards (income, influence on political decisions, and career success). They then show that the negative correlation between commuting time and life satisfaction only exists in the extrinsically oriented group.

Advocates of the multiple goals perspective generally acknowledge that these cognitive biases exist, but question whether these biases represent the complete explanation for behaviors that work against happiness. The multiple goals perspective holds that while happiness is extremely important to people, it is just one of several goals underlying human action (Ahuvia, 2002, 2008). Examples of these other goals include gaining honor or prestige, complying with social expectations, and being sexually attractive. In contrast to arguments that people only want these things because they hope to become happier, the multiple goals perspective holds that people sometimes value these things as ends in themselves, on a par with happiness. As Ahuvia (2002, p. 31) writes, for some people it is just as possible that they "seek social recognition with the ultimate goal of personal happiness," as it is that they "seek happiness with the ultimate goal of getting others to think well of them for having such a pleasant affect." Frijters (2000) looked empirically at this question, and consistent with the multiple goals perspective, found only weak and limited evidence that people try to maximize general satisfaction.

In the multiple goals perspective, then, part of the reason people do not always achieve happiness is that they are implicitly trying to achieve goals that may conflict with happiness. If this is the case, people have multiple motivational systems that at times conflict with each other, rather than just one unified motivational system that maximizes a single goal such as utility. These motivational systems may have evolved at different times in our history and may operate through different neurological mechanisms. Which of these motivational systems eventually wins out and controls our behavior may be the result of factors such as what mood we are in, whether we feel threatened, whether social expectations are momentarily salient to us, or how much alcohol we have consumed, rather than a utility maximizing master algorithm.

10.5 Economic Growth and Happiness

Early studies on economic growth and happiness generally reached the conclusion that economic growth had no impact on people's long-term happiness. Newer studies using more comprehensive data sets are finding that economic growth can, under the right conditions, lead to increased happiness. Veenhoven and Hagerty (2006) found a very slight upward trend in happiness in both the United States and Europe, and a much larger upward trend in happiness in the lesser-developed countries where data were available. This is consistent with Oswald's (1997) and Andrews' (1991) findings for the United States, and Diener and Oishi's (2000) findings for Germany, Denmark, and Italy. Frijters (2004) found that after unification, "East Germans experienced a continued improvement in life satisfaction to which increased household incomes contributed around 12 percent" (p. 649).

A more recent study by Diener et al. (2013) had access to seven years of annual data for 150 countries, allowing for a more comprehensive assessment than in older studies. Consistent with the earlier discussion, they found that economic growth often led to improvements in life satisfaction but not in day-to-day emotional experience. With regard to these improvements in life satisfaction, for these increases to occur three conditions must be met. First, the benefits of the economic growth must be spread around the society enough that many people feel their standard of living to be rising. Second, economic growth must lead to optimism about the future, because this optimism is a major mechanism through which economic growth leads to happiness. But third, the economic growth should not cause people's income expectations to increase so rapidly that they outstrip their actual income improvements, leading to decreased satisfaction with their actual income.

Ahuvia (2001, 2002) argues that to understand one of the key ways that economic development is linked to happiness, one needs to think *very* long run. Economic growth is important for meeting basic human needs. But beyond that, it also creates cultural changes that ultimately have a great influence on happiness. To see the impact of culture on happiness, consider that Helliwell (2003) found that the strong correlation between gross domestic product (GDP) per capita and average national levels of happiness is almost completely eliminated by controlling for region-specific determinants of happiness, such as culture. Ahuvia (2002) argues that "cultures of happiness" are individualistic, not in the sense of selfishness, but individualistic in that they allow people to make major life decisions such as whom they will marry or what their career will be, based on what they will find most personally fulfilling, and thus allow people to achieve higher levels of happiness. This type of individualism is very strongly correlated with happiness (Inglehart et al., 2008; Ng and Diener, 2014; Verme, 2009; Welzel and Inglehart, 2010). Indeed, in a meta-analysis of studies covering sixty-three countries, Fischer and Boer (2011) found that cultural individualism and self-determination were better indicators than wealth at predicting well-being. Historically, this type of individualism has developed slowly through cultural changes linked to economic growth, occurring over hundreds of years. The rate of change in US happiness reported by Veenhoven and Hagerty (2006), where it would take 167 years to move the average happiness level up one point on a ten-point scale, is in line with this type of slow historical transformation.

10.6 Future Directions

The previous discussion has revealed several large questions that remain top priorities for research. Questions about economic growth are high on the list. The need to deal with global warming may make it difficult to maintain high levels of economic growth. And the findings on the negative effects of materialism suggest that a culture less obsessed with economic growth would be not just ecologically healthier, but psychologically and healthier as well (Brown and Kasser, 2005). Many early studies found no relationship between economic growth and happiness, suggesting that low-growth or even zero-growth economies might not be all that bad psychologically. However, more recent studies have found clear and lasting positive effects from economic growth (Diener et al., 2013). This increased happiness comes in part from reductions in poverty that allow more people to meet their basic needs. But economic growth also leads to happiness by increasing optimism about the future (Diener et al., 2013) and by creating cultures in which people have more choice about the big issues in their lives (Ahuvia, 2002). Along these same lines, a zero overall growth level means that for someone to increase his or her income, someone else must lose income. Given that people will still want to get ahead economically, what would the effect of a zero-growth economy be on social trust and harmony (Bell and Mo, 2014)?

Much of the previous discussion revolves around peoples' material aspirations and their link to both income and happiness. In this way, the literature on income is closely linked with people's financial aspirations. But current work has often relied on very approximate proxy measures for these aspirations. The inclusion of good measures for material aspirations in large-scale longitudinal studies would help fill in one of the most problematic lacunae in this area. How material aspirations are set has implications for, among other things, tax policy. If one person's gain in consumption raises the material aspirations of those around him or her, then status consumption has negative externalities (Frank, 1999). Like any good with negative externalities, it will be overconsumed. Thus, Frank (1999) advocates a consumption tax to shift resource allocation away from status consumption and toward leisure, health, education, and other less status-focused pursuits. It is a simple argument, but it has yet to make real headway as a policy.

In future research, it would behoove us to develop effective personal and social strategies for living a happy life in a consumer society (Tatzel, 2014a). We have finally started to see a burgeoning of research in this area, as reviewed in the early sections of this chapter. But work in this area is still in its infancy.

Finally, quality of life is often looked at using a combination of objective (e.g., health, education, safety from crime) and subjective indicators. However, some proponents of subjective measures argue that ultimately, happiness is the only thing that matters. For example, Ng (1997, p. 1849) writes, "We want money (or anything else) only as a means to increase our happiness," and Stutzer and Frey (2004, p. 1) write that "Economic activity is certainly not an end in itself, but only has value in so far as it contributes to human happiness." This position is an intellectual descendent of Aristotle's (Trans. 1999) view that *eudemonia* (roughly translated as happiness) is the proper ultimate goal for all human action (Ahuvia, 2008). Aristotle reasoned that every other goal, such as wealth or power, was only desired because it was hoped to lead to happiness, whereas happiness was desired as an end in itself and not a means to another end. Therefore, other goals were only valuable insofar as they produced happiness.

But is this the position we really want to take? As Veenhoven and Hagerty (2006) point out, at the very least we should be looking at longevity as well as happiness. And Cummins (2000) argues that both objective and subjective measures of quality of life are important to get a full picture of a good life. Diener and Diener (1995) start with the assumption that happiness is just one value among many, and therefore look at numerous measures, such as scientific achievement, which reflect achievement in different societies on a wide range of human values. I applaud the tremendous amount of research now being conducted on happiness, but that's not the same as saying all we should look at is happiness.

10.7 References

Ahuvia, A. C. (2001). Well-Being in Cultures of Choice: A Cross-Cultural Perspective. *American Psychologist*, (January), 2000–2001.

Ahuvia, A. C. (2002). Individualism/Collectivism and Cultures of Happiness: A Theoretical Conjecture on the Relationship Between Consumption, Culture and Subjective Well-Being at the National Level. *Journal of Happiness Studies*, 3(1), 23. Retrieved from 0-proquest.umi.com.wizard.umd.umich.edu/pqdweb ?did=2140482481&Fmt=7&clientId=8511&RQT=309&VName=PQD

Ahuvia, A. C. (2005). Beyond the Extended Self: Loved Objects and Consumers' Identity Narratives. *Journal of Consumer Research*, 32(1), 171–184. Retrieved from www.jstor.org/stable/10.1086/429607

Ahuvia, A. C. (2008). If Money Doesn't Make Us Happy, Why Do We Act as If It Does? *Journal of Economic Psychology*, 29(4), 491.

Ahuvia, A. C. (2011). Dr. Seuss, Felicitator. *International Journal of Wellbeing*, 1(2). doi.org/10.5502/ijw.v1i2.30

Ahuvia, A. C. (2012). Wealth, Consumption and Happiness. In A. Lewis (Ed.), *The Cambridge Handbook of Psychology and Economic Behaviour* (pp. 199–206). Cambridge, England: Cambridge University Press.

Ahuvia, A. C. (2013). Beyond "Beyond the Extended Self": Russ Belk on Identity. In J. Schouten (Ed.), (Vol. Consumer S). Thousand Oaks, CA: Sage.

Ahuvia, A. C. (2015). Nothing Matters More to People than People: Brand Meaning, Brand Love and Social Relationships. *Review of Marketing Research Special Issue on Brand Meaning Management*, 12, 121–149. doi.org/10.1108/ S1548-643520150000012005

Ahuvia, A. C., Bagozzi, R. P., and Batra, R. (2014). Psychometric vs. C-OAR-SE Measures of Brand Love: A Reply to Rossiter. *Marketing Letters*, 25(2), 235–243. doi.org/10.1007/s11002-013-9251-4

Ahuvia, A. C., Batra, R., and Bagozzi, R. P. (2009). Love, Desire, and Identity: A Conditional Integration Theory of the Love of Things. In D. J. MacInnis, C. W. Park, and J. R. Priester (Eds.), *The Handbook of Brand Relationships. New York:* ... (pp. 342–357). New York, NY: M. E. Sharpe. Retrieved from scholar. google.com/scholar?hl=en&btnG=Search&q=intitle:Love,+Desire,+and+Id entity:+A+Conditional+Integration+Theory+of+the+Love+of+Things#0

Ahuvia, A. C., and Friedman, D. C. (1998). Income, Consumption, and Subjective Well-Being: Toward a Composite Macromarketing Model. *Journal of Macromarketing*, 18(2), 153.

Ahuvia, A. C., and Izberk-Bilgin, E. (2012). Well-Being in Consumer Societies. In S. A. David, I. Boniwell, and A. Conley Ayers (Eds.), *Oxford Handbook of Happiness* (pp. 482–497). Oxford: Oxford University Press.

Ahuvia, A. C., and Rauschnabel, P. A. (2015). Is Brand Love Good for Consumers? In *4th Annual Conference for Positive Marketing*. New York.

Ahuvia, A. C., Thin, N., Haybron, D., and Biswas-Diener, R. (2016). Interactionism: A New Skill-Set for Happiness. Project+ Working Paper.

Ahuvia, A. C., Thin, N., Haybron, D. M., Biswas-Diener, R., Ricard, M., and Timsit, J. (2015). Happiness: An Interactionist Perspective. *International Journal of Wellbeing*, 5, 1–18. doi.org/10.5502/ijw.v5i1.1

Aknin, L. B., Barrington-Leigh, C. P., Dunn, E. W., et al. (2013). Prosocial Spending and Well-Being: Cross-cultural Evidence for a Psychological Universal. *Journal of Personality and Social Psychology*, 104(4), 635–652. doi.org/10.1037/a0031578

Albert, N., and Merunka, D. (2013). The Role of Brand Love in Consumer-Brand Relationships. *Journal of Consumer Marketing*, 30(3), 258–266. doi.org/10.1108/07363761311328928

Albert, N., Merunka, D., and Valette-Florence, P. (2008). When Consumers Love Their Brands: Exploring the Concept and Its Dimensions. *Journal of Business Research*, 61(10), 1062–1075. doi.org/10.1016/j.jbusres.2007.09.014

Andrews, F. M. (1991). Stability and Change in Levels and Structure of Subjective Well-Being: USA 1972 and 1988. *Social Indicators Research*, 25(1), 1–30.

Argyle, M. (1996). Subjective Well-Being. In A. Offer (Ed.), *In Pursuit of the Quality of Life* (pp. 18–45). New York: Oxford University Press.

Aristotle. (1999). *Nicomachean Ethics*. (W. D. Ross, Ed. and Trans.) *Ethics*. Digireads. com. Retrieved from socserv.mcmaster.ca/econ/ugcm/3ll3/aristotle/Ethics.pdf

Bagozzi, R. P., Batra, R., and Ahuvia, A. C. (2016). Brand Love: Development and Validation of a Practical Scale. *Marketing Letters*. doi.org/10.1007/s11002-016-9406-1

Batra, R., Ahuvia, A. C., and Bagozzi, R. P. (2012). Brand Love. *Journal of Marketing*, 76, 1–16. doi.org/10.1509/jm.09.0339

Baumeister, R. F., Vohs, K. D., and Tice, D. M. (2007). The Strength Model of Self-Control. *Current Directions in Psychological Science*, 16(6), 351–355. doi.org/10.1111/j.1467-8721.2007.00534.x

Becchetti, L., Castriota, S., Corrado, L., and Ricca, E. G. (2013). Beyond the Joneses: Inter-country Income Comparisons and Happiness. *Journal of Socio-Economics*, 45, 187–195. doi.org/10.1016/j.socec.2013.05.009

Belk, R. W. (1985). Materialism: Trait Aspects of Living in the Material World. *Journal of Consumer Research*, 12, 265–280.

Belk, R. W., and Coon, G. S. (1993). Gift Giving as Agapic Love: An Alternative to the Exchange Paradigm Based on Dating Experiences. *Journal of Consumer Research*, 20(3), 393–417. Retrieved from search.ebscohost.com/login.aspx?direct=true&db=ufh&AN=9409161966&site=ehost-live&scope=cite

Bell, D. A., and Mo, Y. (2014). Harmony in the World 2013: The Ideal and the Reality. *Social Indicators Research*, 118(2), 797–818. doi.org/10.1007/s11205-013-0439-z

Bernthal, M. J., Crockett, D., and Rose, R. L. (2005). Credit Cards as Lifestyle Facilitators. *Journal of Consumer Research*, 32(1), 130–145. doi.org/10.1086/429605

Biswas-Diener, R., and Diener, E. (2001). Making the Best of a Bad Situation: Satisfaction in the Slums of Calcutta. *Social Indicators Research*, 55(3), 329–352. doi.org/10.1023/A:1010905029386

Brown, K. W., and Kasser, T. (2005). Are Psychological and Ecological Well-Being Compatible? The Role of Values, Mindfulness, and Lifestyle. *Social Indicators Research*, 74(2), 349–368.

Brown, S., Taylor, K., and Wheatley Price, S. (2005). Debt and Distress: Evaluating the Psychological Cost of Credit. *Journal of Economic Psychology*, 26(5), 642–663. doi.org/10.1016/j.joep.2005.01.002

Bryant, F. (2003). Savoring Beliefs Inventory (SBI): A Scale for Measuring Beliefs About Savouring. *Journal of Mental Health*, 12(2), 175–196. doi.org/10.1080/0963823031000103489

Campbell, C. (1987). *The Romantic Ethic and the Spirit of Modern Consumerism*. Cambridge, MA: Blackwell.

Cantril, H. (1966). *The Pattern of Human Concerns*. New Brunswick, NJ: Rutgers University Press. Retrieved from mirlyn.lib.umich.edu/Record/000719357 CN – HN 18.C23

Caprariello, P. A, and Reis, H. T. (2013). To Do, to Have, or to Share? Valuing Experiences over Material Possessions Depends on the Involvement of Others. *Journal of Personality and Social Psychology*, 104(2). doi.org/10.1037/a0030953

Carter, T. J., and Gilovich, T. (2010). The Relative Relativity of Material and Experiential Purchases. *Journal of Personality and Social Psychology*, 98(1), 146–59. doi.org/10.1037/a0017145

Carter, T. J., and Gilovich, T. (2012). I Am What I Do, Not What I Have: The Differential Centrality of Experiential and Material Purchases to the Self. *Journal of Personality and Social Psychology*, 102(6), 1304–1317. doi.org/10.1037/a0027407

Carter, T. J., and Gilovich, T. (2013). Getting the Most for the Money: The Hedonic Return on Experiential and Material Purchases. In M. Tatzel (Ed.), *Consumption and Well-Being in the Material World* (pp. 49–62). New York, NY: Springer. doi.org/10.1007/978-94-007-7368-4_3

Caruso, E. M., Gilbert, D. T., and Wilson, T. D. (2008). A Wrinkle in Time: Asymmetric Valuation of Past and Future Events. *Psychological Science*, 19(8), 796–801. doi.org/10.1111/j.1467-9280.2008.02159.x

Chancellor, J., and Lyubomirsky, S. (2013). Money for Happiness: The Hedonic Benefits of Thrift. In *Consumption and Well-Being in the Material World* (pp. 13–47). doi.org/10.1007/978-94-007-7368-4_2

Clark, A. E. (2006). A Note on Unhappiness and Unemployment Duration. *Applied Economics Quarterly*, 52(4), 291–308. doi.org/http://aeq.diw.de/aeq/

Claxton, R. P., Murray, J., and Swinder, J. (1995). Spouses' Materialism: Effects of Parenthood Status, Personality Type, and Sex. *Journal of Consumer Policy*, 18, 267–291.

Csikszentmihalyi, M., and Hunter, J. (2003). Happiness in Everyday Life: The Uses of Experience Sampling. *Journal of Happiness Studies*, 4(January), 185–199. doi.org/10.1023/A:1024409732742

Cummins, R. A. (2000). Personal Income and Subjective Well-Being: A Review. *Journal of Happiness Studies*, 1, 133–158. doi.org/10.1023/A:1010079728426

Demir, M. (2009). Close Relationships and Happiness Among Emerging Adults. *Journal of Happiness Studies*, 11(3), 293–313. http://doi.org/10.1007/s10902-009-9141-x

Diener, E. (2012). New Findings and Future Directions for Subjective Well-Being Research. *American Psychologist*, (November), 590–597. doi.org/10.1037/a0029541

Diener, E., and Biswas-Diener, R. (2002). Will Money Increase Subjective Well-Being? *Social Indicators Research*, 57(September 2001), 119–169. Retrieved from link.springer.com/article/10.1023/A:1014411319119

Diener, E., and Diener, C. (1995). The Wealth of Nations Revisited, Income and the Quality of Life. *Social Indicators Research*, 36, 275–286.

Diener, E., Inglehart, R., and Tay, L. (2012). Theory and Validity of Life Satisfaction Scales. *Social Indicators Research*, 112(3), 497–527. doi.org/10.1007/s11205-012-0076-y

Diener, E., Ng, W., Harter, J., and Arora, R. (2010). Wealth and Happiness Across the World: Material Prosperity Predicts Life Evaluation, Whereas Psychosocial Prosperity Predicts Positive Feeling. *Journal of Personality and Social Psychology*, 99(1), 52–61.

Diener, E., Nickerson, C., Lucas, R. E., and Sandvik, E. (2002). Dispositional Affect and Job Outcome. *Social Indicators Research*, 59(3), 229–259.

Diener, E., and Oishi, S. (2000). Money and Happiness: Income and Subjective Well-being Across Nations. *Culture and Subjective Well-Being*, 185–218. doi.org/10.1.1.208.4409

Diener, E., Tay, L., and Oishi, S. (2013). Rising Income and the Subjective Well-Being of Nations. *Journal of Personality and Social Psychology*, 104(2), 267–276. doi.org/10.1037/a0030487

Dittmar, H., Bond, R., Hurst, M., and Kasser, T. (2014). The Relationship Between Materialism and Personal Well-Being: A Meta-Analysis. *Journal of Personality and Social Psychology*, 107(9).

Douthitt, R. A. (1992). The Relationship Between Measures of Subjective and Economic Well-Being: A New Look. *Social Indicators Research*, 26(June), 407–422.

Duhigg, C. (2012). *The Power of Habit: Why We Do What We Do in Life and Business*. New York: Random House.

Dunn, E. W., Aknin, L. B., and Norton, M. I. (2008). Spending Money on Others Promotes Happiness. *Science (New York)*, 319(5870), 1687–1688. doi.org/10.1126/science.1150952

Dunn, E. W., Aknin, L. B., and Norton, M. I. (2014). Prosocial Spending and Happiness: Using Money to Benefit Others Pays Off. *Current Directions in Psychological Science*, 23(1), 41–47. doi.org/10.1177/0963721413512503

Dunn, E. W., Gilbert, D. T., and Wilson, T. D. (2011). If Money Doesn't Make You Happy, Then You Probably Aren't Spending It Right. *Journal of Consumer Psychology*, 21(2), 115–125. doi.org/10.1016/j.jcps.2011.02.002

Dunn, E. W., and Norton, M. I. (2013). Happier Spending. *New York Times Magazine*, June 22. Retrieved from www.nytimes.com/2013/06/23/opinion/sunday/happier-spending.html

Dunn, E. W., and Weidman, A. C. (2015). Building a Science of Spending: Lessons from the Past and Directions for the Future. *Journal of Consumer Psychology*, 25(1). doi.org/10.1016/j.jcps.2014.08.003

Easterlin, R. A. (2001). Income and Happiness: Towards a Unified Theory. *Economic Journal*, 111(473), 465–484. doi.org/10.1111/1468-0297.00646

Fischer, R., and Boer, D. (2011). What Is More Important for National Well-Being: Money or Autonomy? A Meta-analysis of Well-Being, Burnout, and Anxiety Across 63 Societies. *Journal of Personality and Social Psychology*, 101(1), 164–184.

Frank, R. (1999). *Luxury Fever*. New York: Free Press.

Frey, B. S., and Stutzer, A. (2014). Economic Consequences of Mispredicting Utility. *Journal of Happiness Studies*, 15(4), 937–956. doi.org/10.1007/s10902-013-9457-4

Frijters, P. (2000). Do Individuals Try to Maximize General Satisfaction? *Journal of Economic Psychology*, 21, 281–304. Retrieved from www.elsevier.com/locate/joep%5Cnhttp://www.econ.vu.nl/

Frijters, P. (2004). Investigating the Patterns and Determinants of Life Satisfaction in Germany Following Reunification. *Journal of Human Resources*, 39(3), 649–674.

Galinha, I. C., Garcia-martín, M. Á., and Gomes, C. (2016). Criteria for Happiness Among People Living in Extreme Poverty in Maputo, Mozambique. *International Perspectives in Psychology: Research, Practice, Consultation*, 5(2), 67–90.

Gallup. (n.d.). Wellbeing Lower Among Workers With Long Commutes. Retrieved from www.gallup.com/poll/142142/Wellbeing-Lower-Among-Workers-Long-Commutes.aspx?version=print

Ger, G., and Belk, R. W. (1996). Cross-cultural Differences in Materialism. *Journal of Economic Psychology*, 17(1), 55–77. doi.org/10.1016/0167-4870(95)00035-6

Giesler, M. (2006). Consumer Gift Systems. *Journal of Consumer Research*. doi.org/10.1086/506309

Gilovich, T., Kumar, A., and Jampol, L. (2015). A Wonderful Life: Experiential Consumer and the Pursuit of Happiness. *Journal of Consumer Psychology*, 25(1), 152–165.

Grouzet, F. M. E., Kasser, T., Ahuvia, A. C., et al. (2005). The Structure of Goal Contents Across 15 Cultures. *Journal of Personality and Social Psychology*, 89(5), 800–816. doi.org/10.1037/0022-3514.89.5.800

Guevarra, D. A., and Howell, R. T. (2015). To Have in Order to Do: Exploring the Effects of Consuming Experiential Products on Well-Being. *Journal of Consumer Psychology*, 25(1). doi.org/10.1016/j.jcps.2014.06.006

Helliwell, J. F. (2003, March). How's Life? Combining Individual and National Variables to Explain Subjective Well-Being. *Economic Modelling*, 20(2), 331–360.

Helliwell, J. F., Layard, R., and Sachs, J. (2012). World Happiness Report. New York: United Nations Conference on Happiness on 2 April 2012 (mandated by the General Assembly of the United Nations).

Hudders, L., and Pandelaere, M. (2011). The Silver Lining of Materialism: The Impact of Luxury Consumption on Subjective Well-Being. *Journal of Happiness Studies*, 13(3), 411–437. doi.org/10.1007/s10902-011-9271-9

Hunt, J. M., Kernan, J. B., and Mitchell, D. J. (1996). Materialism as Social Cognition: People, Possessions, and Perception. *Journal of Consumer Psychology*, 5(1), 65–83. doi.org/10.1207/s15327663jcp0501_04

Inglehart, R., Foa, R., Peterson, C., and Welzel, C. (2008). Rising Happiness. *Psychological Science*, 3(4), 264–285. doi.org/10.1111/j.1745-6924.2008.00078.x

Kacen, J. J., and Lee, J. A. (2002). The Influence of Culture on Consumer Impulsive Buying Behavior. *Journal of Consumer Psychology*, 12(2), 163–176. doi.org/10.1207/S15327663JCP1202_08

Kahneman, D., and Deaton, A. (2010). High Income Improves Evaluation of Life but Not Emotional Well-Being. *Proceedings of the National Academy of Sciences of the United States of America*, 107(38), 16489–16493. doi.org/10.1073/pnas.1011492107

Kassam, K. S., Gilbert, D. T., Boston, A., and Wilson, T. D. (2008). Future Anhedonia and Time Discounting. *Journal of Experimental Social Psychology*, 44(6), 1533–1537. doi.org/10.1016/j.jesp.2008.07.008

Kasser, T. (2002a). Sketches for a Self-Determination Theory of Values. In E. L. Deci and R. M. Ryan (Eds.), *Handbook of Self-Detrmination Research* (pp. 123–140). Rochester, NY: University of Rochester Press.

Kasser, T. (2002b). *The High Price of Materialism*. Cambridge, MA: MIT Press.

Kasser, T. (2008). Can Buddhism and Consumerism Harmonize? A Review of the Psychological Evidence. In *International Conference on Buddhism in the Age of Consumerism* (pp. 1–3). Bangkok: Mahidol University. Retrieved from wcbsthailand.com/download/c2_pdf/Tim Kasser.pdf

Koehler, D. J., and Harvey, N. (2014). Utility: Anticipated, Experienced, and Remembered. In G. Keren and G. Wu (Eds.), *Blackwell Handbook of Judgment and Decision Making* (2nd ed., pp. 1–83). Malden, MA: Blackwell Publishing. Retrieved from ssrn.com/abstract=2515535

Kumar, A., Killingsworth, M. A., and Gilovich, T. (2014). Waiting for Merlot: Anticipatory Consumption of Experiential and Material Purchases. *Psychological Science*, 25(10), 1924–31. doi.org/10.1177/0956797614546556

Kumar, A., and Gilovich, T. (2015). Some "Thing" to Talk About? Differential Story Utility From Experiential and Material Purchases. *Personality and Social Psychology Bulletin*, 41(10), 1320–1331. doi.org/10.1177/0146167215594591

Kurtz, J. L., Wilson, T. D., and Gilbert, D. T. (2007). Quantity Versus Uncertainty: When Winning One Prize Is Better than Winning Two. *Journal of Experimental Social Psychology*, 43(6), 979–985. doi.org/10.1016/j.jesp.2006.10.020

Kushlev, K., Dunn, E. W., and Lucas, R. E. (2015). Higher Income Is Associated with Less Daily Sadness but Not More Daily Happiness. *Social Psychological and Personality Science*, 6(5), 483–489. doi.org/10.1177/1948550614568161

Langner, T., Schmidt, J., and Fischer, A. (2015). Is It Really Love? A Comparative Investigation of the Emotional Nature of Brand and Interpersonal Love. *Psychology and Marketing*, 32(6), 624–634. doi.org/10.1002/mar

Lastovicka, J. L., and Sirianni, N. J. (2011). Truly, Madly, Deeply: Consumers in the Throes of Material Possession Love. *Journal of Consumer Research*, 38(2), 323–342. Retrieved from www.jstor.org/stable/10.1086/658338

Layard, R. (2005). *Happiness: Lessons from a New Science*. New York: Penguim Press, 3491. doi.org/10.1007/sl0902-005-0934-2

Lea, S. E. G., Webley, P., and Walker, C. M. (1995). Psychological Factors in Consumer Debt: Money Management, Economic Socialization, and Credit Use. *Journal of Economic Psychology*, 16(4), 681–701.

Lewis, D. M. G., Al-Shawaf, L., Russel, E. M., and Buss, D. M. (2015). Friends and Happiness: An Evolutionary Perspective on Friendship. In M. Demir (Ed.), *Friendship and Happiness*. New York: Springer. doi.org/10.1007/978-94-017-9603-3

Loewenstein, G. (1987). Anticipation and the Valuation of Delayed Consumption. *Economic Journal*, 97(387), 666–684. Retrieved from www.jstor.org/stable/2232929

Lucas, R. E., and Diener, E. (2009). Personality and Subjective Well-Being. *The Science of Subjective Well-Being: The Collected Works of Ed Diener*, 75–102. doi.org/10.1007/978-90-481-2350-6_4

Mitchell, T. R., Thompson, L., Peterson, E., and Cronk, R. (1997). Temporal Adjustments in the Evaluation of Events: The Rosy View. *Journal of Experimental Social Psychology*, 33(4), 421–448. doi.org/10.1006/jesp.1997.1333

Muraven, M., and Baumeister, R. F. (2000). Self-Regulation and Depletion of Limited Resources: Does Self-Control Resemble a Muscle? *Psychological Bulletin*, 126(2), 247–259. doi.org/10.1037/0033-2909.126.2.247

Myers, D. G. (1999). Close Relationships and Quality of Life. In D. Kahneman, E. Diener, and N. Schwarz (Eds.), *Well-Being: The Foundations of Hedonic Psychology* (pp. 353–373). New York: Russell Sage Foundation.

Myers, D. G., and Diener, E. (1995). Who Is Happy? *Psychological Science*, 6(1), 10–19. doi.org/10.1111/j.1467–9280.1995.tb00298.x

Nawijn, J., Marchand, M. A., Veenhoven, R., and Vingerhoets, A. J. (2010). Vacationers Happier, but Most Not Happier After a Holiday. *Applied Research in Quality of Life*, 5(1), 35–47. doi.org/10.1007/s11482-009-9091-9

Neal, D. T., Wood, W., and Drolet, A. (2013). How Do People Adhere to Goals When Willpower Is Low? The Profits (and Pitfalls) of Strong Habits. *Journal of Personality and Social Psychology*, 104(6), 959–975. doi.org/10.1037/a0032626

Ng, W., and Diener, E. (2014). What Matters to the Rich and the Poor? Subjective Well-Being, Financial Satisfaction, and Postmaterialist Needs Across the World. *Journal of Personality and Social Psychology*, 107(2), 326–338. doi.org/10.1037/a0036856

Ng, Y.-K. (1997). A Case for Happiness, Cardinalism, and Interpersonal Comparability. *Economic Journal*, 107(445), 1848–1858. Retrieved from onlinelibrary.wiley.com/doi/10.1111/j.1468-0297.1997.tb00087.x/abstract

Nicholls, J., and Li, F. (2001). Inter-American Perspectives from Mall Shoppers: Chile–United States. *Journal of Global Marketing*, 15, 87–103. doi.org/10.1300/J042v15n01

Nickerson, C., Schwarz, N., Diener, E., and Kahneman, D. (2003). Zeroing in on the Dark Side of the American Dream: A Closer Look at the Negative Consequences of the Goal for Financial Success. *Psychological Science*, 14(6), 531–536. Retrieved from www.jstor.org.proxy.lib.umich.edu/stable/40063908

Nicolao, L., Irwin, J. R., and Goodman, J. K. (2009). Happiness for Sale: Do Experiential Purchases Make Consumers Happier than Material Purchases? *Journal of Consumer Research*, 36(2), 188–198. doi.org/10.1086/597049

Niemiec, C. P., Ryan, R. M., and Deci, E. L. (2009). The Path Taken: Consequences of Attaining Intrinsic and Extrinsic Aspirations in Post-College Life. *Journal of Research in Personality*, 73(3), 291–306. doi.org/10.1016/j.jrp.2008.09.001

O'Guinn, T. C., and Shrum, L. J. (1997). The Role of Television in the Construction of Consumer Reality. *Journal of Consumer Research*, 23(4), 278. doi.org/10.1086/209483

Oishi, S. (2012). *The Psychological Wealth of Nations: Do Happy People Make a Happy Society?* Malden, MA: Wiley-Blackwell.

Oswald, A. J. (1997). Happiness and Economic Performance. *Economic Journal*, 107(445), 1815–1831.

Pieters, R. (2013). Bidirectional Dynamics of Materialism and Loneliness: Not Just a Vicious Cycle. *Journal of Consumer Research*, 40(4), 615–631. doi.org/10.1086/671564

Podoshen, J. S., and Andrzejewski, S. A. (2012). An Examination of the Relationships Between Materialism, Conspicuous Consumption, Impulse Buying, and Brand Loyalty. *Journal of Marketing Theory and Practice*, 20(3), 319–334. doi.org/10.2753/MTP1069-6679200306

Quoidbach, J., Dunn, E. W., Hansenne, M., and Bustin, G. (2015a). The Price of Abundance: How a Wealth of Experiences Impoverishes Savoring. *Personality and Social Psychology Bulletin*, 41(3), 393–404. doi.org/10.1177/0146167214566189

Quoidbach, J., Mikolajczak, M., and Gross, J. J. (2015b). Positive Interventions: An Emotion Regulation Perspective. *Psychological Bulletin*. doi.org/10.1037/a0038648

Read, D., and van Leeuwen, B. (1998). Predicting Hunger: The Effects of Appetite and Delay on Choice. *Organizational Behavior and Human Decision Processes*, 76(2), 189–205. doi.org/10.1006/obhd.1998.2803

Ricard, M. (2015). *Altruism: The Power of Compassion to Change Yourself and the World*. New York: Little, Brown.

Richins, M. L. (1994). Special Possessions and the Expression of Material Values. *Journal of Consumer Research*, 21(3), 522–533. Retrieved from search.ebscohost.com/login.aspx?direct=true&db=ufh&AN=9501161819&site=ehost-live&scope=cite

Richins, M. L. (2004). The Material Values Scale: Measurement Properties and Development of a Short Form. *Journal of Consumer Research*, 31(1), 209–219.

Richins, M. L. (2013). When Wanting Is Better than Having: Materialism, Transformation Expectations, and Product-Evoked Emotions in the Purchase Process. *Journal of Consumer Research*, 40, 1–18. doi.org/10.1086/669256

Richins, M. L., and Dawson, S. (1992). A Consumer Values Orientation for Materialism and Its Measurement: Scale Development and Validation. *Journal of Consumer Research*, 19(3), 303–316.

Ruberton, P. M., Gladstone, J., and Lyubomirsky, S. (2016). How Your Bank Balance Buys Happiness: The Importance of "Cash on Hand" to Life Satisfaction. *Emotion*. Retrieved from psycnet.apa.orgpsycarticles/2016-17475-001

Ryan, R. M., and Deci, E. L. (2000). Self-Determination Theory and the Facilitation of Intrinsic Motivation, Social Development, and Well-Being. *American*

Psychologist, 55(1), 68–78. Retrieved from www.ncbi.nlm.nih.gov/pubmed/11392867

Ryff, C. D. (1989). Happiness Is Everything, or Is It? Explorations on the Meaning of Psychological Well-Being. *Journal of Personality and Social Psychology*, 57(6), 1069–1081. doi.org/10.1037/0022-3514.57.6.1069

Ryff, C. D., and Keyes, C. L. M. (1995). The Structure of Psychological Well-Being Revisited. *Journal of Personality and Social Psychology*, 69(4), 719–727. doi.org/10.1037/0022-3514.69.4.719

Sheldon, K. M., and Kasser, T. (1998). Pursuing Personal Goals: Skills Enable Progress, but Not All Progress Is Beneficial. *Personality and Social Psychology Bulletin*, 24(12), 1319–1331. doi.org/10.1177/01461672982412006

Shiv, B., and Fedorikhin, A. (1999). Heart and Mind in Conflict: The Interplay. *Journal of Consumer Research*, 26(3), 278–292. doi.org/10.1086/209563

Silvera, D. H., Lavack, A. M., and Kropp, F. (2008). Impulse Buying: The Role of Affect, Social Influence, and Subjective Wellbeing. *Journal of Consumer Marketing*, 25(1), 23–33. doi.org/10.1108/07363760810845381

Stutzer, A., and Frey, B. S. (2004). Reported Subjective Well-Being: A Challenge for Economic Theory and Economic Policy. *Schmollers Jahrbuch*, 124(2), 191–231.

Stutzer, A., and Frey, B. S. (2008). Stress That Doesn't Pay: The Commuting Paradox. *Scandinavian Journal of Economics*, 110(2), 339–366.

Sutton, S. K., and Davidson, R. J. (1997). Prefrontal Brain Asymmetry: A Biological Substrate of the Behavioral Approach and Inhibition Systems. *Psychological Science*, 8(3), 204–210. doi.org/10.1111/j.1467–9280.1997.tb00413.x

Tatzel, M. (2014a). *Consumption and Well-Being in the Material World*. (M. Tatzel, Ed.). New York: Springer. doi.org/10.1007/978-94-007-7368-4

Tatzel, M. (2014b). Epilogue – Confessions of a Closet Materialist: Lessons Learned About Money, Possessions, and Happiness. In M. Tatzel (Ed.), *Consumption and Well-Being in the Material World* (pp. 175–194). New York: Springer.

Thaler, R. H., and Sunstein, C. R. (2008). (2008). *Nudge: Improving Decisions About Health, Wealth, and Happiness*. New Haven, CT: Yale University Press.

Thin, N., Haybron, D., Biswas-Diener, R., and Ahuvia, A. C. (2013). Desirability of Sustainable Happiness as a Guide for Public Policy. In F. Boniwell, Ilona (Positran and l'Ecole Centrale Paris) (Ed.), *Report on Wellbeing & Happiness: Contributions Towards the RGOB's NDP Report by IEWG Members of the Wellbeing & Happiness Working Group* (pp. 35–49). New York: United Nations.

Trocchia, P. J., and Janda, S. (2002). An Investigation of Product Purchase and Subsequent Non-Consumption. *Journal of Consumer Marketing*, 19(3), 188–204. doi.org/10.1108/07363760210426030

Vallerand, R. J. (2012). The Role of Passion in Sustainable Psychological Well-Being. *Psychology of Well-Being: Theory, Research and Practice*, 2(1), 1. doi.org/10.1186/2211-1522-2-1

Vallerand, R. J., Blanchard, C., Mageau, G. A, et al. (2003). Les passions de l'âme: on obsessive and harmonious passion. *Journal of Personality and Social Psychology*, 85(4), 756–767. doi.org/10.1037/0022-3514.85.4.756

Van Boven, L., Campbell, M. C., and Gilovich, T. (2010). Stigmatizing Materialism: On Stereotypes and Impressions of Materialistic and Experiential Pursuits. *Personality and Social Psychology Bulletin*, 36(4), 551–563. doi.org/10.1177/0146167210362790

Van Boven, L., and Gilovich, T. (2003). To Do or to Have? That Is the Question. *Journal of Personality and Social Psychology*, 85(6), 1193–1202. doi.org/10.1037/0022-3514.85.6.1193

Van Praag, B. M. S., and Ferrer-i-Carbonell, A. (2010). Happiness Economics: A New Road to Measuring and Comparing Happiness. *Foundations and Trends® in Microeconomics*, 6(1), 1–97. doi.org/10.1561/0700000026

Van Praag, B. M. S., and Frijters, P. (1999). The Measurement of Welfare and Well-Being: The Leyden Approach. In D. Kahneman, E. Diener, and N. Schwarz (Eds.), *Well-Being: The Foundations of Hedonic Psychology* (pp. 413–433). New York: Russell Sage Foundation.

Veenhoven, R., and Hagerty, M. (2006). Rising Happiness in Nations 1946–2004: A Reply to Easterlin. *Social Indicators Research*, 79(3), 421–436.

Verme, P. (2009). Happiness, Freedom and Control. *Journal of Economic Behavior and Organization*, 71(2), 146–161.

Verplanken, B., and Herabadi, A. (2001). Individual Differences in Impulse Buying Tendency: Feeling and No Thinking. *European Journal of Personality*, 15(S1), S71–S83. doi.org/10.1002/per.423

Wallendorf, M., and Arnould, E. J. (1988). "My Favorite Things": A Cross-Cultural Inquiry into Object Attachment, Possessiveness, and Social Linkage. *Journal of Consumer Research*, 14(March), 531–547. doi.org/10.1086/209134

Wang, J., and Wallendorf, M. (2006). Materialism, Status Signaling, and Product Satisfaction. *Journal of the Academy of Marketing Science*, 34(4), 494–505. doi.org/10.1177/0092070306289291

Watson, D., Clark, L. A, and Tellegen, A. (1988). Development and Validation of Brief Measures of Positive and Negative Affect: The PANAS Scales. *Journal of Personality and Social Psychology*, 54(6), 1063–1070. doi.org/10.1037/0022-3514.54.6.1063

Watson, J. J. (2003). The Relationship of Materialism to Spending Tendencies, Saving, and Debt. *Journal of Economic Psychology*, 24(6), 723–739. doi.org/10.1016/j.joep.2003.06.001

Weidman, A. C., and Dunn, E. W. (2015). The Unsung Benefits of Material Things Material Purchases Provide More Frequent Momentary Happiness Than Experiential Purchases. *Social Psychological and Personality Science*, 1948550615619761. doi.org/10.1177/1948550615619761

Welzel, C., and Inglehart, R. (2010). Agency, Values, and Well-Being: A Human Development Model. *Social Indicators Research*, 97(1), 43–63.

Zauberman, G., Ratner, R. K., and Kim, B. K. (2009). Memories as Assets: Strategic Memory Protection in Choice over Time. *Journal of Consumer Research*, 35(5). doi.org/10.1086/592943

Zhang, J. W., Howell, R. T., Caprariello, P. A., and Guevarra, D. A. (2014). Damned If They Do, Damned If They Don't: Material Buyers Are Not Happier from Material or Experiential Consumption. *Journal of Research in Personality*, 50(1). doi.org/10.1016/j.jrp.2014.03.007

Zuzanek, J., and Zuzanek, T. (2014). Of Happiness and of Despair, Is There a Measure? Time Use and Subjective Well-Being. *Journal of Happiness Studies*, 1–18. doi.org/10.1007/s10902-014-9536-1

11 Consumers and Households

Materialism, Nonmaterialism, and Subjective Well-Being

Gerrit Antonides and Chris van Klaveren

11.1 Introduction

Each day, individuals face numerous decisions and choose between many consumption alternatives based on their values and preferences to increase their subjective well-being (SWB). Therefore, it is important to understand decision-making processes as they determine to a large extent the level of SWB or satisfaction resulting from decisions. Up to now, the literature has mainly focused on the role of materialistic factors, while a common finding is that increases in income, or consumption, contribute to increases in SWB only up to a certain level (Delhey, 2009; Inglehart and Baker, 2000; Kahneman and Deaton, 2010). Once this level is reached, nonmaterialistic factors become increasingly important. This situation reflects the importance of higher needs in the determination of levels of SWB, once lower needs have been satisfied.

A plethora of research findings on consumer behavior obtained in the last few decades, and especially in the areas of behavioral economics and economic psychology, shows the importance of nonmaterialistic factors in individual decision-making processes (see, for example, Altman, 2015; Antonides, 2008), and the evaluation of experienced outcomes. This chapter summarizes these findings and outlines which nonmaterialistic factors are of importance in the decision-making process, which may in turn affect levels of well-being. Although earlier the literature has shown the existence of a number of anomalies in economic behavior, the more recent literature has focused more on the implications for such anomalies for the well-being of consumers and households, which explains the focus of this chapter. The findings can be classified into the following three categories: reference effects, effort reduction, and values and experiences. Studies included in the first category suggest that relative outcomes can be more important for individuals than absolute outcomes. Studies in the second category recognize that much of the implemented innovations have the objective to establish effort reductions and therefore increase well-being. Finally, studies included in the third category suggest that individuals may, at a given point, derive well-being from experiences rather than from the (materialistic) consumption itself.

This chapter focuses not only on the individual decision-making process, but also on how nonmaterialistic factors influence this decision-making process within multiperson households. This is of importance, since nonmaterialistic factors can affect the household decision process itself or may lead to a more effective or efficient decision process when choosing between consumption alternatives.

This chapter proceeds as follows. Firstly, we illustrate that observed trends in subjective well-being are indeed driven by nonmaterialistic factors once lower needs have been satisfied. Secondly, we outline which nonmaterialistic factors are important in the individual decision-making process and how they may affect levels of well-being. We briefly summarize the economic models that exist on household decision-making, elaborate how nonmaterialistic factors can affect the household decision process, and pinpoint some differences when we compare this process to the individual decision process. We finish with conclusions and consider future research opportunities. Since the findings in the literature that we describe may also be relevant for policy making, we consider such implications in our final section.

11.2 Large-Scale Trends

A country's SWB is positively related to gross domestic product (GDP) per capita at a marginally decreasing rate, in agreement with the common shape of consumer utility functions (Dolan, Peasgood, and White, 2008; Clark, Frijters, and Shields, 2008). This relationship explains why a higher income may increase SWB relatively quickly for low-income countries (Frijters, Haisken-De New, and White, 2004; Inglehart et al., 2008) and relatively slowly for high-income countries (Easterlin, 2001, 2005). Stevenson and Wolfers (2013) show that SWB increases in *log income* at an even faster rate for high-income countries than for low-income countries. However, their findings still support the idea of a higher marginally decreasing rate of SWB in *income* for high-income countries than for low-income countries. Inglehart et al. (2008) explain these findings from a shift in focus on survival needs to a focus on nonmaterialistic factors, including self-expression values and free choice, as countries become wealthier. As soon as survival needs are fulfilled, further income increases no longer result in much higher SWB. Instead, at higher levels of income, more free choice and control over one's life may result in further increases in SWB. The idea of higher needs emerging after satisfaction of lower needs is consistent with Maslow's need hierarchy (1970). Free choice and self-expression values are part of the long-term trend from materialistic to postmaterialistic consumption values in the Western world (Inglehart, 1990, 1997). Indeed, Delhey (2009) finds that in high-income societies, personal autonomy values are more important in explaining happiness differences than income, whereas the same is true for societies characterized by postmaterialistic values. A related result is that one's job creativity ratings are more important in explaining happiness than income in such societies.

Materialistic values are characterized by traditional and survival values, such as authority, obedience, national pride, economic security, and economic growth. In contrast, postmaterialistic values include secular-rational and self-expression values, such as independence, democracy, freedom of expression, quality of life, and the development of new ideas and environmental values (Inglehart and Baker, 2000). Inglehart et al. (2008) used data from eighty-eight countries included in the World Values Survey, a large sociological survey taking place about every five years, to study changes in SWB. They found that the "sense of free choice" measure positively affected SWB, especially for countries with relatively high GDP per capita. Postmaterialistic factors affecting SWB also include perceptions of relative income and income inequality; consumption styles focused on social responsibility, sustainability, and collaborative consumption; political participation; and gender inequality, to be considered next.

Besides the consumption effect of the level of GDP, also the relative income effect within a country may influence SWB. Research shows that people evaluate their own income relatively to a certain reference level. People's reference level can be, for example, the average income in their country or the average income in their social reference group (Clark et al., 2008). Knight, Song, and Gunatilaka (2009) show that relative income is related more to SWB than the absolute income level. They find that judgments of one's own income as being lower than average resulted in much lower SWB than a higher-than-average income resulted in higher SWB. The latter finding is related to the shape of the SWB/utility function, which is steeper at the lower end of the income scale than at the higher end. Less income inequality obviously will reduce the low/high disparity and will increase SWB at the country level (Clark et al., 2008; Oishi and Kesebir, 2015). Alternatively, one might consider a low income as a loss compared to the average level, and a high income as a gain. Since losses count as heavier than commensurate gains in Prospect Theory (Kahneman and Tversky, 1979), the latter interpretation is qualitatively similar to the first.

In consumer research, consumer values have been related to consumption and life styles. A materialistic consumption style has been characterized by possessiveness, nongenerosity, and envy (Belk, 1985). Richins and Dawson (1992) define materialistic consumption as the importance a person places in acquisition centrality, acquisition as the pursuit of happiness, and possession-defined success. The well-known Values, Attitudes, and Lifestyles (VALS) methodology is also based on measuring consumer value types (Mitchell, 1983). Its latest version includes eight consumer types, whose consumption is driven by three different motivational routes: achievement, ideals, and self-expression. The achievement route seems most related to materialistic values (e.g., "money as source of authority"), whereas the routes of ideals (e.g., "rely on spirituality") and self-expression (e.g., "go against the current mainstream") seem to be based more on postmaterialistic values. Postmaterialistic values seem to be driving consumption into directions of buying brands from companies committed to social responsibility (Nielsen, 2014, 2015); sustainable buying behavior, especially for food (National Geographic, 2014; Greendex, 2014); shared or collaborative consumption (Hamari, Sjöklint, and Ukkonen, 2016); buying services instead of goods; and buying experiences instead of goods (Pine and Gilmore, 1999). Such consumer behaviors appear to have become more common in developed countries where basic needs already have been fulfilled. Also, Verain (2017) found a 10 percent increase in the sustainability-conscious segment of the Dutch population over a period of three years, indicating growth in sustainable food purchases.

Other large-scale trends in which postmaterialistic values may play a role are democratic political participation, which resulted in greater happiness in Switzerland (Frey and Stutzer, 2000), and decentralized political decisions that resulted in increased life satisfaction (Frey and Stutzer, 2002, 2012). Mencarini and Sironi (2012) used the European Social Survey including twenty-six European countries to study the effect of gender inequality on women's happiness ratings. They found that women's share of household work (a proxy for gender inequality) had a strong negative effect on women's happiness, taking into account a number of control variables, including the country Gender Gap (Haussmann, Tyson, and Zahidi, 2010). The latter variable captures a number of differences between men and women, reflecting a kind of reference level for gender inequality in a country. The country Gender Gap tended to increase women's happiness, whereas the household partners' gender inequality in household work tended to decrease it. The results show that the effect of gender inequality in household work is relative with respect to the country Gender Gap.

Sociological research shows a change in the way households have been considered in the welfare state in the Western world (Beck-Gernsheim, 2007). In the middle of the twentieth century, the prevailing model of households comprised married couples of men and women and a strongly gender-based division of labor. However, due to modernization and individualization processes, family structures and labor divisions have changed substantially. These processes have resulted in nontraditional household compositions (Du and Kamakura, 2006), such as remarriage and blended families, and a focus on individual needs and obligations, such as individual benefits and taxes, in governmental policies. Individual freedom and options have replaced traditional social relations, bonds, and beliefs (Beck-Gernsheim, 2007). Van Klaveren and Maassen van den Brink (2007); Carriero, Ghysels, and Van Klaveren (2009); and Van Klaveren, Van Praag, and Maassen van den Brink (2012) furthermore show that the synchronization of labor hours, and, more generally, the intra-household decision process have become increasingly important for these non-traditional household compositions. The development of household economic models, focusing more on household decision-making, or bargaining, seems to reflect these changes in family processes. It has been recognized that nonmaterialistic factors such as altruism, fairness, and equality in decision-making power deserve their place also in economic models of the household. The three main household economic models that have increasingly used such nonmaterialistic factors are unitary models, bargaining models, and collective household models.

11.3 Consumer and Household Behavior

11.3.1 Reference Effects

A general phenomenon studied in economic psychology and behavioral economics is the consumer's sensitivity to changes rather than to absolute outcomes, or states (Kahneman, 2003). It can be argued that the absolute value of income becomes less important as the income level rises and primary consumption needs are satisfied to a greater extent. It follows that consumers are relatively more sensitive to relative income changes when nonmaterialistic factors become increasingly important, and because these changes always occur in relation to a reference state, this phenomenon is referred to as reference effects. We will discuss several such reference effects in relation to SWB, including joint versus separate evaluation of choice alternatives, social comparison effects, effects of past income, aspirations, endowment and status quo effects, the evaluation of a series of outcomes, and the evaluation of the outcomes of household decision-making.

A well-known behavioral economic finding is the influence of reference effects on consumer judgment and SWB. For example, Hsee (1996) and Hsee, Rottenstreich, and Stutzer (2012) have shown that consumer evaluations of goods presented in isolation may be significantly different from those of goods presented jointly. In joint evaluation the goods can be compared, such that one good is evaluated relative to the other good. Such evaluations are important for consumers' SWB. One illustrative finding is an experiment by Yang et al. (2011) where consumers could choose between two digital picture frames. One frame looked ugly but had higher picture resolution, the other frame looked attractive but had lower picture resolution. Under separate evaluation (isolation), 85 percent chose the attractive but less sharp picture, whereas under joint evaluation, where the picture resolution was also stated, 53 percent chose the ugly but sharper model. Isolated choices yielded higher feelings of happiness, whereas choices under joint evaluation resulted in lower feelings of happiness. Hsee et al. (2012) state that most consumer choices are made under joint evaluation mode (e.g., buying a television set), whereas the experienced happiness takes place under a separate evaluation mode, that is, without comparing one's chosen television set with other sets. This situation creates ample opportunities for nonoptimal consumer choice. One possible instrument that may help overcome such nonoptimal choices is customer reviews based on actual experiences after choice. Such reviews may inform consumers about what they can expect after making a choice rather than infer those expectations from comparative information before making a choice. Also, outside of the consumption area, people usually compare a particular alternative with a reference alternative, such as other people's outcomes, one's own previous outcomes, default options, and (sense of) ownership. In general, it has been found that the choice of alternatives that are better than other people's outcomes tend to make people happier. For example, when people were asked whether they preferred A (Your current yearly income is $50,000; others earn $25,000) or B (Your current yearly income is $100,000; others earn $200,000),[1] 56 percent chose A, although its spending power was only half that of B (Solnick and Hemingway, 1998). Similar results were obtained for one's intelligence, attractiveness, education, and holidays. However, the results ranged from 18 percent to 80 percent, indicating that the social comparison effect varies for different issues. This example, although hypothetical, shows that status concerns, or concerns for social comparison, may affect one's preferences. Research on income evaluation shows that the higher the average income in their social reference group, the worse people evaluate their own income (Kapteyn, Van Praag, and Van Herwaarden, 1978; Melenberg, 1992). Ferrer-i-Carbonell (2005) reanalyzed data (1992–1997) from the German Socio-Economic Panel, with social reference group defined as individuals with similar education, age, and living area as the respondent in the survey. People's SWB appeared to be higher the higher their income was compared with the average income in their social reference group. The social comparison effect was found to be larger, and the own-income effect to be smaller, in relatively wealthy West Germany as compared to East Germany, showing that this nonmaterialistic factor was more important in the wealthier country.

Another reference point relevant to SWB is past income. People seem to adapt to income changes just as they adapt to different kinds of sensory experiences, for example, to the taste of sweetness, the sense of darkness, or the pressure of their shoes. Although in the first few years after an income change SWB is affected, the effect seems to level off quickly. Di Tella, Haisken-De New, and MacCulloch (2010) find that after four years, the effect of an income change had no significant effect on SWB any more, due to adaptation. Van Praag and Van Weeren (1988) show that the evaluation of current income is affected by one's own past income, but the effect is much lower for incomes in the more distant past than for incomes in the recent past. Interestingly, the effect is different for people at different ages. For a twenty-year-old individual, 50 percent of the weight given to past income is concentrated between the present and 1.6 years in the past, thus showing a rapid decline in the effect of past income. The income evaluation of a fifty-year-old individual is not affected by past income at all. For a seventy-year-old individual, 50 percent of the weight is concentrated between the present and 0.4 years in the past. Apparently, young people attach somewhat more weight to past incomes than older people because they may lack experience to form clear expectations about the future. Older people attach weight to the past because their future is relatively short. Either way, the effect of past income on current SWB is very limited. Antonides (2007) studied the effect of an income decline up to two years in the past. Although the length of time after the income drop did not affect income evaluation and happiness, information seeking about the consequences of the income decline had a positive effect, whereas not taking precautionary measures to mitigate the effects of the income decline had a negative effect on income evaluation and happiness, given the new (lower) income. This study shows that nonmaterialistic factors, in addition to income, further explain changes in SWB.

An important reason why happiness does not increase so much with a rise in income is the breeding of new aspirations after adaptation to the higher income level (Easterlin, 2005). It appears that, after fulfilling one's current aspirations – for example, obtaining a higher income after graduation from university – new aspirations may develop, such as owning a house. The needs associated with the new level of aspiration are not yet met, so it seems as if the income is not sufficient to satisfy the new needs, leading to a relatively low level of happiness. The ever-repeating cycle of adaptation to new situations and the breeding of new aspirations is called the *hedonic treadmill* (Kahneman, 1999). Easterlin (2005) shows that aspirations change in proportion to income over the consumer's life cycle, thus eroding subjective well-being. This process shows the discrepancy between decision utility, the expected happiness when aspirations are fulfilled, and experienced utility at the moment of evaluating the realized outcomes. It also points to decision errors when consumers take into account materialistic aspirations *ex ante*, the effect of which may disappear *ex post* (see also Section 11.3.3). However, although the hedonic treadmill tends to erode subjective well-being, it does not imply that people cannot be made more happy. That is, they may report relatively low global well-being, although during their actual life episodes, they may experience more happiness if their life circumstances improve.

The endowment effect states that people place more value on their possessions when they own them than when they do not own them (Thaler, 1980; Kahneman, Knetsch, and Thaler, 1990). The endowment effect is evident from a higher compensation demanded to part with a good in one's endowment than willingness to pay to acquire the same good. The implication of the endowment effect is that people may experience more wealth, and possibly happiness, after acquiring material possessions, at least temporarily. The endowment effect reflects a more general effect, associated with the reference point (Kahneman, Knetsch, and Thaler, 1991). In the default situation of non-ownership, any acquisition of a good counts as a gain, which is associated with a moderate increase in utility, or happiness. However, after acquisition, the default situation has become ownership, in which giving up the good counts as a loss, which is associated with a relatively high decrease in utility, or happiness. It has been shown that the endowment effect is even stronger for hedonic types of goods – goods that are emotionally appealing to one's senses – than for utilitarian types of goods – goods of practical value (Antonides and Cramer, 2013; Cramer and Antonides, 2011). The difference in utility, or happiness change, can be explained by the asymmetric value function from Prospect Theory, indicating aversion to losses (Kahneman and Tversky, 1979). Burchardt (2005) finds that an increase in income as compared to the previous year had a moderate positive effect on satisfaction with income, whereas a commensurate income decrease had a relatively strong negative effect, thus supporting the asymmetric evaluation of positive and negative income changes. In order to smooth changes in well-being over time, it appears to be more important (for governments) to avoid negative changes in GDP than to aim for an average increase in GDP over the years (Greenglass et al., 2014).

An extension of the loss aversion effect is the influence of default situations on people's evaluation of their own choices. A default situation generally counts as the status quo, for example, the current practice in the United States of choosing one's own pension contribution, leading to relatively low contributions (Madrean and Shea, 2001). Usually, a deviation from the status quo will be experienced as a loss, and hence will be considered relatively unattractive. So, in the latter situation, people will be reluctant to contribute more to their pension. Conversely, changing the status quo into a new default, for example, a standard pension contribution of 6 percent of one's salary, will result in the relative unattractiveness of contributions less than 6 percent. It has been shown that a change in default status will remain effective at least for several years (Thaler and Benartzi, 2004).

Endowment effects and default effects seem to run counter to the idea of adaptation and the hedonic treadmill. The difference may occur because the two ideas usually refer to two different situations. Adaptation and hedonic treadmill effects usually pertain to gains in income or wealth, whereas endowment and default effects usually occur in situations of losses (parting with a good, or deviating from the status quo). Further research needs to be conducted in order to separate out the two effects across different situations.

Reference effects also may occur in dynamic choices, that is, choices with consequences that occur over time. For example, Hsee (1996) found that people tend to prefer an increasing series of four annual salaries to a decreasing series, although the decreasing series offered $1,000 more salary per year than the increasing series. Obviously, people did not like the year-on-year negative changes in the decreasing series due to loss aversion. For the same reason, people tend to prefer more attractive events to occur later than earlier in a series (Loewenstein and Prelec, 1992; Ross and Simonson, 1991). Such preferences can be explained by the peak-and-end rule, stating that a series of events is mainly evaluated on the basis of the most extreme outcome (the peak) and the final outcome of the series (Kahneman, 1994). Also, the evaluation of single events can be evaluated differently, depending on the timing of such events. Loewenstein (1987) shows people's eagerness to experience unattractive events (e.g., an electric shock) sooner rather than later, thus indicating the effect of dread. Conversely, people value the prolonged anticipation of positive events (e.g., a kiss from one's favorite movie star). Reference effects in dynamic choices have direct implications for the timing of events, and the design of series of events, or even of events during one's entire life. For example, financial planners may advise people to aim for increasing their expenditures over time rather than keeping a stable expenditure flow. Likewise, it is advisable to overcome unpleasant events, such as medical procedures, as quickly as possible. Alternatively, pleasant events such as a round-the-world trip, or the purchase of one's dream car, should be delayed in order to savor these events.

Reference effects may also play a role in household decision-making. In the 1980s and 1990s, Manser and Brown (1980), McElroy and Horney (1981), and, later, Lundberg and Pollak (1993) proposed a cooperative Nash bargaining model (NBM) to describe household behavior, thus recognizing the household partners' interactive decision-making process. The model assumes that partners bargain over the gains of marriage, but if no bargaining agreement is reached, then it is assumed that both partners receive a threshold utility. This threshold level has been defined differently in the literature. Manser and Brown (1980), and McElroy and Horney (1981) refer to the threshold utility level as the utility level obtained if the marriage (or partnership) is dissolved and define this level as the maximum level of utility that can be obtained without considering the family (fall-back situation). Himmelweit et al. (2013) refer to this model as a divorce threat model. Lundberg and Pollak (1993) argued that divorce might be dominated by sharing public goods within an intact but noncooperative marriage and, as a consequence, that the threshold utility levels should be internalized rather than externalized. The latter model is referred to as the separate spheres model (Himmelweit et al., 2013). Threshold utility levels may be considered as reference points against which the partners' realized outcomes are evaluated, rather than evaluating the absolute outcomes of household decision-making. Such models may be considered as complex types of ultimatum bargaining games (Güth and Kocher, 2013) in which lack of a negotiated agreement results in zero outcomes for the negotiation parties. A common finding in ultimatum games are the nonzero offers of the allocators (typically about 40 percent of the total outcome size) and nonminimal demands of recipients (typically not lower than 25 percent). Ultimatum games point to the general preference for fairness, which also plays a part in household decision-making.

11.3.2 Effort Reduction

An important nonmaterialistic factor in creating well-being is effort reduction. Industrialization and product innovations have contributed to the reduction of physical effort, cognitive effort, and the time spent on effort. With respect to physical effort, one can think of consumer product innovations, such as the washing machine and vacuum cleaners, which made life much easier for consumers in addition to creating time savings. Additionally, automatization and robotization have led to a more comfortable work and living environment, leading to increased leisure and work satisfaction (Bii and Wanyama, 2001; Gombolay et al., 2015). Further investments in technological innovations could contribute to increased future SWB levels. Consumer rating websites are also important to mention in this respect, as search efforts are nowadays substantially reduced by these websites when consumers have to decide between consumption alternatives.

Effort reduction also is an important factor in decision-making that is neglected in rational decision-making models. Simplified decision-making is an issue in dual processing theory, precommitments, cognitive scarcity in case of poverty, mental accounting, and household decision-making, to be considered next.

Behavioral economics and economic psychology have come up with distinctions in several types of cognitive effort that may affect consumer decision-making. One class of cognitive effort types is dual processing (Kahneman, 2011), basically consisting of two types of thinking. System I type of thinking is intuitive and fast, using decision heuristics that may produce errors and biases in decision-making. For example, suppose we ask people the following question: "If it takes five machines five minutes to make five widgets, how long would it take 100 machines to make 100 widgets?" The intuitive answer is 100 minutes (Frederick, 2005). However, the answer is wrong. System I type of thinking is the default type of thinking, according to Kahneman (2011), unlike standard economic assumptions. Only when something appears wrong, people engage in System II type of thinking, which is more rational, rule-based and slow, but will lead to the correct answer. The rule-based answer to the preceding problem could be that the number of widgets equals the number of machines times the number of minutes "the number of widgets per machine per minute." The latter term equals 1/5 from the first part of the information. By the same rule, inserting 1/5, we can calculate that it takes five minutes for the 100 machines to produce 100 widgets. A number of cognitive heuristics, or rules of thumb, have been investigated, including, for example, relying on readily available information (availability), plausible representations of the world (representativeness), and arbitrary numbers (anchoring) (see Kahneman, 2011; Kahneman and Tversky, 2000; Kahneman, Slovic, and Tversky, 1982).

System I type of thinking saves cognitive effort and in many cases leads to the correct judgments or decisions, which makes life relatively easy. However, in a number of cases System I leads to systematic errors, the circumstances of which have been investigated in research. Then, by using these insights, practical interventions may be used to avoid the errors or to use System I type of thinking to the benefit of decision makers. The latter type of intervention is also known as nudging (Thaler and Sunstein, 2008). Examples of popular types of nudging (see Antonides, 2011b) are changing the status quo (playing on the default effect), framing (playing on asymmetric valuation), and self-control devices (limiting the effects of impatience). The aforementioned example of pension contribution uses the default effect to the advantage of decision makers using System I type of thinking.

A specific type of cognitive effort is involved in self-control problems, an illustrative example of which is shown in the famous marshmallow experiments at Stanford University (Mischel, Ebbesen, and Raskoff Zeiss, 1972). Children were presented with a few marshmallows and were told that they could obtain more marshmallows if they did not eat them in the absence of the experimenter. Then the experimenter left the room for some time. The children used different techniques for not eating the marshmallows, including not paying attention, counting the marshmallows over and over again, and clapping their hands. This situation is quite similar to economic saving to gain future benefits. Thaler and Shefrin (1981) conceptualized the situation as a principal–agent problem in which a planner (the agent) could influence the behavior of the doer (the principal) by limiting the actions of the latter. The planner is the part of one's personality that may be considered as the ego (acting consciously) in Freudian terminology, whereas the doer is considered the id (acting on instincts). The doer is impatient and wants to gratify immediate desires. The planner is more realistic and oversees the future consequences of the doer. That is why the planner can limit the actions of the doer by, for example, precommitments. Precommitments may be irreversible measures to reduce impatience, for example, a formal contract to arrange monthly saving of a fixed amount of one's salary. Alternatively, a precommitment can be an arrangement that is costly to break, for example, a public promise on the website Stickk.com to pay an amount if one does not meet a certain aim (e.g., losing 10 kilos of weight). The planner–doer distinction has some support in neurological evidence for different brain functions for long-term and short-term types of decision-making (McClure et al., 2004). Although precommitments limit one's free choice, they make life easier because one does not face so many situations in which to exert active self-control.

A factor that increases the cognitive load in making economic decisions is poverty. Mullainathan and Shafir (2013) present evidence for the effects of poverty on the availability of cognitive resources, leading to the so-called scarcity hypothesis. Because the poor focus very much on the fulfillment of immediate needs, they have fewer resources available to pay attention to other issues. Hence, they perform less well on cognitive performance tasks and pay less attention to future consequences of their decisions than wealthier people, even when background factors such as education are controlled. One psychological mechanism behind cognitive scarcity is cognitive depletion, in which cognitive resources are considered as limited (Vohs, 2013). Since the poor have to make many trade-offs in spending limited amounts on necessary goods, their cognitive resources are gradually depleted, and they are unable to use them for other issues such as self-control (Hofman et al., 2012). Increasing the level of social benefits and/or decreasing obligations to secure these benefits might help reduce cognitive scarcity.

Another device to limit one's cognitive effort is mental accounting in which people's expenditures on different categories of goods are separated, such that money reserved for one category will not be spent on another one (Antonides and Ranyard, 2018; Thaler, 1999). The standard microeconomic assumption that consumers' marginal utility of spending is the same for all different ways of spending (e.g., Frank and Cartwright, 2013) cannot be applied in this case, since it requires fungibility of money. Mental accounting facilitates one's overview of expenditures because the marginal utility of a purchase does not have to be compared with that of all other purchases, but only with purchases in the category of interest (Antonides, De Groot, and Van Raaij, 2011). In this respect, mental accounting helps to prevent overspending and serves as a self-control device. Mental accounting may be considered as a financial capability factor contributing to financial management and preventing debts, especially among lower-educated and lower-income consumers. Alternatively, innovations in e-finance may help consumers to manage their mental accounts by making budgeting, and booking and posting of expenses, easier.

A different way of accounting expenses occurs in household decision making. Becker's model of household behavior (1965) is referred to as the *unitary model* because no individual preferences are specified: there are only household decisions that can be accurately described by *one single* household utility function. An immediate consequence of modeling household behavior in this manner is that single- and multiperson households are treated similarly and, as a result, the intrahousehold decision process in multiperson households is considered to be a black box. Furthermore, the *income pooling* assumption of unitary models assumes that *only* the sum of income earned by the household members affects the allocation of goods and time. Thereby, it is irrelevant which member of the household earns the income, and the model predicts that household demand will be similar before and after a change in the division of nonlabor income. The income pooling assumption is rejected by many empirical studies. For example, Lundberg, Pollak, and Wales (1997) examine the effect an exogenous change in the distribution of the nonlabor household income has on the demand for certain goods. The exogenous change was a policy change in the United Kingdom in the late 1970s, which implied that "suddenly" a substantial child allowance was transferred from the father to the mother. The unitary model predicts that this policy change does not affect household demand since the pooled household income does not change at an aggregate level. However, Lundberg et al. (1997) find that the redistribution of income caused a shift toward greater expenditures on women's clothing and children's clothing relative to men's clothing. Pahl (2000) finds that only about half of all couples in the United Kingdom pool their incomes and share management of the pool, whereas in most of the remaining couples either the wife or the husband manages household finance. Burgoyne et al. (2007) find that household partners generally start off managing their finances independently or pooling partially, in order to keep a partnership of equals, and achieving fairness. However, when children are born or a mortgage is required, they shift toward more merging of finances. In general, since many empirical studies have rejected the income pooling assumption, it can thus be argued that this assumption is overly restrictive.

The most general type of household model is the collective model (Chiappori, 1988, 1997; Apps and Rees, 1997), which is less restrictive than the NBM and the unitary model. Household behavior can be described as if the household maximizes a weighted sum of the individual utility functions subject to the budget constraint and two time constraints (one for each partner). An intuitive interpretation of the weight is that it reflects the division of bargaining power between the partners. The division of bargaining power may be related to, for example, divorce laws, the ratio of single (wo)men to nonsingle (wo)men, or the allocation of child benefits to one of the partners. Both Dobbelsteen and Kooreman (1997) and Antonides (2011a) have found that the husband's engagement in financial management and investment decisions is positively influenced by his wage rate, thus providing evidence for the bargaining model and against the standard household economic model (which would predict a negative influence because of the opportunity cost associated with the wage rate).

If no distribution factor is included in the collective model, then household members are assumed to pool their incomes (see, among others, Van Klaveren, Van Praag, and Maassen van den Brink, 2008, 2011; Van Klaveren and Ghysels, 2012). Vogler, Lyonette, and Wiggins (2008) find that 63 to 68 percent of respondents in couple relationships report that major decisions are made jointly, whereas only about 20 percent are either male or female dominated. However, even in joint decision-making, bargaining power may be distributed unequally between the household partners because a larger contribution to the common pool of resources may increase one's entitlement to, and desire to control, spending from it (Burgoyne et al., 2007). Concerning the type of conflicts, Kirchler et al. (2001) report that 23 percent concerned economic matters, and in around 55 percent of these conflicts one or the other partner had more influence. Both the bargaining model and the collective household economic model include nonmaterialistic factors such as reference effects in household economic evaluations, fairness considerations, and bargaining power determinants.

11.3.3 Values and Experiences

In addition to the sociological study of the postmaterialistic trend, economic psychologists have conducted research into the motivational effects of consumption. These effects include the distinction between experiential and material purchases, values and needs associated with sustainability, emotions, consumer participation, and household decision-making, to be considered next.

Van Boven (2005) has made a distinction between *experiential purchases*, defined as "those made with the primary intention of acquiring a life experience: an event or series of events that one encounters, lives through, and 'consumes'" (p. 134), for example, dinners and travel; and *material purchases*, defined as "those made with the primary intention of acquiring a material possession: a tangible object physically retained in one's possession" (p. 134), for example, clothing, jewelry, and televisions. It turned out that people who had purchased any of these items were more happy thinking about experiential than material purchases, and thought that experiential purchases had contributed more to their overall happiness in life, that the money was spent well, and that the money could not have been spent better on something else, than material purchases. In addition to the effect that experiential purchases made people happier than material purchases, the effect was stronger for people at higher income levels. The latter finding seems to support the idea that at higher income levels, other needs have to be satisfied by consumption than at lower income levels. This finding provides opportunities for suppliers to increase the attractiveness of their products and services.

Issues of sustainability and the environment are associated with higher values and higher needs, as opposed to survival values. Also, it is likely that such values become important at higher levels of income, such that sustainability and environmental conditions may affect SWB in developed countries. Indeed, relationships between environmental issues and SWB have been found. Welsch (2007) finds a negative effect of the level of nitrogen dioxide pollution on SWB in fifty-four countries across the world. Nitrogen dioxide pollution may eventually lead to respiratory illness and lung damage. Van Praag and Baarsma (2005) estimate a negative effect of perceived noise from aircrafts around Schiphol Airport in the Netherlands on SWB. Welsch and Kühling (2010, 2011) show that SWB is positively affected by consumers' own consumption of sustainable appliances and lighting, green household products, recycling, and water conservation, given their attitudes toward the environment. Furthermore, Welsch and Kühling (2010) find that these effects are larger for materialistic consumers. They consider these effects as decision errors, since especially materialistic consumers might become happier by consuming more sustainably than they currently do.

Onwezen, Antonides, and Bartels (2013); and Onwezen, Bartels, and Antonides, 2014a) have shown that consumers' anticipated emotions of pride and guilt, being more specific experiences of SWB, guide consumers' sustainable purchase intentions. That is, consumers intend to purchase more organic and fair-trade food products if they expect to be proud of such behavior, or feel guilty if they would not buy such products. The influence of these emotions has been found in both individualistic and collectivistic types of countries (Onwezen,

Bartels, and Antonides, 2014b). Obviously, emotions may be used in the marketing of sustainable consumer food products.

Another factor associated with postmaterialism is consumer participation, which can be accomplished, among other possibilities, in paid labor and volunteer work, household decision-making, and consumer activities, in addition to political participation studied by Frey and Stutzer (2000, 2002, 2012). Warr (1999) points to the effect of having a job on SWB. Especially the fact that work is related to goals that transcend one's own personal goals contributes to SWB (see also Van Raaij and Antonides, 1991). Cantor and Sanderson (1999) state that all kinds of activities in which individuals can freely choose to pursue their personal goals, which are intrinsically valued, performed at a feasible level, and facilitated in their daily life context, lead to SWB. In addition to paid jobs, such activities may include, for example, volunteer work and care giving. In the consumer area, activities such as co-creation (e.g., Van Dijk, Antonides, and Schillewaert, 2014), chat groups, and blogs may provide such features.

Some empirical evidence for bargaining and nonmaterialistic factors in household decision-making has been found. It appears that, in the United States, the influence of household partners in decision-making concerning household expenditures has become more equal over time (Belch and Willis, 2002). That is, the influence of the husband generally has decreased, whereas the influence of the wife has increased in almost all stages of the decision-making process. Vogler et al. (2008) find a strong positive effect of joint decision-making on satisfaction with family life, as opposed to one-partner-dominated decisions. Satisfaction with family life, in turn, positively affected happiness with life in general. Also, cultural values, participation, and negotiation power can be distribution factors that affect SWB of the household partners. Van den Troost et al. (2006) found that the husband's (positive) valuation of traditional roles and tasks in the household negatively affected the wife's marital satisfaction, whereas the wife's familialism – valuing the family's traditional way of life – had a positive effect on her satisfaction. Dia Sow (2010) has found positive effects of women's responsibility in buying food, and managing household finance, on women's income evaluation. Fofana et al. (2015) have shown that women receiving microcredit reported higher decision-making power than women not receiving microcredit. Furthermore, the spouses' perceptions of gains and losses and (behavioral) costs have been found to influence the fairness of decisions taken by husband or wife (Antonides and Kroft, 2005). For example, large expenditures made by one partner are considered relatively fair by the other partner when the former earns more salary, but not in the case where incomes remain the same. As noted previously, marital satisfaction, income evaluations, and fairness all may contribute to general SWB. Policies focusing on gender equality in household decision-making, labor participation, and the performance of household tasks thus might increase SWB of both partners in the household.

11.4 Conclusions, Policy Implications, and Future Research Opportunities

We have argued that nonmaterialistic factors are becoming more important in decision-making beyond a certain income level. This idea seems to be reflected in both the economic-psychological and the economic literature and leads to a number of opportunities for policies aimed at increasing consumer and household welfare. In addition to implications for individual decision makers, and advisors such as financial planners, the research findings presented in this chapter suggest a number of different policy measures that would influence decision-making and the well-being of households and consumers in developed countries. A general conclusion is that behavior frequently deviates from expectations of policy makers and from standard economic models, mainly based on effects of consumption on well-being, because potentially important behavioral mechanisms are not recognized. In the following subsections, we discuss the main conclusions and consider the limitations of this overview.

11.4.1 Conclusions and Policy Implications

Our overview is based on mostly nonmaterialistic decision-making factors that have an influence on SWB of consumers and households, which has become topical in contemporary research in economic psychology and economics. Consulting the ProQuest database, we have observed a sharp relative increase in attention to SWB since the early 1990s. The fraction of publications having "well-being" or "happiness" in the title was 0.5 percent of the total number of publications in scholarly journals from 1981 to 1989, which has increased to 5.5 percent from 2006 to 2015. The tenfold increase shows the relevance of SWB in the study of human behavior, reflected in our overview of the field. It suggests that the study of consumers and households has shifted from showing the existence of economic-psychological and behavioral-economic effects on behavior to assessing the influence of these effects on SWB. Such a shift is important in showing the relevance of these effects to policy makers and is worth studying further in future research.

Policies that have the objective of increasing the quality of decision-making and SWB should acknowledge that not all behavior is driven by attempts at increasing consumption, especially in developed economies, and should take into account nonmaterialistic factors. One type of relatively successful policy measures may be based on postmaterialistic values, such as increasing personal autonomy by promoting free choice, political participation, and creativity; reducing government and employer regulations; and reducing income inequality. It has been shown that a reduction of income inequality can be effectively achieved by a redistributative taxation (Akay et al., 2012). An opportunity to avoid a decline in SWB is preventing income shocks, either by smoothing the development of the national income or by stimulating household precautionary measures against income decline. Also, diminishing gender inequality in household work and in the bargaining power of household partners might increase SWB of an individual within multiperson households, either directly or indirectly (via the partner's SWB). Such policies may be aimed at increasing SWB in a number of different ways, including offering information, providing incentives, and changing the context of choice (Antonides, 2011b), among others.

With regard to product offerings, a trend toward more sustainable, collaborative, and experiential types of consumption seems to exist. It might be the case that breeding more sustainable consumer aspirations may avoid the hedonic treadmill effect. One way of promoting the consumption of experiences is using consumer ratings or likings for such consumption on the Internet and social media. Moreover, government can support, or even develop, rating sites for certain products and services that can have a major impact on levels of well-being (e.g., health care, education, food).

Also, consumer participation might be increased by customer-driven innovations such as co-creation, customization, and crowd-sourcing (Prahalad and Ramaswamy, 2000). An important way of increasing the quality of decision-making and SWB is facilitating consumer information processing by reducing the effort spent on decision-making. This may be accomplished by policies aimed at providing easily accessible information (e.g., labels) and product ratings, nudging (e.g., by employing status quo alternatives), providing self-control devices, and simplifying financial tools.

11.4.2 Future Research Opportunities

A number of issues in assessing the effects of decision-making remain to be investigated. Since adaptation may result in happiness "leaking away," one might ask whether the current focus on happiness is worthwhile at all. Also, some of the variation in happiness is genetically determined or at least stable in the long run. On the other hand, adaptation to life events is incomplete in many cases (Lucas, 2007). The processes of adaptation and the existence of a set point of happiness are still not well understood and deserve future research effort.

Many results concerning decision-making and SWB come from surveys and laboratory experiments, and their validity in the field still has to be assessed. Field studies may comprise a number of different methodologies, including, for example, experiments (Harrison and List, 2004), qualitative methods, and observations (see, for example, Antonides, 2018). A fascinating new methodology in this respect is the study of economic events influencing happiness expressions on social media (Brandwatch, 2015; Dodds et al., 2011).

In addition to showing the existence of factors influencing decision-making, the question of how these factors affect SWB has become topical. Rather than assuming optimal decision-making of consumers and households, as is common in models based on revealed preference, more realistic insights into the effects of decision-making factors should be obtained. In our view, this objective should be pursued by the best possible research methodology, as advocated in this chapter.

Note

1 People were told that prices were the same in states A and B.

11.5 References

Akay, A., Bargain, O., Dolls, M., Neumann, D., Peichl, A., and Siegloch, S. (2012). Happy Taxpayers? Income Taxation and Well-Being. Bonn: IZA Discussion Paper No. 6999.

Altman, M. (2015). *Real-World Decision Making: An Encyclopedia of Behavioral Economics*. Santa Barbara, CA: ABC-CLIO.

Antonides, G. (2007). Income Evaluation and Happiness in the Case of an Income Decline. *Kyklos*, 60(4), 467–484.

Antonides, G. (2008). Comparing Models of Consumer Behavior. In: Lewis, A. (Ed.), *The Cambridge Handbook of Psychology and Economic Behavior* (pp. 227–252). Cambridge, UK: Cambridge University Press.

Antonides, G. (2011a). The Division of Household Tasks and Household Financial Management. *Journal of Psychology*, 219(4), 198–208.

Antonides, G. (2011b). Behavioral Economics Applied: Suggestions for Policy Making. In: P. Martin, F. Cheung, M. Kyrios, L. et al. (Eds.). *The IAAP Handbook of Applied Psychology* (pp. 500–524). Chichester, UK: Wiley-Blackwell.

Antonides, G. (2018). Research Methods for Economic Psychology. In: Ranyard, R. (Ed.) *Economic Psychology: The Science of Economic Mental Life and Behavior*. Chichester, UK: Wiley-Blackwell.

Antonides, G., and Cramer, L. (2013). Impact of Limited Cognitive Capacity and Feelings of Guilt and Excuse on the Endowment Effects for Hedonic and Utilitarian Types of Foods. *Appetite*, 68, 51–55.

Antonides, G., De Groot, I. M., and Van Raaij, W. F. (2011). Mental Budgeting and the Management of Household Finance. *Journal of Economic Psychology*, 32, 546–555.

Antonides, G., and Kroft, M. (2005). Fairness Judgments in Household Decision Making. *Journal of Economic Psychology*, 26, 902–913.

Antonides, G., and Ranyard, R. (2018). Mental Accounting and Economic Behavior. In: Ranyard, R. (Ed.), *Economic Psychology: The Science of Economic Mental Life and Behavior*. Chichester, UK: Wiley-Blackwell.

Apps, P. F., and Rees, R. (1997). Collective Labor Supply and Household Production. *Journal of Political Economy*, 105, 178–190.

Beck-Gernsheim, E. (2007). From 'the Family' to 'Families': How Individualisation and Globalisation Are Changing Our Personal Lives. *Soundings*, 35(1), 105–114.

Becker, G. S. (1965). A Theory of the Allocation of Time. *Economic Journal*, 75, 493–517.

Becker, G. S. (1991). *A Treatise on the Family*. Cambridge, UK: Cambridge University Press.

Belch, M. A., and Willis, L. A. (2002). Family Decision at the Turn of the Century: Has the Changing Structure of Households Impacted the Decision-Making Process? *Journal of Consumer Behavior*, 2(2), 111–124.

Belk, R. W. (1985). Materialism: Trait Aspects of Living in a Material World. *Journal of Consumer Research*, 12, 265–280.

Bii, H. K., and Wanyama, P. (2001). Automation and Its Impact on the Job Satisfaction Among the Staff of the Margaret Thatcher Library, Moi University. *Library Management*, 22(6/7), 303–310.

Brandwatch (2015). *The Twitter Happiness Report*. Brighton, UK: Brandwatch.

Browning, M., Chiappori, P. A., and Lechene, V. (2006). Collective and Unitary Models: A Clarification. *Review of Economics of the Household*, 4, 5–14.

Brickman, P., and Coates, D. (1987). Commitment and Mental Health. In: Brickman, P. (Ed.), *Commitment, Conflict, and Caring* (pp. 222–309). Englewood Cliffs, NJ: Prentice Hall.

Burchardt, T. (2005). Are One Man's Rags Another Man's Riches? Identifying Adaptive Expectations Using Panel Data. *Social Indicators Research*, 74(1), 57–102.

Burgoyne, C. B., Reibstein, J., Edmunds, A., and Dolman, V. (2007). Money Management Systems in Early Marriage: Factors Influencing Change and Stability. *Journal of Economic Psychology*, 28, 214–228.

Cantor, N., and Sanderson, C. A. (1999). Life Task Participation and Well-Being: The Importance of Taking Part in Daily Life. In: Kahneman, D., Diener, E., and Schwarz, N. (Eds.), *Well-Being: The Foundations of Hedonic Psychology* (pp. 230–243). New York: Russell Sage Foundation.

Carriero, R., Ghysels, J., and Van Klaveren, C. (2009). Do Parents Coordinate Their Work Schedules? A Comparison of Dutch, Flemish, and Italian Dual-Earner Households. *European Sociological Review*, 25(5), 603–617.

Chiappori, P. A. (1988). Rational Household Labor Supply. *Econometrica*, 56(1), 63–90.

Chiappori, P. A. (1997). Introducing Household Production in Collective Models of Labor Supply. *Journal of Political Economy*, 105, 191–209.

Clark, A. E., Frijters, P., and Shields, M. A. (2008). Relative Income, Happiness, and Utility: An Explanation for the Easterlin Paradox and Other Puzzles. *Journal of Economic Literature*, 46(1), 95–144.

Cramer, L., and Antonides, G. (2011). Endowment Effects for Hedonic and Utilitarian Food Products. *Food Quality and Preference*, 22, 3–10.

Delhey, J. (2009). *World Values Research*, 2(2), 30–54.

Dia Sow, F. (2010). Intrahousehold Resource Allocation and Well-Being. Wageningen: PhD thesis, Wageningen University.

Di Tella, R., Haisken-De New, J., and MacCulloch, R. (2010). Happiness Adaptation to Income and to Status in an Individual Panel. *Journal of Economic Behavior and Organization*, 76, 834–852.

Dobbelsteen, S., and Kooreman, P. (1997). Financial Management, Bargaining and Efficiency Within the Household: An Empirical Analysis. *De Economist*, 145, 345–366.

Dodds, P. S., Harris, K. D., Kloumann, I. M., Bliss, C. A., and Danforth, C. M. (2011). Temporal Patterns of Happiness and Information in a Global Social Network: Hedonometrics and Twitter. *PLoS ONE*, 6(12), e26752.

Dolan, P., Peasgood, T., and White, M. (2008). Do We Really Know What Makes Us Happy? A Review of the Economic Literature on the Factors Associated with Subjective Well-Being. *Journal of Economic Psychology*, 29, 94–122.

Du, R. Y., and Kamakura, W.A. (2006). Household Life Cycles and Lifestyles in the United States. *Journal of Marketing Research* (February), 121–132.

Easterlin, R. A. (2001). Income and Happiness: Towards a Unified Theory. *Economic Journal*, 111, 465–484.

Easterlin, R. A. (2005). A Puzzle for Adaptive Theory. *Journal of Economic Behavior and Organization*, 56, 513–521.

Ferrer-i-Carbonell, A. (2005). Income and Well-Being: An Empirical Analysis of the Comparison Income Effect. *Journal of Public Economics*, 89, 997–1019.

Fofana, N. B., Antonides, G., Niehof, A., and Van Ophem, J. A. C. (2015). How Microfinance Empowers Women in Côte d'Ivoire. *Review of Economics of the Household*, 13, 1023–1041.

Frank, R. H., and Cartwright, E. (2013). *Microeconomics and Behavior*. London: McGraw-Hill.

Frederick, S. (2005). Cognitive Reflection and Decision Making. *Journal of Economic Perspectives*, 19(4), 25–42.

Frey, B. S., and Stutzer, A. (2000). Happiness, Economy and Institutions. *Economic Journal*, 110(466), 918–938.

Frey, B. S., and Stutzer, A. (2002). What Can Economists Learn from Happiness Research? *Journal of Economic Literature*, 40(2), 402–435.

Frey, B., and Stutzer, A. (2012). The Use of Happiness Research for Public Policy. *Social Choice and Welfare*, 38, 659–674.

Frijters, P., Haisken-DeNew, J. P., and Shields, M. A. (2004). Investigating the Patterns and Determinants of Life Satisfaction in Germany Following Reunification. *Journal of Human Resources*, 39, 649–674.

Gombolay, M. C., Gutierrez, R. A., Clarke, S. G., Sturla, G. F., and Shah, J. A. (2015). Decision-Making Authority, Team Efficiency, and Human Worker Satisfaction in Mixed Human-Robot Teams. *Autonomous Robots*, 39(3), 293–312.

Greenglass, E., Antonides, G., Christandl, F., Foster, G., Katter, J. K. Q., Kaufman, B. E., and Lea, S. E. G. (2014). The Financial Crisis and Its Effects: Perspectives from Economics and Psychology. *Journal of Behavioral and Experimental Economics*, 50, 10–12.

Greendex (2014). Consumer Choice and the Environment: A Worldwide Tracking Survey. Retrieved from environment.nationalgeographic.com/environment/greendex, 14 March 2016.

Güth, W., and Kocher, M. G. (2013). More Than Thirty Years of Ultimatum Bargaining Experiments: Motives, Variations, and a Survey of the Recent Literature. Munich: CESifo Working Paper No. 4380.

Hamari, J., Sjöklint, M., and Ukkonen, A. (2016). The Sharing Economy: Why People Participate in Collaborative Consumption. *Journal of the Association for Information Science and Technology,* 67(9), 2047–2059.

Harrison, G. W., and List, J. A. 2004. Field Experiments. *Journal of Economic Literature*, 42(4), 1009–1055.

Haussmann, R., Tyson, L. D., and Zahidi, S. (2010). *The Global Gender Gap Report 2010*. Geneva: World Economic Forum.

Helliwell, J., Layard, R., and Sachs, J. (2016). *World Happiness Report 2016, Update (Vol. I)*. New York: Sustainable Development Solutions Network.

Himmelweit, S., Santos, C., Sevilla, A., and Sofer, C. (2013). Sharing of Resources Within the Family and the Economics of Household Decision Making. *Journal of Marriage and Family*, 75 (June), 625–639.

Hofmann, W., Vohs, K. D., and Baumeister, R. F. (2012). What People Desire, Feel Conflicted About, and Try to Resist in Everyday Life. *Psychological Science*, 23(6), 582–588.

Hsee, C. K. (1996). The Evaluability Hypothesis: An Explanation for Preference Reversals Between Joint and Separate Evaluations of Alternatives. *Organizational Behavior and Human Decision Processes*, 67(3), 247–257.

Hsee, C. K., Rottenstreich, Y., and Stutzer, A. (2012). Suboptimal Choices and the Need for Experienced Individual Well-Being in Economic Analysis. *International Journal of Happiness and Development*, 1(1), 63–85.

Inglehart, R. (1990). *Culture Shift in Advanced Industrial Society*. Princeton, NJ: Princeton University Press.

Inglehart, R. (1997). *Modernization and Postmodernization: Cultural, Economic and Political Change in 43 Societies*. Princeton, NJ: Princeton University Press.

Inglehart, R., and Baker, W.E. (2000). Modernization, Cultural Change, and the Persistence of Traditional Values. *American Sociological Review*, 65(1), 19–51.

Inglehart, R., Foa, R., Peterson, C., and Welzel, C. (2008). Development, Freedom, and Rising Happiness. *Perspectives on Psychological Science*, 3(4), 264–285.

Kahneman, D. (1994). New Challenges to the Rationality Assumption. *Journal of Institutional and Theoretical Economics*, 150, 18–36.

Kahneman, D. (1999). Objective Happiness. In: Kahneman, D., Diener, E., and Schwarz, N. (Eds.), *Well-Being: The Foundations of Hedonic Psychology* (pp. 3–25). New York: Russell Sage.

Kahneman, D. (2003). A Perspective on Judgment and Choice. *American Psychologist*, 58(9), 697–720.

Kahneman, D. (2011). *Thinking Fast and Slow*. New York: Farrar, Straus and Giroux.

Kahneman, D., and Deaton, A. (2010). High Income Improves Evaluation of Life but Not Emotional Well-Being. *Proceedings of the National Academy of Sciences*, 107(38), 16489–16493.

Kahneman, D., Knetsch, J. L., and Thaler, R. H. (1990). Experimental Tests of the Endowment Effect and the Coase Theorem. *Journal of Political Economy*, 98(6), 1325–1347.

Kahneman, D., Knetsch, J. L., and Thaler, R. H. (1991). The Endowment Effect, Loss Aversion, and the Status Quo Bias. *Journal of Economic Perspectives*, 5, 193–206.

Kahneman, D., Slovic, P., and Tversky, A. (1982). *Judgment Under Uncertainty: Heuristics and Biases*. Cambridge, UK: Cambridge University Press.

Kahneman, D., and Tversky, A. (1979). Prospect Theory: An Analysis of Decision Under Risk. *Econometrica*, 47, 263–291.

Kahneman, D., and Tversky, A. (Eds.) (2000). *Choices, Values, and Frames.* Cambridge, UK: Cambridge University Press.

Kapteyn, A., Van Praag, B. M. S., and Van Herwaarden, F. G. (1978). Individual Welfare Functions and Social Reference Spaces. *Economics Letters*, 1, 173–177.

Kirchler, E., Rodler, C., Hoelzl, E., and Meier, K. (2001). *Conflict and Decision Making in Close Relationships.* Hove, East Sussex: Psychology Press.

Knight, J., Song, L., and Gunatilaka, R. (2009). Subjective Well-Being and Its Determinants in Rural China. *China Economic Review*, 20, 635–649.

Linder, S. B. (1970). *The Harried Leisure Class.* New York: Columbia University Press.

Loewenstein, G. (1987). Anticipation and the Valuation of Delayed Consumption. *Economic Journal*, 97, 666–684.

Loewenstein, G., and Prelec, D. (1992). Anomalies in Intertemporal Choice: Evidence and an Interpretation. *Quarterly Journal of Economics*, 107, 573–597.

Lucas, R. E. (2007). Adaptation and the Set-Point Model of Subjective Well-Being. *Current Directions in Psychological Science*, 16(2), 75–79.

Lundberg, S., and Pollak, R. (1993). Separate Spheres Bargaining and the Marriage Market. *Journal of Political Economy*, 101(6), 988–1010.

Lundberg, S., Pollak, R., and Wales, T. J. (1997). Do Husbands and Wives Pool Their Resources? Evidence from the U.K. Child Benefit. *Journal of Human Resources* , 32(3), 463–480.

Madrian, B. C., and Shea, D. F. (2001). The Power of Suggestion: Inertia in 401(k) Participation and Savings Behavior. *Quarterly Journal of Economics*, 116(4), 1149–1187.

Manser, M., and Brown, M. (1980). Marriage Household Decision-Making: A Bargaining Analysis. *International Economic Review*, 21, 31–44.

Maslow, A. H. (1970). *Motivation and Personality*, 2nd edition. New York: Harper & Row.

McClure, S. M., Laibson, D., Loewenstein, G., and Cohen, J. D. (2004). Separate Neural Systems Value Immediate and Delayed Monetary Rewards. *Science*, 306(5695), 503 507.

McElroy M. B., and Horney, M. J. (1981). Nash-Bargained Household Decisions: Toward a Generalization of the Theory of Demand. *International Economic Review*, 22, 333–349.

Melenberg, B. (1992). Micro-econometric Models of Consumer Behavior and Welfare. PhD thesis, Tilburg University.

Mencarini, L., and Sironi, M. (2012). Happiness, Housework and Gender Inequality in Europe. *European Sociological Review*, 28(2), 203–219.

Mischel, W., Ebbesen, E. B., and Raskoff Zeiss, A. (1972). Cognitive and Attentional Mechanisms in Delay of Gratification. *Journal of Personality and Social Psychology*, 21(2), 204–218.

Mitchell, A. (1983). *The Nine American Lifestyles: Who We Are and Where We're Going.* New York: Macmillan.

Modigliani, F. (1988). The Role of Intergenerational Transfers and Life-Cycle Saving in the Accumulation of Wealth. *Journal of Economic Perspectives*, 2, 15–40.

Mullainathan, S., and Shafir, E. (2013). *Scarcity: Why Having Too Little Means So Much.* New York: Henry Holt.

National Geographic (2014). *Greendex 2014: Consumer Choice and the Environment: A Worldwide Tracking Survey.* London: Globescan.

Nielsen (2014). Nielsen Global Survey. Retrieved from www.nielsen.com, 14 March 2016.

Nielsen (2015). *The Sustainability Imperative: New Insights on Consumer Expectations.* New York: Nielsen.

OECD (Organisation for Economic Cooperation and Development) (2015). *How's Life? 2015. Measuring Well-Being.* Paris: OECD.

Oishi, S., and Kesebir, S. (2015). Income Inequality Explains Why Economic Growth Does Not Always Translate to an Increase in Happiness. *Psychological Science*, 26(10), 1630–1638.

Onwezen, M. C., Antonides, G., and Bartels, J. (2013). The Norm Activation Model: An Exploration of the Functions of Anticipated Pride and Guilt in Environmental Behavior. *Journal of Economic Psychology*, 39, 141–153.

Onwezen, M. C., Bartels, J., and Antonides, G. (2014a). The Self-Regulatory Function of Anticipated Pride and Guilt in a Sustainable and Healthy Consumption Context. *European Journal of Social Psychology*, 44 (1), 53–68.

Onwezen, M. C., Bartels, J., and Antonides, G. (2014b). Environmentally Friendly Consumer Choices: Cultural Differences in the Self-Regulatory Function of Anticipated Pride and Guilt. *Journal of Environmental Psychology*, 40, 239–248.

Pahl, J. (2000). Couples and Their Money: Patterns of Accounting and Accountability in the Domestic Economy. *Accounting, Auditing and Accountability Journal*, 13(4), 502–517.

Pine, J., and Gilmore, J. (1999). *The Experience Economy.* Boston: Harvard Business School Press.

Prahalad, C. K., and Ramaswamy, V. (2000). Co-opting Customer Competence. *Harvard Business Review*, 78(1), 79–87.

Richins, M. L., and Dawson, S. (1992). A Consumer Values Orientation for Materialism and Its Measurement: Scale Development and Validation. *Journal of Consumer Research*, 19, 303–316.

Ross, W. T., and Simonson, I. (1991). Evaluations of Pairs of Experiences: A Preference for Happy Endings. *Journal of Behavioral Decision Making*, 4, 273–282.

Solnick, S. J., and Hemenway, D. (1998). Is More Always Better? A Survey on Positional Concerns. *Journal of Economic Behavior and Organization*, 37, 373–383.

Stevenson, B., and Wolfers, J. (2013). Subjective Well-Being and Income: Is There Any Evidence of Satiation? *American Economic Review: Papers and Proceedings*, 103(3), 598–604.

Stutzer, A., and Frey, B. (2006). Does Marriage Make People Happy, or Do Happy People Get Married? *Journal of Socio-Economics*, 35, 326–347.

Thaler, R. H. (1980). Toward a Positive Theory of Consumer Choice. *Journal of Economic Behavior and Organization*, 1, 39–60.

Thaler, R. H. (1999). Mental Accounting Matters. *Journal of Behavioural Decision Making*, 12, 183–206.

Thaler, R. H., and Benartzi, S. (2004). Save More Tomorrow: Using Behavioral Economics to Increase Employee Saving. *Journal of Political Economy*, 112 (1), S164–S187.

Thaler, R. H., and Shefrin, H. M. (1981). An Economic Theory of Self-Control. *Journal of Political Economy*, 89, 392–406.

Thaler, R. H., and Sunstein, C. R. (2008). *Nudge: Improving Decisions About Health, Wealth and Happiness*. New Haven, CT: Yale University Press.

Van Boven, L. (2005). Experientialism, Materialism, and the Pursuit of Happiness. *Review of General Psychology*, 9(2), 132–142.

Van den Troost, A., Matthijs, K., Vermulst, A. A., Gerris, J. R. M., and Welkenhuysen-Gybels, J. (2006). Effects of Spousal Economic and Cultural Factors on Dutch Marital Satisfaction. *Journal of Family and Economic Issues*, 27(2), 235–262.

Van Dijk, J., Antonides, G., and Schillewaert, N. (2014). The Effects of Co-creation Claim on Consumer Brand Perceptions and Behavioral Intentions. *International Journal of Consumer Studies*, 38, 110–118.

Van Klaveren, C. (2009). *The Intra-Household Allocation of Time*. Amsterdam: Tinbergen Institute Research Series (459), Thela Thesis Academic Publishing Services.

Van Klaveren, C., and Ghysels J. (2012). Collective Labor Supply and Child Care Expenditures: Theory and Application. *Journal of Labor Research*, 33(2), 196–224.

Van Klaveren, C. & Maassen van den Brink, H. (2007). Intra-Household Work Time Synchronization, Togetherness or Material Benefits? *Social Indicators Research*, 84(1), 39–52.

Van Klaveren, C., Maassen van den Brink, H., and Van Praag, B. M. S. (2012). Intra-Household Work Timing: The Effect on Joint Activities and the Demand for Child Care. *European Sociological Review*, 29(1), 1–18.

Van Klaveren, C., Van Praag, B. M. S., and Maassen van den Brink, H. (2008). A Public Good Version of the Collective Model: An Empirical Approach with an Application to British Household Data. *Review of Economics of the Household*, 6(2), 169–191.

Van Klaveren, C., Van Praag, B. M. S., and Maassen van den Brink, H. (2011). *Collective Labor Supply of Native Dutch and Immigrant Households in the Netherlands*. In: Molina, J. A. (Ed.), *Household Economic Behaviors* (pp. 99–119). New York: Springer.

Van Praag, B. M. S., and Baarsma, B. E. (2005). Using Happiness Surveys to Value Intangibles: The Case of Airport Noise. *Economic Journal*, 115(500), 224–246.

Van Praag, B. M. S., and Van Weeren, J. (1988). Memory and Anticipation Processes and Their Significance for Social Security and Income Inequality. In: Maital, S. (Ed.) *Applied Behavioral Economics, Volume II* (pp. 731–751). Brighton: Wheatsheaf.

Van Raaij, W. F., and Antonides, G. (1991). Costs and Benefits of Unemployment and Employment. *Journal of Economic Psychology*, 12, 667–687.

Verain, M. C. D., Sijtsema, S., Dagevos, H., and Antonides, G. (2017). Attribute Segmentation and Communication Effects on Healthy and Sustainable Diet Intentions. *Sustainability*, 9(5), 743.

Vogler, C., Lyonette, C., and Wiggins, R. D. (2008). Money, Power and Spending Decisions in Intimate Relationships. *Sociological Review*, 56(1), 117–143.

Vohs, K. D. (2013). The Poor's Poor Mental Power. *Science*, 341(August), 969–970.

Warr, P. (1999). Well-Being and the Workplace. In: Kahneman, D., Diener, E., and Schwarz, N. (Eds.), *Well-Being: The Foundations of Hedonic Psychology* (pp. 353–373). New York: Russell Sage Foundation.

Welsch, H. (2007). Environmental Welfare Analysis: A Life Satisfaction Approach. *Ecological Economics*, 62, 544–551.

Welsch, H., and Kühling, J. (2010). Pro-environmental Behavior and Rational Consumer Choice: Evidence from Surveys of Life Satisfaction. *Journal of Economic Psychology*, 31, 405–420.

Welsch, H. and Kühling, J. (2011). Are Pro-environmental Consumption Choices Utility Maximizing? Evidence from Subjective Well-being Data. *Ecological Economics*, 72, 75–87.

White, A. (2007). A Global Projection of Subjective Well-Being: A Challenge to Positive Psychology? *Psychtalk*, 56, 17–20.

Yang, A. X., Hsee, C. K., Liu, Y., and Zhang, L. (2011). The Supremacy of Singular Subjectivity: Improving Decision Quality by Removing Objective Specifications and Direct Comparisons. *Journal of Consumer Psychology*, 21, 393–404.

12 An Economic Psychology of the Marketing Firm

Gordon R. Foxall

This chapter contributes to the development of a marketing theory of the firm, one that suggests in behavioural-scientific terms how to define and quantify the links between parties to transactions. In particular, it argues that such interrelationships be conceptualised within an economic-psychological framework that emphasises the bilateral contingencies linking the marketing firm with its publics via networks of reinforcement and response costs. The starting point is Coase's (1937) seminal paper on the nature of the firm, which was in its time revolutionary but which now requires recognition of the changed economic and social circumstances that now prevail. The industrial and commercial forces which were only beginning to emerge when Coase set forth his theory of the firm are now almost ubiquitous stimuli of a style of marketing- and customer-oriented management which has transformed the firm from a unit of production to a market- and marketing-focussed means of responding profitably to customer requirements. By concentrating on the firm as a marketing entity, this chapter seeks to clarify the nature of the modern corporation, and its relationships with other firms and with its customer base, as an inevitable accommodation to the changed socioeconomic circumstances that have intensified since Coase first observed that (essentially production-oriented) firms exist to economise transaction costs by internalising operations.

The resulting interdisciplinary perspective embraces disciplines other than economics, notably psychology and marketing, and raises questions that extend the analysis from the exclusively economic perspective adopted by Coase. The point is not to supersede transaction cost analysis with a behaviour analytical account but to supplement it in order to understand aspects of what is going on that economics cannot capture. This is a key objective of economic psychology. The result is a framework of conceptualisation and analysis the components of which are both empirically available and amenable to research.

After discussing Coase's contribution to the theory of the firm as a device which economises on transaction costs, the chapter draws attention to the demands made by modern marketing conditions on the purpose of the firm and its consequent operations. The limitations of transaction cost analysis in this context lead to a marketing theory of the firm, based on behaviour analysis, a school of psychology which has natural affinities with microeconomics while providing links to human relationships within and across the boundaries of business organisations. An outline of the fundamental tenets of behaviour analysis permits an analysis, first, of consumer choice and, second, of the role of marketing management and marketing-oriented management. The nature of the marketing firm is next explored via a behaviour analytic account of corporate behaviour, marketing transactions and styles of marketing integration. The advantages of this mode of analysis are discussed in the context of interfirm relationships and research agenda.

Before commencing on this agenda, it may be worthwhile to summarise briefly the overall rationale of the chapter and its contribution to economic psychology. The nature of modern firms reflects the circumstances in which they operate, circumstances which impose on them a marketing- or customer-orientation[1] as a central component of their overall corporate philosophy and strategy. Such firms face particular competitive and demand environments that compel them to adopt a marketing orientation and to fulfil certain minimal functions vis-à-vis their customers and other publics. The strategic aims, product-market objectives and externally focussed operations of these businesses mark them out from the production- and sales-oriented firms that dominated the economic landscape prior to the emergence of these more exacting marketing environments (Bartels, 1976). We may, accordingly, designate them *marketing firms*. A marketing firm is a commercial organisation which is obliged by competitive conditions to adopt the strategic philosophy of marketing- or customer-oriented management. A *commercial* organisation in this sense is one that is either committed to making profit or at least avoiding loss – that is, one that has to meet financial goals – so that its long-term future as a business is protected.

Given the conditions that enjoin marketing- or customer-orientation, firms exist, in Drucker's (2007) phrase 'to create a customer'. It may appear self-evident that any commercial organisation must seek to deal satisfactorily with the markets it serves, and that means must be found for the mutually beneficial interaction of the firm and its publics. The proposition is obvious indeed, as is Coase's (1937) observation that firms seek to economise their operations by internalising them rather than contracting with others for their performance. But there can be good reasons for reminding ourselves of such basics if they elucidate the form and function of marketing firms.

It follows that we are unlikely to understand accurately the role of marketing in modern enterprises, let alone the nature of these marketing firms, without first understanding how consumer behaviour is motivated. But it is rare to find a model of one of these behaviours that is matched by a corresponding model of the other that proceeds in similar terms. The models of consumer behaviour and corporate marketing employed in this chapter are behaviour analytic in nature, but they have strong affinity with microeconomics, too, and thus belong to the school of economic psychology which Lea, Tarpy and Webley (1987) propose.[2]

12.2 The Economising Firm

12.2.1 The Coasean Firm

In 'The Nature of the Firm', Coase (1937) advances a microeconomic theory in which the price mechanism is not the sole mechanism of resource allocation. Coase recognises that, within firms, some of which are sufficiently large to carry out extensive tasks of planning and coordination, resource allocation may be affected by managerial authority rather than markets. This raises the question of how and why these alternatives are selected by businesses. What determines whether the entrepreneur relies on external suppliers of products and services with whom bargains must be continually struck or produces them within his or her own business? Why incorporate at all? Coase's response, a view of the firm as an organisation made necessary by the imperative to internalise operations in order to fulfil them more economically, provides a rationale for the very existence of firms as opposed to open contracting within the marketplace. The key lies in the costs of market transacting, of using the price mechanism, such as discovering what prices obtain and writing and policing contracts to govern transacting. Coase argues that managerial economies are possible within the firm through the use of authority to ensure the cooperation of employees.

While prices are given by the market, they remain to be discerned by producers; they may be subject to negotiation and compromise, requiring the formulation of contracts which must not only be properly written but critically monitored and maintained or amended in the face of disputes over their interpretation. The upshot is that the coordinative procedures that transacting requires impose a level of expense on the firm which may be mitigated by the internalisation of these procedures within the organisation. Industrial administration, and corporate management, would therefore supersede the market in these matters. So, an efficient economy requires, in addition to a market mechanism, organisations that are capable of undertaking planning and coordination at lower cost than would be possible in either the marketplace or other firms. As a result of having alternative institutional arrangements for resource allocation, when the costs incurred in repeatedly making deals with other agents reach a certain point, savings are possible through the formation of a firm and the internalising of operations previously performed by the 'invisible hand'. Firms will not undertake exchanges the costs of which exceed the gains likely to flow from them, and as a result the productive gains of the prospective endeavor will not become available.[3]

12.2.2 Transaction Cost Analysis

In *Markets and Hierarchies*, Williamson (1975) takes further the ideas that the transaction is the fundamental unit of analysis and that markets and firms provide alternative means of organisation ('institutions of coordination') and that relative costs of transacting under them determines the chosen mechanism. Williamson's transaction cost analysis is founded on two behavioural principles, Simon's (1976, 1987) idea of *bounded rationality*, and *opportunism*, understood as 'self-interest seeking with guile'. While Coase was primarily interested in the costs incurred in the process of discovering prices, Williamson (1975, 1985) addresses the 'maladaptation costs' that arise when gaps in long-term contracts require 'gap-filling' and realignment of contractual relationships (Medema, 1994). Internal organisation (vertical integration) occurs when costs under internal organisation are lower than those under market organisation. The problems of maladaptation that are not capable of immediate resolution would require costly litigation to resolve. Internal organisation reduces transaction costs, in this case because disputes can be settled by fiat. Internal organisation also makes monitoring easier, as it reduces internal asymmetries; it also increases loyalty and cooperation since both human and nonhuman assets relevant to the transaction are encapsulated within the firm (Williamson, 1975). Importantly, Williamson also sets out to determine *at what point* the costs of internal organisation fall below those of market organisation. First, *transaction frequency* increases transaction costs, especially those involved in opportunistic behaviour; moreover, the recovery of transaction costs incurred in high-frequency transactions is easier and quicker in the case of internal organisation. Second, *uncertainty* with respect to the transaction is a source of augmented transaction costs, for uncertainty increases the possibility of opportunism. Internal organisation permits problems of uncertainty to be worked through and possibly solved by authority. Third, the degree of *asset specificity* demanded by a transaction or series of transactions increases transaction costs since asset specificity, both human and nonhuman, encourages bilateral monopoly, which in turn promotes opportunism.[4]

12.2.3 Beyond Production

Coase's firm is principally a unit of production. It is a reflection of its time, an era when marketing considerations, though in development, were still not central to most firms. The firm of which Coase wrote and which dominated the landscape of his time was principally concerned with production; this was, after all, the age of innovations in manufacturing such as the automation of assembly lines. Competition was among firms in the same industry and, in a sense, over time, within the factory. It is not surprising that this firm was dominated by the need to economise on factor input costs. At a time when customer demand exceeded the capacity to supply it (encapsulated in Henry

Ford's reputed observation that buyers of the Model T could have 'any color they like as long at it's black'), and when consumers' discretionary income was limited and rival manufacturers scarce, competitive advantage inhered in producing ever more economically.

The closest such firms came to marketing took the form of a selling orientation focussed on the firm's interest in using persuasive sales techniques to influence customers to buy whatever it happened to produce. This sales orientation fell far short of what was later known as marketing-oriented management, which treats the customer's viewpoint as paramount and in which the producer's interest lies in discerning consumer wants and responding to them profitably. Much has changed in the interim as far as customer demand and competitive forces are concerned, but considerations raised by Coase in 1937 remain central to understanding the nature and raison d'être of modern marketing management and of marketing firms. The theory of the marketing firm seeks to account for the nature of modern marketing-oriented firms as enduring responses to the circumstances of the marketplace, which were scarcely apparent when 'The Nature of the Firm' was published. It retains and generalises the insights of Coase's work but applies them and other principles of behavioural explanation to an organisation that is existentially distinct from that on which he concentrated.

12.3 Implications of Marketing

12.3.1 Marketing Management and Marketing Orientation

An initial distinction must be made between *marketing management*, consisting in particular functional operations, and *marketing-* or *customer-oriented management*, an overarching corporate philosophy and set of related perspectives. As understood here, marketing management is principally the administration of marketing mixes in the pursuit of profitable consumer response, and it is by and large accomplished by the firm's marketing department. We can identify the mainsprings of consumer behaviour as the response to the scope of the consumer behaviour setting and the pattern of reward or reinforcement offered by consumption. The content of marketing management is therefore conceived as the provision of marketing mixes that offer a persuasive pattern of reinforcement and the management of the consumer behaviour settings in which prepurchase (search and evaluation), purchase and postpurchase (consumption and evaluation) activities occur. However, over and above this, marketing-orientated management is an overall business philosophy (with corresponding business operations) that guides all functions, not only marketing management, in the profitable pursuit of customers (Drucker, 2007).[5] While the marketing department or function is responsible for devising and implementing marketing mixes, these can be optimally directed toward the profitable fulfillment of customer requirements only in the context of a customer-oriented perspective that the marketing firm supplies. Therefore, this chapter refers to the provision of marketing mixes as a corporate-level responsibility of the marketing firm as a whole.

While marketing management is concerned with the planning, implementation and administration of marketing mixes designed to meet consumer wants profitably, marketing orientation is an overall business philosophy in which the entire operations of the firm are oriented toward the profitable fulfillment of consumer wants. Marketing-oriented management is more than a recognition that firms carry out market research or have persuasive sales teams. It is first and foremost a matter of the firm's most senior management accepting intellectually that customer behaviour is logically prior to production: ideally, the investigation of the shape of market demand and the consequent generation of the marketing intelligence on which the profitable servicing of customer requirements depends precedes both production and marketing management.

These circumstances necessitate marketing planning and research; product development; market segmentation strategies (rather than the attempt to satisfy the entire market); and assiduity in planning and producing, implementing and managing integrated marketing mixes that meet corporate goals (Kotler and Keller, 2015). All of these matters are so closely intertwined with the raison d'être of the firm – why it exists, what it does – that the relationship of marketing and corporate strategies is more than alignment: it is coincidence. Both strategic perspectives involve answers to the questions famously raised by Drucker (2007): What business are we in? Who is our customer? Who will be the customer? The shelter of the corporate environment is required to ensure that these tasks are undertaken without their being observed by competitors. Whatever the historical basis for the existence of firms (e.g., Coase, 1937; Nooteboom, 2009; Sautet, 2000), this philosophy of management provides their contemporary rationale. The marketing questions raised here are also essentially strategic management questions; they concern the strategic direction of the firm given its resource base.

12.3.2 Marketing Operations

The theory of the marketing firm identifies three primary kinds of marketing operation, one of which can be readily accommodated by Coase's analysis, the others of which justify an extension to his insight which underpins the concept of the marketing firm. The marketing firm must accomplish three principal tasks.

First, it must acquire appropriate marketing intelligence which enables it to select the segments of the market it plans to serve and how it intends to do so. It may accomplish the acquisition of such intelligence either directly through its own internal capabilities or via an external specialist organisation (to which it is said to commercially delegate the task). This first kind of marketing operation ($MkOp_1$) involves more than just doing market research: it entails all of the information gathering and analysis required for the decision processes inherent in determining the strategic reach of the firm and how this will be addressed through marketing strategy.

This requires, second, that the firm determine its strategic direction in terms of the goals it pursues, its means of achieving them and the criteria of success it applies. These matters entail deciding on the product-market scope of the firm (what markets it seeks to satisfy and with what products/services), and the design and delivery of a marketing mix comprising the product, price, promotion and place with which it will seek to satisfy its consumers or other publics. These strategic marketing operations ($MkOp_2$) are undertaken in some form in all firms but achieve a special significance in the marketing-oriented organisation. Within this framework, the information obtained in the course of $MkOp_1$ can be appraised, developed into marketing intelligence and used in the course of detailed marketing planning and management.

Third, in order to fulfil its strategic purposes, the firm must design and create a suitable marketing mix for the profitable delivery of its products/services to its target consumers/other publics. These marketing-managerial operations ($MkOp_3$) may be integrated into the firm; alternatively, they may be wholly or partially commercially delegated to specialist organisations.

12.3.2.1 *Marketing Intelligence*

$MkOp_1$ are marketing operations concerned with the acquisition and deployment of factor inputs (marketing intelligence, by which is meant more than market research data; it might, for instance, include also consultancy on marketing strategy). However, $MkOp_1$ have an intrafirm focus or orientation, since they are concerned with the acquisition of knowledge and services that assist in the marketing functions carried out by the firm. The planning of what knowledge is required reflects the goals of the firm; hence, the carrying out of $MkOp_2$ is logically prior to this process. The formulation of goals and policies and the conduct of strategic planning are, as a rule, necessarily undertaken exclusively within the firm, but the negotiations with the agencies that provide marketing intelligence and consultancy services, the monitoring of their actions and the receipt of their products are costly operations that involve interactions with other organisations. They do not, for all this, lose their intrafirm orientation since they are concerned with the appropriate acquisition of factors of production. They resemble very well the kinds of market transactions that Coase speaks of. And, as such, they are transactions the cost of which can be minimised by the internalisation of the operations, such as by the firm organising and running its own market research operations.

Marketing intelligence of this kind is a vital input to the selection of market segments to serve and the capabilities of the firm in meeting their requirements.

It is a process in which information is translated into the intelligence which makes decision-making possible. Prices must be discovered not only for factor inputs but also for the goods which are the output of the firm. This makes the creation of market intelligence imperative – over and above market research, this entails the interpretation of data in the context of the decisions that have been made and remain to be made about the firm's strategic direction and chosen approach to the satisfaction of consumer wants. Hence, the tasks involve developing knowledge about consumers and their behaviour that enable the firm to determine which available market segments will form its target markets and then enable an appropriate marketing mix to be constructed to satisfy their wants profitably. The gathering of data is probably the only task involved in the creation of market intelligence that can be commercially delegated. The ensuing tasks, based on such intelligence, are unlikely to be assigned to agencies outside the marketing firm.

There is a range of interactions that the firm may undertake with other organisations in its discharge of $MkOp_1$. It may, first, simply contract with the providers of generic market knowledge for such intelligence. But, second, it is likely, as the required confidentiality of the information involved increases, to employ specialist market research and consultancy agencies. And, third, it may eventually incorporate its own market research and intelligence department as a consequence of the competitive environment which makes not only confidentiality but also flexibility and speed in the access to and use of intelligence imperative. Apart from the first option, these possibilities all entail differing degrees of vertical quasi-integration and vertical integration: even though the firm does not legally take an economic stake in the agency it is sufficient for legal provisions or the research industry's ethical conventions to guarantee the confidentiality of the information. In one sense, the agency–firm relationship is a matter of contracting within the market, as Coase puts it; in another, it is a matter of quasi-internalisation of the relationship.[6]

12.3.2.2 *Marketing Strategy*

Other marketing operations, $MkOp_2$, characteristic of large firms that are organised to plan and coordinate, are of a different kind: they are internalised for different reasons and are concerned with the output of the firm, its corporate behaviour. Although it is common to think of these operations as the peculiar characteristic of large firms that are so organised as to need to plan and coordinate on a large scale, they are central to the functioning of all businesses. They are necessarily internalised for reasons of security but also because they are so central to the raison d'être of the firm itself that they cannot be undertaken by any agency other than the senior executives of the firm itself (e.g., Lynch, 2015). These operations are vitally concerned with answering the questions raised in the preceding section and are logically prior to any other operations the organisation undertakes.

12.3.2.3 *Marketing Mix Management*

These marketing operations, $MkOp_3$, deliver the product or service of the firm to the customer. The content of these operations is suggested by the analysis of consumer behaviour summarised in the preceding. Marketing firms are involved in the attempt to promote their own brands within a product category that contains very many alternatives for consumers to choose among. They seek to do this by changing the scope of the consumer behaviour setting, closing it by making their own brands available and attractive, and opening it by presenting innovative offerings not already available. They also use utilitarian and informational reinforcement to present product, price, promotional and distributive utilities to consumers. In undertaking both of these functions, through the elements of the marketing that they control, they are in competition with other firms doing precisely the same on behalf of the brands for which they are responsible. These operations may be conducted by the firm itself or commercially delegated to specialist agencies such as those engaged in logistics and physical distribution management or through licensing agreements and franchising. These marketing operations go beyond the Coasean analysis of factor input cost minimisation, being concerned with how the firm constructs marketing outputs on the basis of its strategic base and its marketing intelligence. Some of this work of building on market intelligence, whether it is obtained from agencies or through an internal department, might also be undertaken in a similar fashion by an external agency. But it is more probable that the firm will undertake such marketing planning and strategy formulation inhouse. There are several reasons for this. Confidentiality remains crucial within the highly competitive environment that marketing-oriented management involves. Whereas Coase's analysis of economising transaction costs is confined to considerations of the relative expense of contracting or internalising, marketing-oriented management involves the strategic economies that accrue from encapsulation of the firm's $MkOp_3$.

At one level, there is the availability within the firm of knowledge that simply would not be available to an agency including routines, action patterns and history. The need to execute a capabilities analysis in order for the firm to determine which of its market opportunities it should exploit, which can be postponed and which can be abandoned. This does not mean that part of such analyses will not be contracted out. But the ultimate decisions – over what product-market opportunities to exploit, which we take as the fundamental characteristic of marketing-oriented management – will be internal. Indeed, it is difficult to see how this could be otherwise since they are the essence of entrepreneurship. These are all examples of the minimisation of transaction costs since the loss of confidentiality that would ensue from the open acquisition of such information in the marketplace, even if it were available, would impose severe costs on the firm.

Of course, it is not inevitable that these operations are undertaken by an organisation which has the features of the modern firm. The accumulation of market intelligence and its profitable implementation are activities that must be undertaken by any individual working as a sole operator, a professional self-employed accountant, for instance. The point is that when consumers are numerous, distant from the producer, when market segments are many and the problems of researching them not immediately tractable, necessitating delicate decisions over which to exploit and which to ignore, then the coordination requirements of $MkOp_3$ might be more economically pursued by a firm than by individual producers acting as singletons. Moreover, economic coordination of MO_3 becomes, under these circumstances, less expensive if it is the concern of the firm that stands to gain from the successful exploitation of the markets involved. Sole traders cannot obtain sufficient market intelligence, process it, construct marketing plans that provide the products and services required by the selected segments and so on, whether they are acting as individuals or aggregately in the marketplace. From the point of view of the economic system as a whole, optimisation requires the ability to master scale in production and marketing. The cost of such activities are likely therefore to be economised if they are undertaken by corporations.

We must be careful not to oversimplify. It is not the case that *marketing management* inheres in the performance of $MkOp_1$, while *marketing-oriented management* involves $MkOp_2$ and $MkOp_3$. Both types of operation can result in the formulation and implementation of marketing mixes and both may be underlain in various degrees by considerations arising through the pursuit of marketing-oriented management.

12.3.3 Limitations of Transaction Cost Analysis

The transaction costs approach is a blunt/broad brush treatment which attempts to show in gross terms how the firm as a whole incurs costs. It fails to take marketing sufficiently into consideration, especially the importance of marketing-oriented management in contemporary social and economic situations; it is not as useful in the analysis of $MkOp_2$ and $MkOp_3$ as it is in the analysis of factor inputs, including those that contribute to $MkOp_1$; and it deemphasises a number of factors that apply to modern firms and their interrelationships with one another and their customer bases, such as mutuality relationships, the continuity of interfirm relationships and managerial behaviour.

12.3.3.1 *Lack of Marketing Sensitivity*
We have already noted the tendency of Coase's analysis of the firm to emphasise production at the expense of marketing; this is a trend found also in later contributions to transaction cost analysis and the theory of the firm. Demsetz (1995) commendably recognises that the production of the firm is intended for use by others beyond the firm. But his idea of the 'specialised firm' does not take management into consideration. The general tendency is to take a

cost-oriented and specific-cost view which cannot therefore assume a total cost-benefit viewpoint, that is, it does not consider that by incurring higher costs by obtaining inputs from the market ($MkOp_1$) it may be in a position to cut other costs of carrying out $MkOp_2$ and $MkOp_3$ or increasing its revenues from the enactment of $MkOp_3$. It does not consider that, within the firm's limited resource base, it may increase profitability by incurring the costs of purchasing factor inputs from the market as long as this facilitates the production of a more customer-oriented product offering ($MkOp_3$).

In particular, a theory of the modern firm must evince sensitivity to the distinction we have drawn between marketing management and marketing-oriented management, and their implications for the internalisation of marketing operations. This is not a distinction between tactical and strategic operations: it is one between internally oriented sources of profitability and externally oriented sources of profitability. It is a distinction between operations that are economised because they are brought into the firm rather than obtained from suppliers and operations that are economised because they are undertaken within the firm rather than delegated to marketing agencies. Why should a firm maintain these operations rather than appoint specialist marketing agencies to move their goods to the consumer?

While $MkOp_1$ and $MkOp_3$ can be either internalised or effected through the agency of other organisations, it is perhaps inevitable and certainly highly predictable that $MkOp_2$ will be retained within the firm since they concern the intimate intellectual planning that defines the essence of the firm and what it does. These operations include the determination of what business the firm is in, what consumers it is seeking to satisfy and the product-market scope of its entire range of operations. But, there is a core of marketing operations, those we have spoken of as $MkOp_2$, that must be discharged by *any* organisation accorded the title of 'firm', operations that set and maintain its strategic direction and purpose. This is even true of the so-called production-oriented company, often presented in the marketing literature as producing whatever goods it is committed to in the knowledge that customers will be found for them. Even Ford's Model T was a product attuned to the characteristics of the market: the company was as marketing-oriented as it needed to be in the circumstances, and it could not escape decision-making with respect to strategic direction and purpose. Any firm that persists must have in place at least implicit goals about the product-market scope it intends to operate in, its capabilities and its chosen methods for achieving its objectives. Even a firm which delegates its operations concerning both its marketing inputs ($MkOp_1$) and its marketing outputs ($MkOp_3$) must undertake at least a minimal level of strategic planning, monitoring and accommodation to external forces of competition and demand. Such a firm is concerned primarily with the production of particular products and services, buying in its market intelligence or gaining it directly from its customers if they are other firms, and similarly buying in the expertise required to distribute its outputs. Thus such a firm is not 'production-oriented' in the sense that a superficial reading of the history of marketing might suggest. It is highly attuned to the marketplace but optimises its returns by concentrating its efforts on responding to its markets by obtaining accurate market intelligence and the services of external organisations which can more effectively and efficiently undertake the external marketing operations required if a chosen customer segment is to be satisfied profitably.

Transaction cost analysis emphasises, as does economic theory generally, the effects of *price* on production and consumption. In doing this, it fails to embrace the marketing mix, the combined elements that compose the outputs of the marketing firm. But in addition, it is not clear what predictions a transaction cost analysis of firm behaviour would lead to without much more detailed knowledge of the relationships involved between firms.

A further dimension of marketing insensitivity shown by theories of the firm is apparent from their failure to be founded on an underlying theory of consumer behaviour, even though this is central to understanding the modern firm and the circumstances in which it operates.

12.3.3.2 *Scope of Transaction Cost Analysis in the Marketing Firm*

$MkOp_1$ can be readily explicated in terms of transaction cost considerations. Moreover, while Williamson's (1975) observations that integration is more probable the greater the volume of transactions involved in market contracting, the greater the degree of uncertainty and the greater the asset specificity involved do not provide a precise guide to when firms will integrate, they do suggest guidelines for the analysis of decisions to internalise or continue using the market. The ideas of bounded rationality and opportunism are also useful analytic categories in which to analyse decisions of this kind. A role for transaction cost analysis is less apparent in the case of $MkOp_2$, however, since it is very unlikely indeed that these tasks can be delegated. The collectivity that comprises the organisation's executive body must consensually formulate a mission statement, articles of association, strategic objectives and plans, and devise a viable product-market scope for the firm given its asset base. These are at the heart of the firm and cannot be assigned to an outside body. If these functions are not fulfilled by this body, then there is no firm.

$MkOp_3$ ought in principle to be tractable in terms of transaction costs. The tasks involved are in principle delegable to other organisations – advertising and promotions, for instance, can be undertaken by expert agencies as can transportation and the overall management of physical distribution through wholesalers and retailers. But the decisions to delegate these tasks are not tractable in terms of transaction costs. Take, for instance, the marketing firm potentially transacting with a large customer base. Transactions frequency would be very high indeed and because the firm would seek not to integrate $MkOp_3$ but to delegate them; intermediaries would be indispensable and the problems of marketing to many disparate consumers would be delegated to them. At most, there would be a degree of quasivertical integration seeking to control the behaviour of distributors through strict contracting or via such arrangements as franchising retail operations. Uncertainty would also be high since consumer behaviour is volatile and competitive conditions at the retail level high. Again, this calls for delegation rather than integration. Asset specificity is also high in distribution, and again the tendency is for distributors to undertake the tasks in question. The relationships involved in such delegation are less tractable by standard transaction costs analysis, and more tractable by the analysis of bilateral contingencies.

In transaction cost theory, an increase in transaction costs in connection with $MkOp_3$ due to increased transactions frequency ought to result in greater integration of these operations within the firm, but it is actually more likely the firm will in these circumstances seek to use the market in the form of external distributors. Similar pressures may be present in the form of uncertainty about final consumers, which is again met by employing specialist firms to interact with them. The asset specificity involved in distribution may also encourage use of the market. The actual outcome depends of course on trust, experience and ability to predict the behaviour of those one deals with in the market. Firms are boundedly rational and subject to the opportunism of those with whom they transact. Bounded rationality can be made more sensitive to actual market conditions only by the gaining of mutual experience with transactors. Trust depends on the history of reinforcement and punishment demonstrated by trading partners. Increasing the efficacy of one's knowledge of other firms in the market and the degree of trust one can have in them depends on the analysis of a long-term pattern of relationships with them, that is, the analysis of a long-term pattern of bilateral contingencies and the behaviour patterns associated with them. This argues for a much more nuanced interpretation of the behaviour of trading partners which must nevertheless be related to the costs and benefits each (a) receives from and (b) confers on the other.

12.3.3.3 *Mutuality Relationships*

Economics has been characterised as concerned with the analysis of the *no-person group*, 'the study of the movements of commodities and prices in the absence of people' (Boulding, 1970, p. 74). Boulding cautions against imagining that *any* behavioural science can avoid abstraction, so economics is not alone in this, but he warns also against 'mistaking abstraction for reality' (p. 75). One route to examining economic constructs for reality is to at least consider how other social sciences would approach the behaviour of interest and to contrast its outcomes with those of economic analyses. At the very least, this would highlight that there are questions to be asked that are not part of the usual province of economics. The achievement of successful markets relationships is difficult or impossible without the provision of mutuality relationships, the establishment and maintenance of effective medium- to long-term associations between firms and others and the requisite intrafirm relationships among departments and managers. Hodgson (1988) draws attention to the fact that firms engender loyalty and trust, and this insight is applicable not only to relationships within the firm but among firms.

12.3.3.4 *Continuity of Interfirm Relationships*

Transaction cost analysis concentrates on single instances of change in strategic direction rather than the factors that lead to long-term relationships among firms. The transaction-based approach tends to emphasise large, dramatic changes in a firm's relationships rather than to seek the causes of medium to long-term stability in relationships. It is not concerned with the building of sustained associations based on reciprocity of reinforcement. The required analysis can be achieved through consideration of the bilateral contingencies that link firms over time. This can be achieved, however, by the analysis of case study materials that deal with the factors that promote stability and longevity in interfirm relationships: firms do indeed influence the behaviour of their corporate customers by closing the scope of the setting in which they operate; they also influence the behaviour of those with whom they trade by managing the pattern of utilitarian and informational reinforcement they offer; and relationships between trading partners are strengthened by these means over a series of transactions (Vella, 2015; Vella and Foxall, 2011).

12.3.3.5 *Managerial Behaviour*

Transaction cost analysis derives a spurious specificity from its invoking marginal analysis for the identification of the point at which market trading becomes costlier than internal organisation. In practice, the decision to integrate cannot be so sensitive to changing cost structures as the analysis implies. Such decisions must also reflect, at a minimum, aspects of the entrepreneur's resource base (e.g., whether he or she possesses the capacity to organise internally at the present time) and managerial preferences given the entrepreneur's current strategic commitments. There is almost certain to be a time lag before integration can take place. Equally, there are motivations to integrate that arise irrespective of the relative costs of using the market and performing operations within the firm, the entrepreneurial desire for autonomy and independence being a key impetus.

A somewhat naïve picture of industrial relations is apparent in Coase's 1937 paper, typified by his view that part of the savings on transaction costs that would accrue to the firm as a result of its internalising factor production would stem from the ability of managers to redeploy workers at will. There may be occasions when workers are ordered to undertake particular roles or to move from one department to another, but to assume that this is either the norm or a desirable way in which to affect corporate management flies in the face of a century of industrial psychology and sociology, human resource management and trade union intervention. Most changes are likely to be jointly negotiated and mutually agreed, within the ultimate confines imposed by contracts of employment. The closest such analysis comes to assuming the concerns of behavioural science lies in the somewhat simplistic assumption that interpersonal relationships within the business organisation can be understood in terms of principle–agent associations, that human resource management can be reduced to the exercise of authority and that interorganisational associations are reducible to opportunism and bounded rationality. As Alchian and Demsetz (1972) point out, authority relationships within the firm may be as contractually based as extrafirm market transactions. In addition, the richness of organisational psychology and sociology have much to contribute to the analysis of administrative tasks, and interfirm relations are multifacetted and amenable to detailed investigation. This is not to disparage the undoubted progress that transaction cost analysis and modern theories of the firm accomplish, but equally it suggests albeit briefly the scope of the necessary behavioural-scientific contributions to a more comprehensive understanding.

To state this more generally, transaction cost analysis and some modern theories of the firm do not reflect managers' individuality or that their behaviour is ultimately reinforced and punished by emotional reactions based in neurophysiology (Foxall, 2014a). Nor are managerial coalitions within the firm analysed. We need a perspective on the modern firm as a marketing entity that takes account of matters such as these without abandoning the contribution of economics to our understanding of corporate behaviour.

12.3.4 Towards an Economic Psychology of the Firm

In summary, transaction cost analysis is accurate at a broad level but cannot deal in the human relationships involved in transactions and, especially, the emotional consequences of behaviour. We need a more personal level of analysis – transaction cost analysis is firmly superpersonal-level analysis – and possibly also a subpersonal level of analysis.

It is nevertheless important not to deviate entirely from an economics-based approach to the firm: an exclusively psychological account of firm behaviour is unlikely to take economic behaviour sufficiently into consideration. The field of operant behavioural economics (Foxall, 2016c) is apposite, however, for its reliance on a school of psychology, behaviour analysis, which exhibits a natural affinity with microeconomics. In addition, behaviour analysis has proven effective in explicating patterns of consumer choice on which any theory of the firm that is sensitive to marketing must be based. The aim of the following exposition is, therefore, to lay out an alternative mode of analysis, noting empirical research already undertaken and setting an agenda for further investigation.

12.4 The Marketing Firm

12.4.1 Consumer Behaviour Analysis

The underlying explanatory device in behaviour analysis is the 'three-term contingency', which explains the rate at which a response is emitted by an organism in a given context as a function of the kinds of consequence it generates

(Foxall, 2004). Any consequence that has the effect of increasing the behaviour rate is known as a reinforcer, while any which depresses the rate of occurrence is a punisher. The rate of behaviour is thus contingent on the nature of the outcomes of previous instances of this response in similar circumstances. This can be summarised in terms of a two-term contingency: $R \rightarrow S^{r/p}$, in which R is the (behavioural) response, and $S^{r/p}$ denotes the reinforcing or punishing stimulus) that affects its future occurrence. Learning, in this paradigm, is simply a change in the rate at which a response occurs as a result of prior reinforcing and punishing effects. The *three*-term contingency, which forms the basic explanatory device in radical behaviourism, takes its name from the role of an antecedent stimulus in the presence of which learning occurs and which itself exerts control over the emission of the response, even in the absence of the reinforcing/punishing stimuli which brought about learning. Hence, $S^D \rightarrow R \rightarrow S^{r/p}$, in which an S^D is a discriminative stimulus, i.e., an element of the environment in the presence of which an organism performs selectively by emitting a response, R, which has previously been reinforced in the presence of the S^D; S^r is a reinforcing stimulus, and S^p a punishing stimulus.

Another way of describing this mode of explanation is to say that the current probability of a response is determined by the organism's learning history, the manner in which the individual's pattern of previous behaviour and the outcomes it has engendered influence current choice. This basic paradigm is elaborated in consumer behaviour analysis to bring it into service as a means of predicting and interpreting human economic behaviour in naturally occurring settings (Foxall, 2001, 2002). In the Behavioural Perspective Model (BPM), shown in Figure 12.1, the immediate precursor of consumer behaviour is the consumer situation which represents the interaction of the consumer's learning history and the discriminative stimuli that make up the current behaviour setting (Foxall, 1990/2004, 2016b). The essence of the model is the consumer situation–consumer behaviour relationship shown within the dotted ellipse in Figure 12.1.

In this interaction, the consumer's experience in similar contexts primes the setting stimuli so that certain behaviours are made more probable while others are inhibited. Consumer behaviours that are encouraged by the consumer situation are those that have met with rewarding or reinforcing consequences on previous consumption occasions, while those that are discouraged are those that have been punished. The consequences of consumer behaviour, that is, its reinforcing and aversive outcomes, are of two kinds: utilitarian reinforcement and punishment consists in the behavioural consequences that are functionally related to obtaining, owning and using an economic product or service, while informational reinforcement and punishment stem from the social and symbolic outcomes of consumption. Consumer behaviour is therefore a function of the variables that make up the current consumer behaviour setting insofar as these prefigure positive and aversive utilitarian and informational consequences of behaving in particular ways. A more closed consumer behaviour

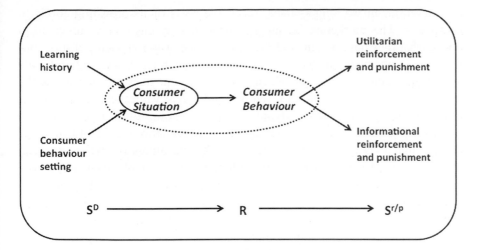

Figure 12.1. *Summative Behavioural Perspective Model.*
Adapted from Foxall (2016b).

setting is one in which one or at most a few behaviours are available to the consumer, while a more open setting is one which presents the consumer with a multiplicity of ways of acting. The topography of consumer behaviour is then predictable from the pattern of utilitarian and informational reinforcement which the setting variables signal to be available contingent on the enactment of specific consumer behaviours.

12.4.2 Marketing Transactions

The transaction is the central element of economic analysis that is also integral to understanding marketing relationships. It entails mutual reinforcement which results from the bartering or trading of goods. These transactions involve literal exchange, not the symbolic interactions that occur when people are said to 'exchange greetings'. In those cases, nothing is actually exchanged in a literal sense, though it is true that such interactions are marked by mutual reinforcement of reciprocated behaviour. In an economic exchange or a marketing relationship, the mutual reinforcement is accomplished by an item-for-item switch of valued items.

The assertion that economic and marketing exchanges are literal transfers, that marketing firms necessarily operate in pecuniary markets, is a necessary prerequisite of their persistence, for unless the reciprocal reinforcement on which such exchanges rest were the case, the firm could not continue to exist as a commercial entity. Each of the parties in a marketing relationship provides the other with utilitarian and informational reinforcement: typically, goods which supply functional and social utilities are swapped for money and marketing intelligence. The financial rewards received by the firm permit its growth and development so long as they exceed the costs of its providing goods to customers. The marketing intelligence provided by customers, information about what they have bought and their experience of it, is a source of informational reinforcement which guides the marketer's strategic planning and marketing management activities. Mutual reinforcement does not mean that the exchanged entities can be said to embody identical values; exchange implies only that each party is sufficiently satisfied with the outputs of the transactions that they maintain a particular pattern of behaviour towards the other.

Although it is easy enough to discern the literalness of exchange when money, say, is given up for a physical product, the question of what is exchanged becomes more difficult in the case of intangibles such as services. What is actually exchanged is legal title to a product or the outcome of a service, whether this be a lawnmower, a manicure, or life assurance. Exchange is the transfer of property rights (see, inter alia, Commons, 1924; Demsetz, 1995; Posner, 1995). Legal entitlement and contractual obligations are elements of the contingencies of reinforcement and punishment which influence behaviour, just as the market itself is ultimately a source of mutually accepted and reciprocally binding contingencies.

Marketing transactions, which require reciprocally reinforcing literal exchanges, are frequently accompanied by other, social relationships, which are characterised by reciprocally contingent reinforcement but not involving literal exchange. These mutuality relationships, fostered by, for instance, trade associations, conventions and dyadic associations between sales personnel and professional buyers, are essential to the negotiation and maintenance of long-term marketing relationships but are qualitatively different, notably in the fact that they do not in themselves constitute economic behaviour or marketing exchanges.

12.4.3 Corporate Behaviour Analysis

12.4.3.1 *Selection by Consequences*

The underlying premise of the marketing firm concept (Foxall, 1999a) is that firms exist in order to market within particular competitive structures, those that enjoin customer-oriented marketing as a general managerial philosophy if these businesses are to survive (avoid loss) and prosper (innovate in ways that encourage a satisfactory level of sales). The structural conditions that compel such marketing orientation include the industrywide availability of sufficient productive capacity to generate supply that exceeds demand; the existence of large levels of discretionary income on the part of consumers engendering interindustrial competition among firms; and an increasingly sophisticated customer base, that is, buyers who are knowledgeable with respect to the products they purchase and the alternative offerings available in the marketplace (Foxall, 2015a). In a nutshell, the marketing firm is that organisation which responds to consumer choice in ways that satisfy both customer requirements and corporate financial goals.

The resulting framework of conceptualisation and analysis understands corporate institutions as organised patterns of behaviour maintained by their consequences, namely the rewards and sanctions that follow them (or, more accurately and avoiding teleology, that have followed them in the past). The behaviour of the marketing firm eventuates in the introduction of marketing mixes that offer product, price and promotion and place utilities to consumers (Foxall, 1999a). The success of the firm, and hence its future behaviour, depends on the reception these marketing mixes receive in the marketplace. This perspective, based on selection by consequences (Skinner, 1981), permits continuity with evolutionary theories of the firm (Hodgson and Knudsen, 2010) by embracing the same explanatory principles of selection by consequences that underlies Darwinian natural selection but extending it to events in the ontogenetic development of individuals and organisations. Van Parijs (1981) refers to these explanation as N-evolution and R-evolution, respectively, noting the role of natural selection (N) in the former and of reinforcement (R) in the latter.

More specifically, the concept of the marketing firm portrays corporate behaviour in marketing-oriented enterprises as the management of the scope of the consumer behaviour setting and the pattern of reinforcement available to the consumer. The relationship of the firm and its consumers is depicted in terms of bilateral contingencies in which the behaviour of marketers is reinforced and punished by consumer behaviours while consumer behaviour is reinforced and punished by managerial actions (Foxall, 2014b).

The theory of the marketing firm also draws a distinction between two kinds of relationship that are relevant to the execution of marketing operations (Foxall, 1999a). The first, between the firm and its customers, between principal and agent within the organisation and between the firm and its suppliers, all of which entail literal exchange of legal rights, are known as 'marketing relationships'. The second comprises relationships that do not proceed on this basis even though they may be essential to forming and maintaining marketing relationships. They include social and trade association contacts among firms and broader noncontractual relationships between managers and other employees. They are known as 'mutuality relationships' (Foxall, 1999a; Vella and Foxall, 2011).

12.4.3.2 *Metacontingency and Macrobehaviour*

The behaviour of an organisation may differ from the aggregated actions of its members but still be amenable to analysis in similar terms. The key to analysing organisational behaviour in behaviour analytic terms lies in envisioning an organisation's structure as a system of interlocking behavioural contingencies. The operant nature of the supra-individual behaviour of the organisation as a whole can then be inferred from the outputs it uniquely produces and their effects on the organisation's subsequent conduct. Biglan and Glenn (2013, p. 256) employ the term *metacontingencies* to 'describe the contingent relations between IBC [interlocking behavioural contingency] lineages with their products, on the one hand, and the consequent actions of their external environment on the other.' In the context of the marketing firm, the suprapersonal behaviour of the organisation comprises the marketing mixes that it generates and offers to the marketplace. Moreover, the emphasis in the theory of the marketing firm on exchange relationships as the heart of marketing transactions provides the mechanism by which the marketing firm and its customer base are bound together, namely the concept of bilateral contingency (Foxall, 1999a, 2014b, 2015b).

The idea of metacontingency enables us to treat the interactions of individual consumers with firms, and of firms with other firms, as based on intertwined contingencies. Each is considered a contextual system in its own right, a system whose behaviour is predictable from its learning history and behaviour setting (Foxall, 1999b, 2015b). The idea of the marketing firm rests, moreover, on a distinction between the behavioural outputs of organisations that are metacontingencies and those of collectivities of persons who may form the firm's customer base (Biglan and Glenn, 2013; Houmanfar, Rodrigues and Smith, 2009.) Hence, the import of a firm as a metacontingency derives from its behavioural output having emerged from, but nevertheless over and above, the combined actions of its members. This renders the output of the metacontingency qualitatively different from the aggregated behaviours of its members. Such metacontingent corporate behaviour evolves in its own right as its consequences are selected or deselected by the environment, in this case by the firm's customers and potential customers, who respond to the marketing mixes it presents. The behavioural output of the firm's consumers is, in contrast, the aggregated consequences of their several actions. While it is possible to perform statistical operations on measures of this behaviour, as though it were an entity in its own right, it remains no more than a combination of individual operant responses (Biglan and Glenn, 2013). Crucially, this combined behavioural entity does not evolve: its future prevalence is not sensitive to any environmental consequences that it generates *in toto* since it produces no behavioural outputs in addition to those of consumers en masse that can be differentially acted on by a selective environment. Such behaviour, the actions of a large collectivity, is termed *macrobehaviour* (Glenn, 2004).

12.4.3.3 *Bilateral Contingency*

Behaviour analysts have traditionally adopted the individual organism as their unit of analysis. However, by treating the organisation that is the marketing firm as a contextual or operant system in its own right, and by assuming that the function of such a firm is to pursue marketing- or customer-oriented marketing, it becomes feasible to interpret the behaviour of its managers in terms of the context provided by its customers.

The relationships between the marketing firm and its customers can be conceptualised in terms of bilateral contingencies (Foxall, 1999a). The essence of this approach is that the behaviour of an organisation is greater than or different from that of the combined repertoires of its members. This conception, which has always been integral to the concept of the marketing firm, is supported by recent thinking in organisational behaviour analysis (Glenn, 2004; Biglan and Glenn, 2013). In both systems of thought, the behaviour of the system is inferred from the outputs it produces. Hence, each element of the marketing mix – product, price, the promotional communications and distribution systems – affects consumer behaviour in such a way as to make the behaviour of the organisation predictable and explicable. To adopt this kind of analysis is to consider the behaviour of an organisation or other collectivity of individuals in operant terms, to understand it as a contextual system.

Consideration of the marketing firm as a contextual system has hitherto been confined to the behavioural analysis, in terms of utilitarian and informational reinforcement, of the relationship between its behavioural outputs and their reception by the market and to the scope of the behaviour settings of the firm and its customers (Vella and Foxall, 2011, 2013). This has entailed the description and explanation of the firm's behaviour in terms of operational measures of behavioural consequences and behaviour setting (Foxall, 2014a, b).

Bilateral contingency analysis concerns the overt relationships between the marketing firm and a customer, either a final consumer or a corporate purchaser (Figure 12.2). The task of marketing management is to plan, devise and implement marketing mixes that deliver satisfactions for the firm's customer base that are profitable for the firm. The components of the marketing mix (product, price, promotion and place utilities) appear in the marketplace initially as discriminative stimuli for the consumer behaviours of browsing, purchasing and consuming.

Purchasing includes the exchange of money for the ownership of the legal right to a product or service, and this pecuniary exchange acts as a source of both utilitarian reinforcement (in the form of resources that can be paid out or reinvested) and informational reinforcement (in the form of feedback on corporate performance) for the marketing firm. The efficacy of Rm (managerial behaviour) in fulfilling the professional requirements of marketing management, namely the creation of a customer who purchases the product at a price level sufficient to meet the goals of the firm, is determined by the generation of profit and reputation for the firm (depicted by the dotted diagonal line in Figure 12.2). This consumer behaviour (Rc) also provides discriminative stimuli for further marketing intelligence activities, marketing planning and the devising and implementation of marketing mixes that respond to the stabilities and/or dynamic nature of the behaviour of the customer base (Foxall, 1999a, 2014a; Vella and Foxall, 2011). At this level of market interaction between the enterprise and its customer base, managerial behaviour can be viewed as maximising a utility function, comprising a combination of utilitarian reinforcement and informational reinforcement (Oliveira-Castro, Cavalcanti and Foxall, 2015, 2016).

THE MARKETING FIRM

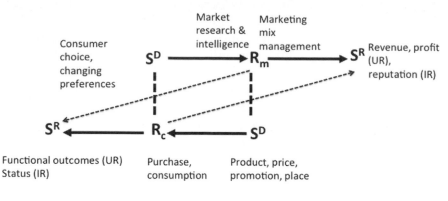

Figure 12.2. *Bilateral contingency between the marketing firm and a customer.*
UR = utilitarian reinforcement, IR = informational reinforcement
Adapted from Foxall (2014b).

12.4.4 Styles of Marketing Integration

Marketing integration may take a number of forms which, in view of what has been said about transaction cost analysis, may prove more or less tractable to analysis by that method.

12.4.4.1 *Minimal Marketing Integration*

Firms differ in the extent to which they are integrated with other organisations with respect to their marketing operations. Figure 12.3 summarises the position of the firm where there is minimal marketing integration. The firm is minimally integrated with respect to its marketing operations, obtains marketing intelligence ($MkOp_1$) from supplier organisations and delegates its externally oriented marketing operations ($MkOp_3$) – physical distribution, for instance – to commercial partners with specialist expertise. It is assumed, however, to retain the strategic managerial functions, which consist in determining marketing considerations such as the product-market scope of the firm ($MkOp_2$) within its own sphere of control. It is by virtue of its retention of these functions that we understand the firm to be a 'marketing firm'.

The firm is minimally integrated with respect to its marketing operations. The firm obtains marketing intelligence ($MkOp_1$) from supplier organisations. It also delegates commercially its externally oriented marketing operations ($MkOp_3$) – physical distribution, for instance – to commercial partners with specialist expertise. However, it is perhaps inevitable and certainly highly predictable that the firm will retain its strategic managerial functions, which consist importantly in marketing considerations such as the product-market scope

Figure 12.3. *Marketing operations and the marketing firm: minimal marketing integration.*

of the firm (MkOp$_2$) within its own sphere of control. 'Customers' may be other firms or final consumers. The dashed lines in Figure 12.3 indicate operations undertaken within the marketing firm. The firm is minimally integrated only with respect to its marketing operations: note that (1) other operations may be supplied by integrated or quasi-integrated organisations, and (2) the marketing operations shown may be supplied by organisations that are quasivertically integrated into the firm.

Even though the ostensible operations of a firm of this kind consist entirely in the physical production of a product or the capacity to deliver a service such as financial brokerage, it is nonetheless a *marketing* firm by virtue of its strategic direction being set by marketing criteria – the selection of a customer base and of the means to satisfy its requirements profitably, and the monitoring of and adaptation to its progress in these regards. Even a professional firm that exists solely to offer, say, legal or accountancy services or to provide consultancy to its clients is as much engaged in marketing as a large, diversified retailer. It employs marketing intelligence, creates marketing mixes to deliver its product to clients and necessarily sets its strategic policies and goals together with its planning of how it will achieve them.

Although such a firm seems to be a self-contained production unit, it is a marketing firm by virtue of the strategic marketing operations it undertakes. But it is not only MkOp$_2$ that the firm retains. It also acts upon marketing intelligence even if this comes solely from discussion with its clients that clarify what they are seeking by way of product or service. It has some responsibility for and control over the way in which it delivers its products or services – the time-honored elements of the marketing mix, namely product, price, promotion and place, remain as necessary to this firm as they are to any more obvious practitioner of marketing management, such as a large retail supermarket or a commercial bank. It is doubtful, therefore, if any firm can entirely avoid the marketing operations inherent in market analysis and market provision. Even if it uses market research and markets distribution agencies for the bulk of these tasks, it still has to select those agencies, ensure they are acting in accord with its own marketing objectives and monitor and control their outcomes

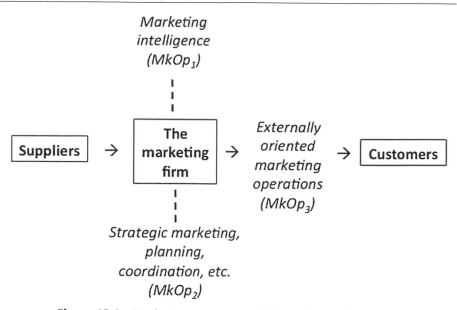

Figure 12.4. *Marketing operations and the marketing firm: partial marketing integration I.*

insofar as they contribute to or impede its own internal marketing policies and procedures. These are all vital marketing considerations and mark the firm out as a marketing firm as previously defined.

12.4.4.2 Partial Marketing Integration

The arrangement depicted in Figure 12.4 shows the firm's marketing operations to be partially integrated: the generation of marketing intelligence is the responsibility of the organisation, but its external marketing operations are conducted by a separate organisation. The firm is still vitally engaged in $MkOp_2$, however; indeed, it is difficult to imagine how these functions could be undertaken by a separate organisation without the firm ceasing to be a marketing firm. It is possible that some wholly owned subsidiaries of larger corporations might have minimal local input to such deliberations and decisions, but they could still be regarded as marketing firms by dint of their operating within a more broadly determined marketing-strategic framework. It is, anyway, unlikely in practice that no inputs to the deliberative and decision processes would be made by the subsidiary. Another solution would be to assume a superordinate level of analysis and see the entire corporation, including its subsidiary, as 'the (marketing) firm'.

The firm is partially integrated with respect to its marketing operations: those relating to marketing intelligence are undertaken within the firm, while those relating to the external marketing of its output are commercially delegated. Supplies are still an integral component of the firm's relationships to allow

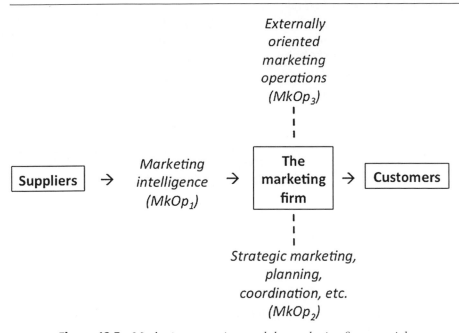

Figure 12.5. *Marketing operations and the marketing firm: partial marketing integration II.*

for the possibility of its obtaining various supplies and nonmarketing factor inputs from external sources. While $MkOp_1$ are fully integrated, the possibility remains that $MkOp_3$ may be supplied by organisations that are quasivertically integrated into the firm.

Similar considerations apply to the state of affairs shown in Figure 12.5, which portrays the reverse situation: the marketing firm obtains its marketing intelligence from external sources but is wholly responsible for its external marketing operations.

The firm is partially integrated with respect to its marketing operations: those relating to marketing intelligence are commercially delegated, while those relating to the external marketing of its output are undertaken within the firm. While $MkOp_3$ are fully integrated, the possibility remains that $MkOp_1$ may be supplied by organisations that are quasivertically integrated into the firm.

12.4.4.3 *Full Marketing Integration*
Figure 12.6 depicts the firm which is fully integrated with respect to its marketing operations: both those relating to marketing intelligence and those relating to the external marketing of its output are undertaken within the firm. The firm is still designated a 'marketing' firm by virtue of the central core of marketing competencies and strategies that are the subject of its strategic marketing operations.

Figure 12.6. *Marketing operations and the marketing firm: full marketing integration.*

12.4.5 Symmetry Versus Asymmetry of Bilateral Contingencies

Empirical research, possibly based on case study investigation, may shed further light on the relevance of the ideas of metacontingency and bilateral contingency to the analysis of firm–customer interactions. A pertinent dimension of these interactions reflects the extent to which they are symmetrical or asymmetrical.

Symmetry denotes the pattern of interaction over time of two organisations each marked by metacontingency whose behaviour forms an overarching metacontingent system. In other words, the two metacontingencies form a superordinate bilateral contingency, depicted in Figure 12.7, in which the transaction comprises the interaction of the integrated marketing mix presented by the marketing firm and the corporate purchasing strategy designed and implemented by the corporate customer: metacontingency meets metacontingency. Symmetrical relationships imply a degree of equality between the transacting parties insofar as each is assumed to possess and implement a strategic marketing plan which takes the behaviour of the other into consideration. The organisational parties to such transactions are predictable on the basis of either the contextual or intentional stance (Foxall, 1999b, 2016b). The behaviour of the metacontingency that is the marketing firm is a discernable marketing mix, and by knowing this the metacontingency that is the buyer can tailor its purchasing strategies accordingly. The marketing firm can similarly tailor its marketing mixes to the purchasing requirements of the firms that

Figure 12.7. *Symmetrical bilateral contingency.*

compose its customer base. The symmetrical relationship between marketing firm and corporate customer is such that each can read the other's behaviour in terms of a unified marketing mix or purchasing policy from which it can infer the strategy of the other and respond to it strategically. As a result, more appropriate marketing mixes and acquisition strategies can be designed and implemented, leading to enhanced efficiency as well as sustained relationships that generate tailored product development. Each organisation enjoys a considerable degree of control of its own behaviour setting. Moreover, each member of the bilateral contingency matters to the other sufficiently for its strategic ends to be taken into consideration. Each party provides the other with marketing intelligence, can assert its strategic aims and, if it chooses not to transact with the other, can wreak tangible effects on the other's fortunes. The result is genuine relationship marketing based on a long-term relationship between the transacting organisations.

Asymmetry, however, is marked by an inequality of interaction in the sense that if only one party to the transaction, the marketing firm, is a metacontingency, then each member of the customer base is individually pitted against an organisation which may use considerable resources to impose a marketing mix on the customer base. This is the transaction depicted in Figure 12.8, in which the transaction comprises the interaction of an integrated marketing mix designed and implemented by the marketing firm, which represents a metacontingency, and the buying behaviour of the individual final consumer or the macrobehaviour of the customer base. The customer base is unlikely to be in a position to develop a strategic stance, let alone to act as a metacontingency that has strategic outputs. As long as the potential customer base is large, the marketing firm need not seek sustained associations with its individual consumers, for it can attain its revenue and profit objectives even if it loses current consumers, so long as it can attract enough new ones. It is hardly under pressure to meet the requirements of each available market segment, let alone each consumer. However, this is a myopic strategy. The high failure rates of new products attest to the power of the customer base to dictate the fortunes of even the largest marketing firms, the constant attraction of a new customer

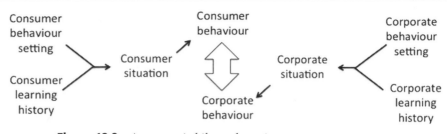

Figure 12.8. *Asymmetric bilateral contingency.*

base is costly – perhaps far more so than the retention of existing buyers – and severe competitive pressures militate against complacency. The relationship remains asymmetrical in the sense defined, but consumers achieve a degree of countervailing power. What this boils down to is that in a market economy marked by the imperatives of marketing-oriented management, bilateral contingencies ensure that consumers' setting scope is sufficiently open to allow them to transfer their business to another supplier.

Bilateral contingencies differ in their stability or fragility where these are understood as the degree to which they motivate orderly exchange between marketers and their customers (Figure 12.9). The consequent relationships have been explored in a study of the bilateral contingencies that characterise marketer–customer interactions in the context of environmentally impacting consumption (Foxall, 2015b), which permits some generalisations to be advanced as the basis for further empirical investigations. Bilateral contingencies at the stable end of the continuum are marked by close or proximal interactions in which the behaviours of marketers and consumers are relatively united. They involve easily read stimulus profiles (the elements of supplier behaviour that act as motivating operations or discriminative stimuli for customer behaviour are very apparent and vice versa), they are immediately acting (especially in the case of metred commodities) and they are reliable. Moreover, stable relationships entail genuine marketing relationships comprising literal exchanges that embrace the whole of the marketing mix. More fragile relationships may, however, be built on contingencies that are more remote or distal, not easily read, featuring delayed and unreliable consequences. They are likely to rely principally on persuasion and to preclude the need for literal exchange.

12.5 Marketing Integration and Bilateral Contingency: Research Agenda

12.5.1 Research Tableau

Figures 12.10 through 12.13 indicate the possible arrays of bilateral contingencies that arise from the associations between the marketing firm and

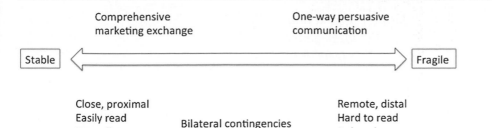

Figure 12.9. *Continuum of stable–fragile bilateral contingencies.*

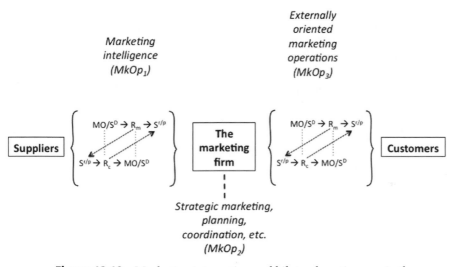

Figure 12.10. *Marketing integration and bilateral contingency in the minimally marketing-integrated firm.*

suppliers of (i) marketing intelligence services on which corporate planning and marketing mix creation depend; and (ii) managerial marketing services, such as distribution, which ensure the delivery of appropriate marketing mixes to customers. In addition, intrafirm relationships marked by bilateral contingencies are shown where they are relevant. The ways in which these bilateral contingencies are managed by the marketing firm depend on the transaction costs they incur in transacting in this way rather than internalising the relevant operations. But they also represent richer social as well as economic interactions that can be captured via consideration of the nature of the bilateral contingencies involved. It is at these junctures that further research would usefully demonstrate the extent to which bilateral contingency analysis may interact with or at least complement transaction cost analysis.

Figure 12.10 depicts the situation in which there is minimal marketing integration. Transaction cost analysis leads to the assumption that marketing transacting is less costly than internal organisation but has little more to

Figure 12.11. *Marketing integration and bilateral contingency in the partially marketing-integrated firm (1): integration of marketing intelligence.*

say about the ongoing relationships involved between the marketing firm and its suppliers and customers. Bilateral contingencies are apparent between the marketing firm and these external organisations and will need to be analysed and managed.

Figure 12.11 shows the integration of marketing intelligence gathering into the marketing firm, which creates a set of bilateral contingencies within the organisation that did not previously exist. Depending on the extent to which the marketing firm practices intraorganisational pricing, this may or may not create significant transaction costs between parts of the organisation.

In Figure 12.12, the integration of aspects of marketing mix management into the marketing firm is shown creating a different set of bilateral contingencies within the organisation that were not previously in operation. Depending on the extent to which the marketing firm practices intraorganisational pricing, this may or may not create significant transaction costs between parts of the organisation.

Finally, Figure 12.13 indicates the bilateral contingencies that mark the interactions of managers within the marketing firm. The firm will still need to

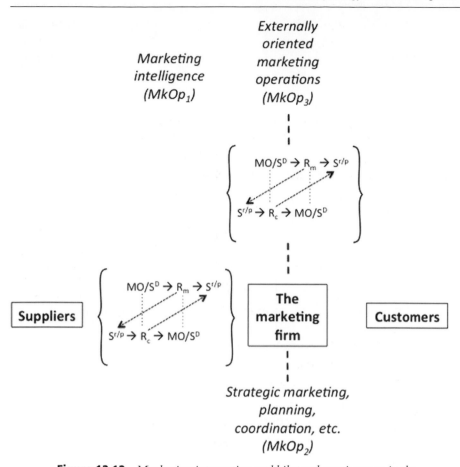

Figure 12.12. *Marketing integration and bilateral contingency in the partially marketing-integrated firm (2): integration of marketing mix management.*

analyse and manage its relationships with its customers through an additional series of bilateral contingencies.

12.5.2 Research Questions

Several avenues for empirical research, possibly case-based but not necessarily exclusively so, can be suggested on the basis of this preliminary analysis. Some answers have already been suggested by the empirical analyses that derive from the theory of the marketing firm (Foxall, 2015a; Vella, 2015; Vella and Foxall, 2011). The following research questions are no more than preliminary suggestions as to how the research might proceed in view of the issues raised in this chapter.

It would be desirable, for instance, to establish the precise patterns of utilitarian and informational reinforcement that sustain the behaviours of (a) the

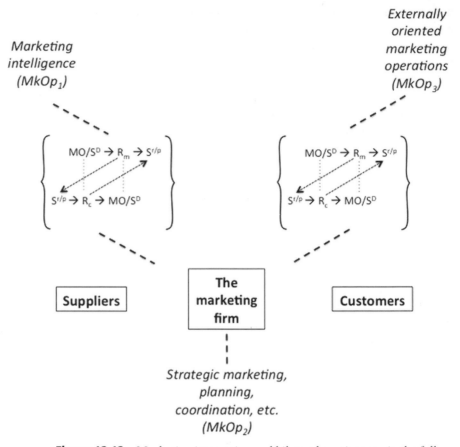

Figure 12.13. *Marketing integration and bilateral contingency in the fully marketing-integrated firm.*

marketing firm and (b) customers in both (i) marketing relationships, that is, literal transfers of legal title to goods; and (ii) mutuality relationships which sustain long-term associations. A similar analysis could be undertaken with regard to the utilitarian and informational punishers in operation in these relationships. Second, we might seek to determine how the behaviours of one party to a transaction or series of transactions act as discriminative stimuli for the other: how are such behaviours monitored and translated into responses? It is also feasible to determine whether there are differences in the bilateral contingencies involved in each of the styles of marketing integration. Are there, for instance, differences in the ways in which bilateral contingencies are established and maintained among the various styles of marketing integration? And how are these differences reflected in (a) marketing relationships and (b) mutuality relationships?

We might, additionally, seek to determine whether there are differences in bilateral contingencies as they arise between, on the one hand, firms which are contractually linked to one another and, on the other, those that arise between managers and other employees within firms. The latter are also contractually bound, of course, but they can be expected to differ from firm–firm relations in that the parties involved are likely to encounter one another on a daily basis, in multiple contexts. Do mutuality relationships assume a more important role in this instance? More specifically, is it possible to detect differences between the marketing mixes generated by metacontingencies operating in the marketing firm when its customer is another corporation and when it is a body of individual consumers?

It would be interesting to know more about the nature of consumers' countervailing power vis-à-vis market firms: for example, (a) consumers' normal market responses, such as their acceptance or rejection of products; and (b) consumers' use of organisation and quasi-organisation through, for instance, social media or consumer boycotts.

Finally, where does transaction cost analysis fit into these areas of investigation? How is transaction cost analysis related to bilateral contingency analysis? Does transaction cost analysis actually explain whether $MkOp_3$ are integrated or delegated? And how do bilateral contingencies fit into this primarily economic pattern of explanation?

12.6 Conclusions

The idea of the marketing firm posits that the primary rationale for firms, given the structural nature of modern markets, is to undertake customer-oriented management – that is, to respond to the general economic and social conditions that make production orientation unprofitable and that compel a customer-oriented strategy on not only the part of the marketing department or function, but of the entire enterprise. Given the competitive structure of modern economies, firms exist primarily to create customers through a series of marketing operations. *Marketing firms* employ marketing intelligence in the formulation of strategic marketing plans, on the basis of which they design and implement marketing mixes that profitably satisfy customer requirements. The first of these operations conforms to the Cosean idea that factors of production may be sourced externally or produced within the enterprise depending on the transaction costs of using the market versus the costs of internalised operations. However, the remaining marketing operations do not so easily fit the transaction costs model. It is proposed that they be understood rather in terms of an economic-psychological framework of conceptualisation and analysis which draws attention to the bilateral contingencies that link the marketing firm with its publics via networks of reinforcement and response costs.

This chapter has taken Coase's approach to the firm as a reference point for several reasons. First is the *level of generality*: neither Coase's theory nor the account of the marketing firm seeks to put forward a particular model of corporate behaviour and its relationship to performance but a general picture of why firms of a particular kind exist. Each seeks to provide a logic for the existence of firms of a particular type rather than a historical account of their coming into being. Coase based his thesis on empirical observation but hardly on the basis of the thorough empirical research that is involved in the testing of specific hypotheses. That is the level of theoretical analysis to which this chapter aspires: specific hypotheses can be derived from the research questions suggested, the testing of which can contribute to the direction of the framework of conceptualisation and analysis advanced here.

Second is the necessity of basing our view of the firm on observations of *changed economic and social circumstances*. It is necessary now to focus attention on the environmental forces that encourage a marketing orientation, which at the time Coase wrote were only beginning to emerge in many industries. That firms must become marketing-oriented in the face of changed economic and social circumstances may be a truism, it is akin to the level of analysis Coase employs in arguing that firms economise transaction costs by internalising operations. That is, it is subject to empirical evaluation but is an observation worth making at the level of theory.

This approach motivates recognition of marketing-oriented management as the expected response of the modern firm. It is possible at the level of generality adopted to see the need for marketing- and customer-orientation that changed circumstances would require without proposing a particular model of such an orientation. The novel emphasis on marketing, the talk of marketing-orientation in textbooks and manuals and the burgeoning literature seeking to quantify the relationship between marketing-oriented management and marketing/corporate performance are all evidence of this. Although all firms exist 'in order to market' (Foxall, 1999a), this is not to say they all do it well or that there is an optimal style of marketing-oriented management.[7]

A further consideration which calls for future research concerns the *empirical availability of marketing-oriented management*. Marketing-oriented management is a logic of corporate behaviour rather than a prescription for microbehaviours that will bring enhanced success. It is not always possible, for instance, to sample consumer opinion before commencing production, since the product (or perhaps more especially the service) may not exist in a form that consumers can easily appraise in terms of its precise functionality. Nevertheless, the logic of marketing-oriented management persists. Hence, to attempt to itemise the components of marketing-oriented management and link them to corporate performance, which has spawned a small industry among marketing researchers, is actually against the true import of marketing-oriented management.

Finally comes the issue of the *delineation of marketing operations*. Coase makes no more than passing reference to marketing and does not appear to see it in terms of anything but sales. That there are some marketing operations ($MkOp_1$) that can be included among the factor inputs that he sees as capable of internalisation in the process of economising transaction costs is worthy of note; so is the delineation of other kinds of marketing operations and the fact that the firm's style of fulfilling these is a response to different imperatives of market conditions from those that attended the firms he observed and on which his ideas are based. The marketing operations which entail the firm's external interventions in customer markets ($MkOp_3$) require analysis in terms of their internalisation or delegation on the basis of transaction cost considerations. The strategic marketing operations that enter into the setting of product-market scope ($MkOp_2$) are also pertinent. The aim is to contribute to the development of a marketing theory of the firm, one that suggests in behavioural-scientific terms how to define and quantify the links between parties to transactions.

Notes

1 These terms are used interchangeably throughout the chapter.
2 These models form part of a broader research programme committed to identifying the place and role of cognitive explanation in the explanation of consumer choice (Foxall, 1990/2004, 2016a,b). This research programme seeks to fulfil these goals by formulating and testing exhaustively parsimonious, non-cognitive models of consumer behaviour and management. The expectation has been that the need for and necessary shape of cognitive explanation will become apparent when these behaviourist models no longer provide satisfactory accounts of the behaviours they concern. In the process of this research programme, which is now sufficiently advanced to allow the development of cognitive theorising (Foxall, 2016a,b), it is possible to understand better the positive contributions of behavioural modelling, and the present chapter is based on the results yielded by this phase of the programme.
3 As Coase points out, transaction cost considerations influence not only the form that contracts take and their rules of implementation but also the nature of the products and services that are produced. This insight generated a revolution in which transaction costs and the consideration to which they give rise, albeit several decades later, came to dominate research and teaching industrial economics and business administration. It was a major factor in Coase's award of the Alfred Nobel Memorial Prize in Economic Sciences in 1991.
4 The resulting principle of action is then to 'organize transactions so as to economize on bounded rationality while simultaneously safeguarding them against the hazards of opportunism' (Williamson, 1985, p. 32; Medema, 1994, p. 30; see also Demsetz, 1995; Easterbrook and Fischel, 1991; Hart, 1995).
5 In Drucker's picturesque estimation, 'Marketing … is a central dimension of the entire business. It is the whole business seen from the point of view of its final result, that is from the customer's point of view' (Drucker, 1977, p. 58.)
6 Networks, which fall between markets and hierarchies and which involve vertical quasi-integration, are also germane here but beyond the scope of the present chapter; see Williamson (1975), and for an exposition in the context of marketing, see Foxall (1988).

7   Kotler and Keller (2015) propose that the societal marketing concept is superior to the corporate marketing concept – but it is practicable only to someone with perfect foresight!

12.7 References

Alchian, A. A. and Demsetz, H. (1972). Production, Information Cost, and Economic Organization, *American Economic Review*, 62, 777–795.

Bartels, R. (1976). *The History of Marketing Thought*. Columbus, OH: Grid.

Biglan, A. and Glenn, S. S. (2013). Toward Prosocial Behavior and Environments: Behavioral and Cultural Contingencies in a Public Health Framework. In G. J. Madden, W. V. Dube, T. D. Hackenberg, G. P. Hanley and K. A. Lattal (Eds.), *APA Handbook of Behavior Analysis* (Vol. 2, pp. 255–275). Washington, DC: American Psychological Association.

Blois, K. J. (1972). Vertical Quasi-Integration, *Journal of Industrial Economics* 20, 253–272.

Boulding, K. E. (1970). *Economics as a Science.* New York: McGraw-Hill.

Coase, R. H. (1937). The Nature of the Firm. *Economica*, 4, 386–405.

Coase, R. H. (1988a). The Nature of the Firm: Origin, *Journal of Law and Economics, and Organization*, ns, 4, 3–17.

Coase, R. H. (1988b). The Nature of the Firm: Meaning, *Journal of Law and Economics, and Organization*, 4, 19–32.

Coase, R. H. (1988c). The Nature of the Firm: Influence, *Journal of Law and Economics, and Organization*, 4, 33–47.

Coase, R. H. (1988d). *The Firm, the Market, and the Law*. Chicago: Chicago University Press.

Coase, R. H. (1994). *Essays on Economics and Economists*. Chicago: Chicago University Press.

Coase, R. H. (1993). Nobel Lecture 1991: The Institutional Structure of Production. In O. E. Williamson and S. G. Winter (Eds). *The Nature of the Firm: Origins, Evolution, and Development* (pp. 227–235). New York: Oxford University Press.

Commons, J. R. (1924). *The Legal Foundations of Capitalism*. Clifton, NJ: Augustus M. Kelley.

Demsetz, H. (1995). *The Economics of the Business Firm: Seven Critical Commentaries.* Cambridge: Cambridge University Press.

Drucker, P. F. (1977). *Management.* New York: Harper.

Drucker, P. F. (2007). *The Practice of Management*. London: Routledge.

Easterbrook, F. H. and Fischel, D. R. (1991). *The Economic Structure of Corporate Law*. Cambridge, MA: Harvard University Press.

Foxall, G. R. (1988). Marketing New Technology: Markets, Hierarchies, and User-Initiated Innovation, *Managerial and Decision Economics*, 9, 237–250.

Foxall, G. R. (1990/2004). *Consumer Psychology in Behavioral Perspective.* London and New York: Routledge. (Reprinted 2004 by Frederick, MD: Beard Books).

Foxall, G. R. (1999a). The Marketing Firm, *Journal of Economic Psychology*, 20, 207–234.

Foxall, G. R. (1999b). The Contextual Stance, *Philosophical Psychology*, 12, 25–46.

Foxall, G. R. (2001). Foundations of Consumer Behaviour Analysis. *Marketing Theory*, 1, 165–199.

Foxall, G. R. (Ed.). (2002). *Consumer Behaviour Analysis: Critical Perspectives in Business and Management*. London and New York: Routledge.

Foxall, G. R. (2004). *Context and Cognition: Interpreting Complex Behavior.* Reno, NV: Context Press/Oakland, CA: New Harbinger.

Foxall, G. R. (2014a). Cognitive Requirements of Neuro-Behavioral Decision Systems: Some Implications of Temporal Horizon for Managerial Behavior in Organizations, *Frontiers in Human Neuroscience*, 8, 184. doi:10.3389/fnhum.2014.00184

Foxall, G. R. (2014b). The Marketing Firm and Consumer Choice: Implications of Bilateral Contingency for Levels of Analysis in Organizational Neuroscience, *Frontiers in Human Neuroscience*, 8, 472. doi:10.3389/fnhum.2014.00472

Foxall, G. R. (2015a). *Strategic Marketing Management.* (Library Edition). London and New York: Routledge.

Foxall, G. R. (2015b). Consumer Behavior and the Marketing Firm: Bilateral Contingency in the Context of Environmental Concern, *Journal of Organizational Behavior Management*, 35, 44–69.

Foxall, G. R. (2016a). *Addiction as Consumer Choice: Exploring the Cognitive Dimension.* London and New York: Routledge.

Foxall, G. R. (2016b). *Perspectives on Consumer Choice: From Behavior to Action, from Action to Agency.* London and New York: Palgrave Macmillan.

Foxall, G. R. (2016c). Operant Behavioral Economics, *Managerial and Decision Economics*, 37, 215–223.

Glenn, S. S. (1991). Contingencies and Metacontingencies: Relations Among Behavioral, Cultural, and Biological Evolution. In P. A. Lamal (Ed.) *Behavioral Analysis of Societies and Cultural Practices* (pp. 39–73). New York: Hemisphere.

Glenn, S. S. (2004). Individual Behavior, Culture, and Social Change, *Behavior Analyst*, 27, 133–151.

Glenn, S. S. and Malott, M. E. (2004). Complexity and Selection: Implications for Organizational Change, *Behavior and Social Issues*, 13, 89–106.

Hart, O. (1995). *Firms, Contracts and Financial Structure.* Oxford: Clarendon Press.

Hodgson, G. M. (1988). *Economics and Institutions.* Philadelphia: University of Pennsylvania Press.

Hodgson, G. M. and Knutsen, T. (2010). *Darwin's Conjecture: The Search for General Principles of Social and Economic Evolution.* Chicago: Chicago University Press.

Houmanfar, R., Rodrigues, N. J. and Smith, G. S. (2009). Role of Communication Networks in Behavioral Systems Analysis, *Journal of Organizational Behavior Management*, 29, 257–275.

Kotler, P. and Keller, K. L. (2015). *Marketing Management.* 15th edition. Harlow, Essex: Pearson.

Lea, S. E. G., Tarpy, R. M. and Webley, P. (1987). *The Individual in the Economy.* Cambridge: Cambridge University Press.

Lynch, R. (2015). *Strategic Management.* 7th edition. Harlow, Essex: Pearson.

Medema, S. G. (1994). *Ronald H. Coase.* London: Macmillan.

Monteverde, K. and Teece, D. J. (1982). Supplier Switching Costs and Vertical Integration in the Automobile Industry, *Bell Journal of Economics*, 13, 206–213.

Nooteboom, B. (2009). *A Cognitive Theory of the Firm*. Northampton, MA: Edward Elgar.

Oliveira-Castro, J. M., Cavalcanti, P. and Foxall, G. R. (2015). What Consumers Maximize: Brand Choice as a Function of Utilitarian and Informational Reinforcement, *Managerial and Decision Economics*. doi: 10.1002/mde.2722. (Published online May 2015.)

Oliveira-Castro, J. M., Cavalcanti, P. and Foxall, G. R. (2016). What Do Consumers Maximize? The Analysis of Utility Functions in Light of the Behavioral Perspective Model. In G. R. Foxall (Ed.), *The Routledge Companion to Consumer Behavior Analysis* (pp. 202–212). London and New York: Routledge.

Posner, R. A. (1995). *Overcoming Law*. Cambridge, MA: Harvard University Press.

Sautet, F. E. (2000). *An Entrepreneurial Theory of the Firm*. London: Routledge.

Simon, H. A. (1976). *Administrative Behavior*. 3rd edition. New York: Macmillan.

Simon, H. A. (1987). Rational Decision Making in Business Organizations. In L. Green and J. H. Kagel (Eds.), *Advances in Behavioral Economics* (Vol. 1, pp. 18–47). Norwood, NJ: Ablex.

Skinner, B. F. (1981). Selection by Consequences, *Science*, 213, (3 July), 501–504.

Van Parijs, P. (1981). *Evolutionary Explanation in the Social Sciences* (London and Totowa, NJ: Rowman & Littlefield.

Vella, K. J. (2015). Selection by Consequences and the Marketing Firm. PhD Thesis, Cardiff University.

Vella, K. J. and Foxall, G. R. (2011). *The Marketing Firm: Economic Psychology of Corporate Behaviour.* Cheltenham, Glouchester, and Northampton, MA: Edward Elgar.

Vella, K. J. and Foxall, G. R. (2013). The Marketing Firm: Operant Interpretation of Corporate Behavior, *Psychological Record*, 62, 375–402.

Williamson, O. E. (1975). *Markets and Hierarchies: Analysis and Antitrust Implications*. New York: Free Press.

Williamson, O. E. (1985). *The Economic Institutions of Capitalism*. New York: Free Press.

Williamson, O. E. and Winter, S. G. (Eds) (1993). *The Nature of the Firm: Origins, Evolution, and Development.* New York: Oxford University Press.

PART IV

Public Sector Consumer Behaviour

13 Tax Psychology

Jerome Olsen, Minjo Kang and Erich Kirchler

13.1 Introduction

Taxation is one of the most fundamental and influential institutions in modern societies (Gaisbauer, Schweiger, and Sedmak, 2015). Taxes are an indispensable source of financing public services to secure social welfare, public order, and national defense. A range of public goods, such as education, health, or infrastructure, cannot be appropriately provided without the government and taxation. Citizens are obliged to pay their taxes imposed by the law. They must pay their tax whatever they may think about the tax system. For law-abiding citizens, paying taxes is a spontaneous prosocial act of contributing to the community. The provision of public goods raises a social contribution dilemma (Dawes, 1980), in which the individual's interest contradicts the collective interest. Hence, individuals can be motivated to free-ride, especially when the opportunity to hide the source of their taxes arises.

Noncompliance represents any failure to meet tax obligations, whether it is intentional or inadvertent. For example, the "tax gap" is an aggregate noncompliance measure, which is defined as the difference between actual tax collected and the potential tax collection under full compliance with the tax code (Gemmell and Hasseldine, 2014); it consists of nonfiling of tax returns, underreporting of tax, and underpayment of tax (IRS, 2012). Estimating the tax gap is challenging given that noncompliant citizens engage in hiding their evasion activities. Moreover, different methods are applied to estimate tax evasion, which makes it difficult to compare data between countries. Nevertheless, the European Commission (2015) regularly publishes the estimated size of the "value-added tax (VAT) gap" (see Table 13.1), indicating that tax noncompliance is prevalent in all European Union (EU) countries. The extent of shadow economy (Schneider, 2015; see Table 13.1), which amounts in part from evading taxes, leads to the same conclusion.

Tax evasion or tax avoidance refer to a deliberate act of noncompliance, while tax evasion or tax cheating refers to intentionally and illegally paying less taxes than the law requires by deliberate nondisclosure (Elffers, Weigel, and Hessing, 1987), tax avoidance is considered a legal response to taxation to reduce one's tax liability, which is however usually in contradiction with the spirit of the law, and thus challenged by tax authorities to be noncompliant. The majority of studies on tax behavior address the problem of individuals'

Table 13.1 *Estimates of the VAT gap (European Commission, 2015) and shadow economy (Schneider, 2015) for twenty-six EU countries*

Country	VAT revenue (2013)	VAT gap (2013)	VAT gap in percent (2013)	Shadow economy as percentage of GDP (2013)
Austria	24,953	3,217	11.4	7.5
Belgium	27,226	3,186	10.5	16.4
Bulgaria	3,775	785	17.2	31.2
Czech Republic	11,694	3,375	22.4	15.5
Denmark	24,360	2,489	9.3	13.0
Estonia	1,558	315	16.8	27.6
Finland	18,848	812	4.1	13.0
France	144,414	14,096	8.9	9.9
Germany	197,005	24,873	11.2	12.4
Greece	12,593	6,497	34.0	23.6
Hungary	9,073	2,930	24.4	22.1
Ireland	10,371	1,225	10.6	12.2
Italy	93,921	47,516	33.6	21.1
Latvia	1,693	721	29.9	25.5
Lithuania	2,611	1,580	37.7	28.0
Luxembourg	3,485	187	5.1	8.0
Malta	586	210	26.4	24.3
Netherlands	42,424	1,852	4.2	9.1
Poland	27,780	10,131	26.7	23.8
Portugal	13,710	1,358	9.0	19.0
Romania	11,913	8,296	41.1	28.4
Slovakia	4,696	2,513	34.9	15.0
Slovenia	3,045	186	5.8	23.1
Spain	61,350	12,094	16.5	25.2
Sweden	39,091	1,776	4.3	13.9
United Kingdom	141,668	15,431	9.8	9.7

Note: Revenue and tax gap refer to Euros in millions.

income tax evasion in the form of underreporting taxable income or over claiming unwarranted deductions.

Why do some people not comply with the fiscal authorities? What is the best policy to establish, maintain, or enhance compliance? In order for the government to implement an optimal fiscal policy, it is important to understand decision processes of taxpayers and the underlying motivations for compliance. Over the last five decades, scholars from various disciplines have investigated behavioral implications of tax compliance that should be considered in the formulation of tax law and policy. Fiscal psychology is concerned with both economic and psychological factors that induce taxpayers' behavioral responses to the tax system. In particular, most studies about tax compliance are centered on individual income tax systems in which taxpayers are given opportunities not to comply, and their tax liabilities are determined by self-declaration and self-assessment of taxable income, while the true income is not observable unless an audit is conducted. Self-employed or workers whose income is not subject to third-party reporting can evade their taxes by understating their true income; or, one can engage in more sophisticated tax sheltering.

This chapter provides a review of research on tax behavior from the perspective of behavioral economics and economic psychology. It is structured into three main sections: rational and irrational decision-making; social representations about taxes; and finally the interaction between tax authorities and taxpayers. The section on decision-making discusses rational choice and tax payments, prospect theory, mental accounting, and framing effects. The section on social representations covers topics such as knowledge and understanding of taxation, attitudes and beliefs, personal and social norms, as well as distributional and procedural justice. The interaction between taxpayers and tax authorities is discussed next with reference to the "slippery slope framework" and empirical investigations regarding the impact of authorities' power and taxpayers' trust in authorities. The chapter concludes with a summary of practical implications of the research surveyed.

13.2 Decision-Making in Tax Compliance

13.2.1 Rational Choice Model

The first economic analysis of tax compliance behavior can be traced back to the pioneering work of Allingham and Sandmo (1972). Their analytic model is a straightforward application of Becker's (1968) economics-of-crime paradigm to individual income tax. Taxpayers are assumed to be motivated *only* to maximize their expected utility from financial outcomes by trading off the potential costs of evasion against the costs of compliance. In this framework, a taxpayer's evasion decision is analogous to portfolio choice between the certain tax position (honest reporting) and the risky prospect of evasion (Sandmo, 2005); the taxpayer is deemed a gambler playing with the tax authority under the risk of being detected. The Allingham and Sandmo (1972) model is often called the standard economic model of tax evasion. In this approach, the key policy parameters affecting tax evasion are the tax rate, the detection probability, and the penalty imposed on evasion. The central point is that an individual pays taxes because of the fear of detection and punishment. Thus, this approach is referred to as the economic deterrence paradigm.

The standard economic model predicts that tax evasion decreases as the economic deterrence factors increase, that is, tax rate, probability of being detected, and penalty rate. These predictions have been extensively examined empirically (Kirchler et al., 2010). First, the size of the relationships between these factors and compliance has proven to be mixed in laboratory experiments. Second, given actual low rates of audits and rather mild penalties in the real world, a taxpayer's rational choice should be to evade most of his or her taxable income, yet it is observed in many countries that the aggregate level of compliance is far higher than would be predicted by the standard economic model (Alm, McClelland, and Schulze, 1992). Lastly, field experiments have revealed that deterrence effects can have mixed results. For instance, in a randomized field experiment manipulating deterrence by threat-of-audit letters, Slemrod, Blumenthal, and Christian (2001) confirmed increased compliance in the group of middle- and low-income taxpayers, but observed adverse responses among high-income taxpayers; high-income taxpayers receiving an audit threat reported lower income than the control group. Kleven et al. (2011) showed that the threat-of-audit letters had significant effects on self-reported income but no effect on third-party reported income.

A model should be evaluated in terms of reasonableness of its assumptions, its predictive power, and its potential usefulness for policy makers. First, the standard economic model assumes that individuals are perfectly rational, selfish, isolated utility maximizers. The underlying assumptions have been criticized by both behavioral economists and psychologists for their lack of reality and humanity (Cullis and Lewis, 1997). Second, neoclassical economists tend to believe that assumptions do not matter as long as the predictions are correct. However, the standard model has failed to explain relatively high levels of actual compliance (Bordignon, 1993). Lastly, the deterrence framework implies enforcement strategy is the only thing that matters to deter the taxpayer from evading. Tax policy based on these assumptions is likely to be inefficient, making it necessary for the tax administration to spend a huge amount of resources monitoring and punishing people.

13.2.2 Behavioral Choice Model

Behavioral choice models deal with the cognitive and contextual aspects in the taxpayer's decision process. It is too burdensome a task for ordinary taxpayers to calculate an optimal concealment of taxable income. Having limited cognitive power, they are susceptible to the ways in which a problem is "framed," and often their judgments and choices are different from those predicted by the standard economic model. For example, whether a tax issue is framed as a bonus for those with children or a penalty for the childless can affect

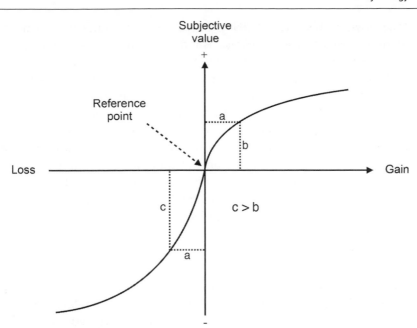

Figure 13.1. *Value function according to prospect theory (Kahneman and Tversky, 1979).*

a taxpayer's attitude toward the tax policy even though the economic consequences are the same (McCaffery and Baron, 2004).

Contrary to the expected utility theory, prospect theory (Kahneman and Tversky, 1979) postulates that an individual's decision outcomes are evaluated by changes in income from some reference point, not by the final state of his or her wealth. The subjective value (Figure 13.1) of gains or losses is determined by a value function that is steeper for losses than for gains, concave for gains, but convex for losses. This implies that the subjective value of a given loss is perceived as more negative than the positive effect of a gain of the same size. As a consequence, people generally try to avoid losses. Depending on whether a potential outcome constitutes a loss or a gain from a person's reference point can thus affect the willingness to take risks; people are risk averse with regards to gains but risk seeking in the domain of losses. Prospect theory provides a framework to understand facets of individual tax behavior that cannot be accounted for by the standard economic model, as for instance framing effects, withholding phenomena, effects of prior audits on subsequent compliance, income nonfungibility, and mental accounting practices.

For instance, taxpayers facing a balance due, generally framed as a loss, tend to be risk seeking, making them more likely to evade (Chang, Nichols, and Schultz, 1987; Kirchler and Maciejovsky, 2001). On the other hand, taxpayers claiming a refund, generally framed as a gain, tend to be risk averse, making them more likely to comply (Elffers and Hessing, 1997; Kirchler and

Maciejovsky, 2001; Yaniv, 1999). The effect of advance tax payment (withholding status) on tax compliance is referred to as the "withholding phenomenon" (Schepanski and Shearer, 1995).

Boylan and Sprinkle (2001) have provided insight into the relation between tax rates and taxpayer compliance by distinguishing endowed income from earned income: when income was endowed, participants responded to tax rate increases by reporting less income, whereas they reported more income for earned income. Kirchler et al. (2009) have confirmed the effect of income source by showing that tax evasion was more pronounced in low-effort conditions. They noted that effort changed the aspiration level (reference point) rather than the slope of the value function, and made high-effort income earners more risk averse and more compliant.

Tax audits constitute not only a reaction to past tax noncompliance, but their consequences represent a cause for future behaviors (Maciejovsky, Kirchler, and Schwarzenberger, 2007). As soldiers would take shelter in bomb craters in the belief that it is unlikely for bombs to fall in the same place twice (which Mittone, 2006, refers to as the "bomb crater effect"), taxpayers may believe that it is safer to evade taxes right after a tax audit has taken place. The effect may be attributable to the misperception of chance, or alternatively taxpayers may attempt to repair their "losses" incurred during the previous audit by engaging in evasion in subsequent tax filings (Andreoni, Erard, and Feinstein, 1998). However there is some support for a contrary "echo effect," where audits, experienced in early stages of taxpaying life cycle, may lead to an increase in compliance (Kastlunger et al., 2009). Experimental evidence suggests that increasing the time lag between tax filing and feedback on audits enhances compliance, mainly due to overweighting of subjective audit probabilities (Kogler, Mittone, and Kirchler, 2015). Field data from the United States (Beer et al., 2015) shows that audits do not affect all taxpayers in the same way. An analysis of Internal Revenue Service (IRS) data by Beer et al. (2015) has revealed that audits increase reported income of sole proprietors substantially if they had additional taxes assessed. Those taxpayers, however, whose audits did not result in an additional tax assessment reported less income in subsequent years. Furthermore, Mendoza, Wielhouver, and Kirchler (2015) have investigated the impact of auditing levels on tax evasion in a comparison of forty-seven countries and found a U-shaped relationship. This means that audits affect compliance positively until a certain auditing level is reached. Thus, simply increasing audits to increase compliance levels is not necessarily the most optimal policy strategy.

Mental accounting describes the set of individuals' cognitive operations to organize, evaluate, and keep track of financial activities (Thaler, 1999). Generally, people have various mental accounts, for instance to pay for their rent, food, or leisure activities. Drawing on this theory in the context of taxes, taxpayers might designate a separate mental account for taxes due in the future. In this case, tax payments would not be mentally deducted from personal income, but from a designated separate account, making it less likely that paying one's taxes will be perceived as a loss. Muehlbacher, Hartl, and Kirchler (2015) have shown that the mental segregation of taxes due from net income affects a taxpayer's reference point in the compliance decision and results in higher tax compliance. However, the effect seems not only to be driven by a shift in reference point to the net income, but because it prevents taxpayers from overspending funds that are needed to pay taxes due later on in the business year. Thus, mental accounting could be regarded as a technique to improve the representation of tax liability without perceiving them as a loss.

13.3 Social Representations of Taxes

Many researchers have pointed out the importance of sociopsychological factors in tax compliance behavior. Individuals are influenced by the social context in which decisions are made. As the tax system builds upon interactions of actors in the field, including taxpayers, tax practitioners, tax authorities, and the government (Alm, Kirchler, and Muehlbacher, 2012), an individual's tax behavior is embedded in the social structures (Pickhardt and Seibold, 2014). Social representations theory (Moscovici, 1961) describes the shared social construction process (rather than individual cognitive processes) of a concept (e.g., tax) that serve as the sociocognitive mental frame to deal with taxes (Moeschler, 2015). Social representations of taxes comprise tax morale, subjective tax knowledge, personal and social norms, fairness perceptions, trust, and interindividual differences of taxpayers (Kirchler, 2007).

13.3.1 Tax Morale

Introducing fiscal psychology as a new field of public finance, Schmölders (1959) maintained that its main task is to analyze the resistance to direct taxation of individuals according to their general "tax mentality," which rests upon the broader tax mentality of their nation. Today, tax morale is used as an umbrella term in the tax literature that refers to all nonmonetary motivations to comply with the tax law (Luttmer and Singhal, 2014). An established definition relates to tax morale as the intrinsic motivation or moral obligation to pay taxes (Alm and Torgler, 2006; Schmölders, 1959, 1960; Torgler, 2005).

Cross-national key findings suggest that tax morale is positively related to direct democracy (Torgler, 2005), institutional quality (Frey and Torgler, 2007), and a progressive tax schedule, while this last effect declines in strength with increasing income (Doerrenberg and Peichl, 2013). Hence, tax morale was found to be especially high among lower-income taxpayers in progressive tax schedules. Moreover, tax morale is negatively associated with perceived tax evasion (Frey and Torgler, 2007) and the shadow economy (Alm and Torgler, 2006; Torgler and Schneider, 2009). Furthermore, regarding the individual

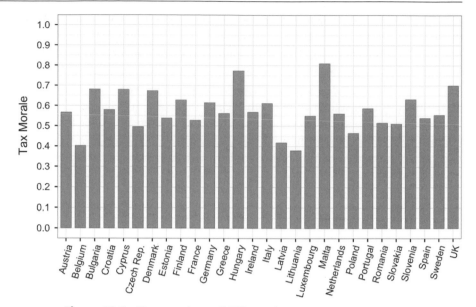

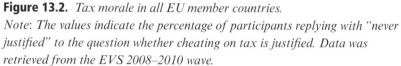

Figure 13.2. *Tax morale in all EU member countries.*
Note: The values indicate the percentage of participants replying with "never justified" to the question whether cheating on tax is justified. Data was retrieved from the EVS 2008–2010 wave.

level, in a number of studies, tax morale was observed to be higher among older taxpayers, more religious people, female taxpayers, people with greater financial experience, taxpayers who trust politicians, and employed taxpayers (Alm and Torgler, 2006; Lago-Peñas and Lago-Peñas, 2010; Torgler, 2004a, Torgler, 2005, Torgler, 2006).

Tax morale is commonly estimated by large-scale surveys such as the World Value Survey (WVS) or the European Value Survey (EVS). The measurement uses a single item, namely: "Please tell me for each of the following statements whether you think it can always be justified, never be justified, or something in between: ... Cheating on tax if you have the chance." The scale ranges from "1 = *never justified*" to "10 = *always justified*," and the observed distribution of answers is usually skewed with a large proportion of participants replying with "1 = *never justified*." A simple measure of tax morale can be obtained by assessing the proportion of participants in a country who believe that cheating on tax is never justified. Torgler and Schneider (2009) have acknowledged that the measurement is not free of bias, as socially desirable answers are likely and it neglects the fact that tax morale is likely to be a multidimensional concept. However, the advantage is an internationally standardized measurement with a wide reach through large-scale surveys and the possibility of cross-national comparisons of intrinsic motivation to comply. Figure 13.2 displays tax morale for all EU member countries using this method with most recent data from the EVS.

The following subsections present specific sociopsychological factors, which all contribute to individuals' social representations of taxes. As all of these factors are nonmonetary and shape intrinsic motives, we regard tax morale as a conglomerate of social representations.

13.3.2 Tax Law Complexity, Tax Knowledge, and Tax Professionals

In most developed countries, tax law is complex and requires a very high reading age to be correctly understood (Lewis, 1982). Commerce Clearing House regularly releases the number of pages contained in their published *Standard Federal Tax Reporter*, a volume covering all aspects of US federal income tax law (Wolters Kluwer CCH, 2015). Figure 13.3 displays the increase in pages over the years, reaching over seventy thousand pages by 2014. Today's income tax code influences a vast range of social and economic domains, which is accompanied by an increase of tax law complexity. In practice, taxpayers facing this complexity are often confronted with uncertainty about their tax liabilities. Complexity may reduce their perceived fairness of the tax system (Cuccia and Carnes, 2001) and result in unintentional noncompliance if they have failed to adequately resolve the uncertainty (McKerchar, 2001). In an experimental study manipulating tax knowledge of student participants, Eriksen and Fallan (1996) found that those who acquired additional knowledge on tax rules evaded less income. Alm et al. (2010) reported experimental evidence indicating that uncertainty reduces compliance, but that the impact is mitigated when the tax agency provides information at low cost to the taxpayer. The results imply that the willingness to pay taxes increases with a greater awareness of tax laws and an improving clarity about the rules.

If tax laws and rules are vague and ambiguous, it may be difficult to fully comply even with no intention to evade. However, there are many tax situations in which their proper treatment is uncertain and the interpretation of facts leads to different tax liabilities. Taxpayers seek practitioners to reduce uncertainty surrounding true tax liability and to save time and effort from understanding complex tax law and preparing their tax returns. They rely upon the guidance of tax experts to cope with the complex compliance procedures or take advantage of legal ambiguities. The role of tax practitioners, therefore, is important in that they can encourage clients to comply with or instigate them to avoid the law: tax practitioners may facilitate taxpayer compliance by reducing their clients' uncertainties about tax liabilities; on the other hand, they can assist their clients with a sophisticated strategy to exploit loopholes in the law. Kaplan et al. (1988) have highlighted the role of tax practitioners in tax compliance by demonstrating that if a tax practitioner provides aggressive tax advice, the taxpayer is likely to take the aggressive tax position that might not be upheld in a tax audit.

Being advocates for their clients as well as intermediaries in the tax system, tax practitioners deal with the interests of both taxpayers and tax authorities.

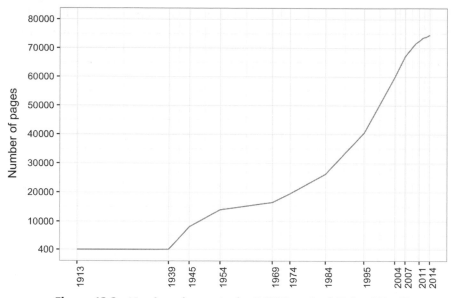

Figure 13.3. *Number of pages in the CCH* Standard Federal Tax Reporter *by selected years (Wolters Kluwer CCH, 2015).*

The dual role of tax practitioners generates a dilemma where interests of the client to minimize the tax burden by straining the law can contradict the obligation to adhere to the tax law. In this situation, an aggressive tax advisor interprets ambiguous tax situations in the taxpayer's favor, whereas a tax auditor, on the other side, is more likely to interpret tax ambiguities to the benefit of the tax authority. In this respect, Frecknall-Hughes and Kirchler (2015) claim negotiation theory to be a conceptual framework for understanding the nature of tax practice and its impact on taxpayer compliance. They argue that the tax advisor and the tax inspector are negotiators who act on behalf of a client and the tax authority, respectively. The negotiation framework has the strength that it not only reconciles the conflict in tax practitioners' work, but fits the different types of work undertaken by tax practitioners encompassing tax inspectors as public sector practitioners. It explains the interaction among taxpayers, tax advisors, tax auditors, and tax authorities at different levels of tax practice.

13.3.3 Personal and Social Norms

Individuals are not only motivated by financial outcomes as they will comply with tax laws if they believe it is the right thing to do. For instance, personal norms significantly moderate the effects of penalty rate and audit probability, indicating that deterrence is only effective when taxpayers' ethics are weak (Wenzel, 2004b). This is especially the case because people with strong personal norms show low tendencies to evade taxes in the first place, and a positive effect of deterrence measures in groups of compliant taxpayers is questionable. Alm and Torgler (2011) have emphasized the impact of tax ethics on compliance decisions as a result of psychological loss that would be incurred by breaking moral standards. Furthermore, individuals are easily influenced by peer behavior. If taxpayers learn that evasion is prevalent among a reference group with which they identify, they would feel less guilty about noncompliance; symmetrically strong social norms against evasion may enhance compliance once taxpayers perceive a threat of social stigma. Wartick and Rupert (2010) reported that student participants who viewed the decision of a noncompliant peer were more likely to cheat than those who viewed the decision of a compliant peer.

Since personal and social norms are interdependent, it could be problematic to completely distinguish the two effects (Onu and Oats, 2015). Nevertheless, Wenzel (2004a) has suggested that the effect of social norms on tax compliance is mediated by personal norms. He holds that personal norms are internalized social norms when the individual identifies strongly with a reference group. In a similar vein, Bobek, Hageman, and Kelliher (2013) investigated the influences of social norms using a hypothetical compliance scenario. In this scenario, participants were asked to imagine preparing an income tax return and to make a hypothetical decision whether to falsely claim a tax deduction that would increase tax savings. Drawing on Cialdini and Trost's (1998) taxonomy of social norms, individuals were asked to respond to a set of questions measuring four specific types of social norms: personal norms (self-based standards), subjective norms (perception of what one's peers think one should do), injunctive norms (perception of what most people think others should do), and descriptive norms (perception of what other people actually do). The results of the study revealed that descriptive norms positively influence injunctive norms. Moreover, these injunctive norms shape subjective norms, meaning that perceived social standards become relevant in taxpayers' perception of his or her closer social environment. Ultimately, these subjective norms become personal norms, thus, behavioral standards for a single taxpayer. The authors reported that both subjective norms and personal norms directly influence tax compliance intentions.

These results suggest that normative appeals to comply should improve tax compliance. However, looking at the effectiveness of normative appeals on the part of tax administrations, results are mixed. In their pioneering field experiment, Schwartz and Orleans (1967) showed that normative appeals may be more effective than legal sanctions in inducing compliance. Bott et al. (2014) observed that including a moral appeal in a letter almost doubled the average foreign income reported compared to a base letter without such an appeal in Norway. Another field experiment by Hasseldine et al. (2007) in the United Kingdom tested the effect of normative appeals and sanction appeals on actual sole proprietors' tax report, and showed evidence of a significant effect for both normative and sanction groups. However, moral suasion had hardly any effect on taxpayers' compliance behavior in a controlled field experiment in Switzerland (Torgler, 2004b), which could be explained by ceiling effects as compliance is assumed to be high already. A similar result was obtained in Israel (Ariel, 2012). Interestingly, in a field experiment conducted in Minnesota, Blumenthal, Christian, and Slemrod (2001) have observed a reversed effect on the highest-income taxpayers, while middle- and upper-income taxpayers were more compliant following the normative appeal. Thus, the effect of normative appeals by tax authorities seems inconclusive. Onu and Oats (2015) have argued that normative appeals must be adjusted to the prevailing norms within a social group. If for instance a person who is late on filing the tax return receives a letter stating that 10 percent of taxpayers do not file a return on time, this person may feel relieved that others are in a similar situation, which could be used as a justification to delay filing the tax return even further. Overall, the importance of norms should not be underestimated in the light of inconclusive field experiment results. Instead, they highlight the subtleties that influence the perception of normative appeals and should encourage policy makers to carefully adjust these (see Onu and Oats, 2015).

13.3.4 Perceived Fairness and Trust

If taxpayers are asked what they think about the tax system, they most frequently mention concerns about fairness (e.g., Braithwaite, 2003; Taylor, 2003). According to Wenzel (2003), the concept of fairness has three main constructs: distributive, procedural, and retributive fairness. Distributive fairness refers to fair exchange of benefits and costs with the government, and the fair distribution of tax burden among taxpayers; procedural fairness involves fair processes of tax collection, such as respectful treatment of taxpayers by tax authorities; and retributive fairness concerns the appropriateness of reward and punishment. There are also concerns about justice where taxpayers weigh up their contributions with any benefits both for themselves and compared with other taxpayers. Wenzel (2002) has argued that taxpayers are more concerned with procedural and distributive justice than purely financial outcomes, given the premise that they strongly identify with the nation.

Justice promotes the legitimacy of political processes that can strengthen trust in the authority (Tyler, 2006). Increasing justice can be achieved by reducing the social distance between taxpayers and tax authorities. One recent attempt by the IRS (2014) was to promote personal taxpayer receipts, containing a detailed overview of which proportion of tax dollars was spent on which public program or service, depending on the size of paid income tax, social security, and Medicare tax. Going one step further from a mere tax contribution feedback system, experimental studies have examined whether tax morale and tax compliance increase when taxpayers can choose what their tax money is being spent on – a concept called "voice." A study by Casal et al. (2016) differentiated between "voice" on contribution, that is, making multiple separate compliance decision for different categories – e.g., defense, pensions, education – and "voice" on distribution, that is, the ability to change the relative amount of tax money spend on each category. Participants assigned to conditions with either high "voice" on contribution or high "voice" on distribution showed higher levels of tax compliance. Thus, individuals were willing to contribute more to public expenditures if they could influence what the money was going to be used for. With regard to majority voting on tax system characteristics, Jun, Cho, and Park (2015) have demonstrated that participants report more income when majority voting determined a tax rate structure compared to when a dictatorship was responsible. In a similar manner, Wahl, Muehlbacher, and Kirchler (2010) confirmed a positive effect of voting on perceived procedural fairness, which increased trust in the government, ultimately leading to higher tax compliance. Moreover, sanctions or punishments can undermine the regulators' legitimacy when perceived as being procedurally unfair. Murphy (2004) has shown that trust in a tax authority and in its procedures plays a key role in determining taxpayers' willingness to comply with the authority's rules and decisions.

Individuals are endowed with civic virtue, which can be crowded out if the government violates norms of fairness (Frey, 1997). Feld and Frey (2007) have claimed that the relationship between taxpayers and the government can be modeled as an implicit contract. Thus, frequent audits or severe penalties that lack legitimacy and credibility may breed distrust and undermine the willingness to cooperate with the authorities. Likewise, tax amnesties devoid of retributive fairness considerations may have a negative impact on subsequent tax compliance by breaching the psychological tax contract. Rechberger et al. (2010) found that the fairer the tax amnesty was perceived to be, the more honestly people reported their income in the filing periods following an amnesty. However, Kastlunger et al. (2011) examined the effect of positive incentives (monetary rewards) on tax compliance and found no evidence of its influence on overall compliance, although they noted that audited compliant taxpayers who were rewarded evaded less in the following period compared with those who experienced no rewards.

Other studies have paid attention to the role of emotions in tax compliance decisions. Relating to the dual system theory of automatic (affective) and reflective (cognitive) processes, Maciejovsky, Schwarzenberger, and Kirchler (2012) investigated how emotional priming affects tax ethics in a series of experimental studies, and showed that information regarding audit probabilities and tax fines are only effective when people are in a state of rational information processing. With regard to general emotional arousal, Coricelli et al. (2010) have reported that higher emotional arousal is associated with lower compliance levels. These presented studies have investigated the effect imposed by emotions on a more general level, while some authors have argued that it is important to study specific emotions as they are linked to distinct motivational system and that emotions of the same valence (e.g., regret and disappointment) can still lead to differences in behavior (Zeelenberg and Pieters, 2006).

Barkworth and Murphy (2015) conducted a series of studies on the effect of procedural justice on experienced emotions and subsequent compliance behavior. They found that low procedural justice leads to anger, which in turn increases tax evasion. Another line of emotion research has focused on shame (Coricelli, Rusconi, and Villeval, 2014), more specifically, whether tax evaders' compliance decreases or increases after public shaming. In the group experiment, which lasted over multiple rounds of paying taxes, shaming was implemented by displaying a tax evader's picture on all screens if the person was audited and caught. However, there were two conditions. In the first condition, the evader's picture was only displayed for a single round. Thus, they were given the opportunity to restore their reputation by not being caught evading taxes again in consecutive rounds. This was not possible in the second condition, where an evader's picture was displayed for multiple rounds. The results indicated that public shaming only increases tax compliance if cheaters are given the opportunity of reintegration immediately, while this is not the case when tax offenders do not get the chance to be socially reintegrated. Another study found that shaming increases compliance effectively when audit procedures are targeted, meaning that taxpayers are not selected for audits randomly, but strategically (i.e., those taxpayers with lowest reported income) (Casagrande, Cagno, and Pandimiglio, 2015).

13.3.5 Motivational Postures

People exhibit great diversity in their behavior. It is assumed that these difference are bound to variations in underlying motives (Ajzen, 1991). In the context of tax behavior, Braithwaite's (2003) defined theses motives as motivational postures, which are interconnected beliefs, evaluations, expectations, and attitudes consciously held by taxpayers. As a consequence, motivational postures reflect the social distance between a taxpayer and the tax authorities and define how taxpayers engage with the authorities. Five motivational postures can be distinguished (see Figure 13.4): commitment; capitulation; resistance; disengagement; and game playing. A committed taxpayer believes in the benefits of the tax system and views taxpaying as morally right; a capitulated taxpayer defers to the tax office when it has legitimate authority; a resistant taxpayer doubts the tax office's intentions and challenges it; a disengaged taxpayer is completely detached from the tax office; and a game-playing taxpayer seeks to take advantage of particular laws and loopholes. While commitment and capitulation represent deferential (positive) attitudes toward tax authorities, resistance, disengagement, and game playing reflect defiant (negative) attitudes toward tax authorities. Since individuals are motivated either by deference motives or by defiance motives, Braithwaite (2009) has claimed that tax authorities should opt for a differential approach where enforcement and regulatory strategies are adjusted in accordance to taxpayers' motivational postures. For instance, it is not necessary to deter a committed taxpayer, who

Motivational postures   **Regulatory strategies**

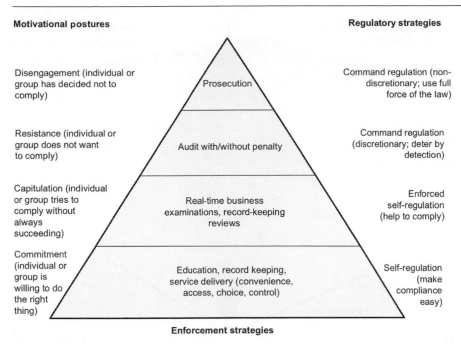

Disengagement (individual or group has decided not to comply)

Resistance (individual or group does not want to comply)

Capitulation (individual or group tries to comply without always succeeding)

Commitment (individual or group is willing to do the right thing)

Prosecution

Audit with/without penalty

Real-time business examinations, record-keeping reviews

Education, record keeping, service delivery (convenience, access, choice, control)

Command regulation (non-discretionary; use full force of the law)

Command regulation (discretionary; deter by detection)

Enforced self-regulation (help to comply)

Self-regulation (make compliance easy)

Enforcement strategies

Figure 13.4. *Australian Taxation Office compliance model.*
Source: Adapted from Braithwaite (2003).

is already compliant. Instead, revenue bodies should make compliance easy by offering services and a transparent filing system. With increasing social distance between tax authorities and taxpayers, the task becomes increasingly difficult. If authorities face a group of disengaged taxpayers, who are not willing to comply, officials must use deterrence measures to enforce compliance.

13.4 The Interaction Between Taxpayers and Tax Authorities

Kirchler, Hoelzl, and Wahl (2008) integrated economic and socio-psychological factors into one comprehensive framework with two dimensions: trust in authorities and power of authorities. The slippery slope framework (SSF), depicted in Figure 13.5, postulates that power and trust determine tax compliance. Power is defined as the capacity of tax authorities to apply deterrence measures. Trust, on the other hand, stems from fairness perceptions, prevalent norms, attitudes, and provided services for taxpayers. On the aggregate level, these two dimensions define the climate between tax authorities and taxpayers. When tax authorities are primarily perceived as powerful, the SSF postulates an antagonistic climate between taxpayers and authorities. If, however, tax authorities are experienced as trustworthy, a synergistic climate is prevalent, where tax authorities are perceived as benevolent. On the individual taxpayer level, these interaction climates lead to different

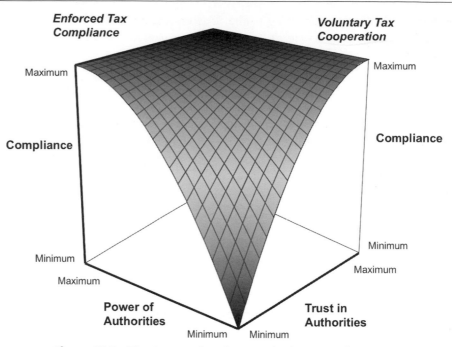

Figure 13.5. *The slippery slope framework of tax compliance (Kirchler et al., 2008).*

motivations to comply with tax law: in an antagonistic climate, taxpayers are presumably compliant with the law because of the fear of detection and fines (enforced compliance); while in a synergistic climate compliance derives from the mindset to contribute to the community (voluntary cooperation).

In the case of enforced compliance, legal coercion may be effective, whereas in the case of voluntary cooperation, social representations of taxes, including subjective tax knowledge, attitudes, norms, and fairness, come into play. The underlying assumptions of the SSF have been confirmed empirically in a number of countries with differing cultural and economic settings (Kastlunger et al., 2013; Kogler et al., 2013; Muehlbacher, Kirchler, and Schwarzenberger, 2011). The largest study was conducted in a total of forty-four countries from five continents (Kogler et al., 2014). Participants were randomly assigned to one of four different scenarios describing a fictitious country with either high or low trust and power. Tax compliance intentions were highest in scenarios where authorities were described as trustworthy and powerful, while intended compliance was lowest in the condition characterized by low trust and low power. On a country level, the results confirmed that trust positively influenced tax compliance intentions in all investigated countries. The effect of power was found for forty-three out of forty-four countries.

The SFF does not only provide a conceptual framework to understand tax compliance research, but also serves as an operational policy tool to devise taxpayers' perceptions of exchange equity simply via information campaigns (Holler et al., 2008). In practice, the Behavioural Insights Team in the United Kingdom and the "I Nudge You" Team in Denmark incorporated the findings of behavioral economics and economic psychology into policies that aim to improve tax compliance. Furthermore, acknowledging the importance of collaborating with tax scholars, tax administrations can provide opportunities for conducting large-scale field experiments in order to develop cost-effective strategies to foster tax compliance with reference to scientific knowledge (e.g., Hallsworth et al., 2014).

The last decade has witnessed the change of research paradigms on tax behavior and regulatory practice in line with the propositions of the SSF (Kirchler, Kogler, and Muehlbacher, 2014). Many countries recognize cooperative compliance as an effective means of achieving tax compliance and establish close relationships between tax authorities and taxpayers that encourage mutual trust in tax matters (OECD, 2013). In 2005, the Dutch Tax and Customs Administration introduced "horizontal monitoring," as an alternative to the traditional "vertical monitoring." Horizontal monitoring allows large companies to enter a partnership with the tax authority, where both work closely together and meet regularly with the key objective of timely and legally accurate tax collections. The advantage for the companies is given by the fact that they have no uncertainty about their tax liabilities and do not have to expect additional tax payments for a concluded accounting period. Thus, companies' compliance costs are reduced and they can benefit from legal security. The partnership is also beneficial for the tax authority because personnel can be shifted to other risk areas (OECD, 2015). Other examples of such programs include the US Compliance Assurance Process, which has existed since 2005; Australia's Annual Compliance Arrangement, which started in 2008; and the South Korean Horizontal Compliance Program, which was established in 2010 (De Simone, Sansing, and Seidman, 2013).

In conclusion, the SSF recognizes the necessity of enforcement, but also stresses the role of tax authorities as service providers for taxpayers based upon trustworthy relationships (Alm et al., 2012). Thus, it is crucial to view tax evasion from different perspectives in order to foster high levels of compliance.

13.6 References

Adams, J. S. (1965). Inequity in Social Exchange. *Advances in Experimental Social Psychology*, 2, 267–299.

Ajzen, I. (1991). The Theory of Planned Behaviour. *Organizational Behaviour and Human Decision Processes*, 50, 179–211.

Allingham, M. G., and Sandmo, A. (1972). Income Tax Evasion: A Theoretical Analysis. *Journal of Public Economics*, 1, 323–338.

regulatory strategies. According to the SSF, tax compliance can be achieved either by increasing power or by building trustworthy relationships. Tax authorities' orientation toward taxpayers and their interaction style create a tax climate: a "cops and robbers" approach stimulates an antagonistic climate in which and taxpayers seek their self-interest, whereas a "service and client" approach stimulates a climate of trust and cooperation.

By implementing measures that increase trust in authorities, tax authorities should be perceived as transparent and capable of handling taxpayers' needs. If deterrence is not used arbitrarily but targeted at high-risk groups, power of the authorities should be perceived as justified and as a protection mechanism against free riders.

13.5 Conclusion

The deterrence model relies heavily on audit probability and penalties as motivators of compliance and neglects the psychological and social aspects of taxation and the interaction dynamics of actors in the field. Taxpayers would feel that they are not trusted as moral agents and refuse to act in moral ways if the tax authority regards all taxpayers as potential criminals. As Cullis and Lewis (1997, p. 310) noted, "If we believe taxpayers are selfish utility maximizers, taxpayers will behave like selfish utility maximizers. If we believe taxpayers have a moral nature, a sense of obligation or civic duty, taxpayers will reveal this side of their nature." Moreover, control and punishment may elicit unintended side effects that crowd out taxpayers' willingness to paying taxes if it is not justly practiced (Feld and Frey, 2002). In short, deterrence may be a necessary condition, but not the sufficient condition for all taxpayer compliance.

While the standard economic approaches stress the relevance of external variables such as tax rate, income, probability of audits, and severity of fines, fiscal psychology has shown the importance of sociopsychological variables that shape higher tax morale and lead to voluntary cooperation. In the tax compliance literature, there was a significant two-step paradigm shift from the exclusive focus on economic factors toward individual psychological and sociopsychological factors (Alm et al., 2012). The SSF reconciles different research paradigms by assigning economic as well as psychological factors to two dimensions: power of authority and trust in authority. In the SSF, the dynamic of power and trust, the tax climate, determines different paths to compliance: enforced or voluntary compliance. The SSF provides an insightful way to apprehend puzzling empirical findings from economic psychological studies of tax behavior.

Concerning practical applications, behavioral nudges may help to construct more efficient tax policies that reduce enforcement costs. For example, Shu et al. (2012) have reported that signing honor codes and tax self-reports before filing taxes triggered more compliant behavior. Or governments could change

Alm, J., Cherry, T., Jones, M., and McKee, M. (2010). Taxpayer Information Assistance Services and Tax Compliance Behavior. *Journal of Economic Psychology*, 31, 577–586.

Alm, J., Kirchler, E., and Muehlbacher, S. (2012). Combining Psychology and Economics in the Analysis of Compliance: From Enforcement to Cooperation. *Economic Analysis and Policy*, 42, 133–151.

Alm, J., and McClellan, C. (2012). Tax Morale and Tax Compliance from the Firm's Perspective. *Kyklos*(1), 1–17.

Alm, J., McClelland, G. H., and Schulze, W. D. (1992). Why Do People Pay Taxes? *Journal of Public Economics*, 48, 21–38.

Alm, J., and Torgler, B. (2006). Culture Differences and Tax Morale in the United States and in Europe. *Journal of Economic Psychology*, 27, 224–246.

Alm, J., and Torgler, B. (2011). Do Ethics Matter? Tax Compliance and Morality. *Journal of Business Ethics*, 101, 635–651.

Andreoni, J., Erard, B., and Feinstein, J. (1998). Tax Compliance. *Journal of Economic Literature*, 36, 818–860.

Ariel, B. (2012). Deterrence and Moral Persuasion Effects on Corporate Tax Compliance: Findings from a Randomized Controlled Trial. *Criminology*, 50, 27–69.

Ayres, I., and Braithwaite, J. (1992). *Responsive Regulation: Transcending the Deregulation Debate*. Oxford: Oxford University Press.

Barkworth, J. M., and Murphy, K. (2015). Procedural Justice Policing and Citizen Compliance Behaviour: The Importance of Emotion. *Psychology, Crime and Law*, 21, 254–273.

Bazart, C., and Bonein, A. (2014). Reciprocal Relationships in Tax Compliance Decisions. *Journal of Economic Psychology*, 40, 83–102.

Becker, G. S. (1968). Crime and Punishment: An Economic Approach. *Journal of Public Economics*, 76, 169–217.

Beer, S., Kasper, M., Kirchler, E., and Erard, B. (2015). Annual Report to Congress: Audit Impact Study. Retrieved from tinyurl.com/zzcouol

Blumenthal, M., Christian, C., and Slemrod, J. (2001). Do Normative Appeals Affect Tax Compliance? Evidence from a Controlled Experiment in Minnesota. *National Tax Journal*, 54(1), 125–136.

Bobek, D. D., Hageman, A. M., and Kelliher, C. F. (2013). Analyzing the Role of Social Norms in Tax Compliance Behavior. *Journal of Business Ethics*, 115, 451–468.

Bordignon, M. (1993). A Fairness Approach to Income Tax Evasion. *Journal of Public Economics*, 52, 345–362.

Bott, K., Cappelen, A. W., Sørensen, E. Ø., and Tungodden, B. (2014). *You've Got Mail: A Randomised Field Experiment on Tax Evasion*. Bergen, Norway: NHH Norwegian School of Economics.

Boylan, S. J., and Sprinkle, G. B. (2001). Experimental Evidence on the Relation Between Tax Rates and Compliance: The Effect of Earned vs. Endowed Income. *Journal of the American Taxation Association*, 23, 75–90.

Braithwaite, V. (2003). *Taxing Democracy: Understanding Tax Avoidance and Evasion*. Aldershot: Ashgate.

Braithwaite, V. (2009). *Defiance in Taxation and Governance: Resisting and Dismissing Authority in a Democracy*. Cheltenham: Edward Elgar.

Braithwaite, V., Murphy, K., and Reinhart, M. (2007). Taxation Threat, Motivational Postures, and Responsive Regulation. *Law and Policy*, 29, 137–158.

Casagrande, A., Cagno, D., Di, Pandimiglio, A., and Spallone, M. (2015). The Effect of Competition on Tax Compliance: The Role of Audit Rules and Shame. *Journal of Behavioral and Experimental Economics*, 59, 96–110.

Casal, S., Kogler, C., Mittone, L., and Kirchler, E. (2016). Tax Compliance Depends on Voice of Taxpayers. *Journal of Economic Psychology*, 56, 141–150.

Chang, O. H., Nichols, D. R., and Schultz, J. J. (1987). Taxpayer Attitudes Toward Tax Audit Risk. *Journal of Economic Psychology*, 8, 299–309.

Christian, R. C., and Alm, J. (2014). Empathy, Sympathy, and Tax Compliance. *Journal of Economic Psychology*, 40, 62–82.

Cialdini, R. B., and Trost, M. R. (1998). Social Influence: Social Norms, Conformity and Compliance. In S. T. Fiske, D. T. Gilbert and G. Lindzey (Ed.), *The Handbook of Social Psychology*. Boston: Oxford University Press.

Coricelli, G., Joffily, M., Montmarquette, C., and Villeval, M. C. (2010). Cheating, Emotions, and Rationality: An Experiment on Tax Evasion. *Experimental Economics*, 13, 226–247.

Coricelli, G., Rusconi, E., and Villeval, M. C. (2014). Tax Evasion and Emotions: An Empirical Test of Re-integrative Shaming Theory. *Journal of Economic Psychology*, 40, 49–61.

Cuccia, A. D., and Carnes, G. A. (2001). A Closer Look at the Relation Between Tax Complexity and Tax Equity Perceptions. *Journal of Economic Psychology*, 22, 113–140.

Cullis, J. G., and Lewis, A. (1997). Why People Pay Taxes: From a Conventional Economic Model to a Model of Social Convention. *Journal of Economic Psychology*, 18, 305–321.

Dawes, R. M. (1980). Social Dilemmas. *Annual Review of Psychology*, 31, 169–193.

De Simone, L., Sansing, R. C., and Seidman, J. K. (2013). When Are Enhanced Relationship Tax Compliance Programs Mutually Beneficial? *Accounting Review*, 88, 1971–1991.

Doerrenberg, P., and Peichl, A. (2013). Progressive Taxation and Tax Morale. *Public Choice*, 155, 293–316.

Elffers, H., and Hessing, D. J. (1997). Influencing the Prospects of Tax Evasion. *Journal of Economic Psychology*, 18, 289–304.

Elffers, H., Weigel, R. H., and Hessing, D. J. (1987). The Consequences of Different Strategies for Measuring Tax Evasion Behavior. *Journal of Economic Psychology*, 8, 311–337.

Eriksen, K., and Fallan, L. (1996). Tax Knowledge and Attitudes Towards Taxation: A Report on a Quasi-Experiment. *Journal of Economic Psychology*, 17, 387–402.

European Commission. (2015). Study to Quantify and Analyse the VAT Gap in the EU Member States. Retrieved from ec.europa.eu/taxation_customs/resources/documents/common/public-ations/studies/vat_gap2013.pdf

Feld, L. P., and Frey, B. S. (2002). Trust Breeds Trust: How Taxpayers Are Treated. *Economics of Governance*, 3, 87–99.

Feld, L. P., and Frey, B. S. (2007). Tax Compliance as the Result of a Psychological Tax Contract: The Role of Incentives and Responsive Regulation. *Law and Policy*, 29, 102–120.

Frecknall-Hughes, J., and Kirchler, E. (2015). Towards a General Theory of Tax Practice. *Social and Legal Studies*, 24, 289–312.

Frey, B. S. (1997). A Constitution for Knaves Crowds Out Civic Virtues. *Economic Journal*, 107, 1043–1053.

Frey, B. S., and Torgler, B. (2007). Tax Morale and Conditional Cooperation. *Journal of Comparative Economics*, 35, 136–159.

Gaisbauer, H. P., Schweiger, G., and Sedmak, C. (2015). Outlining the Field of Tax Justice. In H. P. Gaisbauer, G. Schweiger, and C. Sedmak (Eds.) *Philosophical Explorations of Justice and Taxation* (pp. 1–14). Berlin: Springer.

Gangl, K., Muehlbacher, S., De Groot, M., et al. (2013). "How Can I Help You?" Perceived Service Orientation of Tax Authorities and Tax Compliance. *FinanzArchiv: Public Finance Analysis*, 69, 487–510.

Gemmell, N., and Hasseldine, J. (2014). Taxpayers' Behavioural Responses and Measures of Tax Compliance "Gaps": A Critique and a New Measure. *Fiscal Studies*, 35, 275–296.

Hallsworth, M., List, J., Metcalfe, R., and Vlaev, I. (2014). The Behavioralist as Tax Collector: Using Natural Field Experiments to Enhance Tax Compliance (No. w20007). *SSRN Electronic Journal*. ssrn.com/abstract=2418122

Hasseldine, J., Hite, P., James, S., and Toumi, M. (2007). Persuasive Communications: Tax Compliance Enforcement Strategies for Sole Proprietors. *Contemporary Accounting Research*, 24, 171–194.

Holler, M., Hoelzl, E., Kirchler, E., Leder, S., and Mannetti, L. (2008). Framing of Information on the Use of Public Finances, Regulatory Fit of Recipients and Tax Compliance. *Journal of Economic Psychology*, 29, 597–611.

IRS (Internal Revenue Service). (2012). IRS Releases New Tax Gap Estimates. Retrieved from www.irs.gov/uac/irs-releases-new-tax-gap-estimates-compliance-rates-remain-statistically-unchanged-from-previous-study

IRS. (2014). Your 2014 Taxpayer Receipt. Retrieved from www.whitehouse.gov/2014-taxreceipt

Jun, B.-h., Cho, M., and Park, M.-H. (2015). Procedural Fairness and Taxpayers' Response: Evidence from an Experiment. *Korean Economic Review*, 31, 301–326.

Kahneman, D., and Tversky, A. (1979). Prospect Theory: An Analysis of Decision Under Risk. *Econometrica: Journal of the Econometric Society*, 47, 263–292.

Kaplan, S. E., Reckers, P. M., West, S. G., and Boyd, J. C. (1988). An Examination of Tax Reporting Recommendations of Professional Tax Preparers. *Journal of Economic Psychology*, 9, 427–443.

Kastlunger, B., Kirchler, E., Mittone, L., and Pitters, J. (2009). Sequences of Audits, Tax Compliance, and Taxpaying Strategies. *Journal of Economic Psychology*, 30, 405–418.

Kastlunger, B., Lozza, E., Kirchler, E., and Schabmann, A. (2013). Powerful Authorities and Trusting Citizens: The Slippery Slope Framework and Tax Compliance in Italy. *Journal of Economic Psychology*, 34, 36–45.

Kastlunger, B., Muehlbacher, S., Kirchler, E., and Mittone, L. (2011). What Goes Around Comes Around? Experimental Evidence of the Effect of Rewards on Tax Compliance. *Public Finance Review*, 39, 150–167.

Kim, C. K., Evans, J. H., and Moser, D. V. (2005). Economic and Equity Effects on Tax Reporting Decisions. *Accounting, Organizations and Society*, 30, 609–625.

Kirchler, E. (2007). *The Economic Psychology of Tax Behaviour*: Cambridge: Cambridge University Press.

Kirchler, E., Hoelzl, E., and Wahl, I. (2008). Enforced Versus Voluntary Tax Compliance: The "Slippery Slope" Framework. *Journal of Economic Psychology*, 29, 210–225.

Kirchler, E., Kogler, C., and Muehlbacher, S. (2014). Cooperative Tax Compliance from Deterrence to Deference. *Current Directions in Psychological Science*, 23, 87–92.

Kirchler, E., and Maciejovsky, B. (2001). Tax Compliance Within the Context of Gain and Loss Situations, Expected and Current Asset Position, and Profession. *Journal of Economic Psychology*, 22, 173–194.

Kirchler, E., Muehlbacher, S., Hoelzl, E., and Webley, P. (2009). Effort and Aspirations in Tax Evasion: Experimental Evidence. *Applied Psychology*, 58, 488–507.

Kirchler, E., Muehlbacher, S., Kastlunger, B., and Wahl, I. (2010). Why Pay Taxes? A Review of Tax Compliance Decisions. In J. M.-V. J. Alm and B. Torgler (Ed.), *Developing Alternative Frameworks for Explaining Tax Compliance* (pp. 15–31). London: Routledge.

Kleven, H. J., Knudsen, M. B., Kreiner, C. T., Pedersen, S., and Saez, E. (2011). Unwilling or Unable to Cheat? Evidence from a Tax Audit Experiment in Denmark. *Econometrica*, 79, 651–692.

Kogler, C., Batrancea, L., Nichita, A., Pantya, J., Belianin, A., and Kirchler, E. (2013). Trust and Power as Determinants of Tax Compliance: Testing the Assumptions of the Slippery Slope Framework in Austria, Hungary, Romania and Russia. *Journal of Economic Psychology*, 34, 169–180.

Kogler, C., Batrancea, L., Nichita, A., Olsen, J., and Kirchler, E. (2014). Cross-cultural Research on Tax Compliance, Corruption and Shadow Economy. Paper presented at the 28th International Congress of Applied Psychology in Paris, France.

Kogler, C., Mittone, L., and Kirchler, E. (2015). Delayed Feedback on Tax Audits Affects Compliance and Fairness Perceptions. *Journal of Economic Behavior and Organization* , 124, 81–87.

Lago-Peñas, I., and Lago-Peñas, S. (2010). The Determinants of Tax Morale in Comparative Perspective: Evidence from European Countries. *European Journal of Political Economy*, 26, 441–453.

Lewis, A. (1982). *The Psychology of Taxation*. New York: St. Martin's Press.

Luttmer, E. F. P., and Singhal, M. (2014). Tax Morale. *Journal of Economic Perspectives*, 28, 149–168.

Maciejovsky, B., Kirchler, E., and Schwarzenberger, H. (2007). Misperception of Chance and Loss Repair: On the Dynamics of Tax Compliance. *Journal of Economic Psychology*, 28, 678–691.

Maciejovsky, B., Schwarzenberger, H., and Kirchler, E. (2012). Rationality Versus Emotions: The Case of Tax Ethics and Compliance. *Journal of Business Ethics*, 109(3), 339–350.

McCaffery, E. J., and Baron, J. (2004). Framing and Taxation: Evaluation of Tax Policies Involving Household Composition. *Journal of Economic Psychology*, 25, 679–705.

McKerchar, M. (2001). The Study of Income Tax Complexity and Unintentional Non-Compliance: Research Method and Preliminary Findings. ATAX Discussion Paper. University of Sydney. Australia.

Mendoza, J. P., Wielhouwer, J., and Kirchler, E. (2015). The Backfiring Effect of Auditing on Tax Compliance. *SSRN Electronic Journal*. ssrn.com/abstract=2597479

Mittone, L. (2006). Dynamic Behaviour in Tax Evasion: An Experimental Approach. *Journal of Socio-Economics*, 35, 813–835.

Moeschler, D. (2015). Social Representations of Taxes and Intentions Toward Compliance. *Economies and Finances*. Retrieved from http://dumas.ccsd.cnrs.fr/dumas-01108337.

Moscovici, S. (1961). *La psychanalyse, son image et son public*. Paris: Presses universitaires de France.

Muehlbacher, S., Hartl, B., and Kirchler, E. (2015). Mental Accounting and Tax Compliance Experimental Evidence for the Effect of Mental Segregation of Tax Due and Revenue on Compliance. *Public Finance Review*, 45(1), 1–22.

Muehlbacher, S., Kirchler, E., and Schwarzenberger, H. (2011). Voluntary Versus Enforced Tax Compliance: Empirical Evidence for the "Slippery Slope" Framework. *European Journal of Law and Economics*, 32, 89–97.

Murphy, K. (2004). The Role of Trust in Nurturing Compliance: A Study of Accused Tax Avoiders. *Law and Human Behavior*, 28, 187–209.

OECD (Organization of Economic Cooperation and Development). (2013). *Co-operative Compliance: A Framework from Enhanced Relationship to Co-operative Compliance*. Paris: OECD Publishing.

OECD. (2015). *Tax Administration 2015: Comparative Information on OECD and Other Advanced and Emerging Economies*. Paris: OECD Publishing.

Onu, D., and Oats, L. (2015). The Role of Social Norms in Tax Compliance: Theoretical Overview and Practical Implications. *Journal of Tax Administration*, 1, 113–137.

Pickhardt, M., and Seibold, G. (2014). Income Tax Evasion Dynamics: Evidence from an Agent-Based Econophysics Model. *Journal of Economic Psychology*, 40, 147–160.

Porcano, T. M. (1985). Distributive Justice and Tax Policy. *Accounting Review*, 59, 619–635.

Rechberger, S., Hartner, M., Kirchler, E., and Hämmerle, F. K. (2010). Tax Amnesties, Justice Perceptions, and Filing Behavior: A Simulation Study. *Law and Policy*, 32, 214–225.

Sandmo, A. (2005). The Theory of Tax Evasion: A Retrospective View. *National Tax Journal*, 58, 643–663.

Schepanski, A., and Shearer, T. (1995). A Prospect Theory Account of the Income Tax Withholding Phenomenon. *Organizational Behavior and Human Decision Processes*, 63, 174–186.

Schmölders, G. (1959). Fiscal Psychology: A New Branch of Public Finance. *National Tax Journal*, 12, 340–345.

Schmölders, G. (1960). *Das Irrationale in der öffentlichen Finanzwirtschaft*. Frankfurt am Main: Suhrkamp.

Schneider, F. (2015). Size and Development of the Shadow Economy of 31 European and 5 Other OECD Countries from 2003 to 2015: Different Developments. Retrieved from www.econ.jku.at/members/Schneider/files/publications/2015/ShadEcEurope31.pdf

Schwartz, R. D., and Orleans, S. (1967). On Legal Sanctions. *University of Chicago Law Review*, 34, 274–300.

Shu, L. L., Mazar, N., Gino, F., Ariely, D., and Bazerman, M. H. (2012). Signing at the Beginning Makes Ethics Salient and Decreases Dishonest Self-Reports in Comparison to Signing at the End. *Proceedings of the National Academy of Sciences*, 109, 15197–15200.

Slemrod, J. (1998). On Voluntary Compliance, Voluntary Taxes, and Social Capital. *National Tax Journal*, 51, 485–491.

Slemrod, J., Blumenthal, M., and Christian, C. (2001). Taxpayer Response to an Increased Probability of Audit: Evidence from a Controlled Experiment in Minnesota. *Journal of Public Economics*, 79, 455–483.

Taylor, N. (2003). Understanding Taxpayer Attitudes Through Understanding Taxpayer Identities. In V. Braithwaite (ed.), *Taxing Democracy: Understanding Tax Avoidance and Evasion* (pp. 71–92). Aldershot: Ashgate.

Thaler, R. (1999). Mental Accounting Matters. *Journal of Behavioral Decision Making*, 12, 183–206.

Torgler, B. (2004a). Tax Morale in Asian Countries. *Journal of Asian Economics*, 15, 237–266.

Torgler, B. (2004b). Moral Suasion: An Alternative Tax Policy Strategy? Evidence from a Controlled Field Experiment in Switzerland. *Economics of Governance*, 5, 235–253.

Torgler, B. (2005). Tax Morale and Direct Democracy. *European Journal of Political Economy*, 21, 525–531.

Torgler, B. (2006). The Importance of Faith: Tax Morale and Religiosity. *Journal of Economic Behavior and Organization*, 61, 81–109.

Torgler, B. (2007). *Tax Compliance and Tax Morale: A Theoretical and Empirical Anal ysis*: Cheltenham: Edward Elgar.

Torgler, B., and Schneider, F. (2009). The Impact of Tax Morale and Institutional Quality on the Shadow Economy. *Journal of Economic Psychology*, 30, 228–245.

Tyler, T. R. (2006). Psychological Perspectives on Legitimacy and Legitimation. *Annual Review of Psychology*, 57, 375–400.

Wahl, I., Muehlbacher, S., and Kirchler, E. (2010). The Impact of Voting on Tax Payments. *Kyklos*, 63, 144–158.

Wartick, M., and Rupert, T. (2010). The Effects of Observing a Peer's Likelihood of Reporting Income on Tax Reporting Decisions. *Advances in Taxation*, 19, 65–94.

Wenzel, M. (2002). The Impact of Outcome Orientation and Justice Concerns on Tax Compliance: The Role of Taxpayers' Identity. *Journal of Applied Psychology*, 87, 629.

Wenzel, M. (2003). Tax Compliance and the Psychology of Justice: Mapping the Field. In V. Braithwaite (Ed.), *Taxing Democracy: Understanding Tax Avoidance and Evasion* (pp. 41–70). Aldershot: Ashgate.

Wenzel, M. (2004a). An Analysis of Norm Processes in Tax Compliance. *Journal of Economic Psychology*, 25, 213–228.

Wenzel, M. (2004b). The Social Side of Sanctions: Personal and Social Norms as Moderators of Deterrence. *Law and Human Behavior*, 28, 547–567.

Wolters Kluwer CCH. (2015). Federal Tax Law Keeps Piling Up. Retrieved July 14, 2016, from www.cch.com/TaxLawPileUp.pdf

Yaniv, G. (1999). Tax Compliance and Advance Tax Payments: A Prospect Theory Analysis. *National Tax Journal*, 52, 753–764.

Zeelenberg, M., and Pieters, R. (2006). Feeling Is for Doing: A Pragmatic Approach to the Study of Emotions in Economic Behavior. In D. De Cremer, M. Zeelenberg, and K. Murnighan (Eds.), *Social Psychology and Economics* (pp. 117–137). New York: Psychology Press.

14 New Ways of Understanding Tax Compliance

From the Laboratory to the Real World

Michael Hallsworth

14.1 Introduction

Tax compliance research has been transformed in the twenty-first century. The number of studies has increased dramatically, allowing new methods to be applied to a much wider range of research topics (Slemrod, 2016). Nowhere is the change more obvious than in field experiments on tax compliance. These kinds of studies involve randomly allocating taxpayers to receive or not receive an intervention that aims to influence their tax behaviour in the real world.[1] For example, a tax authority might collaborate with an academic to create an official letter that warns of a possible tax audit, randomly select one group of taxpayers to receive the letter and one not to, and then measure any differences in tax compliance between the two groups.[2] Random selection is important because, if successful, it produces two groups with similar characteristics (for example, age, wealth, attitudes to taxation). This similarity means that we would expect the two groups to have matching levels of tax compliance if treated the same way (Angrist and Pischke, 2008). Any difference in compliance between the two groups can therefore be attributed to receiving the letter, rather than any other cause (Gerber and Green, 2012). Field experiments are therefore different from studies that simply analyse existing datasets (which do not involve randomisation or any direct intervention to influence behaviour) and from laboratory experiments (which, although they randomise direct interventions, do not take place in the real world).

Until 2011, only a handful of tax compliance field experiments had been recorded. Then, more were published in five years than in the preceding fifty (Hallsworth, 2014). From an academic perspective, this development is welcome because the new studies address some of the deficiencies of previous tax compliance research. At the same time, these studies are interesting to practitioners because they concern real interventions rather than hypothetical encounters in simulated environments. This confluence of academic and practitioner interest makes field experiments in tax compliance worth examining in depth. This chapter examines why field experiments have risen to prominence; considers what we can – and cannot – learn from the new wave of studies; and suggests future directions for policy and practice.

14.2 The Increasing Interest in Field Experiments on Tax Compliance

Three main trends have combined to increase the interest of both academics and practitioners in field experiments on tax compliance: a growing challenge to the dominance of the rational actor model in economics and policy making; increased pressure on public finances; and greater willingness by practitioners and academics to adopt experimental approaches. Although these developments are distinct, links exist between them: for example, experimental approaches have been integral to developing the challenge to the rational actor model.[3] Each trend is discussed briefly in the following subsections.

14.2.1 A Growing Challenge to the Dominance of the Rational Actor Model in Economics and Policy Making

The first trend is the move from a rational choice model to a behavioural choice model, as shown in the preceding chapter by Olsen, Kang and Kirchler.[4] Broadly speaking, the main approach to understanding tax compliance has been a rational choice model first put forward by Allingham and Sandmo (1972). In this framework, taxpayers attempt to maximise their expected utility when they have an opportunity to evade tax; they weigh up the potential gain against the probability of punishment, and take the outcome that is likely to benefit them most. A range of studies have now estimated how far the main elements of the Allingham–Sandmo model – probability of audit, size of fine, tax rate and income level – affect compliance decisions (Kirchler et al., 2010). Adopting this framework gives rise to a deterrence-based policy regime, whereby the tax authority focuses on enforcement practices such as extensive monitoring, applying salient penalties and sanctions and removing opportunities for noncompliance. In general, tax authorities have indeed adopted a deterrence-based approach (Feld and Larsen, 2012).

Recent decades have seen growing empirical evidence that individuals often do not behave in line with the predictions of neoclassical economic models (Camerer, Loewenstein and Rabin, 2011). Findings from the behavioural sciences have emphasised the importance of nonconscious processes such as habits and automatic responses to environmental features (Bargh and Chartrand, 1999). The role of these processes helps to explain why studies have found that the relationship between tax attitudes and tax behaviour is not straightforward (Elffers, Robben and Hessing, 1992). Moreover, the identification of various cognitive heuristics – such as loss aversion, mental accounting and framing effects – highlights other ways that decision-making may be influenced by factors not accounted for in standard rational choice models (Kahneman and Tversky, 2000; McCaffery and Baron, 2006).

When considering tax compliance specifically, attention has focused on the influence of factors such as social norms, fairness perceptions and the provision of public goods (Alm, 2012). Some have argued that these factors mean that taxpayers have 'a primary disposition to comply with tax laws', rather than a drive to maximise their utility (Ariel, 2012, p. 32). This perspective suggests that tax authorities should ensure fairness and respect in their dealings with taxpayers, provide clear and timely information to facilitate compliance and persuade taxpayers through tactics such as emphasising the benefits from taxation or that most people comply with their obligations (Kirchler, 2007).

These developments have suggested new approaches that policy makers could take to address compliance issues. But perhaps the most important point is that governments have been increasingly willing to *adopt* these new approaches, usually under the guise of 'behavioural economics' (Thaler, 2015). For example, in 2010 David Cameron's UK government set up the Behavioural Insights Team, a unit that was explicitly given the task of applying behavioural economics to improve public policy and service design (Halpern, 2015). Looking more widely, a recent study found that '51 countries have central state-led policy initiatives that have been influenced by the new behavioural sciences' (Whitehead et al., 2014, p. 8). In other words, governments have shown an increasing appetite to apply these new research findings to real-world policy issues.

14.2.2 Increased Pressure on Public Finances

The second trend is the increased pressure on public finances experienced as a result of the economic slowdown that occurred from 2008. Tax compliance has always been an important issue for governments, since it provides the funding for their actions and is linked to wider social stability. However, the growing need to cut spending and/or raise taxes has naturally led policy makers to consider new options to improve revenue collection – and reassess the effectiveness of existing practices (OECD, 2010; Slemrod, 2016). With finances constrained, policy makers found that their ability to implement deterrence measures such as audits and prosecutions, with their attendant costs, was increasingly limited. In contrast, applying the findings from behavioural sciences offered the possibility of raising compliance at a much lower cost (Halpern, 2015). At the same time, richer countries have taken a renewed interest in increasing tax compliance in poorer countries in order to accelerate their development (European Commission, 2010).

14.2.3 Greater Willingness by Policy Makers to Adopt Experimental Approaches

The final trend is a growing appetite from governments to run experiments in order to evaluate the effectiveness of their actions. This is a crude generalisation, since the willingness to take an experimental approach to government has varied by country. The United States ran several 'social experiments' in the 1960s and 1970s, with many possessing impressive scale and rigour (Burtless, 1995). For example, the RAND Health Insurance Experiment actually created five new health insurance plans, which were then randomly allocated among 2,750 families, in order to establish how cost sharing affected health service use (Newhouse and RAND Corporation Insurance Experiment Group, 1993). Nevertheless, these experiments had only a limited influence on policy making, and their popularity among US policy makers has declined since the 1980s (Oakley, 1998). In contrast, there were few experiments in the United Kingdom prior to the turn of the millennium, but their popularity has grown since – partly driven by an increased emphasis on evidence-based policy making and 'what works' (Ettelt, Mays and Allen, 2015; Sanderson, 2002; Bristow, Carter and Martin, 2015). This trend is mirrored by an increased enthusiasm for the use of randomised controlled trials in international development, driven by an influential group of 'randomistas' who see trialling as a way of challenging assumptions and cutting out waste (Duflo, Glennerster and Kremer, 2007).

This increased willingness by policy makers to test interventions has been mirrored by the greater adoption of experimental approaches by academics engaged in tax compliance research. Given its importance, this development is discussed in more detail in the following section.

14.3 The Evolution of Methods for Analysing Tax Behaviour

Perhaps the most important point to consider is that tax compliance research faces some serious measurement problems (Alm, 2012). There are difficulties in measuring tax behaviour (partly because actors have an incentive to conceal what they are doing); in interpreting whether this behaviour constitutes noncompliance; and in establishing a causal relationship between policy interventions and levels of compliance. Consequently, a recent review concluded that 'we are still trying to answer many *basic questions* on measuring, explaining, and controlling evasion' (Alm, 2012, p. 73).

14.3.1 Econometric Analyses

These problems are evident if we consider one of the standard approaches to analysing compliance: econometric analyses of official statistics and administrative datasets. One obvious and apparently attractive method is to audit a random sample of tax returns in order to estimate levels of evasion in the population. This approach is taken by the US and UK tax authorities, but few others – mainly because the exercise can be both expensive and controversial (Slemrod, 2016). As Hallsworth (2014) points out, there are also methodological issues: '[a]udits are expensive to conduct; officials may not actually discover undeclared income; auditors may not be able to distinguish between fraud and unintentional errors; judgments are not always consistent from one auditor to another; and audits do not address the "ghosts" who simply fail to file a tax return' (p. 666).

Even if studies like these can identify a reliable measure of noncompliance, they still face the challenge of establishing causal links between this measure and the many possible determinants of compliance. The problem is the lack of a reliable counterfactual: what would have happened if a particular policy had not been implemented, or if tax rates had been lower? Creating such a counterfactual after the event is not easy. Even if we can identify taxpayers who did not receive an intervention, this may not be the only way in which they differ from those who did (they may earn more, be older, be geographically distinct and so on).

One response to this challenge has been to use 'quasi-experimental methods' to create such a counterfactual. These methods often exploit the fact that a tax policy may create an eligibility cut-off point and, by looking carefully at behaviour around these thresholds, we can isolate the policy's impact. For example, after tax returns have been submitted, the tax administration may rank them by calculating a risk score and then apply a deterrent to taxpayers with a score just above or below a certain level. A 'regression discontinuity' design would compare the behaviour of those taxpayers who fell just either side of this risk score. The idea is that it is effectively random which side of the threshold these taxpayers fall – and therefore we can find a counterfactual by looking at those who marginally avoided the intervention.

Sánchez (2014) shows how this kind of approach works in practice. His study exploits the fact that Ecuador's tax authority selects some taxpayers to receive a noncompliance notification if it detects probable underreporting of tax. This selection is made by applying a formula that creates an eligibility threshold which – importantly – is unknown to taxpayers.[5] By comparing behaviour either side of the threshold, Sánchez shows that receiving the notification increases taxes paid by around €1,400 (or 70 per cent), and increases taxes reported the following year as well.

Another approach has been to look at 'kinks' or 'notches' created by the design of tax policies. Kinks and notches are similar but distinct; I do not explore the difference for reasons of space, but Kleven (2016) provides an in-depth treatment of the topic. The basic approach here is to identify a point where the marginal tax rate jumps (the kink point) and then examine whether income reporting 'bunches' just below this point. Bunching of this kind offers evidence that taxpayers are underreporting income in order to avoid paying the higher rate – the assumption being that the distribution would be smooth if the kink point were absent. Saez (2010) finds evidence for bunching around a large kink point created by the structure of the US Earned Income Tax Credit. Importantly, the bunching is only present for recipients with self-reported income (rather than wage-only earnings), which suggest that underreporting is the main cause.

14.3.2 Surveys

Another strand of research has tried to use surveys to analyse tax behaviour. These surveys may attempt to estimate levels of noncompliance directly, by asking respondents to report on their tax affairs. They may ask people how they would behave in certain tax-related situations. Or they may focus on beliefs and attitudes towards noncompliance, such as how prevalent or acceptable various practices are seen to be. For example, Lewis (1982) reports the memorable fact that one such survey found that US respondents viewed tax evasion as 'slightly more serious than stealing a bicycle' (p. 145).

There are several well-known problems associated with a reliance on self-reported data. Arguably, the example of tax compliance is just one example of wider problems affecting surveys of economic behaviour, given the concerns over their coverage and data quality raised by Barrett, Levell and Milligan (2014) and Meyer, Mok and Sullivan (2015). One major problem is that people may simply not be able to recall their past tax behaviour accurately or – even if they can – may not recognise that behaviour as noncompliant (Hessing, Elffers and Weigel, 1988; Hessing, Robben and Elffers, 1989). If the survey measures intended behaviours (particularly in response to hypothetical scenarios), it is important to note the copious evidence that such intentions may not be realised in practice (Elffers, Weigel and Hessing, 1987; Webb and Sheeran, 2006). Even small changes to the order and wording of questions can affect respondents' attitudes and attributions about tax behaviour (Hasseldine and Hite, 2003; Hite, 1987; Schwarz, 1999).

These issues are often exacerbated when the behaviour or attitude concerned is seen as socially undesirable. Respondents are likely to engage in what Webley et al. (1991) call 'impression management', whereby 'people act in certain ways to gain social approval and to construct a personal image congruent with their ideal self' (p. 34). Moreover, as Hurst et al. (2014) show, taxpayers may treat household surveys like tax forms. In other words, the illegal nature of tax evasion means that even a small possibility that the survey is not confidential can lead to substantial underreporting of income. Hurst et al. (2014) estimate that the self-employed underreport their income in US household surveys by around 30 per cent. These problems mean that studies usually combine surveys with other methods for measuring compliance.

14.3.3 Laboratory Experiments

One of the most promising of these other methods has been to run laboratory experiments. These experiments usually try to create simplified versions of real-world decisions taken by taxpayers. For example, participants may complete tasks to earn an 'income' that they are asked to declare to a tax authority or some other form of communal fund. Various aspects of the decision can then be manipulated: the size of any punishment, the amount of revenue returned to participants, the visibility of their behaviour and so on. The experimental setting means that these changes can be implemented cleanly and their effects measured precisely. All evasion is known. Given the measurement problems mentioned above, this is a major benefit (Alm, 2012). Moreover, randomisation provides the reliable counterfactual that is often missing from other methods. These advantages mean that 'virtually all aspects of compliance have been examined in some way in experimental work' (Alm, 2012, p. 66).

It is worth emphasising that laboratory experiments permit some inq+uiries that are impossible or highly impractical through other means. Since aspects like tax rates and penalties are often determined at a national or tax system level, there can be few opportunities to vary them orthogonally in the real world. Laboratory experiments can also present new ways of measuring the determinants of noncompliance. For example, Coricelli, Joffily, Montmarquette and Villeval (2010) use data from skin conductance responses to explore the emotional drivers of noncompliance. They find that the emotional intensity occurring before an evasion decision is positively correlated with both the decision to cheat and the proportion of income evaded. The emotional arousal after an audit was heightened by monetary sanctions and, even further, by the risk that a picture of the evader will be displayed (even though this was an artificial environment). This is valuable evidence of the emotional dimension of noncompliance that would be impossible to obtain at the moment of decision in the real world.

Despite these advantages, concerns have grown that tax compliance experiments – and indeed laboratory experiments in the social sciences more generally – may have poor 'external validity' (Camerer, 2011; Elffers et al., 1992; Levitt and List, 2007). External validity here refers to the extent to which a laboratory experiment's findings hold true in real-world settings. I propose that there are four clusters of criticisms that are particularly worth noting: the artificiality of the experimental situation; the low stakes involved; the use of student participants; and the challenges of transferring laboratory interventions to the real world.[6]

14.3.3.1 *The Artificiality of the Experimental Situation*
The main concern here is that the decisions presented to participants in the laboratory do not adequately simulate real-world tax decisions. One common criticism is that the game people are asked to play seems precisely that: a game. Indeed, many early experiments excluded references to tax, thereby making the choices more abstract, in order to better isolate features such as the size and likelihood of a penalty (Spicer and Thomas, 1982). This is a concern because when participants feel that they are merely playing a gambling game, they may be more attracted to risk taking (Webley et al., 1991). Indeed, Choo, Fonseca and Myles (2016) find that experiments that framed the decision in terms of tax produced higher compliance than those using neutral language. Even when studies do use tax-related language, it may be difficult to simulate the complex

range of associations and heuristics triggered by facing tax decisions in the real world.

A related concern is that aspects of the laboratory decisions are fundamentally different from real tax decisions. For example, experiments often provide exact audit probabilities to participants. For most taxpayers in the real world, however, these probabilities are often vague, unknown or greatly overestimated (Kirchler et al., 2010; Alm, McClelland and Schulze, 1992). Or consider the fact that laboratory experiments have to compress multiple tax cycles into rounds that are played within a few hours. Participants therefore find out quickly whether they have been audited, unlike in the real world (where this process may take many years). Although evidence is still limited, it appears that shorter feedback loops may lead to lower tax compliance (Muehlbacher et al., 2012). Finally, there are concerns that tax evasion usually takes place 'out of sight', whereas there is clear and salient oversight by others in laboratory experiments. Participants may therefore comply because they feel it is socially appropriate and expected by the experimenter (Webley et al., 1991).

14.3.3.2 *Low Stakes*

A similar concern is that relatively little is at stake in laboratory experiments, unlike real-world tax decisions. There is no possibility of significant financial loss, let alone criminal sanctions. People have voluntarily chosen to participate and often are simply provided with an unearned windfall income. (More recent experiments have addressed this point by requiring participants to earn income by completing tasks.) In the real world, tax revenues go to fund salient and valued public services and infrastructure. In a tax compliance game, the revenues go to fund an entirely contingent and often hypothetical cause, if they are collected at all.

14.3.3.3 *Student Populations*

A common criticism of laboratory experiments in the social sciences is that their participants are usually students, who may behave differently from the population in general (Levitt and List, 2007). There has been some criticism of tax compliance studies specifically in this regard (Marriott, 2014). Students are generally younger, more intelligent and from wealthier backgrounds than most taxpayers (Torgler, 2007); there is evidence that they may also behave less generously, cooperatively and trustfully in experiments (Exadaktylos, Espín and Branas-Garza, 2013).

Experimental studies that directly compare student and taxpayer samples are rare: two recent ones are worth noting. Alm, Bloomquist and McKee (2015) find that the two groups show 'largely similar' behaviour in laboratory settings. They do not find significant differences between student and taxpayer responses to (a) the provision of information that aided calculation of the tax liability; (b) audit probability; (c) the introduction of a tax credit; or (d) the introduction of an unemployment benefit. (Students did react significantly differently if the size of the liability was uncertain.) In contrast, Choo, Fonseca and Myles (2016) found that there were 'stark behavioural differences' between the student and taxpayer groups (p. 113). Students exhibited much lower compliance than taxpayers, but were also much more responsive to changes in the probability of audit (especially if it was made ambiguous) and the size of the fine for noncompliance. Taxpayers were more compliant and mostly unresponsive to changes in the experimental parameters. One specific concern is that students usually do not have experience of making tax decisions, and thus may not have developed norms of tax behaviour through practice and habit (Kirchler, 1999; Webley et al. 1991). Reinforcing this concern, Choo et al. (2016) concluded that the differences they observed had occurred mainly because taxpayers had developed norms of honesty and compliance through their real-world tax behaviour.

14.3.3.4 *Difficulties with Operationalising Findings*
The final issue is a practical concern, driven by the assumption that one of the goals of tax compliance research is to influence tax administration. A laboratory experiment may be able to implement a concept in ways that are simply not possible in the real world. For example, the preceding chapter mentions a study by Coricelli, Rusconi and Villeval (2014) that concludes that reintegrating cheaters immediately after a public shaming reduces noncompliance, while failing to do so can have the opposite effect. However, there are obvious issues of feasibility and appropriateness in terms of a tax administration 'reintegrating' people (although perhaps not with shaming): it is not clear how this could be done, by whom, over what time frame and with what measures of success.

Despite these concerns, a recent review concludes there is a lack of systemic research comparing tax compliance results in laboratory and field settings (Muehlbacher and Kirchler, 2016). As a result, it is difficult to make firm conclusions on the extent of the external validity problem. One of the most recent studies concludes that 'behavioral patterns of subjects in the laboratory conform to those of individuals making a similar decision in naturally occurring settings' (although the absolute level of evasion was lower in the laboratory) (Alm et al., 2015, p. 1170). Even if the evidence on external validity is not conclusive, the ongoing debate has led researchers to become increasingly interested in running experiments in real-world settings.

14.4 Field Experiments

14.4.1 Advantages of Field Experiments

As previously noted, field experiments apply the process of randomisation from the laboratory to real-world contexts. They therefore address many of the criticisms directed at laboratory experiments while retaining many of their benefits. Randomisation continues to ensure a strong counterfactual, while the real-world setting increases the external validity of the results. A field experiment shows how a concept affects tax compliance *in practice*, taking into account the ways that tax authorities operate, specific questions of policy design and the cues and heuristics that taxpayers apply when making decisions. It is worth noting that, by their very nature, field experiments have overcome problems of translating research into practice. This is not a trivial point, given the extent of these problems and the resources expended to address them (Grimshaw et al., 2012).

Kleven et al. (2011) provides a good example of a field experiment whose findings are of interest to both academics and practitioners. The researchers worked closely with the Danish tax collection agency to select a sample of 42,784 taxpayers, some of whom were subject to third-party reporting, while others self-reported their taxes. Half of this sample were randomly allocated to receive an unannounced tax audit in 2007; the other half received no action. The following year, taxpayers in both groups were randomly allocated to receive one of (a) a letter announcing that their tax return would definitely be audited this year; (b) a letter announcing that there was a 50 per cent chance that their tax return would be audited; or (c) no action.

The experiment therefore provides rare evidence of the effect of exogenously varying the probability of audit: do taxpayers make different decisions with their income when facing a 50 per cent chance of audit, versus a 100 per cent chance? The study concluded that taxpayers do indeed make different decisions – a 100 per cent audit probability had roughly twice the effect on reported income than a 50 per cent probability – but only if they self-reported income. Audit probabilities did not affect those subject to third-party reporting, mainly because the evasion rate was close to zero among this group.

This study offers several advantages. Since it was run in conjunction with a tax authority, the findings were based on actual audit data (thus addressing some measurement issues). Since taxpayers were not aware they were in a study, we can rule out the 'experimenter effects' that may affect laboratory studies. The fact that the audits were random, rather than risk-based, means that their effects can be isolated. The findings provide empirical evidence on the effect of audit probabilities (part of the standard deterrence model), while also informing practical policy decisions about the use of audits versus third-party reporting. These kind of benefits are why field experiments have been seen as one of the main drivers of the recent 'credibility revolution' in applied economics.[7]

One of the more high-profile series of recent tax compliance field experiments was conducted by the UK's Behavioural Insights Team and Her Majesty's Revenue and Customs (HMRC), the UK tax authority (Hallsworth et al., 2017). These field experiments consisted of varying the messages sent by HMRC to individuals and organisations who had failed to pay their liabilities on time. This situation offered several theoretical and practical advantages. Since the target behaviour concerned tax debts, rather than tax evasion, this avoided some of the common measurement problems: noncompliance was clearly identified, and official records unambiguously showed when payments had or had not been made. The field experiment was fully integrated into the business of the tax authority: since the letters had to be sent out regardless of the experiment, the only change it introduced was to the letter wording, which ensured that costs were very low. This integration also meant that experiments could be run over successive years, allowing results to be replicated and incremental improvements to be obtained. Moreover, since the tax authority was dealing with a large developed economy, the sample sizes obtained were very large (200,000+) and any significant results would be of substantive economic importance.

The large sample sizes also meant that the behavioural impact of very small changes in language could be assessed precisely. For example, the two experiments in Hallsworth et al. (2017) focus mainly on the impact of social norm messages. Table 14.1 gives a selection of the results from the second experiment. The first cluster is of four 'descriptive norm' messages, which describe the behaviour of others. The messages indicate that payment levels increase with the introduction of phrases that make the norm more relevant to the recipient (in terms of similar geography or similar debt). The second cluster gives more evidence that the specific phrasing of tax-related messages matters. It concerns the impact of 'injunctive norms', which provide information about others' beliefs (rather than their behaviour) (Cialdini, Kallgren and Reno, 1991). In this case, the injunctive norm is that 88 per cent of respondents to a national survey agreed with the statement that 'everyone should pay their taxes on time'. When this injunctive norm was presented as 'the great majority of people agree that everyone in the UK should pay their tax on time', it did not produce a significant increase in tax payments. However, when presented as 'nine out of ten people agree that everyone in the UK should pay their tax on time', the message increased payment rates by 1.7 percentage points (p < 0.01). Moreover, presenting the exact figure – '88 per cent of people agree that everyone in the UK should pay their tax on time' – resulted in a 3.4 percentage point increase (p < 0.01), which was significantly larger than the 'nine out of ten' message (p < 0.02).

Recall that the messages provide the same information, which suggests that framing effects are driving the differences in behaviour – possibly because the greater message specificity gives the impression of greater message credibility. This example shows that field experiments can investigate hypotheses that are as sophisticated as those in laboratory studies, while also affecting behaviour in the real world: Hallsworth et al. (2017) estimate that their two trials brought forward £11.3 million of revenue in the study period.

14.4.2 Criticisms of Field Experiments

Although field experiments (and randomised controlled trials more broadly) are generally seen as producing the 'gold standard' of evidence, they have also

Table 14.1 *A selection of results from Hallsworth et al. (2017)*

Group name	Test phrase	Payment rates at 23 days after letters issued
0. Control	[None]	33.6%
1. General descriptive norm	The great majority of people in the UK pay their tax on time.	35.0%*
2. Local descriptive norm	The great majority of people in your local area pay their tax on time.	35.8%***
3. Debt descriptive norm	Most people with a debt like yours have paid it by now.	36.6%***
4. Local and debt descriptive norm	The great majority of people in your local area pay their tax on time. Most people with a debt like yours have paid it by now.	38.6%***
5. General injunctive norm	The great majority of people agree that everyone in the UK should pay their tax on time.	37.2%
6. Fraction injunctive norm	Nine out of ten people agree that everyone in the UK should pay their tax on time.	35.3**
7. Percentage injunctive norm	88 per cent of people agree that everyone in the UK should pay their tax on time.	37.0%***

Difference from control is significant at * $p < 0.05$, ** $p < 0.01$, $p < 0.001$.

been criticised. Here I draw out the main objections that are relevant to tax compliance studies.

14.4.2.1 *Lack of Generalisability*

As noted previously, field experiments are thought to provide better external validity than laboratory experiments. However, there is a case that their external validity is still limited: they may only provide information on 'what works *here*', in one particular setting. Since there are a variety of taxes, taxpayers and taxpaying situations, how can we be sure that a certain intervention will produce the same results in a different context (Cartwright and Hardie, 2012)? This is a particular concern given the evidence from the behavioural sciences that the immediate context exerts a powerful influence over decision-making (Kahneman and Tversky, 2000).

One response to this concern is to run more field experiments, so we have broader and richer information about what works where, and for whom. As a recent overview of the tax compliance field puts it: 'In some settings norm-directed letter interventions seem to matter. It now behooves us to understand better why this can work in some settings, but not others' (Slemrod 2016, p. 47). This process may not be quick, since tax compliance experiments are still in their infancy, but we can see some evidence of progress already. For example, Kettle et al. (2016) represents an explicit attempt to translate the messages tested in Hallsworth et al. (2017) from the United Kingdom to Guatemala. The authors find that applying these messages had similar effects on compliance to those observed in the United Kingdom, despite the many differences in context (not least the much lower levels of compliance observed in Guatemala).

There may be practical constraints to constant testing, however, and in some instances it may be necessary to simply implement an existing intervention. The concern here is that, unknown to the researchers, the results from the original field experiment may have been dependent on some aspect of the intervention that is different in the new context (Pawson and Tilley, 1997). For example, it may be that a study concludes that a particular wording of tax notice *alone* produced a certain result, when actually the result was generated by the *combination* of that wording and the fact the notice was issued at the start of the tax year. In this scenario, if the wording is adopted but the notice issued at the end of the tax year (for practical reasons), the same effect will not be obtained. A field experiment may therefore create a 'black box' that does not illuminate why an intervention worked (Burtless, 1995).

There are two main responses to this concern (Bonell et al., 2012), neither of which is wholly satisfactory. One is that the field experiment can be complemented by qualitative research that tries to give a richer account of why the intervention 'worked'. The other is that the trial could test different versions of the intervention, in an attempt to isolate the impact of its constituent elements. To take a simple example, a trial could vary the day of the week on which a compliance note was issued, or the official who signs such a note. However, both these approaches become problematic when the intervention is complex, since this complexity increases the range of potential factors affecting the result, making it difficult to explore or test them comprehensively.

These concerns cannot be dismissed entirely, but they will be minimised if the intervention is simple and the situation is similar to that of the original study. It is also worth pointing out that the generalisability concern applies to all methods; even if field experiments do not address it entirely, arguably they do a better job than most alternatives. Allcott and Mullainathan (2012) analyse results from fourteen energy-saving field experiments in the United States, all of which involved mailing householders reports that compared their energy usage to that of their neighbours. The content and implementation of these interventions were 'almost identical' across the sites (p. 15). The authors used data from thirteen of these sites to predict what the result would be in the other site. If field experiments have perfect external validity, then the results from the other site should perfectly predict the effect in any one site, once we control for the specific characteristics of that site.[8] The study found that there was a significant difference between the predicted and observed effects in 47 per cent of the cases – but, importantly, that using the experimental results produced better predictions than the nonexperimental alternative methods.

14.4.2.2 *Narrowness of Perspective*

Field experiments only examine issues that can be implemented through specific, practical interventions. This means they cannot test more general and diffuse approaches to improving tax compliance, such as improving perceptions of trust in government, or structural factors that cannot be varied experimentally, such as fiscal decentralisation. They therefore risk remaining mute on important drivers of compliance. The pool of potential interventions may be limited even further to a subset that tax administrations feel comfortable testing (whether for ideological, logistical or prudent reasons). While administrations may be open to persuasion on this point, researchers may be unable or unwilling to invest the resources required to persuade them.

A similar concern about the 'narrowness' of field experiments is that they may focus solely on a set of prespecified outcomes. Indeed, not using prespecified outcomes is seen to open the door to poor research practices (Jones et al., 2015). However, the danger here is the field experiment will fail to capture any spillover effects and unintended consequences from the intervention. This may be a particular issue for tax compliance, since taxpayers may seek to claim back elsewhere the money they have 'lost' as a result of a successful intervention – and may have many opportunities to do so. Gillitzer and Skov (2015) report on the unintended consequences of a move to third-party reporting for claims of charitable contributions in Denmark. The changes had two main effects: they reduced compliance costs (by prepopulating tax returns) while also increasing the chances that false claims would be detected. As it turned out, the changes actually led a doubling in the number of claims submitted. It appears that the reduced compliance costs meant people reported more tax-deductible contributions, since it had become easier to do so. The effect of reduced compliance costs outweighed the effects of increased oversight, resulting in a net loss to the tax authority.[9]

14.4.2.3 *Concerns About Ethics and Equity*

A common criticism is that field experiments are unethical because they withhold or impose government action on individuals randomly (Glennerster and Powers, 2016). The argument would be: is it fair to deliberately deny some people a benefit (or subject them to a compliance intervention)? Many countries allow recourse to judicial review if they are seen to be treated arbitrarily by a government authority. Moreover, various researchers have pointed to the importance of 'horizontal equity' (the sense that similar others are treated similarly) and 'procedural justice' (the sense that agreed processes are being applied fairly) for increasing compliance and building trust in a tax system (Moser, Evans and Kim, 1995; Murphy, 2005). Random treatment has the potential to undermine these drivers of compliance.

The standard response to the ethical objection is that randomisation is only appropriate when we cannot be sure that an intervention will actually bring benefits (in a clinical setting, this uncertainty is known as *equipoise*) (Freedman,

1987). Therefore, those in the control group may not actually be losing out. This argument is often made with reference to development initiatives that try to improve the situation of individuals. However, it becomes problematic when applied to policy issues – such as tax compliance – that are collective action problems where the immediate interests of individuals and policy makers are not aligned (Ostrom, 1990). A deterrence intervention (such as auditing) is likely to impose costs on an individual, regardless of whether it increases tax compliance or not. From the individual's perspective, a direct cost is being randomly imposed on them. One response here could be that there is a well-established precedent for the use of random auditing in tax systems.

14.5 Summary and Future Directions

Field experiments offer many advantages over other methods for analysing tax compliance. The twin offer of a robust counterfactual and good external validity remains compelling. The objections I have stated could be applied to many other alternative options. Indeed, arguably the main reasons tax compliance field experiments have remained rare are practical ones, rather than the theoretical objections just outlined. Academics may be daunted by the additional investment required to build trust with tax officials, understand their processes and priorities and wait for the right opportunity. Running a field experiment may create a burden on tax authorities in terms of collecting, storing and transmitting data, since public sector systems are likely to have been designed to address practical challenges, not to allow research. And, of course, administrations may be concerned that the experiment could force them to admit that an intervention actually *reduced* tax revenue (Ariel, 2012). However, as the growth in field experiments shows, sensitive collaboration can make these barriers manageable.

There are many questions that tax compliance field experiments need to explore in the future. Behavioural science highlights the way that many aspects of the design and implementation of tax policies can influence compliance, in often surprising ways. With this in mind, researchers are starting to measure the consequences of apparently mundane choices like whether to post a letter or hand it over in person (Doerrenberg and Schmitz, 2015; Ortega and Scartascini, 2015); much more can be done here to produce gains at relatively low cost. Studies still focus disproportionately on the behaviour of individuals, despite the fact that companies handle the bulk of tax revenue in many countries. The predominance of deterrence-based approaches means that we have little information on the impact of positive incentives, monetary or otherwise (Dwenger et al., 2016; Dunning et al., 2015). Surprisingly few studies have included a reliable cost-benefit analysis of their interventions, despite the value that policy makers place on these kind of analyses. And we still lack a good understanding of how and why tax administrations do (or do not) incorporate the findings from field experiments into policies and standard operating procedures.

14.6 Conclusion

Roth (1995) proposed a well-known classification that divides economic experiments into three categories. 'Speaking to Theorists' covers experiments that attempt to test elements of a theory, thereby providing evidence that could improve future theories. They form part of a dialogue between theorists and experimenters. 'Searching for Facts' groups experiments that test variables that are not incorporated into well-worked theories. In these instances, experimenters are mostly talking to each other, building facts on facts. Torgler (2002) argued that most experiments on tax compliance fall into these two categories; this remains broadly true. Finally, 'Whispering in the Ears of Princes' includes experiments that attempt to simulate the environment in which real tax decisions take place, in order to address policy issues. As the name suggests, this category involves dialogue between experimenters and policy makers.

Field experiments would seem to fit neatly into the third category. But I suggest that they do not and, moreover, represent a challenge to the taxonomy as a whole. 'Whispering in the Ears of Princes' implies that research is taking place away from policy makers, who receive the findings later. This movement from research to policy represents an instance of what Weiss (1979) calls the 'knowledge-driven model' of research utilisation. But a central feature of field experiments is that they are run *in collaboration* with tax authorities, and that experimentation takes place *as a policy intervention*, rather than as an antecedent to government action. Taking this line of thought further allows us to see government action as a site for the production of knowledge rather than a destination for knowledge produced elsewhere. Therefore, if set up carefully, there is no reason why a field experiment cannot answer a theoretical question while also influencing a policy decision. The most impressive field experiments do exactly this (Dwenger et al., 2016). This means that 'collaborating with princes' can become a new way to 'search for facts' or 'speak to theorists', rather than being mutually exclusive with them.

I began by outlining how policy makers have become more interested in field experiments through growing challenges to the rational actor model, increased pressure on public finances and a developing appetite for experimentation. In parallel, academics have increasingly recognised that field experiments can offer both a robust counterfactual and findings with good external validity. This confluence of interests has led to many new field experiments in the past decade. They have helped examine some of the most fundamental questions in theories of tax compliance, while also helping tax officials to find out 'what works'. They therefore exemplify how, in the words of Alm (2012,

p. 56), 'measuring, explaining, and controlling evasion are fundamentally and inextricably bound together'.

The next phase for tax compliance field experiments should be one of consolidation. As noted in the previous section, there are many exciting questions to be answered. But more important is the need to move from 'what works' to 'what works, for whom, when, (and why)'. For any set of results, we need to understand if we are dealing with findings that will not be obtained in different circumstances, or with those that can be formed into general precepts to underpin tax policy. There are two mutually reinforcing ways that this can be done. First, academics and tax administrations need to build a sustained partnership to allow a set of trials to examine issues coherently, in depth and over time. Second, researchers need to be willing to explicitly build on and replicate the work of their peers (recognising that field experiments always represent a compromise between academic priorities and operational exigencies). If those things can be accomplished, the field can take a decisive step towards addressing some of the difficulties it has faced.

Notes

1 Studies of this type have also been defined as 'natural field experiments' (Harrison and List, 2004). They are also sometimes referred to as 'randomised controlled trials'. However, this is a broader term because it refers only to the methods used – i.e., randomisation and the presence of a control group – which could equally be used in a laboratory setting.

2 This chapter takes 'tax noncompliance' to mean 'the intentional or unintentional failure of taxpayers to pay their taxes correctly' (Webley et al., 1991, p. 2). The core elements of compliance are filing tax returns on time, making accurate declarations in those returns, and paying any tax owed when it is due (US Treasury, 2009). While this definition includes legal 'tax avoidance' measures, they are not the primary focus of this chapter.

3 This link is symbolised in the joint award of the 2002 Nobel Prize for Economics to both Daniel Kahneman for 'having integrated insights from psychological research into economic science', and Vernon Smith for 'having established laboratory experiments as a tool in empirical economic analysis'.

4 Given the discussion in Olsen, Kang and Kirchler's chapter, I do not treat this point in great depth here. For a further discussion of this (and other points in this article), see Hallsworth (2014).

5 If taxpayers knew where the threshold would occur, they could aim to fall on one side or the other, by changing what they report. The distribution either side of the threshold would thereby cease to be random. More generally, a regression discontinuity design does not always require individuals to be ignorant of qualifying criteria – as long as they cannot influence the outcome even if they know about it in advance.

6 I found Muehlbacher and Kirchler (2016) a useful source when compiling these criticisms.

7 Hallsworth (2014) gives an overview of the findings from field experiments to increase tax compliance.

8 In other words, if we know that the intervention works less well with (for example) older people, then we would expect it to have a smaller effect if the population of a site is older than other sites.

9 Note here that this is not an issue of compliance versus noncompliance: the loss of revenue was created by taxpayers taking entirely legal and appropriate actions.

14.7 References

Allcott, H., and Mullainathan, S. (2012). External Validity and Partner Selection Bias. National Bureau of Economic Research Working Paper 18373.

Allingham, M. G., and Sandmo, A. (1972). Income Tax Evasion: A Theoretical Analysis. *Journal of Public Economics*, 1, 323–328.

Alm, J. (2012). Measuring, Explaining, and Controlling Tax Evasion: Lessons from Theory, Experiments, and Field Studies. *International Tax and Public Finance*, 19, 54–77.

Alm, J., Bloomquist, K. M., and McKee, M. (2015). On the External Validity of Laboratory Tax Compliance Experiments. *Economic Inquiry*, 53(2), 1170–1186.

Alm, J., McClelland, G. H., and Schulze, W. D. (1992). Why Do People Pay Taxes? *Journal of Public Economics*, 48(1), 21–38.

Angrist, J. D., and Pischke, J. S. (2008). *Mostly Harmless Econometrics: An Empiricist's Companion*. Princeton, NJ: Princeton University Press.

Ariel, B. (2012). Deterrence and Moral Persuasion Effects on Corporate Tax Compliance: Findings from a Randomized Controlled Trial. *Criminology*, 50(1), 27–69.

Bargh, J. A., and Chartrand, T. L. (1999). The Unbearable Automaticity of Being. *American Psychologist*, 54(7), 462.

Barrett, G., Levell, P., and Milligan, K. (2013). A Comparison of Micro and Macro Expenditure Measures Across Countries Using Differing Survey Methods. National Bureau of Economic Research Working Paper 19544.

Bonell, C., Fletcher, A., Morton, M., Lorenc, T., and Moore, L. (2012). Realist Randomised Controlled Trials: A New Approach to Evaluating Complex Public Health Interventions. *Social Science and Medicine*, 75(12), 2299–2306.

Bristow, D., Carter, L., and Martin, S. (2015). Using Evidence to Improve Policy and Practice: The UK What Works Centres. *Contemporary Social Science*, 10(2), 126–137.

Burtless, G. (1995). The Case for Randomized Field Trials in Economic and Policy Research. *Journal of Economic Perspectives*, 9(2), 63–84.

Camerer, C. (2011). The Promise and Success of Lab-Field Generalizability in Experimental Economics: A Critical Reply to Levitt and List. SSRN 1977749.

Camerer, C. F., Loewenstein, G., and Rabin, M. (eds.). (2011). *Advances in Behavioral Economics*. Princeton, NJ: Princeton University Press.

Cartwright, N., and Hardie, J. (2012). *Evidence-Based Policy: A Practical Guide to Doing It Better*. Oxford: Oxford University Press.

Choo, C. L., Fonseca, M. A., and Myles, G. D. (2016). Do Students Behave Like Real Taxpayers in the Lab? Evidence from a Real Effort Tax Compliance Experiment. *Journal of Economic Behavior and Organization*, 124, 102–114.

Cialdini, R. B., Kallgren, C. A., and Reno, R. R. (1991). A Focus Theory of Normative Conduct: A Theoretical Refinement and Reevaluation of the Role of Norms in Human Behavior. *Advances in Experimental Social Psychology*, 24, 201–234.

Coricelli, G., Joffily, M., Montmarquette, C., and Villeval, M. C. (2010). Cheating, Emotions, and Rationality: An Experiment on Tax Evasion. *Experimental Economics*, 13(2), 226–247.

Coricelli, G., Rusconi, E., and Villeval, M. C. (2014). Tax Evasion and Emotions: An Empirical Test of Re-Integrative Shaming Theory. *Journal of Economic Psychology*, 40, 49–61.

Doerrenberg, P., and Schmitz, J. (2015). Tax Compliance and Information Provision: A Field Experiment with Small Firms. ZEW-Centre for European Economic Research Discussion Paper 15–028.

Duflo, E., Glennerster, R., and Kremer, M. (2007). Using Randomization in Development Economics Research: A Toolkit. *Handbook of Development Economics*, 4, 3895–3962.

Dunning, T., Monestier, F., Piñeiro, R., Rosenblatt, F., and Tuñón, G. (2015). *Positive vs. Negative Incentives for Compliance: Evaluating a Randomized Tax Holiday in Uruguay*. SSRN 2650105.

Dwenger, N., Kleven, H., Rasul, I., and Rincke, J. (2016). Extrinsic and Intrinsic Motivations for Tax Compliance: Evidence from a Field Experiment in Germany. *American Economic Journal: Economic Policy*, 8(3), 203–232.

Elffers, H., Robben, H. S., and Hessing, D. J. (1992). On Measuring Tax Evasion. *Journal of Economic Psychology*, 13(4), 545–567.

Elffers, H., Weigel, R. H., and Hessing, D. J. (1987). The Consequences of Different Strategies for Measuring Tax Evasion Behavior. *Journal of Economic Psychology*, 8, 311–337.

Ettelt, S., Mays, N., and Allen, P. (2015). Policy Experiments: Investigating Effectiveness or Confirming Direction? *Evaluation*, 21(3), 292–307.

European Commission (2010). *Communication from the Commission to the European Parliament, the Council and the European Economic and Social Committee: Tax and Development: Cooperating with Developing Countries on Promoting Good Governance in Tax Matters*. Brussels: European Commission.

Exadaktylos, F., Espín, A. M., and Branas-Garza, P. (2013). Experimental Subjects Are Not Different. *Scientific Reports*, 3, 1213.

Feld, L. P., and Larsen, C. (2012) Self-Perceptions, Government Policies and Tax Compliance in Germany. *International Tax and Public Finance*, 19(1), 78–103.

Freedman, B. (1987). Equipoise and the Ethics of Clinical Research. *New England Journal of Medicine*, 317(3), 141–145.

Gerber, A. S., and Green, D. P. (2012). *Field Experiments: Design, Analysis, and Interpretation*. New York: W. W. Norton.

Gillitzer, C., and Skov, P. (2013). Evidence on Unclaimed Charitable Contributions from the Introduction of Third-Party Information Reporting in Denmark.

Working Paper 2013-04, Economic Policy Research Unit (EPRU), University of Copenhagen.

Glennerster, R., and Powers, S. (2016). Balancing Risk and Benefit. In: G. F. DeMartino and D. N. McCloskey (eds.), *The Oxford Handbook of Professional Economic Ethics*. Oxford: Oxford University Press, pp. 367–401.

Grimshaw, J. M., Eccles, M. P., Lavis, J. N., Hill, S. J., and Squires, J. E. (2012). Knowledge Translation of Research Findings. *Implementation Science*, 7(1), 1.

Hallsworth, M. (2014). The Use of Field Experiments to Increase Tax Compliance. *Oxford Review of Economic Policy*, 30(4), 658–679.

Hallsworth, M., List, J. A., Metcalfe, R. D., and Vlaev, I. (2017). The Behavioralist as Tax Collector: Using Natural Field Experiments to Enhance Tax Compliance. *Journal of Public Economics*, 148, 14–31.

Halpern, D. (2015). *Inside the Nudge Unit: How Small Changes Can Make a Big Difference*. London: Random House.

Harrison, G. W., and List, J. A. (2004). Field Experiments. *Journal of Economic Literature*, 42(4), 1009–1055.

Hasseldine, J., and Hite, P. A. (2003). Framing, Gender and Tax Compliance. *Journal of Economic Psychology*, 24(4), 517–533.

Hessing, D. J., Elffers, H., and Weigel, R. H. (1988). Exploring the Limits of Self-Reports and Reasoned Action: An Investigation of the Psychology of Tax Evasion Behavior. *Journal of Personality and Social Psychology*, 54(3), 405.

Hessing, D., Robben, H., and Elffers, H. (1989). *The Relationship Between Self-Reported and Documented Behaviour in the Case of Fraud with Unemployment Benefits*. Madison, WI: 1989 Annual Meeting of the Law and Society Association.

Hite, P. A. (1987). An Application of Attribution Theory in Taxpayer Noncompliance Research. *Public Finance*, 42(1), 105–118.

Hurst, E., Li, G., and Pugsley, B. (2014). Are Household Surveys Like Tax Forms? Evidence from Income Underreporting of the Self-Employed. *Review of Economics and Statistics*, 96(1), 19–33.

Jones, C. W., Keil, L. G., Holland, W. C., Caughey, M. C., and Platts-Mills, T. F. (2015). Comparison of Registered and Published Outcomes in Randomized Controlled Trials: A Systematic Review. *BMC Medicine*, 13(1), 1–12.

Kahneman, D., and Tversky, A. (2000). *Choices, Values, and Frames*. Cambridge: Cambridge University Press.

Kettle, S., Hernandez, M., Ruda, S., and Sanders, M. (2016). Behavioral Interventions in Tax Compliance: Evidence from Guatemala. Working Paper 7690. Washington, DC: World Bank.

Kirchler, E. (1999). Reactance to Taxation: Employers' Attitudes Towards Taxes. *Journal of Socio-Economics*, 28(2), 131–138.

Kirchler, E. (2007). *The Economic Psychology of Tax Behaviour*. Cambridge: Cambridge University Press.

Kirchler, E., Muehlbacher, S., Kastlunger, B., and Wahl, I. (2010). Why Pay Taxes? A Review of Tax Compliance Decisions In: J. Alm, J. Martinez-Vazquez, and B. Torgler, (eds.) *Developing Alternative Frameworks for Explaining Tax Compliance*. London: Routledge, pp. 15–31.

Kleven, H. (2016) Bunching. *Annual Review of Economics*, 8, 435–464.

Kleven, H. J., Knudsen, M. B., Kreiner, C. T., Pedersen, S., and Saez, E. (2011). Unwilling or Unable to Cheat? Evidence from a Tax Audit Experiment in Denmark. *Econometrica*, 79(3), 651–692.

Levitt, S., and List, J. A. (2007). What Do Laboratory Experiments Measuring Social Preferences Reveal About the Real World? *Journal of Economic Perspectives*, 21(2), 153–174.

Lewis, A. (1982). *The Psychology of Taxation*. London: Blackwell.

Marriott, L. (2014). Using Student Subjects in Experimental Research: A Challenge to the Practice of Using Students as a Proxy for Taxpayers. *International Journal of Social Research Methodology*, 17(5), 503–525.

McCaffery, E. J., and Baron, J. (2006). Thinking About Tax. *Psychology, Public Policy, and Law*, 12(1), 106.

Meyer, B. D., Mok, W. K., and Sullivan, J. X. (2015). Household Surveys in Crisis. *Journal of Economic Perspectives*, 29(4), 199–226.

Moser, D. V., Evans III, J. H., and Kim, C. K. (1995). The Effects of Horizontal and Exchange Inequity on Tax Reporting Decisions. *Accounting Review*, 70(4), 619–634.

Muehlbacher, S., and Kirchler, E. (2016). About the External Validity of Laboratory Experiments in Tax Compliance Research. *Die Betriebswirtschaft*, 76(1), 7–19.

Muehlbacher, S., Mittone, L., Kastlunger, B., and Kirchler, E. (2012). Uncertainty Resolution in Tax Experiments: Why Waiting for an Audit Increases Compliance. *Journal of Socio-Economics*, 41(3), 289–291.

Murphy, K. (2005). Regulating More Effectively: The Relationship Between Procedural Justice, Legitimacy, and Tax Non-Compliance. *Journal of Law and Society*, 32(4), 562–589.

Newhouse, J. P., and RAND Corporation Insurance Experiment Group (1993). *Free for All? Lessons from the RAND Health Insurance Experiment*. Cambridge, MA: Harvard University Press.

Oakley, A. (1998). Experimentation and Social Interventions: A Forgotten but Important History. *British Medical Journal*, 317, 1239–42.

OECD (Organisation for Economic Cooperation and Development) (2010). *Understanding and Influencing Taxpayers' Compliance Behaviour*. Paris: Organisation for Economic Cooperation and Development.

Ortega, D., and Scartascini, C. (2015) Don't Blame the Messenger: A Field Experiment on Delivery Methods for Increasing Tax Compliance. Inter-American Development Bank (IDB) Working Paper IDB-WP-627.

Ostrom, E. (1990). *Governing the Commons: The Evolution of Institutions for Collective Action*. Cambridge: Cambridge University Press.

Pawson, R., and Tilley, N. (1997). *Realistic Evaluation*. London: Sage.

Roth, A. (1995). Introduction to Experimental Economics. In: J. Kagel and A. Roth (eds.), *The Handbook of Experimental Economics*. Princeton, NJ: Princeton University Press, pp. 3–110.

Saez, E. (2010). Do Taxpayers Bunch at Kink Points? *American Economic Journal: Economic Policy*, 2(3), 180–212.

Sánchez, G. (2014). The Impact of Low-Cost Intervention on Tax Compliance: Regression Discontinuity Evidence. Texas A&M University Working Paper.

Sanderson, I. (2002). Evaluation, Policy Learning and Evidence-Based Policy Making. *Public Administration*, 80(1), 1–22.

Schwarz, N. (1999). Self-Reports: How the Questions Shape the Answers. *American Psychologist*, 54(2), 93.

Slemrod, J. (2016) Tax Compliance and Enforcement. New Research and Its Policy Implications. SSRN 2726077.

Spicer, M. W., and Thomas, J. E. (1982). Audit Probabilities and the Tax Evasion Decision: An Experimental Approach. *Journal of Economic Psychology*, 2(3), 241–245.

Thaler, R. H. (2015). *Misbehaving: The Making of Behavioral Economics.* New York: W. W. Norton.

Torgler, B. (2002). Speaking to Theorists and Searching for Facts: Tax Morale and Tax Compliance in Experiments. *Journal of Economic Surveys*, 16(5), 657–683.

Torgler, B. (2007). *Tax Compliance and Tax Morale: A Theoretical and Empirical Analysis.* Cheltenham, UK: Edward Elgar.

US Treasury (2009). *Update on Reducing the Federal Tax Gap and Improving Voluntary Compliance.* Washington, DC: US Treasury.

Webb, T. L., and Sheeran, P. (2006). Does Changing Behavioral Intentions Engender Behavior Change? A Meta-analysis of the Experimental Evidence. *Psychological Bulletin*, 132(2), 249–268.

Webley, P., Robben, H., Elffers, H., and Hessing, D. (1991). *Tax Evasion: An Experimental Approach.* Cambridge: Cambridge University Press.

Weiss, C. H. (1979). The Many Meanings of Research Utilization. *Public Administration Review*, 39(5), 426–431.

Whitehead, M., Jones, R., Howell, R., Lilley, R., and Pykett, J. (2014). Nudging All over the World: Assessing the Global Impact of the Behavioural Sciences on Public Policy. *Economic and Social Research Council.*

15 'Individual Failure' and a Behavioural Public Sector Economics

Lory Barile, John Cullis and Philip Jones

15.1 Introduction

Neoclassical welfare economics is the foundation on which the positive and normative prescriptions of public sector economics are premised. Key to this foundation are the preferences and capabilities of the caricature *homo* and *femina economicus*. Both traditional public finance and public choice schools have focused on this 'representative' individual. Following Brennan and Lomasky (1993), this actor is described as (i) 'rational'; (ii) and egoistic; (iii) with egoism predicated on self-interest narrowly defined in terms of income or wealth. Armed with this caricature, public sector economics has undoubtedly made great strides in understanding 'market failure' (in the case of traditional public sector economics) and 'government failure' (in what is called the public choice approach).

What can be said about these very strong facilitating characteristics that were once viewed as harmless and obvious? A vital consideration is the meaning of 'rational' behaviour. 'Rational' behaviour is consistent behaviour. Predictions can be made when *homo* and *femina economicus* face new constraints (relative prices, income). If preferences are assumed exogenous and constant, predictions are premised on the response individuals make to changes in constraints (Stigler and Becker, 1977). This approach can accommodate a broader description of a 'representative' individual. Altruism and malevolence, for example, can be incorporated via interdependent utility functions, but these would be seen as exceptions for the representative individual whose default mode is self-interest in all contexts. Further there is no doubt that defining self-interest narrowly as (expected) utility or wealth maximisation makes many of the examples to be found in economics texts 'work' easily and seamlessly. The motivation of this chapter partly arises because this perspective – or, more grandly, paradigm – may have run its course in terms of the major insights that can be obtained with it and partly from an apparent strong demand for a (public sector) economics based on a more 'real' actor.

The focus is on economic behaviour that is predicated on a different caricature that might be dubbed *homo* and *femina realitus* (see Cullis and Jones,

2009). What are the descriptive characteristics to be employed? This more recently employed actor has a number of characteristics, being reliant on the following:

i.   Bounded abilities that can be subdivided into (a) bounded rationality and (b) bounded self-will.
ii. Bounded self-interest, being concerned with more than pure self-interest narrowly defined – a 'bigger and richer person' than *homo economicus*. Again a subdivision may be helpful: (a) individuals have an internal moral or ethical dimension that shows up in concepts such as intrinsic motivation – a desire to do 'the right thing' for its own sake; and (b) an external dimension where they are wary if they follow their narrow self-interest that they will unjustifiably impose costs on others, or disappoint by failing to act in line with an accepted social norm.
iii. A preference map that is endogenous and malleable (as opposed to the traditionally assumed exogenous and fixed preferences). Here a distinction can be made by (a) looking at transient endogeneity, such as by emotion priming in experiments to affect results or 'micro' framing effects and (b) focusing on more permanent endogeneity, where the actor is responsive to public policy and other signals that affect preferences ('macro' framing effects).

The next section elaborates on the 'individual failure' comprising (i) to (iii) in the preceding.

15.2 *Homo* and *Femina Realitus*

(i)(a) *Bounded abilities*. Both 'traditional public finance' and 'public choice' schools have focused on 'rational' actors in order to predict behaviour. Becker (1971, p. 26) puts it at its starkest: 'The essence of this model of rational behaviour is contained in just two assumptions: each consumer has an ordered set of preferences, and he chooses the most preferred position available to him.' But, if, as Hegel (cited in Knox, 1952, p. 230) profoundly observes, 'The rational is the highroad where everyone travels, where no one is conspicuous', a growing literature now suggests that 'the highroad' is not sign-posted with the axioms required to underpin Becker's definition. The highroad is littered with an array of partially analysed, yet systematic, heuristic responses and the likes of transitivity, strong separability and the usual rules for combining lotteries have to be replaced by something else. Analysis of 'rational' behaviour facilitates prediction (for economists, 'rational' is equivalent to consistent behaviour). If there are departures from 'rational' behaviour, these appear to be *anomalies*. The problem is that, in experiment after experiment, and demonstration after demonstration, anomalies are seen to be ubiquitous and persistent. A very well-established literature now describes such behaviour, but as this behaviour departs systematically from 'rational' behaviour (of *homo economicus*), it is possible to explore the implications for analysis of public finance and public choice. Frey and Eichenberger (1994) are early authors who describe a significant body of evidence drawn from economic psychology and experimental economics. A long list of anomalies that can be drawn up calls into question the extent to which public sector economics can be built on an analysis relying on the rationality of *homo economicus*. It implies that our new actor (*homo realitus* for short) does not have 'unlimited cognitive and information processing capabilities' (Guth and Ortmann 2006, p. 405). Instead, our new 'representative' individual relies on *bounded rationality* (involving 'rules of thumb' and the like), and these should be a feature of behavioural public sector economics.

(i)(b) *Bounded self-will.* An early feature of behavioural economic analysis was the recognition of bounded self-will. As Oscar Wilde famously wrote in Act 1 of *Lady Windermere's Fan*, 'I can resist everything except temptation'. Individuals are tempted and are often impulsive and impatient in their choices. Shefrin and Thaler (1988) have a savings model that involves multiple selves in that the myopic 'doer' in you wants to bring forward all consumption whereas the farsighted 'planner' in you recognises you need to save and spread consumption over all future periods, especially retirement, when you will not be earning. Once this feature of *homo realitus* is recognised, then it becomes natural to have an analysis that involves precommitment devices that may be internal or external. An internal device could involve the use of 'mental accounts' to constrain choices, so that the 'savings account' cannot be raided to bolster the 'entertainments account' this month. Externally problem gamblers may have themselves banned from casinos, or savers sign up to pension schemes that deny any access to your savings until retirement.

(ii)(a) *Internal bounded self-interest.* Individuals have an ethical and moral dimension. They seem to want to do the right thing simply for its own sake – intrinsic motivation. In a 'third-party' punishment game, two players, the dictator A and recipient B, participate in a dictator game. There is a third player, the potential punisher C, who observes how much A gives to B; then C can spend a proportion of his endowment on punishing A. This game measures to what extent 'impartial' and 'unaffected' third parties are willing to stick up for other players at their own expense, enforcing a conventional sharing norm by punishing unfair dictators. A significant number of C players do indeed punish unfair choices by dictators – for them, it is the right thing to do (see, e.g., Fehr and Gächter, 2000a).

(ii)(b) *External bounded self-interest.* There is a vast literature predicated on the notion that individuals demonstrate concern for others in a great variety of ways – so called 'other-regarding' preferences. A number of utility functions have been employed to capture this concern. For example, Fehr and

Schmidt (1999) have a utility function that allows individuals to feel envy and compassion:

$$U_i(x) = x_i - \frac{\alpha_i}{n-1}\sum_{j\neq i}(x_j - x_i) - \frac{\beta_i}{n-1}\sum_{j\neq i}(x_i - x_j) \tag{15.1}$$

n–1 j≠i   n–1 j≠i

so that in Equation (15.1), i's utility depends on i's private outcome xi reduced by an envy term that measures the extent to which there is a set of people who are doing better than i $\sum (x_j - x_i)$, and a compassion term that measures the extent to which there is a set of people who are doing worse than i $\sum (x_i - x_j)$. The coefficient on envy, α_i, exceeds the coefficient, β_i, on compassion; no one's perfect!

(iii)(a) *Transient preference endogeneity.* Lowenstein (2007) suggests economists have been good at picking up insights from cognitive psychology but have missed a large part of what governs individual choices by ignoring emotion. The same individual in different emotional states can behave very differently, being altruistic or selfish, farsighted or myopic, risk averse or risk taking. Lerner, Small and Loewenstein (2004) illustrate the power of 'emotional priming' in the context of the endowment effect explored in Section 15.3. Christian and Alm (2014) find that experimental subjects primed to elicit empathy are more tax compliant than those who do not complete their priming task. What was previously dubbed 'micro' framing can be related to the *reference point effect*: alternatives are evaluated by individuals not in terms of total wealth but relative to a reference point, often the status quo. 'Framing' moves the reference point so that lotteries with the same expected values are treated differently. Lotteries framed as losses invoke risk taking, whilst those framed as gains encourage risk-averse choices.

(iii)(b) *Longer-term preference endogeneity.* It would seem reasonable to accept that cultural, economic and social forces affect individuals' tastes or preferences. This has far-reaching consequences for economics if the test for efficiency (a Pareto optimum) is about a set of economic arrangements that conform to the preferences that, in the extreme, the economic system has itself created. In this chapter, the nature of long-term preference endogeneity is more attenuated than this and will involve 'nudge' type arguments, where government policy intervention may be seen as 'shaping' choices by exploiting what is known about individual decision-making. Here it is an attempt to make preferences endogenous to policy cues to raise individuals' long-term welfare that is the core of the argument. For example, 'opting in/opting out' policy frames that invoke 'status quo' bias seem to make individuals choose to be in a works pension scheme or not.

The upshot of this discussion is that in behavioural public sector economics, the analysis is likely to be more 'messy' than a neoclassical approach and involve the use of heuristics; framing; mental accounts; precommitment devices; exploitation of anomalous choices; intrinsic motivation; and forms of 'other-regarding' preferences.

How sensitive is public finance and public choice analysis to changes in the description of a 'representative' individual and implied internal and external environments is explored in the following section.

15.3 Insights from Behavioural Economics: Implications for Public Expenditure Appraisal

Cost-benefit analysis (CBA) is premised on the neoclassical assumptions that representative individuals are rational and self-interested. However, if insights (i) to (iii) are relevant, is it possible to rely on CBA to appraise public expenditure projects? CBA assesses the welfare implications of projects with reference to individuals' preferences. If the net present value of a project is positive, the implication is that 'willingness to pay' for the project (on the part of the gainers) exceeds 'willingness to pay' not to have the project (on the part of the losers); the project is 'efficient'.[1] But, with evidence of bounded rationality, bounded will power and bounded self-interest, can cost-benefit analysis be premised on individuals' preferences?

15.3.1 Valuations of Costs and Benefits

Should valuations be based on 'willingness to pay' (WTP)? It is also possible to rely on 'willingness to accept' (WTA). WTA is a measure of the compensation required in the absence of the project, to make an individual feel as well off as if the individual had received the net benefits of the project. In neoclassical economics, estimates of WTP differ from estimates of WTA when individuals experience 'income effects' (as a consequence of receipt of the net benefits of expenditure on the project), but the presumption is that differences between valuations based on WTP and on WTA can be ignored because income effects are not expected to be significant (Willig, 1976).

With bounded rationality, individuals are sensitive to framing effects and to reference points. Differences between valuations premised on WTP and valuations premised on WTA are far greater than anticipated.

i. Differences are far greater in experiments. Kahneman, Knetsch and Thaler (1990) focused on the valuations of forty-four undergraduate students in Cornell. Twenty-two students were given Cornell coffee mugs (which sold at $6.00 at the bookstore). The subjects who did not receive a mug were asked to indicate the prices they would be 'willing to pay' for a mug. Those who received a mug were asked to indicate the prices they would be 'willing to accept' to sell their mug. As the mugs were distributed randomly, the expectation was that there would be no difference in the tastes of the twenty-two subjects who received the mug and the tastes of those who did not. The expectation was that approximately eleven mugs would be sold. Only three mugs were sold. WTA was far higher than WTP.

Table 15.1 *Willingness to pay (WTP) and willingness to accept (WTA) in cost-benefit studies (in dollars)*

Study and entitlement	Means			Medians		
	WTP	WTA	Ratio	WTP	WTA	Ratio
Hypothetical surveys						
Hammack and Brown (1974) Marshes	247	1,044	4.2	NA	NA	NA
Banford et al. (1979) Fishing Pier	43	120	2.8	47	129	2.7
Postal Service	22	93	4.2	22	106	4.8
Bishop and Heberlein (1979) Goose-hunting permits	21	101	4.8	NA	NA	NA
Heberlein and Bishop (1985) Deer hunting	31	513	16.5	NA	NA	NA

Source: Adapted from Kahneman et al. (1990).

ii. Differences are far greater in cost-benefit studies. Table 15.1 highlights some illustrative examples (in studies that value environmental assets and activities). The differences are vivid in the ratios of WTA to WTP.

In the experiment described in (i), recipients of mugs acted as if they incorporated their mug into their status quo wealth (Kahneman et al., 1990). With loss aversion, they judged the loss of a mug more seriously than the money that would be paid for the mug. In experiments and in cost-benefit studies, valuations appear to be influenced by an *endowment effect*. Of course, there are other possible explanations. In neoclassical economics, Hanneman (1991) has shown that WTP may diverge significantly from WTA when focusing on a public good (if there are no private goods that are good substitutes for the public good). In behavioural economics, 'anchoring' and 'mental accounting' might also be relevant.[2]

With all of these qualifications, valuations depend on reference points. Cost-benefit analysis is likely to underestimate costs when valuations are premised on willingness to pay. Compensations for losses (in court cases) may fail to fully indemnify individuals when they are based on willingness to pay (Knetsch, 1990). When undertaking cost-benefit analysis, valuations depend on whether individuals view changes (i) with reference to their present status, or (ii) with reference to their status if the proposed changes are to be accepted (Knetsch, 2010).

15.3.2 Discounting Future Costs and Benefits

Neoclassical textbooks suggest that it is 'rational' to discount future gains and losses continuously and exponentially, and to rely on a single discount rate (e.g., Mishan and Quah, 2007).[3] With evidence that individuals rely on bounded self-will, individuals' time preferences appear to be quite different. How relevant are these insights when focusing on: (i) the *way* individuals discount future costs and benefits and (ii) the *rate* at which individuals discount future costs and benefits?

In cost-benefit analysis, costs and benefits are discounted by a discount factor $1/(1 + r)^t$ (where t is a unit of time). This is exponential because the time path of the discount factor follows an exponential function of the form e^{-rt} (where r is the discount rate and t is a unit of time). With a constant discount rate, only the absolute difference between measures of value (V) matters. For example, if benefit Va (due next year) is preferred to benefit Vb (in three years), the ranking should be preserved if (say) twenty years (or any number of years) were added to these two dates. If Va in year 1 is preferred to Vb in year 3, Va in year twenty-one should be preferred to Vb in year twenty-three. However, Thaler and Sheffrin (1981) report that individuals often alter their preference as a function of the time the choice is made (even when the delay between the two sums is held constant, e.g., three years).[4] Even when individuals face the same choice (viewing the choice at different points in the future), there is evidence of preference reversal.

Ainslie (1991) argues that individuals do not discount exponentially. Assessments are based on a hyperbolic curve that is more convex to the origin than an exponential curve. Individuals change their choices over the same prospect when the time span to the availability of a good changes. Individuals have a high time preference for the near future and a lower time preference for events that will take place later in time.[5]

Turning to the *rate* at which individuals discount future costs and benefits, traditional cost–benefit analysis usually relies on *one* rate of discount for costs and for benefits. Insights from behavioural economics indicate that individuals rely on different rates of discount for gains and for losses (e.g., Thaler, 1981; Loewenstein, 1987; Frederick, Loewenstein and O'Donoghue, 2002). The valence of outcomes is important. Discount rates for losses are usually far smaller than discount rates for gains (e.g. Thaler, 1981). One explanation is based on the disutility individuals experience if they 'dread' the future (Lowenstein, 1987). When this is the case, individuals do not discount future losses as heavily as future gains. They prefer to get losses 'out of the way' as soon as possible.

Insights from behavioural economics also question reliance on the same discount rate when assessing the present value of investment in different *domains;* for example, Chapman (1996) compares discount rates in financial and health scenarios. Goodin (1982) argues that individuals rely on different discount rates in different domains because they find it difficult to attach monetary values to nontradables.[6] There is also the question of whether CBA should rely on the same discount rate for *every* period in the future (see Her Majesty's Treasury, 2003, for recommendations in the United Kingdom).

When reflecting on the relevance of these insights from behavioural economics, Robinson and Hammitt (2011, p. 25) argue that '… in choosing a discount rate or set of rates, as well as a functional form … analysts must be clear about what, conceptually, they intend to represent for review by decision makers'.

15.3.3 Other-Regarding Preferences

In neoclassical economics, cost–benefit analysis focuses on *efficiency* as separate from any consideration of distributional *equity*. Is this still possible if there is evidence of bounded self-interest? With bounded self-interest, individuals' preferences are already influenced by *pure altruism*, or by *reciprocity* (individuals' willingness to reward, or to punish others, as a response to their perception of the way that they have been treated by others). In this scenario, it is difficult to separate the influence of other-regarding preferences; for example, it is difficult to separate the influence of altruism because '… altruistic values are typically not quantified when valuing non-market goods …' (Robinson and Hammitt, 2011, p. 27). More extensive information about other-regarding preferences is required because *these* considerations are likely to influence the interpretation of a positive net present value of a project. If altruism varies with outcome (e.g., greater for health than other aspects of well-being), or if it depends on the individuals affected (e.g., greater for the poor than for the wealthy), altruism is likely to influence whether the net present value of a project will be positive or negative.

Insights from behavioural economics also highlight the relevance of *relative* income. Frank and Sunstein (2001) focus on the implications (for CBA) of evidence that individuals are motivated by positional concerns. They question the relevance of estimates of WTP if individuals are asked how much they are willing to pay in isolation. If an individual believes that she is acting in isolation, she will also be concerned that her willingness to pay for the benefits derived from a public expenditure project (e.g., an increase in health or personal safety) will reduce her relative income. Her willingness to pay will be lower than the willingness to pay that she would express if it was clear that the requirement to pay for the project would be the same for all individuals.

An assessment: The overarching problem is how to incorporate evidence that individuals' preferences are likely to be sensitive to cognitive biases and to context endogeneity. With reference to recent research into happiness (life satisfaction), it has been argued that preferences based on self-reported well-being (SWB) may be more informative than preferences based on WTP (e.g., Kahneman and Sugden, 2005). By comparison, Viscusi and Gayer (2016) question 'open-ended justifications' (p. 87) when using narrow insights from behavioural economics (e.g., in laboratory experiments of specific populations) to adjust assessments of the benefits (in a CBA) that will be experienced by a broader population. Referring to 'behavioral transfer' as '… the practice of applying results from a behavioural study in one context to a broader application of policy' (p. 72), the authors call for '… formal guidelines for behavioural transfer practices' (p. 88).

Shogren and Thunström (2016) suggest a different response. A CBA should report a range of benefits (an interval) that encompasses measures of benefits derived from the rational choice model and from behavioural models. If the range of benefits exceeds costs, decision makers are able to proceed with confidence, but if costs are within the 'benefit interval', more discussion is required. Bernheim (2016) suggests a more comprehensive unified approach. The welfare effects of an individual's choice should be explored with reference to each possible decision frame.

With growing consensus that it is no longer possible to rely on the assumption that individuals' preferences are premised on rational self-interest, cost-benefit analysis faces the challenge of how it should embrace the insights delivered by behavioural economics.

15.4 Insights from Behavioural Economics: Implications for Taxation Policy

When applying 'economics' to taxation, the question that usually preoccupies analysts is how different taxes and different tax structures can be assessed – what would 'good' ones look like? Historically, Adam Smith provided a set of criteria for such assessments which are known as Smith's 'canons' of taxation. Smith (1776) argued that a good tax should satisfy four criteria:

1. *Equity*: Individuals ought to contribute 'as nearly as possible in proportion to their respective abilities' (Smith 1776, p. 310). That a tax should be equitable brings into consideration definitions of 'ability to pay' and appropriate tax progressivity.
2. *Certainty*: Tax liabilities should not be arbitrary or uncertain. That is, taxes should be formulated so that taxpayers are certain of how much they have to pay and when they have to pay it. This brings into consideration questions of tax simplicity, visibility (salience) and taxpayer compliance costs.
3. *Convenience*: The manner and timing of tax payment should be convenient to the taxpayer. This brings into consideration the method and frequency of paying taxes; for example, most UK workers will be taxed on their earning automatically as part of the PAYE system.
4. *Economy or efficiency*: The excess burdens or welfare costs of taxation should be minimised. Included in this is the notion that taxes should not be expensive to administer and the greatest possible proportion should accrue as net government revenue. Also included under this would be the administrative, collection and psychic compliance costs of taxation. For further elaboration see Sandford, Godwin and Hardwick (1989).

Subsequently, economists have considered other criteria:

5. Taxes, if the most suitable mechanism, can be *externality correctors*, as in the classic Pigovian tax case.
6. Taxes should facilitate *macro fiscal policy* via a role in economic stabilisation.
7. *Low marginal costs of additional policy delivery*. Once a tax system has been put in place, then a sophisticated administrative and data handling capacity has been created. Its existence may facilitate other public sector policies that require administrative and data handling capacity but are not strictly about raising tax. It may be that a least-cost delivery mechanism for such a policy is to do it via the tax system. An example concerning the provision of US health insurance is provided later in this chapter.

With so many criteria, and the list could be extended, it would not be surprising that they will sometimes conflict. For example, an equitable tax system may be necessarily a complex one. Until relatively recently, the analytical framework in which to couch the previously noted considerations was uncontroversial, being that of neoclassical economics. With the advent of behavioural economics, this has now changed, making the picture much more complicated and familiar 'optimal' solution recipes much less secure. While, as yet, there seems to be no synthesis of behavioural insights on taxation economics, there are plenty of leads to follow up (see, for example, McCaffery and Slemrod, 2006). Some of those leads are illustrated in the following subsections.

15.4.1 Equity

Framing is one of the characteristics of a behavioural analysis, and this can show up in attitudes as to what is deemed as equitable. The tax table can be constructed differently with reference to different default cases. The default is usually a childless family, but the tax table could be described with reference, say, to a two-child family. With a childless family as the default, the tax difference between a childless family and a two-child family is framed as a tax *exemption* (e.g., £1000 deduction from gross income for each child irrespective of family income level). With the default as a two-child family, tax for the childless family would be framed as paying a *tax premium* – extra tax.

Schelling (1981) argues that this difference is important when explaining preference for government intervention. The same tax table is perceived quite differently depending on whether tax arrangements are perceived as a 'loss' or as a 'gain'. When discussing tax premiums and tax exemptions, students' views were sensitive to these perceptions. Schelling tried to sell the generally unpalatable argument that the rich should get a larger tax exemption for their children than the poor, because, for example, they spend more on the bringing up of their children. He reported that students rejected the idea of granting the rich a larger child exemption (in adjusting from gross to taxable income) than the poor in the first frame (when the default was the childless family). The taxable income difference should not, in the students' view, be larger for the rich family than the poor family. However, the default could be the two-child family when the code now needs adjusting for those families without children. A childless premium could now be introduced by, say, cancelling a £1000 exemption for a family with a single child and £2000 exemption for a family without children. In raising the taxable income for the childless, should the rise still be the same for the poor and the rich or should an exemption greater than £2000 be cancelled for the childless rich? When considering this question in the second frame (when the default was the two-child family), views favoured a larger tax premium on the childless rich than on the childless poor (they preferred that the taxable income difference should be larger for the rich family than for the poor family in direct contradiction to what was established under the initial default of childlessness). In one scenario, the rich with children should, for tax purposes, be treated the same as the poor with children, but in the other the rich without children should pay more tax than the poor without children, but all that has happened is that the same income tax has been reformulated. Views of equity seem 'frame' dependent and as such open to manipulation.

15.4.2 Tax Certainty

One of the issues under this heading is the question of tax simplicity. But is there a case for tax complexity? Solving asymmetric information problems is a staple part of any microeconomics course. One solution is to get individuals to voluntarily signal their 'private knowledge' of their type – e.g., high or low ability workers. Typically, a cost is involved in completing a test of some form such that it will involve differentially higher compensation if it is passed. However, set properly, the costs are too high for the low ability worker to incur them and still gain overall from the higher compensation it secures. Only for high ability workers will it be worth incurring the cost and therefore those that do so 'signal' that there are high ability. Congdon, Kling and Mullainathan (2009) provide an example. Suppose there are externalities associated with higher education but they attach to only the ablest (high IQ) type of potential graduate. A tax subsidy to higher education might thus be justified to internalise this externality, but it would only be for the ablest type. How might you be sure that only the ablest make use of a tax subsidy to education? If the tax subsidy is simple and transparent, then all would-be graduates will avail themselves of the subsidy. If, however, the tax code is complex and dense, it will only be the able ones who pass the 'test' of researching the subsidy and therefore apply to receive it. A complex tax system could be an efficient screening device, but it would remain to be shown it was a least-cost screening device.

15.4.3 Convenience *and* Low Marginal Costs of Additional Policy Delivery

A feature of most tax systems is their 'automaticity' which is convenient to most taxpayers so that compliance costs are very low for the majority for most taxpayers. Congdon et al. (2009) combine this feature with the low marginal cost of additional policy delivery to provide a case for tax system provision of a strictly unrelated public policy. Redistributive public policy typically requires an application process involving a 'means test' for qualification. For actors with bounded rationality, the costs of understanding the qualifying conditions, filling in the forms and submitting the application loom so large that they fail to take up benefits to which they are entitled. It is claimed that the poor exhibit more judgemental biases and self-control problems and thus differentially procrastinate, and yet they are the targets of many policies. In a 'behavioural' world, 'take up' is endogenous to the method of delivery. One of Congdon et al.'s, (2009) examples is the possible provision of health insurance in the United States. They note that while 21 per cent of children eligible for Medicaid, or other similar help, remain uninsured, approximately 90 per cent of those children live in families that file a federal income tax return. Given that much of the information that is required to determine Medicaid eligibility is on the tax return, the suggestion is that the processes should be integrated to increase 'take up'.

15.4.4 Economy or Efficiency

A great deal of economics of taxation is devoted to the welfare costs of taxation, which are measured with reference to an assumed stable individual preference map. If this assumed stability is called into question, then so are measures based on this assumption. This issue was illustrated in the previous section. Here, however, the focus is one of the big areas where the insights of behavioural economics are to be found, namely, tax evasion. This affects both net government revenue and the administrative, collection and psychological compliance costs of taxation. In Allingham and Sandmo's (1972) 'standard' tax evasion (as crime) model predictions rely on Von Neuman and Morgenstern indifference curves, detection probabilities and associated fines for evasion. While this model is a 'corner stone' for analysis of tax evasion, there are also some well-known limitations. One of these is that given the likely values of parameters in the model, it predicts much more tax evasion than appears to be observed. Explaining this has proved fertile ground for the behavioural analyst. Weber, Fooken and Herrmann (2014, pp. 25–27) provide a convenient list of possible mechanisms though which three characteristics of the behavioural actor are deemed relevant to increased tax

Table 15.2 *Behavioural concepts and increased tax compliance*

Concept	Mechanism	Trigger
1. Cognitive biases (working through detection and audit probabilities and risk aversion)	Overestimating small probabilities	Part of prospect theory (see decision weights in Section 15.5.4)
	Increasing perceived probabilities	Both threat-of-audit letters and face-to-face contact with a customs official
	Ambiguity aversion	Ambiguous (unknown) audit rates
	Framing effects	Framing tax as 'gains' encourages risk aversion and compliance (prospect theory)
2. Concern about 'self' (internal dimensions)	Intrinsic motivation	'Virtue is its own reward'
	Moral costs	Letters appealing to moral obligation have a muted positive impact
	Guilt costs	Tax amnesties allow 'confession' and guilt reduction
3. Concern about others (social dimensions)	Wider psychological costs of noncompliance	Emotions and public exposure – 'stigma' Redemption for shamed noncompliers
	Social norms of compliance	Letters indicating the majority have already paid their tax
	Fair tax system	Tax system seen as equitable
	Tax morale	Linked to perceived quality of institutions, democratic decision-making and respect for the taxpayer

Source: Adapted from Weber et al., (2014, pp. 25–27).

compliance: cognitive limitations and bounded self-interest (see Table 15.2, which adapts their Table 15.3; Concept 3 reflects what Alm (2014) calls 'group motivations').

If tax analysis is limited to *homo economicus*, it would seem to leave a lot of potential explanatory power about tax compliance and the like completely untapped.

15.4.5 Taxation and Market Correction (Externalities)

An area of economics where externality analysis looms large is environmental economics. Such is the importance of this literature that the following section is devoted to it.

15.4.6 The Tax System and Fiscal Policy

In the simplest macroeconomic models, the multiplier effect on the economy from stimulating aggregate demand is $1/1-c$, where c ($0 \leq c \leq 1$) is the marginal propensity to consume (*mpc*) out of additional income. Early work by Thaler and Shefrin (1981) and Shefrin and Thaler (1988) revealed that individuals have very different *mpc*s depending on how the additional income was assigned to different mental accounts. In their model 'current income', 'current wealth' and 'future wealth' are characterised by successively lower *mpc* values. It suggests, for example, where a tax refund is due to be paid to an individual its form will affect whether it is likely to be spent or saved (see Beverly, Schneider and Tufano, 2006). Sheffrin and Thaler predict that if the tax refund is seen as a bonus, then there will be a lower *mpc* observed than if it were seen as simply returned income. It provides a mechanism through which saving can be encouraged. In the United States since 2007, individuals due refunds have been able to spread them across several accounts, including saving accounts.

An assessment

Measures of the welfare costs of taxation loom large in neoclassical public sector economics, but once preference stability is lost, estimating areas under real-income constant demand curves becomes problematic, as witnessed by the discussion of the previous section. The benefit of losing the theoretical and empirical precision of neoclassical public sector economics seems to be a much more nuanced discussion of the principles of a good tax system that may have much more to offer actual public policy. Sophisticated optimal income tax models often have predictions that seem at odds with policies that are likely to be implemented. For example, it can be shown that the marginal tax rate on the highest income earner should be zero, as it allows that individual the same welfare level and increases his or her tax payment. (see Cullis and Jones, 2009, for an introduction to this literature.) However, such a policy prescription is unlikely to be adopted.

15.5 Insights from Behavioural Economics: Implications for Environmental Policy

Although the effectiveness of environmental policy instruments has long been based mainly upon theoretical inputs provided by standard rational choice theory, behavioural economics has recently attracted the attention of environmental economists. Indeed, there seems to be an increasingly strong consensus in the economics community that behavioural economics can help to understand why people do not respond to environmental policy measures as predicted by rational choice theory. In addition, understanding the motives and driving forces behind prosocial, proenvironmental and cooperative behaviour may help improve environmental policy design (see, e.g., Daskalakis, 2016). A review of the literature recognises at least five different areas where insights from behavioural economics may have implications for environmental policy. These are summarised in Table 15.3 and are discussed in the following subsections.

15.5.1 Conflict and Cooperation in Environmental Policy

Many environmental goods and services are public goods, and policy makers aim to take collective actions to guarantee an efficient allocation/production of these goods. Examples are land use, water pollution, car emissions and global

Table 15.3 *Behavioural anomalies compared with the axioms of rational (expected) utility maximisation*

Environmental issue	Bounded rationality	Bounded self-interest	Bounded willpower
1. Conflict and cooperation in environmental policy		Social norms Self-image Social approval Status concern Reciprocity Fairness	
2. Use of market-based instruments		Intrinsic motivation	
3. Use of CBA	Context-endogenous/ dependent preferences (through, e.g., *framing* and *endowment effects*) and time-inconsistent preferences (through, e.g., *preference reversals*)		Time-inconsistent preferences (through, e.g., *present-biased preferences*)
4. Choice under risk	Risk misperception and ambiguity aversion		
5. Inertia in individual behaviour	Status quo bias or role of defaults		

climate change. Standard utility maximisation theory assumes that behaviour is motivated solely by their material payoffs and that people free-ride when it is in their material self-interest to do so. Behavioural economics suggests that other-regarding preferences (coming from *bounded self-interest*) such as social preferences (e.g., social norms, reciprocity and fairness) and self-identity concerns (e.g., social approval and self-image) can influence human decisions. Several studies have examined the role of other-regarding theories on human behaviour, and a common result in the literature is that people contribute to the provision of public goods to a significant extent. Some studies support the idea that fairness motives or inequality aversion affects people's voluntary contribution to public goods (see, e.g., Fehr and Schmidt, 1999). Others find that reciprocal preferences – the subjects' desire to reward good intentions with good deeds (*positive reciprocity*) and bad intentions with bad deeds (*negative reciprocity*) – are crucial for the provision of public goods (see, e.g., Fehr and Gächter, 2000a, 2000b). Altruistic preferences may also matter for the provision of public goods, as individuals not only tend to take into account the others well-being (*pure altruism*), but may also '… experience a warm glow from having done their bit' (*impure altruism*) (Andreoni, 1989, p. 1448). There is also substantial evidence in the literature that 'others' and 'other's behaviour' matter (see, e.g., Fischbacher, Gächter and Fehr, 2001; Fischbacher and Gächter, 2006). People conform to social norms; imitate, compare with and learn from others; and care about their reputation and self-image. How can these results be generalised to environmental economics?

Most of the literature on international agreements is based on the assumption that each negotiating country cares solely about its own material payoff. International environmental treaties (such as the Kyoto Protocol) generally suffer from weak enforcement and nonbinding voting rules. Therefore, under rational game theory, free-riding should be the dominant strategy (see Shogren and Tylor, 2008). The literature on reciprocal behaviour suggests, for example, that 'the self-enforced rules', such as punishment, represent the dominant strategy to reduce free-riding and increase cooperation and social efficiency, even when this represents a cost for the 'willing punishers' (see, e.g., Fehr and Gächter, 2000a). Thus, policy makers should take into account these kinds of behaviour to promote an optimal level of provision of environmental goods via collective action (Omstrom, 1998). The behavioural-environmental literature on the effect of other-regarding theories on environmental issues is limited but growing rapidly. Efforts have been already made to show the extent to which fairness affects environmental coalitions and cooperation in international climate change policy and the siting of nuclear waste. (See, e.g., Oberholzer-Gee, Bohnet and Frey, 1997 for the latter, and Lange et al., 2010 for the former.) There is also evidence that self-image and social pressure may affect individuals' willingness to recycle (see, e.g., Brekke, Kipperberg and Nyborg, 2007; Czajkowski, Hanley and Nyborg., 2017) and conserve energy (for an overview, see Baddeley, 2011). Although generalising insights from behavioural economics may not be straightforward (especially when this means generalising them from an individual level to a multicountry negotiation level), some of them can be generalised at least qualitatively (Carlsson and Johansson-Stenman, 2012). First, individuals and countries are able to make decisions that are not only based on their own material payoff. This may explain why people tend to recycle on a voluntary basis, or why under certain conditions (such as *small groups*, the possibility of introducing *punishments* or *sanctions*, increasing *interaction* and *communication* and *conditional cooperation*) people and countries may spontaneously manage common goods. Second, individuals and countries are likely to free-ride unless appropriate policy instruments are applied, implying that behavioural economics reinforces conventional environmental economics rather than making it redundant.

15.5.2 Use of Market-Based Policy Instruments

Environmental economics has traditionally been focused on developing solutions to market failures. Market failures are typically associated with externalities, public goods and asymmetric information. Economists refer to these sources of economic inefficiency to design and evaluate public policies for environmental sustainability, which include command and control regulation (i.e., emission standards) as well as market-based instruments (i.e., Pigovian taxes, tradable permits, fines and subsidies; see criterion 5 of Section 15.4), with the latter generally considered superior to the former.[7]

As noted, the standard model of environmental regulation assumes that individuals make consistent decisions on the basis of profit maximisation and their material self-interest. However, behavioural economics provides evidence of systematic deviations from rational choice theory, and one aspect of this is that people may be intrinsically motivated to contribute to a better environment even in the absence of external regulation. A large number of papers in the literature emphasise the role of intrinsic motivation (reflecting *bounded self-interest*) in individual decision-making and more importantly its interaction with external regulation. Understanding the interaction between intrinsic motivation and monetary incentives (such as taxes, subsidies and tradable permits) can be in fact of crucial importance for successful policy implementation, as individuals' morale and motivation can render certain policies more effective (i.e., *crowding-in*) and others less effective (*crowding-out*).[8] The effect of external incentives on individuals' intrinsic motivation has been analysed in many different contexts and areas of research. (For an overview, see Gneezy, Meier and Rey-Biel, 2011.) However, there is little empirical evidence in the environmental literature documenting the existence and implications of intrinsic motivation and its interaction with marked-based instruments. Analysing households' perceptions of recycling activities, Berglund (2006) finds that moral motives significantly lower the costs associated with household recycling efforts. Similarly, investigating the reasons behind households' participation in green electricity programmes, Clark, Kotchenb and Moorea (2003) find that high intrinsic motivation may explain early adoption of green electricity. Feldman and Perez (2009) show how the design of different legal instruments (e.g., deposit, mandatory scheme and voluntary contribution) affect people's motivation to engage in private enforcement to reduce pollution. An increasing number of papers acknowledge the role of intrinsic motivation in the form of environmental morale[9] as a driving force for proenvironmental behaviours (see, e.g., Frey, 1997; Frey and Stutzer, 2006; Torgler, Frey and Wilson, 2009). In this context, Barile et al. (2015) show that the relative efficacy of certain policy instruments depends on the extent to which individuals are motivated by 'environmental morale'. Taken together, what can be learned from behavioural-environmental economics is that marked-based instruments may sometimes be inferior to control and command policies, especially when external interventions are counterproductive. As suggested by Carlsson and Johansson-Stenman (2012, p. 84), 'crowding effects sometimes make such instruments slightly more attractive and sometimes make such instruments slightly less attractive.'

15.5.3 Use of Cost–Benefit Analysis (CBA)

As discussed in Section 5.3, one of the lessons to be learned from behavioural economics is that people's behaviour and preferences are context dependent (reflecting *bounded rationality*). People are affected by the way in which choices are framed (*framing effect*) and are more eager to retain something that they already own than to get something new (*endowment effect*). People show inconsistent time preferences depending on the time the choices are made (i.e., preference reversals) and with choices being dominated by immediate gains (i.e., present-biased preferences). Context-dependent and inconsistent time preferences play an important role in CBA in the areas of intertemporal choices and nonmarket environmental valuation. Most policy recommendations for global warming depend in fact on the choice of the discount rate (see, e.g., Stern, 2007), and contingent valuation methods (CVM) are generally used to estimate how people value certain environmental goods in cost–benefit analysis. As discussed earlier, these findings represent a challenge to fundamental welfare theory and leave the debate about whether researchers should incorporate preference anomalies in cost–benefit analysis or overthrow the standard cost–benefit framework far from over.[10]

15.5.4 Choice Under Risk

Given the nature of the *homo realitus*, prospect theory (Kahneman and Tversky, 1979) is seen by many as a better guide to actual decision-making under risk than the neoclassical standard expected utility theory. As shown in Table 15.2, in prospect theory, 'decision weights' replace probabilities, and the 'value function' replaces the standard utility function. With decision weights, individuals overweight low probabilities and underweight high probabilities. The former will encourage risk aversity in the face of low-probability environmental losses and risk taking for low probability environmental gains. The latter reduces the attraction of high probability environmental gains and reduces the threat of high-probability environmental losses. Given the shape of the value function, individuals are risk averse for gains, are risk seeking for losses and demonstrate loss aversion. An implication is that individuals overestimate low-probabilities/high-loss scenarios such as those found in environmental policy – for example, climate shift in the Gulf Stream.[11] Further individuals are attracted by known probabilities and dislike unknown ones such that they make inconsistent choices. This so-called ambiguity aversion is demonstrated in the Ellsberg paradox (see Knight, 1921; Camerer and Weber, 1992). (This is consistent with ambiguous (unknown) audit rates increasing tax compliance in Table 15.2.)

How can we use this information for policy implementation? Should we rely on the public's risk perception and 'frame' environmental cost and benefit information, use experts' risk perception or adopt other criteria? As suggested by Carlsson and Johansson-Stenman (2012, p. 88), 'the issue of whose risk should ultimately count in public policy is not new', but views vary dramatically. Slovic's (2000) answer to this question is that risk is a social construction and whose definition of risk gets to count in policy is a reflection of political or other power (e.g., a claim to expertise). In the context of environmental policy, risk perception clearly has important consequences for CBA. Despite Slovic's deep concerns the government might prefer to rely on experts' risk judgements rather than those of the public. In fact, if CBA relies on people's valuation, for example, through contingent valuation, one can expect that this is likely to be biased in predictable ways such that individuals misestimate the monetary value of, say, reducing certain environmental risks. However, subjective perceived risk may have important consequences for real welfare effects (via fears) and may induce people to change their behaviour. Therefore, it seems reasonable that governments care also about subjective risks and not only about what some see as objective risks (Carlsson and Johansson-Stenman, 2012). Unfortunately, the question of whether there exists a threshold to separate reasonable from unreasonable beliefs over risky events remains an unresolved dilemma (Shogren and Taylor, 2008).

15.5.5 Inertia in Individual Behaviour

The status quo bias or the role of defaults (reflecting *bounded rationality*) may explain why individuals and/or countries prefer the status quo situation and are reluctant to make changes. Given individuals' *inertia* and preference for the status quo, there exists an increasing number of papers in the literature testing the hypothesis that changing the default option may help in promoting environmentally friendly behaviours. In the context of green energy, Pichert and Katsikopoulosa (2008) and, more recently, Loock, Staake and Thiesse (2013) find that green defaults significantly affect the choice of green energy. According to Sunstein and Reisch (2016, p. 162) 'default rules, and seemingly modest alterations to such rules, can have an exceedingly large impact on environmental quality – potentially larger than that of significant economic incentives or serious efforts toward moral suasion or environmental education.' Again, there is not a general consensus over the use of defaults to change individuals' behaviour; for example, Löfgren et al. (2012), in a natural field experiment to test the role of default effects on the choice of CO_2 emissions offsets for air transport, find that the default has no significant effect on the decision to offset. However, as suggested by Venkatacalam (2008), the existence of the status quo bias may both directly and indirectly affect the efficiency of environmental policies. Thus policy makers should care about this behavioural anomaly when making 'new' environmental policies seeking efficiency in the provision of environmental goods.

An assessment

Although behavioural economics has recently attracted the attention of environmental economists, the explanatory power and the normative implications of behavioural economics are still under critical debate. Shogren and Taylor (2008, p. 13) argue that we are facing a 'new behavioural-environmental second-best problem'. That is, given the presence of market failures (environmental externalities) and behavioural failures (e.g., bounded rationality), environmental policies need to be corrected for both imperfections as correcting one failure without correcting the other will actually reduce overall welfare. They conclude that 'the evidence from behavioural economics remains insufficient to support the wholesale rejection of rational choice theory within environmental and resource economics' (Shogren and Taylor (2008, p. 16).

Similarly, Pasche (2016, p. 117) states that 'the insights of behavioural economics cannot be translated immediately in an improved environmental policy. The social planner will be better informed now, but the institutional setting and the features of political mechanisms are still in place and will shape the decisions.'

15.6 Conclusion

Anomalies feature strongly in this chapter, but Kahlil (2003) seems to suggest there are somehow too many of them: 'The number of uncovered anomalies is as dizzying as the number of sub-atomic particles discovered by physicists' (Khalil, 2003, p. 1). Furthermore, Wittman (1995, p. 54) notes: '… a collection of anomalies does not a theory make'.

Nobel economics laureate Simon (1979), in effect anticipating Wittman's criticism, comments: 'Once a theory is well entrenched, it will survive many assaults of empirical evidence that purports to refute it unless an alternative theory, consistent with the evidence, stands ready to replace it' (Simon, 1979, p. 509).

Thaler (2016) considers the past, present and future of behavioural economics and offers his view on these matters. He asks the question: 'What do you want economic theory to do?' If you want it to be deductive and prescriptive, then the neoclassical paradigm achieves that. However, if you want it to be deductive – evidence based – and predictive, then a behavioural approach dominates. This latter kind of economics is not viewed as a 'paradigm shift' ('an alternative theory'), but rather a 'paradigm rediscovered', as Adam Smith, amongst other early economists, documents cornerstone behavioural traits: 'overconfidence'; 'loss aversion' and 'present bias'. There is no new grand design for economics to be found, as neoclassical economics fits that bill. What there is, however, is the 'engineering' of 'practical enhancements' to that standard theory to increase predictive accuracy. Thaler adds 'testable' to Rabin's (2013) phrase 'portable extensions to existing models' to encapsulate this process as 'portable, testable, extensions to existing models' (PTEEM). It will be this kind of economics that will become the new 'bog standard' economics and the prefix 'behavioural' will atrophy.

Does this chapter fit this picture? As suggested, it patently does not offer a fully articulated alternative theory of public sector economics to rival neoclassical prescriptions. However, on the evidence presented here, it does offer a plethora of examples and instances where bounded abilities, bounded self-will and preference endogeneity matter significantly for an inductive and predictive public sector economics. As such, the key elements in PTEEM seem to be clear. However, it also seems clear that it is difficult, if not impossible, to unify the elements once you have lost the neoclassical anchors of exogenous preference stability and well-defined (budget) constraints. It seems that 'behavioural' public sector economics is necessarily more 'messy' than its elegant neoclassical counterpart. But this is not to say that it may be much more useful for public sector policy than 'clean' theory based on a 'wrong' caricature. The 'tedious, policy relevant, empirical public sector economist', whose seminar questions were an embarrassment to the department, is destined to become the new seminar 'hot shot'!

Notes

1 Willingness to pay not to have the project is a measure of the opportunity cost of resources.

2 With 'anchoring', responses may be sensitive to valuations suggested in questionnaires. With 'mental accounting', individuals might state an amount drawn from the mental account that they assign for expenditure on conservation when they are asked how much they would be willing to pay to prevent the extermination of a particular species. They may then state a much higher amount (with no overall constraint) when they are asked how much they would require to accept this outcome.

3 With this advice, governments have tended to rely on a single discount rate to discount exponentially. (See Henderson and Bateman 1995 for exceptions to this rule.)

4 For example, a majority of individuals preferred £50 immediately to £100 in two years but almost no one prefers £50 in four years to £100 in six years.

5 There are a number of specific hyperbolic forms for discount functions, but for a single good valuation (V), Ainslie advocated using the following formula:

$$(1) \qquad V = A/\xi + \Gamma(T{-}t)$$

where A is the amount involved, T is the time at which each amount is available and t is the time of the behaviour that obtains it, so that (T−t) is the delay for A. The term ξ is an empirical constant that determines the value of zero delay and Γ is an empirical constant that modifies the steepness of the delay gradient. Empirically both ξ and $\Gamma \cong 1$, so the formula simplifies to the following:

$$(2) \qquad V = A/1 + 1(T{-}t)$$

For example, if the delay is three units of time and A is 1, then V = 1/4. If Va = 1 and Vb = 2 and Va and Vb are always separated by three units of time, then, when Va is available, now it is preferred (as Va = 1 and Vb = 0.5). Consider what happens if you add a five-year delay to Va and Vb. Va is now 1/1 + 5 = 1/6 and Vb is 2/ 1 + 8 = 2/9 and is therefore preferred to Va. As time increases, preference for Va passes through indifference to Vb to a preference for Vb.

6 He recommends reliance on a *restricted* form of opportunity cost discounting (changes in nontradables should be compared with future changes in the same good – a 'tree life' today should be compared to 'tree lives' in the future).

7 Compared to command and control instruments, market-based instruments are more cost effective; i.e., if properly designed and implemented, market-based instruments allow any desired level of pollution cleanup to be realised with the least expensive abatement activities and with no need for the government to have information on how to achieve such cost efficiency.

8 In particular, cognitive evaluation theory (see Deci, 1975; Deci and Ryan, 1985) suggests that monetary incentives crowd out moral motivation if and only if they are perceived as *controlling*. However, if individuals perceive external interventions as *acknowledging*, their intrinsic motivation may increase.

9 Environmental morale is generally referred to as the result of the aggregation of internalised norms and intrinsic motivation (Frey, 1997; and Frey and Stutzer, 2006).

10 Some scholars, for example, tried to understand the impact of preference anomalies to the standard cost–benefit framework underlying the application of environmental instruments (see, e.g., Hanley and Shogren, 2005; and, more recently, Robinson and Hammit, 2011). Some others (see Kahneman and Sudgen, 2005; Howarth and Wilson, 2006) offer different approaches to the standard cost–benefit analysis.

11 Behavioural analyses reveal that people tend to overestimate the change of suffering from potentially bad outcomes with very low probability of realisation (i.e., people are loss averse). For a discussion, see Shogren and Taylor (2008).

15.7 References

Ainslie, G. (1991). Derivation of 'Rational' Economic Behaviour from Hyperbolic Discount Curves. *American Economic Review*, 81(2), 334–340.

Allingham, M. G. and Sandmo, A. (1972). Income Tax Evasion: A Theoretical Analysis. *Journal of Public Economics*, 1(3-4), 323–338.

Alm, J. Expanding the Theory of Tax Compliance from Individual to Group Motivations, in Forte, F., Mudambi, R. and Navarra, P. M. (eds.) (2014). *A Handbook of Alternative Theories of Public Economics*. Cheltenham: Edward Elgar, 260–277.

Andreoni, J. (1989). Giving with Impure Altruism: Applications to Charity and Ricardian Equivalence. *Journal of Political Economy*, 97(6), 1447–1458.

Baddeley, M. (2011). Energy the Environment and Behavioural Change: A Survey of Insights from Behavioural Economics, CWPE 1162, University of Cambridge. Available at: www.repository.cam.ac.uk/handle/1810/242028.

Banford, N. D., Knetsch, J. L., and Mauser, G. A. (1979). Feasibility Judgements and Alternative Measures of Benefits and Costs. *Journal of Business Administration*, 11(1), 25–35.

Barile, L., Cullis, J. and Jones, P. (2015). Will One Size Fit All? Incentives Designed to Nurture Pro-Social Behaviour. *Journal of Behavioural and Experimental Economics*, 57, 9–16.

Becker, G. S. (1971). *Economic Theory.* New York: A. A.Knopf.

Berglund, C. (2006). The Assessment of Households' Recycling Costs: The Role of Personal Motives. *Ecological Economics*, 56(4), 560–569.

Bernheim, B. D. (2016). The Good, the Bad and the Ugly: A Unified Approach to Behavioural Welfare Economics. *Journal of Cost Benefit Analysis*, 7(1), 12–68.

Beverly, S., Schneider, D. and Tufano, P. (2006). Splitting Tax Refunds and Building Savings: An Empirical Test, in Poterba, J. M. (ed.), *Tax Policy and Economy*, Cambridge, MA: National Bureau of Economic Research, 111–162.

Bishop, R. C., and Heberlein, T. A. (1979). Measuring values of extramarket goods: Are indirect measures biased? *American Journal of Agricultural Economics*, 61(5), 926–930.

Brekke, K. A., Kipperberg, G. and Nyborg, K. (2007). Reluctant Recyclers: Social Interaction in Responsibility Ascription. Available at: ssrn.com/abstract=1116149 or dx.doi.org/10.2139/ssrn.1116149.

Brennan, G. and Lomasky, L. (1993). *Democracy and Decision: The Pure Theory of Electoral Preference.* Cambridge, UK: Cambridge University Press.

Camerer C. and Weber, M. (1992). Recent Developments in Modeling Preferences: Uncertainty and Ambiguity. *Journal of Risk and Uncertainty*, 5(4), 325–370.

Carlsson, F. and Johansson-Stenman, O. (2012). Behavioural Economics and Environmental Economics. *Annual Review of Resource Economics*, 4(1), 75–99.

Chapman, G. B. (1996). Temporal Discounting and Utility for Health and Money. *Journal of Experimental Psychology: Learning, Memory and Cognition*, 22(3), 771–791.

Christian, R. C. and Alm, J. (2014). Empathy, Sympathy and Tax Compliance. *Journal of Economic Psychology*, 40, 62–82.

Clark, C. F., Kotchenb, M. J. and Moorea, M. R. (2003). Internal and External Influences on Pro-EnviEmpathy, Sympathy and Tax Compliance. ronmental Behaviour: Participation in a Green Electricity Program. *Journal of Environmental Psychology*, 22(3), 237–246.

Congdon, W., Kling, J. R. and Mullainathan, S. (2009). Behavioural Economics and Taxation. National Bureau of Economic Research (NBER) Working Paper No. 15328.

Cullis, J. and Jones, P. (2009). *Public Finance and Public Choice* (3rd Ed.). Oxford: Oxford University Press.

Czajkowski M., Hanley N. and Nyborg, K. (2017). Social Norms, Morals and Self-interest as Determinants of Pro-Environment Behaviours: The Case of Household Recycling. *Environmental and Resource Economics*, 66(4), 647–670.

Daskalakis, M. (2016). Specification Required? A Survey of Scientists' Views About the Role of Behavioural Economics for Assessing Environmental Policy Instruments, in Beckenbach, F. and Kahlenborn, W. (eds.), *New Perspectives for Environmental Policies Through Behavioural Economics*, Berlin: Springer, 69–106.

Deci, E. L. (1975). *Intrinsic Motivation*. New York: Plenum.

Deci, E. L. and Ryan, R. M. (1985). *Intrinsic Motivation and Self-Determination in Human Behaviour*. New York: Pantheon.

Fehr, E. and Gächter, S. (2000a). Cooperation and Punishment in Public Goods Experiments. *American Economic Review*, 90(4), 980–994.

Fehr, E. and Gächter, S. (2000b). Fairness and Retaliation: The Economics of Reciprocity. *Journal of Economic Perspectives*, 14(3), 159–181.

Fehr, E. and Schmidt K. M. (1999). A Theory of Fairness, Competition and Co-operation. *Quarterly Journal of Economics*, 114(3), 817–868.

Feldman, Y. and Perez, O. (2009). How Law Changes the Environmental Mind: An Experimental Study of the Effect of Legal Norms on Moral Perceptions and Civic Enforcement. *Journal of Law and Society*, 36(4), 501–535.

Fischbacher, U. and Gächter, S. (2006). Heterogeneous Social Preferences and the Dynamics of Free Riding in Public Goods. Centre for Decision Research and Experimental Economics (CeDEx) Discussion Paper No. 2006-01. Available at: www.econstor.eu/bitstream/10419/67967/1/506605825.pdf.

Fischbacher, U., Gächter, S. and Fehr, E. (2001). Are People Conditionally Cooperative? Evidence from a Public Goods Experiment. *Economics Letters*, 71(3), 397–404.

Frank, R. H. and Sunstein, C.R. (2001). Cost–Benefit Analysis and Relative Position. *University of Chicago Law Review*, 68(2), 323–374.

Frederick, S., Loewenstein, G. and O'Donoghue, T. (2002). Time Discounting and Time Preference: A Critical Review. *Journal of Economic Literature*, 40(2), 351–401.

Frey, B. S. (1997). *Not Just for the Money*, Cheltenham: Edward Elgar.

Frey, B. S. and Eichenberger R. (1994). Economic Incentives Transform Psychological Anomalies. *Journal of Economic Behaviour and Organisation*, 23(2), 215–234.

Frey, B. and Stutzer, A. (2006). Environmental Morale and Motivation. Available at: www.iew.uzh.ch/wp/iewwp288.pdf.

Gneezy, U., Meier, S. and Rey-Biel, P. (2011). When and Why Incentives (Don't) Work to Modify Behaviour. *Journal of Economic Perspectives* 25(4), 191–210.

Goodin, R. E. (1982). Discounting Discounting. *Journal of Public Policy*, 2(1), 53–72.

Guth, W. and Ortmann, A. (2006). A Behavioural Approach to Distribution and Bargaining, in Altman, M. (ed.), *Handbook of Contemporary Behavioural Economics*. New York: M. E. Sharpe, 379–404.

Hammack, J. and Brown Jr., G. M. (1974). *Waterfowl and Wetlands: Toward Bioeconomic Analysis*. Baltimore: John Hopkins Press.

Hanley, N. and Shogren, J. (2005). Is Cost-Benefit Analysis Anomaly Proof? *Environmental and Resource Economics*, 32(1), 13–34.

Hanneman, W. M. (1991). Willingness to Pay and Willingness to Accept: How Much Can They Differ? *American Economic Review*, 81(3), 635–647.

Heberlein, T. A., and Bishop, R. C. (1985). Assessing the Validity of Contingent Valuation: Three Field Experiments. Paper presented at the International Conference on Man's Role in Changing Global Environment, Italy.

Henderson, N. and Bateman, I. (1995). Empirical and Public Choice Evidence for Hyperbolic Social Discount Rates and the Implications for Intergenerational Discounting. *Environmental and Resource Economics*, 5(4), 413–423.

Her Majesty's Treasury (2003). *Green Book: Appraisal and Evaluation in Central Government*. London: HMSO.

Howarth, R. B. and Wilson, M. A. (2006). A Theoretical Approach to Deliberative Valuation: Aggregating by Mutual Consent. *Land Economics*, 82(1), 1–16.

Kahneman, D., Knetsch, J. L. and Thaler, R.H. (1990). Experimental Tests of the Endowment Effect and the Coase Theorem. *Journal of Political Economy*, 98(6), 1325–1348.

Kahneman, D. and Sugden, R. (2005). Experienced Utility as a Standard of Policy Evaluation. *Environmental and Resource Economics*, 32(1), 161–181.

Kahneman, D. and Tversky, A. (1979). Prospect Theory: An Analysis of Decision Under Risk. *Econometrica*, 47(2), 263–291.

Khalil, E. L. (2003). Behavioural Economics and the Transactional View. *Transactional Viewpoints*, 11(1), 1–8.

Knetsch, J. L. (1990). Environmental Policy Implication of Disparities Between Willingness to Pay and Compensation Demanded. *Journal of Environmental Economics and Management*, 18(3), 227–237.

Knetsch, J. L. (2010). Values of Gains and Losses: Reference States and Choices of Measure. *Environmental and Resource Economics* 46(2), 179–188.

Knight, F. (1921). *Risk, Uncertainty and Profit*. Boston: Houghton Mifflin.

Knox, T. M. (1952). *Hegel's Philosophy of Right: Translated with Notes*. Oxford: Oxford University Press.

Lange, A., Loschel, A., Vogt, C. and Ziegler, A. (2010). On the Self-Interested Use of Equity in International Climate Negotiations. *European Economic Review*, 54(3), 359–375.

Lerner, J. S., Small, D. A. and Loewenstein G. (2004). Heart Strings and Purse Strings. *Psychological Science*, 15(5), 337–41.

Loewenstein, G. (1987). Anticipation and the Valuation of Delayed Consumption. *Economic Journal*, 97(387), 666–684.

Loewenstein, G. (2007). *Exotic Preferences: Behavioural Economics and Human Motivation*. Oxford: Oxford University Press.

Löfgren, Å., Martinsson, P., Hennlock, M. and Sterner, T. (2012). Does Experience Eliminate the Effect of a Default Option? A Field Experiment on CO_2-Offsetting for Air Transport. *Journal of Environmental Economics and Management*, 63, 66–72.

Loock, C.-M., Staake, T. and Thiesse, F. (2013). Motivating Energy-Efficient Behaviour with Green IS: An Investigation of Goal Setting and the Role of Defaults. *MIS Quarterly*, 37(4), 1313–1332.

McCaffery, E. J. and Slemrod, J. (2006). *Behavioral Public Finance*, New York: Russell Sage Foundation.

Mishan, E. J. and Quah, E. (2007). *Cost-Benefit Analysis* (5th Ed.). London: Routledge.

Oberholzer-Gee, F., Bohnet, I. and Frey, B. S. (1997). Fairness and Competence in Democratic Decisions. *Public Choice* 91(1), 89–105.

Ostrom, E. (1998). A Behavioural Approach to the Rational Choice Theory of Collective Action: Presidential Address, American Political Science Association, 1997. *American Political Science Review*, 92(1), 1–22.

Pasche, M. (2016). What Can Be Learned from Behavioural Economics and Environmental Policy? in Beckenbach, F. and Kahlenborn, W. (eds.), *New Perspectives for Environmental Policies Through Behavioural Economics*. Berlin: Springer, 109–126.

Pichert, D. and Katsikopoulos, K. V. (2008). Green Defaults: Information Presentation and Pro-Environmental Behaviour. *Journal of Environmental Psychology*, 28(1), 63–73.

Rabin, M. (2013). An Approach to Incorporating Psychology into Economics. *American Economic Review*, 103(3), 1281–1302.

Robinson, L. A. and Hammitt, J. K. (2011). Behavioural Economics and the Conduct of Benefit-Cost Analysis: Toward Principles and Standards. *Journal of Benefit-Cost Analysis*, 2(2), 1–51.

Sandford, C. T., Godwin, M. R. and Hardwick, P. J. W. (1989). *Administrative and Compliance Costs of Taxation*. Bath: Fiscal Publications.

Schelling, T. C. (1981). Economic Reasoning and the Ethics of Policy. *Public Interest*, 63, 37–61.

Shefrin, H. M. and Thaler, R. H. (1988). The Behavioural Life-Cycle Hypothesis. *Economic Inquiry*, 26(4), 609–41.

Shogren, J. F. and Taylor, L. O. (2008). On Behavioural-Environmental Economics. *Review of Environmental Economics and Policy Advance Access*, 2(1), 26–44.

Shogren, J. F. and Thunström, L. (2016). Do We Need a New Behavioural Benchmark for BCA? *Journal of Benefit-Cost Analysis*, 7(1), 92–106.

Simon, H. A. (1979). Rational Decision Making in Business Organisations. *American Economic Review*, 69(4), 493–513.

Slovic, P. (2000). *The Perception of Risk*, Sterling, VA: Earthscan.

Smith, A. (1776/1937). *The Wealth of Nations*. New York: Random House.

Stern, N. (2007). *The Economics of Climate Change: The Stern Review*. Cambridge, UK: Cambridge University Press.

Stigler, G. and Becker, G. (1977). 'De gustibus non est disputandum'. *American Economic Review*, 67(2), 76–90.

Sunstein, C. R. and Reisch, L. A. (2016). Behaviourally Green: Why, Which and When Defaults Can Help, in Beckenbach, F. and Kahlenborn, W. (eds.), *New Perspectives for Environmental Policies Through Behavioural Economics*. Berlin: Springer, 161–194.

Thaler, R. H. (1981). Some Empirical Evidence on Dynamic Inconsistency. *Economic Letters*, 8(3), 201–207.

Thaler, R. H. (2016). Behavioral Economics: Past, Present, and Future. *American Economic Review*, 106(7), 1577–1600.

Thaler, R. and Shefrin, H. M. (1981). An Economic Theory of Self-Control. *Journal of Political Economy*, 89, 392–406.

Torgler, B., Frey, B. S. and Wilson, C. (2009). Environmental and Pro-Social Norms: Evidence on Littering. *BE Journal of Economic Analysis and Policy*, 9(1), 1–39.

Venkatacalam, L. (2008). Behavioural Economics for Environmental Policy. *Ecological Economics*, 67(4), 640–645.

Viscusi, W. K. and Gayer, T. (2016). Rational Benefit Assessment for an Irrational World: Toward a Behavioural Transfer Test. *Journal of Benefit-Cost Analysis*, 7(1), 69–91.

Weber, T. O., Fooken, J. and Herrmann, B. (2014). Behavioural Economics and Taxation. European Commission Working Paper No. 41.

Willig, R. (1976). Consumer's Surplus Without Apology. *American Economic Review*, 66(4), 589–97.

Wittman D. A. (1995). *The Myth of Democratic Failure: Why Political Institutions Are Efficient*. London: University of Chicago Press.

PART V

Environment

16 Towards Sustainable Lifestyles

Understanding the Policy Challenge

Tim Jackson and Carmen Smith

16.1 Introduction

Amongst the most firmly held *desiderata* of modern liberal society is the notion of individual freedom of choice. It seems almost sacrilegious for governments to assume influence over the complex mix of personal preferences, social expectations and cultural norms which, taken together, constitute 'consumer choice'. Yet this is precisely what the concepts of 'sustainable consumption' and 'sustainable lifestyle' appear to demand of policy. In particular, they seem to call for quite radical changes not just in people's attitudes but in their behaviours, practices and lifestyles.

The aim of this chapter is firstly to outline the emergence of what is essentially a new but rather critical policy discourse secondly, to understand the motivations for engaging in it at all; and thirdly, to develop a basis from social psychological theory with which to provide some policy traction on a seemingly intractable policy domain.

The extent of this task is potentially enormous, and it is certainly beyond our scope to provide an exhaustive account of everything involved in it. Rather, our goal here is to understand the social-psychological and institutional foundations of *unsustainable* consumption, and from these to tease out some of the possibilities for governance in pursuit of lifestyle change. In the following sections, we first explore briefly what is involved in confronting lifestyles and then develop four distinct but related perspectives on the sociocultural basis of modern lifestyles. In the final sections of the chapter, we explore the implications of this discussion for policy makers.

16.2 Contested Terrain

The discourse around sustainable consumption is relatively recent; the concept of sustainable lifestyles more recent still. The terminology of sustainable consumption emerged in 1992 at the United Nations Conference on Environment and Development in Rio de Janeiro. Chapter 4 of *Agenda 21* – the voluminous 'blueprint for action' launched at the conference – was entitled 'Changing Consumption Patterns'. It argued that 'the major cause of the continued deterioration of the global environment is the unsustainable pattern of consumption and production, particularly in industrialized countries', and called for 'new concepts of wealth and prosperity which allow higher standards of living through changed lifestyles and are less dependent on the Earth's finite resources' (UNCED 1992). In so doing, *Agenda 21* provided a potentially far-reaching mandate for examining, questioning and revising consumption patterns – and, by implication, people's behaviours, expectations and lifestyles.

The intervening years have borne witness to some clear tensions over what exactly sustainable consumption is supposed to mean (Jackson and Michaelis,2003; Jackson, 2006; SDC/NCC, 2006; UNEP, 2012). Some people insist that it must involve deep-seated lifestyle changes and clearly entails 'consuming less'. In this camp are those who lament the 'rampant materialism' of modern society and suggest that we could all live better by consuming less. They point to evidence of voluntary 'down-shifting': people who appear to opt for a better work–life balance, more quality time with their families and a low-consumption lifestyle over the conventional model of chasing higher earnings and higher consumer spending (Frank, 1999; Etzioni, 1998; Jackson, 2017; Schor, 2010; Skidelsky and Skidelsky, 2013).

In the second camp are those who suggest that consuming less would restrict choice and reduce the quality of people's lives. They maintain just as fervently that consuming less is not an option and argue instead that sustainable consumption involves 'consuming differently' and, in particular, 'consuming efficiently'. They highlight the transformative power of the market to deliver more with less: greater efficiency in industrial processes, cleaner and greener products, more sustainable consumer choices (DEFRA,2003; UNEP, 2012; Breakthrough, 2015).

The argument over whether or not we should be consuming less often skates over the question of what exactly we should be consuming less of. The 'consumption' of material resources is not necessarily the same thing as the 'consumption' of economic goods and services. But the argument often either proceeds as though it were the same, or else it assumes that the one can easily be 'decoupled' from the other.

Those who argue for a simpler life tend to look at the existing structure of consumer society – built on the ever-increasing accumulation and disposal of material possessions – and assume that the only way to stop the damage is to curb the economic system which feeds it. Not surprisingly, this view alarms those responsible for keeping the economy going, as well as those who have an economic interest in the existing system. Those resisting any notion of consuming less have a tendency to level charges of naivety at the down-shifters, and insist that it is possible to reduce environmental and social impacts without compromising economic consumption. Not surprisingly, this view is seen by the 'down-shifters' as a defence of the status quo, which is unlikely to deliver the radical changes in consumption that appear to be needed. And so the debate has become increasingly polarised.

After two decades of wrangling, two things have become relatively clear. The first is that there is considerable scope for improving the efficiency with which resources are used in delivering human well-being. Reducing resource consumption while increasing economic consumption is certainly possible in principle. It requires us either to reduce the materials needed to deliver a given good or service, or else to shift the balance of people's economic consumption towards goods and services that require fewer material inputs and outputs to start with (UNEP, 2001, 2012; Füchs, 2015; Breakthrough, 2015).

The second is that consuming more efficiently simply does not exhaust the scope or remit of the debate. Sustainable consumption must mean consuming less of certain things. To take only one example, it is clear from the scientific evidence that we must burn fewer carbon-intensive fuels (overall) if we are to stabilise atmospheric concentrations of greenhouse gases at levels that prevent 'dangerous anthropogenic interference' in the climate system.

By 2015, when the Twenty-First Conference of the Parties to the UN Framework Convention on Climate Change met to sign the Paris Agreement, carbon dioxide emissions were over 60 per cent higher than they had been in 1990 and being released into the atmosphere from human activities at a rate unprecedented in the last 66 million years. Temperatures were hotter than in any year since records began in 1850, and the average temperature was for the first time more than 1°C above the preindustrial average (Met Office, 2015; Jackson, 2017, ch. 1).

There was one astonishing outcome from the Paris Agreement. The deal signed in December 2015 committed its two hundred signatories to hold the increase in the global average temperature to 'well below 2°C above pre-industrial levels' and to pursue 'efforts to limit the temperature increase to 1.5°C' (UN FCCC, 2015). This goal represented the culmination of over a quarter of a century of intense international policy, and a series of mammoth negotiating sessions in Paris, which ran through the night for several days in a row before the deal itself was signed. But the hard work of actually achieving emission reductions consistent with an aspiration to restrict global warming to less than 1.5°C has scarcely begun. In fact, it has become clear that to achieve this target, the maximum available 'carbon budget' between now and the end of the century is only 350 billion tonnes. At the current rate of emissions, this budget would be exhausted within a decade. The message from all this is a profoundly uncomfortable one. Global average temperatures are rising inexorably. Dangerous climate change is a matter of decades away. And we are using up the climate 'slack' too quickly. It may take decades to transform our energy systems. Yet we have barely started on that task.

Meeting such 'deep' reduction targets will require more than slight shifts in people's marginal preferences for energy-efficient light bulbs. Policy will need to influence behaviours and practices in a number of different arenas, including supply tariff choices, purchases of energy-using appliances, energy-consuming practices in the home (e.g., personal hygiene, laundry, food preparation), demands for mobility and access (for both work-related and recreational reasons), food consumption behaviours, engagement in recycling and reuse of products, material product choices, home buying, patterns of use of domestic space, choice of leisure pursuits, demand for public services and so on.

In short, it appears that in order to accomplish its own declared environmental and social goals, government now finds itself forced to engage in a terrain which, if the rhetoric of the last two or three decades is to be believed, is not the terrain of government at all. Policy makers must begin to intervene in and to influence people's everyday behaviours and practices and to find ways to encourage lifestyle change.

16.3 Confronting Modern Lifestyles

Few people would disagree that modern society has changed dramatically in the course of only a few decades. These changes can be characterised in a variety of different ways. We can point, for example, to the growth in disposable incomes, to a massive expansion in the availability of consumer goods and services, to higher levels of personal mobility, increases in leisure expenditure and a reduction in the time spent in routine domestic tasks.

We might highlight the gains in technological efficiency provided by an increasingly sophisticated knowledge base. Or the rising resource 'footprint' of modern consumption patterns. Or the intensification of trade. Or the decline in traditional rural industries. Or the translocation of manufacturing towards the developing world. Or the emergence of the 'knowledge' economy.

We should certainly point out that these changes have been accompanied, and sometimes facilitated, by changes in the underlying institutional structures: the deregulation (or reregulation) of key industries, the liberalisation of markets, the easing of international trade restrictions, the rise in consumer debt and the commoditisation of previously noncommercial areas of our lives.

We could also identify some of the social effects that have accompanied these changes: a faster pace of life; rising social expectations; increasing divorce rates; rising levels of violent crime; smaller household sizes; the emergence of a 'cult of celebrity'; the escalating 'message density' of modern living; increasing disparities (in income and time) between the rich and the poor; the emergence of 'postmaterialist' values; a loss of trust in the conventional institutions of church, family and state; and a more secular society (Dunlap et al., 1978; Inglehart, 1991; Jackson, 2004, 2017; Schor, 2010; Skidelsky and Skidelsky, 2013).

It is clear, even from this cursory overview, that no simple overriding 'good' or 'bad' trend emerges from this complexity. Rather, modernity is characterised by a variety of trends that often seem to be set (in part at least) in opposition to each other. The identification of a set of 'postmaterialist' values in modern society appears at odds with the increased proliferation of consumer goods. People appear to express less concern for material things, and yet have more of them in their lives.

The abundance offered by the liberalisation of trade is offset by the environmental damage from transporting these goods across large distances to reach our supermarket shelves. The liberalisation of the electricity market has increased the efficiency of generation, reduced the cost of electricity to consumers and at the same time made it more difficult to identify and exploit the opportunities for end-use energy efficiency.

To take another example, the emergence of the knowledge economy has increased the availability and the value of information. Simultaneously, it has intensified the complexity of ordinary decision-making in people's lives. As Nobel laureate Herbert Simon has pointed out, information itself consumes scarce resources. 'What information consumes is rather obvious: it consumes the attention of its recipients. Hence a wealth of information creates a poverty of attention, and a need to allocate that attention efficiently among the overabundance of information sources that might consume it' (Simon, 1971, pp. 40–41). This consuming effect of information makes the concept of 'informed choice' at once more important and at the same time more difficult to achieve in modern society.

These examples all serve to illustrate that modern lifestyles are both complex and haunted by paradox. This is certainly one of the reasons why policy makers have tended to shy away from the whole question of consumer behaviour and lifestyle change. It is clear nonetheless that coming to grips with consumption patterns, understanding the dynamics of lifestyle and influencing people's attitudes and behaviours are all essential if the kinds of deep environmental targets demanded by sustainable development are to be achieved.

To this end, it is worth at least attempting to impose some structure on this difficult terrain. It is possible to distinguish four somewhat different, but together informative, perspectives on lifestyles and lifestyles change: lifestyles as 'livelihoods', lifestyles as the pursuit of life satisfaction, lifestyles as a social conversation and lifestyles as 'locked in' to the creeping evolution of social norms. Each of these perspectives contributes something to the understanding of unsustainability and has particular implications for policy.

16.4 Lifestyles as 'Livelihoods'

At the most basic level, our lifestyles maintain our lives. In order to live, we need access to food and shelter. We consume food in order to nourish ourselves, housing and clothes to protect ourselves, medicines to keep ourselves and our families healthy and transport services in order to maintain access to these basic goods. In many less developed countries, the underconsumption of these basic resources is itself a problem. In most developed countries, our access to these commodities is so much taken for granted that we sometimes forget how important the structures for securing and providing them are.

Yet, it is clearly not true to say that these basic physical and physiological functions exhaust our personal (or collective) ambitions and goals. Finding a partner, educating our children, developing our friendships, pursuing a full and active life, following our dreams: all of these ambitions and many more characterise modern living. Nor are such goals and dreams confined to modernity. The precise ways in which social and personal ambitions are framed in modern Western society may differ markedly from other times and places. But there are also a number of key similarities between our society and those that have gone before.

Several different kinds of attempts have been made to characterise these 'universal' aspects of the human condition. Some have employed the language of 'human needs' to suggest that people everywhere experience a common set of material, social and psychological needs: the need for shelter, the need for belonging, the need for autonomy and relatedness, the need for meaning and purpose in our lives and so on (Maslow, 1954; Max Neef, 1991; Kasser, 2002; Doyal and Gough, 1991; Jackson, Jager and Stagl, 2004).

The most familiar of these approaches is the 'hierarchy of needs' proposed by Maslow (1968). The model is akin to several theories describing the stages of growth in human developmental psychology, in which certain needs must be met before the individual will desire and be motivated towards fulfilling higher-level needs. A range of 'meta-needs' or 'being needs' are included in the category of self-actualisation, and Maslow coined the term 'meta-motivation' to describe the motivation of those who go beyond satisfying basic needs and strive towards fulfilling their inherent ultimate potential (Engler, 2009).

In his later years, Maslow criticised and reviewed his vision of self-actualisation to suggest that the self only becomes actualised through pursuing some higher goal outside of itself, in altruism and spirituality (Maslow, 1996). Indeed, when a person experiences self-actualisation, much of what he or she accomplishes may benefit others or, 'the greater self', leading to a felt sense of meaningfulness in life (Snyder, Rand and Sigmon, 2005). According to Terror Management Theory (Becker, 1973; Solomon, Greenberg and Pyszczynski, 2014), gaining self-esteem also reduces the 'mortal anxiety' or the fear of death, suggesting that progress up the pyramid towards self-actualisation is driven by the existential motivation to fulfil a higher 'purpose' in life (Greenberg, Pyszczynski and Solomon, 1986).

Fearing that the language of needs is too emotive and too open to manipulation, others have preferred to talk in terms of 'capabilities' or 'functionings', suggesting that people everywhere must have a set of capabilities that will allow them to function properly in whichever society they find themselves (Sen, 1985; Nussbaum, 1998). Other approaches have tended to emphasise the evolutionary, biological nature of our behavioural drives, pointing out how we are all compelled to seek mates, reproduce the species, compete for scarce resources and so on (Wright, 1994; Ridley, 1994; Jackson, 2002; Sterling, 2016).

What unites these different frameworks – aside from the attempt to define something that constitutes a common basis for human motivation – is that they each frame human behaviour in terms of some form of goal-orientation. Human behaviour is regarded as purposive rather than random. People are understood as having underlying motivations, as developing life goals, as actively pursuing improvements in their quality of life (Ajzen and Fishbein, 1975; Bagozzi, Dholakia and Basuroy, 2003). The most recent and widely applied theory of motivation in the field of psychology is Self-Determination Theory (SDT). Initially developed by Edward Deci and Richard Ryan, SDT is concerned with the degree to which an individual's behaviour is self-motivated. Like Social Cognitive Theory, SDT states that, as part of human nature, individuals demonstrate 'inherent growth tendencies', that is, effort, agency and commitment towards growth and development. As a result, behaviours are classified as either intrinsically motivated (to develop oneself) or extrinsically motivated (to obtain an external goal) (Deci, 1971; Deci and Ryan, 2002). Deci and Ryan also proposed three intrinsic needs that are the basis for self-determination: autonomy, competence and relatedness. These provide a framework for human motivation that may be applied to the context of sustainability.

Some of this purposive behaviour is recognised as being influenced by instinctive drives and evolved behavioural patterns. The biological basis for behavioural dispositions is an important reality check on utopian aspirations for radical behaviour change. But even here, in most accounts, humans remain 'reflexive': able to identify and reflect upon their own behaviours and life aspirations and at least partially separate these from unconscious drives and desires.

Bandura (1989, 2001) suggests that behaviours are learnt socially. Social Cognitive Theory (SCT) emphasises the role of 'personal agency' in changing behaviour within particular contexts. Through emphasising the role of cognition, SCT offers an agentic perspective to human adaptation and change where humans are not merely seen as being reactive, driven by impulse or shaped by environmental forces, as had been conceived by behaviourist psychologists during the nineteenth century (Gazzaniga, 2010). 'Agency' refers to the capacity of an agent to act in the world, and according to Bandura (2001) this is the essence of humanness. To be an agent is to influence intentionally one's functioning and life circumstances, and in turn this influences human development, adaptation and change. This view of lifestyles – as the means to achieve a set of purposive goals and ambitions (including basic survival) – is one that has been captured most clearly in recent debates about 'livelihoods' (DfID, 2006; Oxfam, 2006). Interestingly, this debate has emerged mainly from discussions about poverty reduction in developing countries. But the framework is also useful in thinking about livelihoods in developed nations.

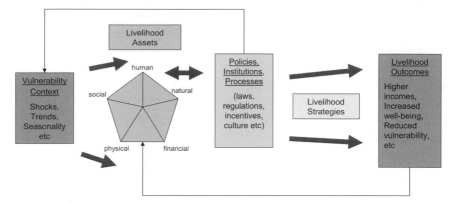

Figure 16.1. *A livelihoods framework: assets, strategies and outcomes. Source: Redrawn from Chambers and Conway (1992).*

Livelihoods have been defined as 'the capabilities, assets (including both material and social resources) and activities required for a means of living' (Chambers and Conway, 1992). Much of the focus of the debate in international development has been on people having the means to survive physically. But the framework recognises explicitly that people's goals potentially involve a wide range of desired 'outcomes', including more food, higher incomes, reduced vulnerability to shocks, better working conditions and lower infant mortality.

In other words, this framework captures quite precisely the notion of lifestyles as strategies for living that are aimed at meeting specific goals and purposes. One of the first elements in applying the livelihoods approach at the local level is to elicit from local people what those goals might be. Livelihoods are characterised (Figure 16.1) by a set of 'livelihood strategies' aimed at achieving specific goals or aspirations ('livelihood outcomes'). But these strategies are themselves mediated by the policies, institutions and processes within which individual or collective action is framed.

The success of livelihood strategies is also dependent on the assets available to people in any given context. In the livelihoods framework, these assets are characterised in terms of a set of five interrelated forms of capital: human, social, physical, financial and natural. In addition, the sufficiency of this asset base in maintaining livelihood strategies is dependent on the 'vulnerability context' within which people operate – the potential shocks, trends or unexpected eventualities which might disrupt their lives.

One of the important aspects of the Sustainable Livelihoods framework is the relationship between different forms of 'capital'. Material (financial, physical, natural) resources are clearly vital in preserving our lifestyles and pursuing our life goals. But social and human resources are not in any sense inferior forms of asset. It has been recognised for a long time by anthropologists, for example, that social networks offer a vital form of resilience in the face of both material and emotional shocks (Douglas, 1976; Douglas and Isherwood, 1979; Wright, 1994). Finding and keeping a good job, coping with economic or emotional loss, weathering natural or unnatural storms: all of these things depend on the strength of our social networks. And this depends in its turn on our personal ability to negotiate and maintain our place in the social group.

Much of the literature on social resilience has looked at the ways in which communities might become more resilient to the effects of climate change and resource depletion (Barr and Devine-Wright, 2012). Indeed, factors supporting resilience play an important role as exposure to risk factors increases, such as the risk of natural disasters, including floods or droughts. However, even when such risks are not immediately perceptible, some individuals actively prepare for emergencies, including possible disruptions in the social or political order (Hammer, 2009). This 'survivalism' movement has, since the 1960s, focussed on emergency and self-defence training, stockpiling food and water and preparing to become self-sufficient, while adherents of the back-to-the-land movement share similar interests in self-sufficiency and preparedness. Importantly, these 'survivalist' strategies have also been suggested as strategies that aim to enhance personal and psychological resilience, allowing individuals to better adapt to stress and adversity on a personal level (APA, 2014).

At the individual level, psychological resilience is defined as the ability to adapt to stress and adversity as a result of family, health or financial problems, for example (APA, 2014). Rather than being a trait of the individual, it is a process of developing and practicing coping techniques (Rutter, 2008; Klohnen,1996). These may be individual coping strategies, or may be supported by families, schools, communities and social policies that make resilience more likely to occur (Leadbeater, Dodgen and Solarz, 2005). Through these factors, psychologically resilient people develop an optimistic attitude that allows them to effectively balance negative emotions with positive ones, enabling them to effectively manage crises (APA, 2014).

In this respect, the distinction between personal and community resilience may be blurred. Tajfel and Turner (1979) proposed that the groups which people belong to, such as family groups, teams or social classes, are an important source of pride and self-esteem as they provide a sense of belonging to the social world, that is, a social identity. The authors therefore introduced the concept of a 'social identity' as the part of one's self-concept derived from perceived membership within a social group (Turner et al., 1987). The authors suggested that, in order to increase self-esteem, one enhances the status of the group to which one belongs, the 'in group', and self-esteem might also be enhanced by discriminating and holding prejudiced views against the 'out group'. A key assumption of Social Identity Theory is that individuals are intrinsically motivated to achieve positive distinctiveness. That is, that people 'strive for a positive self-concept' (Haslam, 2001).

Obviously, the extent to which social positioning is important also depends (at the individual level) on how strong the rest of our asset base is and (at a broader cultural level) on what kind of society we live in. Strong rich people living in society where individuality is prized can afford to ignore social norms. Poorer, weaker people cannot. In societies where the group is prized more highly than the individual, no one can afford to ignore social norms. And somewhere in the middle of all that, the much-maligned practice of 'keeping up with the Joneses' becomes an important livelihood strategy in any society where social position counts.

The Sustainable Livelihoods framework has been useful in thinking through poverty reduction in developing countries. The high vulnerability of poor rural communities to extreme weather events or to changes in the price of basic commodities, for example, places a premium on understanding the assets they possess, and designing policies and institutions that support the strategies they employ to achieve their desired goals.

In most developed countries, people are not quite so obviously vulnerable to the floods, droughts and crop failures that haunt many poorer nations. But even where markets are relatively stable, assets are secure, unexpected mortality is low and shocks few and far between, one does not need to search far to find an undercurrent of fear about the impact that such vulnerabilities might have on our lives (Berger 1967, Jackson 2006, 2013b). Consider, for example, the ferocity of responses to the 'war on terror', or recent 'documentary' examinations of the impacts of sudden unexpected events (global warming, political meltdown, disruptions to the oil and gas markets). When lives, livelihoods and lifestyles are threatened, people tend to react swiftly and sometimes ferociously to try and mitigate the threat (Breakwell, 1986).

In summary, what emerges from this discussion is a view of modern lifestyles that links them closely to fundamental underlying motivations to survive, to reproduce, to live well, to conceive and to pursue basic life goals. This view of lifestyles allows us to approach consumer goods (and people's consumption patterns) as critical components in individual and collective livelihood strategies and to begin to understand processes of lifestyle change – and resistance to change.

16.5 Lifestyles and Life Satisfaction

At the heart of the idea of lifestyles as livelihoods lies the notion of well-being or quality of life. Livelihood strategies are, at some broad level, ways of maintaining or increasing (individual or collective) well-being and improving quality of life. Higher incomes, lower infant mortality, improved health, reduced drudgery, stronger social networks, higher resilience to shocks: these are the kinds of things generally reported as desirable livelihood outcomes.

In fact, the idea that the aim of consumer lifestyles is to improve people's well-being lies at the heart of most modern notions of progress. It is expressed most explicitly in the conventional concept of economic development. Successive governments in most industrialised nations have – at least until recently – taken well-being (or quality of life) to mean more or less the same thing as 'standard of living'. The standard of living in its turn has traditionally been equated with per capita levels of national income – measured conventionally through the gross domestic product (GDP).

The basis for this equation of economic performance with quality of life rests on the idea that (in one formulation at least) the GDP may be regarded as the total of all expenditures made either in consuming finished goods and services or investing money to ensure future consumption possibilities. Since the sum of consumption expenditures is equivalent (under certain conditions) to the value placed by consumers on the goods they consume, then – according to the conventional argument – GDP can be taken as some kind of 'proxy' for the well-being derived from our consumption activities. In a seminal paper in welfare economics, Weitzman (1976) showed that the net domestic product (gross domestic product net of capital depreciation) can be regarded as a proxy for 'sustainable' well-being, since it is formally equivalent to nondeclining consumption possibilities.

Since GDP rose more or less consistently over the last fifty years, the comforting logic of this orthodox view suggests that we have been pretty successful in delivering an increasing standard of living and, by proxy, improving the quality of people's lives over recent decades. Furthermore, if our concern is to ensure that quality of life continues to reach new heights, the conventional view provides a ready and familiar formula for achieving this end: namely, to continue to ensure 'high and stable levels of economic growth' (DETR, 1999).

But this equation of economic growth with increasing quality of life has come under considerable scrutiny over the last few decades, from a number of different quarters and for a variety of different reasons (Douthwaite, 1992; Daly and Cobb, 1989; Daly, 2009; Jackson, 2013). Not least amongst these is the realisation that conventional measures of economic progress fail to account for the depletion of natural resources, and for the environmental and social impacts of consumption and production (Jackson, 2017; Victor, 2008). In addition, this conventional view is faced with what is perhaps the most striking ambivalence involved in understanding modern lifestyles: the so-called life-satisfaction paradox'(Layard, 2005; Jackson, 2013a; Skidelsky and Skidelsky, 2013).

This phenomenon is illustrated in Figure 16.2. The success of conventional development is illustrated by the rise in GDP. Incomes have almost doubled in the United Kingdom since the early 1970s. Yet reported life satisfaction over the same period has scarcely changed at all. This effect is particularly noticeable in the United Kingdom. But it is also observed in a number of other countries. (See, for example, the chapter by Ahuvia in this volume.) Across most developed countries, there is at best a weak correlation between increased income and reported well-being. And for countries with average incomes in excess of

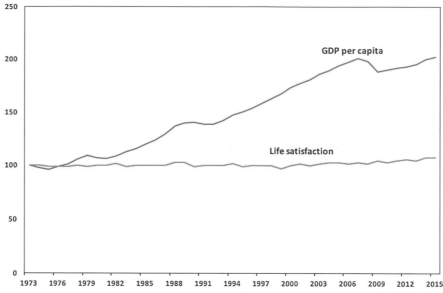

Figure 16.2. *UK GDP per capita versus life satisfaction, 1973–2015.*
Source: Data on life satisfaction from World Happiness Database,
*online at worlddatabaseofhappiness.eur.nl/hap_nat/nat_*
fp.php?cntry=16&name=United%20Kingdom&mode=3&subjects=100
9&publics=121 (accessed 13 January 2017); data on GDP from World
Bank World Database, online at databank.worldbank.org/data/reports.
aspx?source=2&series=NY.GDP.MKTP.KD.ZG&country=#) (accessed 13
January 2017).

around \$15,000 to \$20,000, there is very little correlation at all of increased income with improved happiness (Inglehart, Inglehart and Klingeman, 2000; Inglehart et al., 2008).

If rising consumption is supposed to deliver increasing levels of well-being, these data on stagnant 'life satisfaction' pose a series of uncomfortable questions for modern society (Jackson, 2013a). Why is life satisfaction not improving in line with higher incomes? Is economic growth delivering improved well-being or not? What exactly is the relationship between lifestyle and life satisfaction?

Explanations for the life satisfaction paradox have been sought in a variety of different places (Thompson, Marks and Jackson, 2013). Some authors highlight the fact that relative income has a bigger effect on individual well-being than absolute levels of income (Easterlin, 1974). If my income rises relative to those around me, I am likely to become happier. If everyone else's income rises at the same rate as my own, I am less likely to report higher life satisfaction. Moreover, if my increase in income causes envy in those around me, my increased satisfaction is likely to be offset by dissatisfaction in others, so that aggregate life satisfaction across the nation may not change at all (Layard, 2005).

Others point to the impact of 'hedonic adaptation'. As I get richer, I simply become more accustomed to the pleasure of the goods and services my new income affords me. And if I want to maintain the same level of happiness, I must achieve ever higher levels of income in the future just to stay in the same place (Layard, 2005; NEF, 2004; Offer, 2006).

Humanistic psychologists (and some ecologists and philosophers) have argued that the entire project of income growth rests on a misunderstanding of human nature. Far from making us happier, according to this critique, the pursuit of material things damages us psychologically and socially. Beyond the satisfaction of our basic material needs for housing, clothing and nutrition, the pursuit of material consumption merely serves to entrench us in unproductive status competition, disrupts our work–life balance and distracts us from those things that offer meaning and purpose to our lives (de Boton, 2004; Csikszentmihalyi, 2000; Kasser, 2002; Schor, 1998; Wachtel, 1983; see also the chapter by Ahuvia in this collection).

Others again have suggested a different – but equally radical – explanation for the life satisfaction paradox. In an interesting attempt to construct an international index of quality of life, *The Economist's* Intelligence Unit suggested the explanation for the paradox was that 'there are factors associated with modernisation that, in part, offset its positive impact'. They argued that

> [a] concomitant breakdown of traditional institutions is manifested in the decline of religiosity and of trade unions; a marked rise in various social pathologies (crime, and drug and alcohol addiction); a decline in political participation and of trust in public authority; and the erosion of the institutions of family and marriage (*The Economist*, 2004).

The point about these changes – which have occurred hand in hand with the rise in incomes and the expansion of individual choice – is not that income growth is irrelevant to individual quality of life; all the evidence suggests the contrary. Rather, it is that the pursuit of income growth appears to have undermined some of the conditions (family, friendship, community) on which we know that people's long-term well-being depends.

Is this merely a contingent historical coincidence or is it a necessary consequence of income growth? Do we just happen to have inherited an economic system which risks undermining the conditions of well-being or is it a feature of all such systems to operate in this way? Is it or is it not possible to maintain economic growth without the 'concomitant' erosion of some of the other conditions on which well-being depends?

For the sake of sustainable development, we would certainly want to hope that it is. *The Economist* article appears ambivalent on this point. Some critics of modernity have been far less ambivalent, pointing out that modern economies suffer from a structural need for consumerist values in order to sustain consumption growth (Baudrillard,1970; Baumann, 1998, 2001a, Fromm,

1976; Illich,1977). The question is clearly a vital one to answer, but for the moment must remain beyond the scope of this chapter.

What flows from this discussion is the perhaps surprising insight that lifestyle strategies are not always effective – either because people end up consuming goods that do not contribute to life satisfaction or because there are other (social or institutional) factors at work that prevent individual consumption choices contributing to collective (and future) well-being. This analysis suggests that it is at least a legitimate question to ask whether it is or not possible to live better by consuming less (Jackson 2005, 2017). If at least some of our existing material consumption does not contribute to well-being, can we devise systems of consumption and production which are less resource-intensive but serve our needs better and deliver improved well-being and quality of life?

16.6 Lifestyle as 'Social Conversation'

This discussion raises an obvious question: why, if material consumption fails to satisfy, do we continue to consume? One answer to this is given by a quite specific view of lifestyles that has emerged in recent sociological writings on consumption and lifestyle (Chaney, 1996). Briefly, this idea can be summarised by saying that lifestyles operate partly as 'social conversations': ways of communicating to ourselves and to others what sort of people we are; which kind of groups we belong to; who we like, love and approve of; who we disapprove of; what our social position is, and what we hope that it might be; and what our goals, drives and ambitions are.

(The use of the term 'social conversation' in this context is not typical of sociological writing. Sociology refers more often to 'social practices' – see the next section for details. But it is consistent with the idea that material artefacts constitute what Douglas and Isherwood, 1979, call a 'language of goods' and draws strongly from earlier social psychological theories of symbolic interactionism; Blumer, 1969; Mead, 1934).

This view of lifestyles relies heavily on one of the most important sociological and anthropological understandings about consumption: namely, that material things embody important symbolic meanings for us. As one observer has remarked: 'the currency of lifestyles is the symbolic meaning of artefacts' (Chaney, 1996, p. 43). We value goods not just for what they can do, but for what they represent to us and to others. Without this almost magical potential to speak for us in some sense, it is doubtful that plain 'stuff' could play such a key role in our lives.

This insight clearly has some resonance with popular psychology about our relationship with material possessions. A child's favourite teddy bear, a woman's wedding dress, a stamp collector's prized first day cover, the colours of my favourite football team, the brand name of a pair of trainers, the latest BMW sports car: all these examples suggest that there is much more at stake in the possession of material artefacts than simple functional value.

Over the second half of the twentieth century, this popular wisdom was given much more robust and sophisticated footing. The symbolic importance of consumer goods has been underlined by a wide range of intellectual sources. The evidence from social anthropology is perhaps the most convincing. It suggests that societies throughout the ages have used material commodities as symbolic resources to denote a wide variety of different kinds of meanings in an even wider variety of situations and contexts (Appadurai, 1986; Csikszentmihalyi and Rochberg-Halton, 1981; Dittmar, 1992; Douglas, 1976; Douglas and Isherwood, 1979).

To offer one specific and relevant example, a recent study showed how patterns of lighting design in the home in three different cultures are inextricably linked to underlying social and cultural norms – the way we use space, our emotional attachment to home and hearth and our sense of propriety in entertaining friends and guests. Lighting isn't solely about being able to see in the dark. Rather, it is situated in a complex network of personal and social meanings that must be negotiated in the course of attempting to make domestic lighting patterns more efficient for example (Wilhite et al., 1996).

This symbolic role for material goods is perhaps most obviously put to use in the creation and maintenance of personal identity. I define who I am in part through the symbolic meanings attached to the things that I own, use and display. This has led some sociologists to see modernity quite specifically as characterised by a restless search to define personal identity through one's consumption and lifestyle choices (Giddens, 1991; Featherstone, 1990; Baumann, 2001b; Campbell, 2004; Evans and Jackson, 2007).

Individual choice, the freedom to create one's identity, the ability to construct an 'authentic' personalised lifestyle: all these are highly prized features of modern society. At the same time, there is an irony inherent in this process. In spite of the high emphasis placed on individuality here, the symbols on which the project of self-identity is built are inherently social in nature. The task of constructing and maintaining symbolic meaning is itself a social one.

Symbols are by their nature socially constructed (Hirschman and Holbrook 1980). The symbolic value attached to material artefacts is neither embodied in the artefacts themselves nor entirely open to personal interpretation. This point was made persuasively by the sociologist Georg Simmel (1971) in the early twentieth century. Rather, it is a complex mixture of personal experience, historical tradition, societal values and an evolving process of articulating and elaborating social meaning. Symbolic value is constantly negotiated and renegotiated in modern society through social interactions.

Figure 16.3 illustrates something of how this process works. The left-hand side of the diagram represents the process of personal identity formation. As an individual in modern society (according to this view of modern lifestyles), I am continually involved in constructing a narrative about my own life – a personal

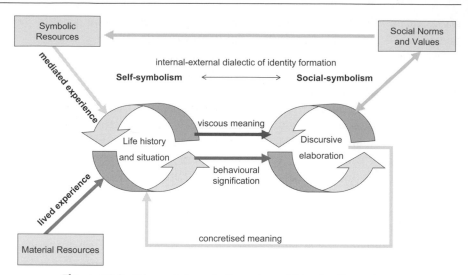

Figure 16.3. *The social-symbolic project of identity formation.*
Source: adapted by the author from Elliott and Wattanasuwan (1998).

project of symbolic 'self-completion' (Wicklund and Gollwitzer 1982). I live in a particular kind of house, drive a certain kind of car, have this kind of job, wear these kinds of clothes, listen to that kind of music and (like most other parents) agonise over which local school to send my children to. Consciously or subconsciously, I see myself and construct my own sense of identity through these lifestyle 'choices'. To the extent that I can achieve it at all, I know how to make sense of my life and pursue my life goals only through continual reference to this evolving narrative.

In pursuit of this narrative, I have at my disposal two distinct sets of resources. The first set is material: the artefacts and commodities that constitute the range of available goods and services. The second is symbolic: the set of meanings, interpretations and associations with which I am constantly surrounded. A specific, simple example of this dual relationship between 'things' and 'meanings' is the relationship between a product and a brand. The product is essentially a material resource; but the brand operates as a symbolic resource carrying or portraying a set of social meanings about use or ownership of the product.

My 'lived experience' of the material resources and my 'mediated experience' of symbolic resources allow me to construct – at a personal level – a kind of semidefined or 'viscous' meaning associated with any particular lifestyle choice. It is only through a social process – illustrated on the right-hand side of Figure 16.3 – of discussing and elaborating on these social meanings with others that I am able to solidify the specific meaning associated with a particular choice and incorporate it into the narrative of my life.

The implication of this rather complex process is that even personal identity – in this view of modern lifestyles – is bound up irretrievably in social

conversations. Individual self-completion is only possible through social interaction with others. Without such social processes, I simply have insufficient
resources to attribute social value to my life choices and to articulate a meaningful sense of personal identity. In short, the most misanthropic individual is
an inherently social creature.

Conversely, of course, the process of discursive elaboration – talking to others about the values attached to material artefacts – is a vehicle for the continual evolution of social meanings. Symbolic meanings of material commodities
don't exist in isolation. Brand loyalty, for example, does not emerge spontaneously out of thin air. The relationship amongst people, meanings and things is
the subject of a continually evolving dialogue over which no single individual,
interest group or company has absolute control.

This is not to suggest that social meanings are immune from manipulation
by powerful interests. On the contrary, an important aspect of this sociological view of lifestyles suggests that modern lifestyles have themselves become
the locus for playing out power discourses, articulating class distinctions and
reinforcing social inequalities (Bourdieu, 1984).

Producers, retailers and marketers have a particular interest in vesting their
products with social value. The art of marketing is quite precisely the process
of attributing social and psychological meanings to individual products. But
the history of brand failures (Haig, 2003) should warn us against any simplistic view on the power of marketers to achieve this end. Rather, lifestyles (and
the power discourses played out through them) are the product of a complex
'social logic' that defies absolute control by individuals or individual interest
groups – or indeed by well-intentioned government departments.

From the point of view of sustainability, this view of lifestyles offers some
interesting insights. In the first place, it positions lifestyles as crucial mediators
amongst resource use, social structure and symbolic meanings. It also points
to the importance of being able to understand – both in general and in specific
situations – how these relationships are constructed and how they change over
time. To attempt to engage in lifestyle change without an awareness of the
social-symbolic processes underlying consumer choices is to invite an almost
inevitable failure.

In fact, the life satisfaction paradox does intimate some 'inefficiencies' here.
But these inefficiencies are rather complex features of the social organisation
of lifestyles, and we cannot expect many 'easy wins' simply by exhorting people to change or tinkering with incentive structures.

Indeed, government attempts to promote sustainable behaviour through
incentive structures have so far failed or only partially succeeded. For example, the NUDGE campaign run by the Behavioural Insights Team of the
UK Cabinet Office employs cognitive and behavioural psychology to 'nudge'
individual consumers into better decision-making through constructing a
premeditated 'choice architecture' at points of consumption (Cabinet Office,
2010). Financial incentives are also offered to encourage individual behaviours

(DEFRA, 2008). However, these approaches have failed to motivate wide-spread change, and recent research in psychology has found that quick-fix policies which aim to 'change behaviour without changing minds' (Dobson, 2010) may actually work to accelerate resource destruction. This occurs as moral responses are crowded out by means of fiscal incentives (Dobson, 2010) and through phenomena such as the 'rebound effect', which offsets the benefits of new measures through greater efficiency (Thøgersen and Schrader, 2012).

In summary, lifestyles are a way of helping us to create the social world and find a creditable place in it. Modernity is characterised by the increasingly important symbolic role played by material goods in this process. In many cases, existing lifestyle choices and consumption patterns are inextricably linked with people's sense of self, social standing and purpose. Teasing apart consumer demand from these social and psychological processes is going to require a concerted effort to understand social values, renegotiate social norms and offer alternative meaning structures. Without such initiatives, attempts to change lifestyles – as we have already noted – can only expect considerable resistance.

16.7 Lifestyles and 'Lock-In'

The modern project of symbolic self-completion – the reflexive construction of personal life narratives – has sometimes been construed in the literature as an inherently creative project in which the individual has a great deal of freedom in deciding on the outcome. It is precisely this promise of immense, inextinguishable personal opportunity on which the consumer society is built. Each new consumer purchase is a small piece of this continual reinvention of possibility. Each lifestyle choice opens the door to a brighter and better future. The opportunity to reinvent ourselves. The chance to realise our dreams. The basis for sustaining hope in the face of adversity. Once again, advertising executives have for decades been alive to these ways of investing mundane goods with a sense of hope. It is part of the art of marketing (Campbell, 2015, 2004; McCracken, 1989; Roberts, 2004).

The reality, of course, is something rather different. At the very least, we would have to admit that choice doesn't always appear possible to people. Though I strive continually for control of my life, it often appears to have a momentum and a pattern of its own. This pattern certainly changes over time. But the change sometimes appears to have less to do with my own decisions and desires than it does with the changing demands on my time, the technologies that shape my existence, the sometimes inescapable efforts of others to persuade me to behave and live in particular ways and the emergence of new social norms and attitudes to which I am expected constantly to adapt if I am to maintain or improve my social standing.

This is one of the most intractable of the paradoxes haunting modern lifestyles. Modern society celebrates choice and personal opportunity; and at the same time, we often find ourselves locked into rather predictable patterns of living, working and consuming. French sociologist Pierre Bourdieu (1977) described social life as 'A constant struggle to construct a life out of the cultural resources one's social experience offers, in the face of formidable social constraints. By living in a society structured by such constraints, and organised by the successful practices of others, one develops predispositions to act in certain ways' (Paterson, 2003, p. 7).

The idea that modern society, and consumerism specifically, operates as a kind of 'iron cage' binding us into certain material dependencies and patterns of behaviour has a long pedigree in the social sciences (Weber, 1930; Ritzer, 2001; Jackson, 2013b). Recent work in sociology has revived this traditional theme as a way of better understanding real consumer behaviours. Social practice theory criticises the individualistic nature of market approaches, arguing instead that practices are deeply embedded within social relations and material infrastructures (Hargreaves, 2011; Southerton, Warde and Hand, 2004; Spaargaren and van Vliet, 2000). These authors argue that too much emphasis has been placed on the conspicuous aspects of modern consumer lifestyles and that a great deal of consumption in fact takes place *inconspicuously* as a part of the everyday decision-making of millions of ordinary individuals. 'Ordinary' consumption, they suggest, is not oriented particularly towards individual display. Rather, it is about convenience, habit, practice and individual responses to social norms and institutional contexts over which the individual has little control (Gronow and Warde, 2001; Shove, 2003; Verplanken and Wood, 2006).

To take one simple and relevant example, the fuel consumption associated with heating our home is determined (amongst other things) by the available fuel supply, the efficiency of the conversion devices, the effectiveness of thermal insulation in the dwelling and the level of thermal comfort programmed into our thermostats. These factors in their turn are constrained by the historical development of the fuel supply and appliance industries, the institutional design of the energy services market, the social norms associated with personal convenience and thermal comfort and our own individual responses to those norms.

The evolution of social and institutional norms is itself complex, often involving incremental changes over long historical periods. Typically, at the point of everyday decision, the ordinary consumer will have little or no control over much of this decision architecture (Guy and Shove, 2000; Sanne, 2002; Shove, 2003).

This message tends to be borne out by empirical studies of consumer attitudes and behaviours. The National Consumer Council, for example, has published a number of studies looking at people's attitudes towards and access to sustainable lifestyle options. They concluded that, for the most part, consumers find their options curtailed by a variety of factors, including time constraints, economic disincentives and the absence or inaccessibility of more sustainable choices (Holdsworth, 2003, 2005; Klein, 2003). This is particularly true of low-income households – for whom restrictions in choice are already onerous (Burningham and Thrush, 2000; Brook Lyndhurst, 2004). Indeed, for many people marginalised through economic scarcity, this reality becomes even more obvious. Choice is restricted in multiple ways. Numerous studies point to social exclusion and lower socioeconomic status as being negatively correlated with proenvironmental behaviour.[1]

At the heart of this concept of 'ordinary consumption' lies the issue of habit. The important role that habit plays in our lives has been acknowledged for some time (Bourdieu, 1984; Camic,1986; Kahneman, 1973; Tversky and Kahneman, 1974). Many of our everyday actions appear to take place with little conscious deliberation at all. Rather, we relegate routine decisions to the realm of semiconscious automaticity. At best, we use a variety of mental short-cuts – what the sociologist Anthony Giddens (1984) has called 'practical consciousness' – to simplify routine choice in our lives.

Habit has both good and bad influences on lifestyle choice. On the one hand, it allows us to free up cognitive resources for more important tasks. But on the other hand, it renders much of our routine decision-making almost invisible, even to ourselves. Changing our behaviour – exercising our ability to choose – becomes more and more difficult as the existing behaviour pattern is repeated.

Resolving the paradox of choice at the heart of modern lifestyles is far from easy. The question of whether consumers are free to make choices about their own actions or whether they are bound by forces outside their control has provoked a long and heated debate in the social sciences. This debate – about the relative influence of human agency and social structure – culminated in the development of Giddens' 'structuration theory', which attempts to show how agency and structure relate to each other (Giddens 1984). Giddens' work provides the basis for a view of lifestyles as a set of *social practices* (Figure 16.4), which are influenced on the one hand by our lifestyle choices and on the other by the institutions and structures of society.

In summary, the message that flows from this subsection is that – in spite of the conscious attempt to construct personal lifestyle narratives – consumers are often far from being free agents in the execution of lifestyle choice. They do have personal priorities. Their lives are in some broad sense (as we discussed previously) goal-oriented. They do exercise deliberative decisions. At the same time, many routine decisions are not deliberative. People often find themselves 'locked in' to unsustainable patterns of living, by a complex mixture of factors: perverse incentive structures, restrictive social norms, institutional constraints or sheer habit.

16.8 Policies for Sustainable Consumption

Perhaps unsurprisingly, lifestyle change is fast becoming a kind of 'holy grail' for sustainable consumption policy (DEFRA, 2005; Swedish Ministry of Sustainable Development, 2005; UNEP, 2005; DEFRA, 2008,

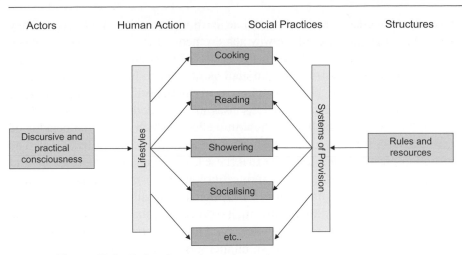

Figure 16.4. *Lifestyles and social practices.*
Source: adapted from Spaargaren and van Vliet (2000).

2012; DECC, 2014). How can we persuade people to behave in more environmentally and socially responsible ways? How can we shift people's transport modes, appliance choices, eating habits, social drinking, leisure practices, holiday plans, lifestyle expectations (and so on) in such a way as to reduce the damaging impact on the environment and on other people? How can we encourage 'sustainable living' and discourage unsustainable living?

These tasks are enormously complex for a variety of reasons. The previous section has highlighted some of these reasons. In particular, the following reasons are clear:

- Lifestyles are a complex aggregation of social practices, the precise nature of which varies widely both within and between population segments.
- Lifestyle practices are interwoven with vital social conversations about status, social affiliation and meaning.
- People often find themselves locked into lifestyle 'choices' by a combination of perverse incentives, institutional rules, habit and deeply engrained social and cultural norms.

In spite of these complexities, it is abundantly clear that lifestyles and consumption patterns do change – indeed, have changed – quite radically over relatively short spaces of time. The uptake of smart phones and mobile apps, 4×4s, digital TV technology, power showers, standby modes in electronic appliances, patio heaters, cheap short-haul holiday flights: these are all examples of technological and behavioural changes which have occurred in the space of only a decade or so in recent Western development. Much further-reaching changes have occurred over only slightly longer time scales.

Several things are significant about these sorts of changes. The first is that many (although not all) of them appear to be in a direction that is moving towards an increase in the energy (and carbon) intensity of lifestyles. They are in fact a part of the reason why achievements in energy efficiency are not matched by overall reductions in the household demand for energy. In this sense, they clearly illustrate how an unconstrained product development market can undermine the best intentions of product-specific policies in one area of that market. Indeed, moral responses are crowded out (Dobson, 2010) through phenomena such as the 'rebound effect', which offsets the benefits of new measures through greater efficiency (Thøgersen and Schrader, 2012). The second interesting point to note is that these kinds of changes represent a kind of 'creeping evolution' of social and technological norms. That is, they occur at a level which is not immediately susceptible to individual control.

This is not to deny that individuals sometimes change their behaviours entirely autonomously. Of course they do. This is illustrated by the emergence of a trend in 'down-shifting' – a spontaneous movement by individuals away from the dominant high-consuming lifestyle and towards voluntary simplicity, exemplified by Transition Towns, ecovillages, Resilience Circles, business barter networks and local currencies, for instance. After the recession in 2009, renting personal assets also became more attractive, leading to the rise of the 'sharing economy': ride sharing, couch surfing and Airbnb, which has reported more than 10 million stays (Schor, 2014). Indeed, the trend towards more resilient forms of economic practice is evident in the growing volume of literature on social enterprises, community investment and corporate social responsibility as well as in the increasing prevalence of the 'sharing economy' within popular culture (Morgan and Kuch, 2015).

Sometimes, moreover, individual behaviour change can initiate new social trends. This is particularly obvious when the individual in question has some kind of celebrity status. The tendency to 'model' our behaviours closely on influential figures around us is a key lesson from social learning theory (Bandura,1977). But it sometimes also occurs from the margins. New mainstream fashions in both clothing and music (for example) are often gleaned from countertrends observed at the margins of society. 'Raiding cool' is one of the new corporate marketing strategies (Klein, 2001; Kotlowitz, 1999).

Those creating and reproducing alternative cultures, often on the fringes of society, make sustainable lifestyle choices as a means of expressing their authenticity. According to Berger (1973), existential authenticity is the state of being in which one is true to oneself and then lives in accord with one's sense of one's self. To be authentic, one must assert his or her will in the choices made when confronted by multiple possibilities (Sartre, 1992). This involves being attuned to one's own experiences rather than interpreting the world through institutionalised concepts and abstractions (Maslow, 1968; Heidegger, 1996). From this definition of authenticity, it may be suggested that self-understanding underlies people's decisions to create and wear unique items of clothing, thereby projecting an 'authentic self' that is in alignment with personal ethical and moral values, as opposed to projecting a 'conformist self', and thereby drawing in the shared possibilities of mainstream consumption.

More often, however, most individuals find themselves responding to societal and technological changes that are initiated elsewhere, at some higher or deeper level. And it is clear from this that we must think of individual behaviour as being 'locked in' not just in a static but also in a dynamic sense. We are locked in to behavioural trends as much as and possibly more than we are locked in to specific behaviours. It is also clear that without policy mechanisms capable of addressing explicitly the underlying trends, it is not going to be a lot of use exhorting individuals to change. Addressing dynamic lock-in is as important as addressing static lock-in.

Conventional responses to issues of behavioural change tend to be based on a particular model of the way that lifestyle choices are made. This 'rational choice' model contends that consumers make decisions by calculating the individual costs and benefits of different courses of action and then choosing the option that maximises their expected net benefits. If it is cheaper for me to travel from A to B by train than by car, I will usually choose to go by train. If it is more costly and time-consuming for me to recycle my household waste than to throw it in the trash, I will tend to do the latter.

There is a familiar and appealing logic to this model. Faced with two clear choices, different in cost but equal in all other respects, it is in my own self-interest to choose the less expensive one. From this perspective, the role of policy appears to be straightforward, namely to ensure that the market allows people to make efficient choices about their own actions.

For the most part, this has been seen as the need to correct for 'market failures'. These failures occur, for example, if consumers have insufficient information to make proper choices. So, according to this view, policy should seek to improve access to information. In addition, private decisions do not always take account of social costs. So on this model, policy intervention is needed to 'internalise' these external costs and make them more 'visible' to private choice.

Sadly, the evidence does not support unrestrained optimism in relation to either of these policy options – at least by themselves. In fact, the history of information and advertising campaigns to promote sustainable behavioural change is littered with failures. In one extreme case, a California utility spent more money on advertising the benefits of home insulation than it would have cost to install the insulation itself in the targeted homes (McKenzie-Mohr, 2000).

The fiscal approach has also faced limited success in encouraging long-term proenvironmental behaviour changes. Although there is evidence to suggest that price differentials (for example) are sometimes successful in persuading people to shift between different fuels, there is much less convincing evidence of the success of economic strategies in improving energy efficiency overall or in shifting behaviours more generally (Verplanken, 2011).

Some have argued that the failure of conventional policy making to foster sustainable behaviours is partly the result of a failure to understand the sheer difficulty associated with changing behaviours. As a review of the residential conservation service – an early energy conservation initiative in the United States – once concluded, most such efforts tend to overlook 'the rich mixture of cultural practices, social interactions, and human feelings that influence the behaviour of individuals, social groups and institutions' (Stern and Aronson, 1984, p. 2). The message is certainly borne out by the overview of modern lifestyles presented in this chapter.

The conclusion to be drawn from this is not that fiscal incentives and information campaigns are irrelevant or inappropriate as policy options to facilitate lifestyle change. People are sometimes self-interested. They do make economic decisions. Their choices are swayed by cost. Adjusting prices to incorporate negative or positive externalities is therefore a legitimate avenue through which to promote proenvironmental or prosocial behaviour and to discourage antisocial or environmentally damaging behaviour. Providing accessible and appropriate information to facilitate proenvironmental choice is also a key avenue for policy.

Social context is key; and it is useful to note that social context is not always a constraining force on behaviour; it can also be empowering. 'Communities of practice' are sites in which behaviours may be learned and reinforced. Wenger (2006) describes these as being formed 'by people who engage in a process of collective learning in a shared domain of human endeavour: a tribe learning to survive, a band of artists seeking new forms of expression, a group of engineers working on similar problems, a clique of pupils defining their identity in the school, a network of surgeons exploring novel techniques, a gathering of first-time managers helping each other cope.' In a nutshell, he suggests, 'communities of practice are groups of people who share a concern or a passion for something they do and learn how to do it better as they interact regularly' (p. 1).

Within dispersed Western communities this tendency towards collaboration forms communities of practice that are not necessarily explicit or formal, may not fit into official teams or social groups and are not limited by geographic proximity. Nevertheless, members are distinguished from nonmembers through competence, and members support each other, share information and develop a shared practice. Mutual engagement in such practices also leads to a shared repertoire of meaning making, which includes 'routines, words, tools, ways of doing things, stories, gestures, symbols, genres, actions or concepts' (Wenger, 1998, p. 83).

Unlike neighbourhood communities in the past, modern communities of practice currently work with the institutions of mass society, occupying various sectors and at various levels of scale, from local groups, to single organisations, partnerships, cities, regions and international communities. New communication technologies such as 'group chats' on social media and remote conferencing through Skype expand the possibility for global communities based on shared practice.

These 'intentional' sites for the initiation and diffusion of alternative practices represent a powerful (if latent) opportunity for lifestyle change. But the evidence does suggest very strongly that these measures are insufficient on their own to facilitate proenvironmental behaviour change of the kind and scale required to meet existing environmental challenges. It is clear from the discussions in the earlier sections of this chapter that achieving lifestyle change demands a sophisticated policy approach, responsive to the social complexity of modern lifestyles. Overcoming lock-in and facilitating alternative avenues of social conversation will be vital. A concerted strategy will be needed to make behaviour change easy for people. This must include the following:

- Ensuring that incentive structures and institutional rules favour more sustainable behaviours
- Enabling access to proenvironmental (and prosocial) lifestyle choices
- Engaging people in initiatives to help themselves
- Exemplifying the desired changes within government's own policies and practices

Most importantly, the evidence suggests that policy plays a vital role in shaping the social context within which we live and act. Governments influence and co-create the culture of consumption in a variety of ways. In some cases, this influence proceeds through specific interventions, such as the imposition of regulatory and fiscal structures. In other cases, it proceeds through the absence of such interventions. Most often, it is a complex combination of the ways in which government does intervene, and the ways in which it chooses not to intervene.

For example, the way in which the energy market was liberalised offers consumers a remarkable choice of energy suppliers who compete vigorously for custom on the basis of the lowest unit price. The same liberalisation process, it could be argued, has actively impeded the development of energy services, by making it difficult (and uncompetitive) for utilities to invest in demand reduction (SDC/UKERC, 2005). At the same time, the UK government has invested millions of pounds in a communications campaign on climate change, and yet it leaves unregulated the advertising of products that threaten the success of its own carbon emission targets.

To take another example, it has been argued that the long-standing failure of successive UK governments to reduce inequalities in the distribution of incomes has the effect of increasing competitive social pressures and reducing affiliative, cooperative and social behaviours (Layard, 2005; James, 1998). Likewise, successive deregulation of retail and trade has tended to erode the cultural space previously afforded by noncommoditised, community-based institutions.

In short, selective policy intervention can have a very significant influence over the institutional and social context of lifestyles. This view of the 'progressive state' (Jackson, 2017) – as a continual mediator and 'co-creator' of the

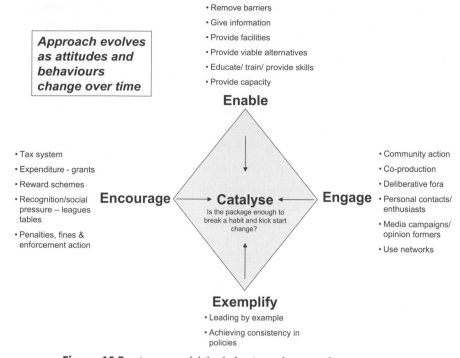

Figure 16.5. *A new model for behaviour change policy.*
Source: *redrawn from DEFRA (2005), chapter 2.*

social and institutional context – opens out a range of possible avenues for policy intervention in pursuit of behavioural change. The complex terrain of human behaviour, as viewed in a social, psychological and cultural context, is not a place devoid of possibilities for state influence. Rather, it is one in which there are numerous possibilities (Figure 16.5) at multiple levels for motivating and encouraging more sustainable lifestyles.

16.9 Conclusions

This chapter has summarised the challenge inherent in recent policy debates about sustainable consumption. It has focussed, in particular, on what might be involved in negotiating the kinds of lifestyle changes that are implied by the radical reductions in carbon emissions required to mitigate climate change.

A preliminary overview of lifestyles in modern society portrays modern lifestyles as being haunted by complexity and paradox. The materiality of our lifestyles – the stuff of everyday living – is deeply woven into the social and psychological fabric of our lives. Our enduring attempts at individuality are confounded by inherently social norms and expectations. Our desire for freedom of choice is continually frustrated by institutional lock-in and force of habit. Our relentless pursuit of the good life is undermined by the breakdown of traditional institutions and the erosion of community and trust.

In these circumstances, the idea of lifestyle change in pursuit of social or environmental goals is immensely challenging. The starting point for any such endeavour has got to be a sophisticated engagement with the material and social basis of lifestyles. This recognition already lies at the heart of commercial consumer engagement strategies. For well over half a century, product designers and marketers have approached the topic of lifestyle in a rigorous and scientific manner: relentlessly unpicking the dimensions of human motivation and desire, carefully exploring the detailed make-up of lifestyle sectors and delving into the dynamics of population segments and social structure.

In one sense, government policy in pursuit of lifestyle change needs to adopt the same rigour. For example, it needs to develop or borrow expertise in lifestyle segmentation analysis and lifestyle sector analysis (Barr, Gilg and Shaw, 2011; Barr and Gilg, 2006; DEFRA, 2008). It needs to build the capability to map (at national, regional and local levels) the resource and environmental implications of different lifestyle sectors and segments – something which the commercial sector has conspicuously avoided doing. And it also needs to be able to develop an understanding of the broader cultural and institutional dynamics which frame these social and material patterns – something which the commercial sector is simply not positioned to do.

It has also been argued that government needs to engage in a more sophisticated way with the dynamics of behavioural change and lifestyle change. The tendency until now has been to fight shy of this difficult terrain and cling to notions of consumer sovereignty and 'hands-off' governance. The evidence reviewed in this chapter suggests that this strategy is neither an accurate reflection of the role of government in lifestyle choice nor particularly helpful. A more useful (and more accurate) view sees government as a 'co-creator' of the culture of consumption, with an integral part to play in negotiating lifestyle change.

One thing is clear from all this: simplistic attempts to exhort consumers to change their behaviours and lifestyles, without taking account of the complexity reviewed here, are almost certainly doomed to failure. On the other hand, the potential for the state to engage creatively in strategies to nurture and support more sustainable ways of life is considerably higher than dominant views of governance often suggest.

Note

1 See, for instance, Martinsson and Lundqvist (2010); Blomquist and Whitehead (1998); Carlsson and Johansson-Stenman (2000); Zelesny, Chua and Aldrich (2000); Jagers (2009). There is a further paradox here. While poverty can lead

to stress, ill-health and addiction, which limit sustainable behaviour (Siegrist, 2000), the high carbon emissions of the most affluent and educated appear to outweigh their more proenvironmental action (Huddart Kennedy, Krahn and Krogman, 2015; Weber and Matthews, 2008; Druckman and Jackson, 2009; Lee, 2010). Understanding the socioeconomic reasons for continued unsustainable behaviour amongst both the wealthy and economically disadvantaged is therefore crucial in developing viable solutions.

16.10 References

Ajzen, I and M Fishbein. 1975. *Belief, Attitude, Intention and Behavior: An Introduction to Theory and Research*. Reading, MA: Addison-Wesley.

American Psychological Association. 2014. *The Road to Resilience*. Available online at: www.apa.org/helpcenter/road-resilience.aspx (accessed 23 December 2015).

Appadurai, A. 1986. *The Social Life of Things: Commodities in Cultural Perspective*. Cambridge: Cambridge University Press.

Bagozzi, R, U Dholakia and S Basuroy. 2003. How Effortful Decisions Get Enacted: The Motivating Role of Decision Processes, Desires, and Anticipated Emotions. *Journal of Behavioural Decision Making* 16, 273–295.

Bandura, A. 1977. *Social Learning Theory*. Englewood Cliffs, NJ: Prentice Hall.

Bandura, A. 1989. Social Cognitive Theory. Chapter 1 in R Vasta (ed.), *Annals of Child Development. Vol. 6. Six Theories of Child Development*. Greenwich, CT: JAI Press, pp. 1–60.

Bandura, A. 2001. Social Cognitive Theory: An Agentic Perspective. *Annual Review of Psychology* 52, 1–26.

Barr, S and A Gilg. 2006. Sustainable Lifestyles: Framing Environmental Action in and Around the Home. *Geoforum* 37, 906–920.

Barr, S, A Gilg and G Shaw. 2011. Citizens, Consumers and Sustainability: (Re)Framing Environmental Practice in an Age of Climate Change. *Global Environmental Change* 21, 1224–1233

Barr, S and P Devine-Wright. 2012. Resilient Communities: Sustainabilities in Transition, Local Environment. *International Journal of Justice and Sustainability* 17, 525–532.

Baudrillard, J. 1970. *The Consumer Society: Myths and Structures*. Reprinted 1998. London: Sage.

Bauman, Z. 1998. *Work, Consumerism and the New Poor*. Buckingham: Open University Press.

Bauman, Z. 2001a. *Liquid Modernity*. Cambridge: Polity Press.

Bauman, Z. 2001b. Consuming Life, *Journal of Consumer Culture* 1, 9–29.

Becker, E. 1973. *The Denial of Death*. New York: Simon and Schuster.

Berger, P. 1967. *The Sacred Canopy – Elements of a Sociological Theory of Religion*. Reprinted 1990. New York: Anchor.

Berger, P. 1973. Sincerity and Authenticity in Modern Society. *Public Interest* 31, 81–90.

Blomquist, G and J Whitehead. 1998. Resource Quality Information and Validity of Willingness to Pay in Contingent Valuation. *Resource and Energy Economics* 20, 179–196.

Blumer, H. 1969. *Symbolic Interactionism: Perspective and Method*. Berkeley: University of California Press.

de Boton, A. 2004. *Status Anxiety*. Oxford: Oxford University Press.

Bourdieu, P. 1984. *Distinction – a Social Critique of the Judgement of Taste*. London: Routledge.

Breakthrough. 2015. *An Ecomodernist Manifesto*. Orlando, CA: Breakthrough Institute.

Breakwell, G. 1986. *Coping with Threatened Identity*. London: Methuen.

Brook Lyndhurst. 2004. *Bad Habits and Hard Choices: in Search of Sustainable Lifestyles*. London: Brook Lyndhurst Ltd.

Burningham, K and D Thrush. 2000. *Rainforests Are a Long Way from Here: The Environmental Concerns of Disadvantaged Groups*. London: Report to the Joseph Rowntree Foundation.

Cabinet Office. 2010. *Mindspace: Influencing Behaviour Through Public Policy: A Practical Guide*. London: Institute for Government. Online at: www.institute forgovernment.org.uk/sites/default/files/publications/MINDSPACE-Practical-guide-final-Web_1.pdf (accessed 11 June 2015).

Camic, C. 1986. The Matter of Habit. *American Journal of Sociology* 91, 1039–1087.

Campbell, C. 2004. I Shop, Therefore I Know That I Am: The Metaphysical Basis of Modern Consumerism, in K Ekstrom and H Brembeck (eds.), *Elusive Consumption: Tracking New Research Perspectives*. Oxford: Berg, pp. 27–44.

Campbell, C. 2015. The Curse of the New: How the Accelerating Pursuit of the New Is Driving Hyper-Consumption. Chapter 2 in K Ekström (ed.), *Waste Management and Sustainable Consumption: Reflections on Consumer Waste*. London: Routledge, pp. 29–52.

Carlsson, F and O Johansson-Stenman. 2000. Willingness to Pay for Improved Air Quality in Sweden. *Applied Economics* 32, 661–669.

Chambers, R and G Conway. 1992. Sustainable Rural Livelihoods: Practical Concepts for the 21st Century. Institution of Development Studies (IDS) discussion paper; No 296. Brighton: IDS.

Chaney, D. 1996. *Lifestyles*. London: Routledge.

Csikszentmihalyi, M. 2000. The Costs and Benefits of Consuming. *Journal of Consumer Research* 27, 267–272.

Csikszentmihalyi, M and E Rochberg-Halton. 1981. *The Meaning of Things: Domestic Symbols and the Self*. Cambridge and New York: Cambridge University Press.

Daly, H 2009. Three Anathemas on Limiting Economic Growth. *Conservation Biology* 23, 252–253.

Daly, H and J Cobb. 1989. *For the Common Good: Redirecting the Economy Towards Community, the Environment and a Sustainable Future*. Boston: Beacon Press.

DECC (Department of Energy and Climate Change). 2014. Understanding the Behaviours of Households in Fuel Poverty: A Review of Research Evidence. Online at: www.gov.uk/government/uploads/system/uploads/attachment_data/file/332122/understanding_behaviours_households_fuel_poverty_review_of_research_evidence.pdf (accessed 27 January 2017).

Deci, E 1971. Effects of Externally Mediated Rewards on Intrinsic Motivation. *Journal of Personality and Social Psychology* 18, 105–115.

Deci, E and R Ryan 2002. *Handbook of Self-Determination Research*. Rochester, NY: University of Rochester Press.

DEFRA (Department of Environment, Food and Rural Affairs). 2005. *Securing the Future: Delivering UK Sustainable Development Strategy*. London: Stationery Office.

DEFRA. 2003. *Changing Patterns: the UK Sustainable Consumption and Production Framework*. London: TSO.

DEFRA. 2008. *Framework for Pro-Environmental Behaviours*. London, DEFRA. Online at: www.defra.gov.uk (accessed 10 June 2015).

DEFRA. 2012. Getting the Message Across: The Role of Social Enterprises as Inspirers of Sustainable Living. Online at: sd.defra.gov.uk/documents/Defra-SESP-Getting-the-message-across-Sep2012.pdf (accessed 26 January 2017).

DETR. (Department of Employment, Training and Rehabilitation) 1999. Towards a Better Quality of Life. London: The Stationery Office.

DfID (Department for International Development). 2006. *Sustainable Livelihoods Guidance Sheets.* London: DfID. Online at: www.livelihoods.org/info/info_guidancesheets.html (accessed 20 July 2006).

Dittmar, H 1992. *The Social Psychology of Material Possessions: To Have Is to Be*, New York: St Martin's Press.

Dobson, A. 2010. Environmental Citizenship and Pro-Environmental Behaviour: Rapid Research and Evidence Review, Sustainable Development Research Network. Online at: www.sd-research.org.uk/post.php?p=1229 (accessed 11 June 2015).

Douglas, M. 1976. Relative Poverty, Relative Communication, in A Halsey (ed.), *Traditions of Social Policy*, Oxford: Basil Blackwell, p. 357.

Douglas, M and B Isherwood. 1979. *The World of Goods: Towards an Anthropology of Consumption*. Reprinted 1996. London and New York: Routledge.

Douthwaite, R. 1992. *The Growth Illusion*. Bideford, Devon: Green Books.

Doyal, L and I Gough. 1991. *A Theory of Human Need.* New York: Guilford Press.

Druckman, A and T Jackson. 2009. The Carbon Footprint of UK Households 1990–2004: A Socioeconomically Disaggregated Quasi-Multi-Regional Input-Output Model. *Ecological Economics* 68, 2066–2077.

Dunlap, R and K van Liere. 1978. The New Environmental Paradigm – a Proposed Measuring Instrument and Preliminary Results. *Journal of Environmental Education* 9, 10–19.

Easterlin, R. 1974. Does Economic Growth Improve the Human Lot? Some Empirical Evidence. Online from: huwdixon.org/teaching/cei/Easterlin1974.pdf (accessed 27 January 2017).

The Economist. 2004. The Economist Intelligence Unit's Quality of Life Index. *Economist Online*. Online at: www.economist.com/media/pdf/QUALITY_OF_LIFE.pdf (accessed 27 January 2017).

Elliott, R and Wattanasuwan, K. 1998. Consumption and the Symbolic Project of the Self. *European Advances in Consumer Research*, 3, 17–20.

Engler, B. 2009. *Personality Theories.* 8th Edition. Boston, MA: Houghton Mifflin.

Etzioni, A. 1998. Voluntary Simplicity: Characterization, Select Psychological Implications and Societal Consequences, *Journal of Economic Psychology* 19, 619–643.

Evans, D and T Jackson. 2007. Towards a Sociology of Sustainable Lifestyles. RESOLVE Working Paper Series 03-07, University of Surrey.

Featherstone, M. 1990. *Consumer Culture and Post-Modernism*. London: Sage.

Frank, R. 1999. *Luxury Fever*. Princeton, NJ: Princeton University Press.

Fromm, E. 1976. *To Have or to Be?* London: Jonathon Cape.

Füchs, R. 2015. *Green Growth, Smart Growth: A New Approach to Economics, Innovation and the Environment*. London: Anthem Press.

Gazzaniga, M. 2010. *The Cognitive Neurosciences*. 4th Edition. Cambridge, MA: MIT Press.

Giddens, A. 1984. *The Constitution of Society: Outline of the Theory of Structuration*. Berkeley and Los Angeles: University of California Press.

Giddens, A. 1991. *Modernity and Self-Identity: Self and Society in the Late Modern Age*, Cambridge: Polity Press.

Greenberg, J, T Pyszczynski and S Solomon. 1986. The Causes and Consequences of a Need for Self-Esteem: A Terror Management Theory. Chapter 10 in R Baumeister (ed.), *Public Self and Private Self*. New York: Springer, pp. 189–212.

Gronow, J and A Warde. 2001. *Ordinary Consumption*. Routledge, London.

Guy, S and E Shove. 2000. *A Sociology of Energy, Buildings and the Environment: Constructing Knowledge, Designing Practice*. London: Routledge.

Haig, M. 2003. *Brand Failures: The Truth About the 100 Biggest Branding Mistakes of All Time*. London: Kogan Page.

Hammer, M. 2009. Suburban Survivalists Stock Up for Armageddon. *Today News*. Online at: www.today.com/id/32108020/ns/today-today_people/#.V9k6YIdwaUk (accessed 9 September 2016).

Hargreaves, T. 2011. Practiceing Behaviour Change: Applying Social Practice Theory to Pro-Environmental Behaviour Change. *Journal of Consumer Culture* 11, 79–99.

Haslam, A. 2001. *Psychology in Organizations*. London: SAGE Publications.

Heidegger, M. 1996. *Being and Time*. Albany: State University of New York Press.

Hirschman, E and M Holbrook (eds.). 1980. *Symbolic Consumer Behaviour, Proceedings of the Conference on Consumer Aesthetics and Symbolic Consumption*, New York: Association for Consumer Research.

Holdsworth, M. 2003. *Green Choice: What Choice? Summary of NCC Research into Consumer Attitudes to Sustainable Consumption*. London: National Consumer Council.

Holdsworth, M. 2005. *Sixteen Pain-Free Ways to Help Save the Planet*. London: National Consumer Council.

Huddart Kennedy, E, H Krahn and N Krogman. 2015. Are We Counting What Counts? A Closer Look at Environmental Concern, Pro-Environmental Behaviour, and Carbon Footprint. *Local Environment: The International Journal of Justice and Sustainability* 20, 220–236.

Illich, I. 1977. *Towards a History of Needs*, New York: Pantheon.

Inglehart, R. 1991. *Culture Shift in Advanced Modern Society*. Princeton, NJ: Princeton University Press.

Inglehart, R, R Foa, C Peterson and C Welzel. 2008. Development, Freedom and Rising Happiness: A Global Perspective (1981–2007). *Perspectives on Psychological Science* 3(4): 264–285.

Inglehart, R R Inglehart and H-D Klingemann. 2000. *Genes, Culture and Happiness*. Boston: MIT Press.

Jackson, T. 2002. Evolutionary Psychology and Ecological Economics: Consilience, Consumption and Contentment. *Ecological Economics* 4, 289–303.

Jackson, T. 2004. *Chasing Progress: Beyond Measuring Economic Growth.* London: New Economics Foundation.

Jackson, T. 2005. Live Better by Consuming Less? Is There a 'Double Dividend' in Sustainable Consumption? *Journal of Industrial Ecology* 9, 19–36.

Jackson, T. 2006. Consuming Paradise? Towards a Socio-Cultural Psychology of Sustainable Consumption. Chapter 24 in T Jackson (ed.), *Earthscan Reader in Sustainable Consumption.* London: Earthscan, pp. 367–402.

Jackson, T. 2013a. *Where Is the 'Wellbeing Dividend'? Nature, Structure and Consumption Inequalities.* Reprinted as chapter 50 in: Victor, P (ed.) 2013 *The Costs of Economic Growth,* Cheltenham: Edward Elgar, pp. 772–791.

Jackson, T. 2013b. *Angst essen Seele auf:* Escaping the 'Iron Cage' of Consumerism. Chapter 2 in U Schneidewind, T Santarius and A Humburg (eds.), *The Economy of Sufficiency.* Wuppertal: Wuppertal Institute for Climate, Environment and Energy, pp. 53–68. Online at: www.sustainablelifestyles.ac.uk/sites/default/files/newsdocs/tj_2014_-_angste_essen_seele_auf_in-_ws_48.pdf (accessed 11 January 2017).

Jackson, T. 2017. *Prosperity Without Growth: Foundations for the Economy of Tomorrow.* London: Routledge.

Jackson, T, W Jager and S Stagl. 2004. Beyond Insatiability: Needs Theory and Sustainable Consumption. Chapter 5 in L Reisch and I Røpke (eds.), *Consumption: Perspectives from Ecological Economics.* Cheltenham: Edward Elgar, pp. 79–110.

Jackson, T and L Michaelis. 2003. Policies for Sustainable Consumption: A Report for the UK Sustainable Development Commission, London. Online at: www.sd-commission.org.uk/publications/downloads/Policies_sust_consumption (accessed 26 January 2017).

Jagers, S. 2009. In Search of the Ecological Citizen. *Environmental Politics* 18, 18–36.

James, O. 1998. *Britain on the Couch: Why We're Unhappier Compared to 1950 Despite Being Richer.* London: Arrow.

Kahneman, D. 1973. *Attention and Effort.* Englewood Cliffs, NJ: Prentice Hall.

Kasser, T. 2002. *The High Price of Materialism.* Cambridge, MA: MIT Press.

Klein, G. 2003. *Life Lines: The NCC's Agenda for Affordable Energy, Water and Telephone Services.* London: National Consumer Council.

Klein, N. 2001. *No Logo.* London, Flamingo.

Klohnen, E. 1996. Conceptual Analysis and Measurement of the Construct of Ego-Resiliency. *Journal of Personality and Social Psychology* 70, 1067–1079.

Kotlowitz, A 1999. False Connections. In R Rosenblatt (ed.), *Consuming Desires: Consumption, Culture and the Pursuit of Happiness.* Washington, DC: Island Press. Reproduced as chapter 10 in Jackson, 2006, pp. 146–151.

Layard, R. 2005. *Happiness: Lessons from a New Science.* London: Allen Lane.

Leadbeater, B, D Dodgen and A Solarz. 2005. The Resilience Revolution: A Paradigm Shift for Research and Policy. Chapter 4 in R D Peters R B Leadbeater and R McMahon (eds.), *Resilience in Children, Families, and Communities: Linking Context to Practice and Policy.* New York: Kluwer, pp. 47–63.

Lee, M. 2010. *By Our Own Emissions: The Distribution of GHGs in B.C.* Vancouver, BC: Canadian Centre for Policy Alternatives.

Martinsson, J and L Lundqvist. 2010. Ecological Citizenship: Coming Out 'Clean' Without Turning 'Green'? *Environmental Politics* 19, 518–537.

Maslow, A. 1954. *Motivation and Personality*. New York: Harper & Row.

Maslow, A. 1968. *Toward a Psychology of Being*. 2nd Edition. Princeton, NJ: Van Nostrand

Maslow, A. 1996. Critique of Self-Actualization Theory. Chapter 3 in E Hoffman (ed.), *Future Visions: The Unpublished Papers of Abraham Maslow*. Thousand Oaks, CA: Sage, pp. 26–33.

Max-Neef, M. 1991. *Human-Scale Development: Conception, Application and Further Reflection*. London: Apex Press.

McCracken, G. 1989. *The Culture of Consumption*. Bloomington and Indianapolis: Indiana University Press.

McKenzie-Mohr, D. 2000. Promoting Sustainable Behavior: An Introduction to Community-based Social Marketing. *Journal of Social Issues* 56, 543–554.

Mead, G. 1934. *Mind Self and Society*. Chicago: University of Chicago Press.

Met Office. 2015. Summer 2015. Online at: www.metoffice.gov.uk/climate/uk/summaries/2015/summer (accessed 27 January 2017).

Morgan, B and D Kuch. 2015. Radical Transactionalism: Legal Consciousness, Diverse Economies, and the Sharing Economy. *Journal of Law and Society*, 42, 556–587.

NEF (New Economics Foundation). 2004. *A Wellbeing Manifesto for a Flourishing Society*. London: New Economics Foundation.

Nussbaum, M. 1998. The Good as Discipline, the Good as Freedom. Chapter 17 in D Crocker and T Linden (eds.), *The Ethics of Consumption*, New York: Rowman and Littlefield, 312–341.

Offer, A. 2006. *The Challenge of Affluence: Self-Control and Well-Being in the United States and Britain Since 1950*. Oxford: Oxford University Press.

Oxfam. 2006. Sustainable Livelihoods – Introduction. Online at: www.oxfam.org.uk/what_we_do/issues/livelihoods/introduction.htm (accessed 20 July 2006).

Paterson, M. 2003. *Anthropology and Mass Communication: Media and Myth in the New Millennium*. Oxford: Bergahn.

Ridley, R. 1994. The Psychology of Perseverative and Stereotyped Behaviour. *Progress in Neurobiology*, 44(2), 221–231.

Ritzer, G. 2001. *Explorations in the Sociology of Consumption*. London: Sage.

Roberts, K. 2004. *Lovemarks: The Future Beyond Brands*. London: Saatchi and Saatchi.

Rutter, M. 2008. Developing Concepts in Developmental Psychopathology. Chapter 1 in J Hudziak (ed.), *Developmental Psychopathology and Wellness: Genetic and Environmental Influences*. Washington, DC: American Psychiatric Publishing, pp. 3–23.

Sanne, C. 2002. Willing Consumers: or Locked In? Policies for a Sustainable Consumption. *Ecological Economics* 42, 273–287.

Sartre, P. 1992. *Truth and Existence*. Chicago: University of Chicago Press

Schor, J. 1998. *The Overspent American: Why We Want What We Don't Need*. New York: Basic Books.

Schor, J. 2010. *Plenitude: the New Economics of True Wealth*. New York: Penguin.

Schor, J. 2014. *Debating the Sharing Economy*, Great Transition. Online at: www.great transition.org/publication/debating-the-sharing-economy (accessed 12 June 2015).

SDC/NNC (Sustainable Development Commission/National Consumer Council). 2006. *I Will If You Will: Towards Sustainable Consumption*. Online at: www.sd-commission.org.uk/data/files/publications/I_Will_If_You_Will.pdf (accessed 27 January 2017).

SDC/UKERC (UK Energy Research Centre). 2005. Unlocking Energy Services: Main Findings of a Joint SDC/UKERC Seminar. Online at: ukerc.rl.ac.uk/UCAT/ PUBLICATIONS/Unlocking_Energy_Services_Main_Findings_of_a_ Joint_SDC-UKERC_Seminar.pdf (accessed 27 January 2017).

Sen, A. 1985. *Commodities and Capabilities*. Amsterdam: Elsevier.

Shove, E. 2003. *Comfort, Cleanliness and Convenience: the Social Organisation of Normality*. London: Routledge.

Siegrist, J. 2000. Place, Social Exchange and Health: Proposed Sociological Framework. *Social Science and Medicine* 51, 1283–1293.

Simmel, G. 1971. The Metropolis and Mental Life. In D Levine (ed.), *On Individuality and Social Forms: Selected Writings*. Chicago: University of Chicago Press, pp. 324–339.

Simon, H. 1971. Designing Organizations for an Information-Rich World. In M Greenberger (ed.), *Computers, Communications, and the Public Interest*. Baltimore, MD: Johns Hopkins Press, 37–72.

Skidelsky, E and R Skidelsky. 2013. *How Much Is Enough? Money and the Good Life*. New York: Penguin.

Snyder, C, K Rand and D Sigmon. 2005. Hope Theory, a Member of the Positive Psychology Family. Chapter 19 in C Snyder and S Lopez (eds.), *The Handbook of Positive Psychology*. New York: Oxford University Press, pp. 257–278.

Solomon, S, J Greenberg and T Pyszczynski. 2014. *The Worm at the Core: On the Role of Death in Life*. London: Penguin.

Southerton, D, A Warde and M Hand. 2004. The Limited Autonomy of the Consumer: Implications for Sustainable Consumption. Chapter 3 in D Southerton H Chappells and B Van Vliet (eds.), *Sustainable Consumption: The Implications of Changing Infrastructures of Provision*. Cheltenham: Edward Elgar, pp. 32–48.

Spaargaren, G and B Van Vliet. 2000. Lifestyles, Consumption and the Environment: The Ecological Modernisation of Domestic Consumption. *Environmental Politics* 9, 50–76.

Sterling, P. 2016. Why We Consume: Neural Design and Sustainability: A Great Transition Viewpoint. Great Transition Network. Online at: www.great transition.org/publication/why-we-consume (accessed 13 January 2017).

Stern, P and Aronson E. 1984. *Energy Use – the Human Dimension*. New York: Freeman.

Swedish Ministry of Sustainable Development. 2005. International Task Force on Sustainable Lifestyles. Memorandum, 25 August 2005. Ministry of Sustainable Development, Stockholm. Online at: www.uneptie.org/pc/sustain/resources/ MTF/Sweden%20TF%20Sust.Lifestyles.pdf (accessed 17 July 2006).

Tajfel, H and J Turner. 1979. An Integrative Theory of Intergroup Conflict. In S Worchel and W Austin (eds.), *The Social Psychology of Intergroup Relations*. Monterey, CA: Brooks/Cole, pp. 33–47.

Thøgersen, J and U Schrader. 2012. From Knowledge to Action: New Paths Towards Sustainable Consumption. *Journal of Consumer Policy Consumer Issues in Law, Economics and Behavioural Sciences* 35(9188), 1–5.

Thompson, S, N Marks, and T Jackson. 2013: Well-Being and Sustainable Development. In: S David I Boniwell and A Conley (eds.), *Oxford Handbook of Happiness*,. Oxford: Oxford University Press, pp.498–517.

Turner, J, M Hogg, P Oakes and M Wetherell. 1987. *Re-Discovering the Social Group: A Self-Categorization Theory*. Oxford: Basil Blackwell.

Tversky, A and D Kahneman. 1974. Judgement Under Uncertainty: Heuristics and Biases. *Science* 185, 1124–1131.

UNCED (United Nations Conference on Environment and Development). 1992. Agenda 21. Online at: sustainabledevelopment.un.org/content/documents/Agenda21.pdf (accessed 27 January 2017).

UNEP (United Nations Environment Programme). 2001. *Consumption Opportunities: Strategies for Change*. Paris: United Nations Environment Programme.

UNEP. 2005. *Talk the Walk? Advancing Sustainable Lifestyles Through Marketing and Communications*. Paris: UNEP/UN Global Compact/Utopies.

UNEP. 2012. *Global Outlook on Sustainable Consumption and Production Policies: Taking Action Together*. Paris: UNEP. Online at: www.unep.org/publications/contents/pub_details_search.asp?ID=6251 (accessed 13 January 2017).

UN FCCC (United Nations Framework Convention on Climate Change). 2015. Paris Agreement December 12th Draft. Online at: unfccc.int/resource/docs/2015/cop21/eng/l09.pdf (accessed 13 January 2017).

Verplanken, B. 2011. Towards More Sustainable Lifestyles: Nudges, Edges, and Opportunities. Institute for Sustainable Energy and the Environment (I-SEE) Seminar Lecture. Online at: www.bath.ac.uk/i-see/pastseminars.html (accessed 11 June 2015).

Verplanken, B and W Wood. 2006. Interventions to Break and Create Consumer Habits. *American Marketing Association,* 25(1), 1547–7207.

Victor, P. 2008. *Managing Without Growth: Slower by Design, not Disaster*. Cheltenham: Edward Elgar.

Wachtel, P. 1983. *The Poverty of Affluence – a Psychological Portrait of the American Way of Life*. New York: Free Press.

Weber, M. 1930. *The Protestant Ethic and the Spirit of Capitalism*. Reprinted 1992/2004. London: Routledge.

Weber, C and H Matthews. 2008. Quantifying the Global and Distributional Aspects of American Household Carbon Footprint. *Ecological Economics* 68, 379–391.

Weitzman, M. 1976. On the Welfare Significance of the National Product in a Dynamic Economy. *Quarterly Journal of Economics* 90, 156–162.

Wenger, E. 1998. *Communities of Practice: Learning, Meaning and Identity*. Cambridge: Cambridge University Press.

Wenger, E. 2006. Communities of Practice: A Brief Introduction. Online at: www.ewenger.com/theory/index.html (accessed 11 June 2015).

Wicklund, R and P Gollwitzer. 1982. *Symbolic Self-Completion*. Hillsdale, NJ: Erlbaum.

Wilhite, H, H Nakagami, T Masuda and Y Yamaga. 1996. A Cross-cultural Analysis of Household Energy Use in Japan and Norway, *Energy Policy* 24(9), 795–803.

Wright, R. 1994. *The Moral Animal: Why We Are the Way We Are*. New York: Vintage.

Zelesny, L, P Chua and C Aldrich. 2000. Elaborating on Gender Differences in Environmentalism. *Journal of Social Issues* 56(3), 443–457.

17 Understanding Residential Sustainable Energy Behaviour and Policy Preferences

Goda Perlaviciute, Linda Steg and Ellen van der Werff

17.1 Introduction

Energy production and use account for two-thirds of the world's greenhouse gas emissions (IEA, 2015), thereby contributing to global climate change (IPCC, 2014). Besides environmental problems, energy production and use pose societal challenges, including energy poverty and geopolitics of energy that threaten global security and prosperity. The Paris Agreement marks a historic event when countries worldwide committed to combat climate change. To achieve these ambitious targets, countries will have to shift towards more sustainable ways of producing and using energy (EC, 2016a).

The residential sector accounts for about 20 to 25 per cent of the total energy consumption in European Union (EU) countries (Eurostat, 2014a) and Organisation for Economic Cooperation and Development (OECD) countries (IEA, 2015). If households used cleaner energy and engaged in more sustainable energy behaviours, this could significantly contribute to combating climate change (Nature Energy, 2016; Stern et al., 2016a). But which factors influence whether individuals and households act sustainably and whether they accept sustainable solutions, such as renewable energy projects? Social sciences have an important role to play in answering these questions (Clayton et al., 2015; Hackmann, Moser and Clair, 2014; Sovacool, 2014; Stern, Sovacool and Dietz, 2016b; Weaver et al., 2014). In this chapter, we take the Integrated Framework for Encouraging Pro-Environmental Behaviour (IFEP; Steg et al., 2014a) as a starting point for understanding and encouraging sustainable energy behaviour and acceptability of sustainable energy projects. More specifically, we argue that people's values influence the likelihood that people will engage in many different sustainable energy behaviours as well as influencing public acceptability of sustainable energy projects. In addition, the IFEP proposes that contextual factors affect the likelihood that people consider environmental consequences of their choices. We review cutting edge psychological literature on factors influencing sustainable energy behaviour and the acceptability of sustainable energy projects from the view of this framework.[1] Notably, sustainable energy projects often introduce new technology and/or require behavioural change, so similar factors are likely to influence sustainable energy behaviours and acceptability of sustainable energy projects. Next, we discuss intervention strategies aimed at promoting sustainable energy behaviour and acceptability of sustainable energy projects. The interventions can change the context to enable and empower people to act sustainably, they can provide information and arguments to help people and motivate them to make sustainable choices and they can motivate people to act consistently. Finally, we discuss how factors related to the implementation of energy projects – in particular, fairness of procedures and people's trust in involved parties – influence public acceptability of these projects. We start with outlining the large variety of sustainable energy behaviours that people need to engage in to realise a truly sustainable energy transition.

17.2 Sustainable energy behaviour

Sustainable energy systems will rely more on low-carbon energy sources, particularly on renewable energy sources such as solar and wind power and hydroenergy, and less on fossil fuels, such as coal, oil and natural gas. The EU aims to raise the share of renewable energy sources to at least 27 per cent by 2030 (EC, 2016b). Currently, households in EU rely to a large extent on fossil fuels, especially natural gas, for their daily energy needs (Eurostat, 2014b). The adoption and use of renewable energy sources and technologies, including public acceptability of renewable energy projects (e.g., wind farms, hydropower plants), are important preconditions for realising a sustainable energy transition.

Shifting to renewable energy sources implies changes in energy systems. For example, energy production will be decentralised and energy supply may be intermittent because availability of wind and solar energy depends on weather conditions. To increase efficiency of renewable energy systems, people need to change their behaviour to reduce their overall energy demand and to match energy demand to availability of energy produced from renewable sources. Energy demand can be reduced by means of energy-efficient technology and energy retrofits in homes, for example replacing heating, ventilation and air conditioning appliances with energy-efficient models, insulating homes and installing water-saving appliances. In parallel, people can adjust their daily behaviours, for example reducing showering times, lowering the heating, turning off lights and appliances not in use and refraining from certain behaviours such as taking a bath. Besides direct energy use, also indirect energy use could be reduced in order to promote a sustainable energy transition. Indirect or 'embodied' energy use refers to the energy required for the production, transportation and disposal of goods and services used by households (Kok, Benders and Moll, 2006; Reinders, Vringer and Blok, 2003). To adjust energy demand to availability of energy supply, households can shift energy use in time, either by themselves or by installing technologies that automatically switch off or on specific appliances in peak or off-peak times (Van der Werff,

Perlaviciute and Steg, 2016). In addition, people could adopt storage technologies such as batteries and electric cars to store surpluses of renewable energy and secure energy supply when renewable energy production is low (Dunn, Kamath and Tarascon, 2011).

In sum, to realise a sustainable energy transition, people could engage in many different behaviours, including (1) adopting and using low-carbon energy sources and technologies, (2) investing in energy efficiency retrofits for buildings, (3) adopting and using energy efficient appliances and (4) changing energy use behaviour as to reduce overall energy use and match energy demand to the available supply from renewables (Steg et al., 2015; Stern et al., 2016a; Van der Werff et al., 2016).[2] An important question is how different energy behaviours are related and to what extent engagement in one sustainable energy behaviour reduces or increases the likelihood of engaging in a subsequent sustainable energy behaviour, phenomena known as negative or positive spillover, respectively. Some studies have found evidence for negative spillover effects. For example, people were more likely to increase their energy consumption after reducing their water use (Tiefenbeck et al., 2013), and people who reduced their electricity consumption as a result of time-off-use tariffs were less likely to adopt energy efficiency measures at home (McCoy and Lyons, 2016). Such effects have been attributed by some to people's feeling that engagement in one sustainable behaviour legitimates not acting sustainably in another occasion (Kaklamanou et al., 2015). Yet, other studies have found positive spillover effects. For example, individuals who recycled were more likely to buy organic food and use environmentally friendly modes of transport one and two years later (Thøgersen and Ölander 2003). Also, green buying promoted subsequent recycling, the use of public transport, carpooling, printing on both sides, saving water, and switching off lights (Lanzini and Thøgersen 2014). Research suggests that positive spillover effects are more likely when people see themselves as environmentally friendly persons, that is, when their environmental self-identity is strong (Van der Werff, Steg and Keizer, 2013, 2014a, b). Specifically, when people see themselves as energy saving and proenvironmental persons, they are motivated to engage in sustainable behaviours in subsequent situations as they want to be or appear consistent.

Which factors influence the extent to which people are willing to engage in many different sustainable energy behaviours and accept sustainable energy projects? Studies suggest that the (perceived) risks, costs and benefits of sustainable energy behaviours and energy projects influence people's actions and acceptability judgements; we review the relevant findings later in this chapter. Importantly, a truly sustainable energy transition requires changes in a wide range of energy behaviours and acceptability of different energy projects. This requires insights into general factors that can explain many different behaviours and acceptability judgements. Based on the IFEP, we argue that people's values and contextual factors play an important role in this respect, as we will explain in this chapter.

17.3 Perceived Risks, Cost and Benefits

People are more likely to engage in energy behaviours and accept energy projects that are seen as having more benefits, less costs and fewer risks. People consider individual as well as collective risks, costs and benefits in their decisions. Additionally, the distribution of these risks, costs and benefits affect people's behaviours and acceptability judgements.

17.3.1 Individual Risks, Costs and Benefits

Individual risks, costs and benefits reflect consequences that affect people's self-interest, for example financial costs, time, pleasure and comfort. People are more likely to engage in sustainable energy behaviours which they believe, have relatively low individual costs and high individual benefits, resulting in overall positive evaluations of the relevant actions. For example, people are more likely to invest in energy-efficiency measures, such as insulation, when they expect financial benefits (rather than costs) and an increase (rather than a decrease) in their daily comfort from such investments (Kastner and Stern, 2015). People may expect renewable energy technology to be costly, which could hinder adoption of such technology. Similarly, expected personal costs such as higher energy bills may hinder the acceptability of renewable energy projects (Leijten et al. 2014; Perlaviciute and Steg, 2014). Similarly, the more concerned people were about energy affordability, the less acceptable they found demand-side management measures in renewable energy systems, such as technology that automatically turns appliances off and on (Spence et al., 2015). Yet, people do not always engage in energy behaviours with the lowest financial costs and the highest financial gains. Indeed, people may not invest in energy-efficiency measures even if this would cut down energy costs in the long run (Darby, 2010; Frederiks, Stenner and Hobman, 2015). People take various other types of costs, risks and benefits into account, and, as we will explain later in this chapter, individual and contextual factors influence which consequences are considered and how people weigh these different costs, risks and benefits.

People are less likely to engage in sustainable energy behaviours and to accept sustainable energy projects if they see such actions as a hassle and as a burden on their daily comfort. This may explain why people sometimes prefer adopting energy-efficient technologies over changing their behaviours to save energy (Poortinga et al., 2003; Steg, Dreijerink and Abrahamse, 2006): the former may be seen as less effortful and demanding than the latter. Furthermore, privacy concerns may inhibit adoption and/or acceptability of sustainability measures, such as energy use monitoring technology at people's homes (Hess, 2014; Krishnamurti et al., 2012). Yet, a study found that privacy concerns were most prominent when people anticipated negative individual consequences (e.g., higher financial costs) from implementing the monitoring technology, while privacy concerns were less strong when people expected to benefit from adopting the technology (Bolderdijk, Steg and Postmes, 2013a).

Besides, people also take into account social costs and benefits. People are more likely to engage in sustainable energy behaviours when they expect that others would approve of them (Harland, Staats and Wilke, 1999; Schultz et al., 2007) and when they think that others engage in these behaviours too (Nolan, Schultz, Cialdini, Goldstein and Griskevicius, 2008). Yet, this is not always the case (Abrahamse and Steg, 2011; Midden and Ritsema, 1983) and may depend on other factors, for example whether people learn about the behaviour from others in face-to-face interactions or anonymously and the extent to which others actually act sustainably (Abrahamse and Steg, 2013). People may also engage in sustainable energy behaviour when they expect that doing so enhances their status, particularly when the behaviour is somewhat costly, as in this case the behaviour signals to others that people have sufficient resources to make altruistic sacrifices (Griskevicius, Tybur and Van den Bergh, 2010). Indeed, people were more likely to accept sustainable energy innovations, such as electric cars and (smart) renewable energy systems, when they evaluated the symbolic aspects of these innovations favourably, that is, when they believed these innovations signal something positive about the owner or user to others and themselves (Noppers et al., 2014, 2015, 2016). Positive symbolic outcomes may thus encourage people to adopt sustainable innovations, even though such innovations may still have some instrumental drawbacks, which is often the case in the early introduction phases. In fact, evaluations of the symbolic aspects of sustainable energy innovations more strongly predicted interest in such innovations when people thought the innovations have some instrumental drawbacks, probably because these drawbacks enhance the signalling function of the relevant behaviour (Noppers et al., 2014, 2015). When engaging in sustainable energy behaviour is somewhat costly or effortful, it is more likely to signal that people care about others and the environment than when it is very easy, convenient or profitable (Van der Werff et al., 2014a).

17.3.2 Collective Risks, Costs and Benefits

Besides individual consequences, people consider collective consequences of their choices, including consequences for others and the environment. Many people care about the environment, and take environmental considerations into account when they make decisions (Steg and De Groot, 2012). People are motivated to see themselves as morally right, which may encourage sustainable energy behaviours, as this indicates that one is doing the right thing (Bolderdijk et al., 2013b). Several studies revealed that moral, and more specifically environmental, considerations affect sustainable energy behaviour, such as using energy-saving light bulbs and reducing meat consumption (Harland et al., 1999), electricity saving at work (Zhang, Wang and Zhou, 2013), energy-saving behaviours at home (Van der Werff and Steg, 2015) and participation in smart energy systems (Van der Werff and Steg, 2015), sustainable energy behaviours at work (Ruepert et al., 2016), investments in energy-efficiency measures (Kastner and Stern, 2015), as well as acceptability of energy projects, such as (further) development of nuclear energy (De Groot and Steg, 2010; Steg and De Groot, 2010) and pricing policies to foster sustainable energy use (Steg, Dreijerink and Abrahamse, 2005). Acceptability of energy policies is higher when people are more aware of energy problems and feel morally obliged to reduce these problems (Steg et al., 2005). Interestingly, engaging in sustainable energy behaviour may make people feel good because they derive pleasure and satisfaction from doing the right thing and doing something meaningful (Bolderdijk et al., 2013b; Venhoeven, Bolderdijk and Steg, 2013; Taufik, Bolderdijk and Steg, 2015). Engaging in sustainable energy behaviour may promote eudaimonic well-being, which is derived from leading a good life and pursuing the right goals (Venhoeven et al., 2013). People may even physically feel warmer by engaging in sustainable energy behaviour; this phenomenon is known as a warm-glow effect (Taufik et al., 2015).

17.3.3 Distribution of Risks, Costs and Benefits

Energy projects aimed at fostering a sustainable energy transition can be seen as unfair (and hence less acceptable) if they are perceived as benefitting some groups in society while burdening other groups (Schuitema and Jakobsson Bergstad, 2012; Sovacool et al., 2016). For example, communities hosting renewable energy projects such as wind farms may experience noise and spoiled views, while the possible benefits, such as reduced CO_2 emissions, affordable energy and energy independence are shared on a national or even global scale. As a consequence, people may be reluctant to accept such projects (Huijts, Molin and Steg, 2012; Perlaviciute and Steg, 2014). When judging the perceived fairness and acceptability of sustainability policies, people also take into account the consequences for nature and the environment and future generations (Schuitema, Steg and Van Kruining, 2011).

17.4 Values

Given that various perceived risks, costs and benefits affect sustainable energy behaviour and acceptability of sustainable energy projects, the next question is which factors determine how people evaluate and weigh different risks, costs and benefits. We propose that values are an important factor in this respect. Values reflect general life goals or ideals that define what is important to people and what consequences they strive for in their lives in general (Rokeach, 1973; Schwartz, 1992). Values are general motivational factors that affect a wide range of evaluations, beliefs and actions (Dietz, 2016; Steg et al., 2014b). Four types of values are particularly important to understand people's evaluations and behaviour in the sustainability domain: hedonic values, which make people focus on pleasure and comfort; egoistic values, which make people focus on safeguarding and increasing their personal resources (e.g., money, status); altruistic values, which make people focus on the well-being of other people and society; and biospheric values, which make people focus on consequences for nature and the environment (De Groot Steg, 2008; Steg and De Groot, 2012; Steg et al., 2014b).

People tend to particularly consider consequences that have significant implications for their important values (Dietz, 2016; Perlaviciute and Steg, 2015; Steg et al., 2014b). Sustainable energy behaviours and projects typically imply positive collective consequences (e.g., reducing CO_2 emissions), and negative individual consequences (e.g., expensive technology). In line with this, research has revealed that, in general, people have more favourable evaluations of and are more likely to engage in sustainable energy behaviours if they have strong biospheric and, to a lesser extent, altruistic values, while they are less likely to do so if they have strong egoistic or hedonic values (Steg and De Groot, 2012). In some cases, strong altruistic values can inhibit sustainable energy behaviour, for example, when altruistic and biospheric goals are in conflict (De Groot and Steg, 2008). Similar results have been found for the acceptability of energy projects. For example, the stronger their biospheric values, the more positively people evaluated development and implementation of renewable energy sources, probably because renewable energy sources are generally seen as having positive (or relatively little negative) consequences for nature and the environment (Bidwell, 2013; Perlaviciute and Steg, 2015). In contrast, stronger egoistic values were related to less positive evaluations of renewable energy sources, probably because renewable energy sources are generally seen as expensive and intermittent (Perlaviciute and Steg, 2015).

People's values not only affect which consequences people find important, but also how people evaluate various risks, costs and benefits. The stronger their biospheric values, the more positively people evaluated renewable energy sources, including personal consequences of these renewable energy sources, such as financial costs (Perlaviciute and Steg, 2015). Similarly, stronger altruistic values led to positive evaluations of wind energy, and more positive evaluations of various pros and cons of wind energy, including effects on the landscape (i.e., wildlife, noise and scenic views) and the local economy (Bidwell, 2013). Thus, people seem to base their evaluations of energy projects on aspects that are most relevant for their important values, which guide their overall acceptability judgements. These value-based judgements may in turn affect the evaluation of various risks, costs and benefits of energy projects that may be less important to people based on their values. In other words, people evaluate energy projects in an overly positive or negative way, in line with their value-based judgements.

Values can influence sustainable energy behaviours via environmental self-identity (Steg et al., 2014a; Van der Werff et al., 2013, 2014b). The stronger people's biospheric values, the more they perceive themselves as a person who acts proenvironmentally. A strong environmental self-identity, in turn, encourages engagement in sustainable energy behaviours, as people are motivated to consistently act in line with how they see themselves (Ruepert et al., 2016; Van der Werff et al., 2013; Whitmarsh and O'Neill, 2010). Besides values, environmental self-identity is also influenced by one's previous behaviours. Having previously engaged in sustainable energy behaviours increases the likelihood that people see themselves as an energy-saving and proenvironmental person, which motivates them to engage in other sustainable energy behaviours (Van der Werff et al., 2014a, 2014b). This can explain why initial sustainable energy behaviour can motivate people to engage in many other sustainable energy behaviours, thereby promoting positive spillover.

In sum, values can influence a wide range of sustainable energy behaviours and acceptability of energy projects. Particularly biospheric values seem to be a stable and reliable basis for sustainable energy behaviours and public support for sustainable energy projects (Steg et al., 2014a). Stronger biospheric values make people prioritise the environmental consequences of energy behaviours and projects and evaluate the related risks and cost less negatively. Furthermore, stronger biospheric values are associated with a stronger environmental self-identity, which, in turn, facilitates engagement in many different sustainable energy behaviours.

In general, people care about the environment and endorse biospheric values relatively strongly. Yet, many people do not consistently engage in sustainable energy behaviour. The IFEP proposes that in addition to individual factors, contextual factors influence sustainable energy behaviours and acceptability of energy projects; contextual factors can influence the extent to which people act upon their biospheric values.

17.5 Contextual Factors

We conceptualise contextual factors broadly as everything that characterises sustainable energy behaviours and projects, for example the characteristics of energy technology, the laws and regulations that apply to energy behaviours and projects and the physical, economic, political and social context within which energy behaviours and energy projects are embedded (Steg et al., 2014a; Perlaviciute and Steg, 2014). Contextual factors define the (distribution of) costs and benefits of energy behaviours and projects, thereby influencing individual motivations and behaviour (Ölander and Thøgersen, 1995; Stern, 1999; Thøgersen, 2005; Lindenberg and Steg, 2007; Steg and Vlek, 2009). The context can influence sustainable behaviour directly, by facilitating or inhibiting sustainable behaviour. The context may introduce barriers that are too strong, that prevent people from acting sustainably even if they want to, or the context can strongly facilitate sustainable behaviour, making everyone act sustainably despite people's values (Corraliza and Berenguer, 2000; Guagnano, Stern and Dietz, 1995; Ruepert et al., 2016). Next, contextual factors can influence the extent to which people are focussed on the environmental consequences of their behaviour (Steg et al., 2014a). For example, the high costs can make people focus particularly on these costs and the values related to these costs, notably hedonic and egoistic values, which makes it less likely that people will act upon their biospheric values (Steg et al., 2014a; Steg, 2015, 2016). Relatedly, the behaviour of others can make people focus on specific values, thereby affecting their behaviour (Keizer, Lindenberg and Steg, 2008, 2013).

17.6 Interventions to Promote Sustainable Energy Behaviour

As explained in the preceding, biospheric values are likely to encourage engagement in many different sustainable energy behaviours and public support for different sustainable energy projects, which is crucial to speed up the sustainable energy transition. For this reason, strategies could be employed to strengthen biospheric values. Yet, values are believed to be relatively stable across time (Feather, 1995; Rokeach, 1973; Stern and Dietz, 1994), and little is known about whether and how biospheric values can be strengthened (Steg, 2016). In this section, we review strategies that can foster sustainable energy behaviour and acceptability of sustainable energy projects by increasing the likelihood that people act upon their biospheric values (Steg et al., 2014a).

17.6.1 Changing the Context

It is important to remove major contextual barriers that prevent people from engaging in sustainable energy behaviours (Steg et al., 2014a). Such interventions can change the actual costs and benefits of sustainable energy choices (Bolderdijk, Lehman and Geller, 2012; Geller, 2002; Steg and Vlek, 2009). For example, major investments in energy efficiency retrofits at home or in renewable energy systems may not be affordable to some people (Kastner and Stern, 2015). Incentives such as subsidies could be implemented in these cases (Bolderdijk and Steg, 2015). Similarly, interventions could make certain energy behaviours easier and less burdening to people. For example, in renewable energy systems, appliances such as washing machines or dishwashers could best be operated at times when energy supply from renewables is abundant, but people may not be able or willing to constantly monitor energy supply or they may simply not be at home to switch on or switch off their appliances. In such cases, technologies can be implemented that automatically switch appliances off and on at different times, thereby making the sustainable behaviour easier and more feasible for people.

Next, it may be important to introduce incentives that enable risks, costs and benefits to be distributed (more) fairly across groups in society. On the one hand, the risks and costs for most affected groups could be reduced as much as possible in order to promote acceptability of energy projects. On the other hand, additional benefits could be provided to those who have to bear most costs and risks. For example, local funds could be established in communities hosting renewable energy projects; the funds could be used to reduce energy bills for local people, to stimulate the local economy or to create or improve local facilities (e.g., sports facilities; Walker, Wiersma and Bailey, 2014). Indeed, offering reductions on energy prices increased people's willingness to host wind farms (Groothuis, Groothuis and Whitehead, 2008). Yet, offering compensations for hosting renewable energy projects can be perceived by people as attempts to buy local support, which can fuel rather than reduce resistance (Ter Mors, Terwel and Daamen, 2012). It has been proposed that collective benefits (e.g., investing in local facilities) may be less likely to be seen as bribes than individual financial compensations (e.g., one-time payments to residents; Ter Mors et al., 2012).

Yet, incentives may be less effective than sometimes assumed, and can sometimes even be counterproductive (Bolderdijk and Steg, 2015). Incentives can make people focus on values related to immediate personal costs and benefits, notably egoistic or hedonic values, which provide a fickle basis for consistent sustainable energy choices (Steg et al., 2014a; Steg, 2015, 2016). Incentives that make people focus on their hedonic or egoistic values will particularly promote engagement in sustainable energy behaviours and acceptability of energy projects when these have clear benefits and when they support their egoistic or hedonic values (Bolderdijk et al., 2011; De Groot and Steg, 2009). In addition, incentives can inhibit positive spillover effects when subsequent actions have no clear personal benefits, which is not uncommon in the energy domain (Thøgersen, 2013). For example, people who were focussed on economic rather than environmental reasons for one proenvironmental act, in this case car-sharing, were less inclined to engage in another sustainable behaviour on a following occasion, in this case recycling (Evans et al., 2013). In addition, incentives will particularly result in behaviour changes when such changes are perceived to be worth the effort (Bolderdijk and Steg, 2015). Many single sustainable energy behaviours, such as unplugging a single coffee machine or microwave, yield small benefits and may therefore be perceived as not worth the effort (Dogan, Bolderdijk and Steg, 2014).

In sum, increasing the benefits and reducing the costs of sustainable energy choices and distributing the risks, costs and benefits fairly across groups in society may be necessary when these choices are too costly and/or too difficult for (some) people. Yet, such strategies should be used with caution since emphasising costs and benefits may make people focus on egoistic and hedonic values, making these values more influential, which may inhibit durable engagement in sustainable energy behaviour.

17.6.2 Social Influence

Social influence strategies, in which other people or groups are used to influence individual choices, can be employed to encourage sustainable energy behaviours (Abrahamse and Steg, 2013). Social influence approaches that make use of face-to-face interaction seem most effective in this respect, such as block leader approaches and behaviour modelling. Block leader approaches, in which local volunteers help inform other people in their neighbourhood about a certain issue, seem to be one of the most effective social influence strategies. Behaviour modelling entails the use of confederates or 'models' who demonstrate a recommended behaviour, thereby potentially helping people to learn the behaviour, as well as demonstrating what others do and what behaviour is socially approved (Sussman and Gifford, 2013; Winett et al., 1985). Social influence strategies that happen in a fairly anonymous way, such as descriptive norm information (i.e., information on the behaviours of others) and social comparison feedback, where people receive feedback about their own performance compared with the performance of others, can also encourage sustainable energy behaviour, although they are less powerful than strategies that rely on face-to-face interactions (Abrahamse and Steg, 2013). Social norm information and social comparison feedback may not be very effective when most (significant) others do not act sustainably. Some studies found that low energy users used more energy after receiving social feedback (Brandon and Lewis, 1999; Schultz et al., 2007), which could potentially be because they found out that others use more and acted in line with the norm. Such undesired effects may potentially be attenuated by additionally showing approval of sustainable energy behaviours and disapproval of unsustainable energy behaviours (Schultz et al., 2007).

17.6.3 Providing Information and Arguments

People may have limited or inaccurate understanding about the environmental impact of their behaviours, as well as about how they could change their behaviours in order to reduce energy use and the related CO_2 emissions (Steg et al., 2015; Stern et al., 2016a). For example, they may overestimate the costs and/or underestimate the environmental benefits of sustainable behaviour or energy projects. In such cases, it is important to change the misperceptions of risks, costs and benefits of sustainable choices via information strategies (Abrahamse and Matthies, 2012; Steg and Vlek, 2009). Next, information can be provided to change people's beliefs about and to increase their awareness of environmental problems caused by their current behaviour, which may enable and motivate them to help reduce these problems by changing their behaviour. There is some evidence to suggest that such information will be particularly effective if people strongly endorse biospheric values. Indeed, an environmental campaign increased knowledge among all exposed to the campaign, but only increased sustainable behavioural intentions and policy acceptability for those who strongly endorsed biospheric values (Bolderdijk et al., 2013c). This suggests that information is more likely to affect policy acceptability and behaviour when it resonates with people's important values. Conversely, information and arguments may not be effective if they do not resonate with people's value-based views. For example, natural gas is often promoted as a relatively clean energy source and an important energy source to facilitate a sustainable energy transition, which implies positive implications for people's biospheric values. Yet, people with stronger biospheric values did not evaluate natural gas more positively when it was promoted as sustainable, probably because they see gas primarily as a fossil fuel and hence not sustainable (Perlaviciute, Steg and Hoekstra, 2016).

People can also be informed about which actions are effective to reduce environmental and energy problems by providing them with feedback about the environmental impact of their energy behaviours. Feedback appears to be an effective strategy for reducing household energy use (Abrahamse et al., 2005), although not always (Fischer, 2008). For example, feedback about environmental and health risks of high energy consumption resulted in a reduction in household energy consumption by 8.2 per cent, thereby outperforming financial feedback, which did not result in a significant reduction in household energy use (Asensio and Delmas, 2015). Participants' willingness to engage in energy-saving programs was higher when environmental benefits were highlighted, compared to when monetary benefits and even both types of benefits were highlighted (Schwartz et al., 2015). Interestingly, however, more participants reported that they would enrol in the energy-saving programs for monetary rather than environmental reasons (Schwartz et al., 2015), and in other studies people preferred to receive financial feedback rather than environmental feedback (Krishnamurti et al., 2013; Karjalainen, 2011). This suggests that people may not know what motivates them most to engage in sustainable energy behaviour. Besides feedback content, the way in which feedback is given may influence the extent to which feedback induces behavioural change. Feedback is more effective when it is given immediately after the behaviour occurs, as this enhances people's understanding of the relationship between the feedback and their behaviour (Geller, 2002). Smart meters offer possibilities for providing immediate and frequent feedback on household energy use and ways to reduce it, via different means such as websites, mobile phones and home displays (Mack and Tampe-Mai, 2016; Van der Werff et al., 2016). Furthermore, it has been advocated that feedback on a more detailed level, for example, on an appliance level, may be more effective than feedback on overall electricity consumption (Fischer, 2008). People indeed indicate they would like to receive information about energy consumption per appliance (Asensio and Delmas, 2015; Karjalainen, 2011; Krishnamurti et al., 2013; Fischer, 2008). Yet, receiving specific information about energy use of many different appliances may cause information overload (Krishnamurti et al., 2013), reducing the effectiveness of such feedback strategies. Given that people may be reluctant and/or unable to process extensive and/or complicated information or feedback on their energy behaviours, ambient persuasive technologies can be offered that promote behaviour change without the need for users' conscious attention and hence with little cognitive effort (Midden and Ham, 2012). For example, processing interactive lighting feedback, such as a light that turns green, may be less cognitively demanding than processing factual feedback, such as statistics on energy use, and may help and motivate people to engage in sustainable energy behaviour even in cognitively demanding situations (Midden and Ham, 2012). Helping people to better envision and understand their energy use via thermal images of their homes proved to be effective in motivating them to reduce their energy use (Goodhew et al., 2015). Furthermore, introducing default options may reduce cognitive load needed to make sustainable choices. Indeed, more people chose 'green' rather than 'grey' electricity when the 'green' option was the default option, possibly because going for the default option requires less time and effort. Additionally, default option may communicate the social norm, which can also be motivating for people (Pichert and Katsikopoulos, 2008).

17.6.4 Motivating People to Act Consistently

Even if people aim to engage in sustainable energy behaviours, they may be tempted to act differently in specific situations. Interventions can be employed that motivate people to consistently engage in sustainable energy behaviours. Commitment strategies are promising in this respect, where people make a promise to engage in sustainable energy behaviour. Additionally, they could indicate how and when they will engage in sustainable behaviour, and how they will tackle any barriers faced in the future; the latter is called implementation intention. Both strategies appear to be effective in encouraging sustainable energy behaviour (Abrahamse et al., 2005; Abrahamse and Steg, 2013; Lokhorst et al., 2013). Commitments are more effective when made in public rather than private (Abrahamse et al., 2005). Although little is known about the processes through which both strategies promote sustainable energy behaviour, one plausible explanation is that people want to be consistent by acting in line with their promise (Abrahamse and Steg, 2013). Evoking cognitive dissonance between individuals' reported attitudes and behaviour is another strategy that is based on people's desire to be consistent, which proved to be effective in promoting sustainable energy behaviour. People who first reported a favourable attitude towards energy conservation, and later were made aware of their relatively high energy usage, significantly reduced their energy use (Focella and Stone, 2013).

Reminding people of their previous proenvironmental actions can promote sustainable behaviour by strengthening environmental self-identity, as previously explained. Environmental self-identity is more likely to be strengthened when people are reminded of a range of sustainable energy actions they engaged in, or when they are reminded of behaviours that were somewhat costly or uncommon, probably because in such cases it is more likely that one engaged in the behaviour out of conviction and not because it happened to be the most attractive option (Van der Werff et al., 2014a). This implies an interesting paradox, when considered together with the previously discussed social influence strategies. On the one hand, it may be beneficial to stress that many others act sustainably, as people are likely to act in line with the behaviour of others. Yet, on the other hand, it seems that stressing that only few people acted sustainably can also encourage sustainable energy choices, via a different process, as engaging in such uncommon behaviour can strengthen one's environmental self-identity. Employing strategies that strengthen people's proenvironmental self-identity could potentially alleviate the possible counter-effects of incentive strategies. If people engage in sustainable energy behaviour because the behaviour is incentivised, the behaviour may have a weaker signalling effect, because people attribute the behaviour to the situation rather than to themselves. In such cases, it may be important to emphasise the environmental benefits of such behaviours, which could potentially strengthen environmental self-identity, thereby decreasing the likelihood of negative spillover and increasing the likelihood of positive spillover effects.

In many cases, the previously described strategies are not implemented separately. Combining interventions may be more effective, as this enables addressing multiple barriers and motivations to engage in sustainable energy behaviour at once. For example, several interventions described in the preceding were combined in an educational programme on household energy use delivered to Girls Scouts in the United States (Boudet et al., 2016). The Girl Scouts received information about sustainable energy behaviours, they rehearsed these behaviours, observed others in the group engage in these behaviours, received items to facilitate sustainable energy behaviours (e.g., reminder stickers), made pledges to engage in sustainable energy behaviours and monitored and reported their energy behaviours. The programme influenced not only Girl Scouts but also their parents to increase their residential energy-saving behaviours immediately after the intervention up to seven months later (Boudet et al., 2016). The study demonstrates that such combined interventions that target children have a high potential in fostering sustainable energy behaviours of households. Another study involving several intervention strategies (e.g., tailored information, commitment) found that interventions may be more likely to enhance sustainable energy behaviour when people recently relocated to another house, making it more likely that they reconsider initial behavioural choices (Verplanken and Roy, 2016).

17.7 Fair Procedures and Trust

How and by whom sustainable energy projects are implemented will affect public acceptability of these projects. In particular, fairness of decision-making procedures and people's trust in parties involved in a sustainable energy transition are important in this respect.

17.7.1 Procedural Fairness

Public engagement in decision-making affects the extent to which procedures of decision-making around energy are seen as fair (see Bidwell, 2016; Huijts et al., 2012; Perlaviciute and Steg, 2014; Sovacool et al., 2016). People may be more likely to accept energy projects if they think that the decision-making process is fair, and if they feel they are sufficiently involved in decision-making and that their interests are considered (Huijts et al., 2012; Perlaviciute and Steg, 2014). However, relatively little is known about how public participation processes should be organised to ensure that procedures are perceived to be fair (Bidwell, 2016). Information provision is a necessary precondition for public involvement: decision-making processes need to be transparent, and people should be fully informed from the beginning, rather than only afterwards when all decisions are already made. Yet, information provision alone is a passive form of public involvement and not sufficient to ensure fair procedures. Collaborative approaches that take people's concerns into account are more likely to be seen as fair than technocratic top-down decision-making processes, which could (partly) explain why the former are evaluated more positively by people than the latter (Walker and Devine-Wright, 2008; Wolsink, 2007, 2010; Wolsink and Breukers, 2010). Importantly, true public engagement means not only that people have an opportunity to express their opinion, but also that their opinion is seriously considered in decision-making and can have an actual impact on decisions around energy (Dietz and Stern, 2008; Hindmarsh, 2010). If people express their opinion but this opinion is eventually not taken into account and will not change energy policies (i.e., 'fake engagement'), this will probably not be seen as fair. Actively engaging people can provide important input to decision-making, which could substantially improve the development and implementation of sustainable technologies and energy projects (Bidwell, 2016). For example, the public could consult on how to develop home technology that is user-friendly and acceptable for direct users. Importantly, however, systematic empirical evidence is lacking on whether and how more public participation leads to higher acceptability of sustainable energy projects. There is even some evidence that more participation may strengthen opposition and social conflict if people are not satisfied with the information given, the neutrality of intermediate parties, the ways opportunities for public voice are organised and the consideration of local context (Colvin, Witt and Lacey, 2016). It is important to study the conditions under which public participation increases acceptability of energy projects, as well as boundary conditions.

17.7.2 Trust

A sustainable energy transition includes complex innovative technology, infra-structure and changes in energy systems, which are difficult to comprehend for the public. Therefore, trust in responsible parties – for example, energy com-panies that site energy technologies and provide energy services, scientists that develop energy technologies and governments that implement energy policies – influences public acceptability of energy projects and people's willingness to change their behaviour and adopt the proposed technology (Frederiks et al., 2015; Huijts et al., 2012; Perlaviciute and Steg, 2014). Trust in involved par-ties will especially affect behaviours and acceptability judgements when people have little knowledge about the proposed energy projects and technology, more likely so when such measures are highly complex (Siegrist and Cvetkovich, 2000). Research puts forward four factors that influence trust, namely (1) perceived knowledge and expertise of responsible parties to carry out their activities; (2) past behaviours of these parties; (3) whether the parties are seen as open, honest and taking people's interests into account; and (4) whether people think these parties endorse values similar to their own values (Earle and Siegrist, 2006; Huijts et al., 2007; Terwel et al., 2009). These factors are closely related. For example, if people think that responsible parties endorse values similar to their own, they also are more likely to think that these parties have sufficient skills and competencies (Huijts, Midden and Meijnders, 2007). As yet, little is known under which conditions specific factors are most pre-dictive of overall trust judgements and about the direction of relationships between these factors and overall trust judgements, since overall judgements could influence evaluations of (some of) these specific factors.

17.8 Conclusion

To achieve a sustainable energy transition, it is important that people engage in a large variety of sustainable energy behaviours and accept differ-ent sustainable energy projects and policies. We proposed the IFEP, a general framework to understand and encourage sustainable energy behaviour (Steg et al., 2014a). We discussed that values influence sustainable energy behav-iours and public acceptability of sustainable energy projects and policies by influencing how people evaluate the related risks, costs and benefits, and by strengthening (or weakening) people's environmental self-identity. Next, con-textual factors can influence sustainable behaviours directly as well as by mak-ing people focus on certain values and enabling them to act upon these values. Various interventions can be implemented to encourage sustainable energy behaviour, by changing the context so as to enable and empower people to act sustainably, providing information and arguments so as to help people and motivate them to make sustainable choices, and by motivating people to act consistently. When developing and implementing sustainable energy projects, it is important to consider procedural fairness and people's trust in parties involved in a sustainable energy transition, to secure responsible decision-making and public support.

Notes

1 This chapter builds on and extends a previous review article on human dimensions of a sustainable energy transition (Steg, Perlaviciute and Van der Werff, 2015).
2 We focus particularly on energy behaviours at home, and will not discuss factors influencing sustainable transportation (e.g., shifting to low-carbon means of transport, sharing transportation, using public transport).

17.9 References

Abrahamse, W., and Matthies, E. (2012). Informational Strategies to Promote Pro-Environmental Behaviour: Changing Knowledge, Awareness and Attitudes. In L. Steg, A. E. van den Berg, and J. I. M. de Groot (Eds.) *Environmental Psychology: An Introduction* (pp. 223–243). Oxford: John Wiley & Sons.

Abrahamse, W., and Steg, L. (2011). Factors Related to Household Energy Use and Intention to Reduce It: The Role of Psychological and Socio-Demographic Variables. *Human Ecology Review*, 18(1), 30–40.

Abrahamse, W., and Steg, L. (2013). Social Influence Approaches to Encourage Resource Conservation: A Meta-analysis. *Global Environmental Change*, 23(6), 1773–1785.

Abrahamse, W., Steg, L., Vlek, C., and Rothengatter, T. (2005). A Review of Intervention Studies Aimed at Household Energy Conservation. *Journal of Environmental Psychology*, 25(3), 273–291.

Asensio, O. I., and Delmas, M. A. (2015). Nonprice Incentives and Energy Conservation. *Proceedings of the National Academy of Sciences*, 112(6), E510–E515002E.

Bidwell, D. (2013). The Role of Values in Public Beliefs and Attitudes Towards Commercial Wind Energy. *Energy Policy*, 58, 189–199.

Bidwell, D. (2016). Thinking Through Participation in Renewable Energy Decisions. *Nature Energy*, 1, 16051.

Boudet, H., Ardoin, N. M., Flora, J., Armel, K. C., Desai, M., and Robinson, T. N. (2016). Effects of a Behaviour Change Intervention for Girl Scouts on Child and Parent Energy-Saving Behaviours. *Nature Energy*, 1, 16091.

Bolderdijk, J. W., Knockaert, J., Steg, E. M., and Verhoef, E. T. (2011). Effects of Pay-as-You-Drive Vehicle Insurance on Young Drivers' Speed Choice: Results of a Dutch Field Experiment. *Accident Analysis and Prevention*, 43(3), 1181–1186.

Bolderdijk, J. W., Lehman, P. K., and Geller, E. S. (2012). In L. Steg, A. E. van den Berg, and J. I. M. de Groot (Eds.) *Environmental Psychology: An Introduction* (pp. 233–242). Oxford: John Wiley & Sons.

Bolderdijk, J. W., and Steg, L. (2015). Promoting Sustainable Consumption: The Risks of Using Financial Incentives. In L. A. Reisch and J. Thøgersen (Eds.) *Handbook of Research in Sustainable Consumption* (pp. 328–342). Cheltenham: Edward Elgar.

Bolderdijk, J. W., Steg, L., and Postmes, T. (2013a). Fostering Support for Work Floor Energy Conservation Policies: Accounting for Privacy Concerns. *Journal of Organizational Behavior*, 34(2), 195–210.

Bolderdijk, J. W., Steg, L., Geller, E. S., Lehman, P. K., and Postmes, T. (2013b). Comparing the Effectiveness of Monetary Versus Moral Motives in Environmental Campaigning. *Nature Climate Change*, 3(4), 413–416.

Bolderdijk, J. W., Gorsira, M., Keizer, K., and Steg, L. (2013c). Values Determine the (In)effectiveness of Informational Interventions in Promoting Pro-Environmental Behavior. *PloS one*, 8(12), e83911.

Brandon, G., and Lewis, A. (1999). Reducing Household Energy Consumption: A Qualitative and Quantitative Field Study. *Journal of Environmental Psychology*,19(1), 75–85.

Clayton, S., Devine-Wright, P., Stern, et al. (2015). Psychological Research and Global Climate Change. *Nature Climate Change*, 5(7), 640–646.

Colvin, R. M., Witt, G. B., and Lacey, J. (2016). How Wind Became a Four-Letter Word: Lessons for Community Engagement from a Wind Energy Conflict in King Island, Australia. *Energy Policy*, 98, 483–494.

Corraliza, J. A., and Berenguer, J. (2000). Environmental Values, Beliefs, and Actions: A Situational Approach. *Environment and Behavior*, 32(6), 832–848.

Darby, S. (2010), *Literature Review for the Energy Demand Research Project*. London: Ofgem (Office of Gas and Electricity Markets).

De Groot, J. I. M., and Steg, L. (2008). Value Orientations to Explain Beliefs Related to Environmental Significant Behaviour: How to Measure Egoistic, Altruistic, and Biospheric Value Orientations. *Environment and Behavior*, 40(3), 330–354.

De Groot, J. I. M., and Steg, L. (2009). Mean or Green: Which Values Can Promote Stable Pro-Environmental Behavior?. *Conservation Letters*, 2(2), 61–66.

De Groot, J. I. M., and Steg, L. (2010). Morality and Nuclear Energy: Perceptions of Risks and Benefits, Personal Norms, and Willingness to Take Action Related to Nuclear Energy. *Risk Analysis*, 30(9), 1363–1373.

Dietz, T. (2016). Environmental value. In T. Brosch and D. Sander (Eds.) *Handbook of Value: Perspectives from Economics, Neuroscience, Philosophy, Psychology, and Sociology* (ch. 6, pp. 329–349). New York: Oxford University Press.

Dietz, T., and Stern, P.C. (Eds). (2008). *Public Participation in Environmental Assessment and Decision Making*. Washington, DC: National Academies Press.

Dogan, E., Bolderdijk, J. W., and Steg, L. (2014). Making Small Numbers Count: Environmental and Financial Feedback in Promoting Eco-Driving Behaviours. *Journal of Consumer Policy*, 37(3), 413–422.

Dunn, B., Kamath, H., and Tarascon, J. M. (2011). Electrical Energy Storage for the Grid: A Battery of Choices. *Science*, 334(6058), 928–935.

Earle, T. C., and Siegrist, M. (2006). Morality Information, Performance Information, and the Distinction Between Trust and Confidence. *Journal of Applied Social Psychology*, 36(2), 383–416.

European Commission (2016a, 22 July). Towards the Paris Protocol. Available from ec.europa.eu/clima/policies/international/paris_protocol/index_en.htm; accessed on 5 August 2016.

European Commission (2016b, 5 August). 2030 Energy Strategy. Available from ec.europa.eu/energy/en/topics/energy-strategy/2030-energy-strategy; accessed on 5 August 2016.

Eurostat (2014a). Final Energy Consumption by Sector. Available from ec.europa.eu/eurostat/data/database; accessed on 5 August 2016.

Eurostat (2014b). Final Energy Consumption in Households by Fuel. Available from ec.europa.eu/eurostat/data/database; accessed on 5 August 2016.

Evans, L., Maio, G. R., Corner, A., Hodgetts, C. J., Ahmed, S., and Hahn, U. (2013). Self-Interest and Pro-Environmental Behaviour. *Nature Climate Change*, 3(2), 122–125.

Feather, N. T. (1995). Values, Valences, and Choice: The Influences of Values on the Perceived Attractiveness and Choice of Alternatives. *Journal of Personality and Social Psychology*, 68(6), 1135.

Fischer, C. (2008). Feedback on Household Electricity Consumption: A Tool for Saving Energy? *Energy Efficiency*, 1(1), 79–104.

Focella, E. S., and Stone, J. (2013). The Use of Hypocrisy for Promoting Environmentally Sustainable Behaviors. In H. C. M. van Trijp (Ed.) *Encouraging Sustainable Behaviour* (203–2015). New York: Psychology Press.

Frederiks, E. R., Stenner, K., and Hobman, E. V. (2015). Household Energy Use: Applying Behavioural Economics to Understand Consumer Decision-Making and Behaviour. *Renewable and Sustainable Energy Reviews*, 41, 1385–1394.

Geller, E. S. (2002). The Challenge of Increasing Proenvironmental Behaviour. In R. B. Bechtel and A. Churchman (Eds.) *Handbook of Environmental Psychology* (pp. 525–540). New York: Wiley.

Goodhew, J., Pahl, S., Auburn, T., and Goodhew, S. (2015). Making Heat Visible: Promoting Energy Conservation Behaviours Through Thermal Imaging. *Environment and Behaviour*, 47(10), 1059–1088.

Griskevicius, V., Tybur, J. M., and Van den Bergh, B. (2010). Going Green to Be Seen: Status, Reputation, and Conspicuous Conservation. *Journal of Personality and Social Psychology*, 98(3), 392–404.

Groothuis, P. A., Groothuis, J. D., Whitehead, J. C. (2008). Green vs. Green: Measuring the Compensation Required to Site Electrical Generation Windmills in a Viewshed. *Energy Policy*, 36(4), 1545–1550.

Guagnano, G. A., Stern, P. C., and Dietz, T. (1995). Influences on Attitude–Behavior Relationships: A Natural Experiment with Curbside Recycling. *Environment and Behavior*, 27(5), 699–718.

Hackmann, H., Moser, S. C., and Clair, A. L. S. (2014). The Social Heart of Global Environmental Change. Nature Climate Change, 4(8), 653–655.

Harland, P., Staats, H., and Wilke, H. A. (1999). Explaining proenvironmental Intention and Behavior by Personal Norms and the Theory of Planned Behavior. *Journal of Applied Social Psychology*, 29(12), 2505–2528.

Hess, D. J. (2014). Smart Meters and Public Acceptance: Comparative Analysis and Governance Implications. *Health, Risk and Society*, 16(3), 243–258.

Hindmarsh, R. (2010). Wind Farms and Community Engagement in Australia: A Critical Analysis for Policy Learning. *East Asian Science, Technology and Society: An International Journal*, 4(4), 541–563.

Huijts, N. M., Midden, C. J., and Meijnders, A. L. (2007). Social Acceptance of Carbon Dioxide Storage. *Energy Policy*, 35(5), 2780–2789.

Huijts, N. M., Molin, E. J. E., and Steg, L. (2012). Psychological Factors Influencing Sustainable Energy Technology Acceptance: A Review-Based Comprehensive Framework. *Renewable and Sustainable Energy Reviews*, 16(1), 525–531.

IEA (International Energy Agency) (2015). *Recent Energy Trends in OECD. Excerpt from: Energy Balances of OECD Countries.* Available from www.iea.org/publications/freepublications/publication/EnergyBalancesofOECDcountries2015editionexcerpt.pdf; accessed on 2 July 2016.

IPCC (Intergovernmental Panel on Climate Change) (2014). *Climate Change 2014: Synthesis Report. Contribution of Working Groups I, II and III to the Fifth Assessment Report of the Intergovernmental Panel on Climate Change* [Core Writing Team, R. K. Pachauri and L. A. Meyer (eds.)]. Geneva, Switzerland: IPCC.

Kaklamanou, D., Jones, C. R., Webb, T. L., and Walker, S. R. (2015). Using Public Transport Can Make Up for Flying Abroad on Holiday: Compensatory Green Beliefs and Environmentally Significant Behavior. *Environment and Behavior*, 47, 184–204.

Karjalainen, S. (2011). Consumer Preferences for Feedback on Household Electricity Consumption. *Energy and Buildings*, 43(2), 458–467.

Kastner, I., and Stern, P. C. (2015). Examining the Decision-Making Processes Behind Household Energy Investments: A Review. *Energy Research and Social Science*, 10, 72–89.

Keizer, K., Lindenberg, S., and Steg, L. (2008). The Spreading of Disorder. *Science*, 322, 1681–1685.

Keizer, K., Lindenberg, S., and Steg, L. (2013). The Importance of Demonstratively Restoring Order. *PLoS ONE*, 8(6): e65137.

Kok, R., Benders, R. M., and Moll, H. C. (2006). Measuring the Environmental Load of Household Consumption Using Some Methods Based on Input–Output Energy Analysis: A Comparison of Methods and a Discussion of Results. *Energy Policy*, 34(17), 2744–2761.

Krishnamurti, T., Davis, A. L., Wong-Parodi, G., Wang, J., and Canfield, C. (2013). Creating an In-Home Display: Experimental Evidence and Guidelines for Design. *Applied Energy*, 108, 448–458.

Krishnamurti, T., Schwartz, D., Davis, A., Fischhoff, B., de Bruin, W. B., Lave, L., and Wang, J. (2012). Preparing for Smart Grid Technologies: A Behavioral Decision Research Approach to Understanding Consumer Expectations About Smart Meters. *Energy Policy*, 41, 790–797.

Lanzini, P., and Thøgersen, J. (2014). Behavioural Spillover in the Environmental Domain: An Intervention Study. *Journal of Environmental Psychology*, 40, 381–390.

Leijten, F. R., Bolderdijk, J. W., Keizer, K., Gorsira, M., Van der Werff, E., and Steg, L. (2014). Factors That Influence Consumers' Acceptance of Future Energy

Systems: The Effects of Adjustment Type, Production Level, and Price. *Energy Efficiency*, 7(6), 973–985.

Lindenberg, S., and Steg, L. (2007). Normative, Gain and Hedonic Goal Frames Guiding Environmental Behavior. *Journal of Social Issues*, 63(1), 117–137.

Lokhorst, A. M., Werner, C., Staats, H., van Dijk, E., and Gale, J. L. (2013). Commitment and Behavior Change: A Meta-analysis and Critical Review of Commitment-Making Strategies in Environmental Research. *Environment and Behavior*, 45(1) 13–34.

Mack, B., and Tampe-Mai, K. (2016). An Action Theory-Based Electricity Saving Web Portal for Households with an Interface to Smart Meters. *Utilities Policy*, 42, 51–63.

McCoy, D., and Lyons, S. (2017). Unintended Outcomes of Electricity Smart-Metering: Trading-Off Consumption and Investment Behaviour. *Energy Efficiency*, 10(2), 299–318.

Midden, C., and Ham, J. (2012). Persuasive Technology to Promote Pro- Environmental Behaviour. In L. Steg, A. E. van den Berg, and J. I. M. de Groot (Eds.) *Environmental Psychology: An Introduction* (pp. 243–254). Oxford: John Wiley & Sons.

Midden, C. J., and Ritsema, B. S. (1983). The Meaning of Normative Processes for Energy Conservation. *Journal of Economic Psychology*, 4(1–2), 37–55.

Nature Energy (2016). That Human Touch [editorial]. 1, 16069.

Nolan, J. M., Schultz, P. W., Cialdini, R. B., Goldstein, N. J., and Griskevicius, V. (2008). Normative Social Influence is Underdetected. *Personality and Social Psychology Bulletin*, 34(7), 913–923.

Noppers, E. H., Keizer, K., Bolderdijk, J. W., and Steg, L. (2014). The Adoption of Sustainable Innovations: Driven by Symbolic and Environmental Motives. *Global Environmental Change*, 25, 52–62.

Noppers, E. H., Keizer, K., Bockarjova, M., and Steg, L. (2015). The Adoption of Sustainable Innovations: The Role of Instrumental, Environmental, and Symbolic Attributes for Earlier and Later Adopters. *Journal of Environmental Psychology*, 44, 74–84.

Noppers, E. H., Keizer, K., Milovanovic, M., and Steg, L. (2016). The Importance of Instrumental, Symbolic, and Environmental Attributes for the Adoption of Smart Energy Systems. *Energy Policy*, 98, 12–18.

Ölander, F., and Thøgersen, J. (1995). Understanding of Consumer Behaviour as a Prerequisite for Environmental Protection. *Journal of Consumer Policy*, 18(4), 345–385.

Perlaviciute, G., and Steg, L. (2014). Contextual and Psychological Factors Shaping Evaluations and Acceptability of Energy Alternatives: Integrated Review and Research Agenda. *Renewable and Sustainable Energy Reviews*, 35, 361–381.

Perlaviciute, G., and Steg, L. (2015). The Influence of Values on Evaluations of Energy Alternatives. *Renewable Energy*, 77, 259–267.

Perlaviciute, G., Steg, L., and Hoekstra, E. J. (2016). Is Gas Perceived as Sustainable? Insights from Value-Driven Evaluations in the Netherlands. *Energy Research and Social Science*, 20, 55–62.

Pichert, D., and Katsikopoulos, K. V. (2008). Green Defaults: Information Presentation and Pro-Environmental Behaviour. *Journal of Environmental Psychology*, 28(1), 63–73.

Poortinga, W., Steg, L., Vlek, C., and Wiersma, G. (2003). Household Preferences for Energy-Saving Measures: A Conjoint Analysis. *Journal of Economic Psychology*, 24(1), 49–64.

Reinders, A. H. M. E., Vringer, K., and Blok, K. (2003). The Direct and Indirect Energy Requirement of Households in the European Union. *Energy Policy*, 31(2), 139–153.

Rokeach, M. (1973). *The Nature of Human Values*. New York: Free Press.

Ruepert, A., Keizer, K., Steg, L., Maricchiolo, F., Carrus, G., Dumitru, A., et al. (2016). Environmental Considerations in the Organizational Context: A Pathway to Pro-Environmental Behaviour at Work. *Energy Research and Social Science*, 17, 59–70.

Schuitema, G., and Jakobsson Bergstad, C. (2012). Acceptability of Environmental Policies. In L. Steg, A. E. van den Berg, and J. I. M. de Groot (Eds.) *Environmental Psychology: An Introduction* (pp. 255–266). Oxford: John Wiley & Sons.

Schuitema, G., Steg, L., and Van Kruining, M. (2011). When Are Transport Pricing Policies Fair and Acceptable? *Social Justice Research*, 24(1), 66–84.

Schultz, P. W., Nolan, J. M., Cialdini, R. B., Goldstein, N. J., and Griskevicius, V. (2007). The Constructive, Destructive, and Reconstructive Power of Social Norms. *Psychological Science*, 18(5), 429–434.

Schwartz, D., Bruine de Bruin, W., Fischhoff, B., and Lave, L. (2015). Advertising Energy Saving Programs: The Potential Environmental Cost of Emphasizing Monetary Savings. *Journal of Experimental Psychology: Applied*, 21(2), 158–166.

Schwartz, S. H. (1992). Universals in the Content and Structures of Values: Theoretical Advances and Empirical Tests in 20 Countries. In M. Zanna (Ed.) *Advances in Experimental Psychology*, Vol. 25 (pp. 1–65). Orlando, FL: Academic Press.

Siegrist, M., and Cvetkovich, G. (2000). Perception of Hazards: The Role of Social Trust and Knowledge. *Risk Analysis*, 20(5), 713–720.

Sovacool, B. K. (2014). Diversity: Energy Studies Need Social Science. *Nature*, 511(7511), 529.

Sovacool, B. K., Heffron, R. J., McCauley, D., and Goldthau, A. (2016). Energy Decisions Reframed as Justice and Ethical Concerns. *Nature Energy*, 1, 16024.

Spence, A., Demski, C., Butler, C., Parkhill, K., and Pidgeon, N. (2015). Public Perceptions of Demand-Side Management and a Smarter Energy Future. *Nature Climate Change*, 5(6), 550–554.

Steg, L. (2015). Environmental Psychology and Sustainable Consumption. In L. A. Reisch and J. Thøgersen (Eds.) *Handbook of Research in Sustainable Consumption* (pp. 70–83). Cheltenham: Edward Elgar.

Steg, L. (2016). Values, Norms and Intrinsic Motivation to Act Proenvironmentally. *Annual Review of Environment and Resources*, 41, 4.1–4.16.

Steg, L., Bolderdijk, J. W., Keizer, K., and Perlaviciute, G. (2014a). An Integrated Framework for Encouraging Pro-Environmental Behaviour: The Role of Values, Situational Factors and Goals. *Journal of Environmental Psychology*, 38, 104–115.

Steg, L., and De Groot, J. I. M. (2010). Explaining Prosocial Intentions: Testing Causal Relationships in the Norm Activation Model. *British Journal of Social Psychology*, 49(4), 725–743.

Steg, L., and De Groot, J. I. M. (2012). Environmental Values. In S. Clayton (Ed.), *The Oxford Handbook of Environmental and Conservation Psychology* (pp. 81–92). New York: Oxford University Press.

Steg, L., Dreijerink, L., and Abrahamse, W. (2005). Factors Influencing the Acceptability of Energy Policies: A Test of VBN Theory. *Journal of Environmental Psychology*, 25(4), 415–425.

Steg, L., Dreijerink, L., and Abrahamse, W. (2006). Why Are Energy Policies Acceptable and Effective? *Environment and Behavior*, 38(1), 92–111.

Steg, L., Perlaviciute, G., and Van der Werff, E. (2015). Understanding the Human Dimensions of a Sustainable Energy Transition. *Frontiers in Psychology*, 6, 805.

Steg, L., Perlaviciute, G., Van der Werff, E., and Lurvink, J. (2014b). The Significance of Hedonic Values for Environmentally Relevant Attitudes, Preferences and Actions. *Environment and Behavior.* 46, 163–192.

Steg, L., and Vlek, C. (2009). Encouraging Pro-Environmental Behaviour: An Integrative Review and Research Agenda. *Journal of Environmental Psychology*, 29(3), 309–317.

Stern, P. C. (1999). Information, Incentives, and Proenvironmental Consumer Behavior. *Journal of Consumer Policy*, 22(4), 461–478.

Stern, P. C., and Dietz, T. (1994). The Value Basis of Environmental Concern. *Journal of Social Issues*, 50(3), 65–84.

Stern, P. C., Janda, K. B., Brown, M. A., Steg, L., Vine, E. L., and Lutzenhiser, L. (2016a). Opportunities and Insights for Reducing Fossil Fuel Consumption by Households and Organizations. *Nature Energy*, 1, 16043.

Stern, P. C., Sovacool, B. K., and Dietz, T. (2016b). Towards a Science of Climate and Energy Choices. *Nature Climate Change,* 6, 547–555.

Sussman, R., and Gifford, R. (2013). Be the Change You Want to See: Modeling Food Composting in Public Places. *Environment and Behavior*, 45(3), 323–343.

Taufik, D., Bolderdijk, J. W., and Steg, L. (2015). Acting Green Elicits a Literal Warm Glow. *Nature Climate Change*, 5(1), 37–40.

Ter Mors, E., Terwel, B. W., and Daamen, D. D. (2012). The Potential of Host Community Compensation in Facility Siting. *International Journal of Greenhouse Gas Control*, 11, S130–S138.

Terwel, B. W., Harinck, F., Ellemers, N., and Daamen, D. D. (2009). How Organizational Motives and Communications Affect Public Trust in Organizations: The Case of Carbon Dioxide Capture and Storage. *Journal of Environmental Psychology*, 29(2), 290–299.

Thøgersen, J. (2005). How May Consumer Policy Empower Consumers for Sustainable Lifestyles? *Journal of Consumer Policy*, 28(2), 143–177.

Thøgersen, J. (2013). Psychology: Inducing Green Behaviour. *Nature Climate Change*, 3(2), 100–101.

Thøgersen, J., and Ölander, F. (2003). Spillover of Environment-Friendly Consumer Behaviour. *Journal of Environmental Psychology*, 23(3), 225–236.

Tiefenbeck, V., Staake, T., Roth, K., and Sachs, O. (2013). For Better or for Worse? Empirical Evidence of Moral Licensing in a Behavioral Energy Conservation Campaign. *Energy Policy*, 57, 160–171.

Van der Werff, E., Perlaviciute, G., and Steg, L. (2016). Transition to Smart Grids: A Psychological Perspective. In A. Beaulieu, J. de Wilde, and J. Scherpen (Eds.)

Smart Grids from a Global Perspective (pp. 43–62). Cham, Switzerland: Springer International Publishing AG.

Van der Werff, E., and Steg, L. (2015). One Model to Predict Them All: Predicting Energy Behaviours with the Norm Activation Model. *Energy Research and Social Science*, 6, 8–14.

Van der Werff, E., and Steg, L. (2016). The Psychology of Participation and Interest in Smart Energy Systems: Comparing the Value-Belief-Norm Theory and the Value-Identity-Personal Norm Model. *Energy Research and Social Science*, 22, 107–114.

Van der Werff, E., Steg, L., and Keizer, K. (2013). It Is A Moral Issue: The Relationship Between Environmental Self-Identity, Obligation-Based Intrinsic Motivation and Pro-Environmental Behaviour. *Global Environmental Change*, 23(5), 1258–1265.

Van der Werff, E., Steg, L., and Keizer, K. (2014a). Follow the Signal: When Past Pro-Environmental Actions Signal Who You Are. *Journal of Environmental Psychology*, 40, 273–282.

Van der Werff, E., Steg, L., and Keizer, K. (2014b). I Am What I Am, by Looking Past the Present: The Influence of Biospheric Values and Past Behavior on Environmental Self-Identity. *Environment and Behavior*, 46(5), 626–657.

Venhoeven, L. A., Bolderdijk, J. W., and Steg, L. (2013). Explaining the Paradox: How Pro-Environmental Behaviour Can Both Thwart and Foster Well-Being. *Sustainability*, 5(4), 1372–1386.

Verplanken, B., and Roy, D. (2016). Empowering Interventions to Promote Sustainable Lifestyles: Testing the Habit Discontinuity Hypothesis in a Field Experiment. *Journal of Environmental Psychology*, 45, 127–134.

Walker, G., and Devine-Wright, P. (2008). Community Renewable Energy: What Should It Mean? *Energy Policy*, 36(2), 497–500.

Walker, B. J., Wiersma, B., and Bailey, E. (2014). Community Benefits, Framing and the Social Acceptance of Offshore Wind Farms: An Experimental Study in England. *Energy Research and Social Science*, 3, 46–54.

Weaver, C. P., Mooney, S., Allen, D., Beller-Simms, N., Fish, T., Grambsch, A. E., et al. (2014). From Global Change Science to Action with Social Sciences. *Nature Climate Change*, 4(8), 656–659.

Whitmarsh, L., and O'Neill, S. (2010). Green Identity, Green Living? The Role of Pro-Environmental Self-Identity in Determining Consistency Across Diverse Pro-Environmental Behaviours. *Journal of Environmental Psychology*, 30(3), 305–314.

Winett, R. A., Leckliter, I. N., Chinn, D. E., Stahl, B., and Love, S. Q. (1985). Effects of Television Modeling on Residential Energy Conservation. *Journal of Applied Behavior Analysis*, 18(1), 33–44.

Wolsink, M. (2007). Planning of Renewables Schemes: Deliberative and Fair Decision-Making on Landscape Issues Instead of Reproachful Accusations of Non-Cooperation. *Energy Policy*, 35(5), 2692–2704.

Wolsink, M. (2010). Near-Shore Wind Power: Protected Seascapes, Environmentalists' Attitudes, and the Technocratic Planning Perspective. *Land Use Policy*, 27(2), 195–203.

Wolsink, M., and Breukers, S. (2010). Contrasting the Core Beliefs Regarding the Effective Implementation of Wind Power. An International Study of

Stakeholder Perspectives. *Journal of Environmental Planning and Management*, 53(5), 535–558.

Zhang, Y., Wang, Z., and Zhou, G. (2013). Antecedents of Employee Electricity Saving Behavior in Organizations: An Empirical Study Based on Norm Activation Model. *Energy Policy*, 62, 1120–1127.

18 Household Production of Photovoltaic Energy

Issues in Economic Behavior

Paul C. Stern, Inga Wittenberg, Kimberly S. Wolske and Ingo Kastner

18.1 Introduction

Photovoltaic (PV) energy offers the technical potential for substantially reducing greenhouse gas (GHG) emissions when it is substituted for fossil fuels (Zhai et al., 2012; Drury, Denholm, and Margolis, 2009). Its rapidly decreasing cost (Barbose and Darghouth, 2015; Bazilian et al., 2013, Wirth, 2016) makes widespread adoption of PV a highly attractive global policy objective. For countries dependent on fuel imports, domestic energy production also offers significant benefits in terms of balance of payments and national security. As the various societal and environmental benefits of PV have become increasingly clear, several governments have offered substantial incentives to make PV adoption financially attractive and thus help achieve these benefits more rapidly (Kumar, 2015).

PV is different from conventional energy technologies in at least two fundamental ways that are relevant to its adoption: the geographic distribution of the resources and the relative lack of economies of scale in production. Unlike fossil and nuclear fuels, the resource (sunlight) is widely distributed geographically, and the economic viability of small-scale PV production units comes closer to that of large-scale ones than is the case for many other energy technologies. These two characteristics make PV technically and economically attractive to small-scale entities such as communities and households in ways that most other energy production systems are not.

The choice to adopt PV technology is also fundamentally different from other technological choices, particularly from the viewpoints of households. For example, energy production is an unfamiliar form of economic activity for most households in high-income countries. Consequently, adopting a PV system is not like acquiring typical household technologies: it has attributes both of a consumer durable and of an investment. The decision process for adopting PV may therefore be different from what would be expected by analyzing it with concepts developed for understanding investments or consumer purchases.

In this chapter, we examine available evidence on PV adoption by households, primarily from Germany and the United States, two countries where large financial incentives have been offered, to attempt to understand rates of adoption and their determinants. Our purposes are twofold: to better inform policies aimed at increasing PV adoption; and to contribute to the understanding of a form of economic behavior that is quite different from the usual household economic activities of outside employment, consumption, and investment in financial instruments. Unlike some analyses, we examine the adoption choice from the standpoint of the householders. Rather than presuming that a particular theory of choice adequately explains this behavior, we seek to build understanding by considering both potentially relevant theories and the available evidence. We use the comparison of Germany and the United States as a further source of insight. In closing, we comment on the roles of behavioral theories in explaining household adoption of PV and in informing efforts to promote adoption.

18.2 The Context of Household PV Choices: Germany and the United States

Household-level PV can be usefully considered as an innovation that is, in most places, early in the process of diffusion (Rogers, 2003). Because the determinants of adoption typically change as an innovation becomes more commonplace, it should not be surprising to find that research studies of adoption conducted more than a few years apart, or in places where adoption has progressed to different degrees, identify different determinants of choice. We consider this possibility in assessing the research evidence.

Germany and the United States have both offered large financial incentives for at least a decade to speed the diffusion of household PV – since at least 1991 in Germany (Hoppmann, Huenteler, and Girod, 2014; Sonnberger, 2015) and 2006 in the United States (Energy Policy Act of 2005). Other than that similarity, they are very different: the solar resource is much stronger in much of the United States than it is in most of Germany; the financial incentives have taken quite different forms in the two countries; the dominant technologies for measuring PV production at the household level have different implications for household choice; the role of subnational governments has been different in structuring and contributing to incentives; and in response to different policy conditions, the roles of nongovernmental institutions, including profit-making entities, in promoting adoption have developed differently. These differences in policies and in the decision contexts they create for households likely hold important keys to understanding the process of diffusion of household-level PV. In this section, we describe the policy and decision contexts facing German and US households that might consider PV adoption, focusing especially on attributes of these contexts that seem likely to be instructive for explaining adoption choices.

We note at the outset that potential adopters may use fundamentally different psychological frames for thinking about adopting PV. (1) They might consider PV as a consumer durable such as a motor vehicle or major household appliance. In this instance, choice might be affected both by financial attributes of the purchase and by various nonfinancial ones, such as consistency with personal values, considerations of status and neighbors' reactions, and processes of social "contagion." (2) They might consider adoption as a financial investment, and thus as an alternative to investing available funds in retirement accounts, securities, or businesses. In this instance, choice might be informed mainly by financial calculations using concepts such as rate of return, payback period, and the like. (3) They might also consider adoption as an activity of economic production, similar to initiating a business at home. In this instance, other implicit or explicit metrics and considerations might come into play. As noted in this chapter, particular policies tend to presume that potential adopters are thinking about PV in certain ways. Given the diverse ways consumers may think about PV, however, policies and marketing efforts may or may not link well with consumer motivations. They may also influence households to think about PV in one or another way, and this could influence adoption choices.

Policies to promote PV in Germany and the United States illustrate this point. The largest financial incentives offered in the United States subsidize the initial cost of PV through tax credits, effectively lowering the price of PV systems and implicitly treating them as consumer durables. Some US installers offer consumers lease arrangements in which consumers can pay the upfront cost (net of the tax credit, which the installer claims) in exchange for a guaranteed rate of production over perhaps twenty years. In this arrangement, the household is making an investment similar to buying a stock or bond, and can compare these two possible uses of funds in terms of rate of return, like an investor. Germany incentivizes adoption by offering a feed-in tariff (FIT), which pays the household a guaranteed price for each kilowatt-hour (kWh) supplied to the grid. This form of incentive treats households as energy producers and encourages them to think about adoption as a business proposition, with themselves as the entrepreneurs.

In Section 1.2, we describe in greater detail the incentives offered in the two countries and the decision contexts that have resulted. In the section that follows, we consider the evidence on adoption in the two countries and elsewhere. Finally, we discuss the implications of the emerging evidence for understanding PV adoption, for informing more effective policies to increase adoption, and for further research.

18.2.1 Choice Context in Germany

18.2.1.1 *Financial incentives.*

Several German government policies have supported the diffusion of renewable energy, particularly PV, and these policies have changed over time (Hoppmann et al., 2014). A central feature of German solar energy policy, which has been widely copied by other countries (Hoppmann et al., 2014), is the FIT. The FIT guarantees owners of PV systems a fixed rate per kilowatt-hour of electricity supplied to the grid for a twenty-year period.

To be eligible for the FIT, PV systems must be grid-connected and registered. The FIT is fixed by German renewable energy law, the Erneuerbare Energien Gesetz (EEG), and takes effect on the date of the PV system's installation. Designed to stimulate initial growth in the market, the FIT has decreased as deployment has proceeded, from more than 0.50 €/KWh in 2006 to about 0.12 €/kWh in 2014. The generated electricity from grid-connected PV systems is either directly fed into the grid while the household consumes electricity from the grid, or is used for the electricity consumption in the household, feeding only the surplus into the grid. In the latter case, households cover their electricity consumption with PV-generated electricity as well as electricity provided by the grid when their PV systems do not generate enough electricity. Independent of the type of grid connection, households receive an account from the grid operator for the PV electricity fed into the grid and another account from the power supply company for the electricity purchased from the grid. Consumption from and production to the grid are metered separately to allow for the separate accounting. Between 2009 and 2012, additional incentives were paid for PV-generated electricity that was directly consumed by the producing households. While the FIT decreased over time, the cost for grid electricity increased, shifting the incentives from producing for the grid toward producing for home consumption. In 2012, grid parity was achieved for households with small PV systems (less than 10 kW of peak [kWp] production; Wirth, 2016). From that point on, most households with new contracts have had to pay more for power from the grid than they could earn from the FIT, so that using PV output for household consumption would lead to economic savings.

Other financial incentives have also been available. Solar loans with advantageous conditions are offered by some banks (e.g., Süd-West Kreditbank, KfW[1]-Bankengruppe) and savings and loan associations (e.g., Schwäbisch-Hall, LBS Hessen-Thüringen) in Germany. Generally, these loans can also be used for a combined investment in a PV system and a battery storage system, which facilitates household consumption of produced power by storing power produced during the day for later use. Some energy supply companies offer additional incentives at a local level. These incentives may be tied to long-term contracts and can consist of an additional FIT or a single payment. In 2015, such incentives were offered by several municipal utilities (e.g., Aachen, Bamberg, and Heidelberg).

Since May 2013, incentives have also been offered for the installation of battery storage systems. The storage program of the KfW-Bankengruppe and the Federal Ministry for the Environment provides low-interest loans and repayment subsidies for new PV installations if a fixed battery storage system is installed (KfW, 2013). PV systems installed since January 2013 can also use these incentives for the retrofitting of battery storage. About half of the PV owners who invest in battery storage systems use this funding (Moshövel et al., 2015; Sterner et al., 2015). About 17,000 battery storage systems were installed between May 2013 and March 2015 (Kairies et al.,2015). The 2013 program ended early in 2016 and was replaced by a new program that will continue until the end of 2018 (KfW, 2016). In the new program, recipients of funding can feed no more than 60 percent of their installed power into the grid (50 percent in the 2016–2018 program). The PV system must also be equipped with options of remote control by the grid operator. Battery storage systems increase the opportunities for owners to consume the power their systems produce, thus keeping within the feed-in limits.

18.2.1.2 *Ownership Options*
In Germany, homeowners can either own or lease PV systems. Few households choose the latter, though, as leasing conditions for small PV systems (<10 kWp) have historically not been very attractive. However, leasing is becoming an option of increased interest, with several municipal utilities (e.g., Aachen and Heidelberg) now offering it.

Because the FIT is not linked to a household's own consumption, households can invest in PV systems by renting a surface (e.g., on the roof of another building) or can participate in energy cooperatives that produce either for the grid or for local use. German law allows for energy cooperatives to take advantage of PV incentives, and 772 such cooperatives have been formed since 2006, with 130,000 members, of which 92 percent are individuals or households (DGRV, 2015).[2] Energy cooperatives can use the generated electricity directly, but other options are more common (Moll et al., 2015). These include selling the produced power to local consumers who may or may not be members of the cooperative, while the cooperative manages the system; leasing the PV system to a user who manages it and uses the power for its own consumption; and locating a cooperative-owned PV system on the roof of a multifamily building and providing power to the tenants (Moll et al., 2015). Energy cooperatives can also use the generated electricity for car-sharing systems with electric cars. By being members of energy cooperatives, private households can contribute to the energy transition by adopting PV even if they own no appropriate PV sites themselves or are prevented by the initial cost.

18.2.1.3 *Social Context and Market Penetration*
In Germany, financial incentives are supplemented by a support system that offers potential adopters individualized energy consulting at low cost. Researchers have noted that household investments in energy systems may be influenced by recommendations from energy consultants who are perceived to be credible sources of information (Achtnicht and Madlener, 2014; Kastner and Stern, 2015; Murphy, 2014; Stern et al., 1986). In Germany, professional energy consulting has been funded at a national level by the German

Ministry of Economics and Energy (BMWi, 2016a).[3] This funding covers up to 60 percent of the costs for in-depth audits, up from 30 percent prior to 2015. Nevertheless, the number of energy audits in Germany has decreased since 2013 (BAFA, 2016).[4] It may be that as PV has diffused more widely, energy consultants are no longer a key information source for households. Some analyses indicate that households prefer to rely on the advice of craftsmen they know, or recommendations from friends who have already made comparable investments (e.g., Kastner and Matthies, 2016). It may also be that households are unaware that energy audits for PV are funded, as there are currently no marketing campaigns promoting them – or PV investments in general. At present, information exchange concerning PV occurs primarily on a private basis in Germany, for instance, through specialized web portals or by nongovernmental organizations, especially nonprofit associations on a local or national level.

German households continue to make PV investments, regardless of the declining FIT, limited marketing, and the decreasing number of energy audits (BSW-Solar, 2016).[5] One reason may be that householders increasingly recognize that PV investments make good economic sense. Also, the rising market penetration may have advanced the diffusion process to a point where government-supported efforts to influence behavior are less critical. By 2012, more than 1.3 million PV systems had been installed in Germany. Market analyses indicate that about 95 percent of those are on residential buildings (BSW-Solar, 2015; BMWi, 2014). Of these, 70 percent were systems less than 10 kWp and 25 percent were systems of 10 to 40 kWp (BMWi, 2014). The market penetration for one- and two-family homes reached 2.4 percent in 2012, with greater diffusion in southern Germany, where the number of sunshine hours is higher (Corradini, 2015). In short, PV diffusion may have reached the early adopter stage in Germany several years ago (Rogers, 2003).

18.2.2 Choice Context in the United States

18.2.2.1 *Financial Incentives*

In the United States, PV-related policies and incentives vary considerably from one state to the next, and sometimes also within states. Only one national-level incentive exists for residential PV: a federal investment tax credit (ITC) that allows PV owners to claim 30 percent of the purchase prices of their systems, including installation costs, as a tax reduction.[6] A parallel corporate investment tax credit allows third-party corporate owners to claim a similar credit (and thereby pass on savings to residential customers).[7] Many states also provide credits against state personal income taxes (see www.dsireusa.org). While tax credits can significantly reduce the upfront costs of solar, and have been credited for spurring the recent increase in PV adoption (Barbose and Darghouth, 2015), they are of limited value to households with low tax liability (Barnes et al., 2012). To further stimulate adoption, many states, electric utilities and local governments offer cash incentives, often in the form of a grant or rebate based on the size of the installed system. An advantage of such incentives is that they are typically tied to quality assurance programs that require installers to meet minimum requirements (Barnes et al., 2012). To further reduce upfront costs, many states exempt or refund the sales tax on PV systems (typically 3–7 percent, depending on the state) (Daniel, Inskeep, and Proudlove, 2015), and some local governments waive or reduce the fees associated with permitting (Barnes et al., 2012). Information on tax incentives at state and local levels in the United States, at the level of postal zip codes, is readily available at www.dsireusa.org. Compared with Germany, the incentive picture is complex. Consequently, the information shared between households in different locations may be less useful, as the incentives for adoption may not be the same for sender and receiver.

Several policies are designed to make PV financially attractive by providing adopters a continuing stream of cost savings over time. As of February 2016, forty-one states have net metering rules that require utilities to credit homeowners for the excess electricity generated by their systems. Bidirectional meters measure the difference between the electricity the household consumes from the grid and the amount it feeds in. Homeowners earn kilowatt-hour credits on their bills when their electricity generation exceeds consumption. If credits remain at the end of the year or some other designated period, homeowners are compensated, often at the retail rate, for their net electricity production. To discourage homeowners from oversizing their systems, however, some states cap how much homeowners can be paid (e.g., at 125 percent of their average electricity consumption prior to installation; DSIRE, 2015). In addition, some states have aggregate statewide caps that limit the total number of PV systems that can participate in net metering.

In states with mandatory Renewable Portfolio Standards (RPS),[8] Solar Renewable Energy Certificates or Credits (SRECs) are another mechanism for lowering PV costs (Burns and Kang, 2012). PV owners earn a SREC for every 1,000 kWh of electricity produced, which can then be sold in an open market to state utilities, often through an SREC aggregator or broker. A typical 5kW residential system is expected to produce about six SRECs a year. The value of SRECs differs considerably by state. In 2015, prices for one SREC ranged from as low as $15 in Pennsylvania to over $400 in Massachusetts (SRECTrade, 2016). To further reduce the total costs of going solar, some states and local authorities exempt or reduce the added value of solar panels from property tax assessments. Some states also offer performance-based incentives (PBIs) that compensate PV adopters over time based on the performance of their PV systems. Like cash rebates, PBIs often come with requirements to ensure proper maintenance of the system in order to maximize its performance (Barnes et al., 2012).

From a purely financial standpoint, the suite of incentives available can significantly reduce the cost of going solar. Gillingham and Tsvetanov (2016) estimate that in Connecticut, for example, average federal and state incentives from 2008 to 2014 reduced the purchasing price of PV by 50 percent. From the perspective of the homeowner, however, navigating the landscape of potential incentives may be overwhelming, as a single installation may be eligible for several different incentives, each with different rules, application processes, and administrators (Vandenbergh et al., 2010). A complex landscape of incentives may deter households from making installations that would be beneficial on financial grounds. It may also make third-party-owned systems attractive, as the installer typically applies for all relevant incentives and can incorporate the savings into a solar lease contract or power purchase agreement.

18.2.2.2 *Ownership Models and Market Penetration*

The US residential PV market has grown dramatically over the last decade from 380 megawatts (MW) of cumulative installed capacity prior to 2010 to 5,644 MW in 2015 (GTM Research, 2016). The great bulk of this growth has been concentrated in a handful of states where policies and financial incentives are favorable and retail electricity rates are high. California has the largest residential PV market in the United States, with 5.7 percent penetration as of March 2016 (State of California, 2016; US Census Bureau, 2015). Much of this growth can be attributed to new ownership models. Third-party-ownership (TPO) financing, in particular, has made PV accessible to households that lack the capital or cash flow necessary to purchase a system outright (Drury et al., 2012; Rai and Sigrin, 2013). Under TPO, solar panels are installed on a homeowner's property but owned and maintained by a third-party company, which thus assumes many risks and responsibilities. Homeowners either lease the system long term (twenty to twenty-five years), paying a set monthly fee for a guaranteed level of production, or purchase the electricity generated at a set per-kilowatt-hour rate for the term of the contract, often with no upfront costs. Households may also have the option of prepaying the entire lease, which yields a predictable rate of return based on guaranteed production levels. Both lease fees and power purchase agreements (PPAs) are designed to be competitive with electricity rates charged by the utility. Whereas nearly 100 percent of PV systems were customer-owned in 2006, 72 percent of new installations in 2014 were TPO (Feldman and Bolinger, 2016; GTM Research, 2015). Some market analysts predict, however, that this trend will soon reverse, with a majority of new adopters choosing to own their systems (Litvak, 2015; PwC, 2015). As of 2015, several of the largest solar companies have begun offering loan products that allow households to own their systems directly while still relying on the solar provider for system maintenance and monitoring. Community solar is another option, still in the early stages of development in the United States. This arrangement allows any individual, regardless of homeownership or property suitability, to purchase shares in a larger, offsite PV installation.

18.2.2.3 *Social and Psychological Context*

While the recent growth in the PV market means more competitive pricing for homeowners, the US system presents households with a mixture of incentives that vary in type and across states and localities; that require multiple and sometimes unfamiliar and complex procedures to take advantage of; and that, compared with Germany, are supported by few accessible and credible information sources. Together, these factors make for complex decisions. Prospective adopters must assess which incentives are applicable for their situations, identify potential installers, get quotes for PV systems, consider the credibility of the production estimates and the reliability of the systems on offer, and weigh the trade-offs of the different options. Technology eases this process somewhat as installers can offer price quotes based on past electricity bills and satellite imagery of the home, without visiting the property in person. Homeowners may struggle, however, to evaluate the resulting quotes, as they may be based on different PV equipment, system sizes, and financial terms. Furthermore, given the relative infancy of the residential PV market, homeowners may be unsure of which companies to trust. Some of the TPO and loan arrangements offered by the PV industry have the effect of simplifying the adoption decision.

Another approach to overcoming these challenges is through community Solarize programs. First started in Portland, Oregon, in 2009, Solarize campaigns seek to reduce decision overload while leveraging the power of collective purchasing. By the end of 2015, more than 230 Solarize campaigns had been conducted in twenty-five states and the District of Columbia (Cook, 2015). Most Solarize programs share a common structure. Typically a lead organization, such as a trusted nonprofit or the local government, will vet one to three solar installers and negotiate a discounted price per kilowatt of installed capacity (e.g., 12–13 percent below market price; Cook, 2015). The discounted solar is then offered within the community for a limited time period. To increase uptake, outreach efforts are designed to take advantage of peer effects. Interested households are encouraged to attend a community workshop, where they not only learn about PV and the benefits of collective purchasing, but also see others in their community who are considering solar. This normative influence is reinforced through solar ambassadors – volunteer community members who have already installed solar and share their experiences with the group. By preselecting contractors through a competitive process and encouraging community members to sign up at the same time, Solarize programs help build consumer confidence and reduce inertia. Evidence from various evaluations suggests that Solarize programs help reach a large number of households, including many that had not previously considered solar (Ulrich, 2015).

18.2.3 Comparison of Germany and the United States

As we have illustrated, the financial incentives for PV, though substantial in both Germany and the United States, are quite different in the ways they are organized and supported. These differences may help explain, in part, the distinct patterns of diffusion observed in each country. As Sovacool (2009) has pointed out, national FITs (as in Germany) are characterized by a degree of harmonization, consistency, and predictability that is helpful to manufacturers, investors, and consumers; based on the experiences of Canada and Germany, FITs seem to be an effective way to quickly facilitate the diffusion of renewable energy technologies. By contrast, the large diversity of financial incentives and procedures for capturing them in the United States has necessitated considerably more effort on the part of the consumer to be well informed. Also, in Germany incentives are production-based, while in the United States, most incentives are aimed at reducing upfront costs for a PV system. These types of incentives place consumers in different psychological situations for the decision process. From a psychological perspective, a national FIT provides a readily understandable long-term promise of financial security that a fixed upfront incentive does not. Some US lease arrangements have a similar effect from the consumer's standpoint, in that by guaranteeing annual levels of production from a PV system, the leases make it easy to calculate annual return on investment by simply multiplying the guaranteed production by the average electricity rate per kilowatt-hour.

As demonstrated by the comparison of the United States and Germany, households in different countries (and states within the United States) are offered a huge variety of financial incentives for PV investments, including FITs, net metering, grants, rebates, low-interest loans, and leasing options. The marketing of these incentives also differs substantially. Multiple approaches have proven somewhat successful, but effectiveness is hard to compare as they have been implemented under different circumstances. Making incentives user-friendly – a strategy that implements recognized principles of program design (Stern et al., 2010; Vandenbergh et al., 2010) – appears to be one key to success, as discussed further later in this chapter. The challenge for policy makers is to identify highly effective approaches for their specific situations. Thus, financial incentives should be assessed not only on the basis of their size, but within the larger decision context. In the next section, we discuss insights from research on factors – financial and otherwise – that have been identified as predictors of the adoption of PV.

18.3 Factors Influencing Adoption

This section reviews available evidence on the factors influencing household adoption of PV systems. We discuss several classes of influences, in order: (a) motives for pursuing solar, including financial, environmental, and technological; (b) social influences; (c) information channels; and (d) other influences. As the previous discussion makes evident, there are major differences between countries in several of these classes of influence. This makes cross-country comparisons a valuable source of information on the determinants of adoption but also makes confident inferences difficult. For example, Germany and the United States offer different types of incentives for adoption, and also different systems for offering information to households. This makes the attribution of any differences in adoption rates to one of these influence types rather than to the other, or to the combination of the two, difficult. We review what is known about the effects of each influence type and then, to the extent we believe the evidence justifies them, we offer tentative conclusions about the importance of particular influencing factors, alone and in combination.

18.3.1 Motives of Potential Adopters

PV is at once a consumer durable, a financial investment, a "green" alternative to fossil fuel-generated electricity, and an innovative technology. The ways households respond to these different attributes of PV may be critical to understanding adoption.

18.3.1.1 *Financial Considerations*
Several studies have surveyed the general population to explore the extent to which financial considerations (among others) predict initial interest in PV. In Germany, Korcaj, Hahnel, and Spada (2015) found that the intention to purchase PV among nonadopting households was strongly predicted by positive attitudes toward PV and subjective norms (i.e., seeing others with PV and believing that one's peers would encourage them to adopt). Positive attitudes, in turn, were strongly correlated with beliefs that solar would lead to personal financial gains; concerns about the costs of solar were also a significant, but a weaker predictor. In a survey of 1,156 nonadopting households in Arizona, California, New Jersey, and New York (four of the largest PV markets in the United States), Wolske, Stern, and Dietz (2017) found that believing PV would be personally and financially beneficial was one of the strongest predictors of intention to talk to a PV installer.

In studies of PV adopters, evidence from the United States suggests that adopters look to PV as a source of financial security. Among early adopters in Wisconsin (US), few participants considered the payback period of their investments when deciding whether to buy PV (Schelly, 2014b). Instead, other economic factors, such as impending retirement, were more important for many participants (Schelly, 2014a). Similarly, planning for retirement and a recent increase in electricity rates were among the most common reasons that adopters in northern California became initially interested in PV (Rai, Reeves, and Margolis, 2016).

In the United States, economic factors have also been found to influence whether homeowners lease or buy their systems. According to Drury et al. (2012), TPO may be more attractive than buying because it reduces or eliminates upfront costs, reduces the risks and uncertainties associated with operating and maintaining a system, and typically reframes the financial benefit of PV into the consumer-friendly concept of monthly savings. From their analysis of California adopters, the authors conclude that TPO opens the PV market to households that would not otherwise invest in a PV system – namely households that are younger, less affluent, or less educated. Other research in California confirms that households that buy their systems are more likely to have greater access to upfront funds and be interested in PV primarily as a financial investment (Rai et al., 2016). Interestingly, research in Texas found no differences between buyers and leasers in terms of income (Rai and Sigrin, 2013). However, households with a tighter cash flow were more likely to lease.

Studies in other countries confirm the importance of financial motivations in pursuing PV (e.g., Haas et al., 1999; Jager, 2006). In a study of Austria's 200 kWp PV-rooftop program (1992–1994), Haas et al. (1999) found that the financial incentive offered played an important role in the decision to adopt; over one-third of the participants reported that they would not have invested in PV without the rebate, and nearly one-third indicated that they would have chosen a smaller system without the incentive. Other studies in the Netherlands (Jager, 2006) and in Hong Kong (Zhang, Shen, and Chan, 2012) have found that the initial cost of PV is an important barrier to adoption.

In sum, financial considerations, particularly the subjective belief that adoption will be financially beneficial, are important to PV adoption. Policies in the United States, Germany, and elsewhere have recognized this and have employed various types of incentives that have had positive financial effects such as lowering initial costs or guaranteeing ongoing financial benefits. Evidence indicates that different financial aspects of adoption matter to different classes of households, according to income, age, and perhaps other factors.

18.3.1.2 *Environmental Motives*

Environmental motives are often self-reported as a top reason for investing in PV, though not necessarily the only motive. This has been found to be true among adopters in Wisconsin (US) (Schelly, 2014b), Austria (Haas et al., 1999), and the Netherlands (Jager 2006). Korcaj et al. (2015) found beliefs about environmental benefits of PV to be a significant predictor of purchase intention, although the predictor was weaker than other ones. In the United States, proenvironmental personal norms were found to indirectly influence interest in PV; individuals who felt a greater moral obligation to address energy issues were more likely to believe that PV would benefit them personally, which in turn predicted interest in talking to a PV installer (Wolske et al., 2017). According to Jager (2006), general environmental problem awareness motivates people to learn more about PV and encourages greater cognitive engagement with the decision-making process. Similarly, Keirstead (2007) found that interest in environmental and energy-related topics motivated participants to become better educated about PV. Nevertheless, evidence from Schelly (2014a,

2014b) suggests that environmental motivations do not always play a role in PV adoption. Forty percent of adopters interviewed indicated that such motivations did not constitute a driver for PV adoption. Consequently, Schelly (2014a) concluded that there is a risk in framing PV in terms of its environmental benefits. Evidence indicates that environmental motives may be more important at earlier phases in the diffusion of innovation than later.

18.3.1.3 Technological Considerations

Evidence also suggests that PV is more likely to be adopted by individuals who are drawn to the innovativeness of the technology and are less averse to its potential risks. This may be especially true among households that adopt early. In Wisconsin, Schelly (2014b) found that early adopters shared a common trait of being interested in energy technologies and tracking their energy consumption. Over a third of participants also expressed a desire to educate others through their PV installations and demonstrate the feasibility of the technology. These results are in line with older research from Austria, where "proving that PV works" was cited as the predominant reason for participating in the 200 kWp PV-rooftop program (Haas et al, 1999). In line with Rogers' (2003) diffusion of innovation theory, participants were interested in the technology and more willing to take on financial risk. Other evidence suggests that consumer innovativeness remains an important factor in the decision to pursue solar in the United States, despite its growing popularity over the last decade. Among nonadopting households in the United States, consumers who, in general, seek out novel products were more likely to express interest in talking to an installer (Wolske et al., 2017). For individuals less technologically inclined, the perceived risks of PV may deter its adoption. In Germany, for example, concerns about increased fire risk and fears of electromagnetic radiation were found to be barriers to adoption (Sonnberger, 2015).

18.3.1.4 Social Influences

An increasing number of studies have looked at the role of social influence in facilitating PV adoption (Palm, 2016). Rai and Robinson (2013) categorized social influences into two types: active peer effects, which occur through peer-to-peer interaction; and passive peer effects, which result from being in close physical proximity to other PV systems.

In the United States, active peer effects such as talking to neighbors with PV have been found to spark interest in PV among eventual adopters (Rai et al., 2016) and significantly speed up the decision to go solar (by 4.6 months) (Rai and Robinson, 2013). Other evidence suggests that social influences are an important determinant of initial interest in PV among the general population. In Germany, for example, Korcaj et al. (2015) found that subjective norms – which measured both perceived social pressure and observed adoption – were the strongest predictor of intention to purchase PV. In the United States, Wolske et al. (2017) similarly found that perceived social support and curiosity about others' PV systems predicted interest in talking to an installer. In the Netherlands, Jager (2006) found that among new PV adopters, those who knew more PV owners prior to adoption were more likely to cite discussions with PV owners as an important motive in their decision to get solar.

Like active peer effects, passive peer effects such as seeing nearby installations have been found to stimulate interest in PV (Rai et al., 2016; Wolske et al., 2017) and shorten the time frame for deciding whether to go solar (by 1.5 months) (Rai and Robinson, 2013). Evidence from California found that each additional installation in a postal zip code area increased the probability of further adoption within that area (Bollinger and Gillingham, 2012). Likewise, PV adoptions in Connecticut were found to be clustered near previously installed systems, not necessarily following income or population distributions (Graziano and Gillingham, 2015). In line with these American studies, evidence of peer effects has been found in Germany. In a case study of the city of Wiesbaden, Müller and Rode (2013) found that people were more likely to get PV if other PV systems were already installed in the neighborhood. Rode and Weber (2016) examined national adoption patterns using a data set of 576,000 German households with PV systems installed through 2009. Similar to Bollinger and Gillingham (2012), they found that existing PV installations significantly increased the probability of new PV installations within a 1 kilometer radius.

Palm (2016) found evidence for both active and passive peer effects in Sweden. PV adopters indicated that local peers as well as observed PV installations nearby had an impact. Installation companies also reported higher interest in PV in areas where a PV system had recently been installed. Additionally, one-third of the households indicated that interest in PV was partially influenced by knowing a person working for a local PV installer.

18.3.1.5 *Information Channels*

Closely related to social influences are the communication channels through which potential adopters learn about PV. As PV is a relatively new technology with ever-changing rules and incentives, potential adopters may struggle to find the information most relevant to their personal situations. Having accessible, trustworthy sources may reduce uncertainties about the technology and shorten the decision period for considering it (Rai and Robinson, 2013). Past research suggests that communities of information (Schelly, 2014b), local electricity utilities (Palm, 2016), and solar community organizations (Noll, Dawes, and Rai, 2014) can be important sources of information. For example, solar community organizations can facilitate active peer effects; leverage trusted information sources; and bring together information about research, policy measures, and technical components (Noll et al., 2014). Rai and Robinson (2013) suggested designing online communication systems for PV that facilitate peer effects, such as online social platforms.

18.3.1.6 *Other Influences*

In addition to the categories of influence already identified, several other factors have been shown to affect the decision to adopt PV. Korcaj et al. (2015) found, for example, that intention to purchase PV was higher among individuals who believed getting PV would enhance their social status and lead to autarky. Independence from the electricity supplier was similarly cited as a moderately important consideration among PV adopters in the Netherlands (Jager 2006). The costs in time and effort of selecting and maintaining PV systems can also be an important influence on adoption. Lessees report spending less time researching PV and finding dependable information than buyers, presumably because the guarantees provided by the third-party owner reduce uncertainty about the decision (Rai and Robinson, 2013). Also, some households that can afford to purchase their systems outright instead choose to lease, in part to avoid the hassle of maintenance (Rai et al., 2016; Rai and Sigrin, 2013).

18.4 Conclusions

It is noteworthy that research on household adoption of PV has, with few exceptions, been conducted quite independently of behavioral theories and concepts from the social sciences that ought, prima facie, to have useful predictive value. Among these theories are diffusion of innovation theory (Rogers, 2003), which is supported by decades of research on adoption of consumer durables; the theory of planned behavior (Azjen, 1991), which offers a broad framework for individual decision-making; and value-belief-norm theory (Stern et al., 1999), which is focused on proenvironmental behavior in particular. Although these social science theories and others have been tested many times on behaviors that involve curtailment of the use of household energy-consuming equipment, they have not been tested frequently on household energy investments, and there is reason to believe that their applicability may not extend readily to these choices (Kastner and Stern, 2015). However, such theories do provide useful and testable hypotheses for study in the context of PV adoption that may help understand these adoption choices and inform efforts to influence adoption. They may also help improve the coherence of research on household energy investments and thus speed the accumulation of knowledge. Empirical tests of such behavioral theories and concepts may also help extend and refine theory by testing applicability in a new domain and pointing to needed refinements or integrations of theory (see, e.g., Wolske et al., 2017).

Research results to date with household adoption of PV seem broadly consistent with those from decades of behavioral research on other household energy investments, that is, adoption of technologies for energy efficiency and conservation (Stern et al., 1986; Gardner and Stern, 2002). Those research findings have been distilled into six basic principles for policy design for reducing greenhouse gas emissions from the household sector (Stern et al., 2010; Vandenbergh et al., 2010). We use these principles here as guideposts for discussing what is known about adoption of PV. They are (1) prioritize high-impact actions; (2) provide sufficient financial incentives; (3) strongly market the program; (4) provide valid information from credible sources at points of decision; (5) keep it simple; and (6) provide quality assurance. We see these principles implemented in some of the policies and programs for promoting PV but not in others. Although strong evidence is not yet in hand, it seems that the design principles likely do apply to PV adoption: policy and program effectiveness increases with the extent to which they embody the design principles. We describe each of the six principles and their applications to PV policy in greater detail in the following subsections.

18.4.1 Prioritize High-Impact Actions

Impact has been analyzed as the product of technical potential and behavioral plasticity (the proportion of people who can be induced to adopt the technology). Adoption of PV has one of the largest technical potentials for reducing greenhouse gas emissions of all household actions, as it can replace most emissions resulting from household electricity use and, in addition, can be used to run heat pumps to substitute for fossil fuel–based heating and to power electric motor vehicles to reduce transportation-related emissions. With community ownership arrangements, the ability of households to adopt PV is also quite large. Such arrangements allow homeowners and renters with inadequate roof space to invest in collectors that are installed elsewhere. Community solar arrangements also allow households to invest in PV that they do not consume themselves. Overall, household PV adoption is an ideal behavioral target for reducing greenhouse gas emissions.

18.4.2 Provide Sufficient Financial Incentives

The high cost of PV was long a major barrier to adoption. Policies in Germany, the United States, and elsewhere have responded to this barrier by providing various sorts of financial incentives. Incentives have likely been necessary to get adoption moving, especially when the cost of PV-generated electricity was not competitive with conventional sources. But even when incentives have been large, they have not been sufficient by themselves. The research on solar energy adoption indicates, as energy efficiency research also did, that although financial considerations are important, they are not by any means the only important factor affecting adoption (e.g., for PV, Korcaj et al., 2015; Rai and Robinson, 2013; Rai et al., 2016; Wolske et al., 2017; for solar thermal energy, Kastner and Matthies, 2016).

One way of providing "sufficient" incentives is to structure them to address the particular financial needs of specific types of potential adopters. For example, loans at any interest rate may not be attractive to low-income households if they cannot afford to borrow, but leases that are paid through saved electricity costs may be compatible with their needs. The qualitatively different kinds of financial incentives that have been offered appear to be aimed at different types of financial needs. For example, financially attractive loans in Germany and the tax credits and leasing arrangements common in the United States aim to reduce the initial cost of adoption, whereas the German FIT policy, US net metering policies, solar renewable energy credits, and some lease arrangements aim to guarantee a stream of financial savings over time. Thus, offering different types of incentive structures to a broad population has potential to increase adoption rates beyond what they would be with only one type of incentive.

A second important effect of financial incentives, according to energy efficiency research, is that they draw attention to the potential benefits of the incentivized investment and thus get potential adopters to consider a choice for the first time. This is another part of the meaning of sufficiency: an incentive needs to be large enough to get householders' attention. The effect of an incentive, however, may not be linear with its size, and may depend on other factors, such as how well the incentive is marketed or how burdensome the process is to apply for it.

Other psychological attributes of incentives can be important, independent of their size and perhaps for reasons other than their fit with users' financial needs and their ability to attract attention. For example, in a study of solar thermal energy systems in Germany, Kastner, Matthies, and Willenberg (2011) found that the psychological framing of an investment in terms of gain versus loss influenced households' choices. The source of the financial incentive may also matter. Past energy efficiency research found that variations in adoption rates of tenfold or more were common when different organizations (e.g., electric utility companies) offered identical financial inducements (Stern et al., 1986; Gardner and Stern, 2002). The variation seems to have been largely due to how well the programs' promoters implemented other design principles. Comparable studies of PV adoption have not been done, but the possibility of a similar phenomenon with PV and the factors responsible for high rates of adoption under particular incentive regimes deserve serious attention.

18.4.3 Strongly Market the Program

This principle seems surely to apply to PV as an emerging technology unfamiliar to most potential adopters. It seems clear that marketing should be tailored to audiences, considering that they vary considerably in their financial ability to invest, their attitudes and motives, their physical situations with respect to installing PV, and their proximity to other adopters. Policies and programs that are tailored in such respects can be expected to be more effective than one-size-fits-all strategies. But very little research can be found directed toward clearly identifying specific target groups and linking them to effective marketing strategies. This is an obvious direction for future research.

18.4.4 Provide Valid Information from Credible Sources at Points of Decision

Evidence of peer effects on adoption from both Germany and the United States suggests that neighbors and other peers can serve as trusted sources of information. The German experience also suggests that the most effective information sources can change as the diffusion process advances. German policy all along has subsidized individualized energy consulting to give potential adopters personalized and credible information. As adoption increased and additional credible sources, such as local installers and neighbors, came into the picture, use of the consulting services has declined, apparently because households were willing to rely on other sources of credible information.

The information consumers need may depend on how they see PV (as a consumer durable like a new roof or automobile, as an investment, as a green good, as a business opportunity) and on their personal values and concerns (e.g., financial motives, proenvironmental motives, attitudes toward novel technology). It would be possible to tailor information to individual consumers' needs through marketing efforts or with online platforms that offer information on different product attributes on request. However, the effectiveness of such approaches has not yet been studied experimentally.

18.4.5 Keep It Simple

This principle flows from the fact that "people economize on cognitive effort, not only on money" (Stern et al., 2010: 4848). In Germany, the FIT has made it easy for potential adopters to calculate the value of PV for them with a straightforward long-term guaranteed price for the electricity they produce. In the United States, by contrast, electricity prices are outside the consumer's control. Moreover, the wide array of available incentives and of associated paperwork in the United States, as well as the differing policies and sources of information, have made the net financial benefits of PV especially hard to estimate. This has likely slowed decision processes and therefore, lowered adoption rates compared with what they could otherwise have been.

More recently in the United States, private-sector solar energy companies have stepped in with programs that markedly reduce cognitive effort for householders with creative leasing arrangements. The companies take on the tasks of shopping for high-quality equipment and of filling out the multiple forms required to reap the available incentives. Lease arrangements can also eliminate the effort of calculating the financial value of PV by guaranteeing a rate for electricity that is lower than what the household is currently paying. Installation companies have economies of scale in doing such calculations and paperwork, and thus lower what may be a major cognitive barrier to adoption. A guaranteed electricity price or level of production also helps reduce the effort of shopping for a reliable installer, while also providing quality assurance (the final design principle). The credibility of such guarantees, however, can be a significant issue (see the following section).

18.4.6 Provide Quality Assurance

Many policies and program features intended to promote PV adoption address this obvious issue. These include the guarantees offered by some private installers, already noted, as well as government efforts to certify energy auditors and installers (in Germany, for example, see BAFA, 2016). In the United States, many state incentive programs are tied to quality assurance requirements to ensure that PV systems perform as promised.

Comparing the experience of Germany and the United States highlights that both governments and private-sector organizations have multiple roles to play in increasing the adoption. Governments can not only provide financial incentives and regulations, but create new types of opportunities for adoption, such as the possibilities for community-based PV installations. And private companies can not only market PV, but create institutional arrangements, such as long-term leases with production guarantees, that embody several design principles at once. Collaborations between different kinds of entities can yield additional opportunities to increase adoption rates, as when PV installers work together with lenders or when government agencies train or certify energy auditors working in the private sector.

18.4.7 Implications for Policy and Research

The design principles developed from research on household energy efficiency provide a good rough guide for policies and programs to promote PV. Each of the design principles clearly applies, and with regard to financial incentives, it is clear that their effectiveness depends not only on size, but on their ability to address specific financial barriers facing specific potential adopters, to get householders' attention, and perhaps to be presented in an attractive psychological framing. Effectiveness also depends on the extent to which policies and programs simultaneously apply the other design principles.

There are policy or program attributes that can embody multiple principles at once. Some of the US leasing arrangements, for example, offer sufficient financial incentives, quality assurance, reduced cognitive effort, and useful information at the point of decision. The best way to apply the design principles in practice has not been defined, however. It is almost surely situation-specific and dependent on factors external to the design principles. These include the policy context (e.g., the types of financial incentives available, rules governing feeding power into the grid); electricity prices and production costs, which vary across countries (Jenner et al., 2013); levels of trust in particular sources of information and systems of quality assurance available to the target populations; the potential adopters' financial positions, consumer concerns, and values as they affect their information needs and interest in the product attributes of PV systems; developments in the technology (e.g., improved performance, changes in cost, emerging issues of grid stability); and the stage of PV diffusion among the target population of potential adopters (Hoppmann et al., 2014). Effective promotion of PV will depend on applying the design principles in ways that also draw on situational knowledge. This is a creative task, and it seems that some promoters of PV have been quite effective in doing this.

So far, there is little scientific evidence available to further elaborate the design principles in the household PV domain and identify highly effective ways to implement them, and the contextual factors that determine effectiveness, let alone measure effectiveness. There is a considerable opportunity for economists, psychologists, marketing researchers, and others to collaborate with government agencies, private companies, and nonprofit organizations to further enlighten efforts to advance adoption of PV in the residential sector. The technical potential is high, the plasticity is considerable, and the time is ripe.

18.4.8 A Final Word on "Economic" and "Psychological" Influences on Adoption

It is tempting, especially in a volume like this one, to draw a sharp distinction between "psychological" and "economic" factors affecting the topic at hand – in this case, adoption of PV by households. The temptation is heightened by the fact that policies to promote adoption have invariably included financial incentives (the quintessential economic motivator) but have only sometimes focused closely on the many nonfinancial factors, some of them familiar to psychological research, that can also affect adoption, either on their own or in interaction with financial incentives. But we do not think a sharp distinction is warranted in an effort to understand and potentially influence adoption. The evidence reviewed here supports the view that multiple factors (psychological, economic, institutional, and other) are involved; that their effects interact; and that the factors that matter most, and the most promising forms of intervention, depend on the stage of the diffusion process in particular communities. Thus, to understand and influence PV adoption, one must be prepared to look at all sorts of possible explanations.

This is not usually done. Economists, psychologists, and for that matter engineers, sociologists, and other disciplinary specialists most typically look for explanations only to the variables and concepts from their home disciplines. Analyses of this type suffer from their disciplinary narrowness. Thus, an economist or an economics-focused policy maker might assume that all one needs to do is get the prices right, and behavior will follow, sooner or later. But it has long been known that responses to identical financial incentives can vary by a factor of ten or more depending on program implementation

(Stern et al., 1986; Kastner and Stern, 2015). Psychologists are prone to study frequently repeated behaviors – in the energy domain, changes in the use of household equipment – and to assume that whatever explains those kinds of behavior will explain the adoption of new equipment, such as PV. But the evidence suggests that this is not the case. For example, although decision makers' dispositions can be important determinants of low-cost, frequently repeated behaviors, they seem relatively unimportant in determining household energy investments (Kastner and Stern, 2015).

As this review indicates, variables favored by economists and psychologists, as well as by other disciplines, may each be influential, both alone and in combination. The review begins to suggest which variables are important to what degree, in what combinations, and in what contexts. It also suggests that to understand and influence PV adoption, researchers need to develop and policy makers and the industry need to use transdisciplinary explanatory frameworks. The design principles discussed in this chapter are a step toward such a framework. The next steps should include efforts to specify and test such transdisciplinary frameworks, so that decisions can be informed by something more precise than the set of general design principles.

Notes

1 KfW = Kreditanstalt für Wiederaufbau (Reconstruction Loan Corporation, Germany).
2 DGRV is Deutscher Genossenschafts- und Raiffeisenverband e.V. (German Cooperative and Raiffeisen Confederation, a regulated association).
3 BMWi is Bundesministerium für Wirtschaft und Energie (Federal Ministry for Economic Affairs and Energy, Germany).
4 BAFA is Bundesamt für Wirtschaft und Ausfuhrkontrolle (Federal Agency for Economics and Export Control, Germany).
5 BSW-Solar is Bundesverband Solarwirtschaft e.V. (German Solar Association).
6 The tax credit is set to phase out after 2021, with the tax credit decreasing to 26 percent for tax year 2020 and 22 percent for tax year 2021.
7 The corporate ITC has a similar phase out as the personal ITC but will continue at a 10 percent rate in tax year 2022.
8 Eighteen states plus the District of Columbia have enacted RPS that require utilities to provide a certain portion of electricity from renewable energy sources. Some states have specific "set asides" or "carve-outs" for solar electricity and have created SREC markets to help with compliance.

18.5 References

Achtnicht, M., and Madlener, R. (2014). Factors Influencing German House Owners' Preferences on Energy Retrofits. *Energy Policy*, 68, 254–263.

Ajzen, I. (1991). The Theory of Planned Behavior. *Organizational Behavior and Human Decision Processes*, 50, 179–211.

Barbose, G., and Darghouth, N. (2015). *Tracking the Sun VIII: The Installed Price of Residential and Non-Residential Photovoltaic Systems in the United States* (No. LBNL-188238). Berkeley, CA: Lawrence Berkeley National Laboratory. Retrieved from emp.lbl.gov/sites/all/files/lbnl-188238_1.pdf

Barnes, J., Gouchoe, S., Haynes, R., and Heinemann, A. (2012). *DSIRE Solar Policy Guide: A Resource for State Policymakers.* (p. 96). North Carolina: NC Solar Center.

Bazilian, M., Onyeji, I., Liebreich, M., et al. (2013). Re-considering the Economics of Photovoltaic Power. *Renewable Energy*, 53, 329–338. doi.org/10.1016/j.renene.2012.11.029

Bollinger, B., and Gillingham, K. (2012). Peer Effects in the Diffusion of Solar Photovoltaic Panels. *Marketing Science*, 31(6), 900–912. doi.org/10.1287/mksc.1120.0727

BAFA (Bundesamt für Wirtschaft und Ausfuhrkontrolle). (2016). Vor-Ort-Beratung. Retrieved from www.bafa.de/bafa/de/energie/energiesparberatung/index.html

BMWi (Bundesministerium für Wirtschaft und Energie) (2014). *Marktanalyse Photovoltaik-Dachanlagen.* Retrieved from www.bmwi.de/BMWi/Redaktion/PDF/M-O/marktanalyse-photovoltaik-dachanlagen,property=pdf,bereich=bmwi2012,sprache=de,rwb=true.pdf

BSW-Solar (Bundesverband Solarwirtschaft). (2016). *Daten und Infos zur deutschen Solarbranche.* Retrieved from www.solarwirtschaft.de/presse/marktdaten.html

BMWi (Bundesministerium für Wirtschaft und Energie). (2015). *Was und wie sanieren? – „Vor-Ort-Beratung" für Wohngebäude.* Retrieved from www.bmwi.de/Redaktion/DE/Publikationen/Energie/energiesparberatung-vor-ort.html

BMWi (Bundesministerium für Wirtschaft und Energie). (2016a). Energieberatung (Publication no. 2016-05-23). Retrieved from www.bmwi.de/DE/Themen/Energie/Energiewende-im-Gebaeudebereich/energieberatung.html

BMWi (Bundesministerium für Wirtschaft und Energie). (2016b). Zeitreihen zur Entwicklung der erneuerbaren Energien in Deutschland. Retrieved from www.erneuerbare-energien.de/EE/Redaktion/DE/Downloads/zeitreihen-zur-entwicklung-der-erneuerbaren-energien-in-deutschland-1990–2015.pdf?__blob=publicationFile&v=6

Burns, J. E., and Kang, J.-S. (2012). Comparative Economic Analysis of Supporting Policies for Residential Solar PV in the United States: Solar Renewable Energy Credit (SREC) Potential. *Energy Policy*, 44, 217–225. doi.org/10.1016/j.enpol.2012.01.045

Cook, R. (2015). *Benchmarking the Solarize Model: A Survey of Campaign Organizers.* Boston, MA: Meisters Consultants Group. Retrieved from solaroutreach.org/wp-content/uploads/2015/09/Solarize.pdf

Corradini, R. (2015). Solarthermie im Gebäudebestand: Notwendiger Schlüssel Energiewende. Retrieved from www.ffe.de/download/article/542/Solarthermie_Notwendiger_Schluessel_zur_Energiewende.pdf

Daniel, K., Inskeep, B., and Proudlove, A. (2015). *Understanding Sales Incentives for Solar Energy Systems: A Fact Sheet for Customers, Industry, and Local Governments.*

Raleigh, NC: NC Clean Energy Technology Center. Retrieved from solaroutreach.org/wp-content/uploads/2015/03/SalesTaxIncentivesFactsheet_Final.pdf

DGRV (Deutscher Genossenschafts- und Raiffeisenverband e.V.) (2015). Energiegenossenschaften: Ergebnisse der DGRV-Jahresumfrage. Retrieved from www.genossenschaften.de/sites/default/files/DGRV-Jahresumfrage_2015.pdf

Drury, E., Denholm, P., and Margolis, R. M. (2009). The Solar Photovoltaics Wedge: Pathways for Growth and Potential Carbon Mitigation in the US. *Environmental Research Letters*, 4(3), 034010. doi.org/10.1088/1748–9326/4/3/034010

Drury, E., Miller, M., Macal, C. M., et al. (2012). The Transformation of Southern California's Residential Photovoltaics Market Through Third-Party Ownership. *Energy Policy*, 42, 681–690. doi.org/10.1016/j.enpol.2011.12.047

DSIRE (Database of State Incentives for Renewables and Efficiency) (2015, December 21). Net Metering in Arizona. Retrieved from programs.dsireusa.org/system/program/detail/3093

Feldman, D., and Bolinger, M. (2016). *On the Path to Sunshot: Emerging Opportunities and Challenges in Financing Solar* (No. NREL/TP-6A20-65638) (p. 109). Golden, CO: National Renewable Energy Laboratory.

Gardner, G. T., and Stern, P. C. (2002). *Environmental Problems and Human Behavior* (2nd ed.). Boston: Pearson Custom Publishing.

Gillingham, K., and Tsvetanov, T. (2016, April 12). Hurdles and Steps: Estimating Demand for Solar Photovoltaics. Retrieved from environment.yale.edu/gillingham/GillinghamTsvetanov_SolarDemandCT.pdf

Graziano, M., and Gillingham, K. (2015). Spatial Patterns of Solar Photovoltaic System Adoption: The Influence of Neighbors and the Built Environment. *Journal of Economic Geography*, 15(4), 815–839. doi.org/10.1093/jeg/lbu036

GTM Research. (2015). *U.S. Utility PV Tracker.* Boston, MA: GTM Research.

GTM Research. (2016). *Solar Marketing Insight Report Q2 2016.* Boston, MA: GTM Research.

Haas, R., Ornetzeder, M., Hametner, K., Wroblewski, A., and Hübner, M. (1999). Socio-Economic Aspects of the Austrian 200 kwp-Photovoltaic-Rooftop Programme. *Solar Energy*, 66(3), 183–191. doi.org/10.1016/S0038-092X(99)00019-5

Hoppmann, J., Huenteler, J., and Girod, B. (2014). Compulsive Policy-Making the Evolution of the German Feed-in-Tariff System for Solar Photovoltaic Power. *Research Policy*, 43(8), 1422–1441. doi:10.1016/j.respol.2014.01.014

Jager, W. (2006). Stimulating the Diffusion of Photovoltaic Systems: A Behavioural Perspective. *Energy Policy*, 34(14), 1935–1943. doi.org/10.1016/j.enpol.2004.12.022

Jenner, S., Groba, F., and Indvik, J. (2013). Assessing the Strength and Effectiveness of Renewable Electricity Feed-in Tariffs in European Union Countries. *Energy Policy*, 52, 385–401.

Kairies, K.-P., Haberschusz, D., Magnor, D., Leuthold, M., Badeda, J., and Sauer, D. U. (2015). *Wissenschaftliches Mess- und Evaluierungsprogramm Solarstromspeicher: Jahresbericht 2015*. Retrieved from www.speichermonitoring.de/fileadmin/user_upload/Speichermonitoring_Jahresbericht_2015_web.pdf

Kastner, I., and Matthies, E. (2016). Investments in Renewable Energies by German Households: A Matter of Economics, Social Influences and Ecological Concern? *Energy Research and Social Science* 17, 1–9.

Kastner, I., Matthies, E., and Willenberg, M. (2011). Chancen zur Förderung nachhaltigkeitsrelevanter Investitionsentscheidungen durch psychologisch basiertes Framing – eine Pilotstudie [Prospects of increasing sustainability-relevant investment decisions through psychologically based framing – a pilot study]. *Umweltpsychologie*, 15 (1), 30–51.

Kastner, I., and Stern, P. C. (2015). Examining the Decision-Making Processes Behind Household Energy Investments: A Review. *Energy Research and Social Science*, 10, 72–89.

Keirstead, J. (2007). Behavioural Responses to Photovoltaic Systems in the UK Domestic Sector. *Energy Policy*, 35(8), 4128–4141. doi:10.1016/j.enpol.2007.02.019

KfW (2013). KfW and Federal Environment Ministry Launch Programme to Promote Use of Energy Storage in Solar PV Installation. Retrieved from www.kfw.de/KfW-Group/Newsroom/Aktuelles/Pressemitteilungen/Pressemitteilungen-Details_107136.html

KfW (2016). Merkblatt Erneuerbare Energien: KfW-Programm Erneuerebare Energien "Speicher"-275 Kredit. Retrieved from www.kfw.de/Download-Center/F%C3%B6rderprogramme-%28Inlandsf%C3%B6rderung%29/PDF-Dokumente/6000002700_M_275_Speicher.pdf

Korcaj, L., Hahnel, U. J. J., and Spada, H. (2015). Intentions to Adopt Photovoltaic Systems Depend on Homeowners' Expected Personal Gains and Behavior of Peers. *Renewable Energy*, 75, 407–415. doi.org/10.1016/j.renene.2014.10.007

Kumar S. B. (2015). A Study on Global Solar PV Energy Developments and Policies with Special Focus on the Top Ten Solar PV Power Producing Countries. *Renewable and Sustainable Energy Reviews*, 43, 621–634. doi.org/10.1016/j.rser.2014.11.058

Litvak, N. *U.S. Residential Solar Financing 2015–2020*. Boston, MA: GTM Research.

Moll, M., Keller, J., Engelmann, R., et al. (2015). *Geschäftsmodelle für Bürgerenergie genossenschaften: Markterfassung und Zukunftsperspektiven*. Energieagentur Rheinland-Pfalz GmbH: Kaiserslautern. Retrieved from www.energiegenossenschaften-gruenden.de/fileadmin/user_upload/Newsletter-Anhaenge/2016_Newsletter_Februar/Buergerenergiegenossenschaften_Broschuere_160210_Small.pdf

Moshövel, J., Kairies, K.-P., Magnor, D., et al. (2015). Analysis of the Maximal Possible Grid Relief from PV-Peak-Power Impacts by Using Storage Systems for Increased Self-Consumption. *Applied Energy*, 37, 567–575. doi:10.1016/j.apenergy.2014.07.021

Müller, S., and Rode, J. (2013). The Adoption of Photovoltaic Systems in Wiesbaden, Germany. *Economics of Innovation and New Technology*, 22(5), 519–535. doi:10.1080/10438599.2013.804333

Murphy, L. (2014). The Influence of Energy Audits on the Energy Efficiency Investments of Private Owner-Occupied Households in the Netherlands. *Energy Policy*, 65, 398–407. doi:10.1016/j.enpol.2013.10.016

Noll, D., Dawes, C., and Rai, V. (2014). Solar Community Organizations and Active Peer Effects in the Adoption of Residential PV. *Energy Policy*, 67, 330–343. doi:10.1016/j.enpol.2013.12.050

Palm, A. (2016). Local Factors Driving the Diffusion of Solar Photovoltaics in Sweden: A Case Study of Five Municipalities in an Early Market. *Energy Research and Social Science*, 14, 1–12. doi:10.1016/j.erss.2015.12.027

PwC. (2015). Financing US Residential Solar: Owning, Rather Than Leasing, Will Bode Well for Homeowners. Retrieved from www.pwc.com/us/en/technology/publications/assets/pwc-financing-us-residential-solar-08-2015.pdf

Rai, V., Reeves, D. C., and Margolis, R. (2016). Overcoming Barriers and Uncertainties in the Adoption of Residential Solar PV. *Renewable Energy*, 89, 498–505. doi.org/10.1016/j.renene.2015.11.080

Rai, V., and Robinson, S. A. (2013). Effective Information Channels for Reducing Costs of Environmentally-Friendly Technologies: Evidence from Residential PV Markets. *Environmental Research Letters*, 8(1), 014044. doi.org/10.1088/1748–9326/8/1/014044

Rai, V., and Sigrin, B. (2013). Diffusion of Environmentally-Friendly Energy Technologies: Buy Versus Lease Differences in Residential PV Markets. *Environmental Research Letters*, 8(1), 014022. doi.org/10.1088/1748–9326/8/1/014022

Rode, J., and Weber, A. (2016). Does Localized Imitation Drive Technology Adoption? A Case Study on Rooftop Photovoltaic Systems in Germany. *Journal of Environmental Economics and Management*, 78, 38–48. doi:10.1016/j.jeem.2016.02.001

Rogers, E. M. (2003). *Diffusion of Innovations* (2nd ed.). New York: Free Press.

Schelly, C. (2014a). Implementing Renewable Energy Portfolio Standards: The Good, the Bad, and the Ugly in a Two State Comparison. *Energy Policy*, 67, 543–551. doi:10.1016/j.enpol.2013.11.075

Schelly, C. (2014b). Residential Solar Electricity Adoption: What Motivates, and What Matters? A Case Study of Early Adopters. *Energy Research and Social Science*, 2, 183–191. doi.org/10.1016/j.erss.2014.01.001

Sonnberger, M. (2015). *Der Erwerb von Photovoltaikanlagen in Privathaushalten: Eine empirische Untersuchung der Handlungsmotive, Treiber und Hemmnisse.* Wiesbaden: Springer.

Sovacool, B. K. (2009). The cultural barriers to renewable energy and energy efficiency in the United States. *Technology in Society*, 31(4), 365–373. doi.org/10.1016/j.techsoc.2009.10.009

SRECTrade. (2016). SREC Markets. Retrieved from www.srectrade.com/srec_markets/

State of California. (2016, January 31). California Solar Statistics. Retrieved from www.californiasolarstatistics.ca.gov/archives/nem_currently_interconnected/

Stern, P. C., Aronson, E., Darley, J. M., et al. (1986). The Effectiveness of Incentives for Residential Energy Conservation. *Evaluation Review*, 10(2), 147–176. doi: 10.1177/0193841X8601000201

Stern, P. C., Dietz, T., Abel, T., Guagnano, G. A., and, L. (1999). A Value-Belief-Norm Theory of Support for Social Movements: The Case of Environmentalism. *Human Ecology Review*, 6(2), 81–97.

Stern, P. C., Gardner, G. T., Vandenbergh, M. P., Dietz, T., and Gilligan, J. M. (2010). Design Principles for Carbon Emissions Reduction Programs. *Environmental Science and Technology*, 44, 4847–4848. doi: 10.1021/es100896p

Sterner, M., Eckert, F., Thema, M., and Bauer, F. (2015). *Der positive Beitrag dezentraler Batteriespeicher für eine stabile Stromversorgung.* Bundesverband

Erneuerbare Energie e.V. (BEE) & Forschungsstelle Energienetze und Energiespreicher (FENES). Retrieved from www.bee-ev.de/fileadmin/ Publikationen/BEE_HM_FENES_Kurzstudie_Der_positive_Beitrag_von_ Batteriespeichern_2015.pdf.

Ulrich, E. (2015, December 29). Making a Difference: Solarize Programs Accelerating Solar Adoption. Retrieved from energy.gov/eere/articles/making-difference-solarize-programs-accelerating-solar-adoption

U.S. Census Bureau. (2015). QuickFacts: California. Retrieved from www.census.gov/ quickfacts/table/PST045215/06

Vandenbergh, M. P., Stern, P. C., Gardner, G. T., Dietz, T., and Gilligan, J. M. (2010). Implementing the Behavioral Wedge: Designing and Adopting Effective Carbon Emissions Reduction Programs. *Environmental Law Reporter*, 40, 10545–10552.

Verbraucherzentrale Bundesverband e. V. (2015). Unser Angebot – Energieberatung der Verbraucherzentrale. Unabhängig, kompeten und nah. Retrieved from www.verbraucherzentrale-energieberatung.de/downloads/Flyer_Unser_ Angebot.pdf

Wirth, H. (2016). *Recent Facts About Photovoltaics in Germany*. Freiburg: Fraunhofer Institut für Solare Energiesysteme. Retrieved from www.ise.fraunhofer .de/en/publications/veroeffentlichungen-pdf-dateien-en/studien-und-konzeptpapiere/recent-facts-about-photovoltaics-in-germany.pdf

Wolske, K. S., Stern, P. C., and Dietz, T. (2017). Explaining Interest in Adopting Residential Solar Photovoltaic Systems in the United States: Toward an Integration of Behavioral Theories. *Energy Research & Social Science*, 25, 134–151.

Zhai, P., Larsen, P., Millstein, D., Menon, S., and Masanet, E. (2012). The Potential for Avoided Emissions from Photovoltaic Electricity in the United States. *Energy*, 47(1), 443–450. doi.org/10.1016/j.energy.2012.08.025

Zhang, X., Shen, L., and Chan, S. Y. (2012). The Diffusion of Solar Energy Use in HK: What Are the Barriers? *Energy Policy*, 41, 241–249. doi.org/10.1016/ j.enpol.2011.10.043

19 Economic and Psychological Determinants of Ownership, Use and Changes in Use of Private Cars

Tommy Gärling and Margareta Friman

19.1 Introduction

In this chapter, we first address two questions: why are automobiles purchased, and why are automobiles, after being purchased, used to such a large extent? We argue that instrumental and economic factors (including time savings) play important roles. Yet, psychological factors appear to also play a decisive role. Following a brief overview of factors accounting for the unprecedented historical increase in automobile ownership (Section 19.2), determinants of private car use will be analysed in the following section, 19.3.

Substantial environmental and societal costs of private car use such as congestion, noise, air pollution, excessive land use crowding out other uses and depletion of material and energy resources are expected future consequences of the worldwide increasing trend in automobile ownership and use (Goodwin, 1996; Greene and Wegener, 1997; van Wee, 2012, 2014). In many urban areas, these consequences are already being felt, leading to various policy measures for reducing or changing private car use being placed high on the political agendas. In Section 19.4, we describe and classify a number of such policy measures. Following this classification, we review in the same section evidence of the policy measures' effectiveness, public acceptability and political feasibility.

19.2 Historical Trends in Private Car Ownership and Use

The automobile has drastically altered the development of the world like few other human inventions. In the developed countries, and now in developing countries, its versatility strongly contributes to why it is chosen for urban, suburban and rural travel (Jakobsson, 2007). Versatility (in this chapter, referred to as instrumental motives) is, however, not a sufficient explanation. As will be argued, the automobile is also chosen because it is fun to drive and ride, provides privacy and security and signals social status (Gatersleben, 2007, 2014; Stradling, 2002).

Even though cars were available at the beginning of the twentieth century, it was only in the years after World War II with the subsequent spread of affluence and the acceleration of automobile mass production that ownership was brought within the reach of a majority of households in the industrialised world. Automobile ownership is related to household socioeconomic characteristics (e.g., income, household composition, employment status), the characteristics of the transport system (e.g., car purchase costs, available road infrastructure, nonaccess to public transport) and attributes of the built environment (e.g., population density, access to services and amenities) (Giuliano and Dargay, 2006).

Bonsall (2000) notes that private car ownership in the United Kingdom rose from 30 per cent of households in 1960 to 70 per cent in 1995. Pucher (1999) reports a similar large increase for the United States: per capita car ownership increased from 0.31 in 1960 to 0.65 in 1996. Considering only licensed drivers, Southworth (2001) calculates that an average of more than one vehicle per licensed driver has already been reached. Such a growth in car ownership is not limited to these Anglo-Saxon countries, to which Australia and Canada can be added with increases in cars per capita for the period 1970 to 1992 from 0.31 to 0.45 and from 0.31 to 0.49, respectively (Dargay and Gately, 1999). Similar trends have been observed for other industrialised countries, including several in the European Union. For instance, Vilhelmson (2005) estimates that in Sweden, almost all growth in daily travel since the 1950s is attributable to increase in car use. Eurostat (2013) estimates that the automobile accounts for more than 80 per cent of the total daily distance of passenger travel; the corresponding figure for the United States is similar (Pucher, 1999). When car use is indexed as the number of trips as opposed to distance travelled, the car accounts for 45 per cent of urban trips in European countries but a staggering 90 per cent in the United States. This implies that in the United States the car is used for shorter distances. Perhaps reflecting a similar European trend, in the United Kingdom Mackett (2001) notes an increase in the number of short car trips.

To some extent, these alarming figures may be offset by recent evidence of a discontinued increase of private car use (Millard-Ball and Schipper, 2011). Thus, referred to as peak car use, stagnation or even a decrease has been observed in eight developed countries (Australia, Canada, France, Germany, Japan, Sweden, the United Kingdom and the United States). Different explanations have been offered. Millard-Ball and Schipper (2011) propose that increasing fuel prices accounts for the peak car use. Litman (2012) highlights a number of additional determinants: automobile saturation, wealth effects, aging populations, increased urbanisation, improved alternative travel options and incentives, changing consumer preferences and increased concerns for health and environment. Goodwin (2012) argues that peak car use should be considered a turning point followed by decline. It remains, however, speculative until a conclusive explanation of peak car use has been offered. Also, current levels of automobile use in developed countries are still not sustainable. Therefore, a decrease would be required – not solely an end to the increase.

Suggesting instead that the future is even darker, sharply increasing automobile ownership and use are observed in countries only beginning the industrialisation process (e.g., China, India) or which are to some extent industrialised such that citizens are beginning to experience income growth and spread of affluence (e.g., South Korea, Taiwan) (Kitamura and Mohamad, 2009). Indeed, according to Sperling and Claussen (2004), the fastest growth has been observed in Latin America and Asia, with vehicle sales in China, for example, having increased annually by more than 50 per cent in recent years (from 700,000 in 2001 to 1.1 million in 2002, and about 1.7 million in 2003).

19.3 Determinants of Car Use

A variety of reasons account for why the private car is such a popular travel mode. Determinants of car use can be broadly classified in terms of whether they are primarily instrumental, economic or psychological. Each is discussed in turn in the following subsections. However, prior to doing so, it is important to note that car ownership (or access) is an important determinant of car use. If individuals own or have access to a car, then they are likely to use it even though there are equal or better alternatives. Wootton (1999) summarises clear evidence of this from the United Kingdom context: the purchase of a household's first car leads to a doubling of the total number of journeys, roughly half the journeys previously made by public transport being transferred to the newly purchased car, and cycling and walking journeys falling slightly. Access to a car may also lead to increases in travel demand, exacerbated by access to additional cars. Wootton (1999) reports that in the United Kingdom families without access to a car made an average of 2.5 journeys per weekday, families with a car an average of 6.4, while families with two or more cars averaged 8.7 journeys per weekday. As another example, Cullinane and Cullinane (2003) showed that 35 kilometres is the average length driven per car per day in Hong Kong. This is despite the fact that Hong Kong is small (50 by 40 kilometres), that very few drivers have permits to drive into mainland China and that public transport accounts for 90 per cent of all motorised journeys. Once a car has been acquired, it appears to quickly become a necessity. As a consequence, car use may become habitual. Yet, there are other factors that also influence car use in addition to the mere access to a car.

19.3.1 Instrumental Factors

Fulfilling biological needs, social obligations and personal desires requires that people move from one place to another place in the environment to perform goal-directed behaviours such as work, maintenance activities (e.g., shopping) and various leisure activities (Gärling and Garvill, 1993). That demand for travel is derived from this requirement constitutes a basic tenet of the dominant activity-based approach to travel behaviour analyses (e.g., Axhausen and Gärling, 1992; Bhat and Koppelman, 1999; Ettema and Timmermans, 1997; Jones et al., 1983; Kitamura, 1988; Recker, McNally and Roth, 1986). It follows that the way a society is spatially organised is an essential determinant of the degree and type of travel demand and that using the car to fulfil such aforementioned obligations, needs and desires can be considered an instrumental reason for car use. The versatility of the automobile has made it the most popular alternative.

This popularity of the automobile is stepped up even further by the fact that from the turn of the twentieth century, a much more extreme spatial separation of activities, never before seen, has evolved. Furthermore, because the spread of affluence subsequent to World War II made automobiles affordable to most people, the rail network has not been maintained at the same level (Crawford, 2000; Maat, 2002). As a result of owning an automobile, people could live farther away from their place of work in locations that had previously not been accessible, giving rise to suburbanisation due to preferences for low-density, single-family homes with a garden in a green setting (Garreau, 1991; Maat, 2002; Muller, 1995). Other contributing factors to suburbanisation include population growth, as well as the high prices of land and construction in city centres (Gordon and Richardson, 1997). Cheaper land for housing, retail and industry frequently available on the outskirts of urban areas has resulted in a gathering momentum of urban sprawl.

The spatial separation due to the decentralisation of activities is generally too large to allow walking or cycling, and the dispersion of people and activities makes it difficult to plan efficient, regular and effective public transport services. Using Los Angeles as an example, Modarres (2003) illustrates how the city centre area is well served by public transport, as are various work subcentres located outside the city centre area. However, while the public transport system is appropriate for connecting workplaces, it is poor at connecting employees to their place of work (particularly if located outside the city centre). Examining the Norwegian context, Aarhus (2000) found that the suburbanisation of work places was associated with increases in commuting by automobile, presumably because suburbanisation is associated with improved access to (free) parking, poorer access to public transport and a smaller share of employees living near enough to work to be able to walk or cycle. This development has negatively affected the demand for public transport. A lack of integrated land and transport policies have further contributed to a lower and less efficient provision of public transport with fewer departures and longer travel times (Cameron, Lyons and Kenworthy, 2004). Some cities even removed public transport during the 1960s and 1970s (one example is the trams in Stockholm, which were all removed), leaving citizens with fewer travel options. In addition, difficulties in subsidising public transport services have increased fare prices without necessarily improving quality. Several negative developments together thus account for a reduced attractiveness and use of public transport.

The versatility of the car is made possible by the advancements made in automobile technology and societies' substantial investments in road infrastructure. Thus, the car, coupled with associated infrastructure investments, assists people in overcoming the natural limitations to their speed of movement and radius of action. This utilitarian tool-function of automobiles can be extended to include comfort, protection or safety and independence (Gatersleben, 2007, 2014; Stradling, 2002). Cars shield people from direct exposure to the elements, and this shielding property also means that direct interactions with people outside the car are limited and that the driver of the car feels secure (Wright and Egan, 2000). The transportation of goods, the chauffeuring of others or time and distance constraints also often make the car a most convenient tool. It also conveys a feeling of independence.

The increasing complexity of individual and household activity agendas is an additional contributing factor to the use of the car. Current travel demand goes far beyond the home-to-work journey on weekdays (e.g., Levinson and Kumar, 1995). In Levinson and Kumar's (1995) work, for example, household travel surveys from the Washington, D.C., metropolitan area for the years 1968 and 1988 were compared and analysed. They found significant increases in the linking of work and nonwork trips, as well as a shift in the peak of non-work trips such that it coincided with the afternoon peak of work trips (i.e., trip chaining with the afternoon commute home). Such trip chaining due to attempts to more efficiently fulfil the ever-growing number of needs, desires and obligations associated with modern life is arguably also a cause of the growth in motorised travel.

Our propositions of instrumental factors determining private car use are summarised in Figure 19.1. Degree and type of travel demand depend on activity choice and the spatial organisation of the environment. Implying that some degree of freedom of choice exists (Timmermans et al., 2003), mediating between travel demand and travel is a choice between whether to travel or not; where to travel; how to travel; and when to travel, which is influenced by attributes of the transportation system such as speed, frequency, reliability, safety and cost.

19.3.2 Economic Factors

Lave (1992) argued that as affluence and incomes rise, the value placed on time increases such that faster modes of travel become attractive. Indeed, research generally shows income to be related to the value of travel time (e.g., Wardman, 2001). Given the complexity of activity agendas, with their tight schedule of activities (e.g., Vilhelmson, 1999) and given the aforementioned pattern of urban sprawl (e.g., Muller, 1995), in most cases the private car is

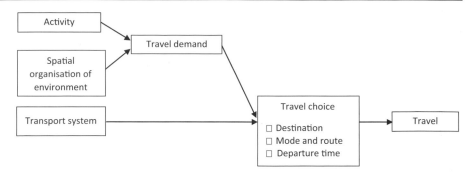

Figure 19.1. *Determinants of travel.*

the fastest mode (i.e., the mode yielding smallest loss of value of time spent travelling). Research by Cullinane (2003) found that the preference for a faster mode of travel (car or public transport) is a major determinant of mode choice in Hong Kong. Despite this and other qualifications (e.g., Priemus, Nijkamp and Banister, 2001), it is nevertheless the case that the spatial separation of activities within the context of mass suburbanisation is a major determinant of car use. Schwanen et al. (2001) illustrated how decentralisation of urban land invariably leads to measurable increases in automobile use and reductions in cycling, walking and the use of public transport. Thus, in sum, travel time and the value of time is such that in the majority of cases it makes 'economic sense' to use the car. Car use is also cheaper in that its full external costs are not paid for. As noted by Steg (2003), the costs of accidents, environmental problems (e.g., air and noise pollution, congestion), traffic safety and infra- structure maintenance are passed from car users to society as a whole. In the majority of places in the world, car users are then able to continue driving without paying for these external costs. It is only in a handful of cities that attempts have been made to internalise such costs, the most obvious example being road pricing in its various forms. The aim of road pricing schemes (e.g., Singapore; see Foo, 1997, 1998, 2000; Goh, 2002) is thus primarily to raise costs so that the congestion externalities are internalised (Emmerink, Nijkamp and Rietfeld, 1995). Yet, road pricing schemes have also been found to have positive effects by improving local environments (Eliasson et al., 2009). Other road pricing schemes have more recently been implemented in London, Oslo and Stockholm (Niskanen and Nash, 2008) closely mirroring the Singapore example (as described in the Appendix).

19.3.3 Psychological Factors

The status and identity associated with being an automobile owner are one source of attraction that has roots in the very early days of the car. Initially, being an automobile owner was an envied and respected position (Sandqvist, 1997), and even since then the automobile has continued fulfilling the role of powerful status symbol, albeit with a slightly different emphasis: the ubiquity of the car has led to it being perceived as an everyday tool, much like a refrigerator, and anyone not owning a car is perceived as being less well-off. Indeed, the norm in many parts of the developed world, particularly in the United States, is for families to own more than one car; not owning a car is interpreted as a sign of poverty (Sandqvist, 1997). The automobile furthermore allows for the expression of one's individuality, identity and personality (Gatersleben, 2007, 2014; Stradling, 2002). The importance of identity and independence varies with sociodemographic variables. Personal identity is particularly important for young drivers and the poor, while independence is particularly important for women over forty years of age. It should thus come as no surprise that advertisers emphasise different aspects of driving dependent on the demographic group to which they are trying to sell their product. As Gatersleben (2007, 2014) noted, status factors are also frequently associated with instrumental factors and therefore difficult to identify. Using direct and indirect methods of assessments, Steg (2005) showed that automobile owners are more willing to reveal instrumental than status motives.

The car may even be perceived to be an extension of the human body, making people more powerful and energetic, with younger car users in particular seeking enjoyment in the ability to travel at great speed. According to Wright and Egan (2000), this is why car design in recent years has emphasised horizontal lines that proclaim power and speed. While designs have changed over the years (e.g., recent designs have given much greater weight to safety because of the increasing number of female drivers), the rationale behind them (i.e., reflecting and communicating personality and as extensions of the human body) has not. Consider, for example, the flamboyant automobile designs of the 1960s, complete with shark fins and teeth, as well as the more contemporary designs associated with many of the larger sport-utility vehicles (e.g., the Hummer), with their massive weight, size and raised bodies. (See also Wright and Curtis, 2005, for a review of the history of car design and its implications.) Clearly, car consumption is not simply an issue of rational economic choice but has also to do with aesthetic, emotional and sensory responses (Sheller, 2004).

A car is also sometimes not purely chosen for the sake of activity participation; car use is thus not purely a derived demand. This is the case when people travel for the sake of travelling or travel to another destination via a more scenic route (Mokhtarian and Salomon, 2001) (or likewise when commuters choose public transport in order to work or read for pleasure; see Lyons and Urry, 2005). Also, in addition to instrumental motives, Jakobsson Bergstad et al. (2011) and Steg (2005) showed that affective (e.g., enjoyment) and symbolic (e.g., prestige) factors are important additional motives for car use. Complementing these findings, Handy, Weston and Mokhtarian (2005) found that excess driving may be due to valuing driving itself. Thus, some people, or all people some of the time, may choose to drive because they like it and not only out of habit, poor planning or poor quality of travel information. Yet, driving is also sometimes stressful or boring (Gatersleben and Uzzel, 2007). Purpose (work or leisure) and length of trip, traffic congestions, road quality and scenery and possibly the type of automobile (a new fancy car or an old one not working properly) may cause the differences in feelings.

The various benefits of the car leading to its frequent use may result in the development of a car-use habit (Fujii and Gärling, 2007). An important pre-requisite for the development of a habit is in general that the behaviour is rewarded, repeated a sufficient number of times under stable circumstances and that the individual is motivated and able to repeat the behavior (Ouellette and Wood, 1998). These conditions appear to apply to car use. Attitudes and the appeal of the automobile contribute to the instigation of driving, often acting as its own reward. Furthermore, the urban environment in which one lives changes very slowly (in terms of road networks, place of residence and work) and, as such, the context in which choices of driving occur is stable. Thus, car use is likely to be repeated and, more importantly, processing of information preceding the choice may change such that the need to travel to an activity automatically activates a script-based choice of the car (Gärling, Fujii and Boe, 2001; Verplanken, Aarts and Van Knippenberg, 1997). The resulting limited information processing makes breaking car-use habits difficult because it requires some incentive to attend to new information (Garvill, Marell and Nordlund, 2003).

19.4 Policies to Reduce or Change Private Car Use

There are several conceivable policy measures that may reduce the adverse effects of private car use. Some measures do not require a reduction in car use (e.g., increased capacity of road infrastructure, improved car technology or limiting speed) if they decrease the environmental impact per car to a sufficient degree. However, a general assessment of the current state is that measures reducing manifest demand for private car use must be implemented in many urban areas (e.g., van Wee, 2012, 2014). Furthermore, it is necessary to change private car use with respect to when and where people drive, particularly on major commuter arteries during peak hours and in city centres. The proposed measures are generally referred to as *travel demand management* (TDM) (Kitamura, Fujii and Pas, 1997) since they focus on changing or reducing travel demand. Other terms with similar meanings include, for instance, transport system management (Pendyala et al., 1997) or mobility management (Kristensen and Marshall, 1999).

19.4.1 Classification

Several attempts have been made to classify TDM measures. At a more specific level, Litman (2003) distinguishes five classes: increasing transport options; provision of incentives to switch mode; land-use management; policy and planning reforms; and support programmes. A partly overlapping set is proposed by May, Jopson and Matthews (2003) as land-use policies, infrastructure provision (for modes other than the private car), management and regulation, information provision, attitudinal and behavioral change measures and pricing. Vlek and Michon (1992) suggest the following classes: physical changes such as, for instance, closing out car traffic or providing alternative transportation; law regulation; economic incentives and disincentives; information, education and prompts; socialisation and social modelling targeted at changing social norms; and institutional and organisational changes such as, for instance, flexible work hours, telecommuting, or 'flexplaces'. At a more general level, Gatersleben (2003) distinguishes measures aimed at changing behavioural opportunities from measures aimed at changing perceptions, motivations and norms. In a similar vein, Jones (2003), Steg and Vlek (1997), Stradling, Meadows and Beaty (2000) and Thorpe, Hills and Jaensirisak (2000) distinguish between push and pull measures. Push measures discourage car use by making it less attractive; pull measures encourage the use of alternative modes to the car by making such modes more attractive.

Partly based on these different systems of classification, Loukopoulos et al. (2006a) proposed that TDM measures may be characterised as varying with respect to *targeting latent versus manifest travel demand, time scale, spatial scale, coerciveness, top-down versus bottom-up process* and *market-based versus regulatory mechanism.* Brief definitions of each are given in Table 19.1 together with assessments on these dimensions of *individualised marketing* (IM), *road pricing* (RP), and *prohibition* (Pn). (Examples of each are described in the Appendix.) Any TDM measure may thus be characterised with respect to whether it targets observed or unobserved travel (e.g., measures reducing congestion targeting manifest travel demand versus measures increasing public transport capacity targeting latent demand), with respect to time and area of operation (e.g., weekday morning peak on major arteries to downtown), and with respect to the degree to which the measure affects voluntary control or freedom of choice. Coercive measures (such as prohibition) target change in manifest travel demand by reducing car users' voluntary control. Other measures are designed to empower car users to increase voluntary control (e.g., by providing individualised information about alternative transportation options) or are designed to make voluntary control costly (e.g., pricing travel). IM is noncoercive and Pn is coercive, whereas RP tends to fall in between the two. It is coercive for those who cannot afford the fees but noncoercive for those who can. As observed in Loukopoulos et al. (2005b), these measures also differ with respect to car users' and non–car users' attitudes, beliefs and evaluations.

It is apparent that devising a TDM measure is in part shaped by the view one holds about determinants of people's behavior in general and car use in particular. The view associated with theories of neoclassical economics that persons or households act in economically rational ways clearly underpins

Table 19.1 *Proposed system of classifying travel demand management (TDM)*
measures

Attribute with definition	IM	RP	Pn
Targeting latent (vs. manifest) demand Changing unobserved (vs. observed) car use	Yes	Partly	No
(Restriction of) time scale Hours of operation	No	Yes	Yes
(Restriction of) spatial scale Area of operation	No	Yes	Yes
Coerciveness Reducing car users' voluntary control	No	Partly	Yes
Bottom-up (vs. top-down) process Empowering car users and increasing voluntary control	Yes	Partly	No
Market-based (vs. regulatory) mechanism Increasing voluntary control at a cost	No	Yes	No

Note: IM = individualised marketing; RP = road pricing; Pn = prohibition.

economic interventions. Coupled with this is the frequently false view that
people have an unlimited capacity to acquire and process information (Bonsall
and Palmer, 1997; Bonsall et al., 2007). The proposal of complex road pricing
schemes to internalise externalities (Ubbels and Verhoef, 2007) is an example.
Yet, in conjunction with the implementation of road pricing schemes, economists also assume that people are concerned about their own unfair (or to a
less extent fair) positions relative to others (Fehr and Schmidt, 1999). Thus,
attempts are made to devise fair measures (Steg and Schuitema, 2007).

Other measures are based on the view that people are concerned about the
collective negative effects of excessive car use, in particular environmental
effects (Gärling and Friman, 2012). Thus, even though this does not preclude
concern for economic incentives or disincentives, it increases effectiveness to
emphasise that the measures will be perceived to be effective. An example is
voluntary change measures that only recruit car users who are motivated to
reduce car use and need to know how to do this (Brög et al., 2009; Richter,
Friman and Gärling, 2011; Thøgersen, 2014). Therefore, households enrolled
in often very extensive behavioral change programmes are, usually through
personal contacts, given different individualised types of advice about how to
reduce their car use (Fujii and Taniguchi, 2006).

A view of people founded in modern cognitive research (Reisberg, 2006)
underlies the belief that the difficulties people have in changing their behavior
does not solely reflect a lack of motivation but also an inability to change. This
view of people would lead to emphasising the importance of devising aids
for providing journey information in advance or en-route intelligent transportation systems (ITS) (Golledge, 2002; Golob, 2001); devising in-vehicle

information systems, for instance, for navigation, gasoline utilisation, and travel time and costs; and devising methods such as individualised marketing to break and build new habits (Gärling et al., 2004).

Information communication technology (ICT) has also begun to transform public transport and change people's travel behaviour by making the service more accessible and personalised (e.g., demand responsive transport services, Hinkle and Grieco, 2004). (See Friman and Gärling, 2017, for a recent extensive review of public transport developments in many different countries.) The development of ICT has furthermore enabled travellers to access reliable and accurate information (e.g., real-time information systems; Zito et al., 2011), which has had an effect on reduced waiting time, reduced uncertainty, simplified use and an increased feeling of security (Dziekan and Kottenhoff, 2007). In addition, ICT has made it possible to pay on-the-go with mobile ticketing services (Mallat et al., 2009), also contributing to accessibility and simplified use. During the trip, ICTs improve the public transport experience by providing possibilities for enjoyment as well as creating opportunities for performing different activities (Ettema et al., 2012). Surfing on the Internet, e-mailing and scheduling appointments are the main ICT activities in public transport in Asia (Ohmori, 2009). In Sweden, Ettema et al. (2012) reported that ICT (mostly smartphones) is used for killing time during morning commutes, which is also confirmed in a US sample (Frei, Mahmassani and Frei, 2015). A study in the United Kingdom showed that mobile technologies, in particular smartphones, allow people to engage in making telephone calls, text messaging, Internet surfing, e-mailing, listening to music and watching videos (Clayton et al., 2016).

An even further degree of advanced use of ICT is represented by the current developments of self-driving cars (or [shared] autonomous vehicles, [S]AV). When interviewed on Swedish radio (23 May 2016), a US professor of robotics expressed the belief that a child born today may never drive a car in the future. Whether or not this forecast is accurate, it is a fact that the technology enabling safe self-driving cars is rapidly developing. Implementing systems of self-driving cars that substitute for travel by private cars or public transport may, however, turn out to be a challenging task. A first step may be to supply taxi companies with self-driving cars (autonomous taxi, or aTaxi) (Kornhaus et al., 2013). Taxis may then become a more important part of public transport services.

What would the benefits be of substituting to private cars? In the European context it has been observed that private cars tend to be parked as much as 90 per cent of the time (Pasaoglu et al., 2012). If fleets of self-driving cars (or taxis or, possibly, instant access to rental cars) were a substitute for private cars, the number of cars in the roads would drastically fall. Land today used for parking could be transformed into attractive places that improve the quality of the urban environment. Fagnant and Kockelman (2014) report an agent-based simulation of a system of self-driving cars serving about

3.5 per cent of all human-driven car trips in a fictitious midsized US city. They estimate that each self-driving car could replace between eight to twelve private cars. The cars are managed by an automatic dispatcher service to pick up users from where they make mobile phone calls. This may still not cause longer waiting times than ten minutes if effective dispatcher decision-making strategies are implemented to relocate the cars in anticipation of travel demand. For this reason, total driving distance would, however, increase by about 10 per cent. Does not an augmented and more flexible system of regular taxis provide the same benefits? What are then the unique benefits of self-driving cars? If traffic volumes decrease and self-driving cars are programmed to not violate traffic rules, traffic safety would increase with substantial gains in reduced costs for society and suffering for victims of traffic accidents. Another benefit is reduced local air pollution if the autonomous cars are electric.

19.4.2 Effectiveness

Given that private car use primarily serves biological needs, social obligations and personal desires to participate in out-of-home activities, car-use reduction should broadly be viewed as an adaptation by car users to changes in travel options that potentially have consequences for their engagement in different activities and the satisfaction they experience. A central issue is whether theories of travel choice that apply in equilibrium are transferable to conditions of change (as when a TDM measure is implemented). In fact, Goodwin (1998) argues that it would take time for a new equilibrium to be reached. Furthermore, theories of choice in equilibrium may not include factors that are important for understanding change processes. For this reason, several recent attempts have been made to conceptualize the *change process* (Arentze, Hofman and Timmermans, 2004; Cao and Moktharian, 2005a, 2005b; Gärling et al., 2002a; Kitamura and Fujii, 1998; Pendyala et al., 1997; Pendyala, Kitamura and Reddy, 1998). In the following, the theoretical framework first proposed by Gärling et al. (2002a) and later expanded by Bamberg et al. (2011) will be briefly described. This theoretical framework aims to analyse the multifacetted nature of car users' responses to TDM measures.

In Figure 19.2, travel options are defined as bundles of attributes describing trip chains (including purposes, destinations, travel modes, departure times, routes and costs), with choices of the trip chains influenced by the bundles of attributes. Another determinant is the reduction or change goals set by individuals or households.[1] Such goals may form a hierarchy from concrete programmes (e.g., cycle to work, walk to the local grocery store) to abstract principles (e.g., reducing car use, being a responsible member of society) functioning as reference values in negative feedback loops regulating changes in behavior (Carver and Scheier, 1998). That is, if a discrepancy is detected between the present state and the change goal as the reference value, then some action is carried out with the aim of minimising the discrepancy. For instance,

Figure 19.2. *Theoretical framework.*
Adapted from Gärling et al., 2002a.

after a road pricing scheme is implemented, a car-use reduction goal may be set if households experience increased monetary travel costs. On the other hand, if other changes are simultaneously encountered such as shorter travel times (due to less congestion) or concomitant reduced living costs (e.g., children moving out, a salary increase), no such goal may be set. In effect, an invariant relationship does not exist between increasing the cost of driving and the setting of car-use reduction goals (Bamberg et al., 2011; Gärling et al., 2002a).

Needs, desires, attitudes and values influence the goals that people set and strive to attain (Austin and Vancouver, 1996). Sociodemographic factors are frequently used as proxies. As shown in Figure 19.2, goals vary in several ways classified as content or intensity (Locke and Latham, 1984, 1990). Content is related to the size of the goal and its difficulty of attainment, the specificity of the goal, the complexity of the goal (the number of outcome dimensions) and the degree of conflict with other goals at the same or higher levels. Intensity refers to the perceived importance and the degree of commitment. Research on goal setting and attainment (e.g., Lee, Locke and Latham, 1989) has shown that specific and challenging goals increase the likelihood that they are attained, provided they are not too difficult or challenging. Skills, commitment to the goal and immediate clear feedback are factors that also increase the likelihood of goal attainment.

After having set a car-use reduction goal, households are assumed to form a plan for how to achieve this goal and to make commitments to execute the plan. This process has been referred to as the formation of implementation intentions (Gärling and Fujii, 2002; Gollwitzer, 1993). The plan that is formed consists of predetermined choices contingent upon specified conditions (Hayes-Roth and Hayes-Roth, 1979). In making plans for how to reduce car use, households may consider a wide range of options (see Figure 19.2), such as staying at home and suppressing trips and activities; using electronic communication means instead of driving; carpooling; or changing the effective set of travel options with respect to purposes, destinations, travel modes, departure times or costs. Households may possibly also consider longer-term strategic changes such as moving to another residence or changing workplace or hours.

It is hypothesised that households seek and select adaptation alternatives that lead to the achievement of their goal. This process does not, however, necessarily entail a simultaneous optimal choice among all alternatives. Consistent with other research (Todd, Gigerenzer and the ABC Research Group, 2012) people use heuristics to simplify choices in sensible ways. In a similar vein, experimental laboratory-based research (Bettman, Luce and Payne, 1998) shows that people make sensible trade-offs between accuracy and (mental and tangible) costs. A crucial difference to microeconomic utility-maximisation theories (e.g., McFadden, 2001) is the assumption that people do not invariably invest the same degree of effort. Whether they do or do not invest effort depends on properties of the goal (e.g., size, importance). As a consequence, if the cost of an effective adaptation is too high, even a small and specific reduction goal to which a household is highly committed may be abandoned or reduced.

Consistent with the notion of bounded rationality (Simon, 1990), a second important difference to microeconomic utility-maximisation theories is that choices are made sequentially over time. This implies that the change process is prolonged and fails to instantaneously result in beneficial outcomes. Furthermore, although both benefits (effectiveness or goal achievement) and costs of chosen alternatives are evaluated, immediately felt costs are likely to be attended to first. Effectiveness is evaluated over time on the basis of feedback. If such evaluations indicate a discrepancy to the goal, more costly changes are chosen. Thus, a sequential cost-minimising principle (Gärling, Gärling and Loukopoulos, 2002b; Loukopoulos et al., 2006a) may dictate the choice of change or adaptation alternatives. Yet, people may not make appropriate accuracy-cost trade-offs in real life when making complex travel choices, in part because car-use habits and related habitual or routine activities cause inertia (Gärling and Axhausen, 2003). Research has also demonstrated that a bias exists such that the current state is overvalued (e.g., Samuelson and Zeckhausen, 1988), thus making changes less attractive. In particular if the car-use reduction goal is vague, evaluating whether or not a change is effective may possibly be biased toward confirming the expectation that it is (e.g., Einhorn and Hogarth, 1978; Klayman and Ha, 1987).

It is claimed that there are three main reasons why TDM measures may not be effective: (1) TDM measures fail to make car use less attractive; (2) TDM measures fail to activate goals to change car use; and (3) TDM measures fail to facilitate the implementation of goals to change car use. Evidence consistent with these claims comes, for example, from analyses of travel diary data reported in Loukopoulos, Gärling and Vilhelmson (2005a), observing that the number of affected trips varied greatly depending on the temporal and spatial specifications of TDM measures, such as prohibition or road pricing. Thus, one cannot assume that prohibition or road pricing makes car use less attractive in a given area without first examining existing travel patterns. Furthermore,

Loukopoulos et al. (2004) demonstrated that individualised marketing may lead to significantly smaller car-use reduction goals being set than either road pricing or prohibition. The same study also revealed that people believe their shopping activities would not be affected because such activities are conducted outside the typical hours of operation of road pricing; that is, car use reduction goals were not activated in this instance. Finally, Loukopoulos et al. (2006b) found evidence that the adaptation to TDM measures takes the form of a change hierarchy, which proceeds according to the cost-minimisation principle, with the less costly adaptation selected first, then the next less costly, and so forth. The exact nature of the hierarchy varied across different trip purposes, indicating that less costly alternatives for one trip purpose (e.g., public transport for work trips) are more costly for another (e.g., public transport for shopping trips) and the reverse. The general implication is that TDM measures will not be effective if the adaptation alternatives are too costly, since then these are unlikely to be chosen.

19.4.3 Public Acceptability

Car users are opposed to TDM measures if they are perceived to be ineffective and limit their freedom to drive; in particular, if they believe that they cannot reduce car use without substantial sacrifices (Bamberg and Rölle, 2003; Jakobsson, Gärling and Fujii, 2000). There may also be opposition because the TDM measure is perceived as unfair if some suffer more than others. Yet, prohibition of car use is perceived as more fair (and also as more effective) than road pricing, presumably because the latter is believed to allow wealthy people to buy their way out (Jones, 1995, 2003). Another possibility is that one believes, perhaps mistakenly (Santos and Rojey, 2004), that predominantly poor people will suffer. Even though minimising differences in outcomes between groups is considered the most important goal (referred to as the equality principle), when this goal implies that unprivileged groups will suffer, a need principle may be perceived as more fair than equality (Steg and Schuitema, 2007).

Other characteristics of a TDM measure such as road pricing include fee level and the allocation of revenues. It has been shown that revenues that benefit the individual car user – for instance, by decreasing road or fuel taxes – are more acceptable compared to revenues that benefit society as a whole, such as general public funds (Steg and Schuitema, 2007). Thus, a possible way of increasing the acceptability of economic sanctions is to let revenues compensate for the infringement on freedom and unfairness.

19.4.4 Political Feasibility

TDM measures may not be politically feasible because they are not acceptable to the public. Yet, there are also other reasons. In political decision-making,

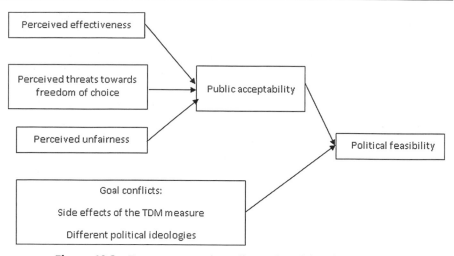

Figure 19.3. *Factors assumed to affect political feasibility.*

it is necessary to resolve conflicts between different goals, either because different political parties (ideologies) prioritise different goals or because a TDM measure in itself leads to conflicting goals. In Europe, reducing car traffic is attractive to environmental and green parties but not to social democratic or conservative parties since they view it as a threat to economic development and, in the longer term, the welfare of society (Johansson et al., 2003). An additional reason for the conservative opposition is trust in deregulation and free-market solutions. A similar goal conflict exists in political decision-making between the municipal and national levels. Although politicians at both levels are sensitive to public opposition, they may be more so at the local, municipal level because of closer ties between politicians and their voters. It may also be the case that public opposition is stronger in a municipality where implementation of the TDM measure is being considered.

A conflict also emanates from the fact that TDM measures have both intended and unintended effects. For instance, road pricing may alleviate congestion if prices are set sufficiently high. At the same time, this may reduce the benefits from faster transportation if less congestion fails to offset the increased costs. In a similar vein, poor households may no longer afford leisure travel that they consider highly desirable, at least not without cutting expenditures for other (perhaps essential) goods and services. Prohibition may have even stronger side effects unless exceptions are made for essential road use.

Figure 19.3 illustrates that political feasibility increases with public acceptability but also that political feasibility is affected by the existence of conflicts between different political goals. Given public acceptability of a TDM measure, its implementation is likely only if such goal conflicts can be resolved so that the goal of private car-use reduction is not compromised.

19.5 Summary and Conclusions

Automobile ownership and use have many determinants, instrumental, economic and psychological. For instance, owning and using a private car is attractive since it makes possible a desired comfortable lifestyle. This is perhaps the most important reason, in conjunction with the spread of affluence, why automobile ownership and use are increasing in developing countries. The increase is a serious threat to human environments on a global scale (Goodwin, 1996; Van Wee, 2012, 2014). In addition, in Western urban areas the excessive car use has already resulted in many urgent problems and continues to do so even if the increase in car ownership and use ends. Policies attempting to reduce current and future problems have been proposed to affect the various determinants of car use. Yet, such measures suffer in many cases from a lack of public acceptability because they reduce speed of travel and freedom of choice. They are also objected to because of strongly held psychological (i.e., noninstrumental) motives associated with automobile ownership and use. The objections voiced by the public in turn influence the political feasibility of implementing the policy measures.

The future does not seem bright for any attempts to alleviate the negative environmental and climate effects of excessive car use given the versatility of the car, the comfortable lifestyle its use makes possible and the complex multi-determined nature of the implementation of policy measures. Are there any policy measures that enable a comfortable lifestyle without private motorised travel? If so, these may possibly satisfy many car users' instrumental motives, but perhaps not their noninstrumental motives. Clearly, the issue is complex, requiring consideration of many factors. Lay people, experts, as well as politicians seem to have faith in that future automobile technology would be the solution. Is a zero-emission, fuel-efficient automobile made from recyclable material a last and only hope? The current assessment is not that new automobile technology will solve all problems. Ogden (2012) therefore argues that a portfolio of solutions is needed and that believing in a single solution is unrealistic. The future would look brighter if people reduce unessential car travel (voluntarily or because it is made more expensive), if travel distances are decreased by changes in the spatial organisation of the environment, if the car fleet worldwide is dominated by low-emission and fuel-efficient automobiles manufactured from recyclable materials and if new attractive and eco-friendly transportation systems are implemented (e.g., fleets of self-driving electric cars). This is obviously not a small agenda.

19.6 Acknowledgements

This is a revision of a chapter published in the former edition of the handbook. Financial support for the preparation of the previous chapter was obtained through grants from the Swedish Agency for Innovation Systems (#2002-00434) and the Swedish Research Council for Environment, Agricultural Sciences and Spatial Planning (#25.9/2001-1763). Revising the chapter was financially supported by the Swedish Agency for Innovation Systems (#2014–05335). We thank our collaborators Satoshi Fujii and Cecilia Jakobsson Bergstad and, in particular, Peter Loukopoulos, whose substantial input to the previous chapter remains substantial in the revised chapter. We also thank Robert Nilsson and Erik Hellsten at Volvo Cars Corporation for inviting the first author to join them in developing an agent-based simulation to investigate the degree to which implementing fleets of self-driving cars would increase efficiency of urban transportation.

Appendix

Table 19A.1 *Appendix*

TDM measure	Description
Prohibiting car traffic in city centre (Cambridge, UK)	The city of Cambridge is a lively historic city in England. Its streets date from the Middle Ages and are not designed for today's traffic flows. Instead of expanding the road network, Cambridgeshire County has chosen another solution. The Council has decided to impose considerable restrictions on private car traffic in the central parts of the city. The policy package is comprised of two parts. Firstly, the area inside the ring road, which is called the Inner Ring Area, has been divided into eight subareas. These eight subareas have only one entry and exit point to and from the inner-ring road. Secondly, pedestrian zones have been created in the liveliest business areas and in residential areas. Parking is not permitted in the pedestrian zones twenty-four hours a day, seven days a week. Car traffic is not permitted between the hours of 10 AM and 4 PM, Monday to Saturday, except for those vehicles that have a special permit. Time-activated traffic barriers have been designed so as to sink into the ground for cars or buses with a special permit in the form of an electronic ID card. This applies, for example, to taxis.
Road pricing (Singapore)	In Singapore, a city-state with about 3.5 million residents, various forms of road pricing in the city centre have been implemented by the government over the past thirty years. The latest system in Singapore is called electronic road pricing (ERP). This means that one has to pay to be able to drive a car within a zone referred to as the 'Restricted Zone', which is about 7 square kilometres in size and has about thirty entry points. All entry points are clearly

Table 19A.1 (*continued*)

TDM measure	Description
	marked with portals over the road, and when the ERP system is in operation, the words 'In Operation' flash on screens situated on the portals. ERP works with the assistance of these portals, an in-vehicle unit which is in every type of vehicle and a smart card system. There are antennae, cameras and optical detectors situated on the portals. When a vehicle approaches the portal, the ERP system communicates with the in-vehicle unit, identifies what type of vehicle it is (i.e., car, taxi, truck, motorcycle, etc.), deducts the appropriate fee from the card which is loaded with money and, if a transgression is detected (e.g., no in-vehicle unit or insufficient funds on the card, etc.), the vehicle and license plate is photographed. The prices vary depending on vehicle type and time of entry into the Restricted Zone. For example, the average price for a private car is SGD 1.00. The price levels are reviewed every three months. If the congestion levels are too high, then the prices are raised, and if the roads are not being sufficiently utilised, then the prices are lowered.
Individualized marketing (Perth, Australia)	The city of Perth, Western Australia, has a population of approximately 1 million. In an attempt to reduce traffic by 10 per cent, a program known as TravelSmart has been introduced. In the suburb South Perth (population 37,000), a part of the TravelSmart programme known as Individualised marketing has been introduced. Individual households are contacted. Information is gathered about the type of car users living in the household and whether they are interested in using alternatives to the car. The decision to participate in the programme is left to the household. Those households that are interested in beginning to use alternative modes of transport to the car are provided with information about the various modes in the Perth area (cycle, buses, walking, etc). They are offered personal advice about their trips. This information consists of personalised timetables, which can be sent by post, received over the phone or by a home visit from a consultant who analyses the household's trips and provides suggestions for alternatives to the car. It has been found that an important reason why people do not refrain from using the car more often is that they believe that the same trip with another transport mode (walking, cycling, public transport) would take twice as long and cost one-third more than is actually the case.

Note

1   We do not discuss the issue of how decisions are made in multiperson households which has been targeted in models of mode choice (Timmermans, 2009). Hence we use the term 'household' without any further specification.

19.7 References

Aarhus, K. (2000). Office Location Decisions, Modal Split and the Environment: the Ineffectiveness of Norwegian Land Use Policy. *Journal of Transport Geography*, 8, 287–294.

Arentze, T., Hofman, F., and Timmermans, H. P. J. (2004). Predicting Multi-Faceted Activity-Travel Adjustment Strategies in Response to Possible Pricing Scenarios Using an Internet-Based Stated Adaptation Experiment. *Transport Policy*, 11, 31–41.

Austin, J. T., and Vancouver, J. B. (1996). Goal Constructs in Psychology: Structure, Process, and Content. *Psychological Bulletin*, 80, 286–303.

Axhausen, K., and Gärling, T. (1992). Activity-Based Approaches to Travel Analysis: Conceptual Frameworks, Models, and Research Problems. *Transport Reviews*, 12, 323–341.

Bamberg, S., Fujii, S., Friman, M., and Gärling, T. (2011). Behaviour Theory and Soft Transport Policy Measures. *Transport Policy*, 18, 228–235.

Bamberg, S., and Rölle, D. (2003). Determinants of People's Determinants of Pricing Measures. In J. Schade and B. Schlag (Eds.), *Acceptability of Transport Pricing Strategies* (pp. 235–248). Amsterdam: Elsevier.

Bettman, J. R., Luce, M. F., and Payne, J. W. (1998). Constructive Consumer Choice Processes. *Journal of Consumer Research*, 25, 187–217.

Bhat, C. R., and Koppelman, F. S. (1999). A Retrospective and Prospective Survey of Time-Use Research. *Transportation*, 26, 119–139.

Bonsall, P. W. (2000). Legislating for Modal Shift: Background to the UK's New Transport Act. *Transport Policy*, 7, 179–184.

Bonsall, P. W., and Palmer, I. (1997). Do Time-Based Road-User Charges Induce Risk-Taking? Results from a Driving Simulator. *Traffic Engineering and Control*, 38(4), 200–208.

Bonsall, P., W., Shires, J. D., Matthews, B., Maule, J., and Beale, J. (2007). Responses to Complex Price Signals: Theory, Evidence and Implications for Road Pricing. *Transportation Research Part A*, 41, 672–683.

Brög, W., Erl, E., Ker, I., Ryle, J., and Wall, R. (2009). Evaluation of Voluntary Travel Behaviour Change: Experiences from Three Continents. *Transport Policy*, 16, 281–292.

Cameron, I., Lyons, T. J., and Kenworthy, J. R. (2004). Trends in Vehicle Kilometers of Travel in World Cities, 1960–1990: Underlying Drivers and Policy Responses. *Transport Policy*, 11, 287–298.

Cao, X., and Mokhtarian, P. L. (2005a). How Do Individuals Adapt Their Personal Travel? A Conceptual Exploration of the Consideration of Travel-Related Strategies. *Transport Policy*, 12, 199–206.

Cao, X., and Mokhtarian, P. L. (2005b). How Do Individuals Adapt Their Personal Travel? Objective and Subjective Influences on the Consideration of Travel-Related Strategies. *Transport Policy*, 12, 291–302.

Carver, C. S., and Scheier, M. F. (1998). *On the Self-Regulation of Behavior*. Cambridge, UK: Cambridge University Press.

Clayton, W., Jain, J., and Parkhurst, G. (2016). An Ideal Journey: Making Bus Travel Desirable. *Mobilities* published on-line.

Crawford, J. H. (2000). *Carfree Cities*. Utrecht, Netherlands: International Books

Cullinane, S. (2003). Hong Kong's Low Car Dependence: Lessons and Prospects. *Journal of Transport Geography*, 11, 25–35.

Cullinane, S., and Cullinane, K. (2003). Car Dependence in a Public Transport Dominated City: Evidence from Hong Kong. *Transportation Research D*, 8, 129–138.

Dargay, J., and Gately, D. (1999). Income's Effect on Car and Vehicle Ownership, Worldwide: 1960–2015. *Transportation Research A*, 33, 101–138.

Dziekan, K., and Kottenhoff, K. (2007). Dynamic At-Stop Real-Time Information Displays for Public Transport: Effects on Customers. *Transportation Research A*, 41, 489–501.

Einhorn, H. J., and Hogarth, R. M. (1978). Confidence in Judgment: Persistence of the Illusion of Validity. *Psychological Review*, 85, 396–416.

Eliasson, J., Hultkrantz, L., Nerhagen, L., and Smidfelt Rosqvist, L. (2009). The Stockholm Congestion Charging Trial 2006: Overview of Effects. *Transportation Research Part A*, 43, 240–250.

Emmerink, R. H. M., Nijkamp, P., and Rietveld, P. (1995). Is Congestion Pricing a First-Best Strategy in Transport Policy? A Critical Review of Arguments. *Environment and Planning B*, 22, 581–602.

Ettema, D., Friman, M., Gärling, T., Olsson, L. E., and Fujii, S. (2012). How In-Vehicle Activities Affect Work Commuters' Satisfaction with Public Transport. *Journal of Transport Geography*, 24, 215–222.

Ettema, D., and Timmermans, H. J. P. (1997). Theories and Models of Activity Patterns. In D. Ettema and H. J. P. Timmermans (Eds.), *Activity-Based Approaches to Travel Analysis* (pp. 1–36). Oxford: Pergamon.

Eurostat (2013). Europe in Figures: Eurostat Yearbook, ec.europa.eu/eurostat. Retrieved 30 May 2016.

Fagnant, D. J., and Kockelman, K. M. (2014). The Travel and Environmental Implications of Shared Autonomous Vehicles, Using Agent-Based Model Scenarios. *Transportation Research F*, 40, 1–13.

Fehr, E., and Schmidt, K. M. (1999). A Theory of Fairness, Competition, and Cooperation. *Quarterly Journal of Economics*, 114, 817–868.

Foo, T. S. (1997). An Effective Demand Management Instrument in Urban Transport: The Area Licensing Scheme in Singapore. *Cities*, 14, 155–164.

Foo, T. S. (1998). A Unique Demand Management Instrument in Urban Transport: The Vehicle Quota System in Singapore. *Cities*, 15, 27–39.

Foo, T. S. (2000). An Advanced Demand Management Instrument in Urban Transport. *Cities*, 17, 33–45.

Frei, C., Mahmassani, H. S., and Frei, A. (2015). Making Time Count: Traveler Activity Engagement on Urban Transit. *Transportation Research Part A: Policy and Practice*, 76, 58–70.

Friman, M., and Gärling, T. (2017). Moving Towards Sustainable Consumption: A Psychological Perspective on Improvement of Public Transport. In C. V. Jansson-Boyd and M. Zawisza (Eds.), *International Handbook of Consumer Psychology* (pp. 524–542). Hove, UK: Taylor and Francis.

Fujii, S., and Gärling, T. (2007). Role and Acquisition of Car-Use Habits. In T. Gärling and L. Steg (Eds.), *Threats from Car Traffic to the Quality of Urban Life: Problems, Causes and Solutions* (pp. 235–250). Amsterdam: Elsevier.

Fujii, S., and Taniguchi, A. (2006). Determinants of the Effectiveness of Travel Feedback Programs: a Review of Communicative Mobility Management Measures for Changing Travel Behavior in Japan. *Transport Policy*, 13, 339–348.

Gärling, T., and Axhausen, K. (2003). Habitual Travel Choice (Introduction to Special Issue). *Transportation*, 30, 1–11.

Gärling, T., Eek, D., Loukopoulos, P., et al. (2002a). A Conceptual Analysis of the Impact of Travel Demand Management on Private Car Use. *Transport Policy*, 9, 59–70.

Gärling, T., and Friman, M. (2012). A Behavioural Perspective on Voluntary Reduction of Private Car Use. In B. Van Wee (Ed.), *Keep Moving, Towards Sustainable Mobility* (pp. 109–134). Hague, Netherlands: Eleven International Publishing.

Gärling, T., and Fujii, S. (2002). Structural Equation Modelling of Determinants of Implementation Intentions. *Scandinavian Journal of Psychology*, 43, 1–8.

Gärling, T., Fujii, S., and Boe, O. (2001). Empirical Tests of a Model of Determinants of Script-Based Driving Choice. *Transportation Research F*, 4, 89–102.

Gärling, T., Gärling, A., and Loukopoulos, P. (2002b). Forecasting Psychological Consequences of Car-Use Reduction: A Challenge to an Environmental Psychology of Transportation. *Applied Psychology: An International Review*, 51, 90–106.

Gärling, T., and Garvill, J. (1993). Psychological Explanations of Participation in Everyday Activities. In T. Gärling and R. G. Golledge (Eds.), *Behaviour and Environment: Psychological and Geographical Approaches* (pp. 270–297). Amsterdam: Elsevier/North-Holland.

Gärling, T., Jakobsson, C., Loukopoulos, P., and Fujii, S. (2004). Roles of Information Technology for Households' Adaptation of Private Car Use to Travel Demand Management Measures. *Journal of Intelligent Transportation Systems*, 8, 189–194.

Garreau, J. (1991). *Edge City: Life on the New Frontier*. Garden City, NY: Doubleday.

Garvill, J., Marell, A., and Nordlund, A. (2003). Effects of Awareness on Choice of Travel Mode. *Transportation*, 30, 63–79.

Gatersleben, B. (2003). On Yer Bike for a Healthy Commute. In L. Hendrickx, W. Jager, and L. Steg (Eds.), *Human Decision Making and Environmental Perception: Understanding and Assisting Human Decision Making in Real-Life Settings* (pp.161–182). Groningen, Netherlands: University of Groningen.

Gatersleben, B. (2007). Affective and Symbolic Aspects of Car Use. In T. Gärling and L. Steg (Eds.). *Threats from Car Traffic to the Quality of Urban Life: Problems, Causes, and Solutions* (pp. 219–233). Amsterdam: Elsevier.

Gatersleben, B. (2014). Psychological Motives for Car Use. In T. Gärling, M. Friman, and D. Ettema (Eds.), *Handbook of Sustainable Travel* (pp. 85–94). Dordrecht, Netherlands: Springer.

Gatersleben, B., and Uzzel, D. (2007). The Journey to Work: Exploring Commuter Mood Among Driver, Cyclists, Walkers and Users of Public Transport. *Environment and Behavior*, 39, 416–431.

Giuliano, G., and Dargay, J. (2006). Car Ownership, Travel and Land Use: A Comparison of the US and Great Britain. *Transportation Research A*, 40, 106–124.

Goh, M. (2002). Congestion Management and Electronic Road Pricing in Singapore. *Journal of Transport Geography*, 10, 29–38.

Golledge, R. G. (2002). Dynamics and ITS: Behavioural Responses to Information Available from ATIS. In H. S. Mahmassani (Eds.), *Perpetual Motion: Travel Behavior Research Opportunities and Application Challenges* (pp. 81–126). Amsterdam: Pergamon.

Gollwitzer, P. M. (1993). Goal Achievement: The Role of Intentions. *European Review of Social Psychology*, 4, 141–185.

Golob, T. F. (2001). Travelbehaviour.com: Activity Approaches to Modelling the Effects of Information Technology on Personal Travel Behaviour. In D. Hensher (Ed.), *Travel Behavior Research: The Leading Edge* (pp. 145–183). Amsterdam: Pergamon.

Goodwin, P. (1996). Simple Arithmetic. *Transport Policy*, 3, 79–80.

Goodwin, P. (1998). The End of Equilibrium. In T. Gärling, T. Laitila, and K. Westin (Eds.), *Theoretical Foundations of Travel Choice Modelling* (pp. 103–132). Amsterdam: Elsevier.

Goodwin, P. (2012). Three Views on Peak Car. *World Transport Policy and Practice*, 17, 8–18.

Gordon, P., and Richardson, H. W. (1997). Are Compact Cities a Desirable Planning Goal? *Journal of the American Planning Association*, 63, 95–106.

Greene, D. L., and Wegener, M. (1997). Sustainable Transport. *Journal of Transport Geography*, 5, 177–190.

Handy, S., Weston, L., and Mokhtarian, P. L. (2005). Driving by Choice or Necessity. *Transportation Research A*, 39, 183–203.

Hayes-Roth, B., and Hayes-Roth, F. (1979). A Cognitive Model of Planning. *Cognitive Science*, 3, 275–310.

Hinkle, J., and Grieco, M. (2004). Scatters and Clusters in Time and Space: Implications for Delivering Integrated and Inclusive Transport. *Transport Policy*, 10 (2003) 299–306.

Jakobsson, C. (2007). Instrumental Motives for Private Car Use. In T. Gärling and L. Steg (Eds.). *Threats from Car Traffic to the Quality of Urban Life: Problems, Causes, and Solutions* (pp. 205–217). Amsterdam: Elsevier.

Jakobsson, C., Fujii, S., and Gärling, T. (2000). Determinants of Private Car Users' Acceptance of Road Pricing. *Transport Policy*, 7, 153–158.

Jakobsson Bergstad, C., Gamble, A., Hagman, O., Polk, M., and Gärling, T. (2011). Affective-Symbolic and Instrumental-Independence Psychological Motives Mediating Effects of Socio-Demographic Variables on Daily Car Use. *Journal of Transport Geography*, 19, 33–38.

Johansson, L.-O., Gustafsson, M., Falkemark, G., Gärling, T., and Johansson-Stenman, O. (2003). Goal Conflicts in Political Decision Making: A Survey of Municipality Politicians' Views of Road Pricing. *Environment and Planning C: Government and Policy*, 21, 615–624.

Jones, P. (1995). Road Pricing: The Public Viewpoint. In B. Johansson and L.-G. Mattsson (Eds.), *Road Pricing: Theory, Empirical Assessment and Policy* (pp. 159–179). Dordrecht, Netherlands: Kluwer.

Jones, P. (2003). Acceptability of Transport Pricing Strategies: Meeting the Challenge. In J. Schade and B. Schlag (Eds.), *Acceptability of Transport Pricing Strategies* (pp. 27–62). Oxford: Elsevier.

Jones, P., Dix, M. C., Clarke, M. I., and Heggie, I. G. (1983). *Understanding Travel Behaviour*. Aldershot, UK: Gower.

Kitamura, R. (1988). An Evaluation of Activity-Based Travel Analysis. *Transportation*, 15, 9–34.

Kitamura, R., and Fujii, S. (1998). Two Computational Process Models of Activity-Travel Choice. In T. Gärling, T. Laitila, and K. Westin (Eds.), *Theoretical Foundations of Travel Choice Modelling* (pp. 251–279). Amsterdam: Elsevier.

Kitamura, R., Fujii, S., and Pas, E. I. (1997). Time-Use Data, Analysis and Modelling: Toward the Next Generation of Transportation Planning Methodologies. *Transport Policy*, 4, 225–235.

Kitamura, R., and Mohamad, J. (2009). Rapid Motorization in Asian Cities: Urban Transport Infrastructure, Spatial Development and Travel Behavior. *Transportation*, 36, 269–274.

Klayman, J., and Ha, Y.-W. (1987). Confirmation, Disconfirmation, and Information in Hypothesis Testing. *Psychological Review*, 94, 211–228.

Kornhaus, A., Chang, A., Clark, C., et al. (2013). *Uncongested Mobility for All: New Jersey's Area-Wide aTaxi System*. Princeton, NJ: Princeton University Press.

Kristensen, J. P., and Marshall, S. (1999). Mobility Management to Reduce Travel: The Case of Aalborg. *Built Environment*, 25, 138–150.

Lave, C. A. (1992). Cars and Demographic access. *Access*, 1, 4–11.

Lee, T. W., Locke, E. A., and Latham, G. P. (1989). Goal Setting Theory and Performance. In L. A. Pervin (Ed.), *Goal Concepts in Personality and Social Psychology* (pp. 291–326). Hillsdale, NJ: Lawrence Erlbaum.

Levinson, D., and Kumar, A. (1995). Activity, Travel, and the Allocation of Time. *Journal of the American Planning Association*, 61, 458–470.

Litman, T. (2003). The Online TDM Encyclopedia: Mobility Management Information Gateway. *Transport Policy*, 10, 245–249.

Litman, T. (2012). Current Mobility Trends: Implications for Sustainability. In B. van Wee (Ed.), *Keep Moving, Towards Sustainable Mobility* (pp. 23–44). The Hague: Eleven International Publishing.

Locke, E. A., and Latham, G. P. (1984). *Goal Setting: A Motivational Technique That Works*. Englewood Cliffs, NJ: Prentice Hall.

Locke, E. A., and Latham, G. P. (1990). *A Theory of Goal-Setting and Task Performance*. Englewood Cliffs, NJ: Prentice Hall.

Loukopoulos, P., Gärling, T., Jakobsson, C., and Fujii, S. (2006a). A Cost-Minimization Principle of Adaptation of Private Car Use in Response to Road Pricing Schemes. In C. Jensen-Butler, M. Larsen, B. Madsen, O. A. Nielsen and B. Sloth (Eds.), *Road Pricing, the Economy, and the Environment* (pp. 331–349). Amsterdam: Elsevier.

Loukopoulos, P., Gärling, T., and Vilhelmson, B. (2005a). Mapping the Potential Consequences of Car-Use Reduction in Urban Areas. *Journal of Transport Geography*, 13, 135–150.

Loukopoulos, P., Jakobsson, C., Gärling, T., Meland, S., and Fujii, S. (2006b). Understanding of Adaptation to Car-Use Reduction Goals. *Transportation Research F*, 9, 115–127.

Loukopoulos, P., Jakobsson, C., Gärling, T., Schneider, C. M., and Fujii, S. (2004). Car User Responses to Travel Demand Management Measures: Goal Setting and Choice of Adaptation Alternatives. *Transportation Research D*, 9, 263–280.

Loukopoulos, P., Jakobsson, C., Gärling, T., Schneider, C. M., and Fujii, S. (2005b). Public Attitudes Towards Policy Measures for Reducing Private Car Use: Evidence from a Study in Sweden. *Environmental Science and Policy*, 8, 57–66.

Lyons, G., and Urry, J. (2005). Travel Time Use in the Information Age. *Transportation Research A*, 39, 257–276.

Maat, K. (2002). The Compact City: Conflict of Interest Between Housing and Mobility Aims in the Netherland. In E. Stern, I. Salomon, and P. H. L. Bovy (Eds.), *Travel Behaviour: Spatial Patterns, Congestions and Modelling* (pp. 3–19). Cheltenham, UK: Edward Elgar.

Mackett, R. L. (2001). Policies to Attract Drivers Out of Their Cars for Short Trips. *Transport Policy*, 8, 295–306.

Mallat, N., Rossi, M., Tuunainen, V. K., and Öörni, A. (2009). The Impact of Use Context on Mobile Services Acceptance: The Case of Mobile Ticketing. *Information and Management*, 46, 190–195.

Mackett, R. L. (2001). Policies to attract drivers out of their cars for short trips. *Transport Policy*, 8, 295–306.

May, A. D., Jopson, A. F., and Matthews, B. (2003). Research Challenges in Urban Transport Policy. *Transport Policy*, 10, 157–164.

McFadden, D. (2001). Disaggregate Behavioural Travel Demand's RUM Side: a 30 Years Retrospective. In D. A. Hensher (Eds.), *Travel Behavior Research* (pp. 17–63). Amsterdam: Elsevier.

Millard-Ball, A., and Schipper, L. (2011). Are We Reaching Peak Travel? Trends in Passenger Transport in Eight Industrialized Countries. *Transport Reviews*, 31, 357–378.

Modarres, A. (2003). Polycentricity and Transit Service. *Transportation Research A*, 37, 841–864.

Mokhtarian, P. L., and Salomon, I. (2001). How Derived Is the Demand for Travel? Some Conceptual and Measurement Considerations. *Transportation Research A*, 35, 695–719.

Morrill, R. L. (1991). *Myths About Metropolis: Our Changing Cities*. Baltimore, MD: Johns Hopkins University Press.

Muller, P. O. (1995). Transportation and Urban Form. In S. Hanson (Ed.), *The Geography of Urban Transportation* (2nd ed., pp. 26–52). New York: Guilford Press.

Niskanen, E., and Nash, C. (2008). Road Pricing in Europe: a Review of Research and Practice. In C. Jensen-Butler, M. Larsen, B. Madsen, O. A. Nielsen and B. Sloth (Eds.), *Road Pricing, the Economy, and the Environment* (pp. 5–27). Amsterdam: Elsevier.

Ogden, J. (2012). Modality and Technical Advancement. In B. Van Wee (Ed.), *Keep Moving, Towards Sustainable Mobility* (pp. 45–93). Hague, Netherlands: Eleven International Publishing.

Ohmori, N. (2009). Connected Anytime: Telecommunications and Activity-Travel Behavior from Asian Perspectives. In R. Kitamura, T. Yoshi, and T.

Yamamoto (Eds.), *The Expanding Sphere of Travel Behaviour Research* (pp. 77–93). Bingley, UK: Emerald.

Ouellete, J. A., and Wood, W. (1998). Habit and Intention in Everyday Life: The Multiple Processes by Which Past Behaviour Predicts Future Behaviour. *Psychological Bulletin*, 124, 54–74.

Pasaoglu, G., Fiorello, D., Martino, A., et al. (2012). *Driving and Parking Patterns of European Car Drivers: a Mobility Survey*. Report EUR 25627. Luxembourg: Publications Office of the European Union.

Pendyala, R. M., Kitamura, R., Chen, C., and Pas, E. I. (1997). An Activity-Based Micro-Simulation Analysis of Transportation Control Measures. *Transport Policy*, 4, 183–192.

Pendyala, R. M., Kitamura, R., and Reddy, D. V. G. P. (1998). Application of an Activity-Based Travel Demand Model Incorporating a Rule-Based Algorithm. *Environment and Planning B*, 25, 753–772.

Priemus, H., Nijkamp, P., and Banister, D. (2001). Mobility and Spatial Dynamics: An Uneasy Relationship. *Journal of Transport Geography*, 9, 167–171.

Pucher, J. (1999). Transportation Trends, Problems, and Policies: An International Perspective. *Transportation Research A*, 33, 493–503.

Recker, W. W., McNally, M. G., and Roth, G. S. (1986). A Model of Complex Travel Behavior: Theoretical Development. *Transportation Research A*, 20, 307–318.

Reisberg, D. (2006). *Cognition*. New York: Norton.

Richter, J., Friman, M., and Gärling, T. (2011). Soft Transport Policy Measures: Gaps of Knowledge and Research Needs. *International Journal of Sustainable Transportation*, 5, 199–215.

Salomon, I., and Mokhtarian, P. L. (1997). Coping with Congestion: Understanding the Gap Between Policy Assumptions and Behaviour. *Transportation Research D*, 2, 107–123.

Samuelson, W., and Zeckhausen, R. (1988). Status Quo Bias in Decision Making. *Journal of Risk and Uncertainty*, 1, 7–59.

Sandqvist, K. (1997). *The Appeal of Automobiles – Human Desires and the Proliferation of Cars* (KFB Report 1997:21). Stockholm: Swedish Transport and Communications Research Board.

Santos, G., and Rojey, L. (2004). Distributional Impacts of Road Pricing: The Truth Behind the Myth. *Transportation*, 31, 21–42.

Schwanen, T., Dieleman, F. M., and Dijst, M. (2001). Travel Behavior in Dutch Monocentric and Polycentric Urban Systems. *Journal of Transport Geography*, 9, 173–186.

Sheller, M. (2004). Automotive Emotions: Feeling the Car. *Theory, Culture and Society*, 21, 221–242.

Simon, H. A. (1990). Invariants of Human Behavior. *Annual Review of Psychology*, 41, 1–19.

Southworth, F. (2001). On the Potential Impacts of Land Use Change Policies on Automobile Vehicle Miles of Travel. *Energy Policy*, 29, 1271–1283.

Sperling, D., and Claussen, E. (2004). Motorizing the Developing World. *Access*, 24 (Spring), 10–15.

Steg, L. (2003). Can Public Transport Compete with the Private Car? *IATSS Research*, 27, 27–35.

Steg, L. (2005). Car Use: Lust and Must. Instrumental, Symbolic and Affective Motives for Car Use. *Transportation Research A*, 39, 147–162.

Steg, L., and Schuitema, G. (2007). Behavioural Responses to Transport Pricing: A Theoretical Analysis. In T. Gärling and L. Steg (Eds.). *Threats to the Quality of Urban Life from Car Traffic: Problems, Causes, and Solutions* (pp. 347–366). Amsterdam: Elsevier.

Steg, L., and Vlek, C. (1997). The Role of Problem Awareness in Willingness-to-Change Car Use and in Evaluating Relevant Policy Measures. In T. Rothengatter and W. Carbonell Vaya, *Traffic and Transport Psychology: Theory and Application* (pp. 465–475). Amsterdam: Pergamon.

Stradling, S. G. (2002). Transport User Needs and Marketing Public Transport. *Municipal Engineer*, 151, 23–28.

Stradling, S. G., Meadows, M. L., and Beatty, S. (2000). Helping Drivers out of Their Cars: Integrating Transport Policy and Social Psychology for Sustainable Change. *Transport Policy*, 7, 207–215.

Thøgersen, J. (2014). Social Marketing in Travel Demand Management. In T. Gärling, M. Friman, and D. Ettema (Eds.), *Handbook of Sustainable Travel* (pp. 113–129). Dordrecht, Netherlands: Springer.

Thorpe, N., Hills, P., and Jaensirisak, S. (2000). Public Attitudes to TDM Measures: A Comparative Study. *Transport Policy*, 7, 243–257.

Timmermans, H. J. P. (2009). Household Decision Making in Travel Analysis. In R. Kitamura, T. Yoshi, and T. Yamamoto (Eds.), *The Expanding Sphere of Travel Behaviour Research* (pp. 159–186). Bingley, UK: Emerald.

Timmermans, H. J. P., van der Waerden, P., Alves, M., et al. (2003). Spatial Context and the Complexity of Daily Travel Patterns: An International Comparison. *Journal of Transport Geography*, 11, 37–46.

Todd, P. M., Gigerenzer, G., and the ABC Research Group (2012). *Ecological Rationality: Intelligence in the World*. New York: Oxford University Press.

Ubbels, B., and Verhoef, E. (2007). The Economic Theory of Transport Pricing. In T. Gärling and L. Steg (Eds.). *Threats from Car Traffic to the Quality of Urban Life: Problems, Causes, and Solutions* (pp. 325–345). Amsterdam: Elsevier.

Van Wee, B. (Ed.) (2012). *Keep Moving, Towards Sustainable Mobility*. The Hague: Eleven International Publishing.

Van Wee, B. (2014). The Unsustainability of Car Use. In T. Gärling, M. Friman, and D. Ettema (Eds.), *Handbook of Sustainable Travel* (pp. 69–83). Dordrecht, Netherlands: Springer.

Verplanken, B., Aarts, H., and Van Knippenberg, A. (1997). Habit, Information Acquisition, and the Process of Making Travel Mode Choices, *European Journal of Social Psychology*, 27, 539–560.

Vilhelmson, B. (1999). Daily Mobility and the Use of Time for Different Activities: The Case of Sweden. *GeoJournal*, 48, 177–185.

Vilhelmson, B. (2005). Urbanisation and Everyday Mobility: Long-Term Changes of Travel in Urban Areas of Sweden. *Cybergeo*, 302, 1–13.

Vlek, C., and Michon, J. A. (1992). Why We Should and How We Could Decrease the Use of Motor Vehicles in the Near Future. *IATSS Research*, 15, 82–93.

Wardman, M. (2001). A Review of British Evidence on Time and Service Quality Valuations. *Transportation Research E*, 37, 107–128.

Wootton, J. (1999). Replacing the Private Car. *Transport Reviews*, 19, 157–175.

Wright, C., and Curtis, B. (2005). Reshaping the Motor Car. *Transport Policy*, 12, 11–22.

Wright, C., and Egan, J. (2000). De-marketing the Car. *Transport Policy*, 7, 287–294.

Zito, P., Amato, G., Amoroso, S., and Berrittella, M. (2011). The Effect of Advanced Traveller Information Systems on Public Transport Demand and Its Uncertainty. *Transportmetrica*, 7, 31–43.

20 Voluntary Individual Carbon Trading

Friend or Foe?

Clive L. Spash and Hendrik Theine

20.1 Introduction

In recent years, the search for regulatory regimes in order to effectively address human-induced climate change, by controlling greenhouse gas (GHG) emissions, has become a prominent political and academic issue. Emission trading schemes have risen in popularity and in the policy community are widely held to be an effective, as well as economically efficient, measure. They have become a favoured government strategy. Although carbon offsets have been developed as serious financial instruments in real markets, evidence has been accumulating as to their pervasive structural problems, negative social and environmental consequences and failure to actually address the reduction of GHGs that is supposed to be their raison d'être (Kollmuss, Zink and Polycarp, 2008; Spash 2010, 2015a, 2015b).

Carbon markets exist in two general types: (i) regulatory markets under a compliance regime with formal rules for both trading and offsetting, and (ii) voluntary offsets sold via typically informal arrangements. Voluntary offsets are a fast-growing market, but they also involve fundamental problems relating to the verification and credibility of the claimed emissions reductions. Proponents of voluntary carbon trading tend to argue, from a purely deductive theoretical perspective, that (re)design to match a market ideal can address all the problems (Caney and Hepburn 2011; Caney 2010; Page 2013). A key aspect is then how voluntary markets operate in practice. The actual projects related to these markets have been the subject of ongoing and unaddressed criticism, including their negative social and ecological impacts that go beyond the carbon-sequestering and GHG-reducing aims. This raises a series of behavioural questions, such as the following: What do individual purchasers think they are doing, do they seek adequate information on consequences and if not why not (e.g., warm glow)? What role do voluntary offsets play in, for example, addressing dissonance? Is ethical concern a major motivator? Are intrinsic motivations enabled or removed? Our aim is not to answer these questions directly but to lay out the terrain and suggest some likely answers through a mixture of theoretical exploration, critical institutional analysis and review of and reflection upon practical and applied experience.

The overall structure of the chapter is to start by reviewing the rise of emissions trading in general, before turning to voluntary markets in particular, and connecting their problems to the psychological and behavioural aspects of offset purchase. The critical review of voluntary carbon markets, their structure and functioning, highlights the divergence between their expected and actual operation in achieving GHG emission reductions. We identify lack of information about and verifiability of actual emissions reductions claimed by offset providers as particularly problematic. Why then are such markets expanding, what role are they performing for individual purchasers and what are their implications for human behaviour? A range of issues arise from engaging individuals in such market-based environmentalism. We focus on three specific topics: the psychology of marketing and purchasing voluntary offsets; commodification and crowding out of intrinsic motivations; and psychological implications of ethical considerations. The final section, before some concluding remarks, concerns the political economy of voluntary carbon markets and their geopolitical implications in terms of the global North–South divide and responsibility for action on human-induced climate change. This raises serious concerns over the individualisation of a collective problem, what can and should be expected of individuals as ethical consumers and how markets operate in practice. Such aspects place individual behaviour within a broader social and institutional context that concerns how market environmentalism impacts upon the expression of value.

20.2 Background to the Establishment of Carbon Trading

The modern idea of controlling pollution emissions via trading in markets can be traced back to academics in the United States writing in the 1960s. In general, the literature developed from the promotion of private property rights as solving 'externalities' in the work of Ronald Coase (1960). More specifically, the idea of pollution permit trading was originally proposed in a paper by Thomas D. Crocker (1966) and later elaborated in a book by John H. Dales (1968). Small-scale markets for emissions trading were later introduced in the United States, but it took until the late 1990s before the idea of trading emissions became generally accepted and began to sideline other proposals such as direct regulation and taxes (MacKenzie 2009; Meckling 2014; Pearse and Böhm 2014).

In the area of human-induced climate change, this approach follows from the more general idea that establishing a price for carbon is the best means of ultimately reducing GHG emissions because it will correct market failures. Mainstream economic theory regards markets as the only institutional arrangement for achieving efficient resource allocation. However, operating efficiently requires that all activities are included in the market system. Thus, where pollution occurs, this is described as a market failure because a lack of property rights means pollution is 'external' to the process of market decision-making. Internalising such 'externalities' is then a matter of getting the prices right and making economic actors pay for the use they make of the environment as a waste sink.[1] This could be achieved by taxes. However, a regular argument is that emissions trading will achieve cost savings because markets are more efficient than government bureaucracies. As Bumpus and Liverman (2008, p. 132) point out, carbon markets can be seen as 'the newest arena for a market environmentalism that assumes that the way to protect the environment is to price nature's service, assign property rights, and trade these services within a global market'. It is then clearly a neoliberal policy instrument. In political economy terms, it has been described as the 'latest incarnation of an ongoing process of commodification and capitalist expansion' (Böhm, Misoczky and Moog. 2012, p. 14).

The idea of a market that buys and sells pollution permits is allied with the concept of offsetting pollution due to one activity by another that reduces pollution (i.e., creating a pollution credit). GHG offsets do not, as Broome (2012, p. 85) notes, 'remove the very molecules that you emit'. Offsetting more precisely refers to the 'balancing out' of some or all of the emissions generated by an organisation or individual (Page, 2013). This occurs through reductions in emissions elsewhere in time and space.

Polluters, whether organisations or individuals, pay a specified price to offset emissions. The market works because the price paid is lower than their willingness to pay for the action causing the emissions, or lower than the cost of reducing emissions directly (Bushnell, 2012). Such trading is regarded as a form of market-based public policy instrument, founded on the idea that the reduction of pollution emissions is particularly efficient – least-cost – when individual actors are brought into situations of arbitrage and exchange.

Carbon trading, in general, refers to the idea of mitigating human-induced climate change through a market for GHGs that buy and sell emissions permits or credits. Such an emissions trading system (ETS) could be restricted to a set of polluters within a given jurisdiction who must either control their emissions directly or buy permits held by other polluters. Offsetting in this model occurs if polluters reduce their emissions enough to allow them to have an excess of permits to sell to others. Typically, offsetting goes far beyond this. A theoretical description is that of Dhanda and Hartman (2011, p. 120): 'if someone performs an act that adds carbon to the atmosphere, then offset providers perform an activity that reduces that equivalent amount of carbon in the atmosphere'. The fundamental idea behind carbon offsetting is that someone else is paid to avoid, absorb or reduce GHG emissions, which compensates for GHG emissions originating from the purchasers actions (Bayon, Hawn and Hamilton, 2009; Kollmuss et al., 2008). These offset providers (or credit traders) may be outside the jurisdiction of the ETS or not be designated as polluters under the ETS. The offset purchasers may be those unable to meet their legal emissions reduction targets under a direct regulation. This is called compliance offsetting.

The Kyoto Protocol, adopted in 1997, but only effective from 2005 after sufficient countries ratified, was a major steppingstone that led to the establishment of both offsetting and ETS. Compliance offsetting was developed under two initiatives: the Clean Development Mechanism (CDM) and Joint Implementation (JI) projects. The CDM and JI have been termed 'flexible mechanisms' that allow industrialised countries (or Global North) to pay others in order to meet their international reduction targets to achieve avoidance of severe disruption to the Earth's climate system. Under Article 2 of the 1992 United Nations Framework Convention on Climate Change (UNFCCC), the 197 countries that are parties to the convention agreed to the 'stabilization of greenhouse gas concentrations in the atmosphere at a level that would prevent dangerous anthropogenic interference with the climate system' (United Nations, 1992, p. 4). Instead of reducing carbon emissions, Annex I countries are allowed to offset emissions via projects in non–Annex I countries.[2] The original aim of these offset mechanisms was to promote technology transfer and assist with sustainable development only where unforeseen failures to reduce emissions occurred. However, the mechanisms have become used more broadly than that and, in contravention with the spirit of the agreement, for planning avoidance of domestic mitigation measures. Both mechanisms and their impacts on the effectiveness of ETSs have been the subject of close examination and criticism (e.g., Kollmuss, Schneider and Zhezherin, 2015; Spash, 2010; Wara and Victor, 2008).

Carbon offsets can be created through investing in a variety of projects. These can be broadly categorised into: (i) forestry and land use, (ii) renewable energy (iii) energy-efficiency, (iv) fuel switching and (v) methane capture (Broderick, 2009; Gössling et al., 2007; Kollmuss et al., 2008). Typically, voluntary offsets for carbon emissions have involved carbon sequestration via reforestation and/or low carbon technologies (Ari, 2013; Bayon et al., 2009; Bumpus and Liverman, 2008). Regulated offsets have, in addition, involved projects that 'destroy' or prevent man-made GHGs such as hydrofluorocarbons. Indeed, projects do not need to reduce CO_2 emissions, but can instead involve reductions in other anthropogenic GHGs such as nitrous oxide (N_2O), methane (CH_4), chloroflurocarbons (CFCs) and hydroflurocarbons (HCFCs). Determining how much an increase in one GHG can be compensated for by the reduction in another requires establishing a common metric and basis of equivalence.

CO_2 equivalent (CO_2e) is a quantity that describes for a GHG the amount of CO_2 that would have the same global warming potential. CO_2 as the numeraire is 1 and other GHGs are then, for example, CH_4 at 25, N_2O at 298 and HCFC-23 at 14,800 times more powerful in their radiative forcing of the climate. This calculation of global warming potential requires a time horizon because different gases have different lifetimes over which they decay in the upper atmosphere; a normal horizon tat has been accepted is one hundred years. These calculations to estimate equivalence are essential to making GHG emissions trading schemes functional; they establish the commensurability of different gases. A typical result is then to describe emissions in terms of tonnes of CO_2 equivalent (tCO_2e) with markets trading certificates representing this artificial quantity.

Regulatory ETS markets are created as mandatory for a set of participants and can operate at regional, national or international levels. In the United States, such markets are termed cap-and-trade systems. The theory is that an overall cap is set by a government authority or regulatory agency. Participants are allocated a certain amount of allowances, or permissions, to emit carbon based on staying under the overall cap. The cap should be binding, meaning that allowances are neither removed nor new ones created, but once created are available for trading. A prominent example of mandatory carbon markets is the European Union (EU) ETS, 'the first large-scale CO_2 emission trading system in the world', often termed the 'cornerstone of EU climate policy' (Knopf et al., 2014, p. 2). Neoliberals and advocates of price-making markets celebrate it as the successful transfer of climate change concerns into the 'logic of the economic system' and an important step in the 'right' direction (Rydge, 2015). However, the scheme has also been highly controversial, subject to fraud, speculation and profiteering and criticised for failing to achieve actual emissions reductions (Brinded, 2012; Elsworth et al., 2011; Inman, 2010; Jacobs, 2013; Seager, 2009; Coelho, 2012; Fullbrook, 2009; Gilbertson and Reyes, 2009; Lohmann, 2012; Spash, 2010). This reveals something of a divergence between idealised 'free' markets in economic theory and the actual operation of a market that requires regulation and enforcement.

Besides schemes targeting firms and corporations, the idea has been floated of creating regulated personal carbon trading. This is defined by Fawcett and Parag (2010, p. 329) as 'a general term used to describe a variety of downstream cap and trade policies, which locate rights and responsibilities for the carbon emissions from household energy use and/or personal travel at the individual level'. Such schemes require mandatory participation by individuals, or households, and none have been implemented so far. This hypothetical idea has been discussed as a means of allocating personal carbon budgets to equitably distribute national, or international, targets on a per capita basis. These may then be traded or kept to offset personal/household emissions (see Capstick and Lewis, 2010; Parag and Fawcett, 2014; Starkey, 2012a, 2012b). The per capita distribution is a key aspect regarded as producing equitable and just outcomes.

20.3 The Development of Voluntary Carbon Markets

Voluntary carbon offsets have developed in parallel with official and regulated ETSs. Guided by faith in the market system, voluntary offsets (like regulated ones) are promoted as creating price incentives for a low-carbon economy based on consumer preferences expressed via willingness to pay. They are also linked with theories of ecological modernisation that promote the corporations as socially responsible agents in society who will freely adopt sustainable, 'green', business models for addressing environmental problems, that is, that business is best at voluntarily controlling its own pollution (Rydge, 2015; Spaargaren and Mol, 2013).

Both regulated and voluntary offset markets have grown considerably since the establishment of the Kyoto Protocol with its promotion of trading as a flexible mechanism, and offsetting via the CDM and JI. By 2015, global trade under regulated ETS is estimated to have reached US$34 billion (World Bank Group and Ecofys, 2015, p. 13). Voluntary offset providers increased from a couple of dozen in 2006 to more than 170 in 2008, while the volume of CO_2 equivalent offsets increased from 24.6 to 123.4 Mt CO_2e over the same period (Dhanda and Hartman, 2011). During 2006 and 2008, the value of trade also increased from approximately US$97 million to US$705 million (Brinkel and Antes, 2011). Peters-Stanley and Yin (2013) agree on the 2006 trade volume, but give a higher 2008 quantity of 135 Mt CO_2e. They acknowledge the fall in annual trade volume, since the financial crisis, to 107 Mt CO_2e in 2009 and 101 MtCO_2e in 2012, and Hamrick, Peters-Stanley and Goldstein (2015) also note the decrease in trade value to US$485 million in 2009 and US$379 million in 2013. Thus, voluntary carbon trading appears to be, like all financial assets, quite sensitive to economic cycles. Trade volume had fallen further by 2013, but increased 14 per cent from 2013 to 2014 to 87 Mt CO_2e, with traded value rising by 4 per cent to US$395 million. Almost 50 per cent of the transacted volume for voluntary carbon offsets in 2014 was attributed to forestry and land use projects, 25 per cent wind power projects, 5 per cent to landfill methane, 5 per cent cooking stove waste heat recovery projects and 10 per cent 'other' (Hamrick et al., 2015).

In contrast to mandatory schemes, voluntary markets are basically unregulated and outside of legally binding frameworks and state emissions control. Voluntary offsets are traded carbon credits issued by companies and civil society groups. Voluntary markets do not entail a finite or regulated supply of allowances, and there is no cap. Carbon credits (and associated offsets) are actualised when a new project is implemented. The created credits can subsequently be bought by polluters (e.g., firms or individuals) to offset their emissions. Companies and individuals freely choose to purchase those credits to offset their emissions.

Voluntary carbon markets are therefore separate from, or go beyond, any legal requirements for individuals or organisations to purchase emissions permits and have been advocated as testing grounds for innovative approaches for GHG reduction (Ari, 2013; Bayon et al., 2009; Perdan and Azapagic, 2011). Their role outside of official schemes has then been seen by some as a positive aspect and a means of taking independent action. In this latter respect, they can extend emissions reduction where regulated markets have not been established (e.g., international flights), and encouraging small projects below the scale of regulated markets (Kollmuss et al., 2008). Indeed, they originated in countries where governments were outside the Kyoto Protocol and/or national policies failed to materialise (e.g., the United States, Australia). Bumpus and Liverman (2008, p. 132) point out that voluntary offsets emerged from 'frustration with the lack of state action – when governmental policies were perceived to be slow, inadequate, or non-existent'. Voluntary carbon markets were, thus, in part promoted by nonprofit organisations providing carbon offsets for proenvironmental individuals or organisations who were attempting to bypass the political blockades around the establishment of Kyoto emissions reductions.

Yet, from the beginning, large GHG-emitting corporations also participated in voluntary carbon trading. Among the first voluntary carbon offsets were investments in agro-forestry and forestry sequestration in Guatemala (1989) and Ecuador (1990) by US and Dutch electricity companies respectively (Bumpus and Liverman, 2008, p. 133). Corporations have also increasingly branded themselves as sustainable, environmentally friendly and 'carbon neutral'. In 2014, globally about 150 corporations claimed that they used a carbon price for internal management purposes with prices ranging from US$6 to US$89 per tCO_2e (World Bank Group and Ecofys, 2015, p. 48). In 2015, this had almost tripled to 435 corporations with internal prices ranging from US$1 to US$357 per tCO_2e. Companies making such public declarations seem stimulated by the existence of government schemes, with 94 per cent located in countries where mandatory pricing (ETS, or tax) is in place or proposed (World Bank and Ecofys, 2016). Appearing 'green' may therefore be a strategic manoeuvre to preempt GHG emission legislation that is expected to be more stringent and costly (Spash, 2010; Spiekermann, 2014).

Green branding, image creation and product marketing are also important drivers for the corporate purchase of voluntary carbon offsets (Brinkel and Antes, 2011; Bayon et al., 2009). Ari (2013, p. 911) points out that 'private companies use the wording "carbon neutral" in their products, events and activities by buying carbon credits to offset their associated emissions'. This helps to neutralise public perception of environmental harm for companies with a large carbon footprint. Offsetting emissions to become 'carbon neutral' can contribute to an image of corporate social responsibility. That corporations promote and advertise carbon neutrality helps normalise the idea that this is both a legitimate response to human-induced climate change and a 'good' thing to do. This then encourages individuals to adopt a similar behaviour and ethical stance.

Three types of buyers can then be distinguished in the voluntary GHG market sector: (i) middlemen; (ii) corporate/business, nongovernmental and local community organisations; and (iii) individual/household consumers. Middlemen purchase carbon offsets to trade them and may put out calls for carbon projects and propose carbon financing to fund projects. They trade permits for profit and may also engage in price speculation. The organisational and individual types of purchasers may have similar motives to each other, from promoting self-image to genuine concern for mitigating GHG impacts. While households and individual consumers are passive purchasers of offsets, organisations may proactively approach offset providers and suggest projects.

There are two forms of voluntary permit trading: direct and via a financial exchange. The majority of voluntary carbon trades are over-the-counter transactions, where buying and selling is conducted directly (Bayon et al., 2009; Peters-Stanley and Yin, 2013). For example, travellers booking a flight might buy offsets directly from an airline along with their plane ticket. The direct character of such transactions means the price is often hidden from customers or hard for them to estimate (Bayon et al., 2009). The other form of trading is via official exchanges and a formal trading platform. The Chicago Climate Exchange is an example of such a system. In this case, price data are typically closely monitored (not least by traders) and recorded. Yet even here, information about what exactly is represented by an offset credit can be far from transparent. As a result, prices for CO_2 vary substantially. Several authors have reported that the cost of offsetting one tCO_2e in voluntary markets generally ranges from a few to around 30 Euros, with some suppliers charging up to €180 per tCO_2e (Brinkel and Antes, 2011; Dhanda and Hartman, 2011; Schiermeier, 2006). What lies behind price differences and more generally what goes on in voluntary markets is often unclear. Comparability of offsets (in addition to any issues of carbon equivalence) is affected by considerable variety in the methods used for offsetting, project types and suppliers.

20.4 Unregulated Carbon Markets: Information and Validity

In this section, we review a range of concerns about how voluntary markets operate. This critical institutional analysis brings to the fore the divergence between a theoretical model of the fully informed consumer and the operation of actual voluntary markets where information on offsets is opaque or lacking, as will be explained. This section sets the stage for the following enquiry into who is prepared to buy such an ill-defined product and what is their justification and motivation for doing so? First, let us establish the extent to which the product is ill-defined.

Voluntary carbon markets lack governmental regulation and oversight – accordingly, they have been termed 'cowboy markets' (Roy and Woerdman 2012, p. 9). Without a regulatory body, various forms of carbon credits have appeared that go under a number of titles (e.g., verified emission reduction, voluntary emission reduction, voluntary carbon unit or just emission reduction units). Providers may engage in product differentiation purely for marketing reasons. This leads to comparability problems. That is, how are consumers meant to understand the differences, if any, between the various offset products? Is expecting the individual purchasers to be, or become, fully informed at all realistic?

A related concern then arises as to quality standards, especially with regard to the conditions ensuring implementation and control mechanisms. Kollmuss et al. (2008) survey different types of standards, which aim to guarantee the credibility and accountability of offsets. However, they found that offset standards differ substantially in accounting, monitoring and verification methods as well as enforcement systems. In a study of over one hundred carbon offset providers, Dhanda and Hartman (2011) come to a similar conclusion that the standards are inconsistent and noncomparable. The attempts to provide a quality control standard covering different providers have also proven problematic. For example, the Voluntary Offset Standard screens and evaluates offset credibility, but this has itself been criticised for having vague screening criteria, an unclear evaluation process and lack of detailed specific information (Kollmuss et al., 2008).

The Chicago Climate Exchange has implemented specific rules in order to ensure the quality and ecological integrity of offset projects. However, in an international survey, Brinkel and Antes (2011) find that market participants vary in their assessment of Chicago Climate Exchange's standards. While some of their respondents state that the requirements laid down are sufficient and ensure the proper working of offsetting mechanisms, others criticise the Exchange's lack of transparency and failure to disclose information. Kollmuss et al. (2008) also reference substantive criticism which questions the additionality of some Chicago Climate Exchange offsets.

Additionality refers to the need for emissions reductions to make a difference over business as usual. That is, if, for example, a reforestation project were going to be undertaken anyway, without the offset funding, then there is no addition of carbon emissions reduction compared to what would have occurred in any case, that is, under business as usual. There is then no justification for payment under economic efficiency criteria and no net reduction in emissions; indeed, exactly the opposite will occur if permits are sold on the basis of a project violating additionality.

Another attempt to provide a quality criteria is the Gold Standard. This was established by the World Wide Fund for Nature to address concerns over the environmental and social integrity of projects. It is the only voluntary standard that has clearly defined additionality rules and requires third-party auditing. Thus, it is 'generally accepted as the standard with the most stringent quality criteria' (Kollmuss et al., 2008, p. 57). As a result, Gold Standard certification requires extensive documentation of the project. However, this also considerably increases the costs for those designing and implementing offset projects. The cost differential, relative to lower-quality offsets, has implications for the adoption of high quality standards in an unregulated price-making market. As Spash (2010) notes, where standards are unenforceable (i.e., voluntary), all certificates are regarded as equally valid, and poor-quality, cheap offsets will drive out the high-quality expensive ones; that is how price-making markets operate. Thus, a general problem with the Gold Standard, and similar schemes, in a competitive price-making market is that they are very likely to be undercut and sidelined.

The majority of offset providers use self-developed offset standards and verification processes instead of adopting the Gold Standard guidelines or other third-party standards. Sterk and Bunse (2004, p. 16) suggest that 'one feature that is indispensable is the auditing of projects by independent third parties; otherwise the compensation cannot be regarded as credible'. Yet, this is not the norm, and the quality and credibility of such self-developed standards have remained unclear and difficult to judge (Taiyad, 2005).

Similarly, the validity of additionality is often highly problematic to establish. Several cases exist where the additionality of projects has been questioned and there is a lack of explicit justification in the project documentation (Bumpus and Liverman, 2008; Dhanda and Hartman, 2011). More fundamentally, Kollmuss et al (2008, p. 89) argue that additionality is based on the idea that

> emission reductions have to be measured against a counterfactual reality. The emissions that would have occurred if the market for offsets did not exist must be estimated in order to calculate the quantity of emissions reductions that the project achieves.

Such a hypothetical reality is always sensitive to determining what would have happened in any case, that is, baseline scenarios. Carbon offsets should be actual reductions of emissions that would not have occurred otherwise, rather than arbitrary paper projections. Worse offset projections are likely to be manipulated by providers to serve their own interests, and this includes claiming consequences are certain and known.

The verification of projected and claimed carbon offsetting is difficult to establish and subject to both considerable wishful thinking as well as deliberate exclusion of risk and uncertainty. For example, the planting of forests to achieve carbon sequestration involves considerable unpredictability. Research has questioned the effectiveness of forestry as a means of carbon sequestration, and it is subject to being overstated (Dhanda and Hartman, 2011). The actual amount of carbon sequestrated depends upon the specific growth rates of the trees, their age, soil conditions and the local climate. Unforeseen events can and do intervene including human activities and natural disasters (e.g., drought, forest fires, hurricanes, flooding) which harm or destroy forests. However, predicting carbon sequestration rates on the basis of future growth projections is necessary in order to sell carbon credits before any actual sequestration has occurred. The promise is that trees will be planted in the future on the basis of payments made for past emissions or emission to be released immediately (Bumpus and Liverman, 2008; Lohmann, 2010).

In general, projects claiming GHG emissions reductions and avoidance face major ambiguities and uncertainties. Projected savings in GHG emissions require ensuring actual implementation as well as maintenance and repair of any associated project equipment and infrastructure. Legislative hurdles and local opposition to projects add political indeterminacy (Brinkel and Antes, 2011). There is additional social indeterminacy due to the difficulty of fulfilling expected outcomes and the vagaries of human behaviour. That is, for example, economists' limited models of human behaviour fail to account for the rich array of potential responses because they assume a single simple causal mechanism (i.e., self-interested greed or more formally utility maximisation and its underlying preference utilitarianism). Actual behaviour results from a mixture of motivators, causal powers and tendencies. Social norms and cultural practices, which are absent from the economic model, are clearly important aspects.

Thus, as with forestry, carbon emission reductions due to renewable energy and energy efficiency are also far from self-evident and dependent upon human practices. Energy-efficiency projects are often small scale and difficult to monitor and evaluate, such as distribution of energy-efficient light bulbs in Australia treated as GHG reducing offsets, although not used, or hoarded, by households (Spash, 2010). Lambe et al. (2015), in their study on cooking stove projects in Kenya, report major uncertainties about the uptake and usage rates of the stoves. Determining the actual amount of carbon saved from distributing cooking stoves depends on several assumptions about cooking behaviour, changes in practices and fuel switches, which the authors find highly arbitrary in existing emissions reduction methodologies. There were several mismatches between the assumptions of international investors compared with local communities and nongovernmental organisations working in the field. For example, Lambe et al. (2015) found divergence between how cooking stoves were used in the Kenya project and the assumed use based on practice in the global North. This led to a mismatch between enforcing the efficiency needs of a carbon project and cultural practices. Such cooking practices might relate to types of food affecting the length of cooking times and intensity of heat during cooking (e.g., cooking food all day on a low heat versus heating food for a short time with more intense heat).

Typically, the energy savings resulting from such projects are calculated by comparing them to a hypothetical baseline scenario of using a fossil fuel–intensive alternative. The investor as well as the project host have an incentive to overstate such scenarios to maximise the claimed gains. The decentralised and geographically distributed sites involved in such projects adds to the difficulty of establishing the baseline scenario necessary to estimate emissions and to monitor the reductions. The emissions reduction of cooking stove projects, for instance, is estimated based on small samples extrapolated to heterogeneous communities (Bumpus, 2011; Kollmuss and Bowell, 2007).

Another issue with respect to the inconsistency of carbon accounting relates to carbon footprint calculators, which are widely employed by individuals to inform themselves about their potential environmental impact relating to the enhanced Greenhouse Effect. They may also be linked to providers' websites or incorporated into the product purchase process. Such calculators vary widely in their estimates of the impact from the same person or activity (Murray and Dey, 2009; Schiermeier, 2006). For example, in a comparison of different carbon credit providers, Schiermeier (2006) found that estimates of carbon emissions for the same flight varied from 2.1 to 6.9 tonnes of CO_2. Emission calculation methods vary so that one company only considered direct emissions emitted per passenger, while another included effects on ozone and climate. Dhanda and Hartman (2011, p. 126) cite the case of a flight from Chicago to Melbourne estimated at anything from 3.8 to 8.0 tonnes of CO_2 costing from \$48 to \$267 to offset.

Brinkel and Antes (2011) argue that pinning down exact numbers is difficult because the actual amount of carbon emitted by companies depends on a variety of factors. For large companies, calculating carbon emissions can be extremely complex due to the extent and variety of their operations, so that producing reliable estimates requires numerous assumptions. In order to go 'carbon neutral', via offsets, a company needs to measure the GHG emissions it is producing. The critical literature on environmental accounting has questioned the data reliability disclosed by companies (Boiral and Henri, 2017; Hopwood, 2009). Based on an in-depth study of Canadian industry using qualitative interviews, Talbot and Boiral (2013) found the complexity of measuring corporate GHG emissions meant claims being made remained highly uncertain, opaque and imprecise. They concluded that: 'The majority of businesses do not have confidence in their own [GHG] inventory and even less in that of their competitors' (Talbot and Boiral, 2013, p. 1082).

The result may be either underestimation or overestimation of GHG emissions, as seems strategically convenient depending upon the institutional and regulatory context. For example, high GHG emissions scenarios may be projected to allow justification for claiming larger than actual reductions are achieved (Downie, 2007). Under regulatory ETS with allocation of permits by grandfathering, exaggeration of emissions is incentivised due to the potential for polluters to obtain free permits that can later be sold on the open market, without any need to actually undertake pollution control (Spash, 2010). In contrast, under unregulated markets, offset providers may claim their projects achieve very low emissions (i.e., underestimate actual emissions) in order to sell more offsets from larger overall emissions reductions than actually occur. As outlined in the preceding, this has indeed been the case for forestry and energy offset projects.

In summary, unregulated voluntary markets incentivise the provision of low-quality offsets. Bushnell (2012) argues that moral hazard is a likely problem because information is essentially an offset project developer's private property. Moral hazard means acting immorally is incentivised. Here the offset provider is incentivised to lie to make profits. Furthermore, adverse selection might be pervasive because offset markets will be particularly attractive to firms whose baseline scenarios prove to be lower than originally estimated or projected. This means projects are selected (moral hazard) or firms opt in (adverse selection), due to the ease of assuming additionality where there is none. Both problems bring into question the claims made for offset markets, but also pose the question as to why do individuals buy offsets. Do they lack information on and awareness of the problems, or do they just not care?

20.5 Effects on Individual Behaviour

As has been explained, there are numerous problems with offsets and their validity as a means for reducing GHG emissions. However, the expectations of voluntary markets is that the consumer, or permit purchaser, will be able to evaluate all relevant information. The foundation for this position is an economic model where consumers have perfect information and make choices on the basis of perfect foresight of all consequences. This is a highly simplified and misleading conceptualisation of human choice in price-making markets and also neglects the interactions between human behaviour and institutional context (e.g., rules, regulations, norms). In this section, we explore how three aspects of voluntary markets impact individuals, namely via playing on their psychology, crowding out intrinsic motivation and promoting a specific ethical approach to environmental problems.

20.5.1 Psychology of Voluntary Offsets

Two issues that have been hypothesised to contribute to greater awareness of personal GHG emissions and incentivising their reduction are 'increased visibility' and 'cognitive availability'. Both are discussed by Capstick and Lewis (2008) for the case of compulsory personal allowances with carbon trading, but seem potentially relevant to voluntary offsetting. Visibility refers to the revelation of information that was previously hidden or difficult to attain, such as displaying the amount of carbon emissions at the point of sale. Cognitive availability is where the display of such information 'has the potential to act as an additional, novel form of feedback' (Capstick and Lewis, 2008, p. 8) leading to a change in behaviour. Such an effect has been claimed for the case of household energy (Capstick and Lewis, 2010; Darby, 2008; Lewis and Brandon, 1999). For example, electricity customers are supplied with a digital display connected to a metre which is meant to be located in a prominent place to encourage reduced energy consumption. However, as has been explained, the information supplied in carbon offsetting is not as reliable as that available from a household electric or gas metring system. Neither does voluntary carbon offsetting involve action to save money on an existing purchase. Voluntary market offsets are marketed products in themselves.

The heterogeneity of consumers explains why voluntary offsets are able to operate within specific market segments and achieve price discrimination between different consumer groups. Take the example of flying, Burns and Bibbings (2009) use the derogatory term 'New Puritans' for people who take a critical stance on environmentally threatening consumption by refraining from flying altogether. More generally, the term 'deep Green' may be used to refer to those who aim to avoid and refrain from certain actions such as fossil fuel combustion and the resulting GHG emissions. The individuals being identified here are not then interested in buying permissions to undertake such actions. Similarly, the climate denialists and those who just 'don't care' will not purchase offsets at all. Spash (2010, p. 186) has therefore hypothesised that this leaves as the primary marketing target the 'moderately environmentally concerned consumer'. This is a person who weighs the consequences and feels a need to assuage guilt over wrongdoing by balancing harmful acts with good acts. The existence and availability of offsets allows the moderately environmentally concerned consumer to purchase permission to perform a specific environmentally harmful action rather than avoid that action. Thus, the widely acknowledged environmentally harmful behaviour of flying can be compensated for by purchasing offsets. Many airlines offer voluntary carbon offsets directly when purchasing tickets. Mair (2011) studied voluntary carbon offset purchasers in the United Kingdom using an online questionnaire. Among those who were offsetting emissions from aviation, most were driven by proenvironmental attitudes. However, frequent reasons for offsetting were the lessening of guilt and the ease of doing so. McLennan et al. (2014), in a survey of international visitors to Australia, found that purchasers of voluntary carbon offsets for aviation are to a large extent 'nature based visitors', that is, travelling to Australia to undertake whale or dolphin watching, rainforest walks and visits to wildlife parks, zoos or aquariums. This supports the hypothesis of Spash (2010) that purchasers of voluntary carbon offsets are 'moderately environmentally concerned consumers'. Yet, despite their apparent environmentalism, some such individuals may actually ignore the implications and outcomes of their offset purchases.

Where individuals are driven by a 'warm glow' and guilt avoidance, there is limited concern for the actual environmental consequences of their purchase (Andreoni, 1989, 1990). Kotchen (2009) notes that it is the 'warm glow' of good feeling and the 'reputational boost' that play an important behavioural role when purchasing carbon offsets. People who buy offsets for such reasons engage in conspicuous consumption and therefore wish to show off their carbon offsets purchases, for example, making use of window stickers. Thus, emissions reduction is transformed into a means of achieving social status as a 'good' person instead of being an end in itself. Carbon providers sell the 'feel good factor' and guilt reductions of carbon credits rather than the actual GHG abatement (Spash, 2010).

Ignorance about the effectiveness of the purchased offset is then unproblematic, and the purchaser is similarly unconcerned over harmful side effects of projects, at least as long as they remain unknown. There is certainly no desire to discover more about such things. This fits well with carbon markets because they do not directly transfer a tangible good or service to the consumer, and there is no actual consumption by the purchaser nor any physical product to inspect for quality. Meanwhile, offset providers are driven by making money, and that means finding the cheapest low-quality offsets and overstating project emissions reductions, which as has been explained is easily done.

Spiekermann (2014) doubts the motivation behind participating in carbon offsetting and argues that the main reason individuals buy offsets is to clear their conscience. As a result, he believes that many of those participating in voluntary schemes would be unwilling to pay higher prices in order to justify their unsustainable consumption practices. They participate because it is cheap and easy to do so. This point is also illustrated by Lohmann (2006a) with reference to an article in the *Daily Telegraph*, a British right-wing newspaper. This recounted the experience of a business executive who was worried to discover that her carbon footprint was about 24 tonnes of CO_2 (i.e., about five times the global per capita average), but relieved to find out the amount necessary to purchase offsets, and achieve carbon neutrality, was trivial and, the article noted, well below her expenditure on lipstick or magazines. As Spiekermann (2014) notes, such offsetting undermines personal carbon emissions reductions and appears to lack strong motivation, as might be related to a moral duty to act. If offsetting successfully increased demand, while reducing carbon emissions, the price would be expected to rise, but then weakly motivated individuals might withdraw. Thus, Spiekermann (2014, p. 927) states that the

> lack of robustness in the offsetting system matters: the system fails as an institution because it would be undermined by its own success. Perhaps even worse, it creates incentives and price signals that convey the impression that climate neutrality could be easy to achieve for everyone without sacrifice.

Hymans and Fawcett (2013, p. 96) basically agree and question the motivation individuals have for participating in carbon offsetting, stating that 'motivation is rather weak, and disappointingly easily defeated by other interests'. They argue that on the basis of such a weak motivational foundation, carbon offsets cannot offer a general solution to human-induced climate change.

Two implications are worth highlighting here. First, such offset purchasers are not particularly motivated to assess the reliability and additionality of offsets. They avoid the psychological costs of questioning offset credibility. Maintaining their belief that offsets are beneficial addresses their cognitive dissonance (Spash, 2010). This conjecture is supported by a survey of green tourism in the context of climate change by Becken (2004, p. 341). She found that

> A preferred way of avoiding the dissonance resulting from actual behaviour and pro-environmental attitudes is to contribute financially (and therefore

internalise externalities), while keeping the privilege of continuing current practices.

If the primary motive is to preserve one's lifestyle, then the extent to which actions have real results is at best secondary. This lack of concern over quality and actual consequences of offset purchases means projections of emissions reductions can more easily 'prove to be illusory' (Hymans and Fawcett, 2013, p. 96). Second, taken together with the dubious foundations of many offset projects, this results in a 'principal–agent problem', that is, the purchaser, or principal, cannot observe the actions of offset provider, or agent (Spash, 2010). The low quality of offsets is hardly noticed and can stay unpunished. The different standards and rating systems of carbon offsets only adds more confusion that makes such an outcome even more feasible.

Ecological modernisation has also been cited as culpable in spreading the ideological commitment to offsetting as a legitimate response from businesses that results in neglecting actual conduct in the marketplace. In a study of the paucity of regulation in the voluntary carbon trading sector, McKie, Stretesky and Long (2015, p. 477) report that activities in the market 'include the false selling of carbon credits, exploitation of weak regulations, tax and security fraud, money laundering and internet crimes'. This has resulted in investigations of such markets by Interpol and the UK Financial Conduct Authority. Trading companies use marketing and advertising techniques that promote sustainability and play on beliefs in ecological modernisation and concerns over ethical conduct in their attempts to cover traditional fraud and theft. McKie et al. (2015, p. 483) argue that 'motivated offenders and victims come together in the marketplace because ecological modernisation ideology is such a strong behavioural driving force'. A world ideologically committed to trust in business and markets appears to create a blindness to how those same markets are used to achieve ulterior motives and fail to fulfil their promises.

On a behavioural level, it is quite likely that carbon offsets solidify and lock in unsustainable consumer practices, rather than changing consumption patterns, because negative effects on the climate are perceived to be neutralised. Gössling et al. (2007, p. 241), for instance, state that voluntary carbon offsets carry the 'risk of encouraging people to believe that they need not change their behaviour, thus creating irreversibility in current consumption and production patterns'. Cohen, Higham and Cavaliere (2011), in reporting interviews with regular air travellers, note the expressions of guilt over conducting behaviour known to have negative consequences for the environment, but that voluntarily offsets relieved this tension and were regarded as a useful neutralisation strategy that enabled interviewees to continue flying on a regular basis. Similarly, in a survey of self-selected green consumers, McDonald et al. (2015) found, when exploring reasons for continuing to fly, that interviewees discussed purchasing carbon offsets instead of changing their behaviour.

Lohmann (2008) argues that carbon offsetting convinces high emissions consumers to see their emissions simply as unavoidable instead of contributing to a consumption pattern that needs to be changed through individual and collective action. In this way, it

> hides the roots of climate change – that is, the historical overuse and skewed use of the Earth's carbon cycling capacity by a global minority – as well as other systemic social and technical processes (Lohmann, 2008, p. 363).

Hence, well-developed carbon offset markets can jeopardise public support for binding limits, carbon taxes and the introduction of cleaner technologies. Carbon offsets carry the risk of locking in unsustainable practices instead of contributing to the actual behavioural changes necessary to reduce carbon emissions in industrialised nations and consumer economies. The argument here is that, while carbon markets might be able to collect some 'low hanging fruits', in doing so they hinder more profound changes (Broderick, 2009; Lohmann, 2008). The availability of carbon offsets individualises and isolates responsibility for human-induced climate change while simultaneously reducing collective psychological controls. This individualisation of responsibility also inhibits serious debate over the necessity of large-scale social ecological transformation.

20.5.2 Commodification of Carbon and Crowding Out

A concern related to the preceding discussion is that transforming emissions into tradable commodities might crowd out intrinsic environmental motivation and erode individual action to protect the climate. In contrast to mainstream economic understanding, several studies have shown – theoretically and empirically – how extrinsic incentives, such as pricing, can crowd out the intrinsic motivations which underlie voluntary actions (Frey and Oberholzer-Gee, 1997; Frey, 1997; Rode, Gómez-Baggethun and Krause, 2015). A central reason for crowding out is that individuals hold a variety of motivations and values other than preference utilitarianism (Spash, 2000a, 2000b, 2006). Decision-making is also recognised as a realm where nonmonetary motivations play an important role, particularly concerning social dilemmas and public goods (Fehr and Fischbacher, 2002).

A major psychological process of crowding out is that external incentives are perceived as a constraint on the possibility to act autonomously. An individual's sense of responsibility and control decreases, replaced by economic rationales and self-interested behaviour (Bowles, 2008; Frey and Stutzer, 2012). Carpenter (2005) finds that decisions which take place in market settings erode social preferences. The anonymous and competitive setting of markets creates an atmosphere that weakens social control to achieve collective action. This is also supported by Kerr et al. (2012), who find that in the case of a low price for buying an offset (as found in voluntary carbon markets), fewer people are likely to participate in collective actions to address the same issue.

Vatn (2005) argues that people only have well-defined preferences for a few types of familiar goods. For others, and in this case particularly environmental 'goods', preferences are often unclear and socially contingent. This means that institutional arrangements that promote autonomy, trust and social preferences are able to crowd in intrinsic motivations (Frey and Stutzer, 2012; Frey, 1997). The institutions of the marketplace are then aimed at promoting exactly the wrong type of values in society (Spash, 2010).

On top of these concerns, the extent to which Nature can be commodified without associated values being destroyed or transformed by market institutions is brought into question. In order for carbon credits to be exchanged on markets, carbon reductions need to be transformed into tradable commodities.

> Offsets are generally commodified into saleable units through the development of specific emissions-reduction projects, the outputs of which can be quantified, owned, and traded (Bumpus and Liverman, 2008, p. 134).

Page (2013, p. 238) argues that the value of carbon offsets cannot be captured by a scheme based on such an economic rationale because this creates a 'false commodity' that lacks the properties of 'goods that can be owned, bought, and sold'. Even if commodification were possible and credible, the atmosphere is not private property but fundamentally owned by either all equally or no one. In either case, transferring emissions into commodified Nature implies a misappropriation of the atmosphere (Bumpus and Liverman, 2008) and a transformation of the associated values from the social to the private. So the institutional setting of private property, competition and individual choice would crowd out the motivations found under social ownership, cooperation and collective decision-making.

20.5.3 Ethical Dimension of Carbon Trading

There is only a small literature on the ethical aspects of carbon trading, and the ethics of offsetting have seldom been explored in any depth. Influential contributions have been made by Goodin (1994) and Sandel (1997), who both raise objections to emissions trading as a general practice. Aldred (2012) discusses whether an idealised ETS could address the ethical objections that have been raised. More specifically, he argues against Caney (2010), who rejects ethical objections on the basis of the standard economists position (also taken by Page, 2013) that in theory redesign can solve all problems.[3] The specific concern for ethical aspects of voluntary carbon trading with respect to individuals is almost absent from the literature; three exceptions are Spash (2010), Dhanda and Hartman (2011) and Hyams and Fawcett (2013).

As already noted there is a strong association in the marketing of voluntary offsets with guilt over wrongdoing. Dhanda and Hartman (2011, p. 126) cite and reference a common argument concerning offsets as being that:

> There is no need to change one's personal lifestyle since consumers can 'purchase forgiveness with money'. In essence, the global emissions market permits countries to trade emissions credits while the carbon credit market permits wealthy individuals or organizations to buy themselves out of responsibility to reduce emission.

The idea of buying one's way out of an ethical responsibility may be seen as objectionable, but emphasising the possibility of forgiveness through a socially approved institution has its own appeal. This appears to be a particularly Christian aspect of the marketing approach employed, where some form of repentance for sin is being coded into the purchasing practice. In a different context, Lopez et al. (2012) provide empirical support for the idea that, in a Christian country, guilt and shame are important mechanisms that strengthen long-term cooperation.

The notion of offsets being like indulgences, where a sinner could buy relief from time in purgatory with a payment to the Roman Catholic Church, was first discussed by Goodin (1994). He reviewed the practice of medieval indulgencies, arguing that these sin offsets enabled the wealthy to pay for their wrongdoing, allowing relief for their conscience, removing the need to change behaviour and avoiding the necessity for completely refraining from sinning. Medieval indulgencies substituted individual action to avoid wrongdoing with monetary transactions justifying immorality. In this way, sinning was actually encouraged because wealthy people were provided with a quick alternative to lengthy penitence. Translated into 'environmental indulgencies', Goodin (1994, p. 579) argues that this is the sale of the unsaleable, transforming the moral duty of (Christian) stewardship for Nature into paying money to offsets sins of environmental destruction. Thus, purchasing GHG offsets permits individuals to commit a sin, justifying environmental harms and removing their moral reprehensibility. Compensating for environmental harm through monetary payments relieves people from feelings of guilt and responsibility. However, the extent to which GHG emissions can be regarded as similar to an act of Christian 'sin' is highly questionable. Spash (2010) criticises the use of this religious perspective as relevant to the emission of GHGs. For instance, consider the range of GHG emitting acts involved that are being regarded as equally sinful, for example, from simply lighting a fire to keep warm or stay alive to flying first class from London to New York to go shopping. There is a flaw in arguing that fundamental necessities of life that lead to GHG emissions should be regarded as a moral sin, such as releasing methane when relieving one's bowels. This changes the emphasis to the ethical distribution of GHG budgets and raises the question as to what emissions are necessary for 'decent' living (Rao and Baier, 2012), or a meaningful/worthwhile life. A useful ethical distinction to draw here is between subsistence and luxury emissions (Shue, 1993). The release of GHG emissions does not then appear morally wrong (or sinful) in and of itself. Instead, as argued by Spash (2002, 2010), a key ethical concern in the context of human-induced climate change is the deliberate creation of harm of the innocent, and the creation of harm through avoidable, and unnecessary, actions. This raises the question as to what is the appropriate ethical basis for judging an act as harmfully polluting.

Hyams and Fawcett (2013, p. 94) argue that carbon offsetting rests on a consequentialist ethics, that is, the claim that acts should be judged only by their consequences. In a consequentialist understanding, purchasing carbon credits to offset emissions is just the same as not emitting carbon emissions beforehand. Different acts, by different people, in different times and spaces are then made commensurable. Sandel (2012) exemplifies the problems this can entail by comparing buying carbon offsets to being allowed to toss a can of beer into the Grand Canyon when paying someone else to collect waste in the Himalayas. When considering offsetting as a general means of addressing harm, or wrongdoing, it can then easily be ridiculed. For example, the website cheatneutral.com satirically collects money from people who cheat on their partners (e.g., having extramarital affairs) to pay others not to cheat, thus supposedly neutralising the acts of betrayal.

In one respect, these examples question what is being valued. That is, the consequences are not being related to the specific act undertaken nor the specific individuals or place involved. There is a misappropriation of the consequences from the specific to the general. In philosophical terms, the confusion relates to conflating the particular (*de re*) with values relating to a general function (*de dicto*), for example, a specific can of beer in the Grand Canyon with waste in general anywhere, or a specific personal act of betrayal with acts of betrayal in general by anyone. In another respect, the applicability of consequentialist ethics itself is being brought into question, and so the foundation of all mainstream economic thinking. This implies that other dimensions of morality and different ethical systems become relevant, such as fairness, justice and rights (Dhanda and Hartman, 2011; Hyams and Fawcett, 2013). Acting virtuously would be another ethical approach and was indeed a reason why Martin Luther, and others, opposed indulgencies, that is, buying them was divorced from the acts required of a virtuous person.

A separate ethical issue concerning GHG emissions is their distributional dimension. Shue (1999) appeals to a concept of fairness in order to claim that contributions to reducing emissions need to be made by those better off, irrespective of whether the existing inequality is justifiable. Yet, the voluntary aspect of offsets implies the exact opposite will occur because the poorest lack the ability to pay their way out of GHG emissions while the rich can pay the poor to undertake such actions. This cost-shifting exercise is indeed the basis for economic efficiency claims and why such carbon offsetting is feasible in the first place. As Hyams and Fawcett (2013,

p. 95) state, offsetting implies that 'the rich are able to continue high rates of emissions at the expense of emissions of the poor'. Furthermore, profits made and wealth created in the development of such markets and business models go to the already rich in the global North (Broderick, 2009; Bumpus and Liverman, 2008). All the aforementioned intensify and solidify the social order responsible for the existing inequalities in the first place (O'Neill, 2007).

20.6 The International Political Economy of Carbon Offsets

In contrast to regulated compliance markets, voluntary offset markets operate without any 'reference to higher institutional levels of governance and free themselves from national boundaries or spatial constraints' (Bumpus and Liverman, 2008, p. 141). As a result, complex international relations can develop. Bumpus and Liverman (2008) exemplify this with the case of the company Climate Care providing funding for the conversion of cow dung to cooking gas used by local communities. A nongovernmental organisation monitors the process and transfers relevant data to Climate Care, which calculates the emission reductions that are then sold to the United Kingdom Cooperative Bank. Multiple actors become engaged in management arrangements with interdependencies between partners from the global North and South (Bumpus and Liverman, 2008). In general, carbon offset projects largely take place in the global South because it is cheap to carry out projects there, while the demand for offsets as well as project developers are typically located in the global North (McKie et al., 2015). This spatial dimension to carbon offsets contains elements of unfair/unequal trade, where economically powerful actors in the North profit from carbon reductions in the South, 'opening the door to a new form of colonialism' (Bachram, 2004, p. 10).

The focus of individual offset purchases is on carbon and this leads to the neglect of other social and ecological impacts arising from projects. There are concerns over the social impacts of carbon forestry projects, especially on local communities. Jindal, Swallow and Kerr (2008) and Lyons and Westoby (2014) provide evidence from Uganda, where international investors enabled by neoliberal policies have built large-scale plantation forestry for carbon sequestration activities. Both studies report that in the course of privatisation of forest areas local communities suffered negative consequences. Local villagers were regularly charged as illegal trespassers, and heavy fines were imposed on people violating the rules. Some local communities reported the destruction of burial sites. Similarly, local communities did not benefit from the carbon revenues from the Forest Rehabilitation Project in Mount Elgon and Kibale national parks in Uganda while being partially excluded from the parks (Lang and Byakola, 2006). Bachram (2004) reports cases where local farmers and fisherfolk have been evicted from their lands for large-scale carbon sink projects in Uganda and Brazil.

Carbon offset projects can therefore add to an emerging 'green grabbing' problem, where land and ecosystem functions are increasingly appropriated for what are stated to be environmentally related projects, such as biofuels, biocarbon sequestration, ecotourism or GHG offsets (Fairhead, Leach and Scoones, 2012). This involves the restructuring of authority and access rules, transforming the use and management of resources. Land is seized in the South for large-scale monoculture plantations (e.g., palm oil), while the poor lose their land and rights to use formerly common property resources. Land grabbing has become a widespread problem due to the incentives provided to carbon project developers to make money (Bachram, 2004; Fairhead et al., 2012; Lyons and Westoby, 2014). Kollmuss et al. (2008, p. 90) conclude that

> although carbon markets ... are intended to deliver development co-benefits for their host countries, these have not been widely realised. In practice, offset projects often rely on relatively conventional technologies, and rarely benefit poor communities with insufficient access to energy services.

Wittman and Caron (2009), in their case study on a solar electrification carbon offset project in Sri Lanka, find that, although communities benefitted from the off-grid solar technology, the projects produced tensions and social inequalities between communities. Such conflict arises due to the replacement of nonmonetary economies by monetary ones and the deliberate undermining of traditional resource management practices.

The total transformation of local ecosystems can also remove traditional practices. This is particularly so where carbon sequestration projects are focussed on fast-growing trees or single-species plantations. Such plantations can create substantial loss of water availability and instream flow as well as increasing salinisation and acidification. Plantations based on exotic species threaten local biodiversity and destroy native species, for example, removing the undergrowth that supports a range of flora and fauna (Jindal et al., 2008). Lohmann (2006a) cites cases where exotic species and monocultures were planted for forest carbon sequestration, resulting in the loss of people's livelihoods, changing soil conditions and increasing fires and droughts. Similarly, he documents several case studies covering a range of offset projects (e.g., biomass, gas and landfill methane combustion) that expose exploitation of local communities.

Drawing on Harvey's concept of accumulation of dispossession, Bumpus and Liverman (2008) argue that offsetting emissions reductions through projects in the global South can be interpreted as a form of neocolonial trade relations. Emission offsets are based on the transformation of former public commons to private commodities and financial assets, implying unequal exchange between companies in the global North and communities in the global South. This reinforces economic inequalities by transforming what was publicly owned (or owned by the poor or even owned by no one) to private ownership of international investors (Lyons and Westoby, 2014). Twyman, Smith and Arnall (2015) claim that carbon trading and offsetting arise from a specifically Eurocentric relationship with Nature, although, in fact, as noted earlier, the concept was developed in the United States (Lohmann, 2006b) and adopted later in Europe (Spash, 2010). Still, the key point is the implications of commodification for the conceptualisation of Nature and the imposition of a specific set of economic relationships, values and understandings. Local and indigenous knowledge of Nature and approaches to forest management are replaced by scientific logic and top-down corporate management (Lyons and Westoby, 2014). In communities where Nature and its elements (such as carbon) are not regarded as commodities, or potential commodities, for trading, offset projects intervene in customary and traditional meanings of Nature and effectively operate to invalidate them.

20.7 Conclusions

The idea of voluntary markets for offsetting individual GHG emissions fits well within a neoliberal ideology. It emphasises the ability of individuals as consumers to change the world through their purchasing decisions. Individual responsibility for environmental harm is highlighted and a means offered to assuage the resulting guilt. In the process, the need for collective action, changing behaviour, new public policies and institutional reform are all undermined.

Despite their fast growth, voluntary carbon markets appear at best a dubious means for addressing human-induced climate change, even if purely a supplement to government policy. Yet there appears to be a lack of critical reflection as to their operation despite a series fundamental problems. We have identified two broad sets of issues. One is the validity of carbon markets in their own terms as a means for achieving the control of GHGs to prevent human-induced climate change. The other is the political economy of such markets and their role as social institutions impacting individual behaviour and embedding it within a capitalist and formal economic logic that has implications for international resource exchange and the geopolitical order.

Clear quality and additionality standards for voluntary carbon offsets are missing. Existing standards vary in scope and rigour and appear inconsistent and/or difficult to assess. There is no mandatory structure that binds offset providers to a particular standard. Purchasers of carbon offsets are unable to obtain reliable information on additionality, as well as the social and ecological integrity of carbon offsets. The average purchaser of offsets is left with a variety of providers and standards with unclear quality differences. The ideal of consumer choice as an informed decision appears highly susceptible to violation, and purchasers also cannot be assumed to have the technical literacy necessary to judge the qualities of different carbon offsets. This raises the question as to why individuals buy offsets.

That the individuals targeted by offset providers are liable to be only moderately concerned environmentalists, who are preoccupied by personal image but feel guilty over their materialist lifestyles, means a further absence of scrutiny as to offset quality. Crowding out of intrinsic motivation means the net outcome may be worse in terms of overall GHG emissions. The ethical critiques of voluntary carbon markets question their basis in consequentialist reasoning and raise the importance of fairness, justice and rights. That voluntary carbon trading also involves concerns over negative effects on indigenous and local communities in the global South, not least through land grabbing, adds to the list of issues.

Overall, the idea that markets can be independently established to address environmental problems appears totally fallacious. Rather, markets are structured institutions that require social regulation like all institutions by which humans attempt to cooperate and coordinate their activities. What the problems we have presented reveal is that other institutions may actually be both more efficient and more effective as well as providing a direct means of achieving social and ecological goals. Perhaps most importantly, the idea of 'solving' the climate crisis through unregulated markets leads to a set of value commitments being adopted in public practice as 'normal' which assuage psychological conflicts but do not address the biophysical reality of climate change. Human behaviour in a price-making market comes with a set of self-justifications that appear to be the antithesis of what is necessary to achieve an informed responsibility for taking joint communal action to implement the social ecological transformation necessary to prevent human-induced climate change.

Notes

1 The concept of externalities has been challenged by Kapp (1978) as being a totally misleading description of how markets and the economy operate. Kapp explains environmental pollution, and a range of other problems, as arising from the deliberate shifting of costs on to others by economic actors. They do so for reasons of personal and corporate gain. The actions are not then external to the market as an institution. Rather than market failures, they are market successes within the context of utility maximisation and profit seeking. Cost shifting is then the correct conceptualisation of the instituted process.

2 'Parties included in Annex I' means a party included in Annex I to the UNFCCC and covered thirty-five countries plus the EU15.

3 The paper by Caney and Hepburn (2011) is a repetition of Caney (2010).

20.8 References

Aldred, J. (2012). 'The Ethics of Emissions Trading,' *New Political Economy*, 17(3), 37–41.

Andreoni, J. (1989). 'Giving with Impure Altruism : Applications to Charity and Ricardian Equivalence,' *Journal of Political Economy*, 97(6), 1447–1458.

Andreoni, J. (1990). 'Impure Altruism and Donations to Public Goods: A Theory of Warm-Glow Giving,' *Economic Journal*, 100(401), 464–477.

Ari, I. (2013). 'Voluntary Emission Trading Potential of Turkey,' *Energy Policy*, 62, 910–919.

Bachram, H. (2004). 'Climate Fraud and Carbon Colonialism: The New Trade in Greenhouse Gases,' *Capitalism, Nature, Socialism*, 15(4), 5–20.

Bayon, R., Hawn, A., Hamilton, K. (2009). *Voluntary Carbon Markets: An International Business Guide to What They Are and How They Work*, 2nd ed, Earthscan: Oxon.

Becken, S. (2004). 'How Tourists and Tourism Experts Perceive Climate Change and Carbon-Offsetting Schemes,' *Journal of Sustainable Tourism*, 12(4), 332–345.

Böhm, S., Misoczky, M. C., Moog, S. (2012). 'Greening Capitalism? A Marxist Critique of Carbon Markets,' *Organization Studies*, 33(11), 1617–1638.

Boiral, O., Henri, J.-F. (2017). 'Is Sustainability Performance Comparable? A Study of GRI Reports of Mining Organizations,' *Business and Society*, 56(2), 283–317.

Bowles, S. (2008). 'Policies Designed for Self-Interested Citizens May Undermine "The Moral Sentiments": Evidence from Economic Experiments', *Science*, 320(5883), 1605–1610.

Brinded, L. (2012). 'Deutsche Bank Chiefs Under Investigation in Carbon Trading Tax Scam', *International Business Times*, www.ibtimes.co.uk/deutsche-bank-carbon-trading-investigation-juergen-fitschen-414318.

Brinkel, S., Antes, R. (2011). 'Voluntary Carbon Offsets: Empirical Findings of an International Survey,' in Antes, R., Hansjürgen, B., Letmathe, P. and Pickl, S. (eds.), *Emissions Trading: Institutional Design, Decision Making and Corporate Strategies*, Springer: Heidelberg, Berlin, 243–262.

Broderick, J. (2009). 'Voluntary Carbon Offsetting for Air Travel,' in Gössling, S. and Upham, P. (eds.), *Aviation and Climate Change: Issues, Challanges and Solutions*, Earthscan: London, 329–346.

Broome, J. (2012). *Climate Matters: Ethics in a Warming World*, Norton: New York.

Bumpus, A. G. (2011). 'The Matter of Carbon: Understanding the Materiality of tCO2e in Carbon Offsets,' *Antipode*, 43(3), 612–638.

Bumpus, A. G., Liverman, D. M. (2008). 'Accumulation by Decarbonization and the Governance of Carbon Offsets,' *Economic Geography*, 84(2), 127–155.

Burns, P., Bibbings, L. (2009). 'The End of Tourism? Climate Change and Societal Challenges,' *Twenty-First Century Society*, 4(1), 31–51.

Bushnell, J. B. (2012). 'The Economics of Carbon Offsets,' in Fullerton, D. and Wolfram, C. (eds.), *The Design and Implementation of U.S. Climate Policy*, University of Chicago Press: Chicago and London, 197–209.

Caney, S. (2010). 'Markets, Morality and Climate Change: What, if Anything, Is Wrong with Emissions Trading?,' *New Political Economy*, 15(2), 197–224.

Caney, S., Hepburn, C. (2011). 'Carbon Trading: Unethical, Unjust and Ineffective?' *Royal Institute of Philosophy Supplement*, (59), 201–234.

Capstick, S. B., Lewis, A. (2008). 'Personal Carbon Trading: Perspectives from Psychology and Behavioural Economics,' University of Bath, Department of Psychology, Paper commissioned for the Institute for Public Policy Research.

Capstick, S. B., Lewis, A. (2010). 'Effects of Personal Carbon Allowances on Decision-Making: Evidence from an Experimental Simulation,' *Climate Policy*, 10(4), 369–384.

Carpenter, J. P. (2005). 'Endogenous Social Preferences,' *Review of Radical Political Economics*, 37(1), 63–84.

Coase, R. H. (1960). 'The Problem of Social Cost,' *Journal of Law and Economics*, 3(1), 1–44.

Coelho, R. (2012). *Green Is the Color of Money: The EU ETS Failure as a Model for the 'Green Economy'*, Carbon Trade Watch.

Cohen, S. A., Higham, J. E. S., Cavaliere, C. T. (2011). 'Binge Flying: Behavioural Addiction and Climate Change,' *Annals of Tourism Research*, 38(3), 1070–1089.

Crocker, T. D. (1966). 'The Structuring of Atmospheric Pollution Control Systems,' in Wolozin, H. (ed.), *The Economics of Air Pollution*, W. W. Norton: New York, 61–68.

Dales, J. H. (1968). *Pollution, Property, and Prices*, University of Toronto Press: Toronto.

Darby, S. (2008). 'Energy Feedback in Buildings: Improving the Infrastructure for Demand Reduction,' *Building Research and Information*, 36(5), 499–508.

Dhanda, K. K., Hartman, L. P. (2011). 'The Ethics of Carbon Neutrality: A Critical Examination of Voluntary Carbon Offset Providers,' *Journal of Business Ethics*, 100(1), 119–149.

Downie, C. (2007). Carbon Offsets: Saviour or Cop-Out? Austrian Institute, Research Paper No. 48.

Elsworth, R., Worthington, B., Buick, M., Craston, P. (2011). *Carbon Fat Cats 2011: The Companies Profiting from the EU Emissions Trading Scheme*, Sandbag Climate Campaign: London.

Fairhead, J., Leach, M., Scoones, I. (2012). 'Special Issue: Green Grabbing: A New Appropriation of Nature?' *Journal of Peasant Studies*, 39(2), 237–261.

Fawcett, T., Parag, Y. (2010). 'An Introduction to Personal Carbon Trading,' *Climate Policy*, 10(4), 329–338.

Fehr, E., Fischbacher, U. (2002). 'Why Social Preferences Matter: The Impact of Non-Selfish Motives on Competition,' *Economic Journal*, 112, 1–33.

Frey, B., Stutzer, A. (2012). 'Environmental Morale and Motivation,' in Lewis, A. (ed.), *The Cambridge Handbook of Psychology and Economic Behaviour*, Cambridge University Press: Cambridge, 406–428.

Frey, B. S. (1997). *Not Just for Money: An Economic Theory of Personal Motivation*, Edward Elgar: Cheltenham.

Frey, B. S., Oberholzer-Gee, F. (1997). 'The Cost of Price Incentives: An Empirical Analysis of Motivation Crowding-Out,' *American Economic Review*, 87(4), 746–755.

Fullbrook, E. (2009). 'Carbon Credits: Britain's Richest Man Cleans Up,' *Real-World Economics Review Blog*, rwer.wordpress.com/2009/12/07/carbon-credits-britain%e2%80%99s-richest-man-cleans-up/.

Gilbertson, T., Reyes, O. (2009). 'Carbon Trading: How It Works and Why It Fails,' *Soundings*, 45, 89–100.

Goodin, R. E. (1994). 'Selling Environmental Indulgences,' *Kyklos*, 47, 573–596.

Gössling, S., Broderick, J., Upham, P., et al. (2007). 'Voluntary Carbon Offsetting Schemes for Aviation: Efficiency, Credibility and Sustainable Tourism,' *Journal of Sustainable Tourism*, 15(3), 223–248.

Hamrick, K., Peters-Stanley, M., Goldstein, A. (2015). *Ahead of the Curve: State of the Voluntary Carbon Markets 2015*, Ecosystem Marketplace: Washington, DC.

Hopwood, A. G. (2009). 'Accounting and the Environment,' *Accounting, Organizations and Society*, 34(3–4), 433–439.

Hyams, K., Fawcett, T. (2013). 'The Ethics of Carbon Offsetting,' *Wiley Interdisciplinary Reviews: Climate Change*, 4(2), 91–98.

Inman, P. (2010). 'Three Britons Charged over €3m Carbon-Trading "Carousel Fraud",' *The Guardian*, www.theguardian.com/business/2010/jan/11/eu-carbon-trading-carousel-fraud.

Jacobs, R. (2013). 'The Forest Mafia: How Scammers Steal Millions Through Carbon Markets', *The Atlantic*, www.theatlantic.com/international/archive/2013/10/the-forest-mafia-how-scammers-steal-millions-through-carbon-markets/280419/.

Jindal, R., Swallow, B., Kerr, J. T. (2008). 'Forestry-Based Carbon Sequestration Project in Africa: Potential Benefits and Challenges,' *Natural Resources Forum*, 32, 116–130.

Kapp, K. W. (1978). *The Social Costs of Business Enterprise*, 3rd ed, Spokesman: Nottingham.

Kerr, J., Vardhan, M., Jindal, R. (2012). 'Prosocial Behavior and Incentives: Evidence from Field Experiments in Rural Mexico and Tanzania,' *Ecological Economics*, 73, 220–227.

Knopf, B., Koch, N., Grosjean, G., et al. (2014). 'The EU ETS: Ex-Post Analysis, the Market Stability Reserve and Options for a Comprehensive Reform,' *Nota di Lavoro* 79.2014.

Kollmuss, A., Bowell, B. (2007). *Voluntary Offsets for Air-Travel Carbon Emissions: Evaluations and Recommendations of Voluntary Offset Companies*, Tufts Climate Initiative, Medford: Boston.

Kollmuss, A., Schneider, L., Zhezherin, V. (2015). 'Has Joint Implementation Reduced GHG Emissions? Lessons Learned for the Design of Carbon Market Mechanisms,' Stockholm Environment Institute, Working Paper July 2015.

Kollmuss, A., Zink, H., Polycarp, C. (2008). *Making Sense of the Voluntary Carbon Market: A Comparison of Carbon Offset Standards*, World Wildlife Fund (WWF) Germany.

Kotchen, M. J. (2009). 'Offsetting Green Guilt,' *Stanford Social Innovation Review*, 7(2), 26–32.

Lambe, F., Jürisoo, M., Lee, C., Johnson, O. (2015). 'Can Carbon Finance Transform Household Energy Markets? A Review of Cookstove Projects and Programs in Kenya,' *Energy Research and Social Science*, 5, 55–66.

Lang, C., Byakola, T. (2006). *'A Funny Place to Store Carbon': UWA-FACE Foundation's Tree Planting Project in Mount Elgon National Park, Uganda*, October, World Rainforest Movement: Montevideo, Uruguay.

Lewis, A., Brandon, G. (1999). 'Reducing Household Energy Consumption: A Qualitative and Quantitative Field Study,' *Journal of Environmental Psychology*, 19, 75–85.

Lohmann, L. (2006a). 'Offsets: the Fossil Economy's New Arena of Conflict,' *Development Dialogue*, 48 (September), 219–328.

Lohmann, L. (2006b). '"Made in the USA": A Short History of Carbon Trading', *Development Dialogue*, 48 (September), 31–70.

Lohmann, L. (2008). 'Carbon Trading, Climate Justice and the Production of Ignorance: Ten Examples,' *Development*, 51(3), 359–365.

Lohmann, L. (2010). 'Uncertainty Markets and Carbon Markets: Variations on Polanyian Themes,' *New Political Economy*, 15(2), 225–254.

Lohmann, L. (2012). 'Financialization, Commodification and Carbon: The Contradictions of Neoliberal Climate Policy,' *Socialist Register*, 48, 85–107.

Lopez, M. C., Murphy, J. J., Spraggon, J. M., Stranlund, J. K. (2012). 'Comparing the Effectiveness of Regulation and Pro-Social Emotions to Enhance Cooperation: Experimental Evidence from Fishing Communities in Colombia,' *Economic Inquiry*, 50(1), 131–142.

Lyons, K., Westoby, P. (2014). 'Carbon Colonialism and the New Land Grab: Plantation Forestry in Uganda and Its Livelihood Impacts,' *Journal of Rural Studies*, 36, 13–21.

MacKenzie, D. (2009). 'Making Things the Same: Gases, Emission Rights and the Politics of Carbon Markets,' *Accounting, Organizations and Society*, 34(3–4), 440–455.

Mair, J. (2011). 'Exploring Air Travellers' Voluntary Carbon-Offsetting Behaviour', *Journal of Sustainable Tourism*, 19(2), 215–230.

McDonald, S., Oates, C. J., Thyne, M., Timmis, A. J., Carlile, C. (2015). 'Flying in the Face of Environmental Concern: Why Green Consumers Continue to Fly,' *Journal of Marketing Management*, 31(13–14), 1503–1528.

McKie, R. E., Stretesky, P. B., Long, M. A. (2015). 'Carbon Crime in the Voluntary Market: An Exploration of Modernization Themes Among a Sample of Criminal and Non-Criminal Organizations,' *Critical Criminology*, 23(4), 473–486.

McLennan, C., Becken, S., Battye, R., So, K. K. F. (2014). 'Voluntary Carbon Offsetting: Who Does It?' *Tourism Management*, 45, 194–198.

Meckling, J. (2014). 'The Future of Emissions Trading,' *Wiley Interdisciplinary Reviews: Climate Change*, 5(5), 569–576.

Murray, J., Dey, C. (2009). 'The Carbon Neutral Free for All,' *International Journal of Greenhouse Gas Control*, 3(2), 237–248.

O'Neill, J. (2007). *Markets, Deliberation and Environment*, Routledge: London and New York.

Page, E. A. (2013). 'The Ethics of Emissions Trading,' *Wiley Interdisciplinary Reviews: Climate Change*, 4, 233–243.

Parag, Y., Fawcett, T. (2014). 'Personal Carbon Trading: A Review of Research Evidence and Real-World Experience of a Radical Idea,' *Energy and Emission Control Technologies*, (2), 23–32.

Pearse, R., Böhm, S. (2014). 'Ten Reasons Why Carbon Markets Will Not Bring About Radical Emissions Reduction,' *Carbon Management*, 5(4), 325–337.

Perdan, S., Azapagic, A. (2011). 'Carbon Trading: Current Schemes and Future Developments,' *Energy Policy*, 39(10), 6040–6054.

Peters-Stanley, M., Yin, D. (2013). Maneuvering the Mosaic: State of the Voluntary Carbon Markets 2013, A Report by Forest Trends' Ecosystem Marketplace and Bloomberg New Energy Finance.

Rao, N and Baer, P. (2012). ' "Decent Living" Emissions: A Conceptual Framework,' *Sustainability* 4, 656–681.

Rode, J., Gómez-Baggethun, E., Krause, T. (2015). 'Motivation Crowding by Economic Incentives in Conservation Policy: A Review of the Empirical Evidence,' *Ecological Economics*, 117, 270–282.

Roy, S., Woerdman, E. (2012). 'End-User Emissions Trading: What, Why, How and When?' University of Groningen Faculty of Law Research Paper Series No. 02/2012.

Rydge, J. (2015). 'Implementing Effective Carbon Pricing. Contributing Paper for Seizing the Global Opportunity: Partnerships for Better Growth and a Better Climate,' New Climate Economy Working Paper Series.

Sandel, M. J. (1997). 'It's Immoral to Buy the Right to Pollute,' editorial article from the *New York Times*, 15 December, 29.

Sandel, M. J. (2012). *What Money Can't Buy: The Moral Limits of Markets*, Macmillan: New York.

Schiermeier, Q. (2006). 'Climate Credits,' *Nature*, 444, 976–977.

Seager, A. (2009). 'European Taxpayers Lose €5bn in Carbon Trading Fraud,' *The Guardian*, www.theguardian.com/business/2009/dec/14/eu-carbon-trading-fraud.

Shue, H. (1993). 'Subsistence Emissions and Luxury Emissions,' *Law and Policy*, 15 (1), 39–59.

Shue, H. (1999). 'Global Environment and International Inequality,' *International Affairs*, 75(3), 531–545.

Spaargaren, G., Mol, A. P. J. (2013). 'Carbon Flows, Carbon Markets, and Low-Carbon Lifestyles: Reflecting on the Role of Markets in Climate Governance,' *Environmental Politics*, 22(1), 174–193.

Spash, C. L. (2000a). 'Ethical Motives and Charitable Contributions in Contingent Valuation: Empirical Evidence from Social Psychology and Economics,' *Environmental Values*, 9(4), 453–479.

Spash, C. L. (2000b). 'Multiple Value Expression in Contingent Valuation: Economics and Ethics,' *Environmental Science and Technology*, 34(8), 1433–1438.

Spash, C. L. (2002). *Greenhouse Economics: Value and Ethics*, Routledge: London.

Spash, C. L. (2006). 'Non-Economic Motivation for Contingent Values: Rights and Attitudinal Beliefs in the Willingness to Pay for Environmental Improvements,' *Land Economics*, 82(4), 602–622.

Spash, C. L. (2010). 'The Brave New World of Carbon Trading,' *New Political Economy*, 15(2), 169–195.

Spash, C. L. (2015a). 'The Politics of Researching Carbon Trading in Australia,' in Stephan, B. and Lane, R. (eds.), *The Politics of Carbon Markets*, Routledge: London and New York, 191–211.

Spash, C. L. (2015b). 'Bulldozing Biodiversity: The Economics of Offsets and Trading-in Nature,' *Biological Conservation*, 192, 541–551.

Spiekermann, K. (2014). 'Buying Low, Flying High: Carbon Offsets and Partial Compliance,' *Political Studies*, 62(4), 913–929.

Starkey, R. (2012a). 'Personal Carbon Trading: A Critical Survey Part 1: Equity,' *Ecological Economics*, 73, 7–18.

Starkey, R. (2012b). 'Personal Carbon Trading: A Critical Survey Part 2: Efficiency and Effectiveness,' *Ecological Economics*, 73, 19–28.

Sterk, W., Bunse, M. (2004). 'Voluntary Compensation of Greenhouse Gas Emissions,' Wuppertal Institute Policy Paper No. 3/2004.

Taiyad, N. (2005). The Market for Voluntary Carbon Offsets: A New Tool for Sustainable Development? Gatekeeper Series 121.

Talbot, D., Boiral, O. (2013). 'Can We Trust Corporates GHG Inventories? An Investigation Among Canada's Large Final Emitters,' *Energy Policy*, 63, 1075–1085.

Twyman, C., Smith, T. A., Arnall, A. (2015). 'What Is Carbon? Conceptualising Carbon and Capabilities in the Context of Community Sequestration Projects in the Global South,' *Wiley Interdisciplinary Reviews: Climate Change*, 6(6), 627–641.

United Nations (1992). United Nations Framework Convention on Climate Change, Fccc/Informal/84.

Vatn, A. (2005). 'Rationality, Institutions and Environmental Policy,' *Ecological Economics*, 55(2), 203–217.

Wara, M. W., Victor, D. G. (2008). 'A Realistic Policy on International Carbon Offsets,' *Program on Energy and Sustainable Development Working Paper*, 74(April), i–24.

Wittman, H. K., Caron, C. (2009). 'Carbon Offsets and Inequality: Social Costs and Co-Benefits in Guatemala and Sri Lanka,' *Society and Natural Resources*, 22(8), 710–726.

World Bank Group, Ecofys. (2015). *State and Trends of Carbon Pricing*, World Bank: Washington, DC.

World Bank Group, Ecofys. (2016). *Carbon Pricing Watch 2016*, World Bank: Washington, DC.

PART VI

Biological Perspectives

21 Neuroeconomics

Ifat Levy and Daniel Ehrlich

How humans and animals make decisions has been the topic of investigation in economics, psychology, and neuroscience for many years. In the last two decades, a synthesis of insights and techniques from these three disciplines has established the field of neuroeconomics – the interdisciplinary research of the mechanisms of valuation and choice.

Economists and psychologists have traditionally employed largely separate approaches to the study of decision-making. Economists of the twentieth century focused on normative models of choice, or on how choices should be made. Paul Samuelson (Samuelson, 1948) and others have recognized that making a small number of simple assumptions, or "axioms," about choice behavior – such as "if a person prefers an orange to an apple she will not also prefer an apple to an orange" – allows one to make strong predictions about choice behavior. Based on such axioms, Von Neumann and Morgenstern (1944) have developed their model for choice between uncertain outcomes, the expected utility (EU) theory. While these economists were developing their models, psychologists preferred to focus on cognitive and behaviorist explanations for choice behavior. The two fields remained largely divided until the "behavioral challenge" to economics began to emerge in the latter part of twentieth century. Based on both thought and actual experiments, a small number of economists and psychologists have started to note that core assumptions of traditional models were often violated. What began to emerge was a more descriptive decision theory, leading to the formation of the field of behavioral economics. This development, best represented by the work of Kahnemann and Tversky in their Prospect Theory (Kahneman and Tversky, 1979), explicitly isolated the question of how humans *actually make* decisions from the question of how they *should make* decisions.

At the time that this was going on in the economics world, neuroscientists have experienced a revolution of their own with the growing accessibility of new sources of neurobiological data. While early work had mainly drawn conclusions from patients who suffered brain lesions or from neural activation patterns observed in anesthetized animals, more recent work has turned to newly developed methods for recording the neural responses of conscious humans and animals. Human neuroimaging, such as positron emission tomography (PET), electroencephalography (EEG), and functional magnetic resonance imaging (fMRI), as well as electrophysiological recording in animals, enabled researchers to examine the neural correlates of behavior during a variety of tasks. Scientists interested in probing the mechanistic basis of decision-making now had an entirely new set of research tools. These new techniques brought novel challenges – they provided increasing amounts of data and required theoretical models for making sense of those data. Searching for such models, neuroscientists turned to cognitive psychology and behavioral economics for guidance. At the same time, some psychologists and economists realized that neuroscientific data could help them improve their models by providing constraints on the types of models that were biologically feasible.

These realizations have led to a series of papers in which neuroscientists, psychologists, and economists joined forces to study decision-making questions. In one of the first papers, for example, Shizgal and Conover (1996) used economic theory to analyze the neurobiology of the behavior of rats pressing a lever to stimulate reward-related neurons in their brains. Employing a similar economic approach, the neuroscientists Platt and Glimcher (1999) showed that neurons in monkey posterior parietal cortex (PPC), a brain area implicated in sensory-motor transformations, can be described as encoding the expected utility – or subjective value – that juice rewards held for the animals. Shortly after the publication of these animal studies, human imaging researchers also began to make use of economic theory in their research design and data analysis (Breiter et al., 2001; McCabe et al., 2001). A growing number of interdisciplinary papers then followed, together with an explicit call, made by Paul Glimcher (Glimcher, 2003), to form an interdisciplinary field of decision-making research. A series of meetings also played an important role in the consolidation of the emerging field. These initial meetings led to the formation of the Society for Neuroeconomics, which has been holding annual, widely attended international meetings for over a decade. The society has published a comprehensive textbook surveying the major advances of the field (Glimcher and Fehr, 2014), making neuroeconomics research accessible to scientists from a variety of backgrounds. While most practitioners still come from a background largely focused on one of the central parent disciplines, increasingly a new generation is trained primarily as neuroeconomists, some even at the undergraduate level. This transition toward a consolidated neuroeconomic program has been a boon for the field in enabling a greater focus on a common intellectual framework for advancing and expanding the scope of inquiry. As decision-making researchers from different fields began to utilize more of the same language, models, and ideas, the opportunity for cross-field investigation and amalgamation continued to grow, leading to important discoveries, some of which are described in this chapter. Neuroeconomists have approached a wide variety of problems, from traditional domains of economics, including decision-making under uncertainty and intertemporal choice, to issues more familiar to neuroscientists and psychologists, such as value normalization and reinforcement learning. In the sections that follow, we provide a brief introduction to the methodology of the field and then survey the main research directions.

21.2 Methods of Neuroeconomic Analysis

As an interdisciplinary field, neuroeconomics is enhanced by the wide variety of research methods inherited from its parent disciplines (Kable, 2011). A grasp of the basic logic and assumptions of each technique is important for understanding existing findings and potential future research directions. Most generally, neuroeconomic studies strive to identify "psychometric-neurometric" matches – correspondences between the modulation of behavioral and neural measures, employing the following behavioral and neural techniques.

21.2.1 Behavioral Methods in Neuroeconomics

Neuroeconomists have utilized a variety of behavioral paradigms borrowed primarily from experimental economics and psychology. Experimental economists employ a "revealed preference" approach to individual preferences and decision traits (Samuelson, 1948). This approach assumes that observed choice behavior provides a more objective account of preferences and traits compared to self-report questionnaires or expert examinations, more popular among other disciplines. For that reason, neuroeconomic experiments often ask participants to make choices with realized outcomes in a controlled laboratory setting. Prominent examples include choices between rewards of various magnitudes received at different times (e.g., $20 today versus $100 in a month) or at different probabilities (e.g., $20 for sure versus a 50 percent chance of $100), choices which involve both potential gains and potential losses, and adaptive choices in changing environments. To examine how decision makers take other intelligent decision makers into account in the choices they make, neuroeconomists also adapt methods from game theory. In all of these experiments, deviations from normative responses can be informative about the heuristics and the mechanistic limitations of decision-making processes.

21.2.2 Imaging and Manipulating Human Neural Function

Neuroeconomics has adopted a variety of methods to link the observed behavior to neural activation patterns in the human (and animal) brain. To this end, neuroimaging methods, including positron emission tomography (PET), electroencephalography (EEG), magnetoencephalography (MEG), and functional magnetic resonance imaging (fMRI), in humans, have been vital.

PET is a method that uses radioactive tracers to image the brain. These tracers can either be linked to glucose analogues, in order to track metabolic activity in the brain, or to molecules that can target specific neurotransmitter receptors in the brain. PET is potentially a very powerful tool for studying neural mechanism of decision-making, but its usability is somewhat limited by high cost and the logistical difficulty of handling and administering the radioactive tracers.

EEG and MEG, in contrast, utilize electrical and magnetic signals recorded on the human scalp to infer the pattern of adjacent cortical activity. These techniques can reveal neural activity on a much finer temporal resolution on the order of milliseconds and are therefore useful for tracking dynamic changes in neural activation. The main limitations of both techniques, however, are low spatial resolution and difficulty in precisely localizing the sources for the measured signals. These techniques are also mostly limited to signals that originate close to the scalp and are inappropriate for measuring signals from deeper brain structures.

fMRI is the most widely used technique to study the human brain, not only in neureconomics, but in cognitive neuroscience in general. fMRI utilizes powerful magnets in conjunction with radiofrequency pulses to measure changes in the oxygenation of blood in the brain, referred to as the blood oxygen level dependent (BOLD) signal. As populations of neurons increase their activity, local blood supply increases, resulting in changes in the concentration of deoxyhemoglobin, which is paramagnetic. This, in turn, results in slight changes to the measured magnetic resonance (MR) signal, which serves as a proxy to neural activity. While resolution is limited, advances in both magnet design and pulse sequences have been making strides in improving both the temporal and spatial precision of fMRI. To date, for most paradigms fMRI provides the best combination of spatial and temporal resolution, with typical spatial resolution at 2 to 3 millimeters and typical temporal resolution at 1 to 2 seconds.

While neuroimaging has granted researchers incredible access to biological measurements of brain function, such methods are limited in what they can tell us about the causal role of specific brain regions and circuits. Traditionally, this limitation has been partly addressed by research in patients with brain lesions, who through disease or accident have lost function in a region of interest (Neylan, 1999). These patients were instrumental in informing researchers whether a given brain region was necessary for a specific cognitive process. More recently, however, promising means of altering the function of neural circuits in conscious humans have entered neuroeconomics laboratories. Among these are transcranial magnetic stimulation (TMS) and transcranial direct current stimulation (tDCS), which allow for activation or deactivation of specific brain regions using magnetic fields and scalp electrodes respectively.

21.2.3 Animal Models in Neuroeconomics

In addition to human work, significant progress has been made using animal models. While the full range of behavioral paradigms is somewhat truncated in animal models, they offer the opportunity for imaging and manipulating single neurons. One of the prominent methods for observing neural activity in animals is in-vivo electrophysiological recordings of voltage changes in or around a neuron or a small subset of neurons. While these recordings allow extremely high temporal resolution, one drawback is that, without complex array implants, only a small group of neurons can be recorded simultaneously. One method that overcomes this limitation is calcium imaging, which relies on a genetically encoded calcium indicator that fluoresces, or gives off light, whenever a neuron fires. This allows researchers to use the fluorescence trace recorded during an experiment as a proxy for that neuron's firing history. In contrast to electrophysiology, however, the fluorescence is delayed and provides a less temporally precise signal.

Animal models also allow active manipulations that are not possible in humans. This includes traditional methods such as electrical stimulation of neurons or pharmacological manipulations, as well as novel genetic tools that allow creation, removal, activation, or inhibition of specific neurotransmitter receptors and imaging of specific populations of neurons in living animals. As these methods improve and new methods for cellular-level control of the animal nervous system develop, they will likely prove fundamental in the search for circuit-level understanding of decision-making processes.

Using all of these techniques, neuroeconomics research has already made several significant contributions to our understanding of the neuroscience of decision-making. A growing number of papers are published every year (Plate 1, see color plate section), raising new research questions and providing new insights. In the following section, we survey some of the major findings of these studies, as well as some of the open questions in the field.

21.3 The Neural Encoding of Value

The computation and comparison of value is so intuitively linked to our lives that it is easy to take them for granted, yet these processes are vital for successful navigation of the world. Standard models of decision-making assert that to make a decision, the value of each available option has to be computed and compared to values of other options. This is not a trivial task, since we often need to choose between options of markedly different nature. Movie or dinner? Steak or apple pie? To facilitate such comparisons, we need some "common currency" for representing the value of qualitatively different options. Indeed, the search for value representation in the brain is a central theme in neuroeconomic research, and the potential benefits of identifying the neural correlates of value are substantial. While economists can identify the relative preferences that individuals place on different alternatives (e.g., "Joe prefers apples to oranges"), and assume that decision makers choose "as if" they aim to maximize the utility, or "subjective value," of their choice, neuro-economists attempt to actually measure the neurally encoded subjective values. Access to a robust measurement of subjective value presents great opportunities for increasing our knowledge of human decision-making. As we will see in this chapter, such measurements can help shape decision models by telling us which models are biologically feasible. Moreover, these measurements provide a *cardinal* estimate of value on a neutral scale (e.g., firing rates, fMRI activation patterns), which cannot be obtained from observing choice behavior. In other words, by measuring neural signals that encode value, we can tell not just that Joe *prefers* apples to oranges, but also *by how much*. Value estimates in turn allow researchers to predict choices between alternatives that were never previously compared by the individual. They also provide a means for tracking dynamic changes in valuation (for example, how the value of apples decreases following the consumption of several apples).

The first studies of value encoding in the human brain occurred in the early twenty-first century. Delgado and colleagues (Delgado et al., 2000) observed higher activity in the striatum, a part of the basal ganglia, when participants received monetary rewards compared to when they incurred monetary losses. A year later, Knutson and colleagues (Knutson et al., 2001) showed that activity in the same brain area scales as a function of the expected value of anticipated rewards. The results of these two studies were consistent with a role for the striatum in value encoding, but were not sufficient for claiming that it encoded *subjective* value. The same monetary amount (e.g., $100) may carry very different subjective values for different individuals (e.g., a rich versus a poor individual) or for the same individual under different circumstances (e.g., when the expectation was to lose $100 compared to when the expectation was to receive $200). In one of the first truly neuroeconomic studies, a group of both neuroscientists and economists (Aharon et al., 2001), including Daniel Kahneman, showed that activity of the striatum is modulated by the participant's expectation, a finding that is compatible with Prospect Theory.

The striatum was not the only brain area implicated in value encoding – at about the same time that these studies were conducted, O'Doherty and colleagues (O'Doherty et al., 2001) identified similar signals in the medial part of the orbitofrontal cortex (OFC). Subsequent studies revealed neural signals that encoded the value of non-monetary rewards and punishments, such as beautiful faces (Aharon et al., 2001), pleasant and unpleasant taste (O'Doherty et al., 2002; Small, Jones-Gotman, and Dagher, 2003), and snack foods (Plassmann, O'Doherty, and Rangel, 2007). Many of these studies pointed to the striatum and the prefrontal cortex, especially its ventromedial section (vmPFC), as important components of the valuation system of the brain, suggesting that these brain areas may constitute the "common currency" valuation system needed to facilitate choice.

In a seminal paper, Kable and Glimcher (2007) provided strong support for this hypothesis by examining how the subjective value of anticipated future rewards is encoded in the brain. Many important decisions involve outcomes that are expected at different times: spend money on a new car now or save more for retirement? Have a chocolate cake now or maintain better health in the future? Much research in neuroeconomics has focused on these types of decisions – how the values of options expected at different times are encoded, and how short- and long-term motivations are integrated in brain and behavior. Early research identified increased activity in response to immediate options in medial areas, including the vmPFC and the striatum, and preferential activity for delayed options in lateral aspects of prefrontal and parietal cortex (McClure et al., 2004). These results were interpreted as consistent with a particular economic theory that viewed intertemporal choices as resulting from a competition between an impatient valuation system, concerned with the here and now, and a patient system that cares about long-term consequences. Kable and Glimcher challenged that view. They employed an experimental economic paradigm, in which participants made a series of choices between immediate and delayed monetary rewards (e.g., $20 now versus $30 in a week) while lying in the magnetic resonance imaging (MRI) scanner. Based on the choices that each participant made, the researchers estimated how patient or impatient the participant was. More patient participants were willing to wait in order to increase the amount of money that they would receive; impatient participants were willing to give up money in order to obtain the reward immediately. Kable and Glimcher then used these estimates together with an economic model, to calculate the subjective value that each option held for each individual participant. These subjective values varied with the individual "discount factor" – the degree to which the participant discounted future rewards. Anticipation of receiving $30 in a week, for example, would carry a higher value for a patient participant than for an impatient one. What the researchers found was that activity in the putative value areas in the brain was associated with the *subjective value* of available rewards, rather than with objective measures of the reward, such as its magnitude or the delay to receive it (Plate 2, see color plate section). Rather than two separate valuation systems, these results pointed to a single system, which encoded the value of both immediate and delayed rewards. Activity in both the vmPFC and the striatum scaled with the subjective values of rewards at various delays. Viewed in this light, the preferential activation for immediate rewards observed earlier in these areas likely reflected the higher value of such rewards, compared to delayed rewards of similar magnitude, rather than unique processing of immediate rewards. While this means that the lateral brain areas probably do not constitute a separate, patient valuation system, these areas may indeed contribute to patient behavior. The dorsolateral prefrontal cortex (dlPFC), in particular, a brain area heavily implicated in working memory and cognitive control processes, is likely to contribute to self-control in the face of temptation. For example, when choosing snacks, based on both their taste and their health, increased activity in this area is associated with increased avoidance of options that are tasty, but unhealthy (Hare, Camerer, and Rangel, 2009). Conversely, reducing activity in this area with the help of transcranial magnetic stimulation lead to less patient choices (Figner et al., 2010). Thus, it is possible that the dlPFC influences value representations in the vmPFC, by reducing the subjective value of options with lesser long-term consequences.

These findings are particularly interesting, because they serve as an interesting example for how neuroscientific data may help shape economic theory – while intertemporal choices may not differ based on whether they result from a single valuation system or from multiple systems, the brain can provide hints about which algorithm is more biologically plausible.

While Kable and Glimcher provided strong support for a unified valuation system, it could be argued that both the immediate and the delayed outcomes were of the same type – monetary rewards. Another highly influential paper published in the same year, however, demonstrated encoding of value, both for potential monetary gains and for potential monetary losses within the same brain areas (Tom et al., 2007), providing additional evidence in favor of a unified valuation system. The next step was to examine value encoding for items from different, nonmonetary, categories of rewards and punishments within the same experiment. Several studies revealed overlapping representations within the vmPFC and the striatum for expectation or receipt of various outcomes (Levy and Glimcher, 2012), including money, snacks, and nonfood items (Chib et al., 2009), money and food (Levy and Glimcher, 2011), money and juice (Kim, Shimojo, and O'Doherty, 2011), and even monetary and social rewards (Izuma, Saito, and Sadato, 2008). Interestingly, activity in these areas also encoded the value of stimuli that participants watched passively and could be used to predict future choices between these stimuli (Lebreton et al., 2009; Tusche, Bode, and Haynes, 2010; Levy et al., 2011). Moreover, in a few studies, activation magnitudes in the same areas in a small group of participants predicted aggregate choice behavior in large populations (Falk et al., 2011; Berns and Moore, 2012). This is important, because while for economists value could be a theoretical concept, neuroeconomists demonstrated the physical encoding of value.

The converging evidence for a unified valuation system in all of these studies, as well as many others, was summarized in two large-scale meta-analyses (Bartra, McGuire, and Kable, 2013; Clithero and Rangel, 2014). Importantly, however, the conclusions of all of these studies were based on the mean activation of large chunks of the brain; this mean activity scaled with the value of stimuli from different categories. It was still possible that these areas contained distributed distinct, but partly overlapping, representations of value signals, each unique for a specific category. To examine this possibility, recent studies employed multivoxel pattern analysis techniques that allow the researchers to unravel spatial patterns of activation within each brain area. Results from these studies (Plate 3, see color plate section) suggest that, at least in the vmPFC, a "common currency" representation coexists with category-specific value signals (McNamee, Rangel, and O'Doherty, 2013; Gross et al., 2014). Finally, while the vmPFC and the striatum are most consistently implicated in value encoding, several other brain structures, including the amygdala, the insula, and the cingulate cortex, are also likely to play a part in valuation. The nature of the various representations, and the manner in which they interact with each other, is the subject of substantial ongoing research.

21.4 Neural Mechanisms of Reinforcement Learning

In the previous section, we reviewed a large number of studies that demonstrated and characterized the neural encoding of value. But how are these values formed in the brain? In an often uncertain, complex, and dynamic world, flexible learning from experience is required in order to form and update the encoded values. The computational algorithms and neural mechanisms that facilitate this "reinforcement learning" have been the topic of substantial research in neuroeconomics and its parent disciplines. Many neurobiological studies point to a major role for the neurotransmitter dopamine, released by neurons in the midbrain, in reinforcement learning (Niv and Schoenbaum, 2008). Animal studies have implicated dopamine in reward processing as early as the 1970s (Mora and Myers, 1977). Their specific role in learning, however, was suggested by Wolfram Schultz and colleagues in groundbreaking work in the late 1990s (Plate 4, see color plate section). These researchers realized that the dopamine neurons did not simply fire in response to a delivered reward, but rather at the initiation of an *unexpected* reward (Schultz, Dayan, and Montague, 1997). Moreover, if a reward were reliably signaled by another stimulus ("CS" in Plate 4), the dopamine spike would temporally shift to the predictive stimulus. What Schultz and his colleagues found was that this pattern of activation could be easily described by a theoretical algorithm from computer science (Sutton and Barto, 1998), in which "reward prediction errors" – or the differences between obtained and expected rewards – drive learning. The firing patterns of dopamine neurons were compatible with the representation of such reward prediction errors.

Subsequent neuroimaging research in humans revealed similar neural signals in several brain areas that receive input from midbrain dopaminergic neurons (McClure, Berns, and Montague, 2003; O'Doherty et al., 2003; O'Doherty et al., 2004; O'Doherty, 2004). Just like the firing of dopamine neurons in the monkey brain, the fMRI signals in these areas of the human brain followed the learned associations between rewards and cues that predicted them and were compatible with signaling predictive errors (O'Doherty, 2004). Such compatibility is of course necessary if dopamine neurons encode subjective value, but is not sufficient to make that claim. To formally test the sufficiency of the observed activity for encoding reward prediction error, Rutledge and colleagues (Rutledge et al., 2010) adopted an "axiomatic" approach. They articulated the basic assumptions – or axioms – that must be obeyed by the dopamine signals if indeed they encode a prediction error that can be used to drive learning, and showed that fMRI signals in the dopamine target areas conform to these axioms.

This simple form of reward learning, termed "model free," is compelling, yet it is unlikely to account for complex human behavior, which involves a series of actions necessary to reach a goal. Recent research, most notably by Nathaniel Daw and colleagues (Daw et al., 2011), hints at a more complex complementary "model-based" reinforcement learning system. To distinguish between model-free and model-based learning, these investigators developed a multistage decision task (Plate 5, see color plate section). Participants first had to make a decision between two alternatives, A or B. Both alternatives led to one of two states, C or D, at the second stage, but at different probabilities. Option A led to state C at a high probability, and to state D at a low probability. Option B had the opposite contingencies, leading to state C at a low probability and to state D at a high probability. Once they reached the second stage, participants made another choice between two options, leading to a probabilistic reward outcome. In a model-free reinforcement context, the receipt of reward would enforce the action taken on that trial, regardless of its likelihood to lead to the rewarding second-stage state (Plate 5c, left). If, however, participants were able to form a model of their environment, a reward following a rare stage transition (e.g., state C following choice of B at the first stage) would reinforce the option that was not taken, because the participant would know that that option was more likely to lead to the rewarding option (Plate 5c, middle). Using this paradigm, Daw and colleagues were able to show that subjects used an intermediate strategy, relying partly on model-free and partly on model-based learning (Plate 5c, right), with individuals varying in the degree of reliance on each type of learning. This mixture was also reflected in the neural patterns, with both model-free and model-based signals observed in dopamine target areas. The mechanism and algorithms underlying reward learning are an active research field in neuroeconomics. While much progress has been achieved in identifying and characterizing potential neural substrates for reinforcement learning, there still remains significant debate regarding the exact role of each component of the reward learning system. For example, it is not clear whether dopamine plays a specific role in reward learning (Fiorillo, 2013), or whether it also has a role in learning from punishments (Bromberg-Martin, Matsumoto, and Hikosaka, 2010). Finally, many innovative studies have extended this research, investigating how we learn from "counterfactual" outcomes, or what would have been had we made a different choice (Coricelli et al., 2005; Lohrenz et al., 2007), and how we identify the relevant objects of learning (Niv et al., 2015).

21.5 Decision Under Uncertainty

An important aspect of most of the decisions we make is that the outcome of a particular choice is seldom certain. Whether we select a cheese from the available variety in the supermarket, decide to accept a job offer, or choose a medical treatment, the outcomes inevitably involve some degree of uncertainty. Just as with time preference, individuals vary substantially in their attitudes toward uncertainty; some accept substantial risks, while others avoid them to a fault. Behavioral economics provides useful tools for studying these attitudes, and its approach has been adapted in many neurobiological studies looking to identify uncertainty processing in the brain. Similarly to intertemporal choice, decision under uncertainty is typically studied by having participants make a series of choices. Consider, for example, the choice between receiving $5 for sure and playing a lottery that offers a 50 percent chance of winning $10 (but also 50 percent of winning nothing). Both options are of the same *expected value* – their average outcome is the same ($5) – but the lottery is uncertain. This form of uncertainty, where the probabilities for potential outcomes are fully specified, is known as "risk." An individual who is not affected by risk (risk neutral) will be indifferent about these options. Conversely, a risk-averse individual would prefer the sure $5, whereas a risk-seeking individual would opt for the lottery.

Neuroeconomic studies of decision-making under risk have implicated several brain areas. Not surprisingly, activity in value-related areas is modulated by outcome probability (Knutson et al., 2005; Tobler et al., 2007). Increasing the probability for obtaining reward (or decreasing the probability for incurring a punishment) increases the desirability, or the subjective value, of that particular option, and thus should be reflected in activation patterns that encode value. Individual risk attitudes also affect subjective value, and indeed these attitudes are reflected in the activation of the same brain areas (Levy et al., 2010) (Plate 6, see color plate section). There is, however, also evidence for neural encoding of the level of uncertainty regarding outcome receipt, which is separate from the encoding of value, and is observed in several parts of the brain, including lateral aspects of the prefrontal cortex (Huettel, Song, and McCarthy, 2005; Tobler et al., 2007) and the parietal cortex (Huettel et al., 2005), as well as in the striatum (Preuschoff, Bossaerts, and Quartz, 2006) and the insula (Huettel et al., 2005). Interestingly, activity in the PPC in response to choices that involved risky options also reflected individual risk preferences (Huettel et al., 2006). The PPC has been studied extensively in the monkey brain and implicated in decision-making processes (Platt and Glimcher, 1999; Sugrue et al., 2004; Louie and Glimcher, 2010; Louie, Gratton, and Glimcher,

2011). The potential role of this area in shaping individual risk attitudes has also been highlighted in a recent study, which demonstrated an association between the volume of gray matter in the same area and individual risk attitudes (Gilaie-Dotan et al., 2014). Individuals with more volume in this area were more tolerant of risk, or less risk averse. Although today we still do not know exactly what this measure of volume translates to at the neural level – it could reflect the number of neurons, the synaptic density, or other physiological properties – this finding raises an intriguing possibility of a link between neural computational capacity and risk attitudes.

Other studies extended the research of decision under uncertainty to more realistic situations, in which the probabilities for different potential outcomes are not precisely known. This situation, known as "ambiguity," has been extensively studied in economics, and is of high interest to neuroeconomists, because it strongly affects decisions (Camerer and Weber, 1992), and because how an individual treats risk (or known probabilities) does not tell us much about how she will treat ambiguity (or unknown probabilities) (Cohen et al., 1987; Tymula et al., 2013), suggesting that these attitudes reflect independent cognitive processes. Similar to time and risk preferences, ambiguity attitudes are also reflected in the activity of value-related areas (Levy et al., 2010) (Plate 6). In addition, there is evidence for preferential response for ambiguous options in the orbitofrontal cortex (OFC) (Hsu et al., 2005) and the neighboring ventrolateral prefrontal cortex (Huettel et al., 2006). The latter area may be especially interesting, because its activity is correlated with individual ambiguity attitudes in an experimental design that enabled participants to reduce the level of ambiguity based on feedback that they received on each trial (Huettel et al., 2006). Other studies have employed dynamic designs specifically focused on learning in ambiguous environments – how individuals use the outcomes of their prior choices to reduce ambiguity about outcome probabilities, and to learn about changes in the probabilistic structure of the environment (Kuhnen and Knutson, 2005; Behrens et al., 2007; Payzan-LeNestour et al., 2013).

21.6 The Neural Correlates of Choice

Evaluating potential outcomes, the likelihood for their occurrence, and the time for their receipt, is essential for decision-making. The decision itself, however, also requires comparisons of available options, either to each other or to some decision criterion. While we know quite a lot about the neural processing of value, the neural mechanisms of choice are a matter of more debate. One possibility is that the brain first computes the subjective value of each available option, by integrating evidence regarding all the attributes of a particular option, and that choice is then implemented, as a second step, based on these integrated values. Another possibility is that valuation and choice are interweaved, such that value comparison is a dynamic process that is carried out as part of the valuation process itself. Such dynamic processes may involve comparisons of single attributes of the available options. For example, when choosing between two cars, it is possible that parallel comparisons of the shape, the safety, the price, and other attributes are carried out, and that the final choice is computed from these multiple comparisons (Hunt, Dolan, and Behrens, 2014).

There is some evidence for implementation of comparatory mechanisms in the vmPFC, the same brain area whose activity encodes the value of available options. Thus, single-unit recordings in monkeys (Strait, Blanchard, and Hayden, 2014) and MEG recordings in humans (Hunt et al., 2012) identified signals in this brain area whose magnitude was correlated with the difference between the values of available options. A growing number of studies have also identified choice-related signals in the PPC (Louie and Glimcher, 2010). The PPC is perfectly situated to accommodate the choice process, because it is spatially organized, such that activity of each neuron is linked to a specific location in space, allowing the simultaneous representation of subjective values of more than one option. Moreover, a choice computed in this brain area can be directly communicated to motor brain areas that can issue the motor commands that will implement the choice (e.g., pointing to the chosen car). Indeed, this brain area has long been implicated in *perceptual* decisions – the choices between different interpretations of sensory information. Recordings from neurons in this area suggest that they accumulate sensory information in favor of a particular interpretation, until enough evidence has been gathered to make a choice (Roitman and Shadlen, 2002). This is consistent with computational models of drift diffusion (Smith and Ratcliff, 2004), which have been successfully used to describe behavioral observations (Ratcliff and McKoon, 2008). Following early studies that demonstrated value encoding in the activity of neurons in the PPC (Platt and Glimcher, 1999; Sugrue, Corrado, and Newsome, 2004), more recent studies describe dynamic signals in the PPC that start out as encoding value and switch to encoding the binary choice that the monkey has made based on these values (Louie and Glimcher, 2010) (Plate 7, see color plate section). Thus, it is possible that similar computational mechanisms underlie both perceptual and value-based decisions, a proposal that is supported by recent human data (Krajbich, Armel, and Rangel, 2010; Krajbich and Rangel, 2011). Interestingly, value encoding in PPC neurons take into account the values of other available options (Louie et al., 2011), a computational feature that is prevalent in sensory neural representations (Carandini and Heeger, 2012) and may explain context-dependent choices in humans and animals (Louie, Khaw, and Glimcher, 2013).

21.7 Social Decision-Making

All the research we have described thus far relies on an implicit assumption – that the decision maker is the sole intelligent agent in the environment; but real decisions are seldom made in isolation. Decision makers often have the interests of other individuals in mind, and, even more importantly, are affected by the actions of other individuals. This complicates the decision process substantially, because it means that to make an optimal decision the decision maker needs to infer the beliefs and intentions of other individuals – beliefs and intentions that, in turn, also depend on the decision maker's own actions. Game theory provides a convenient framework for studying these processes. Von Neumann and Morgenstern (1944), who laid the foundation for expected utility theory, have also developed the basis for game theory, which deals with decisions of multiple players with competing interests. Just like expected utility theory, game theory provides a useful benchmark for quantifying deviations of animal and human behavior from optimal behavior, and for using these quantifications to search for the neural correlates of this type of behavior (Lee and Seo, 2016). Nonhuman primate studies usually employ simple paradigms, such as the well-known *rock-paper-scissors* game. In one study, Barraclough, Conroy, and Lee (2004) have used the somewhat simpler game of *matching pennies* to examine how monkeys' choices are affected by changes in the strategies of their opponent. In matching pennies, each of two players chooses one of two available options. One player wins if both players make the same choice, the other wins if the choices are different. The monkey played the game against a computer opponent, whose game strategy was systematically manipulated by the experimenters. What they changed, essentially, was the degree to which the computer exploited the monkey's choice history in making its own choices. The researchers found that monkeys were able to adapt their behavior, making their choice patterns more random, and thus more difficult to exploit, with each increase in the computer's level of sophistication. While the monkeys were playing that game, the experimenters recorded the activity of neurons in the dlPFC and found that those neurons encoded the monkey's past choices and rewards, providing information that could be used to update the monkey's estimate of future rewards.

Some human studies have used more complex game-theory based experimental paradigms to explore social concepts, including trust, cooperation, and competition, as well as mentalizing – the ability to infer other people's mental states – and preferences for the well-being of others. In the first study to use game theory with fMRI, participants had to decide whether to trust another player (McCabe et al., 2001). Participants who trusted their opponents had higher activation in regions of the medial prefrontal cortex while playing against humans, compared to playing against a computer, suggesting a role for these regions in social processing. A similar design was used in a subsequent study (Kosfeld et al., 2005), which examined the effect of Oxytocin on trust. Oxytocin is a neuropeptide that is thought to play a role in social attachment and related processes. By increasing the brain levels of oxytocin in one group of participants, the researchers were able to increase the level of trust exhibited by these participants, compared to a control group. In another early study, Sanfey and colleagues used fMRI to examine the concept of fairness (Sanfey et al., 2003). They employed a simple paradigm – the Ultimatum Game – where two players are given the opportunity to split a sum of money. One player – the proposer – proposes how the money should be split, and the other player – the responder – can either accept or reject the proposal. If the responder accepts, the money is split as proposed. If the responder rejects the proposal, both players receive nothing. The standard economic solution is for the proposer to offer the smallest possible amount, and for the responder to accept this amount, because any monetary amount is better than none. Yet both intuition and abundant empirical evidence suggest that this is not how most players behave (Thaler, 1988). The majority of proposers offer a fair share of 40 to 50 percent of the total sum, and about half of respondents reject low offers below 20 to 30 percent (Nowak, Page, and Sigmund, 2000), likely because such offers are perceived as unfair (Pillutla and Murnighan, 1996). Sanfey and colleagues examined the neural activity in the brains of respondents and identified several brain areas, including the anterior insula, whose activity in response to unfair offers from human players was higher than activity in response to fair offers or to unfair offers generated by a computer. Moreover, participants with stronger anterior-insula activation to unfair offers rejected a higher proportion of these offers, and activation within individuals was higher for unfair offers that were rejected, compared to those that were accepted, pointing to a potential role of the insula in guiding response to unfairness.

All of these studies were based on one-shot games: participants played only one round with each opponent, and those opponents were unfamiliar to them. This was done in order to prevent effects of reputation, where participants make generous offers, or reject ungenerous ones, in order to affect their opponent's behavior in subsequent games. Other studies, however, did look at dynamic changes in brain and behavior in repeated games. King-Casas and colleagues (2005), for example, used a multiround version of the economic Trust Game. In each round of this game, one player – the investor – receives a sum of money and can invest any portion of it with the other player – the trustee. The invested money is then tripled, and the trustee decides how much of the triple amount to repay. Players maintained their roles across multiple rounds with the same partner, and were thus motivated to build a reputation of trustworthiness. The brains of both players – the investor and the trustee – were simultaneously scanned using two MRI machines. This allowed the researchers to examine not just how the brain signals in one player predicted behavioral changes in the other player, but also the extent of brain-to-brain synchronization, synchronization between signals that may be richer and more subtle than the observed behavior. Results suggested that a model of the investor's behavior was gradually formed in the brain of the trustee, and that this model predicted changes in the trustee's behavior. This was accompanied by a temporal shift in the correlation between brain signals in the two players.

Several studies used game-theory paradigms to investigate mentalizing processes and individual differences in these processes. These studies typically employ games that require participants to compete, rather than cooperate, with another player. For example, Hampton, Bossaerts, and O'Doherty (2008) had participants play the "inspection game" (Plate 8, see color plate section), a version of the aforementioned matching pennies game that was used in the monkey study. In this game, one player is an "employee" and the other is the "employer." The employee can either "work" or "shirk," and the employer can either "inspect" or "not inspect." Both players had to make their choices at the same time, and the payoff structure (Plate 8) was such that the players had competing interests. The employee was incentivized not to work if the employer did not inspect, but to work if she did, while the employer was incentivized to inspect when the employee shirked, but not to inspect if he worked. Hampton and colleagues examined several potential models that could explain participants' behavior. A simple strategy would be to choose the action that led to the highest rewards in the past, similar to the model-free reinforcement learning previously described. While this is a decent strategy for many situations, it is not appropriate here, because the opponent could easily take advantage of this strategy, predict the other player's next choice, and act accordingly. Trying to predict the opponent's action based on their prior actions is therefore a better strategy. An even better and more sophisticated strategy, however, is to not only track the opponent's past actions, but also take into account the influence of one's own actions on those of the opponent. Indeed, this model described participants' behavior and neural patterns better than the other two. These model predictions about expected rewards from a particular action were associated with neural activation in value-related areas and, importantly, activity in a brain area linked to social processes, the superior temporal sulcus (STS), signaled updates to the inferred opponent's strategy. Another well-known game, the Beauty Contest, was used by Coricelli and Nagel (2009) to explore individual differences in the degree of mentalizing. In this game, participants in a group choose a number between 0 and 100, and the winner is the person whose number is closest to two-thirds times the average of all chosen numbers in the group. The most naïve player (level 0) will choose a random number, ignoring the effects of other players' choices on the average. A somewhat less naïve player (level 1) will behave as if other players are naïve and choose randomly. Such a player will assume that the average across the group will be 50, and thus will choose the number 33 (2/3*50). A more sophisticated player will suppose that the rest of the players play at level 1, and will therefore choose the number 22 (2/3*33). This iterative process can go on, until it reaches 0. Most people, however, stop the iterative process at some point, and individuals differ in the number of iterations they go through. Coricelli and Nagel divided participants based on their level of sophistication and identified differences in neural activation patterns between the groups within the medial prefrontal cortex, which correlated with a measure of strategic IQ across participants, suggesting an involvement of this brain area in higher reasoning about others.

Finally, in addition to strategic behavior, several studies have directly examined charitable giving and other-regarding preferences. For example, Harbaugh, Mayr, and Burghart (2007) showed that neural responses in the reward-related striatum in response to mandatory donations predicted the amount of voluntary donations. This result is consistent with an account of "pure altruism," suggesting that people are capable of experiencing rewarding sensations in response to the good fortune of others. Other studies have documented the involvement of social neural processes in charitable giving (Hare et al., 2010) and identified neural signals that are consistent with inequality aversion (Tricomi et al., 2010).

21.8 Summary and Future Directions

Neuroeconomics is a vibrant and developing discipline. We have presented a fraction of existing studies, in an attempt to demonstrate the common theoretical and experimental approaches to some of the main research questions in the field. Major achievements include the characterization of the valuation network in the brain, the identification of multiple neural learning mechanisms, and the use of neuroscientific data to help in shaping prominent economic theories. As we have seen, while there is consensus about some of the findings, many others are under debate, and many questions remain open and are the subject of ongoing research. Past and current studies also open new and exciting research directions. One of the most promising of these directions, in our minds, stems from the focus on individual differences in brain and behavior. Neuroeconomic techniques allow researchers to detect and describe changes in valuation and choice processes within and between individuals, and to relate these variations to other participant characteristics. For example, the neuroeconomic approach is increasingly used to study changes in decision-making across the lifespan, particularly in adolescence (Van Duijvenvoorde and Crone, 2013) and aging (Samanez-Larkin and Knutson, 2015). Similarly, neuroeconomics holds promise for psychiatric research (Sharp, Monterosso, and Montague, 2012; Lee, 2013). For example, intertemporal-choice paradigms can be used to study addiction (Monterosso et al., 2007), and game-theoretical paradigms are of use for studying social deficits in conditions such as autism (Yoshida et al., 2010) and borderline personality disorder (King-Casas et al., 2008). The constant improvement in neuroscientific techniques, together with expending the behavioral paradigms toward more ecological designs, is sure to yield new insights into the neural mechanisms in the healthy brain as well as in disease, and may also point to promising avenues for interventions based on these insights.

Acknowledgments

IL was supported by National Institutes of Health (NIH) grants R21MH102634 and R21AG049293.

21.9 References

Aharon I, Etcoff N, Ariely D, Chabris CF, O'Connor E, Breiter HC (2001) Beautiful Faces Have Variable Reward Value: fMRI and Behavioral Evidence. *Neuron* 32:537–551.

Barraclough DJ, Conroy ML, Lee D (2004) Prefrontal Cortex and Decision Making in a Mixed-Strategy Game. *Nat Neurosci* 7:404–410.

Bartra O, McGuire JT, Kable JW (2013) The Valuation System: A Coordinate-Based Meta-analysis of BOLD fMRI Experiments Examining Neural Correlates of Subjective Value. *NeuroImage* 76:412–427.

Behrens TE, Woolrich MW, Walton ME, Rushworth MF (2007) Learning the Value of Information in an Uncertain World. *Nat Neurosci* 10:1214–1221.

Berns GS, Moore SE (2012) A Neural Predictor of Cultural Popularity. *J Consum Psychol* 22:154–160.

Breiter HC, Aharon I, Kahneman D, Dale A, Shizgal P (2001) Functional Imaging of Neural Responses to Expectancy and Experience of Monetary Gains and Losses. *Neuron* 30:619–639.

Bromberg-Martin ES, Matsumoto M, Hikosaka O (2010) Dopamine in Motivational Control: Rewarding, Aversive, and Alerting. *Neuron* 68:815–834.

Camerer C, Weber M (1992) Recent Developments in Modeling Preferences: Uncertainty and Ambiguity. *J Risk Uncertainty* 5:325–370.

Carandini M, Heeger DJ (2012) Normalization as a Canonical Neural Computation. *Nat Rev Neurosci* 13:51–62.

Chib VS, Rangel A, Shimojo S, O'Doherty JP (2009) Evidence for a Common Representation of Decision Values for Dissimilar Goods in Human Ventromedial Prefrontal Cortex. *J Neurosci* 29:12315–12320.

Clithero JA, Rangel A (2014) Informatic Parcellation of the Network Involved in the Computation of Subjective Value. *Soc Cogn Affect Neurosci* 9:1289–1302.

Cohen M, Jaffray JY, Said T (1987) Experimental Comparison of Individual Behavior Under Risk and Under Uncertainty for Gains and for Losses. *Organ Behav Hum Dec* 39:1–22.

Coricelli G, Critchley HD, Joffily M, O'Doherty JP, Sirigu A, Dolan RJ (2005) Regret and Its Avoidance: A Neuroimaging Study of Choice Behavior. *Nat Neurosci* 8:1255–1262.

Coricelli G, Nagel R (2009) Neural Correlates of Depth of Strategic Reasoning in Medial Prefrontal Cortex. *Proc Natl Acad Sci USA* 106:9163–9168.

Daw ND, Gershman SJ, Seymour B, Dayan P, Dolan RJ (2011) Model-Based Influences on Humans' Choices and Striatal Prediction Errors. *Neuron* 69:1204–1215.

Delgado MR, Nystrom LE, Fissell C, Noll DC, Fiez JA (2000) Tracking the Hemodynamic Responses to Reward and Punishment in the Striatum. *J Neurophysiol* 84:3072–3077.

Falk EB, Berkman ET, Whalen D, Lieberman MD (2011) Neural Activity During Health Messaging Predicts Reductions in Smoking Above and Beyond Self-Report. *Health Psychol* 30:177–185.

Figner B, Knoch D, Johnson EJ, et al. (2010) Lateral Prefrontal Cortex and Self-Control in Intertemporal Choice. *Nat Neurosci* 13:538–539.

Fiorillo CD (2013) Two Dimensions of Value: Dopamine Neurons Represent Reward but Not Aversiveness. *Science* 341:546–549.

Gilaie-Dotan S, Tymula A, Cooper N, Kable JW, Glimcher PW, Levy I (2014) Neuroanatomy Predicts Individual Risk Attitudes. *J Neurosci* 34:12394–12401.

Glimcher PW (2003) *Decisions, Uncertainty, and the Brain: The Science of Neuroeconomics*. Cambridge, MA: MIT Press.

Glimcher PW, Fehr E (2014) *Neuroeconomics: Decision Making and the Brain*, Second edition. Amsterdam: Elsevier/Academic Press.

Gross J, Woelbert E, Zimmermann J, Okamoto-Barth S, Riedl A, Goebel R (2014) Value Signals in the Prefrontal Cortex Predict Individual Preferences Across Reward Categories. *J Neurosci* 34:7580–7586.

Hampton AN, Bossaerts P, O'Doherty JP (2008) Neural Correlates of Mentalizing-Related Computations During Strategic Interactions in Humans. *P Natl Acad Sci USA* 105:6741–6746.

Harbaugh WT, Mayr U, Burghart DR (2007) Neural Responses to Taxation and Voluntary Giving Reveal Motives for Charitable Donations. *Science* 316:1622–1625.

Hare TA, Camerer CF, Knoepfle DT, Rangel A (2010) Value Computations in Ventral Medial Prefrontal Cortex During Charitable Decision Making Incorporate Input from Regions Involved in Social Cognition. *J Neurosci* 30:583–590.

Hare TA, Camerer CF, Rangel A (2009) Self-Control in Decision-Making Involves Modulation of the vmPFC Valuation System. *Science* 324:646–648.

Hsu M, Bhatt M, Adolphs R, Tranel D, Camerer CF (2005) Neural Systems Responding to Degrees of Uncertainty in Human Decision-Making. *Science* 310:1680–1683.

Huettel SA, Song AW, McCarthy G (2005) Decisions Under Uncertainty: Probabilistic Context Influences Activation of Prefrontal and Parietal Cortices. *J Neurosci* 25:3304–3311.

Huettel SA, Stowe CJ, Gordon EM, Warner BT, Platt ML (2006) Neural Signatures of Economic Preferences for Risk and Ambiguity. *Neuron* 49:765–775.

Hunt LT, Dolan RJ, Behrens TE (2014) Hierarchical Competitions Subserving Multi-Attribute Choice. *Nat Neurosci* 17:1613–1622.

Hunt LT, Kolling N, Soltani A, Woolrich MW, Rushworth MF, Behrens TE (2012) Mechanisms Underlying Cortical Activity During Value-Guided Choice. *Nat Neurosci* 15:470–476, S471–473.

Izuma K, Saito DN, Sadato N (2008) Processing of Social and Monetary Rewards in the Human Striatum. *Neuron* 58:284–294.

Kable JW (2011) The Cognitive Neuroscience Toolkit for the Neuroeconomist: A Functional Overview. *J Neurosci Psychol Econ* 4:63–84.

Kable JW, Glimcher PW (2007) The Neural Correlates of Subjective Value During Intertemporal Choice. *Nat Neurosci* 10:1625–1633.

Kahneman D, Tversky A (1979) Prospect Theory: Analysis of Decision Under Risk. *Econometrica* 47:263–291.

Kim H, Shimojo S, O'Doherty JP (2011) Overlapping Responses for the Expectation of Juice and Money Rewards in Human Ventromedial Prefrontal Cortex. *Cereb Cortex* 21:769–776.

King-Casas B, Sharp C, Lomax-Bream L, Lohrenz T, Fonagy P, Montague PR (2008) The Rupture and Repair of Cooperation in Borderline Personality Disorder. *Science* 321:806–810.

King-Casas B, Tomlin D, Anen C, Camerer CF, Quartz SR, Montague PR (2005) Getting to Know You: Reputation and Trust in a Two-Person Economic Exchange. *Science* 308:78–83.

Knutson B, Adams CM, Fong GW, Hommer D (2001) Anticipation of Increasing Monetary Reward Selectively Recruits Nucleus Accumbens. *J Neurosci* 21:RC159.

Knutson B, Taylor J, Kaufman M, Peterson R, Glover G (2005) Distributed Neural Representation of Expected Value. *J Neurosci* 25:4806–4812.

Kosfeld M, Heinrichs M, Zak PJ, Fischbacher U, Fehr E (2005) Oxytocin Increases Trust in Humans. *Nature* 435:673–676.

Krajbich I, Armel C, Rangel A (2010) Visual Fixations and the Computation and Comparison of Value in Simple Choice. *Nat Neurosci* 13:1292–1298.

Krajbich I, Rangel A (2011) Multialternative Drift-Diffusion Model Predicts the Relationship Between Visual Fixations and Choice in Value-Based Decisions. *Proc Natl Acad Sci U S A* 108:13852–13857.

Kuhnen CM, Knutson B (2005) The Neural Basis of Financial Risk Taking. *Neuron* 47:763–770.

Lebreton M, Jorge S, Michel V, Thirion B, Pessiglione M (2009) An Automatic Valuation System in the Human Brain: Evidence from Functional Neuroimaging. *Neuron* 64:431–439.

Lee D (2013) Decision Making: From Neuroscience to Psychiatry. *Neuron* 78:233–248.

Lee D, Seo H (2016) Neural Basis of Strategic Decision Making. *Trends Neurosci* 39:40–48.

Levy DJ, Glimcher PW (2011) Comparing Apples and Oranges: Using Reward-Specific and Reward-General Subjective Value Representation in the Brain. *J Neurosci* 31:14693–14707.

Levy DJ, Glimcher PW (2012) The Root of All Value: A Neural Common Currency for Choice. *Curr Opin Neurobiol* 22:1027–1038.

Levy I, Lazzaro SC, Rutledge RB, Glimcher PW (2011) Choice from Non-Choice: Predicting Consumer Preferences from Blood Oxygenation Level-Dependent Signals Obtained During Passive Viewing. *J Neurosci* 31:118–125.

Levy I, Snell J, Nelson AJ, Rustichini A, Glimcher PW (2010) Neural Representation of Subjective Value Under Risk and Ambiguity. *J Neurophysiol* 103: 1036–1047.

Lohrenz T, McCabe K, Camerer CF, Montague PR (2007) Neural Signature of Fictive Learning Signals in a Sequential Investment Task. *Proc Natl Acad Sci U S A* 104:9493–9498.

Louie K, Glimcher PW (2010) Separating Value from Choice: Delay Discounting Activity in the Lateral Intraparietal Area. *J Neurosci* 30:5498–5507.

Louie K, Grattan LE, Glimcher PW (2011) Reward Value-Based Gain Control: Divisive Normalization in Parietal Cortex. *J Neurosci* 31:10627–10639.

Louie K, Khaw MW, Glimcher PW (2013) Normalization Is a General Neural Mechanism for Context-Dependent Decision Making. *Proc Natl Acad Sci U S A* 110:6139–6144.

McCabe K, Houser D, Ryan L, Smith V, Trouard T (2001) A Functional Imaging Study of Cooperation in Two-Person Reciprocal Exchange. *Proc Natl Acad Sci U S A* 98:11832–11835.

McClure SM, Berns GS, Montague PR (2003) Temporal Prediction Errors in a Passive Learning Task Activate Human Striatum. *Neuron* 38:339–346.

McClure SM, Laibson DI, Loewenstein G, Cohen JD (2004) Separate Neural Systems Value Immediate and Delayed Monetary Rewards. *Science* 306:503–507.

McNamee D, Rangel A, O'Doherty JP (2013) Category-Dependent and Category-Independent Goal-Value Codes in Human Ventromedial Prefrontal Cortex. *Nat Neurosci* 16:479–485.

Monterosso JR, Ainslie G, Xu JS, Cordova X, Domier CP, London ED (2007) Frontoparietal Cortical Activity of Methamphetamine-Dependent and Comparison Subjects Performing a Delay Discounting Task. *Human Brain Mapping* 28:383–393.

Mora F, Myers RD (1977) Brain Self-Stimulation: Direct Evidence for the Involvement of Dopamine in the Prefrontal Cortex. *Science* 197:1387–1389.

Neylan TC (1999) Frontal Lobe Function: Mr. Phineas Gage's Famous Injury. *Journal of Neuropsychiatry and Clinical Neurosciences* 11:280–281.

Niv Y, Schoenbaum G (2008) Dialogues on Prediction Errors. *Trends Cogn Sci* 12:265–272.

Niv Y, Daniel R, Geana A, etc. (2015) Reinforcement Learning in Multidimensional Environments Relies on Attention Mechanisms. *J Neurosci* 35:8145–8157.

Nowak MA, Page KM, Sigmund K (2000) Fairness Versus Reason in the Ultimatum Game. *Science* 289:1773–1775.

O'Doherty J, Dayan P, Schultz J, Deichmann R, Friston K, Dolan RJ (2004) Dissociable Roles of Ventral and Dorsal Striatum in Instrumental Conditioning. *Science* 304:452–454.

O'Doherty J, Kringelbach ML, Rolls ET, Hornak J, Andrews C (2001) Abstract Reward and Punishment Representations in the Human Orbitofrontal Cortex. *Nat Neurosci* 4:95–102.

O'Doherty JP (2004) Reward Representations and Reward-related Learning in the Human Brain: Insights from Neuroimaging. *Curr Opin Neurobiol* 14:769–776.

O'Doherty JP, Dayan P, Friston K, Critchley H, Dolan RJ (2003) Temporal Difference Models and Reward-Related Learning in the Human Brain. *Neuron* 38:329–337.

O'Doherty JP, Deichmann R, Critchley HD, Dolan RJ (2002) Neural Responses During Anticipation of a Primary Taste Reward. *Neuron* 33:815–826.

Payzan-LeNestour E, Dunne S, Bossaerts P, O'Doherty JP (2013) The Neural Representation of Unexpected Uncertainty During Value-Based Decision Making. *Neuron* 79:191–201.

Pillutla MM, Murnighan JK (1996) Unfairness, Anger, and Spite: Emotional Rejections of Ultimatum Offers. *Organ Behav Hum Dec* 68:208–224.

Plassmann H, O'Doherty J, Rangel A (2007) Orbitofrontal Cortex Encodes Willingness to Pay in Everyday Economic Transactions. *J Neurosci* 27:9984–9988.

Platt ML, Glimcher PW (1999) Neural Correlates of Decision Variables in Parietal Cortex. *Nature* 400:233–238.

Preuschoff K, Bossaerts P, Quartz SR (2006) Neural Differentiation of Expected Reward and Risk in Human Subcortical Structures. *Neuron* 51:381–390.

Ratcliff R, McKoon G (2008) The Diffusion Decision Model: Theory and Data for Two-Choice Decision Tasks. *Neural Comput* 20:873–922.

Roitman JD, Shadlen MN (2002) Response of Neurons in the Lateral Intraparietal Area During a Combined Visual Discrimination Reaction Time Task. *J Neurosci* 22:9475–9489.

Rutledge RB, Dean M, Caplin A, Glimcher PW (2010) Testing the Reward Prediction Error Hypothesis with an Axiomatic Model. *J Neurosci* 30:13525–13536.

Samanez-Larkin GR, Knutson B (2015) Decision Making in the Ageing Brain: Changes in Affective and Motivational Circuits. *Nat Rev Neurosci* 16:278–289.

Samuelson PA (1948) Consumption Theory in Terms of Revealed Preference. *Economica-New Series* 15:243–253.

Sanfey AG, Rilling JK, Aronson JA, Nystrom LE, Cohen JD (2003) The Neural Basis of Economic Decision-Making in the Ultimatum Game. *Science* 300:1755–1758.

Schultz W, Dayan P, Montague PR (1997) A Neural Substrate of Prediction and Reward. *Science* 275:1593–1599.

Sharp C, Monterosso J, Montague PR (2012) Neuroeconomics: A Bridge for Translational Research. *Biol Psychiatry* 72:87–92.

Shizgal P, Conover K (1996) On the Neural Computation of Utility. *Curr Dir Psychol Sci* 5:37–43.

Small DM, Jones-Gotman M, Dagher A (2003) Feeding-Induced Dopamine Release in Dorsal Striatum Correlates with Meal Pleasantness Ratings in Healthy Human Volunteers. *NeuroImage* 19:1709–1715.

Smith PL, Ratcliff R (2004) Psychology and Neurobiology of Simple Decisions. *Trends Neurosci* 27:161–168.

Strait CE, Blanchard TC, Hayden BY (2014) Reward Value Comparison via Mutual Inhibition in Ventromedial Prefrontal Cortex. *Neuron* 82:1357–1366.

Sugrue LP, Corrado GS, Newsome WT (2004) Matching Behavior and the Representation of Value in the Parietal Cortex. *Science* 304:1782–1787.

Sutton RS, Barto AG (1998) *Reinforcement Learning: An Introduction.* Cambridge, MA: MIT Press.

Thaler RH (1988) Anomalies: the Ultimatum Game. *J Econ Perspect* 2:195–206.

Tobler PN, O'Doherty JP, Dolan RJ, Schultz W (2007) Reward Value Coding Distinct from Risk Attitude-Related Uncertainty Coding in Human Reward Systems. *J Neurophysiol* 97:1621–1632.

Tom SM, Fox CR, Trepel C, Poldrack RA (2007) The Neural Basis of Loss Aversion in Decision-Making Under Risk. *Science* 315:515–518.

Tricomi E, Rangel A, Camerer CF, O'Doherty JP (2010) Neural Evidence for Inequality-Averse Social Preferences. *Nature* 463:1089–1091.

Tusche A, Bode S, Haynes JD (2010) Neural Responses to Unattended Products Predict Later Consumer Choices. *J Neurosci* 30:8024–8031.

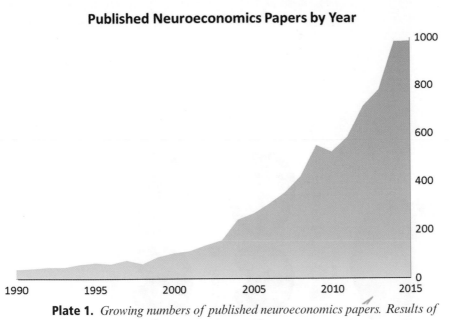

Published Neuroeconomics Papers by Year

Plate 1. *Growing numbers of published neuroeconomics papers. Results of Pubmed search for "decision making" AND "brain."*

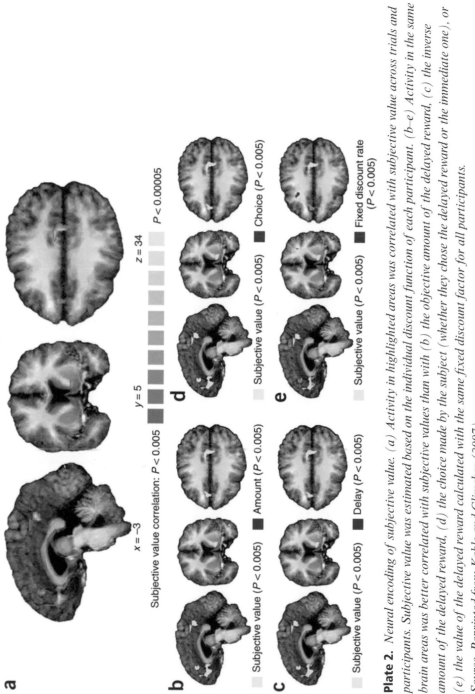

Plate 2. *Neural encoding of subjective value. (a) Activity in highlighted areas was correlated with subjective value across trials and participants. Subjective value was estimated based on the individual discount function of each participant. (b–e) Activity in the same brain areas was better correlated with subjective values than with (b) the objective amount of the delayed reward, (c) the inverse amount of the delayed reward, (d) the choice made by the subject (whether they chose the delayed reward or the immediate one), or (e) the value of the delayed reward calculated with the same fixed discount factor for all participants. Source. Reprinted from Kable and Glimcher (2007).*

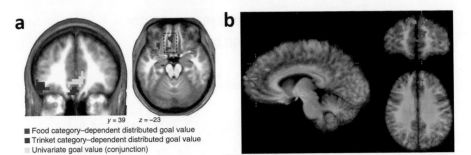

y = 39   z = −23

■ Food category–dependent distributed goal value
■ Trinket category–dependent distributed goal value
▫ Univariate goal value (conjunction)

Plate 3. *Category-general and category-specific value signals in the vmPFC. (a) Value signals specific to snack food items (blue) and consumer goods ("trinkets", red) coexist with category-general value signals (yellow). Adapted from McNamee et al. (2013). (b) Category-general signals for snack foods and pleasant activities. Adapted from Gross et al. (2014).*

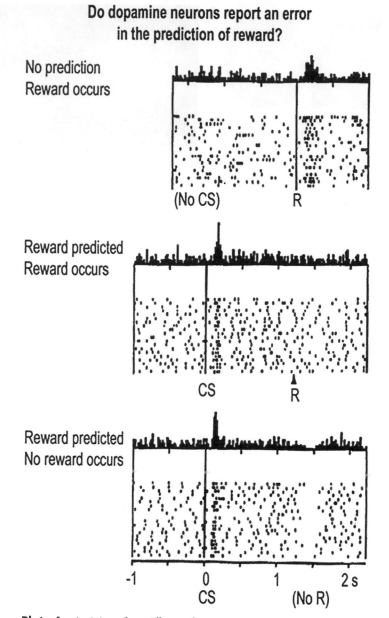

Do dopamine neurons report an error in the prediction of reward?

No prediction
Reward occurs

(No CS) R

Reward predicted
Reward occurs

CS R

Reward predicted
No reward occurs

-1   0   1   2 s
CS   (No R)

Plate 4. *Activity of a midbrain dopamine neuron. Each dot indicates firing by the neuron, and each row depicts the timeline of a single trial. Top: increased firing rate in response to unexpected rewards (R). Middle: after the monkey learned to predict the occurrence of reward based on a conditioned stimulus (CS), the dopamine response shifts to the CS. Bottom: when a predicted reward is not obtained (no R), the firing rate of dopamine neurons is reduced to below baseline levels. This pattern of activation is consistent with encoding a prediction error – the difference between the predicted and obtained rewards.*
Source. Reprinted from Schultz et al. (1997).

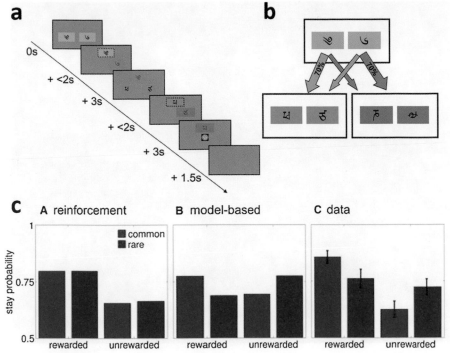

Plate 5. *Experimental paradigm for studying model-free and model-based reinforcement learning. (a) Timeline of events in trial. A first-stage choice between two options (green boxes) leads to a second-stage choice (here, between two pink options), which is reinforced with money. (b) State transition structure. Each first-stage choice is predominantly associated with one or the other of the second-stage states, and leads there 70 percent of the time. (c) Model-free learning (left) predicts that a first-stage choice resulting in reward is more likely to be repeated on the subsequent trial, regardless of whether that reward occurred after a common or rare transition. Model-based prospective evaluation (middle) instead predicts that a rare transition should affect the value of the other first-stage option, leading to a predicted interaction between the factors of reward and transition probability. Actual stay proportions, averaged across subjects (right), display hallmarks of both strategies. Error bars: 1 SEM. Source. Adapted from Daw et al. (2011).*

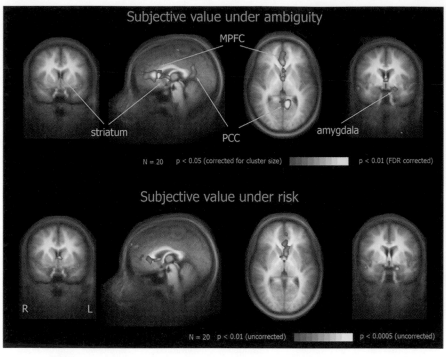

Plate 6. *Subjective values of risky (top) and ambiguous (bottom) options are encoded in the value areas of the brain.*
Source. Reprinted from Levy et al. (2010).

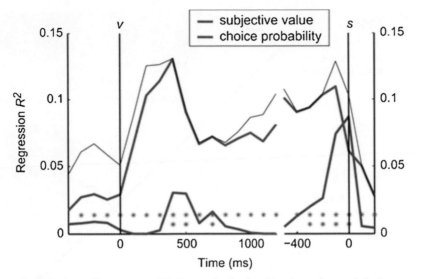

Plate 7. *Neural activity in PPC encodes both subjective value and choice. The graph denotes the contribution of subjective value (blue) and choice probability (red) to the firing rate of the neurons at different time points during the trial. While activity represents subjective value at the beginning of the trial (v), choice is also encoded before the monkey makes his choice(s). Source. Adapted from Louie and Glimcher (2010).*

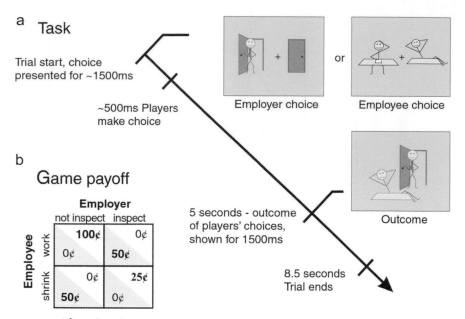

a Task

Trial start, choice
presented for ~1500ms

~500ms Players
make choice

Employer choice   Employee choice

b

Game payoff

5 seconds - outcome
of players' choices,
shown for 1500ms

Outcome

	Employer	
	not inspect	inspect
Employee — work	100¢ / 0¢	0¢ / 50¢
Employee — shrink	0¢ / 50¢	25¢ / 0¢

8.5 seconds
Trial ends

Plate 8. *The inspection game used to probe strategic decision making.*
(a) Two interacting players are each individually given two action choices at
the beginning of each trial. After both players make their choices, the chosen
actions of both players are shown to each player. (b) Payoff matrix used in
Hampton et al. (2008).
Source. Adapted from Hampton et al. (2008).

Tymula A, Rosenberg Belmaker LA, Ruderman L, Glimcher PW, Levy I (2013) Like Cognitive Function, Decision Making Across the Life Span Shows Profound Age-Related Changes. *Proc Natl Acad Sci U S A* 110:17143–17148.

Van Duijvenvoorde ACK, Crone EA (2013) The Teenage Brain: A Neuroeconomic Approach to Adolescent Decision Making. *Curr Dir Psychol Sci* 22:108–113.

Von Neumann J, Morgenstern O (1944) *Theory of Games and Economic Behavior*. Princeton, NJ: Princeton University Press.

Yoshida W, Dziobek I, Kliemann D, Heekeren HR, Friston KJ, Dolan RJ (2010) Cooperation and Heterogeneity of the Autistic Mind. *Journal of Neuroscience* 30:8815–8818.

22 The Importance of Evolutionary Psychology for the Understanding of Economic Behavior

Detlef Fetchenhauer and Anne-Sophie Lang

22.1 What Is Evolutionary Psychology?

For many decades, economists have complained that psychology might offer well-grounded and substantial criticism of economic models of human behavior but lacks any integrative, basic framework that could serve as an alternative to the classical microeconomic theory of human behavior (Brocas and Carrillo, 2003; Levitt and List, 2008). Evolutionary psychology offers such an alternative. In this chapter, we want to first outline the basic premises of evolutionary psychology and its relation to microeconomics. Then, we will discuss how several research areas of economic psychology might be informed by reflecting the many ways in which humans' present behavior is influenced by their evolutionary past.

22.1.1 Evolutionary Psychology in a Nutshell

Evolutionary psychology can be regarded as the systematic attempt to apply Darwin's (1859) theory of natural selection and his theory of sexual selection to the understanding of human cognition, motivation, and behavior (Tooby, Cosmides, and Barkow, 1995).

Darwin's first theory – the theory of natural selection – is founded on three basic observations: (1) organisms of a certain species are not identical but differ from each other (e.g., some antelopes run faster than others); (2) these differences are at least partly heritable (e.g., fast-running antelopes tend to have offspring that also run quickly); and (3) within a given species, only a part of all offspring survive into adulthood and thus have a chance to propagate their genes into future generations.

If the chance of survival is at least partly due to the heritable differences of organisms within a given species, some attributes will be naturally selected (e.g., Bergstrom and Dugatkin, 2012). For example, if fast-running antelopes are better able to evade predators (e.g., lions), they have a higher chance of survival and thus also have a higher chance to sire offspring that will also run quickly. Thus, over the course of evolution, antelopes will run faster and faster (as will lions, who will be under a very similar selection pressure).

There are two distinct ways in which such natural selection can occur: either selection changes the quantitative distribution of already existing traits (e.g., the length of giraffes' necks) or selection is related to genetic mutations (that are maladaptive most of the time but sometimes do increase the fitness of a given organism).

Darwin's theory of natural selection is almost unanimously accepted among biologists. Still, until approximately thirty years ago, it has rarely been applied to human behavior. Since then, the field of evolutionary psychology has been thriving and has now become part of mainstream psychology (Buss, 2015). Its central assumption is that both the human body and the human psyche are adaptations of our evolutionary past. Thus, the way we look (e.g., males being taller and more muscular than females), as well as the way we think, feel, and behave, is shaped not only by our current environment but also by the challenges of survival and reproduction that *Homo sapiens* has faced since its evolution approximately two hundred thousand years ago (McDermott, Fowler, and Smirnov, 2008).

This implies that our bodies as well as our minds are not adapted to our modern twenty-first-century environment, with its long-distance flights, large metropolitan areas with millions of inhabitants and email, Twitter, and Facebook that allow us to communicate twenty-four/seven all around the world with people who we might have never seen before (Cziko, 2000). Instead, humans are adapted to the so-called environment of evolutionary adaptedness (EEA) (Bowlby, 1969) in which our ancestors had to survive as hunters and gatherers for millions of years until the first human settlements appeared approximately ten thousand years ago. Thus, our bodies and minds are adapted to living in small-scale societies that competed with each other for scarce resources (e.g., water and food).

Based on the differences between our modern environments and the EEA, some behaviors of modern humans are maladaptive (i.e., they negatively affect one's health and longevity). One important example is the way we eat. In industrialized countries, the majority of adults are overweight (i.e., have a body mass index between 25 and 30), and a large part of the population is obese (i.e., they have a body mass index of 30 or greater). For example, in the United States, approximately 70 percent of all citizens are overweight, and almost 40 percent of the adult population are obese (Centers for Disease Control and Prevention, 2016). Most weight problems are related to a diet that contains too much sugar and too much fat. To understand this maladaptive eating pattern, one must consider that in the EEA, *Homo sapiens* often lived under adverse conditions with scarce resources. In this environment, it was very adaptive to have a strong preference for food that contained as many calories as possible (Cziko, 2000).

Another example of the way our ancient past shapes our modern preferences can be found in the fact that body length is robustly related to professional success. Tall persons are preferred as managers (Judge and Cable, 2004) as well as political leaders (Murray and Schmitz, 2011; Stulp et al., 2013). In the EEA, this made sense, as body strength was important in the competition for social status. Although in today's industrialized countries, managers in large companies or politicians rarely engage in fistfights about the distribution of scarce resources, they are still more often promoted or elected when they are tall rather than small. Analogously, females prefer tall men as mating partners (Stulp, Buunk, and Pollet, 2013).

An important distinction must be made between proximate and ultimate explanations of a given adaptation (Scott-Phillips, Dickins, and West, 2011). For example, men are known to prefer young women as sexual partners (Cziko, 2000, ch. 8). On a proximate level, this occurs because younger women are perceived as more sexually attractive or more beautiful compared to older women. On an ultimate level, such preferences are adaptive, as the likelihood of a woman getting pregnant when having sex is negatively correlated to her age.

Furthermore, it is important to note that evolutionary psychology sharply distinguishes between an explanatory and a normative level of analysis. To describe a certain behavior (e.g., sexual aggression, egoism, or xenophobia) as "natural" neither implies any ethical evaluation nor legitimates such behavior. (See David Hume, 1739, on the distinction between "is" and "ought".)

Another criticism is related to the suspicion that evolutionary psychologists mainly reanalyze data that are already well known and then interpret these facts retrospectively from an evolutionary perspective (i.e., they are telling "just-so stories") (Gould, 1997). By and large, this criticism is not justified. There are two main tasks for any good theory: to explain data already known and to predict data that are not yet known. In recent years, many studies have been published that have used evolutionary psychology to propose novel and creative new ideas and to experimentally test these hypotheses without knowing the results in advance. In the remainder of this chapter, we will cite some of these studies.

22.1.2 Relation of Evolutionary Psychology to Economics

There are several key differences but also several important similarities between an economic and an evolutionary perspective on the human mind and behavior. We will discuss the similarities first.

Both disciplines emphasize that humans must use their limited means in an adaptive manner to create the greatest possible gains (i.e., "there's no such thing as a free lunch"; Friedman, 1975). Although evolutionary psychologists might be skeptical about the rationality assumption of *Homo economicus* (see the following section), they follow economics in the assumption that humans will not act erratically. Rather, they assume that much of human behavior is motivated by the desire to maximize certain outcomes, taking current constraints into account.

Related to this assumption, competition is vital to both economics and evolutionary psychology: humans compete with each other for scarce resources. For example, evolutionary psychologists often describe human mating as being embedded in complex mating markets in which males and females prefer certain attributes in their potential mating partners and are more able to demand such attributes the more they exhibit the attributes that are preferred by their potential partners (Geary, 2010).

Another similarity between both disciplines relates to the fact that they both aim to explain complexity on a macro level by analyzing it as the result of strategic choices by single individuals. Darwin (1859) explained the existence of thousands and thousands of different species that are well adapted to their local habitats not by the design of an all-knowing creator but by evolution through natural selection. This thought highly resembles Adam Smith's idea that a system of complex and well-functioning economic transactions should not be engineered by any central authority but by the "invisible hand" of free markets (Smith, 1776). Darwin does not cite *The Wealth of Nations*, but in his famous book *On the Origin of Species*, one finds this telling passage: "Though nature grants long periods of time for the work of natural selection, she does not grant an indefinite period; for as all organic beings are striving to seize on each place in the economy of nature, if any one species does not become modified and improved in a corresponding degree with its competitors it will be exterminated" (Darwin, 1859, p. 102).

Another similarity of both disciplines lies in the way they approach the issue of human altruism (Simon, 1992). Both are highly skeptical as to whether something like true altruism exists at all because voluntarily giving up one's own resources for others should decrease one's own level of resources, which would be a negative outcome that organisms should try to prevent (more on that later in this chapter).

However, there are also many differences between evolutionary psychology and economics.

Although some biologists have used economic game theory to understand the strategic behaviors of nonhuman animals (e.g., choosing strategies of predating or intrasexual competition) (Cockburn, 1991; Cowden, 2012), economists themselves are nearly exclusively concerned with *human* behavior. In contrast, evolutionary psychology argues that there is no basic difference between humans and other species, as organisms of all species must solve the same problems (e.g., survival and reproduction). Consequently, on a general level, the behavior of nonhuman animals should follow the same logic as that of humans (Daly and Wilson, 1999).

Another difference relates to the concept of preferences. The economic theory of choice is mostly silent about the content of human desires (for an exception, see Becker, 1976). The only assumption is that preferences are stable over time and that humans try to maximize their expected utility (i.e., the realization of their preferences) when choosing between different alternatives. From an evolutionary perspective, elements of utility functions are not arbitrary, but they serve the function to maximize a person's inclusive fitness (i.e., the number and reproductive success of their great-grandchildren). Thus, all human behavior can be regarded as survival effort, mating effort, or parenting effort. However, as already mentioned, humans are not adapted to their current environments. Therefore, some human behavior appears highly maladaptive (e.g., Cziko, 2000). For example, males (and to a lesser degree, females) spend many hours watching pornography on the Internet, as the graphic representation of female nudity is sufficient to trigger specific sexual reactions in a male's body (Struthers, 2009). To be aroused by an actual naked woman is highly functional, but to be aroused by pictures or videos of a naked woman is not.

Perhaps of most importance from an evolutionary perspective, the idea of a *Homo economicus* being able to process an unlimited amount of information in an infinitesimally small amount of time seems highly unjustified and obscure. The human mind is not a "supercomputer"; it is a biologically evolved organ. As such, it is impressively complex, but it is far from perfect. The cognitive abilities of humans – like those of all other species – have evolved throughout the course of natural selection. The human mind is not a general problem-solving machine, but it consists of a number of highly specific cognitive modules that are very efficient in solving the exact kinds of problems to which they are attached. Thus, the human mind can be regarded as an "adaptive toolbox" (Gigerenzer and Selten, 2001) or a "Swiss Army knife" (Cosmides and Tooby, 1994).

One consequence of this cognitive architecture is the usage of "simple and fast heuristics" (i.e., rules of thumb that need only limited informative input and lead to good decisions most of the time) (Gigerenzer and Todd, 1999; Tversky and Kahneman, 1974). From this perspective, evolutionary psychologists tend to regard many cognitive biases not as anomalies to theories of rational choice but as functional adaptations. For example, status quo bias, loss aversion, or the law of diminishing returns can all be regarded as adaptations to an environment with scarce resources in which it was more important not to lose one's current amount of resources than it was to maximize one's expected outcome (Rubin and Capra, 2012).

22.2 Applications of Evolutionary Psychology

In the remainder of this chapter, we will discuss how evolutionary psychology might broaden our perspective and help to elucidate topics that have been investigated in economic psychology.

22.2.1 Self-Control

The problem of self-control has been of interest for both economists and psychologists for a long time. (See, for example, Ainslie, 1992, 2001; Herrnstein,

1997; Loewenstein, 1996; Logue, 1995; Mischel, 2015; Sutter, 2014); see also the chapter by Read, McDonald, and He in the current volume.)

Self-control problems arise when an organism must choose one of (at least) two alternatives that have the following structure: in the short run, alternative A leads to more positive outcomes than alternative B, but in the long run, the outcomes of alternative B are more positive than the outcomes of alternative A. Everyday knowledge and countless empirical studies demonstrate that in such situations, humans (and nonhuman animals) often fail to maximize their long-term payoff (e.g., Mischel, Ebbesen, and Raskoff Zeiss, 1972; Sutter, Oberauer, and Yilmaz, 2015). People eat too much, they smoke, they drink too much coffee or alcohol, they do not exercise, they miss medical checkups, they do not prepare enough for important exams, they have credit card debt but still buy new things, they fail to use birth control and protect themselves from unwanted pregnancies or sexually transmitted diseases, they postpone writing chapters for handbooks although the deadline is coming closer (or might even have passed), they do not save enough for their retirement … Indeed, this list could go on interminably.

What is one to make of this? Economists sometimes try to work their way around these phenomena, for example by defining addictions as "rational" (Becker, Grossman, and Murphy, 1991, 1994; Becker and Murphy, 1988), but very often both economists and psychologists tend to take a rather normative perspective: not being able to solve one's self-control problems is regarded as deficient and revealing a lack of will power. In a famous long-term study, Mischel and colleagues showed that small children who are able to resist eating a marshmallow that is offered to them and can wait for a second marshmallow for fifteen minutes are more successful in many later stages of their lives (in primary school, high school, college, their jobs, and even their marriages) (Mischel, Shoda, and Rodriguez, 1989). Similarly, criminal behavior is often seen as revealing an offender's lack of self-control in that it leads to small immediate gratification and severe long-term losses (e.g., criminal penalties and prison sentences) (Gottfredson and Hirschi, 1990).

Evolutionary psychologists would not deny all these facts, but they would interpret them from a different angle that might be helpful for future work in economic psychology.

Evolutionary psychology would not consider self-control as the context-free ability of an organism (be it human or nonhuman) to maximize long-term payoffs by being able to forego short-term gratification. Instead, from an evolutionary perspective, self-controlled behavior in different domains would be regarded as a highly context-specific solution to specific challenges related to maximizing one's chance of survival and ultimately one's reproductive success (Logue, 1995). From such a perspective, it would be expected that self-control differs significantly between different life domains and that it is the weakest in those areas in which our modern environments pose challenges to our well-being that have been absent in the EEA. We would argue that this reasoning can be applied to many areas in which we observe self-control problems (e.g., eating too much or any type of addiction).

Thus, it would be surprising if organisms of a given species were to engage in self-harming behavior over an extended period of time if there was sufficient selection pressure on the behavior in question. Indeed, in many areas, we observe all kinds of behaviors that serve an organism's long-term interests although they come with massive short-term costs. Each pregnancy serves the interest of propagating a mother's genes into future generations – a large pay-off indeed. However, in the short run it demands massive physical investments during a nine-month pregnancy, when having to breastfeed a small baby, having to take care of a toddler, and all the way up to paying college fees for one's child (Cziko, 2000; Geary, 2015). Babies have a long-term investment in learning how to stand, walk, and run, but before they are able to profit from these abilities, they fall down again and again. Many nonhuman animals change their habitat from season to season (e.g., they spend the summer in Sweden and the winter in northern Africa). In doing so, they follow an optimal time pattern (e.g., in autumn, they do not stay too long in Europe because of a self-control problem of postponing their flight). Another astonishing example of solving an objective self-control problem is the European eel, which begins its life cycle in the Sargasso Sea (south of Mexico) and is driven to Europe by the Gulf Stream. After having lived in European fresh water for about ten years, it swims all the way back to Mexico to have sex once – and then it dies (Van Ginneken and Maes, 2005).

Thus, self-control problems in humans and nonhumans are observed mainly under circumstances in which new environments create new challenges. Over the course of evolution, such challenges are no longer experienced, as the mind adapts to these challenges by making organisms want what is good for them in the long run (Logue, 1995).

22.2.2 Altruism

For many fields of economic psychology, it is important to know whether human behavior is ultimately selfish or whether it is at least partly governed by altruistic motives. This concern is important for the understanding of tax behavior, donations, cooperation in organizations, and many other areas. Neoclassical economics is very clear on this issue: ultimately, all human behavior is governed by egoistic motives; true altruism does not exist ("scratch an altruist and see a hypocrite bleed"; Ghiselin, 1974, p. 247). Interestingly, a very similar position is taken by evolutionary biology (e.g., Huxley, 1888). If altruistic behavior is defined as voluntarily giving up one's own resources for the sake of increasing the resources of another person without the expectation of any reward for such a behavior in the future, it should not have evolved in humans or in any other species, as those organisms lacking the trait should end up holding more resources than altruists. Consequently, selection pressure will make altruism disappear very quickly (Bergstrom and Dugatkin, 2012; Boehm, 2012; Darwin, 1859, ch. 6; Hamilton, 1996; Pievani, 2011).

Although this may be true on an abstract level, it must be noted that humans are an ultrasocial species and that throughout the course of evolution, individual humans could only be successful if they were able to get along with others. Through the course of evolution, humans developed the ability to empathize with others (e.g., Bowles and Gintis, 2003, 2011). Ultimately, they developed a "theory of mind" (Baron-Cohen, 1999; Leslie, 1987; Premack and Woodruff, 1978), which (a) refers to the insight that other humans perceive their social and physical environment from their own subjective point of view and (b) that this perspective might be different from one's own perspective. This ability does not necessarily lead to altruistic behavior, but it might be used to manipulate others (sometimes referred to as "Machiavellian intelligence") (e.g., Byrne and Whiten, 1988; Cachel, 2006). However, the social mind of *Homo sapiens* and the growing complexity of its social environments enabled human societies to define and enforce moral rules by punishing those who were not willing to follow such norms (e.g., Fehr and Fischbacher, 2003; Sober and Wilson, 1998). Given this complexity, the self-centered *Homo economicus* does not seem like a smart maximizer of his personal utility but rather like a person suffering from Asperger's syndrome.

However, given the evolutionary roots of altruism, it is clear that humans do not reason like moral philosophers. They do not have stable, context-free social preferences, and their reasoning does not follow the mathematical logic of utilitarianism. Instead, human altruism is highly dependent on the situational cues by which it is triggered and by the degree to which a person feels sympathy for a victim. Thus, humans tend to donate more money if they are shown pictures of individual victims instead of merely statistical information – the so-called identifiable victim effect (Jenni and Loewenstein, 1997; Kogut and Ritov, 2005; Schelling, 1968; Small and Loewenstein, 2003), and they donate more money when being shown pictures of small children than when being shown pictures of young men. Humans are more interested in the preservation of animal species that are cute (e.g., baby seals) than those that are "ugly" (e.g., vultures) (Small, 2011; Watt, 2015; for a general review on determinants of donating behavior, see Bekkers and Wiepking, 2011).

As altruism has evolved as a motivational basis for the functioning of small bands and tribes, humans distinguish between members of their "in-group" and members of "out-groups," a phenomenon that has also been described as "parochial altruism" (Bernhard, Fischbacher, and Fehr, 2006). In many languages and cultures, members of other tribes and ethnicities are not even considered to be "human" (Lévi-Strauss, 1952).

Sometimes, economists argue that seemingly altruistic behavior (e.g., donating money to victims of a natural catastrophe) leads to the feeling of a "warm glow" that functions as a reward (Andreoni, 1989). However, from an evolutionary perspective, this argument can only be a proximate explanation of altruistic behavior. The ultimate question would be why people get a warm feeling from helping others if this results in giving up one's own resources.

Any ultimate explanation of human altruism does have to explain why such behavior increases one's inclusive fitness. An important approach in this regard is the theory of kin altruism by William Hamilton (1964). He argues that humans might help their own genes to propagate if they are genetically related to the recipients of their own helpful behavior. To help others is reasonable if the following equation holds:

$$b*r > c$$

where b stands for "benefit for the recipient," r refers to the degree of genetic relatedness between both persons (ranging from 0 for unrelated individuals to 0.5 for parents and their children or for siblings), and c indicates the costs for the helper. This theory is an elegant explanation for helpful behavior among kin, but it has difficulties in explaining altruism between humans who are not genetically related to each other. Still, there is much empirical evidence for this theory, even in today's postfamilial societies. Furthermore, this theory can convincingly explain why Modigliani's (1966) life cycle hypothesis of saving is so often falsified (Banks, Blundell, and Tanner, 1998; Bernheim, Skinner, and Weinberg, 2001). Humans do care about their children and grandchildren even after their own death, which makes sense from the perspective of inclusive fitness.

There are several attempts to explain human altruism between nonrelatives: (1) the theory of reciprocal altruism, which states that altruistic behavior is rational if I can expect the recipient of my help to later help me in return; (2) theories of indirect reciprocity (i.e., others are helped to the degree that they are known to have been helpful to others in the past); or (3) the concept of "altruistic punishment" (i.e., humans are willing to punish others who do not follow the social norms of a given community; De Quervain et al., 2004; Fehr and Gächter, 2002). The famous "ultimatum game" (Güth, Schmittberger, and Schwarze, 1982) is one example of humans' willingness to punish others who do not follow the rules. In this regard, it is important to note that humans have evolved specific cognitive modules to detect cheating by others and that they have a good memory for it (Cosmides, Barrett, and Tooby, 2010; Cosmides and Tooby, 1992; Van Lier, Revlin, and De Neys, 2013).

One weakness of all these theories is that they can hardly explain why at least some humans tend to act altruistically even when nobody is watching (i.e., under conditions of total anonymity) and when there is no "shadow of the future" (i.e., in one-shot interactions).

An important theory to explain such seemingly irrational behavior (e.g., sharing money with another person in an anonymous one-shot dictator game) is the commitment model by the economist Robert H. Frank (1988). He notes that unlike in game-theoretical experiments, humans often choose their interaction partners and that these choices will be based on the assumed trustworthiness of another person (e.g., starting to work at a certain company and believing that one will actually be promoted after a year). Frank argues that true altruism (e.g., being fair even when given the golden opportunity to cheat in an anonymous dictator game) can evolve if others are intuitively able to identify such altruists and prefer them as interaction partners. Indeed, it has been shown that humans are able to predict stimulus-persons' behavior in dictator games after having watched twenty-second mute videos of them (Fetchenhauer, Groothuis, and Pradel, 2010).

Frank's model is able to explain (a) why there is more altruism than would be assumed by both standard biological theory and mainstream economics, (b) why there is interindividual variation in altruism (as the success of altruists versus egoists is frequency dependent), (c) why people are so preoccupied with establishing a reputation as a nice person, (d) why gossip is so important to humans (as gossip provides information about others' trustworthiness), and (e) why humans have developed a "theory of mind" and the ability to empathize with others (i.e., why people are good at predicting other people's behavior).

However, human altruism is always fragile and can easily be overridden by our selfish desires. As Blaise Pascal (1669/1910) said approximately 350 years ago, "man is neither angel nor brute" (p. 122).

22.2.3 Gender

Economics is suspiciously silent about issues of gender. Microeconomic theories traditionally try to model human behavior on a rather abstract and general level and thus try to avoid offering different predictions for males and females. When gender differences are investigated, they are seen in gender-specific constraints rather than gender-specific cognitions, emotions, or preferences (e.g., Gary Becker's (1981) highly influential economic theory of the family).

However, in the economic realm, we observe a number of differences between males and females that might better be explained by taking an evolutionary perspective. For evolutionary psychology, gender differences are to be understood as the consequence of gender-specific reproductive strategies that males and females use to maximize their inclusive fitness (Buss, 1989). Males – if they are lucky – can sire a child within a single sexual act and rightfully hope that their female partner will take care of all further investments. These investments include nine months of pregnancy and years of breastfeeding (under natural conditions, children are usually weaned when they are about four years old). These variations in investments lead to a very different market structure for males and females. While females can choose between a substantial number of willing candidates, males are in fierce competition to get access to young and fertile females (Geary, 2010; Trivers, 1972). Although the average number of children is identical for males and females (as each child has exactly one father and one mother), one consequence of this gender-specific "market structure" is that the variation in reproductive success is much larger for males than it is for females ("some guys have all the luck"). Indeed, genetic studies show that humanity has twice as many female ancestors as male ancestors (Baumeister, 2010; Wilder, Mobasher, and Hammer, 2004).

As a consequence, males have evolved to be more risk-seeking, ambitious, competitive, assertive, and aggressive than females (McDermott, Fowler, and Smirnov, 2008), while females have evolved to be more prudent, empathic, caring, and nurturing than males (Campbell, 2002; MacDonald, 1995). Cross-cultural studies largely confirm the universality of these differences, although they are sometimes moderated by culture (e.g., Costa, Terracciano, and McCrae, 2001; Del Giudice, 2009; Feingold, 1994).

Another consequence of gender-specific reproductive strategies lies in the fact that for many traits, variation among males is larger than among females (e.g., general intelligence) (Archer and Lloyd, 2002; Deary et al., 2003; Pinker, 2008). This is also true for social status: the highest- but also the lowest-ranking positions in society are disproportionally filled by males (e.g., there are both more male top managers and more male prison inmates or homeless people) (Baumeister, 2010).

These general differences are also mirrored in many gender differences that are of interest within economic psychology.

First, at the workplace, females more often than males choose careers and positions that imply having many social contacts with others (e.g., working in the human resources department rather than working in accounting; e.g., PewResearchCenter, 2016). Furthermore, females are more attracted to professions that mainly consist in helping others (e.g., becoming a nurse or a nursery school teacher; Office for National Statistics, 2013).

Second, as having a high-status position increases males' but might even decrease females' sexual attractiveness, males are more ambitious and more competitive in their careers than females. At the workplace, male behavior is often oriented toward climbing the ladder of social hierarchies. Males will be busy establishing good relationships with their supervisors, while females will be more engaged in horizontal networking activities (Baumeister, 2010). Female leadership behavior is less status-oriented than male leadership behavior (Eagly and Johnson, 1990).

Third, females tend to have more communal and egalitarian political attitudes (Gilens, 1988; Kaufmann and Petrocik, 1999; Shapiro and Mahajan, 1986). When thinking about social policies, males tend to follow an ethics of justice (i.e., "rules are rules and have to be followed"), while females tend to follow an ethics of care (Gilligan, 1982; Gilligan and Attanucci, 1988). Thus, females more than males support economic policies that aim to decrease economic inequalities. In the 2016 presidential election, Hillary Clinton won a majority of female voters, while Donald Trump won a majority of male voters (Zillman, 2016).

Fourth, many gender differences in financial and consumer behavior can easily be explained by evolutionary psychology. Males are more risk-seeking than females when investing money (Barber and Odean, 2001). Furthermore, males are more likely to engage in conspicuous consumption than females (i.e., they will use the possession of luxury goods such as expensive cars, suits, or watches as a means of signaling their vocational success) (Sundie et al., 2011). Males use consumption to signal their social status by demonstrating good taste and distinction (e.g., drinking certain kinds of wine, going to the opera, or being interested in abstract art – and being able to knowingly talk about it). Consumption might also directly be used to signal a person's abundance of resources (e.g., expensive sports cars, engagement rings that signal the fiancé's wealth, or flowers that will only last for a few days) (Miller, 2009).

Females are more likely to invest their money in goods and services that directly increase their physical attractiveness (e.g., cosmetics, clothes, visiting a beauty farm) (Pliner, Chaikin, and Flett, 1990). Females more than males invest in looking sexy and younger than their biological age (e.g., wearing uncomfortable high heels).

For both genders, consumption patterns vary with their mating status. For example, consumption might signal commitment to one's current intimate relationship (e.g., selling a convertible and buying a station wagon, buying a house in a suburb, or wearing an engagement ring).

22.2.4 Humans as Herd Animals

Economics traditionally regard actors as solitary agents who are busy maximizing their own utility and do not bother very much about the utility functions of others – as long as others' behavior does not lead to externalities for their own outcome. Evolutionary psychology takes a very different perspective.

Animal species differ considerably in the degree to which they spend their lives in the company of others. Some species are mainly solitary, avoiding contact with conspecifics, only meeting each other for reproductive purposes (but males do not invest any time in rearing their offspring). Primates are generally herd animals, and humans are no exception to this.

Some biologists believe that many of our cognitive abilities mainly evolved to facilitate our functioning in social groups. For example, it has been argued that humans' large brains mainly evolved to keep track of all the other group members and our relations with them and that language mainly evolved as a means to regulate group life. In line with this reasoning, much of human communication consists in gossiping about other group members (Dunbar, 1998).

In the EEA, humans could only reach their goals by cooperating with others (e.g., Bowles and Gintis, 2003). This held true for raising their children, gathering food or hunting game, getting help when ill or defending one's group against hostile tribes. Thus, human behavior from the outset is oriented toward other group members.

Consequently, humans developed a number of cognitive and motivational adaptations that helped them functioning in the groups to which they belonged. Such motivational adaptations entail the "need to belong" (Baumeister and Leary, 1995), the motive to affiliate with others, the fear of being ostracized (Abrams, Hogg, and Marques, 2005), the urge to identify with others, the ability to take pride in other group members' accomplishments, feeling lonely when not with others (Cacioppo, Cacioppo, and Boomsma, 2014), enjoying spending time with friends and family, and feeling embarrassed when not following the social norms that exist within a given group (e.g., Opp and Hechter, 2001).

However, it must be emphasized that our group membership is always ambivalent. From a game-theoretical perspective, our relationship with others can be described as a mixed-motive situation. When humans form social groups (be they families, nations, companies, or sports clubs), there is always a joint interest of all group members, but there are also always conflicts of interest between different group members. One conflict can be described as the problem of collective goods (i.e., it is often rational for each individual to withhold one's own resources and let the others invest in their production) (Olson, 1965). Consequently, humans have developed a number of adaptations to cope with such collective good problems. They are good in detecting cheaters, and they are willing to punish those group members who do not follow a given social norm (e.g., Fehr and Fischbacher, 2003; Sober and Wilson, 1998). It must be noted that hunter-and-gatherer societies have a very egalitarian structure. There are no formal leaders and no formal hierarchies. This might be one evolutionary reason why in many situations we observe *inequality aversion* in humans (i.e., an equal distribution of all resources is both preferred and perceived to be fair; Bolton and Ockenfels, 2000; Fehr and Schmidt, 1999).

Although humans react negatively to (unjustified) inequality, they nonetheless do have a desire to increase their own relative standing within a given group. Even in groups with no formal leaders or hierarchies, group members differ in their informal social status (Boehm, 1993; Lee, 1979). This is even more the case when such formal hierarchies exist. While some members do have much influence on the group's decisions and are often asked for advice, other members would rather follow the lead of others. For males, social status is directly related to their sexual attractiveness and thus their reproductive success (Hopcroft, 2006; Pérusse, 1993). In a study consisting of former students of the military academy at West Point, it was shown that military rank achieved forty years after graduation was positively related to the number of children conceived (Mueller and Mazur, 1997).

Thus, humans have evolved to quickly identify their own and others' social status, and they are highly motivated to gain as much status as possible. This urge for status might be the actual reason for humans' desire to become rich, as in modern societies monetary wealth is an important hallmark of one's social status. Consequently, it can be shown that relative wealth is a stable predictor of life satisfaction (Diener and Fujita, 1997). Furthermore, from an evolutionary perspective, it is not surprising that the absolute wealth of a country (at least beyond a certain threshold) does not influence the life satisfaction of its citizens (Easterlin, 1974). (See also the chapter by Ahuvia in the current volume.)

As humans evolved in small groups, they tend to compare themselves with those around them and not with some abstract level of comparison, thus the saying that to be rich is to earn $50 a month more than the husband of your wife's sister. Consequently, it does not help unemployed people in Western countries that their standard of living might be better than that of most others when compared with mankind in general. Being unemployed is the most robust economic predictor of a low life satisfaction even when taking the financial situation into account (Frey and Stutzer, 2002; Winkelman and Winkelman, 1998).

Much of human consumption can be regarded as an attempt to signal one's social status to others (Miller, 2009). Consequently, one reason why so many people have problems managing their debts is that they do not want to fall behind their peers in terms of conspicuous consumption ("keep up with the Joneses").

22.2.5 Understanding and Misunderstanding the Economy

How do laypeople perceive the economy, and how do they evaluate certain economic measures? This is an important issue because in democratic countries it is ordinary people who elect their government officials, and economic issues often play an important role in voters' decisions (e.g., in the 2016 US election, Donald Trump promised that American jobs would no longer be "stolen" from US workers; NBC News, 2016).

The economy is not the only entity that laypeople have to evaluate without having a proper understanding of its complexities. Other examples would be questions like, "Does global warming actually exist and what should we do about it?" or, "Should I really undergo that chemotherapy to fight my lung cancer?" It has been shown that people try to answer such complex questions by referring to an intuitive kind of "folk physics" or "folk biology" (Geary, 2010). Research has shown that humans understand some basic concepts of physics and biology, but they systematically misunderstand more complicated mechanisms and relations. For example, even small children expect that things fall down to earth when they are held in the air and then let loose; and we know that both the mother and the father of an elephant will be elephants. However, laypeople get it systematically wrong when they try to comprehend very small entities (e.g., atoms or genes) or very large entities (e.g., galaxies). They also have problems understanding processes that are very slow (e.g., the change of continents or the evolution of the universe) or very fast (e.g., the speed of light). Both understanding and misunderstanding certain elements of our physical and biological environment can be traced back to our evolutionary past. Following the logic that "thinking is for doing," we are able to perceive those aspects of our physical environment that are of immediate relevance to our own behavior and decisions.

A similar logic can be applied to the field of economics. When dealing with their own economic decisions as well as when dealing with the economy in general, people follow so-called lay economics. They intuitively understand some basic economic concepts, but they systematically misunderstand complex economic processes. For example, it has been argued that humans follow a certain "trading instinct" in that they spontaneously exchange certain goods with others, but laypeople have trouble understanding the logic of macroeconomic cycles or the functioning of the stock market. Thus, ordinary voters and professional economists very much differ in the way that they evaluate economic measures.

In the following, we want to outline several examples of how being evolved in the EEA has shaped our understanding of the economy.

First, it must be noted that in the EEA, there was rarely a rapid growth of available resources in humans' natural environment. If resources were volatile, their availability went rather down than up (e.g., as consequences of earthquakes, volcanic eruptions, hurricanes, or floods). Consequently, humans tend to neglect compound interest effects when anticipating their own financial future or when evaluating the consequences of different economic policies. For example, when investing 100€ with an interest rate of 5 percent, one holds a total of approximately 340€ after a period of twenty-five years. However, in a study with advanced students of economics and business administration, the average respondent thought it would be less than 190€ (Christandl and Fetchenhauer, 2009).

Second, the production of welfare was mainly dependent on the successful solution of collective good problems (e.g., big game hunting or defending one's tribe against attacks from other tribes). Once such collective goods were produced, their distribution was mainly regarded as a zero-sum game. Therefore, it is not surprising to note that humans have developed a number of adaptations that help them to divide resources evenly among the members of a group (e.g., the aforementioned ability to detect cheaters, inequality aversion, or the willingness to engage in altruistic punishment). As a drawback from such adaptations, humans often have trouble understanding that markets are another and often more efficient way to produce and distribute scarce resources. Consequently, in today's complex economies, many laypeople still regard the goal of economic policy as the distribution of a "fixed pie" that is to be divided fairly among all group members (Bazerman, Moore, and Gillespie, 1999; Bazerman and Neale, 1983, 1994; Thompson and Hastie, 1990). For example, many laypeople are in favor of the minimum wage and the limitation of top salaries, while many economists are against such measures because they fear that both of them will increase unemployment rates (Haferkamp et al., 2009).

Third, our tribal nature leads many people to regard international trade as a *conflict of interest* between different countries. Therefore, many citizens favor import duties to protect jobs and companies, they prefer for their government to subsidize companies that only produce in their home country, and they want to close their borders even to highly qualified foreigners (Jacob, Christandl, and Fetchenhauer, 2011). Contrary to laypeople's thinking, economists favor international trade, and since the seminal work of David Ricardo (1817), they are convinced that free and unrestricted trade is good for both countries involved, at least when both countries engage voluntarily in this transaction and prices are set by markets and not by the government of the stronger country. However, this idea is very difficult to explain to laypeople (Baron and Kemp, 2004), and in the 2016 presidential election, we have seen how successfully Donald Trump used anti–free trade sentiments to instigate the general population (Jacobs, 2016).

To summarize, most humans lack the cognitive resources to intuitively understand complex economic processes and interrelations. When judging economic measures, they instead activate cognitive modules that are adapted to a life as hunter and gatherer. In this regard, they often rely on intuitive judgments of fairness and justness. Ironically, this might lead them to favoring inferior economic policies.

22.3 Why Care About Human Evolution?

In this chapter, we have outlined some of the many ways in which both economics and economic psychology could profit from incorporating the ideas, theories, and empirical results that have been gathered by evolutionary psychologists throughout the last twenty-five years. It is surprising how little impact evolutionary psychology has had on economics and economic psychology so far.

The evolutionary biologist David Sloan Wilson (2016) once described how excited he was "when Richard Thaler and Cass Sunstein called for an economics based on Homo sapiens, not Homo economicus, in their book *Nudge*. Then I searched my kindle edition for the word 'evolution' and came up empty. How can economics be based on Homo sapiens without any discussion whatsoever of Homo sapiens as a product of genetic and cultural evolution?"

We believe that the approach taken by evolutionary psychology could help us to better understand human behavior, not only in its common applications (e.g., mating behavior), but also human behavior in the economy. Unlike so many singular phenomena and narrow-ranging theories within mainstream psychology, it offers an integrative and comprehensive alternative to economic models of man.

22.4 References

Abrams, D., Hogg, M. A., Marques, J. M. (2005). *The Social Psychology of Inclusion and Exclusion*. New York: Psychology Press.

Ainslie, G. (1992). *Picoeconomics: The Strategic Interaction of Successive Motivational States Within the Person*. Cambridge: Cambridge University Press.

Ainslie, G. (2001). *Breakdown of Will*. Cambridge: Cambridge University Press.

Andreoni, J. (1989). Giving with Impure Altruism: Applications to Charity and Ricardian Equivalence. *Journal of Political Economy*, 97, 1447–1458.

Archer, J., and Lloyd, B. (2002). *Sex and Gender* (2nd ed.). Cambridge: Cambridge University Press.

Banks, J., Blundell, R., and Tanner, S. (1998). Is There a Retirement Savings-Puzzle? *American Economic Review*, 88, 769–788.

Barber, B. M., and Odean, T. (2001). Boys Will Be Boys: Gender, Overconfidence, and Common Stock Investment. *Quarterly Journal of Economics*, 116, 261–291.

Baron, J., and Kemp, S. (2004). Support for Trade Restrictions, Attitudes, and Understanding of Comparative Advantage. *Journal of Economic Psychology*, 25, 565–580.

Baron-Cohen, S. (1999). Evolution of a Theory of Mind? In M. Corballis and S. Lea (Eds.), *The Descent of Mind: Psychological Perspective on Hominid Evolution* (pp. 261–277). Oxford: Oxford University Press.

Baumeister, R. F. (2010). *Is There Anything Good About Men? How Cultures Flourish by Exploiting Men*. Oxford: Oxford University Press.

Baumeister, R. F., and Leary, M. R. (1995). The Need to Belong: Desire for Interpersonal Attachments as a Fundamental Human Motivation. *Psychological Bulletin*, 117, 497–529.

Bazerman, M. H., Moore, D. A., and Gillespie, J. J. (1999). The Human Mind as a Barrier to Wiser Environmental Agreements. *American Behavioral Scientist*, 42, 1277–1300.

Bazerman, M. H., and Neale, M. A. (1983). Heuristics in Negotiation: Limitations to Effective Dispute Resolution. In M. H. Bazerman and R. J. Lewicki (Eds.), *Negotiating in Organizations* (pp. 51–67). Beverly Hills: Sage.

Bazerman, M. H., and Neale, M. A. (1994). *Negotiating Rationally*. New York: Free Press.

Becker, G. (1976). Altruism, Egoism, and Genetic Fitness: Economics and Sociobiology. *Journal of Economic Literature*, 14, 817–826.

Becker, G. S. (1981). *A Treatise on the Family*. Cambridge, MA: Harvard University Press.

Becker, G. S., Grossman, M., and Murphy, K. M. (1991). Rational Addiction and the Effect of Price on Consumption. *American Economic Review*, 81, 237–241.

Becker, G. S., Grossman, M., and Murphy, K. M. (1994). An Empirical Analysis of Cigarette Addiction. *American Economic Review*, 84, 396–418.

Becker, G., and Murphy, K. (1988). A Theory of Rational Addiction. *Journal of Political Economy*, 96, 675–700.

Bekkers, R., and Wiepking, P. (2011). A Literature Review of Empirical Studies of Philanthropy: Eight Mechanisms that Drive Charitable Giving. *Nonprofit and Voluntary Sector Quarterly*, 40, 924–973.

Bergstrom, C. T., and Dugatkin, L. A. (2012). *Evolution*. New York: W. W. Norton.

Bernhard, H., Fischbacher, U., and Fehr, E. (2006). Parochial Altruism in Humans. *Nature*, 442, 912–915.

Bernheim, D. B., Skinner, J., and Weinberg, S. (2001). What Accounts for the Variation in Retirement Wealth Among US Households? *American Economic Review*, 91, 832–857.

Boehm, C. (1993). Egalitarian Society and Reverse Dominance Hierarchy. *Current Anthropology*, 34, 227–254.

Boehm, C. (2012). *Moral Origins. The Evolution of Virtue, Altruism, and Shame*. New York: Basic Books.

Bolton, G. E., and Ockenfels, A. (2000). ERC: A Theory of Equity, Reciprocity, and Competition. *American Economic Review*, 90, 166–193.

Bowlby, J. (1969). *Attachment and Loss, Volume 1: Attachment*. New York: Basic Books.

Bowles, S., and Gintis, H. (2003). Origins of Human Cooperation. In P. Hammerstein (Ed.), *Genetic and Cultural Evolution of Cooperation* (pp. 429–443). Cambridge, MA: MIT Press.

Bowles, S., and Gintis, H. (Eds.). (2011). *A Cooperative Species*. Princeton, NJ: Princeton University Press.

Brocas, I., and Carrillo, J. D. (2003). Introduction. In I. Brocas and J. D. Carrillo (Eds.), *The Psychology of Economic Decisions, Volume 1: Rationality and Well-Being* (pp. xiii–xxxii). Oxford: Oxford University Press.

Buss, D. M. (1989). Sex Differences in Human Mate Preferences: Evolutionary Hypotheses Tested in 37 Cultures. *Behavioral and Brain Sciences*, 12, 1–49.

Buss, D. M. (2015). Introduction: The Emergence and Maturation of Evolutionary Psychology. In D. M. Buss (Ed.), *The Handbook of Evolutionary Psychology, Volume 1: Foundation* (2nd ed.) (pp. xxiii-xxv). Hoboken, NJ: Wiley.

Byrne, R. W., and Whiten, A. (Eds.) (1988). *Machiavellian Intelligence: Social Expertise and the Evolution of Intellect in Monkeys, Apes, and Humans*. Oxford: Clarendon Press.

Cachel, S. (2006). *Primate and Human Evolution*. Cambridge: Cambridge University Press.

Cacioppo, J. T., Cacioppo, S., and Boomsma, D. I. (2014). Evolutionary Mechanisms for Loneliness. *Cognition and Emotion*, 28, 10.

Campbell, A. (2002). *A Mind of Her Own: The Evolutionary Psychology of Women*. New York: Oxford University Press.

Centers for Disease Control and Prevention (2016). Obesity and Overweight. Retrieved from www.cdc.gov/nchs/fastats/obesity-overweight.htm

Christandl, F., and Fetchenhauer, D. (2009). How Laypeople and Experts Misperceive the Effect of Economic Growth. *Journal of Economic Psychology*, 30, 381–392.

Cockburn, A. (1991). *An Introduction to Evolutionary Ecology*. Oxford: Blackwell Scientific Publications.

Cosmides, L., Barrett, H. C., and Tooby, J. (2010). Adaptive Specializations, Social Exchange, and the Evolution of Human Intelligence. *Proceedings of the National Academy of Sciences*, 107, 9007–9014.

Cosmides, L., and Tooby, J. (1992) Cognitive Adaptations for Social Exchange. In J. H. Barkow, L. Cosmides, and J. Tooby (Eds.), *The Adapted Mind: Evolutionary Psychology and the Generation of Culture* (pp. 163–228). Oxford: Oxford University Press.

Cosmides, L., and Tooby, J. (1994). Beyond Intuition and Instinct Blindness: The Case for an Evolutionarily Rigorous Cognitive Science. *Cognition*, 50, 41–77.

Costa, P. T., Terracciano, A., and McCrae, R. R. (2001). Gender Differences in Personality Traits Across Cultures: Robust and Surprising Findings. *Journal of Personality and Social Psychology*, 81, 322–331.

Cowden, C. C. (2012). Game Theory, Evolutionary Stable Strategies and the Evolution of Biological Interactions. *Nature Education Knowledge*, 3, 6.

Cziko, G. (2000). *The Things We Do: Using the Lessons of Bernard and Darwin to Understand the What, How, and Why of Our Behavior*. Cambridge, MA: MIT Press.

Daly, M., and Wilson, M. I. (1999). Human Evolutionary Psychology and Animal Behaviour. *Animal Behaviour*, 57, 509–519.

Darwin, C. (1859). *On the Origin of Species by Means of Natural Selection, or, the Preservation of Favoured Races in the Struggle for Life*. London: J. Murray.

Deary, I. J., Thorpe, G., Wilson, V., Starr, J. M., and Whalley, L. J. (2003). Population Sex Differences in IQ at Age 11: The Scottish Mental Survey 1932. *Intelligence*, 31, 533–54.

Del Giudice, M. (2009). On the Real Magnitude of Psychological Sex Difference. *Evolutionary Psychology*, 7, 264–279.

De Quervain, D. J.-F., Fischbacher, U., Treyer, et al. (2004). The Neural Basis of Altruistic Punishment. *Science*, 305, 1254–1258.

Diener, E., and Fujita, F. (1997). Social Comparisons and Subjective Wellbeing. In B. P. Buunk and F. X. Gibbons (Eds.). *Health, Coping, and Well-Being: Perspectives from Social Comparison Theory* (pp. 329–357). Mahwah, NJ: Lawrence Erlbaum.

Dunbar, R. (1998). *Grooming, Gossip, and the Evolution of Language*. Boston: Harvard University Press.

Eagly, A. H., and Johnson, B. T. (1990). Gender and Leadership Style: A Meta-analysis. *Psychological Bulletin*, 108, 233–256.

Easterlin, R. A. (1974). Does Economic Growth Improve the Human Lot? Some Empirical Evidence. In P. A. David and M. W. Reder (Eds.), *Nations and Households in Economic Growth: Essays in Honor of Moses Abramovitz* (pp. 89–125). New York: Academic Press.

Fehr, E., and Fischbacher, U. (2003). The Nature of Human Altruism. *Nature*, 425, 785–791.

Fehr, E., and Gächter, S. (2002). Altruistic Punishment in Humans. *Nature*, 415, 137–140.

Fehr, E., and Schmidt, K. M. (1999). A Theory of Fairness, Competition, and Cooperation. *Quarterly Journal of Economics*, 3, 817–868.

Feingold, A. (1994). Gender Differences in Personality: A Meta-analysis. *Psychological Bulletin*, 116, 429–456.

Fetchenhauer, D., Groothuis, T., and Pradel, J. (2010). Not Only States but Traits: Humans Can Identify Permanent Altruistic Dispositions in 20 s. *Evolution and Human Behavior*, 31, 80–86.

Frank, R. H. (1988). *Passions Within Reason: The Strategic Role of the Emotions*. New York: Norton.

Frey, B., and Stutzer, A. (2002). *Happiness and Economics. How the Economy and Institutions Affect Well-Being*. Princeton, NJ: Prinecton University Press.

Friedman, M. (1975). *There's No Such Thing as a Free Lunch*. LaSalle, IL: Open Court.

Geary, D. C. (2010). *Male, Female: The Evolution of Human Sex Differences* (2nd ed.). Washington, DC: American Psychological Association.

Geary, D. C. (2015). Evolution of Paternal Investment. In D. M. Buss (Ed.), *The Handbook of Evolutionary Psychology, Volume 1: Foundation* (2nd ed.) (pp. 483–505). Hoboken, NJ: Wiley.

Ghiselin, M. T. (1974). *The Economy of Nature and Evolution of Sex*. Berkeley: University of California Press.

Gigerenzer, G., and Selten, R. (Eds.). (2001). *Bounded Rationality: The Adaptive Toolbox*. Cambridge, MA: MIT Press.

Gigerenzer, G., and Todd, P. M. (1999). *Simple Heuristics That Make Us Smart*. New York: Oxford University Press.

Gilens, M. (1988). Gender and Support for Reagan: A Comprehensive Model of Presidential Approval. *American Journal of Political Science*, 32, 19–49.

Gilligan, C. (1982). *In a Different Voice: Psychological Theory and Women's Development*. Cambridge, MA: Harvard University Press.

Gilligan, C., and Attanucci, J. (1988). Two Moral Orientations: Gender Differences and Similarities. *Merrill-Palmer Quarterly*, 34, 223–237.

Gottfredson, M. R., and Hirschi, T. (1990). *A General Theory of Crime*. Stanford, CA: Stanford University Press.

Gould, S. J. (1997). Evolution: The Pleasures of Pluralism. *New York Review of Books*, 44, 47–52.

Güth, W., Schmittberger, R., and Schwarze, B. (1982). An Experimental Analysis of Ultimatum Bargaining. *Journal of Economic Behavior and Organization*, 3, 367–388.

Haferkamp, A., Belschak, F., Enste, D., and Fetchenhauer, D. (2009). Efficiency Versus Fairness: The Evaluation of Labor Market Policies by Economists and Laypeople. *Journal of Economic Psychology*, 30, 527–539.

Hamilton W. D. (1964). The Genetical Evolution of Social Behaviour. II. *Journal of Theoretical Biology* , 7, 17–52.

Hamilton, W. D. (1996). Narrow Roads of Gene Land. *Evolution of Social Behavior*. New York: W. H. Freeman.

Herrnstein, R. J. (1997). Self-Control. In H. Rachlin and D. I. Laibson (Eds.), *The Matching Law: Papers in Psychology and Economics* (pp. 101–188). Cambridge, MA: Harvard University Press.

Hopcroft, R. L. (2006). Sex, Status, and Reproductive Success in the Contemporary United States. *Evolution and Human Behavior*, 27, 104–120.

Hume, D. (1739). *A Treatise of Human Nature*. London: John Noon.

Huxley, T. H. (1888). The Struggle for Existence: A Programme. *Nineteenth Century*, 23, 163–165.

Jacob, R., Christandl, F., and Fetchenhauer, D. (2011). Economic Experts or Laypeople? How Teachers and Journalists Judge Trade and Immigration Policies. *Journal of Economic Psychology*, 32, 662–671.

Jacobs, B. (2016, June 28). Trump Escalates Economic Tirade Against Free Trade, China and Globalism. *The Guardian*. Retrieved from www.theguardian.com/us-news/2016/jun/28/donald-trump-foreign-policy-speech-tpp-china-free-trade

Jenni, K. E., and Loewenstein, G. (1997). Explaining the "Identifiable Victim Effect." *Journal of Risk and Uncertainty*, 12, 235–257.

Judge, T. A., and Cable, D. M. (2004). The Effect of Physical Height on Workplace Success and Income: Preliminary Test of a Theoretical Model. *Journal of Applied Psychology*, 89, 428–441.

Kaufmann, K. M., and Petrocik, J. R. (1999). The Changing Politics of American Men: Understanding the Sources of the Gender Gap. *American Journal of Political Science*, 43, 864–887.

Kogut, T., and Ritov, I. (2005). The "Identified Victim" Effect: An Identified Group, or Just a Single Individual? *Journal of Behavioral Decision Making*, 18, 157–167.

Lee, R. B. (1979). *The !Kung San: Men, Women and Work in a Foraging Society.* Cambridge: Cambridge University Press.

Leslie, A. M. (1987). Pretense and Representation: The Origins of "Theory of Mind." *Psychological Review*, 94, 412–426.

Lévi-Strauss, C. (1952). *Race and History*. Paris: Unesco.

Levitt, S. D., and List, J. A. (2008). *Homo Economicus* Evolves. *Science*, 319, 909–910.

Loewenstein, G. (1996). Out of Control: Visceral Influences on Behavior. *Organizational Behavior and Human Decision Processes*, 65, 272–292.

Logue, A. (1995). *Self-Control: Waiting Until Tomorrow for What You Want Today*. London: Pearson.

MacDonald, K. B. (1995). Evolution, the Five-Factor Model, and Levels of Personality. *Journal of Personality*, 63, 525–567.

McDermott, R., Fowler, J. H., and Smirnov, O. (2008). On the Evolutionary Origin of Prospect Theory Preferences. *Journal of Politics*, 70, 335–350.

Miller, G. (2009). *Spent: Sex, Evolution, and Consumer Behavior*. New York: Penguin.

Mischel, W. (2015). *The Marshmallow Test: Understanding Self-Control and How to Master It*. London: Corgi.

Mischel, W., Ebbesen, E. B., and Raskoff Zeiss, A. (1972). Cognitive and Attentional Mechanisms in Delay of Gratification. *Journal of Personality and Social Psychology*, 21, 204–218.

Mischel, W., Shoda, Y., and Rodriguez, M. L. (1989). Delay of Gratification in Children. *Science*, 244, 933–938.

Modigliani, F. (1966). The Life Cycle Hypothesis of Saving, the Demand for Wealth and the Supply of Capital. *Social Research*, 33, 160–217.

Mueller, U., and Mazur, A. (1997). Facial Dominance in *Homo sapiens* as Honest Signaling of Male Quality. *Behavioral Ecology*, 8, 569–579.

Murray, G. R., and Schmitz, J. D. (2011). Caveman Politics: Evolutionary Leadership Preferences and Physical Stature. *Social Science Quarterly*, 92, 1215–1235.

NBC News (2016, September 27). Trump Opens with Statement on Jobs. Retrieved from www.nbcnews.com/video/trump-opens-with-statement-on-jobs-773617219822

Office for National Statistics (2013, September 25). Women in the Labour Market: 2013. Retrieved from www.ons.gov.uk/employmentandlabourmarket/peopleinwork/employmentandemployeetypes/articles/womeninthelabourmarket/2013-09-25

Olson, M. (1965). *The Logic of Collective Action: Public Goods and the Theory of Groups*. Cambridge, MA: Harvard University Press.

Opp, K.-D., and Hechter, M. (2001). *Social Norms*. New York: Russell Sage Foundation.

Pascal, B. (1910). *Thoughts* (W. F. Trotter, Transl.). New York: P. F. Collier & Son. (Original work published 1660).

Pérusse, D. (1993). Cultural and Reproductive Success in Industrialized Societies: Testing the Relationship at the Proximate and Ultimate Levels. *Behavioral and Brain Sciences*, 16, 267–322.

Pew Research Center. (2016, October 6). The State of American Jobs. Retrieved from www.pewsocialtrends.org/2016/10/06/the-state-of-american-jobs/

Pievani, T. (2011). Born to Cooperate? Altruism as Exaptation and the Evolution of Human Sociality. In R. W. Sussman and C. R. Cloninger (Eds.), *Origins of Altruism and Cooperation* (pp. 41–61). New York: Springer.

Pinker, S. (2008). *The Sexual Paradox*. New York: Charles Scribner's Sons.

Pliner, P., Chaikin, S., and Flett, G. L. (1990). Gender Differences in Concern with Body Weight and Physical Appearance over the Life Span. *Personality and Social Psychology Bulletin*, 16, 263–273.

Premack, D., and Woodruff, G. (1978). Does the Chimpanzee Have a Theory of Mind? *Behavioral and Brain Sciences*, 1, 515–526.

Ricardo, D. (1817). *On the Principles of Political Economy and Taxation*. London: John Murray.

Rubin, P. H., and Capra, C. M. (2012). The Evolutionary Psychology of Economics. In S. C. Roberts (Ed.), *Applied Evolutionary Psychology* (pp. 7–15). Oxford: Oxford University Press.

Schelling, T. C. (1968). The Life You Save May Be Your Own. In Samuel Chase (Ed.), *Problems in Public Expenditure Analysis* (pp. 127–162). Washington, DC: Brookings Institute.

Scott-Phillips, T. C., Dickins, T. E., and West, S. A. (2011). Evolutionary Theory and the Ultimate–Proximate Distinction in the Human Behavioral Sciences. *Perspectives on Psychological Science*, 6, 38–47.

Shapiro, R. Y., and Mahajan, H. (1986). Gender Differences in Policy Preferences: A Summary of Trends from the 1960s to the 1980s. *Public Opinion Quarterly*, 50, 42–61.

Simon, H. A. (1992). Altruism and Economics. *Eastern Economic Journal*, 18, 73–83.

Small, D. A., and Loewenstein, G. (2003). Helping a Victim or Helping the Victim: Altruism and Identifiability. *Journal of Risk and Uncertainty*, 26, 5–16.

Small, E. (2011). The New Noah's Ark: Beautiful and Useful Species Only. Part 1. Biodiversity Conservation Issues and Priorities. *Biodiversity*, 12, 232–247.

Smith, A. (1776). *The Wealth of Nations*. London: W. Strahan and T. Cadell.

Sober, E., and Wilson, D. S. (1998). *Unto Others: The Evolution and Psychology of Unselfish Behavior*. Cambridge, MA: Harvard University Press.

Struthers, W. M. (2009). *Wired for Intimacy: How Pornography Hijacks the Male Brain*. Downers Grove, IL: InterVarsity Press.

Stulp, G., Buunk, A. P., and Pollet, T. V. (2013). Women Want Taller Men More Than Men Want Shorter Women. *Personality and Individual Differences*, 54, 877–883.

Stulp, G., Buunk, A. P., Verhulst, S., and Pollet, T. V. (2013). Tall Claims? Sense and Nonsense About the Importance of Height of US Presidents. *Leadership Quarterly*, 24, 159–171.

Sundie, J. M., Kenrick, D. T., Griskevicius, V., Tybur, J. M. Vohs, K. D., and Beal, D. J. (2011). Peacocks, Porsches, and Thorstein Veblen: Conspicuous Consumption as a Sexual Signaling System. *Journal of Personality and Social Psychology*, 100, 664–680.

Sutter, M. (2014). *Die Entdeckung der Geduld – Ausdauer schlägt Talent [The Discovery of Patience – Persistence Beats Talent]*. Salzburg: Ecowin.

Sutter, M., Oberauer, M., and Yilmaz, L. (2015). Delay of Gratification and the Role of Defaults: an Experiment with Kindergarten Children. *Economics Letters*, 137, 21–24.

Thompson, L., and Hastie, R. (1990). Social Perception in Negotiation. *Organizational Behavior and Human Decision Processes*, 47, 98–123.

Tooby, J., Cosmides, L., and Barkow, J. H. (1995). Introduction: Evolutionary Psychology and Conceptual Integration. In J. H. Barkow, L. Cosmides, and J. Tooby (Eds.), *The Adapted Mind: Evolutionary Psychology and the Generation of Culture* (pp. 3–15). New York: Oxford University Press.

Trivers, R. L. (1972). Parental Investment and Sexual Selection. In B. Campbell (Ed.), *Sexual Selection and the Descent of Man: 1871–1971* (pp. 136–179). Chicago: Aldine.

Tversky, A., and Kahneman, D. (1974). Judgment Under Uncertainty: Heuristics and Biases. *Science*, 185, 1124–1131.

Van Ginneken, V. J. T., and Maes, G. E. (2005). The European Eel (*Anguilla anguilla*, Linnaeus), Its Lifecycle, Evolution and Reproduction: A Literature Review. *Reviews in Fish Biology and Fisheries*, 15, 367–398.

Van Lier, J., Revlin, R., and De Neys, W. (2013). Detecting Cheaters Without Thinking: Testing the Automaticity of the Cheater Detection Module. *PLoS ONE*, 8, e53827.

Watt, S. (2015). *The Ugly Animals: We Can't All Be Pandas*. Stroud, UK: History Press.

Wilder, J. A., Mobasher, Z., and Hammer, M. F. (2004). Genetic Evidence for Unequal Effective Population Sizes of Human Females and Males. *Molecular Biology and Evolution*, 21, 2047–2057.

Wilson, D. S. (2016, January 12). Economic Theory Is Dead: Here's What Will Replace It. [Blog post]. Retrieved from evonomics.com/economic-theory-is-dead-heres-what-will-replace-it/

Winkelman, L., and Winkelman, R. (1998). Why Are the Unemployed So Unhappy? Evidence from Panel Data. *Economica*, 65, 1–15.

Zillman, C. (2016, November 9). Hillary Clinton Had the Biggest Voter Gender Gap on Record. *Fortune*. Retrieved from fortune.com/2016/11/09/hillary-clinton-election-gender-gap/

23 Evolutionary Economics and Psychology

Ulrich Witt

23.1 Introduction

Modern economies are subject to rapid transformations. Their causes ultimately reside in the active and passive change behavior of the economic agents. Innovative and adaptive activities result in an innovation competition. Newly entered ideas, techniques, products, and institutional features compete with one another for successful dissemination. And they compete with incumbent parts of the economy that they try to replace. This form of competition has far-reaching consequences for economic growth, employment, the international division of labor, welfare, and many more aspects of modern economies.

In evolutionary economics, the competitive transformations are interpreted as an evolutionary process. However, this interpretation comes in different forms: a more perfunctory one and a more fundamental one (Witt, 2008). The more perfunctory interpretation remains at the level of analogy. Innovations are seen as a form of variation. Innovation competition is interpreted as an analogue to natural selection (Nelson and Winter, 1982, Metcalfe,1998). The result are neo-Schumpeterian models of competitive industrial dynamics and structural change in which individual economic change behavior plays little, if any, role (see, e.g., Hanusch and Pyka, 2007) and that are therefore of little relevance for economic psychology.

In the more fundamental interpretation, economic evolution is understood as a part of cultural evolution that builds on what natural evolution has endowed humans with. Accordingly, the Darwinian theory of evolution is not a source of inspiration for loose analogies with economic selection processes but rather a meta-theory that helps one to understand the influence of human nature on economic evolution. Active and passive economic change behavior is likely to be contingent in some way on the evolved parts of human nature. The conjectured adaptive value of these parts in ancestral environments and the question of how they match with the rather affluent conditions of modern developed economies can serve as a starting point for hypothesis formation.

Such a starting point is similar to the one in evolutionary psychology also referring to the Darwinian theory of evolution as a meta-theory. However, the focus of evolutionary economics is different from the one of evolutionary psychology. The latter is directed at explaining the human cognitive apparatus (see, e.g., Buss, 2003, and Fetchenhauer and Lang in this volume) and its impact on decision making through framing effects and intuitive decision heuristics (see, e.g., Gigerenzer and Goldstein, 1996; Kahneman, 2011). A similar focus – albeit one that ignores the evolutionary aspects – can be found in the recently emerging field of behavioral economics (see Camerer and Loewenstein, 2004).

In evolutionary economics, in contrast, the motivation and the innate adaptation mechanisms underlying human behavior are at center stage. What drives the innovative and the adaptive activities that transform the economy? What motivational mechanisms induce the search for, and experimentation with, novel ways of acting? How do innovations diffusing throughout the economy change the previously existing motivational structure? Focus is further on the evolved mechanisms of cognitive and noncognitive learning implied by human nature. How do decision makers arrive at the desires and preferences they have and what are the causes of change in them? How does the perception and valuation of action options change as a result of experience and/or observational learning?

Answers to questions like these require theoretical extensions that, though compatible with those pursued by evolutionary psychology and behavioral economics, differ from the research currently conducted there. The questions obviously also transcend canonical theorizing in economics. For a theory in which the characteristics and implications of equilibrium states of the economy are center stage, the complexities of human behavior and its innovative potential are unwelcome complications. In economic textbooks, they are therefore rarely addressed. The present chapter can thus also be read as an outline of how the exchange between the evolutionary and behavioral sciences and evolutionary economics can contribute to broadening the behavioral foundations of economic theory.

In the remainder, the argumentation proceeds as follows. Adaptations in human behavior can be distinguished by the different time scales on which they occur. In rough approximation, three levels can be identified. One level is that of the genes that code certain forms of behavior. Another level is that of innate, noncognitive learning mechanisms that govern instrumental conditioning and conditioned reinforcement. Finally, there is the level of cognitive reflection, creative insight, and observational learning. Adaptations at the genetic level (explicable in terms of the Darwinian theory of evolution) need many generations to appear. Given that, in the economic domain, the bulk of change occurs within single generations, the pace of that kind of behavioral adaptation is too slow to explain the ongoing economic transformation processes.

This fact notwithstanding, it will be argued in Section 23.2 that the Darwinian theory of evolution in general and behavioral ecology and sociobiology in particular are fruitful meta-theories. They contribute to understanding how both cultural evolution and the evolution of the economy are influenced by inherited human behavior dispositions. Elaborating this argument, Section 23.3 explores the influence of the innate, noncognitive learning mechanisms and their motivational underpinnings. To account for these influences within the utilitarian model of economic behavior, a connection to the concepts of utility functions and their logical equivalent, individual preference orderings, needs to be made. Economic theorizing traditionally leaves open how utility is generated or, to put it in that language, what the objects are on which a preference order is formed and for what reasons. As will be explained, to answer these questions it is useful to recognize the influence of innate motivational dispositions and their plasticity.

Section 23.4 turns to the cognitive influences on economic behavior and the systematic changes they are responsible for in interaction with the noncognitive learning processes. In a short digression, the section also discusses what motivates the search for, and experimentation with, new possibilities to act, that is, innovations. Section 23.5 elaborates in an exemplary fashion on what the suggested theory of change behavior can contribute to explaining the economic transformation process using consumption as the case in point. Section 23.6 briefly concludes.

23.2 Setting the Frame: The Role of the Human Genetic Endowment

Over the past three centuries, the transformations of the economy have been accelerating, producing substantial amounts of change within a generation's lifetime. If the ongoing change is understood as an evolutionary process, what relevance does the Darwinian theory of evolution have for its explanation, given that so much of the change occurs just during the life span of single generations? In evolutionary economics opinions on this point are split.[1] If a Darwinian world view is considered the unifying ontological frame for scientific inquiry (Wilson, 1998), a straightforward answer is to interpret the Darwinian theory as a meta-theory. With its help, the conjectural ancestral conditions from which the historical evolution of the human economy started can be reconstructed. Furthermore, it seems possible to derive some constraints from human nature that are binding up to the present day for the way in which the economy is transformed.

Influenced by the Darwinian revolution of his time, this position had already been suggested by Veblen (1898) – who also introduced the label "evolutionary" economics. But his plea for adopting a Darwinian perspective on economic change has not widely been accepted, not even in the school he founded (Hodgson, 2004). Perhaps because of fear of being associated with Social Darwinism, evolutionary reasoning has only been revived in economics half a century later and in the form of the perfunctory interpretation (e.g., in Alchian, 1950; Winter, 1964).[2] Ignoring the common ontological basis of evolutionary biology and the theory of economic change behavior, economists just borrowed key notions and models from natural selection theory to conceptualize, by way of analogy, economic transformation processes.

Analogies to biological modeling approaches such as in population dynamics are characteristic in particular of the so-called neo-Schumpeterian branch of evolutionary economics initiated by Nelson and Winter (1982).[3] However, these analogies detract attention from the crucial role of adaptations at the level of individual behavior and of their underlying motivations.[4] For that reason, the more fundamental, evolutionary interpretation of economic change is adopted in the present chapter.

As in evolutionary psychology, the starting points here are the heritable and, hence, by and large persistent, features of human behavior and their meaning for economic change behavior. There is little doubt that parts of the behavioral repertoire of humans – like that of all animals – are heritable, that is, developed as an expression of their genes. Cases in point are elementary behavior dispositions and adaptation mechanisms such as instrumental conditioning and conditioned reinforcement (Dugatkin, 2003, ch. 4). With their direct or indirect effect on reproductive success, heritable dispositions and adaptation patterns are likely to have been shaped by natural selection in ancestral times in a way that enhanced individual fitness of the organisms carrying the corresponding behavior genes.[5]

This hypothesis is, of course, not meant to imply that economic transformation processes are all governed by innate forms of human behavior. Even in still living, "primitive" societies and presumably also in the early human societies, culturally conditioned and intelligently created forms of behavior play a crucial role as well. Most likely correlated with the rapid ancestral growth of the human brain, they can be seen as the major reason for why the human species has come to master its environment and to develop a highly differentiated economy as no other species has. In fact, this mastery has reduced natural selection pressure on human behavior substantially (at least in present times and in the short and medium run).

Indicative of this effect is the fading correlation between the amount of resources commanded on the one hand and reproductive success on the other.[6] Another indication is that idiosyncratic behaviors with no adaptive value in terms of reproductive success become ever more frequent, and mismatch between inherited behavior dispositions and the increasingly feasible resources for serving them is not wiped out (Burnham et al., 2016). The question then is by what adaptive forces the increasing variety of idiosyncratic behaviors is still kept in check, and what these forces imply for explaining economic evolution more specifically. As will be argued in the next sections, some elementary, non-cognitive adaptation mechanisms have an influence here.

23.3 Explaining What Motivates Economic Behavior and its Adaptations

Motivational hypotheses "… describe why a person in a given situation selects one response over another or makes a given response with greater energization or frequency" (Bargh et al., 2010, p. 286). However, a person's motivation to respond or act belongs to the inner sphere of that person. The same holds for the person's reflections about possible actions serving that motivation. Both cannot be observed in the same way as an action can be that is actually taken. This simple fact is the crux of the long philosophical "other minds" debate. In economics, the repercussion of the debate can be seen in the modifications that utility theory – the economic version of motivational hypotheses – underwent over the centuries.

Starting from Bentham's sensory utilitarianism, these modifications were in the beginning driven by the desire to give utility theory a mathematical expression in terms of the differential calculus of physics (Warke, 2000). As a result, functions were postulated that were first assumed to represent cardinally measurable utility. Later they were reinterpreted as ordinal, subjective utility functions. In the usual textbook representation, they come in the form $u = f(x)$, where the independent variable $x = (x_1, x_2, ..., x_n)$ is a vector defined over quantities of n goods or services and the dependent variable u ("utility") is an index number.

The few empirical implications that can be derived from this version of utility theory all rest on the – unknown – shape of utility function supposed to be held by economic agents. It was found out, however, that a utility function is logically equivalent to a preference order, that is, an ordering over alternative bundles x and x' of the n goods and services, if a transitivity condition is satisfied. Such an ordering is reflected, in turn, in the observable choices made which indicate that either x' is preferred to x or x is preferred to x' or x and x' are equally preferred (indifference). Strikingly similar to the positivist attitude of behaviorism in psychology, it was therefore believed that speculations about the unobservable variable u (belonging to the inner sphere of the economic agents) were obsolete. In "preference revelation" experiments, it is expected to be possible instead to reconstruct the shape of the individual utility functions by focusing exclusively on what ordering over alternatives can be observed in the agents' choices when prices are varied (Samuelson, 1947, chs. I, V).

The proviso in this reconstruction strategy is, of course, the transitivity condition, that is, that the agents' preferences are consistent.[7] However, this is a condition whose empirical validity can only be proved in a preference revelation experiment by means of exactly the same observations required for reconstructing individual preferences. Lacking independent evidence for the assumption results in a logical indeterminacy of the whole approach that made Sen (1977) wonder whether revealed preference theory is more than an "elaborate pun".[8]

In the psychological literature, remnants of sensory utilitarianism (which preceded the formation of psychology as a science) such as the concepts of utility and preferences can hardly be found. Yet, regarding the "other minds" problem, in the form of radical behaviorism, psychological theorizing took a similar positivist stance toward the observability problem as revealed preference theory did in economics. There is one major difference, though. The latter theory was oriented toward deriving abstract logical inferences about demand functions. In contrast, behavioral psychology focused on explaining observable behavior itself – human and nonhuman. With the minimalist theory of operant or instrumental conditioning that focused on conditioned responses, it was possible to identify a narrowly limited number of primary reinforcers. Their existence invites reflections about the underlying motivation to act.

Primary reinforcers are shared, with some variance, by all humans and by many other species (Herrnstein, 1990). This fact and the physiological mechanisms underlying reinforcement that were later discovered in molecular biology point to a genetic basis (Loewenstein and Seung, 2006). In view of the physiological mechanisms, the motivational potential of deprivation and its satiation dynamics can be understood much better. The context in which this kind of response behavior is observed is repeated choices from the same set of actions distributed over a period of time (Herrnstein and Prelec, 1991). Focus is on the relative frequencies of the chosen actions, such as consumption activities (or, alternatively, their shares in the resources allocated by the actions). When behavior is in equilibrium, the frequency distribution of the actions (or resource shares) matches the size distribution of the average rewards experienced as a consequence of choosing these actions. This relationship is called the matching law (Herrnstein, 1997).[9]

If behavior is not in equilibrium, the relative frequencies with which the conditioned responses occur change as a result of reinforcement learning (instrumental conditioning). As a consequence, the frequency distribution of actions converges over time to the matching distribution.[10] Reinforcement learning is an innate mechanism which humans share with many other organisms.[11] It is complemented in the behaviorists' genuinely dynamic approach to motivation by the theory of conditioned reinforcement or conditioning learning, another innate, non-cognitive mechanism of behavior adaptation. Its economic significance lies in the role that it plays in how preferences are formed and change.[12]

The mechanism works as follows (Leslie, 1996, ch. 2.13). A test person happens to carry out two actions in a temporarily coincident fashion. One action is followed by primary reinforcement, the other action by a neutral experience. The longer the coincidence of the two actions last, the more likely the test person learns to associate the rewarding experience of primary reinforcement of the one action with the other action. As a consequence, the initially neutral action is reinforced as well, even if it no longer regularly coincides with the primarily reinforced action. A conditioned or secondary reinforcer is established. This means that the relative frequency with which the initially neutral action is chosen is increased, provided the coincidence of the two actions is occasionally corroborated. In economic terminology, a preference is formed in this way for an action for which there was no preference before (as discussed later in this section).

The innate motivational dispositions and the adaptation mechanism expressed respectively in primary reinforcing events and processes of instrumental conditioning and conditioned reinforcement suggest the following hypothesis: a person derives utility from actions depending on (or prefers them according to) their current potential to induce a rewarding sensory experience[13] either by reducing deprivation with respect to primary reinforcers or through conditioned secondary reinforcement. Thus, if a person's utility function is defined over actions rather than commodities, at least some of the arguments of the function can be connected with the sensory experience of reinforcers.

There is a limited number of innate primary reinforcers shared, with the usual genetic variance, by all humans (Leslie, 1996, chs. 1, 9). Hence, humans widely share the experience caused by the removal or reduction of aversive stimuli such as pain and fear. In numerous experiments, the removal or reduction of deprivation from, among others, aqueous liquids, sleeping, food, body heat, sensory and cognitive arousal of certain kind and strength, social status recognition, sex, care, and affection has also been identified as primary reinforcing instances. Following the preceding argument, utility is generated by actions – often involving goods and services purchased in the markets – that are capable of removing or reducing deprivation in these dimensions (or, to put it that way, such actions represent the objects of preference orderings). Correspondingly, in the short run, the probabilities for choosing actions and the changes of these probabilities reflect the variations in the relative degree of deprivation felt in the respective dimensions.

In addition, based on such innate primary reinforcers, a potentially very long chain of secondary reinforcers emerges over the history of conditioned reinforcement a person goes through. The arguments of the individual utility function therefore also reflect the varying structure of individually acquired secondary reinforcers. Unlike the widely shared primary reinforcers, this structure is highly idiosyncratic, except perhaps for some cultural commonalities in similarly socialized groups. Besides the individual specialization following the idiosyncratic paths of reinforcement learning (i.e., the convergence to an idiosyncratic matching equilibrium over diverse primary reinforcements), it is mainly because of the individually emerging secondary reinforcers that no two individual utility functions or preferences can be claimed to be exactly alike.

23.4 Acknowledging the Role of Cognition

In order to provide a behavioral foundation for the concepts of utility and preferences, and for their inherent dynamics, it has been suggested in the preceding to take recourse to elementary innate behavior dispositions and adaptation mechanisms. This suggestion is not meant to imply that the explanation should be confined to a behavioral approach. Since evolution has endowed humans with a unique cognitive capacity, their behavior can, on the one hand, also be motivated by deprivation of genuinely cognitive needs such as the need for autonomy (Hagger et al., 2006) or the need for a positive self-image and self-esteem (Pyszczynski et al., 2004; Dunning, 2007). On the other hand, cognitive motivational forces can also arise from deliberately setting oneself goals to be pursued (see Bargh et al., 2010). These cognitive motivational forces are no less important than the noncognitive ones for understanding what preferences people have and how they are formed and change.[14]

Goal setting and goal striving induce proactive and often creative behavior instead of the reactive conditioned responses to changing constraints. More precisely, cognitive deliberation intervenes into automatic stimulus-response reaction patterns so that observed behavior can deviate from what is to be expected by the latter. (Put differently, where such cognitive participation is absent, human behavior, particularly repeated routine activities, is guided by the noncognitive default behavior discussed in the previous section.)[15]

A very basic form of cognitively controlled behavior adaptation is model-based reinforcement learning guided by the motivational forces discussed in the previous section. It involves the formation of expectations about likely rewards and their use instead of experienced average reward alone (Daw, et al., 2011). More demanding forms involve declarative cognitive learning such as episodic learning based on recalled episodes and semantic learning based on the semantic representation of content (Burnham et al., 2015). Reflection, insight, inference, and judgment – the characteristics of deliberate decision-making and behavior adaptation – all involve declarative learning.

However, as acknowledged by attribution theory (van Raaij, 1985), the intervening cognitive influences are not only rather complex but also highly idiosyncratic. Moreover, the individual mental states and circumstances are difficult to assess from outside. It is therefore difficult to make them the object of hypotheses about generic effects that human cognition has on the economic transformation processes. But to derive hypotheses particularly with respect to motivational consequences, one can focus instead on the fact that human cognitive capacity is constrained. The reason for the constraint is that, in human perception, only a limited number of sensory stimuli, such as visual and acoustic signals, can spontaneously be processed in parallel into respective stores and be recognized (see Anderson, 2000, chs. 3, 6, 7). Unless attention is quickly paid to any such message, it will, however, be lost from memory.

If, as often, stimuli are offered in abundance to the sensory system, attention must selectively be allocated to competing processing demands. What pieces of incoming information grab attention depends on both their physically based attributes and their meaning-based attributes. The meaning associated with a particular piece of information often has affective connotations of liking or disliking. The latter reflect previous rewarding or aversive experiences ultimately based on reinforcing instances as discussed in the previous section. In the terminology chosen here, the affective connotations therefore relate to a person's preferences or utility function. More specifically, this means that the more a person has developed a preference (or an aversion) for a particular item or event, the more affective weight is attributed to its meaning. Accordingly, it is more likely that attention is allocated to incoming information relating to that item or event.

Concomitantly, there is also an effect on individual knowledge. If information related to a particular item or event attracts more attention, then this information tends to also be more frequently attended and rehearsed in thinking and, hence, to be better cognitively represented in action knowledge. Thus, two mutually reinforcing effects interact. One effect is the affection-driven impact of the current preferences on the selective allocation of attention and the incremental change of knowledge. The other effect is that of selective attention and gradually changing knowledge on the formation of individual preferences.

The more something is valued, the more it is also able to attract attention, to be rehearsed, and to be retrieved in long-term memory. Conversely, what is more often and persistently recognized as a positive stimulus, or as being related to one, tends, in turn, to be preferred increasingly (provided that a positively conditioning setting is maintained). The flip side of the coin in this process with self-augmenting features is the relative neglect of, and the rising ignorance with respect to, other information. The less frequently and the less intensively information has been recalled in the past, the more likely it is lost from long-term memory, that is, from current knowledge.

The implications of these specificities of the human information processing system for economic behavior in general and the transformation processes going on in the economy in particular will be highlighted in the next section. Before, however, a brief digression into a problem may be in order that is of great importance for the explanatory program of evolutionary economics. The problem – also arising at the cognitive level – is how to explain individual innovativeness, that is, the creation of new choice alternatives, and the motivation underlying it. Two different questions are involved: first, how is novelty produced; and second, why.

The second question is epistemologically less problematic and therefore easier to answer than the first.[16] Since neither the outcome of the search endeavor nor the time and effort it will need are known in advance, the search cannot be motivated by the expectation of specific outcomes (as implicitly assumed in optimal search models in economics). Search for novelty is motivated in a different way. In fact, there seem to be different forms of motivation corresponding with different forms of searching. One form is covered by the "satisficing" hypothesis (Siegel, 1957; March and Simon 1958, pp. 47–52). According to this hypothesis, the search motivation is dissatisfaction with the status quo. A person experiences a situation that falls short of the current aspiration level of that person, that is, the level that reflects a balance of the person's earlier successes and failures.

Imagine, to give an example, a producer who has a competitor. If the competitor comes up with an innovative move that causes the producer's revenues to fall whatever feasible reaction she can choose, then such a situation is likely to violate the person's current aspiration level. According to the satisficing hypothesis, a motivation to search for not yet known, better alternatives is triggered, notwithstanding the fact that it is unknown whether the search will indeed lead to better alternatives. The search motivation sooner or later vanishes, however, as search goes on without generating better options. The person's aspiration level gradually declines, and when it eventually converges to the best option presently known, the motivation to search vanishes.

A different motivation to search for novelty, and another form of searching, is highlighted by the taste-for-novelty hypothesis. This hypothesis assumes that humans find the experience of certain kinds of novelty a rewarding experience and deprivation from such sensory or cognitive arousal an aversive experience (Scitovsky, 1981). Hence, the more boring a life becomes, that is, the more deprivation rises in this dimension, the stronger the motivation to either consume (try) new source of sensory arousal, if available, or to actively search for, and generate the experience of, novelty.

Obviously, the two motivational hypotheses refer to different causal contexts and search contexts so that they may be considered complementary hypotheses. The satisficing hypothesis suggests that search for novelty is typically motivated by, and more frequently triggered in, situations of challenge or crisis (where these may be anticipated crises). The taste-for-novelty hypothesis predicts a short-term fluctuation of the search motivation between deprivation and satiation so that, on average, novelty is sought with a perhaps rather low but constant basic rate.

23.5 Pulling Things Together: The Example of Consumption

What follows from the evolutionary approach to economic behavior laid out in the previous sections for explaining the ongoing transformations of the economy? Because of space constraints, this question can only be discussed here in an exemplary fashion. The case to be chosen is that of the transformation of consumption behavior and the growth and structural change that follows from it. The underlying facts are as follows.

In the developed countries, per capita income has risen three to six times in real terms over the past century (Maddison 2001, ch. 1). Consumer spending has grown by a similar magnitude. The enormous expansion of consumer spending was not equally distributed over all consumption categories. To the contrary, there were massive changes in the compositions of goods and services consumed, particularly well documented for the United States (Chao and Utgoff, 2006). As empirical research over the past decades has consistently shown, income elasticities of the demand for different goods and services not only differ but also change over time, resulting in an unequal growth of consumption expenditures across different expenditure categories.[17] Moreover, within each of the consumption categories the quality of existing goods and services has constantly been varied and differentiated. An increasing variety of new goods and services has been introduced to the markets (Bils and Klenow, 2001).

What do these observations tell us? Does consumer spending grow without ever reaching a level of satiation if income continues to rise? What do the differences between the income elasticities (i.e., between the relative growth) of different expenditure categories mean? It is sometimes argued that vicarious entrepreneurs at the supply side of the markets always find ways to offer new or diversified goods and services that appeal to consumer preferences. Can the motivation to consume indeed be upheld in this way so that consumers not only substitute these innovations for previously bought products but also spend more? The reflections in the previous sections can help to answer these questions (see also Witt, 2017).

To recapitulate, one way in which consumers derive utility has been identified in the preceding with the reduction of deprivation in physiologically motivated activities such as drinking, eating, or alleviating pain. Consuming items such as beverages, food, or medicine that serve these purposes is consumption in the literal sense of "eating up" something. A significant feature of this kind of consumption is that it is subject to temporary physical satiation that constrains the amount consumed per period of time. The motivation for additional consumption vanishes as the satiation level is approached, but it reemerges as the organism's metabolism gradually uses up what was consumed. As real income increases, consumption per period of time can sooner or later be expanded so that the satiation level is always reached.[18]

If per capita income continues to grow, and if there is no qualitative change in the composition of consumption, per capita expenditures (per period of time) should therefore converge to an upper bound. Yet, this is not what can be observed. Food consumption is an obvious example. Food expenditures can indeed be shown to be income-inferior (see, e.g., Chao and Utgoff, 2006). However, an upper bound of food expenditures has not been observed so far. All household expenditure surveys show that, in absolute, price-deflated terms, per capita food expenditures still grow despite their relative decline.

There seem to be two main reasons for this phenomenon. First, some qualitative change in the composition of food consumption does occur with rising income. It involves consuming more complex and more expensive food stuff (Manig and Moneta, 2014). Second, wrestling with the satiation problem for decades, the food industry has developed strategies by which it tries to postpone the satiation effect. A prominent strategy consists in creating new products by which the sensory perception of a rewarding consumption experience can be enjoyed without rapidly approaching physiological satiation.[19]

Another strategy takes advantage of the fact that some innate needs are more easily satiable with increasing consumption than others. The innate need for sensory and cognitive arousal that has already been mentioned seems to be one such less easily satiable need (as discussed later in this chapter). If more income can be spent, food consumption does not necessarily only serve the need for calories and other physiologically required elements. It also contributes to satisfying the need for arousal. Cases in point are, for instance, gourmet food or restaurant cuisine sampling.

With rising income, food thus qualifies as a "combination good." If consumption of these goods is growing, satiation levels are usually not reached all at the same time in all need dimensions served by these goods. A motivation to further expand consumption of a combination good is thus upheld as long as not all of the involved needs are satiated. An industry facing signs of market saturation such as the food industry can therefore try to create additional demand by product differentiation and product innovations that add features appealing to not yet, or not at all, satiable needs.

For consumption items other than those directly eaten up, the explanation for a continued motivation to spend more on them is more involved. Consumption items such as, for example, beds or air conditioning facilities serve as means for satisfying physiologically determined needs: getting sleep or conveniently maintaining body temperature. A television set, to give another example, is one tool among many other options that serve the rewarding experience of a pleasant sensory arousal. (In itself, a television set is fairly useless, if it cannot be turned on to emit the entertaining services in the form of a flow of visual and acoustic information.)

Being deprived in the dimension of, say, sleep, body heat, or sensory arousal can thus motivate expenditure on consumption items such as beds, clothes, air conditioning, and television sets respectively which are able to provide the proper service. This means, however, that the motivation to consume the services and the motivation to purchase the means or tools in the first place are two different pairs of shoes. A physiologically conditioned temporary satiation level can only be reached with respect to the services, such as when one feels warm enough, has had enough sleep, or has had enough entertainment. For tools that provide such services, a corresponding upper consumption bound has to be established in the process of goal setting, that is, the cognitive reflection of the instrumental (means and ends) relationship between tools and services.

Accordingly, the motivation for purchasing such tools is strongly cognitively mediated, and deprivation regarding the services may not be the only factor that counts for it. Other factors may result from considerations concerning the securing of a redundant supply or of multiple availability (for instance, at different places in one's home). These factors often come into play through cognitive learning. The reason is that consumers need instrumental information for their purchasing decision: what features of the items service a need, and how do they do so? This is more true the more complex the consumption items with a tool function are (e.g., appliances, electronic equipment, cars, etc.).

Often a rather elaborate knowledge about the consumption technology is necessary and needs to be built up. This knowledge is not least obtained through communication with, and observation and imitation of, other consumers. However, knowledge of the consumption technology is as well offered by the producers through advertisements. If advertisements suggest reasons for acquiring products that consumers have not considered before, but find plausible, producers can succeed in influencing the consumers' cognitive goal setting and, thus, their motivation to spend (the "must-have" effect).

Given the selective nature of individual information processing discussed in the previous section, attention processes tend to shift from information less frequently and less intensely recognize towards information recognized more often and more intensely. At the same time, the perception and, in the longer run, consumption knowledge of items that continue to attract attention tend to become more detailed (the refinement effect). By repeated experience, a conditioned reinforcement is likely to build up that creates secondary reinforcement instances. Individual preferences extend to ever more details and attributes – attracting more attention into the same direction.

Because of the limitations of the individual information processing capacity, the already mentioned consequence of this process is specialization in consumption. One person may develop into a true motor sport fan following up, with an increasing preference and growing expertise, the most recent technical achievements of the motor car industry. Another person may develop into a similarly attentive opera fan with highly differentiated perception of, and preferences for, the qualitative differences in the music performance. Some people may develop into knowledgeable motor sport and opera fans simultaneously, but nobody can be a fan with differentiated perceptions of, and preferences for, everything.

The upshot of specialization and the simultaneous refinement of perception, knowledge, and preferences is that additional reasons can arise for a consumer to purchase, several times over, consumption items with tool functions, if their rising income enables them to do. These reasons may override the fact that the items provide one and the same service (or very similar ones) and that the service of every single item can only less intensely be used per period of time.[20]

In the attempt to explain why and in what way consumer spending is expanding seemingly unboundedly as long as income rises, the following causes have so far been suggested: first, the introduction of innovations by which satiating elements of goods and services are substituted or combined with less easily satiable elements in the form of combination goods; second, the refinement of preferences through consumer learning and the concomitant possibilities of creating ever new consumption motivation at the cognitive level by setting and striving for ever new goals one has happened to learn about. A no less important cause still needs to be addressed that is relevant for both directly and indirectly (toollike) consumed parts of consumption. This is the possibility that, for some innate needs, lasting satiation is not feasible and, hence, the corresponding motivation to consume persists independently of the level of consumption already reached.

One such innate need has already been mentioned, the need for sensory and cognitive arousal. As argued by Scitovsky (1976), it is difficult to remove deprivation in a lasting fashion because of an instability in the underlying deprivation-satiation mechanism. It is caused by hedonic adaptation (Frederik and Loewenstein, 1999), that is, a kind of stupefaction effect: the level of arousal connected with a particular consumption activity that successfully removed deprivation is degraded over time. To again reach a similar level requires new and/or stronger stimuli usually requiring higher consumption expenditures. The consequences of this motivational instability seem characteristic of significant parts of modern consumption such as the expenditures on entertainment and tourism. They have been growing much faster with rising income than average consumption expenditures and are likely to continue to do so (see Chao and Utgoff, 2006).

Another case in point is the motivation for expanding consumption caused by the need for social status recognition. Consumption items whose services are able to signal the desired status by distinguishing oneself from others (i.e., "tools" in the aforementioned sense; see, Witt 2011) may remove or reduce deprivation in this dimension. Yet, with rising average income, lower income groups are enabled to also acquire such consumption items. As a consequence, the status-distinguishing character of the corresponding consumption items is lost and deprivation of the need for social status recognition returns. To continue to be able to signal the desired social status differences by one's own consumption, other, and usually more expensive, status-signaling goods need to be consumed. A level of satiation can, if at all, only be upheld by continuously increasing expenditure on status goods – an unstable condition like in a weapon's race (Hirsch, 1978). This effect can be held responsible for the continuous growth of consumption expenditures on items such as cars, fashion accessories, and housing (Frank, 2011; Frank, Levine, and Dijk, 2014).

23.6 Conclusions

The economy has been changing, and continues to change, dramatically over time. These changes can be interpreted as an evolutionary process. The process is a cultural continuation of evolution in nature. It is driven by the economic agents' active and passive change behavior and enabled by ever-growing human knowledge. Such an interpretation therefore requires a thorough understanding of two questions. First, what inherited and learned motivations underlie active change behavior and the transformations that it causes? Second, how does economic behavior adapt to the ever-changing conditions? Some aspects of economic psychology are fundamentally important for answering these questions. They have been outlined in this chapter.

Like in evolutionary psychology, the present evolutionary approach to economics has started from acknowledging the role of the human genetic endowment. Yet, unlike in evolutionary psychology with its decision-theoretic focus, the focus has been directed here at the motivations and behavioral adaptation mechanisms underlying economic behavior. (This focus also differs from that of the recently emerging field of behavioral economics, which shares the decision-theoretic research interests with evolutionary psychology.) The reason for choosing this focus is that the role of economic behavior in the economic transformation process cannot fully be grasped by exploring the modes and contingencies of human decision-making alone.

Change behavior is based on the interactions between innate motivational dispositions and elementary adaptation mechanisms on the one hand. On the other hand, it is guided by the always selective, cognitive processes of deliberation and learning from experience and observation, both contributing to the ever-increasing and differentiated action knowledge. The implications of this interpretation have been derived in an exemplary fashion when explaining the evolution and growth of consumption.

Notes

1   See, e.g., the special issue of the *Journal of Evolutionary Economics*, 16, 5, 2006, on "Universal Darwinism."

2   In the aftermath of the debate on the relevance of sociobiology, particularly in evolutionary anthropology, and to the explanation of the altruism puzzles, evolutionary game theory has inspired a revival of yet another evolutionary approach; see, e.g., Bowles and Gintis (2011). However, this approach seems to have gained prominence in anthropology more so than in economics.

3   Schumpeter himself considered evolution a Darwinian concept that is irrelevant for the social sciences and opposed the construction of analogies to biology.

4   For example, Nelson and Winter (1982, ch. 5) assume that, because of their bounded rationality, economic agents have to operate on the basis of behavioral routines, particularly in the context of organizations. They submit that organizations such as business firms that have different routines perform well differently. Analogously to the principle of natural selection, less well-performing organizations should therefore be winnowed out until only the best-fit routines survive in the industry. Hence, the competitive transformations in the economy are interpreted as the result of changing relative frequencies in a "population" of more or less inert organizational routines, including routines by which innovations are researched and developed (Metcalfe, 2008).

5   In sociobiology, this hypothesis is extended to the animals' behavior in social interactions, such as the rearing of offspring, the joint stalking of prey, food

sharing, and support of mating and breeding activities (Wilson, 1975). These behaviors and the puzzle of "altruism" observable in the form of self-sacrifices that increase the survival chances of others can be explained in the theory of natural selection by means of either the concept of "inclusive fitness" (Hamilton,1964) or by a group selection hypothesis (Wilson and Wilson, 2007). Since competition for the scarce resources food, habitat space, access to mating partners, etc., is a basic condition of life, it can be argued that behavior genes related to the relevant social behavior have also been selected in early humans and are still part of the genetic endowment of modern humans.

6 In "primitive" human societies (as generally in animals), there is evidence for a positive correlation between the amount of scarce resources commanded and reproductive success; see, e.g., Chagnon and Irons (1979). In developed societies, in contrast, average real income increases and population growth are negatively correlated, as Maddison (2001, ch. 1) shows in a cross-country comparison for the period 1820 to 1998.

7 This means that, if they prefer a bundle x over x' and x' over another bundle x'', then they must not prefer x'' over x for any x, x', and x''.

8 As a matter of fact, revealed preference experiments were rarely conducted and where they were carried out they were rather inconclusive (see the discussion in Wong, 1978). The theory is actually only a platform now to logically deduce "operational" hypotheses about demand functions by which observable prices variations are related to observable variations in quantities demanded (see, e.g., Mas-Colell et al., 1995). As a consequence, individual utility functions and preference orderings now populate economic textbooks, yet it is left unexplained what the index number u represents and what the arguments in the functions stand for, i.e., what it is that people have preferences for.

9 If r_i is the number of times an action $i = 1,..., n$ is chosen over the period of time and R_i the *average* reward obtained from choosing it, the matching law thus postulates $r_i / \sum_i r_i = c_i (R_i / \sum_i R_i)^{\delta_i}$ for all i. $c_i > 0$, $\delta_i > 0$ are constants. The average reward R_i represents a moving average over the last few periods. If the reward related to one of the actions clearly dominates the rewards of all other actions, behavior eventually converges to choosing this action exclusively in a winner-takes-all fashion. See Staddon (2014) for a discussion and Davison and McCarthy (1988) for the experimental evidence for the matching law.

10 By comparison, utility maximization in economics posits that the frequency distribution of actions (or their resource shares) is equated to the distribution of marginal utility associated with the actions. This means that, according to the utility maximization hypothesis, the matching law results in a suboptimal distribution of choices whenever the values of average and marginal utility differ; see Herrnstein and Prelec (1991). However, if an action becomes more costly, its relative frequency decreases in both cases. Hence, reinforcement learning does not conflict with opportunity cost reasoning that is more momentous in economic theorizing than the concept of full rationality. It is sufficient, for example, for deriving the law of demand.

11 See Herrnstein (1989). In its noncognitive form, reinforcement learning is also called model-free reinforcement learning (see Daw and Tobler, 2013). Reinforcement learning can be conjectured to have been genetically fixed because of the behavioral plasticity it entails over an invariable, instinctive behavioral repertoire. However, there is also a variant of reinforcement learning that lacks this plasticity. It is based on a converging rather than moving average of experienced reward and is called habit learning (Glimcher, 2016).

12 Since the term "preference learning" is sometimes used in the neuro-economics literature in the different sense of finding out whether one likes the consequences of an action, given the present state of one's preferences, this term is not used here.

13 Bentham's hedonic interpretation of utility as a sensory perception that is observable and even measurable has recently been revived (Kahneman, Wakker, and Sarin, 1997; Kahneman, Diener, and Schwarz, 1999). However, Bentham's question of what generates utility (and, hence, explaining why people have preferences) has still largely been left out.

14 If goals are not assigned by others, their formation is an idiosyncratic process. Social-cognitive learning by imitation may play a role especially in the context of intergenerational transmission processes; see Volland (2013). The idiosyncratic nature of individual goal formation notwithstanding, communication, indoctrination, and imitation tend to cause a certain amount of interpersonal sharing of goals within interacting groups, i.e., cultural commonalities (Bandura, 1986, ch. 2).

15 In the context of goals striving, mental time traveling (Suddendorf and Corballis, 1997) can result in deliberate postponing of immediate reward by imagining future rewards instead. An instructive example of this kind of "self-efficacy" (Bandura, 1997) given by Kahneman et al. (1997) is voluntary colonoscopy treatment. It can cause patients intense pain – an aversive stimulus triggering a strong motivation to avoid or escape the pain. However, by recognizing the instrumental character of the treatment and by imagining the avoided future malady and risks for life, patients motivate themselves to tolerate the pain.

16 Regarding the first question, the key seems to be the brain's continually ongoing recombination activities of already known cognitive components. How these processes work is, however, still not well understood. Moreover, the inquiry into these issues is complicated by intricate epistemological problems. It may be conjectured that novel cognitive concepts emerge in a recombinatory act of "conceptual blending" (Fauconnier and Turner, 2002). See also the discussion in Witt (2009).

17 See Stone (1954); Houthakker and Taylor (1966); Deaton and Muellbauer (1980); Lebergott (1993). Let I and y denote income and the amount spent on a consumption good respectively. Assuming that a differentiable function $y = y(I)$ exists, the definition of the income elasticity of demand η for that goods is $\eta = (dy/dI) / (y/I)$. The good is said to be income-inferior if $\eta < 1$ (income-superior if $\eta > 1$). This means that, with a marginal increase in disposable income, the percentage change in spending on that good is smaller (larger) than the percentage change of income.

18 If consumption is expanded beyond that level, the purchased items are either no longer completely consumed ("eaten up") in the literal sense but are partly wasted, and/or overconsumption leads to unhealthy consequences such as, e.g., obesity in the case of food.

19 A case in point is calorie intake. Food stuffs in which high-calorie sugar is replaced by artificial, low-calorie sweeteners still contain the motivating sweetness signal yet allow people to consume more of them before satiation in terms of calories is reached (see Ruprecht, 2005). A typical example is Diet Coke. A similar role is played by artificial substitutes such as aromas or non-cholesterol fats replacing easily satiable components, or by a taste-neutral removal of such components like, for instance, alcohol in beer or caffeine in coffee, which tend to delimit their consumption.

20 If there is a satiation level with regard to the services in some deprivation dimension, and if multiple purchases of the same tool or similar ones exceed the number technically necessary to furnish the satiation level in the services, this simply results in a decreasing average rate of using the services provided by each single tool. For example, since only one pair of shoes (a tool for providing pain protection and body warmth as services) can be worn at the same time, purchasing several pairs of shoes means that on average each single pair of shoes is used less intensely.

23.7 References

Alchian, A.A. (1950), "Uncertainty, Evolution, and Economic Theory," *Journal of Political Economy.* 58(4), 211–221.

Anderson, J.R. (2000), *Cognitive Psychology and its Implications.* 5thed., New York: Worth.

Bandura, A. (1986), *Social Foundations of Thought and Action: A Social Cognitive Theory.* Englewood Cliffs: Prentice-Hall.

Bandura, A. (1997), *Self-efficacy: The Exercise of Control.* New York: Freeman.

Bargh, J.A., Gollwitzer, P.M. and Oettingen, G. (2010), "Motivation," in: S. Fiske, D. Gilbert, G. Lindzey (eds.), *Handbook of Social Psychology*, 5th ed., New York: Wiley, 268–316.

Bils, M. and Klenow, P.J. (2001), "Quantifying Quality Growth," *American Economic Review*, 91, 1006–1030.

Bowles, S. and Gintis, H. (2011), *A Cooperative Species: Human Reciprocity and Its Evolution*, Princeton: Princeton University Press.

Burnham, T., Lea, S.E.G., Bell, A., Gintis, H., Glimcher, P.W., Kurzban, R., Lades, L., McCabe, K., Panchanathan, K., Teschl, M., and Witt, U. (2016), "Evolutionary Behavioral Economics," in: D. S. Wilson and A. Kirman (eds.), *Complexity and Evolution: A New Synthesis for Economics*, Cambridge, MA: MIT Press, 113–144.

Buss, D.M. (2003), *Evolutionary Psychology: The New Science of the Mind*, Boston: Allyn and Bacon.

Camerer, C.F. and Loewenstein, G. (2004), "Behavioral Economics: Past, Present, Future," in: C.F. Camerer, G. Loewenstein, M. Rabin, *Advances in Behavioral Economics*, Princeton: Princeton University Press, 3–51.

Chagnon, N.A. and Irons, W., eds. (1979), *Evolutionary Biology and Human Social Behavior: An Anthropological Perspective*, North Scituate: Duxbury Press.

Chao, E.L. and Utgoff, K.P. (2006), *100 Years of U.S. Consumer Spending: Data for the Nation, New York City, and Boston*, Report 991, U.S. Bureau of Labor Statistics, www.bls.gov/opub/uscs/report991.pdf

Davison, M. and McCarthy, D. (1988), *The Matching Law: A Research Review*, Hillsdale: Erlbaum.

Daw, N.D., Gershman, S.J., Seymour, B., Dayan, P., and Dolan, R.J. (2011), "Model-based Influences on Humans' Choices and Striatal Prediction Errors," *Neuron*, 69, 1204–1215.

Daw, N.D. and Tobler P.N. (2013), "Value Learning Through Reinforcement: the Basics of Dopamine and Reinforcement Learning," in: P. Glimcher, E. Fehr (eds.), *Neuroeconomics*, New York: Elsevier, 283–298.

Deaton, A. and Muellbauer, J. (1980), *Economics and Consumer Behavior*, Cambridge: Cambridge University Press.

Dugatkin, L.A. (2003), *Principles of Animal Behavior*, New York: W. W. Norton & Company.

Dunning, D. (2007), "Self-image Motives and Consumer Behavior: How Sacrosanct Self-beliefs Sway References in the Marketplace. *Journal of Consumer Psychology*. 17(4): 237–249.

Fauconnier, G. and Turner, M. (2002), *The Way We Think: Conceptual Blending and the Mind's Hidden Complexities*, New York: Basic Books.

Frank, R.H. (2011), *The Darwin Economy*, New Jersey: Princeton University Press.

Frank, R.H., Levine, A.S., Dijk, O. (2014), "Expenditure Cascades," *Review of Behavioral Economics* 1, 55–73.

Frederik, S. and Loewenstein, G. (1999), "Hedonic Adaptation," in: D. Kahneman, E. Diener, N. Schwartz (eds.), *Well-Being: The Foundations of Hedonic Psychology*, New York. Russell Sage, 302–329.

Gigerenzer, G. and Goldstein D.G. (1996), "Reasoning the Fast and Frugal Way: Models of Bounded Rationality," *Psychological Review*, 103, 650–669.

Glimcher, P. (2016), "Proximate Mechanism of Individual Decision-Making Behavior," in: D.S. Wilson and A. Kirman (eds.), *Complexity and Evolution: A New Synthesis for Economics*, Cambridge, MA.: MIT Press, 85–96.

Hagger, M.S., Chatzisaranti, N.L.D., and Harris, J. (2006), "From Psychological Need Satisfaction to Intentional Behavior: Testing a Motivational Sequence in Two Behavioral Contexts," *Personality and Social Psychology Bulletin*, 32, 131–148.

Hamilton, W.D. (1964), "The Genetical Evolution of Social Behavior I," *Journal of Theoretical Biology*, 7, 1–16.

Hanusch, H. and Pyka, A., eds. (2007), *Elgar Companion to Neo-Schumpeterian Economics*, Cheltenham: Edward Elgar.

Herrnstein, R.J. (1989), "Darwinism and Behaviorism: Parallels and Intersections," in: Grafen, A. (ed.). *Evolution and Its Influence*. Oxford: Clarendon Press, 35–61.

Herrnstein, R.J. (1990), "Behavior, Reinforcement, and Utility," *Psychological Sciences*, 4, 217–221.

Herrnstein, R.J. (1997), *The Matching Law*. Cambridge, MA: Harvard University Press.

Herrnstein, R.J. and Prelec, D. (1991), "Melioration: A Theory of Distributed Choice," *Journal of Economic Perspectives*, 5, 137–156.

Hirsch, F. (1978), *Social Limits to Growth*. Cambridge, MA: Harvard University Press.

Hodgson, G. M. (2004), *The Evolution of Institutional Economics*, London: Routledge.

Houthakker, H.S. and Taylor, L.D. (1966), *Consumer Demand in the United States 1929–1970*, Cambridge, MA: Harvard University Press.

Kahneman, D. (2011), *Thinking, Fast and Slow*. London: Allen Lane.

Kahneman, D., Diener, E., Schwarz, N., eds. (1999), *Well-Being: The Foundations of Hedonic Psychology*, New York: Russell Sage.

Kahneman, D., Wakker, P.P., and Sarin, R. (1997), "Back to Bentham? Explorations of Experienced Utility," *Quarterly Journal of Economics*, 112, 375–405.

Lebergott, S. (1993), *Pursuing Happiness: American Consumers in the Twentieth Century*, Princeton: Princeton University Press.

Leslie J.C. (1996), *Principles of Behavioral Analysis*, Amsterdam: Harwood Academic Publishers.

Loewenstein, Y. and Seung, H.S. (2006), "Operant Matching Is a Generic Outcome of Synaptic Plasticity Based on the Covariance Between Reward and Neutral Activity," *PNAS*, 1003, 15224–15229.

Maddison, A. (2001), *The World Economy: A Millenium Perspective*, Paris: OECD.

Manig, C. and Moneta, A. (2014), "More or Better? Measuring Quality vs. Quantity in Food Consumption", *Journal of Bioeconomics*, 16, 155–178.

March, J.G. and Simon, H.A. (1958), *Organizations*, New York: Wiley.

Mas-Colell, A., Whinston, M.D., and Green, J.R. (1995), *Microeconomic Theory*, Oxford: Oxford University Press.

Metcalfe, J.S. (1998), *Evolutionary Economics and Creative Destruction*, London: Routledge.

Metcalfe, J.S. (2008), "Accounting for Economic Evolution: Fitness and the Population Method," *Journal of Bioeconomics*, 10, 23–50.

Nelson, R.R. and Winter, S.G. (1982), *An Evolutionary Theory of Economic Change*, Cambridge, MA: Harvard University Press.

Pyszczynski, T., Greenberg, J., Solomon, S., Arndt, J., and Schimel, J. (2004), "Why Do People Need Self-Esteem? A Theoretical and Empirical Review," *Psychological Bulletin*, 130, 435–468.

Raaij, W.F. van (1985), "Attribution of Causality to Economic Actions and Events," *Kyklos*, 38, 3–19.

Ruprecht, W. (2005), "The Historical Development of the Consumption of Sweeteners: A Learning Approach," *Journal of Evolutionary Economics*, 15, 247–272.

Samuelson, P.A. (1947), *Foundations of Economic Analysis*, Cambridge, MA: Harvard University Press.

Scitovsky, T. (1976), *The Joyless Economy*, Oxford: Oxford University Press.

Scitovsky, T. (1981), "The Desire for Excitement," *Kyklos*, 34, 3–13.

Sen, A. (1977), "Rational Fools: a Critique of the Behavioral Foundations of Economic Theory," *Philosophy and Public Affairs*, 6, 317–344.

Siegel, S. (1957), "Level of Aspiration and Decision Making," *Psychological Review*, 64, 253–262.

Suddendorf, T. and Corballis, M.C. (1997), "Mental Time Travel and the Evolution of the Human Mind", *Genetic, Social, and General Psychological Monographs*, 123, 133–167.

Staddon, J.E.R. (2014), "On Choice and the Law of Effect," *International Journal of Comparative Psychology*, 27, 569–584.

Stone, J.R.N. (1954), *Measurement of Consumer Expenditures and Behavior in the United Kingdom*, Vol. I, Cambridge: Cambridge University Press.

Veblen, T. (1898), "Why Is Economics Not an Evolutionary Science?" *Quarterly Journal of Economics*, 12, 373–397.

Volland, B. (2013), "On the Intergenerational Transmission of Preferences," *Journal of Bioeconomics*, 15, 217–249.

Warke, T. (2000), "Mathematical Fitness in the Evolution of the Utility Concept from Bentham to Jevons to Marshall," *Journal of History of Economic Thought*, 22, 3–23.

Wilson, D. S. and Wilson, E. O. (2007), "Rethinking the Theoretical Foundation of Sociobiology," *The Quarterly Review of Biology* 82, 327–348.

Wilson, E.O. (1975), *Sociobiology: The New Synthesis*, Cambridge, MA: Belknap Press.

Wilson, E.O. (1998), *Consilience: The Unity of Knowledge*, New York: Knopf.

Winter, S.G. (1964), "Economic 'Natural Selection' and the Theory of the Firm," *Yale Economic Essays*, 4, 225–272.

Witt, U. (2008), "What is Specific about Evolutionary Economics?" *Journal of Evolutionary Economics*, 18, 547–575.

Witt, U. (2009), "Propositions about Novelty," *Journal of Economic Behavior and Organization*, 70, 311–320

Witt, U. (2011), "Symbolic Consumption and the Social Construction of Product Characteristics," *Structural Change and Economic Dynamics*, 21, 17–25.

Witt, U. (2017), "The Evolution of Consumption and Its Welfare Effects," *Journal of Evolutionary Economics*, 27, 273–293.

Wong, S. (1978), *The Foundations of Paul Samuelson's Revealed Preference Theory*, London: Routledge & Kegan Paul.

PART VII

New Horizons

24 Motivation and Awards

Bruno S. Frey and Jana Gallus

24.1 Introduction

Money is necessary to survive. Moreover, income is taken to be an indicator of success. Pay-for-performance has been widely used to incentivize employees to put in more effort at work. Economic theory has been built on the idea that monetary incentives are primordial instruments to induce people to work. Accordingly, the focus has for a long time exclusively been on extrinsic motivation, while intrinsic motivation has either been totally disregarded, attributed to a "do-gooder" ideology, or at best taken to be an irrelevant constant.

With the advent of economic psychology and behavioral economics (for a review of each respectively, see Kirchler and Holzl, 2017, and Thaler, 2016), it has increasingly been understood that for many activities – most importantly in the voluntary sector, but also in normal economic areas – intrinsic motivation is crucial. Even more significantly, it has been understood that intrinsic motivation may be undermined by extrinsic interventions. In particular, this "crowding-out effect" (Frey, 1994), as it is called in economics, applies when monetary payments are used for activities partly or mainly based on intrinsic motivation.

As a consequence, instruments beyond monetary compensation, enhancing rather than destroying intrinsic motivation, have received increasing interest by economists. As individuals are known to crave recognition by their peers and a wider public, awards present a suitable instrument to raise intrinsic motivation: awards specifically honor persons for performing above and beyond the call of duty.

Our chapter presents a survey of the analyses undertaken in economics with respect to human motivation and awards. We focus on empirical work in the form of experiments as well as econometric analyses in the field. The first part is devoted to motivational crowding effects, and the second part focuses on awards.

24.2 Motivation in Economic Theory

The "economic approach to human behavior" (Becker, 1976; Frey, 1999), which has allowed economics to enter and shape the intellectual territory of other disciplines (see also Lazear's discussion of "economic imperialism"; Lazear, 2000a), has skillfully applied the relative price effect. It stipulates that an incentive from outside induces an extrinsically motivated person to act in a predictable manner. All other things being equal, an action becoming more expensive is undertaken less than if the price rise had not occurred. In contrast, psychologists focus more on the intrinsic motives leading a person to action. People are intrinsically motivated when they behave in a certain way because they want to do so by their own volition and inherent interest in the task, or because they are induced to do so due to an internalized social norm.

Economists do not normally differentiate between various sources of motivation. Motivation is assumed to be the underlying preference for the reward that is associated with a particular action. Intrinsic motivation is taken to be an exogenously given constant, and is therefore often neglected. The theory of motivation crowding bridges the gap between the standard economic approach based on extrinsic motivation and psychological theories considering intrinsic motivation. Motivation crowding theory proposes a systematic relationship between extrinsic and intrinsic motivation.

Two different branches of literature in the social sciences suggest that monetary rewards may crowd out intrinsic motivation. In his book *The Gift Relationship* (1970), Richard Titmuss argued that paying for blood undermines intrinsic social values and as a result diminishes or even eliminates people's willingness to donate blood. His proposition was not based on any systematic empirical evidence. A second strand of literature was developed in psychology: under specific conditions, extrinsic rewards undermine intrinsic motivation (Deci, 1971; Deci and Flaste, 1995; Deci and Ryan, 1985). Providing monetary rewards for more and better work may result in people reducing, rather than increasing, their work effort. There are "hidden costs of rewards." These psychologically based theories on intrinsic motivation have over the last decades been integrated into economic theory (Bénabou and Tirole, 2003; Frey, 1992, 1997). The "hidden costs of rewards" have been generalized in two dimensions:

1. Extrinsic rewards (material and symbolic) as well as sanctions may undermine intrinsic motivation. As the polar opposite to intrinsic motivation, high-powered rewards may also lead to manipulation as well as choking under pressure, whereby increased effort leads to lower performance.
2. Extrinsic rewards impair image motivation because they put the motives underlying one's behavior into question; this holds in particular for prosocial behaviors.

The "crowding-out effect" belongs to the most important anomalies in economics. It proposes the exact opposite effect to the relative price effect on which standard economics is founded. In particular, increasing monetary incentives does not necessarily raise effort, but may even decrease effort, thus leading to a counterproductive outcome. The relative price effect may be reversed if there is intrinsic and/or image motivation that is crowded out.

This chapter surveys the theoretical and especially the empirical evidence on crowding-out and crowding-in effects on intrinsic motivation (Section 24.3). Section 24.4 considers awards as an important case of a positive external intervention systematically affecting individual behavior in the economy. The following section looks at awards in the public realm, that is, at awards such as state orders or prizes in the academic sector.

24.3 Crowding Effects

24.3.1 Processes

The possible negative impact of external interventions on intrinsic motivation has been attributed to three psychological processes. Firstly, self-determination can be impaired. Individuals perceiving an external intervention to impair their self-determination experience diminished autonomy. Their intrinsic motivation risks being substituted by extrinsic control. The locus of control is shifted from inside the person to forces outside the person. Individuals following their intrinsic motivation may feel overjustified if they are led to behave in a specific way by an outside intervention, and in response may lower their intrinsic motivation. They can attribute their past behavior to the existence of the reward, even if that behavior had originally emanated from intrinsic motivation to perform the task. Secondly, self-esteem is reduced. A person's intrinsic motivation is rejected if an outside intervention suggests that the actor's motivation (or ability) is insufficient (Bénabou and Tirole, 2003). The person perceives that his or her involvement and competence are either not appreciated or indeed lacking. Related to the undermining of self-esteem is the crowding out of image motivation. People cannot display their involvement if an activity is rewarded from outside, or if they are ordered to do so. Due to the forgone opportunity to gain social esteem, individuals put in less effort. Note, however, that the image motivation being crowded out is distinct from intrinsic motivation. Thirdly, the fact that an extrinsic reward needs to be offered at all may signal that the task as such must be uninteresting.

The first two processes determine the directions in which crowding effects take place:

a. External interventions *crowd out intrinsic motivation* if people perceive them to be *controlling*. Self-determination and self-esteem are impaired. The individuals respond by reducing their intrinsic motivation in the activity.
b. External interventions may *crowd in intrinsic motivation* if people perceive them to be *supportive*. Self-esteem is fostered. Individuals perceive a larger extent of freedom to act, enlarging their self-determination.

24.3.2 Policy Implications of Motivation Crowding

Crowding effects may be important in many different economic realms. An important case is the labor market, where the effect of higher pay on work effort is in question. This holds most strongly in the case of pay-for-performance systems, which have become an almost uncontested instrument for eliciting higher performance from employees. This trend is well supported by the theoretical economic literature. Following principal–agency theory, the incentives of employer and employee can be aligned when the latter's pay is performance-based. Empirical studies for a special work environment (mounting glass windshields in cars) seem to support the effectiveness of pay-for-performance (Lazear, 2000b). However, generalizing these findings to other work contexts, and in particular those involving complex tasks, it was wrongly concluded that price incentives have a general positive effect on work performance. Motivation crowding theory serves as a warning against premature generalizations of conclusions based on effects found in simple task environments, where intrinsic motivation is absent or at least weak. As a consequence, crowding-out effects are far less likely to occur than under complex working conditions.

In environmental policy, pricing instruments, such as pollution charges, may drive out environmental ethics. In social policy, monetary incentives may crowd out the need to assume responsibility for one's own fate. Monetary subsidies may negatively impact entrepreneurship and innovation. Crowding out may also be relevant in contract theory, where relational or "psychological contracts" rely on intrinsic motivation. (Further examples are provided in Frey, 1997, and Osterloh and Frey, 2000). To summarize, standard economics, which largely relies on a skillful application of the price effect, tends to overrate the power of payment-based instruments and policies because it neglects intrinsic motivation and its variability.

24.3.3 Empirical Evidence

The relevance and direction of crowding effects on intrinsic motivation have been analyzed in extensive laboratory and field experiments (see Frey and Jegen, 2001).

24.3.3.1 Laboratory Evidence
Psychologists have undertaken a large number of laboratory experiments on crowding effects.

A meta-study collects the evidence on the "hidden cost" phenomenon in social psychology (Deci, Koestner, and Ryan, 1999). The reported results are based on 128 controlled experiments and suggest consistent effects of extrinsic rewards on intrinsic motivation. Tangible rewards are shown to have a significant negative effect on intrinsic motivation for interesting tasks. On the other hand, supportive verbal rewards have a significant positive effect on intrinsic motivation. However, tangible rewards do not crowd out intrinsic motivation if they are unexpected. The survey concludes that rewards are able to influence people's behavior in a systematic way. On average, rewards tend to undermine self-regulation, and people take less responsibility for motivating themselves.

Economists have also tested motivation crowding theory in laboratory experiments. They find that sanctions may crowd out human altruism (Fehr and Rockenbach, 2003). Crowding effects in contract enforcement have also been analyzed in the framework of evolutionary repeated contract game models (Bohnet, Frey, and Steffen, 2001). The experiment inquired how the participants' motivation and behavior evolved depending on the institutional setting. When contracts were closely enforced, first movers could rely on the fines imposed by the legal system to deter second movers from breaching the contract. Institutional trust replaced personal trust. In contrast, low levels of legal enforcement, that is, a small probability of getting caught when breaching a contract, crowded in the intrinsic motives to treat others fairly. When first movers offered a contract even though both parties were aware that there was only a low probability of being fined for noncompliance, they signaled that they trusted that the second mover would not breach the contract. The analysis reveals that the number of contracts offered rose in the course of the game, which contradicts expectations in standard economics. The possible negative effect on individual intrinsic motivation of externally imposed institutions is also found in a series of other experiments designed as contributions to a pure public good (Frohlich and Oppenheimer, 1998).

24.3.3.2 *Field Evidence*

Barkema (1995) studies the behavior of managers as agents in a firm. When managers are controlled by the parent company, that is, by an impersonal relationship, managers' performance is raised because intrinsic motivation is little or not affected. In contrast, when the firm's chief executive officer controls the managers, there is a personalized relationship that tends to reduce the agents' effort. The external intervention shifts the locus of control toward external motivation. When agents perceive that their superiors do not acknowledge their competence, their intrinsic motivation is crowded out.

Intrinsic motivation is of great importance when it comes to volunteering (Frey and Goette, 1999). Monetary rewards are found to undermine volunteering. The size of the effect is considerable. Interventions giving money or commands were found to backfire, resulting in less volunteering.

Practitioners seem to be aware of the possible traps of pay-for-performance schemes (see the survey by Bewley, 1995). They have experienced that external interventions via monetary incentives can be perceived as controlling, and that they may undermine intrinsic motivations in the form of work morale or creativity (on the latter, see also the research by Amabile, 1998). Managers are aware that workers have so many opportunities to take advantage of employers that it is unwise to only employ coercion and financial incentives as motivators.

This is in particular the case where performance cannot be perfectly observed (e.g., in the case of creative work).

Crowding effects are also of great importance with respect to social and public policies.

Day-care centers face the problem that parents sometimes arrive late to pick up their children. This forces teachers to stay after the official closing time. The economic approach suggests introducing a fine on parents collecting children late. Such a punishment is predicted to induce parents to pick up their children on time. However, in a well-known study, Gneezy and Rustichini (2000a) analyzed the effects of a monetary fine that was introduced by a day-care center to deter parents from collecting children late. The authors found that, contrary to the declared goal, after some time, the number of late-coming parents rose substantially. The monetary fine seems to have transformed the relationship between parents and teachers from a nonmonetary into a monetary one. The parents' intrinsic motivation to respect the time schedules was crowded out. The teachers were now perceived to be "paid" for the disamenity of having to stay longer. Parents' intrinsic motivation seems to have been crowded out for good since the number of late-coming parents remained constant at the lower level even after the fine was removed. (See also Gneezy and Rustichini, 2000b, for another study by the same authors, where low monetary incentives were found to lead to lower performance compared to offering no incentives at all.)

Signs for crowding-out effects were also found in the airline industry (Austin and Hoffer Gittell, 1999). Carriers use a variety of instruments to deal with delays. Principal–agency theory suggests to attribute a single delay as exactly as possible to its source. Evidence shows that this principle is negatively correlated with the airline's on-time flight performance. The most successful company in terms of departing on time was a carrier that used the general term "team delay" to indicate the source of a delay caused by the personnel, independent of whether a single employee, or one specific unit, was in fact responsible. A loose attribution to the source of delay seems to have crowded in the employees' intrinsic motivation to help out other units and groups.

A further study on crowding effects reports results of an econometric test of the consequences of offering communes compensation in return for accepting to host hazardous waste disposal facilities. The dilemma is known as the "Not In My BackYard," or NIMBY, problem. In general terms, there is a wide consensus that such projects are worth being undertaken. However, no commune is prepared to tolerate the vicinity of such projects. Frey and Oberholzer-Gee (1997) analyzed the reaction to monetary compensation offered for a nuclear waste repository in Switzerland. A survey among the population of the community that was chosen as a site by the national government revealed that half of the respondents (50.8 percent) agreed to having the nuclear waste repository built in their community, despite the fact that it was mostly seen as a heavy burden for the residents of the host community. The level of acceptance dropped to 24.6 percent when compensation was offered. The offer of money changed the perceived nature of the siting procedure. It reduced the intrinsic motivation to permit the construction of such a facility. A similar effect was found for the siting of a nuclear repository in Nevada, where higher tax rebates failed to increase acceptance (Kunreuther and Easterling, 1990).

Crowding effects also occur as a result of regulations. An example is provided by a field experiment conducted in Colombia, South America, where a regulatory approach was imposed from the outside with the aim of preserving the local tropical forest. However, this intervention was shown to have produced more egoistic behavior on the part of the population involved, and the destruction of the forest ended up being intensified (Cardenas, Stanlund, and Willis, 2000).

Crowding theory is also relevant to how constitutional and other legal rules affect individual citizens. Intrinsic motivation in the form of civic virtue is supported when public laws convey the notion that citizens are trusted, which is reflected in extensive rights and possibilities for political participation. In contrast, a constitution conveying a fundamental distrust in its citizens, and seeking to discipline them, crowds out civic virtue and the observation of basic laws. The effects of such a distrustful constitution are visible in various ways. The citizens are dissatisfied with the political system and respond by breaking the constitution and its laws whenever they expect to be able to do so at a low cost (Frey, 1997). Distrustful public laws reduce tax morale and, as a consequence, may lead to tax evasion (Feld and Frey, 2002). Econometric research shows that the extent of taxpaying cannot be explained in a satisfactory way without taking tax morale into account. Similarly, government employees in many countries are prepared to work for a significantly lower salary than their peers in the private sector. This may be attributed to the higher intrinsic motivation of people seeking employment in the public sector. There are teachers who want to work in state schools because they believe in the virtue of public education for society. The increasing tendency to closely supervise government employees and to curtail their discretion, however, risks crowding out their work morale.

A cumulative body of research indicates that people's perceptions of how they are treated by the authorities strongly affect their evaluation of authorities and laws, and their willingness to cooperate with them. Citizens considering the constitution and its laws, and the authorities upholding them, to be fair and to treat them respectfully tend to be more compliant than those with more negative perceptions of government (Tyler, 2006). In contrast, the extensive use of adversary institutions for resolving public conflicts tends to crowd out civic virtue (Kelman, 1992).

24.4 Awards

Awards express appreciation in public, and thus simultaneously provide *honor* and *esteem* to the recipient. They can take many different forms, ranging from orders, crosses, medals, decorations, trophies, certificates to honorary titles, and prizes. Awards can be found in virtually all spheres of life, extending their reach far beyond politics and the military. There are awards in the humanitarian sector, architecture, arts and entertainment (film, television, radio, dance, music, literature, design), education, journalism, advertising, games, and sports, as well as in academia.

Awards provide an alternative to the monetary bonuses that over the past few years have come under strong attack in the popular media as well as among scholars (e.g., Frey and Osterloh, 2012). In the top echelons of many parts of society, including the financial and business sectors, medical professions, sports, and academia, performance pay has sharply increased. This has led to grave concerns about the increasingly unequal distribution of income. Awards and public recognition can play a significant role as they offer an alternative to monetary pay.

There are mixed reactions to awards and honors in some quarters. An ironic example is *The Economist* (2004), which featured an article on the British honors system entitled "A Ridiculous, Outdated System That Cannot Be Improved Upon" (p. 31). We argue that it is important to draw a distinction between different forms of awards, and that in several regards awards are an important complement to the incentives normally considered in economics.

Awards have prominent advantages over monetary compensation in several respects. Most importantly, we argue that awards may *support intrinsic motivation* because the giver explicitly expresses that the recipient has performed well and with distinction. For that reason, they are less likely to crowd out intrinsic motivation. Awards have greater *visibility* than bonuses and other monetary rewards since they are given in public and often draw media attention. This visibility makes the signal of recognition more credible as the award givers put their own reputation at risk. We therefore argue that awards express recognition far better than mere transfers of money. These automated money transfers not only lack any emotional and personal context; they are also oftentimes a strictly private matter because many organizations prohibit employees to reveal their salary and bonuses to colleagues. A third advantage of awards is that they can be bequeathed for *broad achievements*, and the performance they honor need only be vaguely specified. With awards, the givers are able to recognize performance that is difficult or impossible to exactly define and measure. This applies in particular to future performance whose content cannot be determined beforehand. Such vagueness is typical for qualified occupations in modern economies. Only menial work can be exactly defined, measured, and given a one-dimensional value.

A further advantage of awards is that they can strengthen *employees' commitment* to the organization honoring them. The intrinsic motivation to perform well and in the interest of the employer is strengthened. In contrast, performance pay conveys the notion to the employees that all that matters is to reach the criteria in order to get the bonus. The content of work becomes secondary. As a consequence, employees are induced to disregard everything not covered by the criteria imposed – even if they know this is bad for the organization they work for. That this matters greatly was well expressed by

Napoléon Bonaparte, who reportedly stated: "Le ruban d'un ordre lie plus fortement que des chaînes d'or." He believed in the capacity of awards to produce loyalty above and beyond material incentives.

Award givers may of course also strategically exploit the bond of loyalty established. They can put designated awardees in an uncomfortable and even dangerous situation by presenting them with an award. This situation occurs when the would-be recipient does not agree with, or even opposes, the donor's ideas, behavior, or policies, and yet has to accept the award in public. Outsiders interpret acceptance as a sign of association and agreement with the donor. However, in particular in authoritarian or dictatorial states, refusal of such an "honor" risks angering the giver and can be denounced as a disloyal action toward the state. Not accepting an award may therefore produce heavy costs for the person refusing the honor. Under such conditions, the giver has a strategic advantage when using awards. However, the *bond of loyalty* between the givers and recipients can also affect the former. The givers are to some extent held accountable for the recipients' conduct as they considered the latter worthy of being honored. At the same time, a public refusal to accept the award has negative reputational effects on the giver if the person refusing the award is held in esteem by others.

Another function of awards is that they can be used to *structure and shape a field*. This applies, for instance, to the Grammy Awards (Anand and Watson, 2004), whose verdict of what is to be deemed high quality has had a great influence on the music industry. In the reasons given for bequeathing an award as well as in the ceremony accompanying the award's conferral, the givers have an opportunity to communicate what is important to them, what should be achieved, and how this should be done. In that sense, awards have an expressive function that givers can use to influence the values people hold. Bequeathing an award also provides a suitable opportunity for *networking* with persons engaged in the same or related fields. As a result, joint actions can be undertaken, therewith furthering the goals of the award-giving organization.

Awards are a *low cost* way to honor persons as well as organizations. The cost can be as low as that of a piece of ribbon given at an award ceremony. While such ceremonies may take an opulent form (such as in the case of the Nobel Prizes), awards are often given in the context of a meeting primarily serving another goal (e.g., an annual assembly or employees and clients). Moreover, awards as such are *not subject to taxation* (they are only taxed if accompanied by money, as is the case, for instance, with the Nobel Prize). In contrast, monetary bonuses and other material rewards, including fringe benefits such as expensive company cars or luxurious apartments, are taxed. This is most relevant when the marginal tax rate that applies is high.

Finally, awards provide *private benefits* to the decision makers (e.g., jury members) and award givers and sponsors. The media and the social attention gained raise their status in society, making them coveted in particular among those who hope to receive the award in the future. Oftentimes, the decision makers also reap private reputational benefits by having their names associated with that of a notable award recipient.

These characteristics of awards put them in contrast to mere pay raises. Income, of course, is a necessary part of work and cannot be dispensed with. However, just relying on money to foster people's motivation is a mistaken approach, in businesses as well as in society.

There are other alternatives to using money as an incentive, besides awards. One is *personal praise* or *positive feedback* given to persons acting in a way desired by the superiors. While this is a form of appreciation often valued by the recipients, it has little or no visibility among coworkers and the public at large. For personal praise and feedback, the status effect and the attention received in the general public are considerably lower than for awards.

Another motivator is *gifts* given to those employees considered to work well and in the interest of the organization. Gift giving confronts the giver with a problem similar to that encountered with monetary pay: the determination of the appropriate size and value of the gift to match the services performed. It is noteworthy that in almost all societies, an effort is made to conceal the price paid for gifts. This moves gifts closer to awards, which have no monetary value as such and are appreciated mainly for their symbolic content. Gifts can be employed to motivate employees, in particular if they signal that the superiors have made an effort to personalize them. Similar to awards, gifts are tangible and can serve as reminders of the recognition received. The effects on motivation can thus be more sustained than in the case of money, where people even tend to forget the exact amount received.

Employees can also be motivated to perform in the interest of an organization by *punishment* of deviant behavior. In most if not all societies, this approach has been extensively used, as the respective criminal law codes show. Such negative sanctions often endeavor to closely monitor and determine human behavior, but it is well known that this is possible only to a limited extent. People often invest a lot of effort and originality in circumventing and cheating on laws and regulations. Tax fraud is a case in point. To react by increasing punishment is only partly effective, as this induces people to move to other areas in order to circumvent the fines. There is an important negative consequence of forcing people to act in a particular way by threatening punishment. Intrinsic motivation in work is crowded out as it becomes unnecessary. Commitment, trust, and loyalty are lost, though they are of crucial importance in all societies, in particular in modern ones based on a large measure of independence at work.

24.5 Awards in the Public Realm

24.5.1 Origins and Literature

Many different principals, ranging from monarchs, presidents, and other public authorities to leaders in public and private organizations, hand out awards, often in large numbers. A science called *phaleristics* is devoted to the study of particular orders, gathering and documenting minute information on their statutes, history, and insignia (e.g., Pedersen, 2009, on the Danish Order of the Elephant). In sociology, there is a rich literature on concepts related to awards, such as fame and esteem, status, and social distinction (e.g., Bourdieu, 1979; Elster, 1985; Sauder, Lynn, and Podolny, 2012). In economics, a first and early endeavor to build a theory of awards was made by Hansen and Weisbrod (1972). Other economists came some time later (Besley, 2005; Frey, 2005; Gavrila et al., 2005). General accounts of awards have subsequently also been developed in Frey (2006, 2007), Frey and Neckermann (2008), Frey and Gallus (2017, 2016), and Gallus and Frey (2016, 2017). For other studies empirically evaluating the effects of awards, see Ashraf, Bandiera, and Lee (2014), Gubler, Larkin, and Pierce. (2016), Kosfeld and Neckermann (2011) on the *ex ante* incentive effects of awards, and Gallus (2016) and Chan et al. (2014) on their *ex post* effects.

The *demand* for distinction and therewith awards seems almost limitless. The First Duke of Wellington, Arthur Wellesley (1769–1852), for example, received an almost uncountable number of titles of nobility and military ranks. In addition to being the first Duke of Wellington, he was also Baron Douro, Viscount, Earl and Marquess of Wellington, Conde de Vimeiro, Duque de Vitoria, and Marques de Torres Veras in Spain, Duque de Ciudad Rodrigo in Spain, and Prins van Waterloo in the Netherlands, to name just a few titles. He received most of the major orders of his time; Knight of the Order of the Garter, Knight of the Most Illustrious Order of the Golden Vlies, and Knight Grand Cross of the Order of the Bath are just some of them. More recent examples of persons accumulating a mass of awards are the German Reichsmarschall Göring or the Soviet Marshal Zhukov, whose uniforms were almost fully covered by orders and medals. Today, this applies, for instance, to generals in North Korea. But it is not only true for the military personnel of dictatorial countries. The American four-star general David Petraeus carried more than twenty decorations on his uniform. Strong demand for awards is also exerted in other areas, including the arts, film, sports, business, and academia.

24.5.2 Confirmatory and Discretionary Awards

Two very fundamental types of awards can be distinguished. *Confirmatory awards* are bequeathed for already well-defined performance. Donors have little leeway whether to give or to withhold a particular award. The people achieving or surpassing a predetermined performance level can be certain to be awarded. Examples of such awards are Knight Bachelors regularly given to Nobel Prize winners. Confirmatory awards are much used in the diplomatic, military, and public services as well as among politicians. They may, however, invite strategic behavior by contenders because the criteria to win an award are made obvious. Much as with monetary incentives, people may be led to focus on meeting these performance criteria while disregarding other important dimensions of performance (see Holmström and Milgrom, 1991). They may even fake their performance and manipulate the criteria in their favor (Osterloh and Frey, 2000).

In contrast, *discretionary awards* allow givers to decide whether, what for, and to whom an award is bequeathed. They provide one of the few cases in which even today the decisions by givers cannot be brought to court. It is, for instance, impossible to go to court in order to be appointed Knight of the Garter. And in any event, the act would almost certainly defeat its purpose.

Discretionary awards are analyzed in the following because they clearly differ from monetary bonuses. An essential question is to what extent discretionary awards influence *subsequent* behavior. Do the recipients raise their work effort and performance, or do they possibly reduce it because they have already been rewarded, start resting on their laurels, or because the external intervention crowds out their intrinsic motivation?

24.5.3 Empirical Evidence on the Effects of Awards

It is not easy to analyze the effect of awards on performance, because it is normally the best performers who receive an award. Is a superior performance after receiving an award due to the increased motivation, or is it because the recipients are just better performers? These two causal relationships are difficult to distinguish, but the research reported in this section takes a significant step into that direction, to find out under what conditions handing out awards indeed raises intrinsic motivation for future performance.

Malmendier and Tate (2009) look at awards given to CEOs by the business press (for instance, Manager of the Year). They conclude that such honors induce their recipients to invest less work effort in the CEOs' original firms, and that recipients rather turn their effort to activities such as writing books or sitting on other companies' boards (see also Siming, 2012). Borjas and Doran (2015) find that the productivity of the recipients of the major award in mathematics, the Fields Medal, subsequently declines compared to the comparison group of similarly brilliant contenders. The authors attribute this result to the winners' stronger inclination to study unfamiliar topics that are less likely to be published.

Chan et al. (2014) use a novel technique to investigate other prestigious honors in academia, such as the John Bates Clark Medal, which is given to the most promising economists in the United States. To distinguish the aforementioned causal relationships, the synthetic control method is used to build a comparison group of nonrecipient researchers with similar profiles (i.e., similar publication and citation performance and comparable time-invariant academic characteristics). This procedure allows the authors to contrast the winners' and control group's performance trajectories after the event of award bestowal. It turns out that the winners publish significantly more articles (their publications were raised by 13 percent after five years) than had they not received the Clark

Medal. The articles published are also cited considerably more (the citations to previously published articles were increased by 50 percent).

The voluntary sector crucially relies on intrinsic motivation for people to engage. Money stands a high risk of crowding out volunteers' intrinsic motivations. A case in point is Wikipedia, whose authors do not receive any monetary compensation and contribute under pseudonyms. While this online public good has been a surprising success, it is now severely struggling with declining retention rates, particularly among new authors. In a large-scale natural field experiment, Gallus (2016) shows that a purely symbolic award without any material or career-related implications increases the retention rate among new Wikipedia authors by 20 percent in the following month. The effect persists for an entire year after the initial award bestowal. Even in the context of for-profit firms, voluntary extra-role behaviors (e.g., helping a colleague) are important. While it would be unsuitable or even impossible to compensate such behaviors financially, feedback and awards can be used to reward employees for such desirable behaviors. Neckermann, Cueni, and Frey (2014) find that an award given to employees at a call center for voluntary work behaviors motivates better performance even on core tasks of the job.

While there is at present only a limited number of serious empirical analyses on the effects of awards, existing research results suggest that meaningful awards indeed tend to raise subsequent performance. If awards are given for meritorious past behavior and kept limited in their numbers, they seem to have a positive effect on people's motivation and behavior. This may be because recipients feel supported, because they are reassured that what they are doing is of value, and/or because they want to live up to the honor received.

24.6 Conclusions

This chapter documents how strongly economics has evolved, from considering money as the major, and often only, motivational instrument, to taking crowding-out effects seriously, and (slowly) to seeing nonfinancial awards as a relevant instrument to maintain and raise intrinsic motivation.

24.7 References

Amabile, Teresa M. 1998. How To Kill Creativity. *Harvard Business Review* 76: 76–87.

Anand, Narasimhan and Watson, Mary R. 2004. Tournament Rituals in the Evolution of Fields: The Case of the Grammy Awards. *Academy of Management Journal* 47: 59–80.

Ashraf, Nava, Bandiera, Oriana, and Lee, Scott. 2014. Awards Unbundled: Evidence from a Natural Field Experiment. *Journal of Economic Behavior and Organization* 100: 44–63.

Austin, Robert D and Hoffer Gittell, J. 1999. Anomalies of High Performance: Reframing Economic and Organizational Theories of Performance Measurement. Working paper, Harvard Business School.

Barkema, Harry G. 1995. Do Top Managers Work Harder When They Are Monitored? *Kyklos* 48: 19–42.

Becker, Gary S. 1976. *The Economic Approach to Human Behavior*. Chicago and London: University of Chicago Press.

Bénabou, Roland and Tirole, Jean. 2003. Intrinsic and Extrinsic Motivation. *Review of Economic Studies* 70: 489–520.

Bender, Keith A. and Theodossiou, Ioannis. 2014. The Unintended Consequences of the Rat Race: The Detrimental Effects of Performance Pay on Health. *Oxford Economic Papers* 66: 824–847.

Besley, Timothy. 2005. Notes on Honours. Mimeo, London School of Economics.

Bewley, Truman F. 1995. A Depressed Labor Market as Explained by Participants. *American Economic Review* 85: 250–254.

Bohnet, Iris, Frey, Bruno S. and Huck, Steffen. 2001. More Order with Less Law: On Contract Enforcement, Trust, and Crowding. *American Political Science Review* 95: 131–144.

Borjas, George J. and Doran, Kirk B. 2015. Prizes and Productivity: How Winning the Fields Medal Affects Scientific Output. *Journal of Human Resources* 50: 728–758.

Bourdieu, Pierre. 1979. *La distinction: Critique sociale du jugement*. Paris: Les Editions de Minuit.

Cardenas, Juan Camilo, Stranlund, John and Willis, Cleve. 2000. Local Environmental Control and Institutional Crowding-Out. *World Development* 28: 1719–1733.

Chan, Ho Fai, Frey, Bruno S., Gallus, Jana and Torgler, Benno. 2014. Academic Honors and Performance. *Labour Economics* 31: 188–204.

Deci, Edward L. 1971. Effects of Externally Mediated Rewards on Intrinsic Motivation. *Journal of Personality and Social Psychology* 18: 105–115.

Deci, Edward L. and Flaste, Richard. 1995. *Why We Do What We Do: The Dynamics of Personal Autonomy*. New York: Putnam's Sons.

Deci, Edward L. Koestner, Richard and Ryan, Richard M. 1999. A Meta-Analytic Review of Experiments Examining the Effects of Extrinsic Rewards on Intrinsic Motivation. *Psychological Bulletin* 125: 627–668.

Deci, Edward L. and Ryan, Richard M. 1985. *Intrinsic Motivation and Self-Determination in Human Behavior*. New York: Plenum Press.

Economist. 2004. Titles. Honour Killings, July 15.

Elster, Jon. 1985. *Sour Grapes: Studies in the Subversion of Rationality*. Cambridge, UK: Cambridge University Press.

Fehr, Ernst and Rockenbach, Bettina. 2003. Detrimental Effects of Sanctions on Human Altruism. *Nature* 422: 137–140.

Feld, Lars P. and Frey, Bruno S. 2002. Trust Breeds Trust: How Taxpayers Are Treated. *Economics of Governance* 3: 87–99.

Frey, Bruno S. 1994. How Intrinsic Motivation Is Crowded Out and In. *Rationality and Society* 6: 334–352.

Frey, Bruno S. 1999. *Economics as a Science of Human Behaviour*. Boston: Kluwer.

Frey, Bruno S. 1992. Tertium Datur: Pricing, Regulating and Intrinsic Motivation. *Kyklos* 45: 161–184.

Frey, Bruno S. 1997. *Not Just for the Money: An Economic Theory of Personal Motivation*. Cheltenham/Brookfield, UK: Edward Elgar.

Frey, Bruno S. 1997. A Constitution for Knaves Crowds Out Civic Virtues'. *Economic Journal* 107: 1043–1053.

Frey, Bruno S. 2005. Knight Fever: Towards an Economics of Awards. CESifo Working Paper No. 1468. www.econstor.eu/handle/10419/18832 (accessed May 17, 2013).

Frey, Bruno S. 2006. Giving and Receiving Awards. *Perspectives on Psychological Science* 1: 377–388.

Frey, Bruno S. 2007. Awards as Compensation. *European Management Review* 4: 6–14.

Frey, Bruno S. and Gallus, Jana. 2017. Towards an Economics of Awards. *Journal of Economic Surveys* 31: 190–200.

Frey, Bruno S. and Gallus, Jana. 2016. Honors: A Rational Choice Analysis of Award Bestowals. *Rationality and Society* 28: 255–269.

Frey, Bruno S and Goette, Lorenz. 1999. Does Pay Motivate Volunteers? IEW Working Paper 7. ideas.repec.org/p/zur/iewwpx/007.html (accessed May 17, 2013).

Frey, Bruno S. and Jegen, Reto. 2001. Motivation Crowding Theory. *Journal of Economic Surveys* 15: 589–611.

Frey, Bruno S. and Neckermann, Susanne. 2008. Awards: A View from Psychological Economics. *Zeitschrift für Psychologie/Journal of Psychology* 216: 198–208.

Frey, Bruno S. and Oberholzer-Gee, Felix. 1997. The Cost of Price Incentives: An Empirical Analysis of Motivation Crowding-Out. *American Economic Review* 87: 746–755.

Frey, Bruno S. and Osterloh, Margit. 2012. Stop Tying Pay to Performance. *Harvard Business Review* (January–February): 51–52.

Frohlich, N. and Oppenheimer, J. 1998. Optimal Policies and Ethical Behaviour: Some Unexpected Contradiction. Unpublished Manuscript. Meeting of the Preferences Network Research Group.

Gallus, Jana. 2016. Fostering Public Good Contributions with Symbolic Awards: A Large-scale Natural Field Experiment at Wikipedia. *Management Science*, Articles in Advance.

Gallus, Jana and Frey, Bruno S. 2016. Awards: A Strategic Management Perspective. *Strategic Management Journal* 37: 1699–1714.

Gallus, Jana and Frey, Bruno S. 2017. Awards as Strategic Signals. *Journal of Management Inquiry* 26: 76–85.

Gavrila, Caius, Caulkins, Jonathan P., Feichtinger, Gustav, Tragler, Gernot and Hartl, Richard F. 2005. 'Managing the Reputation of an Award to Motivate Performance. *Mathematical Methods of Operations Research* 61: 1–22.

Gneezy, Uri and Rustichini, Aldo. 2000a. A Fine Is a Price. *Journal of Legal Studies* 29: 1–17.

Gneezy, Uri and Rustichini, Aldo. 2000b. Pay Enough or Don't Pay at All. *Quarterly Journal of Economics* 115: 791–810.

Gubler, Timothy, Larkin, Ian and Pierce, Lamar. 2016. Motivational Spillovers from Awards: Crowding Out in a Multi-Tasking Environment. *Organization Science*, 286–303.

Hansen, W. Lee and Weisbrod, Burton A. 1972. Toward a General Theory of Awards, or, Do Economists Need a Hall of Fame? *Journal of Political Economy* 80: 422–431.

Holmström, Bengt and Milgrom, Paul. 1991. Multitask Principal-Agent Analyses: Incentive Contracts, Asset Ownership, and Job Design. *Journal of Law, Economics, and Organization* 7: 24–52.

Kelman, Steven. 1992. Adversary and Cooperationist Institutions for Conflict Resolution in Public Policymaking. *Journal of Policy Analysis and Management* 11: 178–206.

Kirchler, E. and Holzl, E. 2017. *Economic Psychology: An Introduction.* Cambridge, UK: Cambridge University Press.

Kosfeld, Michael and Neckermann, Susanne. 2011. Getting More Work for Nothing? Symbolic Awards and Worker Performance. *American Economic Journal: Microeconomics* 3: 86–99.

Kunreuther, Howard and Easterling, Douglas. 1990. Are Risk-Benefit Tradeoffs Possible in Siting Hazardous Facilities? *American Economic Review* 80: 252–256.

Lazear, Edward P. 2000a. Economic Imperialism. *Quarterly Journal of Economics* 115: 99–146.

Lazear, Edward P. 2000b. Performance Pay and Productivity. *American Economic Review* 90: 1346–1361.

Malmendier, Ulrike and Tate, Geoffrey. 2009. Superstar CEOs. *Quarterly Journal of Economics* 124: 1593–1638.

Neckermann, Susanne, Cueni, Reto, and Frey, Bruno S. 2014. Awards at Work. *Labour Economics* 31: 205–217.

Osterloh, Margit and Frey, Bruno S. 2000. Motivation, Knowledge Transfer, and Organizational Forms. *Organization Science* 11: 538–550.

Pedersen, Jørgen. 2009. *Riddere Af Elefantordenen, 1559–2009.* Odense, Denmark: Syddansk Universitetsforlag.

Sauder, Michael, Lynn, Freda, and Podolny, Joel M. 2012. Status: Insights from Organizational Sociology. *Annual Review of Sociology* 38: 267–283.

Siming, Linus. 2012. Orders of Merit and CEO Compensation: Evidence from a Natural Experiment. Available at SSRN: ssrn.com/abstract=2100499; or dx.doi.org/10.2139/ssrn.2100499 (accessed May 17, 2013).

Thaler, Richard H. 2016. Behavioral Economics: Past, Present and Future. *American Economic Review* 106: 1577–1600.

Titmuss, Richard M. 1970. *The Gift Relationship: From Human Blood to Social Policy.* New York: Pantheon.

Tyler, Tom R. 2006. *Why People Obey the Law.* Princeton, NJ: Princeton University Press.

25 Fuzzy-Trace Theory

Judgments, Decisions, and Neuroeconomics

David Garavito, Rebecca Weldon and Valerie Reyna

25.1 Introduction

In psychology and economics, scholars are increasingly combining behavioral and neuroscientific techniques to understand judgment and decision-making. In the following, we describe a major framework that takes this approach: fuzzy-trace theory. Fuzzy-trace theory (FTT) is a theory of judgment, decision-making, and memory and their development across the lifespan. To begin, we define some basic conceptual components of judgment and decision-making that explain economic behavior, including perceptions of probabilities and outcomes (i.e., payoffs or rewards). In this connection, we also briefly describe the evolution of ideas in behavioral economics and neuroeconomics from the perspective of FTT. We then focus on risk preferences and risky decisions, reviewing the theory's explanations for such phenomena as (a) risky choice framing effects (that risk preferences shift depending on whether choices are described as gains or losses); (b) variations on framing effects (e.g., what are called "truncation" effects because pieces of information are systematically deleted from gambles to test alternative theories); (c) time preferences and delay of gratification, including truncation effects also known as hidden-zero effects; and (d) individual and developmental differences among people, such as differences in age and expertise, sensation seeking (the desire for thrills or excitement usually associated with rewards), and numeracy (the ability to understand and use numbers). In each of these sections, we describe both behavioral and brain evidence that illuminates economic behavior. We conclude by summarizing the main tenets of FTT, how it differs from such approaches as prospect theory, and future directions for research on judgments, decisions, and neuroeconomics.

25.2 Economic and Psychological Approaches: Definitions

Economists and psychologists define "risky" decision-making in overlapping but distinct ways. Economists define risk in terms of the variance of possible outcomes (Fox and Tannenbaum, 2011). Risk seeking is preferring an option with a higher variance payoff over a lower variance one, all else being equal (ceteris paribus). For example, stocks are usually more variable in their payoffs than bonds, but they have a greater upside potential, so a risk-seeking person would generally prefer stocks over bonds. When we say "all else being equal," we are referring to the overall expected value of each option: the expected value of an option is the magnitude of each outcome (e.g., the "payoff" if the outcome is monetary gains) multiplied by its probability. Thus, gaining $1,000 for sure is equivalent in expected value to a 0.50 probability of gaining $2,000 (otherwise nothing). When options are equal in expected value, a higher variance payoff implies that the potential magnitude of the payoff is higher, although the probability of receiving that payoff is lower.

With this definition of risk, risk seekers choose risky gambles over equivalent sure options, and they choose more risky gambles over equivalent less-risky gambles. Risk-averse people have the opposite preferences. Risk-neutral people do not make distinctions related to variance in outcomes. These ideas have influenced all subsequent theories of risky decision-making in economics and psychology, and they capture some basic intuitions that most people would agree with, namely, that the desirability of an option depends on both the magnitude of potential outcomes and their probabilities. If two life insurance policies costs exactly the same amount of money, but one pays out $100,000 and the other pays out $200,000, most people would prefer the latter policy (all else being equal).

Although many psychologists who study judgment and decision-making apply the economic definition of risk, clinical psychologists and other professionals (those in public health or management) often define a "risky" decision as a choice that could potentially lead to loss or harm (Fox and Tannenbaum, 2011; Reyna and Huettel, 2014). Consider choosing to smoke cigarettes, engage in unprotected sex, or drive after drinking alcohol. Most people, even adolescents, know that these choices could have harmful – and potentially fatal – consequences. Therefore, psychologists would define these decisions as "risky" because of the potential negative outcomes of these courses of action. Negative outcomes (losses or harms) are uncertain when someone opts for a risky choice in these scenarios: smoking does not inevitably result in lung cancer, unprotected sex does not necessarily result in HIV, and drinking and driving does not always result in an automobile accident or legal sanctions. The willingness to take these kinds of risks is not wrong, according to economists, as long as the potential benefits to that person outweigh the costs. Hence, understanding underlying preferences – what matters to people and why – is essential regardless of the definition of risk. For professionals who wish to reduce social costs or human suffering, understanding underlying preferences is important so that unhealthy risk taking can be reduced (Reyna and Farley, 2006). For economists, it is important to understand whether people's choices are motivated by their values and are consistent with their risk attitudes. FTT builds on these approaches to illuminate the cognitive, social, and personality factors that determine whether people are acting in their rational self-interest (Reyna, 2008).

25.2.1 Basic Conceptual Components of Judgment and Decision-Making

FTT descends from a series of models of judgment and decision-making that have become increasingly "psychological" over time. As noted, classical economic theories of decision-making distinguish between two components, probabilities and outcomes, which are combined multiplicatively to determine the overall value of a prospect. The overall value of $1,000 of the prospect of gaining $2,000 with a 0.50 probability is called "expected value" because the expectation of a 0.50 probability of $2,000 over many trials is $1,000 on average. Theories that followed this mathematical formulation of overall value became successively more subjective or psychological, as we briefly review in this chapter. The upshot with respect to FTT is that this most recent theory emphasizes subjective meaning – the gist – of both probabilities and outcomes, so that mental representations of options can be very different from objective information about those options. It is those mental representations of probabilities and outcomes, combined with background knowledge that fills in gaps, that determines judgments and decisions (see Reyna, 2012, for an overview).

FTT differs radically from earlier approaches that tinkered with perceptions of probabilities and outcomes to capture distortions in perceived magnitudes. One of the most well-known examples of an elegant and powerful theory that attempted to account for psychological distortions is expected utility (EU) theory (von Neumann and Morgenstern, 1944). EU theory amends the concept of expected value by assuming that subjective value is nonlinear; subjective value negatively accelerates as objective value increases. This nonlinearity explains risk aversion given a choice between two prospects, such as the previously described options ($1,000 for sure versus $2,000 with a 0.50 probability). In EU theory, risk aversion is explained because the subjective value of the larger objective value in the gamble ($2,000) is distorted downward more than the smaller objective value in the sure thing ($1,000). Thus, the sure thing has greater subjective value than the risky gamble. Subjective expected utility (SEU) theory adds the idea of nonlinear distortion in the perceptions of probabilities to that of outcomes (Savage, 1954).

Like SEU theory, prospect theory (PT), too, assumes subjective distortions of both probabilities and outcomes. However, it adds the psychological idea of change relative to a reference point, such as the status quo, so that outcomes are perceived as gains (upward change) or losses (downward change) even when they are objectively equivalent (Tversky and Kahneman, 1986). Table 25.1 provides an example of objective gain–loss equivalence that nevertheless elicits very different risk preferences, called a framing effect. Furthermore, losses feel worse than gains of equal magnitude feel good, captured in the steepness of

Table 25.1 *Example of risky-choice framing task options and truncations with PT's and FTT's predictions*

	GAIN frame		LOSS frame		PT's predictions	FTT's prediction
	Sure option	Risky option	Sure option	Risky option		
Gist truncation	Win $1,000 for sure	1/2 chance of winning $0	Lose $1000 for sure	1/2 chance lose $0	Standard framing effect is observed.	Framing effect is strengthened.
Mixed condition: traditional framing task	Win $1,000 for sure	1/2 chance of winning $2,000 and 1/2 chance of winning nothing	Lose $1000 for sure.	1/2 chance of losing $2,000 and 1/2 chance of losing nothing.	Standard framing effect is observed.	Standard framing effect is observed.
Verbatim truncation	Win $1,000 for sure	1/2 chance of winning $2,000	Lose $1,000 for sure	1/2 chance lose $2,000	Standard framing effect is observed.	No framing effect is observed.

Note: PT = prospect theory. FTT = fuzzy-trace theory. In the loss frame, decision makers begin with $2,000 at stake so that gains and losses are equivalent.

the loss function. Thus, loss aversion (feeling worse about losses than comparable gains, regardless of risk) is distinct from risk aversion (but see Yechiam and Telpaz, 2013). Also, low probabilities are overestimated, whereas moderate to high probabilities are underestimated. Once again, the subjective value of the gamble suffers relative to the sure thing because probabilities (as well as outcomes) are perceived as smaller than they objectively are. Because the gamble is smaller, the sure thing is preferred for gains and the gamble is preferred for losses (i.e., a smaller loss is better than a larger loss).

Most recently, PT has been integrated into a more expansive dual-process approach to judgment and decision-making (Kahneman, 2003, 2011), which contrasts rational processes (e.g., deliberation drawing on logic and probability theory) with intuitive processes that foment biases, such as framing effects. Prospect theory laid the foundation for FTT, and FTT encompasses the assumptions of standard dual-process approaches, but it differs from these theories in important ways (Reyna and Brainerd, 2011). Additionally, as neuroeconomics has expanded, FTT has been used as a framework to explain and predict neuroscientific data on decision-making and risk taking, as discussed later in this chapter (Reyna and Huettel, 2014).

25.3 Risk Preferences and Risky Decisions

Like prior approaches, FTT assumes that subjective perceptions of probability and outcomes govern judgments and decision-making. However, rather than simply being less linear than objective values, FTT distinguishes a range of mental representations of probabilities and outcomes from verbatim – the literal words, numbers, or other surface features of information or events – to multiple levels of gist – the bottom-line meaning of the same information or events. A person encodes information into both types of representations separately and simultaneously, and although both gist and verbatim representations are encoded in parallel, these processes are independent and the representations are stored separately. More specifically, gist representations of information are not extracted from the verbatim representations of that same information (Reyna, 2012; Reyna and Brainerd, 2011).

Thus, the gist can be very different from the literal stimulus because it captures subjective interpretation, which is shaped by context, culture, worldview, knowledge, prior experiences, and other factors known to affect meaning (e.g., Reyna and Adam, 2003). The distinction between verbatim and gist representations (and associated thinking) is reminiscent of gestalt theory, which heavily influenced the development of FTT, in which productive nonliteral thinking is contrasted with nonproductive literal thinking (Wertheimer, 1938).

As an example of gist informed by context, a 1 percent chance of an insurance loss (e.g., from a major house fire) could be viewed as high when a person does not have the financial resources to rebuild, and, thus, could be accompanied by feelings of fear rather than complacency. (Note that the probability of 1 percent is the literal verbatim representation.) In this context, being unwilling to take a risk by failing to pay for insurance makes sense (although there is still a maximum cost of insurance beyond which people would not be willing to pay). According to FTT, the crux of this decision turns on a qualitative understanding of the gist of what "high" risk or "too much" money means, in parallel with verbatim analysis of literal numbers. The gist is fuzzy, not an exact number, but it is meaningful to that person in that context; a 1 percent chance of rain, for example, is likely to be viewed as a "low" chance of rain. In FTT, these contextual effects are seen as often a global strength of human cognition, despite producing systematic biases.

Another important tenet of FTT is that a person encodes multiple levels of gist with different amounts of detail, such as categorical versus ordinal gist. A representation described as categorical could include a description of information using a "some" versus "none" distinction, for example, some money as opposed to none or some risk as opposed to none. An ordinal gist representation, on the other hand, would contain a "less" versus "more" distinction, for example, a small as opposed to large amount of money or low as opposed to high risk. The specificity of the question or constraints of the task govern which level of gist is used to make a judgment or decision, but people generally rely on the least detailed level of representation (Corbin et al., 2015).

There is corroborating evidence for verbatim and gist representations in the memory literature (e.g., Reyna et al., 2016). Each type of representation supports a different kind of processing: verbatim representations have the precision to facilitate exact computations, but gist representations facilitate the fuzzy, impressionistic, often unconscious processes of intuition (Reyna, 2012). FTT accounts for behavior in a wide range of cognitive tasks (Reyna and Mills, 2007). To take one example relevant to economic behavior, in FTT, preference reversals are accounted for by different levels of precision imposed by the task: choice, ranking/rating, and numerical judgments (Corbin et al., 2015; Reyna and Brainerd, 1995). A preference reversal occurs when an option is preferred in a choice task (e.g., apartment A is chosen over apartment B as more desirable to rent), but that same option is not preferred in a ratings task (e.g., apartment A is rated as less desirable to rent than apartment B; Fischer and Hawkins, 1993). FTT's explanation is that simpler gist representations can typically be used to discriminate apartment A from B in a choice task, compared to rating the apartments' desirability; the latter requires more precision (see Corbin et al., 2015). In the following, we apply the same principles of FTT to explain risky decision-making for gains and losses.

25.3.1 Fuzzy-Trace Theory and Risky-Choice Framing

Returning to our example in Table 25.1, FTT explains gain–loss framing effects (and similar gist-based biases; Adam and Reyna, 2005; Weldon, Corbin, and

Reyna, 2013) through different means than traditional decision theories, such as EU theory, PT, or standard dual processes. FTT explains the effects found in the decision-making literature by taking into account a person's interpretations of the options in a decision task, which is reflected in their mental representation of gist (Kühberger and Tanner, 2010; Reyna, 2012). According to FTT, the switch in risk preference seen in framing bias occurs because people are deriving the *gist* of their options and applying their values to that gist. The simplest gist in many decision problems is the categorical contrast between some and none. For the example in Table 25.1, the simplest gist of the gains decision would be gaining some money versus gaining some money or gaining nothing. After extracting the gist of their options, participants retrieve and apply general (gist) principles or values to the extracted gist of the decision. An example of one of these gist principles would be "money is good," which supports choosing the sure option because some money is better than no money. These general principles can apply to many decisions because they ignore specific details about the potential risks or benefits (e.g., exact probabilities or magnitudes). In other words, people do not necessarily have "I like $2,000 more than $1,000" stored in long-term memory; rather, they have general principles that apply to a wide array of circumstances stored in a gist format. Therefore, when people represent the categorical gist of options in the risky-choice framing task, and they apply simple gist principles to those representations, they prefer the sure gain over the risky gamble.

The same types of some–none distinctions apply to representations of the loss frame. Using the loss frame that is analogous to our gain-frame example, the gist that one would extract from a sure thing of losing $1,000 and a gamble for a 50 percent chance of losing $2,000 and a 50 percent chance of losing $0 would be "losing some money" versus "losing some money or losing no money." Again, people apply their relevant values or principles (e.g., "Losing money is bad") to the extracted gist of the decision. Because losing money is worse than losing no money, this principle supports the choice of the risky gamble. That is, the gamble is the only option that has a chance of losing no money at all. Laboratory framing tasks have tested this idea that people rely on the gist of choices when making decisions, and supportive results have also been found in real-world decision-making (Broniatowski, Klein, and Reyna, 2015; Kühberger and Tanner, 2010; Reyna et al., 2014; Reyna & Farley, 2006; Reyna and Mills, 2014; Wolfe at al., 2015).

FTT has been extended to explain neuroscientific results regarding risky decision-making and framing (e.g., Reyna & Huettel, 2014). For example, De Martino et al. (2006) conducted the first functional magnetic resonance imaging (fMRI) study of framing behavior. The authors found that framing behavior resulted in increased activation in the amygdala, which they concluded may reflect an affect heuristic driven by an underlying emotional system. A correlation was also found between susceptibility to the framing effect and activation in the medial and orbital prefrontal cortex. However, De Martino et al. (2006), as well as Roiser et al. (2009), confounded gains and losses by including both gain and loss wording in the risky-choice options for both frames. For example, in the gain frame, a safe option would be given: "Keep $20." The risky option was presented in a pie chart that represented the probability of "keep all" and the probability of "lose all." The gist of these options then becomes "keep some money" versus "keep some money" or "lose some money" in the gain frame (and "lose some money" versus "keep some money" or "lose some money" in the loss frame). This different categorical gist of framing options also predicts framing effects, but the preferences would be driven by avoiding the possibility of losing something in the gamble in the *gain* frame and avoiding the sure loss in the loss frame by seeking the possibility of gaining something in the gamble. Thus, the increased activation in the amygdala that has been observed in prior studies when people are framing may have been related to loss aversion rather than framing per se. This explanation aligns with findings from other fMRI framing studies that did not use the gain–loss wording for the risky option in both frames and did not observe amygdala activation (e.g., Gonzalez et al., 2005; Zheng, Wang, and Zhu, 2010).

Additionally, FTT assumes that there is metacognitive monitoring of judgments and decisions (e.g. Liberali et al., 2012). For example, when gain and loss problems are presented to the same person (a within-subjects design), some people notice that they are receiving different versions of similar choices, and there is an inhibition of framing effects (Stanovich and West, 2008; Kahneman, 2003). Supporting this, De Martino et al. (2006) found that, for people who showed less susceptibility to the framing effect, there was increased activation in the anterior cingulate cortex (ACC), right orbitofrontal cortex (OFC), and ventromedial prefrontal cortex (vmPFC) while participants were showing framing effects (choosing a sure gain or risky loss). Activity in the vmPFC and OFC seems to represent the subjective value of options, reflecting verbatim analysis of expected value, as expected in FTT (Reyna and Huettel, 2014; see also Kable and Glimcher, 2007). ACC activation, associated with resistance to framing, may be indicative of heightened decisional conflict inherent in the within-subjects' inhibition of framing that FTT predicts (see also Kahneman, 2003; Stanovich and West, 2008), as ACC activity is often correlated with conflict or error monitoring (Brown and Braver, 2008).

Together, this empirical evidence suggests, and FTT predicts, that framing effects result from a gist-based representation of options (e.g., "Saving some is better than saving none") that can be censored or inhibited when people detect that their responses are inconsistent with one another. Verbatim-based analysis of expected value then competes with gist-based intuition to suppress framing effects. When people resist the framing effect in a within-subjects design, they show greater activation in the neural networks that represent expected value, and, when their decisions are counter to their dominant strategy (i.e., the gist-based simplification of options that drives framing), ACC activation is increased. Conflict signals detected by the ACC are transmitted to the dorsolateral prefrontal cortex (dlPFC), suggesting heightened cognitive demands on executive processes when the nondominant strategy is selected (Reyna and Huettel, 2014).

25.3.2 Variations on Framing Effects

FTT not only predicts basic framing effects, but it also predicts variations on those effects and has predictable implications for decision-making in real-world settings (e.g., Broniatowski et al., 2015; Mills, Reyna, and Estrada, 2008; Reyna and Mills, 2014). One interesting theoretical variation of the standard framing task involves truncating parts of the risky option to emphasize or deemphasize the zero complement in order to manipulate reliance on categorical gist (which pivots on the contrast between zero, or nothing, and something). The zero complement consists of the part of the gamble in a framing task in which nothing is lost (in the loss frame) or nothing is gained (in the gain frame), and this variation was predicted to alter what type of processing (gist or verbatim) is relied on (e.g., Reyna and Brainerd, 1991). Truncating the gamble in this way and changing processing (and the representations associated with that) allows researchers to examine the effects of verbatim versus gist processing on framing effects. Note that if the *non*zero complement from the gamble in the gain frame in our earlier example were removed (e.g., "gaining $1,000 for sure or taking a 50 percent chance of gaining $0"), this would emphasize the categorical difference between the options ("winning some money" versus "winning no money"), favoring the sure option in the gain frame. (This condition is referred to as the "Gist" condition in Table 25.1.) However, if the zero complement were removed (e.g., "gaining $1,000 for sure versus taking a 50 percent chance of gaining $2,000"), this would deemphasize the categorical difference between the choices. This emphasis would, consequently, reduce framing effects because people would tend to choose the risky gamble as opposed to the guarantee in the gain frame. (This condition is referred to as the "Verbatim" condition in Table 25.1.)

It may seem that the effects of the truncations are caused by or confounded by ambiguity. It is important to note, though, that this is not the case. At the outset of the task, participants are given special instructions that remove any potential ambiguity in regard to interpreting the truncated options (e.g., Reyna et al., 2014). For example, they are told that if $2,000 are at stake for a loss, and there is a 1/2 chance that they will lose $1,000, that the omitted part of the gamble must be the complementary outcome and probability, namely 1/2 and $0. They are also tested in order to guarantee that they properly understood these instructions. When these special instructions are given, the effects of these truncations remain and are reliable (Chick, Reyna, and Corbin, 2016).

Although there has yet to be a neuroscientific study examining these specific variations on framing and their neural coordinates, this is an important empirical and theoretical question that should be further examined. From a theoretical standpoint, FTT would predict that the gist-emphasis condition (removing the nonzero complement in the gamble) would result in strengthened framing effects and associated activation in the parietal cortex and lateral PFC, whereas the verbatim-emphasis condition (removing the zero complement) should result in weakened framing effects and be associated with subjective values (e.g., areas in the vmPFC; Reyna and Huettel, 2014). The latter requires that expected value be varied across options, rather than keeping it constant. These neural hypotheses draw on literature on memory for verbatim and gist representations (e.g., Kurkela and Dennis, 2016; Reyna and Mills, 2007; see also Reyna et al., 2016). Although other neuroeconomic approaches take into account analysis of subjective value, they do not take these variations, nor their effects, into account (Rangel, Camerer, and Montague, 2008; Fox and Poldrack, 2009).

25.3.3 Time Preference and Delay of Gratification

The same ideas about representations and gist principles apply to understanding time preferences (Reyna and Wilhelms, 2016). Two tasks that assess time preferences are delay of gratification (DG) and temporal discounting (TD), which have been found to be important in predicting economic behavior (Berns, Laibson, and Loewenstein, 2007; Zayas, Mischel, and Pandey, 2014). DG is typically classified as the ability of a person *to wait for* a larger, later reward (e.g., $1,050 in a year) as opposed to a smaller, sooner reward ($1,000 right now). TD is, alternatively, defined as the degree of discounting of larger, later rewards relative to sooner, smaller ones as assessed using a series of choices with different amounts of reward and time. Both of these tasks describe different aspects of time preference (Doyle, 2013; Frederick, Loewenstein, and O'Donoghue, 2002; Reynolds and Schiffbauer, 2005).

TD, in particular, as well as the index associated with it (i.e., one's discount rate), is thought to be a stable individual difference (Kirby, 2009), although it changes over the lifespan (Green, Fry, and Myerson, 1994; Green, Myerson, Lichtman, Rosen, and Fry, 1996). fMRI studies of delay discounting tasks have typically found that (a) areas and dopaminergic systems associated with impulsivity display higher levels of activation when choosing immediate rewards (Kable and Levy, 2015; McClure et al., 2007), and (b) the areas and system associated with control had higher activation when choosing delayed rewards (e.g., McClure et al., 2007; Meade et al., 2011). These results are consistent with standard dual-process theories (but see Kable and Glimcher, 2010, for a contrasting view) and their explanations that time preference is associated with activation of two systems: one associated with control and the other with impulsivity (Bechara, 2005; Bickel et al., 2011; Jentsch and Taylor, 1999; Kahneman, 2011). However, research on FTT has shown that these dual systems are not sufficient to explain either risk preference or time preference.

FTT incorporates the effects of reward (e.g., the attraction of money) and the inhibition of behavior (Reyna and Mills, 2007). FTT goes further and predicts that intuitive, gist-based reasoning can improve a person's capacity to refrain from unnecessary risk taking (Reyna et al., 2015b) and delay gratification (Reyna and Wilhelms, 2016). This additional aspect differs from standard dual-process models, which conflate intuition and impulsivity under System 1 (or Type 1; Evans and Stanovich, 2013).

More specifically, according to FTT, the ability to delay gratification also involves using the bottom-line gist when making decisions (Reyna and Wilhelms, 2016) rather than trading off verbatim, precise details as is assessed in TD tasks. This explanation for DG and choices between sooner, smaller versus larger, later rewards is analogous to the predictions of FTT for framing tasks and choices between sure options and gambles (e.g., Kühberger and Tanner, 2010; Reyna et al., 2014).

Although research supports the idea that the discounting rate is stable over time, that tendency can be modified (Kirby, 2009; Odum, 2011; Ohmura et al., 2006; Simpson and Vuchinich, 2000). Discounting behavior has been effectively modified using specific manipulations that would be predicted by FTT (Koffarnus et al., 2013). In particular, altering the traditional presentation of discounting tasks to emphasize the "hidden zero" has been effective (Magen, Dweck, and Gross, 2008; Magen et al., 2014). The "hidden zero" in a discounting task is adding zero to standard choices, such as "$1,000 today or $1,050 in one year" so that they become "$1,000 today and $0 in one year or $0 today and $1,050 in one year." This manipulation reduced discount rates significantly, probably by emphasizing good and bad categorical distinctions for each option: some today but none later or none today but some later. Using the standard method of presentation for discounting tasks (in which zeros are hidden) does not facilitate categorical distinctions between different choices using gist representations.

However, adding zeros to both options should be less effective than adding a zero to one of the two options, similar to the truncation effects in framing tasks. (See also FTT's explanation of the Allais paradox in Reyna and Brainerd, 2011.) Returning to our example, adding the hidden zero only to the delayed choice creates a categorical difference equivalent to "something now versus nothing now and something later." This categorical difference, theoretically, would promote choosing the immediate option. In contrast, adding the hidden zero to the immediate choice (i.e., "something now and nothing later or something later") would highlight the categorical distinction "nothing later versus something later," which would result in more frequent delayed choices. Adding zeros would not be expected to affect discount rates in the sense that discounting involves trading off magnitudes of outcomes by magnitudes of time (verbatim processing of trade-offs) rather than comparing qualitative categories (gist processing).

These manipulations of the typical discounting task are based on FTT's predictions involving representations and gist principles, such as some money is better than none. The manipulations and their effects are analogous to the truncation effects that can be used to manipulate framing effects (Reyna et al., 2015b). These manipulations, both in discounting and framing tasks, are not accounted for by other approaches. The choices themselves remain mathematically unchanged, regardless of where the hidden zero is added, and so are not easily explained through discounting functions applied to quantities being traded off (Magen et al., 2014). In decisions involving numbers, FTT assumes that both quantitative and qualitative processing occur in parallel, and effects of zero introduce qualitative distinctions. More specifically, highlighting categorical gist distinctions in these tasks changes how one interprets the options, which results in cognitive reframing and different choices (see also Zayas, Mischel, and Pandey, 2014).

Time preferences also have a social component that have to do with endorsing cultural values, such as self-denial in the present to achieve greater rewards in the future (Reyna and Wilhelms, 2016). Greater endorsement of such gist principles would be expected to better predict behaviors than exact trade-offs, as assessed in delay discounting tasks. This is because gist representations and associated gist principles capture how most people make decisions. These principles are also more general and can therefore be applied to more situations, as opposed to quantitative trade-offs such as "sacrifice X units of pleasure now to enjoy Y units of pleasure later." Therefore, FTT predicts that the gist of delay of gratification – sacrifice now, enjoy later – has greater predictive validity for problem behaviors in real-world settings than verbatim processing about quantitative trade-offs (i.e., problem behaviors can involve borrowing money to have fun rather than for necessities or drinking to excess).

Exploring this predictive validity, Reyna and Wilhelms (2016) compared a twelve-item scale (called DG-Gist) that evaluated individuals' agreement (using a five-point Likert scale ranging from "strongly disagree" to "strongly agree") with qualitative gist principles associated with DG (e.g., "Sacrifice now, enjoy later," and, "I spend money on having fun today and don't worry about tomorrow") to other measures of delay discounting and impulsivity. Having a lower score on DG-Gist signifies having a higher tendency to delay gratification. Reyna and Wilhelms investigated the convergent and divergent validity of DG-Gist along with other potentially related scales (e.g., spendthrift–tightwad, delay discounting, and Barratt impulsiveness). Correlations of these scales with DG-Gist were relatively low, and it also explained unique variance in predicting problem behaviors not accounted for by the other scales (e.g., overdrawing one's bank account). DG-Gist remained a significant predictor of financial and nonfinancial problem behaviors controlling for such dimensions as sensation seeking, cognitive reflection, delay discounting, and Barratt impulsivity. Thus, this simple, short scale outpredicted longer and more precise scales, including those that tap deliberation as posited in dual-process theories (e.g., Frederick, 2005). Furthermore, these findings across four studies provide support for FTT's explanations of economic and health decisions, incorporating mental representations of gist principles such as delay of gratification.

25.3.4 Developmental and Individual Differences

In combination, the aforementioned results provide critical tests of FTT and alternative theories, such as EU, PT, and dual-process theories, supporting predictions that gist-based and verbatim-based mental representations are reflected in the brain and behavior. According to FTT, representational reliance affects judgment and decision-making. Reliance on gist, as illustrated by the strength of the framing effect, grows developmentally (i.e., with age and expertise; Meschkow et al., in press; Reyna and Brainerd, 2011). A person at a later stage of development and expertise (e.g., an adult) is predicted to *rely* more on gist processing (as opposed to verbatim processing) than a person who is younger and has less expertise (e.g., an adolescent). More specifically, studies have shown that adults, more so than children, tend to rely on the simplest gist representation possible that is needed in order to decide on an action, which has been dubbed the "fuzzy-processing preference" (Reyna and Brainerd, 2008; Reyna et al., 2014; Reyna and Lloyd, 2006; Wilhelms, Corbin, and Reyna, 2015). Although children are less able to perform calculations, they tend to nevertheless focus more on literal details, and can make quantitative trade-offs of probabilities and outcomes if amounts are presented using concrete props when making decisions (Reyna, 1996; Reyna and Brainerd, 1994, 1995; Reyna and Ellis, 1994; Reyna and Lloyd, 2006; Reyna et al., 2011; Reyna et al., 2015b).

Adolescents, who are generally less developmentally advanced than adults but more advanced than children, are caught in between the two ends of the continuum and have more variability as a group (Reyna et al., 2011; Reyna and Farley, 2006; Mills et al., 2008). Research on adolescents incorporating eye tracking data also support FTT's predictions. This research suggests that adolescents obtained more information about options and used a more intensive analytical method to trade off quantities compared to adults (Kwak et al., 2015). Verbatim and gist processing both improve developmentally, including improvements in the ability to remember verbatim details and the gist of information, but the extent to which a person *relies* on each type of processing also shifts, from verbatim to gist, with age and expertise (Meschkow et al., in press; Mills et al., 2008; Reyna, 2012; Reyna and Lloyd, 2006).

Ironically, because young children are the most likely to rely on verbatim processing of probabilities and outcomes, "computing" something like expected value, they are the most likely to behave like rational economists. For example, they do not show framing effects, treating gains and equivalent losses similarly (e.g., Reyna and Ellis, 1994). Additional evidence shows that children are sensitive to differences in probabilities and outcomes and combine them roughly multiplicatively (as in expected-value type theories, such as EU theory and PT). They rely on the literal magnitudes of probability and outcome as they are presented. Experiments demonstrating these effects ensure that all probabilities and outcomes are represented with concrete props so that children can understand and remember them.

Adolescents are more sensitive to outcomes, such as rewards, than are children or adults (Reyna et al., 2011). Given that expected values are equal between options in many laboratory tasks, the gamble option will always include a larger possible reward than the sure reward in the opposite option. For example, harking back to our earlier example, $2,000 is larger than $1,000 in the gain frame, and conversely, the $1,000 sure loss in the loss frame is smaller than the $2,000 loss in the gamble. In addition to predicting and finding that framing biases increased from childhood to adulthood, FTT also predicted that adolescents should exhibit reverse framing when differences between outcomes are large (e.g., Reyna et al., 2011; Reyna and Farley, 2006). In reverse framing, a person has a higher preference for the gamble in the gain frame and for the sure option in the loss frame. Reverse framing implies that adolescents are relying more on the quantitative differences between outcomes and less on the simple qualitative gist of options, the latter producing the typical framing effect in adults (Chick and Reyna, 2012; Reyna et al., 2011).

Predictions of FTT allow the theory to explain phenomena in the literature that other theories are not able to account for, such as that framing effects and other gist-based biases become stronger as one ages (e.g., adults are more affected by the framing bias than children; Reyna and Ellis, 1994; Reyna et al., 2011). As a person gains experience and expertise in an area, the effects of framing biases also increase (Reyna et al., 2014). None of the developmental theories, including developmental versions of dual-process theory (Casey et al., 2008; Steinberg, 2008), predict that susceptibility to biases increase as one ages and gains expertise. This increase is classified as a developmental reversal because it reverses the usual expectation of developmental improvement. Because both gist and verbatim processing improve with age, this developmental reversal is not the product of adults or experts losing the ability to determine the expected value of their options (Corbin et al., 2015; Weller, Levin, and Denburg, 2011).

Despite the observations that reliance on gist-based processing increases with age and expertise, relying on gist increases vulnerability to specific cognitive biases (Adam and Reyna, 2005; Reyna et al., 2014). More traditional theories may categorize biases such as framing, and the susceptibility to these biases, as errors in decision-making. However, in FTT, susceptibility to many cognitive biases is the result of the developmental increases in reliance on the gist of information (e.g., Jacobs and Potenza, 1991). Aside from just framing, FTT also predicts that false memories will increase developmentally because, again, these phenomena are based on an increased reliance on gist processing (Brainerd, Reyna, and Ceci, 2008; De Neys, and Vanderputte, 2011; Reyna, 2004). Overall, children and adolescents are less susceptible to gist-based biases than adults, even when controlling for knowledge; verbatim processing impairs decision-making in regard to taking unnecessary risks but lessens the effects of cognitive biases (Reyna and Brainerd, 2011; Weldon et al., 2013).

One clarification that needs to be made, however, is that adults do have the ability to shift to more complex gist representations (and sometimes almost verbatim representations) in decisions that are unable to be made when relying on the simplest gist representation (Reyna, 2012). Imagine, as an example, a person deciding between two choices seen in the Allais paradox: a 11 percent chance of winning $1 million and an 89 percent chance of winning $0 versus a 10 percent chance of winning $5 million and a 90 percent chance of winning $0 (Reyna and Brainerd, 2011). In this instance, an adult would require a more complex representation because the simplest gist representation (e.g., *winning something* versus *winning nothing* in both options) would not provide an answer; options are indistinguishable because both have zeros. Instead, a more precise gist representation would provide the distinction necessary to make a decision (e.g., choosing between "winning less" versus "winning nothing" and "winning more" versus "winning nothing").

The developmental shifts that FTT predicts, and that are supported by the literature, also help to further the understanding of why adolescents (and novices) may be more logical and calculating at times, yet still have higher levels of risk taking. In a similar vein, adults and experts often have lower levels of risk taking for gains and tend to rely more on the gist of the situation (Reyna et al., 2014; Reyna and Lloyd, 2006). As an explanation for these developmental differences, reliance on gist representations and gist-based processing is the foundation for advanced processing and is gradually given precedence over time. This shift toward reliance on gist-based processing also creates a protective effect against unnecessary risks. The preference for gist and the use of gist principles, rather than verbatim processing, to aid in decision-making allows people to rely more on the basic understanding of the decision, which will often result in healthier choices (Chapman, Gamino, and Mudar, 2012; Reyna and Farley, 2006; Reyna and Mills, 2014; Reyna, Weldon, and McCormick, 2015a; Wilhelms, Reyna, Brust-Renck, Weldon, & Corbin, 2015). This is in part due to the nature of many risky scenarios. Often, the benefits of risk taking outweigh the risks. Therefore, verbatim-based decision-making, which results in trade-offs between the exact risks and rewards, favors the risky decisions objectively in more scenarios (Mills et al., 2008). In gist-based processing, which ignores specific details in favor of the bottom-line representation and general principles, these hazardous trade-offs are avoided.

A growing body of evidence suggests that gist and verbatim processing may be characterized by differences in underlying neural circuitry (Reyna et al., 2015b). Venkatraman et al. (2009) examined the neural mechanisms underlying a decision task in which three options were presented: selecting to maximize the probability of winning something (Pmax), minimize losses (Lmin), or maximize gains (Gmax). The authors presented participants with a series of trials. Each trial consisted of five possible outcomes and an associated probability of occurrence (e.g., a 25 percent chance of winning $80, a 15 percent chance of winning $40, a 20 percent chance of winning $0, a 20 percent chance of losing $35, and a 20 percent chance of losing $75). Two alternatives for improving the gambles appeared on the screen, allowing the participant to choose between adding an amount of money (e.g., $20) to one of two outcomes (e.g., to the $0 or to the -$75). The options presented represented one of three possible strategies: gains could be maximized by adding $20 to the magnitude of the highest gain (Gmax); losses could be minimized by adding $20 to the worst loss (Lmin); or the probability of winning anything at all could be maximized by adding $20 to the zero dollar option (Pmax). The Gmax or Lmin strategies involve trading off risk and reward, a "verbatim-based" approach as discussed earlier. The Pmax (gist-based) strategy simplifies the gamble by removing the categorical possibility of winning nothing, clearly a prediction of FTT.

Venkatraman et al. (2009) observed increased activation in the posterior parietal cortex (PPC) and the dlPFC when participants chose the gist-based Pmax strategy. Increased activation in the vmPFC for Gmax choices was also present, as well as increased activation in the anterior insula for Lmin choices. Functional connectivity analyses showed that dmPFC connectivity varied as a function of strategy; there was increased connectivity with the dlPFC and PPC for gist-based (Pmax) simplifying choices, and increased connectivity with the anterior insula for verbatim-based compensatory choices (Gmax or Lmin). Further, cognitive control areas such as the dlPFC may be involved in advanced gist-based thinking (Venkatraman et al., 2009). The notion that gist processing would be associated with higher-level cognitive networks is inconsistent with traditional dual-processing accounts, which assume that intuitive thinking (e.g., as reflected in the simplifying noncompensatory Pmax strategy) is ontogenetically and phylogenetically less advanced (Casey et al., 2008; Evans and Stanovich, 2013). The results described in the preceding sections suggest that distinct neural circuitry underlies the use of gist versus verbatim strategies, consistent with FTT.

25.3.4.1 *Numeracy and Decision-Making*

In some areas of judgment and decision-making, such as medical decision-making, dual-process theorists have emphasized the knowledge of numbers and computation as the paradigmatic example of Type 2 thinking (for overviews, see Peters, 2012; Reyna et al., 2009). Objective numeracy is relevant to many judgments and decisions, but it can have ironic effects when that knowledge is applied by rote using verbatim thinking. For example, the "charity problem" presents a choice between three charitable institutions: one institution that will reduce deaths from a disease from 15,000 to 5,000 per year, a second that will reduce deaths from 160,000 to 145,000 per year, and a third that will reduce deaths from 290,000 to 270,000 per year (Peters, Slovic, and Vastfjall, 2008). The first institution reduces the greatest *proportion* of deaths, whereas the third institution reduces the greatest *absolute number* of deaths. People higher in numeracy tend to select the first institution, probably because they are automatically computing the proportions. People lower in numeracy typically opt for the institution that saves the largest number of lives. Thus, this is an example in which reliance on mindless computation may be beneficial for efficient calculation of proportions, but does not necessarily lead to selecting the best option that saves the greatest number of lives. Liberali et al. (2012) analyzed objective and subjective numeracy, as well as the Cognitive Reflection Test (Frederick, 2005), and found that participants who were more likely to reflect on their initial answers made fewer errors on questions that elicit an automatic (incorrect) answer (e.g., "A bat and a ball cost $1.10 together, and the bat costs a dollar more than the ball. How much does the ball cost?" Liberali et al., 2012). People who used mindless computation came up with the incorrect answer "10 cents" – the automatic answer. However, if the ball costs 10 cents, then the bat would have to cost $1.10, and $1.10 + 0.10 equals a total cost of $1.20. Therefore, when people reflect on and censor their initial responses, they often recognize the error and derive the correct answer (that the ball costs $0.05).

The distinction in FTT between exact computation and approximate intuition of number maps roughly onto neural-based distinctions in numerical cognition (Nieder, 2016; Reyna and Brainerd, 1994, 2008). Neuroscience findings suggest that there are distinct circuits that underlie exact versus approximate number networks in the brain. For example, there is more left-angular gyrus activity for exact than for approximate calculation, perhaps because language-based areas may be involved in memory representations of exact numbers (DeHaene et al., 2003). The horizontal segment of the intraparietal sulcus (HIPS) is involved in approximate numerical estimation and comparing the magnitudes of two numbers (DeHaene et al., 2003, 2004). Furthermore, neurons in the prefrontal cortex (PFC) fire in response to a quantitative representation of zero (lack of stimulus), suggesting that there is a neural representation of "nothing" (Ramirez-Cardenas, Moskaleva, and Nieder, 2016). These recent findings may lend insight into the neural networks of observed framing behavior, namely the categorical comparisons that adults rely on when making a choice (e.g., "winning something" versus "winning nothing").

25.3.4.2 *Reward Responsivity and Decision-Making*

The decision to make a risky choice can also be explained in part by response to reward. For example, some researchers suggest that the reason that risk taking is more prevalent during the adolescent years is because of a greater sensitivity to reward during adolescence (Galvan, 2012). The neural circuitry of response to reward has been well established, consisting of dopamine pathways in the midbrain that project to the striatum. More specifically, the mesolimbic pathways project from the ventral tegmental area to the ventral striatum (nucleus accumbens) and vmPFC. The nigrostriatal pathways project from the substantia nigra to the dorsal striatum (caudate nucleus and putamen). Different parts of the striatum have been recognized as having different roles in the response to reward. The ventral striatum has been implicated in anticipation and evaluation of reward, whereas the dorsal striatum is involved in action selection and initiation by integrating cognitive, motivational, and emotional information (Balleine, Delgado, and Hikosaka, 2007; Diekhof et al., 2012; Hare, Camerer, and Rangel, 2009).

If a person wants or likes a particular reward, he or she may be more likely to take a risk to obtain that reward (or larger amounts of that reward). Neuroscientists have conducted quite a bit of animal research suggesting that there are differences in behavior and in the underlying neural systems that underlie liking versus wanting a reward (Berridge, 2007). For example, disrupting dopaminergic pathways in rodents impairs their motivation to obtain these rewards (wanting), but does not affect how much the animal enjoys the reward. (Liking was measured by orofacial reactions such as tongue protrusions; Pecina and Berridge, 2005.) The differences in wanting versus liking provide further evidence for the notion that these are distinct constructs that should be considered separately. FTT distinguishes effects of reward, and its developmental influence, from effects of representation (Reyna et al., 2011, 2015).

In economics, utility theory (and related theories) suggests that the subjective values of different types of rewards are all mapped onto the same reward value dimension (Samuelson, 1947). In parallel, findings in neuroscience suggest that there may be common neural areas that respond to different types of reward in the striatum and vmPFC (FitzGerald, Seymour, and Dolan, 2009; Kim, Shimojo, and O'Doherty, 2010). For example, Levy and Glimcher (2011) identified distinct areas of activation for different types of reward, also testing the common currency of reward hypothesis (the notion that the same neural circuits respond to different types of rewards; e.g., money versus a palatable food). The authors had participants make choices between sure and risky options for money, food, and water. They found that participants' choices for different reward types were correlated – that is, if a participant was more risk-averse for monetary choices, he or she tended to also be more risk-averse for choices about food or water. (See also the discussion of the DOSPERT risk-taking scale in Reyna and Huettel, 2014.) The authors observed similar areas of activation across reward types, including the vmPFC and striatum. Within the vmPFC, there were differences; they found distinct areas that showed increased activation only to money (posterior cingulate cortex), whereas the dorsal hypothalamic areas showed increased activation only to food (Levy and Glimcher, 2011). A meta-analysis conducted on fMRI studies of reward response supported the conclusion that the vmPFC and medial OFC have a neural signature common to different types of reward (Levy and Glimcher, 2012). Furthermore, Plassmann, O'Doherty, and Rangel (2007) found that the vmPFC/medial OFC signal increased as participants' willingness to pay for rewarding food items increased (see also Kable and Glimcher, 2007). Note that overall subjective value increases with reward, consistent with our earlier comments about these areas. Findings support the notion of a common currency of reward, and although the way people respond to one type of reward does not necessarily perfectly predict response to a different type of reward, they do tend to be correlated (Figner and Weber, 2011; Hanoch, Johnson, and Wilke, 2006; Weber, Blais, and Betz, 2002).

Individuals vary in reward response variables such as sensation seeking, suggesting that individual differences in reward response also explain some of the variance in risky choice. For example, people higher in sensation seeking take more risky choices than people lower in sensation seeking. Cservenka et al. (2013) had participants complete a modified version of the Wheel of Fortune decision-making task in which trials resulted in monetary wins or no wins. Cservenka et al. compared low versus high sensation seeking (SS) groups to understand how neural activation differed between groups in response to the reward outcome. The authors found that those high in SS had greater activation in the bilateral insula and prefrontal cortex than low SS for the Win > No Win contrast. Furthermore, those high in SS showed less activation for No Wins than low SS, indicating that high SS may not be as affected by negative consequences. The authors suggest that this may reflect a lower level of autonomic arousal that may put high SS in dangerous situations in which they are less sensitive to potential negative consequences (Cservenka et al., 2013).

FTT incorporates individual differences in sensitivity to outcomes, particularly rewards, but separates the effects of motivation to approach rewards from gist and verbatim modes of thinking. According to FTT, people higher in sensation seeking have a greater tendency to rely on verbatim processing for reasoning and decision-making, which leads to more computation of risks and rewards, and in turn, less or reverse framing (i.e., more risky choices for gains and fewer risky choices for losses; Reyna et al., 2011; Weldon et al., in press).

In addition to individual difference effects on decision-making, developmental differences in neural activation have also been observed. Adolescent decision-making is characterized by different patterns of brain activation than adult decision-making. Heightened reward sensitivity in adolescence has been associated with overdeveloped reward areas (e.g., ventral striatum) in relation to underdeveloped top-down control areas (PFC and ACC) in the developing brain (Casey, Jones, and Hare, 2008; Steinberg, 2008). According to FTT, increased reward sensitivity to gains along with greater emphasis on verbatim risk-reward trade-offs produces vulnerability to unhealthy risk taking (Reyna et al., 2011; Reyna et al., 2015b).

25.4 Conclusions and Future Directions

In this chapter, we review behavioral and brain evidence supporting FTT as an integrative framework to explain and predict decision-making and economic behavior. FTT incorporates both meaningful and rote representations of information into its predictions, with these representations falling on a spectrum with categorical gist (i.e., some versus none) on one end and precise, verbatim details (i.e., 50 percent chance of winning $2,000) on the other. This key representational aspect goes beyond nonlinear distortion of utilities or values, accounting for a wide range of phenomena in judgment and decision-making that are not fully accounted for by other theories, including false memories, framing effects, reverse framing, truncation effects on framing, sensation seeking and reward sensitivity, metacognitive monitoring and inhibition, hidden-zero effects on delay discounting, delay of gratification, and effects of numeracy. Additional effects, such as base-rate, conjunction, and disjunction effects, are reviewed elsewhere (e.g., Reyna and Brainerd, 2008).

Provided that hypotheses about cognitive strategies and causal mechanisms are tested, identifying the neural circuitry underlying reward sensitivity, subjective value, numeracy, risky choice, and mental representation can lend important insight into decision-making. Economists and psychologists are also becoming increasingly interested in neuroscience because of what can be learned about the neurobiological basis of unwise and irrational behavior, such as spending or borrowing more than one can afford. In this connection, intervention experiments provide additional tests of causal mechanisms and are aimed at reducing unwise and irrational behavior.

As examples, FTT's interventions in the health domain have demonstrated that gist-based processing leads to improved judgment and decision-making (Blalock and Reyna, 2016; Reyna et al., 2015a; Wolfe et al., 2015). Interventions that have involved gist-based training have been successful in improving decisions about sexual risk taking in adolescents (Reyna and Mills, 2014; Reyna et al., 2015a). A gist-based web tutoring system was effective in improving understanding about genetic testing and breast cancer risk (Wolfe et al., 2015). Another study demonstrated the efficacy of a gist-based decision tool in helping rheumatoid arthritis patients understand the risks and benefits of different treatment options (Fraenkel et al., 2012). Given the success of these interventions, it is encouraging that gist-based processing is a way of thinking that can be trained. The same theoretical principles could be applied to interventions to improve financial judgments and decision-making. By building on prior research in many areas, FTT provides a multifaceted approach that links cognition, personality, social, cultural, and neurobiological influences so that researchers can continue to learn more about judgment, decision-making, and neuro-economics.

25.5 References

Adam, M. B., and Reyna, V. F. (2005). Coherence and Correspondence Criteria for Rationality: Experts' Estimation of Risks of Sexually Transmitted Infections. *Journal of Behavioral Decision Making*, 18(3), 169–186. doi:10.1002/bdm.493.

Allais, M. (1953). Le comportement de l'homme rationnel devant le risque: Critique des postulats et axiomes de l'école américaine. *Econometrica*, 21, 503–546.

Balleine, B. W., Delgado, M. R., and Hikosaka, O. (2007). The Role of the Dorsal Striatum in Reward and Decision-Making. *Journal of Neuroscience*, 27(31), 8161–8165.

Bechara, A. (2005). Decision Making, Impulse Control and Loss of Willpower to Resist Drugs: A Neurocognitive Perspective. *Nature Neuroscience*, 8 (11), 1458–1463. doi: 10.1038/nn1584.

Berns, G. S., Laibson, D., and Loewenstein, G. (2007). Intertemporal Choice: Toward an Integrative Framework. *Trends in Cognitive Science*, 11, 482−488.

Berridge, K. C. (2007). The Debate over Dopamine's Role in Reward: The Case for Incentive Salience. *Psychopharmacology*, 191(3), 391–431.

Bickel, W. K., Jarmolowicz, D. P., Mueller, E. T., and Gatchalian, K. M. (2011). The Behavioral Economics and Neuroeconomics of Reinforcer Pathologies: Implications for Etiology and Treatment of Addiction. *Current Psychiatry Reports*, 13 (5), 406–415. doi: 10.1007/s11920-011-0215-1.

Blalock, S. J., and Reyna, V. F. (2016). Using Fuzzy-Trace Theory to Understand and Improve Health Judgments, Decisions, and Behaviors: A Literature Review. *Health Psychology*, 35(8), 781–792.

Brainerd, C. J., Reyna, V. F., and Ceci, S. J. (2008). Developmental Reversals in False Memory: A Review of Data and Theory. *Psychological Bulletin*, 134(3), 343–382.

Broniatowski, D. A., Klein, E. Y., and Reyna, V. F. (2015). Germs Are Germs, and Why Not Take a Risk?: Patients' Expectations for Prescribing Antibiotics in an Inner City Emergency Department. *Medical Decision Making*, 35, 60–67. doi: 10.1177/0272989X14553472.

Brown, J. W., and Braver, T. S. (2008). A Computational Model of Risk, Conflict, and Individual Difference Effects in the Anterior Cingulate Cortex. *Brain Research*, 1202, 99–108.

Casey, B. J., and Caudle, K. (2013). The Teenage Brain: Self-Control. *Current Directions in Psychological Science*, 22(2), 82–87. doi: 10.1177/0963721413480170.

Casey, B. J., Jones, R. M., and Hare, T. A. (2008). The Adolescent Brain. *Annals of the New York Academy of Sciences*, 1124(1), 111–126.

Chapman, S. B., Gamino, J. G., and Mudar, R. A. (2012). Higher-Order Strategic Gist Reasoning in Adolescence. In V. F. Reyna, S. Chapman, M. Dougherty, and J. Confrey (Eds.), *The Adolescent Brain: Learning, Reasoning, and Decision Making* (pp. 123–152). Washington, DC: American Psychological Association.

Chick, C. F., Reyna, V. F., and Corbin, J. C. (2016). Framing Effects Are Robust to Linguistic Disambiguation: A Critical Test of Contemporary Theory. *Journal of Experimental Psychology: Learning, Memory, and Cognition.* 42, 238–256.

Chick, C.F. and Reyna, V.F. (2012). A fuzzy-trace theory of adolescent risk-taking: Beyond self-control and sensation seeking. In V. F. Reyna, S. Chapman, M. Dougherty, and J. Confrey (Eds.), *The Adolescent Brain: Learning, Reasoning, and Decision Making* (pp. 379–428). Washington, DC: American Psychological Association.

Corbin, J. C., Reyna, V.F., Weldon, R.B., and Brainerd, C.J. (2015). How Reasoning, Judgment, and Decision Making Are Colored by Gist-Based Intuition: A

Fuzzy-Trace Theory Approach. *Journal of Applied Research in Memory and Cognition. Journal of Applied Research in Memory and Cognition*, 4, 344–355.

Cservenka, A., Herting, M. M., Seghete, K. L. M., Hudson, K. A., and Nagel, B. J. (2013). High and Low Sensation Seeking Adolescents Show Distinct Patterns of Brain Activity During Reward Processing. *Neuroimage*, 66, 184–193.

Defoe, I. N., Dubas, J. S., Figner, B., and Van Aken, M.A. (2014). A Meta-analysis on Age Differences in Risky Decision Making: Adolescents Versus Children and Adults. *Psychological Bulletin*, 141*(1)*, 48–84. doi: 10.1037/a0038088.

Dehaene, S., Molko, N., Cohen, L., and Wilson, A. J. (2004). Arithmetic and the Brain. *Current Opinion in Neurobiology*, 14(2), 218–224.

Dehaene, S., Piazza, M., Pinel, P., and Cohen, L. (2003). Three Parietal Circuits for Number Processing. *Cognitive Neuropsychology*, 20(3–6), 487–506.

Diekhof, E. K., Kaps, L., Falkai, P., and Gruber, O. (2012). The Role of the Human Ventral Striatum and the Medial Orbitofrontal Cortex in the Representation of Reward Magnitude: an Activation Likelihood Estimation Meta-analysis of Neuroimaging Studies of Passive Reward Expectancy and Outcome Processing. *Neuropsychologia*, 50(7), 1252–1266.

De Martino, B., Kumaran, D., Seymour, B., and Dolan, R. J. (2006). Frames, Biases, and Rational Decision-Making in the Human Brain. *Science*, 313(5787), 684–687.

De Neys, W., and Vanderputte, K. (2011). When Less Is Not Always More: Stereotype Knowledge and Reasoning Development. *Developmental Psychology*, 47(2), 432–441.

Doyle, J. R. (2013). Survey of Time Preference, Delay Discounting Models. *Judgment and Decision Making*, 8, 116–135.

Evans, J. S. B. T., and Stanovich, K. E. (2013). Dual-Process Theories of Higher Cognition: Advancing the Debate. *Perspectives on Psychological Science*, 8(3), 223–241. doi: 10.1177/1745691612460685.

Figner, B., and Weber, E.U. (2011). Who Takes Risks When and Why? Determinants of Risk Taking. *Current Directions in Psychological Science*, 20(4), 211–216. doi: 10.1177/0963721411415790.

Fischer, G. W., and Hawkins, S. A. (1993). Strategy Compatibility, Scale Compatibility, and the Prominence Effect. *Journal of Experimental Psychology: Human Perception and Performance*, 29, 580–597.

Fitzgerald, T. H., Seymour, B., and Dolan, R. J. (2009). The Role of Human Orbitofrontal Cortex in Value Comparison for Incommensurable Objects. *Journal of Neuroscience*, 29, 8388–8395.

Fox, C. R., and Poldrack, R. A. (2009). Prospect Theory and the Brain. In P. W. Glimcher, C. F. Camerer, E. Fehr, and R. A. Poldrack (Eds.), *Neuroeconomics: Decision Making and the Brain* (pp. 145–173). London: Academic Press.

Fox, C. R., and Tannenbaum, D.(2011). The Elusive Search for Stable Risk Preferences. *Frontiers in Psychology*. Published online November 15, 2011. doi: 10.3389/fpsyg.2011.00298.

Fraenkel, L., Peters, E., Charpentier, P., Olsen, B., Errante, L., Schoen, R. T., and Reyna, V. (2012). Decision Tool to Improve the Quality of Care in Rheumatoid Arthritis. *Arthritis Care and Research*, 64(7), 977–985.

Frederick, S. (2005). Cognitive Reflection and Decision Making. *Journal of Economic Perspectives*, 19(4), 25–42.

Frederick, S., Loewenstein, G., and O'Donoghue, T. (2002). Time Discounting and Time Preference: A Critical Review. *Journal of Economic Literature*, 40, 351–401. doi: 10.1257/jel.40.2.351.

Fukukura, J., Ferguson, M. J., and Fujita, K. (2013). Psychological Distance Can Improve Decision Making Under Information Overload via Gist Memory. *Journal of Experimental Psychology: General*, 142(3), 658–665. doi: 10.1037/a0030730.

Galvan, A. (2012). Risky Behavior in Adolescents: The Role of the Developing Brain. In V. F. Reyna, S. B. Chapman, M. R. Dougherty, and J. Confrey (Eds.), *The Adolescent Brain: Learning, Reasoning, and Decision Making* (pp. 267–289). Washington, DC: American Psychological Association.

Gonzalez, C., Dana, J., Koshino, H., and Just, M. (2005). The Framing Effect and Risky Decisions: Examining Cognitive Functions with fMRI. *Journal of Economic Psychology*, 26(1), 1–20.

Glimcher, P. W., Camerer, C. F., Fehr, E., and Poldrack, R. A. (Eds.) (2009). *Neuroeconomics: Decision making and the Brain.* New York: Academic Press.

Green, L., Fry, A. F., and Myerson, J. (1994). Discounting of Delayed Rewards: A Life-Span Comparison. *Psychological Science*, 5(1), 33–36.

Green, L., Myerson, J., Lichtman, D., Rosen, S., & Fry, A. (1996). Temporal Discounting in Choice between Delayed Rewards: The Role of Age and Income. *Psychology and Aging*, 11(1), 79–84.

Hanoch, Y., Johnson, J. G., and Wilke, A. (2006). Domain Specificity in Experimental Measures and Participant Recruitment. *Psychological Science*, 17, 300–304.

Hare, T. A., Camerer, C. F., & Rangel, A. (2009). Self-Control in Decision-Making Involves Modulation of the vmPFC Valuation System. *Science*, 324, 646–648. doi: 10.1126/science1168450.

Jentsch, J. D., and Taylor, J. R. (1999). Impulsivity Resulting from Frontostriatal Dysfunction in Drug Abuse: Implications for the Control of Behavior by Reward-Related Stimuli. *Psychopharmacology*, 146, 373–390.

Kable, J. W., and Glimcher, P. W. (2007). The Neural Correlates of Subjective Value During Intertemporal Choice. *Nature Neuroscience*, 10, 1625–1633. doi: 10.1038/nn2007.

Kable, J. W., and Glimcher, P. W. (2010). An "as Soon as Possible" Effect in Human Intertemporal Decision Making: Behavioral Evidence and Neural Mechanisms. *Journal of Neurophysiology*, 103(5), 2513–2531. doi: 10.1152/jn.00177.2009.

Kable, J. W., and Levy, I. (2015). Neural Markers of Individual Differences in Decision-Making. *Current Opinion in Behavioral Sciences*, 5, 100–107. doi: 10.1016/j.cobeha.2015.08.004.

Kahneman, D. (2003). A Perspective on Judgment and Choice: Mapping Bounded Rationality. *American Psycholigist*, 58, 697–720.

Kahneman, D. (2011). *Thinking Fast and Slow.* London: Penguin.

Kahneman, D., and Tversky, A. (1979). Prospect Theory: An Analysis of Decision Under Risk. *Econometrica*, 47, 263–291. doi: 10.2307/1914185.

Kim, H, Shimojo, S., and O'Doherty, J. P. (2010). Overlapping Responses for the Expectation of Juice and Money Rewards in Human Ventromedial Prefrontal Cortex. *Cerebral Cortex*, 21, 769–776.

Kirby, K. N., (2009). One-Year Temporal Stability of Delay-Discount Rates. *Psychonomic Bulletin and Review*, 16, 457–462.

Koffarnus, M. N., Jarmolowicz, D. P., Mueller, E. T., and Bickel, W. K. (2013). Changing Delay Discounting in the Light of the Competing Neurobehavioral Decision Systems Theory: A Review. *Journal of Experimental Analysis of Behavior*, 99, 32–57. doi: 10.1002/jeab.2.

Kühberger, A., and Tanner, C. (2010). Risky Choice Framing: Task Versions and a Comparison of Prospect Theory and Fuzzy-Trace Theory. *Journal of Behavioral Decision Making*, 23(3), 314–329. doi: 10.1002/bdm.656.

Kurkela, K. A., and Dennis, N. A. (2016) Event-Related fMRI Studies of False Memories: An Activation Likelihood Estimation Meta-analysis. *Neuropsychologia*, 81, 149–167.

Kwak, Y., Payne, J. W., Cohen, A. L., and Huettel, S. A. (2015). The Rational Adolescent: Strategic Information Processing During Decision Making Revealed by Eye Tracking. *Cognitive Development*, 36, 20–30. doi: 10.1016/j.cogdev.2015.08.001.

Levy, D. J., and Glimcher, P. W. (2011). Comparing Apples and Oranges: Using Reward-Specific and Reward-General Subjective Value Representation in the Brain. *Journal of Neuroscience*, 31, 14693–14707. doi: 10.1523/JNEUROSCI.2218-11.2011.

Levy, D. J., and Glimcher, P. W. (2012). The Root of All Value: A Neural Common Currency for Choice. *Current Opinion in Neurobiology*, 22, 1027–1038. doi: 10.1016/ j.conb.2012.06.001.

Liberali, J. M., Reyna, V. F., Furlan, S., Stein, L. M., and Pardo, S. T. (2012). Individual Differences in Numeracy and Cognitive Reflection, with Implications for Biases and Fallacies in Probability Judgment. *Journal of Behavioral Decision Making*, 25(4), 361–381.

Lloyd, F. J., and Reyna, V. F. (2001). A Web Exercise in Evidence-Based Medicine Using Cognitive Theory. *Journal of General Internal Medicine*, 16(2), 94–99. doi: 10.1111/j.1525-1497.2001.00214.x.

Magen, E., Dweck, C. S., and Gross, J. J. (2008). The Hidden-Zero Effect: Representing a Single Choice as an Extended Sequence Reduces Impulsive Choice. *Psychological Science*, 19, 648–649. doi: 10.1111/j.1467-9280.2008.02137.x.

Magen, E., Kim, B., Dweck, C. S., Gross, J. J., McClure, S. M. (2014). Behavioral and Neural Correlates of Increased Self-Control in the Absence of Increased Willpower. *Proceedings of the National Academy of Sciences of the United States of America*, 111, 9786–9791. doi: 10.1073/pnas.1408991111.

McClure, S. M., Ericson, K. M., Laibson, D. I., Loewenstein, G., and Cohen, J. D. (2007). Time Discounting for Primary Rewards. *Journal of Neuroscience*, 27, 5796–5804.

Meade, C. S., Lowen, S. B., Maclean, R. R., Key, M. D., and Lukas, S. E. (2011). fMRI Brain Activation During a Delay Discounting Task in HIV-Positive Adults with and Without Cocaine Dependence. *Psychiatry Research*, 192 (3), 167–175. doi: 10.1016/j.pscychresns.2010.12.011.

Meschkow, A. S., Nolte, J., Garavito, D. M. N., Helm, R. K., Weldon, R. B., and Reyna, V. F. (in press). Risk Taking Across the Lifespan. In M. H. Bornstein (Ed.), *The SAGE Encyclopedia of Lifespan Human Development.*

Mills, B., Reyna, V. F., and Estrada, S. (2008). Explaining Contradictory Relations Between Risk Perception and Risk Taking. *Psychological Science*, 19(5), 429–433. doi: 10.1111/j.1467-9280.2008.02104.x.

Nieder, A. (2016). The Neuronal Code for Number. *Nature Reviews Neuroscience*, 17, 366–382.

Odum, A. L. (2011). Delay Discounting: Trait Variable? *Behavioural Processes*, 87, 1–9. doi: 10.1016/j.beproc.2011.02.007.

Ohmura, Y., Takahashi, T., Kitamura, N., and Wehr, P. (2006). Three-Month Stability of Delay and Probability Discounting Measures. *Experimental and Clinical Psychopharmacology*, 14 (3), 318–328. doi: 10.1037/1064-1297.14.3.318.

Peciña, S., and Berridge, K. C. (2005). Hedonic Hot Spot in Nucleus Accumbens Shell: Where Do μ-opioids Cause Increased Hedonic Impact of Sweetness? *Journal of Neuroscience*, 25(50), 11777–11786.

Peters, E. (2012). Beyond Comprehension: The Role of Numeracy in Judgments and Decisions. *Current Directions in Psychological Science*, 21(1), 31–35.

Peters, E., Slovic, P., Västfjäll, D., and Mertz, C. K. (2008). Intuitive Numbers Guide Decisions. *Judgment and Decision Making*, 3, 619–635.

Pfeifer, J. H., and Allen, N. B. (2012). Arrested Development? Reconsidering Dual-Systems Models of Brain Function in Adolescence and Disorders. *Trends in Cognitive Sciences*, 16, 322–329. doi: 10.1016/j.tics.2012.04.011.

Plassmann, H., O'Doherty, J., and Rangel, A. (2007). Orbitofrontal Cortex Encodes Willingness to Pay in Everyday Economic Transactions. *Journal of Neuroscience*, 27, 9984–9988. doi: 10.1523/JNEUROSCI.2131-07.2007.

Jacobs, J. E., and Potenza, M. (1991). The Use of Judgement Heuristics to Make Social and Object Decisions: A Developmental Perspective. *Child Development*, 62(1), 166–178.

Ramirez-Cardenas, A., Moskaleva, M., and Nieder, A. (2016). Neuronal Representation of Numerosity Zero in the Primate Parieto-Frontal Number Network. *Current Biology*, 26(10), 1285–1294.

Rangel, A., Camerer, C., and Montague, R. (2008). A Framework for Studying the Neurobiology of Value-Based Decision-Making. *Nature Reviews Neuroscience*, 9, 545–556.

Reyna, V. F. (1996). Conceptions of Memory Development with Implications for Reasoning and Decision Making. *Annals of Child Development*, 12, 87–118.

Reyna, V. F. (2004). How People Make Decisions That Involve Risk. *Current Directions in Psychological Science*, 13(2), 60–66. doi: 10.1111/j.0963-7214.2004.00275.x.

Reyna, V. F. (2008). A Theory of Medical Decision Making and health: Fuzzy-trace theory. *Medical Decision Making*, 28, 850–865.

Reyna, V. F. (2011). Across the Lifespan. In B. Fischhoff, N. T. Brewer, and J. S. Downs, (Eds.), *Communicating Risks and Benefits: An Evidence-Based User's Guide* (pp. 111–119). Washington, DC: U.S. Department of Health and Human Services, Food and Drug Administration. Retrieved from www.fda.gov/ScienceResearch/SpecialTopics/RiskCommunication/default.htm

Reyna, V. F. (2012). A New Intuitionism: Meaning, Memory, and Development in Fuzzy-Trace Theory. *Judgment and Decision Making*, 7(3), 332–359.

Reyna, V. F., and Adam, M. B. (2003). Fuzzy-trace theory, risk communication, and product labeling in sexually transmitted diseases. *Risk Analysis*, 23, 325–342.

Reyna, V. F., and Brainerd, C.J. (1991). Fuzzy-Trace Theory and Framing Effects in Choice: Gist Extraction, Truncation, and Conversion. *Journal of Behavior and Decision Making*, 4(4), 249–262. doi: 10.1002/bdm.3960040403.

Reyna, V. F., and Brainerd, C. J. (1994). The Origins of Probability Judgment: A Review of Data and Theories. In G. Wright and P. Ayton (Eds.), *Subjective Probability* (pp. 239–272). New York: Wiley.

Reyna, V. F., and Brainerd, C. J. (1995). Fuzzy-Trace Theory: An Interim Synthesis. *Learning and Individual Differences*, 7(1), 1–75. doi: 10.1016/1041–6080(95)90031–4.

Reyna, V. F., and Brainerd, C. J. (2008). Numeracy, Ratio Bias, and Denominator Neglect in Judgments of Risk and Probability. *Learning and Individual Differences*, 18(1), 89–107. doi: 10.1016/j.lindif.2007.03.011.

Reyna, V. F., and Brainerd, C. J. (2011). Dual Processes in Decision Making and Developmental Neuroscience: A Fuzzy-Trace Model. *Developmental Review*, 31, 180–206. doi: 10.1016/j.dr.2011.07.004.

Reyna, V. F., Chick, C. F., Corbin, J. C., and Hsia, A. N. (2014). Developmental Reversals in Risky Decision Making: Intelligence Agents Show Larger Decision Biases than College Students. *Psychological Science*, 25(1), 76–84. doi: 10.1177/0956797613497022.

Reyna, V. F., Corbin, J. C., Weldon, R. B., and Brainerd, C. J. (2016). How Fuzzy-Trace Theory Predicts True and False Memories for Words and Sentences. *Journal of Applied Research in Memory and Cognition*. 5(1), 1–9. doi: 10.1016/j.jarmac.2015.12.003.

Reyna, V. F., and Ellis, S. C. (1994). Fuzzy-Trace Theory and Framing Effects in Children's Risky Decision Making. *Psychological Science*, 5, 275–279. doi: 10.1111/j.1467–9280.1994.tb00625.x.

Reyna, V. F., Estrada, S. M., DeMarinis, J. A., Myers, R. M., Stanisz, J. M., and Mills, B. A. (2011). Neurobiological and Memory Models of Risky Decision Making in Adolescents Versus Young Adults. *Journal of Experimental Psychology: Learning, Memory, and Cognition*, 37(5), 1125–1142. doi: 10.1037/a0023943.

Reyna, V. F., and Farley, F. (2006). Risk and Rationality in Adolescent Decision Making. *Psychological Science in the Public Interest*, 7(1), 1–44. doi: 10.1111/j.1529-1006.2006.00026.x.

Reyna, V. F., and Huettel, S. A. (2014). Reward, Representation, and Impulsivity: A Theoretical Framework for the Neuroscience of Risky Decision Making. In V. F. Reyna and V. Zayas (Eds.), *The Neuroscience of Risky Decision Making* (pp. 11–42). Washington, DC: American Psychological Association.

Reyna, V. F., and Lloyd, F. J. (2006). Physician Decision Making and Cardiac Risk: Effects of Knowledge, Risk Perception, Risk Tolerance, and Fuzzy Processing. *Journal of Experimental Psychology: Applied*, 12(3), 179–195. doi: 10.1037/1076-898X.12.3.179.

Reyna, V. F., and Mills, B. A. (2007). Interference Processes in Fuzzy-Trace Theory: Aging, Alzheimer's Disease, and Development. In D. Gorfein and C. MacLeod (Eds.), *Inhibition in Cognition* (pp. 185–210). Washington, DC: APA Press.

Reyna, V. F., and Mills, B. A. (2014). Theoretically Motivated Interventions for Reducing Sexual Risk Taking in Adolescence: A Randomized Controlled Experiment Applying Fuzzy-Trace Theory. *Journal of Experimental Psychology: General*, 143(4), 1627–1648. doi: 10.1037/a0036717.

Reyna, V. F., Nelson, W. L., Han, P. K., and Dieckmann, N. F. (2009). How Numeracy Influences Risk Comprehension and Medical Decision Making. *Psychological Bulletin*, 135(6), 943–973.

Reyna, V. F., Weldon, R. B., and McCormick, M. J. (2015a). Educating Intuition: Reducing Risky Decisions Using Fuzzy-Trace Theory. *Current Directions in Psychological Science*, 24(5), 392–398. doi: 10.1177/0963721415588081.

Reyna, V. F., Wilhelms, E. A., McCormick, M. J., and Weldon, R. B. (2015b). Development of Risky Decision Making: Fuzzy-Trace Theory and Neurobiological Perspectives. *Child Development Perspectives*, 9(2), 122–127. doi: 10.1111/cdep.12117.

Reyna, V. F., and Wilhelms, E. A. (2016). The Gist of Delay of Gratification: Understanding and Predicting Problem Behaviors. *Journal of Behavioral Decision Making*. Published online 10 AUG 2016. doi: 10.1002/bdm.1977.

Reynolds, B., and Schiffbauer, R. (2005). Delay of Gratification and Delay Discounting: A Unifying Feedback Model of Delay-Related Impulsive Behavior. *Psychological Record*, 55, 439–460.

Rivers, S. E., Reyna, V. F., and Mills, B. (2008). Risk Taking Under the Influence: A Fuzzy-Trace Theory of Emotion in Adolescence. *Developmental Review*, 28(1), 107–144.

Roiser, J. P., De Martino, B., Tan, G. C., Kumaran, D., Seymour, B., Wood, N. W., and Dolan, R. J. (2009). A Genetically Mediated Bias in Decision Making Driven by Failure of Amygdala Control. *Journal of Neuroscience*, 29(18), 5985–5991.

Samuelson, P. A. (1947). Foundations of Economic Analysis. *Science and Society*, 13(1), 93–95.

Savage, Leonard J. (1954). *The Foundations of Statistics*. New York: Wiley.

Simpson, C. A., and Vuchinich, R. E. (2000). Reliability of a Measure of Temporal Discounting. *Psychological Records*, 50 (1), 3–16.

Stanovich, K. E., and West, R. F. (2008). On the Relative Independence of Thinking Biases and Cognitive Ability. *Journal of Personality and Social Psychology*, 94(4), 672–695. doi: 10.1037/0022-3514.94.4.672.

Steinberg, L. (2008). A Social Neuroscience Perspective on Adolescent Risk Taking. *Developmental Review*, 28(1), 78–106. doi: 10.1111/j.1467-8721.2007.00475.x.

Tversky, A., and Kahneman, D. (1986). Rational Choice and the Framing of Decisions. *Journal of Business*, 59(4), S251–S278.

Venkatraman, V., Payne, J. W., Bettman, J. R., Luce, M. F., and Huettel, S. A. (2009). Separate Neural Mechanisms Underlie Choices and Strategic Preferences in Risky Decision Making. *Neuron*, 62, 593–602. doi: 10.1016/j.neuron.2009.04.007.

Von Neumann, J., and Morgenstern, O. (1944). *Theory of Games and Economic Behavior*. Princeton, NJ: Princeton University Press.

Weber, E. U., Blais, A.-R., and Betz, E. (2002). A Domain-Specific Risk-Attitude Scale: Measuring Risk Perceptions and Risk Behaviors. *Journal of Behavioral Decision Making*, 15, 263–290. doi: 10.1002/bdm.414.

Weldon, R. B., Corbin, J. C., Garavito, D. M. N., and Reyna, V. F. (in press). The Gist Is Sophisticated Yet Simple: Fuzzy-Trace Theory's Developmental Approach to Individual Differences in Judgment and Decision Making. In M. Toplak and J. Weller (Eds.), *Individual Differences in Judgment and Decision Making from a Developmental Context*.

Weldon, R. B., Corbin, J. C., and Reyna, V. F. (2013). Gist Processing in Judgment and Decision Making: Developmental Reversals Predicted by Fuzzy-Trace Theory. In H. Markovits (Ed.), *The Developmental Psychology of Reasoning and Decision-Making* (pp. 36–62). New York: Psychology Press.

Weller, J. A., Levin, I. P., and Denburg, N. L. (2011). Trajectory of Risky Decision Making for Potential Gains and Losses from Ages 5 to 85. *Journal of Behavioral Decision Making*, 24, 331–344. doi: 10.1002/bdm.690.

Wertheimer, M. (1938). Gestalt Theory. In W. D. Ellis (Ed.), *A Source Book of Gestalt Psychology* (pp. 1–11). London: Kegan Paul, Trench, Trubner.

Wilhelms, E. A., Corbin, J. C., and Reyna, V. F. (2015), Gist Memory in Reasoning and Decision Making. In A. Feeney and V. Thompson (Eds.), *Reasoning as Memory* (pp. 93–109). New York: Psychology Press.

Wilhelms, E. A., Helm, R. K., Setton, R. A., and Reyna, V. F. (2014). Fuzzy Trace Theory Explains Paradoxical Dissociations in Affective Forecasting. In Wilhelms, E. A., and Reyna, V. F. (Ed.), *Neuroeconomics, Judgment, and Decision Making* (pp. 49–73), New York: Psychology Press.

Wilhelms, E. A., Reyna, V. F., Brust-Renck, P.G., Weldon, R. B., and Corbin, J. C. (2015). Gist Representations and Communications of Risks about HIV-AIDS: A Fuzzy-Trace Theory Approach. *Current HIV Research*, 13(5), 399–407. doi: 10.2174/1570162X13666150511142748.

Wolfe, C. R., Reyna, V. F., Widmer, C. L., Cedillos, E. M., Fisher, C. R., Brust-Renck, P. G., and Weil, A. M. (2015). Efficacy of a Web-Based Intelligent Tutoring System for Communicating Genetic Risk of Breast Cancer: A Fuzzy-Trace Theory Approach. *Medical Decision Making*, 35(1), 46–59.

Yechiam, E., and Telpaz, A. (2013). Losses Induce Consistency in Risk Taking Even Without Loss Aversion. *Journal of Behavioral Decision Making*, 26(1), 31–40.

Zayas, V., Mischel, W., and Pandey, G. (2014). Mind and Brain in Delay of Gratification. In V. F. Reyna and V. Zayas (Eds.), *The Neuroscience of Risky Decision Making* (pp. 145–176). Washington, DC: American Psychological Association.

Zheng, H., Wang, X. T., and Zhu, L. (2010). Framing Effects: Behavioral Dynamics and Neural Basis. *Neuropsychologia*, 48(11), 3198–3204.

26 Robots, Cyborgs, and Consumption

Russell Belk

26.1 Introduction

Humanoid robots (androids if male; gynoids if female) are becoming increasingly humanlike, not only in appearance, but in responsiveness, emotions, movements, and ability to interact with humans. The counterpart to computerized machines becoming more humanlike is cyborgs (cybernetic organisms) – humans who are becoming more machinelike. Robots and cyborgs are no longer only figures out of science fiction. They are becoming part of our lives as robots move into our homes and as we adopt various internal and external modifications and devices that make us, at least in certain senses, superhuman. If superhuman seems too strong a claim, we have only to reflect on all the things we can do with a smart phone; it puts the world's knowledge instantly at our fingertips and helps us with everything from route finding, to meeting potential partners, to monitoring our health, diet, and fitness, doing our banking, and watching events unfold across the globe (e.g., Bode and Kirstensen 2016).

But these developments are just a taste of things to come. Benford and Malartre (2007, p. 8) observe that:

> Soon robots will be everywhere, performing surgery, exploring hazardous places, making rescues, fighting fires, handling heavy goods. After a decade or two they will be unremarkable as the computer screen is now ... robots will increasingly blend in ... The cyborgs will be less obvious. Many changes will be hidden from view. At first these additions to the human body will be interior, as rebuilt joints, elbows, and hearts are now. Then larger adjuncts will appear, perhaps on people's heads or limbs. Soon we will cross the line between repair and augmentation, probably first in sports medicine and the military, then spreading to everyone who wants to make the body perform better.

Such hybridization and merging of humans and nonhuman devices affects consumer self-definition and raises a number of behavioral, moral, ethical, and legal issues. For example, as machines like automobiles become more autonomous, it has been suggested that they could become not only self-driving, but self-owning vehicles. The plausibility of this forecast will be discussed in this chapter, but it has been predicted that this would mean that such cars might have the legal status of persons, just as corporations can be legal judicial persons (e.g., Calverley, 2011; Casella and Croucher, 2011). This may be a legal issue, but it also has important potential consequences for the economy, as we shall see.

A related concern is that the humanlike appearance of androids and gynoids will not only enhance our willingness to accept them as part of our lives, but may also lead to anthropomorphizing these machines and thinking of them as humans. Even with weak artificial intelligence (AI), which only allows robots to do as they have been programmed to do, we may develop guilty qualms that we are treating these anthropomorphized beings as slaves. There are already movements ready to fight for robot rights and urging that robots be liberated from their slavery. If and when we develop strong AI, in which robots become indistinguishable from humans in their responses, mannerisms, and intellect, these movements are likely to become stronger and be carried out by the robots themselves. But even without strong AI, there are other robotic issues that we will soon need to address. They include the effects of robots on our own identities and our certainty that humans are a superior species, the degree to which semiautonomous robots can act as our agents or have agency of their own, the moral issues raised by battlefield robots and aerial drones, and the degree to which we will trust robots to drive our cars, fly our planes, and care for our children and elderly.

In this chapter, I outline the implications of robots and cyborgs for economic psychology. I discuss how these two entities, the robot and the cyborg, may affect each other. And I summarize a set of consumer research programs that are needed to address issues like those just highlighted. If all this seems like something out of science fiction books, comics, and films, it is! Except that such science fiction is rapidly becoming science fact. And even the more speculative concerns in this arena warrant serious attention because of the severity of their potential consequences.

26.2 Economic and Consumption Issues

26.2.1 Cyborgs

It is perhaps easiest to think of consumption issues with cyborgs. The term cyborg was created by Clynes and Kline (1960) to refer to psychopharmacological and mechanical enhancements that might allow a human to survive in outer space. Haraway (1985) defined the cyborg as "a hybrid of machine and organism." But besides mechanical aids and the pharmacological additions suggested by Clynes and Kline, other cyborgian modifications include plastic surgery, genetic modification, and chip-enhanced cognition (Barfield, 2015). Even more extreme modifications such as uploading our minds into a computer are among the future cyborg scenarios that some scholars and researchers are pursuing (Benford and Malartre, 2007; Broderick, 2014; Chu, 2014; Eth, Foust, and White,2013; Rothblatt 2014).

As the more extreme of these research thrusts suggest, an ultimate aim of cyborg modifications is to enable humans to be smarter, stronger, faster, thinner, and longer-lived. The ultimate aim of the related transhumanist movement is to achieve immortality. That is, they aim to create essentially a new species, the posthuman. And if they fall short during their own lifetimes, a number of transhumanists hope that cryogenic suspension will allow then to be unthawed when medical advances can make them whole again (Bostrom, 2005; Chu, 2014; Clark, 2003; Ranisch and Sorgner, 2014). Beyond that, some transhumanists envision discarding the body altogether and living on as an avatar, computer emulation, or embedded program in a robot (e.g., Badmington, 2004; Bostrom, 2011; Peters, 2011).

Two basic questions in terms of consumption are: who would want to be modified in these ways, and who could afford such a transformation? For more extreme procedures like brain scanning and uploading to a computer, a number of forecasts suggest that the patient would either die in the process or not be preserved as anything like the original human with a personality, history, and feelings (e.g., Corabi and Schneider, 2012, 2014; Rose, 2013; Sirius and Cornell 2015). Thus one forecast is that the terminally ill who are desperate to hang on to some form of life might be the first to attempt such procedures. Given the extremely high cost that is likely to be entailed, another forecast is that such posthumans might create a society of a few privileged superhumans and the rest of us (Bess, 2016; Reddy, 1999). Fears of eugenics also haunt the extreme cyborg modification predictions (Nelkin and Lindee, 1995).

But rather than a sudden jump to superhumanity and immortality, acceptance of cyborg modifications is more likely to come gradually. We are already comfortable with contact lenses, hearing aids, pacemakers, smart phones, and many other prosthetic devices. We take Viagra, Botox, vitamin injections, and similar supplements (Giesler, 2012; Giesler, Luedicke, and Ozergin, 2009). And while one study suggests that those with artificially enhanced intelligence are trusted less than those whose intelligence in unenhanced (Costelo et al., 2015), we do not put such "cheats" in the same currently offensive categories as we do the use of anabolic steroids, blood doping, and other forms of athletic pharmaceutical enhancement among athletes.

The opposite sort of prejudice against artificially enhanced cyborgs is depicted in the film *Gattica* (Niccol, 1997). It depicts a near-future civilization in which babies are genetically engineered to be free of defects and susceptibility to diseases. These are the "valids" who get the important jobs in society, while the "invalids" who have not benefited from eugenics are excluded. Vincent, who dearly wants to be an astronaut on a flight to Saturn's moon Titan, is an invalid who has high probability of several disorders and a predicted lifespan of only 30.2 years. But he finds a valid man who became crippled in a car accident and is willing to provide urine, blood, hair, and skin samples so that Vincent can pass regular tests to be sure that no invalids have sneaked their way into the program. There is more to the plot than this, but in the end Vincent barely escapes detection, leaves a love interest, and boards the spacecraft to Titan. In this film, we see a vision in which genetically altered humans are given elevated status. In a somewhat different take on class-based eugenics, the film Elysium (Blomkamp, 2013) depicts a gigantic orbiting space station on which the rich are able to avail themselves of medical devices that allow them to regenerate body parts, cure diseases, and reverse the aging process, while the poor suffer and die on earth. In a very different vision, modified humans are bred for monotonous work and suffer as status-deprived second-class citizens (see Lai, 2012). In the worries that Lai's research participants discussed, genetic modification was seen as a curse rather than a blessing. Which, if any of these scenarios are more likely is something that we will learn with time. But research such as Lai's examining our reactions, fears, and hopes regarding cyborgs can be conducted now. No doubt these reactions are partly shaped by fictional portrayals such as those of *Elysium* and *Gattica*. These depictions, in turn, are partly driven by what is now technologically feasible.

26.2.2 Robots

Although home robots and service industry robots are beginning to be adopted, robots have thus far had their greatest success in factories. Currently, one out of twenty-five Japanese workers is a robot, and that number is expected to rise rapidly as the Japanese population ages. There are now over a million industrial robots in action (Robertson, 2010a). In manufacturing, it simply makes economic sense to replace humans with robots when a robotic spot welding machine can work for $8 an hour versus a human welder who costs $20 an hour, and who also makes more mistakes, requires a pension plan, and expects to go home after eight hours on the job (Grant, 2015). Not only are robots replacing humans on the assembly line, but also in occupations such as accounting, law, medicine and surgery, and journalism. For example, a robotic algorithm developed at Northwestern University's Medill School of Journalism, Media, and Integrated Marketing Communications writes sports stories and features for newspapers and respected media outlets such as *Forbes*. And readers cannot tell the difference (Levy, 2012). For many delicate surgeries, robotic surgeons do a better job than human doctors (Strickland, 2016). And it makes little sense to hire humans to do legal searches when robotic computer search programs do a better job at a fraction of the cost.

While not everyone agrees (Markoff, 2015), a number of estimates suggest that as much as 50 percent of human jobs could be lost to robots in the next twenty to thirty years (Chace, 2015; Ford 2015; Kaplan, 2015). Although humans have previously adapted to a dramatically changing job market during the industrial and computer revolutions, the pace of forecast change has never been this swift. By one estimate, within fifteen years as many as 90 percent of all newspaper articles may be written by robots (Levy, 2012). Some occupations will be more threatened than others, but robots and computers are already composing music, checking guests into hotels, entertaining us, and answering shopper questions (e.g., Nguyen, 2015; Rajesh, 2015; Smith, 2016; Susskind and Susskind, 2015). Robots are also harvesting crops, building houses, and soothing and helping patients in nursing homes. Robots may even threaten the "Asian Century" as they replace low cost Asian factory workers and allow European and other non-Asian goods makers to re-source their newly robotized manufacturing and reclaim the label of "made in" their home countries (Lee, 2015).

Besides these economic issues, there are also a number of consumer issues with robots. Besides the obvious questions of whether we consumers will accept robots into our homes to clean, control energy use, care for our children, and help our elderly get dressed, bathe, and take their medications, there are additional issues of how else we may use home robots. Some of these issues are explored in the Swedish television series *Äkta Människor* (Real Humans) and the British adaptation *Humans* (Den of Geek, 2015). For example, both series, set in the near future, explore whether humans will bond with robots as family members (yes), whether they will readily replace them with alternative robots (no), whether they will be inclined to have sex with these robots (yes), whether this will be widely accepted (no), whether some robots might be a threat to humans (yes), and whether some humans might be inclined to abuse robots (yes).

Of course, these are just dramatic portrayals like many science fiction stories about robots (Barsani, 2014; Schelde, 1993). However, such fictional portrayals are not far from current reality. For example, there are rudimentary sex robots for sale for between $1,000 and $8,000 (Linden, 2015). There has been a conference on the touristic potential of sexbot prostitution (Yeoman and Mars, 2015). In Japan, where there is a history of sex dolls and robotic sex animations, reportedly sexbot prostitutes are already in business, charging about the same amount as human prostitutes (Orbaugh, 2002; Shaw-Garlock, 2009; Sullins, 2012). It is also argued that as with pornography driving adoption of videotape players, DVD players, and the Internet, sex is likely to play an important role in the adoption of home robots (Levy, 2007; Scheutz, 2012).

Similarly, there is some evidence that some humans may abuse robots (Rosalia et al., 2005). In a replication of Stanley Milgrim's (1963) famous experiments involving subject willingness to shock fellow humans when ordered to do so, Spiegel (2013) found that subjects were much more willing to do so with robots, even when the robots begged them to stop. And even when shopping mall security robots are designed to be friendly, there are some among us who insist on trying to harm and bully them (Wells, 2016).

There are also issues of the degree to which consumers will accept robots in the home and marketplace in the first place. It is generally held that the more humanoid the appearance of the robot, the more likely we will be to engage with it as we might with another human being (Aggarwal and McGill, 2017; Duffy, 2003). But we appear to be willing to anthropomorphize robots and other objects with only vaguely humanoid appearance such as the semblance of a face (Belk, 2016; Goudey and Bonnin, 2016). After having spent two years with the MIT robot Kismet, theology professor Anne Foerst (2011) concluded that Kismet is a person. This is in spite of the fact that the robot has only a head and neck and makes only unintelligible noises. The facts that its gaze follows a person around the room and that it responds to the emotions it senses in people appear to be enough to thoroughly engage us. It is this human emotional recognition and empathy that is a key feature of several commercially available robots such as Nao and Pepper (Woollaston, 2015). Still, when MIT Professor of the Social Studies of Science and Technology Sherry Turkle (2011) was asked by a journalist what she thought of people marrying robots that would satisfy all of their physical and emotional needs for life, she responded with horror that this would be unthinkable since robots cannot really feel.

The acceptance of robots in our homes and lives depends on our ability to trust them. Hassler (2016) asks, for example, "would you trust a robot to give your grandmother her meds?" Strickland (2016) asks "would you trust a robot surgeon to operate on you?" Research is needed to answer such questions, and experimental evidence to date is mixed (LaFrance, 2016; Paeng, Wu, and Boerkoel, 2016; Wang et al., 2015). But if anything, the research suggests that we may trust robots too much, thereby potentially endangering our safety and security. In one study, an "emergency guide robot" ineptly led subjects to the wrong room to complete a questionnaire. When smoke started pouring in under the door, they followed the robot to a dark room filled with furniture rather than following the exit signs (Toenameter, 2016; Toon, 2016). In another study on the Harvard University campus, students readily allowed a robot into secure dormitories when it requested entry (Scharping, 2016).

There are further issues of robot gender and personality that may affect our acceptance and trust of robots. There is some evidence that preferences may depend on the type of application: for example, outgoing female health care robots are preferred, whereas introverted male security robots are seen as more acceptable (Tay, Jung, and Park, 2014). There may also be cultural differences. There is evidence, for example, that partly due to Shintoist and Buddhist beliefs, Japanese consumers readily see robots as friendly and as family members, while Westerners are more likely to scrutinize the utilitarian value of these artificial humans (Hornyak, 2009; Mims, 2010; Robertson, 2007, 2010a, 2010b). This difference may also be seen in a history of friendly robots in Japanese manga and anime in a genre called *mecha* (Bolton, Csicsery-Ronay, and Tatsumi, 2007; Gilson 1998; Hikawa, 2013).

A final illustrative issue requiring consumer research involves the degree to which we see robots as extensions of ourselves versus others against whom or which we might compare ourselves. Nourbakhsh (2013) forecasts that we will operate multiple robots simultaneously as our surrogate agents. While there is some evidence to suggest that we do see robots as self extensions or surrogate selves (Groom et al., 2009; Kamide, Eyssel, and Arai, 2013; Nishio et al., 2013), there is a compelling argument that just as we compared ourselves to animals in the past in order to assure ourselves of our unique human abilities and superiority, we are now more apt to compare ourselves to computers and robots (Geraci, 2010; Kim and Kim, 2013; Scott, 2011). And with each new advance in robotics, we lose a little more of what we once thought made us humans unique. For example, IBM computers have beaten the world's best chess players and *Jeopardy* champions, while a Google computer has taught itself to play Go and then defeat the world's Go champion. A key reason that robots are replacing humans in formerly human jobs is not simply that they are cheaper, they are also better, less error prone, able to work twenty-four/seven in lights-out factories, remember perfectly, and never get sick. Unique human abilities remain, but are becoming fewer and fewer.

26.3 Social Economic Issues

Besides the individual economic and consumption issues that have been considered thus far, there are also broader social economic issues regarding cyborgs and robots. We are not just individual consumers, but citizen-consumers as well. A key area of robot and cyborg development that we fund with our taxes is their military application. While cyborg enhancements such as exoskeletons help soldiers travel farther, faster, and with heavier loads, semi-autonomous military robots not only help carry loads, but also defuse bombs, retrieve wounded soldiers, and perform reconnaissance. More controversially, robotic devices also take the place of soldiers in delivering bombs and lethal gunfire. This includes armed aerial drones, autonomous missile defense systems, and semiautonomous robot tanks with sophisticated sensors and firepower (Singer, 2009). The demilitarized zone between North and South Korea is now patrolled by small semiautonomous tanks that can "see" farther than humans, detect infrared heat signatures, request identification, and shoot to kill. At present, there is also a human in this loop, but there are no international robotic warfare rules to guarantee that this will be the case in the future. Singer (2009) tallies the advance of combat robots over the course of the US war in Iraq: 2003 – 0; 2004 – 150; 2005 – 2,400; 2008 – 12,000. As would be expected, the United States is not alone in military investment in robotics as well as in nanotechnology, biotechnology, posthuman development, and robotic space exploration.

The human is already out of the loop in other military systems such as Israel's "iron dome" missile defense system and the Phalanx missile defense systems owned by some forty countries and focusing mostly on defending ships. In both cases, by the time it would take for a human to decide whether incoming objects are enemy missiles and fire weapons to destroy them, it would be too late. So the systems autonomously act without a human decision maker (Guarini and Bello, 2012; Hellström, 2013; Marchant et al., 2011). There is worry that such killing at a distance with little threat to the soldiers of the robot owner will make it more tempting to go to war. A new robot arms race is also inevitable with such devices. And there is a fear that such impersonal killing is simply immoral. If such weapons fall into the hands of criminals or terrorists, we would likely see them in a different light as well. Although Isaac Asimov (Anderson, 2011; Asimov, 1950/1991) proposed several laws of robotics to protect humans from robots, the first of these laws, "a robot must not harm a human being or, through inaction, cause a human being to come to harm," has already been violated frequently by lethal drone attacks.

Another set of social issues emerges from a robotic economic arena that may at first seem entirely benign. It involves decentralized autonomous organizations (DAOs) or decentralized autonomous corporations (DACs) and digital currencies such as Bitcoin. A simple example was presented by Mike Hearn at the 2013 Turing Festival in Edinburgh (Hearn, 2013; Johnson, 2015; Kelion, 2015). The example involves a combination of self-driving cars and a ride-sharing commercial services similar to Uber and Lyft. The cars use algorithms in bidding based on location, traffic, and a reputation rating takes place for both cars and riders after the trip is completed. But there is a further twist to this scenario in that the self-driving cars would also be self-owning cars after they repaid their original purchase price to a crowd-funding service. They would do so using the money they earned in offering rides. They would operate like Uber, Lyft, and Didi, but they would cut out the middleman. Rather, they would be operating according to their programming to earn just enough revenue to pay for fuel, repairs, and upgrades, with a small amount retained as savings held in digital currency. After repaying the initial loan and setting aside enough money, they would then "have children" by purchasing another car. This child car would operate the same way, repay the parent, and have children of its own. Because these cars could operate twenty-four/seven and have zero labor costs, they would have lower prices and quickly outcompete human drivers. When there got to be too many cars in a particular location, they would spread out to adjacent areas. It is easy to see how this model could also be applied to other areas of the economy involving transportation; banking; cloud servers; retailing (after the model of Amazon); stock trading; venture capitalism; escrow services; real estate services; and, in fact, most any service industry. Deeds, money, and documents would all exist within the network of DAOs, and strict rules would be programmed in to prevent fraud, poor service, censorship, and corruption. DAOs may not be limited only to providing services, but through "smart contracts," they could operate in the supply chains for products as well. The DAOs would hire people, but there would be no hierarchy, board of directors, or boss.

If such DAOs were in fact recognized as corporations, they would have the same legal status as other corporations. They would pay taxes, acquire licenses, and obey the same laws as other corporations, but such an entity would have no human CEO or other officers. Rather, the corporation would be autonomous and be owned by the robots or by a large number of investors across the globe (Banen, 2016; Montevideo, 2014; Morris, 2015; Pangburn, 2015). This is a version of Rifkin's (2014) global Collaborative Commons. Whereas Napster was a centralized organization hosted by humans who were able to be prosecuted and shut down, BitTorrent is a decentralized autonomous organization that has not been successfully curbed or shut down. It is a part of the sharing economy, but without a profit-taking corporation at its heart (Belk, 2010; Sundararajan, 2016; Swan, 2015). This vision, using the blockchain algorithmic mechanism like the one behind Bitcoin, may create a paradigm shift in capitalism and economic organization, in which a much larger number of people are able to participate in the benefits of innovation. Under certain versions of this paradigm shift, everyone would receive a guaranteed minimum income whether they worked or not (Chace, 2015; Ford, 2015; Kaplan, 2015; Markoff, 2015).

Not everyone is so convinced of this, however. Alternative visions hold that a few powerful people would own the robots and control them for profit, while the rest of the population suffers massive unemployment (Morris, 2015; Pangburn, 2015). Despite its transparency, because blockchain technology potentially has a certain amount of anonymity, it might also be used for nefarious purposes, such as hiring assassins. It has already been used for the Silk Road darknet marketplace on which exchanges of drugs, guns, and other illegal purchases took place using Bitcoin (Chacos, 2013). So there is a great range of possible DAO future scenarios ranging from a utopian society in which no one has to work unless they desire to do so to dystopian scenarios in which the powerful and unscrupulous get rich at the expense of everyone else. One thing that is clear is that there is a potential paradigm shift on the horizon that could substantially change our economy and society.

One final social issue to be addressed may in the long run be the most profound as it threatens the continued existence of the human species. As noted earlier, robots and artificial intelligence are becoming more sophisticated and more autonomous. The whole thrust of robotics and AI is to create machines as intelligent as humans – a prospect called artificial general intelligence (AGI). Once this level of machine intellect is achieved, the machines could begin to reprogram themselves and quickly become superintelligent entities that grow exponentially in abilities and soon far exceed human capacities. This development is referred to as the Singularity, and it is forecast to occur within our century and perhaps by midcentury (Barrat, 2013; Bekey, 2005; Kurzweil, 1999, 2012; Moravec, 1999). At this point, humans would be of as little use to the robots, with their superior intellect and strength, as ants are of negligible interest to humans. These scenarios forecast that we will either be exterminated or kept as pets and amusements.

Whatever the likelihood of such scenarios, it clearly behooves us to take precautions to prevent the more sinister potential outcomes now rather than when it is too late. Various preventative measures have been proposed, including striving to create moral robots, keeping them as dumb slaves without sophisticated AI, blackboxing them to preclude access to the Internet and powerful machines, and striving to keep up with AI and robots through human cyborg modification or uploading our minds to computers. The latter solution is appealing, but there is a worry that mechanical and pharmacological cyborg upgrades, genetic engineering, and the progress of mind cloning (uploading our intellect to computers) are either too slow or would become possible too late to be effective. There have been dire forecasts from people such as Stephen Hawking (Dingman, 2014), Bill Gates (Rawlinson, 2015), and Elon Musk (Lewis, 2015) that biological evolution is just too slow to keep up with silicon-based evolution and that the human species is at considerable risk. Films such as *Ex Machina* (Garland, 2015) show the seductive ability of robots with superior intellect to trick inferior humans. For some, the singularity will merely mean that we have created a worthy successor and that the AGI computer will be the last invention we will ever create (Barrat, 2013). Astrobiologists have predicted that if the earth is ever visited by extraterrestrial aliens, they will be robots and come from civilizations millions of years ahead of earth in which machines have eclipsed biological life long ago (e.g., Davies, 2010; Schneider, 2014).

26.4 Conclusions

Other than a common focus on technologies and technological possibilities that are not quite here yet, a common thread in this consideration of robots, cyborgs, transhumanism, and decentralized autonomous organizations is their disruptive potential for the neoliberal capitalist system that now spans the globe. The role of competition versus cooperation is critical to alternative economic systems and DAOs. Competition is the underlying force behind the AI and robotic arms races. The same is true in the commercial realms of industrial and home robotics. And the same is true in efforts to enhance ourselves with cyborg prosthetics, medical procedures, and pharmaceuticals in order to be the best cyborgs money can buy. Visions of cooperation and altruism are evident, however in some of the DAO proposals; work in the areas of computer, robot, or machine ethics (e.g., Anderson and Anderson 2011; Johnson 1985; Lin, Abney, and Bekey 2012); and transhumanism. Thus suppositions about human motivations are ultimately more critical to these discussions than speculations about robot motivations (e.g., Omohundro, 2008). Also not considered here is the role of religion as we try to create artificial life or become gods ourselves (e.g., Cole-Turner, 2011; Geraci, 2010; Rosenfeld, 1966). Some suggest, for instance, that transhumanism is a religion (Mercer, 2015). From a different perspective, it has been suggested that with its focus on immortality, Christianity is equivalent to transhumanism (Redding, 2016).

In economic psychology, we do not often get a chance to contemplate and research topics with such significance. Yet all of these issues are steeped in issues of the marketplace, the economy, and consumption. There are many issues to be grappled with, and we can play a critical part in addressing them. I have only provided a brief outline here, but I have tried to provide a number of references for those who have a desire to dig deeper into some of these issues. I have also expanded on some of these issues elsewhere (Belk, 2014, 2016, 2017). I hope I have been able to provoke the interest of readers to begin to think about these issues, include them in classroom discussions, and carve out research programs in these areas.

26.5 References

Aggarwal, Pankaj and Ann McGill (2017), "Anthropomorphism," in Cathrine V. Jansson-Boyd and Magdalena Zawisza, ed., *Routledge International Handbook of Consumer Psychology*, London: Routledge, 600–617.

Anderson, Michael and Susan Leigh Anderson, ed., (2011), *Machine Ethics*, Cambridge: Cambridge University Press.

Anderson, Susan (2011), "The Unacceptability of Asimov's Three Laws of Robotics as a Basis for Machine Ethics," in Michael Anderson and Susan Leigh Anderson, ed., *Machine Ethics*, Cambridge: Cambridge University Press, 285–296.

Asimov, Isaac (1950/1991), *I, Robot*, New York: Spectra.

Badmington, Neil (2004), *Alien Chic: Posthumanism and the Other Within*, London: Routledge.

Bannon, Seth (2016), "The Tao of 'The DAO' or: How the Autonomous Corporation is Already Here," *TechCrunch*, May 16, techcrunch.com/2016/05/16/the-tao-of-the-dao-or-how-the-autonomous-corporation-is-already-here/, last accessed July 20, 2016.

Barfield, Woodrow (2015). *Cyber-Humans: Our Future with Machines*, Cham, Switzerland: Springer.

Barrat, James (2013), *Our Final Invention: Artificial Intelligence and the End of the Human Era*, New York: Thomas Dunn.

Barsanti, Chris (2014), *The Sci-Fi Movie Guide: The Universe of Film from Alien to Zardoz*, Canton, MI: Visible Ink Press.

Bekey, George (2005), *Autonomous Robots: From Biological Inspiration to Implementation and Control*, Cambridge, MA: MIT Press.

Belk, Russell (2010), "Sharing," *Journal of Consumer Research*, 16 (5), 715–734.

Belk, Russell (2014), "If You Prick Us Do We Not Bleed? Humanoid Robots and Cyborgs as Consuming Subjects and Consumed Objects," *Latin America Advances in Consumer Research*, 3, 3–6.

Belk, Russell (2016), "Understanding the Robot: Comments on Goudey and Bonnin," *Recherche et Applications en Marketing*, 31 (2).

Belk, Russell (2017), "Consumers in an Age of Autonomous Robots," in John Sherry and Eileen Fischer, ed., *Contemporary Consumer Culture Theory*, Routledge, 5–32.

Benford, Gregory and Elisabeth Malartre (2007), *Beyond Human: Living with Robots and Cyborgs*, New York: Tom Doherty Associates.

Bess, Michael (2016), *Super Humans: How the Science of Bio-enhancement Is Transforming Our World, and How We Need to Deal with It*, London: Icon.

Blomkamp, Neill (2013), *Elysium*, Culver City, CA: TriStar Pictures.

Bode, Mathias and Dorthe Kristensen (2016), "The Digital Doppelgänger Within: A Study on Self-Tracking and the Quantified Self Movement," in Robin Canniford and Domen Bajde, ed., *Assembling Consumption: Researching Actors, Networks and Markets*, Abingdon, UK: Routledge, 119–135.

Bolton, Christopher, Istvan Csicsery-Ronay, Jr., and Takyuki Tatsumi, ed. (2007), *Robot Ghosts and Wired Dreams: Japanese Science Fiction from Origins to Anime*, Minneapolis: University of Minnesota Press.

Bostrom, Nick (2005), "A History of Transhumanist Thought," *Journal of Evolution and Technology*, 14 (1), 1–25.

Bostrom, Nick (2011), "In Defense of Posthuman Dignity," in Gregory Hansell and William Grassie, ed., *H± Transhumanism and Its Critics*, Philadelphia, PA: Metanexus, 55–66.

Broderick, Damien (2014), "Introduction I: Machines of Loving Grace (Let's Hope)," in Russell Blackford and Daien Broderick, ed., *Intelligence Unbound: The Future of Uplaoded and Machine Minds*, Chichester, UK: John Wiley & Sons, 1–10.

Calverley, David (2011), "Legal Rights for Machines: Some Fundamental Concepts," in Michael Anderson and Susan Anderson, ed., *Machine Ethics*, Cambridge: Cambridge University Press, 213–227.

Casella, Eleanor and Karina Croucher (2011), "Beyond Human: The Materiality of Personhood," *Feminist Theory*, 12 (2), 209–217.

Chacos, Brad (2013), "Meet Darknet, the Hidden, Anonymous Underbelly of the Searchable Web," *PCWorld*, August 12, www.pcworld.com/article/2046227/meet-darknet-the-hidden-anonymous-underbelly-of-the-searchable-web.html, last accessed July 20, 2016.

Chace, Calum (2015), *Surviving AI: The Promise and Peril of Artificial Intelligence*, New York: 3Cs.

Chu, Ted (2014), *Human Purpose and Transhuman Potential: A Cosmic Vision for Our Future Evolution*, San Rafael, CA: Origin Press.

Clark, Andy (2003), *Natural Born Cyborgs: Minds, Technologies, and the Future of Human Intelligence*, Oxford: Oxford University Press.

Clynes, Manfred and Nathan Kline (1960),"Cyborgs and Space," *Astonautics*, September, 26–27, 75–76.

Cole-Turner, Ronald, ed. (2011), *Transhumanism and Transcendence: Christian Hope in an Age of Technological Enhancement*, Washington, DC: Georgetown University Press.

Corabi, Joe and Susan Schneider (2012), "The Metaphysics of Uploading," *Journal of Consciousness Studies*, 19 (7–8), 26–44.

Corabi, Joe and Susan Schneider (2014), "If You Upload Will You Survive?" in Russell Blackford and Daien Broderick, ed., *Intelligence Unbound: The Future of Uploaded and Machine Minds*, Chichester, UK: John Wiley & Sons, 131–145.

Costelo, Noah, Nicholas Fitz, Bernd Schmidt, and Mikkos Sarvary (2015), "When Enhancing Human Traits Is Dehumanizing, and What to Do About It," *Advances in Consumer Research*, 43, 779.

Davies, Paul (2010), *The Eerie Silence: Renewing Our Search for Alien Intelligence*, Boston: Houghton Mifflin Harcourt.

Den of Geek (2015), "Comparing Humans to Swedish Original, Real Humans," *Den of Geek!* www.denofgeek.us/tv/humans/248234/comparing-humans-to-swedish-original-real-humans, last accessed July 29, 2016.

Dingman, Shane (2014), "Even Stephen Hawking Fears the Rise of Machines," *The Globe and Mail*, December 2, online edition, license.icopyright.net/user/view/FreeUse.act?fuid=MTkwMDg1OTA%3D, last accessed March 24, 2015.

Duffy, Brian (2003), "Anthropomorphism and the Social Robot," *Robotics and Autonomous Systems*, 42 (3/4), 177–190.

Eth, Daniel, Juan-Carlos Foust, and Klaus Schenk-Hoppé (2013), "The Prospects of Whole Brain Emulation with the Next Half-Century," *Journal of Artificial General Intelligence*, 4 (3), 130–152.

Foerst, Anne (2004), *God in the Machine: What Robots Teach us about Humanity and God*, New York: Dutton.

Ford, Martin (2015), *Rise of the Robots: Technology and the Threat of a Jobless Future*, New York: Basic Books.

Garland, Alex (2015), *Ex Machina*, Hollywood, CA: Universal Studios.

Geraci, Robert (2010), *Apocalyptic AI: Visions of Heaven in Robotics, Artificial Intelligence, and Virtual Reality*, Oxford: Oxford University Press.

Giesler, Markus (2012), "How Doppelgänger Brand Images Influence the Market Creation Process: Longitudinal Insights from the Rise of Botox Cosmetic," *Journal of Marketing*, 76 (November), 55–68.

Giesler, Markus, Marius Luedicke, and Berrin Ozergin (2009), "American Self-Enhancement Culture and the Cyborg Consumer: Consumer Identity Construction Beyond the Dominance of Authenticity," *Advances in Consumer Research*, 36, 72–75.

Gilson, Mark (1998), "A Brief History of Japanese Robophilia," *Leonardo* 31 (5), 367–369.

Goudey, Alain and Gael Bonnin (2016), "Must Smart Objects Look Human? Study of the Impact of Anthropomorphism on the Acceptance of Companion Robots," *Recherche et Applications en Marketing*, 31(2), 3–22.

Grant, Tavia (2015), "Rise of the Machines: Robots Poised to Transform Global Manufacturing," *The Globe and Mail*. February 10, www.theglobeandmail.com/report-on-business/rise-of-the-machines-robots-poised-to-transform-global-manufacturing/article22884032/, last accessed July 19, 2016.

Groom, Victoria, Leila Takayama, Paloma Ochi, and Clifford Nass (2009), "I Am My Robot: The Impact of Robot-building and Robot Form on Operators,"

Proceedings of the 4th ACM/IEEE International Conference on Human Robot Interaction, March 9, 31–36.

Guarini, Marcello and Paul Bello (2012), "Robotic Warfare: Some Challenges in Moving from Noncivilian to Civilian," in Patrick Lin, Keith Abney, and George Bekey, ed., *Robot Ethics: The Ethical and Social Implications of Robotics*, Cambridge, MA: MIT Press, 129–144.

Haraway, Donna (1985) "A Manifesto for Cyborgs: Science, Technology, and Socialist Feminism in the 1980s," *Socialist Review*, 80, 65–107.

Hassler, Susan (2016), "Would You Trust a Robot to Give Your Grandmother Her Meds?" *IEEE Spectrum*, June 1, spectrum.ieee.org/robotics/artificial-intelligence/would-you-trust-a-robot-to-give-your-grandmother-her-meds, last accessed July 3, 2016.

Hearn, Mike (2013), "Mike Hearn, Bitcoin Developer – Turing Festival 2013," Turing, Edinburgh International Technology Festival, www.youtube.com/watch?v=Pu4PAMFPo5Y, last accessed March 28, 2015.

Hellström, Thomas (2013), "On the Moral Responsibility of Military Robots," *Ethics, Information, Technology*, 15, 99–107.

Hikawa, Ryusuke, ed. (2013), *Japanese Animation Guide: The History of Robot Anime*, Tokyo: Agency for Cultural Affairs Manga, Animation, Games, and Media Art Information Bureau.

Hornyak, Tim (2009), "Programmed for Combat or for Pleasure: U.S. and Japan Go Separate Ways When it Comes to Robot Technology," *Japan Times*, www.japantimes.co.jp/life/2009/03/25/digital/programmed-for-combat-or-for-pleasure/#.VWctcyTFndk, last accessed July 1, 2016.

Johnson, Amanda (2015), "Self-Owning Computers Can Beat 'Skynet' – Mike Hearn on the Internet of Things," *Coin Telegraph*, February 18, cointelegraph.com/news/self-owning-computers-can-beat-skynet-mike-hearn-on-the-internet-of-things, last accessed July 21, 2016.

Johnson, Deborah (1985), *Computer Ethics*, Upper Saddle River, NJ: Prentice Hall.

Kamide, Hiroko, Friederike Eyssel, and Tatsuo Arai (2013), "Psychological Anthropomorphism of Robots: Measuring Mind Perception and Humanity in Japanese Context," *ICSR 2013*, LNAI 8239, 199–208.

Kaplan, Jerry (2015), *Humans Need Not Apply: A Guide to Wealth and Work in the Age of Artificial Intelligence*, New Haven, CT: Yale University Press.

Kelion, Leo (2015), "Could Driverless Cars Own Themselves?" *BBC News, Technology*, February 15, 2015, online edition, www.bbc.com/news/technology-30998361, last accessed March 12, 2015.

Kim, Min-Sun and Eun-Joo Kim (2013), "Humanoid Robots as 'The Cultural Other': Are We Able to Love Our Creations?" *Artificial Intelligence and Society*, 2, 309–318.

Kurzweil, Ray (1999), *The Age of Spiritual Machines: When Computers Exceed Human Intelligence*, New York: Penguin.

Kurzweil, Ray (2012), *How to Create a Mind: The Secret of Human Thought Revealed*, New York: Viking.

LaFrance, Adrienne (2016), "The Human–Robot Trust Paradox," *The Atlantic*, March 10, online edition.

Lai, Ai-Ling (2012), "Cyborg as Commodity: Exploring Conception of Self-Identity, Body and Citizenship Within the Context of Emerging Transplant Technologies," *Advances in Consumer Research*, 40, 386–94.

Lee, John (2015), "Will Robots Kill the Asian Century?" *National Interest*, April 23, nationalinterest.org/feature/will-robots-kill-the-asian-century-12703, last accessed July 19, 2016.

Levy, David (2007), *Love + Sex with Robots: The Evolution of Human–Robot Relationships*, New York: Harper Perennial.

Levy, Steven (2012), "Can an Algorithm Write a Better New Story than a Human Reporter?" *Wired Magazine*, online edition, www.wired.com/2012/04/can-an-algorithm-write-a-better-news-story-than-a-human-reporter/, last accessed July 19, 2016.

Lewis, Colin (2015), "AI will not Kill Us, Says Microsoft Research Chief," *BBC News*. January 28, online edition, www.youtube.com/watch?v=VuFe8uIZbBU, last accessed March 24, 2015.

Lin, Patrick, Keith Abney, and George Bekey, ed. (2012), *Robot Ethics: The Ethical and Social Implications of Robotics*, Cambridge, MA: MIT Press.

Linden, David (2015), "The Future of Virtual Sex," *Wall Street Journal*, online edition, February 13, http:www.wsj.com/articles/the-future-of-virtual-sex-1423845474, last accessed March 16, 2015.

Markoff, John (2015), *Machines of Loving Grace: The Quest for Common Ground Between Humans and Robots*, New York: HarperCollins.

Marchant, Gary, Braden Allenby, Ronald Arkin, et al. (2011), "International Governance of Autonomous Military Robots," *Columbia Science and Technology Law Review*, 12, www.stir.org/cite.cgl?volume=12&article=7, last accessed July 21, 2016.

Mercer, Calvin (2015), "Introduction: Making the Unknown Known," in Calvin Mercer and Tracy J. Trothen, ed., *Religion and Transhumanism: The Unknown Future of Human Enhancement*, Santa Barbara, CA: Praeger, ix–xiv.

Milgram, Stanley (1963), "Behavioral Study of Obedience," *Journal of Abnormal and Social Psychology*, 67 (4), 371–378.

Mims, Christopher (2010), "Why Japanese Love Robots (and Americans Fear Them)," *MIT Technology Review*, October 12, www.technologyreview.com/view/421187/why-japanese-love-robots-and-americans-fear-them/ last accessed August 25, 2014.

Montevideo, J. M. P. (2014), "Computer Corporations: DAC Attack," *The Economist*, January 28, www.economist.com/blogs/babbage/2014/01/computer-corporations, last accessed July 20, 2016.

Moravec, Hans (1999), *Robot: Mere Machine to Transcendent Mind*, New York: Oxford University Press.

Morris, David Z. (2015), "RoboCorp: Are We Ready for Companies the Run Themselves?" *Aeon*, January 26, aeon.co/essays/are-we-ready-for-companies-that-run-themselves, last accessed July 20, 2016.

Nelkin, Dorothy and M. Susan Lindee (1995), *The DNA Mystique: The Gene as a Cultural Icon*, Ann Arbor: University of Michigan Press.

Niccols, Andrew (1997), *Gattaca*, Hollywood, CA: Columbia Pictures.

Nishio, Shuichi, Tetsuya Watanabe, Kohei Ogawa, and Hiroshi Ishiguro (2013), "Body Ownership Transfer to Teleoperated Android Robot," *Journal of the Robotics Society of Japan*, 31 (9), 854–857.

Nguyen, Trinity (2015), "Metal Machine Music: Tokyo's Robot Restaurant," *Asia Travel Blog*, January 28, http://www.remotelands.com/blog/index.php/metal-machine-music-tokyos-robot-restaurant/, last accessed July 19, 2016.

Nourbakhsh, Illah (2013), *Robot Futures*, Cambridge, MA: MIT Press.

Omohundro, Stephen (2008), "The Basic AI Drives," selfawaresystems.files.wordpress.com/2008/01/ai_drives_final.pdf.

Orbaugh, Sharalyn (2002), "Sex and the Single Cyborg: Japanese Popular Culture Experiments in Subjectivity," *Science Fiction Studies*, 29 (3), 436–452.

Paeng, Erin, Jane Wu, and James Boerkoel, Jr. (2016), "Human-Robot Trust and Cooperation Through a Game Theoretic Framework," *Proceedings of the Thirtieth AAAI Conference on Artificial Intelligence*, 4246–4247.

Pangburn, D. J. (2015),"The Humans Who Dream of Companies That Won't Need Us," *Fast Company*, June 19, www.fastcompany.com/3047462/the-humans-who-dream-of-companies-that-wont-need-them, last accessed July 20, 2016.

Peters, Ted (2011), "Transhumanism and the Posthuman Future: Will Technological Progress Get Us There?" in Gregory Hansell and William Grassie, ed., *H± Transhumanism and Its Critics*, Philadelphia, PA: Metanexus, 147–175.

Rajesh, Monisha (2015), "Inside Japan's First Robot-Staffed Hotel," *The Guardian*, August 14, online edition, www.theguardian.com/travel/2015/aug/14/japan-henn-na-hotel-staffed-by-robots, last accessed July 21, 2016.

Ranisch, Robert and Stefan Sorgner (2014), "Introducing Post- and Transhumanism," in Robert Ranisch and Stevan Sorgner, ed., *Post- and Transhumanism: An Introduction*, Frankfurt: Peter Lang, 7–27.

Rawlinson, Kevin (2015), "Microsoft's Bill Gates Insists AI is a Threat," *BBC News*, January 29, online edition, www.bbc.com/news/31047780?print=true, last accessed March 24, 2015.

Redding, Micah (2016), "Christianity Is Transhumanism," *Huffington Post*, www.huffingtonpost.com/micah-redding/christianity-is-transhuma_b_9266542.html, last accessed June 6, 2016.

Reddy, Raj (1999), "Teleportation, Time Travel, and Immortality," in Peter Denming and James Burke, ed., *Talking Back to the Machine*, New York: Copernicus, 143–153.

Rifkin, Jeremy (2014), *The Zero Marginal Cost Society: The Internet of Things, the Collaborative Commons, and the Eclipse of Capitalism*, London: St. Martin's Press.

Robertson, Jennifer (2007), "Robo Spaiens Japanicus: Humanoid Robots and the Posthuman Family," *Critical Asian Studies*, 39 (3), 369–98.

Robertson, Jennifer (2010a), "Gendering Humanoid Robots: Robo-Sexism in Japan," *Body and Society*, 16 (2), 1–36.

Robertson, Jennifer (2010b), "Robots of the Rising Sun," *American Interest*, 6 (1), 60–72.

Rosalia, Chioke, Rutger Menges, Inèz Deckers, and Christoph Brtneck (2005), "Cruelty Towards Robots," *Proceedings of the Robot Workshop: Designing Robot Applications for Everyday Life*, Grenoble, France: Joint sOc-EUSAI Conference.

Rose, Michael (2013), "Immortalist Fictions and Strategies," in Max More and Natasha Vita-More, *The Transhumanist Reader*, Chichester, UK: John Wiley & Sons, 196–204.

Rothblatt, Martine (2014), *Virtually Human: The Promise and Peril of Digital Immortality*, New York: St. Martin's Press.

Rosenfeld, Azriel (1966), "Religion and the Robot," *Tradition*, 8 (3), 15–26.

Scharping, Nathaniel (2016), "Maybe We Trust Robots Too Much," *Discover D-brief*, May 26, blogs.discovermagazine.com/d-brief/2016/05/26/robot-trust-study/#.V3kWvFfXKOo, last accessed July 3, 2016.

Schelde, Per (1993), *Androids, Humanoids, and Other Science Fiction Monsters: Science and Soul in Science Fiction Films*, New York: New York University Press.

Scheutz, Matthias (2012), "The Inherent Dangers of Unidirectional Emotional Bonds Between Humans and Social Robots," in Patrick Lin, Keith Abney, and George Bekey, ed., *Robot Ethics: The Ethical and Social Implications of Robotics*, Cambridge, MA: MIT Press, 205–222.

Schneider, Susan (2014), "Alien Minds," speech to Library of Congress, September 18, ac.arc.nasa.gov/p39bvbis2q5/?launcher=false&fcsContent=true&pbMode=normal, last accessed July 20, 2016.

Scott, Kristi (2011), "The Human–Robot Continuum of Self: Where the Other Ends and Another Begins," in Rocci Luppicini, ed., *Handbook of Research on Technoself: Identity in a Technological Society*, Hershey, PA: IGI Global, 666–679.

Shaw-Garlock, Glenda (2009), "Looking Forward to Sociable Robots," *International Journal of Social Robotics*, 1, 249–260.

Singer, P. W. (2009), *Wired for War: The Robotics Revolution and Conflict in the 21st Century*, New York: Penguin.

Sirius. R. U. and Jay Cornell (2015), *Transcendence: The Disinformation Enyclopedia of Transhumanism and the Singularity*, San Francisco, CA: Red Wheel Weiser.

Smith, Mark (2016), "What Jobs Will Flying Robots Be Doing in the Future?" *BBC*, online edition, May 17, www.bbc.com/news/business-36301378, last accessed July 21, 2016.

Spiegel, Alix (2013), "No Mercy for Robots: Experiment Tests How Humans Relate to Machines," National Public Radio, January 28, www.npr.org/sections/health-shots/2013/01/28/170272582/do-we-treat-our-gadgets-like-they-re-human, last accessed July 2, 2016.

Strickland, Eliza (2016), "Would You Trust a Robot Surgeon to Operate on You? *IEEE Spectrum*, May 31, spectrum.ieee.org/robotics/medical-robots/would-you-trust-a-robot-surgeon-to-operate-on-you, last accessed July 3, 2016.

Sullins, John (2012), "Robots, Love, and Sex: The Ethics of Building a Love Machine," *IEEE Transactions on Affective Computing*, 3 (4), 398–409.

Sundararajan, Arun (2016), *The Sharing Economy: The End of Employment and the Rise of Crowd-Based Capitalism*, Cambridge, MA: MIT Press.

Susskind, Richard and Daniel Susskind (2015), *The Future of the Professions: How Technology Will Transform the Work of Human Experts*, Oxford: Oxford University Press.

Swan, Melanie (2015), *Blockchain: Blueprint for a New Economy*, Sebastopol, CA: O'Reilly Media.

Tay, Benedict, Younbo Jung, and Taezoon Park (2014), "When Stereotypes Meet Robots: The Double-Edge Sword of Robot Gender and Personality in Human-Robot Interaction," *Computers in Human Behavior*, 38, 75–84.

Toensmeter, Pat (2016), "Should You Really Trust a Robot?" *Aviation Week*, April 8, aviationweek.com/print/defense/should-you-really-trust-rob, last accessed July 3, 2016.

Toon, John (2016), "In Emergencies, Should You Trust a Robot?" *Georgia Tech News Center*, February 29, www.news.gatech.edu/2016/02/29/emergencies-should-you-trust-robot, last accessed July 3, 2016.

Turkle, Sherry (2011), *Alone Together: Why We Expect More from Technology and Less from Each Other*, New York: Basic Books.

Wang, Ning, David Pynadath, and Susan Hill (2015), "Building Trust in a Human-Robot Team with Automatically Generated Explanations," Interservice/Industry Training, Simulation, and Education Conference, Paper No. 15315, people.ict.usc.edu/~pynadath/Papers/iitsec15_15315.pdf, last accessed July 3, 2016.

Wells, Georgia (2016), "Too Cute for Their Own Good, Robots Get Self-Defense Instincts: Droid Designers find Congenial Bots Drawn Pesky Children, Bullies; A Warning Shriek," *Wall Street Journal*, June 19, online edition.

Woollaston, Victoria (2015), "What It's Like to Live with Pepper the 'Emotional' Robot: Humanoid Gives Compliments, Offers Advice and 'Prattles on'," *Mail Online*, July 13, www.dailymail.co.uk/sciencetech/article-3159392/What-s-like-live-Pepper-emotional-robot-Humanoid-gives-compliments-offers-advice-prattles-on.html#ixzz4AukUjFZ7, last accessed June 7, 2016.

Yeoman, Ian and Michelle Mars (2015), "Robots, Men and Sex Tourism," *Futures*, 44 (4), 365–371.

27 End Piece

Behavioural Change and 'Nudge'

Alan Lewis

While this handbook has been dedicated to the psychology of economic behaviour, a number of the contributions have been about behaviour change from a broadly social science perspective, such as Jackson and Smith's work on sustainable lifestyles; encouraging sustainable energy use in the home (Perlaviciute et al.); and increasing tax compliance (Olsen et al.).

Contributors are generally agreed that simple economic models based on incentives and disincentives have their limitations, in, for example, curbing tax evasion and encouraging environmentally friendly behaviour. Even worse, financial incentives may actually 'crowd out' desirable behaviour when driven by implicit rather than explicit motives.

In the past, social psychologists believe (and some still do feel this way) that if you could decipher a person's attitude you could predict his or her behaviour. This was in an era where consistency, congruity, balance and consonance (dissonance) theories prevailed (e.g., Heider,1946; Festinger,1957). It was asserted that people preferred balanced states of mind over dissonant or discordant ones. The task of government then might be to change attitudes through advertising and information campaigns with the idea that changes in behaviour will follow. However, campaigns of this sort have not been especially successful, and within the academic literature the attitude/behaviour link has been heavily criticised from as long ago as 1969 (Wicker, 1969) as well as in more contemporary writings (e.g., Potter and Wetherell, 1987).

A reaction to this, in various forms, was the theory of reasoned action and the theory of planned behaviour (Fishbein and Ajzen, 1975; Ajzen, 1991), which took into account subjective norms and behavioural intentions. The idea was that the approval or disapproval of others matters to us, and our behaviour is not only dependent on our attitudes but our intention to act in one particular way or another; for example, I have a negative attitude towards smoking, other people believe I should stop and I intend to stop. When all these ticks are in place, prediction of behaviour is indeed improved as literature in the area of health psychology has revealed (Conner and Norman, 2005). However, these models remain rather reductionist in nature. In most advanced Western countries, it is now easier not to smoke, not only because it is illegal to smoke in many public spaces, but because there is much wider social disapproval of smoking as the social norm in societies has changed. In a related fashion, Perlaviciute et al. in this volume argue that a combination of environmentally favourable values (which in turn are viewed as more deep-seated and fundamental than attitudes), structural factors (which encourage the translation of values into actions and beliefs) and trust in the institutional will to do something about environmental problems, work together in a complex interaction. An even more macroanalytic approach is at the level of culture, which shows, in the realm of the study of tax compliance, that tax evasion differs between Organisation for Economic Cooperation and Development (OECD) countries in a way which is difficult to explain by tax policies alone: some cultures approve of tax evasion (e.g., Greece and Italy) while others do not (e.g., the United States and the United Kingdom)(Lewis et al., 2009).

Darnton (2008) provides a useful summary of the range of behaviour change models, which begin with those based on economic assumptions; the role of information; values; beliefs and attitudes; norms and identity; behavioural economics; and more community-based interventions, which are mentioned in the current volume by Jackson and Smith.

More recently, there has been some acceptance that there is an interaction between individuals and institutions. In the realm of tax policy, initiatives to encourage compliance are more likely to work if voters trust and respect their government. (See Olsen et al. in this volume.) It also follows that policy makers and citizens to some extent define one another: if tax compliance policies are based solely on the threat of audits and fines, the protagonists are turned into 'cops and robbers' rather than the more desirable 'client and service' relationship. Treating taxpayers as though R.E.M. was a reality helps manufacture that reality.

The link between citizens and policy makers is recognised by the UK's Department of the Environment, Forestry and Rural Affairs (DEFRA) in their '4E's' framework: Encourage (legislation, incentives, information); Enable; Exemplify (leading by example); and Engagement (co-production). The need for politicians, policy makers and government to lead by example is reminiscent of 'demonstration effects' linked to 'crowding in' (rather than 'crowding out'); goodwill, when it comes, in this context, encourages proenvironmental behaviour.

The MINDSPACE, published by the UK Cabinet Office in 2012, condenses social science research in a relatively simple 'noncoercive' list:

Messenger	The credibility and trustworthiness of the source of the message
Incentives	Responses to incentives shaped by heuristics
Norms	Influences from other people, from friends and neighbours to nations and cultures
Defaults	Habitual behaviour and sticking to the easy option of the status quo
Salience	Attention drawn to information of most relevance to us

Priming	Our behaviour can be influenced by subconscious cues
Affect	Emotions influence actions
Commitments	Seeking to be consistent with promises made in public and to reciprocate acts
Ego	Acts which make us feel better about ourselves

One of the authors of MINDSPACE was Michael Hallsworth, a contributor to the current Handbook and previously a member of the Behavioural Insights Team in the UK Cabinet Office (the so-called Nudge team).

Nudge units now shape government policy in the United States, France, the Netherlands, Argentina, Brazil, New Zealand, Germany and the United Kingdom. What makes nudge techniques so attractive is that they do not entail a great deal of complexity, as typified by the MINDSPACE approach, and draw on insights from cognitive psychology rather than social psychology.

This all started with the publication of the influential book *Nudge: Improving Decisions About Health, Wealth and Happiness* by Richard Thaler and Cass Sunstein (Thaler and Sunstein, 2008). Nudges have been mentioned throughout the current Handbook and include heuristics associated with 'anchoring', 'availability', 'loss aversion', 'inertia', 'framing', 'mental accounts', 'self-control' and 'intertemporal choice'. (See, for example, Read, McDonald and He; Antonides and van Klaveren.)

The thesis is predicated by a form of liberal paternalism where people are encouraged to do the right thing by manipulating the 'choice architecture'; for example, people are more likely to save, for retirement and so forth, if the default option is 'opting in' rather than 'opting out' of the saving scheme drawing on the 'status quo' bias. In a similar fashion, employing the framing effect, customers are more likely to buy healthier foodstuffs the closer to eye level they are displayed. Thaler and Sunstein cogently argue that nudges of this sort do not restrict freedom of choice and that surely it is a good thing for governments to create welfare-improving nudges.

These initiatives of course have attracted criticism. For example, Jones, Pykett and Whitehead (2013) describe the nudge 'scientistic' account as follows:

> The story it speaks of ourselves is of irrational, vulnerable citizens in need of correction so that we can become better consumers of choice (the tautology being intentional). Where actual policies are designed for these citizens, it is entirely plausible that the long-term consequences of nudge would render citizens yet more vulnerable and yet more consumerist (p. 171).

Sugden (2009) is particularly concerned with Thaler and Sunstein's claim that their recommendations are designed 'to make choosers better off, *as judged by themselves*' (Thaler & Sunstein, 2008, p.5). Sugden sees the application of liberal paternalism as a trade-off 'between the welfare gains resulting from the reduction of errors in decision-making and the costs that result from restrictions of choice' (Sugden, 2009, p. 369). If the consumer really maintains freedom of choice then, it is argued, they should choose to be nudged (and be aware, one supposes, of the nudge itself). Sugden concludes that the market system works best for the consumers' benefit rather than these interventions.

Some of these criticisms are addressed in Sunstein's *The Ethics of Influence* (Sunstein, 2016). Sunstein provides survey data which seems to show people are not against nudges per se and indeed favour them if the ends are popular (and popularity is dependent upon political affiliation, self-interest, attitudes and values). Sunstein also asserts that only a minority have a negative 'reactance' to nudges. In addition, rather than nudges needing to be covert to work, Sunstein counters 'most nudges are fully transparent and all of them should be …' (Sunstein, 2016, p. 153). Furthermore, he presents some early work which suggests telling people they are being nudged does not change the effectiveness of the nudge.

Supporters of libertarian paternalism point out that nudges are everywhere; examples include car lights turning off when your ignition keys are removed, and ATM's which return your debit/credit card before the cash appears. Yet one wonders, when more members of the public find out about the experts behind these initiatives whether it will make people even more suspicious of the workings of social scientists and psychologists in particular.

27.1 References

Ajzen, I. 1991. The Theory of Planned Behaviour. *Organizational Behaviour and Human Decision Processes*. 50, pp. 199–211.

Conner, M., and P. Norman. (eds). 2005. *Predicting Health Behaviour*. Milton Keynes, UK: Open University Press.

Darnton, A. 2008. *Reference Report: An Overview of Behaviour Change Models and Their Uses*. HM Treasury, London: Government Social Research.

Festinger, L. 1957. *A Theory of Cognitive Dissonance*. Stanford, CA: Stanford University Press.

Fishbein M. and I. Ajzen. 1975. *Belief, Attitiude, Intention and Behavior: An Introduction to Theory and Research*. Reading, MA: Addison-Wesley

Jones, R., J. Pykett and M. Whitehead. 2013. *Changing Behaviours: On the Rise of the Psychological State*. Cheltenham, UK: Edward Elgar.

Heider, F. 1946. Attitudes and Cognitive Organisation. *Journal of Psychology*. 21, pp. 107–112.

Lewis, A., S. Carrera, J. Cullis and P. Jones. 2009. Individual, Cognitive and Cultural Differences in Tax Compliance: UK and Italy Compared. *Journal of Economic Psychology*. 30, 3, pp. 431–445.

MINDSPACE. 2012. UK: Cabinet Office/Institute of Government.

Potter, M., and M. Wetherell. 1987. *Discourse and Social Psychology: Beyond Attitudes and Behaviour*. London: Sage.

Sugden, R. 2009. On Nudging. *International Journal of the Economics of Business*. 16, 3, pp. 365–373.

Sunstein, C. 2016. *The Ethics of Influence: Government in the Age of Behavioural Science*. Cambridge, UK: C.U.P.

Thaler, R., and C. Sunstein. 2008. *Nudge: Improving Decisions about Health, Wealth and Happiness*. London: Yale University Press.

Wicker, A. 1969. Attitudes Versus Actions. *Journal of Social Issues*. 25,4, pp. 41–78.

Index